The Fox Film Corporation,
1915–1935

The Fox Film Corporation, 1915–1935

A History and Filmography

AUBREY SOLOMON

McFarland & Company, Inc., Publishers
Jefferson, North Carolina

The present work is a reprint of the illustrated case bound edition of The Fox Film Corporation, 1915–1935: A History and Filmography, *first published in 2011 by McFarland.*

LIBRARY OF CONGRESS CATALOGUING-IN-PUBLICATION DATA

Solomon, Aubrey.
The Fox Film Corporation, 1915–1935 : a history and filmography / Aubrey Solomon.
  p.   cm.
Includes bibliographical references and index.

softcover : acid free paper ∞

1. Fox Film Corporation — History. 2. Fox, William, 1879–1952.
3. Motion pictures — Catalogs. I. Title.
PN1999.F69S65   2016   791.43 — dc22   2011002126

BRITISH LIBRARY CATALOGUING DATA ARE AVAILABLE

ISBN (print) 978-1-4766-6600-6
ISBN (ebook) 978-0-7864-8610-6

© 2011 Aubrey Solomon. All rights reserved

No part of this book may be reproduced or transmitted in any form or by any means, electronic or mechanical, including photocopying or recording, or by any information storage and retrieval system, without permission in writing from the publisher.

On the cover: *inset* William Fox, 1929; the Fox Hills lot known as Movietone City, circa 1930 (photographs courtesy of Robert S. Birchard)

Printed in the United States of America

*McFarland & Company, Inc., Publishers
Box 611, Jefferson, North Carolina 28640
www.mcfarlandpub.com*

Table of Contents

Preface 1
Introduction 5

Part I. History 9

1. Humble Beginnings 9
2. The Birth of Fox 19
3. A Major Player 37
4. Stability 50
5. Consolidation 68
6. The Rise of Winfield Sheehan 81
7. Talking Pictures 95
8. The Golden Age of Fox Films 112
9. The Fall of William Fox 122
10. Boom to Bust 134
11. Turmoil 156
12. Back from the Abyss 170
13. A Tour of the Studio 182
14. Survival 186
15. 20th Century Pictures 204
16. After the Merger 217

Part II. Filmography 227

Chapter Notes 361
Bibliography 367
Index 369

Preface

Since reading *Upton Sinclair Presents William Fox*, Sinclair's massive 1933 in-depth interview with the Fox Film Corporation founder, as part of my research for a book on the 20th Century–Fox studio, I have been fascinated by how this pioneer of the film industry and the company he founded has been overlooked. Following the merger of Fox and 20th Century Pictures in 1935, the emphasis on the studio output has been largely focused on the post–1935 releases. In fact, the current management of the company recently celebrated its 75th anniversary, totally ignoring the years from 1914 through 1935.

I am as guilty of this oversight as anyone else since I relegated those earlier films to a minimal listing in one of my books, *The Films of 20th Century–Fox*, co-written with Tony Thomas, and skimmed over the early history in *Twentieth Century–Fox: A Corporate and Financial History*. If the complete quantitative output of the studio is considered, however, at least half of its entire library, even to the present day, was produced before 1935. From 1914 (when it was still called the Box Office Attraction Company) through 1935, the Fox Film Corporation distributed 1,173 features (including foreign versions) and many thousands of newsreels and short subjects, an output which represents a sizable contribution to cinema history.

There's a tragic, but understandable, reason for the neglect of this body of work. A major percentage of the Fox releases were produced before the introduction of sound. Once sound arrived, no studio felt any obligation to invest money in preserving obsolete vestiges of the industry's beginning. As well, nitrate-based negatives are prone to deterioration and a catastrophic fire in a film vault in New Jersey in 1937 destroyed three-quarters of Fox features released before 1930. These films no longer exist in any form, so it's impossible to re-evaluate them critically. Whatever still exists of the library might be in fragments, 16 mm prints, or well-used theatrical prints which have luckily survived. These are by no means a complete representation of the early studio's output.

Performers who starred in those films, no matter how popular at the time, are represented to us today mainly in still photos. Theda Bara, who made 40 films at Fox between 1915 and 1919, lives on in only two of these productions, *A Fool There Was* (1915) and *East Lynne* (1916). Only a very brief clip from *Cleopatra* (1917) survives.

Many other contemporary stars like June Caprice, Shirley Mason, Gladys Brockwell, George Walsh, William Farnum, Valeska Suratt, Madlaine Traverse, and Eileen Percy are rarely given credit for the level of popularity they attained. A major director like J. Gordon Edwards, who was compared in his time to D.W. Griffith and was William Fox's most trusted associate, can only be assessed by the occasional feature that still exists since he died suddenly at age 58 in 1925. Distressing, too, is the loss of the early work of major directors like John Ford, Raoul Walsh, William Wellman, Howard Hawks and George Marshall. Fox's contract writers who helped develop the art of screenwriting can only be judged by surviving studio copies of their scenarios, which are almost completely inaccessible to the public. Tom Mix, Fox's most consistently popular star for a decade, is the single best-represented performer, with many of his films still surviving.

The most complete group of films that can be seen includes those made in the early sound period. These were the ones to which I was introduced when I began work at the 20th Century–Fox studio in 1976. At that time, 50 films made between 1929 and 1935 had been preserved from existing studio prints and were being sold to television stations. My first assignment was to screen those films and, admittedly, the conditions for viewing them were less than conducive to any appreciation. I watched them on the small five-inch screen of a 16 mm Moviola film reader.

Nor were they an impressive array of titles. The majority of the package was made up of sluggish dramas, unfunny comedies, and many lacked cinematic dynamism. There were a few exceptions. *The Power and the Glory* (1933) did show a great deal of writing and directorial skill. However, the only pre-print material was a horribly splicy print. It was almost impossible to get a sense of the dramatic effect with words missing and transitions truncated by splices. There was also a group of James Dunn films, all very similar in tone and structure. I imagined these must have been popular since there were so many of them. There were also Janet Gaynor musicals like *Sunny Side Up* (1929) and *Change of Heart* (1934), both with Charles Farrell, and *Delicious* (1931), all of which seemed horribly dated. Early Spencer Tracy titles, aside from historical interest, did not hold up well either.

There were a couple of ambitious films like *Zoo in Budapest* (1933), starring an exquisite Loretta Young. *The Big Trail* (1930) was fascinating in its scope of production but John Wayne's stilted acting did not help. Even the multiple Oscar-winning *Cavalcade*, a massive hit when released in 1933, failed to grab me. There were only a few decent Fox films, mainly those with Will Rogers, that still held up after more than four decades. In general, stories seemed to ramble, moods changed and the level of screenwriting was mediocre. In reviewing some of the films from this package in more recent times, my criticisms remained the same.

There was also a small sub-group of films within this package which were so distinctly different in style and pacing that they stood out from the rest. It included several of the original 20th Century films produced by Darryl F. Zanuck. I knew a lot about Zanuck from previous research and these films confirmed my admiration for his style of picture-making: fast-paced, tightly plotted, if not always logical, and almost always entertaining. Titles like *Advice to the Lovelorn* (1933), *Blood Money* (1933), *Looking for Trouble* (1934), *The Last Gentleman* (1934), *Born to Be Bad* (1934) and *Folies Bergère* (1935) were infinitely more energetic than the Fox films of the same period. Quality aside, these films were structurally very different. It was the differences that led me to wonder what was going on at the Fox studio that resulted in so many misguided projects in the years between 1930 and 1935.

From the Upton Sinclair book, I was well aware that political turmoil and the collapse of William Fox's fortunes after the stock market crash of 1929 led to a coup which forced him out of his company. A few years ago, I decided to look around for the back-story of the company's founding and what finally led to William Fox's loss of his company. No one had ever written a concise history of those years.

I went to trade magazines where I was able to find much long-forgotten material. Different trade papers documented different aspects of the business, so no single publication had everything. *Wid's Daily*, later called the *Film Daily*, *Motion Picture Daily* and *Variety* provided excellent insight into the New York operations with their emphasis on distribution and exhibition as well as a good deal of West Coast coverage. It was *Daily Variety* and the *Hollywood Reporter*, though, with boots on the ground at the studios, that uncovered a good deal of the politics of film production. Piecing together these two elements gave a clearer picture of Fox's successes and failures.

There was not much inside information about studio operations in the late 1910s and 1920s, but one resource provided an invaluable behind-the-scenes look at the Fox operation. Sol Wurtzel's personal correspondence with William Fox, compiled by Lillian Wurtzel Semenov and Carla Winter and published in 2001, gave a detailed representation of how their relationship functioned from 1917 through 1921. The quotes from these letters may seem grammatically odd, but it should be remembered that they were, no doubt, dictated to secretaries and likely reflect train-of-thought dictation.

I have followed the development of the company from beginning to end since the period is so complex that it is easier to follow on a year-by-year basis. Even that gets complicated since films are mentioned when announced, then in production, and finally in release. The industry standard for film release schedules was planned on the basis of a "movie season," which began in September and ran through the next August rather than by a calendar year. For the purpose of clarity and in relation to the filmography, I have considered the studio's releases by calendar years.

Corporate returns were reported in the trades for quarterly periods and the profits from productions for one year did not necessarily figure into a company's returns for that same year.

Films, after all, were in release for up to two years before the final figures were tallied and the profits assessed. I have tried to keep these elements as comprehensible as possible by using the final rental figure to measure a film's success. Box-office rentals, the amount returned to the distributor after the exhibitor cut is removed, gives the best indicator of a film's success. In the last three decades, I have been able to compile reliable financial information from multiple sources, some of which is included in this volume. It is, to the best of my knowledge, accurate, but it appears without footnotes.

Since much of the information has been gathered from articles in the trade papers, I have used original quotes and editorials to preserve their colorful "trade-speak" flavor. Whenever possible, dates have been mentioned to place everything in perspective. I have also tried to point out, where applicable, the various biases specific trade papers held since they shaded the way issues were reported.

Contemporary reviews of films have been quoted to illuminate the reception of those films at the time of release. However, this can be deceiving since recent cinematic re-evaluations have shown that some movies have been given new importance in the development of cinema, whereas others that were considered ground-breaking at first release garner little respect now. The majority of surviving pre-merger Fox films, with the exception of *Sunrise* (1927), is rarely exhibited in any format and is seldom re-evaluated.

Piecing together so much that has been lost is very difficult. Since viewing a majority of the Fox films themselves is impossible, I have assembled in Part II of this book a complete (or as complete as I can determine) filmography listing, in order of release, of all the productions. With a thumbnail description of each movie, it's possible to see the trends in story material; the credits show who was under contract for long periods or just visiting briefly, and who was popular as recurring supporting players but have long since been forgotten; the footage counts sometimes indicate a film's importance since longer pictures cost more and were higher in profile; finally, the release patterns provide a view of the overall annual programs the studio provided its theaters. Landmark or hit releases have been noted with additional information.

The issue of film lengths is also a very fuzzy area. Many lengths are simply listed in terms of reels. However, a five-reel film could technically be anywhere from 3,500' to 4,900'. Also in question, until the late 1920s, is the speed at which film was shot and projected. Some films were cranked at 60-feet per minute, much less than the standard 90-feet per minute of sound films. Since projectors could be run at variable speeds, no matter what the camera speed was, film could be run at anywhere from 60- to 90-feet per minute. From what I can gather, 70- to 84-feet per minute was about right for the mid-1920s based on several reviews of films where the lengths can be documented. I have made a best effort to include footages where they are available. In the silent period, I favor footage to running times since the speeds could be varied. Once sound came in, all running times were standardized but when I could find the footage counts, I used those since they are more accurate than rounding out minutes.

As for photos, I have relied on some long-time collectors and they have come through with a wonderful assortment of rarely seen stills. So, my thanks go to Robert S. Birchard, Mike Hawks and Karl Thiede. A special debt of gratitude is owed to Karl Thiede for proofreading the manuscript and for diligently looking for, and finding, factual or typographical errors. All errors remaining are of course my fault alone. Thanks also to Mandy Tilles, my brother-in-law, who enjoyed my previous Fox history so much that he encouraged me to embark on this project. And of course, thanks to my wife, Gina, who graciously tolerated all the time taken up with the research and writing of this volume.

Introduction

From the first officially recorded public showing of a four-minute motion picture, on May 21, 1895, the public has been fascinated with moving images on a screen. Several years later, in 1902, an amusement house opened that featured moving pictures. Entrepreneurs opened similar establishments, buying films to exhibit. It did not take long before an innovative Harry J. Miles, a San Francisco exhibitor, created the first film exchange by renting out films after he had run them. A constant demand for "new" product began the cycle of production and distribution.

By the time William Fox entered film production in 1914, the business had grown from penny arcades and nickelodeons to something vaguely resembling the fully developed distribution/exhibition industry. The majority of productions were carried out on the East Coast with its proximity to the actors, directors and writers of the New York stage. It was also a time when there was a limit placed on growth by the reluctance of banking interests to risk capital on an enterprise that was evolving so rapidly and with little certainty.

Just having made the transition from one- and two-reel subjects to longer, more sophisticated (for the time) features of anywhere between three and six reels in length, there were questions as to how much audiences really wanted their prime entertainment to be motion pictures. Viewers were still being drawn into theaters for the musical/vaudeville performances that were part of the program. For several years, theater managers considered the live performances as the main attraction. The film portion of the program was still a novelty and not necessarily the future of exhibition.

Soon, the size of theaters increased as it became more profitable to run a film for larger audiences. Admission prices rose at newer theaters that were built with luxury in mind. Gone were the portable chairs or benches of the early years. Architecturally, theaters were built as palaces, places that the average working person could enter in awe. The more plush houses in large cities could charge higher admissions. The question would become "How high?"

The initial store shows charged just a nickel and appealed largely to an immigrant and working-class crowd, places elitist big-city dwellers would never dream of attending. Movie palaces opened up the potential audience to those who could afford to pay admissions of up to two dollars.

From the very beginning of the movies, there were films that were "program pictures" and then there were the "specials." These classifications would always remain a part of the distribution business. Programmers unspooled at less prestigious theaters and returned lower per-venue rentals. The "specials" were given a wider release pattern, beginning with the palaces and finally ending up in the "flea-pits." Rental terms benefitted the producer/distributors of the most popular product.

In 1915, D.W. Griffith promoted a form of exhibition which was known as the "roadshow." His production of *The Birth of a Nation* (1915) debuted in New York City at a top admission of $2. Although exact amounts were never calculated because of the way distribution was set up at the time, the film set a record for rentals, estimated at $10,000,000 worldwide that was held for more than two decades until *Gone with the Wind* opened in the last week of 1939. Roadshows at first played in legitimate theaters for a specified run that vastly exceeded the one-week run of regular films. Through 1920, even certain very popular special films only reached a maximum of four weeks. The extended life of a roadshow meant a limited number of openings for a film that would not hit the smaller theaters for one or two years.

Bankers and investors saw in *The Birth of a Nation* the potential of the movie industry and were more willing to loan capital to legitimate producers who had proven themselves capable of turning a profit. William Fox was one of those able to continuously raise funding to expand his empire.

When audiences demanded to know the identities of their favorite performers and performers insisted that their names be credited onscreen, a star system was developed that would help propel certain films to success. Independent companies that were underfinanced and lacked access to star power fell by the wayside. Dozens of start-ups in the teens never made it to the twenties. Some were absorbed into larger concerns but many simply disappeared. Those companies fortunate enough to sign or nurture stars were rewarded with more investor approval. After all, a star's name attached to a film was as much of a guarantee of success as could be had in the movie business. Charlie Chaplin, Mary Pickford, William S. Hart, John Barrymore, Roscoe "Fatty" Arbuckle, Douglas Fairbanks, Wallace Reid, Theda Bara or Tom Mix translated directly into box-office appeal. The bigger the name, the more money the star demanded, resulting in higher production costs and ultimately higher admission prices. But this was the engine that fueled the industry.

Distribution patterns became established in this period as well, as independently owned chains of theaters sprang up on a regional basis. Theaters in New York were not yet associated with those in Chicago or Los Angeles. It was only in the 1920s that continent-wide exhibition companies were formed. Since producers had to fight for access to theaters, some production companies began buying or building houses to guarantee an outlet for their product.

William Fox presided over his company through the most explosive period of growth in

William Fox (left) at work with an unidentified assistant in New York, ca. 1920s (courtesy Robert S. Birchard).

film history, notably the late 1920s. He saw the expansion of Fox Films from a small exhibition set-up with six exchanges to a massive integrated corporate structure with a reputed value of $300 million in 1930 (probably comparable to $50 billion today). Fox was an entrepreneur par excellence, a member of that narrow range of the immigrant population who were able to build massive corporations from the ground up. Contemporary comparisons with Fox's achievements would rank him with Steve Jobs or Bill Gates. These are men who entered arenas that were in their infancy and created products that fostered industries and empires.

Aside from the sheer volume of films, the ambitious reach of the corporation is impressive indeed. Consider that William Fox, in the early 1900s, successfully challenged the Motion Picture Patents Company. He built an international distribution and exhibition empire that was the envy of every other studio, and almost succeeded in taking over the powerful M.G.M. studio and its parent Loew's, Inc. He promoted newsreels to new heights of popularity. While Vitaphone was capturing headlines with the arrival of *The Jazz Singer* (1927), it was Fox's Movietone system that would prevail as the predominant method of reproducing sound. Fox was also a pioneer in the development of the first wide-screen 70 mm projection system for general use. He was involved in financing a new color process and was also eyeing the fledgling radio industry.

William Fox was one of the many entrepreneurs to enter the new field of "flickers." As an investor, he was obviously interested in profit, and endlessly pursued this goal. Along the way though, he made a considerable number of enemies and developed a reputation for arrogance as reported by *Fortune* magazine in 1930: "Newspapermen have frequently commented upon the fact that on those rare occasions when Mr. Fox consents to meet the Press, he disregards the immediate business of the interview in favor of a long preamble on his Rise from the Ranks, and interruption of which is likely to result in a door slamming upon the departure of an indignant cinema potentate."

Nevertheless, Fox helped pioneer and foster an industry that to this day still manages to entertain, enthrall, excite and educate populations in every corner of the globe. But his vision and relentless hunger for an ever-greater control of motion pictures eventually led to his financial overextension and his downfall. It was an ignominious and probably unavoidable end, but it leaves one wondering about the outcome of the Fox Film Corporation if his tenure had not ended in 1930.

Part I. History

1. Humble Beginnings

"When a man reaches fifty ... three courses lie ahead. He may dream of his past accomplishment, he may rest on his oars, or he may make ambitious plans for the future. The latter of these possibilities appeals to William Fox."[1]

When the Fox Film Corporation announced in July 1929 that revenues from their releases in the first six months of that year had equaled the entire previous year, it was a sign that the arc of economic prosperity enjoyed by the United States following the end of World War I had been especially kind to the motion picture industry. At the helm of the Fox Film Corporation, Fox Theaters and a myriad of ancillary companies strode 50-year-old William Fox, called "the lone eagle of the industry," at the apex of his career as a producer, theater owner, and industry leader.

In the silver anniversary year of his company, he had built up a colossus in the entertainment world. From an initial investment of $1,666 in 1904, by 1929 Fox turned out 53 features, more than 200 newsreels and dozens of short subjects. His theater chain had expanded from a handful of nickelodeons in New York to a worldwide chain of over 1,100 locations, including everything from neighborhood houses to large picture palaces like the 6,214 seat Roxy in Manhattan, New York, the largest theater in the world. He had also, earlier in the year, gained controlling shares of the giant Loew's, Inc., the parent company of Metro-Goldwyn-Mayer and Loew's Theaters. His companies had an estimated value of $300,000,000 and he personally owned 53 percent of Fox Film and 93 percent of the Fox Theaters.

As a pioneer, William Fox financed and spearheaded the development of sound-on-film, a revolutionary and practical process that allowed sound reproduction in motion pictures without the need of a synchronized disc. Fox was experimenting with a color process to rival the dominance of Technicolor and he was about to introduce a new wide-gauge film, projected on larger screens with sharper image resolution and crisper sound.

Fox was a tall man with a stately composure, a large curved nose whose tip dipped slightly over a thick lip which was covered by a black mustache (in early years), bushy eyebrows and a high dome with wisps of receding hair. From humble origins, his staggering success was a tribute to the great opportunities available to immigrants in the United States at the turn of the century.

Born in the village of Tulchva, Hungary, in 1879, to Michael and Anna Fuchs (later Fox), Jewish parents of German descent, William was brought to New York at nine months of age. He grew up in a slum tenement on the East Side and was the oldest of several siblings. At a time when infant mortality was high, Fox's mother gave birth to 12 other children. Only two boys and three girls survived. Fox's father, a machinist, never earned more than $1,000 in a year.

Young Will began school at the age of six, but left when he was 11 years old to help support his brothers and sisters. He would earn money whatever way was available to him. He sold candy in Central Park and dodged police when they were arresting peddlers. Fiercely enterprising, he hired other children to work for him as well and earned $10 to $12 a week during summer months. Working all day and all night was not an unusual occurrence for him.

As a youngster, he fell off a truck, broke his left arm and lost his elbow joint as a result of medical malpractice. This left him unable to bend the arm adequately, but later in life it did not prevent him from excelling at golf.

William Fox's formal career began with jobs in the very active New York clothing industry, a starting point for many future film entrepreneurs of that period, including Samuel Goldfish (later Goldwyn), Marcus Loew, Carl Laemmle and Adolph Zukor. At the age of 13, insisting he was three years older, Fox was promoted to foreman for D. Cohen and Sons in charge of cutting linings. Tall for his age, he was able to get away with the ruse and supervised a dozen workers. His daily routine began at 6 A.M. He worked from 7 A.M. to 6:30 P.M., came home for dinner at 7:30 P.M. then went to classes at night school which he continued until he was fourteen. His salary never increased beyond $8 a week.

Fox's initial interest in the entertainment industry was a matter of happenstance. He learned that storekeepers who put announcements for vaudeville shows in their windows were given free tickets and would sell them to him for five or ten cents. When Fox quit night school, he spent a lot of time going to the theater to see burlesque comedians like the popular Weber & Fields. Rather than merely for entertainment, the expenditure had a purpose. He and a friend worked up a vaudeville routine which they performed for $5 to $10 a night. After a short time, he realized that a performer's life was not to be his road to riches.

The clothing business still offered the best stepladder to financial stability. At age 15, William Fox began working for G. Lippman & Sons: "I can recall going out with boys when I was sixteen, seventeen, or eighteen, and though I wanted to do the things they did, on checking up the cost I usually did without. I knew the soles of my shoes had holes in them and that was the time to have them repaired, but I delayed it by putting pasteboard in them to save the half-soling.... Every penny was something that I denied myself, with the thought in mind that if I was going forward, I had to have money."[2]

He continued working in different clothing firms, earning a top salary of $17 weekly. A practitioner of frugal habits, by the age of 20 he had $580 in the bank. With this financial security, William Fox married Eve Leo, four years his junior, on December 31, 1899, just one day before his 21st birthday. He had met Eve at a party when she was ten and he was 14. Her father was a clothing manufacturer and of higher social standing but that did not deter Will. The newly minted Mr. and Mrs. Fox moved into a five-room flat in Brooklyn with a monthly rent of $11. Three years later they bought a tenement house for $12,000 with a $1,000 down payment that suddenly made William Fox a landlord.[3]

Unhappy with the slow path to wealth and recognizing that company owners would always profit more than workers, Fox decided to go into business for himself. With a partner, he selected the cloth examining and shrinking business since it required little capital and less space in which to work. Fox received cloth directly from the mills, then checked it for imperfections and provided the shrinkage before suits were manufactured. Woolen cloth needed to go through this process so that the seams of a garment would not shrink from dampness when being worn. Limiting his salary to $17 a week to preserve working capital, he allowed his partner to draw $25 weekly. After their second year in business, profits grew to $10,000. Having saved enough once again, he bought out his partner in the Knickerbocker Cloth Examining and Shrinking Company and later sold out, amassing a profit of close to $50,000. The hard work and deprivation never once tempted William Fox to indulge in any luxuries: "I was reaching for a goal, and I enjoyed every moment of it."[4]

The question at this juncture was how to invest his profits. Fox was familiar with the Kinetoscope, built in 1899 by Thomas Alva Edison from designs by W.K.L. Dickson, for a reported expenditure of $24,000,[5] that was drawing crowds of viewers who were dropping their pennies into slots and peering through narrow lenses to see brief moving pictures. But that was already on the way out. The fledgling filmed entertainment industry was quickly metamorphosing and three-to-eight-minute movies like *The Life of an American Fireman* (1903, Edison) were already being projected onto sheets that were used as screens. At the time, those entrepreneurs running picture shows doubted whether anyone would want to see longer films.

The release of Edwin S. Porter's *The Great Train Robbery* (1903, Edison) proved the value of longer films and was one of the earliest American efforts to tell a complete story. Audiences could watch a gang of thieves riding towards a train, boarding it, robbing the safe, then being chased by the law, all in less than ten minutes. There was even hand-tinted coloring to give more realism to the explosion of the safe and in a scene when one of the thieves turns his gun to the camera and fires. For a public unaccustomed to such shock effects, these images created a sensation.

Stories that could be told in one reel of a thousand feet in length or less became more common and ambitious to complement a string of news events, instructional films, and salacious, exploitative subjects like exotic dancers. But it was the story films that held real promise for the movie business. Hundreds were exhibited each year not only from the United States, but also England, France, Germany and Italy.

In 1904, William Fox decided he was in the market for such an operation. He met with J. Stuart Blackton of the Vitagraph Company of America and inspected a Brooklyn nickelodeon in a former store at 200 Broadway that was up for sale. There was a showroom upstairs with 146 seats and some display posters outside informing the public that moving pictures were to be seen. Checking out the property, Fox was struck by the size of the crowds that were there each day he visited. He decided that with such an ample passing trade, it would be easy to fill the seats upstairs and convinced two partners to split the $5,000 cost three ways. For $1,666.67 William Fox now owned a one-third interest in the venture. He learned too late, however, that the crowds had been salted by a slick sales agent and "the Brooklyn public didn't know what moving pictures were and nobody went upstairs. W.F. stood outside for a whole day, gazing anxiously at the public, and regretting that he had no personal charms to lure them into his establishment."[6]

Luckily, a promoter he met hired a coin-trick artist who set up his table at the doorway. When a crowd gathered, the magician said he would finish his performance upstairs and that admission was free. The public learned quickly about moving pictures and within a week, the police had to be called to control the now-paying crowds. Fox configured the route so when audiences left they would pass through a Kinetoscope arcade and drop a few pennies along the way.

With his two partners, William Fox began renting stores all over Brooklyn and ended up with 15 such establishments. Each one had a screen and projector and could not exceed 299 seats because the fire laws became stricter when there were more than 300 seats. Fox found that, in order to get the right location, it often paid to lease the whole building, even though tenants had to be evicted before films could be run due to fire hazards. The storefront theaters attracted immigrants who, through their lack of understanding of English, did not attend live theater performances, but could easily grasp the moving pictures that were shown. Once again, when Fox had saved up enough money, he bought out his partners.

The movie business in those days, however, did not get much respect. In William Fox's own words, "It was a period when, if a boy was arrested for stealing, his attorney found the most convenient defense to be that he learned to commit this crime because he witnesses motion pictures. If a man was arrested for wife-beating, his lawyer said that he had acquired the habit because he was a regular patron of a motion picture theatre. The newspapers throughout the country, without exception to the rule, were its biggest and staunchest enemies. Whether it was because the populace had no liking for motion pictures or because they recognized the fact that the motion picture was some day destined to be of potential value, and perhaps in a competitive way, I don't know."[7] Fox would forever be seeking the respect he felt his company and the movie business deserved.

William Fox bought film prints outright from producing companies like Vitagraph, Biograph, Lubin, Selig, Essanay, Pathé, and Kalem, paying fees on a per-foot basis. He began to combine motion pictures and vaudeville, charging ten cents admission. He would find a manager with a good voice and have him sing popular new songs that were being "plugged" and therefore did not require any royalties. There were also lantern slides for visual accompaniment to the songs and audiences were invited to join the singing with the lyrics appearing on the slides.

The disadvantage to small theaters was the limited number of admissions. Fox recognized that larger theaters could accommodate much larger audiences and return higher revenues. The first theater he purchased was an old 700-seat vaudeville house, the Gaiety: "It was located at 194 Grand Street, Brooklyn, and had been devoted to burlesque. When I went to visit the premises, it was winter and the agent told me to bring along rubber boots. I did, and we walked in snow and water up to the knees; the roof was practically gone and it was the most dilapidated structure I ever saw. When I inquired as to how the building came to be in such a deplorable condition, the agent explained that the building was fifty years old and had been unoccupied for two years.... I think I paid about $20,000 for the land and building.... The theatre did a terrific business, and in a short space of time we paid off the mortgage and declared hundreds of thousands of dollars in dividends."[8]

The format of combining live performances with motion pictures continued to be popular. He leased his next theater, the Folly, which held 2,000 seats. Shows of two hours were performed five times daily, incorporating popular vaudeville acts and short films. In the first ten years, it earned $500,000 to $600,000 in profits. It was clear that William Fox was engaged in the fastest-growing area of entertainment since, by 1907, the gross income from film production exceeded the combined earnings of the legitimate theater and vaudeville.

By 1910, there were approximately 9,000 theaters

in the United States. In that same year, in an attempt to bring prestige to his operation, William Fox leased the New York Academy of Music in Manhattan, New York, a storied venue that was once a famous opera house. He planned to stage a series of plays with a stock company, but attendance for the high-brow offerings was low and resulted in serious financial losses. Doggedly pursuing his career as impresario during three years of live performances at the Academy, Fox acknowledged failure and the theater was converted to a picture house and immediately started to make money again.

Fox bought more theaters and decorated them more lavishly. His concentration on the New York and New Jersey area was logical since both states held at least ten percent of the entire country's population.

As the quality of films improved and increased in length, people were willing to pay higher admissions which increased from the initial five cents to 50 cents in larger venues. Fox prided himself on knowing the number of seats sold each day at each theater, a routine he continued throughout his career.

Becoming more sophisticated in industry methods, William Fox learned that the distribution of films was also a way to make money. Following the example of the first distributor, Harry Miles, who in 1902 began routing films around after he finished with them through his "exchange," Fox bought territorial rights and rented films to others under the name of The Greater New York Film Rental Company.

In December 1908, a group of the most powerful studios, including Edison, Vitagraph, Selig, Méliès, Essanay, Kalem, Lubin, Kleine, Pathé and Biograph, had set up a monopoly called "The Motion Picture Patents Company." In January 1909, the ten partners announced that they exclusively owned all rights to photograph, develop, print and exhibit motion pictures. Claiming patents under the laws of the United States, Great Britain, France, Germany and Italy, they also made it clear that no other entities had the right to duplicate their services. All distributors and producers were forced to sign on to their combine at $2 weekly, guaranteeing the trust an income of $1,250,000 annually. The monopoly set all the rules and pricing guidelines for producers and exhibitors. The maximum fee that could be paid for a scenario was $62.50. Performers were not permitted to be given any screen credits. Films could be no longer than two reels, approximately 20 minutes in length. Rentals were set at ten cents a foot. Distributors could only rent and theaters could only play films made under the Patents Company licenses.

By 1910, this stranglehold spread when the trust partners formed a new entity, the General Film Company, to exert control over the distribution of pictures. General quickly acquired 67 principal exchanges that supplied film to almost all theaters in the United States. Those who refused to sell their exchanges, like Carl Laemmle, later the founder of Universal Pictures, had their licenses canceled. Laemmle continued to produce his own movies in defiance of the trust which ended up filing 240 lawsuits against him.

Of a total 120 distribution licensees to the trust, 119 were bought out or forced out. William Fox was the final hold-out and refused to sell. Fox challenged the trust by offering to buy feature-length films from any producer for distribution in an effort to break the monopolistic grip on motion pictures. When the General Film Company insisted on buying him out, he demanded $750,000 for his exchange. The trust canceled his license. Fox sued General Film under the Sherman antitrust laws for $600,000 and stood to get triple damages if he won the case. The situation played itself out in the courts for the next two years until the trust finally settled without a trial by paying Fox $350,000. In 1913, its grip on the industry was broken. There were no longer limits on film lengths, fixed rental fees, or restrictions against advertising star names. The industry could proceed in a competitive environment with film rentals rising in a free market. Any producer could make films, any company could distribute films and any theater could book these films.

William Fox, savoring his legal victory, was busy building more lavish and beautiful movie palaces, including the Audubon on Broadway near 165th Street and one on Tremont Avenue in the Bronx. He had invested his entire capital of $500,000. When construction on the two theaters was only half done, the projects ran out of money. Fox had to scramble around and place his credit on the line to complete the theaters. He eventually was able to arrange for financing to complete the projects and paid off the loans shortly thereafter. Using this modus operandi, he built up a chain of 125 houses. Although he was always able to pay off debts, his dependence on bank credit would ultimately become his Achilles heel.

In the middle of the second decade of the century, motion pictures, released from the constraints of the General Film Company, were free

One of William Fox's first theaters in New York City, the Academy of Music at 14th Street and Irving Place, in 1915 during the engagement of *The Little Gypsy* (courtesy Robert S. Birchard).

to develop more sophisticated entertainments in whatever lengths producers desired. Adolph Zukor's Famous Players Company had set a new standard in film length by importing a four-reel feature from France, *Les Amours d'Elizabeth* in 1912, starring Sarah Bernhardt, through a special arrangement with the trust. As well, directors like D.W. Griffith and Cecil B. DeMille were bringing a new cinematic language to the motion picture, which had heretofore been nothing more than filmed stage plays. Ironically, the companies of the trust (with the exception of Vitagraph), without the umbrage of a monopoly, could not compete in a free market. Within five years all were out of business.

Beginning in 1914, New Jersey–based William Fox bought films outright from the Balboa Amusement Producing Company in Long Beach, California, for distribution to his own theaters and then for rental to other theaters across the country. Balboa produced more than 1,000 movies between 1913 and 1918 which had been sold to distributors and was run by Herbert and Elwood Horkheimer, pioneers of California-based production. Ultimately Balboa failed by not having its own distribution organization. This was a mistake that William Fox did not make.

Through his Greater New York Film Rental Company, with offices at 116 East Street, Fox set himself up in business as a film distributor for the New York territory. He later changed the business name to The Box Office Attraction Film Rental Company and formed a sales organization that covered 22 cities with its exchanges. Fox bought productions from Balboa that ran between three and five reels in length. Some of the 1914 titles included *The Square Triangle, The Test of Manhood, The Judge's Wife, To Love and to Hold*, and *The Woman He Wronged*.

His many early releases reflected the types of stories he would later produce. *The Criminal Code*, released in September 1914, contained several of what would become tried-and-true plot elements. It tells the story of a 16-year-old girl who escapes abuse at an orphanage and is taken in by a gentleman thief. He tries to enlist her in his crimes but she refuses and stabs him in self-defense. She then moves to a small town and leads an exemplary life until the thief, now caught, names her as his accomplice. Discredited and facing charges, she is only saved by a young lawyer who (along with providing a romantic interest) comes to her defense and restores her good name. The themes of unfair accusations, ruined reputations and knights in shining armor coming to the rescue would recur in many of Fox's films. *The Criminal Code* also starred William Desmond Taylor who would just a few years later become a major director at Famous Players–Lasky, the precursor to Paramount Pictures.

William Fox developed lasting relationships with talent in these early films. *St. Elmo*, a six-reeler released in August 1914, was reportedly directed by Bertram Bracken, who later directed and wrote many Fox films. When Fox decided to make his own films, he sent J. Gordon Edwards to Europe to study methods of film production that could be incorporated into the fledgling American industry. Edwards became Fox's most trusted director until his death, at age 58, on December 31, 1925.

The decision to go into production was a natural progression for William Fox. The theaters he leased and the six distribution exchanges he ran all needed to be supplied with product on a regular basis. By making films, he could rely on his own instincts of what would be popular.

The Eclair studio in Fort Lee, New Jersey, was purchased; contingents of directors, stars and crews were organized, and productions started.[9] Most of the nascent production companies in the early period of five-reelers found source material for movies in novels or plays. In fact, the first 20 William Fox productions, and most others through 1916, were based on established properties, some by popular authors such as Leo Tolstoy and Alexandre Dumas and playwrights Israel Zangwill, David Belasco and Victorien Sardou.

The first official release of a William Fox–produced attraction was *Life's Shop Window* on November 19, 1914. It was based on a popular novel by Victoria Cross and had been purchased for $100. The entire production cost $6,000. The story revolved around an impoverished English orphan who grows up and marries, but almost runs off with another lover before returning to her husband for forgiveness. This, too, became a template for many Fox pictures to come. Fox expunged any suggestive material from the "naughty" book and rendered it moral.[10] *Variety* noted that "without the advance work that the book gave it, [it] would be deemed an ordinary feature, and the renters would have a hard time placing the picture with exhibitors."[11] Reviews aside, the film performed well enough financially.

It was followed one week later by *The Walls of Jericho*, based on a play and starring well-known stage performer Edward José. Having found success with contemporary plays, Fox's next ten releases were also based on stage works. This made sense because the largely immigrant moviegoing public could more easily afford a film's admission than a live performance. And with the heavy concentration of live theater on Broadway, there would be an awareness of the titles in the New York area where Fox had the heaviest concentration of theaters.

Before there was a network of writers dedicated to developing original ideas, scenarios evolved from books and plays. A previously written story that had been worked out in chapters or a three-act structure provided an existing framework and well-developed characters. There were, however, obvious differences between the formats which needed to be addressed. With average films running five reels in length, or approximately one hour, both plays and novels had to be substantially abridged to fit into a film's running time. Much character and thematic development was eliminated in the quest for a simple, coherent plot line. This would continue to be a challenge to screenwriters for decades to come even when films ran longer. Those who could master the skill and write in the language of the cinema would be the ones who prospered in the studio system.

At this time in America, before the growth of a middle class, there were only two extremes in society, the wealthy and the poor. Most of the early William Fox releases were turgid social dramas or even more turgid melodramas, aimed at the masses of less affluence. Almost all stories involved romance, gambling, infidelity, scandal and criminality that interwove the two societal layers. Many elements were mixed and matched over and over again in a never-ending succession of dramatic conflicts. Even when stories were about orphans or the poverty-stricken, there was often a connection to wealth or royalty — either through a secret identity or a last-minute revelation of a higher born birth parent.

Stories made ample use of class differences and the need for "respectable" spouses in marriage. Artists, models, performers, and the idle rich were considered less than desirable. Suicide was also a very common plot device in these films, committed by those too much in love to live or too much out of love to live. Contemporary issues were incorporated as well: a fascination with Russian royalty before the revolution, then anti–Bolshevism after the revolution; the stock market where investors could make or lose large sums even before the great crash of 1929; the belief that hypnotism could make people do things they normally would not do; a trust in modern medicine to heal everything from blindness to criminality; a strong adherence to the ten commandments.

Even before the days of organized censorship, producers incorporated age-old morality plays into their stories. As celebrated and exploited as infidelity and hedonism were in these early films, they were accompanied by a strong moral statement. In *Sins of Men* (1916), a German philosopher becomes famous from his book exalting selfishness and indulgence but his entire family pays the price when they are murdered. When the professor wakes from this nightmare and decides to abandon the book he is writing, the message to audiences was clear.

Fox assessed his audience in retrospect: "The motion picture did not appeal to the native born. He had other forms of recreation and entertainment. The motion picture appealed mainly to the foreign born, who could not speak or understand our tongue, who had no theatre where he could hear his own tongue. He was a Pole, a Russian, a Slav or of some other foreign nationality. He wanted a diversion and found it in the motion picture. It was the money contributed by the foreign born towards the purchase of tickets that enabled the people in the motion picture business at that time to enlarge their scope until the industry grew to such a size that it had a right to expect the respect of the populace of the world."[12]

For the most part, Fox movies gave working class people a keyhole insight into the lives of diplomats, the wealthy and social aristocrats. There were, nonetheless, some anomalies. *Children of the Ghetto* (1915), based on an Israel Zangwill play, dealt with life in the Jewish quarter of New York and depicted the tribulations of an orthodox rabbi who adhered to his religious beliefs even though it led to the dissolution of his family. It was a subject that many Jewish immigrants faced in America from the turn of the century onward and it would appeal to a large audience in the heavily concentrated Jewish communities of New York and New Jersey, where Fox had all his theaters. Nevertheless, *Variety* reviewed it as a picture that would prove a draw "not only among the people with whom it deals, but with anyone who likes a good picture story well played."[13]

Few features risked controversy in the early days of filmmaking, with the notable exception of *The Birth of a Nation* (1915, States Rights), but William Fox produced *The Nigger*, based on a play by Edward Brewster Sheldon, released within a week of the D.W. Griffith production. Aside from its derogatory title, the movie approached its subject in a manner decades ahead of the socially relevant films that would follow in the 1950s and 1960s. It told the story of a well-established Southerner who runs for governor and then, when he wins, decides to sign a bill that would adversely affect powerful vested interests. A businessman who would be impacted by the bill threatens to tell the newspapers that the governor's ancestry includes "Negro" roots. Rather than give in to political adversaries, the governor passes the bill, resigns, and gives up his charmed life to live in the North as one of his own people. It was an unusually progressive and sympathetic story for 1915.

There was also the initial entry of a genre that would become Fox's bread and butter for years to come: the western. *The Girl I Left Behind Me* (1915) was not to be the last story where two rivals fight over a girl. In this case, it was a Cavalry vs. Indians setting with the one of the rival officers for the general's daughter being a villainous coward. The movie version was able to give greater scope to a play written by the legendary and prolific stage writer and producer David Belasco.

One early convention of filmic storytelling was the device of the lookalike, which gave a performer the opportunity of playing two roles in the same film. Theda Bara played two such characters in *Lady Audley's Secret* (1915) as did William Farnum in *The Wonderful Adventure* (1915). Farnum repeated this device in his twin roles in *A Tale of Two Cities* (1917). Meanwhile, Gladys Brockwell played both mother and daughter in *Sins of Her Parents* (1916). Lookalike sisters were also elements of *Sister Against Sister* (1917) with Virginia Pearson, *Tangled Lives* (1917) with Genevieve Hamper, *The Moral Law* (1918) starring Gladys Brockwell in yet another dual role, and *La Belle Russe* (1919) starring Theda Bara. This plot device would be reused many times over the next decade.

With his growing chain of theaters, Fox needed to find enough suitable films for his patrons. His personal tastes influenced his decision to make product for entire families, astutely staying away from off-color subjects, even though some of his critics insisted there were too many sex-drenched stories coming from Box Office Attractions.

William Fox was heavily involved in choosing literary material for his movies: "I was acquainted with every story that was selected by my companies. I read every story they ever produced. I made suggestions in the majority of the stories pro-

An ad for The Box Office Attraction Film Rental Company from a trade magazine in December 1914, several months before the formation of the Fox Film Corporation. Exhibitors are exhorted to "take advantage at once of this chance to work hand-in-hand with master minds of the moving picture world" (courtesy Karl Thiede).

A crowd scene from the William Farnum hit *A Tale of Two Cities* (1917) (courtesy Robert S. Birchard).

duced by our company. In the early years I wrote most of the scenarios. No picture ever produced by the Fox Film Corporation was permitted to be viewed by the general public, until every title it contained had been approved and passed by me, and I don't remember a single picture ever made by the company that the titles contained therein were not corrected, edited and rewritten by me."[14] Fox's assertion that, in the early years, he "wrote most of the scenarios" is highly unlikely. It's more probable that he did view and approve every title card, which was the way silent films communicated descriptions and dialogue to an audience. These could be rewritten after production was completed to clarify the intent of a scene. It is also probable that Fox spent time with the scenarists or directors (sometimes one and the same) and discussed the stories.

Helping Fox was his wife, Eve. A voracious reader, she advised him on which stories to purchase. As Upton Sinclair wrote, "She would tell him a story which she had been reading, and the next day, when he went to the studio, he would talk it off to a stenographer, or maybe tell it to the director, and between them they would put it into continuity, and after they had selected the actors, they would tell it to the actors. All day directors and actors would work, and in the evening, there would be the 'rushes,' and W.F. would inspect them; before long his wife took to coming down and watching these 'rushes,' and helping him to judge whether their dramatic quality had been fully developed." William Fox added, "For five years no one knew the work she was doing, for when the scenarios were submitted, I would pack them up every evening and bring them home to my wife. I remember one story being rejected by her, and the writer of the story then wrote me a letter, saying that his story had just been returned marked 'rejected,' but this was the greatest story he had ever written, and proved that my scenario department was in the hands of incompe-

William Farnum (center, in dark suit and hat) in a lobby card from *A Tale of Two Cities* (1917) (courtesy Mike Hawks).

tents, and he would recommend that I immediately dismiss the party who rejected the story."

There was no doubt, though, that both William and Eve Fox worked very hard to build their business. "It was not a rare occasion that we both left the building at five-thirty or six in the morning. When we were leaving, it was just about the time for the job to open again. Even if we took a brief vacation at Atlantic City, the rushes would be brought down to me every night, and in the morning we would sit in some theatre and view them. I earned what I got; in fact I earned more than I got, because the first year under contract my salary was $1,000, and for the next four years I was to get $10,000 [each year]."[15]

As long as William Fox ran his company, it was a family affair. Brothers-in-law Jack and Joe Leo were assigned to theater operations and another brother, Aaron, was the head of the film lab.

Fox was hiring from non-relatives as well. Winfield R. Sheehan, an overweight jovial Irishman, born in Buffalo in 1883, fought in the Spanish-American War at age 15 before starting out as a reporter on the *Buffalo Courier* in 1901. He then became a police reporter for *New York World* and the *Evening World* between 1902 and 1910. During the administration of New York mayor William J. Gaynor, he was secretary to the fire commissioner, then to the police commissioner.[16] Sheehan built a reputation as a political fixer. Leaving the police as a scandal within the department was about to erupt, Sheehan was hired by Fox on January 1, 1914. The combination of journalism and political smarts allowed Sheehan to exploit a shrewd understanding of human nature. By knowing what people wanted, he was able to gauge what entertainment they would enjoy and later augmented William Fox's showmanship abilities. As entrepreneurial as his boss, Sheehan quickly adapted to the needs of the growing movie industry, exploring opportunities for expanding production and distribution into new areas. He became the company's General Manager and was credited with organizing European and other foreign distribution branches between 1914 and 1921.

Sol M. Wurtzel, another trusted employee for many years to come, was an unemployed bookkeeper who started out as a secretary-stenographer for the Box Office Attraction Company. He worked his way up to private secretary to William Fox. In this capacity, Wurtzel wrote synopses of stories and plays for his boss and studied every aspect of production.

The basic components for what would be a major movie production company were now in place and the future was definitely bright. However, a profile of William Fox in a 1930 issue of *Fortune* magazine pointed out a flaw that would lead to disaster.

> It may be a good thing for a man to start from the bottom, but it is not such a good thing for him to start from the subcellar. For obviously he will be afflicted with a terrible inferiority complex, and although he may make of that very inferiority a driving power forcing him to success, he is bound to do his climbing with a chip on his shoulder and to retain an individualistic and a belligerent attitude long after he has reached the top.[17]

---

2. The Birth of Fox

The Fox Film Corporation was formed on February 1, 1915, with insurance and banking money provided by the McCarter, Kuser and Usar families of Newark and the small New Jersey investment house of Eisele and King. Stock was issued in a 50-50 split between William Fox and his partners. "Two years later, one of the investors decided to cash in on his substantial profits. A delighted William Fox was able to buy this 3 per cent of voting stock, which gave him voting control."[1] John C. Eisele, formerly of Eisele and King, became the company treasurer and remained in that position until his death in 1927. Within 14 years, the original investment of $400,000 in the fledgling company realized dividends of $10,000,000.

William Fox now had the capital to acquire facilities and expand his production capacity. The company leased an old studio in Fort Lee, New Jersey, which became the main hub of activity but, between 1915 and 1919, he also produced films at seven other studios in New Jersey, at Scott's Farm on Staten Island, at four studios in Manhattan and others in Yonkers, the Bronx, and Brooklyn, as well as production work at a rented facility across the street from the Mack Sennett Studios in Edendale, a suburb of Los Angeles.[2]

Fox ramped up his purchases of plays, novels, and the occasional original drama. Of the entire first year of Fox productions, one stood out as a shrewd literary purchase and an even shrewder bit of casting. *A Fool There Was* (1915) had been a popular play based on a poem by Rudyard Kipling. It created a social phenomenon by immortalizing the female "vampire." The term "vamp" entered the cultural lexicon with the story that presented a woman who seduces and ruins a successful, married businessman. Once in her web, she sucks his spirit dry and he ends up a drug addict and alcoholic. His fate is one of torment and suicide. The movie became a milestone by creating the first real star for the Fox Film Corporation. William Fox related the genesis of the casting to Upton Sinclair, an influential novelist and investigative journalist of the 1920s and 1930s.

> Before making "A Fool There Was," I consulted Robert Hilliard, who had produced it on the stage and played the leading role for years. He said, "In my experience, I have had to change my leading lady six times. As soon as one scored a tremendous hit in the part, she believed herself to be a Sarah Bernhardt and became unmanageable, and I had to let her go. My advice would be to put the girl you choose under contract, as the part will make her." We made a test of a girl called Theodosia Goodman, who had no theatrical experience, and decided she would do. She was the daughter of a tailor in Cincinnati. Miss Goodman gave a very remarkable performance in this picture; and then came our problem. If we were going to continue her services, the name didn't have quite the theatrical feeling, and we must find a stage name for her.[3]

The name they chose was Theda Bara.

Bara did become more demanding as her stardom increased and, within six months, William Fox would sign Broadway star Valeska Suratt, at $2,500 weekly, to remind the temperamental Bara that anyone was expendable. But the original vamp's fame could not be equaled between 1915 and 1919, during which time she made 40 films for the Fox Film Corporation. Bara even outlasted Valeska Suratt who left the studio in 1917. Suratt brought along her own set of problems. Her high-strung temperament led William Fox to film the last part of one of her movies first, in case she decided to walk out before production was finished.

There were not a lot of prominent stars in the movies of the mid-teens, with Mary Pickford, Charlie Chaplin, Douglas Fairbanks, William S. Hart and Theda Bara among the most famous, but William Fox concentrated all his efforts on creating "star vehicles" that would make his per-

A very rare original lobby card for *A Fool There Was* (1915), starring Theda Bara, from the Box Office Attraction Company (courtesy Mike Hawks).

formers famous and then exploited their contracts to maximum potential. This was evident in his other releases of 1915. There were *A Celebrated Scandal, Anna Karenina, A Woman's Resurrection,* and *The Song of Hate* all starring Betty Nansen, considered Denmark's Sarah Bernhardt. William Farnum, a seasoned Shakespearean stage actor, could handle drama or outdoor adventure equally well. He appeared in *Samson, A Gilded Fool, The Wonderful Adventure* (in which he played a dual role), *The Broken Law,* and *A Soldier's Oath.* Meanwhile, Theda Bara appeared regularly in Fox Films: *The Clemenceau Case, The Devil's Daughter, Lady Audley's Secret, The Two Orphans, Sin, Carmen, The Galley Slave,* and *Destruction*—almost one a month between January and December 1915.

With a total negative cost of $53,250 for four

Theda Bara in an early publicity photograph, circa 1915, suggesting her dark powers over men (courtesy Robert S. Birchard).

productions in 1914, the Box Office Attraction Rental Company had shown rentals of $272,401. Increased to one release every second week at the beginning of 1915 and ramping up to almost one new release a week by the end of the year, the newly founded Fox Film Corporation was able to turn out 26 features with a negative cost of $767,243. Rentals on those films, however, exploded to $3,208,201. The business was lucrative for Fox Films when a release returned a profit as this sample shows:

Rentals		$100,000
Distribution	less	35,000
Negative cost	less	25,000
Prints and advertising	less	10,000
Returns to producer		$30,000

The industry had determined that a 35 percent distribution fee would cover the costs of keeping a sales staff and exchange office, which amounted to approximately 25 percent of the rentals. A 10 percent profit was built in and the 35 percent fee became pretty much an industry standard over the years. (This fee remained in place until the superstar producer/directors of the 1970s and 1980s, by the names of Lucas and Spielberg, were able to use their earning potential to jawbone down the distribution charges.)

William Fox would carefully watch the outgoing production costs to make sure incoming rentals were greater. Never a profligate spender, he was also very conservative in his choice of film stories and rarely gambled more than he felt he could lose.

It became clear by mid–1915 that there was not an inexhaustible supply of affordable plays and novels to feed the production pipeline. It was inevitable that Fox would have to develop original stories, especially since many of his films would be tailored to the stars under contract. With *Should a Mother Tell?*, Fox embarked on this path. Written by Rex Ingram, later one of the industry's most successful directors, the scenario involved a typical William Fox–supervised story: a mother suffers the guilt of not telling the truth in a murder case to allow her daughter to marry the man she loves. Having been strongly influenced by intense family values, Fox's movies very often reflected the long-suffering efforts of parents to provide for and protect their offspring.

Original stories were less expensive and provided the company with complete ownership. While there were only eight original scenarios for all of 1915, the number increased to 35 the following year. Some directors like Herbert Brenon,

Betty Nansen in a lobby card for *The Celebrated Scandal* (1915) (courtesy Robert S. Birchard).

Raoul Walsh, J. Gordon Edwards, Will S. Davis, Oscar Apfel, and John G. Adolfi received writing credits for their films, some originals and some adaptations.

Scenarists who could craft terse original stories quickly and efficiently could be enlisted from the stage or from novel writing. But some of the most successful came from journalism, as did the most successful writers in the talkies era. E. Lloyd Sheldon, who wrote 18 scripts for Fox between 1917 and 1920, had been a reporter for the *New York Globe* and was later the Washington correspondent for the *New York American*. By 1917, he had contributed 150 short stories, novelettes and articles to national magazines and 48 feature films. Ralph Spence started as the general manager of the *Houston Daily Telegram* before writing for the Fox Studio in 1917. He received credit, after several features, for film editing and title-card writing on a dozen features through 1923. Adrian Johnson, writer of some of Fox's highest-grossing films (including *Checkers* [1919] and many starring Theda Bara, including *Romeo and Juliet* [1916], *The Tiger Woman* [1917], *Madame DuBarry* [1917], *Cleopatra* [1917], *The Soul of Buddha* [1918], *Salome* [1919], and *When Men Desire* [1919]), had not been a journalist but was trained as a commercial secretary. With 28 credits, Jules G. Furthman, formerly a newspaper and magazine writer, was at Fox from 1918 to 1923, and started directing his scripts in 1921 before returning exclusively to writing. With more than 30 scenarios between 1917 and 1924, Charles Kenyon had also initially been a journalist. Starting as a short-story writer and novelist, Denison Clift wrote 23 scenarios for Fox between 1918 and 1920. All of these writers were born in the 1880s and had time to develop their craft just as the movie industry was in need of more original scenarios.

Screenwriting, unlike directing, was not the exclusive domain of men. British-born scenarist Mary Murillo (a pseudonym), who began her Fox career in 1915, turned out 13 scripts in 1916 for a variety of melodramas. Many of these were written for leading ladies like Theda Bara, Virginia Pearson, and Bertha Kalich. Murillo would eventually complete a total of 26 produced scenarios before leaving Fox in 1922 and was one of the early company's most prolific screenwriters.

An inventory of company-owned stories, whether original or purchased, became invaluable when studios recycled previously written material into remakes. When William Fox wanted to remake his 1916 version of *Merely Mary Ann* four years later, he had to renegotiate with playwright Israel Zangwill. By 1920, Fox was savvy enough not to make another one-time deal with royalty payments. He secured the film rights to the play into perpetuity. The deal paid off again when the studio made a third version of the story with sound in 1931.

Aside from purchasing rights to plays or novels and developing original stories, Fox made movies of classics that were in the public domain and not covered by copyright, a good example being *Romeo and Juliet* (1916). Public domain subjects,

Theda Bara emerges from her dressing room with her entourage during the production of *Madame DuBarry* (1917) (courtesy Robert S. Birchard).

however, carried risks as well. They were available to any producer, as William Fox discovered when Metro's $112,930 production of *Romeo and Juliet* (1916) debuted two weeks before his less-extravagant version which cost $39,039. In the days before films were heavily advertised, audiences had only a title and perhaps a star name to lure them into a theater. Audiences that had recently attended the Metro version would not go back to see a Fox version shortly after. However, since film playoff patterns were different and could take many months to cover the entire country, certain venues other than the major cities would run either the Fox or Metro version first. The net result was not advantageous to either company.

Fox was in the same position when he starred Theda Bara in *Carmen* and released it the same week as a Lasky presentation starring operatic soprano Geraldine Farrar. Learning from the results of these two competing productions, Fox and other studios would steer clear of simultaneous versions of the same story.

If 1915 was important to the Fox Film Corporation as its year of incorporation, 1916 had several watershed moments as well. Since production in New York was difficult during the winter months, Fox moved several films to a facility in Kingston, Jamaica. Included in this group were Herbert Brenon's *The Ruling Passion*, J. Gordon Edwards's *A Wife's Sacrifice*, *A Woman's Honor*, and the spectacular *A Daughter of the Gods*. Fox also released his first film shot in Los Angeles, *Fighting Blood*, directed by Oscar Apfel and starring William Farnum.

The motion picture industry was growing in California. Production companies operating in Los Angeles in 1916 included the Universal Film Manufacturing Company, Nestor, Biograph, Reliance Motion Picture Company, and the Famous Players Film Company. The Flying "A" Studios was operating out of Santa Barbara and Balboa Amusement Producing Company was making films in Long Beach.

William Fox wanted to have centralized production facilities on both coasts that would allow for more financial and creative control. In 1916, he traveled to Los Angeles and bought a 13-acre site with production capabilities at the intersection of Western Avenue and Sunset Boulevard for $180,000 from W.C. Frye,[4] a Hollywood pioneer, and Thomas Dixon, author of *The Clansman*, the play which was adapted as *The Birth of a Nation*. The new facility was named the William Fox Studio. Surrounded on two sides by lemon groves, the lot was divided almost in half by Western Avenue, with its original Victorian farmhouse and three bungalows used as office buildings. A sculpted stucco wall designed in Mission Revival style formed a perimeter around the inner production areas. There were two glass stages which allowed in light (but became sweatboxes during peak summer months) as well as two wooden and six open-air stages.

Los Angeles also provided many different environments for location shooting, especially for westerns, a genre that proved to be highly profitable in the next decade. The West Coast studio got around the problems of sending crews to temporary facilities in Miami, Florida or Kingston, Jamaica, when winter precluded outdoor shooting in the northeast.

Fox installed Abraham Carlos as his manager to supervise the production of features on the eastern side of the lot. On the western sector of the lot, two-reel Sunshine Comedies were filmed. Twenty-three of these were released in the 1916-1917 season. With temperate weather for year-round production, the slate of releases could depend more on outdoor stories and less on drawing-room melodramas.

Theda Bara's films continued to be popular and profitable although critics were tiring of her "vamp" persona. Veering from that overused theme, Bara starred in *Her Double Life* (1916) directed by J. Gordon Edwards from an original scenario by Mary Murillo. The story takes place in England during World War I (which was now becoming a more common story element in movies two years into the war). Bara plays a woman who takes on a false identity to escape a war correspondent who previously tried to seduce her. When she falls in love again, the correspondent is about to expose her, but she tells the truth and then ends up happily. This represented a major departure from her more nefarious roles. However, Bara starred in *The Vixen* (1916) just a few months later in which she played a spoiled nymphomaniac.

There were also westerns like *The Mediator* (1916) starring George Walsh, brother of director Raoul Walsh, as a gunfighter who just wants to live a peaceable life in a small town (more than 30 years ahead of the Gregory Peck classic, *The Gunfighter*). Since revolution in Mexico was a contemporary topic, Fox filmed an outdoor adventure, *The Love Thief* (1916), in which a beautiful rebel who, to get even with an American Army officer for spurning her, has him and his

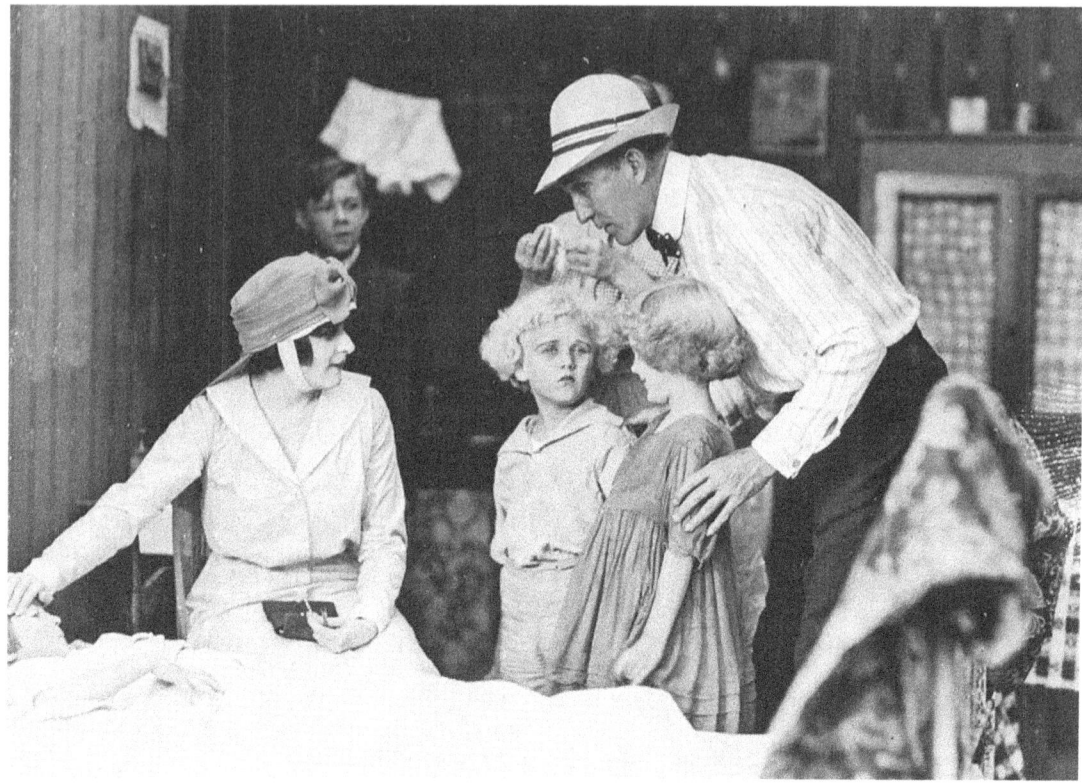

J. Gordon Edwards (right) directing juvenile Jane Lee (center), Theda Bara (left) and an unidentified young actress in *Her Double Life* (1916) (courtesy Robert S. Birchard).

girlfriend arrested. Fortunately, the Americans are rescued when an army raid on the rebel encampment frees them.

One notable failure of the year was *A Daughter of the Gods* (1916), directed by Herbert Brenon and starring Australian champion swimmer Annette Kellerman. The statuesque aquatic star appeared in what were then considered skimpy bathing suits and the film even contained some controversial nudity in an Arabian fantasy setting, complete with sheiks and harems.

Perturbed by the length of production of this film in Jamaica, William Fox sent J. Gordon Edwards to the location to check up on director Herbert Brenon. Edwards came back and reassured Fox that Brenon was handling the assignment well.[5] After editing, though, Fox was so displeased with the final result that he recut the film. There was even a reported rift between Fox and director Brenon that resulted in the latter not being invited to the premiere in New York.[6] The presentation of this two-hour, ten-reel feature, which was culled from a reported 200,000 feet of film, was enhanced by a musical score performed with the picture in major cities. It was a step towards a form of theatrical presentation known as the "road show." While the initial world rentals for *A Daughter of the Gods* reached an extremely high $532,000, it still failed to meet expectations. Fox reissued it one year later but still did not return the production to profitability. So, there was yet another release in February 1920. With all this effort, the film ended up losing $178,000 on its enormous $500,000 cost.

Production costs in this period for an average film ran to about $1,000 per day of shooting. Most films had a production schedule of three to four weeks which placed budgets in the $20,000 to $30,000 range. The Fox Film Corporation, in 1916, was able to turn out 52 features with an average length of five reels for a total negative cost of $1,289,785. Rentals rose once again to $4,244.658, but unnerving to William Fox was the fact that production costs rose to 30.4 percent of rentals, up from 19.5 percent in 1914.

There were many reasons why films were costing more. Talent, always a negotiable commodity, was demanding greater salaries. Even sets and the

Six cameras are ready to roll on location in Florida for the production of *A Daughter of the Gods* (1916). Cameraman J. Roy Hunt is standing at the third camera from the right. Another cameraman, Marcel LePicard, is at the second camera from the right and in the inset (courtesy Robert S. Birchard).

materials to build them were costing more. Ambitious productions swallowed up more shooting days and time was money. Even with all the rises in production expenses, the movie industry was still expanding with greater attendance every year and increased revenues.

Fox purchased the Los Angeles property, and reportedly did not venture back to the West Coast for nearly ten years. However, a New York newspaper article from April 1917 reports that Fox was once again in Los Angeles and purchased an additional 49 acres adjacent to the existing studio where several outdoor stages and one large glass covered stage were added. The additional facilities would allow 12 companies to work simultaneously. There were other changes, as well.

> Mr. Fox did not find the conditions at the studios as he expected and, as a result, made a great many changes in the personnel of the producing forces there. A number of directors as well as actors appearing in Fox comedy productions were given their release.
>
> Raoul Walsh, who has been considered the premier director of the Fox producing organization in California, will move his headquarters from the coast to New York.... William Farnum, considered the leading male star of the Fox organization, will also come East and, in the future, make his productions at the Fort Lee studios. Frank Lloyd, who has been directing the Farnum pictures on the coast, will come East with the star and the rest of the Farnum company.
>
> With the transference of these two directors to the East, two other directors and their companies will take their places in the West. J. Gordon Edwards, who has been directing Theda Bara will, with the completion of a production he is working on at present, proceed to the coast with Miss Bara and her company. This company is to occupy the studios vacated by Walsh.
>
> John G. Adolphi [*sic*], who is directing June Caprice, will also take his company to the coast studios.[7]

In an executive change of this period, William Fox, dissatisfied with Abe Carlos's performance as general manager, sent his personal secretary, Sol M. Wurtzel, to take charge of the Los Angeles facilities in October 1917. Carlos would never

Unidentified actors in a scene from the elaborate *Daughter of the Gods* (1916) (courtesy Robert S. Birchard).

again have a position of such prestige. For the rest of his career, until his death in 1930, he was limited to the periphery of the industry. Wurtzel was made general superintendant of the lot and as such, worked with directors in developing stories, was involved in finding talent, and handled the myriad details of the production unit. There was no doubt that William Fox remained in charge from New York as each film began with the credit "William Fox Presents."

Wurtzel kept his boss apprised of every development in lengthy memos and telegrams regarding the status of productions, costs, and relations with talent. Fox responded in kind and both men discussed the daily operations on a micro-management level. Aside from the occasional West Coast visit by the corporation's General Manager, Winfield Sheehan, the operation of the Los Angeles studio was primarily run by Fox and Wurtzel.

After Wurtzel's arrival, Fox would send existing "companies" out to the coast from New York; these were comprised of a director, star and support staff. At this time, there was a larger pool of talent, largely from the stage, in the East. Since film production had more time to mature in New York, the "companies" would already have experience in shooting films. When Wurtzel had enough story material, custom tailored to a performer or director, another company would be sent. Production at the Sunset-Western studio was increased gradually so that films were shot using the most cost-efficient methods.

The degree of control imposed by William Fox and Sol Wurtzel precluded the company from hiring the more celebrated directors of the period, namely Cecil B. DeMille and David W. Griffith. While considered the foremost creators of cinema, both worked with complete control over the movies they made and little regard to the type of penurious schedules that the Fox Film Corporation allowed. Fox held contracts with directors who were more amenable to management: Raoul Walsh, Bertram Bracken, J. Gordon Edwards, Sidney and Chester Franklin, Edward J. LeSaint, Frank Lloyd, Kenean Buel, Richard Stanton, Harry Millarde, and Carl Harbaugh.

With film production churning away on both coasts, the Fox Film Corporation was able to produce an average of 70 features a year between 1917 and 1920. Perhaps 1917 could be called the year of the original scenario at Fox since an overwhelming majority of films — 53 — were original works, either initiated by film writers or directors. The economics and control of creating a story from the ground up was unavoidably appealing to William Fox.

William Fox launched a series of "kiddie" pictures which he felt would draw in entire families and inoculate youth from the depredations of a Theda Bara or Valeska Suratt. Turning to public-domain subjects, Fox had directors Chester and Sidney Franklin turn out *Jack and the Beanstalk* (1917) and *Aladdin and the Wonderful Lamp* (1917). Both were more expensive than the average production because they took longer to shoot with a cast that was made up mainly of children. Fox also starred five-year-old Jane Lee, who had been in several previous supporting roles, as the lead in *Two Little Imps* (1917) and *Troublemakers* (1917), along with her ten-year-old sister Katherine. The Lee sisters would continue in a series of successful films. Unwilling to give up on the fairy tale series which lost money after *Jack and the Beanstalk*, William Fox authorized other kiddie pictures including *The Babes in the Woods* (1917), *Treasure Island* (1918), and *Ali Baba and the Forty Thieves* (1918). During the production of these Franklin company pictures, the "boys" developed an acrimonious relationship with William Fox.

Sol Wurtzel, who had originally gone to bat for the Franklins, ultimately reported production

A scene from the kiddie production ***Ali Baba and the Forty Thieves*** (1918), with child stars (from left to right) Marie Messinger, Georgie Stone and Gertrude Messinger huddling together (courtesy Robert S. Birchard).

Another kiddie production, *Fan Fan* (1918), starring Buddy Messinger (left) and Francis Carpenter (courtesy Robert S. Birchard).

difficulties with the company as well. Wurtzel came around to agreeing with his boss that the Franklins were more interested in furthering their own careers than in the goals of the Fox Film Corporation. He admitted that he had been wrong in originally disagreeing with William Fox and supplied ample evidence. Determined to escape studio control and against Wurtzel's advice, Chester Franklin, dismissive of the cost involved, had gone on location more than a hundred miles from Los Angeles when the same scenes could have been achieved at the Sunset-Western lot.[8]

Aside from directors going off on location, there was the issue of lengthened production schedules. From the average shoot of 18 to 24 days some films were going far longer. Two films starring young children involved extended production times. *Ali Baba and the Forty Thieves* had a schedule of 35 days and *Fan Fan* (1918), based on *The Mikado*, filmed for a costly 65 days.

One of the more unusual uses of public domain material in 1917 was a modern version of the Victor Hugo classic *The Hunchback of Notre Dame*, first published in 1831. In *The Darling of Paris*, directed by J. Gordon Edwards and starring Theda Bara, a scientist is in love with Esmeralda. Quasimodo is a former hunchback, cured by the scientist who comes to Esmeralda's rescue. Tellingly, Fox felt no allegiance to the original and gave no credit to Monsieur Hugo.

Wife Number Two (1917) was yet another update of a public domain novel, in this case, Gustave Flaubert's *Madame Bovary*, published in 1857, again without any reference to the original. In this version, starring Valeska Suratt as the hopelessly doomed heroine, character names are the same as Flaubert's except the eponymous female lead is known as Emma Bovar. Without taking advantage of the intrinsic classic value of the original, the production raised the ire of the *Variety* reviewer who caustically wrote, "The idea is moss eaten with age and provides a wonderful argument for original screen literature."[9]

Humming along with 70 releases in 1917 meant

June Caprice in a lobby card from *Miss Innocence* (1917) (courtesy Mike Hawks).

that Fox very quickly formularized their productions. Virtually the entire year's slate of releases was simply a pattern of star vehicles. Gladys Brockwell, a leading lady in her second year at Fox, headlined seven films including *One Touch of Sin*, *Her Temptation*, *To Honor and Obey*, *The Soul of Satan* and *A Branded Soul*. It is probably no coincidence that the titles sounded much like Theda Bara films, tapping into the same lucrative audience. Appearing in six features each were action adventure star George Walsh, vivacious young June Caprice, William Farnum and Valeska

J. Gordon Edwards at Theda Bara's feet, circa 1917 (courtesy Robert S. Birchard).

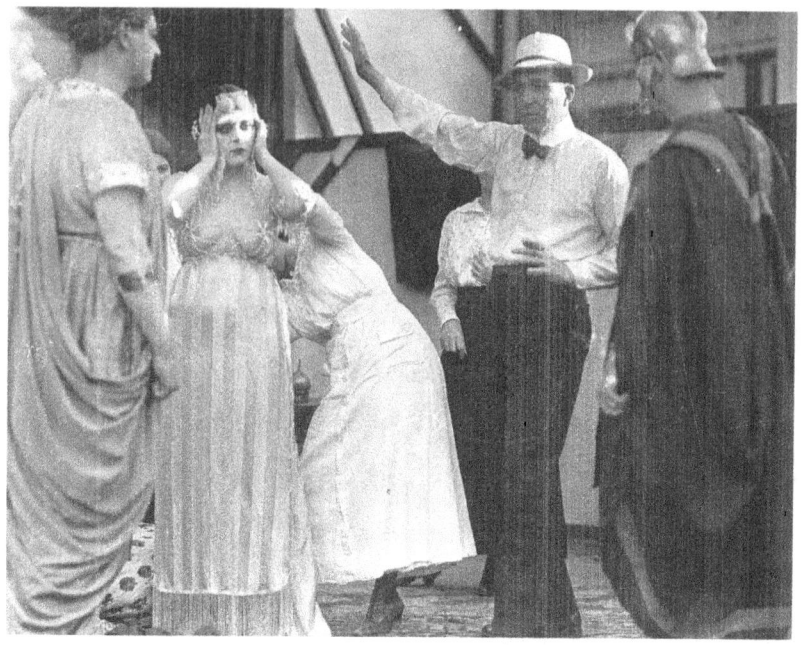

J. Gordon Edwards (right) directing Theda Bara (center) and Thurston Hall (left) during the production of *Cleopatra* (1917). Bara's costume is exposing more than it should in this candid shot (courtesy Robert S. Birchard).

Suratt. Well-respected stage personality Virginia Pearson starred in five films.

Once again, the most ubiquitous Fox star of the year was Theda Bara, the leading lady of eight films, including the high-budgeted (for those days) $300,000 production of *Cleopatra* (1917). Obviously influenced by the spectacle of D.W. Griffith's *Intolerance* (1916), William Fox decided to make an exception to his cookie-cutter method of production and provided an anomalous budget to his trusted director J. Gordon Edwards on the Bara film: "From a scenic standpoint, also, it is quite a triumph. The Sphinx, the pyramids and a goodly section of Rome are duly duplicated, and the larger scenes are handled in a way that suggests D.W. Griffith." Bara's notices were indicative of contemporary acting styles: "The star, by dint of much rolling of eyes and many other manoeuvres contributes a thoroughly successful portrait of 'the serpent of the Nile, the siren of the ages, and the eternal feminine,' in the words of the screen, and thus does the ill-starred Queen of Egypt become the well-starred queen of movies."[10]

Not every film needed a huge budget to be successful. The true story of a humane prison warden who tries to reform the treatment of prisoners came to the screen as *The Honor System*, a film for which story rights cost $250. Starring Milton Sills, a stage actor just beginning his illustrious screen career, and directed by Raoul Walsh, this socially conscious film resulted in hugely successful rentals of $500,000. *Variety* called it "a virile, soul-stirring, heart-interest story, plenty of clean, healthy comedy, natural-unforced scenes of the underworld, life in the wild, untamed west, city political intriguing and some harrowing visualization of prison life and cruelty as it exists in some states without finding it necessary to pile on the agony to an undue degree."[11]

Slapstick comedy, which had been developed by Mack Sennett and comic performers like Charlie Chaplin, Ben Turpin, Mabel Normand, and Harold Lloyd, had become a staple of many theater programs but not generally as feature-length films with the rare exception of the six-reeler *Tillie's Punctured Romance* (1914) starring Marie Dressler and Chaplin. Comedies were generally limited to one or two reels, and at Fox Films this form of entertainment, released as Sunshine Comedies, was allocated to the separate production domain on the eastern side of the Los Angeles studio.

Under the guidance of Henry Lehrman, the first installment, *Roaring Lions and Wedding Bliss*, starring the popular comic actor Lloyd Hamilton, was released in January 1917. *Variety* reviewed it very favorably:

> The Sunshine lives up to its trademark. It not only casts a laughing ray from start to finish, but it also has some uproariously funny scenes in which wild animals have as much prominence as the men and women in the film.... [Henry] Lehrman has staged and directed thousands of funny scenes and directed innumerable camera "bits," but he seems to have outdone himself with his first Sunshine.... All sorts of mixups, confusions, chases, monkeyshines, clashes, jams, roughhouse, slapstick, photographic tricks, illusions, legitimate screen artifice, natural didoes and the Lord knows whatnot are utilized in making the Sunshine subject rank among the best in modern day film comedies.[12]

Theda Bara as Cleopatra with unidentified actors (1917) (courtesy Robert S. Birchard).

There were 23 Sunshine Comedies released in the 1916-1917 season, and 18 in the 1917-1918 season, but only 12 in 1918-1919 when there were organizational changes made in the division as Hampton Del Ruth replaced Lehrman.

A candid photograph of Theda Bara between takes on the production of *Cleopatra* (1917) *(courtesy* Robert S. Birchard).

Since the European market for films was not especially developed in 1917, the war in Europe did not greatly impact the bottom line for American film producers. On April 6, 1917, against the wishes of many Americans who wanted to remain neutral, the United States joined its allies Britain, France, and Russia to fight Germany. There was an immediate effect on American audiences. For a while, some moviegoers stayed away from theaters, feeling the guilt of seeking pleasure while the world was at war. Under the command of Major General John J. Pershing, more than two million U.S. soldiers fought on battlefields in France and as the death toll mounted, the mood of the country darkened.

War or no war, stories, plays and novels were constantly being purchased in both Los Angeles and New York. Sol Wurtzel developed the scenarios that were to be filmed by his companies with directors or writers, just as William Fox and Winfield Sheehan did in New York. When the scenarios were completed in Los Angeles they were sent to New York for William Fox's approval, sometimes after production had begun. This was necessary to keep a steady flow of production in the pipeline. To provide a program of 60–70 features annually, and considering shooting schedules of three to five weeks on average, there had to be several new productions ready to begin every week. When a film completed shooting, it was edited quickly, a negative was cut and both the final positive print and cut negative were sent to New York for approval. On several occasions, William Fox refused to release a picture as it had been cut in Los Angeles and sent it back for reshooting. When a feature was delayed, there were always several others in production at the same time to move into release slots. The Fox Film Corporation had reached a level of providing theaters with at least one new title every week of the year.

For 1917, rentals increased to $7,118,172 on negative costs of $2,964,696 with the help of foreign revenues of $1,114,068 from branch offices in South America, New Zealand, Australia and Cuba, which were unaffected by the war in Europe.

Since Fox Theaters only represented certain territories in the eastern United States, many other theater bookings were needed to allow a film to earn back its costs. The Fox slate had to appeal to independent theater owners in large cities across the country, as well as smaller venues. It was incumbent upon the company to release a regular slate of pictures that could be booked into as many theaters as possible, extracting the maximum rental from each location.

Fox's plans for his release schedule for the movie season of 1918-1919 included three levels of production, all created around the films' stars. The Standard Brand boasted the highest quality and brought in the highest rentals. The Victory Brand was an intermediary level and the Excel Brand was an entry level for acting talent which was contracted to theaters at lower rentals. The schedule called for 26 Standard Pictures, eight with William Farnum, eight with Theda Bara, and ten special pictures without stars to be selected and assigned directors "based on a vitally important subject that is being discussed universally."[13] By William Fox's own description to Sol Wurtzel, the non-star stories "under the STANDARD heading will have to be well planned, well mapped out, and agreed on here in New York before I want you to decide on any picture that will go in under that heading."[14]

The category of "special picture" would not depend on star power but instead on the content and quality of the story as well as the director's skill. The stories for such films would have to be carefully selected to have maximum appeal and be chosen with its audience in mind. Fox was hoping that one of his producing "companies" would find an appropriate story, craft it properly and ultimately complete that film at little cost which would maximize the chance for profits.[15]

Some examples of previous special productions without established stars, enumerated by William Fox in a letter to Sol Wurtzel, were *The Honor System* (1917), based on a timely book, was a success; *Cheating the Public* (1918), a crude melodrama about workers abused by a food monopoly, a subject whose time had passed by the time of release, was a failure; *Jack and the Beanstalk* (1917), a successful venture which ushered in other kiddie pictures; *Woman and the Law* (1918), based on a contemporary legal case but was a financial failure; *Blindness of Divorce* (1918), a financial failure because it did not turn out to be as controversial as William Fox hoped; and *Why I Would Not Marry* (1918), which everyone at the New York office thought would be a remarkable picture, but it turned out to be a flop.[16]

There would also be 26 Victory Brand pictures featuring four films with George Walsh, several with an as-yet undiscovered woman "of especial merit and value who has a splendid reputation, and for whose services the Fox Film Corporation would be willing to pay a handsome price, if she were the woman that all our exchanges would agree on as having special value in their territory."[17]

One member of the Victory Brand was an exceptionally capable horseman named Tom Mix who was already starring in films at the Selig studio in Edendale when Fox leased that facility in 1916.[18] In 1917, William Fox hired Mix at $350 weekly to write, direct and star in two-reel comedies. In his first Fox feature role in 1917, Mix co-starred in the Dustin Farnum vehicle, *Durand of the Bad Lands*. He then took the leap to leading man in *Cupid's Roundup* in January 1918, a film originally slated for George Walsh. Mix's popularity kept growing so that it was to Fox's advantage to star him in six features in the pipeline of product.

The Excel Brand featured films with Gladys Brockwell and Virginia Pearson, each of whom starred in six releases during 1918. Jewel Carmen, an attractive ingénue, started out at Mack Sennett's Keystone Studio in 1912. She began her Fox

Jewel Carmen and William Farnum in *When a Man Sees Red* (1917) (courtesy Robert S. Birchard).

for "vamp" types. In an effort to find an actress comparable to Mary Pickford, he signed graceful, petite June Caprice. She appeared in 16 films for Fox between 1916 and 1919, three of which were released in 1918. Caprice later married the director of many of her films, Harry Millarde.

With the exception of the few non-star special subjects, Fox's output was wholly based upon the acting talent under contract, and the main objective was to develop more stars since audiences responded most vigorously to their favorite performers. Naturally, cost would be a factor in each of the brands. Fox wanted Wurtzel to adhere to budget limits of $15,000 to $18,000 for the Excel Brand and about the same for the Victory Brand. Fox did make an exception, however, in the case of the Victory Brand. Rather than sacrifice the story to budget limitations, he agreed to spend additional money as long as the production would merit it.[21] The Standard Brand, with

career as a female lead in several films, some with William Farnum, then graduated briefly to the lead in five Excel releases in 1918. There was also Peggy Hyland, an English-born actress, in her thirties, who was signed to a Fox contract in late December 1917, after William Fox checked out her popularity with his exchanges. Hyland was hired at $300 weekly, down from the $1,000 salary she received at Vitagraph, and appeared in five 1918 releases.[19]

The purpose of having three different brands of films made it possible to introduce stars to audiences in the lower cost Excel brand then advance them to the Victory brand. If they proved successful in the Victory picture they would advance yet again to the Standard Picture brand. This way, Fox was regularly building up new stars without spending too much money.[20]

Fox did not only search

Peggy Hyland in a lobby card from *Bonnie Annie Laurie* (1918) (courtesy Mike Hawks).

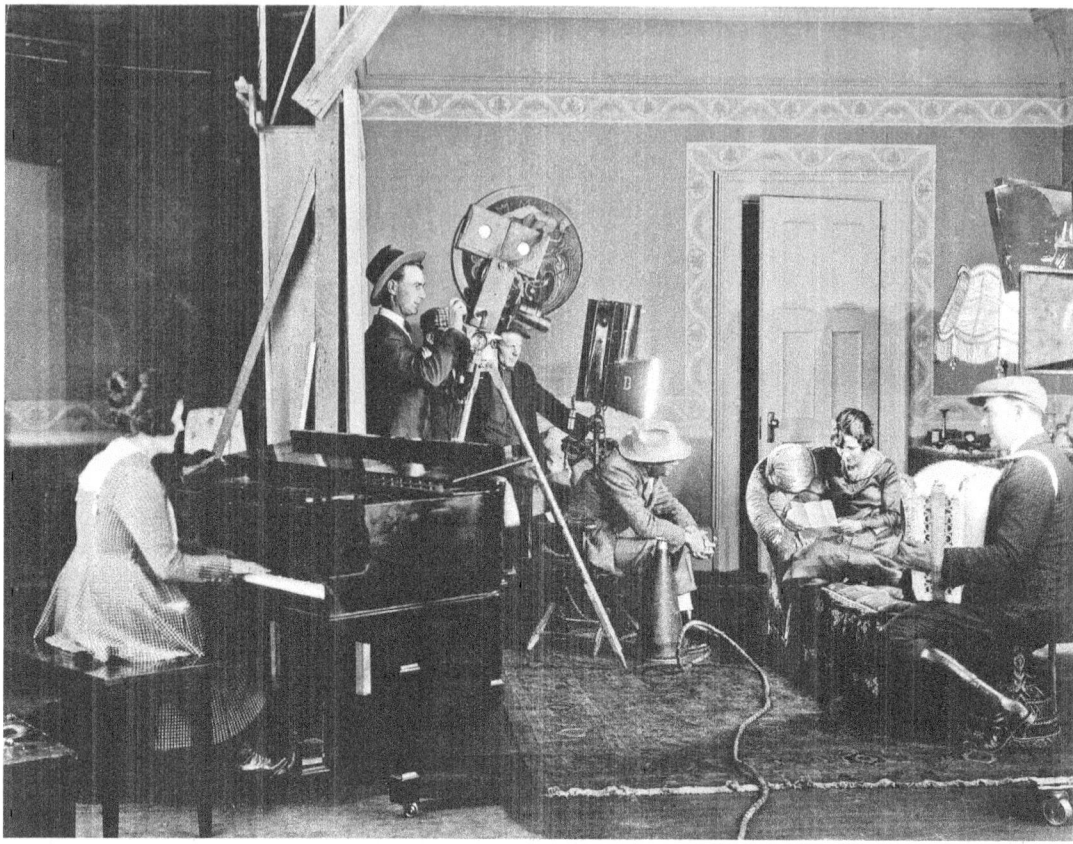

A typical set during filming in the late teens. Notice the musical accompaniment to set the mood (courtesy Robert S. Birchard).

stars like Theda Bara and William Farnum, would be allotted the highest budgets.

One controversial figure William Fox starred in a half dozen movies was Evelyn Nesbit Thaw, a young beauty, infamous as the mistress of famed New York architect Stanford White, who was shot to death in 1908 atop Madison Square Garden by Thaw's jealous millionaire husband. The ensuing "trial of the century" left Thaw penniless and she ended up appearing as a novelty in vaudeville shows as "the girl in the red velvet swing." To add to the morbid curiosity about her, she starred in *The Woman Who Gave* (1918) with her young son, Russell. (In 1955, 20th Century–Fox later made *The Girl in the Red Velvet Swing* about the Thaw-White murder starring Joan Collins as Evelyn Nesbit.)

At a time when productions could be rushed from the writing stage through delivery of a final negative in a matter of several months, there were still pitfalls in pursuing stories dealing with contemporary issues. Four of 1918's releases were not financial successes because they missed the timeliness of a story: *The Caillaux Case* failed because war intervened and audiences were not interested in the case; *The Prussian Cur*, *Why America Will Win* and *Every Mother's Son*, all of which were about the war which ended, shortening their box-office life. Sometimes, it paid to purchase a successful play like *Checkers*, which had been published and read for 25 years. The original story rights cost a considerable $3,000, but rentals on the film reached $500,000.

Yet another unexpected obstacle to box-office grosses hit the industry when, in 1918, there was a global outbreak of Spanish flu, which ended up killing more than 20 million people worldwide. The epidemic hit New York City in March and resulted in theaters closing their doors to avoid the spread of disease. Studios, too, were affected and many, including Fox, trimmed staff to a minimum. Some producers completely shut down operations for a month.

Even with these setbacks, the annual industry-wide grosses continued to climb, albeit less spectacularly. At Fox, with a record 73 features in release in 1918 at a production cost of $3,212,684, an increase of 10 percent over the previous year, revenues rose a minimal 2 percent to $7,300,301.

With the enormous cash outlay for the year's productions, almost half of revenues, William Fox became ever more concerned about the rise in budgets. The cost of everything was increasing due to the wartime economy. A new ½-cent war tax on negative and positive film imposed in January 1918 led Fox to closely watch the amount of film shot on the East Coast and he implored Sol Wurtzel to do the same on the West Coast. Fox insisted that the length of films not exceed 4,500 feet so that the standard release order of 70 prints for the domestic market (U.S. and Canada) would not be excessively costly.

Before there was an adequate technical procedure to duplicate negatives, films were shot with two cameras to provide an extra negative for foreign markets. Fox also issued an edict that the amount of stock to be used should not exceed 20,000 feet for both negatives. This meant that directors would have a shooting ratio of approximately two to one to achieve usable takes. It was a very limiting requirement for production units and one not readily adhered to. Examples of directors who pleased Fox were Edward J. LeSaint who made *Cupid's Roundup* (1918) using 30,000 feet of negative, and Bertram Bracken who brought in *For Liberty* (1917) with just 17,000 feet for two negatives.[22]

Aside from the pressure of dealing with cost controls, Wurtzel found that talent could be uncooperative and temperamental. Jewel Carmen was unreliable and would not show up on production days. Her personal life impinged on her work and occasionally required the services of a private detective hired by the studio.

Most directors who signed with Fox Films for Los Angeles production were quickly subjugated by Sol Wurtzel. However, not all were easily corralled. Chester Franklin, in particular, continued to be a thorn in the side of his bosses. In the case of *The Girl with Champagne Eyes*, Wurtzel had to deal with not only Jewel Carmen, but also Franklin and his writer Bernard McConville. William Fox was especially annoyed with this film because on a negative cost of $38,000 "there is nothing contained in this story that should have cost over $15,000."[23] Fox angrily dismissed Chester Franklin's objections to the New York office's decision to recut his film in a letter to Sol Wurtzel:

The final judgment with reference to any picture made by the Fox Film Corporation, you ought to know, is left with me and not with you or Mr. Franklin.... You know my practice here in New York. You know that there never was a scene that I ever cut out of a picture that met with the director's approval. Each director thinks the scenes he photographs are the most wonderful in the world, and I never followed the policy of consulting with a director when I thought a scene should be eliminated. If I had done that, the Fox Film Corporation would have been on the rocks long ago. The only reason the Fox Film Corporation has made progress is because the power as to what will or will not remain in the film, has been entirely left with me, and I have used it in such a way as to make possible the progress of the Fox Film Corporation.[24]

Shortly after this altercation, both Chester Franklin and Bernard McConville were dismissed from the studio. Chester's brother, Sidney, would not be far behind. However, both Franklins would continue their careers at other studios well into the era of the talkies.

There were other combinations of director and star that made for difficulties. Frank Lloyd, already a successful director, wanted to make higher-budgeted films with the popular William Farnum and tried to use offers from other studios as a wedge. Wurtzel wrote to Fox that he was convinced that Lloyd would never make a William Farnum picture at a reasonable cost again. He suggested instead that Edward LeSaint be given the directorial reins on the Farnum film after Lloyd finished shooting *The Rainbow Trail* (1918) and that Lloyd should be assigned to direct Gladys Brockwell's upcoming production.[25]

In response, William Fox positioned himself and the Fox Film Corporation to be one and the same, and took business relationships personally: "I would be very sorry to see a disagreement between Lloyd and the Fox Film Corporation, for I have a high personal regard for him. I would consider that he is acting dirty and mean if he did anything to disturb the condition of the Fox Film Corporation."[26]

When Raoul Walsh left the studio after four and a half years, William Fox did not lament his departure since an audit of Walsh's productions, artistic value aside, revealed a net loss.

As of mid–1918, Sol Wurtzel wrote to his boss that "everything is going along splendidly at the studios; I am trying hard to get together a good scenario staff so that we will be able to take care of the other companies you will send out here later."[27]

William Fox did not always agree with Wurtzel's

judgment and could become prickly when he saw completed films that disappointed him: "I have likewise reviewed the Tom Mix picture *High Speed*, which I consider impossible for release without destroying all the good work that we have accomplished with Mix. This picture is excellent in the first reel and is excellent in the last reel. The three center reels are long, dragged out, drawn out, unexciting, and cannot be released in its present form."[28]

Wurtzel responded to the blistering criticism with his own explanation. In his defense, he recounted that a Fox newsreel cameraman had been assigned to cover an automobile race held in April 1919 in Santa Monica. However, during the race there was a horrifying accident. One race car came around a curve too quickly and flipped over, killing the driver. The Fox newsreel cameraman happened to be positioned at a vantage point and captured the entire incident.

When Wurtzel happened to see the footage, he was convinced that it was gripping enough to use in a feature film. He got the idea to use this spectacular scene as the climax of a chase in a Tom Mix film. He discussed the matter with Mix and director Edward LeSaint, and everyone agreed that a story structured around a car chase could become an excellent vehicle for the star. Wurtzel hired fledgling writer H.H. Van Loan to construct the story, which would later be turned into a screenplay by the more seasoned Denison Clift.

Regarding a prize fight scene in the picture which Fox objected to, Wurtzel claimed responsibility and admitted that he took the idea from a successful play that had toured theaters a decade earlier. The conceit was that a girl, dressed in male clothing, attends a fight to prevent her fighter boyfriend from being "doped."[29] To Sol Wurtzel's relief, *High Speed* (released as *The Speed Maniac* in 1919) did not sink Tom Mix's career — or his own.

In the days before air conditioning, release schedules were heavier from January through April and September through December because audiences preferred to be elsewhere than in theaters during the sweltering heat of summer. Rather than have low grosses on new movies during the summer of 1918, partly due to the lingering effect of the flu epidemic, William Fox exploited a new phenomenon: the reissue. June saw the reappearance of his early films, including *A Fool There Was* (1915), *The Clemenceau Case* (1915), *The Plunderer* (1915), *The Two Orphans* (1915), *A Soldier's Oath* (1915) and *The Bondman* (1916). August saw the return of *Cleopatra* (1917). In months when business was good, films were released in furious succession. Some weeks saw up to three new films go into distribution.

When Fox decided to reissue some features from the 1916-1917 season in 1919-1920, the main titles were changed which, perhaps advertently, gave audiences the impression they were newly made films. *Dr. Rameau* (1915) became *Infidelity* (1919), *The Serpent* (1916) became *The Wolf's Claw* (1919), *The Love Thief* (1916) turned into *The She Tiger* (1920), and *The Silent Lie* (1917) resurfaced as *Camille of the Yukon* (1920). Trade magazines, which were normally savvy to this kind of chicanery, reviewed the reissue of *The Yankee Way* (1917), with its reincarnated title of *Sink or Swim* (1920), as if it were a new film. Fox was issued a judgment in 1924 by the New York State Superior Court that such practices were illegal. Fox had already ceased doing this in 1920, no doubt as a result of complaints from exhibitors.

The storefront theaters that William Fox first invested in with his partners in 1913 were still in operation and survived well into the 1920s. The average number of seats in a picture house was a fairly stable 500 as late as 1920. "In 1915, many movie theaters still wore the flashy nickelodeon-style ornamentation of an earlier day, bedecked with garish displays of electric lights and gaudy facades in cast iron or terra-cotta, ordered by catalogue from such dealers as the Decorators Supply Company of Chicago.... Projection booths should be fireproof, preferably of brick, terra-cotta blocks, or reinforced concrete."[30]

There were three kinds of projection booths, depending on size. There could be one projector in a small booth. A somewhat larger booth could accommodate one projector and a stereopticon which projected glass slides with song lyrics, paid advertising or promotions for coming attractions. The best-equipped theaters would have two projectors, eliminating the breaks between ten-minute reels which allowed continuous projection, and a stereopticon. Most theaters provided continuous projection by 1919.

Larger movie houses in major cities boasted full orchestras while lower down the chain, music was supplied by smaller accompanist groups, by a pipe organ, or even a single pianist. The quality of the pianist could also vary, depending on talent. For bigger-budget films, entire scores were written and supplied to theaters with scene cues, while flea-pit houses running the same movie relied upon the pianist to play whatever mood was deemed appropriate.

Going to the movies in this period was not a consistent experience across the country. There were so many variables in presenting motion pictures that viewer satisfaction could vary from metropolis to city to town. Since a theater manager custom-tailored films at his own discretion to fit the desired length of the program, cuts were made when a feature ran for too many reels. Long before talent or studios had any say in the final form of a film, some pictures were abridged mercilessly without caution or care.

The best presentation was in the large movie palaces of major cities, but even S.P. Rothafel, the celebrated showman of the Roxy Theater in New York of the 1920s, was known to trim a feature to allow more time for his flashy stage presentations. Not only did the condition of the film print matter, but so did the quality of projection and the skill of musical accompaniment. With pianists in small towns all giving their own interpretations of a musical score, a movie seen with a full orchestra in New York might seem very different at a neighborhood theater in Pittsburgh. Despite all these drawbacks in presentation, the movie industry continued to thrive.

When William Fox started producing his own films in 1914, the average cost was a little over $13,000. In just four years, it had risen to $44,000. Fox felt that he needed to rein in production expenses and especially bring his East Coast unit under one roof. This would be accomplished by a huge new plant in New York, the most modern and spectacular of its kind in the world.

---

3. A Major Player

When Europe was at peace again after World War I, motion picture producers could begin to expand foreign sales. The battles once fought for geopolitical boundaries became a competitive arena for audiences. Silent films were easily exportable with intertitles in any language. American slang and cultural references were converted into comparable expressions, native to the foreign countries. Foreign markets, with reduced production because of the war, readily adopted American-made films as the standard for entertainment.

While on business in Europe, Winfield Sheehan, general manager of the Fox Film Corporation, took advantage of the Armistice to set up an organization to capture news events on film and bring those images home to America. Fox Newsreels would supply the best coverage of events from the far corners of the globe for decades to come. Newsreels had been introduced by Pathé and Vitagraph in 1911 with two issues a week, but when Fox Newsreels began blanketing the United States, they became a valued part of any program that included motion pictures.

Competition for theaters grew fierce in America as well as abroad. A large-scale releasing company like the Fox Film Corporation went head to head with Vitagraph, Selznick, Famous Players–Lasky, Goldwyn Film Company, and to a lesser degree Carl Laemmle and the scores of independent production companies trying to establish a foothold. Their rivalry was over playdates in the approximately 15,000 theaters across the country.

The average film moved along a distribution pattern that was as regimented as an assembly line. Motion pictures were first run at key presentation houses, including the movie palaces of large cities, then neighborhood theaters, and, finally, the less-equipped 10-20-30 circuit, with each number delineating an admission price. Exhibitors, mostly independent operators at the time, were rated by their importance in the playoff of a film. However, the concept of national chains was not unknown. By 1919, First National "controlled 190 first-run theaters and approximately 40 subsequence-run houses, not counting 366 theaters which were controlled under subfranchise agreements."[1]

The average first-run engagement was generally one week. Some theaters changed programs twice or three times weekly. Others, like the Loew's New York, ran double bills to attract customers and had daily program changes. Admissions could range from 25 cents to $1.00 for seats in large-city theaters where audiences would get a live vaudeville show with several acts, a newsreel and a comedy short subject, in addition to the main feature. In many cases, the main five-reel feature was almost irrelevant since audiences came for the entire two-hour show. Program pictures or "programmers" were the type of feature whose initial run went directly to the second- and third-tier theaters or were exhibited on double bills. Theaters paid distributors flat-fee rentals that were set by the company. Large theaters paid the highest rentals for special pictures while other houses paid less for programmers that were made on lower budgets.

The premier attraction of the motion picture industry, though, was the roadshow. These presentations, often run in large non-film venues which were leased for a period of time by the distributor, offered a program made to resemble, as closely as possible, legitimate stage performances with only two shows daily. Promoters advertised them exclusively in the live theater sections of newspapers and appealed to a higher-class audience. Admissions reached $2 in certain cities. The most expensive and elaborate productions were released in this manner to recoup the higher costs. Considering the average production cost in 1919 was $50,000, anything in the range of $200,000 and upwards could be released as a roadshow, or it could simply run at what was called "advanced" (higher) admission. If audiences refused to attend at the increased ticket price, a distributor would have to rethink the release pattern.

Would the public avoid the higher admission prices? There was concern when Douglas Fairbanks's 1922 version of *Robin Hood* was released in New York at $2 tickets while the similar *When Knighthood Was in Flower*, a $1,426,000 film starring Marion Davies, was running in a nearby theater at a 70-cents top. Ultimately, *Robin Hood* was enormously profitable with its $2,101,044 domestic rentals on a cost of $930,043.

The roadshow phenomenon had started in 1911, when the Shubert brothers, through a special agreement with the Motion Picture Patents Company, booked an Italian spectacle, *Dante's Inferno*, into Shubert playhouses to counter the increasingly expensive annual program of stage shows. The competing Frohman and Erlanger circuits then went into filmed roadshow exhibitions in their theaters as well. At the time, the public "was paying for more than a chance to watch a movie in a ritzy theater. This was the one guaranteed place to see a 12- and 13-reel film at its full length, enhanced by state-of-the-art technology, with an orchestra expanded to symphonic proportions.... As the prestige run that came before the normal exhibition cycle, the roadshow's chief benefit was vastly increased circulation for the picture and sky-high visibility. A successful roadshow would play for a year before starting down the regular exhibition ladder."[2]

The enormous rentals of *The Birth of a Nation* (1915), which reached a then-astronomical $10,000,000 on a $110,000 investment, not only solidified the importance of the $2 admission roadshow run, but it also piqued the interest of bankers who now saw motion pictures more as a reliable investment than as an unsavory by-product of vaudeville.

Financial support from banks was the main reason William Fox was able to complete his most ambitious venture to date. With a sizable, although not major, percentage of his features being produced on the east coast, Fox announced, in 1919, the construction of a $2,500,000 structure occupying an entire block at 10th Avenue and 55th and 56th Streets in New York. It was to be the largest motion-picture plant in the world under one roof. No longer would Fox's New York operation be housed in seven rented floors of executive offices separated from production activities.

The building was designed from plans supervised by William Fox himself who gave his architects, not familiar with the particular needs of a film producing center, all the necessary details. The structure included every up-to-date technology for the economical production of films and was designed for a maximum efficiency in administration, a minimum of lost energy and waste, and the greatest safety and comfort for employees.

The new building extended 275 feet along 55th Street. The frontage on 56th Street was 130 feet, with total floor space of 150,000 square feet. Since this location was near the center of the city, and not in the suburbs, the Fox structure was uniquely situated for easy access.

The building with walls of brick, a front of pressed brick, floors of concrete and a main construction of steel and concrete was rated as fire-safe, an important measure at a time when all film was highly flammable. Production also required hot lights near combustible set materials and the processing lab used many chemicals, posing further risk of fire.

Fox insisted on the highest safety standards so that no person in the building would be farther than 100 feet from a fire exit. Fire walls extended through the structure at frequent intervals so that, in the event of a conflagration, any section could be immediately cut off and the spread of fire contained. There was a $60,000 sprinkler system supplied by a 50,000 gallon water tank on the roof in case of fire.

The main entrance to the building on 10th Avenue was decorated with limestone, marble and brick with bronze trimmings. The administration offices were located at the front of the first and second floors with private offices for William Fox, President; Winfield Sheehan, Vice-President of Production; Corporate Vice-President Jack Leo; Treasurer John C. Eisele; Assistant General Manager Herman Robbins; Chairman of the Executive Committee James E. McBride; Casting Director Samuel F. Kingston, and other officials. Other administration departments nearby included contracts, sales, financial, foreign sales, and advertising. There was also to be a scenario department and a library of research books for staff writers. Near the executive offices were the recreation rooms for men and women and a restaurant. The back portion of the second floor held the dressing rooms for extras who were to be "treated" to well-appointed areas—one for men and one for women.

Directors also had private suites close to the administration offices. Conveniently near them were facilities for carpentry, set and scenic design, three prop rooms, wardrobe department and a studio library with source material on locations, costuming and sets.

The lower floor, with an area of more than 45,000 square feet, in addition to housing heating and electrical systems, had quarters for laboratory research work, where a staff of experts devoted its time to devising chemical formulas for the improvement of photography, film developing, tinting and printing.

The rear sections of the first and second floors included the laboratory which could turn out a capacity of 3,000,000 feet of film every week. The floor space of the laboratory comprised 40,000 square feet, and was arranged so that film would be processed with a minimum of wasted effort.

Film editors had their offices in the laboratory section with their editing rooms. This floor also housed 35 fireproof and waterproof vaults, for the storage of negatives and prints. Besides these facilities, there were 12 projection rooms, equipped with every convenience for the comfort of audiences. The comfortably upholstered seats were arranged on a sloping floor, allowing every audience member a good view of the screen. Each projection room had a piano and provision for other music so that films could be seen in an atmosphere approximating that of a theater.

An unusual feature for the time was a large air-conditioning plant which supplied "washed air" for the whole structure, so that the temperature would be a steady 68 to 70 degrees all year long.

The top floor was used exclusively for production studios. Each studio area was designed without posts or other obstructions, since the roof was supported by flying trusses. There were accommodations on this floor for 20 companies working simultaneously. The studio floor was designed with a generous amount of window space and $150,000 worth of lighting equipment to provide illumination for inclement weather or night shooting.

During production, each star was given a dressing room with lockers and toilet facilities, making these quarters "luxurious." There were adjoining darkrooms for cameramen to load their cameras, a restaurant for the actors, a first-aid room, an office for a technical director, and quarters for draftsmen and interior decorators.[3]

William Fox had mentioned in correspondence with Sol Wurtzel that he hoped to have 50 percent or more of all his output produced in New York after the opening of this new facility.[4] Seemingly, every detail was taken into account except the unforeseeable success of the company. Even with all the planning for expansion, the 150,000 square-foot structure was still not large enough to house several offices including the scenario department.

There were only a handful of plays and short stories and a dozen novels that formed the basis for Fox films in 1919. Of the 65 new releases of the year, two-thirds were based on original scripts. It continued to be far easier to develop tailor-made star stories rather than try to find other source material.

After the head of the Los Angeles story department was fired in the summer of 1919, Sol Wurtzel took over as studio story editor since he felt there was no one else capable of handling the position at that time.[5] The need for new stories was a brutal pressure for producers. Since literary material was specifically developed for particular stars, Wurtzel wrote to William Fox soliciting appropriate stories from the New York office for Peggy Hyland and Albert Ray. For some reason, Wurtzel was having more trouble aligning these two stars with good stories. However, he was having more luck with Madlaine Traverse, Tom Mix and Gladys Brockwell.[6]

In a survey of releases for 1919, it becomes clear that William Fox stuck with a production plan that had already proved successful, that of tailoring the vehicle to the star and pigeonholing performers into genres. Only three films were re-

Tom Mix bids farewell to Charles Le Moyne in *Treat 'Em Rough* (1919) (courtesy Mike Hawks).

leased that were not headlined by a Fox contract star.

Tom Mix appeared in eight films, westerns or contemporary action pictures, capitalizing on the use of ever more spectacular stunts. These light family-friendly adventures propelled Mix to new heights of popularity among audience members both young and old. Mix was also credited with popularizing the western genre with younger audiences since his films were more accessible to youth than the dour characterizations of William S. Hart. Mix would remain a big box-office draw for years to come because his films were not just typical westerns but made use of elaborate stunts, different periods and locations, and incorporated every moving object known to exist.

Theda Bara, appearing in eight features, played women of passion, sometimes wicked, sometimes worthy. Wicked roles usually reaped greater grosses. She starred in *When Men Desire*, promoted as "A Theda Bara Super-Production" as well as "A Fox Special Production" of *Salome*, a big-scale film designed to rival *Cleopatra*, directed by J. Gordon Edwards. Nevertheless, audiences were tiring of her and box-office grosses were dropping.

Critically, *Kathleen Mavourneen*, directed by Charles J. Brabin, was apparently not a crowd-pleaser in New York. "Theda Bara, as the Irish Kathleen, played her part well and when she was shown milking cows and dancing the jig the audience seemed to forget Theda Bara 'the vamp.' This picture was also long and tiresome, and in spite of the orchestra, which aided much, and bits of well-played comedy many persons left the theater without learning the end of the play, which was inspired by the Irish song."[7] *Kathleen Mavourneen* lost a substantial amount of money.

Bara also appeared in *The Siren's Song*, *A Woman There Was*, and *Lure of Ambition*, her 40th and final feature for William Fox. She allowed her contract to lapse and left Fox. She was absent from the screen for four years and never recaptured her original level of fame. Theda Bara married director Charles Brabin in 1921.

There were other stars who left the studio as well. Evelyn Nesbit finished out her contract with four turgid dramas, often playing a woman taken advantage of by men, an echo of her own tragic past. Peggy Hyland, in her mid–30s, appeared in a series of eight films, some society dramas and some light adventures, before her contract ended. Juvenile lead Jane Lee and her older sister Kather-

Gladys Brockwell in *Flames of the Flesh* (1919); Brockwell is flanked by Mrs. Rosita Marstini on the left and Mrs. Louise Emmons on the right (courtesy Mike Hawks).

ine left Fox after just one more light comedy, *Smiles*.

There were always other stars on the rise to replace female leads like Bara. Gladys Brockwell, in more domestic melodramas, rivaled Bara's eight releases for the year. Madlaine Traverse, in her 40s, was the oldest star in the Fox stable. Billed as "The Empress of Stormy Emotion," she headed seven dramas, several about taking revenge on the men who wronged her.

The prominent leading man at Fox continued to be William Farnum, starring in six mostly outdoor adventures and westerns with titles like *The Man Hunter*, *The Jungle Trail*, *Wolves of the Night*, and two based on Zane Grey stories: *The Lone Star Ranger* and *The Last of the Duanes*.

George Walsh, brother of director Raoul Walsh, starred in a mixed bag of five light comedies and crime dramas. A review of *Luck and Pluck*, highlighted his skills: "A fast moving story that gives George Walsh all the opportunity necessary for him to display his physical prowess.... Walsh is in his glory scaling walls, climbing trees, foiling cops, etc. There are a couple of corking fights in which he handles anywhere from a dozen to twenty opponents at a time."[8]

New to Fox was 22-year-old Albert Ray, who would only be under contract at Fox for six films, mostly light dramas. The cost of his films represented the entry-level treatment he received from the studio within the moderate limits of the Excel Brand. The progressively lower expenditures may have reflected a lack of interest in Ray's career. *Married in Haste* cost $21,989, *Be a Little Sport* came in at $21,489, *Tin Pan Alley* at $20,213 and *Love Is Love* at $16,000. The trade review of *Love is Love* is a harbinger of the end of his Fox contract: "This Fox feature, like all Albert Ray–Elinor Fair stories is a light comedy type, with more story to it than histrionic ability. Not that

Madlaine Traverse gets help from George McDaniel in *Lost Money* (1919) (courtesy Robert S. Birchard).

William Farnum (right) and an unidentified man in the first version of *The Lone Star Ranger* (1919) (courtesy Karl Thiede).

the cast does not acquit itself creditably, but Mr. Ray appears too weakchinned for a hero type."⁹ Shortly after leaving Fox, Albert Ray gave up acting and enjoyed a long career as a director.

At mid-year, before the upcoming movie season's productions were finalized, there was an annual convention in New York of branch managers from all over the country, who were in direct contact with exhibitors in their territory, and a poll was taken on which performers should stay and which should be eliminated. William Fox made his decision on which contracts were worth keeping and communicated this information to Sol Wurtzel based on the information from his branch managers.

By July 1919, the number of companies shooting in Los Angeles doubled to ten from a year earlier. As smoothly run as the East and West Coast production units may have seemed, William Fox was constantly perturbed by the rising costs involved in filmmaking at the Los Angeles facility. Especially annoying to him was the cost of reshooting scenes for movies that he sent back to Sol Wurtzel. Referring to reshoots of *The Sneak* starring Gladys Brockwell, and *Coming of the Law* with Tom Mix, he wrote, "When I reviewed these pictures after you were supposed to have corrected them, I was unable to find any scenes contained in the original pictures. In fact, the cost of remaking them was as great as the original cost of the making of the pictures.... This is particularly so in the Brockwell subject, where I failed to find a single foot of the original story."¹⁰

Fox was correct in his assessment because *The Sneak* originally cost $16,595 and the reshoot added $24,951 for a final expenditure of $41,600. Wurtzel later explained that one of the performers in many of the scenes was no longer available and to complete the film, the entire production had to be reshot. *Coming of the Law* was not as drastic a reshoot and only added $15,689 to the original $45,829 for a total cost $61,500. Tom Mix films that did come in on or at their budgets were *Six Shooter Andy*, *Western Blood*, *Ace High*, *Fame and Fortune*, and *Hell Roarin' Reform*, each costing around $30,000.

Fox also pointed out to Wurtzel that two 1918 Jane Lee releases that were shot in New York — *Swat the Spy* and *Tell It to the Marines* — cost $16,000 and $19,000 respectively. However, *Smiles*, made at the Los Angeles studio, cost $34,300. Wurtzel explained that Jane Lee had been sick for three weeks and the production fell behind schedule without her, resulting in the cost doubling of her New York films. Such problems were unavoidable and underlined the financial risks involved in making motion pictures.

The Excel program of pictures was a concern

Jane and Katherine Lee in a mischievous pose from *Swat the Spy* (1918) (courtesy Mike Hawks).

to Fox as well. When the company auditors examined the accounting records of the Fox Film Corporation, William Fox claimed that this brand of motion pictures was losing money. He bemoaned the fact that the most Excel pictures could earn in the domestic market was $40,000 per film. For this amount, the company had to supply the cost of production, the positive prints required for distribution, and bear the overhead. The combined costs ended up being thousands of dollars per picture in excess of revenue.[11]

Fox determined the reason costs were so high was because films were 20 percent too long and the sets were too large, requiring directors to fill them with unnecessary furniture and props. Naturally, Fox deduced, if sets were larger by 25 percent, it would be necessary to engage a 25 percent larger number of carpenters, electricians, property men and all other help necessary to build them. Fox insisted that in the Excel Brand, Wurtzel should make certain that interior sets be used for two or three different films, making slight changes and photographing them at a "slightly" different angle.[12] In actuality, as Wurtzel pointed out to his boss, the average length of an Excel picture was 4,545 feet with 220 to 230 scenes.[13] William Fox's incessant cost-cutting would later lead critics to point to the sparse production values in many of his films.

Of all the directors on the lot, William Fox had the most trust for one man, J. Gordon Edwards, and funded the highest budgets to him: "I know that Mr. Edwards does not spend a single penny more than he has to, for he, as you know, has my explicit faith and confidence."[14]

Production was continuing in New York with the East Coast studio at 55th Street and 10th Avenue and two other facilities at College Point, Long Island and Fort Lee, New Jersey.

According to the *Motion Picture Studio Directory and Trade Annual 1920*, the Western Avenue lot's staff included Sol Wurtzel (studio manager), George Teffeau (Superintendant), Denison Clift (scenario editor), Frank Burns (lab superintendant), and E.A. Yerby Smith (technical director). Scenarists under contract included Anthony Roach, H.H. Van Loan and Gus Meins. Directors were Edward J. LeSaint, Scott Dunlap, Howard Mitchell, and Cliff Smith. Cameramen were Fay Durham, Frank Good, Walter Williams, George Schneiderman, Earl Ellis, Irving Rosenberg, Bud Courcier, Frank Heisler, E.B. Schoedsack, P.D. Whitman, and E.B. DuPar. In addition to the main lot, there was a ranch facility located at 2450 Teviot in Los Angeles.

The Sunshine lot had its own staff with directors Eddie Cline, J.G. Blystone, Roy Del Ruth and Del Lord, production manager Lewis Seiler and scenario editor Hampton Del Ruth.[15] Seiler had been brought to the studio in 1917 by his friend from New York who now ran the studio, Sol M. Wurtzel.

With the steady expansion of production in Los Angeles, experienced actors and actresses in 1919, who had been earning $100 to $150 weekly, began demanding $250 weekly. Star performers, like Mary Pickford and Charlie Chaplin, were receiving astronomical salaries, but directors were only receiving between $500 and $1,000 weekly, depending on their stature. There were other considerations that could raise the cost of a production. Tom Mix pictures, for example, which averaged $20,000 to $30,000 on a schedule of four weeks in 1917–1918, were taking five to six weeks by late 1919, a result of more elaborate stunts and costing upwards of $40,000.

Ad art for the 1919 reissue of the 1915 film *The Regeneration*, co-starring Anna Q. Nilsson (courtesy Robert S. Birchard).

Even the budgets of Sunshine Comedies were rising alarmingly. Two short subjects, both directed by John G. Blystone—*A Naughty Wink* (1920), starring Ethel Teare, Billy Franey and Edgar Kennedy and *The Great Nickel Robbery* (1920) with Chester Conklin and Dorothy Lee— averaged $34,000 each. These two-reelers were as expensive to produce as complete five-reel features. After reorganizing the Sunshine program in 1919, with Hampton Del Ruth supervising production, Sol Wurtzel explained to William Fox the need for further expenditures to keep the Sunshine Comedies competitive with rival production companies. Under Henry Lehrman's leadership, the Fox unit had fallen behind other companies and was woefully under-equipped. There were only some flats and a cyclorama, necessitating the building of machinery that would allow quicker and more efficient production of the kinds of elaborate gags and stunts used in the comedies. Wurtzel alerted Fox in advance that the cost of these expenditures would be showing up in the budgets of future comedies. The construction of a "sky backing" cost approximately $3,000. This was necessary in order to do certain trick shots similar to those that the cyclorama allowed and would ultimately result in the saving of large sums of money in the Sunshine Comedies and avoid the cost of going on location. The more production that could be contained to the studio lot was always the objective. As well, Wurtzel authorized the revitalization of a Miniature Department which had been closed down for two years. This would allow the unit to manufacture "trick ducks, horses, carriages, miniature sets, etc." for the comedies.[16]

William Fox strongly insisted on reusing sets from feature productions to save on Sunshine costs but Wurtzel pointed out that was already being done. Wurtzel reminded the mogul that he was attempting to re-use sets whenever possible. A very large set which was constructed for the Tom Mix western *Rough Riding Romance*, released in August 1919, was used in three consecutive Sunshine comedies: *Wild Waves and Women* (1919), *Yellow Dog Catcher* (1919) and *Chicken a la Cabaret* (1920). The set was then re-dressed for an upcoming comedy. A hotel lobby set that was built for the Albert Ray and Elinor Fair feature *Love Is Love*, released in August 1919, was recycled for yet another two-reeler. A log cabin set which was used in the Madlaine Traverse picture *Rose of the West*, released in July, set in the Canadian Northwest, was also used in *Rough Riding Romance* and in *Evangeline*, released in September. It was then re-purposed for a comedy.[17]

Fox's formulaic method of production, necessitated by a demand for regular releases, did not allow more effort in acting or direction and ultimately invited less critical appreciation. Sometimes, the obviously exploitative aspects of a film irked the critics. Even *Variety*, which clearly understood the need for exploitation angles, objected to Evelyn Nesbit in *Woman! Woman!* (1919): "Probably designed for sensationalism.... Usual Fox cast and production. On a par with numerous other 'sex' photoplays turned out by this manufactory, besides having the heavy handicap of Miss Nesbit's 'acting.'"[18]

A review of *The Jungle Trail* (1919) rehashed a comment once directed at William Farnum's acting skills: "There have been times when the effects Farnum has gained by certain of his performances have been nothing if not foolish. 'Like a well-fed St. Bernard dog tearing around a yard and then pulling up and attempting a dignified pose'—so he was once described by one of the cleverest women writing pictures."[19] This was no reflection, however, on his role in *The Jungle Trail*, but it pointed out that his performances were not always reliably good.

What may have been lacking in the artistry of Fox films was compensated for in the technical aspects of visual impact and spectacle. When William Fox spent money on a big production like *Salome*, which premiered in New York in late 1918, even critics took note: "Whether or not the settings are historically correct, there is displayed on the screen a large number of massive sets peopled with soldiers and natives that must represent the investment of a fortune of no mean proportions."[20]

Spending money was necessary as studios competed with one another to top the lavishness of their most impressive productions. But with all the carping about rising costs, William Fox had nothing to complain about. Total expenditures on production in 1919 amounted to $2,929,069 or about $300,000 less than 1918. Worldwide rentals, however, increased by over $2,000,000 to $9,380,883.

As Fox was expanding his organization, the competition was becoming stronger as well, weakening his access to theaters. First National, begun in 1917 along similar lines as Fox's Box Office Attraction Rental Company, bought rights and then distributed films to various theaters. By 1920, it controlled over 600 theaters and had an extended network of several thousand more. In 1918, First National started making its own features and recognizing that top directors and stars were the key to successful films, signed director D.W. Griffith and star talents like Mary Pickford (luring her away from Paramount), Charlie Chaplin, Roscoe "Fatty" Arbuckle, Lillian Gish, and Constance and Norma Talmadge.

Adolph Zukor and Jesse Lasky, who had teamed up to form Famous Players–Lasky, responded to the First National threat by attempting to buy showcase theaters in major cities. Zukor soon had a chain of over 300 first-run showcase theaters. With his roster of star talent, Zukor was able to insist that theaters book blocks of titles, including less desirable films, to be able to play the most popular ones. This practice, later scrutinized by the attorney-general's anti-trust forces, tied up playdates and cut off other distributors' access to certain theaters.

Guaranteed bookings to Famous Players–Lasky, however, were a double-edged sword. When William S. Hart signed a new contract in 1919, Zukor needed to keep the popular western star on the payroll to make his season's release slate more desirable to exhibitors. Hart was able to demand and receive $200,000 per picture with a guarantee of six films per year. Opera star Geraldine Farrar was paid $10,000 weekly. The ripple effect of these extraordinary salaries spread through the entire acting community and performers everywhere began to flex their egos. Each thrust by one company was met with a parry by another. Along the way, the stakes were ratcheted up another notch.

Competition was becoming fiercer in all aspects of the industry for William Fox. In January 1920, Loew's Corp., with a controlling interest in a small chain of nearly 60 theaters, purchased the Metro Pictures Corporation which put them in production and distribution as well. On April 17, 1919, four of the most popular and powerful film people — D.W. Griffith, Mary Pickford, Douglas Fairbanks and Charlie Chaplin — formed their own production company, United Artists, to harness their creative and profit potential.

To combat the new competition, William Fox was forced to spend more money on some of his pictures, while still trying to keep costs at a reasonable ratio to returns. The average industry feature budget had risen from $25,000 in 1915 to $150,000 in 1920 but, fortunately, the rentals paid by theaters had increased by 350 percent. Fox still insisted on keeping within limits on each of his brands.

Excel Pictures	$20,000–$25,000
Victory Pictures	$25,000–$27,000
Mix Pictures	$50,000
Sunshine Comedies	$20,000–$22,000

William Fox's penny-pinching, especially in the Excel Brand, became obvious in his productions as noted in a review of *Molly and I* (1920) starring Shirley Mason and directed by Howard Mitchell. "When the director serving the Fox picture interests will desist in working on an economic schedule that robs them of achieving results they might otherwise secure by the expenditure of a little more money, only then can these features hope to line up alongside other concerns in competitive bidding."[21] Mitchell had actually remained within 1 percent of his budget, so William Fox could not blame his talent this time in the final result.

Further complaints were lodged in a review of *Mother of His Children* (1920) starring Gladys Brockwell. "What is true of many Fox features in viewpoint of economy is also true of this. For example, it is suggested the wife of the sculptor is crossing the Atlantic with her two children to join her successful husband. There is not the slightest suggestion of sea or of leaving land. Instead, an interior of a cabin is shown plus the background of sleeping compartments, one aloft over the other.... In consequence of it all, it is a thought that the director may have been subordinated to a schedule limiting his expense."[22]

Under the yoke of studio guidelines, directors had to maintain fiscal boundaries if they wanted to remain under contract to the Fox Film Corporation. By William Fox's own accounting, the final result of approximate maximum cost to actual cost was not all that drastic, but overages always enraged him.

Director	Title	Budget	Actual Cost
LeSaint #15	The Feud	40,000	68,755
Mitchell #4	Faith	20,000	22,003
Dunlap #6	The Hell Ship	20,000	25,219
Beal #7	Tin Pan Alley	20,000	17,479
Swickard #1	The Square Shooter	20,000	24,513
Smith #1	The Cyclone	40,000	56,885
Mitchell #5	Black Shadows	20,000	24,585
LeSaint #16	Flames of the Flesh	30,000	34,098
Lawrence #11	What Would You Do	20,000	30,116
Smith #2	Three Gold Coins	40,000	39,706
Dunlap #7	Her Elephant Man	30,000	33,008

Director	Title	Budget	Actual Cost
Flynn #2	The Lincoln Highway-Man	35,000	49,228
Clift #1	The Last Straw	20,000	31,001
LeSaint #17	White Lies	30,000	27,930
Mitchell #6	The Tattlers	20,000	25,896
Flynn #3	Shod With Fire	35,000	59,722
Mitchell #7	Molly & I	30,000	30,302
LeSaint #18	Mother of His Children	30,000	34,114
Jaccard #1	Desert Love	40,000	74,163
Clift #2	This Freedom	20,000	25,959[23]

While William Fox would insist that Tom Mix pictures retain their quality, he seemed to lose interest in Gladys Brockwell's career as she neared the end of her contract. One of her later films, *Flames of the Flesh*, released in February 1920, was not well received: "This is probably the worst feature in which Gladys Brockwell ever made her appearance. Even she seems ill at ease in it.... A story stupid and silly to begin with, and told like the worst of the ten, twenty, thirty melos of other times, it neither carries conviction nor affords a sex thrill, the theory justifying Fox's departure from the usual type of feature picture."[24]

A review for *The Devil's Riddle* (1920) confirmed the decline: "Gladys Brockwell is starred in this Fox feature and gives her usual good performance and she is capably supported by William Scott, but the stuff they appear in lacks finish, intelligent plan and first class direction. That's a pity, for Miss Brockwell is one of the few with a punch. She can get a sense of reality into most things, but poor handling has kept her from being a star of the Louise Glaum magnitude."[25]

After 33 starring roles between 1916 and 1920, Brockwell left Fox and continued acting in smaller supporting parts, but did not reach the level of star again. *The Devil's Riddle* was directed by Frank Beal who had guided Brockwell through several previous films. He stayed on to direct just two more films of 1920, one with Vivian Rich and the other with Madlaine Traverse. Vivian Rich had to be let go as well because she would not allow director Scott Dunlap shoot any close-ups for *Would You Forgive?* (1920) since she hated "being photographed at close range."[26]

Along with stars, competent directors were becoming harder to find, especially those who could work efficiently with more temperamental performers. Tom Mix had graduated, with his success, to a weekly salary of $4,000. Such regal earnings tended to inflate the egos of even the most co-operative performers. When it became impossible to find a director Mix could get along with for his next film, *The Hard-Boiled Tenderfoot* (later retitled *The Daredevil*, 1920), Sol Wurtzel allowed the star to take over the reins.[27] William Fox insisted that this practice not be repeated.

Shortly after, William Fox's review of a new director's work with Tom Mix in *Desert Love* (1920) was blistering. He bemoaned Mix's acting performance as "the worst I have ever seen him give." It became clear that Jacques Jaccard, directing his first film for Fox, was capable of creating action but knew little about dramatic sequences. Fox even suspected that Mix may have been directing himself in the dramatic scenes. Once again, the issue of over-stuffing a scene came up as Fox complained about Mix's predilection for insisting on large crowds of people to make things interesting. Calling Wurtzel's attention to the scenes in which Mix's character is elected by the townspeople as sheriff, Fox suggested that this action could have been stated in a title card and would have been just as impressive. Instead, Mix had several hundred people greeting him, which to William Fox did not add up to much dramatic value except "to satisfy and appease Mr. Mix's personal vanity." Fox was biased by having to absorb the $75,000 production costs, $35,000 over budget, as well.[28] Jaccard only stayed at Fox for two more films.

William Fox continued his pattern of screening films before their release and insisting on re-cuts. In the case of the Tom Mix feature, *Rough-Riding Romance*, he was disturbed by the slow pacing of the story and dropped an entire 1,000 feet of film from the story. The production costs were not wasted though. That same footage was incorporated into a story by H.H. Van Loan and became the opening for the Tom Mix vehicle *Three Gold Coins* (1920).

Reminiscent of the hiring of Valeska Suratt when Theda Bara became more difficult, William Fox brought in Buck Jones to star in a series of westerns to coax Tom Mix into giving better performances. Sol Wurtzel was responsible for easing Jones into production without riling Mix.

Even though the Fox Film Corporation had an ironclad contract with Tom Mix, Wurtzel had enough experience, after three years in the picture-making business, to know that it could be very costly if the actor decided to not cooperate with the studio during periods of production. For this reason, the hiring of Jones as a competing cowboy star had to be handled delicately. The biggest concern was to keep Mix from suspecting the studio's ploy by keeping Jones' pictures at a lower level and not assigning the same directors who had handled Mix's films.[29] In the long term, Wurtzel's diplomacy paid off.

In Sol Wurtzel's opinion, the strong relationship between a star and director could poison co-operation with the studio. There was a great deal of animosity between Wurtzel and Mix's new director, Lynn Reynolds, which led to the latter's departure. However, the reliable Reynolds was rehired to direct Mix's studio rival, Buck Jones.

With a dependence on original scenarios and writers taking an average of six to eight weeks to develop and polish their work, the story department had become a much more important component in the production process. Not every script turned out to be a masterpiece and it was the job of the story editor to improve the material as much as possible. For the moment, Sol Wurtzel was not getting satisfactory results from his story editor, established screenwriter Denison Clift, but could not let him go because there was no one to take his place.[30]

Clift was given an opportunity to redeem himself by directing *The Iron Heart* (1920), which he had also written, but the film turned out to be less than expected: "This Fox release with Madlaine Traverse as the star is very far from being a first-class picture. Although its exact status is in a measure difficult to determine, the best recommendation would speed it to a nickelodeon.... Miss Traverse is badly cast.... It is a one-man picture, the story, scenario and direction by Dennison [sic] Clift ... and a great improvement might be made in retitling."[31] Clift left Fox shortly after this debacle to pursue his directing career elsewhere. Several failures later, he eventually returned to writing.

The deficiencies in Fox script supervision showed up in the release of another 1920 production: "Neither cumulative in interest nor contributing that needed essential that would rank it with the better class photoplays, 'The Orphan,' Fox's latest starring vehicle for William Farnum, at best can be recommended as a poorly assembled five-reeler with some melodrama thrown in.... Practically the entire cast, competent to the degree of expression commanded by the director, is wasted on poor material."[32]

Sol Wurtzel, as a matter of necessity, cut back on running the business end of the studio in the spring of 1920 because he found that during the previous six months he was devoting more and more of his time to the actual production of pictures. He supervised the construction of stories and scenarios then oversaw productions as they were being made. He screened the rushes every day and ordered re-takes if the material was of inferior quality. He claimed jurisdiction over what directors did and took it upon himself to be in charge of the editing of films and delivering the final product. There were only two films with which he was not involved and those were 1920 Tom Mix pictures, *The Cyclone* and *3 Gold Coins*, which were taken out of his hands by Winfield Sheehan who was visiting on the West Coast and intervened in some contentious dealings that Wurtzel had with Mix.[33] It is possible that the arrival of Buck Jones may have tainted Mix's relationship with Wurtzel for the moment.

By 1920, William Fox, Winfield Sheehan and Sol Wurtzel had become so preoccupied with grinding out more and more features that the quality of their work had diminished. Aside from Tom Mix, Fox Films no longer had many stars with box-office appeal: "A popularity contest,

Tom Mix as a Mountie with Colleen Moore in *The Cyclone* (1920) (courtesy Mike Hawks).

Buck Jones stars as *Firebrand Trevison* (1920) and wants answers from Frank Clark (courtesy Robert S. Birchard).

inclusion of several features with higher budgets.

Trying to upgrade the quality his release slate, William Fox kicked off the 1920-1921 movie season with four "special" productions released between the end of August and December. *If I Were King* (1920), a period romantic adventure set in France during the reign of Louis XVI, starring Fox's leading thespian, William Farnum, was designed to satisfy the star's desire for more expensive films, and add class to the studio. Critical acclaim was not forthcoming from *Variety*: "It is misdirected, badly imagined, carried out in stilted fashion and its best climaxes lost in the cutting room."[36] However, the $105,000 negative cost was more than offset by a profit of $129,000. But it was *While New York Sleeps* (1920), starring Estelle Taylor, another high-cost production telling three stories of passion and crime in the big city that became the year's most profitable release, clearing nearly $200,000. Two of the specials ended in losses. *The Face at Your Window* (1920), which was cast with lesser-known performers and dealt with immigrant workers, Rus-

conducted by a trade journal, revealed the top fifteen men at the box-office were Wallace Reid, Charles Ray, Thomas Meighan, Eugene O'Brien, Douglas Fairbanks, William S. Hart, William Farnum, Tom Mix, Tom Moore, Harrison Ford, Richard Barthelmess, Bryant Washburn, Charles Chaplin, Earle Williams and Harold Lloyd."[34] Notably, only two of the 15 were at Fox: Tom Mix and William Farnum. The top 15 women were Norma Talmadge, Constance Talmadge, Mary Pickford, Anita Stewart, Dorothy Gish, Clara Kimball Young, Gloria Swanson, Mary Miles Minter, Katherine MacDonald, Pearl White, Marguerite Clark, Ethel Clayton, Elsie Ferguson, Elaine Hammerstein and Enid Bennett.[35] In this group, Pearl White was the sole Fox contract star. Nevertheless, due to the incredible popularity of motion pictures, it was almost impossible to lose money. Fox's film rentals increased, by a substantial 25 percent, between 1919 and 1920, to $12,605,725. The average cost of a feature rose from $42,450 to $60,808. This was, in part, due to the

Jackie Saunders, William Farnum and G. Raymond Nye in *Drag Harlan* (1920) (courtesy Robert S. Birchard).

Betty Ross Clarke and William Farnum in *If I Were King* (1920) (courtesy Karl Thiede).

sian spies and labor unrest, failed to draw and ended up losing $100,000. *Blind Wives* (1920), a follow-up multi-story film to *While New York Sleeps* reunited stars Estelle Taylor and Marc McDermott with director Charles Brabin, but did not repeat the former's success and ended up in the red by $34,000. The catch-line for it was, "Do you ever realize what unhappiness or what tragedy may be connected with the dress you wear?"[37]

The business of turning out a year's slate of releases and the complexities involved in developing, casting, shooting and editing films in Los Angeles had made the process more cumbersome than one man could handle. Sol Wurtzel wanted to initiate a plan to alleviate the bottlenecks: "I believe that in the future the best results will be obtained by having one competent man supervise the production of four companies, these four companies to be under his sole supervision and control; and that another competent man have control of four other companies."[38] Fox resisted this plan, perhaps out of his mistrust of so many others, trying to keep Wurtzel's direct hands-on control in effect as long as possible.

Although the combined attention of William Fox, Winfield Sheehan, and Sol Wurtzel was directed towards the production of feature films, the Sunshine Comedy division, under the direction of Hampton Del Ruth, was an important element of the Fox Film Corporation. With the enormous popularity of Mack Sennett two-reel short subjects and features of Mabel Normand, Fatty Arbuckle, and Charlie Chaplin, slapstick had developed into a wildly successful genre. Looking to cash in on this market as well as augmenting his programs with the Sunshine Comedies, Fox and Wurtzel increased production of the two-reelers from 12 in 1918-1919 to 33 in 1920-1921, representing a considerable investment of nearly $750,000. Stars included Al St. John, Hank Mann, Chester Conklin, Lloyd Hamilton, Mack Swain, Jack Cooper, and Slim Summerville.

Fox was always on the lookout to pick up a relatively inexpensive contract that would yield lucrative returns: "I feel that Clyde Cook will be of great value to the comedy plant as he is a man of extraordinary qualities, and if the picture turns out a hit we can get extraordinary rentals for it and make comedies in which we can star him in addition to the Sunshine Brand, and in that way be in competition with Harold Lloyd and any other comedian who is now featured and sell for high prices."[39]

Australian-born Clyde Cook, at age 29, had only starred in a small part in a feature for Realart but was promoted to star status in a series of 18 Sunshine Comedies. The content of his comedies was easily described by titles such as *Kiss Me Quick* (1920), *The Huntsman* (1920), *The Guide* (1921), *The Sailor* (1921), *The Toreador* (1921), *The Chauffeur* (1921), *The Eskimo* (1922), *The Artist* (1923) and *The Pinhead* (1924). Fox also wanted Cook to eventually appear in Sunshine features.

Sunshine Comedies continued in production through the 1920s, hitting a peak of 52 releases in 1926-1927 before being reduced by half the fol-

A scene from the Sunshine comedy *The Devilish Romeo* (1921) with Big Joe Roberts and Bobby Dunn (courtesy Robert S. Birchard).

lowing season and then being discontinued with the arrival of sound. These two-reelers were not the only short subjects Fox released in 1920-1921; they were augmented by a *Mutt & Jeff* series of cartoons.

In addition to increased competition for theaters, problems with ego-inflated performers, rising costs and keeping the flow of scripts at a level of quality that would attract audiences, there was a tightening of credit as a backlash to federal spending during the World War which grew three times larger than tax collections. When the government cut back spending to balance the budget in 1920 a severe recession resulted.

For William Fox, though, the exploitation of foreign markets increased rentals from those countries almost threefold to $2,817,277, helping profits for 1920 reach $2,029,686 with an after-tax surplus of $1,431,542. Loew's, Inc. showed a surplus of over $2,000,000 while Famous Players–Lasky reported their 1920 surplus of $5,399,089.[40] Estimated box-office receipts in the United States for 1920 were $730,000,000, up from $640,000,000 in 1919 and $502,000,000 in 1918.[41] The postwar economy would continue to solidify and result in an explosion of productivity for certain sectors of the economy — and the motion picture industry would become one of the most profitable.

4. Stability

In the years between 1920 and 1926, production companies that survived and prospered would take on the form that they would keep well into the 1950s. Columbia Pictures started out as a state rights group of franchises, much like the organization William Fox had founded with his Box Office Attraction Rental Company. It took Columbia longer to coalesce as a unified corporation, but Harry and Jack Cohn eventually bought up all the franchises and the company grew to cover every territory in the United States. Expansion into foreign distribution occurred as well.

The four Warner Bros. started in state rights and grew until they purchased Vitagraph, acquiring its network of exchanges, then took on First National (which started out in 1917 as an exhibitors' circuit created to use its size to make better deals with producers)[1] and its studio facility in Los Angeles.

Famous Players–Lasky and Universal kept expanding and, to keep up with the competition, opened their own exchanges around the country.

United Artists expanded its production and distribution organization after its founding in 1919.

The Metro Film Company went through a series of mergers, first with Goldwyn then with Louis B. Mayer's unit to form the legendary Metro-Goldwyn-Mayer in April 1924. The coalescence of the major studios and their concentration of capital and output of production meant that they had a virtual stranglehold on the industry, making it nearly impossible for an independent company to squeeze into their spheres of success.

Since there were few nationwide exhibitors, theater owners were building chains in local territories such as the West Coast Theaters, Inc. takeover of Sol Lesser–Gore Bros. Enterprises. This merger in Southern California involved 30 theaters, four exchanges, real-estate holdings and leases on theaters under construction, as well as plans for several theaters in the future. This was one of the many chains that William Fox would later buy. As these regional chains would cluster together, they would increase their leverage in holding the line on rentals imposed by producers.[2] Studios with the strongest product, biggest stars and best directors would demand the highest rentals. Exhibitors needed comparable bargaining strength.

According to Howard T. Lewis, in his book *The Motion Picture Industry*,

> In January 1920, the total number of theaters controlled by First National had increased to 639; of these 224 were first-run houses, 49 were subsequent-run houses, and 366 were outlets operated by franchise holders.
>
> The Famous Players–Lasky Corporation, too, in order to guarantee adequate representation for Famous Players pictures in certain sections of the country and to secure exploitation through prerelease and first-run houses, became interested in theater control. By August 31, 1921, this company had acquired 303 theaters, 213 of which were included in the holdings of Southern Enterprises, Incorporated a concern which had been organized on April 30, 1919, by the Famous Players–Lasky Corporation. Because of the strong position of the First National franchise holders in the South, Famous Players had experienced some difficulty in disposing of its product at rentals which it considered fair.[3]

There were definite benefits to owning a chain of theaters rather than just a handful, especially for exhibitors with the best-grossing locations in key markets. And even when the major production companies started buying theater chains, there was a simple reality to the production-exhibition equation. No studio could make enough pictures to supply all of its theaters, and no theater chain could keep enough pictures on its screens from just one source. Thus, at some point, a studio would need to make a deal with other studios for their pictures, the same as a theater chain would need to deal with several distributors to keep product on their screens.

The way playdates were determined was that local branch offices, following standards set by the New York head office, would send out their salesmen to negotiate terms which would then be forwarded to division managers who would send them to New York for final approval and the drawing up of signed contracts. If at any stage, a distribution manager felt better rentals could be extracted, the deal would be re-negotiated until both the exhibitor and the distributor came to an agreement. Theaters would try to get films at the lowest rental rates while distributors would want the best price for their pictures.

The practice of "block-booking" arose because distributors found it more practical and cost-efficient to have a salesman make a deal for an entire season of films rather than on a per-film basis. Theaters could sign a contract for perhaps 50 pictures from one source, guaranteeing a flow of product, but with an allowance for some booking cancellations. If a film opened weakly in the major cities, there could be cancellations down the road as other exhibitors decided to not run it. For some theaters, block-booking worked well. Others, such as small independent exhibitors, felt strong-armed by the need to commit, sight unseen, to a large block of films with guaranteed rentals already set. When automobiles became more common, small-town theaters again suffered as their patrons drove to neighboring cities to watch new releases in picture palaces.

Large-scale theater acquisitions by producers began when the First National chain went into production on its own pictures in 1918, in direct competition with the studios. As a defensive move against First National, Adolph Zukor, founder of Famous Players, felt obliged to begin buying and leasing theaters.[4] This put producers in direct competition with theater owners and it gave them more leverage in playdate negotiations. A producing company with its own venues could book its best product into its own houses, withholding such films from other theater owners until as much profit as possible had been obtained. With a fixed number of their own theaters, producers could anticipate a certain number of bookings before films were even made. Based on the average earnings from each house, certain revenue streams could be expected. This took part of the gamble out of making films. Once again, many independents balked at this situation and, from 1922 onward, the issue was examined by anti-trust groups until litigation was finally settled in 1948 in a Consent Decree negotiated by the United States Justice Department with the motion picture industry.

By September 1924, William Fox leased the Central Theater in New York and was looking for another Broadway house. The great theater grab was still a year away, but the incentive was present to begin theater chain acquisitions.

Theater construction continued at a breakneck pace across the country, fueled by investors willing to get into the burgeoning exhibition business and banks more accustomed to dealing with the business model that had been set up. This, of course, would lead to further consolidation for the remainder of the decade when theater chains would bulk up on real-estate holdings and then become ripe takeover targets for major production companies, flush with the banks' readily available cash.

No theater could exist without product, so minor-league distributors flourished in this period by renting their lower-cost independently made films to small-town exhibitors who had less buying power than the chains. A large number of distributors filled the void like Associated Producers, Equity Pictures Corp., Federated Film Exchanges of America, W.W. Hodkinson Corp., Pioneer Film Corp., Robertson-Cole Productions, Lewis J. Selznick Enterprises, and the Stoll Film Corp. Most would disappear or be absorbed into other organizations with the growing power of the major studios.

Box-office grosses were definitely on the increase, benefiting exhibitors, distributors and producers. D.W. Griffith's *Way Down East* (1920) was projected to return rentals of $4,000,000 on an $800,000 negative. This figure was based on the amounts earned from its roadshow run, coupled with its playoff in the rest of the country's theaters. Griffith had originally placed the potential film rental of *Way Down East* at $3,000,000 but, because of the success of the various roadshows that were running the $4,000,000 total was expected.[5] The film showed a profit of $615,736 after just 23 weeks of release on a gross of $2,179,613.[6]

Of course, one of the downside effects to huge grosses was the pressure placed on the cost of story material. To acquire the rights to *Way Down East*, Griffith paid $175,000. Just one year later, Richard A. Rowland, president of Metro, bought the rights to Vicente Ibáñez's *The Four Horsemen of the Apocalypse* (1921) for $190,000. With the presence of Rudolph Valentino, *Horsemen*, based on a popular book, became a top picture of 1921-1922, bringing in a reported $4,500,000 in rentals.

There was also the inflated ego of artistic directors which could rapidly escalate the cost of a film. Robert H. Cochrane, Universal's vice-president, recounted his studio's experience with Erich von Stroheim in 1922: "We were engaged in the production of a picture known as *Foolish Wives*. The director was a temperamental, erratic genius, autocratic in the control of the picture's making. We had not proceeded far with the production before we saw that the cost was going to reach heights unheard of then in the picture field. Frankly, in a day when $300,000 for a single picture was a lot of money, we saw a cool, hard million dollars being spent on *Foolish Wives*."[7]

For a company like First National, a contract with talent could be costly as well. To acquire the distribution rights to *The Kid* (1921), the company advanced Charlie Chaplin $800,000. Costs like these meant that the resulting films had to gross as much as the highest pictures to date to return any profits. Several producing companies would disappear in a financial morass as a result of these inflated costs. Others were able to hang on long enough for another hit.

By January 1921, William Fox, flush with profits from his burgeoning studios, had already outgrown his massive office building in New York. He signed a 20-year lease, at $47,000 monthly, for a four-story and basement fireproof structure at 10th Avenue and 54th Street providing an additional 50,000 square feet of space. Fox also purchased a four-story building on the Southeast corner of 10th and 56th Street which he demolished and planned to build an addition to his main building. The rapid pace of construction was a clear indication of the phenomenal growth of the Fox Film Corporation.

In 1921, Sol Wurtzel surveyed the methods of production in Los Angeles and came up with a suggestion for his boss. It was his opinion that the Fox Film Corporation should follow the example of the Metro Film Company for the 1921-1922 season. This would entail making fewer pictures—only those that were based on hit plays and best-selling books. He felt that the financial returns on only six or seven major films a year would be greater than a program of 50–60 features, many of which were strictly formula pictures. After careful observation of the Metro method of production, Wurtzel faulted their extravagant and, to him, wasteful shooting schedules of eight to ten weeks. It was his strong opinion that any major production based on a play or book should take no longer to shoot than four to five weeks.[8]

William Fox's response was to the point. He emphatically declared that the policy of the Fox Film Corporation for the 1921-1922 season would be business as usual. There would be the same se-

Eileen Percy takes time out to smell the roses as *Her Honor the Mayor* (1920) (courtesy Robert S. Birchard).

ries of star pictures with William Farnum, Pearl White, Tom Mix, George Walsh, William Russell, Buck Jones, and Shirley Mason.[9]

Fox also mentioned a desire to continue making films with Eileen Percy or a "Constance Talmadge type" for a total of eight stars that would fill out the program of 55–65 releases. Fox was still considering special productions, some without stars. These would deal with subjects that had enough audience appeal so as not to need the front-loaded talent. Most of them would be granted large budgets, some almost reaching $500,000.

As the 1921-1922 season rolled along, the priorities did change. Several star series went ahead pretty much as planned as the bread-and-butter releases. Tom Mix, William Russell and Eileen Percy made eight films each for 1921 release and Shirley Mason starred in seven; the remainder of contractees, however, made many less than in previous years. Buck Jones starred in five action films and Pearl White in four light adventures. William Farnum only made two pictures for release that year as did his brother, Dustin, and George Walsh only made one. That left a third of his 65 productions with recently contracted stars and, in several cases, talents hired on a limited basis for just one or two pictures.

Betty Blythe, who had appeared in nearly 30 features but never became a huge star, was given the lead in Fox's most prestigious "special production" of 1921, *The Queen of Sheba*, directed by J. Gordon Edwards. Her short stay at Fox was the highlight of her career. In *The Queen of Sheba*, spectacle and the scantily clad Blythe provided the box-office draw that resulted in Fox's second highest money-making picture of the year with world rentals of $1,121,000. It was also the most expensive to produce at $479,000. Blythe later formed her own production company in 1923 and released her films through Goldwyn.

It was not a star-driven story or an expensive property that brought the Fox Film Corporation the most successful film in its six-year history, but a sentimental drama which was conceived of by William Fox. Upton Sinclair reported, "The story was W.F.'s own idea, and started when he heard a young man recite Will Carleton's poem '*Over the Hill to the Poorhouse*.' The poem made a sensation,

Shirley Mason and Casson Ferguson in a lobby card from the second incarnation of *Merely Mary Ann* (1921) (courtesy Mike Hawks).

George Walsh (right) gets violent in *The Shark* (1920) (courtesy Mike Hawks).

and W.F. was led to read this volume. He was always on the lookout for plots, and this poem brought to mind all the old people left in institutions through the neglect of thoughtless and selfish children."[10]

Fox's recollection of the film's genesis, once again, is not thoroughly credible but partially possible: "We used no script for this picture. The director came to me every morning and I recited the scenes that he would photograph that day. Many times while the story was in progress, he insisted that the material he had finished could not possibly make a motion picture."[11]

The tale of a widowed mother who was denied money by one of her sons and drifted unwelcome from house to house until ending up in the poorhouse, was greeted enthusiastically by *Variety*, "The final analysis leaves you with tears in your eyes and a feeling of reverence, for this is nothing more nor less than a hymn to mother love, depending for dramatic effect on the avenger motive."[12]

The *New York Times* was more cynical in its review: "Its capacity for tear-water and gallery cheers is unlimited. It does a wholesale business in the theatrical commodities of mother-love, filial nobility, the ungratefulness of children, the vengeance of the just, the triumph of right and so on. Without subtlety, without restraint, it pours out its appeal.... Though one is offended by the superabundance of its sentimentality and inclined to resist its overt effort to be heart-rending, it must be admitted that occasionally it does strike a genuine note, sometimes it rings true clearly."[13]

Over the Hill to the Poorhouse (1921), starring Mary Carr (a 44-year-old white-haired actress made to look pathetically frail), was directed by Harry Millarde. The tear-jerker of a tale elevated a mother's suffering to the level of art form but it definitely caught the public's attention. Initially released in big cities in October 1920, it held as a box-office attraction for months and was not given a general release until August 1921. During its run it accumulated world rentals of $2,150,000 on a cost of $99,800, returning a profit of $1,250,000. This was an enormous amount of money for a single film to bring in. *Over the Hill* also solidified William Fox's resolve to deliver popular entertainment without any pretensions to art.

Yet another successful release was the special

Betty Blythe stars as *The Queen of Sheba* (1921) (courtesy Robert S. Birchard).

Betty Blythe is flanked by her minions in *The Queen of Sheba* (1921) (courtesy Robert S. Birchard).

One of the spectacular sets built on the Sunset/Western lot for *The Queen of Sheba* (1921) (courtesy Robert S. Birchard).

An aerial view of the Fox Hollywood lot in 1921 with sets for *The Queen of Sheba* visible near top center. Visible at the lower-left corner of the studio are a large and a smaller glass-roofed stage (courtesy Robert S. Birchard).

production of *A Connecticut Yankee in King Arthur's Court*. Scripted by Bernard McConville, who annoyed Sol Wurtzel greatly when he worked with the Franklin "boys" in the previous decade, the satire adventure updated Mark Twain's story to 1921 and drew some criticism in the use of modern slang in the title cards. The *New York Globe* claimed that the film had "more of the art of Mack Sennett than that of Mark Twain."[14] Nevertheless, the venture was a critical and financial success. Its New York opening began in February and the film entered general release in September. If William Fox needed to be reminded of the importance of owning his own theaters, *A Connecticut Yankee* was yet another lesson. After Fox's ten-week lease on the New York Selwyn Theater expired, the movie had to be moved to another venue. In the next several years, Fox would work to remedy this situation.

With so many comedy stars making the transition from two-reelers to features, including Charlie Chaplin, Fatty Arbuckle, Ben Turpin, Will Rogers, and Mabel Normand, Fox decided to produce a Sunshine feature. *Skirts* (1921) was written and directed by Hampton Del Ruth and featured many of the regular players, including Clyde Cook, Chester Conklin, Polly Moran, Slim Summerville, and Edgar Kennedy. The results met with middling success and limited future interest in the concept. Clyde Cook, who did not reach William Fox's expectations of equaling Harold Lloyd's popularity, went back to two-reelers for the balance of his contract through 1924. There were a few other attempts at Sunshine Features over the next few years, but none were the breakout hits that William Fox or Sol Wurtzel hoped for.

Leaving no segment of the industry unexplored, William Fox was aware of the growing popularity of serials:

Harry C. Myers as *A Connecticut Yankee in King Arthur's Court* (1921) (courtesy Robert S. Birchard).

Allain and Pierre Souvestre, the main character of *Fantomas* was a master criminal who evaded capture for years: "The action is fast and furious from the start, with some good thrills and stunts coming in rapid succession. From the four episodes reviewed it may be judged that this one is a sure bet for exhibitors who use serials. The director Edward Sedgwick has maintained suspense admirably and must also be given credit for the smoothness of the action and the avoidance of confusion in rapidly changing scenes."[16] *Fantomas* starred Edward Roseman, Edna Murphy, and Johnnie Walker. The "episode pictures," however, were abandoned after these first two ventures because of the costs imposed by William Fox's higher production standards which made profitability impossible.

While William Fox and Sol Wurtzel watched over production on both coasts, Winfield Sheehan continued his annual spring travels to Europe to meet with exchange managers and survey developments in the foreign markets. While he was there, plans were made to open a distribution office in Copenhagen to service Scandinavian countries as a prelude to opening other exchanges in Norway, Sweden and Finland.

During this period, Sheehan was also consolidating his power base by bringing two younger brothers into the company. Howard Sheehan owned a small chain of theaters in the San Francisco–Oakland area which he sold in 1919 to become the Fox's West Coast division manager. He would stay with the company until 1929 and was

I am convinced from an observation of the situation, both as a producer and a theater owner, that the public is more than ever eager for serials; but there is this provision — the patrons of the screen, educated by several years' experience of high-class feature pictures, have become keenly discriminating, with an eye for what is thoroughly dramatic, well-staged and, in general, praiseworthy in the films.

The public is no longer the easily pleased gullible throng that formerly uncomplainingly accepted anything offered it. This is universally realized, of course, but cannot be too often stressed, especially with respect to serials.

Not withstanding the strong call for episode pictures — a call that is more insistent than ever — I feel certain that the time has come for a breaking away from the old standards and the elevation of this class of films to a higher level.[15]

Included in Fox's 1921 releases were two serials, the 15-episode *Bride 13* and the more extravagant 20-episode *Fantomas*. Based on detective stories by French authors Marcel

A title card from *Live Wires* (1921) (courtesy Mike Hawks).

ultimately named vice-president of Fox West Coast Theaters. The youngest Sheehan, Clayton, graduated from Harvard Law School and was immediately hired as manager of the Buffalo exchange. With the benefit of nepotism, he rapidly advanced to the position of New York district manager and then to general representative. He would later become the general foreign manager in 1926.

Always on the quest for bigger production values, William Fox considered making films in Europe. He had sent J. Gordon Edwards to analyze European production methods in 1915, at a time when the Continent was far ahead of the United States in technical prowess. However, the long war that occupied Europe's attention had halted the growth of indigenous film production. By 1922, wages in Europe were much lower than in Los Angeles or New York. Once again, Edwards was dispatched to Europe. Fox Films announced that *Mary, Queen of Scots*, produced in England, would be the first of a series of specials to be filmed abroad. Even though Fox promoted *Mary* with a double-page ad in the trades, the company that was supposed to head for England and France ended up being re-routed to Rome.

William Fox had purchased an Italian story written by Charles Sarfer and made arrangements to lease the historical Colosseum, to the dismay of the mayor and council of Rome. J. Gordon Edwards directed all of *Nero* (1922) on location in Italy. It was an elaborate period piece about the mad emperor, and was filmed on a lengthy schedule. Even with reduced wages in Italy, the cost still rose to $358,000. Without any known stars, the film, which ran over two hours, coasted on spectacle, of which it had plenty.

Variety raved: "Fox has done a work certain to reflect credit on the entire industry. It is at once a most engrossing picturization teeming with dramatic intensity of the history of the Roman Empire certain to impress even those opposed to the screen from any angle…. There are many who will say after viewing 'Nero' that Edwards is the only director who has a legitimate claim as a rival of D.W. Griffith, basing their belief on 'The Birth of a Nation' as Griffith's greatest."[17]

Equally impressed was the *New York Times*: "Much of ancient Rome, or the physical appearance of it, has been reproduced. The massive buildings seem genuine. Legions are massed and moved through valleys and across mountain sides. Mobs swarm through the streets and pack the great Roman circus. The chariot races are dizzying, and the burning city is like a city afire."[18]

This was yet another film that would open with advanced prices and then go into wide release, although *Variety* caught the mood of second-rung theater owners in its review: "Exhibitors in the regular run of picture houses need not start figuring on this picture until the Fox organization has managed to skim the cream off the entire country by playing special engagements. When it comes to them [it will be] at prices that will make it next to impossible for them to make any money with the picture."[19] The world rentals on *Nero* hit an impressive $522,000, but it ended up losing nearly $60,000 and became the first and the last of the European specials.

With star salaries rocketing and the impact of onscreen talent eclipsing that of the director there was a response from directors, among them J. Gordon Edwards: "Stars will be secondary in the productions of the days to come…. The progress the cinema has made to this situation where art is foremost has been made in a remarkably short time. It is now at a point where directors by concentration and the right manipulation of personalities must succeed in making hokum-proof, strong and absolutely clean pictures."[20]

Edwards was not quite correct in his assumption, but perhaps coincidentally, one director who would later become well known for his unique style of picture making, had come to Fox from Universal where he had directed some inexpensive westerns. He had a reputation for getting the most production value for his films and would later replace J. Gordon Edwards as Fox's foremost director. Jack (later John) Ford directed a Buck Jones western *Just Pals* (1920), on loan-out from Universal. He returned under contact to William Fox in 1921. His first two films were routine Shirley Mason program pictures. One of them, *Jackie* (1921), reunited Ford with his cameraman from *Just Pals*, George Schneiderman, who would continue to work with Ford on many Fox films well into the 1930s.

Ford was then assigned to co-direct *Silver Wings* (1922) with Edwin Carewe. William Fox brought back Mary Carr, who had played the downtrodden mother in *Over the Hill to the Poorhouse*, in an obvious attempt to recapture the audience of the previous film. Once again, it was a shameless tearjerker, and Ford basked in its success.

Shortly after, Ford was assigned to direct *The Village Blacksmith* (1923). Sharing an attraction to many of the story elements that William Fox held dear, including mother love and the importance of family, Ford turned out yet another successful soap opera: "A real weep-inspiring melodrama that has trials and tribulations piled one on the other until the final scenes.... It is a picture that the majority of picture audiences will love and rave over."[21] Ford would then go on to do the films through which his reputation as a director would flourish. William Fox was not as lucky with other talents.

After signing Jack (John) Gilbert to a contract, Fox, Sheehan and Wurtzel proceeded to star him in a series of films, but not like the standardized type of material tailored to Shirley Mason, Buck Jones, or Tom Mix. The first Gilbert feature, released in October 1921 was *Shame*, in which he played a half-caste who was pursued by a murderer trying to get him into the opium trade. He then appeared in *Gleam O'Dawn* (1922) as an artist in the Canadian woods, entangled in love, jealousy and hatred. It was a misfire.

This was followed by *Arabian Love* (1922), inspired by the fascination with Arab culture spawned by the Rudolph Valentino desert drama, *The Sheik* (1921). The romantic adventure showcased Gilbert well in the role of an American who joins an Arab band after killing a French officer. There was enough action and stormy passion to highlight his talents. Then there was another mediocre programmer, *The Yellow Stain* (1922). This time, Gilbert played a newly arrived lawyer in a small town who goes up against a lumber king. In August, Gilbert starred in *Honor First* (1922), playing twin brothers in a story of usurped identity in post–World War I France. He was teamed with Renée Adorée, with whom he would later co-star in his most memorable film for M.G.M., *The Big Parade* (1925).

After failing to find a proper niche for Gilbert's talents, but having faith in his draw, Fox starred him in a special production of *Monte Cristo* (1922). The trade review in *Variety* was not without criticism: "The story on the screen does not seem to have the romance embodied in the book, nor does the interpretation by Gilbert hold the charm and delight in the performance of James O'Neill on the spoken stage.... The Fox organization cannot hold as much hope for this as for their

John Gilbert in *Monte Cristo* (1922) before being thrown into a dungeon (courtesy Karl Thiede).

Virginia Brown Faire consults a white-haired John Gilbert in *Monte Cristo* (1922) (courtesy Robert S. Birchard).

'Nero.' This is just a picture nothing more, even though it has been elaborately done and undoubtedly represents an outlay of tremendous money."[22]

The *New York Times* was more impressed: "The scenes are impressively set and photographed, the acting in all the important roles is strikingly effective and the action of the story is swift.... John Gilbert's Dantes is at all times interesting and true."[23]

Following *Monte Cristo*, Gilbert went back to a mixture of genres. There were westerns, period pieces, adventures, and turgid melodramas until he landed in a John Ford production, *Cameo Kirby* (1923), as a dashing riverboat gambler. Under Ford's expert direction, the film was a commercial and critical success with rentals of $329,000 on a negative cost of $137,000, yielding a profit of $67,000. But it was not enough to save Gilbert's career at Fox.

By 1924, a review for *A Man's Mate*, in which he played a French artist, noted the difficulty in placing Gilbert in roles that suited him: "John Gilbert appears to be miscast. He has been seen to more advantage in lighter roles."[24] After five more mediocre films in 1924, Gilbert was signed by Louis B. Mayer at M.G.M., where he became one of Hollywood's most popular leading men until the advent of sound.

The example of John Gilbert showed a weakness in the Fox business plan. Although the studio could nurture series stars, it was more difficult to find roles for multi-purpose talent. This became a point which led to Fox's loss of prestige as other studios signed developing talent while Fox, for 1922, continued to recycle Tom Mix, who made nine popular films, including the well-reviewed *Sky High*, *Just Tony*, and *Arabia*, Shirley Mason in eight program pictures, Charles "Buck" Jones in eight action features, and William Russell in seven westerns and adventures. William Farnum appeared in three final films at Fox and Pearl White concluded her contract with three. There was still an aversion on William Fox's part to hire outside stars at elevated salaries. However, this had become an industry practice.

Weekly star salaries, 1923:

Norma Talmadge	$10,000
Gloria Swanson	$6,500
Constance Talmadge	$5,000
Pauline Frederick	$5,000
Lillian Gish	$5,000
Tom Mix	$4,000
Betty Compson	$3,500
Mabel Normand	$3,000
Milton Sills	$2,500
James Kirkwood	$2,500
Wallace Beery	$2,500
Richard Barthlemess	$2,500
Florence Vidor	$2,500
Violat Dana	$2,500
Lon Chaney	$2,500
Harold Lloyd	$1.50 million annually
Charles Chaplin	$1.25 million annually
Douglas Fairbanks	$1 million annually
Mary Pickford	$1 million annually[25]

Responding to complaints about sex and violence in movies, as well as the private behavior of stars like Roscoe ("Fatty") Arbuckle, who was involved in a sensational manslaughter case after the death of an aspiring actress, an organization was formed in 1922 to oversee the content of motion picture productions. The Motion Pictures Producers and Distributors of America boasted a full complement of signatory companies in a non-competitive environment. The association functioned as a clearing house for policy matters relating to the industry and was headed by former United States Postmaster General Will H. Hays. It was also designated as a responsible center for reliable information when banks were looking for investments. Although the issue of film content

The William Fox Studio at Sunset and Western Avenues in Hollywood, circa 1923 (courtesy Robert S. Birchard).

was the primary concern of certain sectors of the public, notably religious leaders, the hue and cry for full censorship did not come until the period of the talkies.

The 1922–1923 season brought the first full-scale attempt by producers to turn out blockbusters with enormously high budgets and box-office potency. This effort returned some startlingly good results on several pictures. United Artists' *The Thief of Bagdad* (1924), starring Douglas Fairbanks, performed exceptionally well with $1,490,419 in domestic rentals, but had a high production cost of $1,135,654. Cecil B. DeMille's production of *The Ten Commandments* (1923) brought in worldwide rentals of $4,169,798 on a cost of $1,464,758 and was highly profitable for the Paramount (Famous Players–Lasky) organization. Another Paramount hit was *The Covered Wagon* (1923), directed by James Cruze and considered the first of the large-scale epics. Originally planned as a Mary Miles Minter film at a budget of $100,000, it was to be sold as a standard release. However, realizing the value of an American epic, the production department decided to raise the negative cost to $601,442 and improve the cast. Paramount's share of the profits was $2,000,000 based on $3,800,000 in world rentals.[26]

Talent and production values were not the only area of inflated costs. In 1924 the average price for a successful play had reached $20,000 and many popular properties sold for well over that.

Turn to the Right (1922)	Metro	$225,000
The Wanderer (1925)	Paramount	$200,000+
Way Down East (1920)	United Artists	$175,000
Winning of Barbara Worth (1926)	Goldwyn	$125,000
A Tailor-Made Man (1922)	United Artists	$105,000
The First Year (1926)	Fox	$100,000
Tiger Rose (1923)	Warner Bros.	$100,000
The Gold Diggers (1923)	Warner Bros.	$100,000
Merton of the Movies (1924)	Paramount	$100,000
The Virginian (1923)	Schulberg	$90,000
Dorothy Vernon of Haddon Hall (1924)	U.A.	$85,000
Tarnish (1924)	Goldwyn	$75,000

Rising costs were a natural result of the increased profitability of the major companies. Agents and talent read the trades and public companies had to report their earnings. In the early 1920s, Famous Players–Lasky, Loew's, Inc. and Goldwyn were listed on the stock exchange and reported their earnings quarterly like any other traded corporations. Fox Films was privately owned and did not report audited earnings. But with trade papers reporting grosses on films, anyone following the business knew that certain movies were earning high numbers. In addition, the enthusiasm of banking firms to invest in both exhibition and production would lead anyone to believe that the movie business was doing very well.

With all the optimism about the industry, there was one area of concern, especially for the ever-frugal William Fox. With high prices for talent and properties, the average cost per film rose from

Alma Bennett lays down the law to William Russell in *Man's Size* (1923) (courtesy Karl R. Thiede).

$73,588 for 65 features in 1921, to $94,538 for only 51 features in 1923. This 22 percent increase in costs was coupled with a 10 percent drop in domestic rentals from 1922 to 1923. A recession which began in 1920, caused by the after-effects of World War I, finally caught up with the film business three years later. The result was a drop in rentals from theaters that carried into 1923. Sensing that drop, most producers cut back on production costs. Goldwyn and Famous Players–Lasky slashed their operating costs by ten to 20 percent beginning in 1921. Other companies waited to see exactly how the lower rentals would play out. After Fox Films returned world rentals of $18,540,109 in 1922 resulting in corporate profits of $3,005,028, 1923 dropped by a third to profits of $2,005,849 on total world rentals of $17,018,623.

As the new 1924-25 productions were about to start, William Fox was still lagging behind other major companies in both stars and directors. John Barrymore was a prestigious draw for Warner Bros. Rudolph Valentino created a sensation for Famous Players–Lasky and Paramount Pictures as did Gloria Swanson and Pola Negri. John Gilbert, after leaving Fox, found his footing at Metro-Goldwyn-Mayer, which also had Lillian Gish, Norma Shearer, and Lon Chaney. First National boasted Norma Talmadge, Milton Sills, Corinne Griffith, and Barbara La Marr.

The industry's top directors were Cecil B. DeMille, James Cruze, Rex Ingram, Frank Lloyd, Henry King, Fred Niblo, Erich von Stroheim and Ernst Lubitsch, none of whom were at Fox.[27]

However, Fox did have John Ford who would prosper and make his mark with critics and audiences alike. Ford was promoted to bigger pictures with the epic western, *The Iron Horse* (1925), Fox's answer to *The Covered Wagon* (1924). Fox also signed Frank Borzage, who started out as an actor and had already directed over 50 features since 1913. He began his long and acclaimed Fox career with a brilliantly directed Buck Jones light drama, *Lazybones* (1925), and a satire about a wife's fight for equality, *Wages for Wives* (1925).

After more than a decade in which directors could develop their craft, Fox no longer had to rely on neophytes starting in the business. There was

Warner Oland (left) in *Curlytop* (1924) appearing as the villainous Shanghai Dan, six years before the Charlie Chan series. Wallace MacDonald (center) co-stars (courtesy Robert S. Birchard).

an adequate pool of directorial talent in Hollywood and it was possible to create better films with these more experienced men. Because directors had not reached the same payroll level as stars, it was also a relatively inexpensive investment.

Fox Films entered into director contracts with many capable talents for the 1924-1925 film season. Among them was Jack Conway, who had made 70 features since 1912. Edmund Mortimer, an experienced actor and director, helmed ten features in his two years at Fox. Emmett J. Flynn, who had been with the studio since 1921, made five films. John G. Blystone was promoted from the Sunshine Comedies to the feature lot, directing eight films in two years. Sol Wurtzel's longtime friend, Lewis Seiler, a production assistant on the comedy lot, moved to directing two-reelers. J. Gordon Edwards, who only made one film, *It Is the Law* (1924), had been elevated to director-general of the Fox Film Corporation, and was based in New York.

Longer shooting schedules and more sophisticated production techniques called for greater directorial skill. Those directors who could bring their films in efficiently and with quality were in great demand. They were also more upwardly mobile and studios were constantly negotiating for their services. Some who worked on the Fox lot and then moved on with productive careers in this period included W.S. (Woodbridge Strong) Van Dyke, William Wellman, Roy William Neill, Victor Schertzinger and George Archainbaud.

The new season would see only 46 new releases from the Fox Film Corporation and fewer series entries. Buck Jones, sometimes billed as Charles Jones, overtook Tom Mix's pace of production and starred in eight program pictures. Mix starred in six, all popular. Shirley Mason's series of five films continued to be less welcome by critics and audiences alike, and her final three releases for Fox would appear in 1925. Two new male stars, Edmund Lowe and George O'Brien, were

George O'Brien clowns around with John Ford on the Fox lot, circa 1925. Edward Piel looks on (courtesy Robert S. Birchard).

cast in a handful of hit films. Lowe was first seen in *Honor Among Men* (1924), and O'Brien, taking over the muscular leads that George Walsh once played, starred in one of the most successful Fox films of the year, *The Man Who Came Back* (1924). He also led the cast of Fox's most prestigious film of the year, *The Iron Horse* (1925). George O'Brien was relatively unknown when given the lead in the high-budget film, but was selected by director John Ford. O'Brien was the son of San Francisco's chief of police and would remain at Fox for the next decade.

The production of *The Iron Horse*, filmed on location in Wadsworth, Nevada, near Reno, was "plagued by problems; intolerable living conditions, bitter cold, winter weather, blizzards, and deep snow drifts.... William Fox began to get nervous and was considering cancelling the picture. He sent Sol Wurtzel to Nevada to find out what was going on. When Wurtzel saw the conditions that the company was working under and the quality of the film that had been shot, he thought that John might be doing his best work. From Wadsworth he went directly to New York and urged Fox to stick with the picture."[28] To underline the immensity of the production, the cast reportedly included a regiment of United States troops and cavalry, 3,000 railway workmen, 1,000 Chinese laborers, 800 Pawnee, Sioux and Cheyenne Indians, 2,800 horses, 1,300 buffalo, and 10,000 Texas steers.

The Iron Horse became John Ford's first important financial success. The reviews were favorable and a William Fox presentation finally got some respect from critics. *Variety* wrote, "John Ford, who directed, put his story over on the screen with a lot of punch.... 'The Iron Horse' is a picture packed with action, a laugh and a tear together with a real heartthrob and thrills. The production is intended as a special, to be road-showed and not reach the motion picture theaters until next year."[29]

The *New York Times* was mightily impressed: "Another stirring chapter in American history was

Tom Mix with Tony, the Wonder Horse, in *Teeth* (1924) (courtesy Robert S. Birchard).

admirable world rental of $1,556,000, resulting in the biggest profit of the year at $650,000.

Other Fox hits for the season included *Dante's Inferno* (1924) which boasted the same type of titillation that William Fox had bestowed on Annette Kellerman's skimpily attired appearance in *Daughter of the Gods* (1916). Containing a lengthy dramatization of the lower depths, *Dante's Inferno* featured some medium-close shots of a nude woman and then wide shots of hundreds of writhing bodies, appearing to be nude as well. However, a press release declared that the other women were wearing proper body stockings, only giving the illusion of nudity. In this period of emerging censor boards and a stern overseer of the industry in Will Hays, this Fox production pushed the

told last night when a picture entitled 'The Iron Horse' was presented at the Lyric Theatre by William Fox.... This ambitious production dwelt on the indomitable energy, resourcefulness and courage of those who spanned the continent with steel.... John Ford, the director of this film, has done his share of the work with thoroughness and with pleasing imagination."[30]

It was exhibitors like H.T. Nolan of First National Pictures in Denver who most appreciated films like *The Iron Horse*. Nolan glowingly endorsed the film in a trade ad stating, "Any exhibitor who cannot make money with 'THE IRON HORSE' ought not to be permitted to run a theatre."[31] With John Ford, William Fox and Winfield Sheehan saw what value a talented director could bring to a film's final critical and financial success. Considering that George O'Brien, the star of *The Iron Horse*, was an unknown, the scope and sweep of Ford's direction, along with a lavish $371,000 production yielded an

On location for *The Iron Horse* (1925). From the left: unidentified, John Stone, Olive Borden, J. Farrell MacDonald, John Ford, Tom Santschi, Frank Campeau, Sol M. Wurtzel, George O'Brien and Lou Tellegen (courtesy Robert S. Birchard).

boundaries of appropriate entertainment. In spite of this, or perhaps because of it, *Dante's Inferno* drew very large audiences. Its $102,000 cost reaped $514,000 in world rentals and a huge profit of $237,000. Rounding out the year's releases, Fox reissued five films in the last half of the year.

Other large-scale efforts of the year from other studios included *Romola* (1925, M.G.M.) starring Lillian and Dorothy Gish; *Monsieur Beaucaire* (1924, Paramount) starring Rudolph Valentino; two Marion Davies costume pictures, *Yolanda* (1924, M.G.M.) and *Janice Meredith* (1924, M.G.M.), both financed by William Randolph Hearst's Cosmopolitan Pictures; the Mary Pickford film, *Dorothy Vernon of Haddon Hall* (1924, United Artists); D.W. Griffith's *America* (1924, United Artists); and Milton Sills's hugely popular adventure, *The Sea Hawk* (1924, First National).

As production expanded at the Sunset-Western lot in Los Angeles, shooting was scaled back in New York.

> The Fox Eastern studio will remain inactive, as soon as Elmer Clifton completes editing "Crossed Wires." Just when additional pictures will be placed in work here is in doubt.
>
> Four productions, all of them now completed have kept the plant quite busy. These were "It Is the Law," directed by J. Gordon Edwards; "The Fool," directed by Harry Millarde and "The Warrens of Virginia" and "Crossed Wires" which Elmer Clifton directed.
>
> It was declared by an individual close to the Fox organization yesterday that cessation of activity in the East presages nothing unusual. He pointed out that when the local plant was built, it was not part of William Fox's plans to make a large number of pictures in the East. Most production was scheduled for the Coast plant where a large number of units are busy. Every year, there occurs a period of inactivity at the Eastern plant and whether it will be of any longer duration this year than before, is a matter yet to be determined.[32]

The writer of this article obviously did not have access to a William Fox letter to Sol Wurtzel in 1919, stating that he wanted to have 50 percent of all production under the New York roof when the new building at 55th Street and 10th Avenue was completed.

The shift to making a greater percentage of films on the west coast was also indicated when Julius Steger, who had been the director general of production in New York for the previous four years, suddenly resigned.

In an adjoining story it was noted that in Los Angeles, about "seventeen units are busy at the Fox studio. In order to relieve the pressure on the indoor stages, two sets which would have ordinarily been built inside have been constructed outdoors."[33] With all this activity, Sol Wurtzel was given extra help with a newly appointed studio manager and another location manager.[34] The growing importance of the west coast production center was underlined during the summer of 1924 when $1,000,000 was spent upgrading and expanding the Western lot.

The move west was not without some animosity from east coast producers, most clearly expressed by Richard A. Rowland, a founder of Metro Pictures and later a head of production at First National: "Production of motion pictures is as simple as A.B.C. as soon as any producer learns the fundamentals.... In fact, it's so easy, it's almost pathetic. And yet, there are a lot of producers and directors out in California who are continually beclouding the production of pictures in an air of mystery. We've got to overcome these clouds of mystery, because there isn't any mystery about it. The trouble with many of these directors is that they get lost in their own fog.... I don't believe in California. The viewpoint is distorted. Out there they think that good motion pictures can't be made anywhere else. But we are not deceived. First National is coming to New York. We're not going to get rooted in California. New York is the greatest story locale in the world and has every advantage to offer. Besides, I consider it impractical to have production and the general office of the company separated by 3,000 miles, so we are going to bring our production to the Atlantic Coast."[35] Some banking interests agreed with this notion and the split between the coasts was repeatedly cited as an unnecessary expenditure over the next decade. However, it had no impact on the Fox Film Corporation.

From the comedy unit on the Western lot, there were 43 shorts made in 1924 to answer the demand by theater owners for more entertainment to accompany feature films. These additional items were sometimes called "program savers" by exhibitors, especially when a feature did not meet audience expectations. Although booked along with Fox features, the Sunshine series never equaled the popularity of the competing one- and two-reelers from Pathé which released films from comedy master Mack Sennett and starring Ben Turpin, Harry Langdon and Ralph Graves. Hal Roach also provided Pathé with comedies featuring Stan Laurel, Snub Pollard, Our Gang, Will Rogers, and Charley Chase. Roach proved the value of his comedy when he signed a new two-year contract with Pathé in 1925 for $9,600,000.

Roach would deliver between 96 and 104 two-reelers, 26 one-reelers and two or three features annually.[36]

In 1924, the average weekly theater attendance hit 46,000,000 with annual admissions amounting to $500,000,000. With about 700 features released in the United States, the average production cost rose from $150,000 to $200,000. The average leading film company was bringing in $1,000,000 in weekly gross income from all sources. About 80 percent of total revenue came from the domestic market, with the balance from foreign markets.

The demand for American films in foreign markets gave rise to a problem which has bedeviled the motion picture industry ever since: film piracy. A London trade paper said, "The success of several films ... on the Continent from their owner's point of view is threatened by the activity of film pirates who are engaged in exploiting their ill-gotten property. One of the features which is suffering badly is 'Scaramouche,' which recently had a successful run at the Tivoli. At least three pirated copies of this are known to be in circulation in Poland. This being the case, there are probably others, not only in Poland, but in Russia and the Balkan States, all three places being apparently beyond the pale of ordinary law."[37]

The problem of piracy did not affect the growth of the industry in the United States at this stage. The industry was too busy expanding its reach to be concerned. American land developers and contractors were also cashing in on the industry's boom. *Architectural Forum* reported in February 1924 that $179,821,700 would be spent on new theater projects for the year.[38]

More theaters meant wider exposure available for a release and the better the venue, the greater the rentals. A typical film made approximately three quarters of its total rentals from its first 20 percent of playdates. These were obviously the largest theaters in the country and charged the highest admission. Here are some examples of first-run houses in the United States in 1924, including those that played roadshows at admissions of $1.50 to $2.00:

Theater	Seats	Price Range	Highest Weekly Gross
Astor, New York	1,131	$1.00–$1.50	$16,102
Cameo, New York	539	.55–.85	$10,053
Capitol, New York	5,300	.35–$1.65	$70,468
Central, New York	960	.50–.75	$19,226
Criterion, New York	608	$1.00–$1.50	$11,960
Cohan, New York	1,100	$1.00–$2.00	$19,550
Cosmopolitan, New York	1,162	.75–$1.50	$19,700
44th Street, New York	1,323	$1.00–$1.50	$16,198
Liberty, New York	1,234	$1.50–$2.00	$22,500
Lyric, New York	1,131	$1.00–$1.50	$12,000
Piccadilly, New York	1,360	.85	$18,650
Rialto, New York	1,960	.35–.99	$26,255
Rivoli, New York	2,200	.35–.99	$30,111
Strand, New York	2,900	.35–.99	$51,460
Chicago, Chicago	2,500	.60	$62,000
McVicker's, Chicago	2,500	.60	$31,000
Monroe, Chicago	987	.40	$12,500
New Orpheum, Chicago	799	.39	$12,000
Randolph, Chicago	686	.50	$9,000
Orchestra Hall, Chicago	1,650	.50–.75	$16,336
Roosevelt, Chicago	1,256	.55	$28,865
Woods, Chicago	1,150	$1.50	$17,200
Aldine, Philadelphia	1,500	$1.65	$16,000
Arcadia, Philadelphia	600	.75 top	$ 7,000
Fox, Philadelphia	3,000	.99	$18,000
Karlton, Philadelphia	1,100	.50	$ 6,000
Stanley, Philadelphia	4,000	.50–.75	$30,000
Stanton, Philadelphia	1,700	.50–.75	$14,000
California, Los Angeles	2,000	.25–.75	$21,500
Criterion, Los Angeles	1,750	.50–$1.50	$20,800
Grauman's Egyptian, L.A.	1,800	.50–$1.00	$29,700
Metropolitan, Los Angeles	3,700	.35–.65	$41,800
Miller's, Los Angeles	850	.75	$ 8,800
Million Dollar, Los Angeles	2,200	.25–.75	$28,900
Mission, Los Angeles	900	.50–$1.00	$12,200
Rialto, Los Angeles	800	.35–.65	$11,500
Loew's State, Los Angeles	2,400	.25–.65	$29,790
Forum, Los Angeles	1,800	.50–$1.10	$11,900
Cameo, Los Angeles	900	.35–.50	$ 5,000
California, San Francisco	2,400	.55–.90	$23,000
Cameo, San Francisco	900	.35–.50	$ 5,300
Granada, San Francisco	2,840	.55–.90	$23,000
Imperial, San Francisco	1,400	.55–.90	$20,000
Strand, San Francisco	1,700	.20–.40	$14,300
Tivoli, San Francisco	2,000	.35–.55	$9,000
Warfield, San Francisco	2,800	.55–.90	$30,000
Loew's Columbia, D.C.	1,200	.35–.55	$18,000
Crandall's, D.C.	1,800	.35–.75	$45,000
Loew's Palace, D.C.	2,400	.35–.75	$22,000
Moore's Rialto, D.C.	1,908	.25–.75	$18,500

Film rentals were no longer the only gauge of popularity. Critics' lists were gaining momentum and importance. Taking all the "Ten Best" lists of 1924, *The Film Year Book 1925* collated the results which revealed the most acclaimed films were:

The Thief of Bagdad (United Artists)
The Sea Hawk (First National)
Monsieur Beaucaire (Paramount)

Beau Brummel (Warner)
Secrets (First National)
The Marriage Circle (Warner)
The Ten Commandments (Paramount)
Girl Shy (Pathé)
Abraham Lincoln (First National)
America (United Artists)

The absence of Fox titles on this list did not bother William Fox. He cared more about box-office results than kudos. While other studios were reaching for spectacle, Fox brought his per-picture cost down from $94,000 to $78,000 and made a tidy profit of $2,224,161 on world rentals of $17,797,568, almost $800,000 higher than 1923. In the same year, Loew's, Inc. showed a profit of $2,949,042 and Famous Players–Lasky ended up with a profit of $9,480,113 due to its heavy involvement in theaters.

There was a good deal of reason for the optimism in the industry in 1924. The comptroller of Famous Players–Lasky outlined many recent positive developments:

1. The film industry had adopted a budget system that would better predict and control cash flow.
2. Large healthy corporations were taking over weaker companies to better absorb losses and sustain a steady output of product.
3. Directors were made to understand the fiscal responsibilities and observe budget limits.
4. Conservative banks recognized the "stabilization" of the industry.
5. The public regarded the industry more favorably.
6. Progress was made in relations between producers and exhibitors enabling distributors to book films in blocks and get favorable rentals.
7. Although several company start-ups lured investors into the business, the failures had not affected the large banking interests.
8. Will Hays' effort to clean up the content of movies was showing positive results.
9. The quality of films was rising.
10. Advertising was reaching a new level of excellence and there had been an adjustment so that all parts of the industry were functioning smoothly.

To sum up, the industry during 1924 gained tremendous STABILITY.[39]

The stability that had settled on the motion picture business was to help William Fox and the Fox Film Corporation accomplish the next level of expansion.

5. *Consolidation*

As movies arrived at the mid–1920s, there was one issue in the film industry which would be making news for the next five years, especially in the pages of trade papers like the *Film Daily*, the self-proclaimed "Bradstreet of Filmdom." In an editorial, composed in his unique trade-oriented syntax, "Danny" (a.k.a. Joe Dannenberg) wrote, "There seems to be an epidemic of theater building and buying. Obviously many theaters make considerable money. Obviously the operator of a chain of ten houses. Can 'talk turkey' to the seller — the producer — much stronger than where an exhibitor owns one or two houses. And the ratio increases. As the holdings grow."[1]

Competition for screens was growing fiercer by the day. Glendon Allvine, publicity director of Famous Players–Lasky, opined, "Just now the principal units in the picture business seem to be engaged in a struggle for theaters. It is a dull week that finds no new alignment of the houses that retail films to the public. And these shifting realignments of theaters represent the working out of the good old law of supply and demand. There are indications that the independent theater owner is going the way of the individual grocer. Sometimes through lack of initiative, sometimes because of an absence of sound showmanship in his operation of theaters, he seems to be losing out in the economic struggle, and chains of theaters to retail amusement are developing just as chain stores have already become firmly established in the retailing of groceries."[2]

The most descriptive way to portray the play for theaters occurring in the mid–1920s was simple — a "feeding frenzy." When there was a mere suspicion of a major company on the move, it threw off the equilibrium of the entire territory. A report that Loew's, Inc. was going to enter the Midwest by purchasing theaters in Iowa and Nebraska, rated a denial in the trades by the company's president Nicholas M. Schenck. Insisting that the company's representation in those territories was adequate, Schenck quelled the speculation.³

The number of theaters in the United States fluctuated according to the level of business. After some closures during the recessionary period of 1921, there were about 15,000 locations running films in 1924. This jumped to over 20,000 in just a few years. Circuits with names that would become familiar in the exhibition industry included Balaban & Katz, West Coast, Stanley, National, Pantages, Saenger, Poli, Hamrick, Ascher, Publix, Moss, Schine, Keith, Skouras, Northwest, Orpheum and Albee. William Fox was well aware that the future lay in theater ownership and the most successful companies would be those with the largest chains. Already Metro-Goldwyn-Mayer, Famous Players–Lasky, and First National were reporting record profits with a good percentage of dollars coming from exhibition.

At the same time, there were some who, not blinded by the over-exuberant optimism, took a more rational view. In an editorial during this period, Joe Dannenberg wrote, "After all, it is the exhibitor who, in the end, must justify the existence of producer, distributor, or both. It is true that each producing and distributing interest can — and might easily — protect themselves against exhibiting difficulties by organizing and operating a chain of their own. It is also quite likely that when the first serious financial depression of nation-wide strength develops that these very chains with their huge size and tremendous cost of operation might easily be the first to weaken under such conditions and break up much more quickly than where an exhibitor owning one or, at best, a few houses, might breast the storm."⁴ Dannenberg was predicting a future that was rapidly approaching.

Realizing not only the importance of theaters, but also a sales force that had the capability of making the best deals, Winfield Sheehan and William Fox hired James R. Grainger away from Metro-Goldwyn to join Fox as domestic general sales manager. "Grainger enjoys the distinction of being one of the most popular sales executives in the country. His friends in exhibiting circles are without number. He has been in turn with Marshall Neilan Prod.; Goldwyn where his sales records reached enviable proportions and then Metro-Goldwyn when the two companies merged interests."⁵ Grainger's job would keep him on the road for a good part of the year, traveling from one end of the country to the other, constantly promoting Fox's pictures and returning with guaranteed booking contracts.

Winfield Sheehan, remarkably absent from the limelight of the press for many years, considering his connections to journalism, finally surfaced in 1925 with a quasi-interview noted in the pages of the *Film Daily* under the heading "Sheehan Talks."

> It's a rarity indeed when any newspaper man gets Winnie Sheehan talking. But this Fox official was trapped by Quinn Martin. Among other things Winnie said: "This business runs in waves, or cycles. It's interesting to watch. You see, what you want to do is to see the next cycle coming. Baby pictures are gone. The biggest flops of the year. The people won't have them.
>
> "You know, the vampire thing was peculiar. It seemed for a time after we brought out Theda Bara that here was a type that would go on eternally. There isn't any such thing any more as a real vampire. Possibly the name had something to do with it. You know, some things about the public's attachment to a person or a fad are unexplainable. I think the name 'Theda Bara' did a great deal for us. We just took two words, 'Death' and 'Arab,' and made 'Theda Bara' out of them. Her first big picture, along about the time we had to get a striking name for her, was placed in Arabia, and the leading woman had to die. That gave us the idea."⁶

Another idea which had been floating around at Fox headquarters in New York was the option to sell shares in the company and raise enough capital to underwrite the purchase of theaters. Loew's, Inc., Famous Players–Lasky, Warner Bros., and Pathé were all publicly traded companies and although William Fox wished to retain complete control of his empire, there was no better way to inject large sums of money into the company than by a stock offering. There would also be the accompanying stringent requirements in accounting practices and the quarterly reporting of income and profits. The company would need to be run in a more transparent manner, something which no doubt made William Fox cringe. Nevertheless, the other companies were successfully using public money and benefitting. There was no reason why Fox could not do the same.

On June 2, 1925, Fox directors, made up of the private investors, voted themselves a 235 percent dividend with the intent of taking the company public and on June 15, it was reported that

> trading in Fox Film stock may be inaugurated on the Exchange today. The application for listing of 165,000 shares of stock has been approved by the Board of Governors. It is anticipated that the opening sale will be at 48.
>
> The Corporation, with its subsidiaries, has issued its first balance sheet showing the effects of the recent readjustment of the company's capital struc-

ture.... The balance sheet shows total assets of $24,509,470, of which one third are cash assets and over one-half current assets.... The company will have an authorized issue of 900,000 shares of Class A stock, which 400,000 shares are outstanding, and 100,000 shares of class B stock, all outstanding.[7]

The offering was intended to raise approximately $25,000,000 in operating capital.

The *Wall Street Journal* looked favorably on the future of Fox because of the way it depreciated its inventory: "Fox has the most conservative policy of carrying film inventories of any of the moving picture companies. New films are written off entirely at the end of ten months or about 40 weeks, although the usual practice is to write off 88 percent of cost in one year. As a result, in Fox's inventory of $6,541,438 there are films which cost a total of around $45,000,000, of which a large proportion are still turning in large weekly rentals, although they are not carried on the books."[8] This additional consideration meant that investors could anticipate a secure and profitable future when purchasing stock since William Fox ran his corporation in a prudent manner. Within three months, Fox Films stock had appreciated in value by 25 percent.

With his company cash-rich, William Fox went on a spending spree, buying an interest in the West Coast theater chain and four houses in Baltimore. He was also planning new multi-thousand seat luxury first-run houses in Los Angeles, San Francisco, Buffalo and Chicago. Meanwhile, Fox was looking at theaters in the northwest, a chain of second-run theaters in St. Louis, and the Stanley chain in Philadelphia and Eastern Pennsylvania. He purchased the Wolfson-Meyer circuit in Miami which operated "several houses for colored patronage,"[9] and was exploring other theaters in Florida. Fox's theaters had previously been clustered in and around New York and the east coast. With 28 exchanges in the United States, he intended to blanket every territory with his Fox Film Corporation releases in company-owned or affiliated theaters.

The ever-competitive Adolph Zukor would take over the Balaban & Katz chain of Chicago in a joint management plan by which Sam Katz would run all of Famous Players–Lasky's theaters as a separate corporate entity, Publix. The massive deal included nine large Chicago picture palaces with total seating of over 30,000, a half-interest in the Lubliner & Trinz circuit of 26 more theaters in outlying areas of Chicago, and a 50 percent interest in 21 houses in nine Illinois towns.[10] The theater division would become so important to the company that it would change its name in 1930 to the Paramount-Publix Corporation. The competition between major producers to build theater chains had begun in earnest.

What had become obvious to all studio executives in preparing their 1925-1926 releases was that audiences responded to higher budget films. Ever since Cecil B. DeMille's *The Ten Commandments* (1923), James Cruze's *The Covered Wagon* (1923), M-G-M's *The Big Parade* (1925), and Fox's own *The Iron Horse* (1925), the exclusive run/roadshow kicked off a release that meant large returns down the road. Since these presentations were more common, it was not practical to lease legitimate theaters as had been done in the past. Now, large movie palaces became a necessity to showcase these "special" engagements.

> To show the more expensive picture in proper form, with fitting prologue, adequate music and impressive surroundings, the small theater became passé in seating capacity, stage room and general appearance. Veritable palaces of marble and bronze are being built both here and abroad. Expert showmen are developing tabloid reviews and choice spectacles! Short subjects of classic beauty are becoming obtainable; architectural designs eliminating posts and providing choice loges and clear vision for all seats are reaching perfection; mechanical devices that automatically reveal vacant seats; cooling plants that make the theater an oasis in the hottest climate or on the warmest summer day; all these mean the investment of vast sums in theater construction.[11]

A reliance on plays and novels, which had been the mainstay of motion pictures when William Fox entered production, originally gave way, due to cost and the necessity of tailoring films to suit contract stars, to original studio-created scenarios. However, there was a swing back to established material by 1925. With fewer star series, there was less need to custom fit as much of the story material. As well, it was becoming more common to hire a star on a per-picture basis so casts could be tailored to the material rather than the reverse. Of the 45 Fox releases that year, fully one-third were derived from novels and almost another third from plays and short stories. By 1926, the number of original scripts had dropped further, making up only a quarter of all story material. The rights to plays had become expensive (as pointed out in the previous chapter), but the value of a well-known property often outweighed the heavy costs. As was always proven, though, there was no such thing as a guaranteed hit in the movie business.

Playwright Winchell Smith sold four of his plays to Fox for the 1925 release year, including *The Fool*. A pedigreed story, it came at high expense and its future did not look promising to *Variety*: "As it stood Sunday night at the Central 'The Fool' was at least half an hour too long, too finely crowded with closeups and unnecessary titles and cluttered with a mass of detail. But Mr. Fox and Winfield Sheehan know that 'The Fool' has some cutting coming its way. With that done, they have a picture which has many more possibilities than its New York showing may indicate."[12]

Another review in the *Film Daily* was less enthusiastic about the film's potential: "'The Fool' enjoyed a long and successful run as a stage play and Fox paid considerably for the screen rights. Just what returns they will reap upon their investment is questionable."[13]

The *New York Times* felt the film was "quite a stirring production which might have been more powerful and satisfying had the director, Harry Millarde, insisted on using the bludgeon less and the rapier more." Nevertheless, the star of the film, Edmund Lowe, received good notices: "Mr. Lowe is restrained and sympathetic throughout his performance. He has a fine face, with a high forehead, a well chiseled nose and a firm mouth. He has been careful with his make-up and in his attire. He has an infectious smile and his eyes radiate sincerity and kindness."[14] *The Fool* (1925), the highest-budget film of the year at $452,000, ended up with a staggering loss of $150,000, the most of any Fox film in 1925.

Another fact stood out which emphasized the importance of story material. Of the 586 features of five reels or more in length during 1924, less than a fourth of them were carried by stars. "Every production of the future, in order to be thoroughly successful, must possess a quality which can be described only as 'heart interest,' bringing a laugh one moment and a tear the next. In the final analysis the story is the thing. No player, no matter how gifted, can succeed unless placed in a good story."[15] So declared Jesse L. Lasky, one of the founding partners of Famous Players–Lasky.

For 1925-1926, a Fox ad promised a slate of releases that was sure to be terrific because "The Biggest Showmen Know the Biggest Product and Book It!" Fox boasted that in Chicago, the Ascher Brothers booked 100 percent Fox product for their 13 theaters and that William James booked the same ratio for his five theaters in Columbus, Ohio. Fox's general sales manager, James Grainger, was able to secure a 100 percent first-run of Fox films for five years with the Interstate Amusement Corp., which controlled theaters in Texas in such cities as Dallas, Fort Worth, San Antonio, and Houston, as well as Little Rock, Arkansas and Birmingham, Alabama. It was the next best thing to owning the theaters and it eliminated the overhead while guaranteeing the screens.[16] This exclusive deal would lure Loew's, Inc., into Texas and create yet another in the endless succession of local skirmishes for the control of territories, either with other major theater-owning studios or other local chains.

A recent development was the day-and-date bookings in more than one local theater. One of the advantages of these simultaneous multiple bookings was that films could be exploited cooperatively among different theaters, cutting down on per-theater advertising costs. In September 1925, 30 sub-run houses in Cleveland were playing five different Fox specials including *The Fool*, *The Iron Horse*, *Havoc*, *Lightnin'*, and *As No Man Has Loved*.[17]

Included in the planned annual release schedule were 24 Fox Supreme Attractions among which were *The Iron Horse* (still running after its exclusive engagement of late 1924), *The First Year*, *As No Man Has Loved*, *Lightnin'*, *Lazybones*, *East Lynne*, *Siberia*, *The Johnstown Flood*, *The Fool*, *7th Heaven*, *Wages for Wives*, and five from a very active John Ford: *Kentucky Pride*, *Lightnin'*, *The Fighting Heart*, *Thank You* and *Three Bad Man*. There were also to be seven Tom Mix productions and a like number of Buck Jones features. Among the short subjects were 20 *Imperial Comedies*, eight *Van Bibber Comedies* starring Earle Foxe, eight *O'Henry* comedies, eight *Married Life of Helen and Warren* comedies, 26 *Fox Varieties* and the twice-weekly *Fox News*. The ad concluded, "See Fox Manager for Your Profit's Sake."[18]

The short-subject division was important enough to Fox's bottom line that it warranted a rare pronouncement from General Manager Winfield Sheehan: "In laying its plans for the coming year, Fox Film Corporation determined upon a $2,000,000 short subject program. This program, in keeping with the program of feature pictures, is unprecedented in magnitude and unequalled in quality. The result is that the Fox sales organization is able to offer every class of exhibitor a complete program second to none in entertainment, variety and box-office value."[19]

Earle W. Hammons, the president of Educational Pictures, a company created to exclusively

Victor McLaglen, George O'Brien and J. Farrell MacDonald (the tallest men from left) in *The Fighting Heart* (1925) (courtesy Robert S. Birchard).

produce and distribute short subjects that were "The Spice of the Program," commented on an irony of his product's evolving importance.

> When I first came into the industry the short-reel pictures, with the exception of those produced by two companies that were making comedies, scenics, and educational pictures, were commonly known as "chasers," and they rightfully deserved that name. If a theatre had an audience and wanted to get another audience in, they put on one of those chasers and it would get the people out. The reason those pictures were chasers was that some assistant cameraman or assistant to the assistant cameraman would take a camera and a thousand feet of film and go out and keep turning and turning. If he took ten feet you might be interested in seeing it, but you would not be interested in fifty feet. Finally we contrived to cut that down and make really interesting pictures by selecting our views and shooting only ten feet where it was required, instead of fifty.
>
> Then our great problem was to try to make the theatre owner understand that these were no longer chasers, that he could run them and have the audience remain in their seats and enjoy the picture. Finally, after years of study in making better pictures, we succeeded so well that now some of the bigger companies like Paramount–Famous Lasky and Metro have determined to go into the releasing of short reels.[20]

While William Fox devoted more time to his theater division, Winfield Sheehan was placed front and center as a spokesman for the Fox Film Corporation, singing praises of the upcoming releases. "With evidence of prosperity in all sections of the country, with bright prospects for the harvesting of large crops in the extensive farming districts, and with the American public constantly increasing its patronage, I believe the forthcoming season will be the greatest the motion picture industry has ever known.... More money, sanely expended, is now going into pictures than ever before and the keen competition that exists among the leading producers makes it imperative that the one who hopes to succeed must produce the best."[21]

Earle Foxe, who appeared in 24 Van Bibber comedy short subjects, also starred in many Fox features between 1924 and 1929, including *The Last Man on Earth* (1924) (courtesy Robert S. Birchard).

The Film Year Book highlighted the 10 Best Pictures of 1925, selected by the "most important motion picture critics of the trade and fan publications, as well as critics of some of the best known daily newspapers."

> *The Gold Rush* (United Artists)
> *The Unholy Three* (MGM)
> *Don Q, Son of Zorro* (United Artists)
> *The Merry Widow* (MGM)
> *The Last Laugh* (Universal)
> *The Freshman* (Pathé)
> *The Phantom of the Opera* (Universal)
> *The Lost World* (Pathé)
> *The Big Parade* (MGM)
> *Kiss Me Again* (Warner)[22]

Notably absent once again from the list were titles released by Fox, a company which had become known for appealing to the general public rather than the critics. In an effort to upgrade the studio's reputation, Maurice Revnes, the company's production manager, announced plans "to eliminate hokum from Fox pictures, assisted by important critics and writers."[23] Before these efforts went into effect, The National Board of Review issued its list of the Forty Best Pictures of 1925 (up to December 1) and not surprisingly, only two Fox films received any mention: *Kentucky Pride*, directed by John Ford, and *Havoc* starring Madge Bellamy. Several films released late in the year would greatly boost Fox Films' presence on critics' lists in the following season, including John Ford's *The Iron Horse* and Frank Borzage's *Lazybones* with Buck Jones, and *East Lynne* starring Alma Rubens.[24]

From the viewpoint of movie fans, Fox was still lagging behind in star power. *Photoplay* magazine chose the six best performances of every month and out of a total of 72 possible awards, the only mention of a Fox star was Tom Mix in *Dick Turpin*. Among the most popular performances were Charlie Chaplin in *The Gold Rush*, Douglas Fairbanks in *Don Q, Son of Zorro*, Raymond Griffith in *Paths to Paradise*, Betty Bronson in *Peter Pan*, Harold Lloyd in *The Freshman*, Lon Chaney in *The Phantom of the Opera* and *The Unholy Three*, Mary Pickford in *Little Annie Rooney*, Gloria Swanson in *Madame Sans-Gene*, Colleen Moore in *So Big* and *Sally*, John Gilbert in *The Big Parade*, and Emil Jannings in *The Last Laugh*.

Many of the Critics' Top Ten selections were huge hits, with the sole exception of *The Last Laugh*, a heavily dramatic German-made film directed by F.W. Murnau. Many exhibitors believed that the propensity of German directors to strive for raw realism and tragic stories made their films unappealing to American audiences which translated into low grosses.

Just because Fox Films did not have any releases in "Ten Best" lists had no bearing on its box-office results. Overall production at Fox was down to its lowest point since 1915 with only 43 features, but domestic rentals rose by a solid 18 percent to $11,750,515. Costs also hit a record average of $121,554 per feature and the total expenditure was $5,226,809.

Audiences had changed considerably since the initial years of the industry and had become more discriminating, as William Fox noted in 1921. While it took more production money to lure crowds into theaters, patrons could be fickle and simply not show up in numbers sufficient to turn a profit. There was still a ceiling for potential rentals and also a floor on how much could be lost. William Fox had long ago figured out this equation and assigned budgets accordingly. These ranges, nevertheless, still allowed the company to be lucrative. Corporate profits for 11 months from December 1924 to November 1925 totaled $2,527,241 with $5.05 in per share earnings on Class A and B stock. Total corporate assets were $26,655,000.[25]

Amidst the influx of profits for major production companies, independent distributors were disappearing at a rapid rate. Within the next few years, companies like East Coast, Atlas, Davis, Artclass, Steiner, Barsky, Chadwick, Rayart, Banner, Truart and dozens of others would fade out permanently, leaving theaters to deal mainly with the major companies which were consolidating their production, distribution and exhibition strength.

As a reminder that some producers' problems never went away, Jewel Carmen returned to William Fox's attention in 1925. When Carmen was under contract to Fox Films in 1917-1918, she created problems for Sol Wurtzel by disappearing without a trace when she was supposed to report for filming. Several times, private investigators were hired to try and find her. Her relations with Wurtzel during this period were almost always antagonistic. In one case, she was spreading rumors about Sunshine director Lewis Seiler propositioning her in the presence of her chauffeur. Wurtzel described the predicament to William Fox: "I called her into my office, confronted her with these statements, and had the chauffeur in my office at the same time. Carmen did not deny that she had made these statements, but I made her admit that at no time had Mr. Seiler or I treated her in anything but a courteous and gentlemanly way. I told her then if she would make any more statements of that kind I would have her arrested."[26]

Carmen's misbehavior continued to the point that Wurtzel declared she "should never be featured in a picture by the Fox Film Corporation; it is also my opinion that she should never be allowed to get out of her contract, that she should be humiliated and belittled in every way so that her reputation, in so far as the screen is concerned, should be forever ruined, and teach her a lesson and through her teach others under contract a lesson."[27]

Unfortunately, the firing had a delayed effect. When Jewel Carmen had signed her contract with Fox Films, she was a minor and was represented through a contract with Frank A. Keeney Pictures Corporation. When she came of age, she "rescinded her contract with Fox and gave notice that she would continue with the Keeney contract. Thereafter, Fox entered into an indemnity agreement with Keeney, induced Keeney to break his contract with Miss Carmen, and the result was that Miss Carmen was unemployed and out of a contract."[28] Apparently, Sol Wurtzel's threat had been carried out. Jewel Carmen then sued Fox Films for interfering with her Keeney deal and preventing her from finding work. In 1925, she was awarded a verdict of $59,406.21 to cover the value of her contract. The award was most likely irksome to the executives at Fox after all the aggravation she had caused them.

By late 1925, Sol Wurtzel was pleased with the slate of films ready for release under his supervision: "It has been a great season ... and I believe, on the whole, the result will be more than we expected. We have turned out some mighty fine pictures here this season and the best of all is that the outlook for next season is even better. We are sparing no expense to get the best of material; stage plays, books, originals. I think it is pretty well known now that we have bought 'What Price Glory' and other big hits. Mr. Fox is more determined than ever that only the best will do for our program, and we are headed for bigger accomplishments all the time."[29] Wurtzel was not unfounded in his optimism. The economy was doing well, money was readily available to the motion picture industry from banking concerns and audience attendance was heading steadily uphill.

William Fox's advertising department echoed the optimism and poured on the salesmanship in a double-page trade ad aimed at theater owners, announcing what appeared to be a record year of grosses.

> Every dollar paid for Fox pictures, in fair and reasonable rentals, is an investment for the protection of your home, your theatre and your independence. Every Fox contract is a first line of defence [sic] to preserve your property rights. The steady progress made by Fox pictures has advanced them to the front rank of box-office attractions; their unprecedented quality has gained public recognition for fine, consistent entertainment. For release in the new season, starting September 1926, Fox takes another great step forward through purchase of the world's best stage plays and popular novels of high screen value. The Fox releases for next year are a stupendous aggregation of box-office attractions.[30]

The company geared up with a splashy ad for exhibitors with the image of an eagle and inset text set off against a rendered vision of the stars and stripes. "FOX HAS THE PICTURES!" it boasted as it listed its special "Nine Golden Nuggets":

> Never before in the history of the industry has there been such an array of sterling box-office attractions by one producer. Never before in the history of the industry has perfection been so nearly reached inasmuch as nothing that is requisite is wanting.
>
> Every picture abounds in thrills, tears and laughs
> Every picture visualizes a successful story or play
> The appeal of the William Fox Nine Golden Nuggets
> Will find a responsive chord in every picturegoer
> *The Ancient Mariner* Based on Samuel Coleridge Taylor's classic poem. Taught in every school in the land. A big Christmas special.
> *The Gilded Butterfly* Based on a Best Seller by Evelyn Campbell. A stirring tale of love and adventure at Monte Carlo.
> *Wages for Wives* Based on the play "Chicken Feed," by Guy Bolton, the popular American playwright. A dramatic comedy which hits every home.
> *Daybreak* Based on last year's stage success, "The Outsider." A story of a great ambition thwarted for a while but triumphant in the end through sublime faith.
> *East Lynne* Known and beloved all over the world. Its publicity started more than fifty years ago. The most poignant love story of all time.
> *The First Year* Based on Frank Craven's amusing play of married life. Adapted to the screen by Frances Marion and probably her best work.
> *The Golden Strain* Based on Peter B. Kyne's Cosmopolitan Magazine story, "Thoroughbreds." This is Kyne at his best.
> *The Palace of Pleasure* Based on the play, "Lola Montez." Depicting the tempestuous career of a beautiful Spanish dancer who left a trail of broken hearts in her wake.
> *When the Door Opened* Based on James Oliver Curwood's novel. Considered by many his greatest. It has the most thrilling flood scene ever screened.
> IT'S A WILLIAM FOX YEAR![31]

The box-office results of these "nuggets" were not as stellar as the sales department and hyperbolic executives had hoped. While *The First Year* (1926) was based on a one of the most successful stage shows of the decade, and trade reviews were positive, the film made a fairly decent showing with $266,000 in world rentals but, because of its $157,000 cost, the profit was only $9,000. *East Lynne* (1925), an anticipated hit as well, showed only a minor profit of $14,000 on a production cost of $176,000. The much-heralded Christmas release, *The Ancient Mariner* (1925), was also a moderately expensive production that lost $33,000. The Cavalry western, *The Golden Strain* (1925), based on a short story by popular author, Peter B. Kyne, who had optioned all his future writing to Fox, performed poorly enough to show a $45,000 loss on a $194,000 negative. *The Gilded Butterfly* (1926) was not golden enough on its $131,000 cost to return more than $205,000 in world rentals to result in an $8,000 loss. None of these vaunted releases performed at anticipated levels.

The meat-and-potatoes series with Shirley Mason and Buck Jones continued to be moderately profitable at their budgets, although an occasional flop occurred. The Mason vehicle *The Star Dust Trail* (1924) cost $40,000 but its world rentals amounted to only $49,000 with a loss of $17,000. The Buck Jones films were generally a third of the cost of the Tom Mix series but profits were a third as well. As an example Jones' *Gold and the Girl* (1925) cost $57,000, brought in world rentals of $150,000 and resulted in a $35,000 profit.

The higher-priced Mix westerns, loaded with action and elaborate stunts were big moneymakers for Fox. After eight years of stardom, the studio's most popular star was also the most profitable. *Riders of the Purple Sage* (1925), with a negative cost of $141,000, showed that Fox was spending more on Mix's films than ever before, but with world rentals of $375,000, it turned a profit of $100,000. Although the studio was placing more effort in developing films with the increasingly popular Edmund Lowe, Alma Rubens, and Madge Bellamy, Mix was still the champion moneymaker.

In the last week of 1925, without much fanfare, Fox announced that actress Janet Gaynor, who had been at Universal, was signed to a long-term contract. She, like Tom Mix, would become a major Fox star.

With Fox Film Corporation stock reaching $84 per share in November 1924, almost doubling in just five months, William Fox announced the formation of a new theater company to handle all exhibition operations which would bring another substantial cash infusion.

> The unit will have an authorized capitalization of $4,000,000. The stock is expected to consist of 3,000,000 Class A shares and 100,000 Class B shares, each class sharing equally in the earnings. Control will rest with the Class B stock which will be held by William Fox and associates.
> The company will begin its corporate existence with assets of more than $20,000,000 of which $11,000,000 will be cash and $9,000,000 in equities in theaters, and the only indebtedness will consist

Tom Mix stars with Clara Bow in *The Best Bad Man* (1925) (courtesy Mike Hawks).

of $1,300,000 represented by real estate brokers.... The equity in these properties is put at $9,000,000 accumulated out of earnings from an original investment of $5,000 by Fox in 1905. In addition it is said this investment has paid Fox and his associates $6,000,000.[32]

Fox's plan was now eminently clear to rival companies. He intended to cover the country with Fox-owned theaters.

With the bankers' announcement that the Fox theater stock issue will appear at an early date comes information of a definite nature that William Fox has set plans to either have representation, or have a big 4,000 or 5,000 seat theater in the key cities of the country. Where it becomes necessary to build Fox necessarily cannot occupy the houses for from 18 months to two years, although some of the present cities will have theaters long before then.... General Sales Manager James R. Grainger, declaring he knew nothing of theater plans of the company, said however, "I know this: that regardless of booking combinations, agreements, or whatever exists Fox product will be played in every key city of this country; we will not be kept out."[33]

Fox was not the only company gobbling up theater chains and building luxury houses. Universal, the perennial runt of the majors, negotiated a deal to take over 93 houses, including ownership in the Hostettler, Sparks and Schine circuits. A publicly traded company was set up, the Universal Chain Theaters Corp. with a capitalization of $2,000,000. Even with concerns surfacing about over-building certain theater districts, the construction contracts continued. In Chicago, 21 houses were being built at a cost of $75,000,000. Names like Lubliner & Trinz, Ascher, Marx, Cooney, and Fitzpatrick & McElroy would be associated with these theaters. Overall, 119 large theaters costing a total of $60,591,660, at an average $466,000 each, were constructed in 1925, eclipsing the previous year's figure of 69.

By 1926, the motion picture industry had evolved to such a point that it became one of the most important businesses in America. While the United States turned out 27 percent of the world's wheat, 63 percent of the world's telephones, 80 percent of the world's automobiles, it produced 85 percent of the world's motion pictures.[34] The domination of foreign markets became so vexing to Italy that Italian producers, in 1925, tried to ban any American films from being shown in their country. The ban failed since Italian audiences enjoyed the imports more than their home-grown films.

Distribution had reached a near-complete penetration of international markets. Famous Players–Lasky and its Paramount Pictures, one of the largest companies, was making a total of 200 positive prints for domestic distribution through 47 exchanges. The largest territorial office was sent eight to 15 prints while the smallest only received one to three prints. For foreign distribution, 142 prints were sent to 115 exchanges in 73 countries and translated into 36 languages.[35]

Paramount considered 13,000 playdates to be the most complete distribution of a release. The company came to this figure by eliminating 7,000 locations because they were competitive houses or below the minimum standards of presentation Paramount allowed. The average circulation of a good picture was 10,000 playdates. The first 1,250 bookings accounted for 75 percent of the revenue a film would bring in and would occur in the initial two to three weeks of release. An average successful film would take the rest of the year to play off the remaining 8,750 to make up average circulation.[36]

Of a total 640 feature-length motion pictures produced in 1925, 540 were filmed in Los Angeles for a total cost of $66,000,000, while New York was the location for only 100 features, with a cost of $15,000,000.[37] The message was clear enough. The future of production lay in the sunny climes of the west coast. Winfield Sheehan spent more time at the Los Angeles plant than in previous years, but Sol Wurtzel was still overseeing the day-to-day operations. Sheehan, meanwhile, was responsible for dealing with foreign operations and spent three months abroad through the summer and fall of 1925. However, he returned to Los Angeles at the end of February 1926 with the intent of staying at the studio until the 1926-1927 slate of films was completed.

There were other changes in production as well. William Fox officially announced in October 1925 that his company was no longer making any pictures in New York, had no further intentions of resuming production there and, after the experience on *Nero*, would have no future plans to shoot abroad. Following the example of Paramount Pictures, M-G-M and First National, in March 1926, Fox instituted a unit system. Winfield Sheehan was in charge of the "super-specials," Edwin C. Hill personally supervised the Tom Mix and Buck Jones westerns, Sol Wurtzel oversaw the "specials,"

and George Marshall was responsible for the two-reel comedies.[38] Reading between the lines, the system elevated Winfield Sheehan to the top production executive on the Los Angeles lot, relegating Sol Wurtzel (who had run the studio operations since 1917), to a secondary position. The lack of success of the expensive 1925 year-end releases may have played a part in the need for more supervision. East Coast production would resume periodically when such a location was necessary to the story but, for the most part, it was the end of active picture-making for Fox in New York.

The outlook for the 1926-1927 booking season was extremely positive. Associated Exhibitors, an independent outfit, announced a schedule of 100 releases, dramatically up from 30 the year before. Universal increased from 50 to 63. Paramount–Famous Lasky would increase its output to 75 features. First National was planning to add an additional ten releases to reach a total of 60. M-G-M scheduled 52 releases, up from 45, and United Artists planned 15, up from ten. Warners, which was experiencing financial difficulties, was the only company to cut back to 34 films from 40 in 1925-1926. Fox announced 49 features for the upcoming season, one fewer than the year before. Factoring in state rights distributors, a total of 811 features were scheduled for release.[39]

Of Fox's 49 releases, there would only be two series of pictures, seven with Tom Mix and the same amount with Buck Jones. The rest would be considered one-off specials. The releases, with some titles ultimately being changed, and two unannounced at this point, were broken down into the following groups:

Giant Specials:
   7th Heaven, *The Music Master*, *3 Bad Men*, *What Price Glory*, *One Increasing Purpose*

Group 1
   Is Zat So?, *Fig Leaves*, *The Auctioneer*, *The Return of Peter Grimm*, *The Lily*, *The Way Things Happen*, *Cradle Snatchers*, *The Monkey Talks*, *The Pelican* (retitled *Marriage License*), *Pigs* (retitled *The Midnight Kiss*)

Group 2
   Mother Machree, *The Family Upstairs*, *Going Crooked*, *The Devil's Master*, *The Holy Terror*, *Wedlock*, *A Temperature Town*, *A Milk White Flag*, *A Black Sheep*, *Married Alive*

Group 3
   The City, *Whispering Wires*, *In Old Virginia*, *Hidden Charms*, *X-Ray Eyes*, *A Paris Divorce*, *Male Flappers*, *Mankind*, *Sins of Humanity*

To provide enough rentals to pay for the constantly rising costs of all films, distribution contracts included clauses that locked in terms guaranteeing that exhibitors would play a certain number of Fox films. A summation of the contractual changes was compiled by the *Film Daily*:

For Super Specials
Article 23: Provides that the exhibitor will play the super-special productions in the order in which they are released by the Fox Film Corp. and in the event the distributor serves a subject out of the released order it shall no(t) be regarded as a release to the exhibitor of the obligation to take all subjects released by Fox under the contract and in such cases the exhibitor shall play all subjects which are released prior and subsequence to the photoplay released out of its order.

For Tom Mix and for "Buck Jones."
Article 6: Provides exhibitor shall start the playing of the Mix and Jones pictures at a specific date, to play a specific number per month and the entire contract shall be completed within a specified period.
Article 24: This provides for the same producer for the Tom Mix and Buck Jones as is provided for super-specials in Article 23.
Article 25: It is understood and agreed by both parties hereto that the "Special Productions 1926-27" in which the aforementioned star plays or will play leading roles, are not included in the above designated pictures.
Article 26: That the number of pictures contracted for hereunder as "Buck" Jones productions (or Tom Mix Productions as the case may be) is approximate only.

For Specials
Article 6a: Same as article 6 above.
Article 24: Same as Article 24, excepting that instead of "special productions" the words Buck Jones are used.
Article 25: Provides that exhibitor has not the right or option to any other pictures produced with Mix and Jones in the stellar role except those specified in the contract. The distributor reserves the right to produce and release other pictures during the period of the contract in which these stars shall appear in addition to the pictures sold.[40]

Upgrading its talent, Fox signed three directors in mid–1926, rating a news flash under the headline "Busy Days at Fox."

"Allen Dwan, Al [Alfred E.] Green and John Stahl join Fox. Each and every one is a box-office director; each record, measured by successful productions, proves that. This is only one of the moves under way at Fox, but its importance augurs much for others to come."[41]

With imports from Germany like F.W. Murnau's *The Last Laugh* (1924) and E.A. Dupont's *Variety* (1925) gaining critical and popular acclaim, William Fox could not ignore the influence of recent developments in German cinema, from technical improvements in cameras to innovative film techniques. Other studios were hiring Germans as the directors *du jour*. Lothar Mendes, signed by Paramount, and Paul Leni at Universal, were offered lucrative deals with larger budgets than in their native land. Studios signed up these representatives of Teutonic cinema in the hope of achieving artistic greatness along with box-office strength.

"William Fox thought that Murnau's *The Last Laugh* was the greatest film ever made, and that Murnau could lead his company into an era of quality productions that would turn around the perception of Fox as a second tier studio."[42] Fox quickly signed F.W. Murnau, on loan from Ufa Studios, to a very generous contract, allowing him to work with the writer and cameraman of his choice. It was an unusual nod to the German director and would be an expensive undertaking.

Fox showered Murnau with receptions in New York befitting a head of state. At a dinner in Murnau's honor, William Fox rose and presented the director with a challenge, "I charge you, sir, with doing your artistic best."[43] Murnau was scheduled to direct *A Trip to Tilsit* starring George O'Brien

An insert advertisement from 1926, boasting Fox's new contract director, F.W. Murnau (courtesy Karl Thiede).

and Margaret Livingston, after which he would return to Germany to fulfill his contract with the Ufa Studio. Even though William Fox had left Sheehan and Wurtzel in charge of most production work, he became a hands-on producer once again, reading script drafts and corresponding with Murnau at great length.

The Fox Film Corporation already had a distribution agreement in place to handle German imports for American release and had set up Europa Fox Produktion mainly to meet that government's requirement to be able to release their pictures in Germany. Although distribution companies could import any number of German films, studio heads felt that having critically acclaimed directors under contract, melding their unique styles with stories designed for American audiences, would be far more productive.

Studios were always jockeying for position as leader of the pack and a telling advertisement placed by M-G-M, made light of the issues facing the quality of production as the golden age of silent movies was under way. Highlighted by a full-page color ad which portrayed a Rube Goldberg cartoon of a sausage-making machine, the next two pages declared: "The Day of Weenies Is Past, Thanks to M-G-M. No more sausages. The day is over when your public can be expected to pay money to see pictures turned out like sausages. Those weenies tasted good once but when you have to serve sausages again and again you'll see empty seats. Two years ago M-G-M killed the sausage idea. In the moving picture business M-G-M attacked the factory system and showed them all how to produce individualized pictures each of which is a product in itself and not part of a machine-made output."[44]

Winfield Sheehan understood the need for further improvement in the quality of Fox Films: "There was a time when audiences would sit through a picture with a mediocre plot, played by mediocre actors. Today they are more discerning. Motion pictures must meet this discernment. The oft told story of the boy who loved a girl, only to fall from grace by being accused wrongfully of a crime and being exonerated in her eyes when the villain is brought to justice, won't suffice any longer. Motion picture themes today must be big and different. And with this change we must have new faces, for, good as they are, a little group of screen idols cannot go on forever. Youth cannot be denied. It must be heard — or seen. Another five years will see dozens of names in lights that today are unheard of. And with this metamorphosis of the picture industry must come new methods of production and presentation."[45]

Stretching the company's horizons for material, Maurice Revnes, head of the production department, spent two months in England, France and Germany and made deals for 14 stories, including six well-known plays. There were plans to introduce the plays in the United States, debuting them on Broadway in the fall of 1926. There is no indication that this plan brought forth any actual performances.

Providing additional production capacity while abandoning the New York studio, William Fox acquired a parcel of land from the Janns Corporation, a major Los Angeles real-estate firm which was in the process of subdividing its holdings on the west side of the city into the planned communities of Westwood, Brentwood, and Bel Air.[46] The land was initially purchased in 1923 on the edge of Beverly Hills and would become known as Fox Hills.[47] Investing over $2,000,000 in a new "location studio" consisting of outdoor standing sets, William Fox planned a facility influenced by Spanish architecture covering 100 acres and accommodating 20,000 people. By comparison, the New York studio covered 30 acres and could accommodate only 1,000 production people.

Opening to the public on August 29, 1926, the "Greatest Outdoor Studio" was dedicated with typical Hollywood pizzazz. There was a flag-raising of the Stars and Stripes by a contingent of Marines to blaring band music, a parade of cowboys and a glittering array of Fox's most popular movie stars. Angelenos could glimpse vivacious Olive Borden presenting the flag to a company of Marines who appeared in *What Price Glory*. Tom Mix, Fox Films' most popular western star, put on a complete horse-riding show. Among the other players present for the occasion were George O'Brien, Anita Stewart, Virginia Valli, Belle Bennett, Alma Rubens, Janet Gaynor, Gladys McConnell, Lou Tellegen, J. Farrell MacDonald, Dolores Del Rio, Bessie Love, Alec Francis, Buck Jones, Kathryn Perry, Florence Gilbert, Richard Walling, Walter McGrail, May McAvoy, May Allison, Robert Frazer, William Powell, Tom Santschi, Frank Campeau, Leslie Fenton, Oscar Shaw, John Roche, and John St. Polis. Among the officials of the Fox Company who attended were Vice-President of Production Winfield Sheehan, Sol Wurtzel, general superintendent of the West Coast studios, and Business Manager Ben Jacks.

The public was allowed to pass through the 12 foot wall that surrounded 40 acres and take a rare

One corner of the new Fox Hills Studio, circa 1926 (courtesy Robert S. Birchard).

tour of the studio grounds, where they could see many of the sets actually used in recent and upcoming productions. Among them were streets in the French villages used in *What Price Glory* (1927); scenes in Bolivian jungles and streets in London for *Upstream* (1927), directed by John Ford; New York and mountain resort scenes of Irving Cummings's *The Country Beyond* (1926); the beautiful garden and conservatories of *The Return of Peter Grimm* (1926), directed by Victor Schertzinger; scenes for *Whispering Wires* (1926), directed by Albert Ray; exterior scenes for *Marriage License* (1926), directed by Frank Borzage; and many other standing stock sets used in Fox comedies.

When the Fox Film Corporation reported its six months' balance sheet it listed the following subsidiaries which showed how truly far-flung it was: William Fox Vaudeville Company, Fox Philadelphia Building Inc., Fox Film Realty Company, Fox Film Ltd. (Canada), Broadway Building Corp., Fox Motion Picture Display Co., Fox Film Corp. (Texas), Fox Chicago Realty Corp., Fox Film de Mexico S.A., Fox Film de la Argentina, Fox Film do Brazil S.A., Fox Film Societé Anonyme, Fox Film Aktiebolaget (Sweden), Fox Film Co. Ltd. (England), Fox Film Corp. (Australia), Fox Film de Cuba S.A., Fox Film Corp. (Italy), Hispano Fox Film S.A.E., Netherlands Fox Film Corp., Deutsch Vereins Fox A.G., Fox Film Corp G.m.b.H. (Austria), Fox Film Corp. G.m.b.H. (Czecho-Slovakia), Fox Film A.G. (Hungary), Fox Film Corp. for Baltic States, Fox Far East Corp. (Japan), Los Angeles Studios, Fox Film Corp. (Poland), and Fox Film Corp. (Egypt).[48]

William Fox, in 1926, was the second-most heavily insured man in the world with a $6,000,000 policy on his life, $4,500,000 of which rested with the company.[49] With two studios in Los Angeles, a firmly established worldwide distribution organization, plans for expansion into studios in Europe and foreign theater chains, and a proven executive leadership firmly in control of the latest developments in the industry, he was positioned to take advantage of the next explosive phase of growth in the motion picture business. While Famous Players–Lasky and First National had led the industry in theaters, M-G-M was building a stable of stars and producing top-grossing movies, and other studios received more critical attention, Fox would ultimately outstrip them all in technology.

6. The Rise of Winfield Sheehan

In the years between 1926 and 1928, Hollywood experienced a maturation which blended art and industry to a level new to cinema. Influenced heavily by the artistry of foreign talents, largely German, new concepts of cinematography, lighting, set design, and special effects known as "trick shots" permeated American filmmaking methods. The somber and sometimes morbid themes of German films also seeped into the American cinema, often to the chagrin of exhibitors who preferred America's exuberant optimism and happy endings.

For Hollywood, the era of the silent star was reaching its apex as well. The importance of a stable of talents was promulgated by M.G.M. with every studio following suit to give more credibility to the value of its films. The celebrity hierarchy which was dominated by just a handful of stars a decade earlier, greatly expanded to encompass dozens of popular performers with new favorites appearing regularly. A younger generation of directors, just entering the business in the mid–1920s, saw their careers blossom. Experimentation became the norm as directors stretched the scope of visual boundaries. The once impossible became possible to portray on the screen with higher budgets and greater photographic skills. Acting styles as well became more subtle and expressive. It was to be the golden age of silent films—albeit a short-lived one.

At the same time, great progress was being made in the showmanship aspects of exhibition. High-budget productions had become hugely successful through their initial exclusive roadshow runs, including *The Ten Commandments* (1923, Paramount), *The Covered Wagon* (1923, Paramount), *The Iron Horse* (1924, Fox), *The Thief of Bagdad* (1924, United Artists), *The Phantom of the Opera* (1925, Universal), and *The Gold Rush* (1925, United Artists). While the concept of an exclusive engagement had been in use for years, studios earmarked their costliest productions for this style of exhibition which became much more formalized.

The roadshow runs of M.G.M.'s *The Big Parade* (1925) and *Ben-Hur* (1925) were cited as templates for the exacting terms of such presentations. A genuine roadshow enterprise demanded a vast organization, attention to detail, and great skill in finding theaters appropriate for such presentations. The one overriding factor was to provide conformity to the program so that the presentation in each location was identical with the one in New York—from music to staging to the mechanical sound and lighting effects. For such engagements, patrons were expected to pay $1.65 to $2.20 admission prices. The importance of the roadshow run was made evident by the grosses of individual pictures on Broadway alone. *The Big Parade* grossed $2,000,000 at the Astor Theater alone (nearly 1,500,000 admissions) and *Ben-Hur* made $625,000 in its initial Broadway presentation. There was the added benefit of building word-of-mouth advertising as a film spread from New York.

The roadshow differed in many respects from the standard policy of the motion picture first-run. In the first place, the attraction was not run continuously, but only in two complete shows daily and all seats were reserved. Astonishingly, drop-in attendance in the middle of the picture was discouraged and tickets were no longer available once a show began. This practice was believed to be in the best interest of the audience and it also allowed a film to be viewed from beginning to end without people arriving and leaving randomly throughout the screening. Secondly, the roadshow concentrated entirely on the production being shown without the addition of newsreels, comedy short subjects, prologues or variety acts. The third vital distinction was the accompanying synchronized music score provided by a touring orchestra that stayed with that particular roadshow unit right through its entire tour. Musical scores were prepared by professional arrangers who had worked in musical theater or opera. Road orchestras were carefully rehearsed by each company unit for two weeks in advance of its first public tryout.

In addition, roadshows were publicized on the merits of the picture itself. Big names—even star values—were secondary. However, if a big star was in the film, it certainly did not hurt the box-office. The style of publicity maintained a certain level of dignity and class. Ballyhoos and publicity "tie-ups" were strictly taboo.

The roadshow company had a seasonal job instead of the all-year-round schedule of the regular theaters. Each company began its tour in August or September and ended around April or May, avoiding the customary summer drop-off in attendance. An entourage moved with a 60-foot baggage car of properties and effects, and a personnel crew of 25 people. The entire equipment package — projection, lighting, shadow box, screen, mechanical effects— was set up in each theater, unless that particular venue happened to have the identical equipment.[1] M.G.M. spent $3,000,000 to operate 20 roadshow companies for the initial releases of *The Big Parade* and *Ben-Hur*. Booking agents, like J.J. McCarthy, were involved in putting together the venues for these runs. William Fox was not one to shy away from a good thing and announced that there would be no fewer than twelve roadshow companies for the 1927 release of *What Price Glory*.

In this period, a multitude of films were poised to stake their claim to a roadshow pedigree based on their expenditures. Paramount Pictures heralded its big-budgeted quartet of releases: *Old Ironsides* (1926 — $2,216,033), *The Rough Riders* (1927 — $1,299,128), D.W. Griffith's *Sorrows of Satan* (1926 — $971,216) and *Beau Geste* (1927 — $902,720). Cecil B. DeMille's Pathé release of *The King of Kings* (1927) ended up costing $2,285,832, nearly $600,000 over its budget. Even Universal was spending $1,763,008 on *Uncle Tom's Cabin* (1927). Certainly, the era of the giant budget had arrived and had nowhere to go but up.

Along with the increased budgets of blockbusters and roadshows came extended running times. An exclusive roadshow engagement of a film like *The Big Parade* (1925, M.G.M.), *Ben-Hur* (1925, M.G.M.), *Wings* (1927, Paramount), *Beau Geste* (1927, Paramount), and *The King of Kings* (1927, Pathé) ran well over two hours and some included an intermission. Running times were often cut before a film went into its general release. When they were not cut, some theater owners objected to such bloated running times and many critics even expressed a desire for further cutting on average pictures which were just 90 minutes long.

In a trade article, Eric T. Clarke, the General Manager of the Eastman Theater in Rochester, New York, which played to an audience over 2,000,000 people per year, voiced his opinion.

> I am still convinced that most feature pictures running over 80 minutes hurts its chances of success by their length. The past year has also seen some improvement in economy of footage, but the relative position of the three major companies remains unchanged. The past year has also seen a reduction in the amount of forced cutting [by exhibitors]. "The Volga Boatman" coming to us 10,600 ft. long had of necessity to be shortened unless we were to sacrifice our overture and weekly film news. This I am unwilling to do for any picture. Meantime another problem in this regard has forced itself upon us. Several pictures produced for road-show length of two-and-one-half-hour performance have been released for regular motion picture presentations. As the two-hour show is standard with most picture houses, the distributors have issued shorter versions. These come to us already cut, and we get blamed by those of our patrons who have seen or heard of sequences exhibited in a road-show and later eliminated. It is a serious question to which, however, I can see no answer at the present time.[2]

This sentiment prompted Richard A. Rowland, head of production at First National to make the pronouncement, "The public has become tired of lengthy pictures — this fact has been demonstrated time and again. Also, with the modern method of arranging programs, with prologues, vaudeville and special features interspersed, too long a picture cuts into the exhibitor's profits. A film running seven reels or more practically cuts out one performance a day — a serious consideration for the exhibitor.... This is a fast-moving age, and the public wants its motion picture entertainment to move at a similar speed.... Henceforth most First National pictures will be limited to approximately 6,000 feet, except in the case of specials."[3] Both Clarke and Rowland were insulated from their audiences and neither opinion carried the day. Roadshows with lengthy running times, when the films were worthy, held a grip on audiences for decades to come.

What types of pictures were popular in the silent film's apex years of 1926-1927? For one thing, Jewish-Irish comedies did well, taking a cue from the stage play *Abie's Irish Rose* (which would not make it to the screen until Paramount's 1929 release) and succeeded as *The Cohens and the Kellys* (1926, Universal), *Private Izzy Murphy* (1926, Warner Bros.), *Kosher Kitty Kelly* (1926, F.B.O.) and *Frisco Sally Levy* (1927, M.G.M.) proved. There were also a number of copycats in this genre, many bordering on bad taste, like F.B.O.'s *Clancy's Kosher Wedding* (1927). Another genre which was finding an audience was the "Crook Pictures." "CROOK PICTURES. Seem to be in demand. At least Coast producers are thinking that way. And looking out for such material. So if you have one up your sleeve dig it out. Female crook stories also wanted. The Evelyn Brent success in such productions has evidently started something. But remember Australia won't admit them." Crooks seemed to be more interesting to audiences than the detectives who solved the mysteries but studios were notified that Australia's censors would not allow the depiction of such behavior in their 1,300 cinemas. "Also wanted are stories with the sea as a background.... Bill Fox wants a historical story with a romance attached. Has a contest on through 'Screenland' for material."[4]

Sports stories proliferated with the countrywide popularity of Jack Dempsey in boxing and Babe Ruth in baseball. Paramount starred Richard Dix in *Knockout Reilly* (1927) and bowing to equal opportunity, *Rough House Rosie* (1927) starring Clara Bow. Universal released *On Your Toes* (1927) with their leading star Reginald Denny. M.G.M. took a comedic look at the sport with Buster Keaton in *The Battling Butler* (1926). Fox, as well, had its share of pugilistic pictures, *The Fighting Heart* (1925) and *Is Zat So?* (1927) and there was major boxing match held on a Navy cruiser in John Ford's *The Blue Eagle* (1926). While M.G.M. produced *Slide, Kelly, Slide* (1927) with William Haines, First National was fortunate to have the "bambino" himself in *Babe Comes Home* (1927), and Paramount competed with *The New Klondike* (1926) and Wallace Beery as *Casey at the Bat* (1927) while Warners had *The Bush Leaguer* (1927).

Studios were also making war-themed pictures with nearly a decade's distance from the battles of World War I. M.G.M. produced *The Big Parade* (1925) and *The Exquisite Sinner* (1926). Fox made *Havoc* (1925) and *What Price Glory* (1927). First National turned out *Dark Angel* (1925), *The New Commandment* (1925), and *The Greater Glory* (1926). Producers Distributing Corporation released *The Crimson Runner* (1925), *Friendly Enemies* (1925), and *The Unknown Soldier* (1926) while Paramount produced *Behind the Front* (1926) and *Wings* (1927). There were even service comedies like *Lost at the Front* (1927, First National) with George Sidney and Charlie Murray in another variation of the Jewish-Irish comedy, and *Spuds* (1927, Pathé) with popular two-reel comedy star Larry Semon.

Flappers were the box-office rage, as were the female stars known for disrobing on camera like Clara Bow, Corinne Griffith and Madge Bellamy. Sex romps and domestic comedies drew well, the steamier the better. Westerns continued their popularity with both the series brand and the super spectacles luring audiences. But popular desert adventures began to fade with the death of Rudolph Valentino in August 1926.

Production increased at the Fox studio in Los Angeles under a new system with units made up of production teams, much like the companies that William Fox originally sent out to Sol Wurtzel in 1916-1917. Eleven companies were using every inch of studio space in the last quarter of 1926. The West Coast production schedule was so crammed that Raoul Walsh was working on two pictures at the same time, completing principal photography on *The Monkey Talks* and sitting with editors and titlers on *What Price Glory*. John Ford was directing *Mother Machree*, and Howard Hawks was shooting *Gaby* (released as *Paid to Love*) starring George O'Brien and Virginia Valli. Frank Borzage was preparing to start on *7th Heaven* and F.W. Murnau had begun his first production for Fox, *Sunrise*.

Two productions were also wrapping up in the reactivated East Coast studio where Allan Dwan was directing *Summer Bachelors* and Irving Cummings was completing *Bertha, the Sewing Girl*. Director Alfred E. Green was in New York preparing to shoot *The Auctioneer* starring George Sidney.

With contract directors like John Ford, Raoul Walsh, Howard Hawks, Frank Borzage, Allan Dwan, and F.W. Murnau, William Fox and Winfield Sheehan had finally corralled talent that would reach the critical acclaim of other major studios. To make the point, Fox Films took an ad in the trades with the banner "They Direct Fox profit pictures— You Play 'Em and reap the benefit

Madge Bellamy in a less glamorous role than usual as **Bertha, the Sewing Machine Girl** (1926) (courtesy Robert S. Birchard).

of their brains and experience." The ad included other contract directors: John Griffith Wray, Victor Schertzinger, Harry Beaumont, Irving Cummings, George H. Melford, J.G. Blystone, Alfred E. Green, Lewis Seiler, R. William Neill, Scott Dunlap, Lambert Hillyer, Ben Stoloff, Eddie Cline, and Albert Ray.[5]

Even with the production capacity of the new studio in Fox Hills, facilities were still being expanded. Ben Jackson, manager of the studios, announced that the building and reconstruction program at both lots would reach an expenditure of $750,000. The Western Avenue improvements included two new stages, each 300 by 150 feet, and a new wardrobe and costume building, 200 by 70 feet. The stages cost $50,000 each and the wardrobe structure cost $45,000. A garage that could service 30 trucks was being built as well as buildings for plastering, carpentering, tinsmithing and blacksmithing departments. There would also be additional dressing rooms and an armory for weapons and explosives. At the Fox Hills lot, a $50,000 structure was built to house four screening rooms, 24 editing rooms and 16 rooms for story readers.[6]

One of the most important changes for the Los Angeles production center was that Winfield Sheehan relocated to the new studio facility to oversee production. The *Film Daily* reported, "Not by accident or snap decision did this come about. The Sheehan move was merely another in a long series of carefully wrought moves by which [William] Fox determined to secure the place in the celluloid sun for which he had set his cap. The Sheehan regime caused no flurries in the beginning. Rather were the other studios prone to smile tolerantly. Their good nature was predicated on the fact that Sheehan's knowledge of production had no practical background."[7]

Nevertheless, Sheehan learned quickly and the *Film Daily* was just as quick to notice.

> Some months ago, "Winnie" Sheehan traveled West. Production was to be his particular job for Fox. Many pictures on the current schedule were in work or planned. That was that.
>
> But Sheehan devoted his full energies to next year's productions. There was where he was to get his chance to put his ideas in work.... Time passed by. The first evidence of the Sheehan regime has arrived. Not only in New York. It has "arrived" in several ways, not the least important of which is the box-office.... The picture is "Fig Leaves." It's a delightful and amusing story. There is a gorgeous style parade in Technicolor, designed, built and concocted for the female contingent. The Adam and Eve episode which introduces the modern version is cleverly done. It has laughs.... Howard Hawks wrote the story and directed. Thereby Mr. Hawks scored for himself a bull's-eye."[8]

Variety praised the film on which Sheehan was supervising producer: "It deals in a fresh way with the husband and wife debate over clothes; has a startling fashion show done in exquisite color; there is a laughable prolog in the Garden of Eden which is a giggle from start to finish, and it winds up in one of those happy finales."[9]

Under Sheehan's guidance, the new unit system of producers installed in March 1926 to boost the quality of Fox productions seemed to have a positive effect on Fox's films. Another release, *The Family Upstairs*, garnered praise for its honest attempt to portray a "truly spiritual comedy of every-day life.... The picture has a wealth of 'class,' another term for literary excellence.... Not a little of the finest passages take real force from the daintily etched characterization of Virginia Valli, a capital actress who has never been so well fitted with a congenial role ... as a creation in the sense of a high class, artistic bit of dramatizing life, it is notable."[10]

Both *Fig Leaves*, on a cost of $193,000, and *The Family Upstairs* returned relatively reasonable profits of around $30,000 each. The critical nod was icing on the cake.

John Ford had distinguished himself with *The Iron Horse* but afterwards had been assigned several films of less importance. By the time *Three Bad Men* was released, he was back in fine form: "John Ford, who directed, has turned out a special in the fullest sense of the word.... There are scenes in it as effective as the wagon train in 'The Covered Wagon,' and the thousands in the mad race across country when the government lands are opened to the public is bigger than anything of its kind that has been shown in a picture.... This is a super-western and every bit as big as 'The Iron Horse' was."[11]

The *Variety* review of *Marriage License* credits the new production imperatives under vice-president and general manager, Winfield Sheehan: "The whole offering is appropriate to the new idea in the Fox establishment to provide high-class screen product of distinction and breaking away from the hokum variety of flicker melodrama. For high intelligence and artistic standards this picture takes its place with the best of the recent output from the Fox studios." The review lauded Alma Rubens "in the emotional role of a mother torn between love of a man and love of her son." It also was a distinct change from the reviews of the past that criticized Fox Films for cheapness.

"The settings are magnificent, with particular emphasis upon fine handling of light and shades in rich pictorial compositions. In this respect the whole picture is de luxe."[12]

Yet another artistic achievement appeared in the form of *The Return of Peter Grimm* (1926). Based on a well-regarded play, the film revolved around the unsettled spirit of a patriarch who returns to straighten out his family's values. "Victor Schertzinger who directed 'The Return of Peter Grimm' for William Fox, has turned out a picture well worth seeing.... In making the picture Schertzinger has worked out some really remarkable bits of photography in visions, and his handling of the 'returned' Peter to walk through the household and right through the other characters of the story is little short of great.... The supporting company is good with Janet Gaynor as the little heroine, standing out as a 'find.' Also, it's a picture that measures up to the artistic standard that has been set for the product this year."[13]

With *Fig Leaves, The Family Upstairs, Marriage License, The Blue Eagle, Womanpower,* and *Three Bad Men* in theaters worldwide, under the sales campaign of "Fox Week," the company set an all-time record in weekly world film rentals of approximately $600,000, according to *The Wall Street Journal.*

Ever since Sol Wurtzel had been sent by William Fox to the Los Angeles studio in 1917, there had been little direct day-to-day contact with Winfield Sheehan. Wurtzel functioned fairly autonomously but always answering to William Fox. After Sheehan arrived in Los Angeles, it was clear he was still the senior executive, taking credit for the most prestigious productions. There are no known reports of animosity between Sheehan and Wurtzel in this period. It is likely Wurtzel accepted Sheehan's presence since William Fox had made the decision to send him to the west coast.

Fox Films seemed to be on a more even keel since Winfield Sheehan had abandoned his supervision of distribution and exhibition for production in Los Angeles. Whether this was a function of Sheehan's skill, or the confluence of rising industry standards, many reporters on the Hollywood scene did lay the credit at his feet. "The result has been that this amusement year, every Fox release has been delivered to exchanges and, therefore to exhibitors, on time. There are not many big organizations which can boast of a similar record. The uncertainties that enter into studio operations are largely the bane of producers' existence. Unforeseen circumstances often wreak havoc with deliveries. It is a common but grievous condition, peculiar to the entire industry. What Sheehan has done to lift production standards is evidenced as each new Fox release appears."[14]

The average theater in 1926 rented approximately 175 features and 350 short subjects from distributors. This represented contracts from 20,000 theaters for 10,500,000 separate shipments every year.[15] The importance of delivering films on schedule becomes evident from this statistic.

Winfield Sheehan boasted about several directors going on location for their films, indicating that the studio was spending more money to achieve realism. Frank Borzage was in Paris to shoot scenes for *7th Heaven*, John Ford was in Ireland for *Mother Machree*, and Harry Beaumont spent time in England for *One Increasing Purpose.*

The influential publication, *Wall Street News*, also took note of Fox's success:

> Fox Film Corp. ranks as one of the foremost producers and distributors of motion pictures. Since incorporation 11 years ago, the company has produced about 962 photoplays and 966 one-reel films, for which rentals and sales returned gross revenue of $130,000,000, with net income of over $14,500,000.
>
> The year 1926 should prove the biggest one in the history of the corporation. It is expected net income after charges and taxes will be equal to about $8 a share on the outstanding common shares, or twice the annual dividend requirements of $4 a share.... Estimates are that the gross turnover of company for current year will aggregate $25,000,000. About 40 percent of this amount will be contributed by its foreign organization.... The foreign business organization has been built up over a period of ten years by the expenditure of between $5,000,000 and $6,000,000."[16]

The report listed both Los Angeles studio properties as being carried on the books at their original valuation of $525,000 even though they had been appraised by a real-estate company at $2,800,000.

The comedy unit for the 1926-1927 season was still churning out 52 two-reelers, the contents of which can be best summarized by a trade review of a Van Bibber subject, *King Bozo*: "The very best laugh in the picture occurs in the lunch room scene where the circus freaks are partaking of their various 'diets' with the 'glass eater' enjoying a plate of chopped glass, the pin swallower devouring a plate of mixed pins— plain and safety — and so on."[17]

The short-subject division, now producing from both the east and west coasts, was turning out a more sophisticated version of the old "scenics" with Fox Varieties, a series of short travel doc-

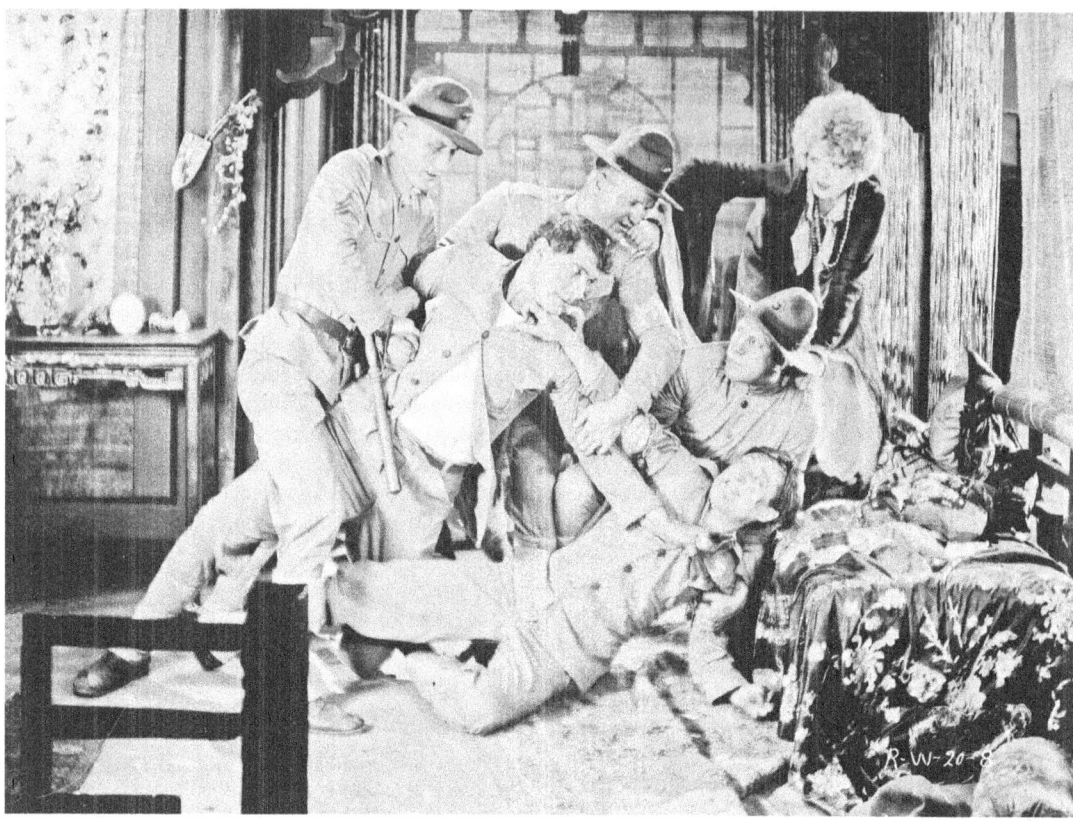

It will take more than three Marines to keep Victor McLaglen from Edmund Lowe in *What Price Glory* (1926). Phyllis Haver looks on (courtesy Robert S. Birchard).

umentaries. There was also a cartoon series and the ever-present Fox Newsreel, based in the east, which was hailed as "Mightiest of All."

Fox's smash hit *What Price Glory*, released in the last weeks of 1926 at the Harris Theater in New York as a roadshow engagement, was accompanied by a 35-piece orchestra with a score written by well-known composer Erno Rapée. Sound effects were recreated backstage for the explosions and gunshots in the battle scenes. The release of *What Price Glory*, which had been held up contractually until the play it was based on ended its run, broke all company records and established the new screen team of Edmund Lowe and Victor McLaglen.

In the "New York Reviews" column of the *Film Daily*, the *Daily Mirror* proclaimed, "This IS a picture! A stirring, vivid drama, humorized and humanized.... McLaglen gives one of the finest performances of its kind ever contributed to the silver sheet.... 'What Price Glory' is a stupendous achievement. An engrossing, grim, vivid war drama, balancing reality with impish humor. Put it on your list and see it quick. You'll want to see it many times."

The Daily News reviewer weighed in with, "But may I marshal a few superlatives to lay at the feet of Victor McLaglen, Edmund Lowe and Dolores Del Rio? This trinity caught and held the spotlight by living, rather than acting, the roles assigned to them."

The Sun reported, "With the most daring, flashing, cinematic war scenes in the history of motion pictures, and with at least two brilliant performances ... the photoplay of the Stallings-Anderson war melodrama, offers as thrilling a show as any theater on Broadway."

The World summed up with, "It is terribly funny, vitally hardboiled and triumphantly free, for the most part, from the sticky slabs of sentiment."[18]

The film's success was considered yet another triumph for Winfield Sheehan. "The resources of the Fox producing organization stand behind Raoul A. Walsh's picture. The tremendous energy which went into the making of 'What Price Glory,' has been reflected to the last iota on the screen. Here you have a picture for which superlatives are indeed in order.... Behind the scenes, to those who know appears the hand of Winfield R. Sheehan. Of him mention should be made since it was he who shaped the course which the production eventually followed." Sheehan had clearly been anointed the creative captain of the studio even though each film still began with "William Fox Presents."

"Winnie Sheehan has been busy," stated the editorial column of the *Film Daily*. "Fox is getting set for next year. There will be 49 pictures, or the same as this season.... There are many interesting developments under way at the Fox studios. A weather eye has been peeled for new talent. Sheehan says he has been successful in signing up many promising players. He is going in for leading men and women. Already the array, he declares is quite formidable. The stars of tomorrow, you know."[19]

The studio was certainly on its way to building a stable of stars. Janet Gaynor had co-starred in such films as *The Johnstown Flood*, *The Shamrock Handicap*, *The Blue Eagle* (with George O'Brien, under John Ford's direction), *The Midnight Kiss* and *The Return of Peter Grimm*, all released in 1926. In the leading man category, there was Charles Farrell, working his way up through smaller parts in *The Wings of Youth* (1925), *Sandy* (1926), and *A Trip to Chinatown* (1926). After seeing Gaynor in *The Midnight Kiss* with Richard Walling, one reviewer suggested that Fox could find an appropriate male lead for her in Charles Farrell. That casting suggestion, whether it was heeded or not, turned out to be prescient. Gaynor and Farrell were co-starred in *7th Heaven* for a late 1927 release.

Along with the still-popular cowboy stars Tom Mix and Buck Jones, the all–American male lead, George O'Brien, and other contract players like Edmund Lowe, Victor McLaglen, Virginia Valli, Alma Rubens, Madge Bellamy, Olive Borden, Dolores Del Rio, and the ubiquitous J. Farrell MacDonald, Fox had finally assembled a considerable number of box-office names.

Next to the acquisition of theaters, star contracts were the most desired components for a top studio. Metro-Goldwyn-Mayer boasted Marion Davies, Lon Chaney, John Gilbert, Ramon Novarro, Buster Keaton, Norma Shearer, Lillian Gish

Madge Bellamy in a more typical role in *Ankles Preferred* (1927), with Allan Forrest (courtesy Robert S. Birchard).

and Mae Murray. First National claimed bragging rights on Milton Sills, Colleen Moore, Corinne Griffith, Dorothy Mackaill, Richard Barthelmess, Norma Talmadge, Constance Talmadge, and Anna Q. Nilsson. Pathé laid claim to Lionel Barrymore, Will Rogers, Mabel Normand, Monty Banks, Glenn Tryon, Blanche Mehaffey, and one-time Fox players Harry Myers, Eileen Percy, Virginia Pearson, Eva Novak, and Theda Bara. Paramount had signed Bebe Daniels, Eddie Cantor, Clara Bow, Richard Dix, Harold Lloyd, W.C. Fields and Adolphe Menjou. Warners showcased John Barrymore, Dolores Costello, Sydney Chaplin, Louise Fazenda, Monte Blue and Rin-Tin-Tin. Universal had Reginald Denny, its top star, Mary Philbin, Conrad Veidt, Laura LaPlante, Belle Bennett, and western stars Hoot Gibson, Jack Hoxie and Art Acord.

The cost of talent had risen so quickly because of studios bidding against one another for the services of stars and directors, that there was industry-wide approval of a plan to halt the practice which was causing production costs to increase steeply. Fox was well versed in such expanding

Olive Borden goes fashionable in *The Joy Girl* (1927) (courtesy Robert S. Birchard).

overhead costs when, in 1926, production ate up a startling 58.3 percent of rentals.

Paramount announced in 1927 that contracts of those talents whose salaries were considered top heavy would not be renewed. The pruning process was expected to hit the "near greats" the hardest, including featured players whose careers had not yet reached appreciable box-office value. Some performers found it difficult to sign new contracts at the same pay level, but those who were worth their star value were not impacted. Sometimes cutbacks had the opposite effect. "More than one player who has been released on the expiration of a contract has surpassed all expectations with some other organization proving suddenly to be a sensational winner."

William Fox needed only to look to John Gilbert as a perfect example. And, in fact, he did so profitably. After Gilbert rocketed to stardom at M.G.M., Fox Films, in 1924 reissued with much ballyhoo *Monte Cristo* (1922) and *Cameo Kirby* (1923) to substantial grosses.

> There is an evident move in many quarters to replace certain high-priced players and directors with newcomers, secured at much reduced figures. How far this will go remains to be seen, but there have been plenty of shifts and changes in the past few months, and an evidently indicated intention of reducing this portion of the costliness of production.[20]

The attempt to rein in star salaries would ultimately fail since a recognizable name was always the closest to a guarantee of success, and no studio would pass it up. New talents who burst into mass public acceptance would remain on lower salaries only as long as their contract lasted and then would demand appropriate compensation which was most often granted.

Additional pay cuts of 10 percent for anyone with a salary above $50 weekly went into effect at Paramount in June 1927 and the concept soon spread to other companies. Paramount, more than any other studio, was responsible for its high overhead costs by boosting production to 80 features a year. The newly formed Academy of Motion Picture Arts and Sciences, which was originally set up to mediate such disputes, intervened and convinced representatives of 12 producing companies, including Fox, M.G.M., Universal, First National, F.B.O., Warners, and Cecil B. DeMille Pictures, Inc., to suspend cuts until August. Paramount–Famous Lasky was the only holdout.

Paramount had more urgent issues to deal with. A government commission found that Paramount's practice of booking its pictures in blocks was a constraint of fair trade and the company, Adolph Zukor and Jesse L. Lasky were judged in violation of interstate and foreign commerce regulations. There was a distinct possibility that Paramount–Famous Lasky would no longer be permitted to own its theaters. An order was given to desist from the practice of block-booking. Paramount refused to obey the order and the litigation which followed left the matter unresolved for the moment. Lawsuits followed but it was not until a major case was brought against all the major studios in 1938 that finally resulted in a consent decree in 1948 in which major producers were forced to abandon block-booking and sell off their theater holdings as well. This, in effect, put an end to the competition between producers and exhibitors which had begun in the 1920s.

Ultimately, in the area of cost control, all branches of production companies agreed to look for economical ways to limit overhead without resorting to pay cuts. Among the many items in

Lawrence Gray and Olive Borden on location in the Canadian Rockies for *Pajamas* (1927) (courtesy Robert S. Birchard).

a pact that covered all branches, actors pledged to "refrain from any display of that unreasonable unnecessary type of temperament that makes only for delay, expense and discomfort of all concerned."[21] This, of course, as many legendary Hollywood egos would prove in the future, was wishful thinking.

Cost-cutting in production became a mantra for exhibitors as well, because the studios would charge higher rentals, reducing theater income. It suddenly became de rigeur for theater owners to criticize the "wasteful" habits of producers. Producers, in turn, blamed exhibitors for spending too much on "overstuffed" pre-show presentations and then trying to save money by paying less for a lower grade of film.

An east coast independent producer, Sam Sax, on the outer edge of the high-flying industry, threw his biased comments into the mix: "Thousands of dollars is [sic] spent on a story and the thousands more paid to adaptors and scenarists to mince the story into hash. Meanwhile, the contract players loll in their porch swings, basking in the California sunlight, receiving enormous salaries for idleness while the scenarists and directors wrangle over the script. And all the while, the production is at a standstill and the bills mount."[22] The entire exercise in blame and counter-blame led nowhere. High-cost quality films still made the biggest bucks.

The box-office results for Fox releases were highlighted by John Ford's *Three Bad Men* with the company's highest world-rental figure for 1926 of $850,000. However, the $500,000 negative cost left profits of only $46,000. Another relatively big-budget film, *Siberia*, starring Alma Rubens and Edmund Lowe and directed by Victor Schertzinger, was a disappointment, barely breaking even on its cost of almost $250,000. The single-biggest loser of the year was *The City*, a crime melodrama, which earned rentals that were less than the cost of the film. Its loss was nearly $100,000.

Tom Mix with Olive Borden in *My Own Pal* (1926) (courtesy Robert S. Birchard).

tention to theaters. Winfield E. [*sic*] Sheehan is directly responsible for production.... Of Grainger, Fox said: 'He brings to this company an invaluable fund of information based on actual observation of the needs of theaters, which he has gained from personal, intimate contact and association in every section of the exhibition field.'" Sheehan had equal praise for him: "During the next five years, under Grainger's progressive leadership, big movements will occur in the distribution of Fox pictures."[23]

Fox Theaters showed a profit as of October 31, 1926 of $654,101. Both of his companies placed William Fox closer to the top of the industry than at any time in his career.

Tom Mix, for yet another year, was the box-office champion at the studio. Two of his films, *My Own Pal* and *The Great K&A Train Robbery* (considered one of the fastest moving action films of all time), were the two most profitable films of the year for Fox. Each had world rentals of over $400,000 and profits of nearly $100,000 each. The Mix unit obviously understood how to make profitable films at a reasonable cost.

On a total of 51 negatives amortized in 1926 for a total cost of $8,328,252, the resulting rentals added up to $14,274,234. This broke down to 58.3 percent of rentals and a per-picture average of $163,299. There was no reason to think costs would ever be contained, but as long as annual revenues rose, these additional expenses could be absorbed. The Fox Film Corporation showed a profit of $3,030,926 for the year ending in December.

A good portion of the increase in profits was attributed to the sales efforts of James Grainger, who had done so well in his two years at Fox that First National was anxious to hire him when his contract expired in 1928. Taking a cue from the competition, Fox signed a new five-year deal with him, running through 1933: "Grainger is one of the triumvirate which controls various Fox enterprises. He has complete charge of sales. William Fox, while maintaining supervision over all company matters, is turning his particular at-

Production at the New York studio had once again dropped drastically and in December 1926, Harold P. Lipsitz, head of the scenario department was transferred to the West Coast studio in a similar capacity. In his place Joseph P. Engel, an original partner of Adolph Zukor and Edwin S. Porter in the company which released the Sarah Bernhardt production of *Queen Elizabeth* (1912), was appointed production manager and was charged with the responsibility of purchasing plays, novels and originals for production on both coasts.

January 1927 began with a flourish for West Coast producers. Total expenditures on filmed entertainment for the year were projected at $197,000,000, a gain of $25,000,000 over 1926. This was a direct result of the centralization of Los Angeles as a production center and the increased costs of manufacturing motion pictures. Annual expenditures by studios had been rising steadily from $156,000,000 in 1923. William Fox was quoted in the trade papers as predicting, "The outlook for 1927 for the motion picture industry could not be better for the individuals and the companies that can measure up to the responsibilities and opportunities that our business now requires and affords."[24]

Winfield Sheehan, sensing a shift in audience taste, offered that "the public is waiting expectantly

for vital, unusual and true-to-life motion pictures in the New Year. The demand in entertainment at the motion picture theaters is turning away from the 'soft pedal' romance and the patrons want virile, red-blooded treatment of life."[25]

Clayton P. Sheehan, manager of Fox's foreign department added his outlook: "Although the strengthening of the motion picture entente cordiale between other nations and the United States has been progressing for some time the speed of this progression during 1926 and the sudden broadening of the movement have given it an impetus and magnitude which bids fair to make the new year an outstanding period of achievement."[26]

The enthusiasm for success was well-founded when, in the last week of January, Fox exceeded its own record of $600,000 in weekly world rentals in October with a total of $800,000 in world rentals, not including any returns from *What Price Glory*.[27]

Just because the Fox Film Corporation was preoccupied with its slate of releases did not mean that William Fox had abandoned his interest in theaters. The acquisition and building program continued at a breakneck pace, in an effort to keep up with Famous Players–Lasky which was aligning itself with the Publix chain, Loew's, Inc., the collaboration of First National, Stanley and West Coast, and the many other circuits that were accumulating properties. Control of theaters in a specific area meant greater access to audiences. William Fox was already in construction on 5,000-seat houses in Philadelphia, Chicago, St. Louis, Brooklyn, Detroit, Washington, Newark and San Francisco. Buffalo would only be a 3,400-seat house.

Fox Theaters also announced, that as a policy, the company would build "the most modern theaters of the largest seating capacity as quickly as it can formulate plans and put them into effect"[28] in every key city where the company was not receiving adequate representation for its product. As a warning shot to competing circuits, Fox general sales manager James R. Grainger said that key city houses would be built in spite of existing combinations of theaters, chains, or distributor exhibitors. Grainger was planning a scouting trip to identify and purchase new locations from Chicago to the west coast, an unusual task for the head sales person. Grainger insisted this was not a selling trip, just an opportunity to acquaint himself with first-run conditions in all western territories in order to have information for a report which he was to submit to Fox upon his return to New York.

The voracious appetite for theaters was evident in a trade editorial: "Day by day it becomes increasingly apparent that the balance of power is swinging toward the factors which are successful in amassing the greatest theater buying power. Mergers in themselves gigantic will give way to larger amalgamations. It is not difficult to foresee three tremendously powerful chains blanketing the country from end to end within a year."[29] William Fox fully intended to control one of those powerful chains. Other companies were already extending their grip on exhibition beyond the United States and into Europe. Famous Players–Lasky, officially called Paramount–Famous Lasky, as of 1927, and M.G.M. had already begun foreign acquisitions.

More financing was necessary for William Fox to keep expanding, and in February 1927, he initiated a relationship with banking giant Halsey, Stuart and Company which offered $1,700,000 in sinking gold bonds issued by the Fox Film Realty Corporation for maturity in 1942. Part of the security of the loan was guaranteed by the Fox Office Building on 10th Avenue and 55th and 56th Streets, which was appraised at $1,853,474 with land valued at approximately $1,100,000.

Although Halsey, Stuart would initially represent Fox's financial deals, it would eventually become a powerful and, for William Fox, a malignant influence on the future of the company. At the time of this offering, however, each party was benefitting from the other. Just two months later, Fox mortgaged his West Coast properties valued at $7,544,920 as collateral for $4,000,000 in a new bond issue. Halsey Stuart would continue to issue bonds and Fox would continue to take advantage of them, getting himself and his company deeper into debt to bondholders.

Ever since plans were announced to build a 6,200-seat Roxy Theater in Manhattan, William Fox had wanted to buy into the project and finally own a Broadway venue. When the construction was funded, Fox waited on the sidelines. He preferred to let the theater proceed as planned under the director of Samuel L. (Roxy) Rothafel, whom he considered a showmanship genius. Rothafel had made his reputation by staging the finest, high-class live shows at first-run houses (including the Capitol on Broadway) and was regarded as the best in his field. His considerable experience in the theater business, coupled with his skill and taste in staging elaborate performances, gave him a unique position in the exhibition market.

The *Film Daily* reported,

> On March 11, 1927, the Roxy opened its doors in the full blaze of a first night, touched perhaps, but never outdone in the history of exhibition. The magnificent theater was the talk of the trade. A few days after the opening, word emanated from Fox's office that something of unusual nature was in store.
>
> That night is well remembered. Newspaper men had gathered in the Fox library. A bit of repast was served when out of the blue from the other end of a Corona, Fox calmly announced he had secured control of America's outstanding theater. The industry stopped right in its tracks in a picture of amazement that approximated the perfect.[30]

In March of 1927, William Fox was able to acquire the entire Roxy circuit, including the newly opened $15,000,000 New York picture palace, the Roxy, which became his base of operations. Fox bought the shares of Herbert Lubin and associates who financed the construction which was still $2,000,000 in debt. Lubin voiced satisfaction with the deal: "This affiliation is an ideal one for all concerned as William Fox will furnish the Roxy Theater with superb attractions and Roxy will give them a most sumptuous presentation. Fox Film Corp. has a series of motion pictures which are not only great box-office attractions, but works of unusual beauty and taste, colossal in their scope and direction."

Under the agreement, Rothafel was to remain the managing director of all the theaters in the circuit. He would have complete control of the Roxy which would give preference to the Fox Film Corporation in bookings, but would also buy films from other studios. Roxy was effusive in his praise of his new boss: "I have known Mr. Fox intimately for 15 years, and have admired his great fearlessness, his vision and his great success in building his corporation to rank as one of the great forces in the motion picture industry."[31]

The editor of the *Film Daily* commented on the acquisition: "The Roxy purchase is significant for several reasons. It is but the first of many moves to come. The scope is national. Roxy and Bill Fox, friends for many years, now become associates. The Roxy style of showmanship will evidence itself in those new Fox houses. It will mean much for those theaters. The Roxy personality — developed by radio — has a definite influence with millions. It is not to be discounted."[32]

William Fox proudly described the entertainment experience at his $15,000,000 showcase theater: "At the Roxy Theatre the motion picture is about one hour of the two-hour performance. The other hour is devoted to an overture by one hundred and ten of the finest musical artists, probably second only to that which would appear at Carnegie Hall. Then there is a ballet of fifty or seventy-five ballet dancers of the type you would see at the Metropolitan Opera House, and a male chorus of about sixty voices. The fourth is a spectacular number in which over two hundred people are on the stage at one time."[33] All this entertainment was available for a dollar, an admission kept low because of the theater's massive seat count.

Now, William Fox had the crown jewel of this theater empire. With its weekly grosses of more than $120,000, it was destined to be a profit center for Fox Theaters. This logic was confirmed when *What Price Glory* hit a record single-engagement gross of $2,216,858 in just 21 weeks. Then, in its 22nd week, the theater broke yet another world record with an unprecedented $144,267 (175,866 admissions) seven-day gross, the highest take ever — and it occurred during a non-holiday period. "Over at Fox, the satisfaction is, of course, great. We can easily imagine how Bill Fox feels. And now, quite naturally, Jimmy Grainger will be harder to stop than ever. Winnie Sheehan, some place overseas, has a real excuse for opening up another bottle and everybody's happy."[34]

Audience access would always be the foremost reason for moving into a market. An example was the theater situation in Minneapolis and St. Paul, Minnesota. Fox had long been dissatisfied with its representation in those cities after having its product jockeyed from one location to another. Before James Grainger joined the company, Fox was locked out of both cities by the Finkelstein and Ruben circuit. Grainger managed to make a deal for exhibition in Minneapolis but had no exposure in St. Paul. When Publix made a deal for the Finkelstein and Ruben theaters, both cities would be cut off from Fox pictures. Fox immediately determined to build 5,000-seat houses in both locations.[35]

The rest of the industry viewed Fox's rapid growth as a threat and exhibitors, especially the smaller circuit owners, considered his entry into new markets as an "invasion." There were trade stories like, "Indianapolis Stirred.... Surprise is expressed locally over proposal of Fox to build a 5,000-seat Roxy theater here."[36] Even though Fox had minimal representation in that city, the impending Roxy was enough to cause consternation in the Indiana exhibition community.

Financially, at this point in time, large theaters were a better investment than smaller houses. The Paramount Theater on Broadway netted Paramount–Famous Lasky $1,250,000 in annual revenues from admissions and film rentals. Of that amount, $750,000 was theater admission profits and $500,000 in film rentals of approximately $10,000 weekly. Weekly overhead was $30,000, made up of $10,000 in building rental, and $20,000 in operating expenses of wages, music rights, and other overhead. An additional $10,000 weekly was paid out for film rentals.

The Fox-owned Roxy Theater, a comparable house, estimated weekly overhead at $50,000, exclusive of film rentals which ranged from $5,000 to $25,000 weekly with the average running at $10,000. On a one-week take of $130,000, Fox Films and Fox Theaters netted a combined $80,000.

Other venues produced much less revenue. In a city of 25,000, average attendance reached 14,800 weekly. In a town of 5,000, average weekly attendance was 3,800. Attendance in a small town of 1,500 yielded approximately 350 admissions weekly with only two nights of shows. Admission prices in small towns averaged 35 cents. The mathematics showed clearly why every company was so interested in establishing their presence in locations that could support large theaters. The average weekly attendance nationwide had grown from 46,000,000 to 65,000,000.

William Fox directly addressed the future at the 1927 annual sales conference where it was announced that the company was planning to have 30 first-run theaters of 5,000 seats each by 1928 and costing a total of between $150,000,000 and $200,000,000. "We are not seeking a battle.... Our theater plans are not to be construed as an invasion of the exhibition field because they are not. Where we have had ample representation we will not build. Where our friends are to be found we will not build."[37] Fox's words may have sounded conciliatory to his sales force, but many in the exhibition end of the business were still wary of his ultimate goals, especially his $69,000,000 immediate building plan which broke down as follows:

City	Capacity	Cost
Boston	5,000	$7,000,000
Brooklyn	5,000	$11,000,000
Detroit	5,000	$10,500,000
Kansas City	4,000	$2,500,000
Los Angeles	5,500	$7,000,000
Newark	4,800	$5,000,000
Philadelphia	4,200	$12,000,000
San Francisco	5,000	$7,000,000
St. Louis	5,000	$10,500,000[38]

It was clear that it was Fox's intention to go head to head with the competition in many markets. Balaban & Katz dominated the Chicago Loop area until James Grainger announced a local Roxy would be built in that market. A further disturbing development occurred when Fox Theaters announced it was entering the small-town field with the construction of a 2,000 seat house in Gloversville, New York. Gloversville and the adjoining town of Johnston were the headquarters of the Schine circuit which was affiliated with Universal Chain Theaters. "Fox's invasion ... marks a hurling of the gauntlet at the Schines, who operate many theaters up-state in association with Universal Theaters.... It is understood that Fox will build in four, and possibly six, New York towns where Schine now operates."[39] The threat was very real because a luxurious new theater would have an advantage over already-existing locations. Other theaters would be forced into expensive upgrades or risk losing patrons. In self defense, Universal made plans to fortify its position in the Greater New York area by purchasing and building new theaters in that market.

Fox was not the only entity considered an invader. The term was used to describe plans by Stanley Company of America and West Coast Theaters to become national circuits and gain footholds in Ohio, with Universal entering the same market. West Coast was spending millions fortifying its position on the coast while Stanley had a building program fund of $10,000,000. Stanley itself became a major player in June 1927, when it joined with the Keith-Albee-Orpheum chain for a nation-wide circuit of 600 theaters, a consolidation with a value of $250,000,000.

The reason each one of these consolidations was considered a threat by the competition was because of the way the industry was organized. The tentacles from Stanley spread out with control of First National while Keith-Albee-Orpheum had similar affiliations with Pathé Exchanges and Producers Distributing Corporation, the Cecil B. DeMille producing concern.

With major companies manning the battle lines on theater acquisitions, a war was shaping up on the production front as well. Each major studio was trying to outdo the other to lock up as many screens as possible for the upcoming movie season of 1927-1928. Paramount planned to flood the market with as many as 80 releases. M.G.M. promised 50 with at least ten specials. Fox announced 52 feature releases, one a week with one special a month, and 156 short subjects, excluding newsreels. Sales conventions were in full swing as a trade-speak editorial made clear:

Look them over. Paramount's meeting in New York. Sid Kent is setting his boys on their toes as never before. On the shores of Michigan Lake, Bob Cochrane, Lou Metzger and the Universalites are busy indeed. Where the Atlantic washed the city named after it, Joe Kennedy, Joe Schnitzer and Lee Marcus are outlining F.B.O.'s plans. Way out West, Earle Hammons is training his lusty youngsters for a tussle in short subjects such as they have never witnessed, we warrant.

Feist's M-G-M round-up is slated for Los Angeles soon. Jimmy Grainger's Fox-es follow in after F.B.O. at the shore. That's not all. The Depinet-Spring contingent, more familiarly known as the First National family, holds forth on the coast simultaneously with M-G-M.[40]

The independents were also in the race with Cohn-Brandt-Cohn at Columbia, Sammy Sax at Gotham Productions, Sam Zierler and Lou Baum at Excellent Pictures, W. Ray Johnson and Dwight C. Leeper of Rayart, and Ike Chadwick of Chadwick Productions. Of all the independents, only Columbia would survive to become a competitor in the major leagues.

Planning a slate of pictures became a lot more complicated as well. Simple announcements of projects no longer meant they would definitely come to fruition, or that they would be released in the season in which originally scheduled. In the spring of 1927, Winfield Sheehan reported that the season's releases would include *Frozen Justice* to be directed by John Ford. When it was finally released more than two years later, its director was Allan Dwan. A well-known David Belasco play, *The Comedian*, was on the slate but was never made. *The Mud Turtle*, written by Elliott Lester, *The Grand Army Man* (which was to be directed by Frank Borzage), and the English stage play, *None but the Brave*, all fell into limbo as well. Although it was not unusual and often unavoidable for some projects to wither and die, abandonment costs were higher when rights were purchased and scripts were developed. Total unproduced Fox properties for 1926 ran up a tab of $785,234.

There were periodic rumblings among talent groups to improve working conditions in the studios. Cameramen got together to promote a plan for a minimum weekly salary of $250. Freelance actors finally received an agreement for a six-day, 48-hour work week. Stars continued to demand higher pay. Amid these pressures, production went on as usual but there was an attempt to contain overhead.

Speed is the order of the day at Coast studios, and in attaining it, producers are dealing a body blow to waste. This is one of the big accomplishments of the economy program, which came to a climax with a general assembling of leaders on the Coast.

Schedules are being trimmed to a point where a specified number of days are prescribed for directors, and they must come within the time allotted. Directors now whip their scenarios into shape before starting production, eliminating necessity for retakes.

Allan Dwan was cited as finishing shooting a production in 14 days and three hours and was bested by Roy Del Ruth, who completed a film in 13 days. "M-G-M is cutting down on time allotted for pictures. In the past the average time for a picture was from four to six weeks, but the studio now is putting pictures on a three weeks' basis. Other companies are setting similar limitations on shooting time."[41]

The one-time edict of William Fox to limit the furniture on a set to cut down on costs had been abandoned years earlier. No longer was there urgency to shorten schedules and limit productions. In fact, production schedules were lengthened to allow location footage to be shot, adding authenticity to stories set in foreign countries. John Ford had already left for Germany to shoot exterior scenes for his upcoming special, *Four Sons* (1928).[42] While Ford was in Berlin, he studied production methods at the Ufa studio. Winfield Sheehan was heading to Europe and would spend some time in Germany at the Fox Studios in Berlin. Germany had become the only country to rival the United States in the quality and quantity of filmmaking. There was even some consideration at the time of Ufa expanding into American production and taking over a studio facility in Los Angeles.

The announcement of eight specials for 1927-1928, with a combined budget of $5,000,000, would require larger crews and tie up studio space at the Fox Hills lot. Further expansion was going on at Fox Hills where two stages were being built near the Pico Boulevard frontage, each measuring 300 feet by 600 feet, twice the size of the new stages built just six months earlier. Electrical engineers were also completing plans for permanent electrical circuits for night shooting on the lot. A central power plant storage and distribution system was installed at a cost of $300,000.[43]

Meanwhile, Sol Wurtzel made a trip to New York, his first vacation since joining the company. Combining business and pleasure, he found time to acquire more story material for the perpetually moving production unit. Wurtzel, although now overshadowed by Sheehan, still was mentioned occasionally in the trades. In August 1927, in his supervision of "specials" at the Western Avenue studio, he assigned Ray Flynn to direct a Buck Jones entry, *Blood Will Tell*, George Marshall to produce a comedy, James Tinling to the Madge Bellamy feature *Very Confidential*, and he promoted actor David Butler to direct *High School Hero* starring Sally Phipps and Nick Stuart. All were undistinguished programmers even though they were under Wurtzel's "specials" aegis.

Due to Winfield Sheehan's strong affiliations in Europe, he anticipated an accelerated level of foreign production: "During the past we have produced a number of British stories. It is my intention to develop units of production which will devote their time exclusively to making pictures based on British stories, and bringing British atmosphere to the screen." There were plans to make features in Spain and Hungary, in collaboration with the respective governments. These films would be partly produced abroad with the remainder filmed in Hollywood. It was more a sound political maneuver since many countries were becoming less accepting of near-total domination of their cinemas by American product.

Sheehan predicted that gross business would double in Europe during the following 12 months. Fox had added many new countries to their foreign market including Italy, Hungary, Czechoslovakia, Bulgaria, Romania and northern Africa. As well, he expected a doubling in revenue from England, Germany, France, Belgium, Holland and Poland. To impress exhibitors of the worldwide reach of the company, it adopted a drawing of a globe with the inset letters spelling out FOX. This logo was carried on all Fox trade ads.

Sheehan was also enthusiastic about the new talent developing in Fox films: "I further believe that, during the coming twelve months, the kinema firmament will be lighted by many newborn stars descending like comets from the celestial blue. The coming of youth, personality and charm is demanded alike in London, Paris, Rome and New York."[44] Sheehan's flowery vision was acknowledged in a trade editorial. "What he has done to elevate production standards at Fox is known, of course, throughout the industry. 'We are building five years ahead,' he said. 'Production is no longer hit and miss, but the result of intensive, hard work year in and year out. We cannot afford to let up.'"[45] As much as Sheehan sounded like a visionary, the reality of the business was that it was still "hit and miss," no matter what genius effort went into a production.

Viewing the Fox Film Corporation at this point in its history, it was rightly considered an incredibly efficient company, with production overseen by Winfield Sheehan who had a fix on the public's taste, James Grainger, a star sales executive, and William Fox, on the prowl to increase his share of the marketplace. Included in the mix was Sam Rothafel, overseeing the stage productions at Roxy theaters, and A.C. Blumenthal, who handled the real estate deals for Fox. But Fox was destined to become an even stronger force in the industry. During the movie season of 1926-1927, a new technological development was being added to the arsenal of motion picture producers—a novelty known as talking pictures.

---

7. Talking Pictures

Prophetically, the *Film Daily* editorial on January 3, 1926 read, "As revolutionary as 1925 proved to be, the coming year promises more radical developments affecting to a marked degree every branch of the motion picture industry."[1] While accurately predicting the continued consolidation of theater chains that would control an entire territory and the further predatory practices of major producers like Fox, Paramount, and Universal to secure their own chains, the comment did not include any mention of the greatest development since the beginning of the movies—talking pictures.

Radio had been introduced in 1920 and became enormously popular through the succeeding five years. For an industry that had evolved with virtually little competition, suddenly there was a popular alternative to going to the movies. William Fox recalled, "Prior to this, on a rainy night our business would be larger than it would be on a clear night. When the radio came in, I made a careful observation and found that on rainy nights we were doing little or no business."[2]

It was inevitable that a technological development would allow motion pictures to recapture those lost audiences and once again exist without equal in entertainment value. Visually, silent films reached their pinnacle of achievement between 1926 and 1928. Films of extraordinary artistry and sensitivity, both American and foreign, were released and audiences responded to the best of them. Cameras became more sophisticated. Moviolas were designed to facilitate better editing. Lenses were improved for clarity and film stocks were finer. Make-up was more natural and acting more restrained. As well, huge sets were used regularly, exotic locations were shown and theatrical presentations had achieved perfection. In 1926, visual enhancement was added when studios began using incandescent lighting instead of carbon arcs to light their sets. Harry Warner, president of Warner Bros., reported, "I saw some of the reels of the first picture, and the lighting is better than with carbon because it is softer. You cannot get as soft a light with carbon as you can get with a regular bulb. You can divide your light better and when you work with carbon you have to work with more powerful electricity."[3] The Technicolor Corporation, under the guidance of Dr. Herbert T. Kalmus, had developed a process that used two negatives to produce an approximation of real color and it was being used frequently for sequences within black and white features and occasionally for entire films. There was not much further the movies could go at this point without a voice. And a voice was what they were about to receive.

There had been many experiments in the synchronization of picture and sound dating back to Thomas Edison, who, in 1910, coupled a phonograph to a projector to achieve synchronized sound effects. The "Cameraphone" was a precursor to the later Vitaphone and was exhibited in theaters over a period of years until the novelty wore off. There were inventors in both Europe and America who had created various systems to marry sound with film, but none of these early techniques caught on with the public, or, more importantly, with financial partners. One such invention was reported in November 1925.

> C.F. Elwell has perfected a process synchronizing motion and sound, according to the "New York Times," in a London cable.
> The first showing occurred before the Radio Society which, according to the Times, was startled to see and hear roosters crowing, dogs barking and sheep bleating.
> The sounds from the loud speakers fit the movement of the mouths with minute accuracy. Dancing with music audible also seems lifelike, reports the paper.
> As with radio, sound is converted by a microphone into electrical waves which are recorded by a sensitive cell of the invention. Elwell asserts that the new method is inexpensive, and that many subjects not effective on the screen are now opened up.[4]

Elwell's invention ended up like so many others before him. But around the same time, several competing processes were being experimented with, three of which would survive.

William Fox was introduced to sound in the spring of 1925 after returning to New York. His brother-in-law, Jack Leo, wanted him to watch some film in the projection room. Fox was expecting to see a silent film but instead he saw an image of a canary on the screen and he could hear it singing. Leo knew Fox's predilection for canaries because the Foxes had a canary in the early days of their marriage. William Fox reported that the scene of the bird was followed by a "Chinaman who had a ukulele and he sang an English song. He sang terribly and played none too well but to me it was a marvel."[5] Fox had just witnessed a test that was made using a new system developed by inventor Theodore Case.

Around the same time, the Warners had been involved with the development of a new sound reproduction system. Vitaphone, which synchronized a record player to a projector, was a co-venture of Warner Bros., Western Electric, Bell Telephone Laboratories and Walter J. Rich, all of whom comprised the Vitaphone Corporation of America.

An early report of the new system described it as making sound recordings on discs in synchronization with film: "A high tension microphone transmits the sound into electrical voltage with the currents in turn passing through an amplifying-reproducer." The discs were then played back on a phonograph machine coupled to the motor which was driving the film projector "and then transmitted into sound through loud-speaking telephones similar to those used in the public-addressing system of the Western Electric Co."[6] The simplicity of Vitaphone meant that equipment could be attached to existing projectors rather than needing to re-equip theaters.

Warner Bros.' plans for Vitaphone at the time were limited to the reproduction of music accompaniment and sound effects for features. Sam Warner envisioned the most important value of sound as providing opening vaudeville acts and musical performances before features and orchestral accompaniments for movies at any theater in the country that would equal the most exclusive presentations in large cities. Sound would also pay a healthy dividend since large theaters would no longer have the expense of maintaining a large orchestra which ran up to $30,000 weekly.

All 16 upcoming Warners releases for the year would utilize Vitaphone for prologues. There was little intent, at this point, to use Vitaphone for talking pictures but there was a lot of excitement being stirred up by the Warner brothers, who had the fiscal health of their entire corporation, which had lost $1,337,826 during the year ending March 31, 1926, riding on this new process.[7]

"Exhibitors!" blared a full page add with blazing orange highlights, "Do you realize that on August 6 motion pictures will have been completely revolutionized by 'VITAPHONE'? On that day 'VITAPHONE' will bring the realization of a new future to the theatres of the world; a future brighter in its aspects, broader in its scope, and greater in its possibilities than any other period in the development of motion pictures. What the telephone means to modern life; what the railroad means to modern travel; what the world's greatest inventions mean to civilization today — that is what Warner Bros. bring to motion pictures in 'VITAPHONE.'"[8]

Making sure that the August 6, 1926 debut of Vitaphone — the world premiere showing of *Don Juan* starring John Barrymore — was viewed as enough of an event, the opening night admission at the Warner Theater in New York was set at $10 a seat. The trade reviews of the first showing, which lasted for four hours, were ecstatic: "Repeated and prolonged applause indicated that both the Vitaphone and the picture thrilled the audience which filled the house. That the Vitaphone marks a new era in entertainment was the opinion generally expressed in the lobby."[9]

Fully half the evening was devoted to the Vitaphone opening numbers, including Mischa Elman playing Dvorak's "Humoresque," Roy Smeck on the banjo, ukulele and guitar, opera singer Marion Talley presenting "Caro Nome," and violinist Efrem Zimbalist playing variations from the "Kreutzer Sonata." There was a brief address by Will H. Hays, president of the Motion Picture Association, then there was an overture and, for the first time in movie history, there was no orchestra in the pit. Although the volume was high enough, the separation of instruments was not as clear as a live orchestra. Nevertheless, the premiere of *Don Juan* was overwhelming enough for Vitaphone to seem like the future of movies.

The potentialities are tremendous. Mediocre music supplanted by the best in the rank and file of the nation's theaters truly makes a rosy picture. Dance and song numbers, vocal selections, violin solos, jazz bands in synchronized form sold on a weekly basis to offset the competition created for the little fellow by presentations at big theaters — that, too, is a potential Utopia for the average exhibitor. Music scores for all features, mechanically timed and perfectly adjusted, are in the offing.[10]

Warners immediately announced the next picture to be given a musical presentation would be the second John Barrymore feature, tentatively titled *Manon Lescaut*, released as *When a Man Loves* (1927). *The Better 'Ole* (1927), a military comedy starring Sydney Chaplin would follow.[11]

William Fox was in attendance at the *Don Juan* premiere and was as intrigued by the possibilities as anyone else. However, he did note some drawbacks at a later showing of Vitaphone.

I went to the Warner Theatre one day, to hear a man sing the introductory number of "Pagliacci." Of course, I went expecting to be thrilled. This was the first person from grand opera who consented to sing for talkies. The picture started, and he was making all the gestures he used on the stage, and the sound I heard was a banjo playing, accompanied by a colored man singing "I Wish I Was in Dixie." Of course the operator had put on the wrong record! And later they ran into this difficulty — they had the problem of shipping the reels to the exhibitor, and if one record was broken, no show could be given. When film gets old you must cut out the brittle part; and of course when this was done, the record and the film did not synchronize. At one time I wrote a paper with 101 definite reasons why it was not possible to have the industry adopt records and film and make them synchronize.[12]

There were other difficulties for exhibitors with Vitaphone. The phonograph needles had to be replaced after every reel otherwise they would cut too deeply into the disc grooves. Discs, as well, had a short life span of 20 uses. With a disc length of only ten minutes Vitaphone reels could run no longer. Projectionists needed to be skilled contortionists to move agilely enough to not only thread the projector, adjust and set the carbons in the arc lamps, but also replace the needle and prepare the disc for synchronization. Eventually, two projectionists were needed in every booth. An industry standard of 2,000 foot reels, lasting approximately 20 minutes, which took the pressure off a projectionist's job, was not adopted until 1936 at which time Vitaphone had given way to sound on film.

Because the roll-out on Vitaphone was slow

and limited to major engagements in large cities, by the end of 1926, it had not made a dent in the business of silent pictures. With hit movies like *The Big Parade* (1925, M.G.M.), *Stella Dallas* (1925, United Artists), *Ben-Hur* (1925, M.G.M.), *The Merry Widow* (1925, M.G.M.), *For Heaven's Sake* (1926, Paramount), *The Winning of Barbara Worth* (1926, United Artists), *What Price Glory* (1926, Fox) and *Aloma of the South Seas* (1926, M.G.M.) all playing to strong returns, there was no shortage of blockbuster successes. But other companies were watching developments in sound very carefully.

A section of *The Film Year Book 1926*, titled "Some Inventions of 1925" listed 13 developments, including a camera that could run at 5,000 frames per second, allowing for extreme slow motion, and the Shuftan Spiegelverahren which Carl Laemmle brought back from Berlin to photograph models and make them look like giants. One unexceptional entry was "Swiss Company Introduces Talking Films":

> Tri-Ergon, Ltd., a Swiss organization, in August introduced a new talking film to the American market. The invention is claimed to be the result of seven years' work on the part of J. Maselle, H. Vogt and Dr. J. Engl, and is owned by Tri-Ergon.
>
> One of the chief technical features of the device, known as the "Kathodophone," is a microphone for which its sponsors claim an ability to obtain pure sounds. There is also an electrical amplifier described as a highly perfected technical achievement and an ultra-frequency lamp which transforms electric current in sound waves into a luminous patch which illuminates the film. The same apparatus which projects ordinary film can be used for the new acoustic film.[13]

Keeping one step ahead of the competition had become a mantra for William Fox and the Tri-Ergon process intrigued him, so he personally purchased the patents for it. Fox was already financing experiments with the Case process that combined both picture and track on the same piece of film. It was commonly referred to as sound-on-film. Fox had become convinced that a successful sound process needed to conform to a system like his. This would side-step the problems created by synchronized discs and the possibility for program interruption every time a reel change occurred. Considering that a theater could have 50 reel changeovers each day, the likelihood of an interruption increased dramatically with Vitaphone.

Jack Leo had spent $12,000, without Fox's consent, to install a production facility for the sound-on-film system at their head office in New York. He had built a soundproof studio on the top floor of the building. "I went up on this temporary stage floor and saw the temporary soundproof room, where everything had to be done. I said that couldn't be right. If the photographing had to be done in a soundproof room, then you are going to rob this camera of seeing nature. They said there was only one way to record sound, and that was in soundproof rooms. I said 'That can't be so — you must be in error.' But they were sure of their position, and it was necessary to build a perfected soundproof room. We let a contract to build our first soundproof stages on 54th Street and 10th Avenue. The contractors said it would take four months to build this studio."[14]

The new sound process, described without any specifics, was first announced on September 20, 1926: "Theodore W. Case, president of the Case Research Laboratories of Auburn, N.Y., is responsible for the statement that talking motion pictures developed in this laboratory have been leased to the Fox-Case Corp., recently incorporated in Albany." Case had been developing the process since 1918 and refined the technique with Earl W. Sponable.

"As noted, the device requires certain adjustments before Fox officials feel that it has reached the perfection point. However, it is understood presentations will be possible — and are actually planned in a few months. The device will be used for synchronizing scores with Fox specials and for prologues with these films. Probably pictures like Fox Varieties and novelties will receive this treatment. It is also planned to make individual numbers featuring famous artists."[15]

There was a definite vagueness about this "new device," but another article less than a month later mentioned another obstacle in Fox's race for a sound-on-film process: Dr. Lee De Forest. De Forest had begun developing a similar process to the Fox-Case system in 1923 called Phonofilm and was in negotiations with Fox for a licensing agreement. When the deal stalled, the inventor took out an injunction against Fox alleging patent infringement on his process. One of the disputed issues involved a patent covering "the 'slit' method of controlling beams of the exciting lamp on reproducing devices."[16] De Forest tried to prevent Fox from marketing its "talking picture device." While the litigation against Fox was in progress, De Forest threatened legal action against anyone who exhibited Fox product in the Phonofilm or Fox process. Fox countersued several months later, claiming De Forest fraudulently took a $100,000 option which he refused to honor.

De Forest claimed in a suit, only made public in late 1930, that on or about September 23, 1926, Western Electric and ERPI dissuaded William Fox from paying the inventor $2,520,000 for the stock of De Forest Phonofilm which had been agreed upon. Fox also agreed to employ De Forest for five years at $50,000 annually. Western Electric and ERPI, the defendants, convinced Fox that De Forest did not control any of the sound patents he claimed. Because of this, Fox failed to exercise his options beyond the $100,000 payment.[17] The litigation was later settled and De Forest was recognized as a pioneer in sound, but Fox's patents were sufficient to keep him from losing rights to his system.

While the legal tangle was being straightened out, William Fox made a deal with Warner Bros. for an exchange of licenses on both their systems. Vitaphone would continue to license exhibitors for their process and Fox-Case planned to distribute films to theaters with Vitaphone. Reciprocally, Fox-Case granted Vitaphone licenses to use its technical developments, now called Movietone. This protected both companies and exhibitors from being shut out of either studio's product. Fox-Case was somewhat behind in setting up theaters for its system and had only produced a handful of Movietone short subjects. Vitaphone, on the other hand, had equipment prepared for any size theater and was installing systems across the country. There was good reason to believe that pictures with sound would be lucrative since Warner Bros., which had substantial losses in 1926, swung to $1,000,000 in projected profits for the year ending August 31, 1927.

There was a lot of money involved in owning the rights to a sound reproduction system. As Warners was equipping the first 300 locations with Vitaphone, it projected royalties of $45,000 weekly by the end of the year and $2,340,000 annually. The contracts for Vitaphone ran for five years with a minimum gross of $11,700,000. However, it was Western Electric and its subsidiary, Electrical Research Products Incorporated, later know as ERPI, which exclusively collected the fees for installations.[18]

Fox began installing Movietone in 25 of its own theaters at the beginning of 1927 and initially planned to reissue *The Queen of Sheba* (1921) with a synchronized score. This idea was later scrapped in favor of premiering the process with a more prestigious new release.

While Fox and Warners were setting themselves up to control the entire sector of sound reproduction, other companies, including M.G.M., First National, Paramount–Famous Lasky, Universal, and Producers Distributing Corporation, formed a committee to examine all the developments in sound and try to arrive at some standardization. "These companies state they hope that further development will follow lines which will keep competition free and open among producers and exhibitors, and make all exhibitors available as customers of all producers, instead of having theaters tied up by the exclusive use of certain devices obtainable only in connection with certain companies' productions."[19]

The committee's investigation ended when it was initially decided to align itself with the De Forest Phonofilm system. This way, these signatory companies could claim some exclusivity to a process and not be at the mercy of either Warners or Fox. What they neglected to consider was that demand alone for Vitaphone and Movietone would dictate the future. The committee collapsed by the middle of 1928 and Paramount, Universal, United Artists and M.G.M. signed up for the ERPI system of Western Electric which would use the Movietone process.

February 25, 1927 brought the announcement, "Movietone — the synchronization of sound and motion photographically is ready. It will shortly make its bow. The Fox-Case group has been working very quietly. Months in time and thousands in dollars have been spent in bringing the component parts up to snuff. There were difficulties with the tonal range. The distribution of sound waves behind the screen was another. Technical problems were numerous but knotty as they were, many have now been met."[20] The similarities between the two systems were minimal — both had been developed by Western Electric. The differences were great. Although both systems could be added to existing projection set-ups at an installation cost of about $8,000 to $15,000, depending on the size of the theater, the advantage of Movietone was what William Fox had wanted. If footage was missing in a reel, there was no loss of synchronization. Movietone prints could be shipped in regular film cans and there was no concern over breakage of discs, replacement of phonograph needles or the wrong accompaniment of sound.

The industry demonstration that was given included a reel of subjects not intended for release which was announced as *Studies in Movietone*.

There were introductory remarks, then a guitar selection, followed by a jazz vocal number at a piano, two string players and comic Charles "Chic" Sale in a vaudeville routine. There was also a selection of musical numbers performed by Raquel Meller.

All the scenes were staged on "elaborate sets" erected in the Movietone studio in New York. There were two stages in which production could go on separately or simultaneously. Both could handle large sets and orchestral accompaniment. The walls were soundproof and each studio was enclosed in a double wall over one-foot thick, including an air space of six inches. On either side of the air space were three-inch walls of gypsum blocks and to the outside of each layer was an additional thickness of cellular textured material. The walls on the inside of the studio were covered with heavy sound-absorbing draperies.[21]

During the production of Movietone, picture and sound were recorded in synchronization onto separate pieces of film, but were printed for exhibition with a soundtrack on the same strip of film. Recording was achieved by converting the sound picked up by a microphone into variations in light intensity. The recording unit was called an "Aeo" light because of an alkaline earth-oxide deposit on the filament. It was contained in a glass tube which was inserted in the back of the camera so that the variations in light were directed at a narrow edge of the film negative at the same time as the photographic image was being captured. A sound reproducing unit, with a photoelectric cell attached to a standard projector, would play back the track and after being fed through an amplifier, would emerge through speakers in the theater.

It was made clear that, with the ongoing De Forest litigation, "The Case laboratories claim to have built up a strong chain of patents covering the crucial points of each step. These patents have been filed in all principal countries. It was acquisition of these patents which led William Fox to affiliate himself in the formation of Fox-Case Corp.... Since the telephonic equipment, which is the principal part of an installation, is common to both Vitaphone and Movietone, reproducing attachments for these two systems now are being designed that both can be put on the one projection machine. This enables the exhibitor, after having secured installation, to reproduce both Vitaphone and Movietone pictures at will over the same machines."[22]

Internationally, there were efforts to invent a sound-on-film system that would compete with American developments. The French, who had pioneered many motion picture techniques at the turn of the century, threw their entry into the ring. Leon Gaumont gave a public demonstration of his talking device, Filmophone, which had been secured through the patents of two Danish inventors. Members of the French Photographic Society witnessed a showing of the process which "worked from the action of rays of light projected upon a cellule of selenium. Sound is registered on the film through the workings of a microphone attached to the source of light. The film is then passed through the projector having a comparatively feeble light and the projection of the film on the selenium, which is contained in a tiny rectangular case, reacts upon a loud speaker which gives the sound.... Gaumont will continue with this phase until the speaker is perfected."[23] Since the bulk of films run in Europe were provided by American companies, it was inevitable that Vitaphone and Movietone would predominate in those markets as well.

Aside from the guarded optimism about sound in motion pictures, it was still considered in the experimental stage, and a vote of non-confidence came from none other than Thomas A. Edison, the then-proclaimed "father of the motion picture." Edison did not believe talking pictures would ever be successful: "Americans prefer silent drama. They are accustomed to the moving picture as it is and they will never get enthusiastic over any voices being mingled in. Yes, there will be a novelty to it for a little while, but the glitter will soon wear off and the movie fans will cry for silence or a little orchestra music.... We are wasting our time by going on with it."[24]

Top-flight director King Vidor tended to agree from the artistic side of filmmaking, although he felt that the accompaniment of music and effects was helpful: "Personally, I can see no advantage in having spoken dialogue in motion pictures. It is something I feel is entirely out of place, and may tend to destroy the quality of the films to be made with its incorporation."[25]

For the moment, production was limited to the new stage atop the Fox head office. William Fox was still dissatisfied with the limitations the system imposed:

> I called for the inventor, Mr. Case, and said, "I am going to give you a million dollars, and you can spend this million dollars in the next four months, any way you like, in experimenting how to make this camera photograph on the outside without a soundproof room." Shortly thereafter they brought the various things they had photographed outside.

One was a rooster crowing and it sounded exactly like a pig squealing. Another was a dog barking which sounded like a cow. They recognized they didn't have it, because of the confusion of sound. About thirty or forty days later, they said, "Here, this time we have it." On the screen there came the rushing before me a train photographed on the Jersey Central tracks, and I heard the whistles blowing and the wheels turning just as though the train were with me in that room. I said, "Now you have it."[26]

Movietone was ready to enter the market in competition with Vitaphone, and its first contract was with the Interstate Amusement Company which owned theaters in Texas, Arkansas and Alabama. Karl Hoblitzelle, president of Interstate, was greatly impressed with the new process: "One of the great problems which the progressive exhibitor has to face is how he can increase his patronage. I believe that Movietone, especially the plans which call for its extensive use in Fox News, will have a definite effect in that direction."[27]

With a public announcement, in late April 1927, that Movietone, equally known as Fox-Case, could be used outdoors as well as in the studio, Fox immediately equipped foreign newsreel offices with Movietone recording devices. This made Fox News more competitive in the very crowded field of newsreels which included the silent Pathé News, Hearst's International Newsreel, Kinograms and the recent entry of M.G.M. and Paramount into the marketplace.

The first foreign sound interview was conducted with the Premier of Italy, Benito Mussolini. The first Movietone newsreel to be shown depicted a drill and parade of West Point cadets with a speech by the post commander. It was screened at the Roxy Theater in New York on April 30, 1927. A trade ad portrayed the showing as "The Greatest Sensation IN ALL SCREEN HISTORY! For the first time in any theatre, before spell-bound audiences in the Roxy, New York, on Saturday, April 30 — FOX NEWS presented the 'talking newsreel,' or motion pictures of current events portrayed IN SOUND, by Movietone. *THE CROWNING TRIUMPH OF SCREEN JOURNALISM!*"[28]

After an initial reluctance to supply Movietone to theaters until it had reached a degree of perfection, the Fox-Case Corporation decided to offer their apparatus to theaters at an installation cost of $2,000, a radical reduction from the original estimated cost of $5,000 and much lower than the cost of Vitaphone. Rather than wait for early purchases to bring down the installation cost, Fox-Case was expecting the demand and high volume to make up for lower prices. As well, smaller theaters would immediately be able to afford to install Movietone. More wired houses meant more venues to play Movietone films.

William Fox declared that Movietone was "as necessary to a picture house as the projector in the booth."[29] The "talking newsreel" had proven successful because of Movietone's practicality. The Movietone news coverage of the Washington celebrations after Charles Lindbergh's non-stop flight across the Atlantic drew praise from audiences and exhibitors alike. "In the parlance of the business, it 'knocked them over,' and at various high points of the Coolidge address and the Lindbergh reply, the applause of the audience was so terrific that the reproduction of the sound was drowned. The theater-going public is not accustomed to such a thrill."[30]

Movietone short subjects available to theaters in January 1928 included the following:

1. The Lindbergh takeoff and reception in Washington
2. Gertrude Lawrence — J. Harold Murray and Rio Rita Girls with the songs "I Don't Know," "Ranger Song," "Doll Dance"
3. Voices of Italy — St. Peter's Vatican Choir, Mussolini — Great Dictator speaks in English and Italian
4. American Legion in Paris — Speeches by Marshal Foch and General Pershing, the Great Parade in Paris
5. Chic Sale — Comedy — "They Are Coming to Get Me"
6. Raquel Meller — Songs — "Flor de Mal," "Corpus Christi Day"
7. Raquel Meller — Songs — "La Mujer del Torero," "Noi de La Mare"
8. Winnie Lightner — Songs — "Nagasaki Butterfly," "Everybody Loves My Girl"
9. Ben Bernie — Orchestra — "A Lane in Spain," "Are You Going to Be Home?," "Scheherezade"
10. West Point Drill — Speech by Maj. Gen. Merch B. Stewart, Drill and Parade of Cadets
11. Kentucky Jubilee Choir — "Old Kentucky Home," "Swing Lo, Sweet Chariot"
12. Nina Tarasova singing "There Once Were Happy Days"
13. Anatole Friedland Ritz Revue — "On the Beach in Atlantic City"

When Movietone News reached peak production by late 1929 with a two-a-week release schedule, it was a vast undertaking to co-ordinate its 60 field crews.

Nearly 200,000 feet of film are shot weekly to provide the approximately 4,000 feet used in the weekly issues of Fox Movietone News. Footage not used is filed in the Fox Movietone News library, which now numbers practically all important world personages, practically every important steamship afloat and a wide variety of subjects which reflect nearly every form of scheduled activity throughout the world.

Forty-four sound trucks are scattered at strategic points throughout the world to gather the pictorial and audible news for Fox and the number is being added to almost weekly. Each has a cameraman and contact man to expedite filming of the news and its dispatch to the New York office with the greatest possible speed.

Here the film is placed in the hands of E. Percy Howard, veteran newspaperman, and newsreel producer, who views nearly every foot of film turned out by Fox Movietone. And because of the exacting big requirements of a four-a-week schedule, subjects to be incorporated into the newsreel must be sent out the same day they are received.

While the film is being viewed by Howard and his corps of assistants piecemeal as it is turned out by the laboratory, title writers are busily engaged in writing the titles in six different ways to make certain that when the final selections are made the titles will also be prepared so that there is no delay. Film editors and cutters are on hand to help figure out just what part of the panorama being unfolded before them is to be used, for the film is screened just as it is received. Sound experts, meanwhile, are passing upon the quality of the recording, while others are determining whether the photographic standards are being measured up to. All this is routine moving like clockwork, so thoroughly grounded in his work is each member of the staff.

Except for the musical accompaniment used with titles, there never has been an attempt made to score a Fox Movietone subject.... The natural sounds are transferred from the film track to discs for theaters thus equipped and no effort is made to doctor it.[31]

With current modern technology and instant news available through various media, it is hard to evaluate the awesome importance of Movietone Newsreels to audiences who only had newspapers and radio. Seeing world events like floods, volcanic eruptions, and other natural disasters, as well as hearing international celebrities like Charles Lindbergh, George Bernard Shaw, King George V of England, and King Alfonso XIII of Spain for the first time was astounding. For the review of *The Red Dance* (1928) in the *New York Times*, one of Fox's biggest releases of the year starring Dolores Del Rio and Charles Farrell, critic Mordaunt Hall took more column space discussing the brief Movietone News interview with George Bernard Shaw than for the main feature: "This Shaw talking picture is a remarkable achievement for besides bringing to this country the utterances of the playwright and author, it also brought his actual voice, with his indubitable charm of intonation."[32] The novelty was something that did not wear off and was a continuing source of fascination to moviegoers around the world.

Newsreels became so popular that one Fox theater in New York, as an experiment, ran a program of only Movietone News subjects. When that was a success, others were planned in Chicago and Los Angeles. Newsreel theaters would become exceptionally important during World War II, after which the introduction of television news stole away their audiences. For all the prestige that Movietone Newsreels brought Fox, "A lot of people think that [William] Fox has too much of an investment in this newsreel. And if it is considered on the basis of 600 or even 2500 houses wired for sound, they be right, for it would take more than 3000 regular bookings to get him out of the bag on this particular piece of entertainment.... So Fox might be taking it on the chin now but with the new sound equipment being set at the rate of 15 to 20 a day ... and all on a five-year contract, things will begin to brighten up after a bit."[33] By now, William Fox was known for placing large bets on long shots and his multi-million-dollar investment in Movietone News would eventually pay off.

Always cognizant of the need for short subjects, Fox immediately set to developing Movietone one- and two-reelers, with 16 titles ready for release by mid-1928.

Movietone's ambitions were grander at the outset than those Harry Warner had envisioned for Vitaphone: "What Movietone purports to do is this: To enhance silent films with meritorious music. Features, comedies, newsreels—all are slated for the same treatment. To broaden the value of motion pictures as an entertainment factor by stressing their importance in the social, educational, political fabric of the nation. Action will not be supplanted by sound, but sound will make action truer by giving to it the ability to say something when there is something to say."[34] The Fox organization may have made their goal sound socially grandiose but the bottom line was its belief that this advance in technology would attract new patrons to theaters.

The first Movietone film released was F.W. Murnau's *Sunrise*, which debuted in New York on September 25, 1927, to rave reviews. "In tonal range and in quality, Movietone has demonstrated its superiority in the field of synchronized sound and action films. The score for 'Sunrise' was intelligently done, a worthwhile complement to a most unusual picture."

The *Film Daily* reported on the company's perspective. "When still pictures took on animation, motion picture cameras came into being.... We hold that another step forward is the giving of voice to motion pictures.... The factor which will supply this voice may be Movietone. Fox thinks so and is making efforts to prepare the device for a permanent niche in exhibition."[35]

Winfield Sheehan estimated that Movietone would be installed in 30,000 theaters internationally within the following two years. Sheehan was also making plans to use the process in talking dramatic films "with the firm's ace directors to be entrusted with the task of introducing the sound pictures."[36]

Building on Movietone's popularity, Fox soon recorded the music score originally written by Erno Rapée for live performance with *What Price Glory* (1926). The Movietone version also featured synchronized sound effects and was followed by a similar revised version of *7th Heaven* in the late fall of 1927.

By September 1927, Fox had installed Movietone in three of its chain theaters, The Academy of Music, which was running *What Price Glory* with a music accompaniment, the Terminal in Newark and the Locust in Philadelphia. Other Fox theaters to add the system by the end of the month included New York houses, Crotona, Japanese Garden, Folly, Ridgewood, Nemo, Jamaica, Star, Audubon, Savoy, as well as the Washington in Detroit, the Liberty in Elizabeth, New Jersey, the American in Patterson, New Jersey and the Tower in Los Angeles. Movietone subjects scheduled for these theaters with either *7th Heaven* or *What Price Glory* featured Ben Bernie and his orchestra, "Chic" Sale, Raquel Meller and Gertrude Lawrence.

In an unusual blow to Vitaphone, the Metropolitan Theater in Atlanta quietly dropped the sound accompaniment process in July 1927. "Vitaphone is declared to have failed to measure up to expectations. It did not catch popular fancy, say observers, and the end of the run was predicted."[37] Since the Met had already abandoned its orchestra, all that was left was an organ to provide music for the movies. This was an ill omen and helped spur the Warners to be more aggressive with their use of the system.

Meanwhile, Electrical Research Products Incorporated, which held the exclusive installation rights for both Vitaphone and Movietone gained ground no matter which system was chosen. Beginning September 1, 1927, exhibitors could install either one or both systems. ERPI additionally charged theaters a weekly servicing fee of $50 to $100 for access to company engineers who kept the device in working condition. By mid–1933, projectionists, now familiar with the set-up, were servicing their own systems and exhibitors filed a lawsuit to cancel the ten-year service contracts since they were paying fees for nothing.

In a further move to consolidate its monopoly over sound reproduction, ERPI contractually insisted that producers and distributors compel theaters to run their pictures only on equipment licensed by Western Electric. It became obvious that once competing systems were available this position was untenable for producer-distributors and was modified by Western Electric president J.E. Otterson. "We have just reached an understanding with the producers licensed by us that they will play their productions on any equipment which in their judgment gives results of satisfactory quality.... To the exhibitors we say, if you can get equipment as good as ours for less money, buy it, but if it is of lower quality, don't buy it at any price.... The success of talking pictures means more to us than the sale or loss of sale of equipment."[38]

Western Electric, by early 1929, had developed a less-costly sound system for smaller theaters. Guaranteed to equal the tonal quality of larger equipment, it carried a price tag of $5,500 for either Vitaphone or Movietone and $7,000 for a dual system. This was not out of a sense of charity but to fend off competition from other companies.[39] Approximately 2,000 theater owners who had installed cheaper "bootleg" devices had to replace them within a year after complaints from patrons. Nearly 1,000 of those turned to Western Electric for their systems.[40]

Undaunted by the impending competition from Movietone, Warner Bros. released *The Jazz Singer* starring Al Jolson on October 6, 1927, recognized as the first film to use dialogue and singing sequences. Although it is heralded as the turning point in the development of sound pictures, the film itself was not considered as revolutionary in its time as its reputation implies. There was no doubt of its financial success as a profit of more than $800,000 indicates. Audiences, however, had become accustomed to musical acts and dialogue in Vitaphone short subjects, so while *The Jazz*

Singer occupies a unique position in the progress of cinema, its initial release was more a part of the transition to sound rather than the cataclysmic event as has been portrayed in film histories. *Variety*, in particular, made this point clear: "But 'The Jazz Singer' minus Vitaphone is something else again. There's really no love interest in the script, except between mother and son. It's doubtful if the general public will take to the Jewish boy's problem of becoming a cantor or a stage luminary as told on celluloid."[41] Ultimately, the film would help promote the Vitaphone process but it would be all-talking films like Al Jolson's next feature, *The Singing Fool* (1928), which helped convince audiences that the talkies had arrived. This popular acceptance showed up in profits for Warners which, for the last three months of 1928, alone totaled $3,000,000.

The competition between Movietone and Vitaphone entered into the studio-owned theater circuits as well. Whenever Fox was planning a new theater, it would be equipped with Movietone. The drama played out in Los Angeles in 1927 when both Fox and Warners were planning to open theaters in Hollywood. Movietone would be a regular feature at the Fox house on Wilshire and Western. "The Warner house on Hollywood Blvd. opens sometime next year. Vitaphone is scheduled to figure in largely at this house. Therefore, a fight on talking films looms on the horizon."[42] Nevertheless, Fox and Warners, by 1929, would begin releasing their sound pictures both on disc and Movietone.

Disgruntled by the sluggish deployment of his Phonofilm system, Lee De Forest publicly claimed that the public had gotten tired of the use of only vaudeville acts in talking pictures: "The chief remaining problems in the talking picture art lie not in the theater or engineering laboratory, but in the motion picture studio. There scenario writers, producers, artists, and cameramen must gradually acquire working knowledge of the new art, and how to take full artistic advantages of the countless and immeasurably rich possibilities which this new art has now brought forth for the entertainment and cultural uplift of the motion picture public."[43]

There were creative problems with the initial use of dialogue. Screen actors were unaccustomed to the requirements of the new process. Lines had to be spoken clearly and distinctly. Directors could not speak to the actors while the camera was rolling. Cameramen had to lock themselves inside small, immoveable, and perilously hot, soundproof booths. There could be no overlapping dialogue since the spoken portions had to begin and end with the take. This resulted in vastly different sound quality from one scene to another and one screen position to another.

Then there was the matter of the written dialogue as was pointed out in a *Film Daily* editorial on Warners' 1928 release of *Tenderloin*, an early part-talkie: "The lines for spoken dialogue represent a new technique. Producers will flounder until they learn what to do with this un-catalogued element. These portions of the 'Tenderloin' dialogue which missed did so not because the idea or the reproduction were poor. The synchronization was excellent, but the conception bad. The innovation suffered because of the utter banality of the words put into the mouths of the characters. The Warners are rightly entitled to credit for taking a bold step in an uncharted direction. Exhibitors and others should bear in mind that there exists no precedent for this type of undertaking. The result, of necessity, will be spotty until experience points the way out of the maze of mediocrity."[44]

Variety was more specific: "Vocally the talking picture will appeal mostly from the trained voices of the stage. Notably here with Mitchell Lewis the best voice of 'Tenderloin,' and Conrad Nagel, both stage trained. Miss Costello is not an elocutionist, nor does she evince more vocal instruction than may have been given her for this film. That she falters at times when speaking cannot be unexpected, from Miss Costello or any other the picture players who find themselves unable to speak in action through not having control of their voice."[45]

The initial criticism was soon countered by producers signing actors, writers, and directors with experience in stage work. Then came the task of converting their talents to the needs of the motion picture. For actors, many had to tone down their flamboyant and oversized stage personas. Playwrights had to abandon flowery and lengthy speeches for snappy dialogue. Once again, the best writers came from journalism as they had a flair for terse storytelling and "street lingo." Stage directors reinvented their styles to take advantage of the camera rather than setting up master scenes in long takes. All of this occurred relatively quickly since audiences had no patience for slow-moving, stodgily told sitting-room dramas.

With a choice of sound systems, studios and exhibitors recognized the greater value in sound-on-film rather than on disc and in mid–1928

Paramount, Universal and M.G.M. signed up for Movietone and began installing equipment in all of their theaters. Not only were Vitaphone and Movietone in competition with each other, two larger entities were lining up producers to use their systems. Western Electric, the dominant supplier of equipment, wanted to convince companies to use its patents which covered both those sound reproduction systems, while Radio Corporation of America (later known simply as R.C.A.) was competing in the same field with its sound-on-film Photophone process. Meanwhile, theater owners were blaming the slow pace of installations as a result of the high costs imposed by both corporations.

With only several hundred theaters initially wired for sound, Fox and Warners still went ahead with production, developing projects that would be dialogue driven and would conform to the restrictions imposed by limited camera mobility, as though there was no question that sound would be adopted by every theater in America. Other major companies were not as enthusiastic and waited for audience reaction to the new technology.

During all this tumult in exhibition, a building expansion program was planned at the Fox Hills lot, soon to be renamed "Movietone City." "C.H. Muldorfer is credited in periodicals and news articles of the period with the design and technological innovation of the first four stages. The massing and detailing of the Period–Influenced production core may be due to him. Little is known of Muldorfer's work outside of the studio, but the striking architectural style and the advanced design of the stages have earned him a place in industry history. H. Keith Weeks served as chief construction engineer on the site."[46]

Four structures containing eight sound stages were built by 2,700 workers on round-the-clock shifts. On this hectic schedule, the first double stage unit was completed in just three months. It

An aerial view of the Fox Hills Studio in 1928. On the left corner of the lot is the original administration building, and prominent in the center are soundproof stages 1&2, and 3&4. The land has already been graded for the construction of four other Movietone stages (courtesy Robert S. Birchard).

was 212 feet long, 165 feet wide and 45 feet high. Stages were equipped with loading rooms, dark rooms, battery rooms, and a camera equipment room. Stage One had a large Wurlitzer organ on its second floor with every appliance and effect possible for use in sound pictures. In addition, there was an electrical control plant that would contain all the recording apparatus necessary for Movietone production.[47] Cables were laid to reach cameras on the soundproof stages. Numerous other structures were completed almost simultaneously, including an administration building, two buildings housing projection rooms, a structure with four rehearsal halls, a spacious negative film vault, storage space for acoustical equipment, an editorial building with numerous cutting rooms, a music library, dressing rooms for 44 featured players and 240 extras, and a make-up department. An old Tom Mix stable was converted into a property room, sound-effects department, carpenter shop and store room. There was also a fully equipped hospital with a physician and surgeon in attendance in case of a medical emergency. Other buildings housed the police and fire departments.

Construction of this "city" took 2,202,712 feet of lumber; 488,000 floor area; 2,100,000 feet of reinforcing steel, including 36 trusses, weighing ten tons each; 240,000 square feet of pavement for streets, driveways and sidewalks; 6,600 feet of cement; 32,000 tons of rocks; 24,000 tons of sand; 51,200 tons of nails; 25,000 feet of water pipe; 15,000 feet of water and sewer mains; 25,000 yards of carpet and 86,000 feet of concrete.[48]

"An unusual feature of Movietone City which gives it a striking, semi–Oriental effect are [sic] three high towers. A decorative column 75 ft. high is silhouetted above the administration building. In the rear of the stages are reared two towers, 100 ft. high, one of them being the gravity tower for the automatic sprinkler system and the other the cooling tower for the air-conditioning system."[49] The stages were to be kept at 67 degrees all year long.

The total outlay for the 30 buildings of Movietone City was in excess of $12,000,000.[50] The new facility was officially dedicated on October 28, 1928 and was cited by the *Los Angeles Times* as cementing Los Angeles as the foremost international production center: "Sensing its coming hold on theatre goers, New York has been making strenuous bids to secure Gotham this valuable productive industry. The Movietone City near Hollywood, puts an end to the hopes of other communities to separate the talkies from the old movie home."[51]

Even though the soundproof stages of Movietone City were hermetically sealed down to their foundations, roofs were painted with warnings for aviators to keep away. Local chambers of commerce even passed resolutions diverting flights from San Diego to San Francisco to detour towards Arizona and bypass Hollywood.[52]

The Western Avenue lot was temporarily shut down and also equipped for sound recording. With these two lots now running at full capacity, production in New York was permanently minimized and the West Coast became the source of all Fox Films releases.

There were further additions made to the Fox Hills lot in 1929 with the construction of The Hall of Music with offices and studios for composers, a rehearsal auditorium and a library. It became the center of the Fox Music Department and was built around a Spanish courtyard with outer columns enhanced by busts of famous classical composers. The Laboratory of Engineering Research building was a "bubbling cauldron" of new cinematographic and sound developments. To provide dining facilities for the entire studio staff, there was the Café de Paris.

In the battle for dominance of sound-reproduction systems, First National adopted a process similar to Vitaphone called Firnatone. Warner Bros., meanwhile, proudly announced that its entire slate of pictures would be released in Vitaphone. As well, the level of production was cut back to 18 releases from 26 without a cut in expenditures. Warners was making their stance clear to exhibitors that their goal was quality rather than quantity.

The first all-talking Vitaphone feature, *The Lights of New York*, was released at a midnight performance on July 6, 1928. The voice quality of a performer suddenly took on importance in film reviews and many critics were unmerciful in their comments. With the industry's best interests at heart, trade reviews were the most brutal.

Variety was quick to point out the deficiencies in performers: "In work in this talker ... the cast of nearly all vaudeville actors who talk the best they may, in lieu of legits or picture actors who can't talk.... Helene Costello, in the fem lead, a total loss. For talkers she had better go to school right away. Cullen Landis opposite, if a juv even in the indies, will never make anyone believe it in this one. He seemed to talk with much effort. Nervousness might be claimed by all excepting the stage trained talent."[53] The *Film Daily* once again published the highlights of the "New York Reviews" and the *Herald Tribune* voiced a similar complaint: "Only its value as a novelty can possibly make the film interesting. It is not, as a matter of fact, even valuable as an experiment, for it was so obviously tossed together in a hurry to take advantage of the current fad for talking pictures that it is really not a fair test for the Vitaphone." The *New York Sun* was even less kind: "[It] would have been laughed off the stage had it been presented without the benefit of Vitaphone." Not every review was negative. The less discriminating *New York Graphic* said, "The audience loved every minute of it, for something new always catches on and the Vitaphone has put across the first long talking picture, which will go down in picture history."[54]

The Lights of New York proved that audiences wanted talking pictures. In its first week at the Strand Theater in New York, it grossed $50,000 which included the midnight performances. Considering that there was excessive heat and rain during its summer debut, that gross was considered phenomenal. Warners quickly made five other Vitaphone talking pictures available to cash in on a market it had exclusively to itself. Warner Bros. designated all upcoming releases as having Vitaphone tracks with at least some dialogue.

Obviously, when audiences heard how their screen idols of the silent era actually sounded, there was some disillusionment. However, Jack Warner minimized the fallout in an interview with the *Film Daily*: "Comparatively few silent screen stars and featured players have fallen by the wayside in the past year which has been marked by sensational strides of the talking picture.... The screen fan public has remained loyal to its stars, and the latter in large measure have justified that loyalty. Fortunately most producers sensed this potential condition a year ago and retained their stellar personnel practically intact. They have not regretted their action."[55]

Audiences turned out to be not quite as forgiving as Warner thought. Major silent stars like Corinne Griffith, May McAvoy and Vilma Banky, were among those done in by their voices. Many others, like Will Rogers, Greta Garbo, Clive Brook, John Barrymore, Janet Gaynor, Marie Dressler, Norma Shearer, Victor McLaglen, Edmund Lowe and Ronald Colman made the transition unscathed and became even more popular with dialogue.

Actors were not the only ones to be at risk in the transition to sound. Musicians who had performed in large theater orchestras viewed the new technology with rightful alarm. They insisted on the retention of orchestras even when films with synchronized music scores were being run. This was a situation in which the odds were stacked against live talent. It was just a matter of time before most musical accompaniment orchestras were released from their employment.

Many of the early talkies were mostly stage-bound efforts with a lot of dialogue. When the lines were skillfully written and acted, audiences were treated to the equivalent of a stage performance with fairly static camera movements and the occasional outdoor shot which was filmed silent and then enhanced by sound effects. Microphone placement became a major issue for directors since the directionality of the actors could affect the quality of the recording. This dilemma was amusingly spoofed in the M.G.M. musical *Singin' in the Rain* (1952). For directors, producers and performers in the late 1920s, it was anything but amusing. A contemporary review of Warners' second all-talking feature made this clear: "Like all other 'talkies,' 'The Terror' resembles a Christmas toy — you have to stop every once in a while and wind it up. And that seems the chief trouble with talking movies. The camera and the 'mike' have to hop around so much, and this makes for disjointed and seamy drama."[56]

The fight between competing sound-reproduction systems would continue for the next several years as the roll-out proceeded at a slow but steady pace. Some systems were designed for low-cost, non-synchronous sound and were merely phonographs that played music along with the projected film. Rival systems came and went like Bristolphone, Vocaphone (used in Educational Films' short subjects), Orchestraphone, Pallotophone, Marveltone, Kinegraphone, Meistertone, Cinephone, Biophone, Cortellaphone and Voiceaphone (later renamed Han-a-phone). The first release in Cinephone, a sound system later abandoned, was the ground-breaking sound cartoon, *Steamboat Willie*, produced by a young animator named Walt Disney. A totally divergent system, Moviephone, utilized sound recorded on a wire spool, a precursor to the earliest audio record/playback machines.

Many film histories characterize this period as a tumultuous and relatively quick change from silent films to talkies. In reality, the transition was much more complex. The films themselves edged into talking gradually, some with selected talking sequences which were inserted into silent films. Some studios, unsure about the future of sound, were reluctant to dive in as wholeheartedly as Warners or Fox. Warners and Fox, by necessity however, were still simultaneously releasing silent versions of the talkies with the obligatory title cards. Universal, which had a closer relationship with small-town theaters than its rivals, in fact, made a promise to continue releasing silent versions on all of its talking pictures.

For the period of the early talkies, Vitaphone was the primary contributing factor to not only the survival, but the incredible success of Warner Bros. With its stock at a record high of $110, Warners was able to finance the purchase of the Stanley Theater Corporation and then gain control of First National Pictures, a company valued at $15,000,000.

The larger battle was which sound system would prevail as the industry standard? At the beginning of 1929, the dust began to settle. Only two companies were still faithful to Vitaphone: Warner Bros. and First National. Paramount, M.G.M., United Artists, Pathé, and the newly formed R.K.O. all opted for sound-on-film because of its superior reproduction results and the elimination of disc breakage and scratching.

In an article entitled "Studio Executive Cite Sound Views," 17 comments were listed. Only two executives voted for Vitaphone and both were with Warner Bros. One was production head Darryl F. Zanuck who claimed that discs offered "the only system which permits music to be synchronized beneath dialogue, thereby allowing the symphony orchestra to play a score throughout a picture.... I favor the disc system because it is the only real commercial system for exhibition as well as the producers and I sincerely believe that all companies will ultimately release their talking pictures on discs."[57] Zanuck was correct in his assessment of the versatility of Vitaphone, but it was only a short time before Movietone was able to accomplish the same flexibility.

In a self-congratulatory trade advertisement, the Fox publicity department reminded exhibitors of the company's forward thinking.

> Now that everybody in the entire amusement world and theatre-goers especially are discussing Movietone, the uncanny foresight and shrewd showmanship of William Fox is on the tip of all tongues.
> While old-fashioned moviemakers were banking on silent films, the Fox Film Corporation was blazing this new trail in entertainment.
> Two years ahead of the field on Movietone, other Fox product continues to set the pace for the industry.
> All the frantic groping for satisfactory audible film has only served to confirm the inevitable choice of William Fox: MOVIETONE, THE FILM YOU HEAR AND SEE.[58]

There was more than a little truth to William Fox's pioneering in sound. As late as mid–1928, M.G.M., the acknowledged industry leader, had only started to convert its facilities to accommodate four stages to shoot sound films. It re-drafted acting contracts to read that players could be used for either silent of sound films. Paramount was scheduled to begin shooting its first dialogue film, *Varsity*, with Charles "Buddy" Rogers, and Universal was still doing sound tests and planning to convert stages to sound.

Companies like F.B.O. had no immediate plans for sound films but assured exhibitors that its "smash hits" of 1928 like *Hit of the Show, Gang War, The Circus Kid, Blockade, Taxi 13* and *The Perfect Crime* would "shortly" be synchronized with music, sound effects and dialogue. *The Perfect Crime* was given a sound prologue in which a husband and wife reunion is interrupted by a radio announcement of the solution of the perfect crime which led into the picture. Then there was a sound epilogue which flashed back to the prologue characters.[59]

Talkies also presented a problem for foreign markets. "Fox will not Movietone foreign prints so far as speaking parts are concerned, it is understood. Making of this type of Movietone production is regarded as unfeasible for the present at least."[60] While sub-titling was possible, it undercut the value of sound if audiences could not understand what was being spoken. Until the technical aspects made the dubbing of voices into foreign languages possible, many companies made foreign language versions of their pictures for the largest marketplaces. Fox, recognizing the sizable audience abroad and in the United States for Spanish-language films had an active company making Spanish versions of some productions.

At the Hal Roach Studio in the early days of talkies, Stan Laurel and Oliver Hardy appeared in French, Spanish and German versions of their two-reelers, speaking foreign languages phonetically. It is astounding to think that Universal made a Spanish version of *Dracula* (1931), considered today by some to be superior to the original Bela Lugosi version, starring Carlos Villarías as Conde Drácula.

By July 1929, there were 5,251 theaters in the

United States wired for sound, most of them in large cities and almost double the amount of installations that had been predicted just one year earlier. The rush for sound was on. For Western Electric, with its control of the two most popular systems, Vitaphone and Movietone, and 80 percent of installations, it was a gold rush. The remaining 20 percent of sound systems were equipped with RCA–Photophone.

William Fox benefitted financially through his control of Movietone and the large number of sound releases in the marketplace. New York, with a population of over six million, had 500 wired theaters. Philadelphia, with over two million people had 125, Chicago had 120 with its population of more than three million. Los Angeles had 87 for its one-and-a-quarter million population. About 15 percent of Canada's 930 theaters were wired. "The millions of dollars spent on wiring theaters, have been distributed among many companies for many different systems, although Western Electric equipment is far and away in the lead, the survey shows. Availability of equipment for speedy installation has been one of the outstanding factors in the rush to install sound reproducing devices, it is emphasized in the national compilation."[61]

R.C.A.–Photophone, meanwhile, still struggling to gain a foothold, brought out new equipment for theaters with fewer than 500 seats for a very low $2,995 installation cost. The cost of sound readers and amplifiers, however, were still comparable to other systems ranging from $4,000 to $16,000. Photophone could read any optical soundtrack making it interchangeable with Movietone, and "the superior tone quality of the Photophone system lies in its superior method of recording sound on film. That is, Photophone processes employ the 'variable width' or 'serrated edge,' and this counts for the very fine tone quality which the Photophone system produces. One other system uses the 'variable density' method of recording, which was abandoned by the Radio group in their experiments some years back."[62] This obvious criticism of the unnamed Movietone system was typical of the proprietary pride exposed in such sniping comments. Eventually, Fox issued permission to exchanges to allow Movietone to be run on Photophone equipment with *Mother Machree* as the first such release in December 1928.

The future of sound films was clear to the industry and especially exhibitors. For 1929, 504 talking pictures were scheduled from West Coast studios. From 521 silent releases in 1929, 17 companies announced the following year would bring only 400 titles. Paramount had the most with 65, Universal 60, Fox 34, Columbia 26, M.G.M. 17, Warners and First National with 35 each, Pathé 20, Radio 13, Rayart 18, and World Wide 16.[63] The balance was made by independent producers. There would also be a drastic reduction in the number of silent short subjects going into release.

As the "soundies" were taking hold, audiences saw various degrees of Movietone tracks. In the 1928-1929 season Fox released many films with synchronized music accompaniment and effects. The first Fox feature with a dialogue sequence, *The Air Circus*, directed by Howard Hawks, was scheduled to begin its run September 1, 1928. The sound portion of the film was a 15-minute scene within the movie's 88-minute running time. Fox publicity director, Glendon Allvine, outlined the method of production: "The former general stage manager of the Shuberts, Charles Judels, staged the dialogue by which Louise Dresser, Sue Carol, Arthur Lake and David Rollins speak their parts. Judels had problems to solve which were worked out with the co-operation of Lew Seiler, director of the studio sequences of the picture."[64]

Winfield Sheehan characterized this intermediate period as "a series of events which further crystallized this trend toward all talking product. Innovations in the form of dialogue sequences introduced into two silent pictures, 'The Air Circus' and 'Mother Knows Best,' aided these pictures materially in going over with the public."[65]

During the transition to sound, the presence of dialogue along with a return to title-cards was confusing to audiences. Douglas Shearer, who was in charge of recording experiments at M.G.M., suggested developing a "fade-out" for dialogue, similar to a visual fade, which could be used to make a transition from talking back into non-talking sequences to smooth the process.[66]

Finally, the fruits of William Fox's quest for outdoor capabilities arrived in the film version of O. Henry's *In Old Arizona* in January 1929. *Variety* said, "A long time ago Winnie Sheehan said Fox would never turn loose a full length talker until the studio was convinced the picture was right…. It's the first outdoor talker and a western, with a climax twist to make the story stand out from the usual hill and dale thesis." Along with the outdoor scenes, there were lengthy stretches (one being 34 minutes) of indoor dialogue but the review considered it "elementary, almost experimental."[67]

Edmund Lowe (center) puts on liederhausen for *Making the Grade* (1929), with Lucien Littlefield (right) (courtesy Robert S. Birchard).

The *New York Times* delineated some of the groundbreaking techniques used in the film: "In this film, for the first time, there is taken into consideration the fact that sounds grow fainter as the object is distanced. Horses hoofs at first are distinct, but as the Cisco Kid or others gallop off the sound becomes fainter and fainter until it dies away."[68] *In Old Arizona* opened its engagement with an astounding two-day gross of $44,000 at the New York Roxy.

To achieve the outdoor sound reproduction for *In Old Arizona*, cameras were wrapped in soundproof coverings. Special vehicles were designed to carry generating apparatus for electricity and sound-recording equipment was constructed to fit in trucks so that it could be moved with ease to locations.[69]

Sheehan again illuminated this development.

> It did much to rout the skeptics who had said previously that dialog films could not be made in the open, and that talking pictures would have to be confined within the cramping limits of a studio. All sorts of difficulties had to be surmounted in making it, which convinced us there was no supposed obstacle to talking pictures which could not be overcome.
>
> Further production of talking pictures bore out this conviction, and showed how flexible the new medium could be. Lois Moran and Clark and McCullough in "The Belle of Samoa" showed us the possibilities of the audible screen in presenting musical shows. "Napoleon's Barber" revealed how much more genuine an historical story became with talk added. "Hearts in Dixie" we consider was another forward step in realism, proving how sensitive talking pictures were in reproducing the fine shades of dialect.[70]

The developments continued with an all-star extravaganza review, *Fox Movietone Follies of 1929*, considered "a pioneer effort.... It's good entertainment all the way and occasionally arresting in its implications of the possibilities to come." The review also pointed out the drawbacks to the nascent process. "Photography seems dead, but here it must be remembered that a cameraman these days is pretty thoroughly handcuffed."[71]

Every opportunity was taken to add sound sequences to a feature. *Chasing Through Europe* (1929), a follow-up to *The News Parade* (1928),

Sue Carol and Nick Stuart go *Chasing Through Europe* (1929), one of Fox's early sound films with talking sequences (courtesy Robert S. Birchard).

depicted the further adventures of a newsreel cameraman, also played by Nick Stuart, who travels around Europe. Scenarists Andrew Bennison and John Stone inserted scenes in which the cameraman photographed Mussolini and the Prince of Wales—existing Movietone sound sequences that were cut into the feature.

With audiences clamoring for talkies, one major casualty of the transition was purely visual comedy. Fox abandoned its $1,000,000 annual program of 26 short feature releases because "the silent comedy had outlived its usefulness." Deluxe theaters never played the shorts anyway. Another consideration was to provide quality entertainment, so it was decided to divert the time and energy spent on the short subjects into features. For short subjects, Fox would still supply 52 Movietone Entertainments, all travelogues and documentaries with sound. Fox was not alone. Mack Sennett, Hal Roach, Christie and Educational Films were forced to begin making their comedies with sound.

Movietone hurtled over yet another obstacle when it released a short subject in Technicolor. "Many have contended that sound and color were impossible to combine on one film. Somewhat crude to be true. That didn't matter, however. That contention has been shattered. Fox has done it and, while the future holds much experimental work in store, the technical knots have been unraveled."[72]

While some production companies were reluctant to take the leap into talkies, there were also recalcitrant exhibitors. Some were ready to leave the business due to the high cost of sound equipment and the impending competition from theaters that had the financial backing to convert immediately. The large chains were siphoning off not only business in their key cities, but with the increasing sales of automobiles, small-town denizens were able to travel to large cities within their range to see movies long before they played in their own towns. Small-town exhibitors saw themselves as being gouged for rentals, flogged by technology and trampled by competition from the major players. Distributors of silent films saw their rentals drop off a cliff. It was not a happy time for all.

Some producers were unrealistically optimistic about the near future of silent films. Victor Halperin, a producer with Inspiration Pictures, insisted that with only one-third of theaters equipped with sound by 1931, there would still be plenty of outlets for non-talkies. He believed that both forms could compete in the marketplace especially if "sound's competitor will be a highly improved type of silent picture — designed for one purpose only — silent entertainment for the 15,000 silent houses. The 'talkies' will force open new avenues for presentation of novelties in silent pictures— greater novelties than have ever before been presented. Among those we are sure to see more foreign subjects, involving foreign locale and casts; more fantasy, more historical and more biographical subjects."[73]

Within a very short period after this prediction was made, it was clear that Halperin was not a reliable prognosticator. The entire industry, from production to distribution to exhibition was completely preoccupied with sound and could not equip itself quickly enough. As if to hammer that point home, Fox took out an ad that stated, "Gone are the days when talking pictures could hope to succeed as novelty alone. The speaking screen has reached maturity — its infant days are over. Noise is through as a box-office attraction. Today the public expects talking features of even better quality than the outstanding successes of the fading silent screen."[74] Winfield Sheehan announced on March 24, 1929, that Fox would make only Movietone features. Silent production had come to an end at Fox Films, although silent versions of sound films would still be available to unwired theaters.[75] Seven silent stages were to be converted to have Movietone capability.

Smaller theaters, unable to afford to make the transition to sound, struggled along with silent-only presentations. Producers continued to make titled versions of their talking pictures as long as it was profitable. There were some genres, particularly musicals, which became very popular in the early sound period that did not translate to silent versions. Although limited to wired theaters, these films brought in enough revenue from those locations to convince other studios to jump on the musical bandwagon. Big-budget releases appeared in rapid succession, including M.G.M.'s *Broadway Melody* (1929), Universal's *Show Boat* (1929), *Broadway* (1929), and *King of Jazz* (1930), Warners' *The Singing Fool* (1928) and *On With the Show* (1929), R.K.O.'s *Syncopation* (1929), Paramount's *The Love Parade* (1929) and Fox's *Movietone Follies* (1929) and *Sunny Side Up* (1929).

While talkies were proliferating around 1930, some independent exhibitors, bypassing the expense and risk of conversion to sound, took the opportunity to sell out because they were uncertain of their future. Some held out until the last of the silent theaters faded away with a whimper in the mid–1930s.

William Fox was one empire builder who continued headlong, buying and building. The compulsion to expand and control would become a heavy financial burden in the very near future.

8. *The Golden Age of Fox Films*

In addition to talking pictures, there were some interesting developments in terms of what drew audiences in the late 1920s. Obviously, the roadshow attractions brought in the highest rentals. *What Price Glory* hit the jackpot with massive world rentals of $2,429,000, the highest figure in the history of the company. Since it was also the most expensive production of the year at $817,000 the profit was still a healthy $796,000, but not equal to the record set in 1921 with *Over the Hill to the Poorhouse*. The emergence of Janet Gaynor and Charles Farrell as a sensational romantic team propelled *7th Heaven* to hit status. World rentals of $1,781,000 were astonishing because the foreign revenue was 65 percent of domestic rentals, much higher than the usual 40 percent. It demonstrated the international appeal of the film and the stars. Profits amounted to $479,000.

As usual, sex appeal was highly marketable. *Loves of Carmen* (1927), starring Victor McLaglen and Dolores Del Rio in the classic tale of passionate love, was definitely considered a better-than-average budget of $366,000, and it returned world rentals of just under $1,000,000 leaving a profit of $277,000. A lower budget production of $94,000 for *Silk Legs* (1927), starring lingerie princess Madge Bellamy, showed a profit of $82,000 with a sizable domestic rental of $207,000.

Pursuing his quest for "vital, unusual and true-to-life motion pictures," Winfield Sheehan chose some story material less certain to be successful. *The Wizard* (1927) was based on a novel by Gaston Leroux, the author of *The Phantom of the Opera* (1925, Universal), which had proven to be massive hit for Lon Chaney and Universal. Yet another macabre revenge tale, *The Wizard* starred Edmund Lowe as a doctor who trains an ape to settle the score for his son's death. With a respectable world-rental figure of $279,000, it showed a profit of $58,000 due to a conservative budget of $117,000.

The Monkey Talks (1927) told a way-off-the-beaten-track story of circus people who disguise one of their own as a talking simian and market him to the gullible public. The animal impersonator, however, becomes involved in a love triangle which results in his death. Not quite true-to-life but certainly unusual, it was perhaps too odd for American audiences. It became an anomaly with its foreign gross almost equaling domestic returns. At a cost of $221,000, it lost $22,000.

Surprisingly, two old-fashioned stories — a for-

The man holding the document is Jacques Lerner, billed at the time as the world's greatest animal impersonator. He also appears as a simian in *The Monkey Talks* (1927). Don Alvarado is at his left and Raymond Hitchcock is far right (courtesy Robert S. Birchard).

mula which years earlier had worked so well for Fox—did not perform as well as expected. The moralistic *One Increasing Purpose* (1927), preaching the virtues of unselfishness, was given considerable production value on a budget of $245,000 and had sufficient domestic appeal, but suffered a lack of foreign interest and was driven into the red with a $43,000 loss. Worse still, the sentimental drama *The Auctioneer* (1927), about a wealthy Jewish pawnbroker who is swindled and has to start over as a peddler, ended up as the biggest loser of the year. Costing $304,000 and earning world rentals of $317,000, it lost $106,000. In the year-end results, losses on those films were easily absorbed and rentals propelled the company to a new corporate record profit of $3,120,557.

Although Tom Mix was maintaining profitability, his costs were rising and exhibitors were experiencing a drop in the revenue from his pictures. The head of sales, James Grainger, notified the production department of the lower grosses. With competition from rival western stars at other studios, the Fox publicity department took a full-page trade ad to squeeze more revenue out of the Mix series. The ad itself was an admission that the cowboy king was being challenged.

> "Westerns" are "Westerns" always—with the exception of Tom Mix productions; they are different! Mix pictures are played and replayed, remembered, talked about, watched for. They are depended on by many exhibitors as "rent payers." Despite the fulsome advertising of other Western stars the fact remains that in the class of Western productions Tom Mix pictures are supreme. Here is one test—infallible—Tom Mix pictures bring the highest price of any Western productions. The crowds that storm your theatre when you play Mix pictures give you the answer. Mix pictures today, as for many years past, are in a class by themselves.[1]

By late 1927, Mix was negotiating with other producers and by 1928, his final Fox release showed a profit of only $14,000. To add injury to insult, Mix was hurt in an accident during the filming of his final film and suffered three fractured ribs, a sprained wrist and leg.[2]

In addition to spectacular grosses from his films, Winfield Sheehan, either through talent, luck or a combination of both, had hit on the winning formula that brought financial and critical success. Reviews were extraordinary for *7th Heaven*. *Variety* crowed, "It is a great big romantic, gripping and red-blooded story told in a straight to the shoulder way and when the last foot of some 11,000 is unwound, if there is a dry eyelash on either man or woman or child, they just have no red blood.... Borzage is entitled to the blue ribbon for this one. He has made a great picture ... he brought to the fore a little girl who has been playing in pictures for two years and made a real star out of her over night ... it took Borzage to take this young woman and let her smack the ball full on the nose by elevating herself into the Lillian Gish grade."[3]

Gaynor was also singled out in the *New York Times* review: "This is an exceptionally well-acted piece of work and Janet Gaynor's performance as Diane is true and natural throughout. This young woman was discovered by Winfield R. Sheehan, general production manager for the Fox Film Corporation. Never once does she falter in her difficult task of reflecting the emotions of the character she portrays ... in her acting there is nothing imitative, but always an earnest and successful effort to impersonate the French girl who is rescued from hardship and cruelty by that 'very remarkable fellow,' Chico."[4]

If *What Price Glory* (1926) and *7th Heaven* (1927) did not convince the industry of Fox Films' role as a purveyor of fine entertainment, the release of *Sunrise* (1927) made the fact undeniable. The F.W. Murnau film introduced many techniques used in German cinema and told its complex story in a simple but entirely visual manner. A city woman seduces a farmer and convinces him to drown his wife. Coming to his senses, the young man realizes the plan is wrong and he comforts his frightened wife. They make their way to the city where they have a daylong second honeymoon. Their rowboat overturns on the home trip and the farmer desperately searches for his wife. When the city girl shows up, the man blames her for his misfortune and is about to strangle her when his wife returns and stops him. "'Sunrise' is a distinguished contribution to the screen.... In its artistry, dramatic power and graphic suggestion it goes a long way toward realizing the promise of this foreign director.... What Murnau has tried to do is to crystallize in dramatic symbolism those conflicts, adjustments, compromises and complexities of man-and-woman mating experiences that ultimately grow into an endearing union.... Murnau reveals a remarkable resourcefulness of effects.... He can convey subtle meanings by trick photography or by treatment of backgrounds."[5]

The *New York Times* showered accolades upon F.W. Murnau for his brilliant direction: "Mr. Murnau shows himself to be an artist in camera studies, bringing forth marvelous results from lights, shadows and settings.... Miss Gaynor, guided by the genius of Mr. Murnau, gives a strangely sympathetic portrait of the Wife.... Mr. Murnau proves by 'Sunrise' that he can do just as fine work in Hollywood as he ever did in Germany."[6]

The *Film Daily* devoted a front page editorial to the film. "The importance of 'Sunrise' cannot be discounted. There will be arguments over its commercial value. That the picture falls into the division of big pictures will be admitted by all who see it. No one can foretell how its box-office valuation is to be rated, for it is a different type of motion picture. There is little precedent by which one may draw a conclusion."[7]

Business for *Sunrise* was initially very strong. "First week's receipts for 'Sunrise' at the Carthay Circle exceeded the house record of any production ever played there by $120, the management reports, and the news has created something of a sensation here. The word of mouth advertising has sent the second week's receipts soaring." The most flattering message was the interest other studios were taking in the film: "It is generally reported that producing organizations have issued instructions to their director and technical staffs to view the picture with a view of absorbing some of the angles that are catching the popular fancy."[8] Fox ads crowed about its hit pictures and had succeeded in elevating its image from the "hokum" of programmers to a purveyor of "$2 specials."

The level of critical respect gained by the Fox Film Corporation was reflected in the list of the 40 Best Films of 1927 chosen by the National Board of Review. The alphabetically arranged list included *The Loves of Carmen, Madame Wants No Children, The Music Master, 7th Heaven,* and *Sunrise,* in a tie with the mighty M.G.M., but both bested by Paramount with seven entries.

Now that Fox executives had writers and directors of esteem under their umbrella, there was good reason to build a structure to house this talent. Located in the southwest portion of the Sunset-Western studio, the building was reportedly Winfield Sheehan's idea. It occupied three sides of a hollow square and boasted an "artistic courtyard."[9] Dedicated by Will Hays on January 27, 1928, it was appropriately called "Park Row," in honor of the New York's historic newspaper district since many Fox directors and writers were formerly newspapermen.

In October 1927, Winfield Sheehan was once again busy supervising the studio's top productions for the upcoming movie season. Among them were two in script stage, *4 Devils* (1928), F.W. Murnau's second assignment and *The Cock-Eyed World* (1929), a sequel to *What Price Glory* that would once again star Edmund Lowe and Victor McLaglen. Filming had commenced on *Lady Cristilinda* (released as *Street Angel*, 1928), reuniting the *7th Heaven* trio of Janet Gaynor, Charles Farrell and director Frank Borzage, as well as the Victor McLaglen comedy drama *A Girl in Every Port* (1928). In his efforts to import more German talent, Sheehan announced that director Ludwig Berger would soon arrive in Hollywood to begin work on *The Dollar Princess* (working title for *Don't Marry*, 1928). Although Berger did make it to the studio and began shooting tests, the project never came to fruition because of a difference of opinion on the story. Fox decided to cancel Berger's contract and made a cash settlement with him. James Tinling was assigned to direct the film. Winfield Sheehan also signed exclusive contracts with Carl Mayer, author of *The Cabinate of Dr. Caligari* (1919), *The Last Laugh* (1924) and *Sunrise* (1927), and Henri Bernstein, a distinguished French dramatist, in an effort to project an aura of prestige.

In the most ambitious launch ever announced, Fox Films scheduled a five-year production program involving a reported $100,000,000 covering the cost of all expenditures through 1932. William

Fox's trio of hits and their talents: Frank Borzage (top), Janet Gaynor (lower left), Charles Farrell (lower right) (courtesy Robert S. Birchard).

Victor McLaglen is surrounded by sweethearts in *A Girl in Every Port* (1928) (courtesy Robert S. Birchard).

Fox made one of his rare trips west to go over the plans for this program. Since no company could project results that far into the future with any accuracy, it seems that it was an effort to convince the competition that Fox had the resources to further increase its market share of rental and theater revenues.

With such an enormous amount of capital being dedicated, Fox was clearly in a dominant industry position. In accordance with this long-term plan, Winfield Sheehan announced that he was making his permanent home in Los Angeles. In a *Time* magazine profile, Sheehan's lifestyle was highlighted. "General Manager Sheehan lives at Beverly Hills in a house of which he supervised the design and building. It has tapestry-covered walls, a sunken garden, a library ceiling imported from Spain. Three butlers serve dinner guests from gold plates and golden goblets. To summon them, Mr. Sheehan keeps on hand a dented, rusty cowbell which he jangles loudly when service is required."[10]

James Grainger expected business to be at least 30 percent better in the coming film season based on the fact of "first, new young faces on the screen, second, the manner in which producers have kept faith with the public, and third the advent of talking films."[11]

As Fox Films and Fox Theaters entered its 13th year of operation, the tentacles were spreading farther and faster, especially in the acquisition and construction of new venues. Fox was reported as being at loggerheads with the Publix and Paramount companies and was tangling with Loew's, Inc. and other organizations, both in the matters of film distribution and theater building.

> Those familiar with William Fox know that once he makes up his mind to proceed in a certain direction he is not easily deterred from his plans. His surprise move in getting hold of the Roxy theater in New York is said to have chagrined the Paramount group to such an extent that it is reported Publix intends to retaliate by erecting a bigger house than the Roxy on the site of Loew's New

York, which the Loew group has under a week-to-week from Publix-Paramount.

Fox loves his independence and isn't going to listen to the dictates of very many in pursuing his course as he has it mapped out. He is convinced that he has the nucleus for a producer-distributor-exhibitor organization that can meet the biggest of them on any terms and come out pretty close to first.[12]

If anyone had doubts about William Fox's searing ambition at the outset of 1928, the acquisition of Wesco Holding Company (West Coast Theaters) with more than 232 houses and a seating capacity of 300,000 in California, Oregon, Washington, Montana, Nevada, and Iowa, more than confirmed it. William Fox, who had previously held 34 percent of the shares, now had a controlling interest in the company and brought the Fox chain to 340 theaters. The purchase of Wesco secured for Fox 28 percent of the capital stock of First National, which would figure importantly for William Fox in the future. Shortly after the purchase, a new Fox offering of 125,000 shares of new Class-A stock at $75 each share was made to the public.

Fox announced that Harold B. Franklin would continue in charge of Wesco's operations with headquarters in Los Angeles. The construction program would continue and involved a financial outlay of about $150,000,000. "Estimated gross for 1928 is $700,000 per week, or $35,000,000 for the year. On the basis of a general admission scale of 33 cents, the houses, he declared, could accommodate 105,000,000 people a year. There are 7,500 employees on the weekly payroll. Combining this figure with the employees of Fox Film and Fox Theaters, it pointed out that there are 27,500 persons on the total weekly payroll of Fox's enterprises."[13]

Just one month later, Fox again made news when he was in negotiations to take over the Finkelstein and Ruben chain which had once shut him out of the St. Paul and Minneapolis. The deal was ultimately unconsummated when there was a dispute about Fox's financing plans. Next, there was talk of the absorption of the Stanley chain of 270 theaters in theaters in Connecticut, Delaware, Maryland, New Jersey, New York, Pennsylvania, West Virginia and Washington, D.C. Again, this deal collapsed in September 1928, so Fox instead took on the 100 neighborhood theaters of the Moss-Sapiro New York circuit. All these acquisitions brought the Fox companies to a valuation of $64,000,000 in 1928 up from $16,000,000 in 1925.[14]

An editorial in the *Film Daily* clarified what was already common knowledge.

Unless the dope sheet is all wrong, Bill Fox's strongest competitors are going to resign themselves to the fact that here is a factor worthy of their own steel. The Wesco deal centers the spotlight on Fox with a brilliancy that refuses to be dimmed. We happen to know some of the inside of the Fox scheme of things. It has been apparent to us for a long time that Fox was set on having his place in the sun, not as small fry but as importantly as anybody else in the industry. He has been building up to this for some time. Indulging in what some call long chances, and operating at odds that often seemed stacked against him, Fox has come through with flying colors. And so in these early days of 1928, you find the Fox banner waving in the breeze as bravely as any and far more vigorously than most.... For, if you please, Mr. William Fox has entered the inner circle of the elect and exclusive, despite the reluctance of some of the charter members. When you hear of industry matters and industry changes from now on, Fox is going to have his say.[15]

Fox himself made this clear in a May 1928 statement. "There is no place under the sun where Fox pictures will not be shown. We have no axe to grind. We feel that this organization has a place in the industry and we are determined to see that we get it."[16] This statement was heard loud and clear through the investment community and pushed the value of Fox stock up to a record high of $113 1/2 per share by September.

Noted in the trades for its smooth continuity, Fox Films was singled out as a well-oiled machine: "There is a harmony prevalent there that is not as widespread through the trade as it should be. Each executive moves through a familiar groove, doing the appointed tasks, sidetracking politics for the advancement of the organization, Bill Fox tops the list of course. Jack Leo, little heard of, is contact on finances — always important. Then Sheehan on the coast. Everybody knows what he's doing at the studio. And Grainger who does more to help the Pullman Co. meet its dividend dates than anybody we know."[17]

William Fox began 1928 with not only the acquisition of the more than 232 house Wesco Holdings chain, but also set a new high weekly record for domestic and foreign receipts of $915,350 for the week ending January 27. The previous weekly high record was $829,000 set for the week ended on January 29, 1927. Movie audiences were growing as the public resistance to content and elitism on the part of socialites both faded. At an average admission of 33 cents, movies were also a lot more economical for the average person than live performances at $4.40.

It was clear there was nothing that would stop William Fox from expanding his theater chain in the United States, and Clayton Sheehan, the foreign manager of Fox Films, announced that theaters would also be bought or built in foreign capitals where representation was lagging.

The Roxy Theater on Broadway proved to be a hugely successful venture with box-office receipts of $5,468,529 in its first year. About half of all the pictures played were Fox releases, and a regular policy was not yet firmly established. Some pictures were first-run, others were films that were already well into their roadshow runs at other houses like Warner's Vitaphone release of *Don Juan* (1926), and Fox's own *What Price Glory* (1926) and *7th Heaven* (1927). By mid–October, the standard policy of one-week first-run higher budget films was established. No film topped the record gross of $144,267 set by *What Price Glory* during the week of August 20, 1927. The year's lowest week was that ending March 2, 1928 with the run of *Silk Legs* (1927) pulling in only $86,000. Average grosses were around $100,000 weekly.[18]

If all this was not enough to create anxiety among Fox's competitors, a headline in the *Exhibitors Daily Review* certainly would. It read "3000 Fox Theatres by 1930." The subsequent article outlined Fox's plan to further expand his theater holdings "to extend from coast to coast and border to border, with theatre outlets in every State in the union. The object of the plan is to make Fox product independent of playdates in theatres of other organizations.... It is the scheme of the originators of this idea to have sufficient theatres to pay the entire production cost of pictures together with a healthy profit, aside from having theatres doing sufficient business to carry themselves and show a profit."[19]

William Fox was apparently trying to create a closed system whereby he never had to rely on other studios for product or chains to book his pictures. This would have made him a monopoly in his own right, independent and powerful.

The animosity within the industry over which Fox's tentacles were spreading further each day finally reached a boiling point.

> In certain high quarters, there is much dissatisfaction and concern over the West Coast Theaters situation in which William Fox is now the dominating and controlling factor. It is understood Joseph M. Schenck and Louis B. Mayer are talking about a survey of the territory with a view to building, if such a step should become necessary.
>
> In 1927, about 70 per cent of the total rentals paid by the West Coast string was divided between Paramount and M-G-M. Now that Fox is in the saddle, the situation gradually will reverse itself. Not that anyone anticipates that Fox will not use Paramount, M-G-M or any other producing unit that turns out worthwhile product ... but Fox is going to get a far better break than he has up to now. That is exactly what is disturbing Paramount and M-G-M. Likewise it is exactly that state of affairs which is spurring Schenck and Mayer into action.[20]

In dollars, Paramount had earned $2,000,000 from West Coast and M.G.M. had received $1,500,000 with other distributors earning $600,000. Those amounts were destined to swing towards Fox's films after the takeover. There would still be some bookings of product from M.G.M. and Paramount since Wesco needed more pictures than Fox alone could deliver. However, Fox Theaters could use its massive buying power to make better deals leaving the other studios with lower rentals. In January 1929, Fox Theaters, with 619 houses in its chain, was estimated to have a total annual gross of $135,000,000.[21]

One area where Fox had always lagged behind M.G.M. and Paramount was in stars. Now Fox bombarded the trades with ads of the company's box-office potency with its new stable of stars. At the time, it was almost comparable in drawing

George O'Brien and Nora Lane in a publicity shot for *Masked Emotions* (1928) (courtesy Robert S. Birchard).

power to M.G.M. Topping the list were Janet Gaynor, Madge Bellamy, Lois Moran, Edmund Lowe, Earle Foxe, Victor McLaglen, Charles Farrell, and George O'Brien.[22] Noticeably missing from the list was Tom Mix, who had already moved on to other, not particularly greener, pastures.

Not every heralded discovery ended up in stardom. Always on the lookout for female pulchritude, Fox Films held beauty contests in many countries to single out possible leading ladies and gave them small parts to test their mettle. Maria Casajuana, winner of Spain's contest appeared in *A Girl in Every Port* (1928) starring Victor McLaglen. The studio quickly changed her name to Maria Alba and she was assigned small parts in English-language films and, when the talkies arrived, larger roles in Spanish language features produced by Fox. Lia Tora from Brazil, was initially luckier with a starring role in *The Veiled Woman* (1929), but earned only a few roles under her one-year contract. Neither woman exploded into stardom, or even near-stardom. Fox was not much luckier with American-born performers. A new cowboy star, Rex Bell, was discovered by Modest Stein, a well-known western illustrator. Bell's career was nowhere near as illustrious as that of Tom Mix or even George O'Brien. He made only three westerns at Fox of the seven that were promised to exhibitors and spent the rest of his contract in supporting roles. Caryl Lincoln was promoted from two-reelers to star in *Wolf Fangs* (1927) and then other features before becoming an uncredited supporting player after 1931.

There were always ample examples that no matter how much studios griped about the high star salaries, they were always giving in to such demands when contracts came up for renewal. "Janet Gaynor has severed her contract with Fox, it is understood," wrote the *Film Daily*. "The youthful player who rose to fame in '7th Heaven,' is said to have refused to sign a new contract with the company, following attainment of her majority age. She was scheduled to play in 'Hangman's House,' which is to mark the return to the screen of William Farnum. Betty Bronson may be assigned the role it is indicated."[23]

"Fox sought to renew the contract at $1,000 weekly, but Miss Gaynor is declared to be holding out for $3,000."[24] Within a week, the studio issued this statement: "Report that Janet Gaynor is to leave Fox is declared to be untrue, with two new vehicles secured for the Gaynor-Charles Farrell co-starring team."[25] Ultimately, Gaynor stayed with Fox without any announcement of her salary, but it was obvious she had gotten pretty much what she wanted. Fox obviously felt she was too valuable to lose.

By this point in time, the production arm of the studio had been almost completely taken over by Winfield Sheehan and James Grainger. Both conferred regularly on the program of pictures, with Grainger feeding information about grosses and star popularity back into the production equation. They conferred in meetings before a slate of pictures was announced. In an effort to quell foreign resistance to playing American films, Sheehan ordered four quota productions from England.

There was a change in the production philosophy at Fox in the fall of 1928. William Fox and Winfield Sheehan had reached the conclusion that program pictures were no longer worth making. "That is program, to the extent of cheap pictures with short shooting schedules and casts of no great consequence. Accordingly, they have decided to supplant these with what has been known as 'specials.' In other words, this organization intends making nothing but big one's [sic], sinking plenty of money in every negative and hoping for the best."[26]

Armed with the capacity for sound films, William Fox decided to use this technology to make musicals, a genre not accommodated by silent films. Fox signed Edward Royce, a celebrated director of stage presentations who was formerly associated with master showman Florenz Ziegfeld. He also hired the popular tunesmith trio of Buddy DeSylva, Ray Henderson and Lew Brown to write the book, words and music for at least two productions. Also brought to the studio were Dave Stamper, another Ziegfeld Follies alumnus; Harland Thompson, a successful composer; and the team of Archie Gottler and Sydney Mitchell. Fox was building up a unit to produce a steady flow of musical productions.

Musical performers like J. Harold Murray (who had starred in the stage version of *Show Boat*), upcoming operatic singer Jeanette MacDonald, and famed Irish tenor John McCormack, were signed to contracts. For the 1928-1929 movie season ample use was made of the new talent. The planned slate of releases was top-heavy with three musical revues, three operettas, four musical comedies and seven other films with music. Not all of these were made, but it demonstrated that Fox Films was now dedicated to using sound to the fullest.

With exhibitors signing contracts for Fox product, it was important that the studio announce the strongest possible slate of pictures. This led to some pie-in-the-sky pronouncements about casts or directors. Some changes in the program were unavoidable and some were beneficial to exhibitor and producer alike. For example, a star like Sally Phipps could start out the year being a moneymaker and then drop off in popularity. With theaters reporting directly to their district managers who then reported back to James Grainger who then discussed the results with Winfield Sheehan, decisions could be made to fine-tune a program of pictures relatively quickly.

The result was that the films released were often not the films promised. Play-off contracts were based on a number of pictures with popular stars and as long as the star still appeared in that number of titles, there were no disputes. Exhibitors had some rights in not playing a picture if it did not perform well in initial engagements or was considered inappropriate for a community, so the production/exhibition relationship was fungible. This loophole in contracts was a necessity since producers could not always deliver what they promised. The occasional bait-and-switch formula could be seen in the nearly fifty pages of color ads for the 1928-1929 slate of films. The publicity department would make the season's program as appealing as possible to exhibitors.

STABILITY
AFTER a quarter century of development, FOX enterprises occupy today an enviable position. Throughout the civilized world, FOX is acknowledged to be the one STABILIZED trade mark in the motion picture industry.
Consistency of performance in the production of exceptional entertainment has been the determining factor in the STABILIZATION of this trade mark. Behind it stands this acknowledged fact— that FOX pictures steadily return the greatest profits.
Anchored on this stability, the exhibitor of FOX pictures is assured a permanent profitable business, a consistent return each week and years of financial prosperity.
Guaranteeing the future product that will rise from the bed-rock of stability of FOX are two facts the exhibitor will do well to consider:
1. A budget of One Hundred Million Dollars has been authorized for the production of FOX box-office attractions during the next five years.
2. The nation's foremost theaters operating in key cities under the FOX banner will depend, for their financial success, upon FOX standard, which cannot and will not fail them.[27]

Unavoidably, of the 42 announced features, ten fell by the wayside including some youth-oriented films with Sally Phipps and Nick Stuart, a couple of Madge Bellamy comedies, and four programmer westerns with Rex Bell. Others, which were announced with top-flight casts, were delivered with lesser names. Some examples include *Romance of the Underworld* (1928), scheduled to star Edmund Lowe and Nancy Drexel ended up with Mary Astor and Ben Bard. *Joy Street* (1929) was to be directed by Irving Cummings with Lionel Barrymore but was filmed with Nick Stuart under the direction of Raymond Cannon. *Me, Gangster* (1928), slated with George O'Brien, Lois Moran and Barry Norton and director Irving Cummings made it to the screen starring Lola Lane and Paul Page with Ben Stoloff directing. *The One Woman Idea* (1929) was to star Charles Farrell, Mary Duncan and Earle Foxe, under director Howard Hawks but, when filmed, it starred Rod LaRoque, Marceline Day and Shirley Dorman with Berthold Viertel directing. In each case, the substituted talents were lesser draws to the ones they replaced. When it came to *The Great White North* (1928), what was advertised as a Lew Seiler–directed drama starring the popular June Collyer and Charles Morton, turned out to be a documentary on the Arctic.

Theater owners had little to complain about Fox's releases since there were many hits in the 1928-1929 season including *Street Angel, The River Pirate, Four Sons, Fazil, Win That Girl, Mother Knows Best, Plastered in Paris, Me, Gangster, The Air Circus, Mother Machree, Sunrise, Making the Grade, The Red Dance* and *Dry Martini*. In October 1928, *Photoplay Magazine* named four of these releases among their six best pictures of the month.

Critical response to the year's films was definitely on an upswing. Aside from the programmers which no longer seemed to attract any attention, the Winfield Sheehan–supervised unit was centering its attention on the "big" pictures. The year started off auspiciously with John Ford's stirring direction of *Four Sons* (1928). *Variety* wrote, "A profoundly moving picture of family life in Germany during the war, giving a sympathetic insight into the effect upon the humble people of rural Bavaria of the great struggle. As an artistic creation the production is magnificent in the amazing effectiveness of its fine realism and in its utter simplicity."[28]

The leading lady, an elderly Margaret Mann, had "worked for ten years as an extra, and her first chance for fame came when Winfield R. Sheehan, general manager of the Fox Studios, chose her to act the principal role in this film.... Mrs. Mann is

Charles Farrell (as an Arab Prince) woos Greta Nissen in *Fazil* (1928) (courtesy Robert S. Birchard).

excellent in her portrayal of Mother Bernle. She looks courageous. She appears to be bearing up in the face of great sorrow, and latterly seems much too exhausted to fight any more. It is an extremely difficult role for an elderly woman, especially before a camera. Yet, Mrs. Mann has succeeded in looking as if she were living the part."[29]

The *Variety* review of *Street Angel* (1928) reuniting Gaynor and Farrell started with "another of those superior program pictures William Fox and Winnie Sheehan are accumulating so rapidly, with each making the heart of the exhibitor playing the Fox stuff beat a little faster every time.... In 'Street Angel' is revealed the rapidly progressing studio ideas. Long and continued shots are in the picture of streets and alleys, that at first glance appear impossible of studio manufacture but doubtlessly were."[30]

Aside from ample praise for the performances, the *New York Times* was also impressed by the production. "The excellence of this feature does not depend on trick photography, but upon genuinely expert composition of the scenes and careful atmospheric effects."[31]

Don't Marry (1928) was nothing more than a comedy entertainment about "a modern flapper encumbered with an old fashioned aunt."[32] As such it was considered skillful and was "nicely photographed, well acted, and there is also opportunity to gaze frequently upon the wholesome beauty of Lois Moran."[33] Moran had several opportunities to appear in skimpy bathing suits, always considered to add audience appeal.

Once again, F.W. Murnau garnered kudos for his inventive direction of a story about circus acrobats: *4 Devils* (1928): "From this sawdust story one gains the impression that Mr. Murnau exerts an amazing influence over his players, and when one might think he is digressing it soon turns out that he has something important to tell.... Without any prismatic effects this picture seems to make an impression of varied colors as it surges along."[34]

Variety noted the commercial prospects of the new Murnau venture. "Murnau made 'Sunrise' and it was not box-office in the sense a picture of its production cost should have been.... Perhaps Winnie Sheehan did the unusual then and followed his belief Murnau could be made box-office. Mr. Sheehan assigned him to 'The Four Devils' and Murnau has come through.... For the classes among the big directors."[35]

In addition to Fox Films appearing on many of the critical "best" lists for the year, the new gold standard in awards made its debut when the Academy of Motion Picture Arts gave out its first statues, known then as "Merit Awards." Out of the eleven categories, Fox, mainly led by *Sunrise*, won in five, including Best Actress (Janet Gaynor for *7th Heaven, Sunrise,* and *Street Angel*); Best Director (Frank Borzage for *7th Heaven*); Best Writing (adaptation) (Benjamin Glazer for *7th Heaven*); Cinematography, (Charles Rosher and Karl Struss for *Sunrise*); and a one-time award given for Artistic Quality of Production for *Sunrise*.

Financially, the calendar year of 1928 was highly profitable with $22,626,747 in rentals from total negative costs of $10,379,365, reflecting a production cost of 45.9 percent against domestic income, the lowest amount since 1925. The average production topped out at a record $188,716. Light-hearted romps like *A Girl In Every Port* helped bring in audiences. On a relatively expensive negative cost of $207,000, world rentals of $460,000 propelled the Victor McLaglen starrer to a profit of $91,000. McLaglen scored once again as a sailor in *The River Pirate*, which brought world rentals of $562,000 and a profit of $72,000. John Ford directed four films, three of which were hits, but *Hangman's House*, starring McLaglen, showed a slight loss and did not connect with audiences. In an attempt to further stretch the popularity of the stars of *What Price Glory*, Fox teamed up Sammy Cohen and Ted McNamara in a comedy with the title *Why Sailors Go Wrong*. A hit gross brought in world rentals of $347,000 and a $63,000 profit. Yet another attempt to lure in the young crowd, *The News Parade*, starring Nick Stuart as a newsreel cameraman and Sally Phipps as his girlfriend, was only a modest hit with mediocre reviews, yet it spawned several similar films. The most successful release of the year for Fox, and one of the industry's highest grossers for 1928, was Frank Borzage's *Street Angel*, with the popular romantic pair of Janet Gaynor and Charles Farrell. On the second-highest Fox budget of the year, $360,000, the film brought in $1,197,000 in domestic rentals and $471,000 in foreign rentals for a profit of $757,000. The most expensive film of the year, and to date, was *Sunrise*, costing slightly over $1,000,000. The Murnau film collected praise but ended up losing over $80,000. For the fiscal year ending September 29, 1928, Fox's net income after taxes had doubled from the previous year to $4,016, 461.

In January 1929, William Fox completed his total domination of the New York marketplace with the acquisition of 200 theaters representing 40 independent units with a seating capacity of 280,000. The houses, secured by purchase and merger would be operated by Fox Metropolitan Playhouses, Inc., a Fox subsidiary. Practically every important independent circuit in Manhattan, Brooklyn, Queens and Kings and Westchester counties, and a number in New Jersey and Connecticut agreed to sell to Fox Metropolitan. Obviously, many exhibitors felt they would be left behind to fight the giant chain if they did not sell and Fox offered top dollar for their theaters.

This deal would practically eliminate independent theaters in Greater New York and would give Fox a buying power for film estimated at $7,000,000. Fox claimed that this purchasing power would greatly improve the quality of neighborhood shows. Competitors saw this as a jawbone to keep Fox's profits high and film rentals from outside companies low.

The added revenue from these acquisitions would increase Fox Theatres Corporation revenue to approximately $100,000,000 annually, yielding Fox about $13,000,000 in profits. The company projected profits for this group alone to be between $7,000,000 and $7,500,000 a year. Under the arrangement, several exhibitors were bought out with the prospect of being made division managers under the Fox Theatres umbrella. The unification of purchasing power was estimated to cut expenses of the new circuit by about 20 percent.[36]

William Fox had reached the apex of his personal success and professional dominance in a brutally unforgiving business. If nothing else than proclaiming his true worth to the industry, he now ranked second among life-insurance holders worldwide, with a policy of $6,400,000. Rodman Wanamaker, the son of department store magnate John Wanamaker, was first.

On the surface, Fox was a smoothly run corporation held together by an executive staff loyal to its president. However, circumstances would change as would the fortunes of the company, and contentious tendencies would surface and eventually play themselves out to the fullest in the saga of the Fox Film Corporation.

9. The Fall of William Fox

With the international success of Fox Films, spearheaded by a slate of popular releases, the coming of sound, and a distribution organization circling the globe with 110 exchange branches, revenues increased dramatically, allowing the corporation access to credit from banks around the world.

William Fox, preoccupied with theater acquisitions, was still the titular head of production at the Fox Film Corporation, but he trusted his executive staff, headed by Winfield Sheehan and Sol

M. Wurtzel, to purchase material and sign talent contracts. At the speed with which Fox was making theater deals, it is hard to imagine that he had any time to devote to the production pipeline. In fact, he visited Los Angeles very rarely, once in 1924, after the purchase of the Fox Hills land, and then again five years later for one day in February 1929, when he was on a theater-buying tour with Winfield Sheehan.

While Fox was putting all the pieces in place for what may have looked to some like a soundly integrated business, to others, especially in the justice department, there was a monopolistic tinge to the Fox companies. Firstly, there was Fox's theater domination in certain sections of the country. Each week brought announcements of the acquisition or construction of new theaters to add to his, as competitors may have phrased it, metastasizing enterprise.

In late 1928, he controlled over 500 houses in the United States covered by the West Coast Theaters, the Fox-Poli circuit of 22 theaters in New England acquired in July 1928, Fox Midwesco in Wisconsin and Illinois, Fox Metropolitan Playhouses in New York and New Jersey, and "deluxe" houses in Brooklyn, Philadelphia, Washington, St. Louis and Detroit.[1] International chains brought the total closer to 700 theaters. The organization was so large that several executives were in charge of various arms of it. John Zanft, vice-president and general manager of Fox Theaters, with years of experience, ran the de luxe operations in more than a dozen key cities. Harold B. Franklin, who came along with West Coast Theaters, continued operating that division.

In early 1929, Isadore Ostrer, a London merchant banker and the principal shareholder of British Gaumont Company (which owned a chain of 300 of the best theaters in England) came to New York. Due to harsh economic conditions in England at the time, Ostrer was looking to sell the chain and William Fox was interested in buying. Fox figured his company was earning a mere $500,000 on his releases in England due to unfavorable terms from Gaumont. Ownership of the chain would yield a more appealing $5,000,000 annually.[2]

Fox went to Halsey, Stuart & Co., the financial firm which was under contract to handle such matters for his companies. With the American Telephone and Telegraph Company (which stood to make an estimated $7,500,000 in sound equipment installations in England) behind him as well, Fox was able to purchase the Gaumont chain for $20,000,000. Within four years, Fox estimated that the investment would pay for itself.

With his Tri-Ergon patents covering Movietone, William Fox held an undisputed grip on the future of sound on film. With the technical drawbacks to Vitaphone, including the difficulties with synchronization, the limited life of discs to 20 plays, and the less-than-practical bulkiness of phonograph players connected to projectors, Fox's Movietone and other compatible sound-on-film processes were to emerge the dominant sound reproduction systems. This control brought envy.

Fox wanted to be a visionary in another development as well. Experimentation had been proceeding, during the 1920s, on a device to watch entertainment in homes via broadcast signals. Predictions were issued that the movie business had nothing to fear in the way of competition for at least five years. Nevertheless, William Fox saw "television" on the horizon and "reached a conclusion that the one thing that would make it possible to compete with television was to use a screen ten times larger than the present screen, a camera whose eye could see ten times as much as at present.... I believed this 'Grandeur' would come closer to the third dimension we hear scientists talking about.... This was an experiment William Fox was making — it was not an experiment of the Fox companies, because there was a great hazard about it, and I always took the hazards myself."[3]

Fox became a leading proponent of a new wide-film system, whose patents he co-owned, called Grandeur. Films would be projected onto much larger, wider screens from 70 mm film that would offer panoramic views and clarity of image. During the development of Grandeur in 1927, Fox brought in a financing partner, Harley L. Clarke, who was president of the Utilities Power & Light Corporation. Clarke had made a fortune in providing electricity to run the nation's new appliances which were proliferating in factories and residences across America. He was also involved in the International Projector Company which manufactured 85 percent of the country's projection equipment. He had merged several companies into National Theatre Supplies which also provided sound equipment, screens, and seating to movie houses around the country including the Fox chain. Clarke wanted to be a part of this new wide-gauge system and manufacture its equipment rather than remain a competitor. Although warned against the trustworthiness of Clarke, William Fox chose to make him a 50 percent partner in the Grandeur Company. Thrown into the deal was the Mitchell Camera Co. which Fox had purchased. Mitchell was the foremost maker of camera equipment for the industry. Clarke, early on, showed an interest in buying into the Fox companies and offered to purchase a half interest in William Fox's shares, an offer which was emphatically turned down. Other studio executives were upset by Fox's new process even though Paramount had experimented with a lens that boosted the size of an image during the roadshow run of *Old Ironsides* (1926).

"They said I was about to make a great mistake: the industry had just changed from silent to sound; a great inventory had to be wiped down, and we were just about catching our breath, and here I was trying to upset it again.... Each company was claiming they had a much finer development at that time, and their purpose was to persuade me not to give the premiere performance."[4] As usual, Fox could not be deterred. On September 17, 1929, at the Gaiety Theater in New York, Courtland Smith of Fox-Case Movietone made the introduction:

> Tonight William Fox presents to you the crowning achievement of his long and magnificent career in motion pictures. It may be unique in the annals of American industry that a real pioneer in a major business lived to become the great pioneer in the second and greater development of that business.... Grandeur has brought another influence actively into pictures. Just as sound brought to us the invaluable aid and friendship of Western Electric Company and such outstanding men as Walter S. Gifford, Edgar S. Bloom and John E. Otterson, now Grandeur brings forward the company responsible for designing and manufacturing the vital part of all pictures, the projection machine. This work has been accomplished by the courage and foresight of Harley L. Clarke and his company, the General Theaters Equipment, Inc. They have worked with the engineers of the Fox organization for three years and the results which you will see tonight could not have been accomplished without them.[5]

The first film in the new process was *Happy Days* (1930), and it was a hit. Fox would produce another Grandeur epic, *The Oregon Trail* (later retitled *The Big Trail*, 1930) budgeted at $2,000,000. The industry suddenly became inundated with new proposals for wide-gauge systems. Whereas the studios were interested in this development, theater owners, especially the smaller independent ones still coping with the financial strains of converting to sound, were less enthusiastic. Once again, roiling the industry waters, William Fox declared that the studio would make three negatives on all future films: standard Movietone, standard silent, and Grandeur wide gauge. A trade paper reported that "a person can sit even in the front row of the Roxy and enjoy the picture without distortion from any angle and that the pictures will be as clear and large as a full-size stage show."[6]

Technicolor, a highly valued and protected monopoly of color reproduction on film was finally gaining acceptance by Warner Bros., Paramount, First National, Universal, United Artists, and M.G.M. when William Fox announced he would spend $1,000,000 to install a laboratory at the Sunset-Western lot for Fox Nature Color film. This new photographic process, which was developed along with Eastman Kodak (the giant in motion picture negative and printing stock), could become a direct threat to Technicolor's stranglehold on color film.

With radio a new competitive force in entertainment (which initially encouraged William Fox to explore talking pictures), there was an opportunity to acquire the bankrupt American Broadcasting Company (not the same ABC network that was formed in 1945 and which exists to today). With a network of 30 stations in the West and Midwest, Fox was considering a purchase of the company which would give him a beachhead in another medium. Like many proposed Fox acquisitions, this one created more anxiety than anything concrete.

An editorial outlined Fox's position and power toward the end of 1928. "Fox has and always will, play a lone hand. He is the boss of the Fox organization and everyone knows that. The Fox backers, and they are numerous, would not have the organization any other way. He has made all of them millions in the picture business. He can get these and other millions by a phone call.... And the word is around the 'street' that 'this fellow Fox is going too far with his theatre buying. He is stepping on too many toes.' But who is going to head him off?"[7] Louis B. Mayer (who had just turned down President Herbert Hoover's offer of an ambassadorship to Turkey) was waiting in the wings to do just that.

Since 1929 started out with economic optimism, Fox, in an acquisitive mood and with seemingly endless bank credit, decided to get in on the merger mania and bit off a major chunk of risk. Perhaps most perplexing to those who feared his over-reaching was the secret purchase, through a consortium of family members and friends, of 401,300 shares of Loew's, Inc. made from February 1 to February 27, 1929, for a total over-market amount of $105,000,000.

> The biggest deal in motion picture history has been closed. William Fox has purchased a controlling interest in Loew's, Inc. which carries with it complete ownership of Metro-Goldwyn-Mayer. The deal, first launched several months ago, came to a successful culmination on Monday and initial payments for the controlling blocks of stock were made late Tuesday night.
> Fox paid $125 a share for the stock held by Nicholas M. Schenck, president of Loew's, Inc.; Mrs. Carrie Loew, widow of Marcus Loew who founded the company; Arthur M. Loew, vice-president; David M. Bernstein, vice-president and treasurer; Louis B. Mayer, vice-president of M-G-M in charge of production and others.
> Previously, Fox had purchased in the open market a large block of Loew common of which 1,400,000 shares are outstanding and in which voting power is vested. In open market buying, the Fox representatives made an investment alone of several million dollars.[8]

The *Film Daily* estimated that unknown buyers for Fox were able to purchase about 250,000 outside shares to give him a 51 percent majority stake.[9]

What was astounding to the industry about the deal, apart from its financial size, was the amount of talent, both executive and on-screen that would be brought together. Fox stars under contract included Mary Astor, Warner Baxter, Marjorie Beebe, Sue Carol, Marguerite Churchill, Robert Clark, Sammy Cohen, June Collyer, Louise Dresser, Mary Duncan, Charles Farrell, Stepin Fetchit, Earle Foxe, Janet Gaynor, Warren Hymer, Dixie Lee, Ivan Linow, Edmund Lowe, Paul McCullough, Victor McLaglen, Farrell MacDonald, Lois Moran, Charles Morton, Paul Muni, George O'Brien, Sally Phipps, Sylvia Sidney, Nick Stuart, and Helen Twelvetrees.

Fox directors included John Blystone, William Beaudine, Frank Borzage, David Butler, Irving Cummings, Allan Dwan, John Ford, Howard Hawks, William K. Howard, F.W. Murnau, Norman McLeod, Robert J. Flaherty, Lew Seiler, George B. Seitz, Benjamin Stoloff, James Tinling, Norman Taurog, Marcel Silver, Berthold Viertel, James Parrott, Raoul Walsh, and Alfred Werker.

M.G.M.'s star roster included Renée Adorée, Nils Asther, Lionel Barrymore, Johnny Mack Brown, Lon Chaney, Joan Crawford, Marion Davies, Greta Garbo, John Gilbert, William Haines, Phyllis Haver, Leila Hyams, Buster Keaton, Bessie Love, Tim McCoy, Joel McCrea, Polly Moran, Robert Montgomery, Conrad Nagel, Anita Page, Aileen Pringle, Norma Shearer, Lewis Stone, Ernest Torrence, and Raquel Torres. Directors were Charles Brabin, Clarence Brown, Tod Browning, Jack Conway, Cecil B. DeMille, William C. DeMille, Jacques Feyder, Nick Grinde, George Hill, Lucien Hubbard, Rupert Julian, Robert Z. Leonard, Fred Niblo, William Nigh, Edward Sedgwick, Victor Seastrom, W.S. Van Dyke, King Vidor, and Sam Wood.[10] Shortly after this announcement, Murnau and Flaherty left Fox to launch an independent company "to produce talking pictures in foreign lands."[11]

A merger could have been the key component in William Fox's plan to control a closed chain of production, distribution, and exhibition. With the Loew's acquisition, Fox planned to close the Sunset/Western studio and move all those companies to M.G.M.'s Culver City lot while continuing production at Movietone City. Another concern was the division of executive responsibilities since there would certainly be overlapping positions. There was also duplication of distribution facilities all over the world although there were a handful of countries where a merger would expand overseas coverage. The Fox Theater chain now controlled 763 theaters in the United States with total domination in New York City, the largest single film-going audience in the world.[12] With an anxious industry awaiting William Fox's next move, he was still carrying out his multi-

Left to right: Dixie Lee, Jean Barry and Sue Carol in *Why Leave Home?* (1929) (courtesy Robert S. Birchard).

pronged effort to acquire more theater properties.

As usual, one thrust from a company deserved a parry from another. Once again, self-defense mechanisms went into overdrive. Paramount and R.K.O. were suddenly talking about a merger. Before Fox swooped in on M.G.M., Warners, also flush with cash, had been covertly planning a move on the studio.

Fox claimed that he had received an approval for the purchase from the Assistant United States attorney general, William J. ("Wild Bill") Donovan.[13] Donovan, through the Department of Justice, had been bringing lawsuits against film companies, questioning the legalities of the collusive rental pricing policies and the validity of exhibition contracts. He was also scrutinizing Fox's merger plan since it was leaked to the *Film Daily* by unnamed sources and was made public on December 10, 1928. William Fox and Nicholas Schenck both vehemently denied any such deal and demanded a retraction by the paper which was "respectfully denied." They were obviously not ready to admit to their private negotiations and explained the rumor as a malicious effort "created possibly with the idea of stock manipulation."[14]

With the enormous studio/distribution/exhibition reach of the two companies, William Fox would have domination of all aspects of the motion picture industry. Having seen only expansion in the moviegoing audience and a rise in theater revenue since he began in 1914, there was no reason to be apprehensive. Fox stock had soared and the assets of the company, although strained, would not snap. "William Fox today stands at the pinnacle of success, occupying a position which now seems well-nigh impregnable," exclaimed the *Film Daily*.[15]

The question about the Justice Department's approval of the deal was seemingly answered. A report appeared in the trades on September 13 that "merging of the Fox enterprises into one unit, with the Fox Film Corp., as holding company has been okehed [sic] by the Dept. of Justice, it is understood. A formal 'no objection' rating, is said to have been given the plan, to combine Loew's with Fox, which was submitted to the department. Other companies to be merged are Fox Theaters, Fox Metropolitan Theaters, M-G-M and Fox Case Corp."[16]

The executives at M.G.M.—Louis B. Mayer, Irving Thalberg and J. Robert Rubin—were annoyed because William Fox had outfoxed them by amassing enough shares through outside sources to gain control of their company. Louis B. Mayer, in particular, did not know he was selling shares that William Fox was buying. After a meeting with President Herbert Hoover, Fox was advised by two prominent Republicans, Claudius Houston and James Burke, to settle with Louis B. Mayer. Fox claimed that he arranged a payment of $2,000,000 to Mayer to settle his contract.[17]

Production co-chief Irving Thalberg issued a statement that "after a conference with my associates Louis B. Mayer, and J. Robert Rubin, in New York, we have completed our plans for 50 talking pictures with complete silent versions ... and I wish to give assurance to the people in our studio that we are to continue to be a progressive separate organization."[18]

Louis B. Mayer was confident he could flex enough political muscle to get the government to prevent the merger from occurring. Mayer had been a guest of President Hoover at the White House on September 6, 1929, no doubt to discuss the interloper William Fox.[19]

No matter how the government's decision was made to pursue the anti-trust efforts, it was clear that Fox would never merge with M.G.M.

"'It's a lotta boloney [sic],' declared Howard Dietz, director of advertising and publicity of M-G-M in commenting upon report in a New York newspaper to the effect that Louis B. Mayer, Irving Thalberg and Harry Rapf are shortly to be dropped from the company's line-up by William Fox."[20] There was no doubt that the Fox organization would remain intact with production reins firmly in the grip of Winfield Sheehan, sales vested securely with James Grainger, finances with Fox's brother-in-law Jack Leo and theater acquisitions, the responsibility of A.C. Blumenthal.

Tellingly, a year-end prediction of the future from Louis B. Mayer was especially uncertain: "Never before in [the] picture industry has it been so difficult to predict which way the industry may jump. There are so many new and thus far, but vaguely appreciated or developed factors, that no one can say with much confidence what the future holds in store."[21]

In this tumultuous period, there was a tangled web of studio relationships. William Fox owned 21,000 shares of First National which he had acquired as part of one of his theater deals. Paramount and M.G.M. had an alliance since President Marcus Loew's son had married the daughter of Paramount's president. The Warners were anxious to see this dissolved because they were interested in acquiring Paramount. Meanwhile, Warners wanted Fox's First National holdings to complete their merger which had begun in 1928. Because of First National's charter, no deal could be made without the consent of a full two-thirds of stockholders. "William Fox — ah, what a man — holds the key to the First National situation. There can be no deal, no sale, no acquirement, no merger with Warner Bros. or anybody else unless they first ask Bill."[22] Anti-trust forces in the Attorney General's office were watching all these developments closely. For the moment, William Fox, believing he had no government opposition to his merger, looked to a bright future.

Luck was not to follow William Fox from this time onward. On July 17, 1929, his regular chauffeur was unavailable to drive the Rolls-Royce to take the ardent golfer to the Lakeview Country Club. Instead, the chauffeur's brother took the wheel. Unfamiliar with the roads, the driver reached a crossing and collided with a vehicle driven by an inexperienced woman. There was a collision and both Fox and his friend, Jacob Rubenstein, were thrown from the car which then rolled over, killing the chauffeur. The 51-year-old William Fox was taken to the hospital suffering from shock, cuts, and a loss of blood. After several transfusions (one of them donated by actor J. Carroll Naish[23]) and a week in the hospital, Fox returned to his Long Island estate, Foxcroft, to recover.

The *Film Daily* editorial column appropriately framed the incident: "An industry held its breath. Over the ticker flashed word of an auto smash-up with Bill Fox the central figure. Mergers, pictures and all else sidetracked. Fox played center stage and down stage all at one time.... Fox, as a major figure within the industry, of course, occupies an unchallenged spot. But it took this incident to demonstrate how importantly he figures in the public eye. Early editions of afternoon paper ribboned the accident story clear across the front page. Every morning paper in New York carried the yarn prominently displayed on page one."[24]

During his recovery, the *Film Daily* editor, Jack Alicoate, wrote for the Fox Film Corporation's Silver Anniversary:

> Twenty-five years in the motion picture business. Each new day full of strife as well as romance.... Each new year invading new worlds to conquer and now reaching his Silver Anniversary with enterprises that span the globe, a world wide organization reflecting a twenty-five year march of dominating progress, and a name that is known in every city, town and hamlet in the civilized world. That's Fox. William Fox who to-day is the active far-seeing and aggressive head of one of the two greatest amusement organizations in the world.
>
> "Bill" Fox will always be known as one of the armored knights of the industry. His career, that of the lone warrior, is as romantic a life as can be found anywhere in pictures. His picture experiences have taken him from the management of the glittering penny arcade and nickel store show of bygone days to the ownership of the largest theater in the world, the Roxy. In production it is generally conceded that William Fox together with the Warner Boys are alone entitled to the credit of completely revolutionizing the industry, through pioneering the advent of sound. His Movietone News marked another forward step in picture progress, and now his Grandeur process bids fair to again turn things literally upside down. As an organizer, he has probably made fewer changes among the executives of his business than any other company. Sheehan, Rogers, Grainger, Leo, Smith and Zanft, old heads who know their stuff and do it. Congratulations to you Bill Fox on your silver Anniversary in pictures. Your idea of starting out to get somewhere in pictures and arriving there without fear or favor from anyone is accomplished.[25]

This tribute was followed by yet another glowing report on William Fox's humanitarian efforts. He intended to use sound film for the instruction of school children, the presentation of sermons in churches and the filming of difficult surgical procedures for the education of medical students. He was preparing to develop 16-millimeter film projectors and make films directly for home and educational use to avoid any conflict with theaters.[26]

For a man of William Fox's age, under enormous financial pressure, the accident did not help. It was three months before he returned to New York City on October 24. Five days after his return "Black Tuesday," October 29, 1929, shattered all preconceptions that the stock market was on an endless upward climb. After rising in value five-fold during the previous six years to 381.17 on September 3, 1929, the Dow Jones Industrial average lost 150 points and $14 billion in value (roughly equivalent of nearly $14 trillion today) in five hours. The losses continued through November 13, when the Dow hit its interim bottom of 198.60. This had a devastating effect on the value of William Fox's companies and his ability to raise further cash to cover the interest payments on his debts.

There were other mitigating factors that would cloud his future. The American Telephone & Telegraph Company, a well-established monopoly itself with $3,000,000,000 in assets and already

William Fox in a rare photograph taken in October 1929, after recovering from his car accident (courtesy Robert S. Birchard).

loaning Fox money, viewed Fox's sound patents as a potential treasure trove and looked to align itself with any entity that would attempt to grab William Fox's empire.

Since he had purchased some of the Loew's, Inc. shares on margin, Fox had to come up with $10,000,000 immediately. The Warner brothers were still very interested in acquiring Fox's 21,000 shares of First National. Fox had resisted selling the shares because First National gave Warners a leg up in the race for industry dominance. The Warners had also consummated deals for former Fox takeover targets, Stanley Theaters and the Finkelstein & Ruben circuit. After some negotiating back and forth, Fox was able to turn the First National shares into an amount to cover his margin call, well above the book value of $3,842,072 at the time, but so important to the Warners, that they were willing to pay the $10,000,000 price. Ironically, this very handy asset was picked up for virtually nothing when Fox bought the Wesco (Fox West Coast) chain.

When more capital was needed, Fox turned to John E. Otterson of Electrical Research Products, Inc. (ERPI), a division of the American Telephone and Telegraph Company (AT&T) with whom he had dealt in the development of sound on film, and the financial firm, Halsey, Stuart & Co., for financial assistance. In December 1929, Fox authorized the formation of a five-year trusteeship to raise capital to meet short-term obligations on debt already incurred. Otterson put up $15,000,000 and Halsey, Stuart financed $12,000,000. As collateral, Fox placed 50,101 shares of "B" voting stock in Fox Film, and 100,000 "B" voting shares of Fox Theaters, on deposit with Bankers Trust Company. This was a fatal mistake for William Fox and would lead to protracted litigation to determine who owned the voting rights on those shares.

In late November 1929, U.S. Attorney General William D. Mitchell was asking Fox and Warners to divest themselves of their Loew's and Paramount holdings in accordance with the Clayton Anti-Trust Act. In the case against Warners, the government alleged that all First National assets had been transferred to a new company, eliminating First National as a competitor of Warner Bros., allowing that company to control one quarter of the industry. The same allegation was made against Fox's purchase of approximately 400,000 shares of Loew's.

By January 3, 1930, Fox shares had dropped to new low of $17 from a previous year's high of $119. Stockholders, fearing a further loss of their holdings, were threatening legal action to put the company into receivership. Rumors spread throughout the industry that William Fox was in financial trouble and, since his holdings so widely influenced the entire industry, there was reason for concern. Fox succeeded in trying to quell the confusion for the moment and the trade papers sided with him: "To date, while there is no question of the Fox situation being complicated, no change of importance has been made in management, directorate or personnel. This in reply to hourly rumors, mostly unfounded, drifting up and down the big street."[27]

While William Fox was assuring shareholders he could meet dividend payments and appealed for patience in arranging for new financing, the Fox Film Corporation was reporting sales of 40 percent more for the 1929-1930 season than in 1928-1929. This was certainly a calming factor to the investing public, but the government was still pursuing anti-trust action over the purchase of Loew's shares on the grounds that it reduced interstate commerce. Of course, much of the government interest in the Fox acquisition was instigated by Louis B. Mayer, who had been out of town when Nicholas Schenck made his deal with

William Fox. Fox had received a tentative approval from Attorney General Donovan in mid-1929, under the outgoing Calvin Coolidge administration. After Herbert Hoover took office on March 4, 1929, there was a new, less-amenable attorney general. Louis B. Mayer, a staunch and influential Republican, also flexed his considerable political muscle with the new Hoover administration. Mayer later told Fox, "You must have known that I have moved heaven and earth to prevent this consolidation. Surely you felt that someone used his influence to have the government change its opinion with reference to these shares. I was responsible."[28]

According to William Fox's testimony before a senate hearing in late 1933, he recounted a meeting with Mayer in which he discussed the anti-trust problems created by the government and Mayer told him, according to reporting in *Time* magazine, "'I know all about that. I caused that record to be changed from a consent to a restriction. That was a perfectly simple matter for me to do.' Mr. Mayer added that getting the record changed back again would not be 'quite so easy.' It was at this point that Mr. Fox told the Committee: 'When I learned that a man had the power to go into the Department of Justice to change the records, I was rather ashamed of being a citizen of this nation.'"[29] The ensuing litigation only created multi-pronged attacks on William Fox's control over Fox and the Loew's shares.

Fox met with independent exhibitors who represented 233 theaters to rally them to support a re-financing plan which he had developed with Bank of America, Lehman Bros., and Dillon, Read & Company, all of which were representing his interests at the time. He assured them that a cash infusion of only $35,000,000 would put the company on a firm footing, not the rumored figure of $91,000,000. The group then issued a statement of support: "The true state of the affairs of William Fox and of these corporations is so different from the stories widely circulated in the press, and the preservation of the Fox interests as an important part of the fabric of this great industry is so vital to the welfare of every exhibitor in the industry, that we deem it our clear duty as exhibitors to forward this information to you."[30]

Fox Films was so determined to boost confidence in its ability to survive the financial debacle a trade article announced that 25 novels and plays had been purchased for production. Under long-term contract were 55 stars, 96 dancers, 23 directors, 23 writers, and 21 composers. William Fox had a proven track record of winning the gambles that he had made up to this point. Unfortunately, his luck would not hold out.[31]

More bad news followed just a few days later when Mrs. Anthony Kuser, wife of Fox's deceased first partner, filed a petition for an equity receivership against Fox and wanted the court to enforce that no corporate money be paid to him. His response was blunt: "Whatever else may happen to me, I propose to maintain my honor. There is not a word of truth in the assertion that I have speculated with the money of Fox Film or Fox Theaters Corporation or with the funds of any company with which I have ever been concerned.... It is also stated that I have received hundreds of thousands of dollars in salary. In point of fact, I relinquished my salary three and a half years ago and never since received a dollar."[32]

Insisting the companies were overwhelmingly solvent, he added that although he was accused of speculating with the company funds in his purchase of Loew's stock, that investment was returning $10 per share and that the savings in merging both companies would amount to $17,000,000 annually. He also pointedly outlined the earnings of the Kuser family since the original investment was made. Between 1918 and 1925, the Kusers received $125,000 annually. Then from 1925 to 1929 they received $332,000 annually. In all, the dividends totaled $2,203,000 on an initial investment value of 200,000 shares. In addition, Fox figured they sold 50,000 shares, based on what they still had, with a selling price between $70 and $100 per share. The total came to between $3,500,000 to $5,000,000, and the balance of approximately 150,000 shares they still held was additional profit. It was clear that the Kuser widow had nothing to complain about.

As a further compromise, Fox proposed the resignation of a majority of the company's Board of Directors and the formation of a new trusteeship to combat demands for a costly receivership. The new board would include William Fox, Jack Leo, Winfield Sheehan, Bernard Baruch, E.R. Tinker, and the president of Bank of America, Edward C. Delafield.[33] Fox felt that this fiscally responsible group would provide stability for the companies. The sticking point quickly became the voting shares for the stock Fox had put up as collateral. He claimed to have the voting rights to 50,101 shares of the Fox Film Corporation and 100,000 shares of Fox Theaters. Halsey, Stuart and John Otterson disagreed and claimed the voting rights for themselves. They knew that as long as they prevented Fox from using those votes, they could control the future disposition of the companies, which by this point was obviously their agenda. This led to a lawsuit and, to defend his interests, Fox hired the prominent 72-year-old attorney Samuel Untermeyer, who took on the case for a then-unheard of $1,000,000.

There was some hope throughout the industry that the dispute would be settled quickly and without disruption to the flow of product to theaters. While this drama was playing out, Winfield Sheehan announced a $20,000,000 slate of releases for 1930-1931, allaying fears on the creative side of the business. Demonstrating the smoothly run

Warner Baxter (in yet another role as a Mexican) woos Mona Maris in *Romance of Rio Grande* (1929) (courtesy Robert S. Birchard).

production machine at the Los Angeles studios, Sheehan added that seven films would begin production in February 1930 including the sequel to the first all-talking outdoor feature, *The Arizona Kid* starring Warner Baxter; *In Love with Love*, later re-titled *Crazy That Way*, with Joan Bennett; *Fox Movietone Follies of 1930*, a star-studded sequel to the Follies film of 1929; and *Born Reckless*, with Edmund Lowe and directed by John Ford.[34] These grandiose plans were greeted enthusiastically by the rest of the industry which was anxiously looking for a stable period after the upheaval caused by the conversion to sound.

Even the publicity department at Fox was sensitive to the turmoil in the company and made note in an ad for a February release of *Such Men Are Dangerous*: "The greatness of the Fox organization has never been better exemplified than by this newest picture."[35]

With an April 1, 1930 deadline of interest payments closing in on William Fox, the Stuart-Otterson team made it clear that the company was hopelessly in debt with over $45,000,000 due in the next six months. In addition, there was over $7,000,000 in judgments from creditors against William Fox. Halsey, Stuart was concerned about the decline in market values of the companies and was unwilling to issue new funding which led to "the immediate cause of the corporation's financial embarrassment."[36]

Desperate to prevent receivership through which he would lose control of the company, William Fox mailed a letter to shareholders on February 20, 1930, which stated,

> Now that you are being called upon to decide between hopeless and inevitable receivership, on the one hand, and acceptance by you on the other hand, of the Plan of financing by which $59,150,000 of cash is to be raised to take the companies out of their financial stress, I feel free to address you in answer to this stream of propaganda by which it is sought to poison your minds against the man who has built the companies from their small beginnings with a cash capital of $1,600 to a present business of $108,128,313 for the past year.... The so-called Plan is, in point of fact, a mere gesture for the purpose of forcing these properties into receivership because these gentlemen find themselves unable to control it.
>
> I am unwilling to desert my stockholders by turning over the companies to these gentlemen at any price.[37]

With litigants fighting out the case in court over receivership issues, the true ownership of William Fox's voting stock, and the validity of the original trusteeship drawn up in December 1929, Fox was able to raise $65,000,000, underwritten by a syndicate of investors. On March 6, 1930, the *Film Daily* reported that stockholders voted for Fox's plan by a margin of 15 to 1: "It was a moral victory and a big personal tribute for Mr. Fox, in addition to the fact that, unless the Stuart-Otterson group have other cards up their sleeve that they can play, it means Mr. Fox will remain in control of his companies."[38] The intimation that Stuart-Otterson may be up to something nefarious was one of the few comments that a trade paper made on the situation. Trade magazines and dailies were dependent upon studio cooperation for information and advertising and the degree of deeply critical reportage was rare indeed. But, anyone knowing all the facts and the players could see there was quite obviously a power-play going on behind the scenes to wrest control of Fox Films and Theaters away from its founder. William Fox was unwilling to give in, harking back to his battles with the Motion Picture Patents Office:

> From 1909 to 1929 I individually carried on a similar fight against a group of men who at that time were trying to create a monopoly in the silent picture industry. If they had succeeded, they would have destroyed the incentive and initiative of those who have since taken part in building up this business. As a result of that fight, the film industry has been free of monopoly and has been conducted on a competitive basis which has made it possible to give the public the best entertainment at the lowest cost. The winning of the present fight again prevents the entrance into the field of a monopoly which the telephone company was trying to establish in talking pictures as a result of certain patents they own. In the last two months I had the choice at one time of accepting $33,333,000 which was offered to me if I would sell my voting shares to make possible this monopoly.[39]

Federal Judge Frank J. Coleman, who had been assigned to the case, made an effort to get both sides to agree in arbitration to settle differences that had clogged the legal machinery. However, injunctions and counter-injunctions were preventing a settlement before the all-important April 15 election of the Board of Directors. It appeared that the Stuart-Otterson group would be able to elect a new board and gain control of the companies.

Judge Coleman's efforts to mediate a quick settlement failed. Coleman was perceived as making judgments too favorable to Fox and was stopped in his tracks. Halsey, Stuart filed affidavits of prejudice and the jurist was restrained from any rulings in the Fox matter. When Fox lawyer Samuel Untermeyer protested to an Appellate Court that there were irregularities in the way the judge was restrained, the Court cited "special conditions," none of which were ever presented.[40]

Coleman resigned on March 23, 1930 and was replaced by Judge John C. Knox, who suddenly had no interest in dealing with the all-important issue of William Fox's voting shares which could have instantly ended the legal battles. The reason he gave for this decision was that Judge Coleman had not turned over the issue to him — mainly because Coleman was restrained from being involved in any of the Fox cases. Knox was willing to deal with the receivership cases. Clearly, he was no friend to the Fox companies and was prejudiced against them. Because political pressure had been applied by powerful vested interests, William Fox was headed for defeat.

William Fox rightly suspected a cabal was organized against him. The final nail was already being hammered in the coffin when Winfield Sheehan, whom Fox had given what turned out to be the opportunity of a lifetime, realized the tide was turning against his boss and sided with Otterson and Halsey, Stuart. It was clear that Sheehan wanted to continue being a production mogul.

To understand how complex and tangled the issues were, the *Film Daily* took to printing a box on its first page titled "Fox Hearings" with daily court assignments. Drawing towards the end of this affair, it may have seemed like the entire New York court system was devoted to William Fox. March 31, 1930 brought this announcement:

> Today, 10 A.M., before Judge Manton, U.S. Circuit Court of Appeals, on order to prohibit Judge Coleman from acting in any Fox cases.
> Today, 10 A.M., before Justice Ford, State Supreme Court, E.C. Krebs vs. Fox, also motion by Fox to withdraw his suit against Stuart and Otterson from the State Supreme Court in view of more comprehensive action brought in Federal Court. These two hearings expected to be put over to Wednesday.
> Today, 4:30 P.M., before Judge Knox in U.S. District Court, on three receivership applications on show cause order to restrain Winfield Sheehan suit against Fox in State Supreme Court.
> Wednesday, 10 A.M., in State Court, Sheehan vs. Fox. Pending: in State Court, Stuart-Otterson vs. Fox; in Federal Court, Fox vs. Stuart-Otterson, over Fox "B" stock. In Brooklyn Supreme Court, Weiss-Otto vs. Fox Theaters.[41]

In a last-ditch effort to save the situation and settle disputes before Fox defaulted on his interest payments, Samuel Untermeyer suggested that Judge Knox preside at an arbitration conference between lawyers. William Fox wanted to expedite minor complaints quickly and not let them tangle larger issues and the issue of whether the trusteeship of December 3, 1929 was valid could do away with many other suits. Knox was uncooperative. William Fox ultimately defaulted on a $12,000,000 loan due April 1. On that same day, yet another suit was filed in state court for holders of $4,668,000 of the Halsey, Stuart-issued notes. This was the end of the road for William Fox's monumental struggle.

Within a week, Fox was able to make a deal with Harley L. Clarke to buy his disputed voting shares. Fox thought that this would allow him to return to the company. Clarke then sided with Halsey, Stuart and J.E. Otterson. Aside from the $15,000,000 his shares brought, William Fox was to continue as Chairman of the Advisory Board for five years and would draw a salary of $500,000 annually. It was a powerless position and everyone knew it would have no impact on the direction of the company Fox had built.

Originally asking for $30,000,000 for his holdings, the situation was no longer the same as when William Fox had the General Film Company in his palm. This time, it was Fox in the hands of Halsey, Stuart, A.T.&T., and Harley Clarke. There was no way he would win this gamble. There was a statement made in a voice-over interview edited into the 2008 documentary *Murnau, Borzage and Fox* which indicated that William Fox had sold his shares to retain some wealth for his family. Perhaps, saying he was doing this for the family was a way of salvaging some victory from defeat, but William Fox was without any other alternatives.

On April 6, 1930, the battle was over and one day later Harley L. Clarke was elected president of Fox Films and Fox Theaters. The only remaining members of the previous Fox board were, not surprisingly, Winfield Sheehan and attorney Saul E. Rogers. James R. Grainger stayed on as vice-president of distribution and Clayton Sheehan, Winfield's brother, remained in charge of foreign sales. Winfield Sheehan crowed, "The war is over and we're back in the amusement business. We feel sure that the stockholders and creditors of the Fox companies will be satisfied that the arrangement now being worked out is the best solution of the existing difficulties. Harley L. Clarke ... has the resources to put the companies in excellent financial position, and there will now be the necessary funds to carry out the theater expansion plans as contemplated."[42]

Clarke admitted, under oath, in a 1933 hearing before a Senate committee, that he had gotten the idea of taking control of the Fox companies when lawsuits were initiated to oust William Fox in early 1930. Fox had rightly claimed that Clarke's moves were premeditated.[43] William Fox even reformulated his thoughts on who had convinced the government to change its position on the Loew's, Inc. merger which further complicated his financial dilemma. Reporting that Fox no longer believed Louis B. Mayer was behind the change, *Time* magazine stated, "Mr. Fox now believes that the record was changed by Harley Lyman Clarke, the man to whom Mr. Fox sold his companies in the spring of 1930 and who is Mr. Fox's special and most bitter hate."[44]

The *Film Daily* echoed industry sentiments when its front-page columnist Jack Alicoate wrote, "The Armistice has been signed. The Fox matter has been washed up, apparently to the satisfaction of all concerned. General Winnie Sheehan calmly suggests that it might not be a bad idea for everybody to get back to work. Sensational publicity such as the Fox matter bred can do nothing but harm. It is now, we hope, off the front page for good. An unfortunate pause in the progress of both a great company and a greater industry."[45]

William Fox would once again be in the trade news in 1931 in relation to several lawsuits. In one, he was required to repay Winfield Sheehan $310,000 for Fox stock that Sheehan had turned over to him. Fox claimed the money was reinvested and showed a loss and then countersued for $190,000. When Fox lost the case, he also dropped his countersuit.[46] There was yet another case which William Fox filed against General Theaters for his share of revenue from Grandeur, of which he owned half. In yet another newsworthy event, Fox held up the construction of the Radio City Music Hall because he owned some of the property for the site. RCA offered $3,000,000 for his holdings, but Fox refused and demanded $10,000,000.[47]

Time magazine reported in July 1932,

> To the cumulative troubles of sick William Fox, hounded onetime film tycoon, two new law suits were added last week. Fox Theatres sued him and six of his friends & kin for $5,000,000 last fortnight. Fox Film Corp, last week sued to recover possibly $10,000,000 from Filman Fox, Jack G. Leo, a former vice president, and partners in M. J. ("Mike") Meehan's brokerage house, which handled many a Fox pool. A sister-in-law, Mrs. Aaron Fox, came forward too, with a $250,000 suit in behalf of her children.
>
> Fox Film seeks to set aside the agreement (made when Filman Fox was ousted in 1930) to pay its founder $500,000 annually until 1935 for his "advisory" services, and to recover what it has already paid him. Demanding an accounting of his alleged secret profits from stock manipulations with an eye to recouping in full, it wants specifically $2,375,000. Mrs. Aaron Fox charged that Brother William "zealously guarded the name Fox as his own trade mark," willingly paid members of the family to refrain from capitalizing on it because, even when he "was obliged to retire," he expected to re-enter the film business and "continue to enjoy, for his sole benefit, the monopoly and prestige of the Fox family name." She said that when her husband incorporated Aaron Fox Film Corp., he "incurred the severe displeasure and disdain" of Brother William, who, with the connivance of a Manhattan alienist, had Brother Aaron whisked away to a sanatorium, the Hartford (Conn.) Retreat. There Brother Aaron still remains, she said, making no effort to get out for fear of further persecution from Brother William. Mrs. Aaron Fox added that Brother William had taken over Brother Aaron's affairs, had forced her children (aged 4 & 6) "to a point where they have no choice between starvation and becoming public charges."[48]

This less-than-flattering portrayal of the dethroned king continued to plague him for the rest of his life. Although still an advisory chairman to the Fox Board of Directors, he never attended any meetings and had no input into the company's operations. His $500,000 annual payment was finally revoked by the Fox board in 1933. Still wealthy and interested in returning to the film industry, there were constant rumors that he would buy controlling shares in one company or another, but nothing ever materialized.

William Fox surfaced again in late 1934, when lawsuits he initiated in 1932 regarding his ownership of Tri-Ergon sound patents threatened the entire industry.

> Last week William Fox, that bald and beady-eyed onetime magnifico of cinema, sprang at his adversaries in eleven directions at once. Alleging "great and irreparable loss, damage and injury," he entered suit in Manhattan for injunction and accounting of profits against Metro-Goldwyn-Mayer Corp., M-G-M Distributing Corp., Columbia Pictures Corp., Consolidated Film Industries Inc., First Division Pictures Inc., Universal Pictures Corp., Monogram Picture Corp., Reliance Picture Corp., Talking Picture Epics Inc., Twentieth Century Pictures Inc., and Ameranglo Corp.
>
> A foundation for these suits had been provided by the U. S. Supreme Court a fortnight ago when it refused to review a lower court ruling and thus, in effect, sustained Mr. Fox's claim that every user of R.C.A. Photophone and Western Electric sound-equipment was infringing on patents owned by his personal holding company. Estimates of the extent to which sanguine Mr. Fox thought he was damaged ranged around $100,000,000. With Mr. Fox out in the open and trying to stage a mighty comeback, spokesmen for the film industry hastened to point out the weaknesses of his position.[49]

Fox Films was contending that William Fox had bought the Tri-Ergon patents abroad with $45,000 of the corporation's money and had no right to them. Finally, it was argued that the "double print" and "sprocket" processes for recording and reproducing sound — the main points of the dispute — were not entirely fundamental and could be circumvented by smart sound engineers. Nevertheless, R.C.A. Photophone and Western Electric's Electrical Research Products were holding conferences behind locked doors and found it necessary to reassure exhibitors that they would be protected according to their contract from having to pay damages to William Fox. Ultimately, the Supreme Court ruled that the Tri-Ergon patents were not valid and the $100,000,000 that William Fox was claiming vanished along with the great amounts he had spent to keep the case in the courts. As of March 6, 1935, J.E. Otterson, president of Electrical Research Products, announced that all Tri-Ergon lawsuits brought by William Fox against every company making or exhibiting sound films were over.[50]

One year later, as a coda to the entire episode,

> Bald, sad-eyed William Fox, onetime film panjandrum, was prevented by a U.S. Supreme Court decision last year from using basic patents that he thought he owned to hoist himself back into the cinema business. Immediately, Fox creditors streamed out in full cry. Harried by many a suit, suave Mr. Fox finally took cover in bankruptcy last May, listing $9,535,261 in claims against assets of $1,600,000. Later he testified that most of the latter had vanished, that even $100 listed as cash in hand had gone. Said he: "I paid it to a lawyer and borrowed another $100."
>
> Of the 43 Fox creditors who sneered at these protestations, there was only one from whom Mr. Fox might conceivably have borrowed another $100. That one, All-Continent Corp., quickly became a target for all the others. All-Continent Corp. was created by Mr. Fox in 1931 as "an irrevocable trust" for his wife and two daughters. Mr. Fox transferred to it securities worth about $6,900,000. Since bankruptcy hearings opened in Atlantic City last June, creditors' lawyers have pooh-poohed All-Continent's present $417,258 claim against Fox, have tried assiduously to show that All-Continent remains his own principal asset.
>
> Last week from their home on Atlantic City's swank Delancey Place the officers of All-Continent went down town to testify. Defiantly Mrs. Eva Fox, All-Continent president, maintained that she knew nothing of All-Continent affairs, had left them all to her lawyers. Ordered to be prepared to answer questions next day, Mrs. Fox took to her bed, sent in a doctor's certificate.
>
> Next up were William Fox's brunette daughters, Mona and Belle. Daughter Mona testified that as All-Continent secretary she had signed minutes without going to meetings. Daughter Belle, vice president, remembered little in a business way except that last year her mother had given her $75,000 which she kept around her room for several months in a black bag. Then she gave it to Fox attorneys.
>
> "I gave them $20,000 at one time, $12,000 another, $15,000 another and so on," said Belle Fox.
>
> "Did they tell you why they wanted the money?"
>
> "No. When I gave it to them, all they would ever say was 'Is that all?'"[51]

William Fox attained some notoriety during his bankruptcy hearing in which he was fighting a government claim of $2,000,000 in taxes. Fox attempted to bribe a judge with a $27,500 "loan." The money, which went to well-known jurist Circuit Court Judge J. Warren Davis, was expected to allow for special consideration in Fox's case. Charges were filed that Fox tried to obstruct justice and defraud the government. He faced a maximum sentence of two years and a $10,000 fine.[52] Fox was sentenced to one year and a day in prison and fined $3,000 on October 21, 1941. He served six months.

William Fox was virtually abandoned by Hollywood. In 1936, he made a rare trip to the west coast and visited the 20th Century–Fox studio. When he toured the lot, no one recognized him.

Fox lived out his remaining years in exile until death came on May 8, 1952, at the age of 73. Sol Wurtzel, who gave a eulogy, was the only member of the Hollywood community who showed up for the sparsely attended funeral. Fox's tax debt was settled after his death for $250,000.

10. Boom to Bust

The 1930s began with a series of blows to the film industry. First of all, stock prices were still dangerously low and although there was some retrenchment, they were not back to the 1929 pre-crash levels that had provided so much working capital to the industry. Production costs, as always, were on the rise. These incrementally higher fixed costs would push the operation of large motion picture enterprises to new heights. Added to Fox Film's overhead were three-year contracts that William Fox insisted on as part of the sale of his shares to Harley Clarke. The contracts covered brothers-in-law Joe Leo at $65,000 annually and Ben Leo at $25,000, Lou Rosenbluth at $40,000, Jack Loeb at $35,000, Alec Kempner at $40,000, Fox's cousin Charles S. Levine, secretary of Fox-Case Corporation, at $26,000, William Freedman at $10,000, William Coneyvear at $25,000, and Alan Friedman at $10,000.[1] Sol Wurtzel was to receive the richest benefit with a guaranteed bonus of $500,000, negotiated by his ex-boss. These were key administrative people in Fox's mind and he wanted them to remain with the company to make his planned return easier. Like Napoleon in exile, William Fox had every intention of regaining control of his empire.

At a time when Fox Films was spending up to $1,000,000 on a feature, it was imperative that audience levels continued to grow. With the proliferation of all-talking pictures and an increase in the number of wired theaters, record-level audiences were drawn to sound pictures in 1929. However, admissions to theaters dropped 25 percent by mid–1930 as the initial novelty of sound began to wear off. Lower movie attendance resulted in the closure of some 500 theaters across the country. This was also a function of a weeding-out process of older houses still running silent films.

Fox Theaters temporarily closed houses that were no longer operating at a profit. Others were nursed back to health by division executives who acted as both managers and publicity men assigned to these "sick" houses. "As the poor houses show results with the new treatment to be given by 'doctors,' the publicity men will be transferred to the next theater in their district which needs a bracing at the box-office." To boost attendance, some Fox theaters in Detroit lowered admission prices to a popular price scale of 25 cents during the day and 50 cents at night. Children were admitted at 15 cents. There was already considerable talk about the nationwide depression, especially in Detroit where auto production had dropped dramatically.[2] The Loew's Theater in Pittsburgh cut its scale from 35 to 50 cents to 25 to 35 cents. Other cities cut admission by half and some chains introduced five-cent matinees, an outrageously low figure for the value of entertainment.

The slump resulted in a plan to convert some of the Fox theaters into "classy" miniature golf courses. The first was located in Kew Gardens, Long Island. Others were planned in Brooklyn, Bronx, and one in New Jersey. The Kew Gardens course was not only thoroughly landscaped but even had an artificial sky. The conversion of other closed houses would depend on the success of these initial ventures.[3] As theaters closed, more conversions were considered by all the circuits. In this period, there were already 70,000 miniature golf courses in the United States.

A trade editorial expressed disdain for this plan: "Miniature golf is on the way to stampeding the theater business. It already seems to have made even some of the major circuits forget that they are in the film business and not in the sporting field. This midget golf thing is just an epidemic. One of those fads like Mah Jong."[4]

The mania certainly faded quickly and original plans for turning several theaters into miniature golf courses were abandoned by Fox Theaters after its first deluxe course in Kew Gardens grossed $620 in its first week, with approximately 1,550 people. The overhead at the location was figured at about $250 weekly, added to the installation cost of $13,000, which did not include the weekly cost of maintaining the building.[5]

An uptick in theater attendance in the fall of 1930 brought a bounce back to the movie business. Of course, with attendance picking up, there were no further conversions. The Fox Corporation reopened 50 of its theaters that had been shuttered. As of September 1930, 5,000 miniature golf courses across the country had closed.

With less than one half of the theaters in the country wired for sound, the upside for producers was that film inventories could be amortized more quickly now because of a shortened "demand period" for talking pictures. A popular silent film would run its cycle of playdates through a maximum of two years, but until enough theaters were wired, talkies received fewer bookings. Major distributors would only need to squeeze a maximum of 200 runs from a sound print, compared to about 300 runs on a silent print. The less wear and tear on a print meant that later playoffs would have a better presentation for their audiences. An average of 175 prints was being made for the worldwide run of each release.[6]

Since the arrival of the talkies, distributors had jettisoned a program of flat-rate rentals in favor of "percentage bookings." The distributor would set a percentage of total box-office revenues as the booking fee, leaving the theater no choice but to pay that rate or lose the film to another circuit. A typical level of between 15 percent–20 percent of the gross brought more revenue to distributors, and then to producers, than the flat rental formula. On an average percentage deal of 17 percent, a film grossed that $50,000 in a week would yield $8,500 to the distributor rather than a flat fee of $5,000 for the same size theater. Fox Films tried to get an additional 25 percent of profits over the weekly house expenses but ran into resistance from exhibitors who felt they were already paying a high enough fee. By late 1930, the number of percentage bookings had risen by 60 percent and were becoming the rule rather than the exception. This practice, begun in roadshow engagements, was now permeating general exhibition. When a film was especially desirable, the terms could be raised enough to leave little profit in an exhibitor's pocket. Charlie Chaplin features, for example, required a 50 percent booking fee. Theater owners often had little choice in the matter.

Another footnote to the changes in movies after the adoption of sound was that, contrary to Richard A. Rowland's declaration that audiences and exhibitors wanted short features, theater owners in 1930 were deploring the short running times of sound films. Producers responded by increasing lengths of many films to around 90 minutes. Since most audiences were now paying exclusively for filmed entertainment and not live opening acts, the films had to be of substantial length to give the paying crowds their money's worth. Vaudeville acts were the victims in this shift, with bookings for working performers 50 percent lower in 1930 than the year before at smaller salaries as well.[7]

As the depression worsened, audience attendance at theaters continued to sag and exhibitors could not afford to pay the prices demanded by distributors for their films. The result was an industry-wide call, issued by Paramount production head B.P. Schulberg in mid–1931, to cut negative costs by 20 percent to 40 percent to make up for the lower revenues.

Although this was a tumultuous period of transition, after the departure of William Fox from the company he created, a sense of calm descended over the studio. For the moment, theater acquisitions ceased and William Fox's presence was quickly eradicated. The introductory credit, "William Fox Presents," was mostly removed from films by mid–1930, and one year later the decision was made to remove Fox's name from Movietone News. Talk of a merger with M.G.M. faded, and Harley L. Clarke, new to the presidency, set about establishing his agenda for the future.

Clarke promised, "During the next few months, with all of the current indebtedness of these companies out of the way, management can devote its entire time to the working out of better operating conditions and carrying out a well-laid expansion program. Large economies are being instituted rapidly in many departments and should save $1,500,000 a year.... The present management believes that the company will have made sufficient strides during the year 1930 to enable it to permanently and economically finance its present one-year obligations, thereby saving millions of dollars as compared with any other plan which has heretofore been put forth."[8]

With these assurances, Clarke was able to arrange a financing plan which belatedly paid for the great theater expansion of 1929. It provided, essentially, that Fox Film would sell to Clarke's General Theatres Equipment, Inc. 1,600,000 shares of new Class A at $30 a share, and would also issue one-year 6 percent notes for $55,000,000. These two transactions would leave the Fox companies well supplied with $103,000,000 of capital. The bankers (who included both the William Fox and the anti–William Fox factions in the recent fight for control) were to receive 300,000 shares of three-year warrants of Film A at $35 a share — a banking profit notably smaller than the commissions formerly proposed by either Halsey, Stuart or the Bancamerica-Blair, Dillon, Read & Co., and Lehman

Harley L. Clarke, president of the Fox Film Corporation, in 1930.

Bros, syndicate. The reality was that the debt was shifted from one entity to another, but it did not go away.

With new financing, came new directors. On the Fox Films Board, William Fox himself was a holdover, as were anti–Fox directors Winfield Sheehan and Saul E. Rogers, general counsel. Gone were William Fox's brother Aaron, his cousin Charles Levine, and his brother-in-law Jack Leo. New directors included: Harley Clarke, Matthew C. Brush of American International, Charles B. Stuart, brother of Harry Stuart of Halsey, Stuart & Company. John Edward Otterson, of American Telephone & Telegraph, was not included. With a new financial plan and a new management, it remained only for Harley Clarke to make another of his announcements about the company getting down to business again and for Winfield Sheehan to see that Fox Films did exactly that.[9]

Part of President Clarke's proposed economizing was to consolidate the work of both studios in Movietone City as of January 1, 1931. This would eliminate double overhead and do away with a great amount of duplication. The project would amount to an investment of $5,500,000 and would be repaid in savings within two years. The Sunset-Western lot would be completely abandoned by June except for the film printing plant and the color laboratory. The 16-acre site was then planned for the development of a modern business center with a "limit height modern hotel, a de luxe theater to be operated by West Coast Theaters, and other buildings." One building would become the new home of Fox West Coast Theaters' executive offices. This was expected to return a substantial commercial income to the company: "All projection and photographic equipment for Movietone City will be supplied by General Theaters Equipment, Inc. and all sound units by Western Electric." General Theaters, of course, was owned by Harley Clarke.

A studio planning committee headed by Sol M. Wurtzel, superintendent of production, with George L. Bagnall, comptroller, as vice-president, is consulting with the architects and builders, working out plans for development of Movietone City to a maximum of efficiency.

With the unification of the studios at Movietone City, an industrial center running from Santa Monica Blvd. to Pico Blvd. along the public golf course, will be constructed. It will house electrical property, scenery, wardrobe, make-up, maintenance, carpenter, machine, sound, and all other departments. They will be so placed that the latest development "time and motion study" will find expression in greater studio efficiency.[10]

Fox West Coast Theaters was immediately involved in cost-cutting by eliminating all unnecessary operation expenses. All house managers were ordered to cut their advertising by at least 10 percent. Fox Theaters, as well, was to eliminate all billboard advertising.[11] While Fox Films had previously placed weekly full-page, double- and triple-page ads for upcoming films in the trades, most advertising was severely curtailed after this announcement.

Another result of economizing was to consolidate the Fox and Loew's Theaters film buying departments which was set to take place by June 1, 1931. However, when the time approached for the plan to be put into effect, Loew's theater executive Charles C. Moskowitz commented that the idea "even hasn't been thought of."[12] M.G.M. wanted to avoid any co-mingling of company activities until the status of the Loew's stock was settled by the government.

Fox Theaters continued to add locations with an aggregate 18,300 seats in seven new houses, mainly in New York and New Jersey. The expansion and scale of the theaters were considerably less ambitious than William Fox's massive 5,000-seat palaces. Most of the new additions were between 2,500 and 3,000 seats, due to a concern about over-building in many cities.[13] Harley Clarke also engineered a deal giving Fox Theaters a substantial interest in the more than 100-house Hoyt chain of theaters in Australia. Many of these theaters were in need of modernization and wiring for sound. For Clarke and his theater-supply company, each of these deals meant more clients. As well, Clarke's co-conspirators against William Fox, Western Electric, picked up more theater installations and royalties for its sound systems. Acquisitions were now geared towards equipment sales rather than a need for exhibitor representation.

Buoying the new administration, Fox had a successful slate of attractions in 1929, profits of which showed up after William Fox's departure. The top industry spot of the year was taken by *Sunny Side Up*, which became Fox Films' most profitable movie up to that time with $1,536,000. The combination of dialogue, music, and stars Janet Gaynor and Charles Farrell added up to record earnings. The next highest-earning Fox film was *The Cock Eyed World*, a sequel to *What Price Glory* (1926), continuing the adventures of Quirt and Flagg, as portrayed by Victor McLaglen and Edmund Lowe. Racking up huge grosses, the film ended up with a profit of $1,083,000. The popularity of musicals and an all-star cast helped bring *Fox Movietone Follies* to a rich surplus of $381,000. Yet, the romanticized plantation musical, *Hearts in Dixie*, only barely made a profit. No big surprise was the hit status of journalist and prominent American humorist Will Rogers in his first talking picture, *They Had to See Paris*, with a profit of $245,000, 30 percent of which came from foreign markets. John Ford's populist drama *Strong Boy* told of the rise of a baggage handler to a higher station and his romance with a pretty girlfriend. It was profitable in the range of $100,000. After the box-office failure of *Sunrise* (compared to its cost), F.W. Murnau was again given the year's highest budget for *4 Devils*. The elaborate circus picture cost $1,023,000 and ended up with a $212,000 loss. *Lucky Star* was another big disappointment, even though it reunited the box-office powerhouse trio of Janet Gaynor, Charles Farrell and director Frank Borzage. Lightning did not strike again for this tear-jerker romance and there was no lucky star to escape a $76,000 loss.

Borzage fared even worse with the moody, German-influenced Charles Farrell drama, *The River*, which was expected to be a hit but went $250,000 into the red. However, the biggest loss was endured by the critically trounced Allan Dwan production of *Frozen Justice* which went a substantial $265,000 in the hole. The year's releases, with an average negative cost of $304,570, totaled $16,142,216 but still returned rentals of $30,803,974.

Assets of the Fox Film Corporation took a leap of 54 percent to $192,524,313, with an earned surplus of $13,627,806, also up by over 17 percent. However, this increase was misleading because some of the profit included 48 percent of the earnings in Loew's, Inc. With the M.G.M. merger uncertain, Fox was still benefiting from that company's record dividends. Harley Clarke predicted a further gain in film rentals for the last six months of the year based on contracts already in hand.

The *Film Daily* editor, Jack Alicoate wrote a column entitled "Concerning Mr. Clarke," in

A publicity photograph for ***The River*** (1929), with (from left) author of ***The River,*** Tristram Tupper, Frank Borzage, Mary Duncan and Charles Farrell (courtesy Robert S. Birchard).

which he presented Harley L. "to be exact. A regular he-man that can look one in the eye and say yes or no and mean it. New generalissimo on the Fox forces is still this side of fifty and one of the youngest really big men in the country. Not unfamiliar with pictures or the show business and with no silly illusions. Graduate of Michigan, one of the biggest utility magnates in the country, and rated well up in the millions. That's Mr. Clarke, formerly of Chicago and now of Fox Films, Inc. It is our guess that he does not seek publicity and does a minimum of talking, but, you're going to hear plenty regarding this young man and his picture activities from now on."[14]

For someone who supposedly did not seek publicity, advertisements for Fox Films' May 1930 release of *The Arizona Kid*, a sequel to the Warner Baxter hit *In Old Arizona* (1929), told a different story. It was the first usage of a new company logo carrying "Harley L. Clarke President" inset in the "O" of FOX. Clarke's new logo would also appear in other Fox advertising.

Demonstrating that all the studio machinery was functioning smoothly, Sol Wurtzel announced that 19 films were in production and eight were being edited. A total of 11 more films were ready to shoot. Wurtzel promised to have more than half the year's releases completed by mid year.[15]

With Fox corporations $100,000,000 in debt, its shares hovering below half of their pre-stock market crash level and dropping, and industry concerns surrounding its future, Harley Clarke had to re-establish confidence in the company. The first in a series of steps to solidify the organization was to sign Sol Wurtzel to a new five-year contract. Having been with the company for 14 years, Wurtzel represented managerial continuity along with Winfield Sheehan. Sheehan also signed a new contract with Fox as head of production and general manager. Previously, when press releases referred to production announcements, only Sheehan was mentioned. Now, both he and Wurtzel were described as chief producing executives. William B. Goetz, following production jobs at M.G.M. and Paramount, was hired as executive assistant to Sol Wurtzel.[16] Shortly after, Goetz married Louis B. Mayer's daughter Edith, which gave him greater upward mobility. In 1933, Goetz left Fox Films and joined Darryl F. Zanuck and Joseph M. Schenck in founding 20th Century Pictures, the start-up company that would eventually merge with Fox Films. John Considine, Jr., the general manager of United Artists was also hired to work with Wurtzel.

It was no longer possible for Winfield Sheehan and Sol Wurtzel to exercise as much hands-on control of each production. To spread responsibility further with the complexities of talking pictures, a system of associate producers was put into place by Sheehan. Some of the experienced people who were trusted with day-to-day preparations were Ralph Block, a former editor-in-chief at Paramount and an associate producer with Pathé; George Middleton, an author of books and plays; James Kevin McGuinness, who had been with Fox since 1928, writing stories and title cards; Al Rockett, former production manager with Universal and First National; Edward W. Butcher, a unit manager at Fox since 1925; Harold Lipsitz, story and script editor at Fox, then supervisor of westerns; and Ned Marin, an executive with Universal and First National. The responsibility of casting was given to Jack Gardner.[17] James McGuinness jumped ship within six months and signed a contract with M.G.M. Marin was not far behind and signed with Paramount.

Meanwhile, there were changes instituted by Clarke that weeded out any former Fox loyalists in the theater division. Oscar S. Oldknow, vice-president of National Theater Supplies, which was controlled by Harley Clarke, was made executive vice-president of all 600 Fox Theaters except the West Coast circuit. In a position once held by Joe Leo, William Fox's brother-in-law, Oldknow now oversaw the Fox-Poli circuit in New England, Fox Midwesco in Wisconsin and Illinois, Fox Metropolitan Playhouses in New York and New Jersey, and deluxe houses in Brooklyn, Philadelphia, Washington, St. Louis and Detroit. Joe Leo's contract would be bought out, but not settled for another year.

Harley Clarke wanted more eastern supervision of the Fox West Coast Theater chain, which was run fairly autonomously by Harold B. Franklin under the William Fox administration. The veteran exhibitor, however, was suddenly offered a contract buy-out to resign from West Coast, which he did with the statement, "The association that I enjoyed with Harley L. Clarke during the past six months has been most pleasant. While my contract as president of Fox West Coast Theaters does not expire until February 1932, Clarke and I have worked out a satisfactory settlement."[18] One day later, Oscar Oldknow was assigned to oversee the West Coast chain, bringing the entire theater operation under Harley Clarke's control.

Within a month after this appointment, Fox Theaters suddenly announced a plan to quicken the return to prosperity by spending approximately $20,000,000 on theater improvements. Low labor and material costs and an optimistic campaign to boost theater attendance influenced the decision to rush into the work. Realistically, there was no immediate need for this program and were it not for Harley Clarke running the show, it probably would not have been started. In retrospect, with the economy on a rocky footing, this expenditure was risky, if not foolhardy. There was also another non-essential but expensive program underway to build new exchange centers in more than a dozen cities. Of course, they would be equipped with the latest projection rooms supplied by Clarke's National Theater Supplies.

In a turnabout from the previous administration's desire to control New York's theaters, Clarke decided to sell 10 percent of the 100 houses, acquired in William Fox's last invasion of that state, back to their original operators. None were rushing to buy back their houses at the prices Clarke wanted.[19]

One of the more blatant firings of the Clarke-Oldknow administration was that of S.L. Rothafel. The managing director of the Roxy, and the genius behind its stage shows, had his contract terminated as of March 1931. Marco Wolf of Fanchon and Marco, also stagers of live entertainment, was named to succeed "Roxy."[20] Shortly after, Harley Clarke was elected President of Roxy Theaters.

Winfield Sheehan also brought his friends on board with the appointment of Joseph Johnson as Fox executive secretary. Johnson, a former commissioner of Public Works in New York and Mayor Jimmy Walker's close advisor for more than 20 years, had started his career as a newspaperman, and both he and Sheehan were in the New York Fire Department from 1910 to 1911.[21] Johnson then hired Frank Prendergast, yet another former co-worker from the Public Works Department as Fox director of publicity.[22] Neither of these men had any previous experience with motion pictures.

As business picked up in the fall of 1930, opti-

J. Harold Murray (left) as *Cameo Kirby* (1930), with Douglas Gilmore and Myrna Loy (courtesy Robert S. Birchard).

Sally Eilers and James Dunn, Fox's youthful team of the early 1930s (courtesy Mike Hawks).

mism returned and Fox appeared to be on a steady winning streak with the release of *Common Clay* starring Constance Bennett and Lew Ayres. As Fox's first entry to its "Greater Talkie Season," it would "spread cheer in other circuit and independent houses. This drawing card is a sample of the aces that are to come, says Winfield Sheehan."[23] *Common Clay* produced a near-record gross of $447,884 in its four weeks at the Roxy in New York City.

With a 40 percent increase in business at Fox Theaters compared to the previous year, there was every reason for Winfield Sheehan to crow. "More than ever before good talkers will enjoy extended run engagements. Where the silent picture played a week, the talking picture can and does play three or four weeks, provided it is a good talking picture. Instead of half a week, audible films will play a full week. Naturally this means new devotees of talking pictures and weekly patrons recruited from those who formerly were only occasional customers."[24]

Buoyed by this rosy outlook, Sheehan and Wurtzel announced a slate of 48 films for the 1930-1931 movie season with a total production cost of $25,000,000 and an average $520,833 budget. They signed a long list of stage performers who would have the acting experience to handle dialogue, including John McCormack, J. Harold Murray, Beatrice Lillie, William Collier, Sr., Kenneth MacKenna, Jillian Sand, Charles Winninger, Constance Bennett, Beryl Mercer, Raymond Hackett, Marjorie White, Paul Muni, Humphrey Bogart, Claire Luce, Ted Healy and his Stooges, Lee Tracy, Mae Clarke, El Brendel, and H.B. Warner. Two new film stars who would serve the company well for a few years were James Dunn, first appearing in *Bad Girl* (1931) and his female co-star in the same film, Sally Eilers. They became fairly popular and appeared in some of Fox's biggest hits of the early 1930s. Of the other stars, only Bennett, Muni, Tracy, Bogart, and Healy's Stooges (later known as The Three Stooges) had any long-lasting impact in motion pictures and not due to pictures made during their Fox period.

Directors with stage experience were David Butler, Guthrie McClintic, Hamilton MacFadden, William K. Howard, and Seymour Felix.

The talking pictures Fox Films made were definitely less distinguished when compared with the strides made artistically and commercially between 1926 and 1928. When it came to handing out the Academy of Motion Picture Arts Awards of Merit for 1929-1930, *In Old Arizona* received nominations for Best Picture, Director, Actor and Cinematography. Only Warner Baxter won as Best Actor. *In Old Arizona*, boosted by its novelty as the first Fox all-talkie, returned the company's third-highest profit of the year at $566,000 on a cost of $314,000. This was a reasonable figure considering that the technique for shooting the film was experimental and that the first footage shot had to be redone. During the early stages of production, director Raoul Walsh, who was also starring as the Cisco Kid, suffered injuries in a car accident, losing an eye, and had to be replaced. Filming began a second time with Warner Baxter in the title role and Irving Cummings behind the camera.

Talking pictures presented new complexities which needed to be addressed. Script writing was not just outlining the action in scenes and then adding title cards afterwards to fill in any story holes. Now, dialogue needed to be honed to perfection before filming. This could entail several different writers preparing a script before it was ready to shoot. Too much dialogue could be seen as padding a thin story and while silent films occasionally stretched a running time with visual action, lengthy talking scenes were downright boring.

Dialogue coaches were often employed to prepare performers for their roles, especially when foreign accents, either those of the fictional characters or the actors themselves, were involved. Musicals were staffed with scores of dancers who needed to be rehearsed and composers who had to prepare songs well in advance of production. There was a great deal more preparation and it required more people to navigate each aspect of production. At the outset of the talking film period, costs went up and producers had to absorb the expenses or become more efficient. Efficiency eventually ruled the day, but it took Fox a while to get to that milestone.

An unusually thick May 27, 1930 issue of the *Film Daily*, which swelled to 80 pages, headlined the story, "Fox Practically Takes Over the Stage." Paying for a lavish 65-page full-color insert with ads for its upcoming releases, Fox received from the *Film Daily*, in return, a virtual testimonial to the studio. This kind of publicity was a necessary move to calm investor and industry fears.

As usual, a percentage of planned productions highlighted in the ads did not come to the screen. In the 1930-1931 announcements, in particular, there was a higher level of project attrition than ever before. Many titles were rushed onto the schedule without enough time for adequate planning because of all the uncertainty during the William Fox stock battles. Of the ads for 47 proposed releases, 17 were never made, a higher-than-average percentage. This exposed an embarrassing inefficiency in production planning. For each announcement, there had to at least be a script or a purchase of story material and some degree of pre-production. To waste time on one-third of the projects that would never be produced created a drain on creative energy and production money. There was also the likelihood that some of the ads were just page fillers, rather than real planned productions.

The reasons for cancellations, or "substitutions" as they were called in exhibition contracts, were not announced in the trades. This was standard practice since studios preferred to let unrealized projects simply disappear. Reasons for dropping a production were legion. A script might not work out, casting conflicts might postpone a film indefinitely, a genre might fall out of favor, or a substituted film might have a better chance at success.

Technically, an exhibitor did not have to play a substitution so studios tried to replace elements that were on a par with what had been promised in the block of releases. Although it did not affect popular films, it could make a big difference in the playoff of lower-budget films without name stars. Fox films usually played in between 3,000 and 10,000 situations. The most popular would be contracted for all 10,000 and play in a fairly high percentage of them. The middle-range films could be contracted in 7,000 theaters and lose as many as 500 of them through cancellations. Since theaters needed a steady flow of product, once they signed a contract and had to pay for a certain number of films, they were less likely to cancel a booking. A theater might decide a film was too spicy for its audience, pay for the film anyway and take the loss to preserve good will within the community.

The musical was a good example of a genre falling out of favor and needing substitution. Fox was leading the other studios with 14 announced musicals when a glut of releases caused popularity for the genre to wane. "If you want our opinion, and nobody up to this minute has asked for it," expressed a *Film Daily* editorial, "on why the abundant crop of Spring filmusicals took almost a collective brody and thereby practically to a filmcan committed box-office hari-kari, we would softly rebut that perhaps it was their own darn fault and to be laid at the door of those who did not pay good money to give them the see and hear. A great majority of these screen musicals that came in like a lion and went out like a lamb were beautiful but Oh! so dumb. We believe the musical talkie still has a chance regardless of the fact that it is now as welcome as measles in most directions."[25]

Among the films planned but not made in the 1930-1931 season was a lavish follow-up to two previous *Fox Movietone Follies* (1929 and 1930), *The New Fox Movietone Follies*. However, after the second installment showed a substantial loss, it signaled the demise of the musical. Its substitution was *Body and Soul* (1931) to which Pete Harrison of *Harrison's Reports*, a trade newsletter designed to protect exhibitors, advised "since the finished product is not such a [musical] picture it is a theme substitution and you are not obliged to accept it. But because no star was promised in the contract and the finished product is delivered with Charles Farrell you will get more than you bargained for if you accept it."[26]

J. Harold Murray's career at Fox also crashed with the musical. Instead of playing to his strengths as a singer, Murray was cast in a few dramas with limited songs. It was a misuse of his talent and two films he was scheduled to star in were canceled, including *Woman Control*, which

Charles Farrell, one of Fox's top stars, romances Madge Evans in *Heartbreak* (1931) (courtesy Mike Hawks).

was to be directed by acclaimed stage director Guthrie McClintic and *Her Kind of Man*. Murray's contract was then terminated.

With stage star Humphrey Bogart under contract at $750 weekly, Fox scheduled him to appear in five films for 1930-1931. *Blondie*, which had him teamed with Lois Moran, was canceled. He was scheduled for but never appeared in *The Spider* (1931), although the film was made with Edmund Lowe and El Brendel. Two more intriguing productions would have been *Sez You, Sez Me*, which would have had Bogart co-starring with Victor McLaglen, and *Barcelona* which was to have co-starred Janet Gaynor and been directed by John Ford. Ford finally directed Bogart in *Up the River* (1930) but by the time of its release, the actor had moved on to Warner Bros. where his career would become legendary.

One release which would have been enticing to exhibitors was *Oh, for a Man* (1930), scheduled to star the popular screen team of Janet Gaynor and Charles Farrell under director David Butler. The romantic pair was replaced with Jeanette MacDonald and Reginald Denny and the director became Hamilton MacFadden. *Oh, for a Man* was not a success. MacDonald left Fox after only three films and became a big star at Paramount and M.G.M. where her voice became an asset in a series of operettas.

Another interesting cast was set for the production of *The Spy* including Milton Sills, Paul Muni, and Marguerite Churchill. A change of cast resulted with the unexpected death of the athletic Sills from a heart attack at the age of 48. When the film was released in 1931, director Berthold Viertel had a less intriguing cast consisting of Kay Johnson, Neil Hamilton and John Halliday.

In some cases, the substitution for exhibitors was better than the film that was expected. For example, for *The Man Who Came Back* (1931), "Holders of a Fox contract are getting more than they bargained for in this picture, for no star was promised in the contract, and Charles Farrell and Janet Gaynor appear in the finished product." This was considered to make up for the changes in *Oh, for a Man*.[27]

One technical development that Fox Films promised for the 1930-1931 season, but never delivered, was color. The New Fox Nature Color process was developed with Eastman Kodak and it was designed to rival the more established Technicolor. A camera was invented by John F. Coneybear, head of the Fox research laboratory, described the process:

> Among the points of superiority which we may fairly put forth for this process, one is the ability to produce uniform and lifelike tints, which audiences will instantly recognize as those of nature herself. Another is that we aim to produce cameras in quantities, both 35 and 70 millimeter, and train a corps of cameramen for color work, so that either color sequences or entire color productions can be made on demand, without being in any way dependent on outside talent.
> It makes use of two lenses instead of one, and makes two frames simultaneously. The two lenses are colored — one red and one green. The red and green images which appear in the two frames, respectively, are — in the final operation — printed on opposite sides of the color position."

The process also has a sound track which is superior to the black and white product with an absence of "ground noise."[28]

To make the most of the new process, Fox Films hired former Ziegfeld Follies set designer

Spencer Tracy, William Collier, Sr., Humphrey Bogart and Warren Hymer in a scene from *Up the River* (1930), directed by John Ford (courtesy Mike Hawks).

Joseph Urban to lend his particular skill to four lavish color productions which included *A Connecticut Yankee in King Arthur's Court* starring Will Rogers, *The Man Who Came Back*, and *Luxury* to be directed by Alexander Korda. *A Connecticut Yankee*, *The Man Who Came Back* and *Luxury* (released as *Once a Sinner*) were produced in standard black and white and the fourth unannounced project was never made. Joseph Urban ended up using his skills in color design for black and white films.

Part of the year's schedule was devoted to foreign versions of standard releases. Fox announced a department headed by John Stone "for the production of talkers in Spanish, with plans for extending the activities later to the making of pictures in French, German, Italian, and the Scandinavian languages." A Spanish version of *One Mad Kiss* had been prepared starring José Mojica, Mona Maris, Antonio Moreno and Tom Patricola with James Tinling directing. Another production was planned with Mojica, *The Love Gambler*, and *The Last of the Duanes* would star George Lewis and Luana Alcañiz. There would also be original two-reel dramatic and comedy subjects.[29]

Just one month later, Winfield Sheehan announced that *Common Clay* and *Last of the Duanes* would be the first films to be made in French and Italian under John Stone's foreign production unit. A group of Italian actors, recruited in Italy and New York, were expected in Los Angeles. Making use of staff already under contract, west coast story department head Al Lewis and Joe Pincus were assigned to making tests of Spanish, Italian and French players in New York. Those performers who made the cut would be sent to Los Angeles to join the international contingent. Although those versions never materialized, the Spanish version of *Common Clay*, *Del mismo barro*, starring Mona Maris, Juan Torena and Luana Alcañiz, became the first release of the foreign language division in August 1930. The following

Joel McCrea and Dorothy Mackaill in *Once a Sinner* (1931) (courtesy Mike Hawks).

year, the Spanish division produced ten foreign versions of English language features and one original title, *Mamá*, starring Catalina Bárcena, who appeared in a series of films over the next few years.

A portion of Movietone City was sectioned off for its foreign players, directors and writers and was named "Latin Quarters." The predominance of Spanish-language features was a result of an estimated $300,000 to $400,000 potential gross per film in that sector of the world audience. The very active Spanish unit also completed three short subjects.[30]

Fox continued a silent division under the direction of John Stone, assisted by R.W. Bischoff, James Tinling, and Louis Loeffler, which provided films for the foreign market. Titles were substituted for dialogue and scenes were remade, when necessary, to help the clarity of the story.[31] John Stone also traveled abroad with the prospect of setting up a unit for foreign production but found that there were not enough wired theaters in those countries to support the cost, according to Fox foreign manager Clayton Sheehan.[32]

By December 1931, the making of foreign language versions, other than Spanish, had been concluded, and a large amount of the staff was dropped. With new dubbing techniques available, there was little need for producing separate German, French or Italian versions.

Spanish films, with a potentially lucrative market, continued to be made by John Stone. Between 1932 and 1935, there would be seven more Spanish-language versions of general releases (some reaching back to the silent period for screenplays) and 19 originals, keeping that division quite active.

Following the corporate turmoil during the first half of 1930, production resumed with the requisite optimism. "Underground reports from the Coast indicate that Mr. Sheehan is again in his best production stride. Steering the good ship 'Fox' through the treacherous waters of the past year and bringing it safely to port was a couple of man-sized jobs. Again, our admiration to Clarke, Sheehan, Grainger & Co., for a great job manfully accomplished."[33]

In a magnanimous nod to the value of story material, Winfield Sheehan assigned $2,000,000 annually for the upcoming four years to acquire plays, novels and screenplays of a quality that would help assure hit movies. Al Lewis, once again focused on the Fox story department, was set to leave for New York on a quest for literary acquisitions. Lewis soon found that purchasing Broadway plays was not very easy with a decline in the number of new stage hits. The economic depression had reduced audiences and Hollywood had lured the better playwrights away from the New York stage. With a drastic decrease in the number of new plays opening on Broadway, this source of material dropped to five percent of all films produced. However, Lewis felt it was the best thing that could happen to Hollywood. Producers would be forced to "call upon their own resources, with a much better product as the result.... Hollywood, Lewis says, is groping about for a new means of expression. New writers must be developed, trained especially in talking picture technique." Fox had only 11 scenarists under contract, down from 21 the year before, and Lewis felt there would be more picture to picture contracts rather than a stable of writers.[34]

In the area of novels, one of the problems preventing some 200 bestsellers from reaching the screen was an avoidance of stories objectionable to censorship groups across the county. The censorship branch of the Hays Office, without any mandate other than industry compliance, had been trying to keep some semblance of propriety in the movies. The subject matter of many books in the late 1920s and early 1930s would prove to be very controversial as films. Illegitimacy, divorce, marital affairs, rape, murder and suicide were all publicly discouraged as plot elements, yet producers could not resist the box-office allure of such stories. The overindulgence of such plot elements would eventually result in a nationwide call for censorship.

When dialogue entered the movies, it became a ripe target for censors. Screenwriters skated over the boundaries imposed by the censors and put in as many suggestive lines and double entendres as allowable. Many early talkies were defined by salacious melodramas and suggestive sex comedies. Society women lounged around in skin-hugging, low-cut, silky gowns. Gigolos plied the upper classes for prey. Gangsters ran amok in the big cities, killing anyone who stood in their way. These popular themes would continue for another year until the jaws of censorship would snap shut around them.

Winfield Sheehan, at age 47 and conservative in his tastes, was no longer in step with contemporary filmmaking trends. There was a roughness and raciness in stories portrayed by Warners' pictures. Fox had no stars comparable to Edward G. Robinson, Bette Davis, James Cagney, or Joan Blondell. Columbia starred Barbara Stanwyck in tough dramas like *Ladies of Leisure* (1930) and *Ten Cents a Dance* (1931). Even Universal Pictures hit upon a series of successful horror films including *Dracula* (1931) and *Frankenstein* (1931) which raised the ire of local censors.

M.G.M. built its films around an array of popular stars like Greta Garbo, Robert Montgomery, Norma Shearer, Marion Davies, Wallace Beery, Marie Dressler and Joan Crawford. Despite the classy sheen to its productions, Metro made plenty of adult melodramas, including *Anna Christie* (1930) and *The Divorcée* (1930) and tough action films like *The Big House* (1930). Paramount made sexually suggestive films like *Morocco* (1930) starring a sensual Marlene Dietrich; a remake of *The Cheat* (1931) in which Tallulah Bankhead sells herself to a rich Oriental man; and the risqué romantic comedies of Ernst Lubitsch, including *One Hour with You* (1932).

Instead of following this new trend, Winfield Sheehan continued to make the kinds of movies he and Sol Wurtzel had made for years. There were more rough and tumble Victor McLaglen films, several with Edmund Lowe. Janet Gaynor and Charles Farrell were still teamed together or with other partners. There was an everyman character that James Dunn would fill in several Fox films of the early 1930s, but there was always a sweetness to his roles, never a dark cynicism. Contemporary audiences wanted fresh talents who reflected the times. Cynicism and gloom were in vogue. Although Fox's grosses from its old-style filmmaking were somewhat stable, the year's total returns were lower.

Following up on William Fox's efforts to introduce a new screen technology to provide a "big screen" experience for audiences as well as being heavily invested in its development, Harley Clarke fully endorsed the release of films in the new Grandeur 70-millimeter process. The enthusiasm for the new process was understandable. Harley Clarke's General Theaters Supplies would benefit by not only owning the patents to Grandeur projection systems but it would also be the exclusive supplier of equipment. So great was Clarke's optimism for the process that, in May 1930, he ordered 40 additional cameras.[35] The theory was sound in principle. The wide-gauge film had a frame size of 21 mm high and 48 mm wide, compared to a standard frame size of 21 mm by 18 mm. The area for the sound track was much wider than standard as well and provided clearer sound reproduction.

The *New York Times* was impressed by the visual image with the first release in Grandeur, *Happy Days*, in early 1930. "William Fox's first Grandeur audible picture ... has the attribute of permitting from three to a half dozen persons to appear in the foreground, quite large enough to carry out the dialogue, without flashing to one person while the others are left off the screen, as is done in the ordinary films."[36]

For the moment, it looked like Clarke's investment might pay off. *Happy Days* received positive reviews for its "let's put on a show"–type story. The highlight, though, was the presence of many of Fox's most popular stars, including Janet Gaynor, Will Rogers, Charles Farrell, Warner Baxter, Victor McLaglen, Edmund Lowe, J. Harold Murray, El Brendel, and just about every other performer under contract. Performing well at the box-office, the film made a profit of $132,000 on a cost of $584,000, not terribly higher than the average Fox budget, even with the additional cost of Grandeur included. The initial success of *Happy Days* was followed by an announcement that there would be color films produced in Grandeur and also Fox Movietone newsreels.

Winfield Sheehan, in particular, was looking forward to the release of Fox's biggest production ever, the Grandeur engagement of *The Big Trail*. Even with the future looking rosy, there was still uncertainty in the halls of Fox sales offices because of diminishing rentals. To boost morale and encourage his staff, James Grainger introduced the "Foxfilm Hall of Merit," whereby outstanding performances by branch managers, salesmen and bookers would be rewarded from $85,000 in prizes. Grainger would make the weekly selections of best performers.[37]

Grainger, too, was anxiously awaiting *The Big Trail*. After watching the film, Grainger declared, "I know positively that 'Common Clay' was just a trailer in comparison with the powerful box-office entertainments we will release."[38] The film was considered to have such enormous worldwide potential that Fox announced that four foreign versions were being prepared by John Stone. There would be a Spanish, French, German and Italian version of the film, each with native casts speaking in their own language for the dialogue scenes. The big action scenes would be filmed once and used in all the versions. Future director Fred Zinnemann, at the time an assistant to director Berthold Viertel, wrote the dialogue for the German version. Expecting Fox's biggest grosses of all time, Grainger elucidated the release pattern of this supposed blockbuster in a letter to exhibitors which was published in the trades.

> THE BIG TRAIL will be given to customers without any attempt made to roadshow it in any city outside of the city of Los Angeles, where it will play a reserved seat engagement at the Chinese Theatre, operated by Fox West Coast Theatres.
> THE BIG TRAIL will be shown solely on percentage and the writer feels confident that every fair minded exhibitor will be only too glad to give to Fox Film Corporation equitable terms to enable us to show a fair return on this huge investment.
> Insofar as I'm personally concerned, I consider road showing of pictures an obsolete practice due to the fact that sound pictures to be properly presented to the public, must be shown in a theatre that uses their sound equipment all the time, and with the finest theatres now situated all over the country, with the very finest kind of equipment, I can see no excuse for road showing THE BIG TRAIL except in any situation that may be so controlled that Fox Film Corporation could not work out a fair and equitable deal."[39]

In other words, if the theaters did not want to pay what Fox thought was a fair rental, the film would be thrown into a roadshow presentation that would deprive the theater of any revenue from the film. This was not exactly a dictionary description of blackmail, but it certainly was a veiled threat. In any case, it turned out to be disingenuous since just five months later, Grainger was considering exhibiting Will Rogers' *A Connecticut Yankee* and *East Lynne* as roadshows and he was studying the advisability of making an exception to his non-roadshow policy.[40]

The further erosion of Fox Films stock, as much a result of investors losing faith in the economy as in the company's future, was countered by Harley Clarke. He announced, "Fox earnings are running ahead of last year and there is no indication that they will not continue to do so for the entire calendar year. The company has completed five pictures for release and a conservative net for these films is $5,000,000. 'The Big Trail' cost $1,500,000 and the company's chart indicates it will gross over $4,000,000."[41] Clarke made this prediction based on the rentals Fox expected to receive from theater contracts.

By the end of 1930, the rest of the rental results from the year's releases were discouraging. While *Common Clay* had become a breakaway hit with a huge profit of $855,000, other films that should have been hits returned lower than expected rentals. A large-scale Jack London maritime adventure, *The Sea Wolf*, starring the very popular Milton Sills (in his last film) was given a substantial budget of $450,000, but did not gross well and ended up with a negligible profit of $13,000. Will Rogers appeared in his second starring role in *So This Is London* and should have broken box-office records based on his enormous following, yet profits amounted to an ordinary $103,000. Among Fox's many remakes was the surefire hit, *Lightnin'*, starring Will Rogers and directed by Henry King. The mix of Rogers's homespun humor and the beloved horse story should have made it a hit. Audiences were not convinced and the film yielded a paltry $31,000 profit.

The concept of remaking silent films with dialogue appealed to all the studios because the properties were already in their inventory. As well, the stories had been worked out and many had a recognition factor with audiences. All that was needed was a little dialogue. Authors of these properties balked at first, expecting to be repaid for the new medium of the talkies. However, courts ruled against the writers and the studios were free to re-use purchased material however they saw fit.[42] Fox made ample use of its properties, especially in the western genre, by remaking many of the films which had starred William Farnum, Tom Mix or Buck Jones.

With audience attendance down overall, even John Ford was not batting up to par. His prison comedy-drama, *Up the River*, starring a pair of former stage actors in their feature film debuts—Spencer Tracy and Humphrey Bogart—returned adequate profits of $142,000. With a miniscule profit, *Oh, for a Man* did not foreshadow a great Fox career for Jeanette MacDonald. Aside from a Quirt and Flagg sequel, there was one other dependable formula for success. Following up on the blockbuster success of *Sunny Side Up* (1929), Janet Gaynor and Charles Farrell reunited in a light romantic comedy, *High Society Blues*, which hit the mark with audiences. It returned the second highest profit of the year at $702,000.

Harley Clarke had to put on a game face in a business where everyone knew from the current releases that Fox Films was no longer the player it once was. Films that would have been considered guaranteed hits were flopping and resulting in huge losses. A big futuristic extravaganza, *Just Imagine*, boasting sets inspired by *Metropolis* and starring Maureen O'Sullivan and popular comedy actor El Brendel, with a script and songs by DeSylva, Brown and Henderson, ended up $280,000 in the red. With its failure, the famous team split up, with Brown and Henderson returning to New York to write and produce stage plays. DeSylva continued under his Fox contract. Other major films with losses included *Liliom*, directed by hit maker Frank Borzage and starring Charles Farrell, which ended up $422,000 in the minus column. The musical special *Song o' My Heart*, starring one of the world's most popular tenors, John McCormack, lost $503,000. *One Mad Kiss*, the first experiment with Spanish-themed films flopped in an English version, losing $263,000. Even F.W. Murnau, in his follow-up to *Sunrise* and *4 Devils*, directed *City Girl* starring Charles Farrell on a $730,000 negative but only showed world rentals of $384,000, resulting in a $517,000 loss. For all the accolades that the Fox Film Corporation had received due to Murnau's genius, the cost of such prestige was a cool $800,000 in three years.

Businessman and entrepreneur Harley L. Clarke knew little about the complexities of running a major film production/distribution company. He had trusted that Winfield Sheehan and Sol Wurtzel would continue to run the production end of the business. What he did not count on were the myriad problems that developed which needed the skill of someone like William Fox, who had weathered the ups-and-downs of production since the early years of the movies. Without the foresight and sensitivity to the vagaries of the business, Clarke was lost.

If nothing else, the average sound picture was more difficult and more expensive to make than silent films. The average cost of a Fox film in 1930 rose from $304,570 in 1929 to $345,153 in 1930, eating up 63.9 percent of rentals, which totaled $31,883,381, up only $1,000,000 from the year before. With costs rising and attendance dropping, Fox was in an unsustainable situation. Since Winfield Sheehan's contract made him the complete head of production at Fox, Harley Clarke was the only executive who could have overruled him. Unfortunately, Clarke did not have enough production experience to do so. He had not followed the theater attendance on a daily basis like William Fox, nor did he have the depth of understanding of the industry that a seasoned producing executive like Fox had.

Regardless of the hype for *The Big Trail*, audiences did not turn out to see it in the numbers Sheehan and Grainger expected. On an enormous negative cost of $1,760,000, the film returned considerably paltry domestic rentals of $945,000. English-language foreign rentals of $242,000 added little more to the total resulting in an extraordinary loss of $1,088,000. Since there were four other foreign versions (made in Spanish, French, German and Italian), the cost of those added $200,234 to the total. In foreign countries, these versions brought in $344,000 and an additional $7,126 in foreign-language theaters in the United States. Surprisingly, this resulted in a Pyrrhic profit of $9,264, not even a dent in the huge overall losses. This was a major embarrassment to the production team that predicted rentals of $4,000,000 just a year earlier.

Another victim of the failure of Grandeur and *The Big Trail* was John Wayne. The young contract actor had been at Fox for several films when he was given the lead in Raoul Walsh's spectacular epic. Walsh and Sheehan expected Wayne to be a new western star in the mold of Tom Mix, but the financial failure of *The Big Trail* and a lack of critics' support for Wayne meant that his next two westerns, *Wyoming Wonder* and *No Favors Asked*, were taken off the production schedule. Wayne left Fox and was relegated to nearly a decade of lower-rank westerns before reaching some degree of stardom with *Stagecoach* in 1939.

When *The Big Trail* had been in release for just a couple of months, Winfield Sheehan and James Grainger were sure that *East Lynne* would be the company's biggest picture of the year.[43] Wrong again, in a major way. The $734,000 production cost of *East Lynne* was substantial enough to make it a contender for blockbuster-level grosses, considering the book on which it was based was hugely popular. However, it reached a domestic level of only $750,000 and a comparatively low $423,000 in foreign markets. What was supposed to be a hit turned out to lose $57,000. What made the gross even worse was that the film was not included in the Fox annual package of 48 films but was booked on a contract-by-contract basis. This meant it did not get full theater coverage across the country. One can only imagine what exhibitors and other studio production chiefs must have thought about Sheehan's ability to predict hits, especially after going out on such a public limb about two highly touted, expensive flops.

By the time returns were in, the "golden goose" promised by Spanish versions was simply laying eggs. These features lost money on a regular basis for Fox, so their continued production through 1935 remains a mystery. RKO abandoned their Spanish-language features in early 1931, using subtitles for Latin America instead. Their producers quickly realized that "native Spanish stars are not wanted. American stars are in demand and as long as titles explain what is transpiring in the film, the natives don't object to listening to a language not understandable to them."[44]

In light of the losses incurred on its films, to keep morale from sinking, Oscar Oldknow, vice-president of Fox Theaters promoted 40 executives and district representatives. This would keep the operation intact and prevent massive defections.

Once again, the nation's leading critics jilted Fox Films with their omission of any Fox product from the annual Ten Best List of 1930. With Universal's *All Quiet on the Western Front* leading the pack with the most votes, Pathé's *Holiday* in second place, M.G.M. was the most represented with *The Divorcée*, *The Big House* and *Anna Christie*. Warners had *Old English* with George Arliss, United Artists had *Abraham Lincoln* and Howard Hughes's World War I epic *Hell's Angels*. Paramount was represented by *With Byrd at the South Pole*, and even the minor independent, Tiffany Pictures, finished with a fourth place *Journey's End*. When the list was expanded to the Top Fifty, Fox had seven titles in the group, including *Common Clay*, *The Big Trail*, *Sunny Side Up*, *Men Without Women*, *Up the River*, *Song o' My Heart*, and *Just Imagine*.

Nevertheless, at the end of year, even after *The Big Trail* had opened to disappointing returns, Harley Clarke announced, "The coming year portends for the motion picture industry a period of substantial artistic and economic development.... Various industry readjustments providing for more efficient and more constructive operation have been effected. Benefits to come from these readjustments will be apparent during the coming year — both in the wide and stronger popular appeal of the industry's attractions and in the more profitable operation of the industry's business."[45]

As of December 1930, gross income broke all previous records at $102,004,009 and yielded a net operating profit of $10,251,827. These figures were what Clarke needed to convince everyone that Fox was now on a firm footing. The production department had imposed budget constraints and was expected to show a savings of $3,000,000 for 1931. Clarke proudly added that administration and distribution costs were more than 45 percent lower compared with 1925. An increase in foreign business and a 21 percent jump in newsreel revenue bode well for the future.

By January 1931, nearly 12,500 theaters had been wired for sound in the United States and 5,400 in Europe. Paramount-Publix declared net profits of $18,370,000 for 1930, 18 percent higher than 1929. RKO profits were up over 100 percent for 1930 at $3,385,628. Success was not being equally spread across the industry. Pathé showed a loss of $1,043,267 in the first 40 weeks of 1930. Fox stock continued to sink further to $27, less than one-fourth of its record high.

Fox still had some high-grossing films like *The Man Who Came Back* (1931), a remake of the 1924 feature with George Walsh, this time starring Fox's box-office duo of Janet Gaynor and Charles Farrell. In its opening week at the Roxy, it reached a gross of $132,000 almost equal to the 1929 opening of *The Cock-Eyed World*. And Winfield Sheehan had an added note of good news; the cost of the average talking picture had been brought down to the same level as the average silent of four years earlier. In the initial period of talkies, costs in some cases doubled, but experience had brought overhead down to "a good commercial foundation and economic basis."[46] But that optimism was not shared by the banks that had invested heavily in motion pictures.

To Harley Clarke fell the responsibility of refinancing some of the debt taken on by William Fox. With $55,000,000 in "gold notes" due April 15, 1931, which he had arranged for a year earlier, Clarke had to deal with a now-reluctant Halsey, Stuart and Company. After collecting all the fees for financing Fox's theater acquisitions over the previous five years, the banking house had suddenly gotten cold feet about the stability of the company. With a foundering stock market, new capital was not an easy task so that "plans for Fox refinancing this month will probably be somewhat different from original expectations. Latest indications are that a short-term note issue, secured by the company's Loew's stock, will be offered publicly, with the remainder of the financing deferred."[47]

As of April 15, 1931, Clarke had lined up a new banking group to take over from Halsey, Stuart. Chase Securities Corporation and Dillon, Read and Company along with Bancamerica and several other participants, formed an investment consortium to assume Fox Films' recapitalization of its debt. The Loew's stock once again came into play with a new company being formed to take over Fox's holdings in Loew's, Inc.[48]

Clarke issued a statement outlining the deal:

> The new financing by Fox Films completes a task of fiscal re-organization taken over by the present management and necessitated by a comprehensive program of expansion and acquisition undertaken by the company during and prior to 1929. This financing program reduces the consolidated funded debt of the corporation by more than $25,000,000 and leaves it with more than $9,000,000 of cash and more than $16,000,000 of working capital.
>
> Film income has increased during the last six months while production costs were declining sharply. There has been a reduction of 24 per cent in production costs compared with film rentals for the six months ended March 28, 1931. Selling and administrative expenses compared with film rentals have been declining steadily for the past five years, the decline being more than 18 per cent during that time.[49]

Costs had indeed dropped, but the revenue stream had not yet reflected the drop in attendance nationwide. Fox Films was still riding on the box-office successes of 1929 and 1930, which were artificially inflating the rental figures.

In yet another corporate move by Harley Clarke, rather than address the problems in production or theater attendance, the president of Fox, who had no experience in those areas, announced that National Theater Supply would handle all the construction, repair and maintenance work of Fox Theaters. The jobs, in turn, would be awarded to a group of preferred contractors. Clarke figured this would save 10 percent–20 percent more than if each job was farmed out separately. All he was doing was increasing National Theater Supply's revenue, a foremost concern of his.

Even following the failure of *The Big Trail* and a general reluctance within the industry to adopt the Grandeur process, Harley Clarke announced in May 1931, that he was equipping all of the company's theaters with dual projectors, adaptable to both standard and widescreen film, with the object of having the entire circuit equipped by the 1932-1933 season. Clarke made this announcement at the Fox sales convention: "Where replacements of projection machines are required in Fox houses from now on, it is understood the new dual purpose machines will be installed in anticipation of the wide-film production schedule.... Camera and sound equipment is reported ready at the Fox west coast studios to take care of production."[50] The only problem with that announcement was that no wide-film production was planned at any studio. Yet, Clarke proclaimed, "It is the opinion of those in close contact with the industry that during the course of the next year or two a large percentage of the theaters of the world will be equipped with this new adjustable apparatus."[51] This flew in the face of logic because the industry had so much as declared the entire experiment a dead issue.

Anxious to avoid tangling with the government's anti-monopoly watchdogs stemming from a suit against the company in 1928, Harley Clarke resolved the issue of the Loew's, Inc. shares by transferring them to a new entity called the Film Securities Corporation that would be controlled by trustees with no interest in either Fox or Loew's or any film-industry association. It was acknowledged that the original acquisition of the stock was a violation of the law and the decree declaring complete divestiture was signed by none other than Judge John C. Knox, who had been so hostile to William Fox. The defendant corporations were perpetually enjoined from having anything further to do with these shares. Louis B. Mayer, J. Robert Rubin and Irving Thalberg had retrieved control of their company, if not the actual ownership of the majority shares.[52]

There were other holdover business deals from the William Fox administration. Jack Leo's contract was finally settled in the summer of 1931 and he was in negotiations to buy all of Fox Theater's 18 venues in Long Island, New York. His brother Joe Leo was to be a part of the new organization along with another brother, Ben Leo, who had already been with the Long Island circuit.[53] The Fox Corporation was also leasing or selling as many theaters as it could all across the country, with the exclusion of the West Coast chain.[54] This had become a necessity in light of losses and dropping revenue. Nevertheless, six Fox theaters in Chicago went into foreclosure in August 1931.

Fox stock, meanwhile, had dropped to $17½ per share, approximately 15 percent of its value from its pre-crash level, and with no bottom in sight. Collateral damage of the decline swamped a banking house, Pynchon & Company, which was declared insolvent because of losses arising from its investment in Fox.[55] Fox, however, was not the only company to drop in value. Although profits at Loew's, Inc. continued to rise, its share value dropped along with Paramount, Pathé and Warners. Overall, film stocks, dragged down by the rest of the weak market, lost 30 percent of their value in April 1931, a total depreciation of $105,134,128. The decline was the carryover effect from the stock market crash of October 1929. The ripple effects of the economic depression were getting worse as unemployment soared and prosperity seemed further away than ever. The country was in the grips of deflation in which fewer dollars were available, shrinking the economy and creating higher unemployment. At the peak of the Great Depression, nationwide unemployment figures reached one-quarter of the workforce.

Investors had nothing to be optimistic about when, in the spring of 1931, Fox postponed its annual stockholders' meeting three times to allow for more preparation of its financial report. When the figures were finally announced by Touche, Niven & Company, at estimated earnings of $12,000,000, the figure was suspect because Price, Waterhouse & Company had previously come up with a figure of $7,000,000, to which Harley Clarke objected. Clarke wanted a new formula for write-offs and depreciation which was different from the more conservative one William Fox followed. Clarke's version gave a rosier picture of profits and disguised the fact that Fox's earnings were dropping. General Theaters Equipment, Inc. also showed a big increase in net income for 1930 to $4,454,405, more than double the 1929 figure. The officially sanctioned statement showed the following results for the Fox Film Corporation:

Rentals '29	$9,232,219	Rentals '30	$11,757,904
Lab sales	441,284	Lab sales	611,460
Total income	$9,673,503	Total income	$12,369,364
Neg & Pos.	$3,630,787	Neg. & Pos.	$ 5,246,894
Participation	917,069	Participation	1,040,186
Dist. & Adm.	2,568,341	Dist. & Adm.	3,063,653
Total costs	$7,116,197	Total costs	$9,323,733
Profit	$2,557,306	Profit	$3,046,631[56]

However, William Fox had another explanation for the operating profits of 1930. He shared his theory with Upton Sinclair:

> I have before me a statement of Fox Film as of December 27, 1930, from which it would appear that the company should have plenty of money. There is made a comparison between the year ending December 28, 1929, under the Fox regime, and December 27, 1930, most of it under the Harley Clarke regime. By manipulation and only by manipulation they were able to reduce the profits of the 1929 Fox regime to $9,469,051, when the fact of the matter is that the profits that I left with that company, earned in 1929, were upwards of $13,500,000, plus the non-recurrent profit for the sale of First National shares to the Warner Company, which, after deducting what these shares had cost the company, gave a net profit of $8,500,000. These two items combined, the Fox Film Corporation earned in 1929 approximately $22,000,000. But here on their statement that I have before me, figures they prepared after I sold out, they show a profit of $9,469,051, and have shifted the difference to the profit made in 1930.... Is it not clear that in correcting these books they have simply taken the profits made in 1929 and deferred them on the statement of 1930?[57]

It would take a forensic audit to determine whether William Fox's theory was correct, but the following years showed that all was not quite profitable within the Fox organization once Harley Clarke took over. William Fox also accused the Clarke contingent of looting the company of $100,000,000 in value, in part by issuing new stock which gave Clarke and the banks a profit of $30,000,000 while diluting existing shares by a like amount. In effect, Fox and Upton Sinclair were accusing the banking interests of perpetrating a massive stock fraud. Again, only a forensic audit at the time could have proved this and no criminal action was taken by the government.

After President Franklin Delano Roosevelt took office in March 1933, the Senate held hearings into the dealings of the film industry. One particular investigation of General Theaters resulted in an admission by Harley L. Clarke that he had artificially inflated the value of dividends that the company paid. While General stock yielded 73 cents a share, Clarke had sold shares claiming the figure was $28.50 with a total stock value of $28,488,000 rather than the actual book value of $2,225,616. Clarke stated that the higher figure was given based on a well-considered estimate of value since his company had developed a new type of projector, referring to Grandeur, which would revolutionize the film industry and would have netted a profit of $3,000,000 to $4,000,000. If nothing else, this confirmed William Fox's accusation that Clarke had a predilection for manipulating figures.[58] Ironically, Clarke hired William Fox's former career-long attorney, Saul E. Rogers, to represent him in these hearings.[59]

To boost industry faith in the company, Fox boasted about its 1931-1932 season emphasizing "personalities" in its line-up. In addition to "old-line" stars, the new pictures would present ten new "recruits" from the stage. Yet, an analysis of the production list shows that the top stars were the same Fox contractees or already established film performers. There were four films with Janet Gaynor and three of those teamed her with Charles Farrell; two others headlined Charles Farrell; Will Rogers was scheduled for three; Victor McLaglen headed five features; Edmund Lowe was to appear in four; Warner Baxter was assigned to four; newly arrived at Fox, Spencer Tracy was starred in four films; the rest were an assortment of films with Maureen O'Sullivan, Warner Oland in additional *Charlie Chan* installments, and El Brendel comedies. There was not much new or revolutionary about the upcoming slate. With the exception of the Gaynor-Farrell vehicle *Delicious* (1931) with a score by the Gershwins, musicals, the original mainstay of the talkies, were out. The only real newcomer was Elissa Landi, an attractive ingénue who would star in a run of unsuccessful films.

Remakes, as well, were falling out of favor with all studios. After making 17 in the 1930-1931 season, Fox announced only six for 1931-1932, including *Skyline* (1931), a remake of *East Side, West Side* (1927), *Riders of the Purple Sage* (1931), *The Yellow Ticket* (1931), *Over the Hill* (1931), *Wild Girl* (1932) originally *Salomy Jane*, and *In Her Arms*, originally *Fazil* (1928), which was not made. Considering that overall production at all other studios combined only amounted to under 20 remakes, Fox was recycling the most story material.

As a sop to the censor-minded who were complaining about the glorification of gangsters and

Warner Baxter romances Miriam Jordan in *Dangerously Yours* (1933) (courtesy Mike Hawks).

gangland activities since the release of *Little Caesar* (1930, Warners) and *The Public Enemy* (1931, Warners), Winfield Sheehan announced that the production of such films was being discontinued at Fox.[60] This left less competition for Warner Bros. which had embarked on a program of tough action films dealing with unsavory male and female characters. These films may have been unappealing to censors, but they amounted to big box-office as audiences showed an insatiable appetite for portrayals of social outcasts.

By mid–1931, not even Harley Clarke's optimism could disguise the fact that business was continuing to fall. While some studios issued calls for salary cuts, Clarke, in a letter sent to all employees, refused to impose any cuts at Fox companies: "We are going through times which fortunately affect our business probably less than it does most businesses, but there is need for continued economy, loyalty and cooperation from everyone in the organization as we are distinctly opposed to cutting wages in any department of the company."[61] This rallying cry for loyalty was necessary to keep Clarke's executive team from abandoning ship.

Even Oscar Oldknow, executive vice-president of Fox Theaters, echoed the necessity to keep a positive outlook at the consumer level: "The theater is the poor man's palace ... and it must be maintained in that attractive light. An atmosphere of brightness and cheerfulness is essential. Members of the staff should not be permitted to talk about the troubles of the motion picture business ... and managers are instructed to not talk about such matters to the staff."[62]

An equally pessimistic vote was cast by the bankers assigned to the Fox board of directors. With new financing in place and austerity on everyone's mind, dividends were cut from $4 per share to $2.50. Elected to the now-conservative board of directors were Harley Clarke, Winfield Sheehan and bankers representing the large institutional investors in Fox. Among them, Edward R. Tinker, president of Interstate Equities Corporation, would play a larger role than Clarke ever expected.

Lower revenue was underlined by a revised statement for the year ending October 26, 1930, for Fox Theaters. A previously issued statement showed a profit of $2,660,261, but the new accounting ended the year with a $3,250,589 loss. The economy had caught up with the high cost of maintaining Fox's extensive theater holdings long before anyone was aware of it.[63]

Another bombshell dropped when the 1931 first-quarter profits were announced and they turned out to be only 25 percent of 1930 profits in the same quarter. While income from all sources totaled $25,458,223, about $1,500,000 lower than the previous year, profits in this period were $1,124,704, down from $4,356,218. The enormous decrease in 1931's first quarter was explained by expenses for the acquisition of 70 theaters which were not included in the 1930 financial statement.[64]

The downside of William Fox's buy-and-build binge was still taking its toll on the bottom line. General Theaters, however, continued to be profitable and benefited further from the dividends paid by Fox stock. But it, too, was not immune to the economy. For the first six months of 1931, profits dropped precipitously to $120,152 from $6,785,897 the year before.[65]

With the Fox Corporation's fortunes tumbling, Harley Clarke, ignoring ethical business practices, issued dividends of more than $4,000,000 and had the board of directors approve his claims of personal loans to the company amounting to $229,000 "for further developing sound pictures."[66]

At a time when Fox productions were losing their luster, Harley Clarke sent story-department head Al Lewis to meet the press. Lewis announced that Fox would accommodate cost-cutting by re-releasing hit movies like *Sunny Side Up* (1929). If this plan worked and generated revenue, it would be followed by *The Cock-Eyed World* (1929). Reissues would lessen the need for as many new films. Of course, Lewis admitted that the grosses on a reissue would be lower than that of a new picture, but there would be no production costs to amortize. What this concept overlooked was that the theater overhead stayed the same and if there were not enough patrons to cover the weekly breakeven figure, the house would lose money.[67] It is possible that Lewis, who generally did not act as company spokesperson, was given this assignment because Sheehan, no doubt, had little faith in this strategy.

Fox abandoned the plan after *Sunny Side Up* flopped in its reissue run at the Roxy Theater in New York City. To make sure Fox Theaters had enough product, deals were being struck with United Artists and RKO for their slates of films.

In an effort to make Fox look like an incubator for new talent, 19 players were being groomed for stardom. None of them made any impact on Fox Films and none had anything resembling a major career. In fact, with the exception of Ralph Morgan, who continued as a character actor for many years, and Helen Mack, who had a few leading roles at other studios, all the others appeared in supporting parts, often without credit.

Desperation was the only way to describe Harley Clarke's hiring of Richard A. Rowland, who had been bouncing from one studio to another. After leaving First National, he ended up at Pathé, then Paramount, then low-end Tiffany and finally Fox, all within four years. His lack of success at these companies should have been a harbinger for any skilled executive. Clarke, however, not trusting the abilities of his production heads Sheehan and Wurtzel, decided to bring aboard the man who had determined in 1927 that no film should be longer than 6,000 feet because audiences did not want longer films, as a vice-president with "general executive duties."[68]

Once Rowland joined the New York office, Sol Wurtzel was conspicuously absent from the west coast lot. He was reportedly on a three-month vacation to Europe. The company denied rumors that Wurtzel had permission to remain away for the remainder of his Fox three-year contract which was signed in April 1930 and had 18 months to go. Wurtzel also reportedly received his bonus of $500,000, at the insistence of William Fox when he left on this vacation. Was he out of the picture?

A trade editorial made the supposition that "while the Fox pictures and the studio were the subjects of much criticism when in a run of lightweight talkers for some time, eastern comment over the Fox studio situation centered largely on Wurtzel. This was supported by coast impressions as well, with neither coast understanding the Sheehan attitude in the face of those criticisms. Sheehan was seemingly willing to personally take the rap for the poor box-office showing." Sheehan was also annoyed by the appointment of Richard Rowland "to head of a story council for Fox, promoted by Rowland. The Rowland appointment is said to have been a personal one made by Clarke, unknown to any of the Fox New York or coast staffs."[69] There was obviously dissension within the executive suites of the Fox Film Corporation.

In an effort to cut down on high-cost salaries, Winfield Sheehan announced in November 1931, the formation of three teams of directors and assistant directors from within the studio. One team included J.M. Kerrigan, an actor in the 1920s, and Bert Sebell, who would work on *The Gay Bandit* with George O'Brien. Sebell had directed Fox's first original Spanish-language feature, *Mamá*, released in September 1931. Edmund Grainger, James Grainger's brother, would be associate producer.

Another team included veteran editor Harold Schuster as director and Samuel Godfrey as his assistant on *Scotch Valley*, with Al Rockett as associate producer. Then there was the team of director Marcel Varnel and assistant director R.L. Hough on *First Cabin*, with associate producer William Sistrom. None of these projects went ahead as announced. Harold Schuster returned to editing and the team of Kerrigan and Sebell never made any films for Fox. Sebell did direct one other Spanish-language feature in 1932. *Scotch Valley* was released under the title *Amateur Daddy* (1932) and starred Warner Baxter under the experienced John Blystone's direction. Varnel and Hough did co-direct a minor film shot in England, *The Silent Witness* (1932).

The financial reason behind these directorial teams was obvious. John Ford had just been let go and his $3,000 weekly salary was cited as the reason.[70] Ford's most recent film, *The Brat* (1931), had lost money, but at least he had a history with the studio. Sheehan was being forced to cut costs so drastically, he had to let one of the studio's most respected directors go elsewhere. Ford would return to Fox two years later.

Vice-president and general manager, Winfield R. Sheehan, circa 1930.

Paul Burger, an executive for United Artists, summed up the industry's problems of the early 1930s:

> There is plenty of business to be had. People haven't stopped eating. They are still wearing clothes. They still drive automobiles. They burn up gas and wear out tires. They still demand entertainment and get it and are still spending some money for luxuries. To be sure, they are not spending as freely as they did in '28 and '29, the tears of paper profits and one-day millionaires.... But buying habits and spending habits have changed for a long while. People are more thrifty, then spend more cautiously and those who are working are saving.... The smart exhibitor gears himself to new trends. He buys cautiously. He employs advertising to a greater extent than ever. His admission prices are geared to represent the values he is presenting. The smart exhibitor throws into discard all his preconceived notions or business habits.[71]

Bad news kept coming. Metro, the best run and most successful of all the companies in the early 1930s, reported that its profit was lower by 33 percent in the first 40 weeks of 1931. Warner Bros. and its subsidiaries reported a net loss of $7,918,604 and a drop in revenues from $52,340,301 to $36,371,383. Amusement stocks hit all-time lows in October 1931, almost two years after the initial market crash. Fox hit $7.50 per share. General Theaters dropped to $1.23. Paramount dropped to $11.50. RKO was at $7.75. Many, many millions in real money had been lost by investors in these companies.[72]

If 1931's box-office results told a story, it was a bitter reminder that business was not running as usual. A big-budget expenditure of $868,000 on the Will Rogers *A Connecticut Yankee*, originally planned in color, was considered to be as surefire a hit as could be imagined. Even on domestic rentals of close to $1,000,000, the film's weak foreign revenues led to a $94,000 loss. *Are You There?*, introducing American audiences to English comedienne Beatrice Lillie, was the most colossal failure of the year, losing almost all of its negative cost of $430,000. Efforts to promote Fox's new male star, Spencer Tracy, fared no better. All of his three pictures of the year were losers. One of those included *Goldie*, in which not even his co-star Jean Harlow, hot from her success in Howard Hughes's *Hell's Angels*, could save the film from going $84,000 into the red.

More surprising, the always popular Quirt & Flagg could not coax enough people into theaters to keep *Women of All Nations* from losing $175,000. Janet Gaynor, however, kept her fans happy and they rewarded her with Fox's two most profitable films of the year. *Daddy Long Legs*, co-starring the popular Warner Baxter, was able to return a surplus of $625,000, the largest of the year, and the next most successful film, *Merely Mary Ann*, pairing Gaynor with Charles Farrell, yielded a profit of $466,000. Frank Borzage regained his position as a profitable director for Fox with a $336,000 surplus from *Bad Girl*. Gaynor and Farrell were together again in the last release of the year, the tuneful *Delicious*, which scored with a profit of $271,000 on a negative cost of $606,000. There was still money to be made in sentiment as *Over the Hill* showed. The remake of the silent 1920 hit did well, but the numbers were nowhere as large as on the earlier film. Still, James Dunn and Sally Eilers made it a winner with world rentals of $1,103,000, yielding a profit of $268,000. Total negative costs had been reduced for the year's slate of films by about $2,500,000 to $17,814,223, with an average film at $329,893. With world rentals of $29,034,364, the production department lowered its annual loss to $8,771.

Jean Harlow and Spencer Tracy share an embrace in *Goldie* (1931) (courtesy Mike Hawks).

Behind the scenes at Fox, there had been machinations by banking interests to wrest control of Fox from Harley Clarke in the interest of protecting their massive investment, totaling $110,000,000. Edward R. Tinker, president of Interstate Equities Corporation and former chairman of Chase National Bank, took over for Clarke in November 1931. This was considered a victory for the Chase bloc on the board of directors. "Both sides are understood to have agreed that this is the only way out for the company, inasmuch as Clarke does not have the time to give the necessary attention to both his utility interests and Fox.

"With that change in the presidency, it is expected that Clarke men will be eliminated from Fox, whose board of directors now represents control by the utility chief. This change has been sought for some time by the Chase group."[73] It was no surprise that anyone with money invested in the Fox companies would be concerned about their holdings, considering its value and future were both on shaky ground.

Harley Clarke gave a face-saving and somewhat disingenuous statement: "I have been hoping for some time that Mr. Tinker would undertake this responsibility and I am delighted he has now accepted it. He comes to the corporation with a long experience in banking and business management."[74]

Tinker had taken over the company to try and salvage what was left of an enormous investment, but he made it clear at the outset that he would step down and hand the position over to a new president from the film industry as soon as possible.

So, here was the once-mighty Fox Films: a production slate in disarray, a company losing theaters to foreclosure and selling off others, dismantling its executive contingent, and failing at every attempt to revive its fortunes. With the economy continuing to swoon, it was becoming less likely that Fox would ever recover.

11. Turmoil

Economic conditions in the early 1930s had hit the film industry, which was previously thought to be immune from the downturn. Audiences had dropped, studios were cutting overhead, and theater chains were facing massive losses and the threat of bankruptcy. Some theaters were resorting to drastic measures like cutting admission to ten cents. Others were initiating a policy of triple bills which distributors did their best to resist on the theory that double bills were destructive enough to moviegoing habits.

A *Variety* editorial summation of 1931 concluded,

> Grosses for individual pictures have dropped to the point where a $750,000 total current rental income is deemed terrific. Outside of Chaplin's last release [*City Lights*] it's doubtful if any distributor ran up $1,000,000 on any one feature throughout 1931. That includes domestic and foreign sales while noting that the Chaplin film never got near its quota (of bookings), due to those demanded 50 percent theatre sharing terms.
>
> Hence, what have $400,000 and $500,000 gross rentals meant to hit pictures which have cost from $300,000 to $800,000 to make? And but recently were released a couple which carry an overhead near that latter figure.
>
> The three, four and $500,000 celluloid clucks which limped around the country probably kept more people away from their own and other circuit theatres than they drew.... Any perusal of figures for '31 ... will tab the approximate 25,000,000 people the picture theatres are estimated to have lost weekly.[1]

Theater circuits controlled by major producers numbered 2,006 houses in the United States and Canada and most of those were large palaces in major cities. In the United States Paramount controlled 971 houses, Warners, 529, Fox 521, of which 470 were Fox West Coast, Loew's, 189, RKO, 161, and Universal, 66.[2]

At a time when 1,000 theaters paid 60 percent–65 percent of all rentals, these first-run situations were very important to the continued health of the studios. When remittances from these sources dropped, the companies which had the largest chains were hurt the most since the overhead of the theaters was enormous. Loew's, Inc., with a relatively small chain and healthy returns from its M.G.M. releases, reported profits of $5,264,729 for the first 28 weeks ending March 1932. Of all the major production/distribution/exhibition entities, Loew's fared the best through the economic depression.

Warner Bros. showed a loss of $1,848,868 for the quarter ending November 28, 1931 against a profit of $1,576,421 in the previous year. Albert

Warner announced that First National, a division of Warners, was trying to keep costs to $200,000 per film, but ultimate costs depended on the needs of the story.[3] By mid-year, Warners would cut star salaries by 30 percent.

RKO reported an operating loss of $2,576,603 for 1931 and also set $200,000 as the average feature cost. Conversely, the Keith-Albee-Orpheum chain, the exhibition arm of R.K.O., showed a profit of $1,620. This was negligible to say the least, but breaking even was a hopeful goal for most companies.

The newly consolidated Columbia Pictures, without the massive overhead of a theater chain and fewer star contracts to service, showed a profit of $276,606 when it became a public company in March 1932.

One company which was still exploiting the installation of sound was Western Electric, with profits of $10,816,387 on sales of $228,956,000 in 1931. However, even that company experienced a downturn from its sales of $361,478,000 in 1930.

To illustrate the problems Fox was having in selling back some of its theaters after William Fox's massive expansion program, the *Film Daily* carried a brief reminder of the troubles at the exhibition level. "Oil City, Pa. Built at a cost of $400,000 less than three years ago, the Latonia Theater was sold at a sheriff's sale yesterday for $36,000."[4]

Feature production was affected by cost cutting and dropped to a 15-year low. Only 550 films were scheduled for the 1931-1932 season, down from a previous high of 747 releases. With the majors producing 396 films, it was their lowest output on record. There were also fewer individual companies in business in 1932 compared with Hollywood's more productive years. Some exhibitors were concerned that there would be a shortage of product and that would increase competitive bidding for the best films, raising rental terms.

The effect of previous consolidations on production was illustrated by the case of Warner Bros. and First National which, in 1926, released 75 and 51 features, respectively, but had dropped to 35 each after merging. Metro put out 40 films and Goldwyn 31 in the season before their merger. However, the combined output was 49. Similar results were expected from the planned Radio Pictures and Pathé merger.[5]

An optimistic *Film Daily* editorial predicted that the worst was over for the film business: "It looks as if that which transpired in 1931 and before will go into industry records as ancient history. The picture business was in for a drubbing and took it. Liquidation has about run its course. It commences to look like efficiency is again in the saddle. The industry can well take care of itself without outside [bank] interference. Off to a promising start, 1932 might well be the year in which the screen led the world from Depression Alley back to Prosperity Boulevard."[6]

In fact, Fox's vice-president of sales, James Grainger, found that business around the country had taken a decided upturn after a tour of exchange centers. He reported that motion picture people were optimistic about the future of the industry and there was a wider feeling that the tide had turned for the better.[7]

Some exhibitors felt that future success lay in the return of vaudeville lead-ins to films. Certainly, live performers were all in favor of that suggestion, but it never did quite catch on. Theaters booked short subjects to fill out programs and only specialized houses like the Roxy continued their stage presentations. The result was that all companies developed a short subject department. Warners entered the already-crowded newsreel business. The continuing success of Walt Disney's cartoon series featuring Mickey Mouse and Silly Symphonies convinced other studios that they, too, should have a branded cartoon character. Universal signed up Walter Lantz who continued making Oswald the Rabbit cartoons which were initially created by Walt Disney; Warners became associated with Harman/Ising which turned out dozens of *Bosko* and *Buddy* cartoons; Paramount with Max Fleischer, known for the *Out of the Inkwell*, *Popeye* and *Betty Boop* series; RKO with Van Beuren studios through its absorption of Pathé; Columbia distributed *Krazy Kat* and *Scrappy* cartoons and originally released Walt Disney short subjects from 1929 to 1932. Disney made a more lucrative distribution agreement with United Artists in early 1932 and continued with that company until moving to RKO in 1937.

Comedy and musical short subjects continued to be made by almost all the studios to provide accompaniment to their features. Columbia, in particular, struck gold with their comedy shorts when they signed vaudeville and screen performers Moe Howard, Curly Howard and Larry Fine, better known as The Three Stooges.

Fox, preoccupied with its own internal problems, only returned to a comprehensive program of short subjects through a distribution deal with Earle W. Hammons's Educational Pictures in 1933. Hammons was having difficulties getting maximum bookings for his productions since all of the studios had their own short subject divisions. Educational supplied comedies with stars Buster Keaton, Andy Clyde, and Harry Langdon. Some future stars had early roles in Educational short subjects, including Bob Hope, The Ritz Brothers, and Danny Kaye. Cartoons were distributed through a deal between Hammons and Paul Terry, who animated his Terrytoons at a studio in New York State. When Educational closed its doors in 1938, Fox continued distributing new Terrytoons annually until 1968. Aside from the annual 104 Newsreels and 26 *Magic Carpet of Movietone* single-reelers which were culled from already-existing footage, Fox distributed no short subjects from 1930 until the merger with Educational.

When the Ten Best Pictures of 1931 were announced, Fox's position as a major provider of critical successes was grossly diminished. RKO's *Cimarron* was in first place. M.G.M. had three on the list, including *Min and Bill*, *A Free Soul* and *The Sin of Madelon Claudet*. United Artists released three in the Top Ten because of deals with Charles Chaplin, Samuel Goldwyn and Howard Hughes, who produced *City Lights*, *Street Scene* and *Hell's Angels*, respectively. Paramount was represented by *Skippy* and First National by *Five Star Final*. Fox received mention for just one film, *Bad Girl*. The Academy Awards of Merit for 1930-31 reflected Fox's lower standing in the film community. No awards were won for this year.

After the departure of President Harley L. Clarke, the truly dismal financial condition he had left the company in was just becoming public. The net loss for the Fox Film Corporation in the first 39 weeks of 1931 was $2,851,996, compared to a profit of $8,280,551 in the previous year. Bad news kept coming with the announcement of a $3,400,000 loss for Fox Theaters as of October 31, 1931.[8] Fox stock hit a new low of $2^1/$_2$. Amusement stocks in general dropped more than 75 percent in 1931.

Amid the red ink, President Edward Tinker declared that, with the consolidation of Fox's producing activities at Movietone City, reductions in production time and costs would result in a $1,000,000 annual saving. In the process, the time required for preparing stories and equipment for filming a picture would be cut at least 25 percent while the time for actual production would be reduced by about 12^1/$_2$ percent. In a period when Fox's films were suffering in the quality department, these cuts would cause the final product to deteriorate further.

To be more efficient, a unit plan of four companies was put in place at Movietone City. Since the same crews would be working together, their efficiency level was expected to increase. Instead of paying salaries while crew members were waiting for a production to begin, the four companies would be kept constantly at work, turning out pictures at the rate of one a week. Each unit would have an individual accountant to keep complete records of all time and money spent in the production. Any time lost or unnecessary expenses would be immediately brought to the attention of the production manager.[9] Tinker's hope was that a more organized factory would curb costs and turn out better pictures. It is unknown how long this unit system lasted, but the quality of Fox releases continued to deteriorate.

The turmoil in the industry as a whole was exacerbated at the Fox Film Corporation. After the toxic struggle for control of the company waged between banking interests and William Fox, and the failed year-long presidency of Harley L. Clarke, the company was now rudderless. Adding to the problems, rumors about changes in management were rampant throughout most of 1932.

> Inside reports that Sol Wurtzel is gradually being disassociated in part from production supervision at Fox are strengthened in the recent move replacing John Stone, former foreign department head, as first assistant on production to Winfield Sheehan.
> Wurtzel is said to have refused a salary cut, having a contract, and was referred to the legal department with his claim.... The shakeup at Fox continued over the weekend. H. Keith Weeks, former prohibition agent who had been executive manager of the Movietone studio at Westwood, is reported out and to be succeeded by William Steincamp, former head of the sound department. E.W. Butcher, production manager, is another dismissal and due, it is said, to an order from New York.
> Sol Wurtzel's brother Ben, who has held various jobs and was recently in charge of the costumes department, was let out Saturday.
> Bert Sebell, former production manager, and J.M. Kerrigan, actor, were removed as a directorial team on "The Gay Bandit" after three days' filming. Marcel Varnel, R.L. Hough, Arnold [sic] Schuster and Samuel Godfrey, other directorial teams appointed at the same time have been given no assignments yet and probably will return to their former positions.[10]

Two weeks later, there were more serious rumors:

> What appeared to be authoritative reports from the Coast on Saturday to the effect that Winfield R. Sheehan, vice-president and general manager of Fox, was leaving the company, were denied by President E.R. Tinker, who said that Sheehan has been

given a three months' leave of absence owing to illness."[11]

Tinker, in an interview with THE FILM DAILY ... said arrangements have been made with Edward Loeb of Loeb, Walker, & Loeb, who handles Sheehan's legal affairs. The leave becomes effective immediately. Sheehan, stated Tinker, has been ill for some time and consequently out of the studio. According to his physicians, said the Fox president, his condition does not permit his return to duty at present.[12]

Sheehan's illness was reported as a nervous breakdown, from which he was recuperating in February and was scheduled to return six weeks later. The 49-year-old executive apparently had been dealing with an enormous amount of stress throughout the year of Harley Clarke's administration. His collapse was considered "authentic" and had been "brought on by the stripping from him of his studio authority."[13]

In March, he was reportedly recovering from his breakdown at a sanitarium in San Francisco and was planning to leave for a vacation in Europe. Sheehan later requested an additional two months' leave which was granted on April 5, 1932. After resting in New York, Sheehan was slated to return to production on the west coast as of June 1.

The Sol Wurtzel situation suddenly did a complete turnaround. With Sheehan gone for so long, Wurtzel, having returned from his three-month "vacation," was now in charge of the studio and was too indispensable to lose. Reports had him traveling to the east coast to meet with the banking interests controlling the company. "The confusion over the status of Winnie Sheehan has at least come to a head in local circles and there is a distinct feeling that the former Fox production chief is out although there is nothing official to verify this local belief."[14]

Wurtzel was not given the absolute authority that Sheehan had, but he was able to handle production matters at Fox until the issue of an executive was sorted out.

It is likely Wurtzel settled his contract dispute, since a trade article pointedly mentioned, "Contract of Sol M. Wurtzel, general superintendent of Fox, has been adjusted amicably. Adjustment provides that Wurtzel will remain under contract as general superintendent until May 25. A mutual understanding has been reached that Wurtzel's connection with Fox after May 25 will be the subject of negotiations at that time."[15] The Tinker administration had no choice but to deal with Wurtzel "amicably," and Wurtzel, no doubt sensing an opening for more responsibility and salary, took the opportunity. John Stone, E.W. Butcher and Ben Wurtzel returned to their previous positions.

Wurtzel was given some assistance when Ben Jackson, who had previously been head of the Fox music department, was promoted to assistant general superintendent of the Fox Studios. Maitland Rice succeeded him as head of the music department.[16]

There were other staff moves during this tumultuous period. Joseph Johnson left as Sheehan's assistant. W.C. Michel resigned as vice-president and treasurer to handle the financial affairs of Fox Films. Theater man Harry Arthur took over as vice-president, and A.D. Shurtleff, formerly comptroller, became treasurer. S.R. Burns, vice-president and secretary, resigned.

More rumors spread about what the company would look like when the dust settled. For the moment, Richard Rowland and Sol Wurtzel were running production. "Richard A. Rowland left on the Century yesterday for the Fox studios on the coast. Although he would make no statement before leaving, it is understood he is going to Movietone City to confer on some production matters that have arisen during the absence of Winfield Sheehan."[17]

Then when Wurtzel was away from the studio, associate producer Al Rockett was made studio manager. This gave rise to more rumors: "Sol Wurtzel is in New York conferring with President E.R. Tinker, it was stated at Fox yesterday, in denying reports that Rockett is succeeding Winfield R. Sheehan as production chief. The rumor apparently had its inception through a misinterpretation of a studio announcement of Rockett's temporary post."[18]

However, Jack Alicoate, editor of the *Film Daily*, added fuel to the speculation. "It is not at all unlikely that when the Fox tangle is straightened out Dick Rowland will play an important part in the future activities of that organization. No one doubts that he knows pretty much what this studio business is all about. His record at Metro and at First National proves this. He is generally recognized as the safest picker of screen material in the business."[19] This was mere speculation and Rowland was not elevated past his position of vice-president.

The Fox board of directors, under Edward Tinker's guidance to achieve financial stability, was disallowing some of the contracts negotiated during the Harley Clarke administration. Among those in dispute was James Grainger's deal. This led to confusion regarding Grainger's position in the company and the deals he had negotiated. Grainger was on a leave of absence and could not address the concerns. A statement was issued by W.C. Michel, executive vice-president of Fox: "We assume that these misleading statements have been inspired by the fact that a comparatively few employment contracts extending over a period of years have been disapproved by the Board, although the great majority of such contracts were authorized and approved. Contracts entered into in the ordinary course of business are not affected by the action of the Board."[20]

There was further confusion caused by the tangle of financial deals since Harley Clarke's General Theaters still owned controlling shares in Fox. Clarke's financial representative was negotiating to turn over the Gaumont circuit in England and the Hoyt's chain in Australia to other investment groups, but these dealings were repudiated by W.C. Michel.[21] Meanwhile, William Fox entered the fray with a suit to recover more than $15,000,000 which he contributed toward the financing of shares in Gaumont British. Litigation following William Fox's departure would continue to plague the company for years.[22]

All the uncertainty must have made exhibitors wonder what exactly was going on at Fox. One of the more distressing rumors concerning one of Fox's biggest box-office stars was immediately suppressed.

> If Will Rogers is quitting pictures when his Fox contract expires, it's news to Fox executives in the East who say plans for his next two pictures are well under way.
>
> A Hollywood dispatch to the *New York Times* declares Rogers told friends he is thinking about quitting pictures to "become the world's airplane reporter." The Times story says Rogers is getting more than $60,000 yearly from Fox but gets $3,000 weekly from daily newspaper writings.
>
> The article also recounts that friends say Rogers prefers newspaper work and that he has considered establishing his residence in either London or Paris.[23]

To add a twist on William Fox's purchase of Loew's there was talk of a reverse takeover: "President Nicholas M. Schenck yesterday said that neither he nor M-G-M has ever had an option on the Fox studios under a reported deal whereby his interests were to take charge of production for Fox. He totally denied a report which said the option had just expired."[24]

To regain some confidence in Fox's ability to keep a steady flow of product, the studio stepped two pictures ahead of its announced January production schedule. Five were being filmed, five were in editing and five more were being prepared for production before the end of January.[25]

What Fox needed most was executive stability and President Edward Tinker created a new management board which consisted of, tellingly, Winfield R. Sheehan as chairman, and including D.E. McIntyre, business manager; Sol M. Wurtzel, general superintendent; George Bagnall, comptroller; Al Rockett, senior associate producer in charge of the business of the studio; Robert North, associate producer; and Richard A. Rowland, vice-president of the New York office. In the absence of Sheehan, W.C. Michel would be acting chairman.[26]

The production committee, created at Richard Rowland's suggestion, was headed by Al Rockett and included Robert North, William Goetz and Edmund Grainger as supervisors. Robert Yost was in charge of the scenario department; David Todd, head of casting; and Victor M. Shapiro, head of publicity. The group would meet weekly to discuss stories, players and ideas. Recommendations would be submitted to the management board for final action.[27]

Replacing the centralized core production people of Sheehan and Wurtzel, projects would now be discussed and decided on by committee. This new team, even with the experienced Wurtzel, was not strong enough to function successfully. The results would show up soon enough.

To rein in the costs of running the Fox theater chain which amounted to about $55,000,000 annually, the Skouras brothers — George, Spyros and Charles — longtime successful exhibitors, made a deal to take over the operation of all 550 houses, including 470 in the Fox West Coast chain as of February 15, 1932. The number of Fox-controlled houses was constantly changing with some leases ending, new ones being acquired, and shifting alliances in the chain.

It was also time for damage control at Fox as the company took out a double-page ad with a statement from the vice-president of sales, James R. Grainger.

> To the 9,078 Exhibitors who have already contracted for Fox pictures and who look to Fox Film Corporation for profitable guidance during 1932 is this frank statement and fact survey of future releases.
>
> Returning to New York from a visit to our production centre at Movietone City, Cal., I submit the following information of particularly timely interest to exhibitors:

1. Fox Film Corporation will positively release to exhibitors the full number of productions announced for 1931-32 availability, namely 48.

2. Twenty-two of these 48 attractions have been released. Nine negatives are at the Home Office in New York. Seventeen are in the course of production or in preparation.

After listing the releases, Grainger continued,

> These releases of box-office promise definitely prove and emphasize the truth of the statement that Fox Film Corporation is delivering to exhibitors a product that is conclusively setting the pace not only for quality of screen entertainment, but, for, what is vitally important, box-office profit.
> We will continue — to the very last letter — our policy of providing exhibitors with only the best and strongest possible box-office attractions for, after all, we profit maximumly only when theatres are enabled to do capacity business.
> In all truth, we can proudly say that a Fox Film playdate is most assuredly a positive pay day for exhibitors.
> Sincerely J.R. Grainger.[28]

Edward Tinker, a banker by profession, had taken over the presidency of the Fox companies out of necessity and always intended to step down when an industry executive could be found. He was finally able to effect a transition in February 1932.

Sidney R. Kent was born in 1886 in Lincoln, Nebraska, and after several years with the Colorado Fuel & Iron Company in Wyoming, he joined the Vitagraph Company. He was appointed, in April 1917, as sales manager of the General Film Company, the distribution end of the Edison combine.[29] Kent helped untangle the monopoly after its indictment under anti-trust laws, then joined Adolph Zukor's organization in distribution in 1916 and was made general sales manager in 1919. He was general manager of Paramount Pictures in 1926 and became vice-president when the corporation changed its name to Paramount-Publix in 1930. After 14 years with Paramount, Kent, whose contract had three years to run, left the company. He had been an extremely effective executive, just the kind of person with enough experience to run Fox. Kent joined the Fox Film Corporation as of April 4, 1932, and was made president of the company on May 15, 1932. Kent said, "There is no doubt in my mind that the company, long one of the leaders in the industry can not only be restored in due time to a position of prosperity, but will be a unit in the business of which everyone, officials, directors, stockholders and those in the industry who appreciate that a clean and healthy company, even as a competitor, is a decided asset to the entire business, may well be proud."[30]

Edward Tinker expressed his confidence in Kent's strength as an executive: "The election of Kent to the presidency of the Fox Film Corporation is a recognition of his ability as an executive and of his position as a leader in the industry. It is in keeping with plans formulated for the future of the company some months ago. It is the best possible assurance of continued improvement in the product of the company and of its restoration to a position of prosperity."[31] Tinker became chairman of the board for several more months but would leave Fox Films in the fall of 1932 to help in the reorganization of West Coast Theaters.[32]

Kent's entry into the company was accompanied by a directors' board vote to reduce the company's per share value to $5, which would bring the capitalization to $12,628,300 from $90,780,000.[33] This would have tax advantages but it would also put up a red flag to investors that the Fox Film Corporation was no longer worth investing in.

Among the immediate problems Sidney Kent had to deal with was the net loss of $4,263,557 for all of 1931 against a profit of $10,251,827 in the previous fiscal year. Theater-operation expenses had been reduced to $50,363,056 from $54,563,268 but were still an enormous burden. The cost of production in 1931 was $19,861,147, down from $26,203,623 in 1930, but it had not resulted in better product, simply less expensive films.

Due to the committee-run production panel, Fox films of the 1932 season were a decidedly lackluster group. Contemporary reviews pointed out a severe failing in the scripts of many films, possibly because they were rushed into production by a company desperate to fulfill its contracts.

After he appeared in several critically and commercially successful films, even Will Rogers was impacted by the new production measures. The review of *Business and Pleasure* slammed the "very choppy and ragged story with Will Rogers trying hard to get the laughs in a mechanical story.... The scenario is one of the most choppy and disconnected affairs offered to the screen fans in a long time."[34]

A reviewer of *She Wanted a Millionaire* pointed out the confusion that existed in a studio trying to throw every emotion into a story: "It is a trivial story with silly dialogue and some strangely absurd ideas. For a while it looks as though it would be a merry production.... Afterward it is thought expedient by the producers to have Norton's life ended by a bullet."[35]

The Devil's Lottery was a "rambling drama of mixed loves poorly motivated.... Director Sam Taylor did wonders with a loose knit drama ... that makes the film look better than it really is on close analysis."[36]

Judging *Cheaters at Play* less than exemplary was also obvious. "As a screen entertainment, it is a somewhat mechanical series of events with dialogue that savors of the old florid subtitles of silent films."[37]

Another in a succession of critical slams was *Careless Lady*, in which the "aimless story rambles mechanically and lacks any definite punch or interest.... The carelessness in the title seems to have drifted into the story construction, for it is weak and arouses no definite interest in any of the characters."[38]

The Trial of Vivienne Ware evoked a similar disdain: "If you stop to analyze the murder plot, it shapes up pretty threadbare, and is rather far-fetched and illogical in spots."[39]

Man About Town was yet another indication that there was no strong guiding force in the story department. "It is a rather involved tale, as if the author had started out with one main idea and got interested in another angle which seems to have led him astray."[40]

Even the much-lauded Frank Borzage could not muster favor in this period: "The director may have thought he could fashion from 'After Tomorrow' a subject comparable with his excellent silent film, 'Seventh Heaven' (1927) but this current contribution possesses none of the dramatic value or the poetic charm of the earlier work."[41]

The *New York Times* reviewer also felt *The Gay Caballero* was "so lacking in suspense," *The Devil's Lottery* was "somewhat weakened by its melodramatic turn in the latter stages," and the story in *Disorderly Conduct* was "a strained and implausible tale." The complaints about the artificiality and incoherence of Fox releases were almost as common as when critics pointed out the cheapness of William Fox's productions in the early 1920s.

However, perhaps a nadir was reached when a review for *Broadway Bad* began with, "The new picture at the Palace is mediocre enough to persuade the disinterested visitor that the title would be a more accurate description if read backward."[42]

The obvious question arises that if a studio is only as good as the man in charge, why was Winfield Sheehan, who had absolute control of production based on his contract signed with Harley Clarke, not relieved of his duties? Sheehan's position was even more questionable because, by now, he had developed a reputation on the lot as a bully who did not tolerate

Lilian Bond and Joan Bennett in *The Trial of Vivienne Ware* (1932) (courtesy Mike Hawks).

criticism or suggestions from others. The answer as to why he remained lies in the contract that Clarke signed. When Sheehan joined the anti–William Fox forces during the fight over company control, Clarke, rather green in the area of production, promised him a long-term play-or-pay deal that relinquished any studio options to fire him. As reported in an issue of the *Hollywood Reporter*, President Edward Tinker would have dismissed Sheehan but for that iron-clad contract.[43]

Without enough time to meet with production teams and devise a strategy that would return the production company to a coherently functioning entity, Sidney Kent was entering the sales period when studios were usually boastfully announcing their upcoming slate of pictures for the 1932-1933 film season.

At the annual sales convention in May, there were heated issues brought forth by branch managers, no doubt having to do with the instability of the company and the diminished quality and drawing power of the releases. With its abandonment of many of its theaters and the expiration of Fox's exclusive franchise for booking the Roxy in New York City, its showcase house, the exchange managers were now responsible for finding appropriate theaters for Fox product.[44]

Sidney Kent, meanwhile, praised the company salesmen, saying, "With all you have been through in the last two years, I don't know how you did it but it is a tribute to you that you have." He then assured the salesmen that he had no desire to tear down and rebuild the organization. He also said that Fox would make pictures "for the masses not the classes."[45]

A trade magazine report on the Fox convention included a startling admission made by Kent: "[The] practice of announcing 'phony' picture titles at the beginning of the selling season was condemned by Sidney R. Kent in speaking to Fox sales department men at their meeting yesterday. He described this policy as 'a thing of the past.' Fox is announcing only actual facts concerning its production plans, he said. Changeable conditions prevent a company from positively setting its lineup at the start of the season, Kent pointed out. 'Play the game on the level,' Kent admonished. Emphasizing the importance of developing exhibitor goodwill he told his auditors to keep their word on all transactions."[46]

Spyros Skouras addressed the convention in his new role, criticizing the "remote control" of theater operations. He endorsed a program that would localize operations and give house managers more latitude in exhibition. He had concluded a complete analysis of operations and came to the conclusion that there was a need to revive a "Barnum & Bailey type of exploitation." Exhibitors had "a moral obligation to exploit product intelligently and to the fullest extent possible."[47]

As astonishing as Sidney Kent's admission that studios tended to "phony up" release schedules, the following letter to exhibitors in the trades was without precedent. It was the end result of a lack of script development during Winfield Sheehan's illness, a rumored power struggle between Sheehan and Sol Wurtzel for control of production, and the ongoing financial woes at Fox.

> Every thinking exhibitor will realize that it is impossible, particularly with trade conditions as they are today, to choose intelligently and to announce in advance a complete list of the titles, stories and casts that will constitute this company's product for the coming year. The public taste changes, world events make new subjects timely, new plays, new books, and original stories which promise much fail to develop under treatment. Frequent changes must be made if showmanship standards are to be maintained.
>
> Our interest is the same as yours. We operate many theatres. It is to our interest as exhibitors as well as to the interest of our exhibitor customers, that we be sure our product is new and timely and that it makes the most of the showmanship opportunities and ideas of the moment. For us to say at this time that we have bought and are prepared to cast and produce for a full and exact list of the pictures we will make during the coming year, would be dishonest and would serve notice on the trade that we are in no position to purchase and produce the best of what becomes available during that year.
>
> With those thoughts in mind we are announcing sincerely and as definitely as humanly possible, a production schedule of approximately two-thirds of next year's output. This list constitutes a well balanced selection of strong stories. It leaves us the opportunity to purchase the best stories that develop during the year and to take advantage of showmanship opportunities as they arise. It is our belief that such a policy frankly stated is the best guarantee for box-office prosperity for ourselves and our customers.[48]

It is possible, but not likely, that Kent's excuse for not announcing a full slate was to leave open the opportunity to acquire "fresh" material. It is much more likely that the studio could not provide him with enough viable projects to fill up an entire season. Rather than opening himself up to accusations from exhibitors, already dissatisfied with Fox product, that he was selling a program that would never materialize, Kent was forced to present the studio's production situation as it really was—in terrible shape.

An interesting example of this was the ill-fated production of *Walking Down Broadway*. The project was originally announced for the new season with an ad that read, "James Dunn ... Sally Eilers ... Irrepressible youth — glorified. Acclaimed the wonder team of 1931-32 and the box-office pacemakers of 1932-33.... A boy and a girl from Main Street whose love conquers the Main stem. Drama of sunlight and shadow ... mirth and misery ... cruelty and caresses ... truth and deception ... understanding and forgiveness."[49]

Sheehan had signed Erich von Stroheim to direct a film based on the unpublished play *Walking Down Broadway*, from which he and Fox staff writer Leonard Spigelgass prepared an outline. Stroheim was dismissed in February 1932 while Sheehan was on sick leave. After shooting for several weeks, the film was in limbo until Sheehan returned in June and reassigned Stroheim. James Dunn and Minna Gombell were set to star at this point. After heading off some censorship issues raised by the Hays Office, the script was approved for shooting. Initial filming began in August and was completed in mid–October 1932. Scheduled for release in November 1932, a double-page trade ad heralded the film with the catchline, "Life itself wrote this story — Genius brings living to your screen." Unfortunately, there was not enough genius, since it was shelved again and Sheehan ordered much re-shooting, this time without Stroheim. The film was finally released in 1933 as *Hello, Sister*, and what may have started out as an artistic attempt ended up a total failure. It was an example of being caught in the Fox production blender that quite apparently was churning out less-than-well-conceived projects in this period. The *Film Daily* commented that the film was "for adults only. Its story is hackneyed and considerably off-color, with dialogue which at times cannot be described as wholesome."[50]

Even with Sidney Kent's "honesty" about the two-thirds of the 1932-1933 slate of films, many were not produced as announced. This is a brief summary:

Promised: Three productions with Janet Gaynor and Charles Farrell: *Precious, Elegant Arms, Untitled*.
Delivered: Two films with Gaynor and Farrell, *The First Year, Tess of the Storm Country*. Three other pictures were substituted for the third Gaynor-Farrell: *Wild Girl* starring Farrell; *Adorable* with Gaynor and Henry Garat; and *State Fair* starring Gaynor.
Promised and delivered: Will Rogers in *Down to Earth*, and *Untitled* which became *State Fair*.
Promised: Four with James Dunn and Sally Eilers: *Walking Down Broadway, Checkers, Born Wild, Okay*.
Delivered: Dunn and Eilers in *Sailor's Luck* and *Hold Me Tight*; Dunn in *Handle with Care* with Boots Mallory; Dunn in *Hello Sister* with ZaSu Pitts; Dunn in *Arizona to Broadway* with Joan Bennett; Eilers in *Hat Check Girl* with Ben Lyon; Eilers in *Second Hand Wife* with Ralph Bellamy; Eilers co-starring in *State Fair*; *Okay* became *Jimmy and Sally* with Dunn and Eilers, but it was released in the next season.
Promised: Three with Joan Bennett: *Bought on Time, Easy, Untitled*.
Delivered: *Weekends Only* with Bennett and Ben Lyon; *Wild Girl* with Bennett and Charles Farrell; *Me and My Gal* with Bennett and Spencer Tracy.
Promised: Three with Warner Baxter: *Desert Flame* with Peggy Shannon and directed by John Francis Dillon, *Trick for Trick*, and *Kiss of Courage* with Marian Nixon (a Cisco Kid story).
Delivered: *Six Hours to Live* with Baxter and Miriam Jordan; *Dangerously Yours* with Baxter and Miriam Jordan; *I Loved You Wednesday* with Baxter and Elissa Landi. *Trick for Trick* starred Edmund Lowe when produced in 1933.
Promised & Delivered: Clara Bow in *Call Her Savage*.
Promised: Five George O'Brien adventures: *The Last Trail, Robbers Roost, Canyon Walls, Arizona Wildcat, Whirlwind Romeo*.
Delivered: *The Last Trail, Robbers Roost, Smoke Lightning, Life in the Raw, Mystery Ranch*.
Promised: Four with Elissa Landi; *Red Dancer* with Ralph Bellamy and directed by John Blystone; *Glamorous; Forgotten Kisses* from the Noel Coward play; *Untitled*.
Delivered: Three with Landi: *A Passport to Hell, The Warrior's Husband, I Loved You Wednesday*.
Promised: Two with Edmund Lowe: *Chandu the Magician, Title to Come*.
Delivered: *Chandu the Magician, Hot Pepper*.
Promised: *Cavalcade; What Price Glory* with Spencer Tracy, Ralph Bellamy, and El Brendel, directed by William K. Howard; *Little Teacher* with Spencer Tracy and Marian Nixon; *The Inside Story* with Ralph Bellamy and Peggy Shannon; *Havoc* with Spencer Tracy and Peggy Shannon, directed by William K. Howard; *Apartment House Love* with El Brendel and Marian Nixon; *Bitter Sweet*, play by Noel Coward; *Shanghai Madness; The Cry of the World; Six Hours to Live* (became Baxter property), *On Parade* with Marian Nixon, directed by Sidney Lanfield; *Bad Boy; Hat Check Girl* with Peggy Shannon, John Boles and El Brendel; *Congorilla; Rackety Rax* with Spencer Tracy, Greta Nissen and El Brendel.
Delivered: *Cavalcade; Shanghai Madness* with Tracy; *Apartment House Love* released as *Olsen's Big Moment; Cry of the World*, documentary; *Hat Check Girl* with Eilers; *Bad Boy* became *Sailor's Luck* with Dunn and Eilers; *Congorilla*, documentary; *Rackety Rax* with Victor McLaglen; *Six Hours to Live* with Warner Baxter; *Face in the Sky* with Spencer Tracy and Marian Nixon; *Trick for Trick* with Edmund Lowe.
Delivered but not announced: *Bachelor's Affairs, Rebecca of Sunnybrook Farm, Almost Married, The*

Painted Woman, Sherlock Holmes, Infernal Machine, Broadway Bad, Humanity, After the Ball, Pleasure Cruise, Bondage, Zoo in Budapest, It's Great to Be Alive, Best of Enemies, The Man Who Dared, The Devil's In Love.

Surprisingly not mentioned in advance, although he appeared in two of the films was Victor McLaglen, who was most likely going through contract negotiations and could not be billed until his deal was signed. In an odd irony, Elissa Landi's film, *A Passport to Hell*, was originally titled *Undesirable Lady*. She indeed proved undesirable at Fox and this film lost $172,000. After two more flops her contract was not renewed.

Sidney Kent was, no doubt, in an awkward position with his first slate of pictures and blamed the lack of definite projects on the company's failure to groom new executives. When he took over the helm, he announced that Fox was looking ahead with a five-year perspective. Winfield Sheehan and Sol Wurtzel were due back at the studio around June 1. Without any further explanation of his absence, Sheehan would assume complete charge of production. No explanation followed Wurtzel, who would resume his duties as general superintendent. Production would continue at a normal pace at that point.

Kent also made it clear that Fox was on an all-out program to develop two new stars each year. The first announcement Winfield Sheehan made when he returned was to sign Lita Grey Chaplin, Charlie Chaplin's ex-wife, and her two sons, to appear in five Fox films over three years.[51] It was an inauspicious beginning to the program because Mr. Chaplin enjoined his wife from putting their sons in front of a camera, and none of the three ever made a Fox Film.

Fox stock sank to yet a new low of $1¼ per share by May 27, 1932. A $1,922,627 loss in first-quarter 1932 compared to profit of $974,704 in 1931 did not help. Charges for the quarter included $714,000 for settlement of contracts entered into in previous years. A.C. Blumenthal settled his lawsuit against Fox for commissions as a broker in a deal whereby Fox acquired a group of metropolitan theaters. The settlement of $700,000 was paid with $50,000 down and $5,000 weekly for two and a half years.[52] William Fox's personal attorney, Saul E. Rogers, who had been legal counsel for the company since its founding, had his contract settled in April 1932. "Though the amount of money involved has not been made known, it is understood to be a substantial amount."[53] Rogers returned to private law practice.

Gross income of Fox's film rentals also dropped precipitously to $19,231,567 from $25,458,223 in 1931.[54] Again, it was not the only company experiencing trouble. By the end of June, RKO showed a nine-month net loss of $4,964,331.[55] Harry M. Warner was surprisingly optimistic when his company reported a net loss of $11,224,550 for 1932 saying, "The company has been equal to every demand made upon it during the period of this depression."[56] Paramount reported the heaviest quarterly losses of $5,900,000 for three months ending in June.[57] Movie attendance nationwide had dropped precipitously from a weekly average of 110,000,000 admissions at its peak in 1929, to 60,000,000 in 1932.

The companies with the heaviest concentrations of theaters were the losers. To reduce overhead, the RKO chain planned to close 35 theaters during the two-week period leading up to Christmas when those houses ordinarily lost more than their rent during that season. Its takeover of the Roxy in New York gave it a $90,000 weekly payout for just this one venue, with a potential $140,000 to $145,000 gross at capacity attendance.[58] Unfortunately, capacity was not reached often enough.

There was still some hope for the motion picture industry. Film stocks were beginning to rise in response to more upbeat reports on the economy. At the outset of August 1932, Loew's touched 24½, up 11 points from its year's low; Paramount closed at 4 up from its low of 1½. Warners, which had been down to ½, reached 2¼. RKO rose to 4 from 1½. Fox was at 2¼ from its low of 1. Edward R. Tinker, still Fox chairman of the board at this point, noted that the optimism in the financial outlook of the company was also noticeable in the overall operation.[59] James Grainger also expressed the feeling that business would get better: "In my travels around the country I find that the exhibitor morale has vastly improved. They confidently look to the studios for product of box-office calibre."[60]

Grainger set up an important deal that would have Fox's entire year of releases play in 100 percent of Publix Theaters. This deal, along with others similar, were what made Grainger so valuable to the company. By late August, Grainger was able to announce that Fox sales were 11 percent ahead of the previous year while also acknowledging the efforts of his sales force. The question was, would Fox deliver films that would perform at the box-office?

Activity at the studio picked up considerably with five features shooting, four nearing completion and two scheduled to start. Two of the films fulfilled the company's commitment for Will Rogers, and there were two more with Janet Gaynor. Fox set an ambitious release schedule of ten films for the last three months of 1932.

Not overlooking the broad Spanish-language market, John Stone was made head of Fox foreign production in June 1932. Director Eugene Forde was Stone's assistant. There were 17–20 Spanish productions planned for the year. José Mojica, discovered in Mexico, would star in three and Argentine Raúl Roulien in two. Sam Wurtzel was appointed business manager for the unit and editor Louis Loeffler became head of the technical department.[61]

In a shake-up of the story department in New York, Albert Lewis, with Fox since 1928, "resigned" in August 1932, even though his contract ran through the end of 1933. Lewis was credited with bringing a number of successful stage writers to Fox, as well as contributing "many successful stories."[62] Richard Rowland and Florence Strauss were assigned Lewis's duties. Former newspaperman and longtime screenwriter, Julian Johnson, was now the west coast scenario editor.

Other studios had problems adjusting to the writing needs of talking pictures, but most were able to overcome them relatively quickly. Paramount, Warner Bros. and M.G.M. hired the best writers, many with journalism backgrounds and a facility for sophisticated dialogue and fast-moving stories. Writers who entered the field at this time learned the techniques associated with sound films and were more adept at merging their talents with the moviemaking requirements of speed and efficiency.

Fox Films had never been known as a writers' studio since there was no strong hand guiding the scenario department. As well, the many recent absences of Winfield Sheehan and Sol Wurtzel meant there was no potent producer supervision comparable to Thalberg and Mayer at M.G.M., David O. Selznick at R.K.O. and Darryl F. Zanuck at Warner Bros. Paramount happened to be lucky to hire skilled writers like Ben Hecht, Herman Mankiewicz, and Joseph Mankiewicz, all of whom worked well with their directors and fashioned clever, sophisticated entertainments. Columbia, for the most part a grade-B studio, was fortunate to have writers like Robert Riskin, Sidney Buchman and Jo Swerling work with Frank Capra on films which propelled that minor company into the major league. Fox still suffered from a haphazard mechanism for purchasing and developing story material.

To make up for a shortage of product, Fox organized a British production arm to experiment with making films for England that could also be marketed in the United States. Not only would these productions qualify under British quota terms, they might also provide Fox with fresh talent.

To fill the gap in domestic production needs, a deal was signed with Jesse L. Lasky, pioneer showman and original partner of Adolph Zukor, with whom Sidney Kent had a long relationship. Lasky had recently left Paramount and was to supply Fox with eight films annually for "a term of years." Fox completely financed all the films and Lasky had his own unit with an executive manager, an associate producer and a story editor. All production would take place at Movietone City and within a reasonable budget.[63] Story ideas had to be submitted to Fox production heads for approval. When that was done, Lasky would carry out production without any interference. Lasky's participation reached a 50-50 split of profits, after Fox took production costs and a 30 percent distribution fee from the total rentals.[64]

Lasky felt that the "old" system of a large program of pictures supervised by a single studio head was over: "There is no other solution to the problem of making good box-office pictures." He firmly believed that formula pictures were without value, and that the public wanted different, unconventional themes. Audiences could no longer be persuaded to see routine pictures. Finally, Lasky wanted to encourage producers to experiment with new types of stories. Titles of the pictures, too, should be unusual in order to attract and arouse public interest.[65]

The reason for Lasky's departure from Paramount only became public a year later when Adolph Zukor went on the record saying that "early in 1932 the company believed the 'production department was spending too much money—pictures didn't measure up to their cost. We wanted to investigate the studio situation ... but were afraid it might embarrass Lasky, so we asked him to take a three months' vacation and then went ahead with the investigation. As a result of that we made some changes and Lasky subsequently stepped out.'" Zukor did not know whether Lasky had ever tendered a resignation. "He just stepped out of the company."[66] This shaky explanation of Lasky's departure after being with Paramount for so many years is obviously open to interpretation. However, it can be inferred that Lasky pictures were costing too much and earning too little.

With Lasky in place, Sidney Kent put to rest the uncertainty over what was to happen with the British-Gaumont theaters in England by settling a dispute with principals Isadore Ostrer and W.J. Gell, confirming that Fox would hold onto the chain. Finally, for the first time since William Fox's departure 2½ years before, there was a president running the company who understood the priorities of Fox Films and Fox Theaters. "Never have we seen the dynamic Mr. Kent in more aggressive form," wrote The *Film Daily*'s Jack Alicoate, "and, as a reflection of his leadership, the morale of the entire Fox outfit is once again at high pitch."[67]

Like Harley Clarke before him, Kent started bringing in people he had worked with at Paramount. However, these were more experienced people in key positions. A major change in the sales division occurred when James Grainger announced his resignation to make way for Kent's selection of John D. Clark as general manager of distribution. Clark had been with Fox since December 1932, when he left his position as western division sales manager of Paramount. Grainger's statement made clear the tension that existed but it was couched in the most "amicable" of terms: "Honest differences of opinion with reference to distribution policies of Fox have arisen between Sidney R. Kent, the president of the corporation, and myself. The exchange of views between us were carried on in the most amicable and understanding manner, and at no time have there been any but the most friendly relations between us. In view of the fact that this discrepancy occurred, it was deemed advisable by Mr. Kent that the corporation and I attempt an amicable adjustment of my contract. And in the interim I take a leave of absence on full pay pursuant to my contract, pending the consummation of such settlement."[68] For Fox, it would be another contract of $2,500 weekly to pay off for two years.

Charles McCarthy, who had been with Paramount for 15 years, abruptly resigned and became director of publicity and advertising at Fox. Harley Clarke's choice of New York story department head, Richard Rowland and his assistant, Florence Strauss, were replaced by former Paramount story executive D.A. Doran. Nevertheless, Rowland stayed on as a vice-president in charge of acquiring story material on the east coast with his responsibilities being further diminished. More Paramount executives would follow to round out the team in New York, but production on the west coast was left to Sheehan, Wurtzel and their units. Kent confirmed this when he told the *Hollywood Reporter* that "anyone who anticipated that he would make revolutionary changes in the company's studio set-up would be disappointed."[69] He did, however, announce a realignment of executive control of the business and physical operation of the studio that placed John J. Gain in the post of studio manager to handle all business details and operation of the plant, with Edward Butcher continuing as production manager and George N. Bagnall as studio treasurer. Sol Wurtzel was relieved of the physical and business ends of the studio for the first time since 1917 to concentrate his efforts in production. Kent added: "I am highly pleased with the progress that has been made under Sheehan, and the changes that are being made are purely in the physical operation of the plant in the perfecting of a studio organization."[70]

Even with industry smiles about the future, reality had a nasty habit of intervening. As a sign of the economic times, the Roxy Theater cut its admission to 25 cents for children at all times and 55 cents to 75 cents for adults. This reflected a 25 percent reduction which would result in comparably lower rentals at the box-office.

Meanwhile, M.G.M. head of production, Irving Thalberg, declared that "cheap pictures are a crime." Thalberg insisted that "stars must be maintained in order to sustain patron interest ... and new stars must be developed. I particularly expect Jean Harlow, Clark Gable and Helen Hayes to acquire big fan followings."[71]

It was the opinion of M.G.M., which was establishing itself as the number-one studio, that each picture was a separate entity and deserved to be treated as such. Metro had, for years, moved away from the cookie-cutter theory of production, and was restating what had always been its policy. As much of a trend-setter as M.G.M. may have been, the industry was not going to budge from reusing what was tried-and-true.

As to the issue of developing new stars, M.G.M. was certainly among the most successful. Fox, on the other hand, was almost the opposite. Considering the financial resources at hand and the talent under contract, Fox was especially inept. Of course, hindsight is always an easy vantage point for criticism. Nevertheless, Sheehan, Wurtzel and William Fox had totally misjudged John Gilbert's potential as a silent star. In the period of the talkies, Fox Films contracted and lost Humphrey Bogart, Jeanette MacDonald, Ralph Bellamy, Maureen O'Sullivan, Joel McCrea, Myrna Loy,

Sally Eilers and James Dunn cut a rug in *Dance Team* (1932) (courtesy Mike Hawks).

and Spencer Tracy to name just a few, yet tried to resurrect Clara Bow several years after she was off the screen. There were misfired attempts to launch Elissa Landi, Victor Jory, Marguerite Churchill, Miriam Jordan, Alexander Kirkland, Greta Nissen, and Lilian Harvey.

When there was a star who had clicked with audiences, the easy route was to keep pumping out similar films, much like the tried-and-true format that Irving Thalberg decried. But that's exactly what Fox did in 1932. As a result, the value of Warner Baxter, Victor McLaglen, Charles Farrell, Sally Eilers, James Dunn, and Joan Bennett decreased measurably as their contracts aged. Not even Will Rogers could be counted on with any regularity. His well-reviewed comedy, *Down to Earth*, lost a surprising $100,000. Another Rogers picture, *Too Busy to Work*, ended up a loser as well. Exemplifying the lack of production finesse at Fox, Rogers's third film of the year, *Business and Pleasure*, noted for its lowercase script, was not only the most expensive picture of 1932 at a cost of $585,000 but it resulted in the largest loss—$219,000.

Janet Gaynor, whose popularity seemed to withstand the repetitive nature of Fox films, starred once again with Charles Farrell in *The First Year* and it was one of the year's profit makers. Another was the duo in *Tess of the Storm Country*, but the level of profit was definitely down from previous years. When Farrell was teamed with Marian Nixon in Frank Borzage's *After Tomorrow*, the results were not nearly as rewarding. The film lost a modest sum.

The most profitable film of the year, *Dance Team*, starred James Dunn and Sally Eilers. But even for the top-profit picture of the year, the return was a meager $187,000. Other notable money losers were *She Wanted a Millionaire* with Spencer Tracy and Joan Bennett. Tracy was nowhere near a moneymaking star as his next film *Me and My Gal*, also with Joan Bennett, lost nearly $100,000. Elissa Landi in *The Devil's Lottery* lost $128,000. Still riding on the coattails of *Daddy Long Legs* (1931), Warner Baxter starred in the profitable *Amateur Daddy*. However, it was not nearly as successful as the previous film. The much-touted production of the classic *Rebecca of Sunnybrook Farm* was only a marginal success with Marian Nixon.

Even though Winfield Sheehan had been able to reduce the average negative cost in 1932 to $293,305 from $345,153 in 1930, rentals had

Warner Baxter is an *Amateur Daddy* (1932) to Marian Nixon (courtesy Mike Hawks).

dropped so dramatically that more than two-thirds of revenue was needed to cover production costs. With the lowest number of releases for any year since 1925, the ratio of production cost was the highest on record since the company was founded. The Fox Film Corporation showed a loss of $1,554,289 on its slate of films for 1932.

In a national movie preference poll conducted by the Hays Office, the most popular genres were exotic jungle stories like *Tarzan*, *Trader Horn* (both M.G.M. films) and *Bring 'Em Back Alive*. Detective stories, sea stories and aviation dramas were also popular.[72] Fox, instead, had a preponderance of melodramas, social dramas, hokey sentimental dramas, homespun Americana, westerns, college comedies, and mysteries. Only the occasional *Charlie Chan* entry or *Congorilla*, a documentary, would fit the profile that the preference poll suggested. *Congorilla* actually proved to be one of the more successful releases of the year, costing only $37,000 and showing a profit of $122,000.

At the beginning of 1933, when the "year's best" lists were published, 152 films were mentioned as contenders by the nation's critics. Paramount scored with 15 on the honor list, while M.G.M. placed with 11, Warner–First National reached the list with nine, RKO took three places, Columbia had two, United Artists, the independent World Wide Pictures and the Fox Film Corporation tied for last place with a single title.[73]

Just five years earlier, Fox was considered the leader in entertainment, with a roster of popular new stars, stories that brought audiences to their local theaters, and grosses that made exhibitors happy. Fox had also been a pioneer in the field of talking pictures, leading the way for the industry. Its once state-of-the-art studio in New York, where Movietone was tested and developed, was taken over by the Western Electric subsidiary, ERPI, for its own theatrical productions. By the end of 1932, the company was a shadow of its once innovative self.

12. Back from the Abyss

Fox Films opened 1933 with a hugely uplifting response to the first release of the year, *Cavalcade*, "A fine, splendid document of the folly and resultant decline of civilization through the tragedies of war."[1] The *New York Herald-Tribune* raved: "The finest photoplay that has yet been made in the English language." The *New York Post* claimed, "For sheer emotional sweep and showmanship the screen has produced nothing quite like it." The raves continued with the *New York Times* adding that it was "a most affecting and impressive picture. Many an eye will be misty after witnessing this production."[2] The *Boston Evening American* chimed in: "A film that is a gold medal for Hollywood. In every respect the peer of the very best films, silent or sound."[3] *Cavalcade* was scheduled to debut in roadshow engagements in 14 major cities.

An interesting sidebar to the release of *Cavalcade* was a trade editorial by W.R. Wilkerson that gave some background on how the movie came to be made.

> At the time this story was purchased by Mrs. Edward R. Tinker, the wife of the president of Fox, there was a lifting of eyebrows throughout the entire show world. And when Winnie Sheehan assured Hollywood that it would be produced by Fox, there were laughs of derision throughout all of the film capital.
>
> Never in the history of the picture business, was a picture so universally relegated to the scrap heap, weeks and months before the production was shown. The consensus of opinion was that Fox would make a picture with an all–British cast for release in the British market, that there was hardly a chance that it would ever see an American release because the story was 100 per cent British and would hold no entertainment for American picture-goers.
>
> Wonder how those "guessers" feel now? All of their talk, all of their logic, all of their shaking of heads in pity for Fox and the "bundle that Mrs. Tinker unloaded in their lap" have been knocked into a cocked hat for the picture as shown in New York and here in Hollywood Thursday night, is one of the finest this industry has ever had and will CERTAINLY return its cost of $900,000 (more or less) to the Fox exchequer with a nice profit, long before its exhibition has been completed.... It should teach them that, regardless of the type of story, IF THERE IS A STORY, it will make a good picture if given the proper production.[4]

The actual cost of *Cavalcade* was $1,116,000 and it was most definitely not a guaranteed success. In fact, if its foreign grosses followed the usual 40 percent of domestic returns, the film would have lost money. In a turnaround, the foreign gross was almost double the $1,000,000 domestic take to reach total world rentals of $3,000,000 and Fox's largest profit of the year at $664,000.

The effusive reception for *Cavalcade* was matched by the release of *State Fair* less than one month later. "Great cast and ace entertainment. Fine human interest story packed with laughs and heart punch," crowed the *Film Daily*. "It is a homey tale, with many an intriguing bit." The *New York Times* enthused, "Mr. Rogers is excellent in his role."[5] Both films carried a credit for Winfield Sheehan as producer.

Finally, with something to boast about, a Fox trade ad carried the upbeat reports that *State Fair* was "headed for a world's attendance record" at the newly opened Radio City Music Hall in Manhattan with 115,822 admissions in the first five days. A little too much ebullience followed as the ad overstated, "All eyes turn to FOX the miracle worker ... as the FOX cavalcade of hits makes the picture habit popular with millions."[6]

State Fair did turn out to be a substantial hit with the help of Janet Gaynor boosting Will Rogers back to the level of money-making star. Its prestige engagements helped rake in a total $1,208,000 in domestic rentals. Surprisingly, in foreign countries unfamiliar with state fairs, it still earned a respectable $429,000. With its total rentals, the film ended up showing a $398,000 profit.

Within days, however, it was back to a release that led the *Hollywood Reporter* reviewer to remark, "It is difficult to believe that the same company, within the same thirty days, could turn out such a masterpiece as 'Cavalcade' and then produce a picture like 'Face in the Sky.' ... In its present form, it is the most amazing conglomeration of unmotivated sequences, gags lugged in by the ears, reminiscences of 'Sunrise' in the wildest Murnau manner and misplaced emphasis on extraneous production values—as they are still called by those who attach importance to them — that has romped across a talking screen."[7] *Face in the Sky* was yet another Spencer Tracy vehicle that flopped at the box-office.

The success of *State Fair* influenced Fox to plan all-star casts for its upcoming "specials." The problem, however, was a shortage of star power. The studio announced that seven new screen personalities would be coming to Fox Films in 1933. They included noted European stars Lilian Harvey

Janet Gaynor, a major Fox star even without Charles Farrell, and Margaret Livingston in *Paddy, the Next Best Thing* (1933) (courtesy Mike Hawks).

There was also an obvious and immediate move afoot at Fox to address the issue of execrable script material. Associate producers William Goetz, Walter Morosco and Lydell Peck, soon to be sued for divorce by Janet Gaynor, were moved into executive positions in the scenario department (under Julian Johnson's guidance) to institute a new policy of concentrating more effort in story preparation. Goetz, dissatisfied with the move, soon left for RKO. Peck left the day Gaynor won her divorce in April 1933, after four years of marriage. The quality of Fox screenplays would remain a hit-and-miss proposition.

and Henry Garat, Heather Angel, stage star Philip Merivale, Una O'Connor and Merle Tottenham, and Henrietta Crosman. Once again, although these performers did show talent, they would not reach the level of box-office stars.

Pressure was mounting from banking interests invested in motion picture companies for studios to cut costs immediately. In effect, bankers were telling producers that there would be no further financing of their companies unless something was done to reverse the huge

Fox's top directors huddle for a publicity photograph. From left: Frank Lloyd, Henry King, John Ford, Frank Borzage, circa 1933 (courtesy Robert S. Birchard).

outflow of capital. Receiverships were announced and both RKO and Paramount were under orders to re-organize their businesses. Paramount-Publix eventually went into bankruptcy, which gave the corporation an opportunity to nullify expensive leases on theaters and renegotiate terms that were more favorable. The bankruptcy resulted in the de-listing of Paramount stock which had fallen to 25 cents per share and was virtually worthless. In a sign of acquiescence to the bankers, Paramount, in its reorganized form, announced that its films would be limited to an average production cost of $250,000.

The Fox West Coast chain would fall into receivership in February 1933. "The strain of heavy rentals, plus a flop in business, estimated at 50 per cent drop below normal, have made it impossible for this big group to function at anything approaching a profit, and the result has been that the group has been taking it on the nose for the past 14 months with terrific weekly losses." The Skouras brothers, operating the chain, hoped that the protection of a receiver would allow leases to be adjusted to permit the heavily burdened houses to break even.[8] Assets were pegged at about $6,500,000, but liabilities totaled $19,011,250. Included in the money owed was $2,456,195 to Fox Films. A sign that every company associated with the film business was in trouble was underlined by Western Electric's loss of $12,625,892 for 1932.

Studio bosses, backed by the Hays Office and the Academy of Motion Pictures, took advantage of this issue to demand compulsory pay cuts to give their companies a chance to balance the books. Anyone who refused the cut would be placed on unpaid leave. The edict would affect everyone in the business, from stars to producers, directors to studio technicians, distribution executives to theater managers. There was considerable fallout from union leaders who felt that the brunt should be carried by the high-paid executives and stars who could more easily afford a drop in income. Some negotiations and compromises were made, but basically everyone would feel the pain for the good of the industry. Darryl F. Zanuck, at Warner Bros., went so far as to declare that anyone who did not comply with this patriotic effort was a person with whom he would not want to work.

Pay cuts only exacerbated relations between everyday workers who felt their bosses were nepotistic fat cats only concerned with taking the lion's share of the industry's lucre. In effect, there was some truth to that belief. This led one anonymous lower-level executive to shift the blame for financial woes back to the highest paid industry leaders in a tongue-in-cheek ad in the *Hollywood Reporter*:

> WARNING — Mr. L.B. Mayer, Mr. A.L. Rockett, Mr. Carl Laemmle, Mr. B.B. Kahane, Mr. Jack Warner, Mr. Harry Cohn, Mr. B.P. Schulberg, Mr. Charles R. Rogers, Mr. Sam Katz, Mr. Emanuel Cohen and all executives: Don't answer this advertisement; because I am a KILLER of inefficiency and waste — because I am poison to yes men, crooked executives and all others who have thrown this industry into its present chaotic condition. I am now employed in an executive capacity next to the head man of a major studio. I have a fine education and reputation, but don't hold it against me. I am white, young, married and abhor Hitler. GOD KNOWS YOU NEED ME LIKE A CRIPPLE NEEDS A CRUTCH.[9]

The result of pressure from the banks was that the studio chiefs came to an agreement to institute across-the-board cuts of 50 percent for anyone with a weekly salary over $50 for a trial period of eight weeks. At the Fox Film Corporation, once again under the threat of receivership, Winfield Sheehan was the first to voluntarily take a cut in his weekly salary of $5,000. This did give the major companies a period of time when revenues could catch up with expenses.

One other result of the salary cut was the creation of the Screen Writers' Guild, which was formed after writers were dissatisfied with their representation in the pay dispute by the Academy of Motion Pictures. The Guild, under the newly elected president, John Howard Lawson, set standards for the elimination of unfair practices and prepared guidelines so that studios gave writers fair recognition for their work in a film's credits. No longer could producers continue the practice of expecting writers to discuss story ideas without pay. Once formed, there was a rush for membership since many writers had long been accustomed to shabby treatment by producers and studios.

Along with other studios, Sheehan set a limit on Fox budgets in a new program of between 20 and 24 pictures. He and Jesse Lasky, assisted by Al Rockett, would supervise eight to ten films budgeted between $250,000 and $300,000 each, all produced at Movietone City. Sol Wurtzel would make 12 to 15 films on the Western Avenue lot, budgeted at a top figure of $100,000, which included all foreign-language productions.[10] The Wurtzel unit consisted of John Stone as associate producer, Jesse L. Lasky, Jr., and R.L. Hough. Robert M. Yost headed the story department, and Harold

Lipsitz was story scout. Eugene Forde supervised foreign versions, with assistance from Max Golden and Sam Wurtzel as business managers. Barney Wolf was the unit's film editor. There were eight writers on the team, including Dudley Nichols, Arthur Kober, Charlotte Miller, Marguerite Roberts and Irene Lee. Foreign-production writers were Gregorio Martinez Sierra, José López Rubio and Paul Perez. Former agent James Ryan was enlisted as casting director. Wurtzel's unit would still have access to all the resources and stages of both lots as well as the roster of players.[11]

As of the February 1933 release of a George O'Brien western, *Smoke Lightning*, Wurtzel was receiving producer credit on some films. Winfield Sheehan had received his first producer credit on the more prestigious Will Rogers film, *State Fair*. Other producers, like Jesse Lasky, would get credit as well on their films. This was a further indication of the decentralization of production at the Fox lots. Executive producers would be responsible for the success or failure of their films.

All the cost-cutting measures were still not enough to satisfy the Chase Bank, which serviced much of Fox's debt. In late February 1933, Sidney Kent issued an order to halt all production and postpone pictures that were scheduled to start. The studio was inactive for an entire week. The face-saving statement to the trades was that there were six features already in the works and Fox was unable to handle more. The trades saw through the ruse and realized the reasons for the halt were due to finances.[12] The trades were correct in their assumptions. The Chase Bank had informed the Fox Film Corporation that it would not provide any further financing. This meant that Fox would have to find money elsewhere, not an easy task in a depression and with a company under such financial pressures. Chase was willing, however, to write off all loans to the company as losses so that Fox could reorganize. Chase had determined that the company no longer had any worthwhile investment potential. Whether Fox did re-emerge as a successful and viable entity was of no concern to Chase. Chase executives withdrew from the board of directors and were replaced with industry-associated persons by Sidney Kent. This move also gave Sidney Kent complete control of the company operations.

Kent immediately announced that there would be no receivership based on a deal he had worked out with Chase for interim financing and the corporation would pay no interest on loans until April 1, 1933. Even with that leeway, it was difficult to find new sources of financing and the bank's patience was running out. As of March 25, 1933, the Chase Bank was preparing to foreclose on Fox for money due the bank, estimated at between $100,000,000 and $150,000,000. If this action was taken, it would mean that Chase would own all of Fox's interest in Loew's, Gaumont and its domestic theaters, the only assets with any value to the bank. Sidney Kent would be given a chance to reorganize the company minus those assets and, if he failed, Fox Films would be liquidated and anything of value would be sold. This was as close to extinction that any company could come.

Probably, no one, not even William Fox, could have prevented the predicament brought on by the depression and its effect on revenues to the industry. However, while Fox Films and Fox Theaters were in the hands of Harley Clarke and the Chase banking interests, $14,000,000 was paid out in dividends to shareholders during 1930 and 1931, based on profits still flowing through from the good times.

With William Fox's experience and the claim that he knew every theater's gross on a daily basis, it is probable that he would have seen the impending disaster and made some adjustments in his theater holdings, financial arrangements and production tech-

The original title card art for *Servant's Entrance* (1934), featuring Winfield Sheehan's producing credit (courtesy Robert S. Birchard).

niques. He might have suspended the payments of dividends as well, retaining that capital for operational expenses. Unfortunately, this is all speculation.

William Fox had weathered other downturns before and somehow pulled through. Even after being forced out of his company, he was still hoping to have a chance to regain control. As creditors lined up, Fox sat on the sidelines with a great deal of cash available from his sale of company stock. "Intimates are certain that the one great ambition of Fox, aside from his health, is to get back Fox Film and believe that the time is ripe now for his grab."[13]

Obviously, some remedies needed to be applied to Fox's dismal condition as a purveyor of quality entertainment. However, the call out came from an unlikely source — a trade paper. The *Hollywood Reporter*, in particular, turned out to be a voice for change in the timid world of trade papers. An astounding, unsigned editorial, obviously written by W.R. Wilkerson, the very independent and outspoken publisher and editor, took Sidney Kent to task and placed blame for the spate of poor films and low studio morale directly on Winfield Sheehan. After chiding Kent for ignoring the editor's pleas to spend some time on the Fox lot to see what was going on, Wilkerson bluntly reminded,

> You stated that politics in the conduct of Fox productions would be thrown out the window. You know, or should know, that never in the history of a production organization or, in fact any organization, has politics run so rampant as on the Fox lot.
> On your general manager's return, the whole dynasty was started all over again. Men or women he thought had opposed him during his absence, or even had talked to his temporary successor, were let out without any ceremony. The old gang was brought back, the conduct of the Fox lot that had been so destructive over a period of two years, since William Fox was shoved out, was immediately resumed.
> The morale on the Fox lot, Mr. Kent, is the poorest of any lot in Hollywood. Every man or woman on that lot is deathly afraid of your general manager, his fancies, his whims. They never know what to expect from him. They are afraid to talk back, afraid to give an opinion, for he has been known to fire men and women on the spot for daring to express an opinion.
> You must have someone on that lot who has a story mind, you must have some one who will listen to ideas, will cause them to be developed. You must have someone on the lot who can and will develop personalities, for they sell tickets, Mr. Kent, and since the start of the talkies, since the departure of William Fox, there has not been ONE personality developed by Fox.

> Those things MUST be done if Fox is to stay in business, if Fox is to contribute its share of successful pictures to this industry. It can and will be done if you can stick here for three or four months and break down that dynasty, that czaristic attitude that reaches every nook and corner of your lot.
> It won't be done, Mr. Kent, if you permit the present head to continue. Fox hasn't a chance under such a guiding hand.[14]

This startling accusation is difficult to assess. There are not enough surviving witnesses to corroborate or deny the statements. However, there is some validity to it since reporters in Hollywood would have gotten first-hand information from people working on the lot. It is likely that there is truth in the allegations since rocky relations between Sheehan and his top producers were made public shortly after this editorial appeared.

The apparent result of the *Hollywood Reporter*'s criticism was that Sidney Kent planned a two-month visit to the studio beginning June 1, coincidentally scheduled while Winfield Sheehan would be on one of his extended trips to Europe. The company also agreed to restore all salaries after seven weeks of the pay cut. It was Sheehan who made the conciliatory statement, perhaps to rehabilitate his reputation: "We feel that the prompt spirit of generosity, and the loyal devotion of our employees so demonstrably given us during this emergency period, entitles them to receive the full share of consideration and reciprocation on our part."[15]

There were typical everyday problems at all studio production departments, but there seemed to be more than usual at Fox. In the early summer of 1933, trade papers covered a never-ending litany of the company's woes. A remake of *5 Cents a Glass*, which was started by director Raoul Walsh, was shut down and turned over to David Butler since Walsh refused the responsibility of "pulling it out of the hole." Rian James was assigned to rewrite the script.[16] Shortly after the announcement, Butler too, refused to shoot the retakes and Fox had to go off the lot to sign director James Cruze.[17] However, the final directing credit ended up with Rian James and adaptation of the script was credited to Sam Mintz with James contributing dialogue. There was obviously considerable turmoil in even this minor production.

In a desperate move to recapture some cash, the studio even tried to unload properties it owned which it had no intention of filming. One was *The Giant Swing* written by the well-known author of *Little Caesar*. The "screen rights to W.R. Burnett's story can be obtained at a bargain, with purchaser also taking one of the several completed scripts which had been prepared at Fox on the yarn.... The first treatment was turned down by the front office. And other scripts were written until the story was shelved. With the original cost and charges for preparation of scripts, Fox has many thousands of dollars tied up in the property."[18] The property was not sold and was made several years later by the "B" division.

On the west coast, the scenario department underwent some changes. Story editor Leonard Spigelgass, who started in New York in 1928 and moved to the coast two years later, resigned his position in June 1933. This came two months after the disastrous release of *Hello, Sister*, which he had helped to write. Under a realignment of duties, Philip Klein became story editor in charge of screenplays and Julian Johnson took charge of the purchase and acquisition of story material in addition to handling the preparation of some pictures.[19] In an obvious acknowledgment that his innovative "production committee" was a failure, Richard A. Rowland, vice-president of Fox in charge of buying all story material, announced his resignation on May 1, 1933. Of course, he was granted leave with all the industry's customary "departure praise" from Sidney Kent.

Longtime Fox comedy director George Marshall was announced at the helm of El Brendel's next film.[20] Between May and the film's release in November, *Olsen's Big Moment*, Marshall only received a story credit and was replaced by Malcolm St. Clair as director.

Preston Foster starred in *The Man Who Dared*, a role he took over after Spencer Tracy refused to play in the film. Fox was planning to build Foster into a star but made a limp effort at it, loaning him out to other companies then finally featuring him in one more picture before he asked for a release from his long-term contract. Fox agreed, but Foster had to pay back $2,000 in salaries when he left for R.K.O., where he was given major parts in important films.[21]

Fox had announced two new films with Clara Bow after she made the moderately successful *Call Her Savage*. *Marie Galante* and *Sandy Hooker* were developed for her, but both projects were shelved as the studio searched for another property. They ended up re-making *The Barker* as *Hoopla* for the fading star. *Marie Galante* was eventually filmed more than a year later with Ketti Gallian, another dismal discovery.

Clara Bow was not the only star Fox could not place. Joan Bennett had signed a contract guaranteeing $130,000 for five pictures. Fox later asked for a reduction and she conceded to lower her salary by $5,000 per picture. Bennett was to receive $1,000 per week and $8,000 for each film completed. Only three of the five films were made before her contract expired, so Bennett demanded the remaining $55,000. She also claimed that Fox flatly refused a loan-out request from Radio Pictures for her appearance in *A Bill of Divorcement* and *The Animal Kingdom*.[22]

In her final film, *Arizona to Broadway*, Bennett suffered the slings and arrows of a Fox production: "Every so often some producer gets an overdose of mental marijuana and decides to make a picture that has everything in it but the kitchen stove.... Joan Bennett had no more business in this hodge-podge.... Her part is the perfect explanation — or ought to be — of why she called it a day with Fox."[23]

There were even problems with loan-outs. Elizabeth Allen, who was borrowed from M.G.M. for a featured role opposite Spencer Tracy in *Shanghai Madness*, refused the part after reading the script and returned to her home lot. Production shut down on the film for a few days until an arrangement was made to borrow Fay Wray for the role.

Fox's big discovery of Elissa Landi had not worked out well either and the British actress announced that she would walk out of her contract, two years early. Considering the grosses on her films, Fox executives did not object. A review of her final film, *I Loved You Wednesday*, did not serve the actress well: "The picture would rate raves, were it not for the fact that Elissa Landi emerges in this film as a full-fledged graduate of the madcap wind-mill school. You know — arms and legs waving and bouncing around all the time.... Miss Landi is far too intelligent an actress to be purposely ridiculous."[24]

Lew Ayres was signed to a contract and anticipated being a "Fox star." His first picture was the unsuccessful *My Weakness* with Lilian Harvey. Ayres actually stayed with the studio and became a leading man until his contract ended in 1935. Unfortunately, in this period, being a leading man at Fox was not really worth much, considering the films that were being made there.

Some production changes were unavoidable. Myrna Loy became ill and caused the postponement of Jesse Lasky's *The Worst Woman in Paris*. Ultimately, the part was recast with Benita Hume, an unfortunate loss for the production since the British-born actress had sophistication but no great charm.

Eugene Pallette and Spencer Tracy in *Shanghai Madness* (1933) (courtesy Mike Hawks).

Highly respected director Frank Lloyd tried to interest Fox in re-making his 1916 version of *A Tale of Two Cities* in sound, but was turned down because of the high cost of a period picture shot in England with an unknown Leslie Howard in the starring role.[25] Three weeks later, there was an announcement that Fox had definitely set the project as one of its "special productions" for the next year with Warner Baxter in the lead and a large cast of box-office names to be added. Lloyd would direct under Winfield Sheehan's supervision. Edwin Burke was assigned to write the screen treatment.[26] After spending considerable time on developing a story treatment, the project was dropped in late 1934, when M.G.M. announced its intention to produce the story. As part of the deal to abandon production plans, Fox was reimbursed by Metro for all its story costs.[27]

The dearth of star power at the studio meant that it was not only difficult to cast one or two players in a film but it was ultimately impossible to have a multi-starred film. M.G.M. was the only studio capable of making *Grand Hotel* with an audience-grabbing cast of Greta Garbo, John and Lionel Barrymore, Wallace Beery, Joan Crawford, and Lewis Stone. *Dinner at Eight* had another all-star cast, with Marie Dressler, Wallace Berry, Jean Harlow, and John and Lionel Barrymore. In the latter case, the production cost was only $391,738 since all the stars were under contract. To assemble a comparable cast of this magnitude without a fully stocked stable of stars, Fox would have to budget a film at well over $1,000,000.

While there were complaints about the level of business at the box-office, other American industries were faring much worse. Steel was 80 percent below its normal levels with an industry-wide loss of $92,000,000. No railroads were making money and 60 percent were on the verge of bankruptcy. More than 1,200 banks closed their doors in 1932 and another 418 followed, less than halfway through 1933. Book publishing had plummeted. Almost 90 percent of all magazines were about to go out of business. Automobile production had dropped by half. Residential properties of all kinds had lost half of their value. Business in almost every industry was down 80 percent from a peak in 1928-1929. Meanwhile, the movie business was still attracting audiences who paid cash for their entertainment, providing some immediate liquidity.

The election of Franklin Delano Roosevelt to the presidency of the United States in November 1932, brought some reason for cheer. As reported in the *Film Daily*, "Leaders in the film industry see renewed hope for the speedy enactment of measures that will restore the country, and motion picture business with it, to normal prosperity.... The screen was an important factor in the success of his presidential campaign, and he is expected to lend a sympathetic ear to this industry's pleas for any relief it may need."[28]

Sidney Kent was among those in the industry welcoming the new president: "In these times of economic stress, diversion is one of the essentials of life and the motion picture industry is doing its best to lighten the load by furnishing popular entertainment for all classes. Our industry pledges a continuance of these efforts and salutes the incoming administration ... with hope of more equanimity and security for the nation."[29]

There were approximately 19,000 theaters in the United States in 1929 with an aggregate daily seating of 10,000,000 people. With the usual operation of three shows a day, this could provide for a maximum weekly patronage of 300,000,000. But the weekly peak of 115,000,000 in 1929 was still less than 50 percent capacity. During the depression, approximately 8,000 theaters closed permanently because film rentals and overhead were too high. Banks were continuing to show concern for their heavy investments in the motion picture industry. Many businessmen felt that having an executive administration in New York and production in Los Angeles made little sense. And logically, it did not. Neither did a total of 459 separate exchanges in 32 cities with all the duplication of labor that this implied. And yet, the industry was able to continue along this path. What saved it was an up-tick in business as the effects of the depression waned and the economy began to show signs of life.

In May 1933, *Upton Sinclair Presents William Fox* was published. In lengthy, candid conversations with the author, Fox outlined the conspiracy he believed had destroyed his corporation. The evildoers consisted of banking interests, the American Telephone and Telegraph Company, Harley Clarke, and Winfield Sheehan. "Its revelations are expected to prove a bombshell in the film industry as well as Wall Street.... Sinclair has proposed that William Fox become a dollar-a-year man at the head of the entire film industry, run by Government for public service instead of private profit. The author calls Fox the 'key man' of the motion picture business because of his patents ownership and organizing ability. Fox says in the book that he would like to put film equipment in every schoolroom in America, even if he received no royalty from the machines."[30]

In a review of the book, the *Film Daily* mentioned that "the dominating tenor of the book is Fox's persistent effort to prove he was framed and double-crossed all-around, that no act of his own was responsible for the difficulties into which his companies found themselves at the height of their expansion activities," although "it appears that man's desire for more money than he can ever use, his ambition for more power than he can wisely exercise — the urge to merge, amalgamate, control, with considering that the more surplus a few men have, the greater is the privation among others — is at the bottom of all catastrophes like the one recounted in this book."[31]

Pete Harrison, the ultra-moralistic publisher of the very independent *Harrison's Reports*, which represented exhibitors' interests, viewed the book differently, especially its swipes at Winfield Sheehan.

> Fortunately, I have been in the picture business since the time Fox started producing and I feel qualified to express an opinion as to whether Fox is justified in his accusation. Contrary to his boasts, the Fox Film Corporation had not occupied a high standing in the industry until Winfield Sheehan took charge of production in 1926. In his early years of production, the name of "Fox Film Corporation" was synonymous with everything that was vile and low, because of the sex pictures William Fox had made.... It was not until Sheehan went to the Coast and brought back such pictures as "What Price Glory," "Seventh Heaven," and "The Cock-Eyed World," that the name "Fox" meant anything. It is, in fact, my opinion that, but for the pictures Sheehan produced Fox would never have reached [the level he did], for after all product is what makes success in this business and Fox was incapable of producing it, as his long production career unmistakably proves.... Fox complains against Sheehan and the Clarke bank group bitterly. In my opinion, instead of complaining against them, he should order statues carved and placed in his bedroom so that he might look at them every morning and thank them for the favors that have done for him, for if it were not for Winfield Sheehan he would not have been able to get for his company today eighteen cents let alone eighteen million dollars.

Harrison then went on with several examples of William Fox's less-than-heroic behavior that were not mentioned to Upton Sinclair.

For instance, he did not say anything about his welching on that $250,000 gambling debt of his, which he contracted at Palm Beach. (I have been informed that years later he was shamed into settling it.) Nor has he mentioned anything about his exacting from D.W. Griffith $100,000 for the foreign rights of "The Two Orphans," which had cost him only $15,000. Griffith overlooked making a deal for these rights when he started "Orphans of the Storm" ("The Two Orphans"), and he had to send to Europe a special representative. Through an oversight, the Griffith New York office failed to pay the $15,000, agreed upon in France, to the New York agent of the rights to the book and the agent, peeved, sold the rights to Fox. All the pleadings that his demand for $100,000 was excessive were of no avail. And Griffith had to pay it.

Harrison also took great exception to the fact that William Fox had curried political favor in helping to elect Herbert Hoover by featuring the candidate in many Movietone News stories since there was a clause in every distributor contract that stated, "Distributor warrants that the photoplays herein provided for will not contain any advertising matter for which compensation is received by the Distributor." Harrison postulated that political favor constituted compensation.[32]

Terry Ramsaye, a journalist with his eye on the film industry, likewise commented on the book's obvious bias: "Like all Sinclair stories and like all Fox arguments there are only two sides, a right side which is theirs, a wrong side which is the other fellow's. The rights are all right and the wrongs are all wrong, utterly, damnably, perniciously and eternally, with malice aforethought and conspiracy without end, until hell freezes over and three days past."[33]

With the new Roosevelt administration investigating the abuses of the banking sector and its role in the economic collapse, there was great interest expressed by members of Congress in the Sinclair book. Representative Brooks Fletcher, an Ohio Democrat, felt that legislation was needed on some of the issues discussed in the book and the author responded by sending a copy to each member of the House of Representatives.[34] The matter was eventually probed by the Senate in hearings in November 1933. However, no further legal action was taken.

By May 1933, Sidney Kent declared that "results from methodical and careful reorganization and revamping and from the application of better business fundamentals are now beginning to show." He added that Fox Film's plans and programs for 1933-1934 had been completed and the company was "on the right road."[35]

Box-office grosses, in general, were racing ahead of the previous eight months, a definitely encouraging sign, but not with any consistency for the Fox Film Corporation. More mediocre films were poor drawing cards. About *Hold Me Tight*, the *New York Herald-Tribune* wrote, "It is simply dull stuff about people leading dull lives. It would, indeed, be difficult to imagine a drabber midst than that which comprises its scenes. The film's greatest merit is the emphasis it lays upon the commendably sleep-inducing chairs at Radio City." The *New York Sun* seconded the sentiment describing it as "typical of the endless little series of romances about the working poor. This latest one, however, gives evidence that some author should take a new attitude."[36]

A trade review castigated the production of *It's Great to Be Alive*, a remake of 1924's *The Last Man on Earth*. "Fox had the opportunity of making one of the funniest films in history ... the beginning of the film is just thirty-five minutes of boredom."[37]

Fox's last hope for quality films was Jesse Lasky. His first release was *Zoo in Budapest*, which the *New York Times* praised as, "A splendid example of cinematic art, in which imaginative direction and lovely photography vie for supremacy." The *New York Post* reported, "It is a plausible, entertaining, well-directed and absorbing movie that should make the Fox people proud of their newly acquired Mr. Lasky." The *New York Herald-Tribune* called it "an engaging combination of sentiment and melodrama." And the *New York News* gushed, "The thrills of the last few scenes are breath-taking."[38] For all the praise, the high cost of *Zoo in Budapest* ended up its undoing. It lost $48,000 and was an inauspicious beginning for the Lasky unit. However, *Zoo in Budapest* did accomplish a similar feat to *Cavalcade*. It ended up almost doubling its domestic rentals in the foreign markets.

Although Lasky's next production of *The Warrior's Husband*, a play-based satire about an early Grecian society where women ruled over men, was a little too high-hat for the average moviegoer, it at least received decent reviews. "The film is filled with witty comedy lines that keep the laughter going right through the reels."[39] However, it too, showed a loss, this time for $129,000.

Failing in local markets, Sidney Kent turned his eyes to Europe and decided to aim at foreign audiences, where a film could earn 40 percent of its total revenue. Kent was pleased with the foreign grosses on *Cavalcade* and *Zoo in Budapest*,

Elissa Landi in the title card for *The Warrior's Husband* (1933) (courtesy Mike Hawks).

which made more money in foreign markets than in the U.S., and was anticipating similar returns on Jesse Lasky's upcoming *Berkeley Square*. Kent believed that there was great value to be had in countries like England, France, Germany, and Australia. R.K.O.'s *King Kong* was projected to earn $500,000 in England alone. Unfortunately, the combined world rentals of *Berkeley Square* increased the losses for the Lasky unit by adding another $174,000 in red ink.

In early April 1933, Robert T. Kane, brother-in-law of Sidney Kent and former head of the Paramount studio in France, joined Fox to produce 12 foreign films in Paris. The French films would be under the supervision of Erich Pommer. Fox also announced that the company would produce 12 films in Germany for worldwide distribution.

Seemingly unconcerned about the political situation in Germany, Fox planned some super-productions to be made at German studios even though the Nazi government had moved in and heavily controlled the film industry of that country. There was also a deal in place to distribute six films made by Gaumont-British. Stories and casts would be subject to Fox approval.

Fox was not the only studio dealing with production turmoil. Warner Bros. lost its head of production, Darryl F. Zanuck, who decided to form his own company, 20th Century Pictures, releasing through United Artists, along with partner Joseph M. Schenck. However, Warners was able to deal with this loss since Zanuck had set up a system of associate producers and an assembly line to follow through in production. Warner Bros. continued to function successfully based on the schematics of the Zanuck administration.

An editorial in the *Hollywood Reporter* reported on this turmoil yet predicted a decided jump in the quality of upcoming releases of 1933-1934. Mention was made that the "new line-up at United Artists, with Zanuck delivering twelve pictures, is a cinch to add plenty of material for the box-office. Warners will come through, even without Zanuck. Metro-Goldwyn-Mayer, if only because of its tremendous star list, is certain to stay at the top of the parade. Paramount, Universal and Radio are not doped to deliver the quality of last year, but they will turn out sufficient moneymakers to cause no great drop in the attractiveness of their output, from a box-office view."[40] No comment was made about the other major producer, the Fox Film Corporation.

When producer Jesse Lasky, credited with delivering quality films, asked for an additional $20,000 for re-takes and added scenes on *The Power and the Glory*, this was "refused at first, but when the studio officials saw the picture, they tore down all bars and placed the entire plant at his disposal."[41]

Opening to universally positive reviews which lauded its then-unique non-linear method of story-telling, later used in the landmark *Citizen Kane*, *The Power and the Glory* certainly stood out as a quality film. "The new treatment which the producer calls 'narratage,' is eminently well-suited to this particular dramatic vehicle.... Mr. [Spencer] Tracy's performance is flawless ... Miss [Colleen] Moore, whose coiffure is quite different from what it was four years ago, gives a splendid performance."[42] Fox might have expected grosses to equal *Cavalcade*, but unfortunately, audiences did not respond to the film. On a respectable negative cost of $319,000, the film lost $52,000.

Another Lasky production, *I Am Suzanne* starring Fox's latest leading lady, Lilian Harvey, and Gene Raymond, the leading man from *Zoo in Budapest*, was heralded in ads as: "The beautiful, ec-

Lilian Harvey, who had more success in Germany than the United States, stars with Gene Raymond in *I Am Suzanne* (1933) (courtesy Robert S. Birchard).

static romance of a '7th Heaven' ... in a brilliant setting of spectacular loveliness ... enticing girls, captivating melodies, glorious dancing.... A picture your patrons will always remember." There were not enough patrons who saw the movie to make it anything but a financial disaster. This was Harvey's final American film for Fox and her next scheduled film, *Lottery Lover*, was temporarily shelved. Still under contract, she returned to Germany and made a film which Fox barely released in the United States.

The balance of Lasky's productions for 1933-1934, including *The Worst Woman in Paris?*, *Berkeley Square*, *As Husbands Go*, *I Am Suzanne*, *Coming Out Party*, *Springtime For Henry*, *Grand Canary*, *The White Parade*, and *Helldorado* resulted in only one film that showed a profit. *The White Parade*, starring Loretta Young and John Boles, was the only winner in the entire group, with $237,000 in profits. This was against an aggregate loss of $1,300,000 on the entire Lasky program of pictures. For all of Lasky's pronouncements about the types of films that should be made, his record appeared to repeat the same problems that Paramount was having with his slate of films. They all cost too much and earned too little.

Nevertheless, the *Hollywood Reporter* seemed to be lobbying for Lasky to take over production by praising his productions to the hilt: "The effort of Jesse Lasky to give us better and higher grade productions as shown in [*The Power and the Glory*] and in *Zoo in Budapest* MUST be supported."[43] It must be remembered that the editorial policy of the *Hollywood Reporter* was adamantly in favor of Winfield Sheehan's removal.

Adding fuel to the rumor mill, Sidney Kent's brother-in-law, Robert Kane, who was made Fox's head of production in London, traveled to New York to confer with Kent on the company's business in Europe. There was some talk that Kane would take over production reins in Los Angeles while Winfield Sheehan would stay at Fox headquarters in London.[44] It was later decided that Kane would produce films in both the United States and Europe, dividing his time between the two continents.[45] There was no further mention of him taking over all production responsibilities.

The Chase Bank announced in May 1933 that it was writing off $55,000,000 in losses from its financial dealings with the Fox Film Corporation. From the $83,000,000 originally invested in both Fox and General Theaters Equipment, the value still left on the books had been written down to $15,000,000.[46]

Fox issued new stock with six shares of the old stock equaling one share of new stock valued at $18.90. This would get the company out from under its staggering debt of $39,746,000. Creditors had the option of agreeing to get back some of their investment or letting the company go into bankruptcy and losing all of it. They opted for reorganization. Even though business was picking up, it would take time to return the company to profitability.

Just in case Fox was to close its doors, Warner Bros. announced that it could fill the gaps left by producers who did not or could not meet the needs of exhibitors. Warners was ready to boost production to 100 films for the year, if necessary, by keeping its studios busy through the summer when it usually shut down in between production cycles. This added capacity, as it turned out, was not called upon.[47]

With refinancing in place, production running somewhat capably, movie attendance on the upswing and the worst of the economic depression over, Fox Film shares rose again to $15 by the early fall of 1933.

New talent was still an issue. Fox took out a full-page trade ad to announce that Joe Cook, the "merry maestro of nonsense and cock-eyed machinery," had signed with the company for two films a year, the first to start production in the spring of 1934. Cook was going to join the "ever-growing 'who's who' of Fox manpower!" Some manpower! Cook never made a feature because the story department could not find any material for him[48] and he was cast in a single Educational short subject in 1935.[49]

The "manpower" theme continued as Fox promoted Clara Bow "in her second hit for Fox," *Hoopla*. Bow's previous "hit" *Call Her Savage*, which showed the skimpiest of profits, was certainly nothing close to a hit. *Hoopla* emphasized Bow's diminished fan base by losing $70,000. This was Fox's last effort to resurrect her career.

There was a custom-designed Fox ad referring to the industry's acceptance of the federal government's National Recovery Act just in time for the upcoming Christmas entries. "Here's some Recovery action. Fox manpower ready ... as usual ... with six releases ... brimming with box-office ... brilliant with stars ... sparkling with entertainment."[50] Those box-office titles? *Smoky, Mr. Skitch, I Am Suzanne!, As Husbands Go, Jimmy and Sally*, and *Hoopla*. This package of "Recovery action" did not recover any great profits. Will Rogers's *Mr. Skitch* showed the best returns with a $98,000 profit. *Jimmy and Sally* showed a moderate profit and *Smoky* just broke even. The losses outweighed the profits by over $150,000 for the Christmas pictures.

There was, nevertheless, good news awaiting Fox management for the first time in three years. For the 26-week period ending September 30, 1933, the Fox Film Corporation actually showed a profit of $330,777, excluding West Coast Theaters. Gross income for the period totaled $15,449,322. The six-month report indicated a steady improvement in the company's position. The first three months of the current fiscal year showed a profit of $74,716. It was not the massive profits that the company experienced under William Fox, but it was a step in the right direction.[51] For all of 1933, the production program had resulted in higher rentals and greater profits. On a total negative cost of $24,382,000 for 52 films, excluding foreign-language features, there were profits of $846,435. The average feature cost $245,000 to produce, $50,000 per film less than a year before. Fox was beginning to regain some profitability but it paled in comparison to Loew's, Inc., the most successful production-distribution organization, which showed a solid corporate profit of $4,034,289.[52]

On November 8, the trades announced that, although Winfield Sheehan had been listed as an Associate Producer on his return from England, he was at the Fox studio continuing in the capacity as vice-president and general manager. Perhaps it was the company's fortuitous turnaround to a profit position that preserved his position. The other listings of studio personnel included J.J. Gain as studio manager; George L. Bagnall, treasurer; eight associate producers; ten departmental heads; 17 directors; 25 writers; 20 contract male and 19 female players. These numbers hit a new low for permanent contract people on the lot.[53]

November 27, 1933, was the court date to settle the matter of the Fox Corporation's control of Loew's stock. The 660,900 shares, which William Fox had purchased for $105,000,000 to gain control of that company, had been sold for $55,000,000 to the Film Securities Corporation in 1931. The shares were then lost because of a default by Film Securities on a $20,000,000 bond used to finance the $55,000,000 purchase and were now up for auction by the court.[54] However, when the auction was over, there had been no bids for the shares, which meant that they were turned over to the underwriters of Film Securities Corporation. Heading this group was Chase National Bank which would now control the stock. Ironically, Chase still controlled General Theaters Equipment and, thus, the Fox corporations. The Loew's and Fox companies were once again controlled by a single interest, which was the situation that had gotten the anti-trust forces involved in the first place. Judge Knox had the case returned to his court and commented derogatorily, "In the meantime, I must allow the 'Shylocks' their 'pound of flesh.'"[55] The stock was purchased a short time later by an investment house for $18,604,335, much less than the $105,000,000 that William Fox had paid.

This brought to an end yet another aspect of the William Fox era. But questions about his company's survival still remained.

13. A Tour of the Studio

In 1933, three years after William Fox had left the company, and following two years of heavy losses and a disastrous drop in revenue, the Fox administration was undertaking a public relations effort to overcome the studio's battered image. In a remarkably descriptive press release of December 1933, an indelible record of what the studio looked like was preserved.

Movietone City embraces a greater number of standing "sets," [sic] exteriors, sound stages, technical laboratories, and other essential adjuncts for the filming of sound photoplays than any other enterprise extant. Every inch of space on the "lot," every structure regardless of its practical use, is susceptible of being utilized as a "set" and for adaptation in the making of pictures. The mechanical units may provide factory scenes; the huge stages can be rigged to depict great buildings; the wide streets are available as busy thoroughfares; even the flower-beds and decorative gardens, nursed by a staff of Japanese gardeners, are frequently called into service to provide "shots" necessary in different productions.

Uniformed police, of the Department of Safety, are on duty at the Tennessee Gate, the main entrance to the studio, in the south "lot." Passing through the gate, along Tennessee Avenue, the first building on the right is the bungalow of George White, stage producer whom Robert T. Kane recently brought west to produce the first motion picture of "George White's Scandals." This building was formerly occupied by Frank Lloyd, who made "Cavalcade" and who is now in England on leave. On the left is the time-clock for employees. Next to the "White house" is the headquarters of the Police Department, which safeguards the property with regular rounds of inspectors and watchmen, night and day.

We turn right into Avenue A, the principal street in Movietone City, and pass several directors' bungalows, including those of Henry King, who did "State Fair" and "Carolina," and John Blystone, who made "My Lips Betray" and "Coming Out Party."

Across the street is the "dressing room" of Will Rogers, a bungalow in desert style — plain, almost severe — but artistic and comfortable. Cacti, century plants, mesquite and greasewood are in the

The Fox Hills lot, known as Movietone City, circa 1930 (courtesy Robert S. Birchard).

Writers got their own building, but not much respect, at the Fox Hills lot in 1932 (courtesy Robert S. Birchard).

"garden." Here Will keeps his portable typewriter and here he grinds out his daily squibs for a newspaper syndicate.

At the south end of Avenue A, which forms an impasse, we face the new Writers' Building, and through the archway dividing the two wings, we get a glimpse of the dazzling Jesse L. Lasky unit quarters beyond.

The graceful, rambling old Norman chateau, with a clock tower and pigeon cotes in the eaves, housing blooded birds, was built to accommodate the writing staff which has become so important since the advent of sound and dialogue and the passing of silent pictures. It houses the Story Purchasing Department, the Story Editor, the Script and the Stenographic Departments and the Secretarial Bureau. There are offices for about thirty writers on the two floors. In the basement are vaults containing thousands of scripts and scenarios.

Bronze plaques dedicating the building are at the entrance, and in front are three distinctive lampposts, the highest from Rome, the centre one from Berlin, and the other from London. In the archway hangs a bracket street lamp from Madrid, and beyond the building is a "bec de gaz" from Paris.

Turning east on Fifth Street, we see on the right the bungalow of Sammy Lee, dance director, then on the opposite corner the house occupied by B.G. de Sylva, song writer and producer, who has just completed "Bottoms Up." Next door is the rococo, sky blue and white cottage of Lilian Harvey, with ultramarine and scarlet chimney pots and a white picket fence and arched entrance. It has a salon, bedroom and bath, and an electric kitchen for the imported actress to enjoy the special regimen provided by her personal cook.

We turn right at this corner and face the Pico end of the "lot," getting a full view of the Jesse L. Lasky building. We continue on to the Berkeley (pronounced Barclay) Square location, with its row of old English mansions frowning down on the historic park, and the "To Be Let" signs so delightfully British, hanging at the windows.

As we turn left, we pass the three huge lions, formerly crouching at the base of the Nelson Monument in the Trafalgar Square scene in "Cavalcade," but now gazing stonily into the high stucco wall along Pico Boulevard.

We face a cheap, East End district in London, with a typical grimy "pub" on the corner, then pass south in Jewel Street, flanked by dingy little shops, to emerge in a large square. On the right, St. Paul's cathedral has been removed and in its place is a row of Fifth Avenue residences, used in "Coming Out Party." Around the corner and behind the section of London's shopping centre, Regent Street, is the Mexican hacienda, a faithful replica of a typical ranch beyond the Rio Grande.

Turning left, we pass a row of London town houses facing Grosvenor Square in classic Mayfair. Street lamps, letter boxes, grille work and other adjuncts are exact copies of those used in England. From a balcony on one of the mansions the family group in "Cavalcade" watched the funeral cortege of Queen Victoria "five kings riding behind her."

Around the prim, well-groomed park, meeting place of governesses and nurse maids wheeling their "prams," we pass, and we turn sharp left into Avenue D to face the ship, a scale model of the Italian queen of the Atlantic, the "Rex," which recently established a new ocean record between Europe and New York. The "Rex" has all five upper decks. The superstructure towering high in air, carries the regulation lifeboats mounted on the new improved davits used by the Italians. There is the forward deck with ventilators, booms, derricks and hatches, and amidships, portholes bristle from the lower decks. On the upper and promenade decks, protected by plate glass, deluxe cabins suites, and the ship's recreation halls, open.

Turning right behind the ship, to E Street, we pass a long line of dressing-rooms and the "hot dog" lunch counter on the right. On the left are rear entrances to buildings on the street beyond.

We reach a concrete wall, separating the "north lot" from the "south lot," and make a hair-pin turn left, passing the Sound Engineering Building, where electrical research and experiments for the perfection of synchronization of sound goes on continually by laboratory experts.

Ornate landscaping and handsome gardening effects are seen in the boulevard strip between D and C Streets.

Next is the Café de Paris, the principal restaurant for the personnel of the studio. It is a handsome structure, reminiscent of the elegant eating-places of the Bois de Boulogne outside Paris. The chef and his staff provide daily repasts to tempt the most exacting palate. A perambulator, or traveler, exactly like those in Simpson's in London and Ciro's in Paris, dispenses the plat du jour.

The walls of the café are covered with murals depicting representative scenes typifying the principal cities of the world, arranged in an orderly fashion as one would make a trip around the globe. The series of characteristic scenes is treated in the vivid impressionistic style of post-modernism and forms a unique decorative scheme for the restaurant.

The murals also serve as a background for the studio Hall of Fame. Fresco portraits done after the European style depict the most distinguished stars of Movietone City in life-like action poses. Janet Gaynor is shown riding a surfboard at Waikiki, her favorite vacation haunt. Will Rogers is shown at Claremore, Oklahoma, with "Blue Boy," the prize porker of "State Fair." Warner Baxter is portrayed in the Madrid panel as "The Cisco Kid." To be admitted to this galaxy, an artist must appear as a star or co-star in ten "hits" produced by Fox Film Corporation. Beside the entrance to the restaurant is a great bronze bell which in 1917 tolled the outbreak of the Red Revolution in Petrograd. Through fire it fell and was shattered. Shipped to Germany it was re-cast in Westphalia and later acquired by the studio.

Next door is the still portrait gallery, with the plumbing department and water-cooling plant above, and on the right are the powerful dynamos where electricity is generated.

On the left, is the Ladies' Wardrobe Department, presided over by Miss Rita Kaufman. The stylist, long a resident of Paris, creates the modern confections which array the stars. A staff of artists aids Miss Kaufman in designing gowns, wraps, hats and novelties. Thousands of costumes, complete with chapeaux, coats and slippers, are on the long racks, carefully preserved from dust and moths. Behind are the workrooms where seamstresses make up the costumes.

Next door is the Men's Wardrobe containing garments for all occasions; dress, business and sports. Here are stored a collection of uniforms of all ranks as worn by armies and navies of the principal powers.

Turning left onto Fifth Street, we find on the right side of Stage 9 and next to it, the row of steel vaults where raw film is kept. Across the street on the corner is the Scenic Studio presided over by Fred Sersen and Ralph Hammeras. Next door is the Urban Art Studio, named in honor of Joseph Urban who died last year. Half a dozen art directors have their offices here. Here they sketch and draft scenes for productions; beyond, architects make blue prints of "sets" and skillful craftsmen construct miniatures of forthcoming scenes.

Across the street, as we turn, are the Special Effects and Sound Effects Departments, lodged in what was once Tom Mix's stable, preserved for sentimental reasons. Every conceivable sound from the squeak of a mouse to the hissing roar of a volcano in eruption is on record here. The vast property room contains thousands of articles used in "set dressing."

Adjoining in the Arsenal, presided over by Lou Witte, a veteran of the World War. He specializes in creating smoke screens, gas clouds, barrages and bombardments, and in camouflage effects. He has several batteries of artillery, field guns, howitzers and mortars, as well as anti-aircraft guns, machine guns, automatic rifles, flame throwers, trench mortars, anti-tank rifles and pistols of all kinds. There are stacks of steel helmets of the German, French and British patterns, hand grenades, gas masks, and all the necessary paraphernalia of war, including rifles and side arms of the type in use in the United States and various European armies.

We swing around into Avenue B and pass the thatched roofed, Irish cottages of Janet Gaynor. It has a huge, raftered living room, bedroom, bath and dressing room. Here removed from the bustle of the "set," Miss Gaynor rehearses dramatic scenes; there is a piano to provide music for auditions of her song numbers; she may practice dance steps on the hardwood floor of the salon. Rose bushes line the fence and nestle against the lowflung eaves of the straw roof.

Continuing, we pass around the Park, a decorative square, with two field guns, relics of the Great War, emplaced on opposite corners. In the centre is a fountain; restful benches surround it.

Opposite across A Street is the Hall of Music. There is a marble statue to the spirit of harmony in the patio and a bronze bust of Victor Herbert to the left of the entrance. Here originals and copies of every important piece of music are filed. Here ballets and choruses are trained by Sammy Lee.

Skirting the Park, we enter again on Tennessee Avenue from B to C to D Streets passing on the right long lines of dressing rooms and villas for featured and contract players whose names are household words throughout the world. Oranges hang ripe on squat little trees, natural carbonic water gushes from a spring. The streets are lined with flower beds.

At the head of the street after passing the Precision Machine Shop and Electrical Engineering Department we turn sharp left again in a right about face, and emerge in a wide street with the backs of Sound Stages 1, 2, 3, and 4 on the right, and on the left, a long row of two-story stucco dressing rooms. These contain the barber shop and bootblack, the hairdresser and coiffeur for women, the wig department, the beauty shop and make-up department and the dermatologist. Upstairs is a school room for children employed in productions, and rest rooms and showers for "extras."

As we progress toward the far corner we pass a block of villas for featured and contract players, then turn left on Avenue A finding on our right a battery of projection rooms, where the daily "rushes" are shown night and morning for inspection of the progress of films in the making. The word was derived from the marking of this newly made film "rush," for development and printing and showing. Next door is the cutting room where film is edited and sequences trimmed by expert cutters to proper length, pieced, spliced and dovetailed. Beyond is the Library and Research Department containing thousands of books and volumes on every subject, maps and photographs and other material for investigation.

Next door is the projection room for executives.

Turning right on Third Street, we pass on our right the first battery of sound stages constructed since the advent of sound. There are 1 and 2 and 3 and 4, coupled into two mammoth structures, windowless, like a sultan's harem, insulated with double walls, floor and ceilings to make them impervious to noise. Constructed of steel and reinforced concrete when sound pictures were first produced and the recording apparatus had not been refined and perfected, it was then necessary to eliminate every extraneous sound, and maintain absolute silence in the building, as the crude microphones of those days picked up every unwanted and foreign noise, along with the dialogue.

Opposite these are the trio of units of the air conditioning plants, where the air is cooled or heated as the atmosphere requires, then washed and purified in a liquid bath and piped into the sound stages. Vitiated air is drawn off through the roof.

At the top of the street is the power plant with giant dynamos and generators with gleaming rows of switches to provide electricity for the studio. Enough power to supply a small city is developed here. Walter Quinlan is chief engineer in charge of electrical development.

We turn left and proceed down Second Street, on the other side of the air conditioning units, and facing on our right, the gigantic newer Sound Stages 5 and 6, coupled by an archway. These later stages are adapted to the latest modern sound recording and are built of steel and stucco. Development in synchronization and recording, improvement in microphones, with their long, sliding, antenna-like blooms [sic], and perfected film, enable sound men to blot out much foreign sound from the aural effects desired.

The entire series of interior "sets" required in a picture can be "dressed" on these huge stages. Inside the aspect presents a heterogeneous view of corners and angles, rooms and walls to embrace every scene in a production.

Back again at Avenue A we face the Executive wing of the Administration building. The end suite is occupied by the offices of Winfield Sheehan. He designed and supervised the creation of Movietone City, from grading and filling and laying out of streets, to the construction of the various improvements, buildings, parks, exterior "sets," etc.

The Administration Building houses the studio business manager, the comptroller, the casting department, the telephone switchboard, paymaster's office, the publicity department, the telegraph and cable room, the main post office, legal counsel, and transportation and location departments. There is a handsome general reception room for visitors, and beyond that the casting gate for "extra" actors and actresses.

Turning right in First Street, we pass "tin pan alley," where song writers for musical productions are housed. And next door is "Park Row," where a number of directors and their assistants are quartered. Beyond is the parking lot with accommodations for 250 automobiles. On the right are the backs of Sound Stages 5 and 6.

Swinging round to the left, we pass through the gate in the concrete wall separating the South from the North "lot." Beneath us will eventually pass a prolongation of Olympic Boulevard through a tunnel, as the municipal authorities intend to extend this thoroughfare directly beneath Movietone City and through to the Pacific Ocean at Santa Monica.

On our left we find a gully, with a hamlet deep down in the ravine. On the plateau to the right is the bed of a lake and beyond the rambling old mansion, used in the new Gaynor vehicle, "Carolina." The huge columns are in true Colonial style, set outside the broad piazza, and supporting the sloping roof like a great canopy over the frame of the building.

Turning right through a stone gateway we face an imposing chateau, with a large swimming pool in front. Flanking it is the Garden of All Nations containing flora from all parts of the world; trees, shrubs, bushes, vines and other plants and flowers from the four quarters of the globe.

Continuing on to the right we reach the wild west sets of "In Old Arizona," the first outdoor talking picture ever made. Here are typical scenes of frontier hamlets with hitching posts, jails, saloons, "the Paris store," a Chinese laundry and the Wells Fargo Express office.

Turning left, we go down the hill past where "Sherlock Holmes" was made. On the right is a section of a Mississippi River steamboat, on the left a view of Singapore harbor with sampans and native craft in the murky waters, and beyond is a glimpse of the jungles of equatorial Africa. "Sea Wolf," "Painted Woman," and "Devil's Lottery" were made here. There is also a Nicaraguan scene used in "The Cock-Eyed World."

Continuing we see the grilled gates and sentry boxes used in "Zoo in Budapest" and around the corner is a new large Sound Stage, No. 15, installed in what was formerly "King Arthur's Court," used in "The Connecticut Yankee" with Will Rogers.

We turn right to the cavernous entrance of an Old World Cathedral, with a German schloss across the street, and then we traverse the tortuous streets of typical European capitals, the representative gabled buildings encroaching and stifling the narrow alleys reach through the arches. Bits of a score of cities of as many lands are faithfully reproduced to show the populous quarters of these communities.

Through a double arch we emerge into the municipal square in Geneva with its artistic fountain topped by an equestrian statue. Opposite is the Secretariat of the League of Nations, used in "Six Hours to Live" with Warner Baxter. Beside it are handsome chalets and town houses of the thrifty Swiss burghers.

Out through another arch and we plunge into Germany, Bavaria, a Munich street, where "Adorable" with Miss Gaynor and Henry Garat was made.

On the right is seen the distinctive entrance to the harem of the Sultan of Morocco at Fez, and we continue to a corner of Egypt on the right, with a view of Algiers on the left. Next is Stockholm with the harbor jammed with Swedish shipping in the background.

We turn right and encounter Sutter Street, San Francisco, then continue to the New York "set" with a subway kiosk in the foreground and the Columbus Avenue elevated railroad structure in the distance. The "Tenderloin" police station in West 47th Street is shown, and across the street is Engine Co. 54 of the New York Fire Department. In the extreme background the mountains give the illusion of the Palisades across the Hudson River.

Traffic lights, lamp-posts, fire-hydrants, mailboxes, manhole covers and similar material are all genuine articles from New York City. So is the inlaid glass in a drug store window on the corner where once newspaper reporters "covering" the Tenderloin, telephoned their "beats" and "scoops" to fretful city editors in Park Row.

Beneath the segment of the "L" are New York street cars, with underground contact rails and slots. We continue along a section of Park Avenue, Manhattan, and then turn right into the New England Village "set."

This is a permanent exterior with real trees, and a town square with a heroic statue of a Civil War veteran in the centre. Smooth bore, muzzle loading cannon flank the entrance to the park. Round about are the town hall, post office, drug store and general store and behind is the stone church. Here Will Rogers was in "Dr. Bull."

We pass a railroad depot, part of which represents Epsom Downs where the Derby is run annually; the other end is a Russian railway station.

We sweep around right and pass the Irish village used in the Janet Gaynor–Warner Baxter picture, "Paddy, the Next Best Thing," turn right over a bridge spanning a brook and see the cemetery. Then we face the blackened, shell-shattered, devastated war zone of Belgium.

Passing through a replica of Sing Sing Prison gate, we turn left into a French provincial street, edged by farm houses, and used in "Pilgrimage." Past a "set" used in "What Price Glory" we find the inn of "Berkeley Square," and then beyond the artificial gardens and hot houses, the Cafeteria, a third eating place on the "lot."

The Grand Canyon, with its typical rusty, red rock formation, is seen to the right, with a "shot" of Boulder Dam in the distance.

Interminable stalls of scenery and property docks are on the left, as we climb the hill and pass the Hospital, where a surgeon and trained nurse are constantly on duty.

Near the top of the hill on the right are Spanish and Italian streets, with a bit of Athens in old Greece, and a scene used in "Shanghai Madness."

Across the gulch and we are back in the South "lot."

Without ever leaving Movietone City, we have covered more than five miles in a trip around the world in less than sixty minutes.[1]

14. Survival

With all the adversity the Fox Film Corporation had endured for nearly four years, the beginning of 1934 offered a new beginning with some hope for the future. Following a film season of mainly bad reviews, dismal grosses and aspersions hurled at the company management, the Academy Awards of Merit offered some comfort. Out of nine categories for 1933, Fox films *Cavalcade*, *Berkeley Square*, and *State Fair* were nominated in seven. Frank Lloyd won a Best Director Award and *Cavalcade* was deemed Best Picture of the year. It also won an award for Art Direction.

The economic disaster which had befallen the country was on its way toward a resolution as well. When President Franklin Delano Roosevelt came into office, he established the National Recovery Act to help businesses reorganize under better practices that would prevent the kind of economic meltdown that brought on the Great

Depression. It was run by General Hugh Johnson and its aim was to set reasonable profit levels for industries and fair wages for workers. Codes of fair competition were set up for all businesses, including the motion picture industry. Deputy NRA Administrator Sol A. Rosenblatt was charged with investigating the motion picture industry and its practices. Some of the national requirements of the new business code encompassed an agreement for buyers to pay fair prices for products, for employers to provide a minimum wage to their workers, to stop the exploitation of children and to allow trade unions. A thorough analysis of film industry practices was made through government investigations, focusing mainly on the high cost of stars and the practice of block-booking. One of the new rules which producers and distributors applauded was the abolition of double bills in mid–1934 because the NRA felt it diminished the fair play-off of films.[1] This ban did not hold for long and in no time, theaters were once again playing double bills.

Each industry protested some, if not all, of the requirements of the code. In Hollywood, studio heads objected to a proposed $2,000 weekly salary for talent. In his comprehensive overview of the film industry Rosenblatt found, "A large portion of the problem with respect to salaries is raised by the fact statistics show that of the total cost of salary and labor expense in producing pictures, an average of 466 persons received 51 per cent of the total salary and labor payrolls, although more than 12,000 are salary and general labor employes [sic]."[2]

Producers felt there would be no way to bid for stars if they were limited by salary, even though the spending cap was supported by President Roosevelt himself. The sweeping legislation covered by the code would also set standards for license fees, cancellation clauses, free-lance contracts, and it imposed a 30-day moratorium on offers to stars whose contracts had expired. Agents were most affected by measures that prohibited false representation, kickback deals with producers, or intimidation of clients. Strict penalties would be in place for those who refused to comply, including a $10,000 fine for the payment of excessive salaries.[3] When finally adopted, the most controversial aspect of the code dealing with the limit on star salaries was put on hold for further study. It was never implemented. However, the Federal Trade Commission's report on salaries to the Senate resulted in a proposed 80 percent tax of all income over a salary of $75,000. Some of this recommendation did find its way into law.

If a company signed up to abide by the Code, it was permitted to display a blue eagle on its products to show the public it was helping the New Deal. By the end of 1933, 22 million workers nationwide were covered by the New Deal and most studios were in compliance. The blue eagle symbol was carried on the end credits of many motion pictures (in black and white) from 1933 and into the war years. Six major studios agreed to "contribute" an annual $20,000 each to cover the administrative costs of NRA code's motion picture supervision.[4]

The NRA was meant to spread sacrifice through all levels of industries. The only sacrifice Winfield Sheehan had suffered for presiding over a nearly bankrupt company that continued to deliver mediocre product, was a cut in salary from the astronomical level of $459,655 in 1930 to $250,000 in 1933. He would stay at that pay level through 1935. His new contract, signed by Harley Clarke in the giddy days after William Fox's expulsion, had left him well protected. Any efforts to remove him were thwarted by his ironclad deal.

As a comparison of annual executive salaries in 1933, the best-compensated writer received $93,500; highest paid composer $57,000; cameraman, $46,000; sales manager, $43,000; top exhibiting company president, $94,750; and the highest paid actor earned $150,000 per picture.

With the imposition of the new code, the ubiquitous Jesse L. Lasky summed up the objectives.

> In signing the motion picture code of practice and ethics, the President of the United States has effectively forced upon producers an instrument of mutual cooperation. The basic idea behind the code is sound. It will end many evils under which the industry has labored for many years with no prospect of remedy. As I see it, this code will classify all branches of the industry, outline their specific duties as a basis for just wages and, more important still to the rank and file, it provides adequate compensation and working hours for all classes of employees.
>
> I can't help but think that the industry will be benefited by the mutual cooperation the code imposes. Under a temporary arrangement many more workers were given jobs and fairer remuneration.
>
> The code, however, will not solve all the ills of the business. Only good pictures can return the industry to the prosperity it once enjoyed. I believe that we are reaching out into novelties for our product, films that have meaning and purpose. The last two months have witnessed a great improvement in screen entertainment — and the chief reason for all this is that we are no longer afraid of taboos. We're doing things.[5]

Evidence that the New Deal was having a positive effect was provided by Will Hays who announced that by the end of 1933, overall motion picture industry employment had returned to its 1929 level of 300,000 jobs.[6]

Winfield Sheehan returned to Fox in his post as production chief and Sidney Kent informed all producers of the lot that he would have "complete power of story selection from that point on." Sheehan's return would not affect the right of associate producers to determine what vehicles they wanted to produce, but he would have the final say on what went into production.

> I believe we are going to return to an era of honest stories dealing with human emotions and issues. Above all, clean stories with wholesome humor will find favor with the public. The cynical sophisticated screen play, whose characters are unreal, synthetic sinners is passé. The public's taste turns to the real problems and actual struggles of regular people who lead clean lives.
>
> It is the great mission of motion pictures to take the lead in this campaign. Literature and the stage have given themselves over to decadence; the screen must have a renaissance in clean entertainment for the whole family.

Sheehan then addressed a genre which was considered overexposed and dated.

> Musicals with a good story, catchy music and interesting personalities, will make money. But a hackneyed narrative with poor music and cast lacking in talent will "flop." The world's political unrest demands a reaction in its entertainment to optimism, comedy and wit.
>
> The coming year will produce a new crop of personalities. Young actors and actresses, recruited from all over the world, have been tested, coached, tried out and developed to a point where they are ready for presentation to the public in featured parts. Not all will make the grade, but from this group our future and increasingly talented stars will emerge.[7]

Sidney Kent outlined a plan that would help the quality of Fox films. "To insure the best in story material, the Fox studio has set up a centralized board of control for all story material to be produced on the lot. This board control consists of three: the producer who will make the picture, also Winfield Sheehan in all cases, and another producing executive. This producing executive may be the story head, another associate producer or an executive with a particular knowledge regarding the definite story in question. This board of three with Mr. Sheehan as chairman has the final say in the selection and approval of stories." Ray Long and Fred Collins were charged with the responsibility of searching for story material.[8]

What happened behind the scenes was fraught with more drama and it exposed the major tensions between Sheehan and his producers. According to the *Hollywood Reporter*, which was editorially no fan of Sheehan's, when the production head returned from Europe he was irked that stories spread that he had been demoted to head of a single unit, equal to Jesse Lasky, Al Rockett and Edward Butcher. He had also heard the rumors that Jesse Lasky might succeed him as production head.

> He demanded a showdown. He went to Kent and Kent passed the buck on to the Chase board looking after their interests. On reaching that point Sheehan reminded them that he holds a contract giving him prior rights to the contract they signed with Jesse Lasky, granting the latter non-interference with his productions. Sheehan demanded the full force of his contract or that Chase settle with him on the basis of the unexpired term of the ticket which had $3,000,000 more to run.
>
> Chase had little thought of settling any contract. They tried that during Tinker's term, with very bad results.... It is understood that Sheehan knowing of the terms of the Lasky deal has been laying low waiting for the full flop of Lasky's efforts and although the Lasky pictures have not set the world on fire they have done a better business and have given Fox whatever legs it still has to stand on. Finding that Lasky's operas were improving instead of flopping, Sheehan demanded this showdown.[9]

In this period of strangled finances, the Chase board of directors decided once again to keep Sheehan.

There was no doubt that Fox's two most prestigious films of the year, *Cavalcade* and *State Fair*, were Sheehan productions and together had brought in more profits than the ten best-grossing Fox films of the previous two years. No matter that it was Edward Tinker's wife who instigated the development of *Cavalcade* or the fact that Philip Stong's bestseller had been given an irresistible cast of Janet Gaynor, Will Rogers, Lew Ayres and Sally Eilers, Sheehan fit the Hollywood adage of "you're only as good as your last picture." Luckily, Sheehan, who was still receiving $250,000 annually, was golden at this point.

Jesse Lasky, though, was reported as being ready to walk out of his contract if Winfield Sheehan seriously interfered with his unit: "It is stated definitely here that Lasky's loyalty to S.R. Kent caused him to agree to playing along with Sheehan as boss, but with the stipulation about what would happen at the first interference."[10]

The big question throughout the industry was, would Sheehan be capable of holding together the Fox production unit and restoring its luster with the exhibition end of the business? In 1933, the film with the most contracts played was *State Fair*, which was run at 9,490 locations. The lowest number of the year came in for a British-made release, *After the Ball*, with a scant 2,531 playdates. As a comparison, Paramount Pictures played 10,012 locations for its most heavily booked film of the year, the Mae West comedy *She Done Him Wrong*, and the lowest number of theaters was still 4,151 for the Carole Lombard film *Supernatural*.[11]

At the time there were 18,371 theaters in operation across the country with locations affiliated with large chains down to 1,954.[12] There was a catch, though. The number of bookings had little correlation with the ultimate gross. If a playdate yielded low rentals, even the maximum number of bookings could not make it profitable. Nevertheless, it was still preferable to have as many bookings as possible.

With Fox still churning through the backlog of product that was produced during its most recent executive turmoil, reviews for many of the resulting films were negative, again largely due to a lack of polished writing. For Jesse Lasky's light society drama, *Coming Out Party*, directed by John Blystone, story material seemed to be a major drawback: "It is unfortunate that a picture as exquisitely presented in all departments as 'Coming Out Party' is, should be burdened with a plot that inspires giggles in the audience.... The preview audience was always about ten jumps ahead of the story and it was vocally dissatisfied with some of the more hackneyed and threadbare formulae which were dragged in."[13]

Not even the well-intentioned Lasky could escape the enmity of the rest of the reviewing community. The *New York News* averred, "The plot ... has been worn so threadbare that, in spite of its glittering settings in its Park Avenue locale, it presents a shabby appearance on the Roxy screen." The *New York Herald Tribune* was not willing to sugarcoat a bad movie even from this distinguished producer: "Jesse Lasky's latest effort as an individual producer is, for some reason, disappointing."[14] The film fared no better at the box-office, losing almost half its $304,000 negative cost.

Comments about Fox's lower quality production standards occasionally reached insulting proportions: "Those little theatres specializing in unproduced plays by unknown authors might have brought forth something such as 'I Believed In You.' It smacks of the amateur in nearly every department.... The direction of Irving Cummings and the photography of Barney McGill are both uneven. Cutting hasn't helped."[15]

For *Frontier Marshal*, the *Herald-Tribune* commented, "This story could have been made into a good, exciting, colorful show had it not been done on quite such elementary terms of dialogue, character and plot manipulation." The *New York Post* concurred: "It is hard to believe that 'Frontier Marshal' was not a product of the 'Great Train Robbery' era, brought up to date in addition of sound effects and dialogue." The *New York Times* gave the creators the benefit of the doubt: "'Frontier Marshal' being a frank melodrama, does not bother about plausibility, and one gathers it was produced with the adaptor and the director having their tongues in their cheeks."[16]

Orient Express received a critical drubbing from the *Herald-Tribune*: "Due either to bad cutting or an assumption on the part of the producers of clairvoyance it remains a veiled mystery. The story is a tangle of loose ends and rough edges which grows increasingly obscure as the tale unwinds." The *New York World Telegram* added a further negative review: "Mediocre entertainment, lazily put together and amateurishly acted and directed." The *New York News* chimed in, "The earlier sequences are pieced together in a crude way, and the latter ones are unbelievable."[17]

The *New York Post* especially took exception to *Such Women Are Dangerous* saying, "When Henrietta Crosman intimates to Herbert Mundin that he is something less than a half-wit, that still leaves him at the head of the class that participates in the latest Fox product."[18]

The *Hollywood Reporter* hammered away mercilessly at the deficiencies of the story department:

> *Wild Gold*: It seems doubtful that there was an actual script for this picture. It has all the earmarks of something that they made up as they went along.[19]
>
> *Call It Luck*: Unfortunately it took five credited writers to get the idea on the screen and the outcome is somewhat muddled. Couldn't they have thought of any more novel racket than a variation of the badger game?[20]
>
> *Grand Canary*: An unbelievable story, unbelievably slow, which the gorgeous photography of Bert Glennon strives desperately to save by giving it some visual movement at least.... As a matter of fact, the holes in the script are far larger than the story itself and there is practically no action.[21]
>
> *Three on a Honeymoon*: It seems too bad that such a fine actress as ZaSu Pitts should have to carry the load in such a mediocre picture as this one.[22]

An editorial in the *Hollywood Reporter* suggested why all studios were turning out less-than-satisfying product: "Pictures are being rushed into production with the casts all screwy. The director or the writer has NOTHING to say, that is, what they say means nothing. The producers throw any person that is available into spots that ruin the picture even before it gets started and then we wonder why most pictures are so bad."[23]

Not all reviews of Fox Films were negative. Some were downright positive when the film was deserving. Considering that musicals were out of favor, there was one surprise: "The new Fox picture 'Bottoms Up' is just plain, downright, and excitingly good. In fact, it is so good that it must be something new in the way of entertainment."[24]

When *Stand Up and Cheer* was previewed under the title *Stand On Your Feet*, the *Reporter* was highly complimentary: "It is undoubtedly a standout picture, with a credible cast, plenty of action, an opportune theme that carries a punch, catchy music and spectacular settings."[25] Surprisingly, there was no mention of young Shirley Temple's brief appearance in this review or many others, but the *New York Journal* did take notice: "It is all very light and gay and diverting. Despite the fact that the cast contains plenty of high-powered names, an individual triumph is scored by four-year-old Shirley Temple."[26]

Handy Andy (previewed as *Happy Andrew*) received kudos as "the best [Will] Rogers comedy in years and years and years."[27]

Surprisingly, one of the best-reviewed films of early 1934 was immune from the Fox staff writers. The low-budget documentary, *Devil Tiger*, received a rave review from the *New York American*: "Sensational is the word to describe this thrilling animal picture." The *Herald-Tribune* agreed, "A realistic, well-photographed, and no doubt, informative chronicle of jungle adventure." So did the *New York Journal*. "There's plenty of excitement in the piece."[28]

One of the few writers who later rose to acclaim within the Fox stable was Dudley Nichols, with credits on two John Ford films (*The Seas Beneath* and *Pilgrimage*), as well as the Quirt and Flagg reunion in *Hot Pepper*. "His two year contract expiring, Dudley Nichols has been awarded a new deal with Fox, a group picture arrangement. Dud-

John Ford directing *The Seas Beneath* (1931) (courtesy Karl Thiede).

ley, regarded as one of the company's aces, foregoes his usual weekly pay check in preference to a lump sum per picture deal with Sol Wurtzel giving him a sizable tilt over his old contract." His next assignment was reported as *Grand Canary*, which was a Lasky film. Luckily for Nichols he did not write that script, which received unanimously negative reviews, and he stayed with the Wurtzel unit. Nichols's non-exclusive contract with Fox gave him the option to follow John Ford to R.K.O. for several high-quality productions like *The Lost Patrol* (1934), *The Informer* (1935, a multi–Oscar winner), and *Mary of Scotland* (1936). Nichols was a much-in-demand writer in the 1930s and capped the decade with his tersely effective screenplay for John Ford's iconic western, *Stagecoach* (1939). After Nichols won a Best Screenplay Academy Award for *The Informer*, he only wrote one more screenplay for Fox, the 1935 John Ford–Will Rogers teaming of *Steamboat Round the Bend*. The Fox lot, at the time, was not a place where a talented writer could thrive.

There were only two reliable writers who stayed with the company through this uncertain period. William M. Conselman had been plying his craft around Hollywood since 1921. With experience and skill, he managed to deliver satisfactory screenplays for comedy and drama. Lamar Trotti had just begun his screenwriting career with the arrival of sound. A fine ear for dialogue and considerable ability to shape characters defined the films he wrote. He would stay with the company for his entire career and later became known for his portrayals of rural America.

As usual, Fox was still having problems staffing the story department, an issue which dated back to the 1920s when Sol Wurtzel wrote about the dilemma to William Fox. Story editor and successful screenwriter Philip Klein left Fox and was replaced by Malcolm Stuart Boylan, who had written title cards for many earlier Fox films. Julian Johnson was still head of the story department and Ray Long was continuing to search for material.[29] In less than a month, Boylan requested to be released from his executive position and returned to screenwriting.[30]

Julian Johnson announced later in the year that he had made a deal with popular writer-humorist Damon Runyon to acquire all his story material for one year.[31] It seemed to be a promising source for story material, but whatever Runyon was paid, Fox saw no immediate benefit since none of his stories were produced until 1936.

Some of the problems keeping authors and inspiring them to create may have been caused by Fox's disregard for those who plied the craft. A peek behind the curtains of the story department was offered in "The Low Down" column of the *Hollywood Reporter* in early 1934: "There's a very simple way of finding out whether or not 'you figger' on the Fox lot. At a story conference the other day in a certain exec's office, were one director, one supervisor and a couple of writers. After the conference was over, the exec opened his desk drawer, carefully pulled out a box of cigars, offered them to the director and the supervisor, took one himself and carefully replaced the cigars in the desk drawer. When the writers got outside the exec's office they stopped the director and asked him how come they didn't rate a cigar. And the director gave it to them straight with 'He only offers the cigars to IMPORTANT people.'"[32] An anecdote, perhaps, but it was probably more the case than the exception. Writers were generally considered the most expendable talents in the Hollywood community.

In an effort to add prestige to its slate of films, Ray Long agreed to the purchase price of $25,000 for Sinclair Lewis' latest book, *A Work of Art*.[33] Lewis, a highly regarded author, had written the novels upon which *Arrowsmith* (Goldwyn-U.A., 1931), *Ann Vickers* (Radio, 1933) and *Babbit* (Warners, 1934) were based. "The price is understood to be very high because of the independent attitude taken by Sinclair Lewis on all of his works for the screen, and despite the fact that there was no active bidding because other story heads had passed the story up as not adaptable to the screen."[34] In fact, the story was not adaptable and it was shelved while the high purchase price was amortized in the annual abandonment costs.

The front-page trade announcements did not end with Sinclair Lewis: "As an indication of how Fox is bulling the story market in a rush to get better stories at any cost comes news of Ray Long's latest purchase — the payment of $20,000 for a story in the Ladies' Home Journal, and by an anonymous author at that."[35] *Impersonation of a Lady* was not made, either.

The years-long problems with developing acting talent persisted at Fox. In 1934, an effort was made to boost second-tier performers into starring roles. The comedy team of Frank Mitchell and Jack Durant, under contract to Fox, had appeared as comic relief in several films when the company decided to launch the duo's first feature. Joel Sayre was writing the script when the project was announced. It was never made and Mitchell and Durant continued appearing as supporting players for the duration of their contract.

Other efforts were made to elevate one-dimensional supporting players to leads in films. Edward Butcher, former studio manager, was promoted to associate producer and assigned to handle the first Stepin Fetchit vehicle. The story, which was untitled, was based on the flight of a "colored aviator" to Honduras, which had taken place several years earlier.[36] It, too, was never made.

Another leading role was planned for El Brendel, but perhaps after reviewing the lack of success of *Olsen's Big Moment* and *Mr. Lemon of Orange*, saner thinking prevailed and his contract was not renewed.

Herbert Mundin, a narrow-shouldered British actor usually in the role of a butler, took the lead in *Call It Luck*, which did make it to production but not to success.

For most of 1934, there were constant announcements of Fox adding performers to a film's cast, but there were never any major names signed, just more supporting players. Although the announcements made it look like there was great activity going on at Fox, little had changed and most of the films retained a mediocre quality, even when competent stars were in the leads.

A report in the trades announced that Fox was trying to buy the Gregory Ratoff story *I Loved an Actress* from Radio Pictures, which had been unable to find a star for it. Fox reportedly wanted the property for Lilian Harvey, although she had already returned to Germany and would not return to make another Fox movie. Sidney Kent and Winfield Sheehan mutually agreed with Harvey to tear up her contract a few months later.[37]

Fox bought the rights to *The Seal Poachers* by Norman Reilly Raine, and were planning to shoot it as an Edmund Lowe–Victor McLaglen vehicle. It became yet another un-filmed property, although Lowe and McLaglen did make two more films for Fox the following year. Neither, though, was *Oriental*, another project developed for Lowe and McLaglen, and proudly announced as an original screenplay by Gene Towne and Graham Baker, and was to be directed by Raoul Walsh.[38]

There was yet another Fox announcement that director Richard Wallace was on his way to Scotland to film background shots for his production of *Marigold*, which was to begin production in July. Neither the project nor Wallace ever made it to the screen at Fox.

Finally recognizing a perfect fit of star and material, Fox wanted to buy the rights to playwright Eugene O'Neill's *Ah, Wilderness!* George M. Cohan had starred in the lead on Broadway and then Will Rogers successfully took over the part. It was widely thought that it would make a perfect film for Rogers. Unfortunately, Fox found the asking price for the property too high. M.G.M., however, had the foresight and the funds to buy the screen rights for $100,000, the highest amount paid for any play of the 1933-1934 stage season.[39] When George M. Cohan demanded $150,000 for the screen performance, Metro had second thoughts but still held on to the property. It was later recast with Wallace Beery and became one of the top-grossing films of 1935.

Avoiding the high costs of current properties, Fox went back to the practice of utilizing public domain material in its announcement that the Alexander Dumas novel *The Corsican Brothers* would be filmed. However, with budget limitations, the studio was not going to make any elaborate costume dramas. Dumas's story remained in the unproduced files with so many others.

There was a noticeable timidity in the film subjects that the Fox development people were choosing, certainly following the edicts of Winfield Sheehan. It was an industry-wide problem as characterized by W.R. Wilkerson: "In the first place (with the exception of MGM) there is not a plant in the business which would take a chance of the making of a GREAT PICTURE, they would not care to risk that money, they would not give the time for the writing or the adaptation or sufficient time to shoot such a picture. And because of this, writers are not writing in that direction, they are attempting to deliver what the producers want and it does not seem to be GREAT PICTURES."[40]

In early 1934, Col. Jason Joy, a former executive secretary of the Red Cross and liaison officer with Will Hays's Motion Picture Producers and Distributors organization, joined the Fox story department. Initially hired to search out story material, Col. Joy would later become the company's point man with the Hays Office as the censorship code was strengthened to limit the degree of frank adult material in motion pictures.

While other studios were recovering their financial footings, an article in the *Hollywood Reporter*, "Receivers On Way Out — Pic Business Likely to Stage First Miracle of Recovery," paid tribute to advances resulting from the National Recovery Act in the movie business. However, not all studios were in the clear.

Fox alone has the Wall Street forecast uncertain. Sidney Kent put over a great deal when he got bondholders and creditors to accept new paper for their debts, but the new deal was based largely on expectancy of money-making pictures to come. "Cavalcade's" foreign profits, particularly in England and not forgetting the change in the dollar's status, have helped a lot, but most of that money had been spent on expensive Hollywood musicals, and the answer now awaits on how the public accepts those offerings.[41]

No matter what the future brought, the present was starting to look better for the Fox Film Corporation. For the 39-week period ending December 1, 1933, the company showed a profit of $1,410,793, largely due to the success of Cavalcade in the United Kingdom, which had brought in a significant portion of its nearly $2,000,000 foreign take. The profit for this period compared with a loss of $595,100 for the same period the year before. The gross take was $24,288,824, with an increase of $4,058,924.[42]

Continuing on an upward climb, Fox net profits for the first quarter of 1934, amounted to $805,376 compared with a loss of $557,122 previous year. Even the continuing return to profitability of the company could not keep the Chase National Bank from divesting itself of one-third of its Fox holdings. A total of 583,135 shares were sold to a New York financial group which had the influential British investment group of Balfour, Boardman and Company associated with it. The per-share price worked out to $15, which put a heavy loss on Chase's books. After holding onto the stock from when it was nearly worthless, the bank decided that it was time to sell off some of its holdings. The new investment group would replace Chase's representation on the Fox board of directors.[43] Balfour, Boardman and Company had plans to make Fox and Gaumont-British a gigantic international film enterprise while returning complete control of Gaumont-British to England rather than have a 65 percent interest in an American company's hands.[44] This deal, however, like many others associated with Fox, fell through.

The lack of long-term relationships with talent was made clear when Frank Lloyd, who had directed films for Fox since 1917, and most recently had made Cavalcade, was reported to be in a salary dispute for a production starring Janet Gaynor. Winfield Sheehan, who had produced Cavalcade should have been able to woo Lloyd back considering the many times they had worked together, but the director's $150,000 per-film fee on a deal for two features was a sticking point. Lloyd ended up directing one more film in 1934, Servants' Entrance, with Gaynor and Lew Ayres. Lloyd then went to M.G.M. and made the critically acclaimed, Academy Award–winning Mutiny on the Bounty.

Considering that the United States government spent so much time fuming over the lavish star salaries paid by Hollywood, little was done to cut them back. Samuel Goldwyn broke rank with other producers by going public in a Saturday Evening Post article where he revealed confidential information about the stars' weekly salaries:

Greta Garbo	$9,000
Will Rogers	$7,000
Maurice Chevalier	$7,000
Constance Bennett	$7,000
John Barrymore	$6,500
Norma Shearer	$6,000
Richard Barthelmess	$6,000
Ann Harding	$6,000
Wallace Beery	$5,000
William Powell	$4,500
Joan Crawford	$4,000
Janet Gaynor	$3,750
Edward G. Robinson	$3,000
James Cagney	$2,800
Clark Gable	$2,500[45]

Fox Films turned to Europe for acting talent and found Charles Boyer, who was already considered a major star in France. He was cast in Caravan, a big-budget film directed by a groundbreaking German talent, Erik Charell. It became yet another production nightmare for Fox. Winfield Sheehan was so dissatisfied with the finished film that he insisted on remaking part of it before it could be released. When the retakes were to be shot, the leading lady, Loretta Young, was in the hospital, the supporting lead, Phillips Holmes, was at Universal starring in Million Dollar Ransom, and star Charles Boyer was trying to get out of his contract. The studio faced a considerable delay before the desired retakes could be made.[46] After Caravan was completed, Boyer refused to star in his next film, Serenade, because he disapproved of the role. His contract was for $25,000 per film, but Caravan was the only Fox project he completed before continuing his career at other studios. Boyer ended up paying back $9,000 which he had received as an advance on the second picture.[47] Serenade became a Buddy DeSylva musical which was released as Welcome Home. It starred James Dunn and was directed by James Tinling. Boyer would not return to the Fox lot until 1942, at which point he was a major international star.

Caravan was expected to be a big hit and, in an

ad testimonial to Erik Charell, Fox lavished praise on the director:

> The industry owes you a debt of gratitude ... which the box-office will collect. Your genius has blazed a new trail ... marked a new milestone. Your daring originality, soaring imagination, are reflected in every scene of "Caravan." You have inspired a cast of many stars to give you the grandest performances of their lives. You have assembled mass effects involving thousands of people ... and infused them with swinging, colorful rhythm.... Above all, you have given us something in your first production for FOX definitely new and significant that will be studied in every studio ... and welcomed by a public that has been begging for a newer, truer use of the motion picture.[48]

The only debt that was realized was red ink on Fox's ledger pages. At a cost of $709,000 for the

Erik Charell shoots a scene for *Caravan* (1934). Charles Boyer sits at the head of the table with Loretta Young (courtesy Robert S. Birchard).

English version and $116,000 for the French version, *Caravan* yielded a $333,000 loss. As much as Charell was lauded, his contract was not renewed by Fox or any other company and his genius accompanied him back to Europe.

The age-old problem of developing stars to preclude the outrageous salaries was continuing to plague the Fox studio. Even when there was a star in the making, she could go unnoticed. In this case the "she" was Shirley Temple. Appearing in Educational kiddie two-reelers in 1932 and 1933, which were distributed by Fox, executives had a chance to see her talents.

Temple was reportedly hired by Winfield Sheehan at an audition for *Stand Up and Cheer*. "Standing in Sheehan's office with thirty or forty other children, she grew impatient at the tests that Sheehan was making and, walking out of line, she approached Sheehan's desk with 'Do I get the part or not? I'm tired of standing.' And she got the part."[49]

Shirley was given a small role in the 1934 Fox feature *Carolina*, and then was loaned to Warners for small parts in two films. She returned to Fox and was introduced as a five-year-old singing and dancing performer in two scenes of *Stand Up and Cheer*, based on a story by Will Rogers and Winfield Sheehan. Although the feel-good movie was a series of musical and comedy numbers designed to lift the spirits of America, a perfect antidote to the gloom and doom, it was barely profitable, through no fault of Shirley Temple's. The tot then went into yet another supporting role in the Gaynor-Farrell film, *Change of Heart*. Evidently, no one at Fox thought of her as having enough box-office strength to carry an entire film. It took a loan-out to Paramount for the title role of *Little Miss Marker* to prove her value as a star.

Even after she was given a starring part by Paramount, Fox put her into yet another small role in *Now I'll Tell*. This was the last supporting part she would play. Fox announced that Shirley Temple would star in a special production tentatively titled *Million Dollar Baby*. It was a prophetic title because that was exactly what she became for Fox — a prime property who would be the most consistent audience lure for the next five years. Her salary leaped from $150 weekly to $1,250 when a new seven-year contract was signed. Fox had already been receiving much more than the lower amount when she was loaned to Paramount.[50] Temple's mother, Gertrude, who coached her with dialogue, received $100 weekly.[51]

The fact that it took interest from other studios to convince Fox to promote Temple to larger roles made it apparent that no Fox star builders had the foresight to see her prodigious talent early on.

Meanwhile, back at the studio, there were renewed reports of creative tension between Winfield Sheehan and producers on the lot. In one case, there was a public feud with *Scandals* creator George White. Two different cuts of the *Scandals* film were screened for test audiences before release, one championed by the producer, the other by studio head Sheehan. "The battle reaches its climax at the studio today (Monday, February 26, 1934) when both forces return with their individual preview cards. White's contract specifies that he is the boss of his own picture. Sheehan interprets that up until the time the picture is ready to be cut and previewed. The present battle is what to cut and what to leave in, with both holding out for different versions of the musical.... Fox people are laying the odds that White wins his battle, and if this is the case the silence that has existed between himself and Sheehan for the past few weeks will be made permanent."[52]

A headline in the *Hollywood Reporter* played up a "Lasky-Sheehan Battle" that was ready to break out.

> Battlefront reports yesterday were that the Jesse Lasky-Winnie Sheehan situation was reaching the point of open warfare. Argument has grown up over new stories being considered, suggestions for casting, etc.
>
> The understanding is that the arrival of Sidney Kent before the end of this month is the only thing holding off the shooting. Lasky, it is stated, feels that he wouldn't want to start something without a first opportunity to talk with Kent.[53]

If Jesse Lasky did not have a champion in Sidney Kent, there is a good chance he would have had his deal canceled. He continued to turn out one clunker after another and this trend continued into his 1934 program. Even *Springtime for Henry*, modestly-budgeted for a Lasky unit feature at $250,000, brought in the lowest rentals of the year at $126,000 and suffered a loss of $167,000.

Sheehan had rocky relations with other talents as well. Buddy DeSylva, who produced big-budget films like *Sunnyside Up* and *Just Imagine*, and Sheehan were at odds over creative control clauses in his new contract, so the songwriter-producer went back to New York with plans to produce Broadway plays.[54] Lew Brown, who had arrived at the studio with DeSylva, signed with Fox for two years at $2,500 per week for the first year and $3,500 for the second. Brown was to be in complete control of musicals made on the lot which eliminated DeSylva from future projects.[55] Two months later, DeSylva signed with M.G.M. for three films.[56]

Shortly after, though, more problems arose.

> "Winnie Sheehan" has given Lew Brown the air and behind it is a swell story.
> Of the three musicals made by Fox, the only one having any appearance of success is "Stand Up and Cheer," which was produced by Brown. "[George] White's Scandals" checked in as a flop at a $650,000 production cost, and the Buddy DeSylva yarn, "Bottoms Up," the cheapest of the three at $400,000, was not so hot.
> After the Brown picture was previewed, Sheehan started talking more pictures with Lew, but Lew was considerably burned by Sheehan demanding all the credit for the picture. Accordingly, the "other picture" question was left until after the release of "Stand Up and Cheer," and that's cold now, as Sheehan is supposed to have heard that Brown was doing a lot of talking around New York, telling listeners how little he (Sheehan) had to do with the picture.[57]

Perhaps sensing that Sheehan's slate of pictures was not meeting expectations, Sol Wurtzel lobbied to add prestige to his Western Avenue unit: "As a result of conferences with Sidney Kent the official okay has been given to include a number of more expensive pictures in the Western Avenue output, with stars, directors, etc. on a par with the output from the Sheehan fortress at Westwood Hills."[58]

The first big-budget film to be produced at the lot under Wurtzel's guidance was announced as "Dante's 'Inferno...' Harry Lachman was selected yesterday as director, and will immediately begin looking for a big-name cast.... No date has been set for the start of production, but work will begin at once on the many unusual settings to be used."[59]

Attempting to resolve the dilemma of providing adequate screenwriting talent, Sol Wurtzel established a junior writing staff for his unit at the Western Avenue studio including Sally Sandlin, Harry Fried, and Robert Cummings. They were all under the supervision of Robert Yost. Wurtzel's efforts amounted to little. Sandlin wrote the story for one of his films while Fried and Cummings ended their contract without any writing credits. Yost received a screenplay credit on the 1935 Spencer Tracy feature *Dante's Inferno*, but the actor said it was one of the worst pictures ever made anywhere, anytime. Yost left the studio within a year and wrote B-westerns at other studios. Wurtzel later hired his daughter, Lillian, to contribute to screenplays. She never received on-screen credit and no public announcement of her employment was ever made. Once again, efforts to improve the writing of Fox films ended in failure.

While Fox was trying to deal with all of its problems, one aspect of production would not affect it as much as other major studios. Censorship would become the bane of every studio production chief. However, Winfield Sheehan had already sworn off a program of exploitative sex and violence.

Although the Catholic Church, Will Hays, several of the editorial boards of trade magazines and various citizens' and women's groups had decried "smut" in the movies, little had been done within the other studios to clean up content. The racy language of the talkies erupted into an overheated issue and added to the moralists' general discontent. While many exhibitors did not mind the adult subjects, figuring that it sometimes added to attendance, the pro-censorship groups were massing their strength. Frank Capra, known for intelligent, quality films, added his voice to the mix, "Smutty pictures have done more harm to the exhibitors' business. While they temporarily attract a certain class, they definitely repel others to whom this type of production is repulsive. The harm is not confined to that picture alone; those who dislike smut stay away from all moving picture theatres for some time after they, or their children, witness such a picture."[60]

Sidney Kent reiterated Winfield Sheehan's position on this matter with a further promise that Fox would not release any objectionable pictures in the next season. "We need no pictures which have dirt dragged into them."[61] With its major stars like Warner Baxter, who had just signed another two-year contract, Will Rogers and Shirley Temple, the studio's films were not known for appealing to "baser instincts."

The Federation of Women's Clubs, representing over 2,000,000 women, issued a list of the most offensive films. Warner Bros., having released a series of tough melodramas and crime thrillers, mostly initiated by production head Darryl F. Zanuck, was a clear target for censorship groups with 15 objectionable films, including the notorious *Baby Face, Lily Turner, The Mayor of Hell, Three on a Match* and the overly suggestive costuming of *Footlight Parade*. Paramount was in second place with 13 objectionable films, characterized by spicy Maurice Chevalier musicals, "salacious" Mae West comedies and sordid adult dramas like *The Story of Temple Drake*. The latter was so castigated that it is almost single-handedly credited with bringing about the Motion Picture Code's censorship guidelines and the Catholic Church's Legion of Decency. The chairwoman of the Federation of Women's Clubs even endorsed Fox, Radio, Columbia and Universal for "the progress they have made in dispensing clean pictures."[62]

Activating the moral supervision of motion pictures began in earnest in July 1934, when a new division of the Hays Office under Joseph I. Breen opened for operation. "A distinctive seal has been adopted to identify all pictures which have been approved by the Code Administration. This will be shown after the main title on all pictures as evidence of the industry's compliance with the production code of our organization," stated Will Hays.[63] Theater owners, as well, pledged to only run films with the code seal. Producers were now obliged to bend to the censorship imposed on them.

Breen made it clear that the sanitizing of screenplays was the producers' responsibility. His office would only approve or turn down final films. However, producers who did not want to take the chance until productions were completed could submit screenplays or even outlines for Breen's perusal and comments before filming began. Breen said, "It will be our aim to have films reasonably acceptable to all classes of society, and to be sure that nothing downright lewd and offensive reaches the screens."[64]

The first film to be certified as a 100 percent clean picture was Fox's John Ford production of *The World Moves On*. As a consequence of the sudden rush to "clean" films, the major distributors gave exhibitors a three-day window to cancel any films against which there was protest on moral grounds. Cancellation rights would cover releases of 1932, 1933 and 1934, or a two-year period which the Hays Office called the life of a picture. In that two-year period nearly 1,000 films were released at a production cost of approximately $260,000,000. The industry stood to lose $10,000,000 in canceled bookings for films that would no longer comply with the new code standards, based on an average admission price of 19½ cents. The new standards also meant that many of the films made before 1934 would never be reissued because they could not qualify for code seals without drastic cutting. Some films were abridged, in many cases with large chunks removed, including *Mata Hari* (1931, M.G.M.), *The Public Enemy* (1931, Warners), *Dr. Jekyll and Mr. Hyde* (1932, Paramount), *A Farewell to Arms* (1932, Paramount), *The Eagle and the Hawk* (1933, Paramount), *Scarface* (1932, United Artists), *King Kong* (1933, Radio), and *Manhattan Melodrama* (1934, M.G.M.).

Staff writers at Fox were gathered together by Col. Jason Joy for a briefing and were told that "their stories would have to be 100 per cent pure or else." Joy announced he was calling them together at the request of Sidney Kent and Winfield Sheehan.

"Fox has no intention of showing a scene or having a word uttered that could bring a blush, Col. Joy indicated. He remarked on the current agitation about the subject matter of motion pictures on the part of Catholic leaders, and gave the assembled talent to understand that the individual writers who worked on a picture would be held responsible for any moral criticism that might be leveled at any Fox production."[65]

In mid–1934, Fox still had a weak story department, few big stars under contract and distinctly second-tier directors. Aside from one film each from John Ford, Henry King, William K. Howard and two from James Cruze, the mainstay directors were competent but uninspired. This lesser group included David Butler, John Blystone, George Marshall, Hamilton MacFadden, Kenneth MacKenna, and James Tinling. Directors who made lasting films in this period were all at other studios. M.G.M. had Clarence Brown, Richard Boleslavsky, W.S. Van Dyke and Sam Wood. Paramount could call on the services of Henry Hathaway, Norman Z. McLeod, Norman Taurog and Edward Sutherland, all under the supervision of Ernst Lubitsch. Warners, thanks to Darryl Zanuck, was top-heavy with directors, including Lloyd Bacon, Busby Berkeley, Michael Curtiz, Roy Del Ruth, Alfred E. Green, Mervyn LeRoy, Archie Mayo, and William Wellman.

The result of delivering consistently lower quality product to exhibitors finally had its public airing, precipitated by Sidney Kent's insistence that Fox salesmen sell eight of the upcoming season's films strictly on a percentage basis. This aroused the ire of one of the leaders of the Independent Theatre Owners organization who remarked, "That's the funniest thing I ever heard of. If it had come from any outfit other than Fox, there would be little surprise, but from the organization that delivered us more bad pictures last year than all the companies combined, it sounds like a gag.... Where there is some guarantee of the quality of the product from an organization, the percentage angle has some value to both distributor and theatre owner, but where a company continually delivers flop attractions, under the percentage plan the picture must be played, and that's where the rub comes in. If it were a straight rental proposition, the showman could pay for the picture and shelve it, taking his loss in an effort to play fair with his audience."[66]

Doubly confirming the exhibitors' feelings was the result of a *Harrison's Report* survey which had Fox in seventh place of eight distributors ranked for their money-making product. The only reason exhibitors had booked Fox's product "was due to the great confidence exhibitors held in Sidney R. Kent as a 'doer' and organizer." The result for exhibitors was "to pay heavily for the play of the pictures, most of which resulted in heavy losses, due to the poor quality of the product as turned out under Sheehan's direction."[67]

Nevertheless, Fox announced a slate of 55 films for the upcoming movie season, of which 46 would be in English, eight in Spanish and one in French. The budget for all the films would be $18,000,000. Eight of the productions were to be personally supervised by Winfield Sheehan and Sol Wurtzel would produce 17. Edward Butcher and Al Rockett were assigned four each and Erich Pommer, who came to the United States when production in Germany was thwarted by the Nazi government, would produce two. Jesse Lasky, would be responsible for seven films, including *Redheads on Parade* and *Casanova — The Immortal Lover*, with production starting in September. Beyond that were *The Apple Tree* by John Galsworthy, *Flight of the Swan* and *Aces Down*.[68]

Aware that his previous films had not fared well at the box-office, Lasky came up with a publicity tie-in for *Redheads on Parade*. He selected eight redheads to play chorines in the film and planned to send them on a personal appearance tour in key locations similar to the tour of the "Goldwyn Girls," conceived of by producer Samuel Goldwyn.[69] This was also a very personal project for the producer since he once had a vaudeville act called "Lasky's Redheads." However, like many hapless Fox films of the period, this one ran into trouble when Lasky was unable to find enough genuine redheads to stock his cast, a unique reason to postpone a black and white film. The fact that the script was not ready, either, played into the postponement.[70]

As enterprising a publicity idea as Lasky had, it did not help the gross of the film, which ended up being one of the biggest Fox losers of 1935, following along the trail of other Lasky films. With a hefty production cost of $633,000, it left a loss of $326,000. Lasky never made *Casanova* or the other three films that were announced. His final two Fox releases were also duds. *The Gay Deception*, a sophisticated comedy starring Francis Lederer and Frances Dee, deceived no one with a loss of $274,000, and few toasted *Here's to Romance* introducing Nino Martini, which pulled Lasky's unit $226,000 further into the hole.

In July, just as 11 of the new season's films were about to go into production within the following eight weeks, Winfield Sheehan left the studio for a combined business trip and vacation to New York and Europe that was scheduled to last three months.[71] "Fox production chief will go first to London where he will work on negotiations for a couple of film spectacles to be made later in the year.... Sheehan will spend considerable time at Carlsbad and return here in September, in time to put into production the Janet Gaynor–Warner Baxter special 'One More Spring.'"[72] Sheehan did not return to the studio until October 5, 1934. Buttressing the impression that Sheehan was traveling abroad to sign up new performers, he was accompanied by Fox talent scout Paul Frawley who was to scour English and continental live theaters for prospective stars.[73]

Sidney Kent arrived in Los Angeles three weeks after Sheehan's departure to check up on the production status of future releases. While at the studio, he investigated the overboard production costs on *Lottery Lover*. The film's over-runs resulted in the immediate departure of producer Al Rockett.[74]

Ultimately, the great expenditure on *Lottery Lover* was hardly worth the effort. A *Variety* review hammered the film: "An obese story, faltering continuity, a forced brand of comedy and half-hearted performance in the top spot (Lew Ayres, Pat Paterson) are handicaps which make 'Lottery Lover' sag at the knees. Heroic recutting ... may help some but the offering will have to fight for every dollar."[75]

Sidney Kent was offered a new three-year contract shortly after Sheehan returned in the fall of 1934. Concurrent with the new contract, word went out to start building up the studio's stock of players. "Admitted [sic] weak in names, studio will now go after stage, air and opera people who look like potential picture attractions. To this end, producers have been instructed to give all junior players first opportunity in preference to outside players. Studio has an idea that several of the youngsters have a chance to get over on the screen if given an opportunity, but feels that producers have been unwilling to give the embryos a break."[76]

New talent became imperative. Even seasoned performers with potentially productive careers ahead could become problematic. Spencer Tracy, a heavy drinker known to disappear from town, was a prime example. When Tracy went AWOL for more than two weeks, during the filming of *Marie Galante*, production was suspended. Fox was about to replace him with Edmund Lowe but Tracy returned and filming resumed with two weeks of production remaining. Tracy agreed to reimburse Fox for losses incurred during the hiatus and had the severest fine ever levied against a performer in pictures. Fox abandoned a $125,000 lawsuit against Tracy in lieu of a penalty of $25,000 plus half his $2,500 weekly salary for 17 weeks. Tracy agreed that if the studio picked up his option, he would get half his pay for the first picture with the remainder due upon completion of his second under the option.[77]

Tracy again failed to show up for the start of the Jesse Lasky production of *Helldorado* in September 1934, and his continued absence led to him being dropped from the film. Fox immediately entered into negotiations with Richard Arlen to step into the part. Tracy was to remain off payroll for the next four weeks unless a part opened up for him and was threatened with indefinite suspension. Nevertheless, a new contract was drawn up for him, one which would last into 1936.

Like many previous Fox films, the script development of *Helldorado* was blamed for hobbling its chances at success: "Stupid and unbelievable story plus situations and characterizations that are annoying, 'Helldorado' has little to offer any audience. Main trouble is that producers have three stories in one.... Stepin Fetchit drools his way through the picture, becomes tiresome with his inane mutterings."[78] The *Film Daily* was not negative but did concur that this was not top-rank fare which "turns out to be just a moderately satisfying yarn about a western gold rush."[79]

Stung by films poorly reviewed in the trades after sneak previews, Fox tried to screen films away from local theaters, easily reached by prying trade papers. The studio decided to try out its films at houses at least 40 miles from Los Angeles. Not only did executives feel this would inoculate them from the trades, but audiences would not be as jaded. Huntington Park was chosen for a few months and then San Bernardino. The studio would continue to have its final screening for cast and executives in local theaters.[80]

Talent was no doubt costly and Fox dropped its Spanish stock players Raúl Roulien, Juan Torena and Julio Peña, as well as director John Reinhardt. The studio figured it would be less expensive to engage players as needed for the Spanish pictures rather than carry a stock company.[81] Roulien, however, was re-signed three weeks later with a pay hike.

Sol Wurtzel, having been recently elevated in status, had produced Will Rogers's latest film *Judge Priest* at the Western lot. With a great success anticipated for that film, and in Winfield Sheehan's extended absence, Wurtzel was announced as producer of the next two Rogers films which would be made before the end of the year. Having been elevated to higher budget films, he was now turning out productions in the $300,000–$400,000 range.[82]

John Stone, who had been working his way up the ladder from writer to story editor then to producer for the previous 11 years had never held a contract.[83] Having been brought in under his original name of Jack Strumwasser by Sol Wurtzel in early 1921, he wrote 22 scenarios between that year and October 1923, many of them for Buck Jones, Dustin Farnum and then Tom Mix. Then the efficient Strumwasser reportedly ran into a problem, most likely with Winfield Sheehan, who insisted on his termination. In an anecdote recounted by Sol Wurtzel's son, Paul, shortly after Wurtzel carried out these orders, a new writer appeared on the lot named John Stone (really Strumwasser) who continued his writing career on Tom Mix films. Under Wurtzel's personal guidance, Strumwasser/Stone remained on the lot but without a contract. The lack of a contract continued for 11 years until Sheehan left on vacation and suddenly, Stone was handed a long-term deal by Sol Wurtzel. It is only speculation, but there may have been some connection between Sheehan's declining importance at Fox and Wurtzel's ascendancy, that the time was right to offer Stone a contract.

Wurtzel's successful Will Rogers films helped propel revenues with their box-office strength. The consolidated net profit of Fox Films for first half of 1934 was $1,199,241. There was an earned surplus of $2,913,312 which had accumulated since the company's reorganization on April 1, 1933. Theater operations of Wesco were not included since principal operating subsidiaries of the company were still in bankruptcy.[84] The lingering financial and corporate problems of the West Coast theater chain were on their way to resolution by November 1934, when Sidney Kent announced that the company in its reorganized status would be known as National Theatres Corporation. Kent would be president, with Spyros Skouras as first vice-president and his brother Charles as vice-president and general manager. Fox Films and the Chase bank, owed $20,000,000, were the two largest creditors and would have joint control of the new chain.[85] Only the Fox Metropolitan Theaters, which had once formed the nucleus of William Fox's control of the New York City market, remained a financial headache which still needed to be resolved.

Buddy De Sylva, setting aside previous disagreements, returned to Fox with a contract for four films, two musicals and two dramatic vehicles. De Sylva would have complete control over story, cast, director and an assurance of no interference from any other executives.[86]

In December 1934, for the benefit of exhibitors who subscribed to his newsletter, Pete Harrison recounted his visit to all the studios in Los Angeles, and his comments were highly critical of the Fox organization and one producer in particular.

> One would think that a producer with the background of Jessie [sic] Lasky would produce wonders; but he has made one good picture in ten pictures. My conjecture is that Mr. Lasky does not know good story material, for after all it is story material that makes good pictures.
>
> The employment of Mr. Lasky does not [sic] any discredit on him as a producer; he used to make good silent pictures but he has not yet learned the talking picture technique; the demerits should go to Sidney Kent, who has employed him, sacrificing hundreds of thousands of dollars of the Fox money. Kent should have known if Mr. Lasky possessed a, what Hollywood calls, "story sense," but in my opinion, Kent has no story sense himself, for if he had he would not have let Mr. Lasky continue.

After chastising Kent further for having hired his brother-in-law for $2,500 weekly, Harrison added, "Incidentally, Bob Kane produced for Fox 'Caravan,' that $900,000 box-office failure and 'East River' (*Under Pressure*), another mediocrity; also 'George White's Scandals,' which the churches banned."

Referring to Winfield Sheehan, Harrison had praise. "Few producers in Hollywood have had the experience Mr. Sheehan has had.... Although nominally the head of the Fox Film Corporation's production activities on the Coast, Mr. Sheehan has confined himself to producing a small number of pictures, preferring to make few pictures but good, than many but mediocre."

Sol Wurtzel "is very intelligent, a square shooter, and has the courage of his convictions. But he is driven too much, like a good horse; he is made to produce too many pictures. That is why frequently he produces poor pictures. In addition to this he is handicapped by the releasing system which often compels him to put into production stories he knows that cannot make good pictures."[87]

Pete Harrison's accusation of Sidney Kent's lack of story sense was proven out by the turmoil within the writing department. Continuity of talent and leadership was the most pressing issue. Julian Johnson had remained in charge of the department, but there was a constant turnover of those within his domain, best characterized by the musical chairs played in late November 1934. Robert Bassler, Johnson's assistant, who later became a prominent producer, was moved from Los Angeles to the New York story department. There, he was to work under the guidance of department head, Thomas Costain, who would also rise to prominence as a best-selling writer of historical novels. The New York story department was not immune to staff changes since Costain had replaced Hunter Lovelace. John Mott, former secretary to Winfield Sheehan, was appointed as assistant to Costain. Robert Bassler was replaced in Los Angeles by Karl Tunberg who became Julian Johnson's new assistant. Tunberg also developed into a prominent screenwriter only a few years later. Gordon Wiles, a former art director, left the story department and was returned to his previous position on the next installment of *George White's Scandals*.[88] Under Julian Johnson, there was definitely a respectable pool of writing talent and there would be some improvement in the quality of Fox films in 1935.

Writers, however, were limited by the literary material that was purchased for Fox productions in this period. Competition and out-bidding by other companies left Fox at a disadvantage when funds were tight. The only major purchase made in 1934 was $65,000 for the screen rights to *The Farmer Takes a Wife*, by Max Gordon, which happened to be the highest sum any studio paid for a novel that year. Most of the other story acquisitions were for less popular novels and plays. In the case of *Farmer*, so much of the budget was expended on the material that Winfield Sheehan decided against shooting any of the film on location in Erie, Pennsylvania, as originally planned. Instead, the exteriors were shot on the banks of the Sacramento canal.[89]

Fox acquired the remake rights to *Ramona*

from director Edwin Carewe, who had made the most recent version in 1928, and assigned one of the studio's top writers, Sonya Levien, to prepare the screenplay from Helen Hunt Jackson's novel. Production, which would include a Spanish version, was scheduled under John Stone's supervision.[90] The script would undergo many changes until it came to the screen two years later.

Without strong screenplays and sufficient pre-production supervision, many productions ended up in need of retakes. *Under Pressure*, yet another boisterous Victor McLaglen–Edmund Lowe romp (this one about subway diggers, known as "sandhogs") was one of those seriously troubled productions. After having spent many weeks in production under Raoul Walsh's direction with Grace Bradley as the female lead, major changes were ordered when Winfield Sheehan returned to the studio. Story revisions were made and Bradley was replaced by Florence Rice. James Tinling was assigned to three weeks of re-shooting but it was ultimately Irving Cummings who directed the added scenes, contributed by writers Lester Cole and Noel Pierce.[91] Costs were mounting on the picture since $400,000 had already been spent on the production, and the re-shoot was expected to cost another $200,000.[92]

The pressure that studios were under to assign massive budgets to major pictures was underscored by the rise in the average cost of films. M.G.M., which had been spending more than any other studio, finally hit a new level for the Depression era with an expenditure of $1,525,826 on *The Merry Widow*. The French version cost $227,287. It was Metro's most lavish effort since *Ben-Hur* and the budget covered both an English and French version. "Part of the huge cost was due to shooting scenes for four different prints at the same time. Certain sequences involving royalty were cut out of the English and Belgian prints, because these countries have kings. Scenes were made using military heads in these parts, so royalty wouldn't be offended. However, for the American and French versions, the king and queen stuff was okay."[93]

Star salaries, too, at M.G.M., set new post–Depression industry records. Greta Garbo received $270,000 for *The Painted Veil*, while her agent was negotiating a new deal for two films the next year at $300,000 each.[94]

Other studios, forever in a competitive upward spiral, were compelled to put more money into their productions. In the 1934-1935 season, this would result in Warners investing large sums to make *Wonder Bar*, *Dames*, and *Captain Blood*. R.K.O. spent lavish sums on *The Little Minister*, *She*, *The Three Musketeers*, *The Last Days of Pompeii*, *Roberta* and *Top Hat*. Paramount spent big on *Cleopatra*, *Belle of the Nineties*, *The Devil Is A Woman*, *The Big Broadcast of 1936*, *The Lives of a Bengal Lancer*, *Peter Ibbetson* and *The Crusades*. Universal assigned major budgets to *Sutter's Gold*, *Imitation of Life*, *Magnificent Obsession*, and *Showboat*. United Artists had its share of expensive releases because of the high-class production values promulgated by producer Sam Goldwyn who made *Kid Millions*, *Barbary Coast* and *We Live Again*. M.G.M., though, topped them all with *Tarzan and His Mate*, *David Copperfield*, *Anna Karenina*, and the $1,899,973 production of *Mutiny on the Bounty*.

Forging ahead, Fox announced the start of production on "four biggies," including *Dante's Inferno* starring Spencer Tracy, *Life Begins at 40* with Will Rogers, *George White's Scandals* and Shirley Temple's new film, *The Little Colonel*.[95]

Buoying the production executives at Fox were the box-office results of several hit pictures in 1934. Shirley Temple in *Bright Eyes*, co-starring James Dunn, racked up a stupendous world-rental figure of $3,296,000 and profits of $1,228,000. The expenditure on the production was a mere $233,000. *Baby Take a Bow*, released in the same

Warner Oland as the Oriental sleuth in *Charlie Chan in Shanghai* (1935) (courtesy Mike Hawks).

year, brought in over $500,000 in profits. Will Rogers regained his popularity and became a major attraction whose films could generate considerable revenue. *Handy Andy* and *Judge Priest* returned combined profits of $750,000. Janet Gaynor was still drawing audiences in *Change of Heart, Carolina* and *Servant's Entrance*. The infusion of box-office dollars from these stars, as well as two *Charlie Chan* installments, and *The White Parade* helped Fox Films amass total world rentals of $29,582,800 on a total negative expenditure of $14,503,100. The profits were able to erase large losses from the Lasky unit and films like *Music in the Air*, the year's biggest loser with $389,000 in the red, John Ford's *The World Moves On* a loser to the tune of $372,000, *Marie Galante*, another Spencer Tracy flop, losing $298,000, and *All Men Are Enemies*, with a loss of $223,000.

With the average Fox film costing $259,000, gross revenue ending December 29, 1934 reached $37,546,586 compared with $33,285,767 in 1933. Profits regained some ground at a level of $1,273,069 compared with a loss of $557,122.[96] Fox shares, however, were languishing. After rising to $13½ in mid–1934, they had dropped back to $9 in the spring of 1935. Fox West Coast Theaters had been reorganized and had no funded debt or bank loans.

Sidney Kent, nevertheless, was pleased with the company's progress: "Subsequent to the closing of the Corporation's fiscal year, the most important group has been taken out of bankruptcy and it is hoped that by the end of 1935 the entire system will have been reorganized. Fox Films' former ownership of Wesco Corp. has been reduced to 42 per cent but that the elimination of the large debts formerly existing ahead of Fox Film's 100 per cent ownership has brought the present 42 per cent interest in National Theaters much nearer the actual theater properties and, in the judgment of the management, has improved Fox Film's position with respect to the entire theater chain."[97]

With many of the financing obstacles removed, 1935 looked like a banner year for the motion picture industry. Paramount, which had re-emerged from bankruptcy, showed net earnings of $6,360,000 for 1934. Even its theaters contributed $1,282,000 to the figure. Loew's Incorporated's quarterly profits rose 30 percent to $2,001,308 for the period ending November 22, 1934. Weekly attendance had risen back to 70,000,000 persons each week, an increase of 5,000,000 admissions. Worldwide audiences brought weekly attendance to 200,000,000.[98]

The Fox Film Corporation would also ride the wave of prosperity. "Fox is expected to set the production pace right after the holiday by launching a schedule calling for 14 pictures to be put before cameras during January, only two of which will be carry overs from month of December ... 'Dante's Inferno' and 'Scandals.'"[99]

Not all of those scheduled for production went before the cameras as planned. There were some that were filmed quickly and released within months, such as *Man-Eating Tiger* which began shooting on January 2, 1935 and was in theaters by mid–April. Even quicker, *Recipe for Murder* with Lowe and McLaglen started January 3 and was released as *The Great Hotel Mystery* March 8. Some films took longer. *Tabloid*, a James Dunn feature went before the cameras on January 16 and was released by the end of May under the title *The Daring Young Man*. January 7 was supposed to be

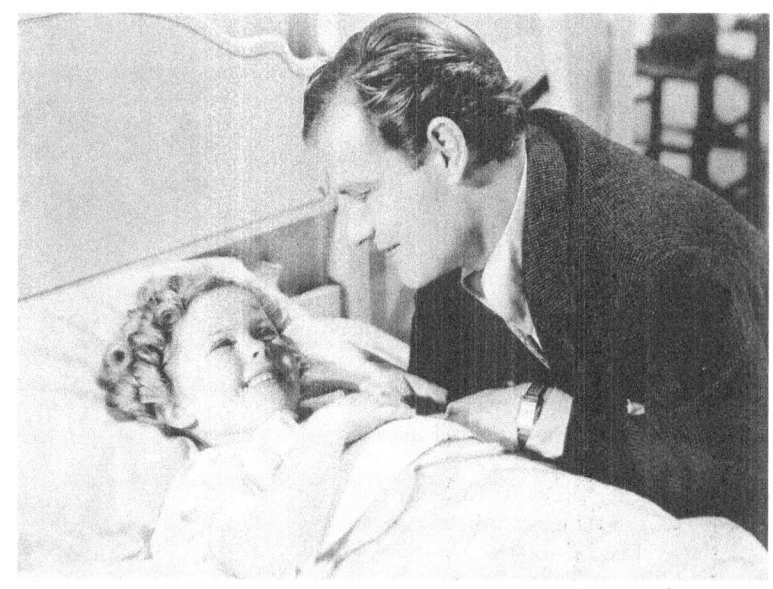

Joel McCrea puts Shirley Temple to bed in *Our Little Girl* (1934) (courtesy Mike Hawks).

the start of Jesse Lasky's *Redheads on Parade*, but it was postponed again until the end of February and was not filmed until the end of April; it was released in late August. The prestigious Winfield Sheehan production of *The Farmer Takes a Wife* went before the cameras in early March and was on screens by the beginning of August. *Our Little Girl*, another Shirley Temple vehicle, was filmed in February and rushed into theaters by mid–May.

The stability which had finally been achieved in setting productions in motion did not always hold steady. The Buddy De Sylva production of

An aerial view of the Fox Hills Studio looking north from Pico Boulevard, after the merger in 1935, with standing sets clearly visible on the backlot (courtesy Robert S. Birchard).

Nymph Errant, starring Alice Faye and Jack Haley, was to start production January 21, but did not begin until July by which point Haley had been replaced by Ray Walker and De Sylva was no longer producer. *Thunder in the Night* was to start on January 14 with Warner Baxter and Ketti Gallian in producer Erich Pommer's second feature. Before it did, though, Baxter and Gallian were assigned to *Under the Pampas Moon* which began filming in February. They were replaced by Edmund Lowe and Karen Morley with George Archainbaud as director and John Stone producing when the film went into production in February. *Work of Art*, based on the Sinclair Lewis book, had a start date of January 14 at the Western lot. It never began. The fluidity of the production schedule is illustrated by how interchangeable film projects were at studios in this period. There was always enough contract talent around to mix and match projects so that the total number of a year's films could be met. However, quality could suffer just as easily when there was so much shifting around of talent.

Sol Wurtzel's corporate profile also rose during this period as he continued to be a reliable source of Fox product.

> Fox's Hollywood studio, which has been under Sol M. Wurtzel's command since it reopened in May 1933, will hereafter be in every way on an equal footing with the company's Movietone City studio, and will share on the same basis in the services of the company's stars, directors and writers as well as having equal access to story material, it is announced by Winfield Sheehan, vice-president and general manager of production. The action comes as a result of Wurtzel's work in the last 12 months, during which he produced, among other films, "Judge Priest," "Handy Andy," "Life Begins at 40," and "Bright Eyes." Wurtzel now is making "Dante's Inferno," one of the company's big films of the year. Will Rogers' "Steamboat Round the Bend" and others are in preparation.
>
> John Stone continues as Wurtzel's chief aide. He made "Baby Take a Bow," and the Charlie Chan films, in addition to supervising all the Spanish productions. Joseph Engel and Edward T. Lowe recently were promoted to associate producers by Wurtzel.[100]

In a continuing effort to build up a talent pool, the Fox Film Stock Company was formed under the guidance of Edward Curtis, Broadway stage director. Curtis was signed to also direct screen tests and coach young players.[101] Fox also signed 14 new female players from around the country. Of the group, only Lynn Bari was able to establish a career.

From April through June, Fox was about to start production on 21 films from its 1935-1936 program. With great fanfare, Winfield Sheehan signed Tutta Rolf, Scandinavian stage, screen and operatic star to play in a piece tentatively titled *The Dressmaker* co-starring with Clive Brook. The film was to be adapted by Samson Raphaelson from a French stage comedy by Alfred Savoir. It was to be produced by Robert T. Kane under the direction of Harry Lachman. Sheehan's talents missed more often than succeeded and Rolph was no exception. She made just this one American film, released as *Dressed to Thrill* before returning to Europe.[102]

Even though the Fox Film Corporation was about to see some of its most profitable films in years with the emergence of Shirley Temple as an audience grabber, all the announcements and pronouncements of Winfield Sheehan would soon prove to be academic. Sidney Kent was already pursuing a deal that would change the future of the Fox Film Corporation.

15. 20th Century Pictures

Concurrently with William Fox taking his company public, beginning to buy theaters and solidify his empire in 1925, a two-line entry in the "Hollywood Happenings" column of the *Film Daily* simply stated, "Darryl Francis Zanuck has re-signed a long-term contract with Warner Bros."[1] It might have seemed inconsequential to even the most avid reader of trade magazines, but nobody could have known what it portended.

Darryl Zanuck, born in Wahoo, Nebraska, in 1902, was to become a genuine Hollywood wonder boy. Although initially overshadowed by the proclaimed moviemaking genius of Irving Thalberg, Zanuck grew into an outsized role from his earliest days. An adventurer and self-promoter, he developed as a skilled screenwriter and motion picture executive with very little formal education or journalistic background. What Zanuck possessed was a vivid imagination, razor-sharp story sense, boundless energy and complete enthusiasm for the film industry.

At age 21, after being published under the sponsorship of a hair tonic company, the whippet-thin, buck-toothed five-foot-six-inch tyro parlayed his limited experience into a writing assignment at Warner Bros. One year later, he was writing screenplays for the canine star of the lot, Rin-Tin-Tin. His speed and acuity in screenwriting led to other assignments and he was promoted to more prestigious projects involving some of the studio's top talent, including stars like Dolores Costello, Louise Fazenda, Sydney Chaplin and May McAvoy. Zanuck was so prolific that in 1923 and 1924 he wrote 20 screenplays. In 1925, at Jack Warner's request, he began adopting pseudonyms so exhibitors would not complain about the studio's frugality in hiring writers. For the next four years, he turned out 36 stories, adaptations and screenplays under aliases Gregory Rogers, Melville Crossman and Mark Canfield as well as his own name. These mystery screenwriters were occasionally sought out by agents for work at other studios.

While he was at Warners, Zanuck spent a great deal of time in the lot's editing rooms, absorbing how a film was cut together and learning the tricks of saving bad films. So obviously attuned to all aspects of filmmaking, Zanuck was named head of production at Warner Bros. in October 1928. Still relatively young and unknown to the industry at large, his name was misspelled in a the *Film Daily* article as Daryl Zanuck.[2] In his executive position, he was reportedly responsible for inserting actual dialogue for Al Jolson into *The Jazz Singer*.

Not only the benefactor of a terrific story sense, Zanuck had a producer's intuition about what the public wanted to see. He revolutionized the early talkies with a cycle of tough gangster films, including *Doorway to Hell*, *Little Caesar* and *The Public Enemy*. It was under his supervision that an all-out effort for new faces brought stars like Al Jolson, Edward G. Robinson, James Cagney, Bette Davis, Ruby Keeler, George Arliss, Joan Blondell, Loretta Young, Aline MacMahon, Warren William, and Dick Powell to the screen. Trusted by actors and respectful of writers, Zanuck forged professional and personal relationships that would last decades in a business known for short careers and shorter friendships.

In May 1931, Zanuck was named as the executive in charge of both Warner Bros. and First National by Jack L. Warner. Hal Wallis and Lucien Hubbard became his associate producers. By now, all trade journals knew how to spell Zanuck's name.[3] From then on, he made front-page copy. Darryl Francis Zanuck also became known in the business as a fearless polo player and avid adventurer, always ready to spend his vacation in the wilds, hunting or fishing.

In his executive position, never being one to shy away from controversial material, Zanuck set a pattern for the socially relevant films that Warner Bros. would produce for the next decade, when he enthusiastically backed the production of Mervyn LeRoy's *I Am a Fugitive from a Chain Gang* and Michael Curtiz's *20,000 Years in Sing Sing*, in 1932. Zanuck's success was unprecedented. No writer had ever made the transition so quickly to control the entire output of a major studio. Even when compared to Thalberg, Zanuck stands out as a capable hands-on executive who was willing to be involved in every stage of production. In January 1933, Warners–First National signed Zanuck to a new three-year contract as production chief.[4]

Zanuck did not abide by any particular formula for films, but his productions tended to move swiftly and smartly along in a coherent manner. Characters were well defined and there was seldom an endless amount of dialogue (a common fault of many early talking pictures). No scenes in a Zanuck film went longer than necessary to make a story point and there were introductory and periodic montages that tended to add pacing to a film. Brevity and story movement were the most telling aspects of the movies Zanuck supervised.

In January 1933, during the period of Zanuck's ascendancy at Warners, the Fox Film Corporation was struggling to produce worthwhile, money-making entertainment. There were trade rumors of a merger between Fox and Warner–First National.

> Understood here that the whole motivation of the deal is the opportunity of Fox to get the advantage of Warner–First National production organization. If that is worth $63,000,000, which is supposed to be the price set on the Warner–First National outfit, then production brains are at a new high in the picture market.
>
> The feeling around town is that the deal, if and when made, will provide for a substantial cash payment to the Warners, plus a participating interest, places on the board, etc., with Kent heading both groups and Zanuck in charge of production for the joint companies.[5]

Within a week, any potential deal with Fox was off.

It's no secret that the Warners went to the merger market. Burdened with some 300 theatres that were driving them almost insane with the weekly losses, they went to offer the best production organization in pictures. But they found that no other company could match their properties and offer a deal that had any semblance of being to their own advantage and the advantage of the merged companies.

The Warner productions are making and have made for the past two years, better than $100,000 weekly profit. The theatres during that time have lost them twice that amount each week. They now have deals to turn individual houses and groups of houses over to independent operators and are ready and willing to enter into any pooling arrangement of producer-owned circuits for the betterment of their own condition and that of the entire industry.[6]

Although this merger never occurred, it was highly prescient that Zanuck was suggested as the man to take over Fox's ailing production department. One vote in favor of the merger was the outspoken editor of the *Hollywood Reporter*, W.R. Wilkerson: "Fox's greatest need at present is a competent, economical production organization. Warners can give it the best in the business. What Warners requires most is financing. Fox, through its Chase affiliation, can supply that."[7]

Zanuck was also known for listening to suggestions from everyone, especially in script development.

> Few studio executives put themselves on the spot as does Darryl Zanuck. At story conferences Zanuck has a transcription made of all conversations anent the story with all suggestions, no matter who makes them, recorded. Following the confab everyone who attended receives a copy of what transpired. Transcriptions are dragged out after the preview with all concerned with the picture's production at the conference.
>
> Zanuck then reads the suggestions with the credit for the picture's high spots going to the one who made the original contribution and the panning for the bad spots going likewise.
>
> Often Zanuck has to take his share of the panning.[8]

Even with his importance to the company, Zanuck was well aware that the strong Warner family ties at the core of the company would be an impediment to him ever becoming a full partner at the studio. Nevertheless, he was a loyal company man. During the period of salary cutbacks in early 1933, Zanuck encouraged fellow workers to agree to these emergency measures even though he did not believe in them himself.

Having earned the trust of studio workers at all levels, the Warners made him their spokesperson when there were concerns about the financial condition of the company: "Darryl Zanuck, production chief of Warners, called practically all contract writers, directors and stars into his office Monday (Jan. 30) and assured them confidentially that the Warner company was not involved in either a merger or receivership, and there was nothing for anyone connected with the organization to worry about."[9]

Having been so instrumental in the success of Warner Bros. during the coming of sound and still being shut out from a full partnership rankled the young dynamo. He was even held up as the standard other studio heads should follow by W.R. Wilkerson, editor and publisher of the *Hollywood Reporter*: "Zanuck has proven that a studio can turn out a good program of pictures with a minimum of executive power. Warners are making, have made, 60 pictures a year for the three years, with a top of four executives and now just about three. And those 60 pictures are made in eight months, with plenty of time in between for those executives to play and rest. If Zanuck and Warners can do it, why can't the other studios?"[10]

Then, in mid–April 1933, came a trade paper headline, "ZANUCK OUT OF WARNERS." Once again, he was front-page news. This bombshell exploded when Harry Warner refused to accept the ruling of the Emergency Committee of the Academy on the date that Warner employees would revert to full pay. Harry Warner had promised to abide by the committee's decision and Darryl Zanuck resented the fact that Warner broke his promise. It was Zanuck, at the Warners' bidding, who had told the staff that the terms of the salary cut would be fairly administered. He claimed he could not tolerate anyone making him look like a liar. There were some industry figures who suspected that, since Zanuck could not get much farther at Warners, the salary-cut issue paved the way for an exit from his contract.

Harry Warner announced, "Due to a disagreement of policy in company management, Darryl Zanuck today tendered his resignation to Warner Bros. Pictures Inc., which the company accepted. The resignation is effective Saturday, April 15. The future business policies of the company will be handled by Jack L. Warner."[11]

W.R. Wilkerson continued his analysis of this industry-shaking event: "This was probably the most astounding single announcement that has ever been voiced in the long history of the picture business, and one that will furnish food for conversation for days to come…. That Warners would have precipitated anything that would lead up to his resignation and the acceptance of that resignation is plenty cause for astonishment."[12]

In this same issue, Wilkerson once again laid praises at Zanuck's feet.

> Gentlemen of the Motion Picture Industry, we present for your approval this morning the greatest piece of motion picture property living today — we offer you Darryl Francis Zanuck, former production head of Warner–First National Pictures. How much are we offered for this prized property?
>
> We offer with Mr. Zanuck a guarantee of as many pictures as one organization could handle in a single year and more successful pictures on that program than any other producing organization.[13]

Zanuck's contract had four more years to run and his release was signed in the presence of Will Hays, as well as an attorney for the Producers Association and counsel for both parties of the agreement. Zanuck insisted on this procedure to be certain the Warners had no claim on him or any say in what he could do beyond this point. After the resignation, Zanuck issued a terse statement: "I have nothing to add to the statement that has already been given you. You know as much about my future plans as I do. For the present I am going to take a rest."[14] It was a rare event in Hollywood when someone with a four-year signed contract did not demand a financial settlement.

The resignation was the talk of the town. When Winfield Sheehan was a guest at a wedding two days later, he was reportedly approached by another guest who, not knowing who he was, inquired, "Don't you think Darryl Zanuck would be a good man to head production at Fox?"[15]

With the departure of Zanuck, Jack Warner called in all executives, writers and directors to assert themselves as to whether they wanted to remain at the studio. None, other than Raymond Griffith and William Dover who had left with Zanuck, departed. Hal Wallis took charge of writers preparing stories and Henry Blanke took over for Raymond Griffith.[16]

After he left the studio, Darryl Zanuck was concerned about rumors of re-cutting on his last two productions, *Gold Diggers of 1933*, and *Captured*. When both films were released, their box-office results left Zanuck's sterling reputation intact. *Gold Diggers*, in particular, became a smash success and led to a series of similarly titled musicals.

Joseph M. Schenck, the Russian-born 55-year-old entrepreneurial president of United Artists who already knew Darryl Zanuck, immediately arranged for a meeting. He produced a $100,000 check signed by none other than Louis B. Mayer. Schenck proposed setting up a production company in partnership with Zanuck. The only catch to the investment from Mayer was that they take in William B. Goetz, Mayer's son-in-law, as an executive, to which Zanuck readily agreed. Mayer's participation would also provide access to M.G.M.'s stable of stars.[17] Mayer's total financing amounted to $1,400,000 and it was augmented by $3,000,000 invested by Dr. A.H. Giannini, president of Bank of America. Consolidated Film Laboratories also kicked in $750,000.[18]

With high-paying offers of employment coming from every major producing company in the business, Zanuck announced on April 17, 1933, two days after his resignation, that he would be heading his own organization in partnership with Joseph M. Schenck, producing from eight to twelve pictures a year. Banking interests were ready to fund whatever he wanted to do. He would be guaranteed his Warner salary plus a 50 percent ownership in the company. Moving with incredible speed, the deal would be signed and sealed within 48 hours.

With Schenck's long-standing relationship with United Artists, it was inevitable that the lot on Santa Monica Boulevard in Hollywood would be a natural location for the new company. Ten story readers were immediately hired and began looking for material. The films that resulted would be released by United Artists. Until production was ready to start, Zanuck left for a month-long vacation. He traveled to British Columbia to packhorse for four days, then to canoe to the headwaters of the Columbia River. Joining him were Lloyd Bacon, Raymond Griffith, Michael Curtiz, Ray Enright, John Adolfi and Samuel G. Engel. Unfortunately, putting a damper on the proceedings, 45-year-old Adolfi, Zanuck's close friend, suffered a cerebral hemorrhage on the trip and died in the wilds. The body was transported back to civilization by packhorse then returned to Los Angeles for interment.[19]

In celebration of the new venture the *Hollywood Reporter* featured 48 pages of congratulatory ads for Zanuck with best wishes expressed by many of the people with whom he had worked at Warners, including directors, writers, actors, executives, management companies, agents, and even other producers. There were no congratulations from any of the Warner brothers.

On April 28, 1933, the new Joseph Schenck–Darryl Zanuck production company was given a name, suggested by Sam Engel — 20th Century Pictures.[20] Zanuck said, "The reason for selecting

Darryl Francis Zanuck, circa 1933 (from the collection of Aubrey Solomon).

Twentieth Century Pictures Inc. was because it seems to exemplify the types of pictures we intend to produce. Our stories, with but few exceptions, will be modern headline types of stories, packing a punch aimed at the box-office. We intend to carry to the box-offices a spirit as modern and as vital as the company's name."[21]

The deal with United Artists was for eight features, budgeted between $210,000 to $225,000 each. Zanuck received $100,000 as a bonus upon signing (although Mayer's signature on the check was not made public) and $4,500 weekly plus 50 percent of the net profits of the pictures produced. United Artists' distribution fee was set at 26 percent, the same rate given to Sam Goldwyn for his films, but below the standard 33 percent charged by the company. Zanuck's executive personnel went under contract, but there were separate deals made with writers, directors and actors for individual pictures.[22]

William Goetz, Mayer's son-in-law who was a one-time story editor at Fox Films, and Raymond Griffith, a silent-screen actor whose on-screen career disappeared with the coming of sound, were the first to join 20th Century Pictures. Goetz came from Radio Pictures and was made vice-president while Griffith became Zanuck's supervisor of production. Upon their arrival Joseph Schenck stated, "Pictures must have new blood. The film industry needs men with modern ideas, men not handicapped by ideas of the past. Producers of old have a hangover of ideas, and the present generation will not accept them. The reason that costume pictures are a failure today is because people of the present day cannot enter into the spirit of past generations. Zanuck has youth and great ideas, and his mind is a perfect blend of artistry and practicability. Goetz and Griffith are youthful, too, in addition to being fully experienced."[23] It was somewhat ironic that Griffith was already 38 years old but to the older Schenck that was considered "young."

The first star contract signed by the company was with Constance Cummings who would be under Zanuck's guidance for two years.[24] Cummings was a mid-level star under contract to Columbia since 1931, but in a contentious disagreement with the studio's boss, Harry Cohn, over the cancellation of her deal. She had gone to First National as a leading lady opposite Warren William in *The Mind Reader*, a film supervised by Zanuck, and then to England to make two pictures for British-Gaumont.

Zanuck also signed an exclusive deal with George Arliss, considered a feather in the cap of the fledg-

Zanuck signs George Arliss to a contract with 20th Century Pictures in 1933, leading to considerable animosity with the Warner Bros. (from the collection of Aubrey Solomon).

ling company, since he was such a potent box-office draw. Another catch was Loretta Young, whom Zanuck had starred in countless Warner pictures. The first three directors under contract to 20th Century were Gregory La Cava, Sidney Lanfield and Walter Lang. La Cava signed for two pictures and the others for three each. Harry Brand, who had been Joseph Schenck's press agent for many years, became the head of studio publicity for 20th Century Pictures in June 1933. Zanuck later added Harold Long, his former secretary, and Laird Doyle from M.G.M., to the scenario department. He even hired his former barber from the Warner lot to work at the United Artists studio.

Requests made to other studios for loan-outs were refused outright, possibly due to pressure from the Warners who had no interest in seeing Zanuck succeed. Especially galling to Schenck and Zanuck was the fact that the loan-outs were requested on performers who were not scheduled to work at the time of the request. The company needed immediate casts for 12 productions to be made between June 1933 and January 1934.

Schenck and Zanuck finally delivered an ultimatum about the lack of co-operation. Both men made it clear that, if some consideration was not forthcoming within 24 hours, they would feel free to sign up whatever talent they wanted when their contracts expired.[25] There was an agreement among signatory companies of the Motion Picture Producers Association that forbade poaching other studios' stars. Since the new company was not yet a member of the Producers Association, it was under no legal obligation to abide by the standard rules and regulations. Zanuck and Schenck were changing the status quo, much to the Warners' chagrin.

Jack L. Warner called an immediate meeting of the Producers Association after Zanuck signed George Arliss, insisting that the actor had not yet been freed from Warners' contract. Zanuck felt Warner had no cause for concern since Arliss's contract had expired before any overtures were made. Of course, part of the problem was the persistent bad blood between the Warners and 20th Century Pictures.

In an issue of the *Hollywood Reporter*, a humorous column stated, "There has been a story going the rounds of Hollywood for days that when Jack Warner was notified that the Schenck-Zanuck organization had signed George Arliss, he hit the house-tops and had to send home for a fresh set of linen."[26]

Schenck went on record by notifying other studios that 20th Century was in business to stay and must have actors. The new company would take them on loan or in the open market, but it pledged not to raid contract people. Schenck added that he and Zanuck had no intention of offering increased salaries to lure talent and that they hoped to get some people on percentage deals, whereby the artists would be paid according to the box-office success of their pictures.[27]

When word leaked out that Zanuck had already received a loan-out arrangement for Wallace Beery and Clark Gable from M.G.M. and George Raft from Paramount, Jack Warner insisted on an investigation into whether some unannounced collusion was at work. Adolph Zukor was singularly unmoved by these complaints since he was still upset by Warners' raiding tactics in snaring Ruth Chatterton, William Powell and Kay Francis two years earlier. Zukor was quoted as saying, "Now you ask for my help when someone is doing it to you?"[28] There was never any collusion proven and eventually 20th Century joined the Producers Association and was treated as an equal member.

Warners unofficially severed all goodwill ties with other studios in the area of loan-outs. It became that studio's policy to not even consider such deals largely because it would mean dealing, as well, with 20th Century Pictures. Burned by the George Arliss signing and the acquisition of similar story properties, Warners closed the studio gates on their talent pool. "The only way the Warner company can defend itself is by ignoring inter-studio relations and concentrating on its own problems, confident that it is self-sustaining and independent of other majors."[29]

Zanuck was determined to avoid the friction that existed in major companies between the home offices in New York and production in Hollywood, so he eliminated the idea of having a New York office. He had much experience with the wasted time, money, and energy on the disagreements between the two branches so he concentrated all business in one location. He made arrangements to have all agencies deal through his office at the United Artists lot. All negotiations for talent and literary material would be dealt with in Los Angeles. William Dover was the contact man for talent and Howard Smith was handling story material.[30]

Mary Pickford, one of the founders of United Artists, was flattering to the association with the Zanuck company and looked forward to a long relationship: "I consider the contract with Darryl

Zanuck of the greatest possible advantage to United Artists and to all its production and distribution members. Mr. Zanuck is one of the greatest producers in the business and I only hope that he may find time to supervise some of my productions."[31] Samuel Goldwyn, another partner who had been the top producer at United Artists, was not as enthusiastic about the addition of 20th Century because the new company was getting more than its share of attention.[32]

There were others, aside from the Warners and Goldwyn, who were not initially excited by Zanuck's new company. Pete Harrison, of the independent New York–based *Harrison's Reports*, offered his perspective.

> For days and days there was a discussion as to whether Zanuck was or was not responsible for the production of the Warner successes last season, the majority opinion inclining to give him credit for them.
> HARRISON'S REPORTS had formed no opinion; pictures at the large studios are the product of a combination of talents, and it felt that no one far away from the studio could determine, and that Zanuck's ability could be demonstrated only after he made several pictures on his own.
> Since good pictures depend by about ninety percent on good story material, the ability of Darryl Zanuck to select such material would be the best proof of his ability to make good pictures.
> Since the two books Darryl Zanuck has announced for production are the worst any new producer could have selected (*The Mighty Barnum* and *Miss Lonelyhearts*), I now wonder whether he was the water boy for Warner Bros., instead of the great genius, responsible for the good Warner Bros. pictures, he was painted by the trade papers![33]

The first film scheduled for release by the new company was *The Bowery*, directed by Raoul Walsh, who was borrowed from Fox because they could not find a picture for him. Howard Estabrook, recently released from Fox, and James Gleason were writing the screenplay based on *Chuck Conners*, a novel by Martin L. Simmons and B.R. Solomon. It was a raucous story about the rivalry between Conners and Steve Brodie, the bridge jumper at the turn of the century. *The Bowery* would start shooting in July and would star Wallace Beery and George Raft.

Within days of this announcement there was further rancor from Warner Bros. Warners claimed that Zanuck was infringing on their rights with three pieces of material. One was *Chuck Conners*, which the Warners story department had considered but then dismissed because it was not appropriate for Edward G. Robinson, for whom it had been submitted to the studio. Zanuck optioned the book when he felt he could cast someone like Wallace Beery. *Trouble-Shooters* was another disputed property, a story which had been purchased from J.R. Bren who was already in the 20th Century writing department. Bren threatened to sue Warners if they went ahead with another story with the same title. The final property riling the Warners was a story about the Rothschilds. There had already been 64 stories and seven plays produced about the famous banking family. In this case, Warners owned one of the many stories, so they used this as yet another reason to antagonize the new company. Zanuck referred to the story battles in a statement: "I am not interested in any mud-slinging campaign with Warners or anyone else, as I have noticed that candidates who did the slinging always checked up on the short end in the election. I feel sure that, should Warners have any just claim to the three stories in question, the courts of the United States will recognize that claim. And, anyhow, I am too busy trying to make good pictures to take up my time in argument."[34]

The animosity continued to be reported in the trades, still centered on Zanuck's acquisition of George Arliss. *The Hollywood Reporter* wrote,

> New York — At the meeting of the Hays' members held here Monday night, the proceedings were greatly enlivened with a threat made by Harry Warner that unless the alleged "raiding" activities of Darryl Zanuck, Joseph Schenck and their Twentieth Century Productions were instantly regulated, the Warner membership in the Hays group would be withdrawn immediately.
> Hays replied that, so far as he knew, the Twentieth Century crowd had done nothing illegal, unethical or unlawful and until Mr. Warner brought him facts that breached the code of ethics of the organization, some proof of something illegal, there seemed nothing he could do. Mr. Warner was also reminded of a similar complaint made by Paramount some months ago about Warner activities.[35]

The feud, which went on for another six months, was finally settled when 20th Century released actor Paul Kelly, a former Warners player, from his contract and allowed him to return to Warners to appear in a film with Aline MacMahon. Kelly wanted the part, and the casting chiefs at both Warners and 20th Century got together and worked out a series of loan-outs that would follow.[36]

Darryl Zanuck was rightly concerned about limited stage space on the U.A. lot. There were only two large stages and a couple of small ones. Samuel Goldwyn was shooting an Eddie Cantor film on one and an Anna Sten picture on the other.

The best Zanuck could hope for was to get one of the big stages and a smaller one. For this reason a big musical he was planning would have to be shot at another studio so that it would be ready for the fall. Zanuck's presence on the lot also meant that every inch of studio space was now taken up. Space for several of the writers was made in dressing rooms.[37] Writers ended up in offices on the adjacent Educational Studios lot while construction was rushed on an addition to the administration building on the U.A. lot to provide 16 new offices.

In need of permanent studio space, 20th Century acquired the studio owned by United Artists at the beginning of December 1933 from principal owners Douglas Fairbanks and Mary Pickford. The deal reportedly involved around $750,000.[38]

The Bowery started the company off with a hit. It bowed to terrific reviews and remarkable business, boasted an ad in *Motion Picture Daily*. "A smash. Has everything a picture should have," raved the *Hollywood Reporter*. "Tab this as a record wrecker. A cinch to sell! They've handed you everything," crowed the *Motion Picture Herald*. "Gets the new company away to a grand start! A money magnet at any theatre," predicted *Variety*.[39] The final box-office results lived up to all the hyperbole as *The Bowery* became one of the industry's top-grossing films of the year, showing a profit to the new company of $304,286.18.[40]

After the rowdiness of *The Bowery* came a gangster melodrama, *Broadway Through a Keyhole*, from a story by Walter Winchell, featuring Constance Cummings, Paul Kelly and the latest crooner, Russ Columbo. Another tough gangster picture followed in *Blood Money*, the twist in this one being a female gang leader played by Judith Anderson.

Zanuck expressed his expectations for 1934 in a year-end trade article.

> The most significant development for 1934, to my mind, is the impending change from mass production to individual production. In my opinion mass production is due for the discard because the day of "cycles" is over. Practically every new type of picture has been made, and there has been no background or type of story left untouched. Producers who play a game of "Follow the Leader" must now depend on their own resources and ingenuity.
>
> Each picture, henceforth, must be made as big and as good as possible. This can only be accomplished by full concentration on one picture at a time. Stars must be supported by stars, in strong stories, produced on a lavish scale. That is what I mean by individual production.[41]

Zanuck was echoing a thesis put forward by M.G.M. many years earlier, and he was in the best position to take advantage of it. Without any pre-existing production patterns in place, he could easily model 20th Century on this thesis.

Heeding the public moral objections by *Harrison's Reports* to the sordidness of *Miss Lonelyhearts* by Nathanael West, Zanuck abandoned most of the original story, retitled his film *Advice to the Lovelorn* and starred Lee Tracy as a fast-talking, wisecracking reporter who is assigned to a Lonelyhearts column as a punishment. It did not help the returns on *Advice*, which became the company's first flop with only $384,000 in world rentals on a negative of $226,000.

With large box-office returns flowing in from his other releases, Zanuck took time off to have new material developed.

> Twentieth Century will have a three month shutdown on or about May 1, at which time Darryl Zanuck and Joseph Schenck will wind up the first year's work of the new company with the completion of twelve pictures.
>
> Darryl Zanuck and William Goetz will leave for Europe at that time with their families and Darryl Zanuck will continue on to Africa on a big game hunt while Goetz will remain in Paris.[42]

Zanuck always rewarded himself with an outdoors adventure during a hiatus.

What may have seemed a truce with Warners after the settlement of loan-out issues did not carry over to the distribution operation. In late January 1934, Warner unexpectedly booked their new release, *I've Got Your Number*, to open at the Roxy Theater in early February. "The official explanation given is that the Warner boys are filled up with pictures for their Strand and Hollywood theatres, but the undercover story is that the deal is intended to beat Darryl Zanuck to Broadway on his picture with a similar theme, the telephone company trouble shooters. Zanuck's picture 'Looking For Trouble' will probably have to wait its turn at the United Artists Rivoli, which won't be in the near future because of the success made by 'Gallant Lady.'"[43]

Continuing his streak of successful releases, *Gallant Lady* was a change of pace from the period adventures or contemporary melodramas. The change did not hurt 20th Century's chances for a hit movie as various reviews were quoted in the *Hollywood Reporter*: "Being singularly fortunate, this time, in having an excellent story, Miss Harding rises gallantly to the occasion and gives a performance that is earnest and real," wrote the *World Telegram*. "The picture rings true in all its poignant sequences and is exquisitely played by a cast of theatrical craftsmen," issued the *American*. The *New York Times* stated that "there is a good deal of well-written dialogue ... results in the rather prosaic story being frequently quite interesting."[44]

By the release of the sixth 20th Century picture, *Looking for Trouble*, reviewers already had an idea of what to expect. "In the full swing of the Zanuck stride of pictures with action, humor and plenty of the well-known audience appeal comes 'Looking for Trouble.' ... Still on the lookout for the human interest story and the punch in every day drama, Zanuck has put on the screen the story of the 'trouble-shooters' of the telephone company.... J.R. Bren has written a swell yarn made a hundred percent better by some of the snappiest dialogue written by Leonard Praskins and Elmer Harris we have heard for many a day."[45] Zanuck obviously had carried over his emphasis on script development to the new company. It was exactly what was so lacking at the Fox Film Corporation since the advent of the talkies.

Although there had been financial successes for 20th Century Pictures, it was not until *House of Rothschild* hit the screens that rave reviews poured in unanimously from the New York papers: the *News*, *Post*, *World-Telegram*, *Journal*, *American*, *Herald-Tribune*, *Sun*, *Times*, and *Mirror*.

Opening its New York engagement at $2 roadshow prices, seats were sold out two weeks in advance of opening performances. *Rothschild* played at the Astor Theater on Broadway, and it grossed $21,600, which was $2,160 beyond the maximum capacity of the theater.[46] In the second week it grossed $22,340. In making these amounts, it had to play to full capacity for two shows a day (four on Saturday and three on Sunday), and then provide for over $4,000 worth of customers with standing room only. In its seventh week, it was still reaching a $20,000 gross. The film was projected to run for six months and take in $400,000 at the Astor box-office. It was estimated that another $400,000 would come in from circuits in neighborhood runs. This would yield a total of $800,000 for just the one city of New York.[47] This very popular film was taking the lead in grosses in every city it opened. Its Hollywood premiere at Grauman's Chinese Theater charged a $5 admission.

"The staggering business that is being done by 'The House of Rothschild' at every engagement has led experts to the belief that the picture is headed for a gross of $3,000,000." The film was banned in France, though, according to Zanuck because of "resentment by the French Rothschilds against the Napoleonic angle."[48] The run of 20th Century's hit movies was not lost on news magazines. Adding to the film's prestige, George Arliss as Rothschild was featured on the cover of the March 26, 1934 issue of *Time* magazine.

Every indication showed movie profits increasing in 1934, backed by foreign revenue, which was more dramatically valuable because of the weakness of the U.S. dollar. The *Hollywood Reporter* estimated that M.G.M. was collecting almost $750,000 weekly in foreign markets. Paramount was averaging $400,000; Warners was doing $400,000 weeks' worth of business; Fox had weeks of $400,000 and none less than $250,000; Universal and Radio Pictures averaged $175,000 to $200,000. With those figures added to the bottom line, M.G.M. was expected to show a profit of $4,000,000 for the year. Paramount and Warners would make better than $2,000,000. Fox and Radio would run between $1,500,000 and $2,000,000. Columbia would hit $1,000,000. "The most astounding success that will be shown by any company for a twelve month business will be that of Twentieth Century. On returns in so far and with only four more pictures to complete for their year's output, it is estimated that that organization will net well over $2,000,000 for their efforts."[49]

It was impossible to ignore the incredible results that this fledgling, independent company — with no studio of its own, limited contract talent and no previously owned literary material — could explode to profitability so quickly. In just seven months after its initial film went into production, 20th Century had placed itself among the most profitable major studios that had been in operation for two decades. It also helped boost United Artists' bottom line with all the revenue from the distribution of the Zanuck films.

After his first wave of films was complete, Zanuck took advantage of his star contracts by loaning out Loretta Young, Constance Bennett and Fredric March to M.G.M. while 20th Century was on its three-month hiatus. Directors on loan-out included William Wellman, Walter Lang, and Sidney Lanfield. George Arliss and Ronald Colman were not put on loan.[50]

Meanwhile, grabbing publicity, Zanuck offered acting contracts to Prince Sigvard of Sweden and his fiancée and blonde German film star, Erika Patzek. Nothing ever resulted, other than some ink in the trades.[51]

The 20th Century production model involved

> **Greetings:**
>
> We, the Screen Stars of Hollywood, join in extending felicitation and Birthday Greetings to 20th Century Pictures and to Joseph M. Schenck and Darryl F. Zanuck, on the occasion of this First Anniversary Celebration.
>
> We also extend Best Wishes for the Great Success of its First Anniversary Picture, George Arliss in "The House of Rothschild".
>
> signed:
>
> *[numerous signatures]*

A congratulatory declaration from many in Hollywood wishing Zanuck success on the first anniversary of 20th Century Pictures. The top signatures belong to Mary Pickford, Charlie Chaplin, Harold Lloyd, and Marie Dressler. Others include Douglas Fairbanks, Fredric March, Sylvia Sidney, Jackie Cooper, Gloria Swanson, Clark Gable, Charles Laughton, George Raft, Loretta Young, Eddie Cantor, Ronald Colman, Gary Cooper, Jack Oakie, Constance Cummings, Fay Wray, Claudette Colbert, Irene Dunne, Carole Lombard, Bruce Cabot, Ben Lyon, Ramon Novarro, Colleen Moore, Bing Crosby, Richard Dix, Robert Montgomery, W.C. Fields, Joel McCrea, Pert Kelton, John Boles, Jeanette MacDonald, Edmund Lowe, Spencer Tracy, Johnny Weissmuller, and others. One can only imagine what the original document would be worth (courtesy Karl Thiede).

astute script preparation, efficient planning and compact shooting schedules. For the largely interior set-based filming of *The Affairs of Cellini*, director Gregory La Cava was able to finish all production within 24 days. The elaborate sets and costumes, though, brought production costs up to $549,000, which was not covered by the $852,000 in world rentals. Nevertheless, the losses were ultimately not critical since the profits from the hits vastly swamped the small number of flops.

Virtually all of Zanuck's productions proceeded smoothly, from filming through editing. Following his practice at Warners, Zanuck was able to deliver his films on time and either on or below budget. His selection of seasoned and trustworthy directors and casts delivered reliable performances and mostly problem-free films.

The motion picture world was always wondering what subjects Zanuck would tackle next. On his hiatus tour of Europe, where he visited all the United Artists exchanges on the continent, he was asked this very question. The answer was surprising. The purveyor of rowdy, action packed films and contemporary melodramas said that he wanted to bring Shakespeare and opera to the screen. Then, when asked about the foremost development in technology, color films,

> he said that he did not believe they would ever become popular. He felt they could not be as good photographically as black and white.
> His prediction as to the public taste in pictures is that, this year, he thinks productions of great scope are desired. He cited, as examples, productions dealing with British rule in India, or war pictures with a definite anti-war slant and with a distinct patriotic angle.
> He is not at all worried over the future of the industry. Its troubles now, he said, are due to past huge real estate and theatre commitments.
> "This resulted," he said, "in producing companies being obliged to make too many pictures, only a few of which were good, and so they lost money, both on the pictures and in their theatres."[52]

For Zanuck, the future, as the past, was a great adventure leading only to amazing success. Several days after this interview, Zanuck was reported as having purchased the rights to *Clive of India*, a play that was running in London which starred Leslie Banks.

Zanuck had a close relationship with writers, developed in his earliest years as an independent producer, and had great respect for the craft. "When Gene Fowler made his deal with Darryl Zanuck to write the story of 'Barnum,' he was to get one-third of his huge stipend when he started to work, one-third when the story was finished, and the last third when they started shooting. But when Fowler turned in his 'manuscript,' Zanuck was so delighted with the thing that he paid the scribe his remaining two-thirds dough pronto and signed him all over again to do the script and dialogue for his brainchild. What's more, Zanuck asked Fowler's permission to have copies made of his 'Barnum' story for all the other writers on the lot to get a good healthy glance at — as a perfect example of an A-1 picture story."[53] Compare the writer's status at 20th Century to the attitude at Fox that these talented people did not count as important, and therein lays the reason Zanuck was able to coax more creativity from his screenwriters.

Another writer who joined Darryl Zanuck and 20th Century Pictures was a Georgia-born former journalist. The qualities he possessed were highlighted in a trade article, pointing out the best in new writing talent: "The latest one to make good is Nunnally Johnson, who, in two short years in the picture business, has established himself as an invaluable writing asset to that industry, and the real basis for that success has been not alone his writing talent (which is something), but his enthusiasm for the medium in which he works. It is reflected both in the pictures he has written, which are all way above average, and in his own personal success."[54] Johnson would spend most of his career working with Darryl Zanuck, whom he considered the best executive in the business. The films that resulted included *The House of Rothschild* (1934), *The Prisoner of Shark Island* (1936), *Jesse James* (1939), *The Grapes of Wrath* (1940), *Roxie Hart* (1942), *The Desert Fox* (1951), *How to Marry a Millionaire* (1953) and many more.

The explosive hit-making machine that was 20th Century Pictures was showered with kudos once again in the columns of the *Hollywood Reporter*.

> Joe Schenck made the bid that won Zanuck and we have from Schenck's own lips "It was the best buy I have ever made in the business," for Darryl Zanuck, guiding Twentieth Century production, will turn in a profit in excess of FOUR MILLION DOLLARS for the first twelve months of its operation. With that profit it is easy to estimate what the profits elevated United Artists nearly to the top of the best money-makers of the year among major distributors.
> He just happens to be a "down-to-earth" individual, whose purpose in life is to make good entertainment, whose days and nights (when he is not playing polo or going on long jaunts in the jun-

gles on shooting and fishing trips) are spent in devising entertainment, surrounded by a collection of men and women who respect his judgment, and are anxious to join with him in making that entertainment.

Zanuck's success is the result of sincere effort. Instead of trying to make the production of pictures a tough task, he fights to make it easy, AND IT IS EASY for those who know what it is all about and who are not bound by studio policies and political situations that make the task almost impossible.[55]

Even with Zanuck unbound by studio politics, there were still production minefields around which to maneuver. Although critical of the censorship restrictions imposed by the recent Motion Picture Code, Zanuck's films were still impacted by Joseph Breen's supervision. When *Born to Be Bad* (1934, with Cary Grant and Loretta Young) was filmed before the censorship code became mandatory, it was intended to be a biting and racy portrayal of a careless woman who wrecks an honest man. By the time the film was completed, it was caught up in the tangle of morality policing that was pervading the industry. Forced to give in to Breen's pressures, Zanuck recut the film which rendered it an incoherent mess. Reviewers who were not told of the production problems, chalked up the film's lack of quality to a 20th Century misfire. "This one simply doesn't make the grade," said the *American*. "The picture starts out well enough.... That promise dies early," agreed the *Sun*. "Contains some of the saddest and sometimes most unbearable characters, as well as the most feeble and unreal dialogue imaginable," complained the *World-Telegram*.[56] It was also born to fail in its adulterated version, bringing in rentals of $333,000 which was not enough to offset a cost of $252,000.

A small number of productions still did not mean they all came to the screen as planned. Zanuck, like his counterparts at every other studio, had to deal with the realities that affect a project between concept and final release. Zanuck and Schenck purchased the rights to the play, *The Red Cat*, which Bess Meredyth scripted for Fredric March and Constance Bennett. March did not end up in the cast and was replaced by Maurice Chevalier who was teamed with Merle Oberon in the re-titled *Folies Bergère*. Zanuck planned to shoot *Folies Bergère*, budgeted at a reported $800,000, with the original French Can-Can dancers, all the production props, scenery as well as the chorus brought over from Paris under the supervision of Max Weldie and M. Duval, owners and directors of the Folies in France. Cole Porter was signed to write the music for the film.[57] The involvement of the Folies Bergère also brought some legal problems which had to be resolved before the production went ahead.

There was an announcement by 20th Century of a re-teaming of Clark Gable and Claudette Colbert in *It Had to Happen* to cash in on the success of *It Happened One Night* (1934 — Columbia). It did not happen as planned, although the script was eventually filmed in 1936 with George Raft and Rosalind Russell. The finished product was not quite as exciting with the replacement cast.

Zanuck forged ahead fearlessly with all the pressures and difficulties in buying properties and bringing stories to the screen. After the failure of *Born to Be Bad*, he was fortunate enough to not suffer any further disappointments. On the contrary, his films gained an almost charmed cachet. An amazing run of hits followed including *Bulldog Drummond Strikes Back* (1934) with Ronald Colman, *The Last Gentleman* (1934) starring George Arliss, *The Mighty Barnum* (1934), *Clive of India* (1935), *Folies Bergère* (1935), another Arliss starring role in *Cardinal Richelieu* (1935), then topping off the release schedule, *Les Miserables* (1935) starring Fredric March and Charles Laughton, and the Clark Gable–Loretta Young teaming in *The Call of the Wild* (1935). These films were released to the delight of exhibitors who booked them, to United Artists which distributed them, and to the private shareholders of 20th Century, not the least of whom were Joseph Schenck and Darryl Zanuck. This led Schenck to recollect, "When we started Twentieth Century Pictures, all we had was a desk, a pen, a pencil and a Darryl Zanuck."[58]

When Fox Films president Sidney Kent arrived in Los Angeles on August 21, 1934, for a ten-day stay to check on productions for the upcoming year, Darryl Zanuck and Joseph Schenck coincidentally returned to Los Angeles on the same day from their summer hiatus. This was one month after Fox production head Winfield Sheehan had left on his three-month trip to Europe. But it seems more than just coincidence that Fox's distribution executives were also in town.[59] Although none of these dots were connected in the trades, it is odd that Sidney Kent, who had been steadily on the job for two years without a break, was suddenly taking a "weekend fishing trip."[60] Chances are this was an opportunity for the Fox and the 20th Century people to meet without the prying eyes of the press.

Once again, this is speculation, but another coincidence played into this exact period. Darryl Zanuck, the most successful producer in the business whose films were topping the charts with their grosses, rather than announcing an expansion of his slate of films for the coming year, said he was cutting back his schedule to ten features for the 1934-1935 program. The company appropriated $6,500,000 for the entire slate, which was $2,000,000 more than the previous year. But here is the catch — included in the United Artists distribution deal was a clause that allowed 20th Century to make fewer or more than the ten films. This gave Zanuck and Schenck the leeway to end their relationship at any point with United Artists.[61] It is likely that preliminary talks about merging 20th Century and Fox Films were already taking place.

In early December 1934, Winfield Sheehan hosted the president and directors of the Chase National Bank at the Café de Paris on the Movietone City lot, an affair hosted by Will Rogers and other studio talent. The group spent an entire day surveying the studio.[62] Chase National had long been seeking a buyer for the remaining 72 percent holdings in the Fox Film Corporation since they had ceased providing further financing to the debt-ridden venture. Although it is further speculation, there is a good chance that the suspected conversation between Schenck, Zanuck, and Sidney Kent on the "fishing trip" in late August had progressed to figuring out the financial implications of a merger.

There is an expression commonly associated with successful ventures in the movie business— "timing is everything." This was never truer than in the case of 20th Century Pictures and there was never a better time for a merger. Certainly, Darryl Zanuck's skill in choosing literary material, in gauging the public's taste, and his astuteness in gathering talent under budgetary limitations came into play. However, that all-important timing was a considerable factor as well. The major effects of the economic depression had passed, theater attendance was up, admission prices were slowly on the rise, and those companies in fiscal distress were being reorganized. One factor, not generally attributed to the expansion of the movie business in the mid- to late–1930s, was the newly restored interest by Wall Street in the industry. Due to the bankruptcies and the reorganizations, banking interests were able to get a clearer picture of how the motion picture business operated.

From the earliest days of the studios, the banks rushed into financing companies like the Fox Film Corporation without fully understanding the underpinnings of where all the profits or losses came from. Until massive losses were suffered by Fox, Warners, Paramount and R.K.O. between 1930 and 1933, the banks felt confident that their investments would always be recouped. By 1934, the two best-faring companies in the downturn, Columbia Pictures and M.G.M., offered examples of entities that were run efficiently and profitably when others were failing. The companies that had lost the most readjusted their expenditures to show bigger profits by lowering overhead and production costs. Following these examples, a new business model was created for the banks and their interest in financing major studios was renewed.[63] At the time, 20th Century was in need of financing for its expansion, Bank of America was willing to underwrite Zanuck and Schenck.

There is no doubt that 20th Century Pictures' publicity department, buoyant on its wave of hits, was getting cocky when it announced in a trade ad: "You could gross $30,000,000 on CLIVE OF INDIA if you played to the 60,000,000 people who will read the FULL-PAGE ADS soon to appear in the nation's leading magazines on this 20th CENTURY PICTURE!"[64]

Without any rumors about a merger between Fox and 20th Century, Darryl Zanuck completed work on his last three productions for release in the 1934-1935 season through United Artists. *Les Miserables* went into release April 21, *Cardinal Richelieu*, April 28, and *The Call of the Wild*, May 6.[65]

In early March 1935, Joseph Schenck visited Florida where he met with Sidney Kent, ostensibly to investigate the construction of a $10,000,000 Florida studio. At least, that is what was reported in *Time* magazine. What they really discussed was the continuing plans for a merger. Their subterfuge, however, kept the real purpose of the meeting secret.[66]

Zanuck, carrying on as if the company would continue with United Artists, announced ten films for the 1935-1936 season of 20th Century releases. They included *Ivanhoe, The Man Who Broke the Bank at Monte Carlo* starring Ronald Colman, *Sing Governor Sing* with Phil Baker, *Diamond Horseshoe* starring Lawrence Tibbett, *Shark Island* starring Fredric March, *Professional Soldier* starring Wallace Beery, *Nile Patrol, Gentlemen, the King!, Earthbound,* and *It Had to Happen.* Twentieth Century directors signed for the new season were Gregory LaCava, Roy Del Ruth, John Ford and Rowland V. Lee. Stars already contracted included George Arliss, Loretta Young, Fredric March, Wallace Beery (on loan-out from M.G.M.) and Ronald Colman.[67]

Zanuck, having attained a statesman-like status in the industry, akin to Irving Thalberg, expressed similar views when it came to the value of high-quality productions. Like Thalberg, Zanuck berated producers who made Class-B features, in this case for the express purpose of playing them on double bills: "Pictures of this type are the curse of the business ... they keep audiences away from the theaters." He felt that after a filmgoer saw a succession of mediocre films that were given a huge publicity build-up, interest would wane in seeing any films. Zanuck also recognized the value of making longer films of 10,000 feet, because they froze out a second feature on a program.

Zanuck expressed his feeling that *Les Miserables* would be popular with the public because "its leading character is kicked around by life much in the 1935 depression fashion."[68]

On May 28, 1935, a little more than a month after expounding his views for the trades, the *Film Daily* featured a headline that would herald a major change in the industry, "Framing Details of Fox-20th Century Merger." Behind closed doors and without so much as the slightest leak to the press (most likely since August 1934), Joseph Schenck, Darryl Zanuck, Sidney Kent, the Chase National Bank and Dr. A.H. Giannini's Bank of America, had ironed out all the details for the consolidation of the two companies.

> The merger will include the personal services of Schenck as chairman of the Fox board, while Darryl Zanuck, 20th Century production chief, will become a Fox vice-president. Schenck resigns his United Artists post, but remains as head of the U.A. theater circuit. He will make his headquarters on the coast, working in close contact with Winfield Sheehan and Darryl Zanuck.
> A minimum of 55 to 60 pictures a year will be made under the new affiliation, and there will not be any shakeup in the Fox organization, but merely a rearrangement of the executive and producing work.[69]

The deal would not affect films made by 20th Century for United Artists that were still unreleased. However, the merged company would retrieve distribution rights from United Artists to the 18 films after seven years. Fox would not start releasing new 20th Century pictures until the fall of 1935, when the Zanuck product would be ready.[70] Darryl Zanuck and Joseph Schenck had just pulled off one of the greatest coups in Hollywood history.

16. After the Merger

After the May 28, 1935, announcement about a merger between the massive Fox Film Corporation and the upstart 20th Century Pictures, heads were being scratched throughout the industry. How was such a merger possible? There had been previous rumored mergers between Fox and M.G.M., Paramount and Warners, Fox and Warners, but these all involved major companies with studios, theater chains and international distribution organizations. Zanuck's 20th Century Pictures, a privately owned corporation, had no studio of its own, limited talent contracts, no theaters, and only a distribution deal with an outside company.

Fox Films could produce and release 50–60 features annually as well as dozens of short subjects and newsreels. Fox had access to hundreds of theaters in prime locations. It employed thousands of people and owned two studio facilities, one of which was the largest in the world. However, Fox was saddled with a sclerotic production system which had taken five years to return to profitability. Its stable of stars was limited, but included Shirley Temple, Will Rogers, Warner Baxter, and newcomers Alice Faye and Henry Fonda who, to date, had not been exploited to the fullest by Winfield Sheehan or Sol Wurtzel.

Yet, 20th Century's greatest asset, Darryl F. Zanuck, was the one man who could jump-start Fox's production department and, along with Sidney Kent, run the company to much higher profits. The Fox companies, which at one time were appraised at having a value between $200,000,000 and $300,000,000, were now worth $36,000,000 with an annual earning power of $1,800,000. The value of 20th Century Pictures was placed at $4,000,000 with annual returns of $1,700,000, in effect almost equal in profits to the massive Fox Film Corporation. Kent had originally wanted to buy out 20th Century and call the new entity Fox–20th Century, but Zanuck refused. The agreement

Fox musical star Alice Faye with James Dunn in *George White's Scandals of 1935* (courtesy Mike Hawks).

called for a merger with 20th Century being the top dog.

To get a sense of the enormity of the organization that 20th Century merged with, the number of film exchanges and the global penetration of the Fox distribution division was considerable. In the United States alone, there were 31 local offices including: Albany, New York; Atlanta, Georgia (District Manager); Boston, Massachusetts (District Manager); Buffalo, New York; Charlotte, North Carolina; Chicago, Illinois; Cincinnati and Cleveland, Ohio (District Manager); Dallas, Texas; Denver, Colorado; Des Moines, Iowa; Detroit, Michigan; Indianapolis, Indiana; Kansas City, Missouri (District Manager); Los Angeles, California; Memphis, Tennessee; Milwaukee, Wisconsin; Minneapolis, Minnesota; New Haven, Connecticut; New Orleans, Louisiana; New York City, New York; Oklahoma City, Oklahoma; Omaha, Nebraska; Philadelphia, Pennsylvania (District Manager); Pittsburgh, Pennsylvania; Portland, Oregon; St. Louis, Missouri; Salt Lake City, Utah; San Francisco, California (District Manager); Seattle, Washington; and Washington, D.C.

In Canada there were exchanges in Calgary (Alberta), Montreal (Quebec), St. John (New Brunswick), Toronto (Ontario—District Manager), Vancouver (British Columbia) and Winnipeg (Manitoba).

There were also South American exchanges in Bahia Blanca (Argentina), Buenos Aires (Argentina—District Manager), Concordia (Argentina), Cordoba (Argentina), Mendoza (Argentina), Rosario (Argentina), Montevideo (Uruguay), Bahia (Brazil), Juiz de Fora (Brazil), Porto Alegre (Brazil), Recife (Brazil), Ribeirao (Brazil), Rio de Janeiro (Brazil—District Manager), Santiago (Chile), Valparaiso (Chile), and Lima (Peru).

Great Britain was covered in England through Birmingham, Leeds, Liverpool, London (Head Office), and Manchester. There were also offices in Dublin (Ireland), Glasgow (Scotland), and Cardiff (Wales).

Scandinavia had offices in Stockholm (Sweden), Copenhagen (Denmark), Helsingfors (Finland), and Oslo (Norway).

Southern Europe included Algiers (Algeria), Brussels (Belgium), Bordeaux, Lille, Lyons, Marseilles, Paris, Strasbourg (France), Casablanca (Morocco), and Geneva (Switzerland). Italian exchanges were situated in Bologna, Catania, Florence, Genoa, Milan, Naples, Padua, Rome, Trieste, and Turin. Representation in Spain was through Barcelona, Bilbao, Madrid, Seville, Valencia and Portugal had one office in Lisbon.

In addition, there were nine offices in the central European countries of Germany, Estonia, Holland, Latvia, Lithuania, and Poland. Eastern Europe had seven exchanges in Austria, Czechoslovakia, Hungary, Jugo-Slavia, and Romania. The Near East was covered in Bulgaria, Egypt, Greece, Palestine, Iraq, Syria and Turkey. Eight offices represented Fox in Australia and New Zealand, while there were four in Malaysia, four in India, and ten in the Far East countries of China, Manchuria, Manchukuo, Japan, Korea and the Philippines. The Caribbean offices were in Panama, Colombia, Venezuela, Cuba, Mexico, and Puerto Rico.[1] William Fox had always boasted that his pictures were seen in every corner of the globe, every hour of the day, and his penetration of distribution proved him to be correct.

The formation of 20th Century–Fox, which was official on May 31, 1935, would have a valuation of $40,000,000 and about 1,600,000 shares of common stock at a par value of $30, according to the Dow Jones financial service. Preferred stock would be convertible into one-and-a-half shares of new common stock. "There are 2,419,759 shares of Fox Class A common stock outstanding and 16,650 shares of Class B common so that approximately 1,218,000 shares of the new $1.50 preferred will be issued to Fox holders or about $36,000,000 at par, and about 600,000 shares of the new common."[2] Shares of common stock in the company were divided equally between previous Fox shareholders and the 20th Century partners. Joseph Schenck and William Goetz received 214,642 shares each and Zanuck was given 183,979 shares. Schenck resigned his presidency of United Artists and was replaced by Al Lichtman, but stayed on as president of the theater circuit. At 20th Century–Fox, he would receive $130,000 a year as chairman of the board. Sidney Kent would remain in his position of president with a salary of $180,000 annually with an additional $25,000 as president of National Theaters Corporation. Zanuck was made vice-president in charge of production, and given a contract for $260,000 a year and 10 percent of the profits of his films that would bring him, along with stock dividends up to a take-home pay of $500,000. This was a major undertaking for Zanuck and he approached it like he did everything else, fearlessly. Sam Engel said, "I would think that Zanuck, at age two, thought he'd be great. I don't think he ever had a doubt in his mind about his own capabilities. He wasn't just an optimist, he was completely and totally without fear."[3]

Schenck sold 20th Century's participation in the United Artists studio for $250,000 to Sam Goldwyn who became the sole owner of the stages and equipment, even though Douglas Fairbanks and Mary Pickford still owned the real estate upon which the studio stood.[4]

The annual Fox sales conference was held just two days after the earthshaking announcement of changes within the company. The big loser in this deal would be United Artists, which had seen its percentage of hit movies soar since Darryl Zanuck's arrived on the lot. *Time* magazine reported,

While Fox executives were gloating over the merger at their annual sales convention last week for which the announcement had been carefully timed, United Artists heads were frantically trying to deal with the situation caused by Twentieth Century's departure. A loosely organized group of producers, set up 16 years ago by actors who felt that they were being exploited by their employers, the company's only active producing members now are Sam Goldwyn, Charlie Chaplin, whose new, unnamed "Production No. 5" will be released in August, and Mary Pickford, who plans six pictures next year. In Hollywood last week, Producers Goldwyn, Pickford and Chaplin held all-day meetings, lunched for five hours, arguing about whom to elect president to replace Producer Schenck, and where to find a new producing organization to replace Twentieth Century.[5]

Rather than admit that Fox was merging from a position of weakness, the production department put on a show of strength, setting forth a program of 54 features, not including the 20th Century output. There would be "a trend toward spectacular productions and an increased use of music" in the new program.

> Pictures of a spectacular nature include such massive productions as "Dante's Inferno," Eugene Sue's "Mysteries of Paris," "Under Two Flags," "Ramona," "Hawk of the Desert," "Way Down East," and "Farmer Takes a Wife" ... there will be productions based on the works of many contemporary authors, including Booth Tarkington, Kathleen Norris, Clarence Buddington Kelland, Sophie Kerr, Cornelius Vanderbilt, Jr., Vina Delmar, Ben Lucien Burman, Courtney Riley Cooper, Zane Grey and others.
>
> New personalities added to the roster of players this season include Nino Martini, Metropolitan Opera and radio star; Tutto [sic] Rolf, Scandinavian movie stage and opera star; Tito Guizar, popular radio baritone; Simone, the vivacious actress who has been acclaimed in both British and French motion pictures the past year, and Madame Ernestine Schumann-Heink, who will make her debut in "Here's To Romance."[6]

Of these new personalities the only one to remain under contract to Fox was Simone Simon, who was a capable dramatic actress. The others disappeared quickly after the merger.

The *Film Daily* reported in mid–June that the quota of 1935-1936 pictures would be scheduled with Sol Wurtzel producing 14, Winfield Sheehan with nine; Robert T. Kane, five; B.G. De Sylva, four; Jesse Lasky, three; Edward Butcher, three; John Stone, three as well as Spanish pictures; Edward T. Lowe, three Charlie Chans; Sol Lesser, four westerns through his Atherton Productions; and Joseph Engel was assigned to the still-planned, but ultimately doomed *Work of Art*.

When Darryl Zanuck and his staff moved into their new offices on the Westwood lot in June 1935, no one had yet discussed the matter of what would happen to contract talent, properties, the production schedule and most importantly, the previous heads of production, Winfield Sheehan and Sol M. Wurtzel.

Sheehan and Wurtzel optimistically announced their release schedule for the following six months in an almost futile effort to lock in the projects they had developed. The schedule held pretty much intact through November, but by then Zanuck had already evaluated all of Fox's development and decided that many projects were not worthy of production. The first to be dropped was *Ramona* with Gilbert Roland and Rochelle Hudson, originally set for release on November 22. It was finally made in 1936 as 20th Century–Fox's first all-Technicolor production starring Loretta Young and Don Ameche. The December 6 release of *Thanks to You* was dropped as were *Hawk of the Desert* with Warner Baxter and Rochelle Hudson for December 13, *Meal Ticket* with Jane Withers and Jackie Searl for December 20, *Twins* with Shirley Temple for January 10, *Broadway Co-Ed* with Alice Faye and Jack Haley for January 17, and *Farewell to Fifth Ave.*, for January 24. The planned January 31, 1936 release of *Shoestring Charley* with Will Rogers had to be canceled because of the humorist's untimely death in a plane crash on August 15, 1935.[7]

Other productions to be nixed by Zanuck included *Efficiency Edgar* which would have been an Edward Everett Horton vehicle based on a Clarence Buddington Kelland story. *Police Parade* would have re-united James Dunn with Alice Faye, along with co-stars Mona Barrie and Herbert Mundin, under director Lewis Seiler. *Matinee Idol*, a vehicle for John Boles, and *Argentina*, an all-star musical for which second-unit footage had already been shot, were both canceled. *Impersonation of a Lady* with Mona Barrie was scrapped, as were an adaptation of Eugene Sue's *Mysteries of Paris* and *Caesar the Great* with Warner Baxter and Jane Withers. Additionally in the trash bin were *Hard to Get*, *Brief Rapture*, *Stranger in the Night* and three untitled projects. Yet another Will Rogers production, *The Man from Home*, had to be dropped from the schedule. *Song and Dance Man*, a musical to star Jack Haley and Alice Faye, based on a play by George M. Cohan, was shunted over to the Wurtzel unit where it was cast with Claire Trevor and Paul Kelly.

Zanuck also screened the films that were already completed, including John Ford's *Steamboat Round the Bend* (1935). He recut the film, picking up the pace and eliminating some of the broader sight gags. Ford, who tended to let his films meander and was accustomed to complete autonomy under the Sheehan-Wurtzel administration, complained that Zanuck "ruined my picture." He criticized Zanuck for "showing off" and being more interested in showing that he was in charge more than for releasing a good film. When the film opened, edited by Zanuck, it received rave reviews and excellent box-office results.[8]

With Darryl Zanuck fully in charge of production, Winfield Sheehan's future had been decided. He announced his resignation from the $7,000-a-week job in mid–June, effective with the completion of *Way Down East* (1935), which had been in production for a month. Sheehan left his position at a company he had seen grow from its humble beginnings in 1914. About the resignation, Sidney Kent said with typical Hollywood aplomb as reported in *Time* magazine, "'It was accepted with regret. I and the corporation extend our best wishes to Mr. Sheehan.... This matter has been settled amicably....' Producer Sheehan ... said he had no plans except a holiday abroad. That last week's settlement might really have been amicable was indicated by the terms revealed. Producer Sheehan kept his fat block of Fox stock, got something like $360,000 for his contract which had 14 months to run."[9] Sheehan actually received $375,000 with the last payment due in 1937, according to court documents.[10]

While there was general excitement and optimism about the dynamic, young Zanuck taking over the production reins, not all industry critics were pleased. Pete Harrison of *Harrison's Reports* raised what were, to him, serious issues about the merger and especially Sheehan's departure. Harrison asked,

> Will Mr. Sheehan's resignation harm the interests of those exhibitors who have already signed a 1935-36 Fox contract?
>
> Mr. Sheehan has, as every one of you knows, a long record of box-office successes. Starting in 1926 with "What Price Glory?" he produced one moneymaking picture after another.... Mr. Sheehan's position has been filled by Mr. Zanuck, a capable producer, having produced several box-office successes while with United Artists.
>
> But when he was releasing his pictures through United Artists he was making only twelve and was devoting all his time to those twelve pictures. As general manager of production for Fox, he will have to devote his time to Fox pictures.
>
> And here is where the interests of the Fox customers come in: Neither the Twentieth Century

A happy event on the set of *Steamboat 'Round the Bend* (1935). From left to right in foreground: Will Rogers, John Ford, Anne Shirley, Sol M. Wurtzel. Behind Shirley is Francis Ford (John's brother) and behind Wurtzel is humorist/actor Irvin S. Cobb (courtesy Karl Thiede).

pictures nor the Fox pictures will receive the same attention as these pictures received before the reshuffling. The realignment of producers, therefore, does not serve the interests either of the Fox Film Corporation or of the exhibitors. If anything, it leaves Fox in a weaker position. Consequently, the Twentieth Century pictures, which are sold on a separate contract, are not worth the money they were worth when Zanuck was producing for United Artists, and the Will Rogers, Shirley Temple, and Janet Gaynor pictures are not worth the money they were worth when they were receiving the individual attention of Mr. Sheehan.

The Fox and Twentieth Century pictures will suffer also in another way: Movietone City is a vast plant — the most beautiful and perfect studio in Hollywood. Before Mr. Zanuck will learn its "ins" and "outs" he will require considerable time.

HARRISON'S REPORTS hopes that these deductions are wrong, and that under Mr. Zanuck neither the Twentieth Century nor the Fox pictures will suffer. But only time can tell.[11]

The atypically skeptical Harrison followed up his report with yet another swipe at the new company while questioning the value of the contracts that Fox salesmen were presenting to exhibitors.

He added the additional qualifier that "the name 'Fox' is an asset, not only because it has a history, whatever that history may be, but also because it is easily pronounced and easily remembered. The name 'Twentieth Century' is not known as advantageous. It was satisfactory as long as it was a producing unit, releasing its pictures through a well-known distributing concern; but when it is made the foundation, the matter differs. Until the name Twentieth Century–Fox becomes as well known as the name Fox, or as the name of any of the other companies, it will not be as good an asset."[12]

These plainly stated exhibitor issues were addressed aggressively by Darryl Zanuck two weeks later in a response to Pete Harrison.

> You most assuredly have a short memory if you fail to recall that I served at Warner Bros. and First National for ten years. During the last five years I alone single-handed managed Warner Bros. and First National and supervised an average of fifty pictures per year, still finding time each year to contribute four or five original stories, among them

42nd STREET, UNION DEPOT and a few fairly successful films. Of course, I cannot expect to go away for four or five months' vacation each year as I have done during the existence of 20th Century Pictures, but to me the job of handling the entire studio's product from a supervisory capacity is certainly no more difficult than specializing in a few important pictures.

In the first place, I have many more assets and I am enabled to purchase many more assets from the standpoint of writers, directors, associate producers and capable assistants. You state that I will be unable to devote as much time to Will Rogers and Shirley Temple as Mr. Sheehan did. I would like to call your attention [to] the fact that Mr. Sol Wurtzel produced the following Will Rogers pictures, which were his most successful ones; JUDGE PRIEST, LIFE BEGINS AT FORTY, STEAMBOAT 'ROUND THE BEND, HANDY ANDY. Mr. Edward Butcher produced IN OLD KENTUCKY. These gentlemen are now under contract to 20th Century–Fox.

Now we come to the subject of Shirley Temple. The picture that brought Shirley Temple to the position she now enjoys was made, not in the Westwood studios, but at the Fox Western Avenue Studios, by Sol Wurtzel. It was called BRIGHT EYES. Since then her most successful picture was THE LITTLE COLONEL which was made by Buddy DeSylva who has just signed a long-term contract to become one of our associate producers. I feel sure if you would sit down and reconsider your analysis of the Temple-Rogers situation, you will most assuredly revise it.

Please don't get the idea that I am endeavoring to take anything away from Mr. Sheehan's management of the Fox producing company, but these are actual facts and you have misstated them, and I feel, because you are in my opinion very fair and honest, you would like to know the real lowdown on the situation.

I also call to your attention the fact that the scenarios of eight of the twelve 20th Century Pictures for 1935-36 release were already completed and in shooting script form before the consolidation was announced. Therefore, we came to the Fox Studio with two-thirds of our program practically in the bag.

Right now three of the pictures are actually being photographed: METROPOLITAN, THANKS A MILLION and MAN WHO BROKE THE BANK AT MONTE CARLO.

I am sure that in six months from now you will have to admit that the entire general tone of 20th Century–Fox pictures will show a definite improvement at the box-office and in quality. It is our positive determination to put no picture into production henceforth, regardless of the cost, unless it has, in our opinion, the scenario and cast requirements to make it a success. In other words, we refuse to be satisfied in allowing Shirley Temple and Will Rogers to carry a program of fifty pictures. We are determined to bring at least fifteen more pictures up to the level of the Temple-Rogers grosses and elevate the other pictures to a position where they may at least show a healthy return for the exhibitor and the producer. This is no idle sales talk on my part; as you know I realize that the final results of our plans will have to eventually be accounted for at the box-office, so I want you to get on our bandwagon as 20th Century–Fox is a company that is going a long, long way in the motion picture business.[13]

Once again, Darryl Zanuck's enthusiasm and self-confidence were well represented in the films that were released. He replaced Sheehan projects with those that had already been prepared at 20th Century, including the musical comedy *Thanks a Million* (1935) starring the popular lead of Warner Bros. musicals, Dick Powell; *Show Them No Mercy* (1935), a tough, gangster film in the tradition of his Warner melodramas; *Professional Soldier* (1936) teaming Wallace Beery with juvenile favorite Freddie Bartholomew; and John Ford's directorial debut under Zanuck, *The Prisoner of Shark Island* (1936), starring Warner Baxter. Following Ford's initial animosity over the editing of *Steamboat Round the Bend* (1935), he and Zanuck got along well and turned out memorable films like *The Grapes of Wrath* (1940), *How Green Was My Valley* (1941) and *My Darling Clementine* (1946).

When Zanuck took over the reins of the company, he oversaw, and would continue to oversee, the Class-A productions at the Westwood lot. Sol Wurtzel, already running the Western Avenue lot, continued to produce films but never again was given the resources he had gotten during the Sheehan administration. The Western Avenue studio became the permanent home of the Charlie Chan series, the Mr. Moto series, the Michael Shayne series, the Jane Withers series, the Jones Family series, and any and all other Class-B films, usually made on tight budgets of $125,000 to $250,000. Wurtzel stayed at Fox until the demise of the "B" film in the mid-1940s.

The irony of the takeover, which has heretofore never been written about, is that the Fox Film Corporation was actually beginning to produce high-profit films and probably could have survived with the upward draft of the economy. Fox's average of hit films was rising once again, but the most successful films were still those of Shirley Temple and Will Rogers and the profits from these two stars contributed the most to the success of the 20th Century–Fox's releases of 1935. Production profits for the year were $5,938,000 on rentals of $34,739,000, an increase of nearly 20 percent over 1934. Temple's films alone — including *The Little Colonel* (1934), *Our Little Girl* (1934), *Curly Top* (1935) and *The Littlest Rebel*

An unusually mischievous Shirley Temple in *The Littlest Rebel* (1935) (courtesy Mike Hawks).

and Sol Wurtzel could have continued on their winning streak without the box-office punch of a Shirley Temple or Will Rogers film. That formula would have unraveled with Will Rogers's death and Shirley Temple's maturation. Aside from these two talents, Sheehan had placed his bet on *The Farmer Takes a Wife* (1935), a $736,000 production anchored by Janet Gaynor and newcomer Henry Fonda. It was one of the few recent Gaynor films to lose money, a figure reaching $202,000. Sheehan's other major production of the year, a remake of *Way Down East* (1935), lost $273,000. Sol Wurtzel's much-ballyhooed production of *Dante's Inferno* (1935), given a huge Western Avenue budget of $749,000, lost $270,000. Accounting for these losses, it is understandable that Sidney Kent felt new blood was needed to kick-start his company's production unit.

But no Hollywood story concludes without problems. There was yet another obstacle to the finalization of 20th Century–Fox's incorporation. A lawsuit was filed by the All-Continent Corporation, the holding company for Mrs. Eve Fox, which contained all the assets owned by William Fox,

(1935)—threw off over $5,000,000 in profits. When Will Rogers's hit films *The County Chairman* (1935), *Doubting Thomas* (1935), *Steamboat Round the Bend* (1935) and *In Old Kentucky* (1935) are included, this was a fortunate year for Darryl Zanuck and Joseph Schenck to merge the companies. More ironic is the failure of the first Zanuck 20th Century–Fox production, *Metropolitan* (1935), a backstage opera story with the popular tenor Lawrence Tibbett which lost $117,000 on a $536,000 negative. However, Zanuck came roaring back with a string of hits in 1935, including *Thanks a Million*, *The Man Who Broke the Bank at Monte Carlo* and *Show Them No Mercy*.

There is considerable doubt, however, that Winfield Sheehan

A more sedate Shirley with Lionel Barrymore in *The Little Colonel* (1935) (courtesy Mike Hawks).

charged that Fox directors were wasting the assets of the company in merging with 20th Century and the rights of Fox stockholders were being prejudiced in the transaction. Mrs. Fox owned 37,000 shares of the outstanding Class-A Fox Film stock and 25,000 shares of Fox Film B-stock and was the largest individual shareholder fighting the consolidation. Another litigant angrily referred to reports that A.C. Blumenthal, once William Fox's real-estate developer, engineered the merger at a regal fee of $1,000,000.[14]

At the company's annual meeting, a stockholder complained about the high salaries being paid Sidney Kent, Joseph Schenck, and Darryl Zanuck, and the fact that 20th Century had no tangible assets. In response, Kent rallied in defense of the merger.

> This is a business of creation and imagination.... The best company in the industry is Loew's, Inc.— because some time ago they bought Metro-Goldwyn-Mayer Corporation and the services of Louis B. Mayer, Irving Thalberg and J. Robert Rubin. Without those three men I wouldn't give ten cents for the stock. We pay stars $8,000 or $9,000 weekly and make money on them. Mr. Zanuck, who directs these stars and creates stars, is worth $5,000 a week.
>
> The first step necessary when I took hold of this company three years ago was to save it.... The second step is to make a good company of it. When I took this company in April 1932, it had $37,000,000 in past due debts. I could have written my own ticket.

Kent said that he cut his salary by half the first year to $66,000 and returned the rest to the company. During his second year he drew $77,000. This was justification for his current $130,000 salary, now that the company was once again profitable.

He also offered some background into his considerations for Fox Films: "We considered a lot of deals to build up the company, but most of the others involved taking over debts. We took Twentieth Century, first, because it had no dead studios we did not need and because it had no distribution facilities. It had five or six stars and directing personnel that we needed."

Kent then revealed that of all the unamortized negative assets being acquired from Twentieth Century, only one would show a loss of $75,000 while one or two others would show losses of less than $75,000. The average return on Twentieth's films in two years had been two and a half times their negative cost which he described as "the best record in the industry." Kent added, "Their pictures have been especially good abroad and ours have not.... Janet Gaynor is weak outside this country. Twentieth's record in England is the best I have ever looked at."

Wrapping up his feelings for the shareholders Kent added, "This is the finest deal ever put together in the industry and I talk as a stockholder as well as president of the company, because I have many times more stock than all that has been spoken against the plan at this meeting and it was bought with my own money."[15]

The Fox litigation against the merger was overturned, after several appeals, by a court decision which paved the way for the consolidation of the two companies. On May 31, 1935, 20th Century–Fox Film Corporation was incorporated in the state of Maryland. Darryl F. Zanuck would continue as the creative head of the studio, with his offices on the Westwood lot for two decades, during which time he created stars like Tyrone Power, Betty Grable, Don Ameche, Sonja Henie, The Ritz Brothers, Carmen Mi-

Will Rogers and Frank Albertson in *Doubting Thomas* (1935) (courtesy Mike Hawks).

randa, Linda Darnell, Richard Widmark and Marilyn Monroe. He also propelled Fox Films contractees Alice Faye and Henry Fonda to stardom. Year in and year out for twenty years, he produced the Class-A films; frothy musicals, zany comedies, period spectacles, rousing adventures, flag-waving wartime stories and later controversial social dramas that brought 20th Century–Fox to be one of the most respected companies in the industry.

Just as Darryl Zanuck had predicted, six months after the merger, 20th Century–Fox released films that were "a definite improvement at the box-office and in quality." Zanuck brought his own unique skills as production head to the company, along with his hand-picked team of stars, writers, producers, and directors to elevate the Fox studios back to where they been in the glory days of William Fox. Although the company never achieved the glossy prestige of Metro-Goldwyn-Mayer, Zanuck carved out a niche for 20th Century–Fox very close to the top of the industry. He invigorated its management and distribution, regained exhibitor faith in the company and ushered it into the future, a future which has lasted to the present day.

Part II. Filmography

The filmography is designed to give the main credits and a brief synopsis of the story. These synopses were gathered from various sources, some of which were conflicting with others, so a best effort was made to be accurate. All films are listed in order of their general release. Mention is made when there was a pre-release date or a roadshow engagement. The pre–Fox Corporation films, released by William Fox's Box Office Attraction Rental Corporation, are denoted as such. When it is known that a production was released under the aegis of a producer with a special contract, such mention is made. The determination of Fox Films for its final year of releases in 1935 was made by the production dates. All films shooting before the first 20th Century–Fox production, Metropolitan, which went before the cameras on July 29, 1935, are considered as Fox Films even though they may have been released after the official date of the merger and distributed by 20th Century–Fox. Some feature lengths have two entries since there were conflicting running times. The key includes: SP: Supervising Producer; P: Producer; AP: Associate Producer; D: Director; AD: Assistant Director; W: Writer; SCR: Scenario/Screenplay; ST: Story; ADPT: Adaptation; DIAL: Dialogue; C: Cinematographer; E: Editor; M: Music; UC: Uncredited

1914 Releases

LIFE'S SHOP WINDOW (Nov. 19, 1914) Box Office Attraction; D: J. Gordon Edwards; W: Mary Asquith (synopsis), Victoria Cross (novel); C: Harry A. Fishbeck; Cast: Stuart Holmes, Claire Whitney • An impoverished English orphan (Whitney) grows up and marries a man (Holmes) who moves her to Arizona. She almost runs off with another lover but returns to her husband for forgiveness. 5 reels

THE WALLS OF JERICHO (Nov. 23, 1914) Box Office Attraction; D: Lloyd B. Carleton; W: Alfred Sutro (play); Cast: Edmund Breese, Claire Whitney, Stuart Holmes, Edward José • An English rake (Holmes) tells an obsessive woman gambler (Whitney) that her husband (Breese) murdered a man in America, but the truth is revealed that the amorous rake is the murderer. 5 reels

THE THIEF (Dec. 7, 1914) Box Office Attraction; D: Edgar Lewis; W: Edgar Lewis (scr), Henri Bernstein (play); Cast: Dorothy Donnelly, Richard Buhler, Harry Spingler, George De Carlton, Edgar L. Davenport, Ivy Shepard • Marie, a free-spending Frenchwoman (Donnelly), cannot pay for an expensive dress she ordered to lure Richard Voysin (Buhler) into marriage and steals jewels from a wealthy family; she later confesses her guilt. 5 reels

THE IDLER (Dec. 21, 1914) Box Office Attraction; D: Lloyd B. Carleton; W: C. Haddon Chambers (play); Cast: Charles Richman, Catherine Countiss, Claire Whitney, Walter Hitchcock, Stuart Holmes, Maude Turner Gordon, William T. Carleton, Harry Spingler • A wealthy Englishman (Richman) leaves for America's western goldfields and becomes involved with a fortune-hunting bank clerk (Hitchcock) who worked for him in England. 5 reels

1915 Releases

SAMSON (Jan. 4, 1915) Box Office Attraction; D: Edgar Lewis; W: Henri Bernstein (play); Cast: William Farnum, Maude Gilbert, Edgar L. Davenport, Agnes Everett, Harry Spingler, Charles Guthrie, Carey Lee, George De Carlton, Elmer Peterson • A poor Parisian, Maurice (Farnum), rises to financial success in the copper market and marries Marie, an aristocratic woman (Gilbert) whose family is on the verge of financial ruin. However, Marie has an affair with the polished Jerome (Guthrie) whom her husband later ruins even though it causes his downfall as well. Marie eventually returns to him. 5 reels

A FOOL THERE WAS (Jan. 14, 1915) Box Office Attraction; D: Frank Powell; W: Roy L. McCardell, Frank Powell, Peter Emerson Browne (play), Rudyard Kipling (poem); Cast: Theda Bara, Edward José,

Mabel Fremyear, May Allison, Runa Hodges, Clifford Bruce, Victor Benoit, Frank Powell, Minna Gale, Creighton Hale • On a ship to England, John Schuyler (José), a New York businessman falls for a vampire (Bara) who brings him to ruin. When he begs her to leave him in peace, she laughs and says "Kiss me, my fool." 6 reels • This was Theda Bara's first appearance in a Fox Film and established her as the ultimate "vamp."

THE GIRL I LEFT BEHIND ME (Jan. 25, 1915) Box Office Attraction; D: Lloyd B. Carleton; W: David Belasco and Franklyn Fyles (play); Cast: Robert Edeson, Stuart Holmes, Irene Warfield, Claire Whitney, Walter Hitchcock, J. Albert Hall • Two rival cavalry officers, Hawkesworth (Edeson) and Parlow (Holmes), are sent to quell a Blackfoot uprising. Parlow proves to be a coward and Hawkesworth, the hero, marries the general's daughter (Whitney). 5 reels

A GILDED FOOL (Feb. 1, 1915) Box Office Attraction; D: Edgar Lewis; W: Edgar Lewis, Henry Guy Carleton (play); Cast: William Farnum, Maude Gilbert, Margaret Vale, Charles Guthrie, Harry Spingler, George De Carlton • Chauncey Short (Farnum) inherits $5,000,000 and spends it frivolously because his mother died before they had enough money for her medical care. He meets Margaret (Gilbert), a banker's daughter, who rejects him for his extravagance. He later uses his wealth to make profitable investments and exposes a swindler in her father's bank. 5 reels

CHILDREN OF THE GHETTO (Feb. 8, 1915) Box Office Attraction; D: Frank Powell; W: Edward José, Israel Zangwill (play); Cast: Wilton Lackaye, Ruby Hoffman, Ethel Kauffman, Frank Andrews, Luis Alberni, Irene Boyle, Victor Benoit, David Bruce, Riley Hatch, J. Albert Hall • Reb Shemuel's (Lackaye) children bring him tragedy. His blaspheming son dies after a brawl. Then, he insists his daughter, Hannah (Hoffman), obtain a religious divorce after a friend puts a ring on her finger in jest. As a result of the divorce Hannah is unable to marry the man she loves within the orthodox religion and has a civil ceremony, estranging herself from her father. Years later, when the lonely rabbi conducts a Passover Seder, his widowed daughter and her two children are warmly welcomed back. 5 reels

THE CELEBRATED SCANDAL (Feb. 11, 1915); D: James Durkin; W: Elaine Sterne, José Echegaray y Eizaguirre (play); Cast: Betty Nansen, Edward José, Walter Hitchcock, Stuart Holmes, Wilmuth Merkyl, Helen Robertson • A scandal develops when Teodora (Nansen), the young wife of Don Julian (José), a Spanish diplomat, is rumored to be carrying on an affair with Ernesto (Merkyl), the newly arrived son of a friend. Don Julian challenges the rumor monger (Holmes) to a duel and is fatally wounded, but he is convinced by Ernesto that his wife has been faithful. 5 reels • Along with the distribution name of the Fox Film Corporation, this also carried a title of "William Fox Photoplays Supreme."

KREUTZER SONATA (March 1, 1915); D: Herbert Brenon; W: Herbert Brenon, Jacob Gordin (play); Cast: Nance O'Neil, Theda Bara, William E. Shay, Mimi Yvonne, Henry Bergman, Sidney Cushing, Maude Turner Gordon, John Daly Murphy, Anne Sutherland • Miriam (O'Neil), a pregnant Orthodox Jewess in Russia, is convinced by her father to marry a conceited man (Shay) and move to New York after her lover's suicide. Miriam's sister (Bara) follows and begins an affair with her new, abusive husband. Miriam kills both of them in a rage, then shoots herself. 5 reels

THE NIGGER (March 22, 1915); D: Edgar Lewis; W: Edgar Lewis, Edward Brewster Sheldon (play); Cast: William Farnum, Claire Whitney, George DeCarlton, Henry Armetta • A Southern Governor of Negro ancestry (Farnum) is threatened with exposure of his roots by a political boss. Nonetheless, he signs a bill that will bring his political ruin and resigns his office. After the newspaper story is published, he leaves his sweetheart (Whitney) and moves north to improve the plight of his people in America. 5 reels

FROM THE VALLEY OF THE MISSING (Apr. 1, 1915); D: Frank Powell; W: Clara Beranger, Grace Miller White (novel); Cast: Jane Miller, Vivian Tobin, Harry Spingler, William Bailey, Riley Hatch, Robert Cummings, Kate Cummings, Arline Hackett, Clifford Bruce, George Tobin • This complicated plot covers the misdeeds of two sea dogs, Crabbe (Cummings) and Cronk (Hatch), and the custody of Crabbe's natural child and the twins of a district attorney, kidnapped by Cronk. 5 reels

ANNA KARENINA (Apr. 5, 1915); D: J. Gordon Edwards; W: Clara Beranger, L.N. Tolstoy (novel); Cast: Betty Nansen, Edward José, Richard Thonton, Stella Hammerstein, Mabel Allen • Anna (Nansen), the beautiful wife of Baron Alexis (José), becomes the mistress of a handsome Prince Vronsky (Thornton). Expelled from her home and unable to see her beloved son, she then loses her lover to a younger woman. In despair, she throws herself in front of a moving train. 5 reels

THE CLEMENCEAU CASE (Apr. 19, 1915); D: Herbert Brenon; W: Herbert Brenon, Alexandre Dumas, fils (novel), Martha Woodrow (play); C: Philip E. Rosen; Cast: Theda Bara, William E. Shay, Stuart Holmes, Frank Goldsmith, Mrs. Allen Walker, Jane Lee, Saba Raleigh, Sidney Shields • Pierre (Shay), an artist in Paris, marries Iza (Bara), a Russian model who was betrothed to a wealthy duke (Goldsmith). After the marriage, Iza has an affair with the duke who is killed by Pierre in a duel. Pierre travels to America with a newly married friend, Constantin (Holmes), but Iza later follows and entices Constantin into an adulterous affair. To save his friend's marriage, Pierre stabs Iza to death. 5–6 reels

PRINCESS ROMANOFF (May 10, 1915); D: Frank Powell; W: Clara Beranger, Victorien Sardou (play); Cast: Nance O'Neil, Clifford Bruce, Dorothy Bernard, Stuart Holmes • Russian princess Fedora (O'Neil) tracks down Ipanoff (Bruce), the murderer of her betrothed (Holmes), to New York. Unaware of his identity, she falls in love with Ipanoff and forgives him. She eventually sacrifices her honor to keep Ipanoff from being killed. Later remorseful, she attempts suicide but is saved. 5 reels

A WOMAN'S RESURRECTION (May 16, 1915); D: J. Gordon Edwards; W: Leo Tolstoy (novel); Cast: Betty Nansen, William J. Kelly, Edward José, Bertha Brundage, Arthur Hoops, Stuart Holmes, J.B. Williams, Edgar Davenport, Ann Sutherland • A Russian peasant girl, Katusha (Nansen) and companion of Countess Sophia, is seduced by Sophia's nephew, Prince Dimitri (Kelly), who then goes to war. Pregnant, Katusha leaves town and becomes known for her loose morals. Katusha is sentenced to Siberia for the poisoning of a wealthy merchant, but Dimitri follows her and tries to make amends. Katusha ends up by shielding him in a duel, during which she is killed. 5 reels

THE PLUNDERER (May 31, 1915); D: Edgar Lewis; W: Garfield Thompson, Louise Keller, Roy Norton (novel); C: Frank C. Kugler; Cast: William Farnum, Harry Spingler, William Riley Hatch, Claire Whitney, Elizabeth Eyre, William J. Gross, George DeCarlton, Henry Armetta • Miners Bill (Farnum) and Dick (Spingler) head west only to find the owner of the adjacent property, Bully (Hatch), is tapping into a low level of their mine and promoting a strike among the miners. After Dick falls in love with Bully's daughter Joan (Whitney), she forces her father to confess his plundering and repay the value of what he had taken. 5 reels

WORMWOOD (June 7, 1915); D: Marshall Farnum; W: Garfield Thompson, Marie Corelli (novel); C: W.C. Thompson; Cast: John Sainpolis, Ethel Kauffman, Charles Arthur, Edgar Davenport, Stephen Grattan, Philip Hahn, Lilian Dilworth, Frank De Vernon, Bertha Brundage • A young Frenchman, Gaston (Sainpolis), learns that his fiancée, Pauline (Kaufman), is in love with his best friend (Arthur). On the altar, he denounces her in an absinthe-induced rage. Pauline ends up in the streets of Paris and Gaston kills his rival, then dies from the absinthe. 5 reels

THE DEVIL'S DAUGHTER (June 21, 1915); D: Frank Powell; W: Garfield Thompson, Gabriele D'Annunzio (play); C: David Calcagni; Cast: Theda Bara, Paul Doucet, Victor Benoit, Robert Wayne, Jane Lee, Doris Heywood, Jane Miller, Elaine Evans, Edouard Durand, Elaine Ivans • Gioconda (Bara) enchants a famous sculptor (Doucet) and ruins his family before deserting him. He shoots himself and is nursed back to health by his wife (Heywood), but returns to the vamp. When his wife is maimed for life as a result of Gioconda, he and the vamp go insane. 5 reels • Playwright D'Annunzio insisted on Theda Bara for the lead role before he would sign a contract with Fox.

SHOULD A MOTHER TELL? (July 5, 1915); D: J. Gordon Edwards; W: Rex Ingram; C: Arthur D. Ripley; Cast: Betty Nansen, Stuart Holmes, Runa Hodges, Jean Sothern, Stephen Grattan, Grace Everett, Ralph Johnston, G. Baldwin, Kate Blancke, Claire Whitney • Rose, a French woman (Nansen), keeps her silence in a murder to allow her daughter (Sothern) to marry. However, as the wrongfully accused man is led to the guillotine, Rose confesses the truth and the real murderer, Gaspard (Holmes), commits suicide. 5 reels

DR. RAMEAU (July 15, 1915); D: Will S. Davis; W: Will S. Davis, Gerald Thompson, Georges Ohnet (novel); C: Arthur D. Ripley; Cast: Frederick Perry, Stuart Holmes, George Allison, Dorothy Bernard, Jean Sothern, Edith Hallor, Bertha Brundage, Mayme Kelso, Graham Velsey • Dr. Rameau (Perry), the most famous surgeon in Paris, has lost his faith in God and is further disillusioned when his wife dies in childbirth. Years later, bringing up his daughter (Sothern), he discovers letters that the child was sired by his wife's lover. He drives the girl into a storm and she becomes deathly ill. He finally realizes his love for her and prays for her recovery. 5 reels

LADY AUDLEY'S SECRET (Aug. 4, 1915); D: Marshall Farnum; W: Mary Asquith, Mary Elizabeth Brandon (novel); C: Norton (Doc) Davis; Cast: Theda Bara, Riley Hatch, Clifford Bruce, Stephen Grattan, Warner Richmond • Assuming her adventurer husband, George (Bruce), has abandoned her, Helen Talboys (Bara) marries an aristocrat (Richmond) and becomes Lady Audley. Her look-alike maid dies suddenly and she passes off the corpse as Helen Talboys. George returns from Australia rich in gold and wants to reclaim his wife. Lady Audley throws him down a well. When George is rescued and shows up again, Audley dies from the fright. 5 reels

THE TWO ORPHANS (Sept. 6, 1915); D: Herbert Brenon; W: Herbert Brenon (adpt), Adolphe d'Ennery & Eugene Cormon (novel); C: Philip E. Rosen; Cast: Theda Bara, Jean Sothern, William E. Shay, Herbert Brenon, Gertrude Berkeley, Frank Goldsmith, E.L. Fernandez, Sheridan Block, Sarah Raleigh • In Paris, a beautiful orphan, Henriette (Bara), is kidnapped by a libertine marquis (Goldsmith), leaving her blind friend Louise (Sothern) wandering the streets to beg for food. Henriette is rescued by a noble family and discovers that Louise is a long-lost daughter of the countess (Raleigh). Both girls end up happily, marrying the men they love. 5–7 reels

THE SONG OF HATE (Sept. 13, 1915); D: J. Gordon Edwards; W: Rex Ingram, Victorien Sardou (play); Cast: Betty Nansen, Arthur Hoops, Dorothy Bernard, Claire Whitney • Baron Scarpia (Hoops), an Italian police official, loves Floria Tosca (Nansen), a beautiful opera singer, engaged to an artist. Her fiancé is tortured by Scarpia to reveal information about a suspected Austrian spy. Unable to hear her lover's screams, Floria reveals the whereabouts of the friend. Now spurned by the artist, she later offers herself to Scarpia, then stabs him to death. The artist is executed and Floria, trying to escape from the prison, falls to her death. 5–6 reels

REGENERATION (Sept. 20, 1915); D: Raoul Walsh; W: Raoul Walsh (adpt), Carl Harbaugh (adpt), Owen Frawley Kildare (autobiography); C: Georges Benoit; Cast: Rockcliffe Fellowes, Anna Q. Nilsson, William Sheer, Carl Harbaugh, James Marcus, Maggie Weston,

H. McCoy, John McCann, Peggy Barn • After growing up motherless and with an abusive father, Owen (Fellowes) heads his own gang. He later rescues Marie (Nilsson), a socialite, and her date, the district attorney (Harbaugh), from gangsters at a café. Marie teaches Owen to read and write, but she is accidentally shot by a thug who wanted to kill Owen. As Marie dies, she makes Owen promise not to take revenge. 5 reels

THE WONDERFUL ADVENTURE (Sept. 27, 1915); D: Frederick A. Thomson; W: Rex Ingram, Wilbur Lawson (play); C: Arthur D. Ripley; Cast: William Farnum, Dorothy Green, Mary G. Martin • Mazora (Green), an exotic mystic, seduces Wilton Demarest (Farnum), a wealthy contractor, and introduces him to the pleasures of opium. Demarest becomes a hopeless addict and has a look-alike friend (Farnum) take his place. The double, however, keeps a safe distance from Demarest's wife (Martin). Mazora discovers the deception and threatens to expose it, but is killed in a freak electrical accident. Demarest dies from an overdose, leaving the double and his wife together. 5 reels

SIN (Oct. 4, 1915); D: Herbert Brenon; W: Herbert Brenon; C: Philip E. Rosen; Cast: Theda Bara, William E. Shay, Warner Oland, Henry Leone, Louis Rial • Rosa (Bara), an Italian peasant girl, is followed by her fiancé, Luigi (Shay), to New York where he finds her in love with Pietro (Oland), head of a New York crime syndicate. To outdo the gangster, Luigi decides to steal the jewels of the Madonna for her, but Rosa ends up overcome by religious guilt. After returning the jewels, Luigi kills himself on the church steps. 5 reels

THE LITTLE GYPSY (Oct. 11, 1915); D: Oscar Apfel; W: Mary Murillo, J.M. Barrie (novel); C: Alfredo Gandolfi; Cast: Dorothy Bernard, Thurlow Bergen, Raymond Murray, W.J. Herbert, B. Barker, Mrs. Hurley, Riley Hatch • A gypsy girl (Bernard), abandoned at birth but brought up by a Scottish lord, becomes involved in a weaver's strike and is arrested for inciting a riot. Escaping from jail, she seeks protection with a young minister (Bergen), who secretly loves her. She eventually learns her true parentage and weds the minister. 5 reels

THE SOUL OF BROADWAY (Oct. 18, 1915); D: Herbert Brenon; W: Herbert Brenon; C: Philip E. Rosen; Cast: Valeska Suratt, William E. Shay, Sheridan Block, Mabel Allen, Jane Lee, George W. Middleton, Gertrude Berkeley • A young woman, Grace (Suratt), is shot in the neck by admirer William (Shay), who will not tolerate her taking money from an elderly, wealthy suitor. After serving three years in prison, William falls in love with June (Allen), the daughter of a gambler (Block) posing as a businessman. Grace, now a Broadway star, pursues William and threatens to expose his past and the truth about the gambler. Before she does so, Grace falls to her death. 5 reels • This film marked the screen debut of stage star Valeska Suratt, who, according to publicity articles, wore 150 different costumes in this production, at a cost of $25,000.

THE FAMILY STAIN (Oct. 25, 1915); D: Will S. Davis; W: Will S. Davis, Joseph H. Trant, Emile Gaboriau (novel); Cast: Frederick Perry, Einar Linden, Walter Miller, Stephen Grattan, Carey Lee, Dixie Compton, Helen Tiffany, Frank Evans, Edith Hallor, Mayme Kelso • In a French town, Detective Tabaret, investigating a woman's murder, unravels a family's tawdry past involving the payment by a wealthy man to switch his wife's baby with that of his mistress. When one of the switched siblings discovers the truth, he murders the woman who could keep him from his undeserved title and inheritance. 5–6 reels

CARMEN (Nov. 2, 1915); D: Raoul Walsh; W: Raoul Walsh, Prosper Merimée (novella); C: Georges Benoit, George Schneiderman; Cast: Theda Bara, Einar Linden, Carl Harbaugh, James A. Marcus, Emil De Varny, Elsie MacLeod, Fay Tunis, Joseph P. Green • Don José (Linden), a young Spanish soldier, arrests Carmen (Bara), an alluring tobacco worker, for slashing another woman in the factory. After allowing her to escape, he is imprisoned; and later kills his captain (De Varny) in a duel. Carmen helps him escape and their love affair becomes more passionate while on the run. She later deserts Don José for a famous toreador (Harbaugh), and he stabs her. After Carmen dies, Don José rides his horse over a cliff. 5 reels • Fox had the temerity to release this version at the same time as the Lasky production starring operatic soprano Geraldine Farrar. Ironically, the Fox version hewed closer to the opera but was compared unfavorably to the other production.

BLINDNESS OF DEVOTION (Nov. 9, 1915); D: J. Gordon Edwards; W: J. Gordon Edwards (scr), Rex Ingram (st); C: Arthur D. Ripley; Cast: Robert B. Mantell, Genevieve Hamper, Stuart Holmes, Claire Whitney, Henry Leone, Charles Young, Jack Standing • The wealthy Count de Carnay (Mantell) adopts his 17-year-old niece Bella (Whitney). She later marries an officer, Pierre (Holmes), to keep him from exposing an affair he had with Renée, the count's wife (Hamper). To win Pierre back, Renée tries to poison the count but, by accident, poisons herself. Pierre finds out and shoots himself. Before Renée dies, the count strangles her and throws her body across Pierre's. 5 reels

A WOMAN'S PAST (Nov. 15, 1915); D: Frank Powell; W: Rex Ingram, John King (play); Cast: Nance O'Neil, Clifford Bruce, Alfred Hickman, Carleton Macy • Jane (O'Neil), an aspiring writer, rejects the advances of her editor, Howard (Hickman), and marries Captain Stanley (Bruce). While her husband is abroad for three years, Howard tries to make amends with Jane, and her father-in-law banishes her. Years later, Jane is accused of killing Howard and is defended in court by her son, Harrison (Hickman), who is unaware of her real identity. Jane is about to be sentenced when Captain Stanley confesses to the murder and reveals Harrison to be Jane and Howard's son. 5 reels

THE BROKEN LAW (Nov. 22, 1915); D: Oscar Apfel; W: Monte M. Katterjohn, Oscar Apfel, George Borrow (novel); Cast: William Farnum, Dorothy Bernard,

Mary Martin, Bertram Marburgh, Richard Neill, Nicholas Dunaeu, Lyster Chambers, Christine Mayo • A novelist, Daniel Esmond (Farnum), learns that his father sired an illegitimate Gypsy child. Searching for the girl, Daniel joins a Gypsy group and becomes their leader; he later falls in love with a socialite, Isobel (Martin). After the beautiful Ursula (Bernard) is seduced by a lord, she accuses Daniel of the seduction. They are both flogged under Gypsy law. Before Ursula dies, she reveals the truth to a hunchback, who kills the lord. Daniel marries Isobel. 5 reels

THE GALLEY SLAVE (Nov. 28, 1915); D: J. Gordon Edwards; W: Clara Beranger, Bartley Campbell (play); Cast: Theda Bara, Claire Whitney, Lillian Lawrence, Ben Hendricks, Stuart Holmes, Jane Lee, Hardee Kirkland, Henry Leone, A.H. Van Buren • Antoine (Holmes), the husband of Francesca (Bara), inherits a fortune that his uncle intended for Francesca and her child. Antoine then deserts her and plans to marry an American heiress (Whitney). After Francesca and an American artist she has posed for are unjustly sent to the galleys for theft, Antoine is revealed as Francesca's husband. When he tries to kidnap their child, Francesca shoots him, and the socialite marries the artist. 5 reels

THE UNFAITHFUL WIFE (Dec. 6, 1915); D: J. Gordon Edwards; W: Mary Murillo; C: Phil Rosen; Cast: Robert B. Mantell, Genevieve Hamper, Stuart Holmes, Runa Hodges, Doris Wooldridge, Warner Oland, Lawrence White • In Naples, unfaithful Juliet (Hamper) entombs her husband, Count Romani (Mantell), but he escapes and seeks revenge by disguising himself and winning her affections. Her lover, Arturo (Holmes), challenges Romani to a duel, during which Arturo is killed. Juliet later marries Romani, still unaware of his disguise. He leads her into a tomb and locks her in to die. 5 reels

HER MOTHER'S SECRET (Dec. 13, 1915); D: Frederick A. Thomson; W: Martha Woodrow; Cast: Ralph Kellard, Dorothy Green, Jule Power, Jane Meredith, Edwards Davis • Seth Cartwright (Kellard) returns to his wife and son after abandoning his mistress (Power). Seth's wife adopts the mistress's illegitimate daughter Lorna (Green), but then both parents are killed in a shipwreck that reunites Lorna with her real mother. Several years later, a romance develops between the unsuspecting half-siblings. When their love cannot be consummated because of their relation, Lorna commits suicide. 5 reels

A SOLDIER'S OATH (Dec. 20, 1915); D: Oscar Apfel; W: Oscar Apfel, Mary Murillo; Cast: William Farnum, Dorothy Bernard, Kittens Reichert, Alma Frederic, Henry Hebert, Ruth Findlay, Walter Connolly, Louise Thatcher, Benjamin Marbaugh • Pierre (Farnum), a French soldier, returns from battle to deliver a box of jewels to a dead soldier's family. A war correspondent (Herbert) who knows about the valuables steals them and kills Pierre's wife (Bernard). Pierre is unfairly sentenced to life imprisonment but is exonerated when the true criminal is exposed. 5 reels

DESTRUCTION (Dec. 27, 1915); D: Will S. Davis; W: Will S. Davis (scr), Nixola Daniels (scr), Bernard Chapin (st); Cast: Theda Bara, James Furey, Warner Oland, J. Herbert Frank, Carleton Macy, Gaston Bell, Frank Evans, Esther Hoier, Master Tansey, Arthur Morrison • Ferdinande (Bara) is a temptress who marries a wealthy mill owner (Furey) to the dismay of his son, Jack (Macy), who had also proposed to her. During a mill strike and a riot, Jack befriends another worker's wife, Josine (Hoier), and urges his father to settle the strike. Ferdinande tries to poison her husband, continues affairs with other men, and after being raped by a worker, she meets her end in a fire. Jack marries Josine, recently a widow. 5 reels

1916 Releases

THE GREEN-EYED MONSTER (Jan. 3, 1916); D: J. Gordon Edwards; W: Mary Murillo; C: Arthur D. Ripley, Philip E. Rosen; Cast: Robert B. Mantell, Genevieve Hamper, Stuart Holmes, Pauline Barry, Henry Leone, Charles Davidson • Two brothers are rivals for their cousin Claire's (Hamper) hand in marriage. Raimond (Mantell) loses out and leaves for India. After many years, he returns to France and still jealous, secretly poisons brother Louis (Holmes) and hides the corpse. When Claire refuses to marry him, already insane with guilt, he reveals where he's hidden his brother's body. Claire dies of shock when she sees Louis's body. Years later, Raimond makes a deathbed confession to Claire's son. 5 reels

A PARISIAN ROMANCE (Jan. 10, 1916); D: Frederick A. Thompson; W: Mary Murillo, Octave Feuillet (play); Cast: H. Cooper Cliffe, Dorothy Green, Dion Titheradge, Margaret Skirvin, Angelica Spier, Isabel O'Madigan, Clarence Heritage, Harold Hartzelle, Mrs. Cecil Raleigh • The aging roué, Baron Chevrial (Cliffe), has affairs with various women, including Rosa (Green), a ballet dancer, but marries Thérèse (Skirvin), the respectable daughter of a businessman who is really in love with Henri (Titheradge). Distraught by the marriage, Henri marries Marcelle. The Baron tries to seduce Marcelle, who later runs away with an opera singer. When the singer leaves her, Marcelle commits suicide and, soon after, the Baron dies. Finally free from spouses they never loved, Henri and Thérèse make plans for their marriage. 5 reels • Twenty years earlier, the role of Baron Chevrial became a signature stage performance for Richard Mansfield and made him one of the country's premier actors. William Fox obtained permission from Mansfield's widow to use the actor's name in the film's advertising, even though the part was played by H. Cooper Cliffe.

THE FOURTH ESTATE (Jan. 17, 1916); D: Frank Powell; W: Frank Powell, Joseph Medill Patterson (play); Cast: Clifford Bruce, Ruth Blair, Victor Benoit, Alfred Hickman, Samuel J. Ryan, Aline Bartlett, Stacey Van Patten, Jr. • Noland (Bruce), the leader of a city-wide strike, out of jail on bail, leaves for Canada while his wife (Blair) is held behind by corrupt Judge Bertelmy

(Hickman), who has designs on her. After making a fortune in Canada, Noland returns, buys a newspaper, and crusades against the evil Bertelmy, who is arrested for a murder he committed years before. 5 reels

THE SERPENT (Jan. 23, 1916); D: Raoul A. Walsh; W: Raoul A. Walsh (scr), Philip Barthomolae (st); C: Georges Benoit; Cast: Theda Bara, Lillian Hathaway, James Marcus, Charles Craig, Carl Harbaugh, George Walsh, Nan Carter, Marcel Morhange • A Russian peasant, Vania (Bara), after being raped by Duke Valanoff (Craig) and seeing him kill her boyfriend (Walsh), becomes a success on the London stage. She is admired by Valanoff, who does not recognize her. She encourages his advances and then makes his son Leo (Harbaugh), fighting at the front, fall in love with her. She marries Leo and then has an open affair with his father. Leo commits suicide and Vania then reveals her true identity to the duke. However, it all turns out to be the dream of the peasant girl. 5 reels

THE RULING PASSION (Jan. 31, 1916); SP: Herbert Brenon; D: James McKay; W: Herbert Brenon; Cast: William E. Shay, Claire Whitney, Harry Burkhardt, Edward Boring, Thelma Parker, Florence Deschon, Stephen Grattan, Katherine Gilbert, Violet Rockwell • A young Englishwoman in India, Claire (Whitney), marries a British officer. She refuses the advances of a rajah (Shay) who uses his hypnotic power to make her love him and become a part of his harem. Her husband leaves her but she finally escapes the rajah's brutality. The rajah is killed in an unsuccessful coup against the royal governor, and, with his death, the spell is broken. Claire is reconciled with her husband. 5 reels • Filmed in Kingston, Jamaica

THE FOOL'S REVENGE (Feb. 14, 1916); D: Will S. Davis; W: Will S. Davis, Tom Taylor (play); Cast: William H. Tooker, Maude Gilbert, Richard Neill, Warner Oland, Kittens Reichert • Anson (Tooker), a clown, kills his unfaithful wife (Gilbert) and gets away with the murder; he then devotes his life to taking care of his daughter, Ethel (Findlay). He also plots revenge against the man, Randall (Neal), who was having the affair. However, his plan to encourage and then expose an affair between Mrs. Randall and Randall's friend backfires, and Anson ends up kidnapping and drugging Ethel, ruining her chances for marriage. 6 reels

MERELY MARY ANN (Feb. 17, 1916); D: John G. Adolfi; W: John G. Adolfi, John W. Kellette, Israel Zangwill (play); C: Hugh C. McClung; Cast: Vivian Martin, Edward Hoyt, Harry Hilliard, Laura Lyman, Isabel O'Madigan, Sidney Bracy, Niles Welch • A young penniless girl, Mary Ann (Martin), wandering through London, meets a musician (Hilliard), who finds her lodging. Mary Ann later learns that she has inherited a fortune, but the musician parts company because of their different financial positions. A few years after, at a party for Mary Ann, she reunites with the musician, now a famous composer. They eventually fall in love and marry. 5 reels

FIGHTING BLOOD (Feb. 21, 1916); D: Oscar C. Apfel;

W: Oscar C. Apfel; C: George Richter; Cast: William Farnum, Dorothy Bernard, Fred Huntley, Henry Hebert, H.A. Barrows, Dick Le Strange, Willard Louis • A lumberman, Lem Hardy (Farnum), is jailed on a trumped-up payroll robbery charge because he is in love with Evie (Bernard), the owner's daughter. Evie, unaware of the truth, marries Harry (Herbert), the superintendent who falsely accused Lem. Released from prison, Lem becomes a minister in the town where Harry and Evie live. Harry tries to murder Evie in a drunken rage, but is killed. Evie is moved by Lem's sermons and the two decide to get married. 5 reels • This is the first Fox Film made in Los Angeles.

THE WITCH (Feb. 28, 1916); D: Frank Powell; W: Frank Powell, Victorien Sardou (play); Cast: Nance O'Neil, Alfred Hickman, Frank Russell, Macey Harlam, Ada Neville, Jane Miller, Sadie Gross, Stuart Holmes, Harry Kendall, Robert Wayne, Jane Janin • In a Mexican village, Zora (O'Neil) is banished as a witch because of her hypnotic skills. She falls in love with Riques, unaware that he is engaged to Dolores (Miller), the daughter of the governor (Hickman). She puts a sleeping spell on Dolores to keep Riques to herself. Their affair is exposed and Zora is sentenced to die by fire. However, the governor realizes that only Zora can bring his daughter out of her spell and grants her freedom to leave the town. 5 reels

THE MARBLE HEART (March 6, 1916); D: Kenean Buel; W: Herbert Brenon, Emile Zola (novel); Cast: Violet Horner, Louise Rial, Walter Miller, Rhy Alexander, Henry Armetta, Walter McCullough, Harry Burkhardt, Hal De Forrest, Mademoiselle Marcelle • A girl in a small French town, Thérèse (Horner), marries her mentally weak cousin Camille, but falls in love with Laurent (Miller). The lovers drown Camille while boating and claim it was an accident. Thérèse and Laurent marry and live in Thérèse's aunt's (Rial) house. When the aunt overhears their counter-accusations about the murder, she becomes paralyzed. Haunted by the aunt's constant accusatory stare, the couple commits suicide. 5 reels • When the play version of Zola's Thérèse Raquin was on stage 20 years earlier, it was stopped by police because it contained an undressing scene. This scene was not re-enacted for the film version.

GOLD AND THE WOMAN (March 13, 1916); D: James Vincent; W: Mary Murillo; Cast: Theda Bara, Alma Hanlon, H. Cooper Cliffe, Harry Hilliard, Carleton Macy, Chief Black Eagle, Julia Hurley, Carter B. Harkness, Caroline Harris, Ted Griffin • Hester Gray (Hanlon) inherits land that her ancestor stole from the Indians. She wants to marry an Indian descendant to restore half the land to its rightful owner. Hester's guardian (Cliffe) marries her but is under the influence of a Mexican adventuress, Juliet (Bara), and hands the deed over to her. The swindle is exposed, Hester's husband dies and she is free to marry the man she loves. 6 reels

THE BONDMAN (March 20, 1916); D: Edgar Lewis; W: Louis Kellar, Edgar Lewis, Hall Caine (novel); Cast:

William Farnum, L.O. Hart, Dorothy Bernard, Charles Graham, Doris Wooldridge, Charles Brooke, Julia Hurley, Cathy Lee, Harry Spingler • Jason Orry (Farnum), vowing revenge against Sunlocks (Spingler), a half-brother he does not know, because of an injustice to his mother, tracks him to Iceland. There, Jason ends up in jail shackled to another man. After the two escape, Jason realizes that he is chained to his enemy and both are in love with the same woman, Greeba (Bernard). Jason is pardoned, but Sunlocks is sentenced to execution. Visiting Sunlocks, Jason realizes Greeba loves his half-brother and he stays in the cell to be executed in his place. 5–6 reels

A WIFE'S SACRIFICE (March 27, 1916); D: J. Gordon Edwards; W: J. Gordon Edwards; C: Philip E. Rosen; Cast: Robert B. Mantell, Genevieve Blinn, Claire Whitney, Louise Rial, Henry Leone, Genevieve Hamper, Stuart Holmes, Walter Miller, Walter McCullough, Jane Lee • Brother and sister, Peppo (Holmes) and Gorgone (Hamper), assume the identities of a deceased brother and sister in order to inherit their fortune. They convince a count (Mantell) that his wife's (Blinn) meeting with an illegitimate sibling (McCullough) is a romantic encounter which results in the young man being shot to death. The count then marries Gorgone. The pair is later exposed as imposters and Peppo takes poison, while Gorgone accidentally stabs herself to death trying to kill the count. 5 reels • This film was made on location in Kingston, Jamaica.

BLUE BLOOD AND RED (Apr. 3, 1916); D: Raoul Walsh; W: Raoul Walsh; C: Georges Benoit, Leonard S. Powers, George Richter; Cast: George Walsh, Martin Kinney, Doris Pawn, James Marcus, Jack Woods, Augustus Carney • Expelled from Harvard and thrown out by his millionaire father, Algernon DuPont (Walsh) goes west and falls in love with the daughter (Pawn) of a wealthy rancher. The "blue blood" proves his grit when he defends himself against a jealous cowboy who plots to have him lynched. He marries, returns home with twins, and is reconciled with his father. 5 reels

SLANDER (Apr. 10, 1916); D: Will S. Davis; W: Will S. Davis; C: Lloyd Lewis; Cast: Bertha Kalich, Eugene Ormonde, Mayme Kelso, Edward Van Sloane, Robert Rendel, Warren Cook, C. Peyton, T. Jerome Lawler • Richard Tremaine (Ormonde) convinces a man that his wife, Helene (Kalich), is cheating on him so he can marry her. Before the wedding, Helene discovers Richard wrecked her marriage and seeks revenge by making his son (Van Sloane) fall in love with her. Richard threatens suicide and he accidentally shoots and kills his son. Helene testifies against Richard, but she later reveals that the murder was accidental. She is then reconciled with her husband. 5 reels

A MODERN THELMA (Apr. 17, 1916); D: John G. Adolfi; W: John G. Adolfi, Marie Corelli (novel); C: Hugh C. McClung; Cast: Vivian Martin, Harry Hilliard, William H. Tooker, Albert Roccardi, Maud Sinclair, Elizabeth Kennedy, Allen Walker, Stuart Russell, Richard Neill • Sir Philip (Hilliard) meets Thelma (Martin) while on a mountain-climbing vacation in Norway, marries her and returns home to London high society. When Philip's jealous former sweetheart starts spreading rumors of his infidelity, Thelma returns to Norway. Philip follows her and is reconciled with Thelma after proving the rumors are false. 5 reels

A MAN OF SORROW (Apr. 23, 1916); D: Oscar C. Apfel; W: Oscar C. Apfel, Henry Arthur Jones & Wilson Barrett (play); C: A. Gandolfi; Cast: William Farnum, Dorothy Bernard, Willard Louis, Mary Ruby, Fred Huntley, Harry DuRoy, Henry J. Hebert, H.A. Burrows, Thelma Burns, William Scott, Robert Wayne • A husband (Farnum), determined to drown himself because of his wife's infidelity, saves a woman (Bernard) from jumping into the water. She turns out to be his wife's gypsy half-sister who was hired by a man who was in love with the wife to make it look like she was unfaithful. The husband tracks down the man, who is also wanted for a murder, and has him arrested. The husband apologizes to his wife. 5 reels

BLAZING LOVE (May 1, 1916); D: Kenean Buel; W: Mary Murillo; C: Phil Rosen; Cast: Virginia Pearson, Frank Burbeck, Wilmuth Merkyl, Lew Stern, Frank Goldsmith, George Selby, Louis Huff, Mattie Ferguson • Margaret (Pearson), a widow whose husband died in a polar expedition, marries a much older man (Burbeck) and then falls in love with Stephen (Merkyl), who is much younger than she. Her husband commits suicide because of unfair rumors. Margaret marries Stephen, who then falls in love with a woman his own age. Finally, like her previous husband, Margaret commits suicide to allow her young husband to be with the woman he truly loves. 5 reels

THE ETERNAL SAPHO (May 8, 1916); D: Bertram Bracken; W: Mary Murillo, Alphonse Daudet (novel); C: Rial Schellinger; Cast: Theda Bara, James Cooley, Walter P. Lewis, Hattie Delaro, Einar Linden, Mary Martin, Kittens Reichert, George MacQuarrie, Warner Oland, Frank Norcross • Laura (Bara) becomes notorious after posing as Sapho for a sculptor and loses two suitors. She gives up a married man (Linden) for the sake of his daughter, and the other suitor drops her because of rumors that she was responsible for her father's murder. She discovers the sculptor has committed suicide after losing her and Laura then goes insane and dies. 5 reels • By this point in Theda Bara's career, critics were tiring of her "vamp" role and it was rumored that this would be the last time she reprised the part.

SINS OF MEN (May 15, 1916); D: James Vincent; W: Mary Murillo; C: René Guissart; Cast: Stuart Holmes, Dorothy Bernard, Tom Burrough, Alice Gale, Stanhope Wheatcroft, Hattie Burks, Louis Hendricks, Stephen Grattan, Kittens Reichert • An obscure German philosopher (Burrough) becomes famous and wealthy from his book which preaches selfishness and hedonism, but suffers the consequences when his daughters, Elsie (Bernard) and Bertie (Wheatcroft), follow his doctrine and the family ends up being murdered. Waking up and realizing it was all a dream, the philosopher burns the manuscript he has been writing. 5 reels

THE BATTLE OF HEARTS (May 22, 1916); D: Oscar Apfel; W: Oscar Apfel (scr), Frances Marion (st); Cast: William Farnum, Elda Furry, Wheeler Oakman, William Burrs, Willard Louis • Martin (Farnum), the owner of a fleet of fishing boats, is in love with Maida (Furry), who prefers the lighthouse keeper's son Jo (Oakman). However, Jo becomes a smuggler and causes the lighthouse to go dark during a raid, causing Maida's boat to crash. Martin rescues her and captures the smugglers. 5 reels

THE SPIDER AND THE FLY (May 29, 1916); D: J. Gordon Edwards; W: Franklin B. Coates; C: Phil Rosen; Cast: Robert B. Mantell, Genevieve Hamper, Stuart Holmes, Genevieve Blinn, Franklin B. Coates, Claire Whitney, Walter Miller, Henry Leone, Stephen Grattan, Jane Lee • In France, Delano (Mantell) falls in love with Blanche (Hamper), a vamp, and becomes an alcoholic. Blanche abandons him for another man, and, while she is ruining more lives, Delano dies from alcohol. As a result, Blanche finds religion and helps others. 5 reels

HYPOCRISY (June 5, 1916); D: Kenean Buel; W: Hugh C. Weir; Cast: Virginia Pearson, Alfred Swenson, John Webb Dillon, Ida Darling, Henry Leone, Lydia Dickson, Adella Barker, Gladys Morris • To cover her huge debts, a woman (Darling) arranges for her daughter Virginia (Pearson) to marry millionaire Morgan Hutchins (Dillon). Virginia, however, marries Warren (Swenson), who lost his money in stocks. Virginia accepts money from Hutchins, which leads to her separation. She later clears Warren in a fraudulent stock scheme carried out by Hutchins. Happily, her husband's worthless stock regains its value. 6 reels

A WOMAN'S HONOR (June 12, 1916); D: Roland West; W: Donald I. Buchanan, George L. Knapp (article); C: Ed Wynard; Cast: Bradley Barker, José Collins, Armand Cortes, Arthur Donaldson, Ruby Hoffman, DeVore Palmer, Saba Raleigh, Anna Reedor • Helena (Collins) returns to Italy from New York, with the financial help of a wealthy Italian lawyer, to take revenge on Count Tochetti (Donaldson), who raped her when she was young. The lawyer helps her with the revenge even though he discovers the count is his uncle. They both return to America. 5 reels • Some scenes for this movie were shot in Jamaica.

EAST LYNNE (June 19, 1916); D: Bertram Bracken; W: Mary Murillo, Ellen Wood (novel); C: R. Schellinger; Cast: Theda Bara, Ben Deeley, Stuart Holmes, Claire Whitney, W.H. Tooker, Loel Stewart, Eldean Stewart, Eugenie Woodward, Stanhope Wheatcroft • Isabel (Bara) leaves her husband (Deeley) and children because she mistakenly believes that he loves Barbara (Whitney). Her husband, hearing a report that Isabel was killed in a train wreck, marries Barbara. Isabel misses her children and disguises herself as their governess. She reveals herself when her son becomes ill and calls out for his mother. Her husband forgives Isabel, but she dies of grief. 5 reels • This was the first of three Fox film versions of the English novel.

AMBITION (June 25, 1916); D: James Vincent; W: Mary Murillo; C: René Guissart; Cast: Bertha Kalich, Kenneth Hunter, William H. Tooker, W.W. Black, Kittens Reichert, Gilbert Rooney, Barnett Greenwood, May Price • An assistant district attorney (Hunter) arranges a love match between his wife (Kalich) and a political boss (Tooker) to gain a candidacy. The wife eventually realizes the plan and throws her husband out of the house. 5 reels

THE MAN FROM BITTER ROOTS (July 3, 1916); D: Oscar C. Apfel; W: Oscar C. Apfel, Caroline Lockhart (novel); C: Alfred Gandolfi, Harry W. Gerstad, J.C. Cook; Cast: William Farnum, Charles Whitaker, H.A. Barrows, Willard Louis, William Burress, Henry De Vere, Betty Schade, Betty Harte, Ogden Crane • After striking gold, Bruce (Farnum), a prospector, seeks out his deceased partner's daughter, Helen (Schade), to give her a share of the strike. A villain (Barrows) wants the gold and convinces Helen that Bruce murdered her father. However, a dance hall girl ferrets out the truth, allowing Bruce and Helen to marry. 5 reels

CAPRICE OF THE MOUNTAINS (July 10, 1916); D: John G. Adolfi; W: Clarence J. Harris; C: Hugh C. McClung; Cast: June Caprice, Harry Hilliard, Joel Day, Lisle Leigh, Richard Hale, Albert Gran, Tom Burrough, Robert D. Walker, Sara Alexander, Harriet Thompson • A mountaineer's daughter (Caprice), forced into a shotgun wedding with a big city playboy (Hilliard), finds the city lifestyle unbearable. She moves back to the mountains and is later followed by her husband, who realizes how much he loves her. 5 reels

A TORTURED HEART (July 17, 1916); D: Will S. Davis; W: Will S. Davis; C: Lloyd Lewis; Cast: Virginia Pearson, Stuart Holmes, Fuller Mellish, Stephen Grattan, Frances Miller, Joseph Levering, Glen White, Georg Larkin, Marian Swayne • Lucille (Pearson), who abandoned her baby years before, tries to dissuade the now-grown girl, Liza (Miller), from doing what she did, eloping with a notorious scoundrel. The girl does not listen and ends up with an abusive husband (Holmes), who is later killed in a fight, allowing Liza to marry a respectful man (Larkin). 5 reels

THE BEAST (July 24, 1916); D: Richard Stanton; W: Richard Stanton; C: F. Granville, J.C. Cook; Cast: George Walsh, Anna Luther, Herschel Mayall, Edward Cecil, Henry De Vere, Clyde Benson • Mildred Manning (Luther), touring the West with her sweetheart, Sir Charles Beverly (Cecil), wants to experience frontier life firsthand. While Charles gambles, ranch owner Del Burton (Walsh) saves Mildred from two drunken cowboys, falls in love with her, and follows her back east. He takes on the manners of an easterner and changes Mildred's low opinion of him into love. 5 reels

UNDER TWO FLAGS (July 31, 1916); D: J. Gordon Edwards; W: George Hall, Ouida (novel); C: Phil E. Rosen; Cast: Theda Bara, Herbert Heyes, Stuart

Holmes, Stanhope Wheatcroft, Joseph Crehan, Charles Craig, Claire Whitney • Bertie Cecil (Heyes), an Englishman, leaves his sweetheart, Venetia (Whitney), and joins the French Foreign Legion in Algiers, taking the blame for a crime committed by his brother. He becomes a hero, but runs afoul of his commanding officer (Holmes) and is condemned to death. Cigarette (Bara), who loves Bertie, rides through a sandstorm with a pardon and shields Bertie from the firing squad. Exonerated, Bertie returns to Venetia. 6 reels

THE END OF THE TRAIL (Aug. 7, 1916); D: Oscar C. Apfel; W: Oscar C. Apfel (scr), Maibelle Heikes Justice (st); C: Alfredo Gandolfi, J.C. Cook; Cast: William Farnum, Gladys Brockwell, Willard Louis, Eleanor Crowe, H.A Barrows, William Burress, Harry De Vere, Hermoina Louis, Henry J. Hebert, Ogden Crane • A Canadian trapper, Jules (Farnum), marries Adrienne (Brockwell) who believes her previous husband Cabot (Louis) is dead. Cabot shows up alive, kidnaps her and is enraged when she gives birth to a baby. Adrienne returns to Jules, but dies from the traumatic events. Years later, Cabot shows up again and attacks the daughter, but Jules kills him first. 5 reels

SPORTING BLOOD (Aug. 14, 1916); D: Bertram Bracken; W: Bertram Bracken; C: R. B. Schellinger; Cast: Dorothy Bernard, Glen White, De Witt C. Jennings, George Morgan, Madeleine Le Nard, Claire Whitney • James Riddle (White) and Mary Ballard (Bernard) plan to take revenge on a gambler, Dave Garrison (Jennings), who has seduced and cheated both their siblings. Mary agrees to sleep with Dave if his horse wins a race and receive $10,000 if he loses. The pair manages to get a look-alike horse in the race, get even with the crook and then decide to marry. 5 reels

DAREDEVIL KATE (Aug. 21, 1916); D: Kenean J. Buel; W: Clarence J. Harris, Philip Batholomae (play); C: Frank Kugler; Cast: Virginia Pearson, Victor Sutherland, Mary Martin, Kenneth Hunter, Alex Shannon, Leighton Stark, Fred R. Stanton, Jane Lee, Katherine Lee, Minna Philips • Orphaned sisters, Kate (Pearson) and Irene (Martin), live in the same boom town munitions camp, but are unaware of their identities. Kate's pursuit of Cliff (Sutherland), Irene's adopted brother, creates hostility between the two women until they discover that each has half of their mother's ring, which leads to a reconciliation and Irene's approval of Kate pairing with Cliff. 6 reels

LITTLE MISS HAPPINESS (Aug. 28, 1916); D: John G. Adolfi; W: Clarence J. Harris; C: Hugh C. McClung; Cast: June Caprice, Harry Hilliard, Zena Keefe, Sara Alexander, Sidney Bracy, Leo Kennedy, Robert Vivian, Lucia Moore, Genevieve Reynold, Grace Beaumont • Sadie (Keefe) leaves her husband (Hilliard) in the city and returns to her village with a child. Afraid to tell her father she plans to raise her daughter as a single parent, Sadie turns the child over to Lucy (Caprice), who then is ostracized for allegedly having a baby out of wedlock. Sadie is finally reunited with her baby when she reconciles with her husband. 5 reels

HER DOUBLE LIFE (Sept. 11, 1916); D: J. Gordon Edwards; W: Mary Murillo; C: Philip E. Rosen; Cast: Theda Bara, Stuart Holmes, A.H. Van Buren, Madeleine Le Nard, Walter Law, Katherine Lee, Jane Lee, Carey Lee, Lucia Moore • An English nurse at the front, Mary (Bara) poses as someone else to keep away from Lloyd, a war correspondent (Holmes) who tried to seduce her. Under this identity, she falls in love with a nobleman, Elliot (Van Buren), but is almost exposed by Lloyd. Confessing the deception, she is able to retain Elliot's respect and earn his mother's forgiveness. 6 reels

THE UNWELCOME MOTHER (Sept. 14, 1916); D: James Vincent; W: Mary Murillo; C: René Guissart; Cast: Valkyrien, Violet de Biccari, Walter Law, Frank Evans, John Webb Dillon, Warren Cook, Tom Burrough, Lillian Devere, Jane Lee, Katherine Lee • Elinor (Valkyrien) is abandoned by a sailor (Law) who tricked her into a phony marriage ceremony. She then falls in love with a rich widower, John Hudson (Dillon), and agrees to marry him, but is not accepted by his grown children. Eventually, John's oldest daughter, Ann (de Biccari), realizes that her father will be hurt if Elinor leaves, and convinces her to stay with them. 5 reels

WHERE LOVE LEADS (Sept. 18, 1916); D: Frank C. Griffin; W: Frank C. Griffin; C: Robert Newhard; Cast: Ormi Hawley, Rockcliffe Fellowes, Royal Byron, Haydn Stevenson, Charles Craig, Hebert Evans, Albert Gran, Maud Hall Macey, Dorothy Rogers • Marion (Hawley) is forced into marriage with an older man (Craig) by her parents, even though she loves someone else. Years later, afraid of her husband's bad influence, she sends her daughters to America, unaware they have been turned over to a white slaver (Rogers). The girls are rescued by Marion's true love (Fellowes) and all ends happily with the lovers marrying. 5 reels

THE FIRES OF CONSCIENCE (Sept. 26, 1916); D: Oscar Apfel; W: Henry Christeen Warnack (st); Cast: William Farnum, Gladys Brockwell, Nell Shipman, H.A. Barrows, H.J. Herbert, William Burress, Eleanor Crowe, Willard Louis, Brooklyn Keller, Fred Huntley • Falling in love with a woman (Brockwell) in a small western town, George Baxter (Farnum) finally turns himself in for the murder of his adulterous wife's boyfriend. The dead man's father (Burress) turns out to be the presiding judge and star witness as well. The judge is honest and claims he saw the murder and declares George innocent because he simply followed the "unwritten law." 5–6 reels

THE STRAIGHT WAY (Oct. 2, 1916); D: Will S. Davis; W: Will S. Davis; C: A. Lloyd Lewis; Cast: Valeska Suratt, Herbert Heyes, Glen White, Claire Whitney, Elsie Balfour, Richard Turner, Richard Rendell • Falsely accused of infidelity by her husband, John (Heyes), Mary (Suratt) leaves home to have her baby. There is a train wreck on the way, and John, thinking she has died, takes custody of their daughter. Years later, after recovering from amnesia, Mary returns to avenge John by disgracing his daughter, but discovers that the girl is really her child. 5 reels

THE WAR BRIDE'S SECRET (Oct. 9, 1916); D: Keenan Buel; W: Mary Murillo; C: Frank Kugler; E: Alfred De Gaetano; Cast: Virginia Pearson, Walter Law, Glen White, Stuart Sage, Henry Hallam, Olive Corbett, Robert Vivian, Billy Lynbrook • Scottish lass Jean (Pearson), secretly married to Colin (White), a soldier she thinks has been killed, weds an elderly farmer, Robin (Law), so her baby will have a father. When Colin recovers and returns from battle, Robin realizes Jean still loves him and steps aside. 6 reels

THE RAGGED PRINCESS (Oct. 16, 1916); D: John G. Adolfi; W: John W. Kellette (scr), Frederic Chapin (st); C: R. B. Schellinger; Cast: June Caprice, Harry Hilliard, Richard Neill, Tom Burrough, Florence Ashbrook, Sid Bracy, Caroline Harris, Jane Lee, Katherine Lee • A runaway orphan, Alicia (Caprice), is adopted by wealthy mine owner Thomas Deigan (Neill). Harry (Hilliard), whom Alicia loves, follows her and discovers that Deigan is his half brother and stole the property from a young girl who was placed in an orphanage. Harry saves Alicia from Deigan's advances and returns the mine to her. 5 reels

A DAUGHTER OF THE GODS (Oct. 17, 1916); SP: J. Gordon Edwards; D: Herbert Brenon; W: Herbert Brenon; C: J. Roy Hunt, Andre Barlatier, Marcel Le Picard, A. Culp, William C. Marshall, C. Richards, E. Warren; E: Hettie Grey Baker; Cast: Annette Kellerman, William E. Shay, Hal De Forrest, Mademoiselle Marcelle, Edward Boring, Violet Horner, Jane Lee, Katherine Lee, Stuart Homes • A mysterious beauty, Anitia (Kellerman), is abducted and taken to the harem of the sultan (De Forrest). Her dancing so arouses the sultan that she is locked in a tower by the jealous Zarrah (Horner). Anitia escapes into the sea and ends up in Gnomeland. To save the kingdom she leads the gnomes to rescue her lover, Omar (Shay), but is only united with him in death. 10 reels • This lavish spectacle, filmed in Jamaica, was an expensive venture which failed financially and critically and was known mostly for the various states of undress of swimming champion Kellerman. A musical accompaniment was written by Robert Hood Bowers.

ROMEO AND JULIET (Oct. 23, 1916); D: J. Gordon Edwards; W: Adrian Johnson, William Shakespeare (play); C: Philip E. Rosen; Cast: Theda Bara, Harry Hilliard, Glen White, John Webb Dillon, Einar Linder, Elwin Easton, Edwin Holt, Alice Gale, Victory Bateman, Helen Tracy • Romeo (Hilliard) and Juliet (Bara) have an ill-fated romance because of their feuding families in medieval Italy, ending with the death of both. 7 reels • The William Fox version was in direct competition with an 8-reel Metro version released four days earlier, starring Francis X. Bushman and Beverly Bayne.

LOVE AND HATE (Oct. 30, 1916); D: James Vincent; W: Mary Murillo (scr), James R. Garey (st); C: René Guissart; E: Alfred De Gaetano; Cast: Bertha Kalich, Stuart Holmes, Kenneth Hunter, Madeleine Le Nard, Jane Lee, Katherine Lee • George (Holmes) covets Robert's (Hunter) wife, Helen (Kalich), and makes him believe she has been unfaithful so he will divorce her. When George fails to win over Helen, he kidnaps her daughter (Lee). Helen finally consents to spend the night with George, then kills him. Robert reconciles with her when he learns the whole truth. 6 reels

SINS OF HER PARENT (Nov. 6, 1916); D: Frank Lloyd; W: Frank Lloyd (scr), Tom Forman (st); C: William C. Foster; Cast: Gladys Brockwell, William Clifford, Carl von Schiller, George Webb, Herschel Mayall • Valerie (Brockwell), unhappy with her husband, gives up her daughter for adoption and moves to Alaska, where she works in a saloon dance hall. Years later, her daughter Adrian (Brockwell) is refused permission to marry Richard (Schiller) because his father (Clifford) wants information about her parents. Richard goes to Alaska to track down Valerie and is finally allowed to marry. Before the wedding, however, Valerie is killed in a fight with the saloon owner (Mayall). 5 reels

THE MEDIATOR (Nov. 13, 1916); D: Otis Turner; W: Otis Turner (adpt), Ethel Webber (adpt), Roy Norton (novel); C: Dev Jennings; Cast: George Walsh, Juanita Hansen, James Marcus, Lee Willard, Pearl Elmore, Sedley Brown • Lish Henry (Walsh), a gunfighter who wants to retire to a small town, ends up being a mediator since he is the toughest person there. He keeps killing gang members until everyone agrees to a peace settlement. One final gunfight with an old enemy, Big Bill (Marcus), brings his career to an end and he marries Maggie (Hansen), his true love. 5 reels

JEALOUSY (Nov. 20, 1916); D: Will S. Davis; W: Will S. Davis; Cast: Valeska Suratt, Lew Walter, Charline Mayfield, Curtis Benton, Joseph Granby, George M. Adams • Anne (Suratt), whose bankrupt father commits suicide, enters a mutually approved loveless marriage with Carney (Benton), a wealthy stockbroker. Anne is sued for divorce when Carney believes she is having an affair with an artist. Anne goes on stage as a dancer, then marries a millionaire (Walter). She tries to wreck Carney's happiness, but her scheme fails. 5 reels

THE MISCHIEF MAKER (Nov. 27, 1916); D: John G. Adolfi; W: John G. Adolfi (scr), Alfred Solman (st); C: Rial Schellinger; Cast: June Caprice, Harry Benham, John Reinhard, Margaret Fielding, Inez Marcel, Minnie Milne, Tom Brooke, Nellie Slattery • Effie (Caprice), sent to a French boarding school because she refused to marry the man her mother had chosen, is expelled when the principal erroneously believes she posed for a nude statue by sculptor Jules (Reinhard). Effie marries Al Tournay (Benham), who rescues her from Jules' advances and returns her to her mother. As it turns out, Effie married the man her mother had selected in the first place. 5 reels

THE VIXEN (Dec. 4, 1916); D: J. Gordon Edwards; W: Mary Murillo; C: Philip E. Rosen; Cast: Theda Bara, A.H. Van Buren, Herbert Heyes, Mary Martin, George Clarke, Carl Gerard, George Odell • Elsie (Bara), a spoiled nymphomaniac, woos away the boyfriend of her sweet sister Helen (Martin), Wall Street businessman named Martin (Van Buren), but leaves him when he loses his money. She repeats the indignity with statesman Knowles Murray (Heyes), then marries him. Years later, Elsie returns to entice Martin, who has regained his fortune. By now, he knows what Elsie the vixen is like and marries Helen. 6 reels

THE BATTLE OF LIFE (Dec. 11, 1916); D: James Vincent; W: Adrian Johnson (scr), James R. Garey (st); C: Rene Guissart; Cast: Gladys Coburn, Art Acord, Richard Neill, William Sheer, Frank Evans, Violet De Biccari, Alex Shannon • Mary (Coburn), the daughter and accomplice of a crook, is involved in a crime, even though she is trying to go straight. Her lover, Dave (Acord), also a crook, steals some jewels, including a necklace which she takes for herself. The gang members accuse each other of hiding the necklace. Dave kills one of the gang in a fight, but discovers Mary has the necklace. He leaves it with the dead man, clears himself of murder, and decides to go straight. 5 reels

THE LOVE THIEF (Dec. 19, 1916); D: Richard Stanton; W: Ben Cohn (scr), M.P. Niessen (st); C: Dal Clawson; Cast: Gretchen Hartman, Alan Hale, Frances Burnham, Edwin Cecil, Willard Louis, Jack McDonald, Charles Ehler • Juanita (Hartman), a Mexican rebel leader, falls in love with American Captain Boyce (Hale), who rejects her. In retaliation, she has him arrested on a false murder charge. After Boyce is cleared, Juanita kidnaps Clare (Burnham), his lover, and later puts her and Boyce in front of a rebel firing squad. However, the cavalry comes to the rescue in time and kills Juanita. 5 reels

THE VICTIM (Dec. 25, 1916); D: Will S. Davis; W: Will S. Davis; C: A. Lloyd Lewis; Cast: Valeska Suratt, Herbert Hayes, Claire Whitney, John Charles, Joseph Cranby, Oscar Nye, Charles Edwards • After serving an unjust sentence for burglary, Ruth (Suratt) starts a new life. She falls in love and marries wealthy Dr. Boulden (Heyes). Ruth's father, the true criminal in the burglary, tracks her down but is followed by corrupt Detective Higgins (Charles), who blackmails Ruth. The father accidentally kills Higgins in a fight and flees. Ruth is once again accused, but when her father is burned in a fire, Boulden saves him and he confesses everything. 5 reels

1917 Releases

THE ISLAND OF DESIRE (Jan. 1, 1917); D: Otis Turner; W: Otis Turner, J. Allen Dunn (short story); C: Charles Kaufman; Cast: George Walsh, Margaret Gibson, Anna Luther, Herschel Mayall, William Burress, William Clifford, Sam Searles, Hector Sarno, Marie McKeen • A newspaper reporter, Bruce Chalmers (Walsh), finds a South Sea treasure of pearls in the possession of Leila (Gibson), shipwrecked since she was a girl. Two adventurers (Mayall, Burress) challenge him for the jewels, but end up killing each other, leaving Bruce with Leila and the treasure. 5 reels

A MODERN CINDERELLA (Jan. 8, 1917); D: John G. Adolfi; W: Florence Auer; C: Rial B. Schellinger; Cast: June Caprice, Frank Morgan, Betty Prendergast, Stanhope Wheatcroft, Grace Stevens, Tom Brooke • A mother (Stevens) keeps young Joyce (Caprice) away from Tom (Morgan) to allow for a romance with the older Polly (Prendergast). When Polly flirts with Harry (Wheatcroft), Joyce moves in on Tom and real love develops. To test Tom's love, Joyce jumps into shark-infested waters. Tom rescues her. 5 reels

THE PRICE OF SILENCE (Jan. 8, 1917); D: Frank Lloyd; W: Frank Lloyd (scr), Mildred Pigott (st), William Pigott (st); C: Billy Foster; Cast: William Farnum, Frank Clark, Vivian Rich, Brooklyn Keller, Charles Clary, Ray Hanford, Gordon Griffith • In order to protect the reputation of Judge Vernon (Clark) and his daughter Grace (Rich), Senator Deering (Farnum) accepts a bribe of bonds stolen from the judge and goes to jail to keep the news of worthless value of the bonds from becoming public. 5 reels

THE BITTER TRUTH (Jan. 15, 1917); D: Kenean Buel; W: Mary Murillo; C: Frank Kugler; Cast: Virginia Pearson, Jack Hopkins, William H. Tooker, Alice May, Sidney D'Albrook • Anne (Pearson) seeks revenge against Judge Marcus (Tooker), who unfairly sentenced her to jail, by setting him up in a compromising situation. However, she actually does fall in love with him and decides not to go through with her plan. 6 reels

THE DARLING OF PARIS (Jan. 22, 1917); D: J. Gordon Edwards; W: Adrian Johnson, Victor Hugo (novel); C: Philip E. Rosen; Cast: Theda Bara, Glen White, Walter Law, Herbert Heyes, Carey Lee, Alice Gale, John Webb Dillon, Louis Dean • Esmeralda (Bara) is admired by scientist Claude Frallo (Law), who has cured a hunchback, Quasimodo (White). Esmeralda is accused of stabbing Captain Phoebus (Heyes) to death, but Quasimodo testifies that it was another. 5 reels • This is a modern adaptation of the Hugo classic, *The Hunchback of Notre Dame*.

THE PRIMITIVE CALL (Jan. 22, 1917); D: Bertram Bracken; W: Bertram Bracken; C: Rial B. Schellinger; Cast: Gladys Coburn, Fritz Leiber, John Webb Dillon, George Alan Larkin, Lewis Sealy, Velma Whitman, Kittens Reichert • A society girl (Coburn), whose father (Larkin) was trying to cheat an Indian tribe, seduces the tribal leader (Lieber) to get the deed to his land. She then spurns him and he kidnaps her, taking her to live in his wigwam. She falls in love with him, but he prefers an Indian maiden and sends the society girl back. 5 reels

ONE TOUCH OF SIN (Jan. 29, 1917); D: Richard Stanton; W: L. Genez (st); C: J.D. Jennings, Dal Clawson, George Richter; Cast: Gladys Brockwell, Jack Standing, Willard Louis, Sedley Brown, Carrie Clark Ward, Frankie Lee, Charles Edhler, Jack MacDonald • Traveling west, Mary (Brockwell), unable to earn a living, is forced to become a thief. She then marries Watt Tabor (Louis) to avoid prison. Richard Mallaby

(Standing), the lover who deserted her, also comes west and insists on taking her back. The two men have a fight in a mine shaft over Mary. Watt saves Mallaby from an ensuing flood and wins her love. 5 reels

THE NEW YORK PEACOCK (Feb. 5, 1917); D: Kenean Buel; W: Mary Murillo; C: Frank C. Kugler; Cast: Valeska Suratt, Harry Hilliard, Eric Mayne, Alice Gale, Claire Whitney, W.W. Black, John Mackin, Frank Goldsmith • Billy (Hilliard), visiting New York to invest $100,000 of his father's money, is lured into a gambling house, becomes romantically involved with the seductive Zena (Suratt), and ends up losing all his money. Zena tries to repay his money by seducing and then extorting a businessman (Mayne), who turns out to be Billy's father. 5–6 reels

THE SCARLET LETTER (Feb. 12, 1917); D: Carl Harbaugh; W: Carl Harbaugh, Nathaniel Hawthorne (novel); C: Georges Benoit; Cast: Mary Martin, Stuart Holmes, Dan Mason, Kittens Reichert, Edward N. Hoyt, Robert Vivian, Florence Ashbrooke • Hester Prynne (Martin) is forced to wear a scarlet "A" on her clothing when she has an out-of-wedlock child (Reichert). The father is kept secret, but turns out to be the Rev. Arthur Dimmesdale (Holmes). 5 reels

MELTING MILLIONS (Feb. 19, 1917); D: Otis Turner; W: Joseph Anthony Roach; Cast: Sidney Dean, Cecil Holland, Velma Whitman, George Walsh, Frank Alexander, Anna Luther, Charles Gerrard • Jack (Walsh), an irresponsible young man, must prove his business acumen to inherit his late uncle's fortune. He goes out West where he rescues Jane (Luther) from a gang of outlaws and later proves himself by saving her from being kidnapped by his father's former secretary (Whitman). 5 reels

THE TIGER WOMAN (Feb. 26, 1917); D: J. Gordon Edwards; W: Adrian Johnson (scr), James W. Adams (st); C: Philip E. Rosen; Cast: Theda Bara, Ed F. Rosenman, Louis Dean, Emil DeVarny, John Webb Dillon, Glenn White, Mary Martin, Kittens Reichert, Herbert Heyes, Edwin Holt • Princess Petrovich (Bara) is a vamp who drains men of their money. She forces young Edwin (White) to rob, resulting in the death of his father (Holt). She then goes after the man's brother, Mark (Heyes), but her villainy comes to an end when one of her victims stabs her to death. 5–6 reels

A CHILD OF THE WILD (Feb. 26, 1917); D: John G. Adolfi; W: John W. Kellette (scr & st), John G. Adolfi (scr); Cast: June Caprice, Frank Morgan, Tom Brooke, Richard Neill, Jane Lee, John W. Kellette, John G. Adolfi, Tom Cameron • Tomboy June (Caprice) is romantically attracted to new teacher Frank (Morgan), to the chagrin of her boyfriend, Bob (Neill), who leads her to believe that Frank's sister and child (Lee) are his wife and daughter. The plot is exposed and June is happily reunited with Frank. 5 reels

SISTER AGAINST SISTER (March 5, 1917); D: James R. Vincent; W: Mary Murillo; C: Rene Guissart; Cast: Virginia Pearson, Maud Hall, Walter Law, Irving Cummings, Calla Dillatore, William Battista, Archie Battista, Jane Lee • Anne (Pearson) and Katherine (Pearson), each brought up by one of their separated parents, marry men who end up running for governor. Katherine, who lacks integrity, tries to lure Anne's husband (Cummings) into a compromising position, but a murder occurs and confusion follows regarding the identities of the girls. 5 reels • Irving Cummings, who started out as an actor, became a major director for Fox.

LOVE'S LAW (March 12, 1917); D: Tefft Johnson; W: Mary Murillo; C: Maxwell Held; Cast: Joan Sawyer, Stuart Holmes, Olga Grey, Leo Delaney, Richard Neill, Frank Goldsmith • Innocence (Sawyer) is sent away by her wealthy uncle, then taken prisoner by Andre, a gypsy leader (Holmes). She escapes to the city and becomes a famous dancer, but is pursued by Andre, whom she realizes she loves. 5 reels

A TALE OF TWO CITIES (March 12, 1917); D: Frank Lloyd; W: Frank Lloyd, Charles Dickens (novel); C: Billy Foster, George Schneiderman; Cast: William Farnum, Jewel Carmen, Charles Clary, Herschell Mayall, Rosita Marstini, Josef Swickard, Ralph Lewis, William Clifford, Marc Robbins, Olive White, Willard Louis • During the French Revolution, Englishman Sidney Carton (Farnum) unselfishly changes places with aristocrat Charles Darnay (Farnum) and goes to the guillotine so his lookalike can escape to be with Lucia (Carmen), the woman they both love. 7 reels

THE BLUE STREAK (March 19, 1917); D: William Nigh; W: William Nigh; C: Joseph Ruttenberg, A. Lloyd Lewis; Cast: William Nigh, Violet Palmer, Ruth Thorp, Martin Faust, Ned Finley, Edward Rosenman, Tom Cameron, Danny Sullivan, Ed Kennedy, Bert Gudgeon • Quick on the trigger, the "Blue Streak" (Nigh) prevents a forced marriage, but then realizing the girl (Palmer) is pregnant, reunites her with the gambler he believes violated her. When a posse comes after "Streak," the girl realizes she loves him, and the two ride off together. 5 reels

HIGH FINANCE (March 26, 1917); D: Otis Turner; W: Anthony F. McGrew Willis (scr), Larry Evans (st); C: Charles Kaufman; Cast: George Walsh, Doris Pawn, Willard Louis, Charles Clary, Herschell Mayall, Rosita Marstini, William Marr • Thrill-seeking Preston (Walsh), disowned son of a millionaire (Mayall), heads out West to prove he can make money. He concocts a plan to make a mine look like a rich lode and sells stock before he reveals the hoax. However, through the stock sale he has made enough to impress his father and be reinstated. 5 reels

HER GREATEST LOVE (Apr. 2, 1917); D: J. Gordon Edwards; W: Adrian Johnson, Ouida (novel); C: Philip E. Rosen; Cast: Theda Bara, Marie Curtis, Walter Law, Glen White, Harry Hilliard, Callie Torres, Alice Gale, Grace Saum • A naïve French girl, Vera (Bara), goes to live with her unprincipled, amoral mother, Lady Dolly (Curtis). Vera falls in love with Correze (Hilliard), an opera singer, but Lady Dolly insists she marry Russian Prince Zuroff (Law). When Vera discovers that Zuroff has a mistress, Jeanne (Torres), he sends her to a monastery. She is found by Correze. When her husband shows up, he gets into a duel and is killed, leaving Vera to marry Correze. 5 reels

TANGLED LIVES (Apr. 2, 1917); D: J. Gordon Edwards; W: Mary Murillo, Wilkie Collins (novel); Cast: Genevieve Hamper, Stuart Holmes, Robert B. Mantell, Walter Miller, Harry Leone, Claire Whitney, Genevieve Blinn, Louise Rial, Millicent Liston, Jane Lee; C: Philip E. Rosen • Ann (Hamper), half sister of wealthy Laura (Hamper), tries to talk her out of marriage to Roy (Holmes), a wastrel. Ann is kidnapped by Roy but refuses to sign over control of the estate. When Ann dies, a cousin (Whitney) retrieves Laura from the asylum where Roy placed her. Roy's conscience later tortures him to death. 5 reels

HER TEMPTATION (Apr. 9, 1917); D: Richard Stanton; W: Ben Cohn (scr), Norris Shannon (st); C: J.D. Jennings; Cast: Gladys Brockwell, Bertram Grassby, Ralph Lewis, Beatrice Burnham, James Cruze • Shirley (Brockwell) consents to marry the aged friend (Lewis) of her late father because she discovers he has been supporting her financially. She soon meets Gerald (Grassby), her former sweetheart, who hypnotizes her to disobey her vows and poison her husband. The will leaves the estate to Shirley's sister, who then gets Gerald's attention. However, a doctor (Cruze) who understands hypnosis, is able to figure out what went on. 5 reels • James Cruze later directed the epic western *The Covered Wagon*.

THE DERELICT (Apr. 16, 1917); D: Carl Harbaugh; W: Carl Harbaugh; C: George Benoit; Cast: Stuart Holmes, Mary Martin, June Daye, Carl Eckstrom, Dan Mason, Wanda Petit, Olive Trevor • Dissolute husband Teddy (Holmes) fakes his own suicide, thus freeing Rose (Martin) and her daughter. Rose remarries. Years later, Teddy, a derelict, sees a young girl being accosted and learns that she is his daughter Helen (Petit). In the ensuing fight, he strangles the assailant and then flees. Helen is arrested for the murder, but is acquitted when Teddy confesses to the crime. 5 reels • This film was Stuart Holmes's first movie for Fox.

SHE (Apr. 23, 1917); D: Kenean Buel; W: Mary Murillo, H. Rider Haggard (novel); C: Frank G. Kugler; Cast: Valeska Suratt, Ben L. Taggart, Miriam Fouche, Wigney Percival, Tom Burrough, Martin Reagan • Leo (Taggart), the direct descendant of an ancient Egyptian priest, carries on a 3,000-year-long quest to avenge the priest's death by Queen Ayesha (Suratt). He meets the ageless Ayesha, who recognizes Leo and declares her love for him. She wants to make him immortal, but as Ayesha bathes in the Flame of Life, her beauty begins to shrivel and she emerges a hideous ape. Leo flees the city. 5 reels

ROYAL ROMANCE (Apr. 30, 1917); D: James Vincent; W: Adrian Johnson; C: L.E. Taylor; Cast: Virginia Pearson, Royce Coombs, Irving Cummings, Charles Craig, Nora Cecil, Grace Henderson, Nellie Slattery, Alex K. Shannon, Emil De Varney • Princess Sylvia (Pearson) refuses a proposal from the Emperor Maximilian (Cummings) because it is not from his heart. She disguises herself as a commoner, and, when they meet, Maximilian falls in love with her. She saves him from an assassin and he offers to marry her. The prime minister is upset by the idea of marriage to a commoner, but Sylvia is revealed as the princess. She knows the emperor's proposal is sincere and accepts. 5 reels

AMERICAN METHODS (Apr. 30, 1917); D: Frank Lloyd; W: F. McGrew Willis, Frank Lloyd, Georges Ohnet (novel); C: Billy Foster; Cast: William Farnum, Jewel Carmen, Bertram Grassby, Willard Louis, Lillian West, Genevieve Blinn, Alan Forrest, Florence Vidor, Mortimer Jaffe, Marc Robbins • William (Farnum), an American of French descent, inherits an iron mine in France and marries Claire (Carmen). Her previous fiancé, Gaston (Grassby), now jealous, places her in a compromising position. In a fight, Gaston tries to shoot William, but is fatally wounded himself. Claire begs for, and receives, William's forgiveness. 5 reels

THE SMALL TOWN GIRL (May 7, 1917); D: John G. Adolfi; W: John G. Adolfi (st), Adrian Johnson (st); C: Rial B. Schellinger; Cast: June Caprice, Jane Lee, Bernard Delaney, Ethyle Cook, Tom Brooke, Lucia Moore, Inez Marcel, Howard D. Southard, John Burkell • A country girl, June (Caprice), comes to a New York tenement to take care of her young niece Jane (Lee) and meets Frank (Delaney), her sweetheart from home. A band of thieves in the building hide a stolen jewel, which is found by the niece. The crooks realize who has the jewel, but the police arrive in time and make an arrest. June and Frank then return home for their honeymoon. 5 reels

THE BOOK AGENT (May 14, 1917); D: Otis Turner; W: F. McGrew Willis (scr), Otis Turner (scr), Walter Woods (st); C: R.E. Irish; Cast: George Walsh, Doris Pawn, William Burress, Reginald Everett, Willard Louis, Josef Swickard, Velma Whitman, Phil Gastrock • A book peddler, Harry (Walsh), meets nurse Mollie (Pawn) who cares for wealthy invalid Crandall (Burress). Harry shields Crandall from three men (Everett, Louis, Swickard) who are trying to swindle him out of his money. After an abduction attempt is foiled, Harry establishes Mollie as the old man's long-lost granddaughter, and she becomes the beneficiary of an inheritance. 5 reels

HEART AND SOUL (May 20, 1917); D: J. Gordon Edwards; W: Adrian Johnson, H. Rider Haggard (novel); C: Philip E. Rosen; Cast: Theda Bara, Edwin Holt, Claire Whitney, Walter Law, Harry S. Hilliard, Glen White, Alice White, John Webb Dillon, Margaret Laird, Kittens Reichert • Jess (Bara) and Bess (Whitney), sisters living with their uncle on his plantation in Puerto Rico, both meet and fall in love with John (Hilliard). Jess, the elder, sacrifices her own happiness for that of her sister. During a revolution by planters, the property is captured. Jess rides for help, but is mortally wounded. Her dying words include a blessing for Bess and John. 5 reels

THE FINAL PAYMENT (May 21, 1917); D: Frank Powell; W: Frank Powell; C: David Calcagni; Cast: Nance O'Neil, Jane Miller, Clifford Bruce, Leslie Austin, Alfred Hickman, Dorothy Bernard • Two fishermen, Neccola (Austin) and Cesare (Bruce), are best friends until they fall in love with Nina (O'Neil). When Neccola is killed by Alfredo (Hickman), owner of the fishing fleet, Cesare is found guilty of the murder and hanged. Nina eventually discovers the truth and, in a struggle with Alfredo on a boat, a fire starts and the killer dies. 5 reels

THE SILENT LIE (May 28, 1917); D: R.A. Walsh; W: C.B. Clapp, Larry Evans (short story); C: Dal Clawson; Cast: Miriam Cooper, Ralph Lewis, Charles Clary, Monroe Salisbury, Henry A. Barrows, Howard Davies, William Eagle Shirt • A stranger (Salisbury) who is secretly in love with Lady Lou (Cooper), a dance hall girl at a lumber camp, helps her escape to a neighboring camp. She marries Conahan (Clary), a lumberjack, without telling him of her past. When it is discovered, Conahan turns from her in disgust. The stranger appears again and reveals that she was forced into the dance hall by her brutal foster father (Lewis). 5–6 reels • Raoul Walsh took his crew to Truckee, Arizona, to shoot winter scenes for this film.

THE SLAVE (June 3, 1917); D: William Nigh; W: William Nigh; C: Joseph Ruttenberg; Cast: Valeska Suratt, Violet Palmer, Eric Mayne, Herbert Heyes, Edward Burns, Edwin Rosenman, Dan Mason, Tom Brooke, Martin Faust, Martin Hunt • A New York shop girl, Caroline (Suratt), is urged by her mother to marry a wealthy old man. She then dreams that she is in a novel called *The King's Favorite*. The king insists she not have a child. When one is born, she is thrown out and it ruins her chances with a young man she loves after the king has died. When Caroline wakes from the dream, she is convinced not to marry the old man. 5 reels

THE BROADWAY SPORT (June 10, 1917); D: Carl Harbaugh; W: Carl Harbaugh; C: Georges Benoit; Cast: Stuart Holmes, Wanda Petit, Dan Mason, Mabel Rutter, W.B. Green, J. Sullivan, Mario Majeroni, Jay Wilson • A bookkeeper (Holmes) dreams of being a "Broadway sport" and wooing the boss's daughter Sadie (Petit). He discovers two crooks breaking into the company safe, locks them in the vault and takes the bankroll to New York. There, he ends up getting involved in a plot to acquire a large inheritance. He wakes up to discover it has all been a dream. However, he has really captured the crooks and Sadie proclaims him a hero. 5 reels

SOME BOY! (June 17, 1917); D: Otis Turner; W: William Parker; C: R.E. Irish; Cast: George Walsh, Doris Pawn, Herschel Mayall, Caroline Rankin, Hector Sarno, Velma Whitman, N.A. Myles • After being expelled from college, a young man (Walsh) becomes a publicity agent for a hotel and creates several stunts that backfire. He later follows Marjorie (Pawn) back to her Texas cattle ranch and is hired to manage the ranch, ultimately defeating a hostile takeover bid for the property. The bidder turns out to be his father (Mayall), who is impressed by his son's abilities. 5 reels

THE SIREN (June 24, 1917); D: Roland West; W: Donald I Buchanan (scr), Walter Archer Frost (st); C: Edward Wynard; Cast: Valeska Suratt, Clifford Bruce, Robert Clugston, Isabel Rea, Cesare Gravina, Armand Kalisz, Rita Scott, Curtis Benton • In a western town a dance hall worker known as "The Siren" (Suratt), impersonates a doctor's daughter to get a $25,000 inheritance. However, her wicked past catches up with her. A stranger, who previously committed murder for her, shows up and kills her, lifting the spell she has over Burt (Clugston), who was enamored with her. 5 reels

PATSY (July 1, 1917); D: John G. Adolfi; W: Joseph F. Poland; Cast: June Caprice, Harry Hilliard, John Smiley, Edna Munsey, Ethyle Cooke, Alma Muller, Fred Hearn, Jane Lee • John (Smiley) sends his daughter Patsy (Caprice) east for refinement. She ends up staying with her father's friend's son, Dick (Hilliard), who lives the high life. Patsy falls in love with Dick, who is tricked into marriage by Helene, a vamp (Munsey). Helene is later exposed as already having a husband, leaving Dick alone for Patsy. 5 reels

TWO LITTLE IMPS (July 9, 1917); D: Kenean Buel; W: Mary Murillo; Cast: Jane Lee, Katherine Lee, Leslie Austen, Edna Hunter, Edwin Holt, Stuart Sage, Sidney D'Albrook, William Harvey • Two mischievous sisters, Jane (Lee) and Katherine (Lee), are left at a summer resort in the care of their bachelor uncle, Billy (Austen). At the hotel, Billy falls in love with Betty (Hunter). His romance is disrupted when Betty's brother Bob (Sage) is ordered by a burglar (D'Albrook) to rob their father (Holt). The young sisters upend the thieves' plan, and Billy marries Betty. 5 reels

TO HONOR AND OBEY (July 15, 1917); D: Otis Turner; W: F. McGrew Willis (scr), Olga Printzlau (st); C: Charles Kaufman; Cast: Gladys Brockwell, Bertram Grassby, Charles Clary, Josef Swickard, Willard Louis, Jewel Carmen • Lorrie (Brockwell) marries flamboyant playboy Richard (Grassby), who loses his fortune in stock market speculation, then wants Lorrie to get money from wealthy former suitor Marc (Clary). Lorrie ends up sacrificing her virtue, but, when they are wealthy again, Richard throws her out. Marc gets revenge by ruining Richard in a stock battle. Richard commits suicide, freeing Lorrie to be with a man who really loves her. 5 reels

THE INNOCENT SINNER (July 23, 1917); D: R.A. Walsh; W: R.A. Walsh (scr), Mary Synon (st); Cast: Miriam Cooper, Charles Clary, Jack Standing, Jane Novak, Rosita Marstini, Johnny Reese, Jennie Lee • Mary Ellen (Cooper), a country girl, is newly married to Benton (Standing), a city man with underworld connections. Mary Ellen helps reform a burglar (Parsons), who escapes and joins the Navy after being unjustly accused of Benton's murder. Mary Ellen is then forced to live in shame until she meets Benton's cousin, Dr. Graham (Clary), with whom she falls in love. She is abducted by the thug who killed her husband, but Graham rescues her. 5 reels

WIFE NUMBER TWO (July 30, 1917); D: William Nigh; W: William Nigh; C: Joseph Ruttenberg; Cast: Valeska Suratt, Erin Mayne, Bertha Brundage, John Goldsworthy, Martin J. Faust, T.J. Lawler, Peter Lang, Dan Mason, William Burton, Dan Sullivan • Bored by her country life, Emma (Suratt) marries Dr. Charles Bovar (Mayne), an older widower. She enjoys the company of young men and has an affair with Rudolph (Goldsworthy). Unhappy with her marriage, she tries to commit suicide at the river, but the bank gives way and she drowns. 5 reels • Fox used all the elements of Gustave Flaubert's *Madame Bovary*, even character names, without attributing any credit.

WRATH OF LOVE (Aug. 6, 1917); D: James Vincent; W: Mary Murillo (scr), James R. Garey (st); C: L.E. Taylor; Cast: Virginia Pearson, Louise Bates, Irving Cummings, Nellie Slattery, Frank Glendon, Johnny McCann • Roma (Pearson), the author of a book called *Jealousy*, becomes trapped by suspicions when her husband Bob (Cummings) is seen with Ethel (Bates), a mutual female friend. Roma threatens Bob with divorce, but since Ethel's boyfriend enlisted in the secret service, an intrigue with spies is the reason for the misunderstandings. 5 reels

DURAND OF THE BAD LANDS (Aug. 13, 1917); D: Richard Stanton; W: Maibelle Heikes Justice (st); C: J.D. Jennings; Cast: Dustin Farnum, Winifred Kingston, Tom Mix, Babe Cressman, Lee Morris, Amy Jerome, Frankie Lee • After rescuing three children from an Indian attack, a young outlaw, Dick Durand (Farnum), places them in the care of Molly (Kingston). Durand is later blamed for the attack and pursued by the sheriff (Mix). He also saves the governor's daughter, who was kidnapped by Indians, earns a complete pardon and settles down with Molly. 5 reels • This is Tom Mix's first appearance in a Fox feature after appearing in five two-reel comedies.

THE SPY (Aug. 19, 1917); D: Richard Stanton; W: George Bronson Howard; C: J. Dev Jennings; Cast: Dustin Farnum, Winifred Kingston, William Burress, Charles Clary, William E. Lowry, Howard Gaye • Mark (Farnum) accepts a challenge, joins the Secret Service and sets sail for Germany to secure a list of spies in the U.S. working for the enemy. German spy Greta (Kingston) falls in love with Mark and helps him get the information. Eventually, both are caught by the Germans and tortured. Sentenced to death, they march together to the executioner. 6–8 reels • The length of this film varies in different sources, most likely because of censorship. The film was banned in Chicago for its graphic violence.

THE SOUL OF SATAN (Aug. 20, 1917); D: Otis Turner; W: Randolph Lewis; Cast: Gladys Brockwell, Bertram Grassby, Charles Clary, William Burress, Josef Swickard, Gerard Alexander, Norbert Myles, Lucille Young, Frankie Lee • A woman in New York, Miriam (Brockwell), is tricked into a phony marriage with Valdez (Grassby), a notorious gambler, who uses her as a lure at his high-class gambling house. She is sent to swindle "Lucky" Carson (Clary), who realizes the scheme and confronts Valdez. When Valdez is killed, Miriam discovers her illegal marriage; nevertheless, she has Carson's genuine love. 5 reels

THE HONOR SYSTEM (Aug. 26, 1917); D: Raoul A. Walsh; W: Raoul A. Walsh (scr), Hettie Gray Baker (titles), Henry Christeen Warnack (st); C: Georges Benoit, George Richter, Len Powers; Cast: Milton Sills, Mrs. Cora Drew, James A. Marcus, Arthur Mackley, Miriam Cooper, George Walsh, Charles Clary, Gladys Brockwell, Roy Rice, Pomeroy J. Cannon • Joseph Stanton (Sills), convicted of a self-defense murder, calls on the governor (Marcus) to investigate the deplorable conditions in the prison. An honor system is implemented improving the living conditions. Crooked Senator Harrington (Clary) refuses to pardon Stanton, but gives him three days' leave from prison. Harrington then schemes to kidnap him so he will not return on time and the honor system will be abolished. 10 reels • As a publicity stunt for the premiere, a convict serving a life sentence was temporarily released on the honor system and escaped to Canada.

EVERY GIRL'S DREAM (Aug. 26, 1917); D: Harry Millarde; W: Adrian Johnson (scr), Clifford Howard (st); C: David Wills; Cast: June Caprice, Kittens Reichert, Harry Hilliard, Margaret Fielding, Marcia Harris, Dan Mason • In a Dutch village, Gretchen (Caprice) is in love with Carl (Hilliard), the foundling son of impoverished parents. An old man (Mason) offers to pay off Gretchen's guardian's mortgage in return for her hand in marriage. Fortunately, Carl is actually the heir to the throne, who was stolen from the king and queen as a baby. Carl becomes king and makes Gretchen his queen. 6 reels

BETRAYED (Sept. 2, 1917); D: R.A. Walsh; W: R.A. Walsh; C: Dal Clawson; Cast: Miriam Cooper, James Marcus, Hobart Bosworth, Monte Blue, Wheeler Oakman • Carmelita (Cooper), a young Mexican girl, is attracted to the bandit Juares (Bosworth) when he takes refuge in her house. She then becomes enamored of William, an American officer (Oakman) on the bandit's trail. She leads him to Juares, who discovers her plan and dresses her in his clothes. William shoots Carmelita and is ordered to be executed. Carmelita then awakens from her dream to discover that United States troopers are arresting Juares, who is hiding there. 5 reels

JACK AND THE BEANSTALK (Sept. 2, 1917); D: C.M. & S.A. Franklin; W: C.M & S.A. Franklin (scr), Mary Murillo (st); C: Frank Good, Harry Gerstad, Walter E. Williams; Cast: Francis Carpenter, Virginia Lee Corbin, Violet Radcliffe, Carmen Fay De Rue, J.G. Traver, Vera Lewis, Ralph Lewis • Young Jack (Carpenter) sells his mother's cow for a sack of magic beans which turn into a vine that reaches up above the clouds. Jack climbs the vine and encounters a land where the people are held prisoner by a huge giant (Traver). Following his fairy godmother's advice, Jack kills the giant, frees the people and wins the princess (Corbin). 10 reels

WHEN FALSE TONGUES SPEAK (Sept. 9, 1917); D: Carl Harbaugh; W: Carl Harbaugh (scr), George Scarborough (st); C: Georges Benoit; Cast: Virginia Pearson, Carl Harbaugh, Hardee Kirkland, Claire Whitney, Carl Eckstrom, William E. Meehan • Married to a philanderer, Mary (Pearson) refuses to divorce Fred (Harbaugh), who is in love with his mistress (Whitney). Organizing a settlement house in the slums, Mary meets Eric (Eckstrom), a reporter with whom she is seen by her husband's lawyer (Kirkland), who then files a suit for divorce. Eric threatens him with disbarment unless the suit is dropped. Fred is later murdered by a burglar. 5 reels

THE YANKEE WAY (Sept. 16, 1917); D: Richard Stanton; W: Edward Sedgwick (st), Ralph Spence (st); Cast: George Walsh, Enid Markey, Joe Dowling, Charles Elder, James O'Shea, Ed Sedgwick, Count Hardenberg, Edward Cecil, Tom Wilson • Having left Chicago for Lithuania after defending a girl's honor in a restaurant brawl, Dick Mason (Walsh) meets the girl (Markey) again. She turns out to be Princess Alexia. He later thwarts a revolution led by disgruntled Lithuanian Count Vortsky (Cecil) and wins Alexia's heart. 5 reels

THE CONQUEROR (Sept. 16, 1917); D: R.A. Walsh; W: R.A. Walsh (scr), Henry Christian Warnack (st); C: Dal Clawson; Cast: William Farnum, Jewel Carmen, Charles Clary, J.A. Marcus, Carrie Clarke Ward, William Chisholm, Robert Dunbar, Owen Jones, William Eagle Shirt • Sam Houston (Farnum) enters politics and climbs his way to the office of governor of Tennessee, winning the hand of Eliza Allen (Carmen). He discovers Eliza is more interested in the status of First Lady, but he later rescues her from a marauding band of Mexicans and, together, they start over to seek happiness and fame. 8 reels

NORTH OF 53 (Sept. 23, 1917); D: Richard Stanton; W: Gardner Hunting (scr), Bertha Muzzy Sinclair (st); Cast: Dustin Farnum, Winifred Kingston, William Conklin, Edward Alexander, Rex Downs, Frank Lanning • "Roaring" Bill Wagstaff (Farnum), looking to avenge his partner's (Downs) death, discovers Hazel (Kingston), the newly arrived school teacher, lost in the woods. He takes her to his cabin, where he declares his love and ignores previous unfair accusations of scandal made against her. After taking care of his partner's murderer, he returns to Hazel, who finally accepts his love. 5 reels

CAMILLE (Sept. 30, 1917); D: J. Gordon Edwards; W: Adrian Johnson, Alexandre Dumas, fils (novel); C: Rial Schellinger; Cast: Theda Bara, Albert Roscoe, Walter Law, Alice Gale, Claire Whitney, Glen White • Camille (Bara), a Parisian model, becomes the mistress of a Count de Varville (Law); she later meets Armand (Roscoe), with whom she falls in love. Armand's father convinces Camille to give him up for the benefit of his sister (Whitney). Angrily, Armand denounces her. However, as Camille lies dying, Armand realizes that his father was responsible for breaking off the affair. 5 reels

A RICH MAN'S PLAYTHING (Sept. 30, 1917); D: Carl Harbaugh; W: Carl Harbaugh (scr), Randolph Lewis (st); Cast: Valeska Suratt, Edward Martindel, John T. Dillon, Charles Craig, Robert Cummings, Gladys Kelly • A multi-millionaire, "Iron" Lloyd (Martindel), looking for a woman who will love him for himself, goes incognito to a small New England town, where he meets Marie (Suratt), who cares for him. Lloyd arranges with his lawyer to give her a million dollars to see what she will do with the money. Marie uses the money to go to New York and lures a financier, Deneau (Dillon), who had previously swindled her aunt out of a fortune, to a roadhouse. Marie's aunt gets back her fortune and Deneau is ruined. When Lloyd reveals his scheme to Marie, she realizes he has used her, but reconciles with him. 5 reels

CONSCIENCE (Oct. 7, 1917); D: Bertram Bracken; W: Adrian Dawson (scr), J. Searle Dawley (st), E. Lloyd Sheldon (st); Cast: Gladys Brockwell, Marjorie Daw, Eugenie Forde, Eve Southern, Genevieve Blinn, Douglas Gerrard, Edward Cecil, Harry G. Lonsdale, Bertram Grassby • Following John Milton's "Paradise Lost," a society girl, Ruth (Brockwell), prepares to marry the wealthiest man (Gerrard) in town. Ruth is summoned to the Court of Conscience, where the witnesses, Lust, Avarice, Hate, Revenge and Vanity (all played by Brockwell), testify about Ruth's history of seducing and abandoning men. The Court dooms Ruth to live with the torment of remembrance. Left alone at the altar, Ruth kneels and repents. 5–6 reels

WHEN A MAN SEES RED (Oct. 7, 1917); D: Frank Lloyd; W: Frank Lloyd, Larry Evans (short story); C: Billy Foster; Cast: William Farnum, Jewel Carmen, G. Raymond Nye, Lulu May Bower, Coca Drew, Marc Robbins, A. Burt Wesner • A sailor, Larry (Farnum), is at a South Sea port when he learns that his former captain, Sutton (Nye), abducted and violated his sister and was responsible for her death. Larry later catches up with the captain, who is trying to sell Violet (Carmen), with whom Larry has fallen in love, to the natives. Larry kills Sutton and rescues Violet. 5–7 reels

THOU SHALT NOT STEAL (Oct. 14, 1917); D: William Nigh; W: Adrian Johnson, Emile Gaboriau (short story); C: Joseph Ruttenberg; Cast: Virginia Pearson, Claire Whitney, Eric Mayne, Bertha Brundage, John Goldsworthy, Robert Elliott, Martin Faust, Lem F. Kennedy, Danny Sullivan • Mary Bruce (Pearson) steals money from her father's (Mayne) safe that he had gotten as payment for her pending marriage to Lord Haverford (Goldsworthy). Mary is overcome by another unseen thief. When the theft is discovered, Mary, her father, and her father's secretary, Roger Benton (Elliott), whom she loves, are suspects. Haverford turns out to be a real thief, impersonating a lord. 5 reels

ALADDIN AND THE WONDERFUL LAMP (Oct. 14, 1917); D: C.M. & S.A. Franklin; W: Bernard McConville; Cast: Fred Carpenter, Fred Turner, Virginia

Lee Corbin, Alfred Paget, Violet Radcliffe, Buddy Messinger, Lewis Sargent, Gertrude Messinger, Marie Messinger • The daughter (Corbin) of the sultan (Paget) falls in love with Aladdin (Carpenter) and rejects evil alchemist al-Talib (Messinger). Unable to get his magic lamp, al-Talib hires Aladdin, who keeps the lamp and gets his wishes of wealth and position. Al-Talib retrieves the lamp and gets a palace, from which he threatens to throw the princess to the lions unless she marries him. Aladdin and soldiers arrive in time to rescue her and recover the lamp. 8 reels

THIS IS THE LIFE (Oct. 21, 1917); D: R.A. Walsh; W: Ralph Spence, R.A. Walsh; C: Dal Clawson; Cast: George Walsh, James A. Marcus, Wanda Petit, Ralph Lewis, Jack McDonald, W.H. Ryno, Victor Sarno • Movie-struck Billy (Walsh), leaving for South America for his father's munitions company, spots a beautiful woman (Petit) on board his ship. Also on board is Count Von Nuttenburg (Lewis), who has stolen a movie camera, thinking that it is a new type of machine gun. Billy perceives the count as a director, the woman as a star, and the ship as a movie set. However, they all end up in a war and Billy finally accepts reality when he and the woman are caught and threatened with death. By a clever ruse, Billy escapes from his captors, defeats the count and wins the girl. 5 reels

THE ROSE OF BLOOD (Nov. 4, 1917); D: J. Gordon Edwards; W: Bernard McConville (scr), Richard Ordynski (st); C: Rial Schellinger, John W. Boyle; Cast: Theda Bara, Richard Ordynski, Charles Clary, Herschel Mayall, Bert Turner, Joe King, Marie Kerman, Genevieve Blinn, Hector V. Sarno • Lisza (Bara), governess of a Russian royal family, is not permitted to marry Prince Arbassoff (Clary), so she leaves for Switzerland, and joins revolutionaries. The prince eventually decides to marry Lisza, but she continues her revolutionary activities, assassinating government officials and leaving a red rose on each of her victims. When the revolutionaries order her to slay the prince, her devotion to the cause triumphs and she dynamites her house. Lisza dies along with Arbassoff. 5 reels

MISS U.S.A. (Nov. 4, 1917); D: Harry Millarde; W: Randolph Lewis; C: Henry A. Leach; Cast: June Caprice, William Courtleigh Jr., Frank Evans, Tom Burrough, Al Hall • June (Caprice), the ward of Major Warfield (Burrough), escapes death at the hands of Uncle Gabriel (Evans), who wants her fortune. She returns to her old home town and falls in love with Herbert (Courtleigh Jr.). Gabriel tries to kill her again and turns out to be in league with spies, one of whom is captured by June. Herbert joins the American forces in France and proposes to June before he leaves. 5 reels

THE PAINTED MADONNA (Nov. 11, 1917); D: Oscar A.C. Lund; W: Oscar A.C. Lund (scr), George Scarborough (st); C: Joseph Ruttenberg; Cast: Sonia Markova, Sidney Mason, William Lampe, David Herblin, Albert Tavernier, Anita Navaro, Edith Reeves, Julia Stuart • Dishonored by a playboy (Lampe), Stella (Markova), a simple country girl, flees to the city, gets a job in a chorus line and lives a profligate life, amassing great wealth from many suitors. She meets Milton (Mason), an artist who knew her from her innocent home town days, and she poses as his model of the Madonna. When he discovers her reputation, his illusions are shattered. Repentant, she converts her mansion into a refuge for foundlings and returns to her home town, where she is reconciled with Milton. 5 reels

ALL FOR A HUSBAND (Nov. 18, 1917); D: Carl Harbaugh; W: Carl Harbaugh (scr), George Scarborough (st); Cast: Herbert Evans, Virginia Pearson, Dorothy Quincy, Gladys Kelly, Carl Moody, William W. Crimans • Wanting her mayoral candidate brother Henry (Evans) to marry her college friend, Celeste (Kelly) concocts a plan to have Henrietta (Pearson) pose as an escaped lunatic. The real lunatic (Quincy) is convinced the candidate is her long-lost lover, so confusion ensues. Police and doctors sort out the situation and Henry is smitten with Henrietta. The movie ends nonsensically, with a studio director throwing a tantrum to get an actor to break his contract. 6 reels

A BRANDED SOUL (Nov. 25, 1917); D: Bertram Bracken; W: Franklyn Hall (scr), Bertram Bracken (scr), E. Lloyd Sheldon (st); Cast: Gladys Brockwell, Colin Chase, Vivian Rich, Willard Louis, Lewis J. Cody, Gloria Payton, Fred Whitman, Barney Furey • After a prologue set in ancient Rome, a millionaire oil man John Rannie (Cody), whose oil fields have displaced the peasants, desires the lovely Conchita (Brockwell). He threatens to expose that her fiancé, Juan (Chase), has been employed by a German spy. Conchita agrees to give herself to Rannie to save Juan. Rannie, moved by her sacrifice, begs her forgiveness. Juan sees them together and uses Conchita's cross to brand a mark of shame on her. The spy incites the villagers to set the oil fields on fire, and Conchita saves Rannie from being burned. 5 reels

THE SCARLET PIMPERNEL (Nov. 28, 1917); D: Richard Stanton; W: Ben Cohn, Baroness Emmuska Orczy (novel); C: J.D. Jennings; Cast: Dustin Farnum, Winifred Kingston, William Burgess, Bertram Grassby, Bert Hadley, Howard Gaye, Willard Louis, Jack Nelson • During the French Revolution, Englishman Sir Percy Blakeney (Farnum) comports himself as a fop, but is really a hero. His wife, Lady Marguerite (Kingston), shares the opinion of most that Sir Percy is useless, until she discovers his secret identity. 5 reels

DAUGHTER OF THE GODS (Dec. 2, 1917) Reissue

THE BABES IN THE WOODS (Dec. 2, 1917); D: Chester M. and Sidney A. Franklin; W: Bernard McConville, Jakob & Wilhelm Grimm (fairy tale); C: Harry Gerstad; E: Della Conley; Cast: Francis Carpenter, Virginia Lee Corbin, Violet Radcliffe, Carmen de Rue, Herschell Mayall, Rosita Marstini, Robert Lawler, Scott McKee, Teddy Billings • A millionaire (Mayall) stipulates that his money will go to his children, Roland (Carpenter) and Rose (Corbin). He learns from the butler (McKee) that his wife (Marstini) and brother (Lawler) are planning to kill the children. He then tells his children the story of Hansel and Gretel, as a warning. Meanwhile, his wife overhears the story and realizes the evil she was planning. 5 reels

UNKNOWN 274 (Dec. 9, 1917); D: Harry Millarde; W: Adrian Johnson (scr), George Scarborough (st); C: David Mills, Ollie Leach; Cast: June Caprice, Kittens Reichert, Florence Ashbrook, Inez Marcel, Dan Mason, Richard Neill, Tom Burroughs, Jean Amour, William Burns, Alexander Shannon • Dora, an orphan (Caprice), is registered as "unknown 274" after her violinist father is kidnapped and taken back to his native country. Years later, Mme. Gordon (Armour), an opportunist, decides to provide Dora with music lessons, then sell her to a young millionaire. The music teacher turns out to be her father, and the millionaire really falls in love with her. 5 reels

TROUBLEMAKERS (Dec. 9, 1917); D: Kenean Buel; W: Kenean Buel; C: Leo Rossi; Cast: Lillian Concord, Jane Lee, Katherine Lee, Richard Turner, Robert Vivian, William T. Hayes, Stuart Sage, Frances Miller • Widowed Mrs. Lehr (Concord) returns to the family estate with her two mischievous daughters Jane (Lee) and Katherine (Lee). Their pranks annoy townspeople, but they end up proving a slow-witted handyman (Vivian) innocent of a murder charge stemming from a barn fire, and save him from execution. 5–7 reels

THE HEART OF A LION (Dec. 16, 1917); D: Frank Lloyd; W: Frank Lloyd, Ralph Connor (novel); C: Billy Foster; Cast: William Farnum, Mary Martin, William Courtleigh Jr., Wanda Petit, Walter Law, Marc Robbins, Rita Bori • Self-sacrificing Barney Kemper (Farnum), disgusted by his brother Dick's (Courtleigh Jr.) selfishness, goes west and becomes a doctor in a lumber town. Dick finally repents and is ordained a minister and assigned to the same lumber town. Barney's hometown sweetheart, Margaret (Martin), follows him as well to start a hospital. Realizing that Dick has changed, Barney defends him against resentful lumbermen, one of whom, Tex (Law), mortally wounds Dick. Barney later kills Tex and returns to Margaret. 5 reels

THE PRIDE OF NEW YORK (Dec. 16, 1917); D: Raoul Walsh; W: Raoul Walsh, Ralph Spence; C: Dal Clawson; Cast: George Walsh, James A. Marcus, William Bailey, Regina Quinn • Two young men are drafted into the Army during wartime. Harold (Bailey) is a rich idler and Jim (Walsh) is a hard-working contractor's son. Harold loses his fiancée, Mary (Quinn), over his cowardice, and when she becomes a Red Cross nurse in France, she tends to the brave aviator Jim. Later, Mary is abducted by a German prince, but Jim comes to her rescue and they both escape in an airplane. 5 reels

THE KINGDOM OF LOVE (Dec. 23, 1917); D: Frank Lloyd; W: W. Doty Hobart; Cast: Jewel Carmen, Nancy Caswell, Genevieve Blinn, L.C. Shumway, Fred Milton, Ernest Wade, Joseph Manning, G. Raymond Nye, Murdock MacQuarrie • Violet Dale (Carmen), a dancehall girl in Alaska, becomes involved with Frank (Milton), who turns out to be a brother she never knew she had. Keeping her identity secret from Frank, she learns that their mother needs an expensive operation. To raise money, Violet selflessly offers herself to the highest bidder. The Reverend Cromwell (Shumway), who loves Violet and wants to keep her virtue intact, offers the highest bid. Buck (MacQuarrie), the dancehall owner, loans Cromwell the money. 5 reels

FOR LIBERTY (Dec. 30, 1917); D: Bertram Bracken; W: Bennett Cohen; C: Charles Kaufman; Cast: Gladys Brockwell, Charles Clary, Bertram Grassby, Willard Louis, Colin Chase, Clara Graham, Norbiq Miles, Ryno William, George Routh • Marcia (Brockwell), an American expatriate in Berlin for years, uses her connections to General Von Lentz (Grassby), who is attracted to her, to help the U.S. during the war. An American spy, Frank Graham (Clary), thinks she has become a traitor. When Frank is caught, Marcia gives herself up to win his freedom. He returns to save her as well. 5 reels

MADAME DU BARRY (Dec. 30, 1917); D: J. Gordon Edwards; W: Adrian Johnson, Alexandre Dumas (novel); C: Rial Schellinger, John Boyle; Cast: Theda Bara, Charles Clary, Fred Church, Herschel Mayall, Genevieve Blinn, Willard Louis, Hector Sarno, Dorothy Drake, Rosita Marstini, Joe King • Du Barry (Bara) gains status in the court of Louis XV (Clary) and becomes his favorite. When she falls in love with a soldier (Church), her affair is exposed, but Louis refuses to believe it. After the king dies, and the revolution breaks out, Du Barry is sentenced to the guillotine. 7 reels

1918 Releases

STOLEN HONOR (Jan. 6, 1918); D: Richard Stanton; W: Adeline Leitzbach, George Scarborough; C: M. Kellermann, Harry W. Forbes; Cast: Virginia Pearson, Clay Clement, Ethel Hallor, Walter Law, Dorothy Rogers, Edward Roseman, George Majeroni, John Ardrizonia • Jealous Italian Countess Collona (Rogers), in love with Capt. Mackin (Clement), conspires with a count to frame the officer's American girlfriend, Virginia (Pearson), for art theft. Virginia accepts the blame because exposing the truth would implicate her father's new young wife, Betty (Hallor), in an affair. Later, Virginia is able to trap the count and countess into revealing the plot. 5 reels

CUPID'S ROUNDUP (Jan. 13, 1918); D: Edward J. LeSaint; W: Charles Kenyon, George Scarborough; Cast: Tom Mix, Wanda Hawley, Edwin B. Tilton, Roy Watson, Verna Mersereau, Alfred Padgett, Frederick R. Clark, Eugenie Forde • Larry (Mix) decides to have a final fling before marrying Helen (Petit), the woman his father has chosen for him sight unseen. Not realizing he has become interested in his intended, he takes a job on a ranch next to hers. Helen poses as a maid to learn more about her fiancé. Larry exposes a group of cattle thieves, but is accused of murder and makes a run for it. Everything is explained and Larry realizes he has been courting his wife-to-be. 5 reels •

This was Tom Mix's first starring role in a feature film, which was originally intended for George Walsh.

A HEART'S REVENGE (Jan. 19, 1918); D: O.A.C. Lund; W: O.A.C. Lund, George Scarborough; C: Joseph Ruttenberg; Cast: Sonia Markova, David Herblin, Frank Goldsmith, Eric Mayne, Bradley Barker, Helen Long, Stanley Heck, Fred Ratcliffe, J. Alling • A Russian baron (Goldsmith), in love with Vera (Markova), drugs Jim Harding (Herblin), an American officer Vera loves, and puts him on a ship to China. The baron then tries to convince Vera that Jim committed suicide. Vera is able to learn the truth and finds her lover in China, but the drugging has driven him insane. In a fight, he receives a blow to the head, which restores his sanity. He returns home with Vera. 5 reels

CHEATING THE PUBLIC (Jan. 20, 1918); D: Richard Stanton; W: Mary Murillo, Richard Stanton, Edward Sedgwick; C: J.D. Jennings; Cast: Enid Markey, Ralph Lewis, Bertram Grassby, Tom Wilson, Edward Peil, Sr., Charles Edler, Wanda Petit, Carrie Clark Ward, Fanny Midgely, Frankie Lee • Mary Garvin (Markey) pleads with John (Lewis), a hard-hearted factory owner, to compromise with his striking employees, but John attacks her and is shot. Mary is convicted for his murder, and, just before her execution, a factory foreman (Wilson) admits to shooting John. 7 reels

TREASURE ISLAND (Jan. 27, 1918); D: C.M. Franklin & S.A. Franklin; W: Bernard McConville, Robert Louis Stevenson (novel); C: Frank Good, Harry Gerstad; E: Della Conley; Cast: Frances Carpenter, Eleanor Washington, Virginia Lee Corbin, Herschel Mayall, Elmo Lincoln, Charles Gorman, Ed Harley, Frances Carpenter • A young Englishman, Jim Hawkins (Carpenter), gets possession of a pirate's treasure map and, with his young girlfriend (Corbin), sets out to find the mysterious island on a chartered ship. On the island, he befriends a former crew-mate of the pirate, who leads him to the treasure. After several fights between pirates and the honest crew members, the ship sets sail for England. 6 reels

THE HEART OF ROMANCE (Feb. 3, 1918); D: Harry Millarde; W: Adeline Leitzbach, Frances Crowley; Cast: June Caprice, Bernard Thornton, George Bunny, Joseph Kilgour, Lilian Page, Jack Martin, Jack Raymond • Eloise (Caprice) spends her wealthy uncle's money on extravagant parties for her friends. She falls in love with Harvey (Thornton), a penniless writer. To test Harvey's love, the uncle (Bunny) claims that he is bankrupt. All of Eloise's friends abandon her except Harvey, who convinces the uncle that he is not after her money. 5 reels

THE FORBIDDEN PATH (Feb. 3, 1918); D: J. Gordon Edwards; W: Adrian Johnson, E. Lloyd Sheldon; C: John W. Boyle; Cast: Theda Bara, Hugh Thompson, Sidney Mason, Walter Law, Florence Martin, Wynne Hope Allen, Alphonse Ethier, Lisle Leigh, Reba Porter • Mary Lynde (Bara) gets involved with an artist's wealthy friend, Robert (Sinclair), and becomes pregnant. Robert refuses to marry or support her. Mary ends up living in a dive, but later forces Robert to cancel his engagement to another woman (Martin) and marry her. She gets revenge by exposing him publicly at the altar. 6 reels

LES MISERABLES (Feb. 10, 1918); D: Frank Lloyd; W: Frank Lloyd, Marc Robbins, Victor Hugo (novel); C: William C. Foster, George Schneiderman; Cast: William Farnum, George Moss, Hardee Kirkland, Sonia Markova, Kittens Reichert, Jewel Carmen, Harry Spingler, Dorothy Bernard, Anthony Phillips • After serving prison time, Jean Valjean (Farnum) becomes a respected citizen, but is hounded by the mean-spirited Inspector Javert (Kirkland). Finally, after many encounters, the inspector, in a rare moment of kindness, grants Valjean his freedom. 9–10 reels

JACK SPURLOCK, PRODIGAL (Feb. 10, 1918); D: Carl Harbaugh; W: Ralph Spence, George Horace Lorimer (novel); Cast: George Walsh, Dan Mason, Ruth Taylor, Robert Vivian, Mike Donlin, Jack Goodman • Jack's (Walsh) wild student escapades get him expelled from college and cut off from his family's money. His girlfriend, Anita (Taylor), introduces him to a professor (Vivian) who has developed a health tonic made from onions. Buying up an onion surplus to meet demand for the tonic, Jack becomes a success and regains his family's favor. 6 reels

THE MORAL LAW (Feb. 17, 1918); D: Bertram Bracken; W: Charles A. Kenyon, E. Lloyd Sheldon; C: Charles Kaufman; Cast: Gladys Brockwell, Rosita Marstini, Joseph Singleton, Colin Chase, Bertram Grassby, Ora Rankin Drew • Isobel (Brockwell) searches for her long-lost sister Anita (Brockwell) in Buenos Aires, but is wrongly imprisoned for a crime committed by Anita under Isobel's identity. Anita returns to Florida, takes over the family home and is set to marry Isobel's fiancé, Robert (Chase), when her scheme is exposed. 4,300'

SIX SHOOTER ANDY (Feb. 24, 1918); D: Sidney A. Franklin, Chester M. Franklin; W: Bernard McConville; C: J.D. Jennings; E: Della Conley; Cast: Tom Mix, Bert Woodruff, Sam De Grasse, Charles Stevens, Pat Crisman, Bob Fleming, Enid Markey, Jack Plank, Ben Hammer, Georgie Stone, Lewis Sargent • Andy (Mix), a young prospector, vows to get rid of a gang that is preying on the town with the help of a corrupt Sheriff Slade (De Grasse). Andy forms a vigilante committee which captures the gang and then rescues his girlfriend, Susan (Markey), from Slade. Andy becomes the new sheriff. 5 reels

THE GIRL WITH THE CHAMPAGNE EYES (March 3, 1918); D: C.M. Franklin; W: Bernard McConville; E: Della Conley; Cast: Jewel Carmen, L.C. Shumway, Charles Edler, G. Raymond Nye, Alfred Padget, Charles Gorman, Eleanor Washington, Francis Carpenter, Gertrude Messinger • Gold-digging Nellie (Carmen) feels shame for having sent an innocent man, James (Shumway), to prison, so she enlists Milligan (Edler) to help him escape. The trio heads for Alaska, where they prospect for gold. Nellie ends up offering herself to a saloon owner (Nye) to keep James from being sent back to prison, but James rescues her just in time. 5 reels

THE DEBT OF HONOR (March 10, 1918); D: O.A.C. Lund; W: O.A.C. Lund, Eve Unsell; C: Joseph Ruttenberg; Cast: Peggy Hyland, Eric Mayne, Irving Cummings, Frank Goldsmith, Hazel Adams • Honor (Hyland), an orphan, is adopted by a wealthy U.S. senator, Middleton (Mayne). When war breaks out, Honor is accused of being a German agent. However, it is the senator's wife (Adams) who is passing government papers, and Honor is cleared of the charge. 5 reels

THE DEVIL'S WHEEL (March 17, 1918); D: Edward LeSaint; W: Charles Kenyon; C: Friend F. Baker; Cast: Gladys Brockwell, William Scott, Lucille Young, Bertram Grassby, T.D. Crittendon, Pietro Buzzi, Andrew Robson • Blanche (Brockwell), daughter of a marquis (Buzzi), is kidnapped from her home in Paris and taken to live in an underworld slum with a gang leader, the "Stag" (Scott). She has no recollection of her previous life, but when she is found, a brain operation saves her from prison and restores her memory. She starts a new life with the "Stag," who goes straight. 5 reels

WOMAN AND THE LAW (March 17, 1918); D: Raoul A. Walsh; W: Raoul A. Walsh; C: Roy Overbaugh; Cast: Miriam Cooper, Ramsey Wallace, Peggy Hopkins, Jack Connors, George Humbert, Agnes Neilsen, Lewis Dayton, John Laffe, Lillian Satherwaite • A South American heiress (Cooper) is tortured emotionally by her philandering ex-husband, Jack (Wallace), who refuses to return their son (Connors) after a custody visit. She shoots and kills Jack, but is acquitted by a jury because she committed the crime to protect her son. 7 reels

ROUGH AND READY (March 24, 1918); D: Richard Stanton; W: Richard Stanton, Edward Sedgwick; C: Harry Forbes; Cast: William Farnum, Violet Palmer, Alphonse Ethier, Jessie Arnold, David Higgins, Frank Newton, Mabel Bardine, Frank McGlynn • Bill (Farnum) and Jack (Ethier), two rivals, fight over a woman in an Alaska mining town. Bill is honorable, but Jack wants to take advantage of Evelyn (Palmer). Bill prevails and kills Jack in a fierce fight, thus winning the girl. 6 reels

A DAUGHTER OF FRANCE (March 24, 1918); D: Edmund Lawrence; W: Betta Breuil, Adrian Johnson, Benjamin S. Kutler; C: Frank C. Kugler, William M. Zollinger; Cast: Virginia Pearson, Hugh Thompson, Herbert Evans, George Moss, Ethel Kaufman, Anthony Merlo, Maude Hill, Nadia Gray • During World War I, a French girl, Louise (Pearson), endures the German invasion and fights off the advances of two officers, von Knorr (Thompson) and von Meyring (Evans). When von Meyring tries to attack Louise, von Knorr kills him. Louise then stabs von Knorr, but later discovers he is a French agent and was trying to save her. When von Knorr recovers, both flee across French lines. 5 reels

A CAMOUFLAGE KISS (March 31, 1918); D: Harry Millarde; W: Ralph H. Spence, Stephen Fox, Julius Grinnell Furthman (short story); C: H. Anderson Leach; Cast: June Caprice, Bernard Thornton, Pell Trenton, George Bunny, Lola May • A series of mix-ups at a society party occurs when a kiss is exchanged in the dark. Martha (Caprice) thinks she has been kissed by someone more interesting than her fiancé (Trenton). When it has all been straightened out, she finally ends up with the fiancé. 5 reels

THE BRIDE OF FEAR (Apr. 7, 1918); D: S.A. Franklin; W: S.A. Franklin (scr), Bennett Cohen (st); C: J.D. Jennings; Cast: Jewel Carmen, Charles Gorman, L.C. Shumway, Charles Bennett • Ann Carter (Carmen) is saved from suicide by Hayden (Gorman), a crook, whom she marries out of fear. When Hayden is arrested and she believes he was killed in a prison break, she agrees to marry wealthy Martin Sterling (Bennett). Hayden turns up and demands Ann's help in robbing the Sterling mansion. Hayden is about to kill her new husband when she shoots him. A jury rules the shooting was done in self defense. 5 reels

THE BLINDNESS OF DIVORCE (Apr. 7, 1918); D: Frank Lloyd; W: Frank Lloyd; C: Billy Foster; Cast: Charles Clary, Rhea Mitchell, Nancy Caswell, Bertram Grassby, Marc Robbins, Willard Louis, Fred Church, Al Fremont, Bertha Mann • Florence (Mitchell) is arrested in a gambling house raid while trying to determine whether her mother, Claire (Mann), is running the operation. The arrest leads to Florence's divorce, but Claire confesses she went into crime out of desperation after being unfairly accused of having an affair and being divorced by her society husband (Clary). 6 reels

WESTERN BLOOD (Apr. 14, 1918); D: Lynn F. Reynolds; W: Lynn F. Reynolds (scr), Tom Mix (st); Cast: Tom Mix, Victoria Forde, Frank Clark, Barney Furey, Pat Chrisman, Buck Jones • Tex (Mix), a rancher visiting Los Angeles, does not fit in comfortably at a society party. Nevertheless, he invites the host, Colonel Stephens (Clark), and his daughter Roberta (Forde) to his ranch to inspect horses for the war effort. Tex makes his horrified cowboys wear formal evening attire to welcome the visitors. During the party, German agents kidnap Roberta and Tex has to rescue her. 5 reels • This was Buck Jones's first Fox Film. He would later be starred in stories very similar to those of the studio's top star, Tom Mix.

THE SOUL OF BUDDHA (Apr. 21, 1918); D: J. Gordon Edwards; W: Adrian Johnson, Theda Bara; C: John W. Boyle; Cast: Theda Bara, Hugh Thompson, Victor Kennard, Anthony Merlo, Florence Martin, Jack Ridgeway, Henry Warwick • Bava (Bara), a sacred Japanese dancer with a roving eye, runs off with British officer Sir John Dare (Thompson). Ysora (Kennard), the high priest, follows her to Scotland and kills her baby to avenge her insult. In Paris, Bava is hired as a dancer and begins an affair with Count Romaine (Merlo). Distraught, Sir John kills himself in her dressing room and she hides the body. During Bava's dance performance, Ysora stabs her to death. 4–5 reels

AMERICAN BUDS (Apr. 21, 1918); D: Kenean Buel; W:

Kenean Buel, M. Strauss; C: Leo Raffi; Cast: Jane Lee, Katherine Lee, Albert Gran, Regina Quinn, Lucille Southerwaite, Leslie Austin, H.D. Southard, Nora Cecil, William Hays, Maggie Weston • In the South, Captain Bob Dutton's (Austin) engagement to Cecile Harding (Quinn) is broken after he accepts responsibility for two orphaned sisters, Jane (Lee) and Katherine (Lee), suspected as being from a previous relationship. Jane exposes an Austrian spy who is shot and confesses that he is actually the girls' father. With Dutton's past cleared, he is free to marry Cecile. 6 reels • Filmed on location in Georgia.

HER ONE MISTAKE (Apr. 28, 1918); D: Edward J. LeSaint; W: Charles Kenyon, George Scarborough; Cast: Gladys Brockwell, William Scott, Willard Louis, Charles Perley, Mark Fenton, Helen Wright • Harriet (Brockwell), an heiress, falls in love and elopes with a crook, Chicago Charlie (Scott), who abandons her. Harriet marries district attorney John Mansfield (Perley), but Charlie shows up later to commit robbery. In the process he attacks Harriet, who stabs him to death. However, Detective Scully (Louis), who has been trailing Charlie, takes responsibility for the death. 5 reels

BRAVE AND BOLD (May 5, 1918); D: Carl Harbaugh; W: Carl Harbaugh, Perley Poore Sheehan (short story); C: Ben Struckman; Cast: George Walsh, Francis X. Conlon, Dan Mason, Mabel Bunvea, Regina Quinn, A.B. Conkwright • On his way to negotiate a million-dollar war contract with a foreign prince, Robert (Walsh) is kidnapped by a rival businessman, Chester Firkins (Conlon). The daring Robert escapes and, through a series of adventures, not only wins the contract but saves his fiancée Ruth (Quinn) as well. 4,368'

TRUE BLUE (May 5, 1918); D: Frank Lloyd; W: Frank Lloyd; C: Billy Foster; Cast: William Farnum, Francis Carpenter, Charles Clary, Katherine Adams, Genevieve Blinn, Harry De Vere, Barney Furey, G. Raymond Nye, Buck Jones • Two half brothers, Bob (Farnum) and Stanley (Scott), come together in Chicago to reunite with their father, English nobleman Gilbert (Clary). Their parents had divorced years before because the father was embarrassed by his American wife. Bob has become an industrious rancher while the spoiled younger Stanley has remained a weakling. Gilbert is more impressed with Bob and offers him his title and wealth which Bob turns down and returns to his sweetheart, Ruth (Adams), in Arizona. 5,620'

PEG OF THE PIRATES (May 12, 1918); D: O.A.C. Lund; W: O.A.C. Lund (scr), W.L. Randall (st); Cast: Peggy Hyland, Carleton Macy, Sidney Mason, Frank Evans, James Gunnis Davis, L. Walheim (Wolheim), Ajax Carrol, Eric Mayne • Peg (Hyland) escapes death when pirates attack her father's (Macy) estate and carry her off to their ship. She is later rescued by Terry (Mason), the man she loves, who finds the pirate treasure and impresses her father enough to let him marry her. 5 reels • Filmed on location in Charleston, South Carolina.

CONFESSION (May 19, 1918); D: S.A. Franklin; W: S.A. Franklin; C: J.D. Jennings; Cast: Jewel Carmen, L.C. Shumway, Fred Warren, Jack Brammall, Charles Gorman, Andrew Arbuckle • Bob Anderson (Shumway) is arrested and sentenced to death for a woman's murder on his wedding night at a hotel. His bride, Mary (Carmen), and her father (Warren) set a trap for the real murderer, who turns out to be the hotel clerk (Brammall). However, Mary is unable to stop the execution, but awakens and realizes that it was all a dream. 5 reels

THE FIREBRAND (May 26, 1918); D: Edmund Lawrence; W: Adrian Johnson (scr), E. Lloyd Sheldon (st); Cast: Virginia Pearson, Victor Sutherland, Carleton Macy, Herbert Evans, James Courtney, Willard Cooley • During the Russian Revolution, Princess Natalya (Pearson) falls in love with a prisoner, Julian (Sutherland), who later assassinates her uncle, Prince Rostoff (Macy) and his son Boris (Evans), for collaborating with the German Kaiser. Natalya shoots Julian in revenge, but he is able to prove Rostoff was guilty. Julian recovers from the wound and marries Natalya. 5 reels

BLUE-EYED MARY (June 2, 1918); D: Harry Millarde; W: Adrian Johnson (scr), Frances Crowley (st); C: H. Anderson Leach; Cast: June Caprice, Helen Tracy, Blanche Hines, Bernard Randall, Thomas Fallon, Jack McLean, Florence Ashbrooke, Henry Hallam • A society woman, Mrs. Du Bois (Tracy), disowns her son and signs her estate over to a nephew, Cecil (Randall), instead. Years later, granddaughter Mary (Caprice) is able to bring about reconciliation between her father and grandmother after Cecil tries to rob Mrs. Du Bois's safe. 4,605 ft.

THE BONDMAN (June 6, 1918) Reissue

ACE HIGH (June 9, 1918); D: Lynn Reynolds; W: Lynn Reynolds; C: J.D. Jennings, George Richter, William Reinhart; Cast: Tom Mix, Lloyd Perl, Lewis Sargent, Kathleen Connors, Virginia Lee Corbin, Lawrence Peyton, Colin Chase, Jay Morley, Pat Chrisman • Annette (Connors), who was sent away to school years before, returns to her adoptive father Dupre (Chase), owner of the Ace High saloon. Jack Keefe (Peyton), the town's corrupt sheriff, decides he wants to marry Annette and kidnaps her, but she is rescued by an officer, Jean Rivard (Mix) of the Royal Canadian Mounted Police, who then becomes her husband. 5 reels

A FOOL THERE WAS (June 16, 1918) Reissue

WE SHOULD WORRY (June 16, 1918); D: Kenean Buel; W: Kenean Buel; C: Leo Rossi; Cast: Jane Lee, Katherine Lee, Ruby De Remer, William Pike, Edward Sturgis, Tammany Young, Henry Clive, Charles Craig, George Humbert, Henry Hallam • Little Jane (Lee) and Katherine (Lee) get involved in the romances of their rich and beautiful aunt, Miss Ashton (De Remer). One of her suitors, Percival (Clive), is a bank robber whose gang kidnaps the girls. The sisters torment the crooks with their pranks and are willingly released. When the thieves decide to rob the local bank, the sisters help the police catch them. 5 reels

UNDER THE YOKE (June 16, 1918); D: J. Gordon Edwards; W: Adrian Johnson (scr), George Scarborough (st); C: John W. Boyle, Harry Gerstad; Cast: Theda Bara, G. Raymond Nye, Alan Roscoe, Edwin B. Tilton, Carrie Clark Ward • Maria (Bara), a young Spanish woman, returns to her father's plantation in the Philippines. Her father (Tilton) is killed by a group of rebels and she is kidnapped until a handsome American army captain (Roscoe) rescues her. 5 reels • Some scenes were shot in the San Jacinto Mountains in California.

THE SCARLET ROAD (June 23, 1918); D: Edward J. LeSaint; W: Charles Kenyon; C: Friend Baker; Cast: Gladys Brockwell, Betty Schade, L.C. Shumway, Charles Clary, William Scott • Mabel (Brockwell), once a Puritan, goes to New York and is pursued by John (Shumway), a magazine editor, and Raymond (Clary), a womanizing stockbroker. Mabel agrees to marry Raymond to repay John a large amount of money he loaned to her brother Dick (Scott). Raymond turns out to be a relentless liar who had abandoned another wife and whose check to John was worthless. The loveless marriage ends with a fight in which Raymond falls to his death, leaving Mabel free to marry John, whose wife has just died. 5 reels

THE CLEMENCEAU CASE (June 23, 1918) Reissue

THE PLUNDERER (June 23, 1918) Reissue

THE KID IS CLEVER (June 30, 1918); D: Paul Powell; W: Randolph Lewis; C: John W. Leezer; Cast: George Walsh, Doris Pawn, Ralph Lewis, A. Burt Wesner, Don Likes, Clyde Hopkins, James Marcus • George Walsh has hired a French director, Monsieur Hoe Beaux, for his new film and they watch the completed results. In the film, a college graduate encounters adventures with a group of revolutionaries and is rescued, along with his sweetheart Doris (Pawn), by the United States Marines. After watching the film, Monsieur Hoe Beaux is fired. 4,458 ft.

THE TWO ORPHANS (June 30, 1918) Reissue

A SOLDIER'S OATH (June 30, 1918) Reissue

OTHER MEN'S DAUGHTERS (July 7, 1918); D: Carl Harbaugh; W: E. Lloyd Sheldon; C: Ben Struckman; Cast: Peggy Hyland, Eric Mayne, Elizabeth Garrison, Regina Quinn, Riley Hatch, Frank Goldsmith, Robert Middlemas • Shirley (Hyland) tries to prevent her mother (Garrison) from filing for divorce by breaking up her father's relationship with his girlfriend, Lola (Quinn). Lola's father (Hatch) decides to get revenge by hiring a lecherous friend, Trask (Goldsmith), to ruin Shirley's reputation. Shirley's boyfriend, Richard (Middlemas), is able to rescue her and she convinces her mother to forgive her father. 5 reels

HER PRICE (July 14, 1918); D: Edmund Lawrence; W: Adeline Leitzbach (scr), George Scarborough (st); C: Frank Kugler; Cast: Virginia Pearson, Edward F. Rosen, Victor Sutherland, Henri Leone, Charles H. Martin, Paul Stanton • Aspiring singer Marcia (Pearson), in exchange for a year of training in Italy, agrees to be Philip Bradley's (Rosen) mistress. Philip soon abandons her. Marcia later becomes a success in Paris, but Robert (Stanton), whom she loves, deserts her when she confesses her past. Since Philip has died, she vows to take revenge on his brother John (Sutherland), who falls in love with her and promises to make amends for Philip's transgressions. 4,644'

MISS INNOCENCE (July 21, 1918); D: Harry Millarde; W: Thomas Fallon (scr), Hazel Corker (st); C: Nat Leach; Cast: June Caprice, Marie Shotwell, Robert Walker, Frank Beamish, Carleton May, Mrs. Garrison • Romance and tragedy befall young Dolores (Caprice) after she escapes from a convent. She takes up with a high society crowd and Lawrence (Walker), whom she loves, is accused of murdering another suitor, Kale (Beamish), who has threatened to blackmail Dolores. Dolores's father confesses to the crime, reuniting his daughter with Lawrence. 5 reels

THE FALLEN ANGEL (July 28, 1918); D: Robert Thornby; W: Bennett R. Cohen, Gouvernor Morris (short story); C: Frank B. Good; Cast: Jewel Carmen, Charles Clary, L.C. Shumway, Herbert Heyes, Daisy Robinson, Lavine Monsch • Jill (Carmen), a department store salesgirl, becomes her boss's (Clary) mistress to provide for her penniless sisters. She is left a fortune when the boss dies and becomes engaged to Harry, a society man (Heyes). When Harry learns of her past from her late boss's son (Shumway), he suggests they continue to live under the same arrangement, but Jill opts for a life on her own. 5 reels

DOING THEIR BIT (Aug. 4, 1918); D: Kenean Buel; W: Kenean Buel; C: Joseph Ruttenberg; Cast: Jane Lee, Katherine Lee, Franklyn Hanna, Gertrude Le Brandt, Alex Hall, Beth Ivins, Kate Lester, William Pollard, Jay Strong, Aimee Abbott, R.R. Neill • Orphans Kate (Lee) and Janie (Lee) are sent to live with their wealthy American uncle (Hanna), a munitions plant owner during World War I. They expose and trap spies who are reporting on the plant's operations to Germany. 5 reels

THE BIRD OF PREY (Aug. 11, 1918); D: Edward J. LeSaint; W: Charles Kenyon, Albert G. Kenyon, Guy de Maupassant (short story); C: Friend Baker; Cast: Gladys Brockwell, Herbert Heyes, L.C. Shumway, Willard Louis • Adele (Brockwell) falls in with a group of bandits in Mexico when she is abandoned by Robert (Heyes), an American mine owner, because he blames her for his friend's (Shumway) suicide. Adele later has to join forces with Robert as they plot an escape from the bandits. She offers herself to Pedro (Louis), the bandit leader, to save the lives of other Americans. This gains Robert's respect, leading to marriage. 5 reels

CLEOPATRA (Aug. 12, 1918); D: J. Gordon Edwards; W: Adrian Johnson; C: Rial Schellinger, John W. Boyle, George Schneiderman; Cast: Theda Bara, Fritz Leiber, Thurston Hall, Albert Roscoe, Herschel Mayall, Dorothy Drake, Dell Duncan, Henri de Vries, Art Acord, Hector Sarno • Julius Caesar (Leiber) falls in love with Cleopatra (Bara), and when he is assassinated, Marc Antony (Hall) becomes her next lover. Antony joins forces with Cleopatra, but is defeated by Octavius (de Vries) and stabs himself. When Cleopatra learns of Antony's death, she kills herself with an asp bite. 11 reels (running time 155 minutes) • This version of the story was loosely based on, but not credited to, plays by William Shakespeare and Victorien Sardou and Emile Moreau. The production cost almost $300,000 with a profit of $60,000. It was pre-released on Oct. 14, 1917.

THE LIAR (Aug. 18, 1918); D: Edmund Lawrence; W: Katherine Kavanaugh; Cast: Virginia Pearson, Alexander Frank, Edward F. Rosenman, Victor Sutherland, Eugene Borden, Albert Roccardi, Liane Held Carrera, Myra Brooker • Sybil (Pearson), daughter of a sugar plantation owner (Frank), is prevented from marrying John Carter (Sutherland) by her late father's personal secretary, Franklin (Rosenman), who wants her for himself. Franklin reveals that Sybil is part black. While John fights with Franklin, Sybil apparently shoots herself. Remorseful, Franklin confesses his lie and Sybil reappears unharmed. 5 reels

LAWLESS LOVE (Aug. 25, 1918); D: Robert Thornby; W: Olga Printzlau, Max Brand (short story); C: Frank Good; Cast: Jewel Carmen, Henry Woodward, Edward Hearn • Two stranded vaudeville performers, LaBelle (Carmen) and Freddie (Hearn), hatch a scheme to impersonate a wanted bandit, Black Jim, in order to collect a big reward. Before they can do so, Geraldine is taken by Black Jim (Woodward), who falls in love with her. She falls for him, too, and discovers his gang's plot to kill him. After a shoot-out, they escape together. 5 reels

BONNIE ANNIE LAURIE (Sept. 1, 1918); D: Harry Millarde; W: Leila Leibrand (scr), Hamilton Thompson (st); C: A. Leach; Cast: Peggy Hyland, Henry Hallam, William Bailey, Sidney Mason, Marion Singer • Scottish Annie Laurie (Hyland) is torn between two soldiers during World War I. She becomes a Red Cross nurse and is at the hospital when both men are wounded. She eventually decides to marry the man she was engaged to before he left to fight. 5 reels

THE PRUSSIAN CUR (Sept. 1, 1918); D: R.A. Walsh; W: R.A. Walsh; C: Roy Overbaugh; Cast: Miriam Cooper, Sidney Mason, Capt. Horst von der Goltz, Leonora Stewart, James Marcus, Patrick O'Malley • In pre-war America, a notorious German spy, Otto (Goltz), and his co-conspirators cause factory explosions and transportation disasters. Otto marries an American, Lillian (Stewart), and treats her brutally. Lillian's death is later avenged by an American soldier (Mason) who is in love with her sister Rosie (Cooper). The film ends with America's entry into the war. 8 reels • A good portion of this film made use of footage from Fox Newsreels.

QUEEN OF THE SEA (Sept. 1, 1918); P: William Fox; D: John G. Adolfi; W: John G. Adolfi (scr), George Bronson Howard (st); C: Carl Gregory, Frank D. Williams; Cast: Annette Kellerman, Hugh Thompson, Mildred Keats, Walter Law, Beth Ivins, Philip Van Loan, Fred Parker, Louis Dean, Carrie Lee, Minnie Methol • A prince (Thompson) rescues and falls in love with Merilla (Kellerman), the queen of the sea, who is on a mission to become mortal by saving the lives of four persons. She completes her ordeal by saving a princess (Keats) who was betrothed to her lover, but Merilla wins the prince for herself. 5,360' • Scenes were filmed in Maine, Bermuda, Jamaica, Florida, Mexico, and California.

RIDERS OF THE PURPLE SAGE (Sept. 1, 1918); D: Frank Lloyd; W: Frank Lloyd, Zane Grey (novel); C: Billy Foster; Cast: William Farnum, William Scott, Marc Robbins, Murdock McQuarrie, Mary Mersch, Katherine Adams, Nancy Caswell, J. Holmes, Charles Clary, Jack Nelson, Buck Jones • After taking revenge on Dyer (Robbins), who abducted and killed his sister, Lassiter (Farnum), a Texas Ranger, is pursued by a gang. Lassiter, along with Jane (Mersch) and Fay (Caswell), is chased to a valley where he dislodges a huge boulder, blocking the exit to the valley and trapping him and the women inside. 6,470'

MR. LOGAN, U.S.A. (Sept. 8, 1918); D: Lynn F. Reynolds; W: Lynn F. Reynolds (scr), Jay Coffin (st); C: J.D. Jennings; Cast: Tom Mix, Kathleen Connors, Dick La Reno, Charles Le Moyne, Jack W. Dill, Val Paul, Maude Emery • Jim Logan (Mix), a cowboy drifter, arrives at a tungsten mine in New Mexico in time to thwart Gage, a spy for the Germans (Paul), who is inciting a strike. Jim wins the love of the mine owner's daughter, Suzanne (Connors), and then prevents a German plan to blow up the mine. Gage tries to escape with Suzanne as hostage, but Jim captures him after a wild car chase. 4,135'

LAND OF THE FREE (Sept. 8, 1918) Alternate title — Why America Will Win; D: Richard Stanton; W: Adrian Johnson; C: H. Cronjager; Cast: A. Alexander, Harris Gordon, Olaf Skavian, Ralph C. Faulkner, W.E. Whittle, Miss Irving, Frank McGlynn, Betty Grey, Ernest Maupain, Harry Warwick • This is a dramatization of the story of John J. Pershing from his graduation at West Point to fighting Apaches, the Battle of San Juan Hill, then as commander of the American Expeditionary Forces in France during World War I. 6,060'

THE CAILLAUX CASE (Sept. 15, 1918); D: Richard Stanton; W: Adrian Johnson; C: Henry Cronjager; Cast: Madlaine Traverse, Henry Warwick, George Majeroni, Eugene Ormonde, Philip Van Loan, Emile La Croix • In turn of the century Paris, Henriette (Traverse), an ambitious woman, gets a divorce so she can marry Joseph Caillaux (Warwick), the Minister of Finance. A reporter, Leo Claretie (Van Loan), learns that Caillaux, now France's premier, plans to unite with Germany to oppose war. Claretie is killed by Mme. Caillaux, who is acquitted, but a confederate in the plot is executed and Joseph Caillaux is imprisoned for treason. 7 reels

THE QUEEN OF HEARTS (Sept. 15, 1918); D: Edmund Lawrence; W: Adrian Johnson (scr), Harry O. Hoyt (st); C: John Urie; Cast: Virginia Pearson, Joseph Smiley, Victor Sutherland, Edward J. Burns, Peggy Sahnor,

John Webb Dillon, James A. Furey, Adelaide Lawrence • Pauline (Pearson), a French girl, takes over her father's (Smiley) New York gambling house to find out who murdered him. Of the three suspects, guilt appears to fall on Jimmie (Sutherland), whom Pauline has come to love. However, the murderer turns out to be her father's servant (Furey). 5 reels

KULTUR (Sept. 22, 1918); D: Edward J. LeSaint; W: J. Grubb Alexander, Fred Myton; C: Friend F. Baker; Cast: Gladys Brockwell, Georgia Woodthorpe, William Scott, Willard Louis, Charles Clary, Nigel de Brulier, William Burress, Alfred Fremont • Just prior to World War I, the Emperor's mistress, Countess Griselda (Brockwell), has her servant (de Brulier) assassinate Austria's Archduke Franz Ferdinand (Clary), who has plotted her death. The murder is covered up by Baron von Zeller (Louis), who loves the countess. When Griselda goes to Berlin, she falls in love with a Frenchman, René (Scott), and instead of exposing him as a spy, she helps him escape. The countess is shot for her treachery. 6 reels

SWAT THE SPY (Sept. 29, 1918); D: Arvid E. Gillstrom; W: Raymond L. Schrock (scr), Hamilton Thompson (st), Arvid E. Gillstrom (st); C: Al Leach; Cast: Jane Lee, Katherine Lee, Charles Slattery, P.C. Hartigan, Florence Ashbrooke • Jane (Lee) and Katherine (Lee), both mischievous daughters of a munitions inventor (Slattery), are unaware their housekeepers, Karl (Hartigan) and Lena (Ashbrooke), are German spies. The girls inadvertently steal their father's plans for a new explosive and prevent the Germans from getting the formula. 5 reels

WHEN A WOMAN SINS (Sept. 29, 1918); D: J. Gordon Edwards; W: E. Lloyd Sheldon (scr), Betta Breuil (st); C: John W. Boyle; Cast: Theda Bara, Josef Swickard, Albert Roscoe, Ogden Crane, Alfred Fremont, Jack Rollens, Genevieve Blinn • Michael West (Roscoe), a divinity student, blames his father's (Swickard) death on a seductive young nurse, Lillian (Bara). Disillusioned, Lillian then pursues a dissolute life as the dancer Poppea and becomes involved with Michael's cousin, Reggie (Rollens), who is driven to suicide. Michael finally realizes neither of the deaths were Lillian's fault and he rescues her as she is about to sacrifice her virtue. 7 reels

ON THE JUMP (Oct. 6, 1918); D: Raoul A. Walsh; W: Ralph A. Spence (scr), Raoul A. Walsh (st); C: Roy Overbaugh; Cast: George Walsh, Frances Burnham, James Marcus, Henry Clive, Ralph Faulkner • Jack (Walsh), a reporter, quits his paper when German sympathizer Otto Crumley (Clive) takes control of it. Jack later exposes Crumley as a German agent who has stolen the formula to a secret gasoline substitute invented by the father (Marcus) of his girlfriend, Margaret (Burnham). Jack rescues Margaret from Crumley and is able to sink a German submarine in the process. 6 reels

THE RAINBOW TRAIL (Oct. 13, 1918); D: Frank Lloyd; W: Charles Kenyon, Frank Lloyd, Zane Grey (novel); C: Billy Foster; Cast: William Farnum, Ann Forrest, Mary Mersch, William Burress, William Nye, Genevieve Blinn, George Ross, Buck Jones • In a sequel to *Riders of the Purple Sage*, Lassiter (Farnum), the Texas Ranger, and the two women he was trapped with in the "secret valley," Fay (Forrest) and Jane (Mersch), are rescued by his cousin, who thwarts the gang that is still after them. 6 reels

MARRIAGES ARE MADE (Oct. 13, 1918); D: Carl Harbaugh; W: Raymond L. Schrock (scr), E. Lloyd Sheldon (st); Cast: Peggy Hyland, Edwin Stanley, George Clarke, Al Lee, Dan Mason, Ellen Cassidy, William H. Boyd, Ed Begley, George Halpin • Susan (Hyland), daughter of a retired financier Cyrus Baird (Mason), is not permitted to marry James Morton (Stanley), the man she loves, because of a family feud. However, James proves his worth when he rescues Susan from Max (Boyd), a German spy, who has planned to mine the local harbor. 5 reels

WHY I WOULD NOT MARRY (Nov. 14, 1918); D: Richard Stanton; W: Adrian Johnson; C: H.G. Plimpton; Cast: Lucy Fox, Ed Sedgwick, William Davidson • Young Adele Moore (Fox) sees her future with four men who have proposed to her in a crystal ball. All end in miserable marriages. Instead of marrying, she moves to Vermont and opens a store where she meets a salesman who becomes her husband. 6 reels

FAN FAN (Nov. 17, 1918); D: Sidney A. & Chester M. Franklin; W: Bernard McConville, Gilbert & Sullivan (operetta); C: Frank B. Good, George Richter; Cast: Virginia Lee Corbin, Francis Carpenter, Carmen De Rue, Violet Radcliffe, Bud Messinger, Joe Singleton, Gertie Messinger, Louis Sargeant • Hanki Pan (Carpenter), the Japanese emperor's son, elopes with Fan Fan (Corbin) rather than marry the hag, Lady Shoo (DeRue), his father has chosen for him. Fan Fan's rejected suitor, the Executioner (Radcliffe), and Lady Shoo soon snare the young lovers with plans to behead Hanki Pan. Learning of the plot, the emperor (Singleton) allows Hanki Pan and Fan Fan to reunite. 5 reels • This is another of the Kiddie Pictures.

TELL IT TO THE MARINES (Nov. 17, 1918); D: Arvid E. Gillstrom; W: Adrian Johnson, Arvid E. Gillstrom; C: A. Leach; Cast: Jane Lee, Katherine Lee, Charles Slattery, Edward Bagley • After a busy day of playing pranks on the guests and servants of their father, Harry Williams (Slattery), Jane (Lee) and Katherine (Lee) tumble into bed and fall asleep. After seeing a movie depicting World War I battles, little Jane dreams that two armies, consisting entirely of mechanical dolls, are advancing against each other in battle. The German dolls, guilty of committing atrocities, battle the Allied army, which ultimately wins the war. 5 reels

THE WOMAN WHO GAVE (Nov. 17, 1918); D: Kenean Buel; W: Kenean Buel (scr), Izola Forrester (st), Mann Page (st); C: Joseph Ruttenberg; Cast: Evelyn Nesbit, Irving Cummings, Robert Walker, Eugene Ormonde, Dorothy Walters, Russell Thaw (son of Evelyn Nesbit) • A beautiful model, Colette (Nesbit), agrees to marry

Balkan Prince Vacarra (Ormonde) when he threatens to rape her. After the war, they move to the Adirondack Mountains with their young son Rudolph (Thaw). Vacarra treats Colette brutally and kills her previous lover (Cummings), then threatens to throw Rudolph over a steep cliff. Another former lover, Don (Walker), shoots the prince and Colette promises to marry him. 6 reels • Some scenes were filmed in the Adirondack Mountains of New York. Evelyn Nesbit was infamous for being the mistress of prominent New York architect Stanford White, who was shot in 1912 by Nesbit's jealous millionaire husband, Harry Thaw. The resulting murder trial was a "crime of the century" affair. Her story was later told in the 1955 "The Girl in the Red Velvet Swing" produced by 20th Century-Fox.

ALI BABA AND THE FORTY THIEVES (Nov. 24, 1918); D: S.A. & C.M. Franklin; W: Bernard McConville, Antoine Galland (short stories); Cast: George Stone, Gertrude Messinger, Lewis Sargent, Buddy Messinger, G. Raymond Nye, Raymond Lee, Charles Hincus, Marie Messinger, Jack Hull • Ali Baba (Stone) discovers a thieves' cave filled with treasure opens with the command, "Open Sesame." He falls in love with slave girl Morgianna (Messinger) who saves him from the forty thieves. Ali Baba overcomes the leader of the thieves and marries his true love. 5 reels • This is another of the Kiddie Pictures.

FAME AND FORTUNE (Nov. 24, 1918); D: Lynn F. Reynolds; W: Bennett R. Cohen, Charles Alden Seltzer (short story); C: J.D. Jennings; Cast: Tom Mix, Kathleen Connors, George Nicholls, Charles McHugh, Annette DeFoe, Val Paul, Jack Dill, E.N. Wallock, Clarence Burton • A wandering cowboy, Clay (Mix), returns home to find Big Dave Dawley (Nicholls) has stolen his late father's bank by a forged will. Clay's girlfriend, Della (Connors), a ranch owner, allows him to enlist her crew to fight off Dawley's gang and retrieve his property. 5 reels

BUCHANAN'S WIFE (Dec. 1, 1918); D: Charles J. Brabin; W: Adrian Johnson, Justus Miles Forman (novel); Cast: Virginia Pearson, Marc McDermott, Victor Sutherland, Ned Finley • Beatrix (Pearson) has been forced into marriage with Herbert (McDermott) while under a trance. When Herbert learns that Beatrix really loves Harry (Sutherland), he disappears. Beatrix falsely identifies a corpse as her husband and marries Harry. Herbert, who has teamed up with a vagrant (Finley), shows up again and the vagrant tries to blackmail Beatrix. Herbert, dying of tuberculosis, convinces him to not go through with the plot. 5 reels

THE SHE-DEVIL (Dec. 1, 1918); D: J. Gordon Edwards; W: George James Hopkins; C: John W. Boyle, Harry Gerstad; Cast: Theda Bara, Alan Roscoe, Frederick Bond, George A. McDaniel • Lolette (Bara), a beautiful Spanish peasant girl, prefers French artist Maurice (Roscoe) to a local bandit, the Tiger (McDaniel). Returning to Paris with Maurice, Lolette becomes a famous model. Fleeing France for Spain to escape arrest for questionable business deals, Lolette is imprisoned by the Tiger, but she and Maurice are able to escape. 6 reels

THE STRANGE WOMAN (Dec. 8, 1918); D: Edward J. LeSaint; W: J. Grubb Alexander, William J. Hurlbut (play); C: Friend F. Baker; Cast: Gladys Brockwell, Charles Clary, William Scott, Harry Depp, Ruby Lafayette, G. Raymond Nye, Ada Beecher, Eunice Moore, Grace Wood, Margaret Cullington • In Paris, after her wealthy, abusive husband is killed in a brawl, Inez (Brockwell) swears off marriage but falls in love with John (Scott), an American student. He is shocked by her "modern" views and reluctantly agrees to live with her, but when they return to Iowa, Inez is made a pariah. However, she is touched by the forgiveness of John's mother (Lafayette), and she finally agrees to marry. 6 reels

CAUGHT IN THE ACT (Dec. 15, 1918); D: Harry Millarde; W: Raymond L. Schrock (scr), Fred Jackson (st); C: Ben Struckman; Cast: Peggy Hyland, Leslie Austen, George Bunny, Mrs. Carlotta Coer, Jack Raymond, Wally McKeown, Elizabeth Garrison, Ellen Cassidy, Mr. Martin, Henry Hallam • Priscilla (Hyland), a society girl, rejects the man her father (Bunny) has selected for her and runs off. She falls in love with journalist Langdon Trevor (Austen), who once exposed her father as a food profiteer. When her father tries to frame Trevor, Priscilla helps him escape scandal and they get married. 5 reels

I WANT TO FORGET (Dec. 15, 1918); D: James Kirkwood; W: James Kirkwood (scr), Harry O. Hoyt (st), Hamilton Smith (st); Cast: Evelyn Nesbit, Russell Thaw (son of Evelyn Nesbit), Henry Clive, Alphonse Ethier, William R. Dunn, Jane Jennings • During the war, an exotic dancer from Austria, Varda (Nesbit), falls for Lieutenant John Long (Clive). While John is away on a mission, Varda agrees to use her former contacts to get information for the American secret service. While allowing a German agent (Ethier) to seduce her, John finds her in a compromising situation and thinks she is unfaithful. Later, she helps John escape and he finally understands her mission. 5 reels

I'LL SAY SO (Dec. 22, 1918); D: Raoul A. Walsh; W: Ralph Spence; E: Ralph Spence; Cast: George Walsh, Regina Quinn, William Bailey, James Black, Ed Keeley, May McAvoy • Rejected from enlistment when war is declared, Bill Durham (Walsh) falls in love with Barbara (Quinn), whose guardian, August (Bailey), is a German spy. Bill is able to subvert a plot to stir up trouble on the Mexican border with the United States. When he returns to New York, he arrives in time to stop Barbara from entering into a marriage with a German spy (Black), engineered by August. 5 reels

FIGHTING BLOOD (Dec. 29, 1918) Reissue

THE DANGER ZONE (Dec. 29, 1918); D: Frank Beal; W: Adrian Johnson (scr), Denison Clift (scr), Marshall Bruce Bennington (st); C: Harry Gerstad, J. Dev Jennings; Cast: Madlaine Traverse, Thomas Holding, Fritzie Ridgeway, Edward Cecil • Abandoned by her lover, Philip (Cecil), Lola Dupre (Traverse) becomes a famous opera singer and marries a wealthy senator (Holding). Philip returns and threatens Lola with blackmail, then convinces the senator's daughter Marie (Ridgeway) to elope with him. Before he leaves, he attacks Lola, who stabs him to death. Marie is accused of murder, but Lola confesses and wins her freedom because "a woman's honor is her life." 5 reels

FOR FREEDOM (Dec. 29, 1918); D: Frank Lloyd; W: E. Lloyd Sheldon (st), Florence Margolies (st); C: Billy Foster; Cast: William Farnum, C. Albertson, Ruby De Remer, Anna Lehr, Herbert Frank, G. Raymond Nye, John Slaven, Marc Robbins • Robert Wayne (Farnum) steals letters Stratton (Frank), a blackmailer, is using against his married sister Edith (Lehr) and fatally shoots him. When war breaks out, Robert is released from prison to fight in France. His bravery wins him a pardon and he reunites his sister with her husband (Albertson). 6 reels

1919 Releases

TREAT 'EM ROUGH (Jan. 5, 1919); D: Lynn Reynolds; W: Lynn Reynolds, Charles Alden Seltzer (novel); C: J. Devereaux Jennings; Cast: Tom Mix, Jane Novak, Val Paul, Charles Le Moyne, Jack Curtis • A daredevil cowboy, Ned Ferguson (Mix), is hired to hunt down cattle rustlers but arouses jealousy in the ranch foreman (Le Moyne) over the affections of Mary (Novak), who is writing a western novel. The foreman accuses Ned of shooting Mary's brother (Paul) in the back. After rescuing Mary from a cattle stampede and pinning her brother's murder on the foreman, Ned becomes Mary's real, rather than fictional, hero. 5 reels

THE WOLF'S CLAW (Jan. 5, 1919) Reissue Title — The Serpent

THE REGENERATION (Jan. 12, 1919) Reissue

THE LIGHT (Jan. 12, 1919); D: J. Gordon Edwards; W: Adrian Johnson (scr), Charles Kenyon (scr), Luther Reed (st), Brett Page (st); Cast: Theda Bara, Eugene Ormonde, Robert Walker, Georges Renavent • Blanchette (Bara), "The wickedest woman in Paris," gives up cavorting with her wealthy lover, Chabin (Ormonde), and takes up with young sculptor Etienne (Walker), who has returned from the war without his sight. Blanchette nurses Etienne and he sculpts her image by touch. A jealous Apache dancer, Auchat (Renevant), tries to kill Etienne, but Blanchette kills him first. Chabin is touched by Blanchette's kindness towards Etienne and tells police he killed Auchat. 5 reels

THE BROKEN LAW (Jan. 19, 1919) Reissue

THE CALL OF THE SOUL (Jan. 19, 1919); D: Edward J. LeSaint; W: Denison Clift (scr), Julia Burnham (st); C: Friend F. Baker; Cast: Gladys Brockwell, William Scott, Lydia Yeamans Titus, Charles Clary, Nancy Caswell • Marooned on an island after a picnic, Barbara (Brockwell), a nurse, is victimized by Dr. Clayton (Scott), the head of the hospital where she works. Later rescued, Barbara secretly gives birth to Clayton's daughter. She falls in love and marries explorer Neil (Clary), who eventually learns of the daughter. The young girl becomes seriously ill but is saved by her natural father's medical skills and is accepted by Barbara's husband. 5 reels

UNDER TWO FLAGS (Jan. 26, 1919) Reissue

WOMAN, WOMAN! (Jan. 26, 1919); D: Kenean Buel; W: Kenean Buel, Norma Lorimer (novel); C: Joseph Ruttenberg; Cast: Evelyn Nesbit, Clifford Bruce, Gareth Hughes, William H. Tooker, William R. Dunn, Frank Goldsmith, Anna Luther, Nora Cecil, Henry Hallam, Florence Flinn • Small-town girl Alice Lindsay (Nesbit) becomes part of Greenwich Village Bohemian life. She resists advances from an advocate of free love (Hughes) and marries civil engineer Samson (Bruce). Alice later goes to wealthy former suitor Roy (Tooker) for financial assistance and ends up pregnant with his baby. Samson divorces her and she is turned away from her hometown. Alice accepts Roy's marriage proposal to assure her son's future. 5 reels

THE GIRL WITH NO REGRETS (Jan. 26, 1919); D: Harry Millarde; W: Raymond L. Schrock (scr), Evelyn Campbell (st); Cast: Peggy Hyland, Charles Clary, Eugene Burr, Betty Schade, Jack Nelson, Al Fremont, Harry Von Meter, Dort Clark, William Ellingford • Small town girl Signa (Hyland) joins her sister, Janet (Shade), in New York only to find that she is a shoplifter married to a burglar, Jim (Burr). After covering for them with the police, Signa becomes secretary to young millionaire Olney French (Clary), who falls in love with her. When Jim tries to heist Olney's jewels, Signa is implicated, but finally exonerated. 5 reels

LUCK AND PLUCK (Feb. 2, 1919); D: Edward Dillon; W: Adrian Johnson (scr), Raymond Schrock (scr), George Scarborough (st); Cast: George Walsh, Virginia Lee, Joseph W. Smiley, George Fisher, Corene Uzzell, George Halpin • A master crook, Joe Grim (Walsh), falls in love with a society lady, Laura (Lee), whose friend, Countess Briand (Uzzell), is really the leader of a German spy ring. Joe is tricked by Briand into stealing plans for a new airplane, but steals them back, breaks up the spy ring and rescues Laura, whom he plans to marry. 5 reels

SALOME (Feb. 2, 1919); P: William Fox; D: J. Gordon Edwards; W: Adrian Johnson, Flavius Josephus (book); C: George Schneiderman, John W. Boyle, Harry Gerstad; Cast: Theda Bara, G. Raymond Nye, Albert Roscoe, Herbert Heyes, Bertram Grassby, Genevieve Blinn • Salome (Bara) uses her seductive charms in the court of the tyrannical King Herod (Nye) to destroy her enemies, including John the Baptist (Roscoe). At Herod's birthday feast, Salome performs a sensuous dance and receives John the Baptist's head as a reward. A fierce storm frightens Herod and he orders Salome's execution. 8 reels • This film was pre-released in August 1918.

INFIDELITY (Feb. 2, 1919) Reissue title — Dr. Rameau

THE LOVE AUCTION (Feb. 9, 1919); D: Edmund Lawrence; W: Raymond L. Schrock (scr), Julia Burnham (scr), Edmund Lawrence (scr), May Edginton (st); C: Al Leach; Cast: Virginia Pearson, Elizabeth Garrison, Gladys McLure, Hugh Thompson, Edwin Stanley, Thurlow Bergen, Charles Mason • Lea (Pearson) opts to marry Dorian (Thompson) for his money rather than love and discovers that he is an alcoholic. Lea's solace is in spending time with Jack Harley (Stanley), whom she really loves. When Lea gives birth to a child, Dorian attempts to overcome his alcoholism. A blackmailer (Bergen) threatens to reveal that Lee's child is Jack's, but an enraged Dorian strangles him and then shoots himself. Lea then marries Jack. 5 reels

THE SOUL OF BROADWAY (Feb. 9, 1919) Reissue

HELL-ROARIN' REFORM (Feb. 16, 1919); D: Edward J. LeSaint; W: Charles Kenyon (scr), Joseph Anthony Roach (st); C: Friend Baker; Cast: Tom Mix, Kathleen O'Connor, George Berrell, Bowditch M. Turner, Jack Curtis, Kewpie Morgan • Tim (Mix), a good-hearted cowboy, disguises himself as a preacher to clean up a town preyed upon by a gang of robbers. Through many daredevil adventures, he accomplishes his goal and marries Doris (Connors), whom he saved from the gang. 5 reels

THE DARLINGS OF PARIS (Feb. 16, 1919) Reissue

SMILES (Feb. 23, 1919); D: Arvid E. Gilstrom; W: Arvid E. Gilstrom (scr), Albert Glassmire (scr), Ralph Spence (st); Cast: Jane Lee, Katherine Lee, Ethel Fleming, Val Paul, Carmen Phillips, Charles Arling, Katherine Griffith • With their father missing in battle, Jane (Lee) and Katherine (Lee) are sent to stay with their aunt Lucille (Fleming). Lucille is romantically involved with Lt. Tom Hayes (Paul), who is making her jealous because of his interest in another woman. Tom is actually a Secret Service agent and is on the trail of a spy. The sisters' pranks help Tom capture the spy and they are able to reunite him with Lucille. 5 reels

EVERY MOTHER'S SON (Feb. 23, 1919); D: Raoul Walsh; W: Raoul Walsh; Cast: Charlotte Walker, Percy Standing, Edwin Stanley, Ray Howard, Gareth Hughes, Corona Paynter, Bernard Thornton • After sending two sons to battle in the war, an English mother (Walker) keeps her youngest (Hughes) from enlisting, against her husband's (Standing) wishes. She takes the boy to their seaside home, where they witness survivors of a ship sunk by a German U-boat coming ashore. Both mother and son are awakened to the importance of enlisting. The story ends with all three sons returning home at Christmas. 5 reels • This was pre-released on Dec. 1, 1918.

THE MAN HUNTER (Feb. 23, 1919); D: Frank Lloyd; W: Frank Lloyd; C: Billy Foster; Cast: William Farnum, Louise Lovely, Charles Clary, Marc Robbins, Leatrice Joy • George (Farnum), a wealthy bachelor in London, is swindled out of his money by Henry Benton (Clary) and serves a year in prison for assaulting him. George follows Benton to New York and starts another fight with him aboard ship to save Helen Garfield (Lovely) from being swindled. After a shipwreck, the trio ends up on a deserted island, where Benton meets his death. When they are rescued, George marries the wealthy Helen. 6 reels

THE FORBIDDEN ROOM (March 2, 1919); D: Lynn Reynolds; W: W.S. Van Dyke; Cast: J. Dev Jennings, Gladys Brockwell, William Scott, J. Barney Sherry, Harry Dunkinson, Al Fremont, William Burress, T.S. Guide, Louis King, Robert Dunbar, Lillian West • An honest district attorney, Anthony (Scott), falls in love with his stenographer, Ruth (Brockwell), and is blackmailed by corrupt officials who are trying to discredit him. He fires Ruth, thinking that she framed him. Ruth then risks her reputation to get the officials to admit to the plot. 5 reels

WHEN MEN DESIRE (March 9, 1919); D: J. Gordon Edwards; W: Adrian Johnson (scr), E. Lloyd Sheldon (st), J. Searle Dawley (st); C: John W. Boyle; Cast: Theda Bara, Fleming Ward, G. Raymond Nye, Florence Martin, Maude Hill, Edward Elkus • Marie (Bara), an American visiting her uncle in Germany, assumes the identity of a dead German spy to escape after war is declared. Marie stabs a German officer (Nye) who is trying to seduce her. Robert (Ward), her American aviator boyfriend, rescues her and, after a chase, they fly safely over the border. 5 reels • This film was billed as a "Theda Bara Super-Production."

GAMBLING IN SOULS (March 9, 1919); D: Harry F. Millarde; W: Denison Clift (scr), Samuel J. Warshawsky (st); C: Harry Gerstad; Cast: Madlaine Traverse, Herbert Heyes, Murdock McQuarrie, Lew Zehring, Mary McIvor, Henry A. Barrows, Marion Skinner, William Clifford • Marcia (Traverse) vows revenge against a Wall Street broker (MacQuarrie), who led to the suicide of her husband (Clifford). She takes a job at a gambling den and leads the broker's son Dick (Philborn) into great losses, which bring his father to ruin. When Marcia learns that her daughter has secretly married Dick, she manages to use her position at the gambling house to reverse the damage she has done. 6 reels

NEVER SAY QUIT (March 16, 1919); D: Edward Dillon; W: Raymond L. Schrock, Ralph Spence (titles); C: R. Schellinger; Cast: George Walsh, Florence Dixon, Henry Hallam, William Frederic, Frank Jacobs, Joseph W. Smiley, Jean Acker • Reginald Jones (Walsh), born on Friday the 13th, has been unlucky his entire life, is conned out of his money and loses his million-dollar inheritance. He meets wealthy, treasure hunting Professor Lattimore (Holland) and his daughter, Helen (Dixon), aboard a schooner. Finally breaking his jinx, Reginald disrupts a plot to kidnap Lattimore and wins Helen's love. 5 reels • Some scenes were shot in Miami, Florida.

THOU SHALT NOT (March 23, 1919); D: Charles J. Brabin; W: Charles J. Brabin; Cast: Evelyn Nesbit, Ned Burton, Florida Kingsley, Gladden James, Crauford Kent, Edmund Lawrence • A well-bred New England girl, Ruth (Nesbit), elopes with railroad worker Alec (James) to New York, but they never marry. When he throws her out without a penny, Ruth is found at a charity home by a minister (Kent), who was in love with her. Returning home, her parents forgive her, but the community considers her a pariah. The minister, repelled by the town's bigotry, leaves with Ruth to start over elsewhere. 6 reels

THE REBELLIOUS BRIDE (March 23, 1919); D: Lynn Reynolds; W: Charles Kenyon (sc), Joseph Anthony Roach (st); C: Friend Baker; Cast: Peggy Hyland, George Nichols, George Hernandez, Pell Trenton, Charles Le Moyne, Kathleen Emerson, Lillian Langdon, Harry Dunkinson • A rebellious Ozark girl, Cynthy (Hyland), refuses to marry Tobe (Hernandez), whom her grandfather (Nicholls) has chosen, so she must marry the first man she meets. It happens to be Arthur (Trenton), a stranded aviator who is forced to marry her at gunpoint. After being locked up for days, Arthur escapes and flies home. He later realizes that he misses Cynthy, who follows him. They now acknowledge their love for each other. 5 reels

FIGHTING FOR GOLD (March 30, 1919); D: Edward J. LeSaint; W: Charles Kenyon, William MacLeod Raine (novel); Cast: Tom Mix, Teddy Sampson, Sid Jordan, Jack Nelson, Harry Lonsdale, Robert Dunbar, Hattie Buskirk, Frank Clark, Lucille Young • Jack (Mix), a British co-owner of a goldmine in the West, spends most of the time getting his partner, Curly (Nelson), out of trouble and protecting their claim from Lord Farquhar's (Dunbar) British mining company. Jack falls in love with Farquhar's daughter, Moya (Sampson), and ends up saving her from a dishonorable suitor (Lonsdale). 5 reels

MARRIED IN HASTE (Apr. 6, 1919); D: Arthur Rosson; W: Charles Kenyon (scr), E. Lloyd Sheldon (st), J. Searle Dawley (st); C: Roy Klaffki; Cast: Albert Ray, Elinor Fair, Robert Klein, Don Bailey, Bowditch M. Turner, Thomas Jefferson, William Carroll, William Elmer • Sam Morgan's new wife, Constance (Fair), tries to break the millionaire of his spendthrift ways by getting Downer (Jefferson), the trustee of his inheritance, to pretend to steal all the money. On their honeymoon, Sam finds they have no money and he gets various jobs, using his ingenuity to figure a way out of their debts. Constance confesses the arrangement with Downer, and Sam is wealthy again. 5 reels

PITFALLS OF A BIG CITY (Apr. 13, 1919); D: Frank Lloyd; W: Bennett Cohen; Cast: Gladys Brockwell, William Scott, William Sheer, Neva Gerber, Al Fremont, Ashton Dearholt, Janis Williams • Molly (Brockwell) is trying to go straight, running a restaurant in the underworld district. Two former friends, Jerry (Scott) and Spike (Sheer), released from prison, show up. Spike threatens her daughter Marion's (Gerber) future by planning to rob her fiancé's house. Spike then threatens to expose Molly's past if she does not help them. Molly is later mistakenly arrested as a part of the plot, but with Jerry's help, Spike is apprehended. Molly is freed and marries Jerry. 5 reels • Some scenes were shot at San Quentin prison in California.

THE JUNGLE TRAIL (April 20, 1919); D: Richard Stanton; W: Adrian Johnson (scr), George V. Hobart (st); C: Horace Plimpton, Jr.; Cast: William Farnum, Anna Luther, Lyster Chambers, Sara Alexander, Anna Schaefer, Edward Roseman, Henry Armetta, G. Raymond Nye, Anna Lehr • Mrs. Lamar (Schaeffer) prefers that daughter Mary (Luther) marry wealthy Philip (Chambers) rather than Robert (Farnum), who is just well off. Philip arranges for Robert to go to Africa, where he plans to have him killed. However, Robert escapes and becomes a god to the natives. With the help of a jungle princess (Lehr), he returns to New York and stops Mary's marriage to Philip. 5 reels • Some scenes were filmed in Miami and the Everglades, Florida.

THE LOVE THAT DARES (Apr. 20, 1919); D: Harry F. Millarde; W: Denison Clift (scr), Elmer Harris (st); C: Frank Good; Cast: Madlaine Traverse, Tom Santschi, Frank Elliott, Mae Gaston, Tom Guise, George B. Williams • A marital misunderstanding leads to an iron tycoon Perry Risdon (Santschi) being forced to repay a large loan to Ned (Elliott), a rival for his wife, Olive (Traverse). Ned then lures Olive to his apartment, but she is saved from seduction by Ned's mistress, Marta (Gaston), who alerts Perry to what is happening. Marta then kills Ned and drowns herself. 5 reels

HELP! HELP! POLICE! (Apr. 27, 1919); D: Edward Dillon; W: Raymond L. Schrock (scr), Irving McDonald (st); Cast: George Walsh, Eric Mayne, Henry Hallam, Marie Burke, Alice Mann, Alan Edwards, Evelyn Brent, Joseph Burke • George (Walsh) is in love with Eve (Mann), but has to get over her father's (Hallam) objections because of a business rivalry between families. In trying to apprehend another suitor, Arthur (Edwards), who is a thief, George is arrested but released on Eve's pleas. He is wrongly charged again after saving a woman from a fire that Arthur started. Finally, George captures Arthur and recovers money stolen from Eve's father. Both families become partners in business with the marriage of George and Eve. 5 reels

MISS ADVENTURE (May 4, 1919); D: Lynn F. Reynolds; W: Joseph Anthony Roach; C: J. Dev Jennings; Cast: Peggy Hyland, Gertrude Messinger, Edmund Burns, Lewis Sargent, Frank Brownlee, George Hernandez, George Webb, Alice Mason • Jane (Hyland), adopted years earlier by sea captain Barth (Hernandez), has become an adventure-seeking tomboy. Barth's nephew, Albert (Webb), pays smuggler Bog (Brownlee) to kidnap Jane so he will not have to marry her. When Bog drowns, Jane is left on a deserted island. Richard (Burns) rescues Jane and tells her of a huge inheritance from her late father. Albert now kidnaps Jane to marry her for her money. Richard rescues Jane again and reveals himself as the person charged with her care when her father died. 5 reels

THE SIREN'S SONG (May 4, 1919); D: J. Gordon Edwards; W: Charles Kenyon; C: John W. Boyle; Cast: Theda Bara, Al Fremont, Ruth Handforth, Alan Roscoe, Lee Shumway, Carrie Clark Ward, Paul Weigel, Carrie Clark Ward • Marie (Bara), a French fisher girl, has a beautiful singing voice but her father (Fremont) considers it a gift from the Devil. When she attempts suicide, a singer (Weigel) from Paris, rescues her and helps her become famous. She falls in love with Gaspard (Roscoe), a married man, and later loses her voice. She lives life as a peasant again until Gaspard is freed from marriage after his wife dies. 5 reels

THE COMING OF THE LAW (May 11, 1919); D: Arthur Rosson; W: Denison Clift, Arthur Rosson, Charles Alden Seltzer (novel); C: Le Roy Granville; Cast: Tom Mix, Agnes Vernon, Jack Curtis, Sid Jordan, Bowditch M. Turner, Charles Le Moyne, Pat Chrisman, Lewis Sargent, Jack Dill, Harry Dunkinson • Kent (Mix), an Easterner, brings law and order to a small southwestern town. A cattle rustler, Big Bill (Nicholls), orders him to leave town but Kent refuses. After a beating, he is nursed by Nellie (Vernon), who is also desired by Bill. Kent wins the town's election for sheriff and then is victorious in a shootout with Bill. 5 reels

A FALLEN IDOL (May 18, 1919); D: Kenean Buel; W: E. Lloyd Sheldon; C: Joseph Ruttenberg; Cast: Evelyn Nesbit, Lillian Lawrence, Sidney Mason, Lyster Chambers, Pat Hartigan, Harry Semels, Thelma Parker, Marie Newton, Fred C. Williams • Princess Laone (Nesbit), a Hawaiian composer staying in Santa Barbara, falls in love with a society matron's nephew, Keith (Mason). Mrs. Parrish (Lawrence) forbids Keith from marrying Laone because of her ethnicity. While Keith is out of town, Laone leaves for Hawaii with Brainard (Chambers), a smuggler. Keith finds out his aunt told Laone that he had deserted her. Keith heads to Hawaii, where he is accused of a theft committed by Brainard. Laone clears him and the two reunite. 5 reels

WORDS AND MUSIC BY— (May 18, 1919); D: Albert Ray; W: Charles Kenyon (scr), William Charles Lengel (article); C: Roy Klaffki; Cast: Albert Ray, Elinor Fair, Robert Bolder, Eugene Pallette, Edwin Booth Tilton • Impresario Sullivan (Tilton) discovers country girl Millicent (Fair) and makes her a Broadway star. Her bookkeeper boyfriend, Brian (Ray), follows her to New York with an opera he has written. Gene (Pallette), a playwright, is unable to come up with a new vehicle for Millicent and steals Brian's opera. However, the truth is finally revealed and Millicent and Brian reunite. 5 reels

THE DIVORCE TRAP (May 25, 1919); D: Frank Beal; W: Denison Clift (scr), Jasper Ewing Brady (st); C: Fred Leroy Granville; Cast: Gladys Brockwell, Francis McDonald, William Sheer, John Steppling, Betty Schade, William Scott, Herschel Mayall • Eleanor (Brockwell), a hotel telephone operator, marries Jim Drake (MacDonald), who has been disinherited by his wealthy father (Mayall). While she works to support Jim, he carries on with another woman. Hoping to get a divorce and be reinstated by his father, Jim makes Eleanor look like an adulteress. A lawyer (Scott) with whom Eleanor was previously in love comes to her rescue and arrests the plotters. 4,800'

A WOMAN THERE WAS (June 1, 1919); D: J. Gordon Edwards; W: Adrian Johnson, Neje Hopkins (short story); C: John W. Boyle; Cast: Theda Bara, William B. Davidson, Robert Elliott, Claude Payton, John Ardizoni • A South Sea pearl diver, Pulke (Elliott), is in love with Zara (Bara), the Chief's daughter. Zara is happy until she becomes infatuated with Winthrop (Davidson), a missionary. Pulke attacks Winthrop and Zara steals a sacred black pearl to bring him back to health. When Winthrop recovers and leaves, Zara dies as angry natives try to retrieve the pearl. 5 reels

WHEN FATE DECIDES (June 1, 1919); D: Harry F. Millarde; W: Denison Clift (scr), Evelyn Campbell (st); C: Frank Good; Cast: Madlaine Traverse, William Conklin, Clyde Fillmore, Claire DuBrey, Henry J. Herbert, John Cossar, Genevieve Blinn, Cordelia Callahan • Vera (Traverse), an unhappily married society woman, is advised to divorce her womanizing husband, Herbert (Conklin), by Donald (Fillmore). Herbert, who is on a date with Mrs. Alicia Cateret (DuBrey), gets into a fight with Donald. Herbert is later found dead and Donald is accused, but Vera proves the murderer was really Alicia. 5 reels

MY LITTLE SISTER (June 15, 1919); D: Kenean Buel; W: Kenean Buel, Elizabeth Robins (novel); C: Joseph Ruttenberg; Cast: Evelyn Nesbit, Leslie Austin, Lillian Hall, Kempton Greene, Lyster Chambers, Herbert Standing, Caroline Lee, Amelia Summerville, Ben Hendricks, Louise Rial • The older of two sisters (Nesbit) writes about the younger one's tragedy. She and Bettina (Hall) were to be introduced into London society by their aunt (Rial). However, they were intercepted by a woman disguised as their aunt who led them to a brothel. The elder sister, helped by a male companion, escaped, but was unable to rescue Bettina. She then devoted her life to saving other women by writing this story. 5 reels

COWARDICE COURT (June 15, 1919); D: William C. Dowlan; W: Joseph Anthony Roach, George Barr McCutcheon (novel); C: J. Dev Jennings, King D. Gray; Cast: Peggy Hyland, Jack Livingston, Arthur Hoyt, Kathryn Adams, Burton Law, Bull Montana, Harry Lonsdale, Bertram Grassby, Gung Wong, Mrs. Jack Mulhall • Lord (Hoyt) and Lady Bazelhurst (Adams), who live on an estate in the Adirondacks, want to develop the adjoining acreage on which Randolph Shaw (Livingston) has his shack. A feud develops in which Randolph is shot and then becomes engaged to the lord's sister, Penelope (Hyland). The feud ends when the nobles realize the property will be in the family. 5 reels

PUTTING ONE OVER (June 22, 1919); D: Edward Dillon; W: Raymond L. Schrock, Mary Imlay Taylor (short story); C: Al Leach; Cast: George Walsh, Edith Stockton, Ralph J. Locke, Frank Beamish, Robert Lee Keeling, Matthew Betts, Jack Dillon, Mrs. Elizabeth Garrison, Marcia Harris • Jack Trevor (Walsh), a car salesman, bears a striking resemblance to millionaire Horace Barney (Walsh), who is traveling on the same train. After a wreck, Jack awakens to find that he's been given Horace's identity by the dead man's unscrupulous guardian, Maurice (Locke). Jack falls in love with Horace's cousin, Helen (Stockton), who is in line for the inheritance, and tries to save her estate. However, Horace was on his way to a sanitarium, so Maurice tries to commit Jack. There are fights and chases before the situation is resolved. 5 reels

THE LONE STAR RANGER (June 29, 1919); D: J. Gordon Edwards; W: Charles Kenyon, Zane Grey (novel); C: John W. Boyle; Cast: William Farnum, Louise Lovely, G. Raymond Nye, Charles Clary, Lamar Johnstone, Frederic Herzog, Irene Rich • Steele (Farnum), a Texas Ranger seeking revenge for the murder of his best friend, is hired by Cyrus (Clary), a rancher who is secretly the leader of a gang of rustlers. Steele falls in love with Cyrus's daughter, Ray (Lovely), and discovers that Cyrus was blackmailed into continuing on as a rustler. Steele routs the gang and marries Ray. 5–6 reels • This was the first of four versions of the Zane Grey novel, all made under the same title, between 1919 and 1942.

BE A LITTLE SPORT (June 29, 1919); D: Scott R. Dunlap; W: Joseph Anthony Roach (scr), Hale Merriman (st); C: Ray Klaffki; Cast: Albert Ray, Elinor Fair, Lule Warrenton, George Hernandez, Leota Lorraine, Eugene Pallette • Salesman Gerald (Ray) is in love with chorus girl Carlotta (Lorraine). His uncle (Hernandez) offers him $100,000 to get married the following Saturday. Carlotta, having flirted with the uncle, postpones the date. With the help of stenographer Norma (Fair), Gerald sets up a phony wedding. Gerald is surprised when he and Norma are really married. There are comic complications, but in the end the husband and wife realize they love each other. 5 reels

THE WILDERNESS TRAIL (July 13, 1919); D: Edward J. LeSaint; W: Charles Kenyon, Francis William Sullivan (novel); C: Friend F. Baker; Cast: Tom Mix, Colleen Moore, Frank Clark, Lulu Warrenton, Sid Jordan, Pat Chrisman, Jack Nelson • Unfairly accused of leading a group that steals furs from the Hudson Bay Company, Donald (Mix) sets out to capture the gang. Sergius (Jordan), the half-breed leader of the thieves, kidnaps Donald's girlfriend, Jeanne (Moore), but her father (Clark) accuses Donald of the crime. Donald has to escape capture to rescue Jeanne and kill Sergius. 5 reels

ROSE OF THE WEST (July 20, 1919); D: Harry F. Millarde; W: Denison Clift; C: Frank B. Good; Cast: Madlaine Traverse, Frank Leigh, Beatrice La Plante, Tom Santschi, Henry J. Hebert, Minna Prevost, Jack Nelson • Northwest Canadian trapper Pierre (Leigh) returns after being presumed dead in an avalanche just as his wife, Rose (Traverse), is to marry Lt. Bruce Knight (Santschi). Pierre abuses Rose and sells his daughter, Angela (La Plante), for some land to Jules (Nelson). Rose retrieves Angela and kills Jules. Natoosh (Prevost), a half-breed servant, then kills Pierre and takes responsibility for Jules's death as well. Rose marries Bruce. 5 reels

THE SNEAK (July 27, 1919); D: Edward J. LeSaint; W: Ruth Ann Baldwin (scr), J. Grubb Alexander (st); C: Friend F. Baker; Cast: Gladys Brockwell, William Scott, Alfred Hollingsworth, John Oaker, Harry Hilliard, Irene Rich, Mrs. Gerrard Grassby • When Rhona (Brockwell), daughter of a gypsy king (Hollingsworth), chooses Wester (Scott) over Francisco (Oaker) for her husband, passions are inflamed. Rhona makes the situation worse by posing for an artist, Roger (Hilliard), as penance for having stolen his valuables on Francisco's orders. Found at Roger's home, Rhona is expelled from the camp. The king later realizes that Rhona is innocent, and she is allowed to return. Francisco stabs Wester, and Rhona challenges him to a knife duel, during which he is killed. Rhona then marries Wester. 5 reels

CHEATING HERSELF (Aug. 3, 1919); D: Edmund Lawrence; W: Ruth Ann Baldwin (scr), Mortimer Peck (st); C: King Gray; Cast: Peggy Hyland, Harry Hilliard, Mollie McConnell, Mrs. Jack Mulhall, William Elmer, Edwin Booth Tilton, Edward Jobson • In a scheme to get her millionaire father (Tilton) to enjoy life without all his money, Patience (Hyland) enlists their butler (Elmer), an ex-burglar, to advise her in blowing open her father's safe. The butler has two thieves steal the securities. The family is driven to a life of hard work. Patience's boyfriend (Hilliard) tracks down the crooks and recovers the money, winning Patience's hand in marriage. 5 reels

WOLVES OF THE NIGHT (Aug. 10, 1919); D: J. Gordon Edwards; W: E. Lloyd Sheldon; Cast: William Farnum, Louise Lovely, Lamar Johnstone, Charles Clary, Al Fremont, G. Raymond Nye, Carrie Clark Ward, Irene Rich • Bruce (Farnum), a mining engineer, is lured into investigating a copper mine in Chile so his scheming neighbor, Edmund (Clary), can get control of his ranch. A mine explosion leaves Bruce with amnesia. Edmund and his partner, Burton (Johnston), hearing he has died, financially ruin Bruce's wife Isabel (Lovely) so that she will sell the ranch and marry Burton, who has always desired her. When Bruce recovers his memory and returns, he gets revenge on the two men by ruining them and regaining Isabel's love. 5–7 reels

LOVE IS LOVE (Aug. 17, 1919); D: Scott R. Dunlap; W: Joseph Anthony Roach (scr), Scott Dunlap (scr), Richard Washburn Child (st); C: George Schneiderman; Cast: Albert Ray, Elinor Fair, William Ryno, Hayward Mack, Harry Dunkinson, John Cossar • Gerry (Ray), a locksmith, is so weak willed that he allows his employer Nick (Ryno) to order him to be a safecracker. When he realizes it is wrong, his girlfriend, Polly (Fair), gets him a job at a hotel, where he is framed for thefts by a crook Red Devlin (Mack). Gerry is bailed out by Devlin and takes a job on the lam as a typesetter at a newspaper. Polly exposes the crooks and is reunited with Gerry when he turns himself over to the police. 5 reels

ROUGH-RIDING ROMANCE (Aug. 24, 1919); D: Arthur Rosson; W: Charles Kenyon; C: Fred Leroy Granville; Cast: Tom Mix, Juanita Hansen, Pat Chrisman, Spottiswoode Aitken, Jack Nelson, Sid Jordan, Frankie Lee • Dairyman Phineas Dobbs (Mix) becomes wealthy when oil is discovered on his ranch. He rescues a woman visitor (Hansen) and follows her back to San Francisco to discover she is really a princess being forced into marriage. Dobbs rides to her hotel and performs daring stunts to rescue the princess, after which they return to his ranch to marry. 5 reels

CHECKERS (Aug. 31, 1919); D: Richard Stanton; W: Adrian Johnson, Henry Martyn Blossom (novel); C: Harry G. Plimpton; Cast: Thomas Carrigan, Jean Acker, Ellen Cassity, Robert Elliott, Tammany Young, Bertram Marburgh, Edward Sedgwick, Peggy Worth, Frank Beamish • Checkers (Carrigan), a man who loves horses, becomes a rival for Pert Barlow (Acker), the daughter of a wealthy Southern judge (Marbaugh). When he enters Pert's horse in a race, his rival, Kendall (Elliott), conspires to have the horse's train car set on fire. Checkers rescues the horse, and, when Pert is kidnapped, Checkers saves her, too. Pert rides her horse to victory against Kendall's entry. 7 reels

THE SPLENDID SIN (Sept. 7, 1919); D: Howard M. Mitchell; W: Denison Clift (scr), Emil Forst (st); C: Walter Williams; Cast: Madlaine Traverse, Charles Clary, Jeanne Calhoun, Wheeler Oakman, Elinor Hancock, George Hackathorne, Edwin Booth Tilton • An English explorer, Sir Charles (Clary), and his American wife, Marion (Traverse), are unable to have children. Charles's sister, Gertrude (Calhoun), who was not able to marry before she died in childbirth, leaves behind a child. Marion tells Charles the child is theirs, but when he returns from an expedition she has to explain the truth to prevent him from killing Stephen Hartley (Oakman), whom he suspects of having an affair with Marion. 5 reels

BROKEN COMMANDMENTS (Sept. 14, 1919); D: Frank Beal; W: Ruth Ann Baldwin (scr), John B. Clymer (st); C: Friend F. Baker; Cast: Gladys Brockwell, William Scott, Tom Santschi, G. Raymond Nye, Spottiswoode Aitken, Margaret McWade, Lule Warrenton • A young woman, Nella Banard (Brockwell), shelters two escaped convicts, Austin (Scott) and Berger (Nye), at her home in the Redwoods. Austin makes love to her and marries Nella, but is re-arrested and sent to prison. Nella is pregnant and marries John (Santschi), a novelist. On a research visit to prison, John is intrigued by one man's story and invites him home upon his release. The man turns out to be Austin, and the truth comes out. John offers to release Nella, but Austin suggests they toss dice for her, and lets John win by using loaded dice. 4,600'

EVANGELINE (Sept. 21, 1919); D: Raoul Walsh; W: Raoul Walsh, Henry Wadsworth Longfellow (poem); C: J.D. Jennings; Cast: Miriam Cooper, Albert Roscoe, Spottiswoode Aitken, James A. Marcus, Paul Weigel • The story of Longfellow's poem is dramatized, as an 18th century marriage is broken up by British soldiers. The groom, Gabriel (Roscoe), is exiled to Louisiana, but cannot forget his Evangeline (Cooper). Years later, Gabriel is nursed by his long-lost love, and dies in her arms. The tale is book-ended by a modern couple who stop quarrelling after hearing the poem. 5,200'

LA BELLE RUSSE (Sept. 21, 1919); D: Charles J. Brabin; W: Charles J. Brabin, David Belasco (play); C: George Lane; Cast: Theda Bara, Warburton Gamble, Marian Stewart, Robert Lee Keeling, William B. Davidson, Alice Wilson, Robert Vivian, Lewis Broughton • Phillip (Gamble), an English aristocrat, is disowned by his family when he marries a French dancer, Fleurette (Bara). Phillip enlists during the war but returns from France and is unable to find his love at the family castle. There is a misunderstanding when another dancer, known as La Belle Russe (Bara), shows up, bearing a striking resemblance to Fleurette. La Belle Russe turns out to be Fleurette's twin who hoped to replace her ailing sister in Phillip's aristocratic family. 5,400'

THE MERRY-GO-ROUND (Sept. 21, 1919); D: Edmund Lawrence; W: Douglas Bronston (scr), Richard Washburn Child (st), Philip E. Hubbard (st); C: Frank B. Good; Cast: Peggy Hyland, Jack Mulhall, Edward Jobson, Edwin B. Tilton, Vera Lewis, Robert Walker, Willard Louis, Lule Warrenton • A financial wizard driven to bankruptcy, Jack (Mulhall), serendipitously becomes owner of a failing circus and turns it into a success. He falls in love with the teenaged ticket-taker (Hyland), who turns out to be Susie Pomeroy, kidnapped as a baby from the financier (Tilton) who ruined Jack's fortune. Returning Susie to her family proves to be a miserable experience for her. However, on her 18th birthday, Jack rescues her with marriage. 5 reels

THE WINNING STROKE (Sept. 28, 1919); D: Edward Dillon; W: Raymond L. Schrock (scr), Edward Sedgwick (st); C: Al Leach; Cast: George Walsh, Jane McAlpine, John Leslie, William T. Hayes, Louis Estes, John Woodford, Sidney Marion, Byron Douglas • A jealous Yale student, Paul Browning (Leslie), tries to keep Buck (Walsh) from participating in a boating race. He plants a letter on Buck about a deal to throw the race, which is found by the coach. Buck's girlfriend, Aida (McAlpine), the dean's niece, is able to straighten things out. After Yale wins the race, Buck repays Browning in a bruising fight. 5 reels • The scene of the Yale varsity race on the Thames River in Connecticut was filmed from a seaplane by Howard Plimpton, considered Fox's daredevil cameraman.

THE LOST PRINCESS (Oct. 5, 1919); D: Scott R. Dunlap; W: Scott R. Dunlap (scr), Joseph Anthony Roach (st); C: George Schneiderman; Cast: Albert Ray, Elinor Fair, George Hernandez, Maggie Fisher, Edward Cecil, A. Burt Wesner, H.C. Simmons, Fred Bond • Sam (Ray), a farm worker, goes to the city to become a newspaper reporter. Ethel (Fair), a sympathetic columnist, introduces him to her editor, who is in love with her. All Sam has to do is come up with a story. Ethel suggests he find the lost princess of Burvania. Ethel turns out to be the princess and Sam has to rescue her from a trap. Sam wakes up to realize he has dreamed the story, but he is able to write another, which earns him success and Ethel. 5 reels

SACRED SILENCE (Oct. 12, 1919); D: Harry F. Millarde; W: Thomas F. Fallon (scr), Roy Sommerville (adpt), Robert Peyton Carter (play), Anne Alice Chapin (play); C: George W. Lane; Cast: William Russell, Agnes Ayres, George McQuarrie, James Morrison, Tom Brooke • Lt. Ralph Harrison (Morrison) is having an affair with the wife of Major Marston (MacQuarrie). Capt. Jim Craig (Russell) intervenes with Mrs. Marston to save Ralph from dishonor. Marston discovers Harrison with her and kills him, placing the blame on Craig. Craig flees to avoid a scandal but is tracked down by Secret Service agent Madge Summers (Ayres), who falls in love with him. Craig is arrested. Mrs. Marston continues to be unfaithful until the Major murders her then confesses to killing Harrison. Craig and Madge find happiness together. 6 reels

LAST OF THE DUANES (Oct. 12, 1919); D: J. Gordon Edwards; W: Charles Kenyon, Zane Grey (short story); C: John W. Boyle; Cast: William Farnum, Louise Lovely, Frances Raymond, Harry De Vere, Charles Clary, G. Raymond Nye, Clarence Burton, Lamar Johnstone, Henry J. Hebert • Buck Duane (Farnum), the son of an outlaw, kills in self-defense and hides out in the hills. Rescuing Jenny (Lovely) from the dreaded Bland gang, Buck is wounded. Nursed by Jenny, Buck falls in love with her. Buck is then arrested, but agrees to help the Texas Rangers find a gang of outlaws. The gang is captured during a bank robbery and Buck is pardoned. He and Jenny marry. 7 reels • This was the first of four versions of the Zane Grey novel, all filmed under the same title, between 1919 and 1942.

KATHLEEN MAVOURNEEN (Oct. 12, 1919); D: Charles J. Brabin; W: Charles J. Brabin, Dion Boucicault (play); Cast: Theda Bara, Edward O'Connor, Jennie Dickerson, Raymond McKee, Marc McDermott, Marcia Harris, Henry Hallam, Harry Gripp, Morgan Thorpe • Kathleen (Bara), a poor Irish girl, reluctantly gives in to a marriage proposal from Squire Traise (McDermott) when he threatens to evict her family from his land. Years later, Traise, short of funds, wants to marry wealthy Lady Clancarthy (Harris) and get rid of Kathleen. Blacksmith Terence (McKee), Kathleen's true love, rescues her from a plot, but is sentenced to hang for killing one of the conspirators. Kathleen awakens to find it was all a dream. She turns down Traise's offer of marriage and accepts Terence's. Her family is permitted to stay on the squire's land. 5–6 reels

THE SPEED MANIAC (Oct. 19, 1919); D: Edward LeSaint; W: Denison Clift, (scr), H.H. Van Loan (st); C: Fred Granville; Cast: Tom Mix, Eva Novak, Lee Shumway, Helen Wright, Jack Curtis, George Stone, George H. Hackathorn, Buck Jones • Ranch owner Billy (Mix), who has invented a new car engine, is fleeced in San Francisco and ends up helping a prizefighter, McClusky (Shumway). Billy bets on McClusky in a big fight, but finds out he has been drugged. Billy gets in the ring and knocks out Tiger Doran. Billy is reunited with his father (French), who owns a motor corporation and ends up using his invention in an exciting car race, which he wins along with the love of Pearl Matthews (Novak), whom he rescued along the way. 5 reels • The inspiration for this story came from Sol Wurtzel, who saw footage of a spectacular car crash a Fox News cameraman had filmed.

SNARES OF PARIS (Oct. 19, 1919); D: Howard M. Mitchell; W: Denison Clift; C: Walter Williams; Cast: Madlaine Traverse, Charles Arling, Frank Leigh, Jack Rollens, Josef Swickard • Marguerite (Traverse), the wife of French diplomat Emile (Arling), protects her past by agreeing to help a villain, Belloc (Leigh), obtain secret information about a trade agreement her husband is about to sign. Marguerite's son Fernand (Rollens), the result of Belloc's seduction when she had just left the convent, gets into a fight which results in Belloc's death. When the truth is exposed about her previous relationships, Emile forgives her. 5 reels

CHASING RAINBOWS (Oct. 26, 1919); D: Frank Beal; W: Ruth Ann Baldwin, Karl Harriman (novel); C: Friend F. Baker; Cast: Gladys Brockwell, William Scott, Richard Rosson, Harry Dunkinson, Irene Aldwyn, Walter Long, Claire McDowell • Sadie (Brockwell), a railroad station waitress, takes a job at a desert town restaurant after discovering her boyfriend Jim (Long) is married. She falls in love with Billy (Scott), the manager, who goes prospecting for gold so he can afford to marry Sadie. Meanwhile, Jim, running from the law, promises never to return if Sadie gets him enough money to go east. Jim reveals the man he shot was Billy, but, to Sadie's relief, Billy returns and they marry. 4,151'

A GIRL IN BOHEMIA (Nov. 2, 1919); D: Howard M. Mitchell; W: Denison Clift, H.B. Daniel (play); C: Frank Good; Cast: Peggy Hyland, Josef Swickard, L.C. Shumway, Betty Schade, Edward Cecil, Melbourne MacDowell, Winter Hall, J. Montgomery Carlyle • With her manuscript on Bohemian life in Greenwich Village rejected, aspiring author and society girl, Winifred (Hyland), elopes with De Lancy (Cecil), an unemployed actor who is plotting to steal her money. De Lancy gets into a fight with Cleo (Schade), his partner in the scheme, in which Cleo dies. Winifred is accused, but her ex-fiancé Richard (Shumway) is able to get the truth from De Lancy. Winifred wakes up and realizes it was all a dream. She marries Richard and her novel becomes a success. 4,800'

SHOULD A HUSBAND FORGIVE? (Nov. 9, 1919); D: R.A. Walsh; W: R.A. Walsh; C: J.D. Jennings; Cast: Miriam Cooper, Mrs. James K. Hackett, Eric Mayne, Vincent Coleman, Lyster Chambers, Peggy Standing, Charles Craig, Martha Mansfield, James Marcus • Mary Carroll (Hackett) is thrown out by her husband's wealthy family after she has had an affair that led to her husband's (Mayne) death in a duel. John Jr. (Coleman), the son Mary has not seen in many years, falls in love with Ruth Fulton (Cooper), daughter of a horse trainer who is now Mary's secretary. Ruth discovers that Mary is John's mother and convinces her to confess everything to her son. Not ready to forgive his mother, John is angry with Ruth until she rides his horse to victory in a race. 6 reels

VAGABOND LUCK (Nov. 16, 1919); D: Scott Dunlap; W: Scott Dunlap (scr), J. Anthony Roach (scr), James Frank Tinney (st); C: George Schneiderman; Cast: Albert Ray, Elinor Fair, Jack Rollens, John Cossar, William Ryno, George Millum, Al Fremont, Lloyd Bacon, Johnny Ries • Jimmie (Ray), a jockey fired for being overweight, is in love with penniless Joy (Fair), whose family desperately needs money. Joy enters the aging Vagabond, the last of the family's racehorses, in a big race. Her brother Harry (Rollens), convinced by a crooked bookie (Fremont) to place a big bet, mortgages his half of the family home to bet on Vagabond. Jimmie discovers that Vagabond goes into a wild dash on wet ground, and a prayer for rain allows Vagabond to win the race. Jimmie, meanwhile, wins Joy's love. 5 reels

LURE OF AMBITION (Nov. 16, 1919); D: Edmund Lawrence; W: Julia Burnham (scr & st), Edmund Lawrence (st); C: H. Alderson Leach; Cast: Theda Bara, Thurlow Bergen, William B. Davidson, Dan Mason, Ida Waterman, Amelia Gardner, Robert Paton Gibbs, Dorothy Drake, Peggy Parr • A nobleman, Cyril Ralston (Davidson), provides Olga (Bara), a poor stenographer, with a suite at a fashionable New York hotel. He promises to marry her, but returns to England. Olga vows revenge and follows him, but finds out that he is already married. While Ralston continues to pursue Olga, she becomes the Duke of Rutledge's (Bergen) private secretary and stops his insane wife (Waterman) from killing him. The duchess dies of a heart attack and Olga marries Rutledge. 5 reels • This was the final film Theda Bara made for William Fox.

EASTWARD HO! (Nov. 16, 1919); D: Emmett J. Flynn; W: Roy Somerville, William MacLeod Raine (st); C: George Lane; Cast: William Russell, Lucille Lee Stewart, Johnny Hines, Charles A. Stevenson, Mary Hay, Thomas Delmar • Arizona ranchers choose Buck (Russell) to get them out of a cattle-options swindle by Easterners. In New York, Buck enlists the help of syndicate head Casper Whitford (Stevenson) and falls in love with his daughter Beatrice (Stewart). After Beatrice assumes the worst when she sees Buck with another woman (Hay), she accepts a proposal from Clarendon Bromfield (Cain), who swindled the ranchers. Buck is framed for a murder by Bromfield, but is bailed out by Whitford and is able to retrieve the ranchers' property. 5 reels

THIEVES (Nov. 23, 1919); D: Frank Beal; W: Douglas Bronston (scr), Will C. Beale (st); C: Friend F. Baker; Cast: Gladys Brockwell, William Scott. Howard Mack, Jeanne Calhoun, Spike Robinson, Bobby Starr, John Cossar, Yukio Aoyama, Marie James • After Mazie (Brockwell), a thief trying to go straight, is arrested for shoplifting, Allison Cabot (Calhoun), who charged her, becomes her benefactor. Mazie and her ex-thief boyfriend, Jimmy (Scott), arrange to retrieve documents from Henry (Mack), the leader of their previous gang, so they can exonerate Allison's lover, who has been jailed. The couple then goes straight for good. 5 reels

LOST MONEY (Nov. 30, 1919); D: Edmund Lawrence; W: Denison Clift; C: Walter Williams; Cast: Madlaine Traverse, George McDaniel, Henry Hebert, Edward B. Tilton • Wealthy Ox Lanyon (McDaniel) entrusts his South African diamond field to neighbor Graham Atherstone (Tilton). When Graham believes Ox is dead, he takes over the property. For revenge, Ox takes Graham's daughter Judith (Traverse) to the desert, but has a change of heart and saves her from death by giving her their only water. Grateful to Ox by the time they are rescued and understanding his anger, Judith saves him by saying they have married. Graham's house is later attacked by Kaffirs and Ox brings soldiers to quash the revolt. Graham allows Judith to marry Ox. 5 reels

WINGS OF THE MORNING (Nov. 30, 1919); D: J. Gordon Edwards; W: Charles Kenyon, Louis Tracy (novel); Cast: William Farnum, Herschel Mayall, Frank Elliott, G. Raymond Nye, Clarence Burton, Harry De Vere, Louise Lovely, Genevieve Blinn • A British captain in Singapore, Robert (Farnum), is caught up in an affair between the wife of his colonel (Mayall), Lady Costabel (Blinn), and Lord Ventnor (Elliott). To protect the wife's reputation, Robert takes blame for the affair, leaves the army and works as a sailor. He rescues Iris (Lovely), a ship owner's daughter, after a wreck and they fall in love on a desert isle. They fight off pirates and are rescued by Ventnor, Iris's suitor. Ventnor exposes Robert, but Costabel clears him. Robert is restored to the service, and he marries Iris. 6 reels

THE FEUD (Dec. 7, 1919); D: Edward LeSaint; W: Charles Kenyon; C: J. Dev Jennings, John Leezer, Irving Rosenberg; Cast: Tom Mix, Eva Novak, Claire McDowell, J. Arthur Mackley, John Cossar, Mollie McConnell, Lloyd Bacon, Joseph Bennett, Jean Calhoun, Frank Thorne • Before the Civil War, Jere (Mix) and Betty (Novak) are children of feuding Kentucky families. Betty's father (Cossar) threatens to kill Jere if they speak again. After Betty's brother (Bacon) kills Jere's father in a duel, Jere leaves and plans to send for Betty. Jere's sister writes that Betty married another, and tells Betty that Jere is dead. Jere and Betty then marry others. After Jere and his wife die during an Indian massacre, their baby grows up and marries Betty's daughter. The birth of their son ends the feud. 5–6 reels • Lloyd Bacon became a prominent director of films from 1924 through 1953.

THE BEAST (Dec. 7, 1919) Reissue

THE WEB OF CHANCE (Dec. 14, 1919); D: Alfred E. Green; W: Donald Bronston, Edgar Franklin (novel); C: Frank Good; Cast: Peggy Hyland, Harry Hamm, E.B. Tilton, William Machin, George Dromgold, Sam Appel • Dorothy (Hyland), niece of a detective, uses disguises to shadow Arthur (Hamm), the suspect in a million-dollar contract theft. Arthur, however, is himself under an alias and turns out to be the head of the company and is operating this way to fulfill his father's will. After chases and adventures, Dorothy and Arthur apprehend the thief and then get married. 5 reels

THE LINCOLN HIGHWAYMAN (Dec. 21, 1919); D: Emmett J. Flynn; W: Emmett J. Flynn (scr). Jules Furthman (adpt), Paul Dickey (play); C: Clyde De Vinna; E: C.R. Wallace; Cast: William Russell, Lois Lee, Frank Brownlee, Jack Connolly, Edward Piel, Harry Spingler, Edwin Booth Tilton • While Marian (Lee) travels along the California coast with her society family to a weekend party, they are robbed of their jewelry by the infamous Lincoln Highwayman. At the party, Marian suspects Jimmy (Russell), but soon falls in love with him. Steele (Piel), a Secret Service agent in love with Marian, is unable to nab the gang, but Jimmy captures them and gets a financial reward and Marian's love. 5 reels • Some scenes were shot on the Lincoln Highway in the Rocky Mountains.

TIN PAN ALLEY (Dec. 28, 1919); D: Frank Beal; W: J. Anthony Roach, William Charles Lengel (article); Cast: Albert Ray, Elinor Fair, George Hernandez, Louis Natho, Kate Price, Ardito Mellinino, Frank Weed, Thomas A. Persee • Tommy (Ray), an unemployed violinist, is inspired by June (Fair), a cigarette girl in his boardinghouse, to write a hit song. Suddenly popular, Tommy forgets about June and falls for Mona (Mellonino), a musical performer. His publisher requests a new song but Tommy is not capable of writing it. His money spent, his newfound friends gone, he marries June, moves to a home and writes the hit his manager requested. 5 reels

1920 Releases

FLAMES OF THE FLESH (Jan. 4, 1920); D: Edward J. LeSaint; W: Dorothy Yost (scr), Forest Halsey (st), Clara Beranger (st); Cast: Gladys Brockwell, William Scott, Harry Spingler, Ben Deely, Charles K. French, Louis Fitzroy, Mme. Rosita Marstini, Josephine Crowell, Nigel De Brulier • Candace (Brockwell), ruined by an old man, Simon Eastcoat (French), sets out to take revenge on all men. She goes to Paris and is taught by a courtesan (Crowell) how to become a seductress. She changes her name to Laure, but actually falls in love with Simon Eastcoat's son, Bruce. When Simon shows up in Paris, Laure commits suicide rather than disgrace Bruce, the man she loves. 5 reels

WHAT WOULD YOU DO? (Jan. 11, 1920); D: Edmund Lawrence; W: Denison Clift; C: Walter E. Williams; Cast: Madlaine Traverse, George McDaniel, Frank Elliott, Charles K. French, Lenore Lynard, Bud Geary, Edwin Booth Tilton, Cordelia Callahan • Claudia (Traverse) marries an old friend, Curtis (Elliott), after her husband, Hugh (McDaniel), entangled in a stock swindle by his partner, is thought to have committed suicide in South America. The unfaithful Curtis falls from a horse and is paralyzed. He eventually commits suicide, allowing Claudia to be happily reunited with Hugh, who returns after having made a fortune. 5 reels

THE SHARK (Jan. 18, 1920); D: Dell Henderson; W: Thomas F. Fallon; C: Joseph Ruttenberg; Cast: George Walsh, Robert Broderick, William G. Nally, James Mack, Henry Pemberton, Marie Pagano, Mary Hall • Shark Rawley (Walsh), a sailor aboard a tramp steamer, rescues society girl Doris (Hall), trapped on the ship by one of the crew. Shark battles the brutal Captain Sanchez (Nally) and his men, then abandons ship with Doris when a fire breaks out. By the time the rescue ship reaches them, Shark and Doris have fallen in love. 5 reels

THE CYCLONE (Jan. 25, 1920); D: Cliff Smith; W: J. Anthony Roach (scr), Col. Todhunter Marigold (st); C: Frank Good; Cast: Tom Mix, Colleen Moore, Henry Herbert, William Ellingford • Sergeant Tim Ryerson (Mix) of the Northwest Mounted Police is visiting his girlfriend, Sylvia (Moore), when he discovers the ranch foreman, Baird (Hebert), is leading a gang that smuggles Chinese laborers into the U.S. Baird kidnaps Sylvia and Tim pursues him to Vancouver's Chinatown, where he breaks up the gang and rescues Sylvia. 3,984'

FAITH (Jan. 25, 1920); D: Howard M. Mitchell; W: Joseph Anthony Roach; Cast: Peggy Hyland, J. Parks Jones, Edward Hearn, Winter Hall, Edwin B. Tilton, Milla Davenport, Frederick Herzog • In a Scottish village, Peggy (Hyland), the niece of wealthy Sir Kent MacGregor (Tilton), is in love with David (Jones), the shepherd son of a faith healer (Hall). A conniving Dr. Kyle (Hearn), however, is scheming to marry her. Unaware he is being used in the plot, MacGregor has David and his father placed in jail so Peggy will marry Kyle. When Peggy becomes ill and no one can cure her, the faith healer is released and brings her back to health. Kyle is arrested for his scheme and Peggy is allowed to marry David. 4,241'

HEART STRINGS (Jan. 25, 1920); D: J. Gordon Edwards; W: E. Lloyd Sheldon (scr), Henry Albert Phillips (st); C: John W. Boyle; Cast: William Farnum, Gladys Coburn, Betty Hilburn, Paul Cazeneuve, Robert Cain, Rowland G. Edwards, Kate Blancke • Pierre (Farnum), a gifted and good-hearted French violinist, attracts New York socialite Kathleen (Coburn) whose jealous fiancé, Rupert (Cain), joins forces with a former grudge holder against Pierre. They set Pierre up to look like a jewel thief. However, the co-conspirator crumbles when confronted by Pierre and reveals Rupert's plans. 6 reels

HER ELEPHANT MAN (Feb. 1, 1920); D: Scott Dunlap; W: Isabelle Johnston, Pearl Doles Bell (novel); C: George Schneiderman; Cast: Shirley Mason, Albert Roscoe, Henry J. Hebert, Ardito Mellonino, Harry Todd, Dorothy Lee • Philip (Roscoe) travels to Africa when he learns his wife (Mellonino) married him only for money. Joining circus men on an elephant hunt, he finds Joan (Mason), a missionary's orphaned daughter. Years later, Joan, a bareback rider in the circus, is in love with Philip, who tends to the elephants. He rejects her advances and leaves the circus. When he finds out his wife has divorced him, he returns to Joan amidst a torrential storm that destroys the circus tent. 5 reels

THE LAST STRAW (Feb. 8, 1920); D: Denison Clift; W: Denison Clift, Harold Titus (serial story); C: Vernon

Walker; Cast: Buck Jones, Vivian Rich, Jane Tallent, Colin Kenny, Charles Le Moyne, Bob Chandler, William Gillis, H.W. Padgett, Hank Bell, Zeib Morris, Lon Poff • Tom (Jones), a ranch-hand romantically involved with his boss, Jane (Rich), suspects that her foreman, Hepburn (Le Moyne), is part of a gang of rustlers. Setting out to round up the gang, Tom is captured by the outlaws and left to die. Freeing himself, he returns to shoot it out with the gang and win Joan. 4,822' • This was Buck Jones's first leading role for Fox. The storyline was cut from the same cloth as the Tom Mix westerns.

THE STRONGEST (Feb. 15, 1920); D: R.A. Walsh; W: R.A. Walsh, Georges Clemenceau (novel); Cast: Renee Adorée, Carlo Liten, Harrison Hunter, Florence Malone, Madame Tressida, Jean Gauthier De Trigny, Georgette Gauthier De Trigny, Hal Horne • A French businessman, Harle (Hunter), wants his daughter Claudia (Adorée) to marry a count, but she is in love with Maurice (Horne), an American. When her father's disgruntled employees kidnap Claudia, Marquis Henri (Liten), who is her real father through an affair with her mother, is killed in a rescue attempt. Maurice finally helps her escape abduction. The truth about her real father frees her to travel to America and marry. 5–6 reels

SHOD WITH FIRE (Feb. 15, 1920); D: Emmett J. Flynn; W: Anthony J. Roach, Harold Titus (novel); E: C.R. Wallace; Cast: William Russell, Helen Ferguson, Betty Schade, Robert Cain, George Stewart, Nelson McDowell, Jack Connolly • A cowboy, Bruce (Russell), takes Ned (Cain), a drunk, to his ranch to reform him. When Ned's wife, Ann (Ferguson) shows up, he accuses her of an affair with Bruce and sends her to a mine he swindled from another man. Aware of the swindle, Bruce warns Ann to keep Ned away from the mine. When Ned goes to the mine, Bruce is unable to save him from the avenger. When Ned is killed, Ann is free to marry Bruce. 4,840'

A DAUGHTER OF THE GODS (Feb. 15, 1920) Reissue

CLEOPATRA (Feb. 15, 1920) Reissue

A TALE OF TWO CITIES (Feb. 15, 1920) Reissue

THE HONOR SYSTEM (Feb. 15, 1920) Reissue

SALOME (Feb. 15, 1920) Reissue

THE HELL SHIP (Feb. 22, 1920); D: Scott R. Dunlap; W: Denison Clift; C: George Schneiderman; Cast: Madlaine Traverse, Alan Roscoe, Betty Bouton, Dick La Reno, Jack Curtis, Frederick Bond, William Ryno • Paula (Traverse) has taken over a tramp ship after her father is killed in a mutiny. She rescues and falls in love with John (Roscoe), the survivor of a shipwreck. After helping her put down another mutiny, John goes ashore at San Francisco and retrieves Paula's long-lost sister, Glory (Bouton). Once again at sea, the crew rebels and sets fire to the ship. John and the women escape in a raft. Paula, believing that John is in love with Glory, is about to kill herself, but is surprised by John's love for her. 5 reels

THE DEVIL'S RIDDLE (Feb. 29, 1920); D: Frank Beal; W: Ruth Ann Baldwin (scr), Edwina Levin (st); C: Sam Landers; Cast: Gladys Brockwell, William Scott, Richard Cummings, Claire McDowell, Easter Walters, Nicholas Dunaew, Kate Price, Louis Fitzroy, Chance Ward, Vera Lewis • Separated for a long time from Dr. Jim Barnes (Scott), whom she saved in a snowstorm, Esther (Brockwell) joins a theatrical troupe. When Jim finds her again, a jealous member of the troupe speaks badly of Esther's morals. Jim, believing this, leaves Esther, who goes to New York and becomes engaged to an artist. Sam (Fitzroy), a friend of Esther's, brings Jim back to save her from an unhappy marriage. 5 reels

THE DAREDEVIL (March 7, 1920); D: Tom Mix; W: J. Anthony Roach (scr), Tom Mix (st); C: L. Dev Jennings; Cast: Tom Mix, Eva Novak, Charles K. French, L.C. Shumway, Sid Jordan, Lucille Younge, L.S. McKee, Pat Chrisman, George Hernandez, Harry Dunkinson • An Eastern railroad magnate (Hernandez) sends his son Timothy (Mix) to Arizona to keep him out of trouble. Tim falls in love with Alice (Novak), whose father is a superintendent of the railroad (French). Tim tracks down bandits who have been robbing trains and threatening Alice's father's job security. When Alice is kidnapped by the gang, Tim rescues her, returns the stolen money and is redeemed in his father's eyes. 5 reels

BLACK SHADOWS (March 7, 1920); D: Howard M. Mitchell; W: Joseph Anthony Roach (scr), Natalie S. Lincoln (st); Cast: Peggy Hyland, Alan Roscoe, Correan Kirkham, Henry Hebert, Edwin Booth Tilton, Estelle Evans, Cora Drew • Marjorie (Hyland), heiress Janet Fordyce's (Kirkham) companion, is suspected in the theft of jewels. When Marjorie sees Janet in the process of stealing, she keeps it to herself. Janet's brother, Duncan (Roscoe), enamored of Marjorie, discovers that Janet has been hypnotized and is under the control of the villainous Chester Barnard (Hebert). Duncan clears Marjorie, and they marry. 5 reels

THE ADVENTURER (March 14, 1920); D: J. Gordon Edwards; W: E. Lloyd Sheldon; C: John W. Boyle; Cast: William Farnum, Estelle Taylor, Paul Cazeneuve, Kenneth Casey, Dorothy Drake, Harry Southard, Pat Hartigan, James Devine, Sadie Radcliffe • Don Caesar (Farnum), a penniless nobleman in 17th century Spain, in love with a dancer at court, Maritana (Taylor), is imprisoned for fighting a duel during Holy Week. He becomes a pawn in the corrupt Prime Minister Don José's (Cazeneuve) efforts to have Maritana lure the king (Southard) with her wiles. Don José gets her into the court by having her marry Don Caesar just before he is executed. But Don Caesar escapes, rescues Maritana from the king and exposes Don José's plan. 6,062'

A MANHATTAN KNIGHT (March 14, 1920); D: George A. Beranger; W: George A. Beranger (scr), Paul Sloane (scr), Gelett Burgess (novel); C: Charles Gilson; Cast: George Walsh, Virginia Hammond, William H. Budd, Warren Cook, John Hopkins, William T. Hayes, Cedric Ellis, Charles Slattery, Louis Wolheim • John Fenton

(Walsh), an athletic Manhattanite inadvertently solves his parentage when he stumbles upon an attempted suicide. He helps Belle (Hammond) protect the reputation of her wounded half-brother (Budd), who has stolen jewels from their uncle (Cook), by concealing the shooting from the police. John recovers the jewels from a crooked butler (Hopkins) and finds out he is a distant relative of Belle, having been kidnapped by thieves when he was an infant. John and Belle become engaged. 4,855'

DURAND OF THE BADLANDS (March 21, 1920) Reissue

MOLLY AND I (March 28, 1920); D: Howard M. Mitchell; W: Isabel Johnston, Frank W. Adams (novel); C: George Schneiderman; E: Carr Himm; Cast: Shirley Mason, Alan Roscoe, Harry Dunkinson, Lilie Leslie • Shirley Brown (Mason) idolizes Philip (Roscoe), a brilliant novelist who lives at her boardinghouse. When she learns he is losing his eyesight and needs money to have an operation in Italy, she convinces him to marry her, sight unseen, so she can receive a $5,000 legacy and pay for the surgery. Philip regains his sight, and, on his return, Shirley uses an alias to rekindle his interest in her. 5,250'

THE TATTLERS (Apr. 4, 1920); D: Howard M. Mitchell; W: Denison Clift, Henry Clifford Colwell (play); C: Walter E. Williams; Cast: Madlaine Traverse, Howard Scott, Jack Rollens, Ben Deeley, Genevieve Blinn, Elinor Hancock, Correan Kirkham, Frank Whitson, Edwin Booth Tilton • Bess Rutherford (Traverse), humiliated by her drunken husband, Tom, leaves him so that she may live out of wedlock with long-time admirer Jim (Deeley). Bess's son, Jack (Rollens), has his engagement broken off because his fiancée's mother (Hancock) disapproves of Bess's scandalous behavior. Jack ends up killing a rival. Bess, at a breaking point, is about to drink poison but awakens from this nightmare. Husband Tom promises never to drink again. 5 reels

THE MOTHER OF HIS CHILDREN (Apr. 11, 1920); D: Edward LeSaint; W: Charles J. Wilson (scr), Barbara La Marr Deely (st); C: Harry Harris; Cast: Gladys Brockwell, William Scott, Frank Leigh, Nigel De Brulier, Golda Madden, Nancy Caswell, Jean Eaton • Richard (Scott), a sculptor in Paris, and the visiting Princess Yve (Brockwell) fall in love. Count Tolstoff (Leigh), also in love with the princess, tries to destroy Richard's prize-winning statues, but Yve's loyal servant, Hadji (de Brulier), kills him. When Richard is arrested for the crime, the princess discovers he is married. However, the servant confesses his guilt and Richard is told his wife had died on an ocean voyage. Richard marries Princess Yve. 4,503'

DESERT LOVE (Apr. 11, 1920); D: Jacques Jaccard; W: Jacques Jaccard, Tom Mix; C: Frank Good; E: Lloyd L. Nosler; Cast: Tom Mix, Francelia Billington, Eva Novak, Lester Cuneo, Charles K. French, Jack Curtis • Buck (Mix), a newly appointed sheriff, quickly sets out to avenge the bandits who murdered his parents and succeeds in killing most of the gang. A rancher (French), whose daughter, Dolly (Novak), is Buck's fiancée, thinks she has been having an affair with the bandit leader's son and forces her to marry him. Buck rescues her in time and kills the remaining outlaws. 5 reels

WOULD YOU FORGIVE? (Apr. 18, 1920); D: Scott Dunlap; W: Jules Furthman; C: Vernon Walker; Cast: Vivian Rich, Tom Chatterton, Ben Deely, Lilie Leslie, Nancy Caswell • John (Chatterton) and Mary (Rich) want nothing more than a family. Mary secretly adopts a baby girl who is cared for by another woman, Clare (Leslie). Mary's former suitor, ex-con Paul (Deely), discovers the child and blackmails Mary out of valuable jewelry. John reports the theft and the police arrest Paul. In the process, John believes the infant is his wife's illegitimate child. However, Mary produces proof that the child is the offspring of John and his mistress. John begs for Mary's forgiveness. 5,670'

THE ORPHAN (Apr. 18, 1920); D: J. Gordon Edwards; W: Roy Somerville, Clarence E. Mulford (novel); C: John W. Boyle; Cast: William Farnum, Louise Lovely, Henry Hebert, Earl Crain, G. Raymond Nye, George Nichols, Harry De Vere, Olive White, Al Fremont, Carrie Clark Ward • A bandit known as The Orphan (Farnum) joins forces with Sheriff Shields (Nichols), fends off an Indian attack, and then rescues Shields's niece Helen (Lovely). Local ranchers oppose the alliance and create tension with Shields. When The Orphan recognizes one of the ranchers, Tex (Hebert), as his father's killer, he gets his revenge in a gun duel. With no further reason to be an outlaw, he settles down to a peaceful life with Helen. 5,696'

LEAVE IT TO ME! (Apr. 25, 1920); D: Emmett J. Flynn; W: Jules Furthman (scr), Arthur Jackson (st); C: Clyde De Vinna; Cast: William Russell, Eileen Percy, Marcella Daly, Hallam Cooley, Lucille Cavanaugh, William Elmer, Harvey Clark, Milla Davenport • To convince his fiancée Madge (Percy) that he is not just a wealthy idler, Dick (Russell) buys a clientless detective agency. He then hires some crooks to steal valuables from his rich friends. A friend, Tom (Cooley), who is engaged to Dick's sister Dot (Daley), engages him to retrieve sensitive letters from a vamp, Viola (Cavanaugh). Viola kidnaps Tom, and Dick has to rescue him. By retrieving all the goods stolen by his hired crooks, Dick changes Madge's opinion of him. 5 reels

THE SHE TIGER (May 2, 1920) Reissue title — The Love Thief

THE DEAD LINE (May 9, 1920); D: Dell Henderson; W: Paul H. Sloane; C: Charles Gilson; Cast: George Walsh, Irene Boyle, Baby Anita Lopez, Joseph Hanaway, Al Hart, Henry Pemberton, James Milady, Gus Weinberg, G.A. Stryker, Virginia Valli • In mountain country, Clay (Walsh) is in love with Mollie (Boyle) but cannot marry because of a feud between their families. Clay, branded a coward because he refuses to take up arms, protects a woman from moonshiners. During the fight, Mollie's family members are arrested, which frees her and Clay to live in peace. 5,019'

FORBIDDEN TRAILS (May 16, 1920); D: Scott R. Dunlap; W: Scott R. Dunlap, Charles Alden Seltzer (article); C: Vernon Walker; Cast: Buck Jones, Winifred Westover, Stanton Heck, William Elmer, George Kunkel, Fred Herzog, Harry Dunkinson, Edwin Booth Tilton • Quinton (Jones), a rancher, goes on a search to find and protect his late partner's daughter, Marion (Westover). Believing Marion is in league with Carrington (Heck), who is plotting to steal the ranch, Quinton investigates. Marion eventually turns to him when she realizes what Carrington is up to. A Mexican is bribed to testify against Quinton in a murder case, and Carrington then tries to kidnap Marion. Quinton rescues her and kills the villain. 5 reels

THE TERROR (May 16, 1920) Tom Mix Series; D: Jacques Jaccard; W: Jacques Jaccard (scr), Tom Mix (st); C: Frank Good; Cast: Tom Mix, Francelia Billington, Charles K. French, Lucille Younge, Joseph Bennett, Wilbur Higby • Deputy Marshal Bat Carson (Mix), investigating gold-shipment robberies at a mine, falls in love with Phyllis (Billington). Bat learns that Phyllis's brother (Bennett) is unknowingly leaking information to the thieves through his girlfriend, Fay (Younge). The leaders of the gang are saloon owner Con (Cuneo) and Sheriff Canby (French). Con kidnaps Phyllis before she can testify against the thieves. After a thrilling chase, Bat rescues her and races back to court to win both Phyllis's hand in marriage and her brother's freedom. 5 reels

LOVE'S HARVEST (May 23, 1920); D: Howard M. Mitchell; W: Isabel Johnston, Pearl Doles Bell (novel); C: George Schneiderman; Cast: Shirley Mason, Raymond McKee, Edwin B. Tilton, Lilie Leslie • Jane Day (Mason) is turned over to wealthy cousin Jim (McKee) after her stepfather's death then runs away to the city with her dog. She meets a theatrical producer, Allen Hamilton (Tilton), who discovers her musical talent and sends her to study in Paris. Jane meets cousin Jim there and falls in love with him. Torn between Hamilton and Jim, she realizes Jim is her true love. 5 reels

THE IRON HEART (May 30, 1920); D: Denison Clift, Paul Cazeneuve; W: Denison Clift; C: Walter Williams; E: Della Conley; Cast: Madlaine Traverse, George A. McDaniel, Edwin Booth Tilton, Melbourne MacDowell, Ben Deeley • Heiress to a steel mill, Esther Regan (Traverse) carries out her late father's wishes to protect his workers. A financial group, trying to gain control of the company, sends Darwin McAllister (McDaniel) to do the deed, but he is so impressed with the way the company is run that he helps Esther fight for the trust. Dan Cullen (Deely) is hired by the trust to sabotage a shipment, but Esther and Darwin, now romantically involved, rally the workers to complete the order on time. 5 reels

WHITE LIES (June 6, 1920); D: Edward J. LeSaint; W: Charles J. Wilson, Charles Reade (novel); C: Harry Harris; Cast: Gladys Brockwell, William Scott, Josephine Crowell, Evans Kirk, Violet Schram, Charles K. French, Howard Scott, Lule Warrenton • French Col. Raynal (French) claims that he will not foreclose on the Beaurepaire estate if daughter Josephine (Brockwell) marries him. Josephine, believing her boyfriend, Lt. Camille Du Jordin (Scott), has committed treason, agrees and they marry. Camille is cleared of treason and decorated for bravery. When Josephine believes Raynal has been killed in battle, she marries Camille and gives birth to a child. Reynal reappears and demands to know who fathered Josephine's baby. After discovering the truth, Reynal agrees to annul his marriage. 4,332'

A WORLD OF FOLLY (June 13, 1920); D: Frank Beal; W: Louis Stevens (scr), Jane Grogan (scr & st); C: R.E. Yeager; Cast: Vivian Rich, Aaron Edwards, Philo McCullough, Daisy Robinson, Augustus Phillips • A dashing playboy, Duke Tremaine (McCullough), rescues children from a car accident and befriends their mother, Helene Blair (Rich). This threatens to split up Helene's happy marriage to Raoul (Edwards) when he catches Duke in her bedroom. However, a friend (Phillips) of Raoul's uncovers the truth, that Duke forced his way into the bedroom, and that Helene is innocent. 5 reels

TWINS OF SUFFERING CREEK (June 20, 1920); D: Scott R. Dunlap; W: Jules G. Furthman, Ridgwell Cullum (novel); C: Clyde De Vinna; Cast: William Russell, Louise Lovely, E. Alyn Warren, William Ryno, Henry Hebert, Joe Ray, Florence Deshon, Malcolm Cripe, Helen Stone • Honest saloon owner Bill Lark (Russell) crosses paths with a cheater, Pemberton (Hebert), and instead of shooting it out right there, they play cards. Lark draws a losing hand and Pemberton gives him three days to live. Pemberton is also a bandit leader and persuades Jess (Deshon) to leave her husband, Scipio (Warren). Lark bravely retrieves Jess for Scipio, and, by the time the showdown arrives, he discovers Pemberton has been killed by Scipio. 5 reels

THE JOYOUS TROUBLEMAKER (June 27, 1920); D: J. Gordon Edwards; W: Charles Kenyon, Jackson Gregory (novel); C: John Boyle; Cast: William Farnum, Louise Lovely, Henry Hebert, Harry DeVere, G. Raymond Nye, Clarence Morgan, George Nichols, Sedley Brown, John Underhill • A wealthy lover of weekend outings, William (Farnum), buys a resort but runs into opposition from Beatrice (Lovely), who claims the property is on her land. They make an agreement that if he can build a cabin on the land, he can stay. Beatrice hires Joe Embry (Hebert) to prevent the construction, but the unsavory Embry ends up kidnapping her. William rescues her and they merge their holdings through marriage. 6 reels

CAMILLE OF THE YUKON (June 27, 1920) Reissue Title — The Silent Lie

THREE GOLD COINS (July 4, 1920); D: Clifford Smith; W: Alan J. Neitz (scr), H.H. Van Loan (st); C: Frank Good; Cast: Tom Mix, Margaret Loomis, Frank Whitson, Bert Hadley, Disk Rush, Margaret Cullington,

Sylvia Jocelyn, Bonnie Hill, Sid Jordan, Walt Robins, Frank Weed • A sure-shooting cowboy, Bob Fleming (Mix), wins three gold coins from millionaire Luther Reed (Whitson). Two swindlers, Ballinger (Hadley) and Berry (Rush), make Bob's ranch look like it is oil rich and sell stock to the townsfolk. Bob is held responsible for the swindle and arrested for being a notorious outlaw. After several adventures, Bob sets things straight and wins Reed's daughter, Betty (Loomis). 5 reels

A SISTER TO SALOME (July 4, 1920); P: William Fox; D: Edward J. LeSaint; W: Jules Furthman; C: Harry Harris; Cast: Gladys Brockwell, William B. Scott, Edwin B. Tilton, Ben Deeley • A famous opera singer, Elinore (Brockwell), has weird dreams while undergoing an operation. She becomes a siren of ancient Rome in love with Paul (Scott), a heretic for whom she poisons the high priest (Deely). She has other dreams of love triangles then awakens and finds the men in her dreams are part of her real life. 4,072'

SINK OR SWIM (July 18, 1920) Reissue Title — The Yankee Way • Although this was a reissue, it was reviewed in *Variety* as a new release with no mention of the 1917 version. It is possible some slight changes were made to the film as well.

THE SPIRIT OF GOOD (July 25, 1920); D: Paul Cazeneuve; W: Denison Clift (scr), Clifford Howard (st), Burke Jenkins (st); C: Walter Williams; Cast: Madlaine Traverse, Fred R. Stanton, Dick La Reno, Charles Smiley, Clo King • Deserted by her husband, showgirl Nell Gordon (Traverse) goes west and works in a dance hall. She and saloon owner Chuck (La Reno) conspire to get rid of a minister, Josiah (Smiley), who threatens their business. Nell pretends to join the congregation and converts Neal Bradford (Stanton), who falls in love with her. Nell becomes a convert, joins the congregation and, after vanquishing the saloon owner, starts a new life. 5 reels

THE ROSE OF NOME (Aug. 1, 1920); D: Edward J. LeSaint; W: Paul Schofield (scr), Barbara La Marr (st); C: Harry B. Harris; Cast: Gladys Brockwell, William Scott, Herbert Prior, Gertrude Ryan, Edward Peil Sr., Stanton Heck, Frank Thorne, Lule Warrenton, Georgie Woodthorpe • Rose Donnay (Brockwell) escapes her abusive husband, Tim (Peel). She is accompanied by Jack (Prior), who killed Tim and stole his money. In Nome, where Rose performs in Jack's dance hall, she discovers his unfaithfulness. Jack then shoots a Canadian Mountie (Heck) who is tracking him. Rose, an accomplice, is forced to accompany Jack, but Anatole (Scott), who has fallen in love with her, comes to the rescue with his sled dog and kills Jack. 5 reels

THE WHITE MOLL (Aug. 8, 1920); D: Harry F. Millarde; W: E. Lloyd Sheldon, Frank L. Packard (novel); C: Edward Wynard; Cast: Pearl White, Richard Travers, Jack Baston, Walter P. Lewis, Eva Gordon, John Woodford, George Pauncefort, Charles J. Slattery, John P. Wade • Rhoda (White) is forced by circumstance to help her once-wealthy father (Pauncefort), rob their church's poor box, whereupon he is shot and killed. The man who ruined her father is now penitent and vows to have Rhoda return his ill-gotten gains to all the people he robbed. She has several adventures in the underworld as an angel of mercy (the White Moll) and brings the leader (Baston) of a notorious gang to justice. 7 reels

THE SQUARE SHOOTER (Aug. 8, 1920); D: Paul Cazeneuve; W: Denison Clift; C: Vernon L. Walker; Cast: Buck Jones, Patsy De Forest, Charles K. French, Al Fremont, Fred Starr, Edwin Booth Tilton, Ernest Shields, Charles Force, Lon Poff, Orpha Alba • Chick Crandall (Jones), half-owner of a ranch, returns home after five years to find his foreman, Sam (Fremont), is a cattle rustler who has forced Barbara Hampton (De Forest) and her mother from their home. Disguising himself, Chick exposes and expels Sam and is rewarded with full ownership of the ranch. He then marries a grateful Barbara. 5 reels

THE LITTLE WANDERER (Aug. 15, 1920); D: Howard M. Mitchell; W: Denison Clift; C: George Schneiderman; Cast: Shirley Mason, Raymond McKee, Cecil Van Auker, Alice Wilson, Jack Pratt • Larry Hart (McKee), son of a newspaper publisher, upset that his father exploits the poor in his stories, sets out to reform a slum dweller. He meets and falls in love with a young girl, Jenny (Mason). She turns out to be the daughter of his father's crooked ex-partner Joe (Van Auker). Joe surfaces with a plan to blackmail Larry's father. Larry is able to correct the situation and gets his father's permission to marry Jenny. 5,240'

HER HONOR THE MAYOR (Aug. 22, 1920); D: Paul Cazeneuve; W: Denison Clift, Arlin Van Ness Hines (play); C: Walter Williams; Cast: Eileen Percy, Ramsey Wallace, Charles Force, Edwin Booth Tilton, William Fletcher • Julia Kennedy (Percy) is elected mayor over the animosity of her male opponent, District Attorney Frank Stanton (Wallace). Ward boss Jerry McGrath (Force) blackmails her by accusing a family member, John (Tilton), of embezzlement. Julia is able to turn the tables on Jerry with a similar charge. Julia finally earns the respect and love of her former opponent Stanton. 5 reels

IF I WERE KING (Aug. 22, 1920); D: J. Gordon Edwards; W: E. Lloyd Sheldon, Justin Huntly McCarthy (play); C: John W. Boyle; Cast: William Farnum, Betty Ross Clarke, Fritz Leiber, Walter Law, Henry Carvill, Claude Payton, V.V. Clogg, Harold Clairmont, Renita Johnston, Kathryn Chase • François Villon (Farnum), a vagabond poet, is released from prison and appointed as a constable for one week. If he can earn the love of Katherine (Clarke), King Louis's (Lieber) ward, his life will be spared. In the week, he overcomes the Grand Constable's (Law) forces and foils a plot to abduct the King, earning Katherine's love. 8 reels • The cost of this Special was $105,000, but world rentals of about $500,000 led to a profit of $129,000.

THE MAN WHO DARED (Aug. 29, 1920); D: Emmett J. Flynn; W: Jules Furthman; C: Clyde De Vinna; Cast:

William Russell, Eileen Percy, Frank Brownlee, Fred Warren, Lon Poff, Joe Ray • Corrupt sheriff Ed Cass (Brownlee) gets Mamie (Percy) to agree to marry him for exculpating her father (Warren) from a forgery charge. Cass then robs a saloon and frames Mamie's suitor, Jim (Russell). In jail, Jim has a religious experience and converts to Christianity. Mamie then finds a confession to the saloon robbery written by Cass, who has committed suicide. Mamie and Jim are free to marry. 6,320'

THE UNTAMED (Sept. 5, 1920); D: Emmett J. Flynn; W: H.P. Keeler, Max Brand (novel); C: Frank Good, Irving Rosenberg; Cast: Tom Mix, Pauline Stark, George Siegmann, Philo McCullough, James O. Barrows, Charles K. French, Pat Chrisman, Sid Jordan, Maj. J.A. McGuire • Whistling Dan (Mix), found in the desert as a boy, grows up to be an untamed man. He gets into a saloon brawl with Jim (Siegmann), an outlaw, and vows to kill him. His girlfriend, Kate (Starke), tries to prevent this, but is kidnapped by Jim. After a spate of abductions on both sides, Dan eradicates the gang in a blaze of violence. Somewhat tamed after this explosion, Dan settles down with Kate. 5 reels

FIREBRAND TREVISON (Sept. 5, 1920); D: Thomas N. Heffron; W: Denison Clift, Charles Alden Seltzer (novel); C: Vernon Walker; Cast: Buck Jones, Winifred Westover, Martha Mattox, Stanton Heck, Frank Clark, Joe Ray, Pat Hamman, Fong Hong • Trevison (Jones) owns a ranch which the railroad tries to acquire by sending representatives to negotiate. He takes an immediate dislike to Corrigan (Heck), who is traveling with his sweetheart, Rosalind (Westover), the company president's daughter. Corrigan conspires with a crooked judge to get the property for the railroad. After a series of misunderstandings with Rosalind and some adventures, Firebrand is able to keep his land and the girl. 5 reels

THE SKYWAYMAN (Sept. 5, 1920); D: James P. Hogan; W: Julius G. Furthman; Cast: Lt. Ormer Locklear, Louise Lovely, Sam DeGrasse, Ted McCann, Jack Brammall • Aviator and hero Captain Craig (Locklear) returns from war an amnesiac. Dr. Leveridge (DeGrasse) tells Craig's sweetheart, Virginia (Lovely), of a plan to restore Craig's memory. Leveridge suggests a fake robbery, but it is really a ruse to steal Virginia's family's jewels. As the robbery proceeds, Craig pursues the thieves by plane and hits his head in a crash, restoring his memory. Leveridge's crooked scheme is exposed and the thieves are arrested. 5 reels • Famed aviator Ormer Locklear died in a crash while filming a scene for this movie.

BRIDE #13 (Sept. 5, 1920) Serial; D: Richard Stanton; W: Edward Sedgwick (adpt. & scr), Thomas F. Fallon (scr); C: Horace C. Plimpton; Cast: Marguerite Clayton, Mary Christensen, Greta Hartman, William H. Lawrence, John O'Brien, Lyster Chambers, Edward F. Roseman • Episode #1: Snatched from the Altar. Episode #2: The Pirate Fangs. Episode #3: The Craft of Despair. Episode #4: The Vulture's Prey. Episode #5: The Torture Chamber. Episode #6: The Tarantula's Trail. Episode #7: Tongues of Flame. Episode #8: Entombed. Episode #9: Hurled from the Clouds. Episode #10: The Cavern of Terror. Episode #11: Greyhounds of the Sea. Episode #12: Creeping Peril. Episode #13: The Reefs of Tragedy. Episode #14: The Fiendish Tribesman. Episode #15: Thundering Vengeance.

WHILE NEW YORK SLEEPS (Sept. 12, 1920); D: Charles J. Brabin; W: Charles J. Brabin, Thomas F. Fallon; C: George W. Lane; Cast: Estelle Taylor, William Locke, Marc McDermott, Harry Southern, Earl Metcalf • Three episodes recount the melodramatic stories, each one revolving around unhappy married couples who become enmeshed in infidelity and murder. 8 reels • This was the big profit maker of the year, with $192,000.

MERELY MARY ANN (Sept. 12, 1920); D: Edward J. LeSaint; W: Edward J. LeSaint, Israel Zangwill (play); C: Friend F. Baker; Cast: Shirley Mason, Casson Ferguson, Harry Spingler, Georgia Woodthorpe, Babe London, Kewpie Morgan, Jean Hersholt, Paul Weigel • A London house worker, Mary Ann (Mason), meets Lancelot (Ferguson), a baronet's son with aspirations to be a musician. When Mary inherits a fortune, Lancelot breaks off the relationship from a sense of pride. Years later, when he finally becomes a successful musician, he returns to marry Mary. 4,555' • This is a remake of the 1916 film.

HUSBAND HUNTER (Sept. 19, 1920); D: Howard M. Mitchell; W: Joseph F. Poland, F. Scott Fitzgerald (short story); C: Walter Williams; E: Ralph Spence; Cast: Eileen Percy, Emory Johnson, Jane Miller, Evans Kirk, Edward McWade, John Steppling, Harry Dunkinson • Kent (Johnson) and Bob (Kirk) concoct a scheme to teach a flirtatious young socialite Myra (Percy) a lesson. Kent, her "boyfriend du jour," invites her to meet his family, but he presents a crude and obnoxious group. When Myra finds out it was a ruse, she retaliates by hiring a fake minister, then pretends to marry Kent and tells him the ceremony was all a joke. Kent, chastened, suggests they get married for real. 4,800'

FROM NOW ON (Sept. 26, 1920); D: Raoul Walsh; W: Raoul Walsh (scr), Frank L. Packard (st); C: Joseph Ruttenberg; Cast: George Walsh, Regina Quinn, Mario Majeroni, Paul Everton, J.A. Marcus, Tom Walsh, Cesare Gravina, Robert Byrd • Dave (Walsh), heir to a fortune, is fleeced out of $100,000 by race-track crooks. Dave steals back money from their safe and hides it. He is later caught and sentenced to prison. When he is freed five years later, the police are waiting for him to go to his hiding place. Capriano (Majeroni), a bomb maker, drugs him and steals the money for himself. Dave is helped by Capriano's daughter (Quinn), with whom he has fallen in love, retrieves the money and turns it over to the police, then vows to go straight. 5 reels • Variety wrote, "From now on and forever R.A. Walsh and George Walsh ... should decide on making better productions than 'From Now On.'"

SUNSET SPRAGUE (Oct. 3, 1920); D: Thomas N. Heffron, Paul Cazeneuve; W: Clyde C. Westover; C: George Schneiderman; Cast: Buck Jones, Patsey De Forest, Henry J. Herbert, Gloria Payton, Edwin Booth Tilton, Noble Johnson, Jack Rollens, Gus Saville • Sunset Sprague (Jones) saves a rancher and his niece, Rose (De Forest), from outlaws who killed the girl's father to steal his mine. Sprague discovers that Rose's sweetheart, Mace (Hebert), is the leader of the bandits and is blackmailing her half-brother (Rollens). Sprague has several battles with the gang and finally wipes them out, winning Rose's love. 5 reels

THE TIGER'S CUB (Oct. 10, 1920); D: Charles Giblyn; W: Paul Sloane, George Goodchild (novel); C: Joseph Ruttenberg; Cast: Pearl White, Thomas Carrigan, Jack Baston, John Davidson, Frank Evans, John Woodford, Ruby Hoffman, Albert Tavernier • Searching Alaska for his father, David (Carrigan) is rescued by a woman, known as Tiger's Cub (White), with whom he falls in love. However, Cub has been promised to a villain, Bill (Baston), who cheated and killed David's father (Woodford). After the marriage, Bill attempts to rape Cub, but David intervenes and Bill is killed by Hilda (Hoffman), a previous wife he had deserted. 6 reels

THE CHALLENGE OF THE LAW (Oct. 10, 1920); D: Scott Dunlap; W: Denison Clift (scr), E. Lloyd Sheldon (st); C: Clyde De Vinna; Cast: William Russell, Helen Ferguson, Arthur Morrison, James Farley, Robert Klein, D.J. Mitsoras, Fred Malatesta • Two Mounties, Capt. Bruce Cavanaugh (Russell) and Tom Wallace (Morrison), are sent to Fort Qu'Appelle to arrest fur smugglers. When Bruce arrests Pere Du Barre (Farley), father of Madeline (Ferguson), with whom he has fallen in love, she joins up with the smugglers. The smugglers break Du Barre out of jail, killing Wallace. Cavanaugh pursues the group and finds Madeline and Du Barre wandering in a desert. A witness testifies that the other smugglers killed Wallace, clearing Madeline and her father of the crime. 5 reels

BEWARE OF THE BRIDE (Oct. 17, 1920); D: Howard M. Mitchell; W: Joseph Franklin Poland, Edgar Franklin (short story); C: Walter Williams; Cast: Eileen Percy, Walter McGrail, Hallam Cooley, Harry Dunkinson, Jane Miller, Ethel Shannon, George W. Banta • Mary Emerson (Percy), distracted from her honeymoon with Billy (McGrail) by a friend's invitation to a masquerade ball, is scandalized when a cousin (Banta) recognizes her. Mary disguises herself in a suit of armor and she evades several misunderstandings to be reunited with her husband. 5 reels

THE GIRL OF MY HEART (Oct. 24, 1920); D: Edward J. LeSaint; W: Edward J. LeSaint, Mildred Considine, Frances Marian Mitchell (novel); C: Friend Baker; Cast: Shirley Mason, Raymond McKee, Martha Mattox, Al Fremont, Cecil Van Auker, Calvin Weller, Hooper Toler, Alfred Weller • Joan (Mason), a young runaway, rescues an ailing Rodney (McKee) from suicide. Rodney then takes her to the West in an attempt to regain his health. On an Indian settlement, they discover Maj. Philips (Fremont) selling whiskey to the Indians. Philips hires an Indian (Toler) to kill Rodney and kidnap Joan. Rodney escapes death and rescues Joan. Now cured, Rodney and Joan realize they are in love. 4,340'

DRAG HARLAN (Oct. 24, 1920); D: J. Gordon Edwards; W: H.P. Keeler (scr), Charles Alden Seltzer (st); Cast: John Boyle, William Farnum, Jackie Saunders, Arthur Millett, G. Raymond Nye, Herschel Mayall, Frank Thurwald, Kewpie Morgan, Al Fremont, Erle Crane • Drag Harlan (Farnum) avenges his partner's killer and shoots a bandit. At the same time, he saves miner Lane Morgan (Mayall), who begs him to look after his daughter, Barbara (Saunders). Barbara is threatened by Luke (Nye) and his gang, who want to take over Morgan's ranch. Drag defeats the gang and finds a gold mine from a map Lane gave him. 5,038'

THE LITTLE GREY MOUSE (Oct. 31, 1920); D: James P. Hogan; W: James P. Hogan (scr), Barbara LaMarr Deely (st); C: William O'Connell; Cast: Louise Lovely, Sam DeGrasse, Rosemary Theby, Philo McCullough, Wilson Hummel, Miss Gerard Alexander, Willis Marks, Thomas Jefferson • Beverly (Lovely), a legal secretary, is courted by two lawyers at her firm, John (DeGrasse) and Stephen (McCullough). She marries Stephen and helps him become a famous writer. When Stephen becomes bored with Beverly, he divorces her for another woman. Beverly then becomes a successful writer, and, when Stephen decides to return to her, she has fallen in love with John. 5 reels

THE TEXAN (Oct. 31, 1920); D: Lynn F. Reynolds; W: Lynn F. Reynolds (scr), Jules G. Furthman (scr), James S. Hendryx (st and novel); C: Frank Good; Cast: Tom Mix, Gloria Hope, Robert Walker, Charles K. French, Sid Jordan, Pat Chrisman • Cowboy Tex Benton (Mix) meets Alice (Hope), an Easterner, when a train stalls on the tracks. Tex decides she is the woman he wants to marry. He finds there is another Easterner, Winthrop (Walker), vying for Alice's affection. Tex decides to move in quickly but Winthrop wins Alice's favor. Tex gives up on the idea of marriage. 5 reels

THE FACE AT YOUR WINDOW (Oct. 31, 1920); D: Richard Stanton; W: Edward Sedgwick (scr), Max Marcin (st); C: Horace G. Plimpton Jr.; Cast: Gina Reilly, Earl Metcalf, Edward Rosenman, Boris Rosenthal, Walter McEwen, Diana Allen, Alice Reeves, Fraser Coulter, William Corbett, Henry Armetta • Frank (Metcalfe), the son of a factory owner, falls in love with a Russian immigrant, Ruth (Reilly), who works for his father. When Frank is stabbed in the back, Ruth is arrested. Released for lack of evidence, Ruth agrees to spy on fellow Russians and discovers a jealous labor agitator, Koyloff (Rosenthal), is responsible for the stabbing. Frank later helps quell workers during a violent revolt and ends up with Ruth. 7 reels • The combination of topical issues and politics resulted in a loss of $100,000.

THE PLUNGER (Nov. 7, 1920); D: Dell Henderson; W: Thomas F. Fallon; C: Charles Gilson; Cast: George

Walsh, Virginia Valli, Byron Douglas, Richard R. Neill, Edward Bouldon, Inez Shannon, Irving Brooks, Robert Vivian, W.S. Harkins • One-time Wall Street office boy and now a wealthy broker, chance-taker Schuyler (Walsh) buys the estate of John Houghton (Douglas), who has been blackmailed out of his money by a former employee, Yates (Neill). Yates has convinced Houghton he was responsible for a murder. The Houghtons still live at the estate and Schuyler ends up saving Houghton's daughter Alice (Valli) from Yates. Schuyler forces Yates to admit he was the real murderer. When he clears Houghton, Schuyler marries Alice. 5 reels

JUST PALS (Nov. 15, 1920); D: Jack Ford; W: Paul Schofield (scr), John McDermott (st); C: George Schneiderman; Cast: Buck Jones, Helen Ferguson, George Stone, Duke R. Lee, William Buckley, Edwin Booth Tilton, Eunice Murdock Moore, Bert Apling, Slim Padgett, Ida Tenbrook • A good-natured ne'er-do-well, Bim (Jones), is in love with Mary (Ferguson), who is engaged to Harvey (Buckly), a bank teller. When Mary puts her reputation on the line by lending Harvey some money from a school fund, Bim discovers that Harvey is embezzling bank funds. Bim disrupts Harvey's robbery attempt and is given a reward. He then buys a farm for Harvey and Mary. 5 reels • Jack (John) Ford directed this film on loan-out from Universal. He returned to Fox under contract the following year.

THE IRON RIDER (Nov. 21, 1920); D: Scott Dunlap; W: Jules G. Furthman (scr), Frank L. Packard (st); C: Clyde De Vinna; Cast: William Russell, Vola Vale, Arthur Morrison, Wadsworth Harris, George Nicholls • After a shooting in Angel City, Larry (Russell) puts on the signature robe and mask of a vigilante group, the Iron Riders, which his father founded. Corrupt Sheriff Donovan (Harris) blames a saloon robbery on the Rider. Larry knows Donovan is implicated, but will not expose him to protect his daughter, Mera (Vale), whom Larry loves. After rescuing Mera from villainous Jim Mason (Morrison), Larry clears his name and restores order to Angel City. 5 reels

THE THIEF (Nov. 28, 1920); D: Charles Giblyn; W: Max Marcin, Paul H. Sloane, Henri Bernstein (play); C: Joseph Ruttenberg; Cast: Pearl White, Charles Waldron, Wallace McCutcheon, George Howard, Dorothy Cummings, Eddie Featherstone, Sidney Herbert, Anthony Merlo • Mary Vantyne (White), married to Andrew (Waldron), a man of little means, decides to get a new wardrobe and is romanced by the impressionable Fred Lenwright (Featherstone), son of a millionaire. Fred is accused of stealing $3,000 from his father (Howard) to pay for Mary's clothing bills. Andrew finds out about the whole deal and is out for revenge when Mary confesses that she stole the money and has now learned her lesson. 6 reels

THE LAND OF JAZZ (Nov. 28, 1920); D: Jules Furthman; W: Jules Furthman (scr), Barbara LaMarr Deely (st); C: Walter Williams; Cast: Eileen Percy, Ruth Stonehouse, Herbert Heyes, George Fisher, Franklyn Farnum, Hayward Mack, Rose Dione, Carry Ward, Blanche Payson, Wilson Hummel • Nina (Percy), pretending to be unbalanced, gets herself committed to a sanitarium on a French island to help win back a doctor's affection for her friend Nancy (Stonehouse). She joins the other inmates in their odd behavior, and, in a twist, she and the doctor end up falling in love. 3,699'

FLAME OF YOUTH (Dec. 5, 1920); D: Howard M. Mitchell; W: Frank Howard Clark (scr), Barbara LaMarr Deely (adpt); C: Friend F. Baker, George Schneiderman; Cast: Shirley Mason, Raymond McKee, Philo McCullough, Cecil Van Auker, Adelbert Knott, Betty Schade, Karl Formes • Beautiful but naïve Belgian peasant girl Beebe (Mason) is lured into loving immoral Parisian artist Victor Fleming (McCullough) to the dismay of Jeanot (McKee), who loves her. Deeply in love with the artist, Beebe's illusions are shattered when she discovers Victor in the midst of a wild orgy at his studio. She returns to her village and Jeanot. 5 reels

THE SCUTTLERS (Dec. 12, 1920); D: J. Gordon Edwards; W: Paul H. Sloane, Clyde C. Westover (novel); C: John Boyle; Cast: William Farnum, Jackie Saunders, Herschel Mayall, G. Raymond Nye, Arthur Millet, Harry Spingler, Manual Ojeda, Erle Crane, Kewpie Morgan • Lloyds of London investigator Jim Landers (Farnum) goes after Captain Machen (Mayall), suspected of scuttling his ships to collect the insurance. Jim is shanghaied aboard a ship on which he meets Machen's daughter, Laura (Saunders). The ship is legitimately abandoned and Machen confesses on his deathbed that he had previously scuttled a ship because it was transporting weapons to Mexico. 6 reels

NUMBER 17 (Dec. 12, 1920); D: George Beranger; W: Louis Tracy (st); Cast: George Walsh, Mildred Reardon, Charles Mussett, Lillian Beck, Louis Wolheim, Harold Thomas, Charles Slattery, Jack Newton, Spencer Charters, Lillian Griffith • A fiction writer, Frank Theydon (Walsh), gets involved in New York's Chinatown Tong wars in his research. He also ends up rescuing his girlfriend, Evelyn (Reardon), from a kidnapping attempt when a Manchu leader, Wong Li (Thomas), is trying to settle a score with her father (Mussett). 5 reels

FANTOMAS (Dec. 19, 1920) Serial; D: Edward Sedgwick; W: Edward Sedgwick (adpt & scr), George Eschenfelder (adpt & scr), Marcel Allain & Pierre Souvestre (story); C: Horace G. Plimpton Jr.; Cast: Ed Roseman, Ben Walker, Edna Murphy, Eve Balfour, J. Thornton Barton, Lionel Adams, Henry Armetta, Rena Parker, Johnny Walker, Irving Brooks • Episode #1: On the Stroke of Nine. Episode #2: The Million Dollar Reward. Episode #3: The Triple Peril. Episode #4: Blades of Terror. Episode #5: Heights of Horror. Episode #6: Altar of Sacrifice. Episode #7: Flames of Destruction. Episode #8: At Death's Door. Episode #9: Haunted Hotel. Episode #10: Fatal Card. Episode #11: The Phantom Sword. Episode #12: The Danger Signal. Episode #13: On the Count of Three. Episode #14: The Blazing

Train. Episode #15: The Sacred Necklace. Episode #16: The Phantom Shadow. Episode #17: The Price of Fang Wu. Episode #18: Double Crossed. Episode #19: Hawks Prey. Episode #20: The Hell Ship.

TWO MOONS (Dec. 19, 1920); D: Edward J. LeSaint; W: Edward J. LeSaint (scr), Robert Welles Ritchie (st & novel); C: Friend F. Baker; Cast: Buck Jones, Carol Holloway, Gus Saville, Bert Sprotte, Slim Padgett, William Ellingford, Louis Fitzroy, Edward Pell, Edwin Booth Tilton • A Wyoming feud between sheep herders and cattlemen results in the murder of five sheepmen. The cattlemen have secretly hired corrupt Sheriff Agnew (Sprotte) to settle the feud. Honest Bill Blunt (Jones) plays by the rules for the sheep men and ultimately resolves the conflict. He also falls in love with a sheepman's tough, girl-of-the-plains daughter, Hilma (Holloway). 5 reels

BLIND WIVES (Dec. 19, 1920); D: Charles J. Brabin; W: Charles J. Brabin, Edward Knoblock (play); C: George W. Lane; Cast: Marc McDermott, Estelle Taylor, Harry Southern • Anne's husband (McDermott) cuts off his indulgent wife's credit so she can no longer buy so much clothing. Anne (Taylor) has four dreams in which the desire for clothes result in sacrifice and tragedy. The dreams cure her of the passion for clothes. 8,376' • An attempt to cash in on the success of *While New York Sleeps* resulted in one of the biggest flops of Fox's five-year-old company.

PRAIRIE TRAILS (Dec. 26, 1920); D: George Marshall; W: Frank Howard Clark (scr), James B, Hendry (st); C: Frank B. Good; Cast: Tom Mix, Charles K. French, Kathleen O'Connor, Robert Walker, Gloria Hope, Sid Jordan, Harry Dunkinson, William Elmer • Tex (Mix), a cowboy in love with Janet (O'Connor), will be allowed to marry her if he tends sheep on her father's (French) ranch. Tex refuses and returns to a life of adventure, rescuing a woman (Hope), whom he is accused of kidnapping, then retrieving Janet, abducted by an outlaw. Janet's father finally allows Tex to marry her. 6 reels

1921 Releases

PARTNERS OF FATE (Jan. 2, 1921); P: William Fox; D: Bernard J. Durning; W: Robert Dillon, Stephen Chalmers; C: Glen MacWilliams, Otto Brautigan; Cast: Louise Lovely, William Scott, Rosemary Theby, Philo McCullough, George Siegmann, Richard Cummings, Eileen O'Malley • Helen (Lovely) and Frances (Theby) are on their respective honeymoons when a shipwreck leads to a mix-up of the two couples. This results in one adulterous relationship before they are rescued. 5 reels

THE CHEATER REFORMED (Jan. 9, 1921); P: William Fox; D: Scott Dunlap; W: Jules Furthman (scr), Scott Dunlap (scr), Jules Furthman (st); C: Clyde De Vinna; Cast: William Russell, Seena Owen, John Brammall, Sam De Grasse, Ruth King • Luther (Russell), a minister, is killed in a train wreck and his embezzler twin brother, Lefty (Russell), takes his place. Carrying on as a minister, Lefty experiences a genuine conversion and wins the love of his brother's wife, Carol (Owen). 5 reels

WHY TRUST YOUR HUSBAND? (Jan. 16, 1921); D: George E. Marshall; W: William M. Conselman (scr), George E. Marshall (st), Paul Cazeneuve (st); C: Lucien Andriot; Cast: Eileen Percy, Harry Myers, Ray Ripley, Harry Dunkinson, Milla Davenport, Jane Miller, Hayward Mack, Bess True • Elmer (Myers) and Gilbert (Mack) tell their wives, Eunice (Percy) and Maud (Miller), they have a business engagement, then attend a masquerade. Their spouses find out and complications result when costumes and identities are confused. 5 reels

THE MOUNTAIN WOMAN (Jan. 23, 1921); D: Charles Giblyn; W: Ashley Locke; C: Joseph Ruttenberg; Cast: Pearl White, Corliss Giles, Richard C. Travers, George Barnum, Warner Richmond, John Webb Dillon, J. Thornton Baston, Charles Graham • When her lumberman father, Aaron (Barnum), is wounded in a fight, Kentucky girl Alex (White) takes his logs to market and encounters various suitors along the way, including Jerry (Giles), Jase (Baston) and Jack (Travers). She is captured by Jase, but escapes and returns home to marry Jerry. 6 reels

THE BIG PUNCH (Jan. 30, 1921); D: Jack Ford; W: Jules G. Furthman; C: Frank B. Good; Buck Jones, Barbara Bedford, George Siegmann, Jack Curtis, Jack MacDonald, Al Fremont, Jennie Lee, Edgar Jones, Irene Hunt, Eleanore Gilmore • Buck (Jones), preparing for the priesthood, is sent to prison for two years for helping his brother Jack (Curtis) who is a fugitive from justice. In prison, he meets Salvation Army worker Hope Standish (Bedford). When Buck returns home be becomes a circuit rider and is once again involved with Jack who escapes from prison. Buck converts Jack and is reunited with Hope. 5 reels

THE RAINBOW TRAIL (Jan. 30, 1921) Reissue

WING TOY (Jan. 30, 1921); D: Howard M. Mitchell; W: Thomas Dixon, Jr. (scr), Pearl Doles Bell (st); C: Glen MacWilliams; Cast: Shirley Mason, Raymond McKee, Edward McWade, Harry S. Northrup, Betty Schade, Scott McKee • Wing Toy (Mason), who was brought to a Chinese laundryman as an infant by a former convict, is set to marry Chinatown boss Yen Low (Northrup). Bob (McKee), a cub reporter, is able to get her released from the pending marriage and becomes engaged to her himself. Wing Toy turns out to be the daughter of the district attorney. 5–6 reels

WHEN A MAN SEES RED (Jan. 30, 1921) Reissue

WHILE THE DEVIL LAUGHS (Feb. 13, 1921); D: George W. Hill; W: George W. Hill; C: Friend Baker; Cast: Louise Lovely, William Scott, G. Raymond Nye, Edwin Booth Tilton, Wilson Hummell, Molly Shafer, Oleta Ottis, Coy Watson, Jr., Helen Field • Mary (Lovely), a hostess at a café, supports her family by lifting jewelry from her dancing partners. She is eventually convinced to go straight by her boyfriend, Billy (Scott), who is framed by the café owner McGee (Nye), but all is straightened out by a confession from McGee. 4,200'

THE ROAD DEMON (Feb. 20, 1921); D: Lynn Reynolds; W: Lynn Reynolds; C: Frank Good; Cast: Tom Mix,

Clare Anderson, Charles K. French, George Hernandez, Lloyd Bacon, Sid Jordan, Charles Arling, Harold Goodwin, Billy Elmer, Frank Tokawaja, Lee Phelps • Hap Higgins (Mix), a cowboy, transforms a broken-down car into the fastest racer and heads for the west coast. There, he becomes a champion driver and his girlfriend Patricia (Anderson) convinces her father, John O'Malley (Hernandez), to invest in his car design. Hap enters a race and wins a contract for O'Malley. 5 reels

DYNAMITE ALLEN (Feb. 20, 1921); D: Dell Henderson; W: Thomas F. Fallon; C: Charles E. Gilson; Cast: George Walsh, Edna Murphy, Dorothy Allen, Carola Parsons, Byron Douglas, J. Thornton Baston, Nellie Parker Spaulding, Frank Nelson, Billy Gilbert • A blind child, Betty (Murphy), witnesses the murder of a mine owner, and based on her erroneous testimony, Sid Allen (Royce) is convicted. When her sight is restored years later, Betty returns home and befriends Dynamite Allen (Walsh), the convicted man's son. Dynamite rescues her from a kidnapper, Bull Snide (Douglas), who was responsible for the original murder. Dynamite, with Betty's help, is able to convict the real culprit and release his father. 4,494'

THE BLUSHING BRIDE (Feb. 27, 1921); D: Jules G. Furthman; W: Jules G. Furthman; C: Otto Brautigan; Cast: Eileen Percy, Herbert Heyes, Philo McCullough, Jack La Reno, Rose Dione, Harry Dunkinson, Bertram Johns, Herschell Mayall, Sylvia Ashton, Earl Crain • A series of mix-ups result when follies dancer Beth Rupert (Percy) marries a wealthy suitor, Kingdom Ames (Heyes), who believes she's the niece of a duke. Beth is really the niece of the Ames family butler (Dunkinson). A ruse evolves in which the butler's cousin poses as the Duke of Downcastle, but the real duke is finally revealed. It turns out that Beth really is the niece of a duke. 4,200'

OLIVER TWIST, JR. (March 13, 1921); D: Millard Webb; W: F. McGrew Willis, inspired by *Oliver Twist* by Charles Dickens; C: William C. Foster; Cast: Harold Goodwin, Lillian Hall, George Nichols, Harold Esboldt, Scott McKee, Wilson Hummell, G. Raymond Nye, Hayward Mack, Pearl Lowe, George Clair, Fred Kirby • A modernized version of the classic story with a 17-year-old Oliver (Goodwin) who falls in with a gang of thieves headed by Jim Cleek (Nye). During a robbery, Oliver is shot and wounded, but his possession of a locket later identifies him as the grandson of a wealthy man. 4,200' • Messing with the classics was not looked upon favorably by critics. *Wid's Daily* mentioned in its review, "The general opinion... will likely be a wish that it had been done in the original setting and atmosphere." *Variety* concurred: "The thing was not worth doing in the first place and to make it complete has been done badly."

KNOW YOUR MEN (March 20, 1921); D: Charles Giblyn; W: Paul H. Sloane; C: Joseph Ruttenberg; Cast: Pearl White, Wilfred Lytell, Downing Clarke, Harry C. Browne, Estar Banks, Byron Douglas, William Eville • A young woman, Ellen Schuyler (White), abandoned by her socialite boyfriend, Roy (Lytell), because of a financial fiasco blamed on her father (Clarke), marries John Barrett (Browne) from her small Eastern town. However, an irritating mother-in-law (Banks) almost sinks the marriage for Ellen, but after a brief separation, she returns to Barrett. 5,315'

BARE KNUCKLES (March 20, 1921); D: James P. Hogan; W: James P. Hogan (scr), A. Channing Edington (st); C: George Schneiderman; Cast: William Russell, Mary Thurman, Correan Kirkham, George Fisher, Edwin Booth Tilton, Charles Gorman, Jack Roseleigh, John Cook, Joe Lee, Charles K. French, Jack Stevens • An underworld brute, Tim McGuire (Russell), rescues young girl Lorraine (Thurman) from hoodlums and is given a construction job by her father (French). He saves her again from a rival company gang that kidnaps her and then tries to blow up the construction site. 3,861'

THE ONE-MAN TRAIL (March 27, 1921); D: Bernard J. Durning; W: William K. Howard (scr), Jack Strumwasser (st), Clyde C. Westover (st); C: Frank B. Good; Cast: Buck Jones, Beatrice Burnham, Helene Rosson, Jim Farley • Tom Merrill (Jones) sets out on the trail to avenge his murdered father and find his kidnapped sister, Grace (Rosson), who has been taken by the killer, Crenshaw (Farley). When Tom catches up with Crenshaw at a saloon he owns, he falls for Cressy (Burnham). A lot of fisticuff action follows as Tom gets even with Crenshaw. 4,200'

RIDERS OF THE PURPLE SAGE (Apr. 3, 1921) Reissue

HANDS OFF (Apr. 3, 1921); D: George E. Marshall; W: Frank Howard Clark (scr), William MacLeod Raine (st); C: Ben Kline; Cast: Tom Mix, Pauline Curley, Charles K. French, Lloyd Bacon, Frank Clark, Sid Jordan, William McCormick, Virginia Warwick, J. Webster Dill, Marvin Loback • Tex (Mix) rescues Ramona Wadley (Curley) from a gang of rustlers and is given a job by her rancher father, Clint (French). Ramona's brother, Ford (Bacon), is involved with the rustlers and their leader, Pete Dinsmore (Jordan). When Ford is killed by the gang, Tex is accused of a holdup and has to fight the gang to clear his name. 4,158'

THE LAMPLIGHTER (Apr. 10, 1921); D: Howard M. Mitchell; W: Robert Dillon, Marie Susanna Cummins (novel); C: Glen MacWilliams; Cast: Shirley Mason, Raymond McKee, Albert Knott, Edwin Booth Tilton, Iris Ashton, Philo McCullough, Madge Hunt • A waif is given to a sailor by Malcolm Graham (Tilton), who believes his granddaughter was born out of wedlock. Mistreated, the child, Gertie (Mason), runs away and is taken in by a kindly lamplighter (Knott). She eventually ends up back at Graham's house and becomes a companion to the woman who is actually her blind mother (Ashton). Gertie also meets and falls in love with the lamplighter's assistant, Willie (McKee). When Gertie's father returns from India, the family is reunited and she is saved from a fire by the sailor who had raised her. 5,450'

SKIRTS (Apr. 10, 1921); D: Hampton Del Ruth; W: Hampton Del Ruth; Cast: Clyde Cook, Chester Conklin, Polly Moran, Jack Cooper, Billy Armstrong, Ethel Teare, Glen Cavender, Slim Summerville, Harry McCoy,

Bobby Dunn, Tom Kennedy • Peter Rocks, Jr. (Cook) works in a circus along with his mother, who is the bearded lady. He tries to get at his estranged father's fortune, but is outsmarted by the strong man. There are many large-scale slapstick sequences as a result. 4,950' • This was an attempt by Sunshine Comedies to produce a feature. It did not meet with great success.

THE TOMBOY (Apr. 10, 1921); D: Carl Harbaugh; W: Carl Harbaugh; C: Otto Brautigan; Cast: Eileen Percy, Hal Cooley, Richard Cummings, Paul Kamp, Byron Munson, Harry Dunkinson, James McElhern, Leo Sulky, Grace McLean, Walter Wilkinson • The village tomboy, Minnie (Percy), declares war on local bootleggers and their leader, Pike (Munson), after she finds her father intoxicated. She then joins a newspaper as a sports writer to expose their activities. A handsome stranger (Cooley) helps her combat the forces of evil. 4,630'

HIS GREATEST SACRIFICE (Apr. 17, 1921); D: J. Gordon Edwards; W: Paul H. Sloane; C: Harry L. Keepers; Cast: William Farnum, Alice Fleming, Lorena Volare, Evelyn Greeley, Frank Goldsmith, Charles Wellesley, Edith McAlpin Benrimo, Henry Leone • A successful but jealous writer, Richard Hall (Farnum), kills James Hamilton (Goldsmith), who helped his wife, Alice (Fleming), become an opera singer. When released after 20 years in prison, Richard meets his daughter, Grace (Volare), who convinces him to live with her and her philanthropist husband, Reed (Wellesley). 6,295'

COLORADO PLUCK (May 1, 1921); D: Jules G. Furthman; W: Jules G. Furthman, George Goodchild (novel); C: George Schneiderman; Cast: William Russell, Margaret Livingston, William Buckley, George Fisher, Helen Ware, Bertram Johns, Ray Berger • Jim (Russell), a Colorado millionaire living in England, falls in love with Angela Featherstone (Livingston), who is pressured by her family to marry him. When she agrees, it is to be a marriage in name only. Angela spends all of Jim's money and they return to Colorado, but Angela is followed by Philip (Fisher), who desires her. Jim finds outlaws living on his ranch and engages in a gun battle to remove them. Wounded, he is cared for by Angela, who now genuinely loves him. 4,700'

HEARTS OF YOUTH (May 8, 1921); D: Tom Miranda; W: Millard Webb, E.D.E.N. Southworth (novel); C: Walter Williams; Cast: Harold Goodwin, Lillian Hall, Fred Kirby, George Fisher, Iris Ashton, Glen Cavender, Grace Goodall, Colin Kenny • The tribulations of Ishmael Worth (Goodwin) begin with him renouncing his young sweetheart, Beatrice Merlin (Hall), over doubt as to his legitimacy because of his mother's uncertain marital status. Through a series of events, another woman (Ashton) his father was concurrently married to, appears and turns out to be a bigamist, which invalidates her marriage, removing the stigma from Ishmael. 5 reels

BEYOND PRICE (May 8, 1921); D: J. Searle Dawley; W: Paul H. Sloane; C: Joseph Ruttenberg; Cast: Pearl White, Vernon Steel, Nora Reed, Arthur Gordini, Louise Haines, Maude Turner Gordon, Byron Douglas, Ottola Nesmith, Dorothy Walters, Dorothy Allen • Leaving her marriage over neglect, Sally (White) writes a note of her three wishes: to be a millionaire's wife, to be famous, and to have a child. She does not realize that they will all come true and she will return to reconcile with her husband, Philip (Steel). 5–6 reels

GET YOUR MAN (May 22, 1921); D: George W. Hill; W: John Montague (scr), Alan Sullivan (st); C: Frank B. Good; Cast: Buck Jones, William Lawrence, Beatrice Burnham, Helen Rosson, Paul Kamp • A Scottish coal miner, Jock McTier (Jones), goes to Canada to join the Royal Canadian Mounted Police. He is attracted to Lenore De Marney (Burnham), whose father is a reputed fur smuggler. A friend from Scotland, Arthur Whitman (Lawrence), now an embezzler, shows up and plans to rob De Marney, but Jock prevents it. De Marney is killed in the shoot-out, but Whitman is caught with Lenore's help. She and Jock decide to marry. 5,400'

A RIDIN' ROMEO (May 22, 1921); D: George E. Marshall; W: George E. Marshall (scr), Tom Mix (st), Ralph Spence (titles); C: Ben Kline; E: Ralph Spence; Cast: Tom Mix, Rhea Mitchell, Pat Chrisman, Sid Jordan, Harry Dunkinson, Eugenie Ford • Jim Rose (Mix) is thwarted from romancing a rancher's daughter, Mabel (Mitchell), by being banned from the Brentwood ranch. Jim, however, breaks up a stagecoach robbery, rescues an abandoned baby and finally gets King Brentwood's (Dunkinson) permission to marry Mabel. 4,700'

THE MOTHER HEART (May 29, 1921); D: Howard M. Mitchell; W: Frank Howard Clark (scr), Howard M. Mitchell (st); C: Glen MacWilliams; Cast: Shirley Mason, Raymond McKee, Edwin Booth Tilton, Cecil Van Auker, William Buckley, Peggy Eleanor, Mrs. Raymond Hatton, Lillian Langdon • When John Howard (Van Auker) is falsely arrested for stealing food at a grocery store, his daughter, May (Mason), is sent to live on George Stuart's (Tilton) farm while her siblings are taken to an orphanage. Stuart, owner of grocery stores, finally realizes that his manager, Cliff Hamilton (Buckley), was dishonest and was responsible for May's father being arrested. The Howard family is reunited. 4,806'

BIG TOWN IDEAS (June 5, 1921); D: Carl Harbaugh; W: John Montague; C: Otto Brautigan; Cast: Eileen Percy, Kenneth Gibson, Jimmie Parrott, Lon Poff, Laura La Plante, Leo Sulky, Harry De Roy, Lefty James, Larry Bowes, Paul Kamp, Paul Cazeneuve • Fan (Percy), a railway junction waitress, meets handcuffed Alan Dix (Gibson), who has been unfairly convicted of stealing bonds and is on his way to the nearby state prison. Fan gets a job inside the prison, and helps Alan escape. She then proceeds to the real crook's house and climbs a slender tree to enter a second-story window, retakes the bonds and, after a wild chase, proves Alan innocent. 4,200'

STRAIGHT FROM THE SHOULDER (June 9, 1921); D: Bernard Durning; W: John Montague (scr), Roy

Norton (st); C: Frank B. Good; Cast: Buck Jones, Helen Ferguson, Norman Selby, Frances Hatton, Herschell Mayall, Yvette Mitchell, G. Raymond Nye, Glen Cavender, Dan Crimmins, Albert Knott, Lewis King • The Mediator (Jones) is hired to replace Big Ben Williams (Nye), a crooked gold mine superintendent in Peaceful Valley, by the owner, Joseph (Mayall). To get even, Williams instigates a workers' strike, which the Mediator averts. After foiling a gold robbery, The Mediator wins the heart of local waitress Maggie (Ferguson). 5,527'

CHILDREN OF THE NIGHT (June 26, 1921); D: Jack Dillon; W: John Montague; C: George Schneiderman; Cast: William Russell, Ruth Renick, Lefty Flynn, Ed Burns, Arthur Thalasso, Wilson Hummell, Helen McGinnis, Edwin Booth Tilton, Frederick Kirby, Herbert Fortier • Brokerage house clerk Jerrold Jones (Russell), who is in love with his stenographer, Sylvia (Renick), falls asleep and dreams that he is a worldly adventurer who is mistaken for the leader of a criminal enterprise, "Children of the Night." When the real leader (Flynn) shows up, Jones is drugged with a cigarette and thrown into a cellar. He comes to in time to save Sylvia, who has given herself up for him. When Jones awakens, he is fired for sleeping on the job. 5,011'

LIVE WIRES (July 3, 1921); D: Edward Sedgwick; W: Jack Strumwasser (scr), Charles E. Cooke (st), Edward Sedgwick (st); C: Victor Milner; Cast: Johnnie Walker, Edna Murphy, Alberta Lee, Frank Clark, Bob Klein, Hayward Mack, Wilbur Higby, Lefty James • Just before an important game, Bob (Walker), a college football star, returns home and finds his mother (Lee) has been swindled out of her property, for which the railroad is willing to pay $25,000. His sweetheart Rena's (Murphy) father (Higby), who has been tricked and blackmailed by the villain, steals back the deed. The villain has Bob tied up in a barn, but he escapes and leaps from the roof of a moving train to a rope ladder suspended from an airplane. He is then airlifted back to the field in time to save his team from defeat. 4,290' • Fox News clips were inserted into this film for the football game.

BIG TOWN ROUND-UP (July 3, 1921); D: Lynn Reynolds; W: Lynn Reynolds, William MacLeod Raine (novel); C: Ben Kline; Cast: Tom Mix, Gilbert Holmes, Ora Carew, Harry Dunkinson, Laura La Plante, William Buckley, William Elmer, William Crinley • Arizona rancher Larry McBride (Mix) rescues Alice (Carew), a San Francisco lady, from a pretended snake bite and becomes enamored of her. Larry follows her to the big city and meets Rodney (Buckley), who is also in love with Alice and in league with gangster Jerry Casey (Elmer). Larry is framed for murder, but Alice's father reveals that Rodney is the killer. Alice and Larry end up together. 4,249'

MAID OF THE WEST (July 17, 1921); D: Philo McCullough; W: John Montague (scr), W.E. Spencer (st); C: Otto Brautigan; Cast: Eileen Percy, William Scott, Hattie Buskirk, Charles Meakin, June La Vere, Jack Brammall, Frank Clark • Texas heiress Betty (Percy) is sent to New York society on her 20th birthday to keep her away from aviator Bert (Scott). Undaunted, Bert follows her, masquerades as her aunt's chauffeur, and gets involved with jewel thieves who are caught, with Betty's help. 4,193'

LOVETIME (July 24, 1921); D: Howard M. Mitchell; W: Dorothy Yost (scr), Hubert La Due (st); C: Glen MacWilliams; Cast: Shirley Mason, Raymond McKee, Frances Hatton, Edwin B. Tilton, Mathilde Brundage, Wilson Hummell, Harold Goodwin, Charles A. Smiley, Correan Kirkham • Arthur (McKee), the son of a French marquis, is in love with peasant girl Marie (Mason), but his mother (Brundage) secretly pledges him to the daughter of Count de Beaudine (Hummell). The villainous count also has his eye on Marie. Marie's parents send her to Paris for her safety, but Arthur follows and allows her to use his apartment. The count scandalizes Marie, and her father (Tilton) is distraught over his daughter's downfall. Ultimately, Arthur offers to marry Marie. 4,533'

AFTER YOUR OWN HEART (Aug. 7, 1921); D: George E. Marshall; W: John Montague (scr), Tom Mix (adpt); C: Ben Kline; Cast: Tom Mix, Ora Carew, George Hernandez, William Buckley, Sid Jordan, E.C. Robinson, Bill Ward • A college athlete, Herbert Parker (Mix), returns to his modern-day ranch in Arizona and finds himself in the middle of a dispute over water rights with neighbor Luke (Hernandez). Enamored of Luke's daughter, Loretta (Carew), Parker takes a job on his ranch and ends up fighting a gang headed by Luke's former foreman, Tex (Jordan). Working together with Luke, Larry foils Loretta's kidnapping and then defeats the gang. 4,244'

PLAY SQUARE (Aug. 14, 1921); D: William K. Howard; W: Jack Strumwasser; C: Victor Milner; Cast: Johnnie Walker, Edna Murphy, Hayward Mack, Laura La Plante, Jack Brammall, Wilbur Higby, Nanine Wright, Harry Todd, Al Fremont • A young pickpocket, Johnny (Walker), working the big city, is persuaded to reform by a judge (Higby) who remembers him from his hometown. Returning home, Johnny takes a job in a grocery store owned by the father (Todd) of his former girlfriend, Betty (Murphy). Johnny's old gang returns and forces him to rob the store, but he refuses. With Betty's help, the thieves are arrested. 4,163'

OVER THE HILL TO THE POORHOUSE (Aug. 14, 1921); D: Harry Millarde; W: Paul H. Sloane, Will Carleton (poems); C: Hal Sintzenich, George Schneiderman; Cast: Mary Carr, William Welch, Sheridan Tansey, Noel Tearle, Stephen Carr, John Dwyer, Jerry Devine, John Walker, James Sheldon, Wallace Ray, Rosemary Carr, Maybeth Carr • Selfless mother Ma Benton (Mary Carr) slaves for her six children in spite of her shiftless husband (Welch). It is the black sheep, John (Walker), who shines 20 years later when he saves his mother's pride by taking the blame for a crime his father committed. After leaving prison and making his fortune, John sends money for his mother to his brother Isaac (Tearle), who then steals it. Ma Benton is relegated to living in the poorhouse. Returning to punish Isaac, John restores the homestead and redeems himself. 10,700' later cut to 6,800' for general release • *Over the Hill to the Poorhouse* was a phenomenal success, reportedly earning $2,150,000 in world rentals on a cost of $99,800, returning a profit of $1,250,000. It was remade as a talkie in 1931.

SINGING RIVER (Aug. 21, 1921); D: Charles Giblyn; W: Jules Furthman (scr), Robert J. Horton (st); C: George Schneiderman; Cast: William Russell, Vola Vale, Clark Comstock, Jack Roseleigh, Arthur Morrison, Jack McDonald, Jack Hull, Louis King, Charles L. King • A homesteader (Russell), facing foreclosure, refuses to take part in a robbery. He is then lured into a gunfight and kills his antagonist (Morrison), but later makes a silver strike, clears his name and rescues the sheriff's daughter (Vale). 5 reels

TO A FINISH (Aug. 21, 1921); D: Bernard J. Durning; W: Jack Strumwasser; C: Frank B. Good; Cast: Buck Jones, Helen Ferguson, G. Raymond Nye, Norman Selby, Herschell Mayall • Rancher Jim Blake (Jones) is accused of rustling by an unscrupulous landowner, Bill Terry (Nye), who not only wants Jim's land but is also his rival for the sheriff's daughter Doris (Ferguson). Doris hides Jim when he's wounded in a gun battle with outlaws in league with Terry, but he returns to defeat the gang and its leader (Selby). 5 reels

EVER SINCE EVE (Aug. 21, 1921); D: Howard M. Mitchell; W: Dorothy Yost (scr), Joseph Ernest Peat (st); C: Glen MacWilliams; Cast: Shirley Mason, Herbert Heyes, Eve Gordon, Mrs. Vin Moore, Charles Spere, Frances Hancock, Ethel Lynn, Louis King • Wealthy French bachelor and artist, Carteret (Heyes), is visited by Celestine (Mason), believed to be the war orphan he adopted six years earlier. In a case of mistaken identity, he begins to fall in love with her, but she appears to elope with a stranger. However, it is revealed that the girl who eloped is the adopted daughter and Celestine is really her cousin, facilitating marriage to Carteret. 5 reels

HICKVILLE TO BROADWAY (Aug. 28, 1921); D: Carl Harbaugh; W: Carl Harbaugh, Ralph Spence (titles); C: Otto Brautigan; E: Ralph Spence; Cast: Eileen Percy, William Scott, Rosemary Theby, John P. Lockney, Margaret Morris, Ray Howard, Paul Kamp, Ed Burns • Small-town druggist Virgil Cole (Scott) meets and becomes so obsessed with Broadway actress Sibyle Fane (Theby) that he sells his store and follows her to New York. Sibyle offers to tutor Virgil's girlfriend, Anna Mae (Percy), to become a "vamp" to win Virgil back. Meeting the denizens of the New York social set, Anna Mae discovers that Virgil is not worthy material for marriage and instead chooses an artist (Burns). 4,219'

CARMEN (Sept. 4, 1921) Reissue

A VIRGIN PARADISE (Sept. 4, 1921); D: J. Searle Dawley; W: Hiram Percy Maxim; C: Joseph Ruttenberg, Bert Dawley; Cast: Pearl White, Robert Elliott, J. Thornton Baston, Alan Edwards, Henrietta Floyd, Grace Beaumont, Mary Beth Barnelle, Lynn Pratt, Lewis Seeley, Charles Sutton • The young survivor of a South Seas volcanic eruption, Gratia Latham (White), who grew up among the jungle animals, is returned to civilization on an ocean liner. She has been retrieved by a cousin as part of a plan to steal the estate she inherited from a wealthy uncle. Nearly forced into a shipboard marriage with her cousin Bernard (Edwards), Gratia is rescued by Bob (Elliott) and his buddy Slim (Baston). Swimming ashore in New York, the trio resides in a house on Gratia's property, where her jungle sensibilities make her the talk of society. She evades another attempt to force her into marriage to Bernard and marries Bob. 8 reels

THE PRIMAL LAW (Sept. 11, 1921); D: Bernard J. Durning; W: Paul Schofield (scr), E. Lloyd Sheldon (st); Cast: Dustin Farnum, Mary Thurman, Harry Dunkinson, Philo McCullough, William Lowery, Charles Gorman, Glen Cavender, Frankie Lee, Rosita Marstini, Allan Cavan, Edwin Booth Tilton • A shifty operator, Walter Travers (McCullough), is luring a couple of Easterners, Peter Webb (Tilton) and his daughter Janice (Thurman), into fraudulently buying a ranch owned by Brian Wayne (Farnum). Brian is the guardian of Bobbie (Lee), the son of a partner who was killed by a gang of outlaws. Both Brian and Travers have their eye on Janice. Travers tricks Brian into selling his land for a low price, but Bobbie reveals that oil has been discovered on the property. Brian retrieves the property and marries Janice. 5,320'

WHAT LOVE WILL DO (Sept. 11, 1921); D: William K. Howard; W: Jack Strumwasser (scr), L.G. Rigby (st); C: Victor Milner; Cast: Edna Murphy, Johnnie Walker, Glen Cavender, Barbara Tennant, Richard Tucker, Edwin B. Tilton • Goldie Rowan (Tennant) is abandoned by Herbert Dawson (Tucker), who enticed her to elope and leave her husband (Cavender) and young son. Years later, Johnny Rowan (Walker) has grown up, works in a grocery store, is in love with the minister's daughter (Murphy) and is treasurer of the church's funds. Dawson shows up again as a traveling evangelist with plans to steal the church's money. His scheme ends in his death and the reunion of Johnny and his mother, who has kept her presence in the congregation a secret from her son. 4,252'

A CONNECTICUT YANKEE IN KING ARTHUR'S COURT (Sept. 11, 1921); D: Emmett J. Flynn; W: Bernard McConville (adpt), Mark Twain (novel); C: Lucien Andriot; E: C.R. Wallace; Cast: Harry Myers, Pauline Starke, Rosemary Theby, Charles Clary, William V. Mong, George Siegmann, Charles Gordon, Karl Formes, Herbert Fortier, Adele Farrington • While reading about the Age of Chivalry, Martin Cavendish (Myers) is knocked unconscious by a burglar and dreams he is back in 6th century England. He meets King Arthur (Clary) and comes into conflict with Merlin (Mong). Eventually knighted, he uses his knowledge of modernity to improve the castle. He falls in love with Sandy (Starke) and then awakens to realize she is his mother's secretary, Betty, and his true love.

8,291' • Reportedly, every motorcyclist in Los Angeles was enlisted for the big battle scene in which 370 pounds of nitroglycerine were used to blow up a castle. Fox's release competed with Chaplin's *The Kid* for audiences in its opening engagements.

THE NIGHT HORSEMEN (Sept. 18, 1921); D: Lynn F. Reynolds; W: Lynn F. Reynolds, Max Brand (novel); C: Ben Kline; Cast: Tom Mix, May Hopkins, Harry Lonsdale, Joseph Bennett, Sid Jordan, Bert Sprotte, Cap Anderson, Lon Poff, Charles K. French • Whistling Dan (Mix), an eccentric, dreamy cowboy, heads north following a flock of wild geese just before his wedding, leaving his sweetheart, Kate Cumberland (Hopkins), behind. He later gets involved in a gunfight and wounds Jerry (Anderson), whose brother, Mac (Sprotte), follows for revenge. When Mac burns down the Cumberland barn, Dan is about to shoot him, but Kate intervenes and dissuades him. 4,970'

THE LONE STAR RANGER (Sept. 18, 1921) Reissue

LITTLE MISS HAWKSHAW (Sept. 25, 1921); D: Carl Harbaugh; W: Carl Harbaugh; C: Otto Brautigan; Cast: Eileen Percy, Francis Feeny, Frank Clark, Vivian Ransome, J. Farrell MacDonald, Fred L. Wilson, Glen Cavender, Eric Mayne, Leslie Casey • Patsy (Percy), whose mother died after giving birth en route from England to America, works at Mike Rorke's (Clark) newsstand on the Bowery. Sir Stephen (Mayne), trying to make amends for losing track of his daughter 18 years earlier, sends his nephew Arthur Hawks (Feeney), from England to find his granddaughter. Hawks locates Patsy and, thinking she is as close to the description as he is going to get, convinces her to impersonate the missing girl. However, Sir Stephen recognizes her, and Patsy turns out to be the real heiress. She and Hawks also fall in love. 4,106'

BLUE BLOOD AND RED (Oct. 2, 1921) Reissue

THUNDERCLAP (Oct. 2, 1921); D: Richard Stanton; W: Paul H. Sloane; C: George W. Lane; Cast: Mary Carr, J. Barney Sherry, Paul Willis, Violet Mersereau, Carol Chase, John Daly Murphy, Walter McEwen, Maude Hill, Thomas McCann • Lionel Jamieson (Sherry), a brutal gambler who beat his wife (Carr) to a paralytic state, takes his stepdaughter Betty (Mersereau) out of a convent to lure men to his club. Lionel's horse trainer, Tommy (Willis), who is preparing Thunderclap for the big race, is sympathetic to Mrs. Sherry and Betty, and rescues the daughter from a kidnapping attempt. He then rides Thunderclap to victory, even though Jamieson does his best to throw the race to a competing horse to settle a large gambling debt. 6,745'

BAR NOTHIN' (Oct. 2, 1921); D: Edward Sedgwick; W: Jack Strumwasser (scr), Clyde C. Westover (st); C: Frank B. Good; Cast: Buck Jones, Ruth Renick, Arthur Carew, James Farley, William Buckley • Duke (Jones), a foreman, gets money from crooked cattle buyers. Before he can turn the money over to the ranch's owners, Bess (Renick) and her invalid brother Harold (Buckley), Duke is robbed by the con men, led by Stinson (Carew), and left to die. Duke catches a stray horse and returns to keep Bess from marrying Stinson. 4,311'

THE LADY FROM LONGACRE (Oct. 2, 1921); D: George E. Marshall; W: Paul Schofield, Victor Bridges (novel); C: Ben Kline; Cast: William Russell, Mary Thurman, Mathilde Brundage, Robert Klein, Jean Dr Briac, Francis Ford, William Brunton, Douglas Gerard, Lillian Worth, Arthur Van Sickle • Princess Isabel (Thurman) flees her country to escape an arranged marriage. When she arrives in England, a nobleman, Lord Anthony (Russell), comes to her aid and assumes she is the actress Molly Moncke, whom she closely resembles. Isabel falls in love with Lord Anthony, but returns to her country only to find the king she was to marry in the neighboring country has fallen in love with the actress Molly Moncke (Thurman), leaving Isabel free to marry Anthony. 5 reels

QUEENIE (Oct. 9, 1921); D: Howard M. Mitchell; W: Dorothy Yost (scr), Wilbur Finley Fauley (novel); C: George Schneiderman; Cast: Shirley Mason, George O'Hara, Wilson Hummell, Aggie Herring, Lydia Titus, Adolphe Menjou, Clarissa Selwynne, Pal the dog • Queenie (Mason), who has a difficult life, is employed by her housekeeper, Aunt Pansy (Herring), in the residence of aged recluse Simon (Hummell). By chance, Queenie meets Vivian Van Winkle (O'Hara), the poetic son of a noodle king, and the two strike up a friendship. Vivian disappears, but returns in time to save Queenie from an arranged marriage with Count Michael (Menjou). 5,174'

SHAME (Oct. 16, 1921); D: Emmett J. Flynn; W: Emmett J. Flynn, Bernard McConville, Max Brand (novel); C: Lucien Andriot; Cast: John Gilbert, Micky Moore, Frankie Lee, George Siegmann, William V. Mong, Rosemary Theby, Doris Pawn, "Red" Kirby • William Fielding (Gilbert) is murdered in Shanghai by Foo Chang (Siegmann) because he desires the woman who takes care of Fielding's son David (Lee). A family secretary, Li Clung (Mong), brings David to his wealthy grandfather in San Francisco. When David (Gilbert) is married and has his own son, Foo Chang returns and tries to blackmail him into smuggling opium by telling him his mother was Chinese. Believing he is a half-caste and a social disgrace, David flees with his son to Alaska. Li Clung kills Foo Chang and tells David his mother was not Chinese. David returns to San Francisco. 8,322'

ROSE OF THE WEST (Oct. 16, 1921) Reissue

CINDERELLA OF THE HILLS (Oct. 23, 1921); D: Howard M. Mitchell; W: Dorothy Yost, John Breckenridge Ellis (novel); C: George Webber; Cast: Barbara Bedford, Carl Miller, Cecil Van Auker, Wilson Hummel, Tom McGuire, Barbara La Marr Deely • Norris Gradley (Bedford), who refuses to accept her father's (McGuire) divorce and re-marriage, falls in love with an oil worker, Claude Wolcott (Miller), on her father's payroll. With him, Norris exposes her stepmother's (Deely) infidelity, reunites her parents and marries Claude. 4,800'

THE ROUGH DIAMOND (Oct. 30, 1921); D: Edward Sedgwick; W: Edward Sedgwick (scr & st), Tom Mix (st), Ralph Spence (titles); C: Ben Kline; E: Ralph Spence; Cast: Tom Mix, Eva Novak, Hector Sarno, Edwin J. Brady, Sid Jordan • Ranch hand Hank (Mix) flirts with Gloria Gomez (Novak) from a foreign country, impresses her ex-president father, Emeliano (Sarno), and ends up as a counter-revolutionary in the Republic of Bargravia, to restore Gomez to the presidency. 4,458'

PERJURY (Oct. 30, 1921); D: Harry Millarde; W: Mary Murillo (scr), Ruth Comfort Mitchell (adpt), Julius Steger (play); C: Edward Wynard; Cast: William Farnum, Sally Crute, Wallace Erskine, Alice Mann, Gilbert Rooney, Grace La Vell, Jack Crane, Frank Joyner, Frank Shannon, John Webb Dillon • Robert Moore (Farnum) is wrongfully sentenced for the murder of his boss, John Gibson (Erskine). When he is set free 20 years later, after the real murderer confesses, Moore finds out that his wife, Martha (Crute), has remarried an abusive man, and he saves her from an attack by shooting in self defense. 8,372'

THE SCARLET LETTER (Oct. 30, 1921) Reissue

BUCKING THE LINE (Nov. 6, 1921); D: Carl Harbaugh; W: Frances Lynde (novel); C: Frank B. Good; Cast: Maurice B. Flynn, Molly Malone, Norman Selby, Edwin Booth Tilton, Kathryn McGuire, J. Farrell MacDonald, James Farley, Leslie Casey, George Kerby • John (Flynn), a small town bank clerk, is forced to leave town and gets a job on a railroad construction project. After rescuing the project boss's daughter, Corona Baldwin (Malone), from a runaway handcar and preventing a train from going over an open drawbridge, John is promoted to foreman. 4,544'

THE KINGDOM OF LOVE (Nov. 13, 1921) Reissue

RIDING WITH DEATH (Nov. 13, 1921); D: Jacques Jaccard; W: Agnes Parsons (scr), Jacques Jaccard (st); C: Frank B. Good; Cast: Charles Jones, Betty Francisco, Jack Mower, J. Farrell MacDonald, H. von Sickle, William Steele, William Gettinger, Bill Gillis, Artie Ortega, Tina Mendotti • Texas Ranger Steve Dorsey (Jones) vows to get even with the murderer of his pal Val Nelson (Mower). Steve tangles with a gang headed by Sheriff Garrity (MacDonald), who covets Steve's girlfriend, Anita (Francisco). Jailed by Garrity, Steve is freed by the Rangers, who shoot it out with the gang, leaving Steve to have a showdown with Garrity. 4,110'

DESERT BLOSSOMS (Nov. 13, 1921); D: Arthur Rosson; W: Arthur J. Zellner (scr), Kate Corbaley (st); C: Ross Fisher; Cast: William Russell, Helen Ferguson, Wilbur Higby, Willis Robards, Margaret Mann, Dulcie Cooper, Charles Spere, Gerald Pring • The collapse of a bridge, caused by the employer's son (Spere), is wrongfully blamed on a young engineer, Steve (Russell), who leaves for an irrigation project in the desert, under an assumed identity. The manager's daughter Mary (Ferguson) recognizes Steve, but keeps his secret and marries him after his exoneration. 4,500'

CAPRICE OF THE MOUNTAINS (Nov. 13, 1921) Reissue

FOOTFALLS (Nov. 13, 1921); D: Charles J. Brabin; W: Charles J. Brabin, Wilbur Daniel Steele (short story); C: George W. Lane; Cast: Tyrone Power, Tom Douglas, Estelle Taylor, Gladden James • Hiram (Power), a blind cobbler, is present when his son Tommy (Douglas) is murdered by a lodger (James) who escapes after starting a fire that burns Hiram beyond recognition. The old man has to wait several years for the murderer to return, but Hiram gets his revenge when he recognizes the footfalls and strangles him. 8,068'

THE DEVIL WITHIN (Nov. 20, 1921); D: Bernard J. Durning; W: Arthur J. Zellner, George Allen England (novel); C: Don Short; Cast: Dustin Farnum, Virginia Valli, Nigel De Brulier, Bernard Durning, Jim Farley, Tom O'Brien, Bob Perry, Charles Gorman, Otto Hoffman, Kirk Incas, Evelyn Selbie • In the 1870s, tyrannical Captain Briggs (Farnum) is cursed by islanders after stealing an idol. This results in his wife and son being killed. Bad luck continues on in his nephew Hal's (Durning) life. A sailor, Hal steals Briggs's savings, which disappoints Laura (Valli), his sweetheart. After a brush with death from a poisonous sword, Hal reforms and he settles down with Laura. 5,997'

THE JOLT (Nov. 20, 1921); D: George E. Marshall; W: Jack Strumwasser (scr, st), George E. Marshall (st); C: Jack MacKenzie; Cast: Edna Murphy, Johnnie Walker, Raymond McKee, Albert Prisco, Anderson Smith, Wilson Hummell, Lule Warrenton • A young soldier, Johnnie (Walker), returns to New York with his French wife, Georgette (Murphy), but is unable to find work and is persuaded by pal Jerry (Prisco) to join up with his old gang. During the commission of a theft of military papers, Johnnie is saved in the nick of time, while the thieves are captured. 4,800'

THE LAST TRAIL (Nov. 27, 1921); D: Emmett J. Flynn; W: Jules Furthman, Paul Schofield, Zane Grey (novel); C: Lucien Andriot; Cast: Maurice B. Flynn, Eva Novak, Wallace Beery, Rosemary Theby, Charles K. French, Harry Springler, Harry Dunkinson • A stranger (Flynn) rides into a small frontier town and is mistaken for a bandit, "The Night Hawk." Sheltered from the sheriff (French) by Winifred (Novak), the stranger turns out to work for a construction firm and prevents an engineer (Berry) from stealing the company payroll and dynamiting the dam they are building. 6,355'

JACKIE (Nov. 27, 1921); D: Jack Ford; W: Dorothy Yost, Countess Helene Barcynska (novel); C: George Schneiderman; Cast: Shirley Mason, William Scott, Harry Carter, George Stone, John Cook, Elsie Bambrick • Jackie (Mason), a Russian waif in London, has talent as a dancer but must escape the advances of her manager (Carter). She and an accordion-playing friend (Stone) run away and perform in the streets of London. Jackie is "discovered" by a wealthy American (Scott) who falls in love with her and provides her chance to become famous. 4,943'

THE QUEEN OF SHEBA (Dec. 11, 1921); D: J. Gordon Edwards; W: Virginia Tracy (st); C: John W. Boyle; Cast: Betty Blythe, Fritz Leiber, Claire De Lorez, George Siegmann, Herbert Heyes, Herschell Mayall, G. Raymond Nye, George Nichols, Genevieve Blinn, Pat Moore, Joan Gordon • The Queen of Sheba (Blythe) and King Solomon (Leiber) fall in love but are forbidden from marriage by a threat of war from the King's father-in-law. Adonijah (Nye) marches in war against his brother, Solomon, but is repulsed by Sheba's armies. 8,279' • Tom Mix is credited as the supervisor of the chariot race sequence. This was Fox's second-highest money-making picture of the year with world rentals of $1,121,000, but it was also the most expensive to produce, at $479,000.

TRAILIN' (Dec. 11, 1921); D: Lynn F. Reynolds; W: Lynn F. Reynolds (adpt), Max Brand (novel); C: Ben Kline; Cast: Tom Mix, Eva Novak, Bert Sprotte, James Gordon, Sid Jordan, William Duvall, Duke Lee, Harry Dunkinson, Al Fremont, Bert Handley, Carol Holloway • Anthony Woodbury (Mix), living in the East with his wealthy father, John (Sprotte), wants to know more about his mother. When John is killed, Anthony swears revenge and returns to Idaho, where he gets involved with scoundrels. He discovers that two men were in love with his mother, but John kidnapped Anthony as an infant. John later marries Sally (Novak), a hotel waitress. 4,355'

WHATEVER SHE WANTS (Dec. 11, 1921); D: C.R. Wallace; W: Edgar Franklin (article); C: Otto Brautigan; Cast: Eileen Percy, Herbert Fortier, Richard Wayne, Otto Hoffman • Enid (Percy) takes a business course and secretly gets a job at her fiancé John's (Wayne) manufacturing plant. She suspects John is carrying on with another worker so she takes up with Amos (Hoffman), a married man, and gets into trouble before reuniting with John and begging his forgiveness. 4,616'

ROUGH AND READY (Dec. 11, 1921) Reissue

WHY I WOULD NOT MARRY (Dec. 11, 1921) Reissue

DAREDEVIL KATE (Dec. 25, 1921) Reissue

THE ROOF TREE (Dec. 25, 1921); D: John Francis Dillon; W: Jules Furthman, Charles Neville Buck (novel); C: Sol Polito; Cast: William Russell, Florence Deshon, Sylvia Breamer, Robert Daly, Arthur Morrison, Al Fremont • A Kentucky man, Ken (Russell), escapes after the murder of his sister's husband and is presumed to be guilty. Ken later meets and is about to marry Dorothy (Breamer), when he is arrested for the murder, but his sister Sally (Deshon) confesses to the crime. 4,409'

1922 Releases

ANY WIFE (Jan. 1, 1922); D: Herbert Brenon; W: Julia Tolsva; C: Tom Malloy; Cast: Pearl White, Holmes Herbert, Gilbert Emery, Lawrence Johnson, Augustus Balfour, Eulalie Jensen • An unhappy woman (White) dreams about an extramarital affair in which she marries her new lover (Herbert), but when the marriage fails she drowns herself. Luckily, she wakes from the dream. 4,597'

WINNING WITH WITS (Jan. 8, 1922); D: Howard M. Mitchell; W: Jack Strumwasser, Dorothy Yost, H.H. Van Loan (original); C: Max Dupont; Cast: Barbara Bedford, William Scott, Harry S. Northrup, Edwin Booth Tilton, Wilson Hummel • Mary Sudan (Bedford), an aspiring actress, poses as wealthy widow Mary Wyatt to gain a partnership in the investment company where her father (Tilton) has been charged with theft. She befriends Corday (Northrup), the president, and stages a séance, which frightens Corday into confessing to the crime. Mary later marries the young vice-president (Scott), and her father is exonerated. 4,435'

LITTLE MISS SMILES (Jan. 15, 1922); D: Jack Ford; W: Jack Strumwasser, Dorothy Yost, Myra Kelly (novel); C: David Abel; Cast: Shirley Mason, Gaston Glass, George Williams, Martha Franklin, Arthur Rankin, Alfred Testa, Richard Lapan, Sidney D'Albrook, Baby Blumfield • The poor, New York tenement-dwelling Aaronson family suffers with a mother (Franklin) going blind and an aspiring prizefighter son (Rankin), who shoots a gangster after he insults his sister. The son is cleared of the crime but the pride of the family is the always cheerful Esther (Mason), who falls in love and marries a doctor (Glass). 4,884'

SKY HIGH (Jan. 15, 1922); D: Lynn Reynolds; W: Lynn Reynolds; C: Ben Kline; Cast: Tom Mix, J. Farrell MacDonald, Eva Novak, Sid Jordan, William Buckley, Adele Warner, Wynn Mace, Pat Chrisman • Grant (Mix), an immigration officer on the Mexican border, is charged with investigating a gang that is smuggling Chinese laborers into the United States. He sets up camp in a canyon and meets Estelle (Novak), who is lost. Later, Grant is captured by Bates (Jordan), the leader of a gang. He escapes with Estelle's help in a thrilling series of dangerous stunts. 4,546' • Tom Mix incorporated a jump from an airplane into a stream to rescue the girl.

GLEAM O'DAWN (Jan. 22, 1922); D: Jack Dillon; W: Jules G. Furthman, Arthur Frederick Goodrich (novel); C: Don Short; Cast: John Gilbert, Barbara Bedford, James Farley, John Gough, Wilson Hummel, Edwin Booth Tilton • An artist (Gilbert) confronts his family past when he encounters various visitors who show up in the Canadian woods, leading to jealousy and the desire for revenge. 4,178'

THE STRENGTH OF THE PINES (Feb. 5, 1922); D: Edgar Lewis; W: Louise Lewis (adpt), Edison Marshall (novel); C: Sol Polito; Cast: William Russell, Irene Rich, Lule Warrenton, Arthur Morrison, Les Bates • Bruce (Russell), a college graduate, goes west to help his sister Linda (Rich) regain an estate that had been seized by swindlers. He discovers the girl is not really his sister, which allows for a romance between them. 4,382'

SMILES ARE TRUMPS (Feb. 5, 1922); D: George E. Marshall; W: Delbert F. Davenport, Frank L. Packard (magazine story); Cast: Maurice B. Flynn, Ora Carew,

Myles McCarthy, Herschel Mayall, Kirke Lucas, C. Norman Hammond • A railroad paymaster, Jimmy (Flynn), discovers his superior, Slevin (McCarthy), is cheating the company, but Jimmy is assaulted and forced to resign. Later, he foils an attempted takeover of the company's train, and, in a locomotive chase, routs the gang and wins the love of the vice-president's daughter (Carew). 4,049'

THE BROADWAY PEACOCK (Feb. 19, 1922); D: Charles J. Brabin; W: Julia Tolsva; C: George W. Lane; Cast: Pearl White, Joseph Striker, Doris Eaton, Harry Southard, Elizabeth Garrison • A Broadway hostess, Myrtle (White), is opposed by Harold Van Tassel's (Striker) blueblood family and becomes jealous when he takes a liking to her friend Rose (Eaton). Myrtle seeks revenge through Mrs. Van Tassel (Garrison), but finally relents and leaves Harold to Rose. 4,380'

CHASING THE MOON (Feb. 26, 1922); D: Edward Sedgwick; W: Tom Mix (st), Edward Sedgwick (st), Ralph Spence (titles); C: Ben Kline; E: Ralph Spence; Cast: Tom Mix, Eva Novak, William Buckley, Sid Jordan, Elsie Danbric, Wynn Mace • Dwight (Mix) is told by his girlfriend Jane's (Novak) brother, Milton (Buckley), that he has been poisoned from a cut suffered in his shop and has 30 days to live. Dwight must track down a Russian professor who has the antidote. Milton later finds out that Dwight did not really get any poison, and the antidote will kill him. Adventures ensue as Milton and Jane race against time to find Dwight. 5,092'

PARDON MY NERVE! (March 5, 1922); D: B. Reaves Eason; W: Jack Strumwasser, William Patterson White (novel); C: George Schneiderman; Cast: Charles Jones, Eileen Percy, Mae Busch, G. Raymond Nye, Joe Harris, Otto Hoffman, William Steele, Robert Daly • A skilled gunman, Dawson (Jones), befriends a rancher's daughter, Molly (Percy), whose father (Daly) was cheated out of his property. Dawson pursues the villain, McFluke (Nye), and is accused of murdering him, but is later exonerated. 4,093'

A STAGE ROMANCE (March 5, 1922); D: Herbert Brenon; W: Paul H. Sloane, Alexandre Dumas (novel); C: Tom Malloy; Cast: William Farnum, Peggy Shaw, Holmes Herbert, Mario Carillo, Paul McAllister, Etienne Gerardot, Bernard Siegel, Hal De Forrest, Edward Kipling • The great Shakespearean actor Edmund Kean (Farnum) becomes involved in a romantic intrigue and suspects the Prince of Wales (Herbert) of being a rival for his love, Anna Damby (Shaw). 6,416'

EXTRA! EXTRA! (March 5, 1922); D: William K. Howard; W: Arthur J. Zellner (scr), Julien Josephson (st); C: George Webber; Cast: Edna Murphy, Johnnie Walker, Herschel Mayall, Wilson Hummell, John Steppling, Gloria Woodthorpe, Theodore von Eltz, Edward Jobson • Cub reporter Barry (Walker) disguises himself as a butler to get access to industrialist Edward Fletcher (Mayall), who is about to merge his company. Meanwhile, Myra (Murphy) is after the same story so she can restore her father's reporting job. While competing for the same scoop, the opposing sides eventually unite in romance. 4,160'

IRON TO GOLD (March 12, 1922); D: Bernard J. Durning; W: Jack Strumwasser (scr), George Owen Baxter (st); C: Don Short; Cast: Dustin Farnum, Marguerite Marsh, William Conklin, William Elmer, Lionel Belmore, Glen Cavender, Robert Perry, Dan Mason • An outlaw, Tom Curtis (Farnum), rescues Anne (Marsh) from highwaymen and realizes that her husband, George (Conklin), had robbed him of his claim. Tom plans to take revenge on Anne but follows her East after George is killed. 4,513'

THE RAGGED HEIRESS (March 19, 1922); D: Harry Beaumont; W: Jules Furthman; C: Lucien Andriot; Cast: Shirley Mason, John Harron, Edwin Stevens, Cecil Van Auker, Claire McDowell, Aggie Herring, Eileen O'Malley • Lucia Burke (Mason), whose father, James (Van Auker), has been in prison since she was very young, works as a housekeeper for Sam Moreton (Stevens). Sam turns out to be Lucia's uncle, and he confesses that he and his wife, Sylvia (McDowell), were to take care of Lucia when James went to prison, but they were cruel and Lucia ran away and changed her name. Lucia and her James are reunited when he is released from prison. 4,888'

UP AND GOING (Apr. 4, 1922); D: Lynn Reynolds; W: Lynn Reynolds (scr & st), Tom Mix (st); C: Ben Kline, Dan Clark; Cast: Tom Mix, Eva Novak, William Conklin, Sidney Jordan, Tom O'Brien, Cecil Van Auker, Pat Chrisman, Carol Holloway, Helen Field, Paul Weigel, Marion Feducha • David (Mix), a Canadian, moves to England when his father Albert (Van Auker) inherits a fortune, but returns to Canada and becomes a member of the Royal Canadian Mounted Police. In his exploits he nabs bootleggers, romances Jackie (Novak) and finds his long-lost mother. 4,350'

ELOPE IF YOU MUST (Apr. 4, 1922); D: C.R. Wallace; W: Joseph Franklin Poland, E.J. Rath (novel); Cast: Eileen Percy, Edward Sutherland, Joseph Bennett, Mildred Davenport, Mary Huntress, Harvey Clarke, Larry Steers • A hick actor, Jazz Hennessy (Sutherland), and his girlfriend, Nancy (Percy), are stranded in a small town and are trying to make some money to get home. They meet rich Mr. Magruder (Clarke), who has just received word from his wife (Huntress) that his daughter Elizabeth (Davenport) is about to marry Willie (Bennett), a sap. Magruder hires Nancy and Jazz to bring about a breakup while directing Elizabeth to Warren (Steers), the man Magruder approves of. 4,995'

ARABIAN LOVE (Apr. 9, 1922); D: Jerome Storm; W: Jules Furthman; C: Joe August; Cast: John Gilbert, Barbara Bedford, Barbara La Marr, Herschel Mayall, Robert Kortman, William H. Orlamond, Adolphe Menjou • Nadine Fortier (Bedford) is taken prisoner by bandits in the Arabian Desert. One of the bandits, Norman Stone (Gilbert), an American, falls in love with her. Stone is later revealed by Themar (La Marr), the sheik's jealous daughter, as the murderer of Nadine's husband (Menjou). Stone explains that he confronted Fortier while he was meeting secretly with Stone's sister, and Fortier pulled a gun on him. There was a scuffle, and death was accidental. Stone fled to keep his sister out of the scandal. Nadine then returns with Stone for America. 4,440'

WITHOUT FEAR (Apr. 16, 1922); D: Kenneth Webb; W: Paul H. Sloane; C: Tom Malloy; Cast: Pearl White, Robert Elliott, Charles Mackay, Marie Burke, Robert Agnew, Macey Harlam • Aristocratic Ruth Hamilton (White) rebels against convention and meets John (Elliott), a nouveau riche gentleman, whom her father (Mackay) insists she must marry after being seen in a compromising situation. Ruth refuses at first but later consents since John really loves her. 4,406'

MONEY TO BURN (Apr. 22, 1922); D: Rowland V. Lee; W: Jack Strumwasser, Sewell Ford (novel); C: David Abel; Cast: William Russell, Sylvia Breamer, Hallam Cooley, Harvey Clark, Otto Matieson • Wealthy Lucky Garrity (Russell), who made his fortune on Wall Street, buys a Long Island mansion, hoping to retire. However, he finds Countess Vecchi (Breamer) living there with her dying husband (Matieson). The countess later helps Garrity fight rival investors and the two are united after the count dies. 4,850'

WESTERN SPEED (Apr. 23, 1922); D: Scott Dunlap, C.R. Wallace; W: Scott Dunlap, William Patterson White (novel); C: George Schneiderman; Cast: Charles Jones, Eileen Percy, Jack McDonald, J.P. Lockney, Jack Curtis, Milton Ross, Walt Robbins, Charles Newton • Cowboy Red Kane (Jones) befriends Dot Lorimer (Percy) and shields her father, Ben (Lockney), who is unjustly wanted for a robbery at a Colorado express office. Kane rounds up the men who committed the crime and brings them to justice. 5,002'

VERY TRULY YOURS (Apr. 30, 1922); D: Harry Beaumont; W: Paul Schofield (scr), Hannah Hinsdale (st); C: John Arnold; Cast: Shirley Mason, Allan Forrest, Charles Clary, Otto Hoffman, Harold Miller, Helen Raymond, Hardee Kirkland • After Marie (Mason), a stenographer, marries Bert Woodmansee (Forrest), a man who thinks she has money, Marie discovers it is Bert's uncle (Clary) who is a wealthy lumberman. Nevertheless, the uncle takes a liking to her and although Marie leaves Bert briefly, the uncle's generosity reunites them. 5,000'

SHACKLES OF GOLD (May 7, 1922); D: Herbert Brenon; W: Paul H. Sloane, Henri Bernstein (play); C: Tom Malloy; Cast: William Farnum, Al Loring, Marie Shotwell, Myrtle Bonillas, Wallace Rey, C. Elliott Griffin, Ellen Cassity, Henry Carvill • A former dockworker, John Gibbs (Farnum), who has risen to wealth, marries Marie (Bonillas). Her blueblood family members, particularly her mercenary mother (Shotwell), are only interested in John's money to keep their position in society. Marie raises John's ire by admitting to seeing socialite Donald Valentine (Griffin), who has made a lot of money by getting John's stock tips from her. John takes revenge on Donald by driving down the stock in which he invested, but also ruins himself financially. Marie decides to stay with John and start all over again. 5,957' • Based on the play and 1915 film *Samson*.

THE FIGHTING STREAK (May 14, 1922); D: Arthur Rosson; W: Arthur Rosson, George Owen Baxter (novel); C: Dan Clark; Cast: Tom Mix, Patsy Ruth Miller, Gerald Pring, Al Fremont, Sidney Jordan, Bert Sprotte, Robert Fleming • Forced to flee his town, Andy Lanning (Mix), a blacksmith, takes up with outlaws when the sheriff is paid to eliminate him by Charles Merchant (Pring), who wants his girlfriend, Ann (Miller). In a shootout, Andy kills the sheriff, but later saves the new sheriff's life and explains it all to him. Ann hires a lawyer to clear Andy. 4,888'

THE MEN OF ZANZIBAR (May 21, 1922); D: Rowland V. Lee; W: Edward J. LeSaint, Richard Harding Davis (short story); C: David Abel; Cast: William Russell, Ruth Renick, Claude Peyton, Harvey Clarke, Arthur Morrison, Michael Dark, Lila Leslie • Hugh Hemingway (Russell) and George Sheyer (Peyton) are each suspected by American Consul Wilbur Harris (Clarke) of being a fugitive thief in Zanzibar. Harris's secretary, Polly (Renick), becomes involved with Hemingway, who, although suspicious, finds the final evidence that proves Sheyer is the fugitive. 4,999'

THE YELLOW STAIN (May 21, 1922); D: Jack Dillon; W: Jules Furthman; C: Don Short; Cast: John Gilbert, Claire Anderson, John P. Lockney, Mark Fenton, Herschel Mayall, Robert Daly, Mace Robinson, James McElhern, Frank Hemphill, May Alexander • A young lawyer in Michigan, Donald Keith (Gilbert), represents worker Daniel Kerstin (Daly) in a case against a powerful lumber king, Quartus Hembly (Lockney). Olaf Erickson (Fenton), father of Thora (Anderson), whom Keith loves, is complicit in swindling Kerstin. A deathbed confession resolves the matter, even though Keith is attacked and the jury is bribed. 5,006'

STRANGE IDOLS (May 28, 1922); D: Bernard J. Durning; W: Jules Furthman (scr), Emil Forst (st); C: Don Short; Cast: Dustin Farnum, Doris Pawn, Philo McCullough, Richard Tucker • A lumberman, Angus (Farnum), marries New York cabaret dancer Ruth (Pawn) and takes her back to the Northwest. Bored, Ruth returns to the cabaret. Six years later, Angus reconciles with her and their daughter. 4,300'

ROUGH SHOD (June 4, 1922); D: Reeves Eason; W: Jack Strumwasser, Charles Alden Seltzer (novel); C: Lucien Andriot; Cast: Charles Jones, Helen Ferguson, Ruth Renick, Maurice B. Flynn, Jack Rollins, Charles Le Moyne • "Steel" Brannon (Jones), who is the foreman of Josephine Hamilton's (Renick) ranch, is still on the trail of his father's killer years after the murder. There is much horse stealing in the area, and wealthy rancher "Satan" Latimer is a suspect. Betty (Ferguson), a cultured Easterner, is kidnapped by Latimer, and Brannon gives chase. In a fight, Brannon discovers, from a tattoo, that Latimer is his quarry. Latimer is pushed over a cliff in the fight. 4,486'

LIGHTS OF THE DESERT (June 11, 1922); D: Harry Beaumont; W: Paul Schofield (scr), Gladys E. Johnson; C: Frank Good; Cast: Shirley Mason, Allan Forrest, Edward Burns, James Mason, Andree Tourneur, Josephine Crowell, Lillian Langdon • Yvonne (Mason), a member of a theatrical troupe stranded in a western town, decides to stay when she is romanced by an oil company foreman (Burns), but later falls in love with an oil well owner (Forrest) and opts for his love. 4,809'

FOR BIG STAKES (June 18, 1922); D: Lynn Reynolds; W: Lynn Reynolds, Ralph Spence (titles); C: Dan Clark; E: Ralph Spence; Cast: Tom Mix, Patsy Ruth Miller, Sid Jordan, Bert Sprotte, Joe Harris, Al Fremont, Earl Simpson, Tony the Wonder Horse • "Cleanup" Sudden (Mix) rides into town with his identity as a ranch owner hidden from everyone. He starts by cleaning out the thieves and capturing crooked Sheriff Blaisdell (Fremont). He then saves Dorothy (Miller), daughter of the previous ranch owner (Sprotte), when she is tied to a tree by arch-villain Scott Mason (Jordan). Mason returns to burn down the ranch house and barn. All ends well for Sudden and Dorothy. 4,378'

A SELF-MADE MAN (June 25, 1922); D: Rowland V. Lee; W: Rowland V. Lee, Monte M. Katterjohn, Ralph Spence (titles), George Horace Lorimer (novel); C: David Abel; E: Ralph Spence; Cast: William Russell, Renee Adorée, Mathilde Brundage, James Gordon, Richard Tucker, Togo Yamamoto, Harry Gribbon • Jack Spurlock (Russell), an indolent son, is disowned by his magnate father, Jonas (Gordon), and abandons his fiancée, Anita (Adorée), but she eventually helps save Jonas financially and restores the son's self-respect. 4,920'

TROOPER O'NEIL (July 16, 1922); D: Scott Dunlap, C.R. Wallace; W: William K. Howard, George Goodchild (novel); C: Lucien Andriot; Cast: Charles Jones, Beatrice Burnham, Francis McDonald, Claude Payton, Sidney Jordan, Jack Rollins, Karl Formes • A Northwest Mountie (Jones) falls in love with Marie (Burnham), a woman he has arrested on suspicion of murder. The real murderer, Pierre (McDonald), also in love with Marie, attempts to free her and dies at the hands of the Mountie, but not before confessing to the murder. 4,862'

OATH-BOUND (Aug. 13, 1922); D: Bernard J. Durning; W: Jack Strumwasser (scr), Edward J. LeSaint (scr, st), William Locke (novel); C: Don Short; Cast: Dustin Farnum, Ethel Grey Terry, Fred Thomson, Maurice B. Flynn, Norman Selby, Aileen Pringle, Bob Perry, Herschel Mayall • Lawrence (Farnum) is a wealthy steamship owner whose liners are being robbed of cargo. He sends his younger brother Jim (Thomson) to trap the thieves, but a Secret Service man (Flynn) exposes Jim as the ringleader of silk thieves. 4,468'

THE NEW TEACHER (Aug. 20, 1922); D: Joseph Franz; W: Dorothy Yost (adpt), Margaret Elizabeth Sangster (novel); C: Frank B. Good; Cast: Shirley Mason, Allan Forrest, Earl Metcalf, Otto Hoffman, Ola Norman, Pat Moore, Kate Price • A society girl, Constance (Mason), becomes a school teacher on New York's Lower East Side, and keeps her job a secret from fiancé Bruce (Forrest). When Bruce discovers this, he becomes a policeman in the same area and convinces her that she needs a husband and protector. 4,453'

THE FAST MAIL (Aug. 20, 1922); D: Bernard J. Durning; W: Agnes Parsons, Jacques Jaccard, Lincoln J. Carter (unpublished play); C: George Schneiderman, Don Short; Cast: Charles Jones, Eileen Percy, James Mason, William Steele, Adolphe Menjou, Harry Dunkinson • A cowboy, Stanley Carson (Jones), is tricked out of winning a racehorse by crooked gamblers who kidnap his girlfriend, Virginia (Percy). Stanley uses a train, boat, and car to rescue her. 6 reels

MOONSHINE VALLEY (Aug. 27, 1922); D: Herbert Brenon; W: Mary Murillo (scr, st), Herbert Brenon (scr), Lenora Asereth (st); C: Tom Malloy; Cast: William Farnum, Sadie Mullen, Holmes Herbert, Dawn O'Day, Jean the dog • Ned (Farnum), a drunkard wandering in the forest, finds a child, Nancy (O'Day), and takes her home. When Nancy becomes ill, Ned takes her to Dr. Martin (Herbert). The doctor recognizes Nancy as his wife's (Mullen) daughter. Martin is killed by Ned when he tries to kidnap Nancy, and Ned is reunited with the woman who had left him to marry Dr. Martin. 5,679'

HONOR FIRST (Aug. 27, 1922); D: Jerome Storm; W: Joseph Franklin Poland, George Gibbs (novel); C: Joseph August; Cast: John Gilbert, Renee Adorée, Hardee Kirkland, Shannon Day, Wilson Hummel • French twin brothers, Jacques (Gilbert) and Honoré (Gilbert), fight in the Great War. Due to a mix-up in uniforms, credit for a heroic act goes to Honoré, the coward, who later takes Jacques's identity and tries to have him killed, but is killed himself. 5,075'

SILVER WINGS (Aug. 27, 1922); D: Edwin Carewe, Jack Ford; W: Paul H. Sloane; C: Robert Kurrie, Joseph Ruttenberg; Cast: Mary Carr, Claude Brook, Percy Helton, Joseph Striker, Jane Thomas, Roy Gordon, Florence Haas, Roger Lytton, Ernest Hilliard • A mother (Carr) is forced to live in poverty after one son (Helton) leaves town, accused of embezzling the family's money which was stolen by another son (Striker). A magazine story causes the family to be happily reunited after all is straightened out. 8,271'

JUST TONY (Aug. 30, 1922); D: Lynn F. Reynolds; W: Lynn F. Reynolds, Max Brand (novel); C: Dan Clark; Cast: Tony the Wonder Horse, Tom Mix, Claire Adams, J.P. Lockney, Duke Lee, Frank Campeau, Walt Robbins • A wild man-hating mustang (Tony) learns to appreciate a cowboy, Ferris (Mix), who saves him from mistreatment. Tony rescues Ferris and a rancher's daughter (Adams) when they are in trouble. 5,233'

MONTE CRISTO (Sept. 3, 1922); D: Emmett J. Flynn; W: Bernard McConville (scr), Alexander Salvini (st), Charles Fechter (addl. st), Alexandre Dumas (novel); C: Lucien Andriot; Cast: John Gilbert, Estelle Taylor, Robert McKim, William V. Mong, Virginia Brown

Faire, George Siegmann, Spottiswoode Aitken, Ralph Cloninger, Albert Prisco, Gaston Glass • Edmond Dantes (Gilbert) is separated from his bride, Mercedes (Taylor), and placed in a dungeon on false charges. He ingeniously escapes from his island prison to become a wealthy man by finding a treasure and takes revenge on the three men (Prisco, Cloninger, McKim) who wronged him. 9,828'

WEST OF CHICAGO (Sept. 3, 1922); D: Scott Dunlap, C.R. Wallace; W: Paul Schofield (scr), George Scarborough (st); C: Lucien Andriot; Cast: Charles Jones, Renée Adorée, Philo McCullough, Sidney D'Albrook, Charles French, Marcella Day, Kathleen Key • After he learns that his uncle has been killed, Conroy (Jones), a cowboy, shows up at the uncle's ranch using a false identity. In league with Della (Adorée), he exposes a ranch-hand (McCullough) who has kidnapped the still-alive uncle and taken over the property. 4,694'

NERO (Sept. 7, 1922); D: J. Gordon Edwards; W: Virginia Tracy, Charles Sarver; C: Harry Plimpton; E: Hettie Grey Baker; Cast: Jacques Gretillat, Violet Mersereau, Alexander Salvini, Guido Trento, Enzo De Felice, Nero Bernardi, Adolfo Trouche, Nello Carolenuto, Americo De Giorgio, Paulette Duval • Nero (Gretillat) rises to power, becomes infatuated with a young Christian (Mersereau) who is romancing a Roman soldier (Salvini), and is betrayed by the Empress Poppaea (Duval). 12 reels (approx. 135 min.) • This high-budget film included a chariot race in the Circus Maximus, the burning of Rome and a charge of Roman legionnaires. Although it was planned as Fox's biggest picture of the year, because of its cost, it turned out to be a disappointment and showed a loss.

A FOOL THERE WAS (Sept. 10, 1922); D: Emmett J. Flynn; W: Bernard McConville, Porter Emerson Browne (play), Rudyard Kipling (poem); C: Lucien Andriot; Cast: Estelle Taylor, Lewis Stone, Irene Rich, Muriel Dana, Marjorie Daw, Mahlon Hamilton, Wallace MacDonald, William V. Mong, Harry Lonsdale • Englishman John Schuyler (Stone) abandons his wife (Rich) and daughter (Dana) to be with Gilda Fontaine (Taylor), who sucks the life out of him and turns him to alcohol. In his attempt to strangle Gilda, John falls to his death. 6,604' • This is a remake of the 1915 Theda Bara "vamp" story of the same title.

THE CRUSADER (Sept. 10, 1922); D: Howard M. Mitchell; W: William K. Howard, Jack Strumwasser, Alan Sullivan (article); C: David Abel; Cast: William Russell, Gertrude Claire, Helen Ferguson, Fritzi Brunette, George Webb, Carl Grantvoort • An honest young miner, Peter (Russell), believes he has struck silver and gets involved with a crooked entrepreneur (Webb) who swindles townspeople into buying worthless stock in the mine. Peter is later trapped by a mine cave-in caused by the swindler's cohorts, but a neighbor (Ferguson) and her father come to the rescue. 4,780'

THE YOSEMITE TRAIL (Sept. 24, 1922); D: Bernard J. Durning; W: Jack Strumwasser, Ridgwell Cullum (novel); C: Don Short; Cast: Dustin Farnum, Irene Rich, Walter McGrail, Frank Campeau, W.J. Ferguson, Charles French • Jim (Farnum) and his cousin Ned (McGrail) are rivals for Eve (Rich), but Ned wins her. Jim goes to South America, but returns and eventually gets the girl when Ned turns out to be a criminal and an abuser. 4,735'

YOUTH MUST HAVE LOVE (Oct. 1, 1922); D: Joseph Franz; W: Dorothy Yost; C: George Schneiderman; Cast: Shirley Mason, Cecil Van Auker, Wallace MacDonald, Landers Stevens, Wilson Hummel • Earl Stannard (MacDonald), accused of murder, escapes from jail and tracks down the people who framed him, including his girlfriend's (Mason) father, Marvin (Van Auker). Marvin eventually reveals that he was covering up for his friend's guilt. 4,368'

DO AND DARE (Oct. 1, 1922); D: Edward Sedgwick; W: Edward Sedgwick, Ralph Spence (titles); C: Dan Clark; E: Ralph Spence; Cast: Tom Mix, Dulcie Cooper, Claire Adams, Claude Peyton, Jack Rollins, Hector Sarno, Wilbur Higby, Bob Klein, Gretchen Hartman • Henry Boone (Mix) listens to his grandfather's (Mix) stories about life as an Indian fighter. Drawn to the romance of adventure, Boone is later arrested as a spy when he is caught carrying a military message to a South American revolutionary leader (Rollins), but he escapes and rescues the leader's daughter, Juanita (Adams). 4,744'

CALVERT'S VALLEY (Oct. 8, 1922); D: Jack Dillon; W: Jules Furthman, Margaret Prescott Montague (novel); C: Don Short; Cast: Jack Gilbert, Sylvia Breaker, Philo McCullough, Herschel Mayall, Lule Warrenton • James Calvert (McCullough) is pushed off a cliff and his drunken lawyer, Page Emlyn (Gilbert), is accused of murder. In jail, Page believes Calvert committed suicide over Hester Reynal (Breamer), with whom Page has fallen in love. An old woman (Warrenton), who was a witness, eventually clears the lawyer by naming her half-witted son as the culprit. 4,416'

BELLS OF SAN JUAN (Oct. 15, 1922); D: Scott Dunlap; W: Rex Taylor, Jackson Gregory (novel); C: Dev Jennings; Cast: Charles Jones, Fritzi Brunette, Claude Peyton, Harry Todd, Kathleen Key, William Steele, Otto Matieson, Sid Jordan • Sheriff Norton (Jones) is lured into a trap when his girlfriend, Dorothy (Brunette), is kidnapped by Jim Garson (Peyton), who is suspected in the murder of Norton's father. In the pursuit and rescue of Dorothy, Norton suffers a head injury and turns to crime, but is cured by an operation and extracts confessions from the guilty man. 4,587'

MIXED FACES (Oct. 22, 1922); D: Rowland V. Lee; W: Paul Schofield, Roy Norton (novel); C: David Abel; Cast: William Russell, Renée Adorée, De Witt Jennings, Elizabeth Garrison, Charles French, Aileen Manning, Harvey Clarke • A traveling salesman, Jimmy Gallop (Russell), who is a dead ringer for a Judge Woodworth (Russell), is convinced by opponents in a political race to impersonate the candidate. Woodworth is kidnapped and Jimmy is almost murdered before their identities are straightened out. The judge's girlfriend, Mary (Adorée), falls for Jimmy. 5 reels

WITHOUT COMPROMISE (Oct. 29, 1922); D: Emmett J. Flynn; W: Bernard McConville, Lillian Bennett-Thompson and George Hubbard (novel); C: Dev Jennings; Cast: William Farnum, Lois Wilson, Robert McKim, Tully Marshall, Hardee Kirkland, Otis Harlan, Will Walling, Alma Bennett, Eugene Pallette, Fred Kohler, Jack Dillon • Sheriff Dick Leighton (Farnum) is tested when forced to stand his ground against the leader of political corruption in his town. 5,173'

MY FRIEND, THE DEVIL (Oct. 29, 1922); D: Harry Millarde; W: Paul H. Sloane, Georges Ohnet (novel); C: Joseph Ruttenberg; Cast: Charles Richman, Ben Grauer, William Tooker, Adolph Milar, John Tavernier, Myrtle Stewart, Barbara Castleton, Alice May, Peggy Shaw, Robert Frazer, Mabel Wright • A prominent surgeon, George Dryden (Richman), who is an atheist, endures all kinds of personal tragedies. When his daughter (Shaw) cannot be cured by science, he turns to prayer and she is miraculously cured. 9,555'

THE LOVE GAMBLER (Nov. 12, 1922); D: Joseph Franz; W: Jules Furthman, Lillian Bennett-Thompson and George Hubbard (article); C: Joe August; Cast: John Gilbert, Carmel Myers, Bruce Gordon, Cap Anderson, William Lawrence, James Gordon, Mrs. Cohen, Barbara Tennant, Edward Cecil, Doreen Turner • A ranch hand, Dick Manners (Gilbert), marries a dying woman, Kate (Tennant), just to give her child a name, but the woman survives and keeps Dick apart from his true love, Jean (Myers), until Kate commits suicide. 4,682'

SHIRLEY OF THE CIRCUS (Nov. 12, 1922); D: Rowland V. Lee; W: Robert N. Lee; C: G.O. Post; Cast: Shirley Mason, George O'Hara, Crauford Kent, Alan Hale, Lule Warrenton, Maude Wayne, Mathilde Brundage • A young French circus girl, Nita (Mason), is sent to school by an American artist (Kent), but later runs away and arrives at the artist's home in the United States. She rejoins her circus troupe while they perform in America, and is reunited with her former sweetheart, Pierre (O'Hara). 4,668'

ARABIA (Nov. 19, 1922); D: Lynn Reynolds; W: Lynn Reynolds (st and scr), Tom Mix (st), Hettie Grey Baker (titles); C: Don Clark; E: Hettie Grey Baker; Cast: Tom Mix, Barbara Bedford, George Hernandez, Norman Selby, Edward Piel, Ralph Yearsley, Hector Sarno • A dashing horseman, Billy Evans (Mix), swaps clothes with an Arabian prince who is being pursued and is then abducted and taken to Arabia. He ousts a pretender to the throne, restores the sultan to power and rescues Janice Terhune (Bedford), who has also been kidnapped. 4,448'

WHILE JUSTICE WAITS (Nov. 19, 1922); D: Bernard J. Durning; W: Edwin Booth Tilton (scr), Jack Strumwasser (scr), Charles A. Short (st), Don Short (st); C: Don Short; Cast: Dustin Farnum, Irene Rich, Earl Metcalf, Junior Delameter, Frankie Lee, Hector Sarno, Peaches Jackson, Gretchen Hartman • A gold miner, Dan (Farnum), returns from Alaska and joins up with a gang of criminals to find out who kidnapped his wife, Nell (Rich), and their son. On the trail, he is joined by a boy (Delameter) who has lost his mother. When he finally tracks down Nell, Dan has a shootout with the villain and is told that the boy is his son. 4,762'

THE BOSS OF CAMP 4 (Nov. 26, 1922); D: W.S. Van Dyke; W: Paul Schofield, Arthur Preston Hankins (novel); C: Ernest Miller, Dev Jennings; Cast: Charles Jones, Fritzi Brunette, G. Raymond Nye, Francis Ford, Sid Jordan, Milton Ross • A war veteran, Chet Fanning (Jones), arrives in a small town and gets a job on a construction crew when he spies the boss's daughter Iris (Brunette). Chet rescues Iris from a falling boulder and later frustrates the plot of a gang trying to impede the completion of a road under construction so that the owner (Ross) will default on his schedule and lose his right to the land. The road is completed and Chet ends up with Iris. 4,235'

WHO ARE MY PARENTS? (Nov. 26, 1922); D: J. Searle Dawley; W: Paul H. Sloane, Merle Johnson (novel); C: Bert Dawley; Cast: Roger Lytton, Peggy Shaw, Florence Billings, Ernest Hilliard, Robert Agnew, Adelaide Prince, Niles Welch, Marie Reinhardt, Florence Haas, Jimmie Lapsley • When Betty (Shaw) and Bob (Agnew) are eloping, Bob is killed in a car accident. Betty's father (Lytton) discovers she is pregnant and puts her baby in an orphanage. Having been told by her father that the baby died, Betty marries Ken (Tyler). While visiting the orphanage with her sister (Billings), who is looking to adopt a child, Betty finds her daughter. At first angry with her, Ken finally agrees to adopt the daughter. 8,361'

THE GREAT NIGHT (Dec. 3, 1922); D: Howard M. Mitchell; W: Joseph Franklin Poland; C: David Abel; Cast: William Russell, Eva Novak, Winifred Bryson, Henry Barrows, Wade Boteler, Harry Lonsdale, Earl Metcalfe • Besieged by women willing to marry him for his fortune, Larry Gilmore (Russell), who must find a wife to gain an inheritance, becomes a police officer, falls in love with Mollie (Novak), a waitress, and nabs a gang of jewel thieves. Larry and Mollie arrive at the altar just seconds before the expiration of his inheritance. 4,346'

THE LIGHTS OF NEW YORK (Dec. 10, 1922); D: Charles J. Brabin; W: Charles J. Brabin; C: George W. Lane; Story #1: Clarence Nordstrom, Margaret Seddon, Frank Currier, Florence Short, Charles Gerard; Story #2: Marc McDermott, Estelle Taylor • Two separate New York stories: (1) a foundling (Currier) is adopted but led astray by evil friends; (2) a Wall Street financier (McDermott) plunges into despair when his fiancée (Taylor) leaves him. 5,581'

A CALIFORNIA ROMANCE (Dec. 24, 1922); D: Jerome Storm; W: Charles E. Banks (scr), Jules Furthman (st); C: Joseph August; Cast: John Gilbert, Estelle Taylor, George Siegmann, Jack McDonald, Charles Anderson • A young girl, Dolores (Taylor), in 1840s California, pledges herself to a Mexican army officer Juan Diego (Siegmann), who is really the leader of a renegade band. However, Juan Diego imprisons her. A rival for her love, Patricio (Gilbert), ends up rescuing her. 3,892'

PAWN TICKET 210 (Dec. 31, 1922); D: Scott Dunlap; W: Jules Furthman, David Belasco and Clay M. Greene (unpublished play); C: George Schneiderman; Cast: Shirley Mason, Robert Agnew, Irene Hunt, Jacob Abrams, Dorothy Manners, Fred Warren • Meg (Mason), a young girl left at Harris Levi's (Warren) pawn shop and never reclaimed, is later turned over to Levi's influential friend. When Meg's mother, Ruth Sternhold (Hunt), returns after 15 years, Meg learns that the man she's living with is really her father. With the family reunited, Meg also introduces them to her sweetheart (Agnew). 4,871'

CATCH MY SMOKE (Dec. 31, 1922); D: William Beaudine; W: Jack Strumwasser, Joseph Bushnell Ames (novel); C: Dan Clark; Cast: Tom Mix, Lillian Rich, Claude Peyton, Gordon Griffith, Harry Griffith, Robert Milash, Pat Chrisman, Cap Anderson, Ruby Lafayette • A World War I veteran, Bob Stratton (Mix), thought to be dead, returns to learn his ranch is now owned by Mary Thorne (Rich), whose deceased father was Stratton's executor. Stratton fights off some shady characters and regains the ranch when he marries Mary. 4,070'

1923 Releases

A FRIENDLY HUSBAND (Jan. 1, 1923) Sunshine Comedy; D: John Blystone; W: John Blystone (scr), Hampton Del Ruth (st), Ralph Spence (titles); C: Jay Turner; E: Ralph Spence; Cast: Lupino Lane, Alberta Vaughn, Eva Thatcher • A husband (Lane) and his wife, Tootsie (Vaughn), go camping in their trailer, equipped with beds, stove, shower bath, dishwasher and other weird and amusing devices. They are joined by Tootsie's man-eating mother (Thatcher), who makes the husband the sap of the family tree. After doing all the work and enjoying none of the fun, the husband becomes a hero when he rescues his wife from a gang of bandits. 4,527'

THE CUSTARD CUP (Jan. 1, 1923); D: Herbert Brenon; W: G. Marion Burton, Florence Bingham Livingston (novel), Ralph Spence (titles); C: Tom Malloy; E: Ralph Spence; Cast: Mary Carr, Myrta Bonillas, Miriam Battista, Jerry Devine, Ernest McKay, Peggy Shaw, Leslie Leigh, Frederick Esmelton, Henry Sedley, Louis Hendricks, Edward Boring • A widow (Carr) with three children, and a couple of counterfeiters, Frank Bosley (Sedley) and his wife, Gussie (Bonillas), all live in a tenement neighborhood known as the "Custard Cup." While trying to destroy evidence, the Bosleys start a fire on a boat excursion and the widow is accused of passing phony bills. A detective proves she is innocent and nabs the Bosleys. 6,166' • This was yet another attempt to capitalize on the popularity of "Over the Hill to the Poorhouse."

THE FACE ON THE BARROOM FLOOR (Jan. 1, 1923); D: Jack Ford; W: G. Marion Burton, Eugene B. Lewis, Hugh Antoine D'Arcy (poem); C: George Schneiderman; Cast: Henry B. Walthall, Ruth Clifford, Walter Emerson, Frederick Sullivan, Alma Bennett, Norval MacGregor, Michael Dark, Gus Saville • In a series of flashbacks, artist Robert (Walthall), engaged to society girl Marion (Clifford), becomes infatuated with a fisherman's (Saville) daughter, who has been dishonored by Marion's brother (Emerson). The daughter commits suicide and Robert is wrongfully imprisoned. After being released, he hangs around in a barroom, where he is eventually found by Marion. 5,787'

THE VILLAGE BLACKSMITH (Jan. 1, 1923); D: Jack Ford; W: Paul H. Sloane (adpt), Henry Wadsworth Longfellow (poem); C: George Schneiderman; Cast: William Walling, Virginia True Boardman, Virginia Valli, Ida McKenzie, David Butler, Gordon Griffith, George Hackathorne, Pat Moore, Tully Marshall, Francis Ford • The trials and tribulations of a blacksmith, John Hammond (Walling), whose grown children each get into trouble but come to a happy ending through their father's or each other's help. 7,540'

THREE WHO PAID (Jan. 7, 1923); D: Colin Campbell; W: Joseph Franklin Poland, George Owen Baxter (article); C: Don Short; Cast: Dustin Farnum, Fred Kohler, Bessie Love, Frank Campeau, Robert Daly, William Conklin, Robert Agnew • Riley (Farnum), a cowboy, sets out to avenge his brother's death by hunting down the three men who killed him. Each is killed by others and the cowboy ends up exonerating a woman (Love) accused of murder. 4,859'

SALOME (Jan. 14, 1923) Reissue

THE FOOTLIGHT RANGER (Jan. 14, 1923); D: Scott Dunlap; W: Dorothy Yost, William Branch; C: Dev Jennings; Cast: Charles Jones, Fritzi Brunette, James Mason, Lillian Langdon, Lydia Yeamans Titus, Hanrey Barrows • Cowboy Bill Moreland (Jones) follows Janet (Brunette), an actress, back to New York, rescues her from a lecherous producer, marries her, and returns to the West. 4,729'

MAN'S SIZE (Jan. 21, 1923); D: Howard M. Mitchell; W: Joseph Franklin Poland, William MacLeod Raine (novel); C: George Schneiderman, Ernest Miller; Cast: William Russell, Alma Bennett, Stanton Heck, Charles K. French, James Gordon, Carl Stockdale • Tom Morse (Russell), visiting his uncle (Gordon), a Canadian northwest trading magnate, to learn the business, falls in love with Jessie McRae (Bennett). Jessie is the ward of an old Scottish trapper, Angus (French). Because of a feud between the Morses and McRaes, Jessie is "sold" to a bootlegger, Bully West (Heck). Tom rescues Jessie and sets everything straight. 4,316'

BRASS COMMANDMENTS (Jan. 28, 1923); D: Lynn F. Reynolds; W: Charles Kenyon, Charles Alden Seltzer (novel); C: Dev Jennings; Cast: William Farnum, Wanda Hawley, Tom Santschi, Claire Adams, Charles Le Moyne, Joe Rickson, Lon Poff, Al Fremont, Joseph Gordon, Cap Anderson • A cowboy (Farnum) returns from the East to end cattle rustling in his town, but is lured into a trap in which two female rivals for his love, Gloria (Hawley) and Ellen (Adams), are kidnapped by the leader (Santschi) of the rustlers. 4,829'

THE TOWN THAT FORGOT GOD (Feb. 11, 1923); D: Harry Millarde; W: Paul H. Sloane; C: Joseph Ruttenberg; Cast: Bunny Grauer, Warren Krech, Jane Thomas, Harry Benham, Edward Denison, Grace Barton, Raymond Bloomer, Nina Casavant • Distraught by his true love, Betty (Thomas), marrying Harry (Benham), a surveyor, village carpenter Eben (Krech) leaves town. He returns years later and befriends Betty's son, David (Grauer), now an orphan, who has run away from a cruel foster father (Denison). A ferocious storm destroys the town, but the boy and his new mentor survive. Twenty-five years later, David (Bloomer) returns to rebuild the town. 8,500'

ROMANCE LAND (Feb. 11, 1923); D: Edward Sedgwick; W: Joseph Franklin Poland, Kenneth Perkins (novel); C: Dan Clark; Cast: Tom Mix, Barbara Bedford, Frank Brownlee, George Webb, Pat Chrisman, Wynn Mace • "Pep" Hawkins is a western hero dressed in a knight's suit of armor and carrying a lance. He rescues Nan (Bedford), whose uncle is looking for a suitable mate for her since she is about to come of age and will have to take over the family ranch. The uncle (Brownlee) has mismanaged the accounting and needs someone he can control to cover his mistakes. Nan is a romantic and sets up a rodeo with three events in which the victor will win her hand in marriage. There is a chariot race, a pony express race, and an all-vehicle race. Hawkins is the victor, but before the wedding, the uncle has Nan kidnapped, which leads Hawkins into chases, stunts and fist fights. 3,975'

TRUXTON KING (Feb. 18, 1923); D: Jerome Storm; W: Paul Schofield, George Barr McCutcheon (novel); C: Joe August; Cast: John Gilbert, Ruth Clifford, Frank Leigh, Micky Moore, Otis Harlan, Henry Miller, Jr., Richard Wayne, Willis Marks, Winifred Bryson, Mark Fenton • Truxton (Gilbert), an American visiting a foreign land, foils a plot against the Prince (Moore) and prevents an attack on his castle while winning the heart of the Prince's aunt (Clifford). 5,613'

THE BUSTER (Feb. 18, 1923); D: Colin Campbell; W: Jack Strumwasser, William Patterson White (novel); C: David Abel; Cast: Dustin Farnum, Doris Pawn, Francis McDonald, Gilbert Holmes, Lucille Hutton • A rancher, Bill Corvell (Farnum), tries to impress Charlotte (Pawn), the city girl he loves, by faking a kidnapping, from which he will rescue her. The tables are turned when she ends up rescuing him. 4,587'

GOOD-BY GIRLS! (March 11, 1923); D: Jerome Storm; W: Joseph Franklin Poland, George Foxhall (article); C: Joe August; Cast: William Russell, Carmel Myers, Tom Wilson, Kate Price, Robert Klein • An author, Vance McPhee (Russell), on the verge of a nervous breakdown, discovers Florence (Myers) hiding from a gang led by Tom Wilson (Jordan) at his aunt's country home. Vance defends her from the pursuers who are after her father's valuable patents. His doctor later appears and pronounces Vance cured of his ailments. Vance later marries Florence. 4,746'

THREE JUMPS AHEAD (March 25, 1923); D: Jack Ford; W: Jack Ford; C: Dan Clark; Cast: Tom Mix, Alma Bennett, Virginia True Boardman, Edward Piel, Joe Girard, Francis Ford, Margaret Joslin, Harry Todd, Buster Gardner • Cowboy Steve McLean (Mix) and his uncle make a deal to be freed by outlaws, but they have to track down another captive, John Darrell (Girard), who has escaped. When Darrell is found, Steve realizes that John is the father of his girlfriend, Annie Darrell (Bennett). Steve now has to rescue John from the outlaws. 4,854'

BUCKING THE BARRIER (Apr. 1, 1923); D: Colin Campbell; W: Jack Strumwasser (scr), George Goodchild (st); C: Lucien Andriot; Cast: Dustin Farnum, Arline Pretty, Leon Bary, Colin Chase, Hayford Hobbs, Sidney D'Albrook • An Alaskan miner, Kit Carew (Farnum), travels to England to claim an inheritance from Frank Farfax (Chase), but must fend off Frank's step brothers, Luke (Bary) and Cyril (Hobbs). Kit falls in love with Frank's step-sister, Blanche (Pretty), but his intentions are misunderstood. Kit returns to Alaska without the inheritance, but is reunited with Blanche years later. 4,566'

MADNESS OF YOUTH (Apr. 8, 1923); D: Jerome Storm; W: Joseph Franklin Poland (scr), George Frank Worts (st.); C: Joseph August; Cast: John Gilbert, Billie Dove, Donald Hatswell, George K. Arthur, Wilton Taylor, Ruth Boyd, Luke Lucas, Julanne Johnston • A youthful crook, Jaca (Gilbert), posing as an evangelist, falls in love with Nanette (Dove), the daughter of one of his targets for robbery, Theodore Banning (Taylor). Nanette awakens Jaca's better nature. 4,719'

LOVEBOUND (Apr. 15, 1923); D: Henry Otto; W: Josephine Quirk (scr), Jules Furthman (scr), George Scarborough (st); C: David Abel; Cast: Shirley Mason, Albert Roscoe, Richard Tucker, Joseph Girard, Edward Martindel, Fred Kelsey • Bess (Mason), the daughter of reformed criminal David Belwyn (Girard), marries District Attorney John Mobley (Roscoe) and later has to fend off blackmail attempts because she had inadvertently committed a crime to protect her father. 4,407'

SNOWDRIFT (Apr. 22, 1923); D: Scott Dunlap; W: Jack Strumwasser (scr), James B. Hendryx (st.); C: George Schneiderman; Cast: Charles Jones, Irene Rich, G. Raymond Nye, Dorothy Manners, Lalo Encinas, Lee Shumway, Charles Anderson, Bert Sprotte, Gertrude Ryan, Colin Chase, Evelyn Selbie • A mining engineer in Alaska, Carter Brent (Jones), has lost all his money through gambling and cures himself of an addiction to liquor. He heads north to re-develop his mine and falls in love with Snowdrift (Manners), an orphan of white parents reared by an Indian squaw (Selbie). Snowdrift is kidnapped by dancehall manager Johnnie Claw (Nye), and Brent engages in mortal combat to rescue her. 4,617'

BOSTON BLACKIE (May 6, 1923); D: Scott Dunlap; W: Paul Schofield, Jack Boyle (article); C: George Schneiderman; Cast: William Russell, Eva Novak, Frank Brownlee, Otto Matieson, Spike Robinson, Frederick Esmelton • Released from prison, Boston Blackie (Russell) threatens the warden (Brownlee) for using torture methods. He is pursued and returned to prison but the warden is prevented from torturing him because Blackie's girlfriend, Mary (Novak), enlists the governor's help. 4,522'

STEPPIN' FAST (May 13, 1923); D: Joseph J. Franz; W: Bernard McConville; C: Dan Clark; Cast: Tom Mix, Claire Adams, Donald MacDonald, Hector Sarno, Edward Peil, George Siegmann, Tom S. Guise, Edward Jobson, Ethel Wales, Minna Redman, Tony • Rancher Grant Malvern (Mix), on his way to visit his mother in San Francisco, rescues a scientist (Guise) who is being accosted by three men. When the scientist (Guise) is fatally stabbed, he gives Grant a map ring to take to his daughter, Helen (Adams), in China. The villains catch up with him and throw him into San Francisco Bay. Grant still makes his way to China, meets up with Helen and they race back to America, pursued by the villains, to find the gold mine on the map ring. 4,608'

SKID PROOF (July 22, 1923); D: Scott Dunlap; W: Harvey Gates (scr), Byron Morgan (st); C: Don Short; Cast: Charles Jones, Laura Anson, Fred Eric, Jacqueline Gadsden, Peggy Shaw, Earl Metcalf, Claude Peyton, Harry Tracey • A race car driver (Jones) loses a transcontinental challenge when a competitor shoots him from an airplane. He ends up becoming a movie star, falls in love with an actress (Anson), whom he saves from a bad marriage, and then wins the next race. 5,565'

ALIAS THE NIGHT WIND (Aug. 19, 1923); D: Joseph Franz; W: Robert N. Lee, Varick Vanardy (novel); C: Ernest Miller; Cast: William Russell, Maude Wayne, Charles K. French, Wade Boteler, Donald MacDonald, H. Milton Ross, Charles Wellesley, Mark Fenton, Otto Matieson, Bob Klein • Bing Howard (Russell), a fugitive stockbroker, is hunted by private detective Clifford Rushton (MacDonald), who teams up with female investigator Kate Maxwell (Wayne). Kate later proves Rushton framed both Howard and her father for bond robbery. 4,145'

IF WINTER COMES (Aug. 19, 1923); D: Harry Millarde; W: Paul Sloane, Arthur Stuart-Menteth Hutchinson (novel); C: Joseph Ruttenberg; Cast: Percy Marmont, Arthur Metcalfe, Sidney Herbert, Wallace Kolb, William Riley Hatch, Raymond Bloomer, Russell Sedgwick, Margaret Fielding, Ann Forrest, Gladys Leslie • This is the sprawling tale of a soldier, Mark Sabre (Marmont), who returns with wounds from the war to find that the young woman, Effie (Leslie), whom he had engaged to keep his wife, Mabel (Fielding), company, has been dismissed. Later, the snobbish, unpleasant Mabel leaves Mark when he offers to help Effie and her baby. Scandal follows when Effie kills her baby and commits suicide. Mark finally attains some happiness when the woman he has always loved, Lady Tybar (Ann Forrest), comes to his side after her husband has been killed. 12,000' • The original length of this melodrama was 14 reels, almost three times as long as a standard release.

THE MAN WHO WON (Aug. 23, 1923); D: William A. Wellman; W: Ewart Anderson, Ridgwell Cullum (novel); C: Joseph August; Cast: Dustin Farnum, Jacqueline Gadsden, Lloyd Whitlock, Ralph Cloninger, Mary Warren, Pee Wee Holmes, Harvey Clark, Lon Poff, Andy Waldron, Ken Maynard • A gambler, Wild Bill (Farnum), lures a bandit (Whitlock) by driving a coach filled with gold, to help a miner (Cloninger) find the bandit's lair and retrieve his runaway wife (Gadsden). 5,050'

SOFT BOILED (Aug. 26, 1923); D: J.G. Blystone; W: J.G. Blystone (scr & st), Edward Moran (st); C: Dan Clark; Cast: Tom Mix, Joseph Girard, Billie Dove, L.C. Shumway, Tom Wilson, Frank Beal, Jack Curtis, Charles Hill Mailes, Harry Dunkinson, Wilson Hummell, Tony • Under the threat of being disinherited by his wealthy uncle (Beal), cowboy Tom Steele (Mix) has been able to control his short temper. But when his girlfriend (Dove) is insulted, he loses control and destroys everything in sight and avenges the insult with comical consequences. 7,054'

SECOND HAND LOVE (Aug. 26, 1923); D: William Wellman; W: Charles Kenyon (scr), Shannon Fife (st); C: Don Short; Cast: Charles Jones, Ruth Dwyer, Charles Coleman, Harvey Clark, Frank Weed, James Quinn, Gus Leonard • A roving, worry-free vagabond handyman, Andy (Jones), comes to a small town to fix fences and houses. He ends up helping Angela (Dwyer), who is married to an abusive bootlegger (Coleman), and finishes off the villain in a ferocious fight on the limb of a tree, hanging over quicksand. The villain is dispatched into the quicksand and dies. 5,000'

THE ELEVENTH HOUR (Sept. 2, 1923); D: Bernard J. Durning; W: Louis Sherwin, Lincoln J. Carter (unpublished play); C: Don Short; Cast: Shirley Mason, Charles Jones, Richard Tucker, Alan Hale, Walter McGrail, June Elvidge, Fred Kelsey, Nigel De Brulier, Fred Kohler • The mad Prince Stefan (Hale) intends to take over the world. Herbert Glenville (Tucker), a villainous executive with the company where a new explosive is being made, co-operates with Stefan, but factory owner Barbara Hackett (Mason) joins forces with one of her workers, Brick McDonald (Jones), actually the head of the U.S. Secret Service, to defeat the prince. Many action sequences involving airplanes, submarines, and motor boats follow before victory is at hand. 6,820'

THE GUNFIGHTER (Sept. 2, 1923); D: Lynn F. Reynolds; W: Lynn F. Reynolds, Max Brand (article); C: Dev Jennings; Cast: William Farnum, Doris May, L.C. Shumway, J. Morris Foster, Virginia True Boardman, Irene Hunt, Arthur Morrison, Cecil Van Auker, Jerry Campbell • A years-long feud is caused between two mountain families when Nell Camp is abducted to replace a dead child in the Benchley family. Stranger Bill Buell (Farnum) arrives, falls in love with Nell and restores her to her rightful family, averting a shootout. He ends the feud when he marries Nell. 4,700'

THE SILENT COMMAND (Sept. 9, 1923); D: J. Gordon Edwards; W: Anthony Paul Kelly (scr), Rufus King (st); C: George W. Lane; Cast: Edmund Lowe, Alma Tell, Martha Mansfield, Betty Jewel, Florence Martin, Bela Lugosi, Carl Harbaugh, Martin Faust, Gordon McEdward, Byron Douglas • Foreign agents hire Peg Williams (Mansfield) to vamp Captain Decatur (Lowe) to gain information about mine positions in the Canal Zone. Decatur, alerted to the deceit, plays along, thwarts the saboteurs and saves the Panama Canal from destruction. 7,809'

THE LONE STAR RANGER (Sept. 9, 1923); D: Lambert Hillyer; W: Lambert Hillyer, Zane Grey (novel); C: Daniel Clark; Cast: Tom Mix, Billie Dove, L.C. Shumway, Stanton Heck, Edward Peil, Frank Clark, Minna Redman, Francis Carpenter, William Conklin, Tom Lingham, Tony the Wonder Horse • Duane (Mix), an outlaw, is pardoned by the Texas Rangers when he promises to capture a gang of cattle rustlers, even though the leader of the gang is the father (Conklin) of his sweetheart (Dove). 5,259' • Tom Mix stars in the role originally played by William Farnum in the 1919 version.

MONA VANNA (Sept. 16, 1923) German-made; D: Richard Eichberg; W: Helmuth Orthmann (scr), Olga Alsen (scr), Maurice Maeterlinck (play), Niccolo Machiavelli (st); Cast: Lee Parry, Paul Wegener, Hans Sturm, Paul Graetz, Hans Hurka, Emil Rameau, Max Pohl, Toni Zimmerer, Alb. Steinrueck, Lydia Salmonova, Olaf Fjord, Viktor Gehring • A spectacle set in Italy at the time of Machiavelli. 8,648'

HELL'S HOLE (Sept. 23, 1923); D: Emmett J. Flynn; W: Bernard McConville (scr), George Scarborough (st); C: Lucien Andriot; Cast: Charles Jones, Maurice B. Flynn, Eugene Pallette, George Siegmann, Ruth Clifford, Kathleen Key, Hardee Kirkland, Charles K. French, Henry Miller Jr., Fred Kohler • After being thrown off a train by a conductor, cowboy Tod Musgrave (Jones) dreams that his partner, Dell Hawkins (Flynn), robs the train, plants the money on Tod, who is then thrown into prison. After an escape, Tod tracks down Dell and brings him to justice. When Tod awakens, he and Dell are still friends. 5,488'

ST. ELMO (Sept. 30, 1923); D: Jerome Storm; W: Jules G. Furthman, Augusta Jane Evans (novel); C: Joe August; Cast: John Gilbert, Barbara La Marr, Bessie Love, Warner Baxter, Nigel De Brulier, Lydia Knott • After shooting his friend Murray Hammond (Baxter) in a jealous rage over his fiancée, Agnes (La Marr), St. Elmo Thornton (Gilbert) travels the world with a hatred of women. He returns home and falls in love with a blacksmith's daughter, Edna (Love), who redeems him and inspires him to become a minister. 5,778'

TIMES HAVE CHANGED (Oct. 7, 1923); D: James Flood; W: Jack Strumwasser, Elmer Holmes Davies (novel); C: Joseph Bretherton; Cast: William Russell, Mabel Julienne Scott, Charles West, Martha Mattox, Edwin Booth Tilton, George Atkinson, Allene Ray, Dick La Reno, Gus Leonard, Jack Curtis • Mark O'Rell (Russell), a hero of the World War, is dispatched to New York by his wife's (Scott) aunt Cordelia (Mattox) to retrieve a quilt, a family heirloom, which Mark had carelessly loaned to friends. Mark is pursued by crooks who have since sewn diamonds inside the quilt, and also by a high school flapper, Irene (Ray), who has designs on him. The crooks are arrested, the flapper is resisted, and Mark returns home with the quilt. 5,082'

DOES IT PAY? (Oct. 7, 1923); D: Charles Horan; W: Howard Irving Young (scr), Julius Steger (st); C: Joseph Ruttenberg; Cast: Hope Hampton, Robert T. Haines, Florence Short, Walter Petri, Peggy Shaw, Charles Wellesley, Mary Thurman, Claude Brooke, Pierre Gendron, Roland Bottomley • John Weston (Haines) divorces his wife, Martha (Short), for their household helper, Doris (Hampton). However, Doris cheats on him with a music teacher (Bottomley), which causes John to have a nervous breakdown. Weston loses his memory and returns to Martha, who agrees to help restore him to health. 6,652'

THE EXILES (Oct. 14, 1923); D: Edmund Mortimer; W: Fred Jackson (scr), John Russell (adpt), Richard Harding Davis (short story); Cast: John Gilbert, Betty Boulton, John Webb Dillon, Margaret Fielding, Fred Warren • District Attorney Henry Holcombe (Gilbert) heads to Tangiers to bring back an innocent woman, Alice Carroll (Boulton), who fled as a murder suspect. Alice has fallen into the hands of an unscrupulous gambling den owner (Dillon). Holcombe rescues her and returns to America to clear her of charges. 4,719'

THE GRAIL (Oct. 14, 1923); D: Colin Campbell; W: Charles Kenyon (scr), George Scarborough (st); C: Joseph Bretherton; Cast: Dustin Farnum, Peggy Shaw, Carl Stockdale, Frances Raymond, James Gordon, Jack Rollins, Frances Hatton, Alma Bennett, Leon Barry • By pretending to be a preacher, Texas Ranger Chic Shelby (Farnum) tricks an outlaw, James Trammell (Gordon), and his son John (Rollins), who are wanted for the murder of a cattleman. Chic's sermon is so convincing that he brings fanatical religious devotion into John's life. When James is killed by Sam Hervey (Barry), Shelby is blamed, but the guilty man is eventually captured. 4,617'

BIG DAN (Oct. 21, 1923); D: William A. Wellman; W: Frederick Hatton, Fanny Hatton; C: Joseph August; Cast: Charles Jones, Marian Nixon, Ben Hendricks, Trilby Clark, Jacqueline Gadsden, Charles Coleman, Lydia Yeamans Titus, Monte Collins, Charles Smiley • Dan O'Hara (Jones), a boxer, returns from the war and finds that his wife has left him. He becomes a fight trainer and turns his home into a gym for boys. He shelters Dora Allen (Nixon) by getting into a fistfight with her abusive suitor. Falling in love with Dora, Dan marries her after he learns his wife has died at an Arizona sanitarium. 5,934

CAMEO KIRBY (Oct. 21, 1923); D: John Ford; W: Robert N. Lee, Booth Tarkington and Harry Leon Wilson (play); C: George Schneiderman; Cast: John Gilbert, Gertrude Olmstead, Alan Hale, Eric Mayne, William E. Lawrence, Richard Tucker, Phillips Smalley, Jack McDonald, Jean Arthur, Eugenie Ford • Gambler Cameo Kirby (Gilbert) gets into a card game and wins the deed to a property to keep it from crooked Colonel Moreau (Hale). The loser of the deed, Randall (Lawrence), kills himself before Kirby can return it. Moreau accuses Kirby of causing Randall's death, and the two shoot it out with Moreau being killed. Kirby then has to deal with Randall's heirs, who want revenge. Kirby is able to explain the incident to Randall's sons; he later falls in love with Randall's daughter, Adele (Olmstead). 6,931'

NO MOTHER TO GUIDE HER (Oct. 28, 1923); D: Charles Horan; W: Michael O'Connor, Lillian Mortimer (play); C: Thomas Malloy; Cast: Genevieve Tobin, John Webb Dillon, Lolita Robertson, Katherine Downer, Dolores Rousse, Frank Wunderlee, Maude Hill, Ruth Sullivan, J.D. Walsh, Jack McLean • Kathleen Pearson (Rousse) has grown up in a privileged home. Mary Boyd (Tobin) had a brutal father and no mother. Yet, it is Mary who turns out to be the most self-sacrificing. Kathleen discovers that she has entered into a fraudulent marriage with Donald Walling (McLean). She returns home with a child and Mary pretends to be the young girl's mother. When Kathleen's "husband" dies in an auto accident, she discovers the marriage was actually legitimate and she can marry the man she loves. 6,650'

SIX CYLINDER LOVE (Nov. 4, 1923); D: Elmer Clifton; W: Carl Stearns Clancy (adpt), Ralph Spence (titles), William Anthony McGuire (play); C: Alexander G. Penrod; E: Ralph Spence; Cast: Ernest Truex, Florence Eldridge, Donald Meek, Maude Hill, Anne McKittrick, Marjorie Milton, Thomas Mitchell, Ralph Sipperly, Berton Churchill, Harold Mann • Two families, the Sterlings and the Burtons, share in the cost of an expensive automobile and it almost ruins their happiness. When they are financially wiped out, their apartment janitor buys the car from them. 6,659'

THE TEMPLE OF VENUS (Nov. 11, 1923); D: Henry Otto; W: Henry Otto, Catherine Carr; C: Joe August; Cast: William Walling, Mary Philbin, Mickey McBan, Alice Day, David Butler, William Boyd, Phyllis Haver, Leon Barry, Celeste Lee, Señorita Consuella, Robert Klein, Marilyn Boyd • Venus (Lee) sends Cupid to Earth to see if romance still exists, and he visits the cottage of a fisherman who has two daughters, Moira (Philbin) and Peggy (Day). An artist from the city, Dennis (Walling), comes to the seaside and falls in love with one of the daughters, but is lured back to the city momentarily by a socialite widow who throws lavish, jazzy parties. Dennis ends up returning to his seaside love. 6,695'

NORTH OF HUDSON'S BAY (Nov. 18, 1923); D: Jack Ford; W: Jules Furthman; C: Dan Clark; Cast: Tom Mix, Kathleen Key, Jennie Lee, Frank Campeau, Eugene Pallettte, Will Walling, Frank Leigh, Fred Kohler • Rancher Michael Dane (Mix) goes to Northern Canada to join his brother (Pallette), who has made a gold strike with his partner, Angus McKenzie (Walling). On his way, Dane falls in love with Estelle MacDonald (Key). When Michael is informed that his brother has been killed and McKenzie is the murderer, Dane sees red. However, when McKenzie is sentenced to a torturous "death trail" involving starvation and exposure, Dane takes pity and tries to help him against the code of the north. Dane is likewise sentenced to the same torture. Surviving the odds, Dane returns and exposes Estelle's uncle, Cameron (Campeau), as his brother's murderer. 4,973'

MILE-A-MINUTE ROMEO (Nov. 18, 1923); D: Lambert Hillyer; W: Robert N. Lee, Max Brand (novel); Cast: Tom Mix, Betty Jewel, J. Gordon Russell, James Mason, Duke Lee, James Quinn, Tony the Wonder Horse • Lucky Bill (Mix) approaches the refined Molly (Jewel) on behalf of his friend, to whom she is betrothed, but when he finds out his friend has tricked him, he decides to land her himself. Through skillful horsemanship and pure determination, he easily shows up his rival in Molly's eyes. Then, to prove his assertiveness, Bill picks the meanest justice of the peace in the state and has to use the point of a gun to finally bring him to perform the marriage. 5,306'

THE SHEPHERD KING (Nov. 25, 1923); D: J. Gordon Edwards; W: Virginia Tracy (scr), Wight Lorimer and Arnold Reeves (play); C: Bennie Miggins; Violet Mersereau, Edy Darclea, Virginia Lucchetti, Nero Bernardi, Guido Trento, Ferrucio Biancini, Alessandro Salvini, Mariano Bottino, Samuel Balestra, Adriano Bocanero • After David (Bernardi) slays Goliath (Balestra), King Saul of Israel (Trento) sends him to fight against the Philistines, believing he will be killed. David returns victorious but leaves the court after Saul attempts to kill him. David organizes an army and when the Philistines attack Saul, David saves the kingdom. Saul is killed in the battle and David becomes king, marrying Saul's daughter, Michal (Mersereau). 9 reels

WHEN ODDS ARE EVEN (Nov. 25, 1923); D: James Flood; W: Dorothy Yost; C: Joseph Bretherton; Cast: William Russell, Dorothy Devore, Lloyd Whitlock, Frank Beal, Allan Cavan • Jack Arnold (Russell) and Clive Langdon (Beal) are competing for an opal mine on an exotic island and simultaneously for the affection of Caroline (Devore). Langdon tries to sabotage Jack, but fails in both efforts. 4,284'

KENTUCKY DAYS (Dec. 2, 1923); D: David Solomon; W: Dorothy Yost (scr), John Lynch (st); Cast: Dustin Farnum, Margaret Fielding, Miss Woodthrop, Bruce Gordon, William De Vaull • Don Buckner (Farnum), a Southerner, goes west in search of gold and loses his wife to a jealous cousin, who insists Don has died. Don returns and kills his cousin in a duel and orders his wife out for infidelity. He finally realizes she was misled and agrees to take her along to California. 4,508'

THE NET (Dec. 2, 1923); D: J. Gordon Edwards; W:

Olga Linek Schnoll, Virginia Tracy, Maravene Thompson (novel); C: Bennie Miggins; Cast: Barbara Castleton, Raymond Bloomer, Albert Roscoe, Peggy Davis, William H. Tooker, Helen Tracy, Eliah Nadel, Claire De Lorez, Arthur Gordini • After killing his wife Allayne's (Castleton) cousin after a quarrel, gambler Bruce Norman takes the identity of an amnesiac (Roscoe). He has Allayne convince the police that the innocent man is the murderer. When Bruce dies, the amnesiac regains his memory, is cleared, and marries Allayne. 6,135'

YOU CAN'T GET AWAY WITH IT (Dec. 9, 1923); D: Rowland V. Lee; W: Robert N. Lee, Gouverneur Morris (short story); C: G.O. Post; Cast: Percy Marmont, Malcolm McGregor, Betty Bouton, Barbara Tennant, Grace Morse, Clarissa Selwyn, Charles Cruz • A department store clerk, Jill (Bouton), begins an illicit affair with the owner Charles Hemingway (Marmont) when his wife refuses to grant a divorce. When Hemingway dies, Jill inherits a sum of money, falls in love with another young man, but refuses his offer for the same kind of relationship as she had with Hemingway. 6,152' or 6,019'

CUPID'S FIREMAN (Dec. 16, 1923); D: William A. Wellman; W: Eugene B. Lewis (scr), Richard Harding Davis (st); C: Joseph August; Cast: Charles Jones, Marian Nixon, Brooks Benedict, Eileen O'Malley, Lucy Beaumont, Al Fremont, Charles McHugh, Mary Warren, L.H. King • Andy McGee (Jones), whose father died as a fireman, longs to become a "smoke eater" as well. Against his mother's (Beaumont) wishes, he joins the department, then meets and is smitten with Agnes (Nixon), who is married to worthless drunkard Bill (Benedict). When Bill, in a drunken haze, starts a fire at their house, Andy rescues Agnes. Her decision to stay with Andy is simplified when Bill dies in the fire. 4,204'

HOODMAN BLIND (Dec. 16, 1923); D: John Ford; W: Charles Kenyon, Wilson Barrett and Henry Arthur Jones (play); C: George Schneiderman; Cast: Marc McDermott, Gladys Hulette, Regina Connelly, Frank Campeau, Trilby Clark, Jack Walters, David Butler, Eddie Gribbon • A father with wanderlust tendencies, John Linden (McDermott), walks out on his wife (Clark) and daughter Nancy (Hulette). He goes west, accompanied by Jessie Walton (Connelly), with whom he has another daughter, Jessie (Hulette). John then leaves them as well and makes his way to South Africa, where he finds his fortune. While he is away, both mothers die. Nancy marries a fisherman (Butler), and Jessie earns her living on the streets. When John returns he has to deal with a lawyer (Campeau) who has been embezzling money for the girls. He also heroically rescues Nancy from a sinking boat during a storm. 5,434'

GENTLE JULIA (Dec. 23, 1923); D: Rowland V. Lee; W: Donald W. Lee (scr & adpt), Booth Tarkington (novel); C: G.O. Post; Cast: Bessie Love, Harold Goodwin, Frank Elliott, Charles K. French, Clyde Benson, Harry Dunkinson, Jack Rollins, Frances Grant, William Irving, Agnes Aker • Attractive Julia (Love) is a queen bee in her home town and believes she will be as successful in Chicago. Lured there by an older man, she finds that she is out of her league, especially when the man turns out to be married. Julia returns home, chastened, to marry her sweetheart (Goodwin). 5,837'

EYES OF THE FOREST (Dec. 30, 1923); D: Lambert Hillyer; W: LeRoy Stone (scr), Shannon Fife (st); C: Daniel Clark; Cast: Tom Mix, Pauline Starke, Sid Jordan, Buster Gardner, J.P. Lockney, Tom Lingham, Edwin Wallock, Tony the Wonder Horse • Bruce Thornton (Mix), a forest ranger pilot patrolling for lumber thieves, meets Ruth (Starke), wrongly accused of murdering her stepfather. Bruce helps Ruth prove that her husband, Horgan (Jordan), a timber thief, is the murderer and rounds up his gang. 4,408'

THIS FREEDOM (Dec. 30, 1923) British-made; D: Denison Clift; W: A.S.M. Hutchinson (scr & novel); Cast: Fay Compton, Clive Brook, John Stuart, Athene Seyler, Nancy Kenyon, Gladys Hamer, Fewlass Llewellyn, Adeline Hayden Coffin, Mickey Brantford, Bunty Fosse • A cleric's daughter, Rosalie (Fay Compton), takes a husband (Brook), but devotes her life to a career, utterly neglecting her home life and causing her children to grow up with emotional problems. One daughter dies and a son is sent to prison. She then realizes that all the misfortunes her family has suffered were her fault. 7,220'

THE GOVERNOR'S LADY (Dec. 30, 1923); D: Harry Millarde; W: Anthony Paul Kelly, Alice Bradley (novel); Cast: Robert T. Haines, Jane Grey, Ann Luther, Frazer Coulter, Leslie Austen • A wealthy miner, Daniel (Haines), acquires social standing and runs for political office, but his wife (Grey) is unable to adjust to their new station in life. Daniel plans to get a divorce, but later realizes that he really loves his wife. 7,669'

1924 Releases

JUST OFF BROADWAY (Jan. 20, 1924); D: Edmund Mortimer; W: Frederic Hatton, Fanny Hatton; C: G.O. Post; Cast: John Gilbert, Marian Nixon, Trilby Clark, Pierre Gendron, Ben Hendricks, Jr. • A failed Broadway stage actress, Jean (Nixon), is rescued by gangster's moll, Nan Norton (Clark), and becomes involved with a counterfeiting ring. Jean falls in love with millionaire Stephen (Gilbert), disguised as a counterfeiter; he rounds up the gang and introduces himself to her. 5,544'

NOT A DRUM WAS HEARD (Jan. 27, 1924); D: William A. Wellman; W: Doty Hobart, Ben Ames Williams (st); C: Joseph August; Cast: Charles Jones, Betty Bouton, Frank Campeau, Rhody Hathaway, Al Fremont, William Scott, Mickey McBan • Bud Loupel (Scott) and Jack Mills (Jones), friends from childhood, are rivals for Jean (Bouton). When Bud wins her love, Jack leaves but first asks Bud to name his firstborn after him. Years later, Bud, needing money, steals from the bank where he works. His friend Jack, having returned, protects Jean by staging a fake bank robbery and pretending to take the money Bud stole. In the robbery, Bud shoots the bank owner (Campeau) and is fatally wounded. Bud admits his guilt and Jack takes over his responsibilities for Jean and Jack Jr. (McBan). 4,823'

THE BLIZZARD (Feb. 3, 1924) Swedish-made

LADIES TO BOARD (Feb. 3, 1924); D: J.G. Blystone; W: Donald W. Lee (scr), William W. Pelley (st); C: Daniel Clark; Cast: Tom Mix, Gertrude Olmstead, Philo McCullough, Pee Wee Holmes, Gertrude Claire, Dolores Rousse • Cowboy Tom Faxton (Mix) inherits an old ladies home after the former owner, whom he saved from a car accident, dies. He induces his cowboy friend Bunk (Holmes) to accompany him. Tom has to woo a pretty nurse Edith (Olmstead) away from her boyfriend, Evan (Carmichael), and Bunk teams up with a housekeeper. 6,100'

LOVE LETTERS (Feb. 10, 1924); D: David Solomon (a.k.a. David Selman); W: Doty Hobart, Fred Jackson (article); Cast: Shirley Mason, Gordon Edwards, Alma Francis, John Miljan, William Irving • Evelyn (Mason) tries to retrieve the passionate love letters she and her sister Julia (Francis) wrote to Thomas Chadwick (Miljan) when they were young. Chadwick is killed by the brother of an abandoned lover, and Evelyn discovers that the letters had been destroyed. 4,749'

THE WOLF MAN (Feb. 17, 1924); D: Edmund Mortimer; W: Frederick Hatton (scr), Fanny Hatton (scr), Reed Heustis (st); C: Don Short, Michael Farley; Cast: John Gilbert, Norma Shearer, Alma Francis, George Barraud, Eugene Pallette, Edgar Norton, Thomas R. Mills, Max Montisole, Charles Wellesley, Richard Blaydon • Englishman David (Gilbert), who becomes violent when intoxicated, leaves for Canada and becomes a lumberjack because his brother has convinced him he killed Phil (Montisole), his fiancée's (Francis) brother. David does not touch a drop of liquor until he learns that his brother has married Beatrice. In a rage, he kidnaps a young tourist, Elizabeth (Shearer), and escapes with her by canoe; he finally has to save her when they capsize in rapids. Caught and almost lynched, Elizabeth intercedes on David's behalf and saves his life. 5,145'

THE SHADOW OF THE EAST (Feb. 27, 1924); D: George Archainbaud; W: Frederic Hatton, Fanny Hatton, Edith Maude Hull (novel); C: Jules Cronjager; Cast: Frank Mayo, Mildred Harris, Norman Kerry, Bertram Grassby, Evelyn Brent, Edythe Chapman, Josef Swickard, Lorimer Johnsson • Former sweethearts Barry (Mayo) and Gillian (Harris) meet in India but Barry is already married. His native wife, Lolaire (Brent), commits suicide and he returns to England to marry Gillian, his true love. A vengeful Indian servant, Kunwar (Grassby), casts a spell on Barry, which sends him to the Algerian desert. Gillian follows, and, when Kunwar is killed, the spell is broken. 5,874'

THE VAGABOND TRAIL (March 9, 1924); D: William A. Wellman; W: Doty Hobart, George Owen Baxter (novel); C: Joe August; Cast: Charles Jones, Marian Nixon, Charles Coleman, L.C. Shumway, Virginia Warwick, Harry Lonsdale, Frank Nelson, George Reed, George Romain • Donnegan (Jones), a Westerner looking for his long-lost brother, is taken in by Colonel Macon (Lonsdale) and his daughter Lou (Nixon). Donnegan discovers that his brother, known as Lord Nick (Shumway), is the colonel's dishonest partner and Lou's fiancé. Nick ends up relinquishing his fiancée to Donnegan and repays the colonel. 4,302'

THE ARIZONA EXPRESS (March 23, 1924); D: Thomas Buckingham; W: Fred Jackson (scr), Robert N. Lee (scr), Lincoln J. Carter (st); C: Starke Wagner; Cast: Pauline Starke, Evelyn Brent, Anne Cornwall, Harold Goodwin, David Butler, Francis McDonald, Frank Beal, William Humphrey • David (Goodwin) is unfairly sent to prison for the murder of his uncle, a bank president. Katherine (Starke), his sister, reaches the governor just before the execution and proves that a member of a gang planning to rob the bank was responsible for the murder. 6,316'

A MAN'S MATE (March 23, 1924); D: Edmund Mortimer; W: Charles Kenyon; C: G.O. Post; Cast: John Gilbert, Renee Adorée, Noble Johnson, Wilfrid North, Thomas Mills, James Neill, Jack Giddings, Patterson Dial • Famous artist Paul Bonnard (Gilbert) loses his memory during a fight at an Apache café. Paul hangs around with the Apache crowd and falls in love with a dancer, Wildcat (Adorée). Paul paints her portrait and it becomes his masterpiece. Wildcat realizes who Paul is and brings him back to his family for an operation to restore his memory, even at the risk of losing him. Surprisingly, Paul remembers his love for Wildcat and he searches her out at the Apache café. 5,041'

THE PLUNDERER (March 30, 1924); D: George Archainbaud; W: Doty Hobart (scr), Roy Norton (st & novel); C: Jules Cronjager; Cast: Frank Mayo, Evelyn Brent, Tom Santschi, James Mason, Peggy Shaw, Edward Phillips, Dan Mason • Mining engineer Richard (Phillips) heads west with his friend Bill (Mayo) to develop his father's gold mine. Bill discovers from The Lily (Brent), a saloon owner with whom he becomes romantically involved, that the mine is being plundered by Presbey (Santschi), the father of Richard's girlfriend, Joan (Shaw), through secret tunnels. After a variety of action-packed events, the stolen gold is returned and Bill and The Lily find happiness. 5,812'

THE TROUBLE SHOOTER (May 4, 1924); D: Jack Conway; W: Frederic Hatton, Fanny Hatton; C: Daniel Clark; Cast: Tom Mix, Kathleen Key, Frank Currier, J. Gunnis Davis, Mike Donlin, Dolores Rousse, Charles McHugh, Al Fremont • Tom Steele (Mix), a lineman for a power company, meets Nancy (Key), the daughter of a corporate rival. The two companies are in a race to claim a piece of land which, the government has ruled, goes to the first claimant. Tom rescues Nancy during a storm, escaping on his horse from a turbulent stream. Nancy later helps him claim the rights to the land for his company. 5,702'

THE CIRCUS COWBOY (May 11, 1924); D: William A. Wellman; W: Doty Hobart (scr), Louis Sherwin (st); C: Joseph Bretherton; Cast: Charles Jones, Marian Nixon, Jack McDonald, Ray Hallor, Marguerite Clayton, George Romain • Buck (Jones) is called away from home and, when he returns, he visits his ex-girlfriend (Clayton) who is now married to the wealthy but grouchy and very jealous Ezra Bagley (McDonald). Bagley, seeing Buck near his wife, fires a shot and inadvertently hits his son Paul (Hallor). Buck is accused of the crime and leaves with a posse in pursuit. He is helped by Bird Taylor (Nixon), who invites him to join a circus with her. Bird is a wire walker. A jealous animal trainer who is in love with her, cuts her rope but Buck rides underneath on his horse and catches her in his arms. Buck later proves his innocence in the attempted murder accusation. 4,175'

THE LONE CHANCE (May 18, 1924); D: Howard Mitchell; W: Charles Kenyon (scr), Frederick J. Jackson (st); C: Bart Baldridge; Cast: John Gilbert, Evelyn Brent, John Miljan, Edwin Booth Tilton, Harry Todd, Frank Beal • Jack (Gilbert), a penniless inventor, assumes guilt for a murder in exchange for $20,000 and a pardon after one year in prison. The agreement is not fulfilled and Jack breaks out of jail and confronts the governor, whose daughter Margaret (Brent) committed the crime in self-defense. Margaret then realizes that Jack is her lost love. She clears him and is herself exonerated. 4,385'

WESTERN LUCK (June 22, 1924); D: George André Beranger; W: Robert N. Lee; C: Joseph Brotherton; Cast: Charles Jones, Beatrice Burnham, Pat Hartigan, Tom Lingham, J. Farrell MacDonald, Edith Kennick, Bruce Gordon • Two brothers, separated at birth in the West, are raised by different parents. One is with his Wall Street banker father and the other, rescued by a rancher, is in love with his guardian's daughter. The rancher is in danger of being foreclosed upon by the banker's representative. When oil is discovered on the land, the evil capitalist moves in to seize it. However, the two brothers reunite and their differences are reconciled. 5,020'

ROMANCE RANCH (June 29, 1924); D: Howard M. Mitchell; W: Dorothy Yost (scr), Jessie Maude Wybro (st); C: Bert Baldridge; Cast: John Gilbert, Virginia Brown Faire, John Miljan, Bernard Siegel, Evelyn Selbie • Carlos (Gilbert) finds out he owns a ranch that is in the possession of the Hendley family. Rather than evict them, because he is in love with Carmen Hendley (Faire), he marries the girl and becomes the ranch's legal co-owner. 4,471'

THE MAN WHO CAME BACK (July 17, 1924); D: Emmett Flynn; W: Edmund Goulding, John Fleming Wilson (novel), Jules Eckert Goodman (play); C: Lucien Andriot; Cast: George O'Brien, Dorothy Mackaill, Cyril Chadwick, Ralph Lewis, Emily Fitzroy, Harvey Clark, Edward Piel, David Kirby, James Gordon, Walter Wilkinson • Henry Potter (O'Brien), who has been banished from his home in New York for unregenerate behavior, leaves for San Francisco, then ends up in Shanghai. There, he meets an American girl, Marcelle (Mackaill), a morphine addict. Henry's growing love restores her health. The regenerated couple returns home and Henry effects a reconciliation with his family. 8,293' • This was George O'Brien's first Fox feature and the beginning of a studio contract that would last for the next ten years.

THE HEART BUSTER (July 20, 1924); D: Jack Conway; W: John Stone (scr), George Scarborough (st); C: Daniel Clark; Cast: Tom Mix, Esther Ralston, Cyril Chadwick, William Courtwright, Frank Currier, Tom Wilson • Rose (Ralston), cowboy Tod Walton's (Mix) childhood sweetheart, is about to marry Edward (Chadwick), who had eloped years earlier with another woman. Believing Rose to be in danger of marrying a bounder, Tod holds the sheriff and several ministers hostage until he can establish Edward's dishonorable reputation. 4,500' • John Stone is the reincarnation of Jack Strumwasser, who was ordered fired by the New York office, most likely at the behest of Winfield Sheehan, but was rehired by his friend Sol Wurtzel, the Los Angeles studio general manager, under a new name.

AGAINST ALL ODDS (July 27, 1924); D: Edmund Mortimer; W: Frederic Chapin, Max Brand (article); C: Joseph Bretherton; Cast: Buck Jones, Dolores Rousse, Ben Hendricks, Jr., William Scott, Thais Valdemar, William N. Bailey, Bernard Siegel, Jack McDonald • Chick Newton (Jones) is trying to save the life of his friend Bill Warner (Scott), who has been accused of murdering his uncle (McDonald). Chick resorts to force to free Bill from deputies as he is being led to his execution. He then unravels a complicated plot in which the victim was never murdered, but is laying low in a conspiracy with a blackmailer who was trying to collect insurance on the uncle's life to pay off his creditors. 4,809'

THAT FRENCH LADY (Aug. 17, 1924); D: Edmund Mortimer; W: Charles Kenyon (scr), William Hurlbut (st); C: G.O. Post; Cast: Shirley Mason, Theodore von Eltz, Harold Goodwin, Charles Coleman • John (von Eltz), an American architecture student in Paris, falls in love with a youthful widow, Inez (Mason), who has written a book which warns women against marriage and promulgates the idea of free love. Inez is willing to join John in returning to his Midwest home three years later, but refuses his offer of marriage. The locals shun Inez, especially after they acquire a copy of her book. Ultimately, wedding bells ring for the couple. 5,470'

THE DESERT OUTLAW (Aug. 24, 1924); D: Edmund Mortimer; W: Charles Kenyon; C: Joseph Brotherton; Cast: Buck Jones, Evelyn Brent, De Witt Jennings, William Haynes, Claude Payton, William Gould, Bob Klein • On the run from a posse, Sam Langdon (Jones), a prospector, is unfairly accused of murdering McTavish (Klein), a religious fanatic. Sam is accompanied by an outlaw, Tom Holloway (Haynes), who was forced, by difficult circumstances, to hold up the express office just as his sister May (Brent) arrived from the East. Langdon clears up the situation, wins a pardon for Tom and marries May. 5,576'

WOLVES OF THE NIGHT (Aug. 24, 1924) Reissue

THE LAST OF THE DUANES (Aug. 24, 1924); D: Lynn Reynolds; W: Edward J, Montagne; C: Dan Clark; Cast: Tom Mix, Marian Nixon, Brinsley Shaw, Frank Nelson, Lucy Beaumont, Harry Lonsdale • Buck Duane (Mix), a cowboy who wants to hang up his guns, is forced into a gunfight with Cal Bain (Shaw). In his escape, he helps a dying cattle rustler, rescues a girl who is being held hostage, and rounds up the members of the rustling gang. 6,942'

IT IS THE LAW (Aug. 31, 1924); D: J. Gordon Edwards; W: Curtis Benton, Elmer Rice and Hayden Talent (play); C: George W. Lane; Cast: Arthur Hohl, Herbert Heyes, Mimi Palmeri, George Lessey, Robert Young, Florence Dixon, Byron Douglas, Olaf Hytten, De Sacia Mooers, Guido Trento, Byron Russell • Albert Woodruff (Hohl) and Justin Victor (Heyes) are in love with the same girl, Ruth (Palmeri). Ruth chooses Justin, and Albert swears revenge against his friend. On the wedding night, Albert calls Ruth and threatens blackmail, which brings Justin to his apartment. Albert has found a vagrant who is his double (Hohl) and shoots him to make it appear that he's been murdered by Justin. Justin is sentenced to prison and Albert assumes a new identity. However, Ruth is able to see through the disguise and gets Justin released from a life sentence. Free again, Justin commits the murder he was accused of — and gets off since he cannot be convicted for the same crime twice. 6,895'

DANTE'S INFERNO (Sept. 7, 1924); D: Henry Otto; W: Edmund Goulding (adpt), Cyrus Wood (st); C: Joseph August; Cast: Lawson Butt, Harold Gaye, Ralph Lewis, Pauline Starke, Josef Swickard, Gloria Grey, William Scott, Robert Klein, Winifred Landis, Lorimer Johnston, Lon Poff, Bud Jamison • A millionaire, Mortimer Judd (Lewis), refuses to repair his tenements and a friend, Eugene Craig (Swickard), sends him a copy of "The Inferno" along with a curse. In a delirious dream, Judd goes through a tour of hell and witnesses punishments for his kind of sins. He wakes up and makes amends for what he has done. 5,484'

THE CYCLONE RIDER (Sept. 14, 1924); D: Thomas Buckingham; W: Thomas Buckingham (scr), Lincoln J. Carter (st); C: Sidney Wagner; Cast: Reed Howes, Alma Bennett, William Bailey, Margaret McWade, Frank Beal, Evelyn Brent, Eugene Pallette, Ben Deeley, Charles Conklin, Bud Jamison, Ben Hendricks, Jr. • A skyscraper worker, Richard (Howes), loves the building owner's daughter, Doris (Bennett), and invents a carburetor that helps him win a car race in spite of efforts by his rival, an underworld king (Bailey), to kill him. With the prize money, he impresses the girl's father (Beal) enough to win the girl. 6,472'

THE CONQUEROR (Sept. 14, 1924) Reissue

OH, YOU TONY! (Sept. 21, 1924); D: J.G. Blystone; W: Donald W. Lee; C: Daniel Clark; Cast: Tom Mix, Claire Adams, Dick La Reno, Earle Foxe, Dolores Rousse, Charles K. French, Pat Chrisman, Miles McCarthy, Mathilda Brundage, May Wallace, Tony the Wonder Horse • Tom Masters (Mix), a ranchers' representative in Washington is deceived by a group of crooked lobbyists, headed by Jim Overton (Foxe), who are trying to acquire his ranch because the property is rich in oil. Betty Faine (Adams) helps him uncover the plot and Tom ultimately saves his property by betting all his money that his horse, Tony, will win a race. 6,302'

HONOR AMONG MEN (Sept. 28, 1924); D: Denison Clift; W: Denison Clift, Richard Harding Davis (novel); Cast: Edmund Lowe, Claire Adams, Sheldon Lewis, Diana Miller, Frank Leigh, Fred Becker, Paul Weigel, Hector Sarno, Fred Malatesta, Walter Wilkinson • An attractive American heiress, Patricia (Adams), fends off the attention of the treacherous King Louis of Messina (Lewis) because she is in love with the Prince Kaloney (Loew), son of the deposed king. Betrayed by a jealous mistress, the pretender, King Louis, is forced to abdicate, and Kaloney sets out to regain the throne for his family. 4,600'

THE PAINTED LADY (Sept. 28, 1924); D: Chester Bennett; W: Thomas Dixon Jr., Larry Evans (article); Cast: George O'Brien, Dorothy Mackaill, Harry T. Morey, Lucille Hutton, Lucille Ricksen, Margaret McWade, John Miljan, Frank Elliott, Lucien Littlefield • After serving a prison sentence for a crime her sister committed, Violet (Mackaill), traveling on a South Seas cruise, meets a sailor, Luther (O'Brien), who is looking to avenge his sister's death. Violet later falls into the clutches of Captain Sutton (Morey), who was responsible for Luther's sister's death. She is rescued by Luther, who gets revenge for both of them at the same time. 6,398'

HEARTS OF OAK (Oct. 5, 1924); D: John Ford; W: Charles Kenyon, James A. Herne (play); C: George Schneiderman; Cast: Hobart Bosworth, Pauline Starke, Theodore von Eltz, James Gordon, Francis Powers, Jennie Lee, Francis Ford • Chrystal (Starke) is about to marry elderly sea captain Terry Dunnivan (Bosworth) when her sweetheart, Ned (von Eltz), is rescued after being missing at sea for two years. Dunnivan realizes that the two young people should marry. He takes a ship assignment to the Arctic, leaving them together. 5,336'

THE GREAT DIAMOND MYSTERY (Oct. 5, 1924); D: Denison Clift; W: Thomas Dixon Jr., (scr), Shannon Fife (st); Cast: Shirley Mason, Jackie Saunders, Harry von Meter, John Cossar, Philo McCullough, Hector V. Sarno, William Collier, Jr., Eugenia Gilbert, Mary Mayo, Hardee Kirkland • An author, Ruth Winton (Mason), tests the basis of her book in real life to clear her sweetheart Perry (Collier Jr.) of murder. She hires the people who worked with a murdered diamond merchant, Graves (Cossar), and recreates the set-up for the crime. She proves her point — a murderer will return to the scene of the crime. In the process, Graves's butler (Sarno) is shot and confesses to killing his boss, exonerating Perry. 5,069'

WINNER TAKE ALL (Oct. 12, 1924); D: William S. Van Dyke; W: Ewart Adamson, Larry Evans (novel); C: Joseph Brotherton, E.D. Van Dyke; Cast: Buck Jones, Peggy Shaw, Edward Hearn, Lilyan Tashman, William Norton Bailey, Ben Deeley, Tom O'Brien • Perry (Jones), who is fired for fighting at work, enters the boxing ring, guided by promoter Charles Dunham (Deely). He becomes a star boxer but refuses to fight a crooked match. Later, he's coaxed back into the ring for a winner-take-all match, which he wins, and convinces his girlfriend (Shaw) he is not a coward. 5,949'

THE END OF THE TRAIL (Oct. 12, 1924) Reissue

THE WARRENS OF VIRGINIA (Oct. 12, 1924); D: Elmer Clifton; W: William C. DeMille, (scr & play); Cast: George Backus, Rosemary Hill, Martha Mansfield, Robert Andrews, Wilfred Lytell, Harlan Knight, James Turfler, Helen Ray Kyle, Lieut. Wilbur Fox, J. Barney Sherry, Frank Andrews • A Union officer, Lt. Burton (Lytell), is purposely captured by Confederates in his sweetheart's home so that false dispatches will be found. After Betty (Hill), his girlfriend, misinterprets his motives, she saves him from execution as word arrives that the war is over. 6,356' • This film was released without any cast credits because 24-year-old Martha Mansfield burned to death in a freak accident shortly before the film's release.

GERALD CRANSTON'S LADY (Oct. 19, 1924); D: Emmett J. Flynn; W: Edmund Goulding, Gilbert Frankau (novel); Cast: James Kirkwood, Alma Rubens, Walter McGrail, J. Farrell MacDonald, Lucien Littlefield, Spottiswoode Aitken, Templar Saxe, Marguerite De La Motte, Eric Mayne • A successful English financier, Cranston (Kirkwood), marries Hermione (Rubens) to gain social acceptance. His wife, however, has married him for financial independence. While there is no love in the marriage, Hermione socializes with Gordon (McGrail) and Gerald is involved with his wife's cousin, Angela (De La Motte). The threat of financial ruin finally unites the couple. 6,674'

DARWIN WAS RIGHT (Oct. 26, 1924) Sunshine Feature; D: Lewis Seiler; W: Edward Moran; C: Jay Turner; Cast: Nell Brantley, George O'Hara, Stanley Blystone, Dan Mason, Lon Poff, Bud Jamison, Myrtle Sterling, Nora Cecil, David Kirby • After scientist Henry Baldwin's (Mason) staff has him committed to an asylum for experimenting with an elixir of youth, three escaped chimpanzees enter his house. The scientist's sister (Cecil) and daughter (Brantley) think he took an overdose of the elixir and has proved Darwin's theory of human evolution from monkeys. There is little time to theorize as the chimps create havoc until they are finally caught. 4,992'

THE LAST MAN ON EARTH (Nov. 2, 1924); D: J.G. Blystone; W: Donald W. Lee, John D. Swain (article); C: Allan Davey; Cast: Earle Foxe, Grace Cunard, Gladys Tennyson, Derelys Perdue, Maryon Aye, Clarissa Selwynne, Pauline French, Jean Johnson, Buck Black, Maurice Murphy, William Steele • Elmer Smith (Foxe) is rejected for marriage by his sweetheart, Hattie (Perdue), and becomes a hermit in the forest. In 1954, an epidemic kills all males except the hermit; he is discovered and then becomes wanted by every woman. He finally meets up with Hattie and selects her for marriage. 6,637'

TEETH (Nov. 2, 1924); D: John Blystone; W: Donald W. Lee, Claude Stagg (article), Virginia Hudson Brightman (novel); Cast: Tom Mix, Lucy Fox, George Bancroft, Edward Piel, Lucien Littlefield, Tony the Wonder Horse, Duke the dog • Dave (Mix), a prospector, finds an injured dog that has been thrown from a train's baggage car. The villainous baggage master, Dan (Bancroft), is fired and kills a postmaster, framing Dave. Dave escapes with the dog and his owner, Paula Grayson (Fox), who is then in danger from the murderer. The dog, named Teeth, saves them both, and when each claims ownership of him, marriage settles the issue. 6,190'

THE SCUTTLERS (Nov. 9, 1924) Reissue

DAUGHTERS OF THE NIGHT (Nov. 9, 1924); D: Elmer Clifton; W: Willard Robertson; Cast: Orville Caldwell, Alyce Mills, Phelps Decker, Alice Chapin, Warner Richmond, Bobbie Perkins, Clarice Vance, Claude Cooper, Willard Robertson, Charles Slattery • Two disinherited brothers, Billy (Caldwell) and Jimmy (Sands), take different paths. Billy becomes a telephone lineman, while Jimmy joins a gang of crooks. After a robbery, the gang ends up in the phone building, where Billy's girlfriend, Betty (Mills), is working the switchboard. Billy rescues her from a fire, in which Jimmy dies. 5,740'

MY HUSBAND'S WIVES (Nov. 16, 1924); D: Maurice Elvey; W: Dorothy Yost (scr), Barbara La Marr (st); C: Joseph Valentine; Cast: Shirley Mason, Bryant Washburn, Evelyn Brent, Paulette Duval • Two former female schoolmates, Vale (Mason) and Marie (Brent), get together without Vale knowing that her husband, William (Washburn), was previously married to Marie. Marie tries to rekindle the romance, making for a lot of tension. Finally, William sends Marie away and reconciles with Vale. 4,609'

THE BRASS BOWL (Nov. 17, 1924); D: Jerome Storm; W: Thomas Dixon Jr., Louis Joseph Vance (novel); Cast: Edmund Lowe, Claire Adams, Jack Duffy, J. Farrell MacDonald, Leo White, Fred Butler • Sylvia (Adams), who has just robbed the safe at a country home, turns the jewels over to their actual owner, Dan (Lowe), whom she mistakes for Anisty (Lowe), a thief who is a double for Dan. There is a lot of confusion as both men's identities are mistaken. They take each other's place until Dan declares his love for Sylvia, who was originally searching the safe for papers that would incriminate her father. 5,830'

THE MAN WHO PLAYED SQUARE (Nov. 23, 1924); D: Al Santell; W: John Stone (scr), William Wallace Cook (st); Cast: Buck Jones, Ben Hendricks, David Kirby, Hank Mann, Howard Foster, William Scott, Wanda Hawley • Matt Black (Jones), heir to half ownership in a gold mine, conceals his identity from his young female co-owner Bertie (Hawley), since the previous owners had mortally wounded each other while fighting over the property. After rescuing Bertie from a mine fire and getting rid of a dishonest foreman (Hendricks, Jr.), Matt relinquishes his claim. Both partners finally realize they love each other and decide to marry. 6,500'

FLAMES OF DESIRE (Nov. 30, 1924); D: Denison Clift; W: Denison Clift, Reginald G. Fogwell, Ouida (novel); C: Ernest G. Palmer; Cast: Wyndham Standing, Diana Miller, Richard Thorpe, Frank Leigh, George K. Arthur, Jackie Saunders, Frances Beaumont, Hayford Hobbs, Charles Clary, Eugenia Gilbert • Daniel (Standing), a man of wealth and influence, falls for a beautiful adventuress (Miller) and accidentally kills a friend in an argument over the woman. Daniel takes responsibility for the friend's daughter, who eventually falls in love with him and forgives his past. 5,439'

THE ROUGHNECK (Nov. 30, 1924); D: Jack Conway; W: Charles Kenyon, Robert William Service (novel); C: George Schneiderman; Cast: George O'Brien, Billie Dove, Harry T. Morey, Cleo Madison, Charles A. Sellon, Anne Cornwall, Harvey Clark, Maryon Aye, Edna Eichor, Buddy Smith • Jerry (O'Brien), a boxer who thinks he killed his opponent in the ring, stows away on a ship to the South Seas run by the brutal Captain McCara (Morey). On board, Jerry falls in love with Felicity (Dove), a painter, but he jumps ship rather than involve her in his disgrace. He ends up on an island and is reunited with his mother. When McCara's ship docks, Jerry ends up saving Felicity from the captain's unwanted advances. McCara also once made a promise of marriage to Jerry's mother, then abandoned her on the island. Jerry kills the captain in a fight. He then returns to San Francisco and finds out his boxing opponent did not die. He marries Felicity. 7,619'

THE MAN HUNTER (Dec. 7, 1924) Reissue

TROUBLES OF A BRIDE (Dec. 7, 1924); D: Thomas Buckingham; W: John Stone, Thomas Buckingham; Cast: Robert Agnew, Mildred June, Alan Hale, Bruce Covington, Dolores Rousse, Charles Conklin, Lew Harvey, Bud Jamieson • A smooth crook, The Baron, goes to the house of a Southern colonel (Covington) after the family fortune, just as the colonel's daughter Mildred (June) is to marry Robert (Agnew). The Baron robs the safe and kidnaps Mildred from her wedding. There are many cliffhanging episodes, including a horse and train chase, a fight down a long hillside, and Mildred's rescue from a burning train car. 4,915'

THE DEADWOOD COACH (Dec. 7, 1924); D: Lynn Reynolds; W: Lynn Reynolds, Clarence E Mulford (novel); C: Dan Clark; Cast: Tom Mix, George Bancroft, De Witt Jennings, Buster Gardner, Lucien Littlefield, Doris May, Norma Wills, Sid Jordan, Nora Cecil • Preventing a stagecoach holdup, Jimmie Gordon (Mix), a cowboy known as the "Orphan," reluctantly lets outlaw Tex Wilson (Bancroft), who killed his parents, escape. On the stage is the sheriff's daughter Helen (May), who falls in love with Jimmie. During their wedding, Wilson shows up, kidnaps Helen and escapes in the Deadwood Coach. Jimmie catches up and he and Wilson fight it out on the edge of a cliff, where the villain falls to his death. 6,346'

CURLYTOP (Dec. 28, 1924); D: Maurice Elvey; W: Frederick Hatton, Fanny Hatton, Thomas Burke (novel); C: Joseph Valentine; Cast: Shirley Mason, Wallace MacDonald, Warner Oland, Diana Miller, George Kuwa, Ernest Adams, Nora Hayden, La Verne Lindsay • Curlytop (Mason), who works in a London department store, falls in love with Bill Brannigan (MacDonald). Bill's previous girlfriend, Bessie (Miller), tries to break up the romance by cutting off Curlytop's curls. When Curlytop disappears, Bill finds her shorn curls among his girlfriend's belongings and forces her to tell him what happened. He then rescues Curlytop from a sinking barge owned by a nefarious half-caste Chinese hypnotist, Shanghai Dan (Oland). 5,828' • A good part of Warner Oland's career involved playing Chinese characters, including the notable Charlie Chan.

IN LOVE WITH LOVE (Dec. 28, 1924); D: Rowland V. Lee; W: Robert N. Lee, Vincent Lawrence (play); Cast: Marguerite De La Motte, Allan Forrest, Harold Goodwin, William Austin, Mary Warren, Will Walling, Allan Sears, Mabel Forrest • Ann Jordan (De La Motte) is bored with her fiancé Robert (Goodwin) so she becomes engaged to Frank Oaks (Sears). Meanwhile, her father (Walling) has an engineer, Jack Gardner (Allan Forrest), whom he feels is a good match for Ann. Ann agrees, but Jack thinks she is after him so her father can get the plans to a bridge he has designed. After the confusion is explained, the couple is reconciled. 5,677'

1925 Releases

GOLD HEELS (Jan. 4, 1925); D: William S. Van Dyke; W: John Stone, Frederic Chapin, Henry Martyn Blossom (novel); C: Arthur Todd; Cast: Robert Agnew, Peggy Shaw, Lucien Littlefield, William Norton Bailey, Carl Stockdale, Fred Butler, Harry Tracey, James Douglas, Winifred Landis, Katherine Craig • A down-on-his-luck racetrack gambler, Boots (Agnew), ends up in a small town, where he takes a clerk job. He buys a broken-down racehorse, Gold Heels, from the store owner, Barlow (Stockdale), and falls for his daughter Pert (Shaw). While training his horse for the big race, some charity money is stolen and Boots is accused of the crime. Boots later proves that the thief is a young gambler (Bailey). When Gold Heels wins the race, Boots reconciles with Pert, who thought he was a crook. 6,020'

THE ARIZONA ROMEO (Jan. 4, 1925); D: Edmund Mortimer; W: Charles Kenyon (scr & st), Edmund Mortimer (st); Cast: Buck Jones, Lucy Fox, Maine Geary, Thomas R. Mills, Hardee Kirkland, Marcella Daly, Lydia Yeamans, Harvey Clark, Hank Mann • To escape an unwanted fiancé, Richard Barr (Geary), chosen by her wealthy father, John (Kirkland), Sylvia Wayne (Fox) runs away to Arizona and meets a local rancher Tom (Jones). Tom defends her from unwanted advances, and falls in love. Knowing that Sylvia will do the opposite of what John says, Barr shows up at the ranch and tells her John is now against the marriage. To spite her father, Sylvia suddenly agrees to marry Barr, but when Tom realizes she doesn't really love him, he goes after her for himself. 4,694'

PORTS OF CALL (Jan. 4, 1925); D: Denison Clift; W: Edfrid Bingham (scr), Garrett Elsden Fort (st); Cast: Edmund Lowe, Hazel Keener, William Davidson, William Conklin, Bobby Mack, Lilyan Tashman, Alice Ward, Mary McLean • Kirk (Lowe), a society man, is disowned by his father (Conklin) and rejected by his girlfriend, Marjorie (Keener), after a show of cowardice during a fire at a charity bazaar. Kirk ends up in Manila, and becomes a derelict. He finds love with a fellow lady drifter, Lillie (Tashman), and they get work on a plantation owned by Marjorie's husband, Randolph (Davidson). Randolph is killed during a native uprising, and Kirk saves Marjorie's life. Even though Marjorie now acknowledges his bravery, Kirk stays with Lillie. 5,500'

THE DANCERS (Jan. 11, 1925); D: Emmett J. Flynn; W: Edmund Goulding, Hubert Parsons (novel); C: Ernest G. Palmer, Paul Ivano; Cast: George O'Brien, Alma Rubens, Madge Bellamy, Templar Saxe, Joan Standing, Alice Hollister, Freeman Wood, Walter McGrail, Noble Johnson, Tippi Grey • The owner of a dancehall in South America, Tony (O'Brien), falls in love with Maxine (Rubens), one of his dancers. When Tony inherits a fortune and returns to London alone, he reunites with his childhood sweetheart, Una (Bellamy), who has been living a wild life. Una agrees to marry, but before the wedding, with a heavy conscience, she reveals her indiscretions and dies from poison she has taken. Tony returns to his South American love. 6,583'

ROUGH AND READY (Jan. 18, 1925) Reissue

DICK TURPIN (Feb. 1, 1925); D: John G. Blystone; W: Charles Kenyon (scr & st), Charles Darnton (st); C: Dan Clark; Cast: Tom Mix, Kathleen Myers, Philo McCullough, James Marcus, Lucille Hutton, Alan Hale, Bull Montana, Fay Holderness, Jack Herrick, Fred Kohler • A roguish English highwayman, Dick Turpin (Mix), saves aristocratic Alice (Myers) from a coach attack. Alice is unhappily engaged to Lord Churlton (McCullough), whom Turpin once robbed, so he helps her get away to London. Caught and about to be hanged, Turpin escapes into a sympathetic crowd, goes to Churlton's residence, where Alice is being held against her will, and rescues her. The couple then escapes to France, where they marry. 6,176'

THE FOLLY OF VANITY (Feb. 8, 1925); D: Maurice Elvey, Henry Otto; W: Edfrid Bingham (scr), Charles Darnton (st); C: G.O. Post, Joe August, Joseph Valentine; Cast: Billie Dove, Jack Mulhall, Betty Blythe, John Sainopolis, Fred Becker, Otto Matieson, Consuelo, Jean La Motte, Bob Klein, Ena Gregory, Lola Drovnar, Paul Weigel • Alice (Dove) and Robert (Mulhall), are giving a party. A gift of a pearl necklace to Alice from Robert's wealthy client (Sainopolis) leads to a domestic misunderstanding. Alice later dreams in a fantasy sequence that she jumps into the sea and is guest of honor at Neptune's (Klein) court. When Neptune discovers the pearl necklace has left a mark of vanity on her neck, he banishes her from the deep. When Alice awakens, she returns the necklace and makes up with her husband. 5,250'

THE STAR DUST TRAIL (Feb. 8, 1925); D: Edmund Mortimer; W: Dorothy Yost (scr), Frederick Hatton (st), Fanny Hatton (st); C: Joseph Valentine; Cast: Shirley Mason, Bryant Washburn, Thomas R. Mills, Richard Tucker, Merta Sterling, Shannon Day • A beautiful cabaret dancer, Sylvia (Mason), marries an actor, John (Washburn), but a spurned theatrical producer (Benton) spreads rumors about her fidelity. From stress, John turns in bad performances and is unable to get more work. He is about to ask Sylvia for a divorce when he is run down by a taxi, but she comes to his side and they make up. 4,800'

THE CHAMPION OF LOST CAUSES (Feb. 22, 1925); D: Chester Bennett; W: Thomas Dixon Jr., Max Brand (article); C: Ernest Palmer; Cast: Edmund Lowe, Barbara Bedford, Walter McGrail, Jack McDonald, Alec Francis • An author, Loring (Lowe), looking for a story, visits a gambling club and witnesses a murder. The accused is the father (Francis) of Loring's secret love (Bedford). Loring gets involved with a gang of thugs and, after several attempts on his life, discovers that the club owner (McGrail) was the murderer. 5,115'

DRAG HARLAN (Feb. 22, 1925) Reissue

THE TRAIL RIDER (Feb. 22, 1925); D: William S. Van Dyke; W: Thomas Dixon, Jr., George Washington Ogden (novel); C: Reginald Lyons; Cast: Buck Jones, Nancy Deaver, Lucy Fox, Carl Stockdale, Jack McDonald, George Berrell, Jacques Rollens, Will Walling • A fast-draw cowboy, Tex (Jones), gets a job as a trail rider but is fired when a villainous banker (Stockdale) stampedes diseased cattle into his herd. When Tex finds out who caused the stampede, he forces the banker to sign a confession which clears him in everyone's eyes, including his girlfriend (Deaver). 4,752'

RIDERS OF THE PURPLE SAGE (March 15, 1925); D: Lynn Reynolds; W: Edfrid Bingham, Zane Grey (novel); C: Dan Clark; Cast: Tom Mix, Beatrice Burnham, Arthur Morrison, Seesel Ann Johnson, Warner Oland, Fred Kohler, Charles Newton, Joe Rickson, Mabel Ballin, Charles Le Moyne • Lassiter (Mix), a Texas Ranger, sets out to find the lawyer (Oland) who kidnapped his sister (Burnham) and niece (Johnson). He takes a job on Jane Witherstein's (Ballin) ranch and learns that his quarry goes by the name of Judge Dyer. Lassiter kills Dyer and leaves town with Jane. On the run from a posse, Lassiter and Jane are trapped for life when he rolls a boulder down a mountainside, sealing off the valley. 5,578'

THE SCARLET HONEYMOON (March 22, 1925); D: Alan Hale; W: E Magnus Ingleton (scr), Edmund Goulding (st); C: Joseph Valentine; Cast: Shirley Mason, Pierre Gendron, Allan Sears, J. Farrell MacDonald, Rose Tapley, Maine Geary, Eugenie Gilbert, Eric Mayne, Eulalie Jensen • A young Argentine man, Pedro (Gendron), is sent by his wealthy father, Fernando (Mayne), to work in their New York office, where he falls in love with stenographer Kay (Mason). Fernando arranges to have Pedro accused of embezzling to test Kay's loyalty. After she pleads for Pedro's job, Fernando is convinced that she really loves Pedro and the couple returns to wed in Argentina. 5,080'

THE HUNTED WOMAN (March 22, 1925); D: Jack Conway; W: Robert N. Lee, Dorothy Yost, James Oliver Curwood (novel); C: Joseph August; Cast: Seena Owen, Earl Schenck, Diana Miller, Cyril Chadwick, Francis McDonald, Edward Piel, Victor McLaglen • A writer, John Aldous (Schenck), goes to an Alaskan gold mining settlement and gets involved with Joanne (Owen), searching for her husband who disappeared. When John finds that the husband, Rann (Chadwick), is dead, he marries Joanne, only to learn that Rann is really alive and a partner of ruthless dancehall owner, Quade (McLaglen). Quade kidnaps Joanne and Rann claims her as his wife, but Quade kills him and is then killed by another miner (McDonald). This clears the way for John and Joanne to reunite. 4,954'

MARRIAGE IN TRANSIT (March 29, 1925); D: R. William Neill; W: Dorothy Yost (scr), Grace Livingston Hill Lutz (st); C: G.O. Post; Cast: Edmund Lowe, Carol Lombard, Adolph Milar, Frank Beal, Harvey Clark, Fred Walton, Wade Boteler, Fred Butler, Byron Douglas, Fred Becker, Edward Chandler • A government agent, Cyril Gordon (Lowe), who closely resembles Holden (Lowe), the leader of a gang, impersonates him to retrieve important documents. Gordon has to marry the gangster's girl, Celia (Lombard), to keep his identity secret, and then fights off the gang when they realize who he is. Celia, who was apprehensive about putting in with a crook, is relieved that Gordon is working for law and order. 4,800'

GOLD AND THE GIRL (Apr. 5, 1925); D: Edmund Mortimer; W: John Stone; C: Allen Davey; Cast: Buck Jones, Elinor Fair, Bruce Gordon, Claude Peyton, Lucien Littlefield, Alphonse Ethier • Dan (Jones), an undercover agent for a mining company, decides to trap thieves by driving a gold shipment himself. He befriends Ann (Fair), who realizes her uncle (Ethier) and her suitor (Gordon) are behind previous robberies, and tips off Dan. The sheriff's posse captures most of the gang, but Dan goes after the two ringleaders himself. 4,512'

WINGS OF YOUTH (Apr. 12, 1925); D: Emmett Flynn; W: Bernard McConville, Harold P. Montayne (article); C: Ernest G. Palmer; Cast: Ethel Clayton, Madge Bellamy, Charles Farrell, Freeman Wood, Robert Cain, Katherine Perry, Marion Harlan, George Stewart, Douglas Gerard • To tame her three wild daughters, Betty (Harlan), Madelyne (Bellamy) and Gwen (Perry), Katherine Manners (Clayton) goes abroad and marries a much younger husband. Katherine returns and indulges in the same vices as her daughters. When Madelyne berates her mother for being reckless, she explains it was all an act to bring the girls back to their senses. 5,340'

SHE WOLVES (Apr. 12, 1925); D: Maurice Elvey; W: Dorothy Yost, Ruth Chatterton (adapted play), Andre Picard (original play); Cast: Alma Rubens, Jack Mulhall, Bertram Grassby, Harry Myers, Judy King, Fred Walton, Diana Miller, Josef Swickard, Helen Dunbar, Charles Clary • Germaine (Rubens) is distressed by her parents' plans for an arranged marriage to the rough-edged Lucien (Mulhall). To please her, Lucien goes to Paris to make himself into a gentleman. Before Germaine sees the new Lucien, he learns that she has rejected him. Despondent, he wastes his fortune. When Germaine finally meets up with Lucien, he is penniless and holds a menial position, but he is so refined that she declares her love for him. 5,783'

THE RAINBOW TRAIL (May 24, 1925); D: Lynn Reynolds; W: Lynn Reynolds, Zane Grey (novel); C: Daniel Clark; Cast: Tom Mix, Anne Cornwall, George Bancroft, Lucien Littlefield, Mark Hamilton, Vivian Oakland, Thomas Delmar, Fred De Silva, Steve Clements, Doc Roberts, Carol Halloway • John Shefford (Mix) joins a wagon train to rescue his uncle, Lassiter (Roberts), trapped in a valley with no way out. John rescues Fay Larkin (Cornwall), the adopted daughter of Jane (Halloway), who is trapped with his uncle, and then goes to the valley. After fighting off a gang of outlaws, John frees Lassiter and Jane. 5,251' • This story picks up where *Riders of the Purple Sage* left off. The "uncle" character was played by Tom Mix in the previous film.

SCANDAL PROOF (May 24, 1925); D: Edmund Mortimer; W: Charles Kenyon; Cast: Shirley Mason, John Roche, Freeman Wood, Hazel Howell, Frances Raymond, Ruth King, Edward Martindel, Joseph Striker, Billy Fay, Clarissa Selwynne • Enid Day (Mason) becomes a governess in the Hollister home, but a chance visit by Herbert (Roche), the man who testified in her defense at a murder trial, reveals a tawdry past. Even though she knew she was innocent and acquitted, Enid is forced by the Hollisters to leave her job. Before she does, she saves the reputation of Lillian Hollister (King), who has been having an affair with Dick Thornbeck (Striker), by compromising herself with Thornbeck. Mr. Hollister (Martindel) expels her, but she is offered the hand of Herbert, who still believes in her. 4,400'

THE KISS BARRIER (May 31, 1925); D: R. William Neill; W: E. Magnus Ingleton (scr), Frederick Hatton (st), Fanny Hatton (st); Cast: Edmund Lowe, Claire Adams, Diana Miller, Marion Harlan, Thomas Mills, Charles Clary, Grace Cunard • An actor, Richard Marsh (Lowe), meets a nurse, Marion (Adams), who tended to him in France during the war. When Marion suspects Richard is having an affair with Suzette (Miller), she snubs him. To win her back, Richard writes a play which explains the situation and Marion realizes she misjudged him. 5,000'

EVERY MAN'S WIFE (June 7, 1925); D: Maurice Elvey; W: Lillie Hayward (scr), Ethel Hill (st), Enid Hilbert (st); Cast: Elaine Hammerstein, Herbert Rawlinson, Robert Cain, Diana Miller, Dorothy Phillips • Jealous newlywed Mrs. Randolph (Hammerstein) makes her husband's (Rawlinson) life miserable because she wrongly suspects him of carrying on with a neighbor, Mrs. Bradin (Phillips). To expose him, she has a party and invites the Bradins. While Mr. Randolph is the model of fidelity, Mrs. Bradin's husband (Cain) makes a play for Mrs. Randolph. The Randolphs are later reunited with new trust in each other. 4,365'

HEARTS AND SPURS (June 7, 1925); D: William S. Van Dyke; W: John Stone, Jackson Gregory (novel); C: Allen Davey; Cast: Buck Jones, Carol Lombard, William Davidson, Freeman Wood, Jean La Motte, J. Gordon Russell, Walt Robbins, Charles Eldridge • Cowboy Hal Emory (Jones) rescues Sybil (Lombard), an Easterner, from a landslide. He then covers for her brother, Oscar (Wood), by taking the blame for a stagecoach robbery Oscar was forced into because of gambling debts. Hal catches up with Dufresne (Davidson), a notorious gambler, and keeps him from killing Oscar. Hal wins Sybil's love when he exonerates Oscar and pins the robbery on Dufresne. 4,600'

GREATER THAN A CROWN (July 26, 1925); D: R. William Neill; W: Wyndham Gittens, Victor Bridges (novel); Cast: Edmund Lowe, Dolores Costello, Margaret Livingston, Ben Hendricks, Paul Panzer, Anthony Merlo, Robert Klein • Tom (Lowe), a wealthy American in London, helps Isabel (Costello) and her friend, Molly (Livingston), escape assailants. Molly then needs Tom's help in figuring out the disappearance of her jewels and Isabel. Isabel turns out to be a princess who ran away from her country rather than marry King Danilo (Merlo). Tom ends up rescuing Isabel and Danilo from kidnappers and takes them back to their country. When Danilo reveals he is married to Molly, Tom marries Isabel. 5,000'

LIGHTNIN' (Aug. 23, 1925); D: John Ford; W: Frances Marion, Winchell Smith and Frank Bacon (play); C: Joseph August; Cast: Jay Hunt, Madge Bellamy, Wallace MacDonald, J. Farrell MacDonald, Ethel Clayton, James Marcus, Edythe Chapman, Otis Harlan, Brandon Hurst, Richard Travers • Real estate hucksters try to get control of a hotel from Mother Jones (Chapman) that is on land to be developed by the railroad. Lightnin' Jones (Hunt) refuses to allow the sale, so the schemers persuade his wife to divorce him. Mother Jones eventually changes her mind, following the advice of lawyer John Marvin (Wallace MacDonald), who is in love with her daughter, Millie (Bellamy). The swindlers are arrested. 8,050'

THE LUCKY HORSESHOE (Aug. 30, 1925); D: J.G. Blystone; W: John Stone (scr), Robert Lord (st); C: Dan Clark; Cast: Tom Mix, Billie Dove, Malcolm Waite, J. Farrell MacDonald, Clarissa Selwynne, Ann Pennington, J. Gunnis Davis • Ranch foreman Tom Foster (Mix) takes over a property after the death of its owner. The owner's daughter, Eleanor (Dove), whom Tom loves, is taken to Europe by an aunt (Selwynne) and returns with a fiancé, Denman (Waite). Denman kidnaps Tom, who is knocked out and dreams that he is the fabled lover Don Juan. When Tom regains consciousness, he races off in time to prevent the wedding. 4,949'

KENTUCKY PRIDE (Sept. 6, 1925); D: John Ford; W: Dorothy Yost, Elizabeth Pickett (titles); C: George Schneiderman; Cast: Henry B. Walthall, J. Farrell MacDonald, Gertrude Astor, Malcolm Waite, Belle Stoddard, Winston Miller, Peaches Jackson • A Kentucky horseman, Beaumont (Walthall), loses his fortune after betting heavily on his last horse, which falls and breaks a leg. The horse is nursed back to health, is sold and gives birth to a colt that is trained and entered in the big race. Beaumont bets every penny he has on the race and wins enough to buy back the offspring. 6,597'

THE MAN WITHOUT A COUNTRY (Sept. 13, 1925) Alternate title — As No Man Has Loved; D: Rowland V. Lee; W: Robert N. Lee, Edward Everett Hale (novel); C: G.O. Post; Cast: Edward Hearn, Pauline Starke, Lucy Beaumont, Richard Tucker, Earl Metcalf, Edward Coxen, Wilfred Lucas, Francis Powers, Harvey Clark, William Walling, George Billings • Lt. Nolan (Hearn) is court-martialed in the Aaron Burr (Tucker) conspiracy of the early 19th century and placed on a warship, never again to set foot on American soil. He spends years on ships in battle and is finally pardoned by President Lincoln (Billings), but dies before he can return to America. 10,000'

THE WHEEL (Sept. 20, 1925); D: Victor Schertzinger; W: Edfrid Bingham, Winchell Smith (play); C: Glen MacWilliams; Cast: Margaret Livingston, Harrison Ford, Claire Adams, Mahlon Hamilton, David Torrence, Julia Swayne Gordon, Clara Horton, Georgie Harris, Erin La Bissoniere, Russ Powell • Ted Morton (Ford), the gambling son of a wealthy banker (Torrence), is disinherited when he marries a milliner, Kate (Adams), against his parents' wishes. Taking a job as a car salesman, Ted is lured back to gambling and loses company funds. When he sees Kate taking money from an acquaintance (Hamilton), he shoots at the man, slightly wounding his wife. The misunderstanding is explained and the couple is finally accepted by the wealthy parents. 7,264'

TIMBER WOLF (Sept. 20, 1925); D: William S. Van Dyke; W: John Stone (scr), Jackson Gregory (st); C: Allan Davey; Cast: Buck Jones, Elinor Fair, David Dyas, Sam Allen, William Walling, Jack Craig, Robert Mack • After staking an old prospector, Joe Terry (Allen), Bruce Standing (Jones), known as the Timber Wolf, finds out a gang of swindlers, led by Babe Deveril (Dyas), has been trying to claim Terry's gold strike. The gang first has Terry arrested and then gets Renée (Fair) to use her feminine wiles to find out where the mine is. The Timber Wolf breaks up the gang and wins over Renée. 4,809'

HAVOC (Sept. 27, 1925); D: Rowland V. Lee; W: Edmund Goulding, Henry Wall (novel); C: G.O. Post; Cast: Madge Bellamy, George O'Brien, Walter McGrail, Eulalie Jensen, Margaret Livingston, Leslie Fenton, David Butler, Harvey Clark, Wade Boteler, Edythe Chapman • During the World War, two officers in the British Army, Dick (O'Brien) and Roddy (McGrail), fall in love with the same girl, Violet (Livingston). Roddy, the senior ranking officer, is jilted and sends Dick off on a mission to certain death. Dick returns alive, but blinded, and Roddy commits suicide. After the war, Dick, too, is jilted and marries the late officer's sister Tessie (Bellamy). 9,283'

THE IRON HORSE (Oct. 4, 1925); D: John Ford; W: Charles Kenyon (scr & st), John Russell (st), Charles Darnton (titles); C: George Schneiderman; M: Erno Rapée; Cast: George O'Brien, Madge Bellamy, Cyril Chadwick, Fred Kohler, Gladys Hulette, James Marcus, J. Farrell MacDonald, James Welch, Walter Rogers, George Waggner • Davy Brandon (O'Brien), surveyor for the Union Pacific, meets Miriam (Bellamy), his childhood sweetheart, while working on the railroad. He also discovers that his father's murderer is Deroux (Kohler), the leader of a band of renegades disguised as Indians that attacks rail workers. After dispensing justice, Davy joins the Central Pacific and is present for the joining of the two lines with a golden spike. 10,424'

THUNDER MOUNTAIN (Oct. 11, 1925); D: Victor Schertzinger; W: Eve Unsell, Pearl Franklin (play); C: Glen MacWilliams; Cast: Madge Bellamy, Leslie Fenton, Alec B. Francis, Paul Panzer, Arthur Houseman, ZaSu Pitts, Emily Fitzroy, Dan Mason, Otis Harlan, Russell Simpson, Natalie Warfield • Illiterate Sam Martin (Fenton) is persuaded by the preacher (Francis) to leave Thunder Mountain and get an education. When Sam returns, he is determined to raise enough money to build a schoolhouse. He is caught up in a family feud and becomes involved with a fleeing circus performer, Azalea (Bellamy), and is accused by a lynch mob for the murder of the local moneylender, Si Pace (Simpson). The preacher defuses the mob by igniting dynamite in the mountain, and the real murderer (Houseman) confesses. 7,537'

THE EVERLASTING WHISPER (Oct. 11, 1925); D: J.G. Blystone; W: Wyndham Gittens, Jackson Gregory (novel); C: Dan Clark; Cast: Tom Mix, Alice Calhoun, Robert Cain, George Berrell, Walter James, Virginia Madison, Karl Dane • Rescued from her runaway horse, Gloria (Calhoun), a society heiress, marries her savior, prospector Mark King (Mix). She soon misses the city life and resents her new husband. Moving back to San Francisco, she realizes the depth of her love for Mark, and the couple is reunited under the everlasting whisper of the pine trees. 5,611'

THE FIGHTING HEART (Oct. 18, 1925); D: John Ford; W: Lillie Hayward, Larry Evans (novel); C: Joe August; Cast: George O'Brien, Billie Dove, J. Farrell MacDonald, Victor McLaglen, Diana Miller, Bert Woodruff, Francis Ford, Hazel Howell, Edward Piel, James Marcus • Heavy drinking Denny Bolton (O'Brien), scorned by the townsfolk and his girlfriend, Doris (Dove), leaves for New York. His objective is to fight boxing champion Soapy Williams (McLaglen), who had caused his grandfather to go blind by selling him bootlegged whisky. Soapy's girl, Helen (Miller), vamps Denny, and he loses the fight. Some time later, he meets the champ on the street and is goaded into a rough and tumble fight, which he wins. He returns to his town, victorious, and is reunited with Doris. 6,978'

THE WINDING STAIR (Oct. 25, 1925); D: John Griffith Wray; W: Julian La Mothe, Alfred Edward Woodley Mason (novel); C: Karl Struss; Cast: Alma Rubens, Edmund Lowe, Warner Oland, Mahlon Hamilton, Emily Fitzroy, Chester Conklin, Frank Leigh • Paul (Lowe), a French Foreign Legionnaire, seemingly deserts his regiment to save his men and his sweetheart (Rubens) from a native massacre. Disgraced, he organizes a regiment of natives to fight for France during the Great War and restores his honor in the battle of Flanders. 6,100'

DURAND OF THE BAD LANDS (Nov. 1, 1925); D: Lynn Reynolds; W: Lynn Reynolds (scr & adpt), Maibelle Heikes Justice (st); C: Allan Davey; Cast: Buck Jones, Marian Nixon, Malcolm Waite, Fred De Silva, Luke Cosgrove, George Lessey, Buck Black, Seesel Ann Johnson, James Corrigan, Carole Lombard • A rancher, Dick Durand (Jones), returns home to find that crimes have been committed under his identity. Vindicating himself, he falls in love with Molly (Nixon) an invalid rancher's (Corrigan) daughter, rescues children from an attack on a wagon carrying gold, and frees a banker's daughter (Lombard), imprisoned in a mine by an outlaw. 5,844'

THANK YOU (Nov. 1, 1925); P: John Golden; D: John Ford; W: Frances Marion, Winchell Smith and Tom Cushing (play); C: George Schneiderman; Cast: Alec B. Francis, Jacqueline Logan, George O'Brien, J. Farrell MacDonald, Cyril Chadwick, Edith Bostwick, Marion Harlan, Vivian Ogden, James Neill, Billy Rinaldi • The Reverend Lee (Francis) has spent 30 underpaid years ministering to his town's people, with little appreciation. When his niece, Diane (Logan), arrives from Paris and gets the attention of a young millionaire (O'Brien), tongues start wagging. The Reverend Lee is ousted from his post when he refuses to send Diane away, but the hypocritical townspeople later reform and all is settled amicably. 6,839'

LAZYBONES (Nov. 8, 1925); D: Frank Borzage; W: Frances Marion, Owen Davis (play); C: George Schneiderman; Cast: Charles "Buck" Jones, Madge Bellamy, Virginia Marshall, Edythe Chapman, Leslie Fenton, Jane Novak, Emily Fitzroy, ZaSu Pitts, William Norton Bailey • At the turn of the century, shiftless but goodhearted Steve Tuttle, nicknamed Lazybones (Jones), saves Ruth (Pitts) from committing suicide in the river. He also adopts her infant daughter because Ruth's mother (Fitzroy) does not believe that she was married to a sailor who drowned. The adoption causes Lazybones's girlfriend Agnes (Novak) to leave him. Years later, after fighting in France during the war, Lazybones returns home, hoping to marry his grown stepdaughter (Bellamy), but she has fallen in love with another (Fenton). 7,234' • This was the first film of Borzage's illustrious career at Fox.

THE FOOL (Nov. 15, 1925); D: Harry Millarde; W: Edmund Goulding, Channing Pollock (play); C: Joseph Ruttenberg; Cast: Edmund Lowe, Raymond Bloomer, Henry Sedley, Paul Panzer, A.J. Herbert, Downing

Clarke, George Lessey, Blanche Craig, Fred C. Jones, Brenda Bond, Anne Dale • An assistant rector, Daniel (Lowe), is dismissed for his views against worldly possessions and is deserted by his fiancée (Bond). He starts a mission where his former fiancée, now married, seeks solace because of her abusive husband (Lessey). Daniel is later accused of infidelity with Pearl Hennig (Thurman), who is beaten by a mob led by her husband (Herbert). A child (Dale), crippled since birth, walks over to help Daniel and the mob declares it has witnessed a miracle. 9,453' • The film's New York opening was in May 1925, and its rapid descent into regular release reflects its disappointing box-office returns in exclusive engagements. It lost $150,000, the most for any Fox picture of 1925.

EAST LYNNE (Nov. 22, 1925); D: Emmett Flynn; W: Lenore J. Coffee (adpt), Emmett Flynn (adpt), Mrs. Henry Wood (novel); C: Ernest G. Palmer; Cast: Alma Rubens, Edmund Lowe, Lou Tellegen, Frank Keenan, Marjorie Daw, Leslie Fenton, Belle Bennett, Paul Panzer, Lydia Knott, Harry Seymour, Richard Headrick • Archibald Carlyle (Lowe), a wealthy young Englishman, buys a debt-ridden estate and marries Lady Isabel (Rubens). A former sweetheart, Barbara (Daw), visits Archibald to enlist his help and Isabel is persuaded that her husband has been unfaithful. Isabel goes abroad with Sir Francis (Tellegen), who lied to her, and is later reported dead in a car accident. Archibald marries Barbara. Isabel returns when one of her children becomes ill. She contracts the disease and dies, but is recognized by her husband. 8,975' • This is a modernized version of the 1861 novel, which was originally produced in 1916.

THE BEST BAD MAN (Nov. 29, 1925); D: J.G. Blystone; W: Lillie Hayward, Max Brand (article); C: Dan Clark; Cast: Tom Mix, Buster Gardner, Cyril Chadwick, Clara Bow, Tom Kennedy, Frank Beal, Judy King, Tom Wilson, Paul Panzer, Tony the Wonder Horse • Ranch owner Hugh Nichols (Mix) returns to his property in disguise and finds his agent, Frank (Chadwick), has been cheating him and preventing the construction of a dam. Frank is also trying to marry Peggy (Bow), who falls in love with Nichols. Frank dynamites the dam, trapping Peggy in a flood, but Nichols, with help from his horse, rescues the girl and arrests Frank. 4,983'

WHEN THE DOOR OPENED (Dec. 6, 1925); D: Reginald Barker; W: Bradley King, James Oliver Curwood (article); C: Ernest G. Palmer; Cast: Jacqueline Logan, Walter McGrail, Margaret Livingston, Robert Cain, Frank Keenan, Roy Laidlaw, Diana Miller • Clive (McGrail), a man of the Canadian Northwest, thinking he has killed his wife's (Livingston) lover, Morgan (Cain), flees into the woods. He meets and falls in love with Teresa (Logan), whose grandfather (Keenan) initially does not take to Clive. When Morgan shows up and tries to lure Teresa away from him, Clive discovers Morgan is married to his now-divorced wife. This leaves Clive free to remarry as well. 6,515'

WAGES FOR WIVES (Dec. 13, 1925); D: Frank Borzage; W: Kenneth B. Clarke, Guy Bolton and Winchell Smith (play); C: Ernest G. Palmer; Cast: Jacqueline Logan, Creighton Hale, Earle Foxe, ZaSu Pitts, Claude Gillingwater, David Butler, Margaret Seddon, Margaret Livingston, Dan Mason, Tom Ricketts • Nell (Logan) agrees to marry Danny (Hale) provided he will split his paycheck with her. Danny refuses after they are wed and Nell goes on strike, getting her mother and sister (Pitts) to join her, making it difficult for all three husbands. A vamp enters the picture, but all is straightened out with each side meeting the other halfway. 6,650'

THE DESERT'S PRICE (Dec. 13, 1925); D: W.S. Van Dyke; W: Charles Darnton, William MacCleod Raine (novel); C: Reginald Lyons; Cast: Buck Jones, Florence Gilbert, Edna Marion, Ernest Butterworth, Arthur Houseman, Montague Love, Carl Stockdale, Harry Dunkinson, Henry Armetta • Nils McCann (Jones), a cattle rancher, goes to work for Julia Starke (Gilbert), whose father was murdered during a range war. The Starke crew has been unfairly accused of crimes committed by a gang headed by Jim Martin. Martin has Julia arrested for his brother's murder, and Nils has to save her from a lynch mob and bring the guilty parties, including her father's murderer, to justice. 5,709'

THE ANCIENT MARINER (Dec. 20, 1925); D: Henry Otto, Chester Bennett; W: Eve Unsell, Tom Miranda (titles), Samuel Taylor Coleridge (poem); C: Joseph August; Modern Sequences: Clara Bow, Earle Williams, Leslie Fenton, Nigel De Brulier; Ancient Mariner sequences: Paul Panzer, Gladys Brockwell, Robert Klein • A wealthy roué, Victor (Williams), tries to carry off an innocent country girl, Doris (Bow), from her fiancé, Joel (Fenton). To stop him, an old seaman (De Brulier) tells him the story of the ancient mariner who shot the albatross. After the shooting, all the misfortunes of the world descended on him and, only when he repented, did he get a break. Victor is touched by the story and leaves Doris behind so she can marry Joel. 5,548'

THE GOLDEN STRAIN (Dec. 27, 1925); D: Victor Schertzinger; W: Eve Unsell, Peter Bernard Kyne (article); C: Glen MacWilliams; Cast: Hobart Bosworth, Kenneth Harlan, Madge Bellamy, Lawford Davidson, Ann Pennington, Frank Beal, Frankie Lee, Coy Watson, Robert Frazer, Oscar Smith • Major Mulford (Bosworth), a cavalry officer, takes a detachment after Apaches who have been cheated by Major Gaynes (Davidson), an Indian agent. Mulford is put to the test and fails to lead. He loses his commission and his fiancée, Dixie (Bellamy), until he later proves his courage. 5,989'

MONTE CRISTO (Dec. 27, 1925) Reissue

1926 Releases

THE GILDED BUTTERFLY (Jan. 3, 1926); D: John Griffith Wray; W: Bradley King, Evelyn Campbell; C: Frank Good; Cast: Alma Rubens, Bert Lytell, Huntly

Gordon, Frank Keenan, Herbert Rawlinson, Vera Lewis, Arthur Hoyt, Carolynne Snowden • A spoiled woman (Rubens), whose fortune has been dissipated, goes to Monte Carlo with borrowed money and falls in love with Brian (Lytell), an American. When she returns, she resorts to insurance fraud and, by fortunate circumstance, is given a chance to leave for South America with Brian. 6,202'

THE PALACE OF PLEASURE (Jan. 10, 1926); D: Emmett Flynn; W: Bradley King (scr), Benjamin Glazer (adpt), Adolf Paul (original, "Lola Montez"); C: Ernest Palmer; Cast: Edmund Lowe, Betty Compson, Henry Kolker, Harvey Clark, Nina Romano, Francis McDonald, George Siegmann • Lola Montez (Compson) is kidnapped by an accused traitor (Lowe) and forced to marry him. She is persuaded to lead her husband into a trap, but realizes she loves him before he is caught. 5,467'

THE YANKEE SEÑOR (Jan. 10, 1926); D: Emmett Flynn; W: Eve Unsell, Katherine Fullerton Gerould (novel); C: Daniel Clark; Cast: Tom Mix, Olive Borden, Tom Kennedy, Francis McDonald, Margaret Livingston, Alec B. Francis, Kathryn Hill, Martha Mattox, Raymond Wells, Tony the Wonder Horse • An aging Spanish rancher, Don Fernando (Francis), finds his long-lost grandson, Paul Wharton (Mix), but Paul is resented by Juan (McDonald), an adopted son who tries to get him out of the way. Paul ends up thrashing Juan and marries Manuelita (Borden). 4,902'

THE OUTSIDER (Jan. 17, 1926); D: Rowland V. Lee; W: Robert N. Lee (adpt), Dorothy Brandon (play); C: G.O. Post; Cast: Jacqueline Logan, Lou Tellegen, Walter Pidgeon, Roy Atwell, Charles Lane, Joan Standing, Gibson Gowland, Bertram Marburgh, Crauford Kent, Louis Payne • Famous English dancer Leontine (Logan) meets a mystic Ragatzy (Tellegen) at a gypsy camp in Hungary while looking for new material. When she is injured in a fall, Ragatzy follows her to London and offers his help, but she considers him a fraud. After doctors fail to cure her, she relents. The mystic is able to help her walk again, and she realizes she loves him. 5,424'

THE FIRST YEAR (Jan. 24, 1926); D: Frank Borzage; W: Frances Marion, Frank Craven (play); C: Chester Lyons; Cast: Matt Moore, Kathryn Perry, John Patrick, Frank Currier, Frank Cooley, Virginia Madison, Carolynne Snowden, J. Farrell MacDonald • A newly married small-town couple, Tom (Moore) and Grace (Perry), goes through a humorous but rocky first year as the ambitious wife, bored with Tom's lack of success, is finally impressed when he signs a big deal. Tom also learns a baby is on the way. 6,038' • This is a film version of one of the biggest stage hits of the decade.

THE COWBOY AND THE COUNTESS (Jan. 31, 1926); D: R. William Neill; W: Charles Darnton (scr), Maxine Alton (st), Adele Buffington (st); C: Reginald Lyons; Cast: Buck Jones, Helen D'Algy, Diana Miller, Harvey Clark, Monte Collins, Jr., Fletcher Norton, Chappell Dossett, Jere Austin, White Eagle • Cowboy Jerry Whipple (Jones) helps Countess Justina, who gets involved in a car accident while visiting the West. Justina returns to her native land to marry a duke (Norton), but Jerry, touring with a Wild West show, saves her from the duke who is really the leader of a gang of thieves. 5,345'

THE ROAD TO GLORY (Feb. 7, 1926); D: Howard Hawks; W: L.G. Rigby (scr), Howard Hawks (st); C: Joseph August; Cast: May McAvoy, Leslie Fenton, Ford Sterling, Rockcliffe Fellowes, Milla Davenport, John MacSweeney • Judith Allen (McAvoy), who has lost her sight in a car accident, breaks off her engagement with David Hale (Fenton), renounces her faith and retreats to a mountain lodge. When David is injured while trying to find her, she prays for his recovery. With her renewed faith, she also regains her sight. 6,038'

OVER THE HILL TO THE POORHOUSE (Feb. 14, 1926) Reissue

A CONNECTICUT YANKEE IN KING ARTHUR'S COURT (Feb. 14, 1926) Reissue

MY OWN PAL (Feb. 28, 1926); D: John G. Blystone; W: Lillie Hayward, Gerald Beaumont (novel); C: Daniel Clark; Cast: Tom Mix, Olive Borden, Tom Santschi, Virginia Marshall, Bardson Bard, William Colvin, Virginia Warwick, Jay Hunt, Hedda Nova, Tom McGuire, Helen Lynch • A cowboy, Tom O'Hara (Mix), moves to the city, rescues Alice Deering (Borden) from a runaway horse and is made a police officer. He arrests a gang of jewel thieves and again rescues Alice after she is kidnapped by the leader of the gang. 6 reels

THE JOHNSTOWN FLOOD (Feb. 28, 1926); D: Irving Cummings; W: Edfrid Bingham, Robert Lord; C: George Schneiderman; Cast: George O'Brien, Florence Gilbert, Janet Gaynor, Anders Randolf, Paul Nicholson, Paul Panzer, George Harris, Max Davidson, Walter Perry, Sid Jordan • Tom O'Day (O'Brien), an engineer, warns a logging camp owner, Hamilton (Randolf), that the dam at Johnstown has been weakened by using it for floating logs. Not heeding the warning, catastrophe hits the town when the dam bursts. Tom escapes with his girlfriend, Hamilton's daughter Gloria (Gilbert). Young Anna (Gaynor) tries to warn the townsfolk; she is killed when the town is destroyed. 6,357'

THE DIXIE MERCHANT (March 7, 1926); D: Frank Borzage; W: Kenneth B. Clarke, John Barry Benefield (novel); C: Frank B. Good; Cast: J. Farrell MacDonald, Madge Bellamy, Jack Mulhall, Claire McDowell, Harvey Clark, Edward Martindel, Evelyn Arden, Onest Conly, Paul Panzer • After losing his home, J.P. Fippany (MacDonald) sets out with his family and their racehorse, Marseillaise. Jimmy Pickett (Mulhall), who falls for daughter Aida (Bellamy), ends up buying the horse. The mother (McDowell), in a misunderstanding about Marseillaise, takes Aida and leaves. However, Fippany rides Marseillaise and wins a race, which reunites everyone. 5,126'

HELL'S 400 (March 14, 1926); D: John Griffith Wray; W: Bradley King, Vaughan Kester (novel); C: Karl Struss; Cast: Margaret Livingston, Harrison Ford, Henry Kolker, Wallace MacDonald, Rodney Hildebrand, Amber Norman • A chorus girl, Evelyn (Livingston), marries a rich man, Marshall (MacDonald), against the wishes of her boss, Gilmore, who is then killed by Marshall. District Attorney John North (Ford), a foe of Gilmore, is arrested, and Evelyn is reluctant to clear him because she would incriminate her husband. Evelyn's guilt gets to be unbearable, but then she awakens. The whole thing has been a dream. 5,582' (Technicolor sequence)

SIBERIA (March 28, 1926); D: Victor Schertzinger; W: Eve Unsell (scr), Nicholas A. Dunaev (adpt), Bartley Campbell (play); C: Glen MacWilliams; Cast: Alma Rubens, Edmund Lowe, Lou Tellegen, Tom Santschi, Paul Panzer, Vadim Uraneff, Lilyan Tashman, Helen D'Algy, James Marcus, Daniel Makarenko • A woman of the revolution, Sonia (Rubens), is exiled to Siberia, and her previous boyfriend, Petroff (Lowe), a Russian officer helps her escape even though they have different political views. They are pursued across the frozen wastelands by wolves and a revolutionary leader (Tellegen). 6,950'

THE FIGHTING BUCKAROO (Apr. 4, 1926); D: R. William Neill; W: Charles Darnton (scr), Frank Howard Clark (st); C: Reginald Lyons; Cast: Buck Jones, Sally Long, Lloyd Whitlock, Frank Butler, E.J. Ratcliffe, Ben Hendricks, Jr., Ray Thompson, Frank Rice • Hoping to purchase a ranch on which gold has been found, Larry Crawford (Jones), heads to Los Angeles, but gets mixed up with attractive young Betty (Long) and a gang of thugs, in a succession of comic situations. 5,095'

RUSTLING FOR CUPID (Apr. 11, 1926); D: Irving Cummings; W: L.G. Rigby, Peter Bernard Kyne (article); C: Abe Fried; Cast: George O'Brien, Anita Stewart, Russell Simpson, Edith Yorke, Herbert Prior, Frank McGlynn, Jr., Sid Jordan • The romance between a rancher, Bradley Clatchford (O'Brien), and a schoolteacher, Sybil (Stewart), is complicated when her criminally inclined brother creates a rustling problem in the town, which is first blamed on Bradley's father (Simpson), but then is revealed to be the fault of Sybil's brother. 4,835'

SANDY (Apr. 11, 1926); D: Harry Beaumont; W: Eve Unsell (adpt), Elenore Meherin (novel); C: Rudolph Bergquist; Cast: Madge Bellamy, Leslie Fenton, Harrison Ford, Gloria Hope, Bardson Bard, David Torrence, Lillian Leighton, Charles Farrell, Charles Coleman, Joan Standing • A jazz baby, Sandy (Bellamy), grudgingly marries a wealthy suitor to please her father. The cruel husband causes the death of her child and she then moves through a tawdry love life, entering a romance with her sister (Hope) Judith's boyfriend, Douglas (Fenton). Sandy's story ends when another lover, Ramon (Ford), shoots her fatally and then kills himself. 7,850'

TONY RUNS WILD (Apr. 18, 1926); D: Thomas Buckingham; W: Edfrid Bingham (scr), Robert Lord (scr), Henry Herbert Knibbs (st); C: Daniel Clark; Cast: Tom Mix, Tony the Wonder Horse, Jacqueline Logan, Lawford Davidson, Duke Lee, Vivian Oakland, Edward Martindel, Marion Harlan, Raymond Wells, Richard Carter • Tom Trent (Mix) is a modern cowboy who captures, trains, then releases a wild horse. He is framed and arrested for a stage holdup, but when his girlfriend, Grace (Logan), is abducted, he escapes his captors and brings the guilty party (Davidson) to justice with the help of the wild horse. 5,477'

A MAN OF SORROW (Apr. 24, 1926) Reissue title — Hoodman Blind

YELLOW FINGERS (Apr. 25, 1926); D: Emmett Flynn; W: Eve Unsell, Gene Wright (novel); C: Ernest G. Palmer, Paul Ivano; E: Joseph Kane; Cast: Olive Borden, Ralph Ince, Claire Adams, Edward Piel, Otto Matieson, Nigel De Brulier, Armand Kaliz, Josephine Crowell, May Foster, John Wallace, Charles Newton • A Far East trader, Capt. Shane (Ince), is loved by Saina (Borden), a half-caste he's raised, and Nona (Adams), an English girl he rescued in his travels. Saina jealously tries to deliver Nona to Chinese merchant Kwong Li (Piel), but has a change of heart and leads Shane to rescue her. 5,594'

EARLY TO WED (Apr. 25, 1926); D: Frank Borzage; W: Kenneth B. Clarke, Evelyn Campbell (article); C: Ernest G. Palmer; Cast: Matt Moore, Kathryn Perry, Albert Gran, Julia Swayne Gordon, Arthur Housman, Rodney Hildebrand, ZaSu Pitts, Belva McKay, Ross McCutcheon, Harry Bailey • A young couple, Tommy (Moore) and Daphne (Perry), pretend to be prosperous, but their plan backfires. Tommy loses his job and their furniture is repossessed. By chance, they show a millionaire some kindness and Tommy is rewarded with a job. 5,912

THE SHAMROCK HANDICAP (May 2, 1926); D: John Ford; W: John Stone (scr), Peter Bernard Kyne (st), Elizabeth Pickett (titles); C: George Schneiderman; Cast: Janet Gaynor, Leslie Fenton, J. Farrell MacDonald, Louis Payne, Claire McDowell, Willard Louis, Andy Clark, Georgie Harris, Ely Reynolds, Brandon Hurst • Sir Miles Gaffney (Payne), an Irishman facing financial ruin, and his daughter, Sheila (Gaynor), come to America when the girl's boyfriend, Neil (Fenton), a jockey, is injured in a race. They bring their horse with them and Neil later rides it to victory. 5,685'

A MAN FOUR-SQUARE (May 9, 1926); D: R. William Neill; W: John Stone, Charles Darnton, William MacLeod Raine (novel); C: Reginald Lyons; Cast: Buck Jones, Marion Harlan, Harry Woods, W.E. Lawrence, Jay Hunt, Sidney Bracey, Florence Gilbert, Frank Beal • A rancher, Craig (Jones), is implicated and pursued by a posse for cattle rustling. His friend suspects him as well of horning in on his sweetheart, Polly (Harlan). When Craig heroically rescues his friend and Polly, he regains their respect. 4,744'

BLACK PARADISE (May 30, 1926); D: R. William Neill; W: L.G. Rigby; C: George Schneiderman; Cast: Leslie Fenton, Madge Bellamy, Edmund Lowe, Edward Piel, Harvey Clark, Paul Panzer, Marcella Daly, Samuel Blum, Doris Lloyd, Patrick Kelly, Mary Gordon • Graham (Lowe), a detective, is shanghaied by a smuggler and taken to a South Seas island where he is forced to work at a sulfur mine by master crook Murdock (Piel). Graham falls in love with Sylvia (Bellamy), the sweetheart of Callahan (Fenton), a criminal he is pursuing. A volcanic eruption destroys the island, allowing Graham and Sylvia to escape. 4,962'

HARD BOILED (June 6, 1926); D: J.G. Blystone; W: Charles Darnton (scr), John Stone (scr), Shannon Fife (st), Ralph Spence (titles); C: Dan Clark; Cast: Tom Mix, Helene Chadwick, William Lawrence, Charles Conklin, Emily Fitzroy, Phyllis Haver, Dan Mason, Walter "Spec" O'Donnell, Ethel Grey Terry, Tony the Wonder Horse • Cowboy Tom Bouden (Mix) is mistaken for a fashionable doctor at a health resort run by his friend. He increases the resort's popularity by putting on a Wild West show and attracts a gang of thieves who rob the hotel safe, but Tom rounds them up and wins a girl's affection (Chadwick). 5,679'

A TRIP TO CHINATOWN (June 6, 1926); SP: George E. Marshall; D: Robert P. Kerr; W: Beatrice Van, Charles Hale Hoyt (play); C: Barney McGill; Cast: Margaret Livingston, Earle Foxe, J. Farrell MacDonald, Anna May Wong, Harry Woods, Marie Astaire, Gladys McConnell, Charles Farrell, Hazel Howell • Millionaire hypochondriac Welland Strong (Foxe) believes he only has six months to live, so he decides to travel. He ends up in San Francisco's Chinatown, where he meets a charming widow (Livingston), who cures him. 5,594'

MORE PAY, LESS WORK (June 13, 1926); SP: Kenneth Hawks; D: Albert Ray; W: Rex Taylor, Peter Bernard Kyne (st); C: Sidney Wagner; Cast: Albert Gran, Mary Brian, E.J. Ratcliffe, Charles "Buddy" Rogers, Otto Hoffman, Heinie Conklin, Frank Cooley • The Ricks family and the Hinchfields are business rivals. Complications arise when Betty Ricks (Brian) falls in love with Willie Hinchfield (Rogers) and they try to carry on a secret romance. When the couple decides to marry, the fathers, Cappy Ricks (Gran) and Dad Hinchfield (Ratcliffe), decide to become partners. 6,027'

THE SILVER TREASURE (June 13, 1926); D: Rowland V. Lee; W: Robert N. Lee, Elizabeth Pickett (titles), Joseph Conrad (novel); C: G.O. Post; Cast: George O'Brien, Jack Rollins, Helene D'Algy, Joan Renee, Evelyn Selbie, Lou Tellegen, Otto Matieson, Stewart Rome, Hedda Hopper, Daniel Makarenko, Fred Becker • Based on the Conrad classic *Nostromo*, this is the story about a man (O'Brien) who tries to protect his treasure from pirates, and his desire for a woman (Renee) other than one he is to marry (D'Algy). 5,386'

THE GENTLE CYCLONE (June 27, 1926); D: William S. Van Dyke; W: Thomas Dixon, Jr., Frank R. Buckley (article); C: Chester Lyons, Reginald Lyons; Cast: Buck Jones, Rose Blossom, Will Walling, Reed Howes, Stanton Heck, Grant Withers, Kathleen Myers, Jay Hunt, Oliver Hardy, Marion Harlan • A lawyer, Absolem Wales (Jones), is hired to resolve a feud involving two uncles, Marshall (Walling) and Wilkes (Heck), whose orphan niece, June (Blossom), has inherited a strip of valuable property between their farms. A truce is agreed upon when Wales adopts June. 4,825'

HONESTY—THE BEST POLICY (Aug. 8, 1926); D: Chester Bennett, Albert Ray (additional sequence); W: L.G. Rigby (scr), Howard Hawks (st); C: Ernest G. Palmer; Cast: Rockcliffe Fellowes, Pauline Starke, Johnnie Walker, Grace Diamond, Mickey Bennett, Mack Swain, Albert Gran, Dot Farley, Heinie Conklin • A struggling author, desperate to sell a story, concocts his own "true" past for a publisher, involving robberies, pursuits, captures, escapes and eventual reform. His wife finds out that he has included her in his story and spoils his finale. 4,200'

FIG LEAVES (Aug. 22, 1926); SP: Winfield R. Sheehan; D: Howard Hawks; AD: James Tinling; W: Hope Loring (scr), Louis D. Lighton (scr), Howard Hawks (st); Cast: George O'Brien, Olive Borden, Phyllis Haver, Andre de Beranger, William Austin, Heinie Conklin, Eulalie Jensen • The story of Adam and Eve is retold in modern times with a struggling plumber, Adam (O'Brien), and his wife, Eve (Borden), longing for luxury. Both encounter the temptation of seductions and end up reconciling with each other. 6,498' (Technicolor sequence)

THE FAMILY UPSTAIRS (Aug. 29, 1926); D: J.G. Blystone; W: L.G. Rigby, Harry Delf (play); C: Reginald Lyons; Cast: Virginia Valli, Allan Simpson, J. Farrell MacDonald, Lillian Elliott, Edward Piel Jr., Dot Farley, Cecille Evans, Jacqueline Wells • A mother discourages Charles (Simpson), a bank teller, who is romancing her daughter Louise (Valli) with stories about the girl's need for luxury. Louise is upset by her mother's nosiness and goes to Coney Island. She is followed by Charles, who is struck down by two of her friends who take him for a masher. The story ends with the couple reunited. 5,971'

NO MAN'S GOLD (Aug. 29, 1926); D: Lewis Seiler; W: John Stone (scr & adpt), J. Allen Dunn (novel); Cast: Tom Mix, Eva Novak, Frank Campeau, Forrest Taylor, Harry Grippe, Malcolm Waite, Micky Moore, Tom Santschi, Tony the Wonder Horse • A dying prospector, shot by Frank Healy (Campeau), gives Tom Stone (Mix) and his sidekick, Lefty (Grippe), a map to his mine. Rescuing Jane Rogers (Novak) from the notorious Krell (Waite), who ordered Healey's death, Tom sets out for the mine, but must battle the gang once more. 5,745'

THE FLYING HORSEMAN (Sept. 5, 1926); D: Orville O. Dull; W: Gertrude Orr, Max Brand (article); C: Joseph August; Cast: Buck Jones, Gladys McConnell, Bruce Covington, Walter Percival, Silver Buck, Hank Mann, Harvey Clark, Vester Pegg, Joseph Rickson • A wandering cowboy, Mark (Jones), turns some bullied kids into Boy Scouts, then helps young June Savary

(McConnell) save her father's (Covington) ranch. Mark is framed for murder by Bert Ridley (Percival), who wants June and the property, but he is able to overcome adversity with help from his horse. 4,971'

MARRIAGE LICENSE? (Sept. 5, 1926); D: Frank Borzage; W: Bradley King, Elizabeth Pickett (titles), F. Tennyson Jesse and Harold Marsh Harwood (play); C: Ernest Palmer; Cast: Alma Rubens, Walter McGrail, Richard Walling, Walter Pidgeon, Charles Lane, Emily Fitzroy, Langhorne Burton, Edgar Norton, George Cowl, Lon Poff • Wanda (Rubens), divorced from English nobleman Marcus Heriot (McGrail) in a split instigated by Lady Heriot (Fitzroy), Marcus's mother, sacrifices her happiness to remarry her repentant ex-husband so that her son, Robin (Walling), declared illegitimate years earlier, will have an honorable name. 7,168'

THE BLUE EAGLE (Sept. 12, 1926); D: John Ford; W: L.G. Rigby, Gerald Beaumont (article); C: George Schneiderman; Cast: George O'Brien, Janet Gaynor, William Russell, Robert Edeson, David Butler, Phil Ford, Ralph Sipperly, Margaret Livingston, Jerry Madden, Harry Tenbrook, Lew Short • George (O'Brien) and Tim (Russell), two rivals over Rose (Gaynor), fight between themselves through the World War. They have a boxing match on the deck of a battleship to settle their differences. After the war, they team up when narcotics smugglers kill George's brother and Tim's friend. 6,200'

WOMANPOWER (Sept. 19, 1926); D: Harry Beaumont; W: Kenneth B. Clarke, Harold McGrath (article); C: Rudolph Bergquist; Cast: Ralph Graves, Kathryn Perry, Margaret Livingston, Ralph Sipperly, William Walling, David Butler, Lou Tellegen, Anders Randolf, Robert Ryan, Frankie Grandetta • A rich idler, Johnny (Grave), goaded by his father's (Randolf) contempt and a vamp's (Livingston) sneers, retires to a boxing camp. He meets the camp owner's daughter, Jenny (Perry), who gives him the encouragement to become a successful fighter. 6,240'

THREE BAD MEN (Sept. 26, 1926); D: John Ford; AD: Edward O'Fearna; W: John Stone (scr & adpt), Ralph Spence (titles), Malcolm Stuart Boylan (titles), Herman Whitaker (novel); C: George Schneiderman; Cast: George O'Brien, Olive Borden, Lou Tellegen, J. Farrell MacDonald, Tom Santschi, Frank Campeau, George Harris, Jay Hunt, Priscilla Bonner, Otis Harlan, Walter Perry • Three horse thieves, Mike (MacDonald), Bull (Santschi) and Spade (Campeau), band together to protect a young woman (Borden) and her sweetheart (O'Brien) after her father is killed by a rival gang. The trio guards a mountain trail to allow the couple to reach a valuable claim, while being pursued by a crooked sheriff (Tellegen). 8,710'

THE LILY (Oct. 3, 1926); D: Victor Schertzinger; W: Eve Unsell, Pierre Wolff and Gaston Leroux (play); C: Glen MacWilliams; Cast: Belle Bennett, Ian Keith, Reata Hoyt, Barry Norton, John St. Polis, Richard Tucker, Gertrude Short, James Marcus, Lydia Yeamans Titus, Thomas Ricketts • A French count (St. Polis) forces his daughter Odette (Bennett) into a loveless marriage, but the younger Christiane (Hoyt) defiantly marries an artist, Arnaud (Keith), and makes her father furious. However, the count is chastised by Odette for selling furnishings to support his mistress. The hypocrisy allows both daughters to find and keep the husbands they love. 6,268'

THE MIDNIGHT KISS (Oct. 10, 1926); D: Irving Cummings; W: Alfred A. Cohn (scr & adpt), Anne Morrison and Patterson McNutt (play); C: Abe Fried; Cast: Richard Walling, Janet Gaynor, George Irving, Doris Lloyd, Tempe Piggot, Gladys McConnell, Herbert Prior, Gene Cameron, Arthur Housman, Bodil Rosing • The Atkins family lives with some oddball relatives. Their son, Thomas (Walling), is concerned with all the sick animals in the village. When Thomas Sr. (Irving) needs money, Junior buys 250 pigs and sells them for a large sum. He elopes with his true love, Mildred (Gaynor), and returns home. 5,025'

THE GREAT K&A TRAIN ROBBERY (Oct. 17, 1926); D: Lewis Seiler; W: John Stone, Paul Leicester Ford (novel); C: Dan Clark; Cast: Tom Mix, Dorothy Dwan, William Walling, Harry Grippe, Carl Miller, Edward Piel, Curtis McHenry, Tony the Wonder Horse • A railroad detective, Tom Gordon (Mix), disguises himself as a bandit to track down thieves. With the help of his horse Tony, he rounds up a gang led by the railroad president's (Walling) secretary and wins the love of the president's daughter (Dwan). 4,800'

THE COUNTRY BEYOND (Oct. 17, 1926); D: Irving Cummings; W: Irving Cummings, Ernest Maas, Katherine Hilliker (titles), H.H. Caldwell (titles), James Oliver Curwood (novel); C: Abe Fried; Cast: Olive Borden, Ralph Graves, Gertrude Astor, J. Farrell MacDonald, Evelyn Selbie, Fred Kohler, Lawford Davidson, Alfred Fisher, Lottie Williams • A Canadian Northwest man, Roger (Graves), takes the blame for the murder of a white slaver to protect an innocent backwoods girl, Valencia (Borden), whom he loves. Valencia goes to New York and becomes a Broadway dancing star, but returns to Roger, who is cleared of wrongdoing by a confession from the murderer's wife. 5,363'

WHISPERING WIRES (Oct. 24, 1926); D: Albert Ray; W: L.G. Rigby (scr), Henry Leverage (adpt), William Conselman (titles), Kate L. McLaurin (play), Henry Leverage (novel); C: George Schneiderman; Cast: Anita Stewart, Edmund Burns, Charles Clary, Otto Matieson, Mack Swain, Arthur Housman, Charles Conklin, Frank Campeau, Scott Welsh, Mayme Kelso • Two incompetent detectives, Cassidy (Swain) and McCarthy (Housman), and a hero, Barry (Burns), save Doris Stockbridge (Stewart), who has been threatened with murder over the telephone by a vengeful ex-convict and his inventor pal. 5,906'

30 BELOW ZERO (Oct. 31, 1926); D: Robert P. Kerr, Lambert Hillyer; W: John Stone; C: Reginald Lyons; Cast: Buck Jones, Eva Novak, E.J. Ratcliffe, Frank Butler, Paul Panzer, Harry Woods, Fred Walton, Henry

Murdock, Howard Vincent • Don Hathaway (Jones), traveling in Alaska to escape a Follies girl, is taken in by Ann Ralston (Novak) and then accused of being a bootlegger by a jealous rival. Don proves his innocence and wins Ann's affections. 4,691'

THE RETURN OF PETER GRIMM (Nov. 7, 1926); D: Victor Schertzinger; W: Bradley King (adpt), David Belasco (play); C: Glen MacWilliams; Cast: Alec B. Francis, John Roche, Janet Gaynor, Richard Walling, John St. Polis, Lionel Belmore, Elizabeth Patterson, Bodil Rosing, Mickey McBan, Sammy Cohen • Peter Grimm (Francis) defeats selfishness and rewards virtue by coming back as a spirit after his death to set things straight with his family and their flower business. 6,961'

THE CITY (Nov. 14, 1926); D: R. William Neill; W: Gertrude Orr, Clyde Fitch (play); C: James Diamond; Cast: Nancy Nash, Robert Frazer, George Irving, Lillian Elliott, Walter McGrail, Richard Walling, May Allison, Melbourne MacDowell, Bodil Rosing, Fred Walton • After the death of George Rand (Irving), a wealthy reformed criminal, the Rand family moves to the city to pursue their lives. Unfortunately, they all face misfortunes and complications as a result of their patriarch's past; they eventually move back to their small-town lifestyle. 5,508' • The biggest loss of the year, $92,000, with a cost of $178,000 and world rentals of $152,000. There may have been production problems, since five months before release, this production was advertised with a completely different director, screenplay and cast.

WINGS OF THE STORM (Nov. 28, 1926); D: J.G. Blystone; AD: Jasper Blystone; W: Dorothy Yost, L.G. Rigby, Elizabeth Pickett (titles), Lawrence William Pedrose (article); C: Robert Kurrle; Cast: Thunder the Dog, Virginia Brown Faire, Reed Howes, William Russell, Hank Mann • Thunder, a police dog, runs away from Anita Baker's (Faire) lumber camp and is adopted by a forest ranger (Howes). A thug, Bill Martin (Russell), who wants Anita's land, attacks her, but Thunder comes to the rescue. 5,374'

THE CANYON OF LIGHT (Dec. 5, 1926); D: Benjamin Stoloff; W: John Stone, William Conselman (titles), Kenneth Perkins (novel); C: Dan Clark; Cast: Tom Mix, Dorothy Dwan, Carl Miller, Ralph Sipperly, Barry Norton, Carmelita Geraghty, William Walling, Duke Lee, Tony the Wonder Horse • Soldier Tom Mills (Mix), whose buddy Ricardo (Norton) was killed in France, visits his friend's family on the Mexican border, where he encounters a bandit (Miller) who is perpetrating crimes while posing as Tom. There is a runaway rescue, a near hanging, a rodeo, and river riding before Tom wins Concha (Dwan), Ricardo's sister. 5,399'

GOING CROOKED (Dec. 12, 1926); D: George Melford; W: Keene Thompson, Albert Shelby Le Vino, Winchell Smith and William Collier (play); C: Charles G. Clarke; Cast: Bessie Love, Oscar Shaw, Gustav von Seyffertitz, Ed Kennedy, Leslie Fenton, Lydia Knott, Bernard Siegel • A murder is committed during a daring jewel robbery and a young man, Rogers (Fenton), is sentenced to death. Marie (Love), who was a member of the gang, saves Rogers's life by getting a confession from the real killer, Mordaunt (von Seyffertitz). District Attorney Banning (Shaw), who is romantically involved with Marie, gets a pardon for her as well. 5,345'

BERTHA, THE SEWING MACHINE GIRL (Dec. 19, 1926); D: Irving Cummings; W: Gertrude Orr, Theodore Kremer (play); C: Abe Fried; Cast: Madge Bellamy, Allan Simpson, Sally Phipps, Paul Nicholson, Anita Garvin, J. Farrell MacDonald, Ethel Wales, Arthur Housman, Harry Bailey • A sewing machine girl, Bertha (Bellamy), loses her job and goes to work for a lingerie company. She attracts unwanted attention from Jules Morton (Nicholson), the wealthy manager, who entices her onto his yacht. When he makes advances on Bertha, she is rescued by a shipping clerk, Roy (Simpson), who turns out to be the owner of the company. 5,245'

SUMMER BACHELORS (Dec. 26, 1926); D: Allan Dwan; W: James Shelley Hamilton, Warner Fabian (novel); C: Joseph Ruttenberg; Cast: Madge Bellamy, Allan Forrest, Matt Moore, Hale Hamilton, Leila Hyams, Charles Winninger, Clifford Holland, Olive Tell, Walter Catlett, James F. Cullen • A secretary, Derry Thomas (Bellamy), organizes a club for flirtatious husbands who step out while their wives are away for the summer. When she falls in love with Tony Landor (Forrest), who turns out to be single, she needs to undergo hypnosis before she admits her feelings for him. They are married while she is in a trance. 5,500' or 6,727'

DESERT VALLEY (Dec. 26, 1926); D: Scott R. Dunlap; W: Randall H. Faye, Jackson Gregory (novel); C: Reginald Lyons; Cast: Buck Jones, Virginia Brown Faire, Malcolm Waite, J.W. Johnston, Charles Brinley, Eugene Pallette • A roaming cowboy, Fitzsmith (Jones), saves some cattle during a water war and teams up with rancher Tim Dean's (Johnston) daughter (Faire) to exonerate her on charges of breaking a pipeline. Fitzsmith also exposes the villains, led by Jeff Hoades (Waite), who are trying to drive out honest ranchers. 4,731'

1927 Releases

ONE INCREASING PURPOSE (Jan. 2, 1927); D: Harry Beaumont; W: Bradley King, Arthur Stuart-Menteth Hutchinson (novel); C: Rudolph Bergquist; Cast: Edmund Lowe, Lila Lee, Holmes Herbert, May Allison, Lawford Davidson, Emily Fitzroy, George Irving, Huntley Gordon, Josef Swickard, Jane Novak • A young English soldier (Lowe) returns home after the war to find his brothers Charles (Herbert) and Andrew (Gordon) have lost their moral bearings. He realizes his purpose in life is to set them on a more meaningful road. Later, he and his wife travel around England, preaching unselfishness. 7,677' • "The Best-Selling Novel by a Modern Master of Fiction! Presented as a William Fox screen attraction."

STAGE MADNESS (Jan. 9, 1927); D: Victor Schertzinger; W: Randall H. Faye (scr), Polan Banks (st); C: Glen MacWilliams; Cast: Virginia Valli, Tullio Carminati, Virginia Bradford, Lou Tellegen, Richard Walling, Tyler Brooke, Lillian Knight, Bodil Rosing • A ballet dancer, Madame Lamphier (Valli), returns to the stage, but her husband, Andrew (Carminati), disappears with her young daughter, Dora (Bradford). Years later, after an injury, Lamphier is jealous of her young replacement and frames the girl for the murder of her manager (Tellegen). She dies after discovering the girl is really her daughter, Dora. 5,620'

THE AUCTIONEER (Jan. 16, 1927); D: Alfred E. Green; W: L.G. Rigby, John Stone, Charles Klein and Lee Arthur (play); C: George Schneiderman; Cast: George Sidney, Marian Nixon, Gareth Hughes, Doris Lloyd, Ward Crane, Sammy Cohen, Claire McDowell • A Jewish immigrant, Simon Levi (Sidney), builds a successful pawnbroker-auction business. His adopted daughter, Ruth (Nixon), falls for a stockbroker (Hughes), but when her father invests all his money, a crooked broker (Groode) at the firm defrauds him. Starting over again as a peddler, Simon eventually catches the crook and retrieves his fortune. 5,500' • Janet Gaynor and Charles Farrell were originally set for supporting roles in this film.

THE MUSIC MASTER (Jan. 23, 1927); W: Philip Klein (adpt), Charles Klein (novel); C: George Webber, William Miller; Cast: Alex B. Francis, Lois Moran, Neil Hamilton, Norman Trevor, Charles Lane, William B. Tilden, Helen Chandler, Marcia Harris, Kathleen Kerrigan • Viennese orchestra leader von Barwig (Francis) searches for his daughter, who has been lost since his wife ran off with another man. By chance, a society girl (Moran) seeks music lessons from him and she eventually recognizes von Barwig as her father. 7,754'

THE LAST TRAIL (Jan. 23, 1927); D: Lewis Seiler; W: John Stone, Zane Grey (novel); C: Dan Clark; Cast: Tom Mix, Carmelita Geraghty, William Davidson, Frank Hagney, Lee Shumway, Robert Brower, Jerry the Giant, Oliver Eckhardt, Tony the Wonder Horse • Tom Dane (Mix) singlehandedly helps a stagecoach owner get a contract by winning a race, saving the old man's business, winning his daughter Nita (Geraghty), and foiling the leader (Davidson) of a gang of bandits. 5,190'

UPSTREAM (Jan. 30, 1927); D: John Ford; W: Randall H. Faye, Wallace Smith (article); C: Charles G. Clarke; Cast: Nancy Nash, Earle Foxe, Grant Withers, Lydia Yeamans Titus, Raymond Hitchcock, Emile Chautard, Ted McNamara, Sammy Cohen, Judy King, Lillian Worth, Francis Ford • An egotistical actor (Foxe), living in a boardinghouse with vaudeville performers, makes good in a West End revival of *Hamlet*, but becomes the victim of his own conceit when he wrongly assumes a wedding reception is for him and his girlfriend (Nash). Instead, he is kicked out, but regains his composure for photographers. 5,510'

THE WAR HORSE (Feb. 6, 1927); D: Lambert Hillyer; W: Lambert Hillyer (scr), Buck Jones (st); C: Reginald Lyons; Cast: Buck Jones, Lola Todd, Lloyd Whitlock, Stanley Taylor, Yola d'Avril, James Gordon • A horseman, Buck Thomas (Jones) enlists to fight in France when his horse is conscripted into the army. He falls in love with a beautiful ambulance driver (Todd) and ends up saving a detachment of American soldiers. 4,953'

MARRIAGE (Feb. 13, 1927); D: R. William Neill; W: Gertrude Orr, Elizabeth Pickett (titles), H.G. Wells (novel); C: Rudolph Bergquist; Cast: Virginia Valli, Allen Durant, Gladys McConnell, Lawford Davidson, Donald Stuart, Frank Dunn, Edwards Davis, James Marcus, Billie Bennett • An English lady (Valli) elopes with an idealistic inventor (Durant) and persuades him to market his ideas. In Africa, she begins an affair with a nobleman (Davidson) and is thrown out by her husband. However, she returns to nurse him back to health after he is mauled by a lion. 5,458'

THE MONKEY TALKS (Feb. 20, 1927); D: Raoul Walsh; W: L.G. Rigby, René Fauchois (novel); C: L. William O'Connell; Cast: Olive Borden, Jacques Lerner, Don Alvarado, Malcolm Waite, Raymond Hitchcock, Ted McNamara, Jane Winton, August Tollaire • Jocko (Lerner), a member of a stranded circus troupe, is disguised as a talking monkey to earn back some money. His rival (Alvarado), meanwhile, moves in on his sweetheart (Borden), with whom he performs. A chimpanzee is substituted by the jealous lion tamer (Waite) and the monkey-man dies while rescuing his love from the attacking chimp. 5,500' • Jacques Lerner was billed as "The world's foremost animal impersonator." The catchline: "Monkey or Man — love was his ruling passion."

ANKLES PREFERRED (Feb. 27, 1927); D: J.G. Blystone; W: James Shelley Hamilton (scr), Kenneth Hawks (st), J.G. Blystone (st), Philip Klein (st); C: Glen MacWilliams; Cast: Madge Bellamy, Lawrence Gray, Barry Norton, Allan Forrest, Marjorie Beebe, J. Farrell MacDonald, Joyce Compton, William Strauss, Lillian Elliott, Mary Foy • A department store clerk, Nora (Bellamy), gets a job modeling because of her attractive ankles. She is promised a trip abroad if she can arrange a loan for the shop from a financier (Forrest). Unwanted advances from the financier bring her young suitor (Gray) to the rescue. 5,498'

LOVE MAKES 'EM WILD (March 3, 1927); D: Albert Ray; W: Harold Shumate, Florence Ryerson (article); C: Chester Lyons; Cast: Johnny Harron, Sally Phipps, Ben Bard, Arthur Housman, J. Farrell MacDonald, Natalie Kingston, Albert Gran, Florence Gilbert, Earle Mohan, Coy Watson, Jr. • A put-upon office worker (Harron), who has been saving every penny until he is independent, is told he has only six months to live. He then uses his last months to settle scores with the assistant boss, the janitor and elevator man, all of whom have been browbeating him. He takes a room at the Ritz, ready to spend his savings of $4,000. A real doctor reveals that his only health problem is that he is in love with a stenographer (Phipps) and should marry his sweetheart. 5,508'

THE BRONCHO TWISTER (March 13, 1927); D: Orville O. Dull; W: John Stone (scr), Adela Rogers St. Johns (st); C: Dan Clark; Cast: Tom Mix, Helene Costello, George Irving, Dorothy Kitchen, Paul Nicholson, Doris Lloyd, Malcolm Waite, Jack Pennick, Otto Fries, Tony the Wonder Horse • Tom Mason, a Marine (Mix), returns home to find a villainous neighbor, Brady (Nicholson), is trying to take over his father's ranch. He goes through numerous adventures while saving his father (Irving) and sister (Kitchen) from a gang of henchmen, then rescues Brady's daughter (Costello) from a forced marriage. 5,435'

WHISPERING SAGE (March 20, 1927); D: Scott R. Dunlap; W: Harold Shumate, Harry Sinclair Drago and Joseph Noel (novel); C: Reginald Lyons; Cast: Buck Jones, Natalie Joyce, Emile Chautard, Carl Miller, Albert J. Smith, Joseph Girard, William A. Steele, Ellen Winston, Hazel Keener, Enrique Acosta • A cowboy (Jones) becomes an ally of Basque immigrants against Acklin (Girard), the villainous owner of an adjoining ranch. He falls in love with Acklin's daughter (Joyce) and discovers that Acklin was responsible for his brother's death. 4,873'

MADAME WANTS NO CHILDREN (Apr. 3, 1927) German-made; P: Karl Freund; D: Alexander Korda; W: Bela Balazs, Adolf Lantz, Clement Vautel (novel); C: Robert Baberske, Theodor Sparkuhl

HILLS OF PERIL (May 1, 1927); D: Lambert Hillyer; W: Jack Jungmeyer, Winchell Smith and George Abbott (play); C: Reginald Lyons; Cast: Buck Jones, Georgia Hale, Albert J. Smith, Buck Black, William Welch, Marjorie Beebe, Duke Green, Charles Athloff, Robert Kortman • A cowpuncher, Laramie (Jones), rescues a sheriff and later joins a gang of bootleggers while working for the law. He helps capture the gang, is elected sheriff and wins the affection of a lady (Hale) who has been trying to reactivate an abandoned mine. 4,983'

OUTLAWS OF RED RIVER (May 8, 1927); D: Lewis Seiler; W: Harold Shumate (scr), Gerald Beaumont (st), Malcolm Stuart Boylan (titles); C: Dan Clark; Cast: Tom Mix, Marjorie Daw, Arthur Clayton, William Conklin, Duke Lee, Francis McDonald, Lee Shumway, Ellen Woonston, Jimmy Downs, Virginia Marshall • A Texas Ranger (Mix) searches for the bandit leader who killed his parents. He poses as a stagecoach robber to infiltrate a gang and meets an orphan girl (Daw). They team up to destroy the gang's stockade with the help of other rangers. 5,327'

THE HEART OF SALOME (May 8, 1927); D: Victor Schertzinger; W: Randall H. Faye, Allen Raymond (novel); C: Glen MacWilliams; E: Margaret V. Clancey; Cast: Alma Rubens, Walter Pidgeon, Holmes Herbert, Robert Agnew, Erin La Bissoniere, Walter Dugan, Barry Norton, Virginia Madison • Monte Carroll (Pidgeon) falls in love with Helene (Rubens) in Paris, but then turns away from her when he discovers she has stolen some of his valuable papers. To get even with Monte, Helene promises to marry her employer (Herbert) if he will, like the stepfather of Salome, kill Monte. When Monte is imprisoned in a dungeon, Helene eventually has a change of heart. 5,615'

IS ZAT SO? (May 15, 1927); D: Alfred E. Green; W: Philip Klein, James Gleason and Richard Taber (play); C: George Schneiderman; Cast: George O'Brien, Edmund Lowe, Kathryn Perry, Cyril Chadwick, Doris Lloyd, Dione Ellis, Richard Maitland, Douglas Fairbanks, Jr., Philippe De Lacy • Chick (O'Brien), a fighter, and his manager, Hap (Lowe), lose a fight, befriend a millionaire (Fairbanks, Jr.) and take the place of his servants. After a misunderstanding, Chick wins the championship and also exposes the millionaire's brother-in-law as a crook. 6,950'

RICH BUT HONEST (May 22, 1927); D: Albert Ray; W: Randall H. Faye, Arthur Sommers Roche (article); C: Sidney Wagner; Cast: Nancy Nash, Clifford Holland, Charles Morton, J. Farrell MacDonald, Tyler Brooke, Ted McNamara, Marjorie Beebe, Ernie Shields, Doris Lloyd • Two department store clerks, Florine (Nash) and Maybelle (Beebe), talk their way into performing on stage. Maybelle achieves success with her clowning, but Florine has trouble with her boyfriend (Holland) after appearing as Lady Godiva. 5,480'

THE CRADLE SNATCHERS (June 5, 1927); D: Howard Hawks; W: Sarah Y. Mason, Malcolm Stuart Boylan (titles), Russell G. Medcraft and Norma Mitchell (play); C: L. William O'Connell; Cast: Louise Fazenda, J. Farrell MacDonald, Ethel Wales, Franklin Pangborn, Dorothy Phillips, William Davidson, Joseph Striker, Nick Stuart, Arthur Lake, Dione Ellis • Three wives, Susan (Fazenda), Ethel (Wales) and Kitty (Phillips), concoct a plan to keep their husbands from flirting with flappers by arranging with three college boys, Henry (Stuart), Oscar (Lake) and Joe (Striker), to flirt with them. Complications arise when the husbands, George (MacDonald), Howard (Pangborn) and Roy (Davidson), show up at the same party with their flapper friends. 6,281'

SLAVES OF BEAUTY (June 5, 1927); D: J.G. Blystone; W: William M. Conselman (scr & adpt), James K. McGuinness (titles), Nina Wilcox Putnam (article); C: L. William O'Connell; E: Margaret V. Clancey; Cast: Olive Tell, Holmes Herbert, Earle Foxe, Margaret Livingston, Sue Carol, Richard Walling, Mary Foy, Mickey Bennett • Anastasia (Tell), running a shop that sells her husband's beauty products, has become very successful. However, she tires of husband Leonard (Herbert) and falls for the dashing young shop manager, Paul (Foxe). She neglects the business and sells out to a mysterious buyer, who turns out to be Leonard. He makes an even greater success and also acquires youthfulness by diet and exercise. Anastasia later returns to him after being disappointed by Paul. 5,412'

GOOD AS GOLD (June 12, 1927); D: Scott Dunlap; W: Jack Jungmeyer, Murray Leinster (article); C: Reginald Lyons; Cast: Buck Jones, Frances Lee, Carl Miller, Charles French, Adele Watson, Arthur Ludwig, Micky Moore • Buck (Jones), a cowboy, grows up vowing revenge against the man who stole his father's mine. He robs the mine's payroll but later falls in love with Jane (Lee), the owner. However, it is the crooked foreman (Miller) who is really guilty and is finally brought to justice in a fight at the edge of a cliff. 4,545'

THE SECRET STUDIO (June 19, 1927); D: Victor Schertzinger; W: James Kevin McGuinness, Hazel Livingston (serialized novel); C: Glen MacWilliams; Cast: Olive Borden, Clifford Holland, Noreen Phillips, Ben Bard, Kate Bruce, Joseph Cawthorn, Margaret Livingston, Walter McGrail, Lila Leslie, Ned Sparks • An ambitious girl, Rosemary (Borden), poses for an artist (Bard), who makes the painting look like she was nude. This creates a scandal for Rosemary's reputation when the picture is published. A wealthy suitor (Holland) is able to save her from public scorn, and Rosemary gives up ambition for love. 5,870'

THE CIRCUS ACE (June 26, 1927); D: Ben Stoloff; W: Jack Jungmeyer (scr), Harold Shumate (st); C: Dan Clark; Cast: Tom Mix, Natalie Joyce, Jack Baston, Duke Lee, James Bradbury, Stanley Blystone, Dudley Smith, Buster Gardner, Tony the Wonder Horse • A cowboy (Mix) rescues a circus performer (Joyce) parachuting from a balloon over his ranch. He rescues her a second time to the chagrin of the circus manager (Baston), who has him framed for murder. The cowboy exonerates himself and captures the villain. 4,810'

COLLEEN (July 3, 1927); D: Frank O'Connor; W: Randall H. Faye; C: George Schneiderman; Cast: Madge Bellamy, Charles Morton, J. Farrell MacDonald, Tom Maguire, Sammy Cohen, Marjorie Beebe, Ted McNamara, Tom McGuire, Sarah Padden • An Irish couple squabbles and experiences romantic difficulties because the husband is the son (Morton) of an impoverished lord (MacDonald), and the wife (Bellamy) is the daughter of a wealthy neighbor (Maguire). All this is set against the backdrop of horse racing. 5,301'

MARRIED ALIVE (July 17, 1927); D: Emmett Flynn; W: Gertrude Orr, Ralph Strauss (novel); C: Ernest Palmer; Cast: Lou Tellegen, Margaret Livingston, Matt Moore, Claire Adams, Gertrude Claire, Marcella Daly, Henry Sedley, Eric Mayne, Charles Lane, Emily Fitzroy • A college professor meets a man (Tellegen) who claims to be married to four women. The professor sets out to tell each of the wives about the man's dastardly behavior, and meets with varying responses. The fourth woman turns out to be a lady of royalty whom the professor discovers is not really married to the man. He ends up marrying her himself. 4,557' • *Variety* noted, "A hopeless combination of tragedy and comedy."

CHAIN LIGHTNING (Aug. 14, 1927); D: Lambert Hillyer; W: Lambert Hillyer, Malcolm Stuart Boylan (titles), Charles Alden Seltzer (novel); C: Reginald Lyons; E: Louis Loeffler; Cast: Buck Jones, Dione Ellis, Ted McNamara, Jack Baston, William Welch, Marte Faust, William Caress, Gene Cameron • A rancher, Steve Lannon (Jones), returns home to find a gang of rustlers have been stealing his horses, including his favorite. He tracks down the rustlers, retrieving his horses and rescuing a young lady (Ellis). 5,333'

PAID TO LOVE (Aug. 14, 1927); D: Howard Hawks; W: William M. Conselman (scr), Seton I. Miller (scr), Benjamin Glazer (adpt), Harry Carr (st); C: L. William O'Connell; Cast: George O'Brien, Virginia Valli, J. Farrell MacDonald, Thomas Jefferson, William Powell, Merta Sterling, Hank Mann • An American banker, Pete Roberts (MacDonald), befriends a Balkan king (Jefferson) and becomes a matchmaker for Crown Prince Michael (O'Brien), who is more interested in cars than girls. Roberts brings an Apache dancer, Gaby (Valli), back from Paris and nurtures the young man's interest in women. 6,888' • Howard Hawks was influenced by F.W. Murnau's style around this time, but, according to Todd McCarthy, said, "It isn't my type of stuff... at least I got over it in a hurry."

TUMBLING RIVER (Aug. 21, 1927); D: Lewis Seiler; W: Jack Jungmeyer, Jesse Edward Grinstead (novel); C: Dan Clark; Cast: Tom Mix, Dorothy Dwan, William Conklin, Stella Essex, Elmo Billings, Edward Pell Sr., Wallace MacDonald, Buster Gardner, Harry Gripp, Tony the Wonder Horse • While cowboy Tom Gier (Mix) is away from his ranch, rustlers steal his horses. In trailing them, he saves Edna (Dwan) from a runaway. She has a habit of bringing heroes home to meet her father, who summarily dismisses them. However, when the rustlers raid the father's ranch, Tom gives chase, rescues Edna from the rapids and breaks up the gang, achieving respect from the old man. 4,675'

SINGED (Aug. 21, 1927); D: John Griffith Wray; W: Gertrude Orr, Adela Rogers St. Johns (article); C: Charles G. Clarke; Cast: Blanche Sweet, Warner Baxter, James Wang, Alfred Allen, Clark Comstock, Howard Truesdale, Claude King, Ida Darling, Mary McAllister, Edwards Davis • A Wall Street oil investor, Royce Wingate (Baxter), is socially frowned upon because of his association with a notorious dancehall girl, Dolly (Sweet), who tries to take revenge on him when he decides to marry a society belle (McAllister). In an attempt to throw acid on Wingate, Dolly is shot. She later recovers and reconciles with him. 5,790'

CAMEO KIRBY (Aug. 28, 1927) Reissue

WHAT PRICE GLORY (Aug. 28, 1927); D: Raoul Walsh; W: James T. O'Donohoe, Malcolm Stuart Boylan (titles), Lawrence Stallings and Maxwell Anderson (play); C: Barney McGill, John Marta, John Smith; M: Erno Rapée; Cast: Victor McLaglen, Edmund Lowe, Dolores Del Rio, William V. Mong, Phyllis Haver, Elena Jurado, Leslie Fenton, August Tollaire, Sammy Cohen • This establishes the hard-boiled, fierce Marine rivals, Sergeant Quirt (Lowe) and Captain Flagg (McLaglen), as they fight in France and fall in love with the same woman (Del Rio), attempting to outsmart each other at every turn. 11,400' • The New York opening was Nov. 26, 1926. Box-office rentals hit an astounding $2,000,000, making it Fox's most popular movie of the year.

LOVES OF CARMEN (Sept. 4, 1927); D: Raoul Walsh; W: Gertrude Orr, Katherine Hilliker (titles), H.H. Caldwell (titles), Prosper Merimee (play); C: Lucien Andriot; E: Katherine Hilliker, H.H. Caldwell; Cast: Dolores Del Rio, Victor McLaglen, Don Alvarado, Nancy Nash, Rafael Valverda, Mathilde Comont, Jack Baston, Carmen Costello, Fred Kohler • Carmen (Del Rio), a gypsy working in a cigar factory, is desired by a soldier, José (Alvarado), who helps her escape from jail. However, Carmen returns to her other lover, a hard-hearted toreador (McLaglen), prompting the love-crazed José to kill her. 8,538'

2 GIRLS WANTED (Sept. 11, 1927); D: Alfred E. Green; W: Randall H. Faye (scr), Seton I. Miller (scr), Gladys Unger (st), Malcolm Stuart Boylan (titles); C: George Schneiderman; Cast: Janet Gaynor, Glenn Tryon, Ben Bard, Joseph Cawthorn, Billy Bletcher, Doris Lloyd, Pauline Neff, C.L. Sherwood, Alyce Mills, William H. Tooker • Marianna (Gaynor) and Edna (Mills), rivals for the affection of the same man, Dexter (Tryon), take jobs as cook and maid in the country house of Dexter's uncle. While both women vie for Dexter's interest, Marianna learns of a plan to swindle his uncle. As a result, Dexter's affections shift from Edna back to her. 6,293'

HONOR FIRST (Sept. 18, 1927) Reissue

THE JOY GIRL (Sept. 18, 1927); D: Allan Dwan; W: Frances Agnew (scr), Adele Camondini (adpt), Malcolm Stuart Boylan (titles), May Edginton (article); C: George Webber, William Miller; Cast: Olive Borden, Neil Hamilton, Marie Dressler, Mary Alden, William Norris, Helen Chandler, Jerry Miley, Frank Walsh, Clarence J. Elmer, Peggy Kelly • Jewel Courage (Borden), looking for a wealthy suitor, rejects John Fleet (Hamilton), who is really a millionaire, because she thinks he is a chauffeur. Jewel instead marries Vicary (Miley), a chauffeur she believes is a millionaire. She is discouraged when Vicary turns out to be a chauffeur who is already married to a wealthy widow (Dressler), so Jewel's marriage is annulled. She then realizes she actually loves John, and is happy to learn that he is wealthy. 5,877' or 6,162' (Technicolor sequence)

BLACK JACK (Sept. 25, 1927); D: Orville O. Dull; W: Harold Shumate, Johnston McCulley (article); C: Reginald Lyons; Cast: Buck Jones, Barbara Bennett, Theodore Lorch, George Berrell, Harry Cording, William Caress, Buck Moulton, Murdock MacQuarrie, Frank Lanning • A shiftless gambler, Phil Dolan (Jones), has one of three pieces of a silver dollar, on which is engraved a mine map. Another is held by Nancy (Bennett), whom he helped out, and a rustler has the third piece. Phil and Nancy team up to get the final piece of the coin from the rustler and his gang. 4,777'

THE GAY RETREAT (Sept. 25, 1927); SP: George E. Marshall; D: Ben Stoloff; W: J. Walter Ruben (scr), Murray Roth (adpt), Edward Moran (adpt), William Conselman (st), Edward Marshall (st), Malcolm Stuart Boylan (titles); C: Sidney Wagner; Cast: Gene Cameron, Betty Francisco, Judy King, Sammy Cohen, Holmes Herbert, Ted McNamara, Charles Gorman • A wealthy sleepwalker (Cameron) joins an ambulance unit during the war. He, his chauffeur (Cohen), and valet (McNamara) accidentally end up in France as members of the U.S. Army. Interspersed with comedic and romantic interludes, they capture a detachment of German soldiers. 5,524'

PUBLICITY MADNESS (Oct. 2, 1927); D: Albert Ray; W: Andrew Bennison (scr), Anita Loos (st), Malcolm Stuart Boylan (titles); C: Sidney Wagner; Cast: Lois Moran Edmund Lowe, E.J. Ratcliffe, James Gordon, Arthur Housman, Byron Munson, Norman Peck • A publicity manager, Pete Clark (Lowe), puts up $100,000 of his company's money as a reward for a then-impossible flight from California to Hawaii. When Lindbergh flies across the Atlantic, Pete suddenly has to make the flight himself to save his company from having to pay out the money. When he succeeds in flying to Hawaii, he also wins the boss's daughter, Violet (Moran). 5,893'

SILVER VALLEY (Oct. 2, 1927); D: Ben Stoloff; W: Harold B. Lipsitz (scr), Harry Sinclair Drago (st), Malcolm Stuart Boylan (titles); C: Dan Clark; Cast: Tom Mix, Dorothy Dwan, Philo McCullough, Jocky Hoefli, Tom Kennedy, Lon Poff, Harry Dunkinson, Clara Comstock • Cowboy Tom Tracey (Mix), who causes destruction when he tries to fly a plane, becomes the sheriff of a town that is preyed upon by a gang of outlaws. He finds the gang near a dormant volcano, but later rescues a kidnapped girl (Dwan) and escapes an eruption in a plane. 5,011'

ST. ELMO (Oct. 9, 1927) Reissue of the 1923 John Gilbert version

EAST SIDE, WEST SIDE (Oct. 9, 1927); D: Allan Dwan; W: Allan Dwan (adaptation), Felix Riesenberg (novel); C: George Webber; Cast: George O' Brien, Virginia Valli, J. Farrell MacDonald, Dore Davidson, Sonia Nodalsky, June Collyer, John Miltern, Holmes Herbert, Frank Dodge • Parentless John Breen (O'Brien) is rescued from toughs and becomes successful as a prize-fighter. Becka (Valli), the girl whose family took him in, gives him up because marriage would hurt his career. When John is mentored by Gil Van Horn (Herbert), a millionaire, he leaves boxing, becomes engaged to Josephine (Collyer), a society girl, but eventually rescues Becka from a nightclub owner and reconciles with her. 8,154'

HIGH SCHOOL HERO (Oct. 16, 1927); D: David Butler; W: Seton I. Miller (scr), David Butler (st), William M. Conselman (st), Delos Sutherland (titles); C: Ernest Palmer; Cast: Nick Stuart, Sally Phipps, William N. Bailey, John Darrow, Wade Boteler, Brandon Hurst, David Rollins, Charles Paddock • Pete (Stuart) and Bill (Darrow), two rival high school students, feud over Eleanor (Phipps), and their enmity threatens to disrupt the basketball team. School loyalty wins out, but Eleanor chooses a student (Rollins) devoted to education over sports. 5,498'

PAJAMAS (Oct. 23, 1927); D: J.G. Blystone; W: William Conselman, Malcolm Stuart Boylan (titles); C: Glen MacWilliams; Cast: Olive Borden, John J. Clark, Lawrence Gray, Jerry Miley • A young woman (Borden) takes her father's pilot's place and crashes a plane with a young Canadian (Gray) who has come to close a business deal. Although she dislikes the man at first, their comedic adventure in the wild brings them together. 5,876'

TRUXTON KING (Oct. 30, 1927) Reissue

7TH HEAVEN (Oct. 30, 1927); D: Frank Borzage; W: Benjamin Glazer, Katherine Hilliker (titles), H.H. Caldwell (titles), Austin Strong (novel); C: Ernest Palmer; E: Katherine Hilliker, H.H. Caldwell; Cast: Janet Gaynor, Charles Farrell, Ben Bard, David Butler, Marie Mosquini, Albert Gran, Emile Chautard, George Stone, Jessie Haslett • A Parisian sewer worker, Chico (Farrell), rescues a victimized street waif, Diane (Gaynor), takes her to live on his seventh-floor apartment, and falls in love with her. Their marriage is interrupted by war, and, although Chico is thought to be dead after the Armistice, he does return, blinded. He manages to restore his wife's faith and love. 10,350' • *Variety* reported the cost of this film as $1,300,000. The actual cost was $692,000.

VERY CONFIDENTIAL (Nov. 6, 1927); D: James Tinling; W: Randall H. Faye (scr), James Kevin McGuinness (st); C: Joseph August; Cast: Madge Bellamy, Patrick Cunning, Mary Duncan, Joseph Cawthorn, Marjorie Beebe, Isabelle Keith, Carl von Haartmann • A fashion model, Madge (Bellamy), impersonates a famous sportswoman in the hope of winning her ideal husband, Roger (Cunning). She finds it difficult to live up to her "reputation" in handling a speed boat and a race car, but she triumphs and wins the man of her dreams. 5,620

BLOOD WILL TELL (Nov. 13, 1927); D: Ray Flynn; W: Paul Gangelin (scr), Adele Buffington (sc); C: Reginald Lyons; Cast: Buck Jones, Kathryn Perry, Lawford Davidson, Robert Kortman, Harry Gripp, Austin Jewel • After rescuing Sally Morgan (Perry), a cowboy, Buck (Jones), gets a job on the ranch in which she has invested her fortune. He and his 11-year-old sidekick later pursue the villains who plot to take Sally's money and leave her to the advances of a treacherous foreman. Buck and his horse set everything straight. 4,556' • This was Jones's final film for Fox.

LADIES MUST DRESS (Nov. 20, 1927); D: Victor Heerman; W: Reginald Morris (scr), Victor Heerman (st), Malcolm Stuart Boylan (titles); C: Glen MacWilliams; Cast: Virginia Valli, Lawrence Gray, Hallam Cooley, Nancy Carroll, Earle Foxe, Wilson Hummell, William Tooker • Eve (Valli) and Joe (Gray) break up when Joe is distressed by their drab clothes. Eve, meanwhile, becomes a ravishing beauty with help from her friend Mazie (Carroll), and Joe regrets his decision. When he gets back together with Eve, he suspects she's carrying on with her boss, but later discovers she is still an innocent. 5,599'

THE ARIZONA WILDCAT (Nov. 20, 1927); D: R. William Neill; W: John Stone (scr), Adela Rogers St. Johns (st); C: Dan Clark; Cast: Tom Mix, Dorothy Sebastian, Ben Bard, Gordon Elliott, Monte Collins, Jr., Cissy FitzGerald, Doris Dawson, Marcella Daly, Tony the Wonder Horse • Tom Phelan (Mix) meets his childhood sweetheart, Regina (Sebastian), who is a target of society crooks. The crooks also arrange the defeat of her brother's (Elliott) polo team, but Phelan gets to the field, with help from his horse, Tony, in time to win the game and save Regina from the swindlers. 4,655'

WOLF FANGS (Nov. 27, 1927); D: Lewis Seiler; W: Seton I. Miller (scr & st), Elizabeth Pickett (st & titles); C: L. William O'Connell; Cast: Thunder, Caryl Lincoln, Charles Morton, Frank Rice, James Gordon, White Fawn, Zimbo, Oswald • A sheepherder's dog, Thunder, is driven to the wilderness by brutal treatment of his master (Gordon) and becomes the leader of a wolf-dog pack. He later rescues his master's kind daughter (Lincoln) when she is attacked by the pack. 5,331'

SHAME (Nov. 27, 1927) Reissue

THE WIZARD (Dec. 11, 1927); D: Richard Rosson; W: Harry O. Hoyt, Andrew Bennison, Malcolm Stuart Boylan (titles), Gaston Leroux (novel); C: Frank Good; Cast: Edmund Lowe, Leila Hyams, Gustav von Seyffertitz, E.H. Calvert, Barry Norton, Oscar Smith, Perle Marshall, Norman Trevor, George Kotsonaros • A doctor (von Seyffertitz), whose son was electrocuted for murder, trains an ape to avenge his son's death. A newspaper reporter (Lowe) investigating the case, stumbles on the bizarre situation and saves a judge (Trevor) and his daughter (Hyams) from the ape. 5,629'

SILK LEGS (Dec. 11, 1927); SP: William Conselman; D: Arthur Rosson; W: Frances Agnew (scr), Frederica Sagor (st), Delos Sutherland (titles); C: Rudolph Bergquist; Cast: Madge Bellamy, James Hall, Joseph Cawthorn, Maude Fulton, Margaret Seddon • Two hosiery sales agents, Phil Berker (Hall) and Ruth Stevens (Bellamy), who represent rival companies, try to sell their wares to the same buyers. Phil sweet-talks the women buyers and his attitude is to "feed 'em, flatter 'em, fondle 'em and forget 'em." Ruth decides to use her physical assets to sell to the male buyers, modeling the goods herself. In the end, the hosiery companies merge and the couple consolidates in marriage as well. 5,446'

COME TO MY HOUSE (Dec. 25, 1927); D: Alfred E. Green; W: Marion Orth (scr), Philip Klein (adpt), Malcolm Stuart Boylan (titles), Arthur Somers Roche (novel); C: Joseph August; Cast: Olive Borden, Antonio

Moreno, Ben Bard, Cornelius Keefe, Doris Lloyd, Richard Maitland • A society girl, Joan (Borden), engaged to Maurtaugh Pell (Keefe), is seen by a blackmailer when she is invited to the home of lawyer Floyd Bennings (Moreno). Unless Joan pays heavily, the blackmailer threatens to expose the indiscretion to her fiancé. Bennings takes care of the blackmailer and, when brought to trial for murder, refuses to reveal the reason for his crime. Joan tells all, risking her reputation to set Bennings free. 5,430'

1928 Releases

THE GATEWAY OF THE MOON (Jan 1, 1928); D: John Griffith Wray; W: Bradley King, Katherine Hilliker (titles), H.H. Caldwell (titles), Clifford Bax (novel); C: Chester Lyons; Cast: Dolores Del Rio, Walter Pidgeon, Anders Randolf, Leslie Fenton, Noble Johnson, Virginia LaFonde, Ted McNamara, Adolph Millar • A ruthless railroad construction crew foreman (Randolf) in Bolivia attempts to kill an English job inspector (Pidgeon). The foreman's niece (Del Rio) discovers the plot and saves the Englishman after he has been shot by her uncle's accomplices. 5,038'

THE BRANDED SOMBRERO (Jan. 8, 1928); D: Lambert Hillyer; W: Lambert Hillyer, James K. McGuinness (titles), Cherry Wilson (article); C: Reginald Lyons; Cast: E: J. Logan Pearson, Buck Jones, Leila Hyams, Eagle the horse, Jack Baston, Stanton Heck, Francis Ford, Josephine Borio, Lee Kelly • On his deathbed, a ranch owner (Heck) confesses to two sons that he had rustled cattle, with the number stolen from each outfit branded on his sombrero. The elder son (Jones) makes amends and repays each outfit and saves his younger brother (Kelly) from prison. 4,612'

WOMAN WISE (Jan. 8, 1928); D: Albert Ray; W: Randall H. Faye (scr), Andrew Bennison (adpt), Douglas McGibney (st), James K. McGuinness, Malcolm Stuart Boylan (titles); C: Sidney Wagner; E: Ralph Dixon; Cast: William Russell, June Collyer, Walter Pidgeon, Theodore Kosloff, Ernie Shields, Raoul Paoli, Duke Kahanamoku, Josephine Bario, Carmen Castillo • The American consul (Pidgeon) in Persia and his rakish friend (Russell) are rivals for a pretty consular secretary (Collyer), but both men team up when the ruling Pasha (Kosloff) sets his sights on the girl as well. 5,050'

SHARP SHOOTERS (Jan. 15, 1928); D: John G. Blystone; W: Marion Orth (scr), Randall H. Faye (st), Malcolm Stuart Boylan (titles); C: Charles G. Clarke; Cast: George O'Brien, Lois Moran, Noah Young, Tom Dugan, William Demarest, Gwen Lee, Josef Swickard • George (O'Brien), a sailor, makes ardent love to a French dancing girl, Lorette (Moran), in Morocco, and, believing his sincerity, she follows him to the United States. George then tries to avoid her, but his two friends shanghai him aboard a vessel and force him to marry her. 5,573'

DAREDEVIL'S REWARD (Jan. 15, 1928); D: Eugene Forde; W: John Stone; C: Dan Clark; Cast: Tom Mix, Natalie Joyce, Lawford Davidson, Billy Bletcher, Harry Cording, William Welch, Tony the Wonder Horse • Texas Ranger Tom (Mix) rounds up a gang of highwaymen headed by the uncle (Welch) of his sweetheart, Ena (Joyce). Ena is later abducted by the villains, and Tom rescues her from an automobile speeding out of control down a mountainside. 4,987'

SOFT LIVING (Feb. 5, 1928); D: James Tinling; W: Frances Agnew (scr), Grace Mack (st), Malcolm Stuart Boylan; C: Joseph August; E: J. Edwin Robbins; Cast: Madge Bellamy, John Mack Brown, Mary Duncan, Joyce Compton, Thomas Jefferson, Henry Kolker, Olive Tell, Maine Geary, Tom Dugan, David Wengren • Nancy Woods (Bellamy), secretary to a divorce lawyer, marries Stockney Webb (Brown) with the sole object of receiving alimony. Webb, who really loves her, figures out her plan and decides to teach her a lesson in humility by taking her to his cabin in the wilderness. 5,629'

A GIRL IN EVERY PORT (Feb. 26, 1928); D: Howard Hawks; W: Seton I. Miller(scr), James K. McGuinness (st), Howard Hawks (st), Malcolm Stuart Boylan (titles); C: L. W. O'Connell; E: Ralph Dixon; Cast: Victor McLaglen, Maria Casajuana, Natalie Joyce, Dorothy Mathews, Elena Jurado, Louise Brooks, Francis McDonald, Phalba Morgan, Robert Armstrong • Spike Madden (McLaglen), a sailor, meets and becomes a pal of Salami (Armstrong), his rival for women at various ports of call. When Spike believes he's fallen in love with a gold-digging French girl (Brooks), his friend dissuades him and they continue their adventures. 5,500'

SQUARE CROOKS (March 4, 1928); P: Philip Klein; D: Lewis Seiler; W: Becky Gardiner, Malcolm Stuart Boylan (titles), James P. Judge (play); C: Rudolph Bergquist; E: Jack Dennis; Cast: Robert Armstrong, John Mack Brown, Dorothy Dwan, Dorothy Appleby, Eddie Sturgis, Clarence Burton, Jackie Coombs, Lydia Dickson • Two crooks, Eddie (Armstrong) and Larry (Brown), decide to go straight but have difficulty keeping jobs when Detective Welsh (Burton) finds them. After losing their jobs as chauffeurs for the wealthy Carson family, jewels are stolen from the Carsons and Welsh wants to pin the crime on Eddie and Larry. Luckily, another crook is nailed and Eddie and Larry resume their jobs as chauffeurs. 5,397'

A HORSEMAN OF THE PLAINS (March 11, 1928); D: Benjamin Stoloff; W: Fred Myton (scr), Harry Sinclair Drago (st); C: Dan Clark; Cast: Tom Mix, Sally Blane, Heinie Conklin, Charles Byer, Lew Harvey, Grace Marvin, William Ryno, Tony the Wonder Horse • A sheriff (Mix) is enlisted to catch a band of swindlers and later ends up acting as a wagon driver for a female ranch boss (Blane) in an obstacle race. He also nabs the crooked leader of the gang (Byer). 4,399'

DRESSED TO KILL (March 18, 1928); D: Irving Cummings; W: Howard Estabrook (scr), William M. Conselman (st), Irving Cummings (st), Malcolm S. Boylan (titles); C: Conrad Wells; E: Frank Hull; Cast: Edmund

Lowe, Mary Astor, Ben Bard, Robert Perry, Joe Brown, Tom Dugan, John Kelly, Robert E. O'Connor, R.O. Pennell, Ed Brady, Charles Morton • Against the backdrop of a nightclub that is used as a rendezvous by the mob, a well-dressed master crook, Mile-Away Barry (Lowe), invites Jeanne (Astor), with whom he is in love, to his mansion for the night. Jeanne goes because she wants Barry to help get her boyfriend out of jail. Coyly locking the bedroom door, she forces Barry to sleep on a couch. Later, Barry is shot down by gangsters while saving Jeanne. 6,566'

WHY SAILORS GO WRONG (March 25, 1928); D: Henry Lehrman; W: Randall H. Faye (scr), William Conselman (st), Frank O'Connor (st), Delos Sutherland (titles); C: Sidney Wagner; E: Ralph Dietrich; Cast: Sammy Cohen, Ted McNamara, Sally Phipps, Carl Miller, Nick Stuart, Jules Cowles, Noble Johnson, E.H. Calvert, Jack Pennick • Two cabbies, Sammy (Cohen) and Mac (McNamara), are hired by a wealthy would-be suitor (Miller) to work on his yacht and keep a fiancé (Stuart) apart from his girlfriend (Phipps). The fiancé discovers the plan, and the cabbies are overcome. They wake up on the island of Pago Pago. They escape from lions, alligators, monkeys and angry natives before being rescued by an American warship. 5,112'

LOVE HUNGRY (Apr. 8, 1928); D: Victor Heerman; W: Randall H. Faye (scr), Victor Heerman (st), Frances Agnew (titles); C: Glen MacWilliams; E: Alexander Troffey; Cast: Lois Moran, Lawrence Gray, Marjorie Beebe, Edythe Chapman, James Neill, John Patrick • Struggling writer Tom Harver (Gray), who lives with Ma Robinson (Chapman), convinces her discouraged chorus girl daughter, Joan (Moran), to marry his friend, wealthy Lonnie Van Hook (Patrick). Joan ultimately chooses Tom and accepts the "be happy-at-$40-per" concept. 5,792'

THE PLAY GIRL (Apr. 22, 1928); D: Arthur Rosson; W: John Stone, Norman Z. McLeod (titles); C: Rudolph Bergquist; E: Ralph Dietrich; Cast: Madge Bellamy, John Mack Brown, Walter McGrail, Lionel Belmore, Anita Garvin, Thelma Hill, Harry Tenbrook • A flower shop clerk, Madge (Bellamy), is sent to deliver and arrange a bouquet at lawyer David Courtney's (McGrail) apartment. She does not realize that Courtney's client, Bradley Lane (Brown), is taking a bath and loses her job when her co-worker Millie (Garvin) suggests she has become a playgirl. Madge works herself into that lifestyle to check into Millie's associations and finds out that she has been carrying on an affair with Courtney. Madge puts aside the life of a playgirl when Lane proposes marriage. 5,200'

THE ESCAPE (Apr. 29, 1928); D: Richard Rosson; W: Paul Schofield, Garrett Graham (titles), Paul Armstrong (play); C: H. Kinley Martin; E: J. Logan Patterson, Edwin Robbins; Cast: William Russell, Virginia Valli, Nancy Drexel, George Meeker, William Demarest, James Gordon • A hospital intern, Jerry (Russell), loses his position for drinking on the job. He goes to work bartending at a mob nightclub, where he meets May (Valli), a hostess whose bootlegger father was killed in a raid. A gunfight in the nightclub on New Year's Eve kills off all the mobsters. Jerry and May, sobered by the experience, escape just before the police break in. 5,109'

HONOR BOUND (May 6, 1928); D: Alfred E. Green; W: C. Graham Baker, Philip Klein, William Kernell (titles), Jack Bethea (novel); C: Joseph August; E: J. Edwin Robbins; Cast: George O'Brien, Estelle Taylor, Leila Hyams, Tom Santschi, Frank Cooley, Sam De Grasse, Al Hart, Harry Gripp, George Irving • Evelyn (Taylor), married to wealthy mine-owner Mortimer (Santschi), is having an affair with her chauffeur, John (O'Brien), whom she had paroled. John selflessly took the rap when Evelyn accidentally killed her previous husband. Mortimer learns of the affair, sends John into the mines to dig coal and later attempts to kill him. John ends up in jail again, but after another convict sets fire to the building, he escapes, goes to the governor and is given a full pardon. 6,188'

HELLO CHEYENNE (May 13, 1928); D: Eugene Forde; W: Fred Kennedy Myton (scr), Harry Sinclair Drago (st), Dudley Early (titles); C: Dan Clark; E: Robert W. Bischoff; Cast: Tom Mix, Caryl Lincoln, Jack Baston, Martin Faust, Joseph Girard, Al St. John, William Caress, Tony the Wonder Horse • Tom Remington (Mix) is on one of rival telephone crews trying to establish service between Rawhide and Cheyenne. His foreman (Girard), who is the father of his girlfriend, Diana (Lincoln), needs the victory. The rival foreman (Faust) kidnaps Diana, but Tom rescues her and wins the race. 4,618'

HANGMAN'S HOUSE (May 13, 1928); D: John Ford; W: Marion Orth (scr), Willard Mack (scr), Philip Klein (adpt), Malcolm Stuart Boylan (titles), Brian Oswald Donn-Byrne (novel); C: George Schneiderman; E: Margaret V. Clancey; Cast: Victor McLaglen, June Collyer, Earle Foxe, Larry Kent, Hobart Bosworth, Joseph Burke, Eric Mayne, Jack Pennick, Belle Stoddard, John Wayne (UC) • An Irish girl, Connaught (Collyer), turns down Dermot's (Kent) offer of marriage for D'Arcy, an informer (Foxe), just to please her dying father (Bosworth). Her husband, hunted by an Irish freedom fighter (McLaglen), later meets his death in a fire, leaving her free to marry Dermot, her childhood sweetheart. 6,518'

THIEF IN THE DARK (May 20, 1928); D: Albert Ray; W: C. Graham Baker (scr), Albert Ray (st), Kenneth Hawks (st), Andrew Bennison (st), William Kernell (titles); C: Arthur Edeson; E: Jack Dennis; Cast: George Meeker, Doris Hill, Gwen Lee, Marjorie Beebe, Michael Vavitch, Noah Young, Charles Belcher, Raymond Turner, Erville Anderson • A young man (Meeker), traveling with a troupe of fake spiritualists in a carnival, falls in love with the leader's (Vavitch) granddaughter (Hill) and exposes the old man as the murderer of a rich old woman. The leader dies when a jewel case, wired for burglars, explodes when he opens it. 5,937'

THE NEWS PARADE (May 27, 1928); D: David Butler; W: Burnett Hershey (scr), David Butler (st), William M. Conselman (st), Malcolm Stuart Boylan (titles); C: Sidney Wagner, Joseph A. Valentine; E: Irene Morra; Cast: Nick Stuart, Sally Phipps, Brandon Hurst, Cyril Ring, Earle Foxe, Franklin Underwood, Truman Talley • A newsreel cameraman (Stuart) follows a camera-shy millionaire (Hurst) and his daughter (Phipps) to various vacation spots and saves both of them from a kidnapping plot in Havana. He also gets the footage he needs. 6,679'

DON'T MARRY (June 3, 1928); D: James Tinling; W: Randall H. Faye (scr), Philip Klein (st), Sidney Lanfield (st), William Kernell (titles); C: Joseph August; Cast: Lois Moran, Neil Hamilton, Henry Kolker, Claire McDowell, Lydia Dickson • A flapper, Priscilla (Moran), masquerades as her Victorian "cousin," dressed in clothes from the 1890s, to capture strait-laced lawyer Henry (Hamilton) with old-fashioned ideas. Henry discovers, however, that he prefers the flapper persona. 5,708'

NO OTHER WOMAN (June 10, 1928); D: Lou Tellegen; W: Jessie Burns (scr), Bernard Vorhaus (scr), Polan Banks (st), Katherine Hilliker (titles), H.H. Caldwell (titles); C: Ernest Palmer, Paul Ivano; E: J. Edwin Robbins; Cast: Dolores Del Rio, Don Alvarado, Ben Bard, Paulette Duval, Rosita Marstini, Andre Lanoy • A South American heiress, Carmelita (Del Rio), jilts Frenchman Maurice (Alvarado) for his fortune-hunting friend, Albert (Bard), who turns out to be a no-good husband. Carmelita eventually divorces Albert and returns to her first love. 5,071'

WILD WEST ROMANCE (June 10, 1928); D: R. Lee Hough; W: Jack Cunningham (scr), John Stone (st), Delos Sutherland (titles); C: Sol Halprin; E: Barney Wolf, J. Logan Pearson; Cast: Rex Bell, Caryl Lincoln, Neil Neely, Billy Butts, Jack Walters, Fred Parke, Albert Baffert, George Pearce, Ellen Woodston • A ne'er-do-well cowboy, Phil O'Malley (Bell), in love with a minister's daughter, Ruth (Lincoln), proves that his rival for her was responsible for a robbery. Phil joins the sheriff (Walters) to round up the gang of thieves. 4,921'

CHICKEN A LA KING (June 17, 1928); D: Henry Lehrman; W: Izola Forrester, Mann Page, James A. Starr (titles), Wallace A. Mannheimer & Isaac Paul & Harry Wagstaff (play); C: Conrad Wells; E: Frank Hull; Cast: Nancy Carroll, George Meeker, Arthur Stone, Ford Sterling, Frances Lee, Carol Holloway • Horace (Sterling), a stingy businessman with a drab wife, Effie (Holloway), spends time with two gold-digging chorus girls, Maisie (Carroll) and Babe (Lee). The ladies then visit Effie and make her aware of her drabness. Effie spends a lot of Horace's money to make herself look young and "modern." When Horace sees her, he promises to reform his ways. 6,417'

FLEETWING (June 24, 1928); D: Lambert Hillyer; W: Elizabeth Pickett (scr & st), Lambert Hillyer (st); C: Frank Good; E: Alexander Troffey; Cast: Barry Norton, Dorothy Janis, Ben Bard, Robert Kortman, Erville Anderson, James Anderson, Blanche Frederici • Jaafor (Norton), a young Arab, loses his horse, Fleetwing, and slave girl, Thurya (Janis), to a cruel sheik (Bard), who is later killed in an enemy attack. Jaafor then marries Thurya. 4,939'

PAINTED POST (July 1, 1928); D: Eugene Forde; W: Buckleigh F. Oxford (scr), Harry Sinclair Drago (st), Delos Sutherland (titles); C: Dan Clark; E: Robert W. Bischoff; Cast: Tom Mix, Natalie Kingston, Philo McCullough, Al St. John, Fred Gamble, Tony the Wonder Horse • Sheriff Tom Blake (Mix) and his girlfriend, Barbara (Kingston), outwit a desperado gang that has carried out a robbery. They recover the money but not before Barbara's life is placed in jeopardy and she must be rescued. 4,952'

ROAD HOUSE (July 5, 1928); D: Richard Rosson; W: John Stone (scr), Philip Hurn (st); C: George Schneiderman; Cast: Maria Alba, Warren Burke, Lionel Barrymore, Julia Swayne Gordon, Tempe Piggott, Florence Allen, Eddie Clayton, Jack Oakie, Jane Keckley, Joe Brown • Larry (Burke) is the son of permissive parents, Henry Grayson (Barrymore) and his wife (Gordon), who hypocritically preach civic virtue while carousing in private at roadhouses. When Larry visits a roadhouse, he becomes involved with an underworld gang and falls in love with a vamp, Maria (Alba). He is thrown out of the house by his father and joins up with the gang. The gang sets Larry up as a fall guy in a hold-up, and a murder results. The trial ends in a light sentence for Larry, but a strong rebuke to his overindulgent parents. 4,991'

THE COWBOY KID (July 15, 1928); D: Clyde Carruth; W: James J. Tynan (scr), Harry Sinclair Drago (st), Seton I. Miller (st), Delos Sutherland (titles); C: Sol Halprin; E: Milton Carruth; Cast: Rex Bell, Mary Jane Temple, Brooks Benedict, Alice Belcher, Joseph De Grasse, Syd Crossley, Billy Bletcher • Cowboy Jim Barrett (Bell) becomes involved with the town banker's (De Grasse) daughter, Janet (Temple), captures a gang of thieves that has been preying on his bank, and saves the family from financial ruin. 4,385'

NONE BUT THE BRAVE (Aug. 5, 1928); D: Albert Ray; W: Dwight Cummins (scr), Frances Agnew (scr), Fred Stanley (st), James Gruen (st), Norman Z. McLeod (titles); C: Charles Van Enger, Edward Estabrook; E: Alex Troffey; Cast: Charles Morton, Sally Phipps, Sharon Lynn, J. Farrell MacDonald, Tom Kennedy, Billy Butts, Alice Adair, Tyler Brooke, Earle Foxe, Gertrude Short • A college hero, Charles Stanton (Morton), fails at business, becomes a lifeguard, falls in love with a concessionaire, Mary (Phipps), helps an injured swimmer and is rewarded for his valor. 5,034' (Technicolor sequence)

STREET ANGEL (Aug, 19, 1928); D: Frank Borzage; W: Marion Orth (scr), Philip Klein (adpt), Henry Roberts Symonds (adpt), Katherine Hilliker (titles), H.H. Caldwell (titles), Monckton Hoffe (novel); C: Ernest Palmer; E: Barney Wolf; Cast: Janet Gaynor, Charles Farrell, Guido Trento, Henry Armetta, Natalie Kingston, Louis Liggett, Milton Dickenson, Helena Herman, David Kashner, Gino Conti • A poor Neapolitan girl, Angela (Gaynor), fleeing from the police, finds refuge with a circus and meets a painter, Gino (Farrell), who has her pose for a portrait. She is tracked down and serves time in prison. When Angela is released she recognizes the portrait in a church and is reunited with Gino, who has always loved her. 9,221' (Part-talkie, with music and sound effects)

THE RIVER PIRATE (Aug. 26, 1928); D: William K. Howard; W: John Reinhardt, Benjamin Markson, Malcolm Stuart Boylan (titles), Charles Francis Coe (novel); C: Lucien Andriot; E: Jack Dennis; Cast: Victor McLaglen, Lois Moran, Nick Stuart, Earle Foxe, Donald Crisp • At reform school, a waterfront urchin, Sandy (Stuart), meets a sailor, Fritz (McLaglen), a convict who has been sentenced to teaching sail-making. Fritz helps Sandy escape and the pair embarks on a career of warehouse theft. Although Marjorie (Moran), a detective's daughter, tries to get Sandy to go straight, it isn't until Fritz is captured again in a robbery that the boy reforms and marries Marjorie. 6,937' (Music track)

FOUR SONS (Sept. 2, 1928); D: John Ford; W: Philip Klein (adpt), Katherine Hilliker (titles), H.H. Caldwell (titles), Ida Alexa Ross Wylie (article); C: George Schneiderman, Charles G. Clarke; E: Margaret V. Clancey; M: S.L. Rothafel; Cast: James Hall, Margaret Mann, Earle Foxe, Charles Morton, Francis X. Bushman, Jr., George Meeker, Albert Gran, Frank Reicher, Hughie Mack, Michael Mark, August Tollaire, June Collyer, Wendell Phillips Franklin, Ruth Mix, Jack Pennick, Leopold Archduke of Austria, Robert Parrish, L.J. O'Connor, Capt. John Porters • German Grandma Bernle (Mann) has lost three of her four sons in war. Her surviving son (Hall) moves to America, where he marries, starts a family and lives through the Great War by fighting on the allied side. After the Armistice, he returns to America and invites his mother to live with his family. 9,412' (Music and sound effects)

FAZIL (Sept. 9, 1928); D: Howard Hawks; W: Seton I. Miller (scr), Philip Klein (adpt), Pierre Frondaie (play); C: L. William O'Connell; Cast: Charles Farrell, Greta Nissen, Mae Busch, Vadim Uraneff, Tyler Brooke, Eddie Sturgis, Josephine Borio, John Boles, John T. Murray, Erville Anderson, Dale Fuller, Hank Mann • Prince Fazil (Farrell), an Arab chieftain, casts his eye on a carefree Parisienne, Fabienne (Nissen), and takes her away from her boyfriend (Boles). Fazil marries Fabienne and expects to exert complete control over her. Their cultural differences clash immediately. Fabienne rebels, so Fazil returns to the desert and establishes a harem. Fabienne locates the harem and disperses the other women, which annoys Fazil. A rescue party, searching for Fabienne in the desert, arrives. Fazil is mortally wounded, but manages to poison Fabienne, so they will die together. 7,217' (Music and sound effects)

WIN THAT GIRL (Sept. 16, 1928); D: David Butler; W: John Stone, Dudley Early (titles), James Hopper (article); C: Glen MacWilliams; E: Irene Morra; Cast: David Rollins, Sue Carol, Tom Elliott, Roscoe Karns, Olin Francis, Mack Fluker, Sidney Bracey, Janet MacLeod, Maxine Shelly, Betty Recklaw • The third generation of a college football rivalry plays out between two families, the Nortons and the Brawns, as they battle on the field. The Nortons, defeated for the past two generations, finally raise a son, Johnny (Rollins), who leads his team to victory and wins the lovely Gloria (Carol). 5,337' (Music and sound effects)

PLASTERED IN PARIS (Sept. 23, 1928); D: Benjamin Stoloff; W: Harry Brand (scr), Andrew Rice (scr), Harry Sweet (st), Lou Breslow (st), Edwin Burke (dial), Malcolm Stuart Boylan (titles); C: Charles G. Clarke; Cast: Sammy Cohen, Jack Pennick, Lola Salvi, Ivan Linow, Marion Byron, Michael Visaroff, Albert Conti, August Tollaire • Sammy Nosenblum (Cohen) and Bud Swenson (Pennick) return to Paris for an American Legion convention ten years after the Great War. They are later drafted by mistake into the French Foreign Legion and rescue a general's (Visaroff) daughter, Marcelle (Salvi), from a harem in North Africa. 5,641' (Music and sounds effects)

THE AIR CIRCUS (Sept. 30, 1928); D: Howard Hawks, Lewis Seiler; W: Norman Z. McLeod (scr), Seton I. Miller (scr), Graham Baker (st), Andrew Bennison (st), Hugh Herbert (dial), William Kernell (titles); C: Dan Clark; E: Ralph Dixon; Cast: David Rollins, Arthur Lake, Sue Carol, Charles Delaney, Heinie Conklin, Louis Dresser, Earl Robinson • Two pals, Buddy (Rollins) and Speed (Lake), set out to become pilots, but Buddy has a panic attack and almost crashes. Speed and a girlfriend, Sue Manning (Carol), later take off in a plane with defective landing gear, and Buddy has to overcome his fear to save them. 7,702' (Part-talkie, with music and sound effects)

DRY MARTINI (Oct. 7, 1928); D: H. D'Abbadie D'Arrast; W: Douglas Doty, John Thomas (novel); C: Conrad Wells; E: Frank E. Hull; M: Erno Rapée, S.L. Rothafel; Cast: Mary Astor, Matt Moore, Jocelyn Lee, Sally Eilers, Albert Gran, Albert Conti, Tom Ricketts, Hugh Trevor, John Webb Dillon, Marcelle Corday • Elisabeth (Astor), the daughter of Willoughby Quimby (Gran), a divorced American in Paris, arrives to live with her father. While Willoughby gives up his carousing, Elisabeth is interested in a wild time and takes up with a French artist. Freddie (Moore), a drinking friend of Willoughby's, lures her away from the artist and they eventually return to America together. 7,176' (Music and sound effects; also released as a silent)

ME, GANGSTER (Oct. 14, 1928); D: Raoul Walsh; W: Charles Francis Coe, Raoul Walsh, William Kernell (titles); C: Arthur Edeson; E: Louis Loeffler; Cast: June Collyer, Don Terry, Anders Randolph, Stella Randolff, Al Hill, Burr McIntosh, Walter James, Gustav von Seyffertitz, Herbert Ashton, Harry Cattle • A young gangster (Terry) commits armed robbery and hides $50,000 before he goes to jail. When he is paroled, he decides to go straight and return the money, but his old gang tries to get it first. With the help of a young woman (Collyer), he outwits the gang. 6,042' (Music and sound effects)

MOTHER MACHREE (Oct. 21, 1928); D: John Ford; W: Gertrude Orr, Katherine Hilliker (titles), H.H. Caldwell (titles), Rida Johnson Young (article); C: Chester Lyons; E: Katherine Hilliker, H.H. Caldwell; Cast: Belle Bennett, Neil Hamilton, Philippe De Lacy, Victor McLaglen, Pat Somerset, Ted McNamara, John MacSweeney, Eulalie Jensen, Constance Howard • A poor Irish immigrant to America, Ellen McHugh (Bennett), is persuaded to enter a circus sideshow by an Irish carnival strongman (McLaglen). When it is revealed that she appears as a "half-woman," Ellen is forced to surrender her young son, Brian (De Lacy), to the school principal's care. She loses track of her son and becomes a housekeeper, raising her employer's daughter, Edith (Howard). Years later, Edith falls in love with the adult Brian (Hamilton), who finds out his mother is still alive. All are reunited. 6,807' (Music and sound effects)

THE FARMER'S DAUGHTER (Oct. 28, 1928); D: Arthur Rosson; W: Frederica Sagor (scr), Henry M. Johnson (st), Harry Brand (st), Garrett Graham (titles); C: Joseph August; E: J. Logan Pearson; Cast: Marjorie Beebe, Arthur Stone, Lincoln Stedman, Jimmie Adams, Harry Dunkinson, Sam de Grasse • A country girl, Margerine Hopkins (Beebe), drops her boyfriend and falls for a city slicker, who cons her out of her money. Her boyfriend, an inventor, later sells his invention to a milk baron and wins her back. 5,148'

MOTHER KNOWS BEST (Oct. 28, 1928); D: John Blystone; W: Marion Orth (scr), Eugene Walter (dial), William Kernell (titles), Edith Bristol (titles), Edna Ferber (article); C: Gilbert Warrenton; E: Margaret V. Clancey; Cast: Madge Bellamy, Louise Dresser, Barry Norton, Albert Gran, Joy Auburn, Stuart Erwin, Lucien Littlefield, Dawn O'Day, Annette De Kirby, Aaron De Kirby • An overbearing stage mother (Dresser) pushes her daughter Sally (Bellamy) from vaudeville to Broadway, but strictly forbids any romantic life. When Sally has a nervous breakdown, her doctor convinces the mother to reunite her with the boy (Norton) she loves. 10,116' (Part-talkie with music and sound effects)

THE DEADWOOD COACH (Nov, 4, 1928) Reissue — Silent

SUNRISE: A SONG OF TWO HUMANS (Nov. 4, 1928); D: F.W. Murnau; W: Carl Mayer, Katherine Hilliker (titles), H.H. Caldwell (titles), Hermann Sudermann (novel); C: Charles Rosher, Karl Struss; E: Katherine Hilliker, H.H. Caldwell, Harold Schuster; M: Hugo Riesenfeld; Cast: George O'Brien, Janet Gaynor, Margaret Livingston, Bodil Rosing, J. Farrell MacDonald, Ralph Sipperly, Jane Winton, Arthur Housman, Eddie Boland • A city lady (Livingston) persuades a farmer (O'Brien) to murder his wife (Gaynor). He cannot bring himself to commit murder and renews his vows in a church. Rowing home, a storm hits their boat and the husband swims to get help. While fishermen search for his wife, he goes to the city and is about to strangle the woman who started it all when word comes that his wife has been found and is safe. 9,900' (Music and sounds effects) • New York opening Nov. 4, 1927

ROMANCE OF THE UNDERWORLD (Nov. 11, 1928); D: Irving Cummings; W: Douglas Doty (scr & st), Sidney Lanfield (st), Garrett Graham (titles), Paul Armstrong (novel); C: Conrad Wells; E: Frank Hull; Cast: Mary Astor, Ben Bard, Robert Elliott, John Boles, Oscar Apfel, Helen Lynch, William A. Tooker • Judith (Astor), a country girl in the city, is reduced to soliciting in a dancehall, where she meets and marries Stephen Ransome (Boles), a man of excellent quality, who knows nothing of her lifestyle. Her former pimp, Dan (Bard), learns of the marriage and blackmails Judith until a detective (Elliott) puts him behind bars. 6,162' (Music and sound effects)

PREP AND PEP (Nov. 18, 1928); D: David Butler; W: John Stone, Malcolm Stuart Boylan (titles); C: Sidney Wagner, Joseph Valentine; E: Irene Morra; Cast: David Rollins, Nancy Drexel, John Darrow, E.H. Calvert, Frank Albertson, Robert Peck • Cyril (Rollins), the son of a military academy's greatest athlete, is unable to live up to his father's record until he distinguishes himself in horsemanship and rescues the commandant's daughter (Drexel) from a fire. 6,806' (Music track)

TAKING A CHANCE (Nov. 18, 1928); D: Norman Z. McLeod; W: A.H. Halprin, Bret Harte (article); C: Sol Halprin; E: J. Logan Pearson; Cast: Rex Bell, Lola Todd, Richard Carlyle, Billy Butts, Jack Byron, Martin Cichy, Jack Henderson • The exploits of rodeo cowboy Joe Courtney (Bell) and his pursuit of bandit Jessie Smith (Todd) are highlighted by gunfights, romance and adventure, in this colorful portrayal of the Wild West. 4,876'

RILEY THE COP (Nov. 25, 1928); D: John Ford; W: Fred Stanley, James Gruen; C: Charles G. Clarke; E: Alex Troffey; Cast: Farrell MacDonald, Louise Fazenda, Nancy Drexel, David Rollins, Harry Schultz, Mildred Boyd, Ferdinand Schumann-Heink, Del Henderson, Mike Donlin • Riley (MacDonald), a lifelong cop, is assigned to bring back a bakery worker, Joe Smith (Rollins), who has been unjustly accused of embezzlement. Joe has gone to Europe in search of his wealthy girlfriend, Mary (Drexel). Meanwhile, Joe falls in love with Lena (Fazenda), a German girl, who turns out to be the sister of Riley's beat cop nemesis. Riley brings Joe back to America, where he is proven innocent. 6,132' (Music and sound effects)

THE RED DANCE (Dec. 2, 1928); D: Raoul Walsh; W: James Ashmore Creelman (scr), Pierre Collings (adpt), Philip Klein (adpt), Eleanor Browne (st), Malcolm Stuart Boylan (titles), Henry Leyford Gates (novel); C: Charles G. Clarke, John Marta; E: Louis Loeffler; M: S.L. Rothafel; Cast: Charles Farrell, Dolores Del Rio, Ivan Linow, Boris Charsky, Dorothy Revier, Andrés de Segurola, Demetrius Alexis • A peasant girl (Del Rio) in Czarist Russia is persuaded to shoot the Grand Duke

(Farrell), whom she secretly loves, on the eve of his marriage. After the Revolution, she becomes the Red Dancer and saves the Grand Duke from a firing squad, and is reunited with him. 9,250' (Music and sound effects; also released as a silent)

BLINDFOLD (Dec. 9, 1928); D: Charles Klein; W: Ewart Adamson, Robert Horwood (adpt), Charles Francis Coe (story), William Kernell (titles); C: Lucien Andriot; E: Jack Dennis; Cast: Lois Moran, George O'Brien, Maria Alba, Earle Foxe, Don Terry, Fritz Feld, Andy Clyde, Crauford Kent, Robert E. Homans, John Kelly, Phillips Smalley • Mary Brown (Moran) goes into shock after her boyfriend is gunned down by gangsters. A master criminal, Dr. Cornelius Simmons (Foxe), uses her shock to persuade her to commit crimes. A discharged detective, Robert Kelly (O'Brien), goes after the gang and meets Mary, whom he shocks back to normalcy. Together, they bring down the gangsters. 5,598' (Music and sound effects)

HOMESICK (Dec. 16, 1928); D: Henry Lehrman; W: John Stone, William Kernell (titles); C: Charles Van Enger; E: Ralph Dixon; Cast: Sammy Cohen, Harry Sweet, Marjorie Beebe, Henry Armetta, Pat Harmon • A servant girl (Beebe) in California puts an ad in a newspaper, looking for a suitable husband. Two men, Ambrose (Sweet) and Sammy (Cohen), answer the ad and enter a transcontinental bike race to win her. 5,153'

RED WINE (Dec. 23, 1928); D: Raymond Cannon; W: Andrew Bennison (adpt), Charles Condon (adpt), Raymond Cannon (st), Garrett Graham (titles); C: Daniel Clark; E: Malcolm Stuart Boylan (supervisor); Cast: June Collyer, Conrad Nagel, Arthur Stone, Sharon Lynn, E. Alyn Warren, Ernest Hilliard, Ernest Wood, Marshall Ruth, Dixie Gay, Margaret La Marr, Bo Ling • An upstanding married man, Charles Cook (Nagel), goes on the town with friends, has too much to drink and passes out. As a joke, his friends arrange for him to think that he was unfaithful to his wife. Charles and his wife, Alice (Collyer), celebrate their anniversary the next night at the same restaurant and Charles has to explain a series of misunderstandings that result from the prank. 6,194' (Music and sound effects)

THE GREAT WHITE NORTH (Dec. 30, 1928); D: Sydney Snow, H.A. Snow; W: Sydney Snow, H.A. Snow, Malcolm Stuart Boylan (titles), Barney Wolf (titles); C: Sydney Snow, H.A. Snow; E: Kenneth Hawks • This is a documentary record of Arctic life, including a walrus hunt, a bear hunt, and the harpooning of a whale. 5,560' (Music, sound effects & talking prologue)

1929 Releases

SKY HIGH (Jan. 6, 1929) Reissue — Silent

CAPTAIN LASH (Jan. 6, 1929); D: John Blystone; W: John Stone (scr), Daniel G. Tomlinson (scr & st), Laura Hasse (st); C: Conrad Wells; E: James K. McGuinness; Cast: Victor McLaglen, Claire Windsor, Jane Winton, Clyde Cook, Arthur Stone, Albert Conti, Jean Laverty, Frank Hagney, Boris Charsky • A ship stoker, Captain Lash (McLaglen), saves attractive Cora Nevins (Windsor) from a broken steam valve and she has him unknowingly take stolen jewels ashore. When he meets her to return the jewels, they have been replaced with coal by a co-worker (Cook). Lash is set upon by her henchmen, but overcomes the gang and turns them over to the police, then retrieves the jewels. 5,454' (Music and effects; also released as a silent)

IN OLD ARIZONA (Jan. 20, 1929); D: Raoul Walsh, Irving Cummings; W: Tom Barry; C: Arthur Edeson; E: Louis Loeffler; Cast: Edmund Lowe, Dorothy Burgess, Warner Baxter, Farrell MacDonald, Fred Warren, Henry Armetta, Frank Campeau, Tom Santschi, Roy Stewart • The Cisco Kid's (Baxter) flair for daring thievery and dangerous trysts leads him into trouble. His Mexican sweetheart, Tonia Maria (Burgess), is double dealing with Sgt. Mickey Dunn (Lowe), a law enforcement officer and the Kid is almost captured, but frames Tonia so that Dunn shoots her by accident. The Kid rides off, laughing. 8,724' (First Fox all-talkie; also released as a silent) • This was the first outdoor all-talkie released by any studio.

TRUE HEAVEN (Jan. 20, 1929); SP: Kenneth Hawks; D: James Tinling; W: Dwight Cummins (adpt), Malcolm Stuart Boylan (titles), Charles Edward Montague (article); C: Conrad Wells; Cast: George O'Brien, Lois Moran, Phillips Smalley, Oscar Apfel, Duke Martin, Andre Cheron, Donald MacKenzie, Hedwig Reicher, Will Stanton • Lt. Gresson (O'Brien), a British soldier in Belgium, falls in love with a café entertainer, Judith (Moran), and later discovers that she's an enemy agent. Torn between love and duty, Judith turns Gresson in as a spy behind enemy lines, but he is saved by the Armistice. 5,331' (Sound effects; also released as a silent)

FUGITIVES (Jan. 27, 1929); SP: Kenneth Hawks; D: William Beaudine; W: John Stone, Malcolm Stuart Boylan (titles), Richard Harding Davis (short story); C: Chester Lyons; Cast: Madge Bellamy, Don Terry, Arthur Stone, Earle Foxe, Matthew Betz, Lumsden Hare, Edith Yorke, Jean Laverty, Hap Ward • A nightclub singer (Bellamy) is accused of murdering the club owner (Foxe). The District Attorney (Terry) sends her to prison, but a friend (Stone) helps her escape and she proves her innocence after rescuing the D.A. from a gang of crooks. 5,356' (Music; also released as a silent)

JUST TONY (Feb. 2, 1929) Reissue — Silent

THE SIN SISTER (Feb. 10, 1929); D: Charles Klein; W: Harry Behn (scr), Andrew Bennison (scr), Frederick Hazlitt Brennan (st), Becky Gardiner (st); C: Charles Clarke, George Eastman; Cast: Nancy Carroll, Lawrence Gray, Josephine Dunn, Myrtle Stedman, Anders Randolf, Richard Alexander • A girl (Carroll) pays fur traders a great sum of money to help her father off an ice-bound ship and deposit him in a desolate hut. The traders also want to take the daughter as payment. The father grabs the girl and they escape in sleds. 6,072' (Music and sound effects; also released as a silent) • *Variety* said, "From the title up this thing is a freak. One minute it's slapstick, then there is a serious interlude... Hopelessly boring even to grind audiences."

NAPOLEON'S BARBER (Feb. 17, 1929) Short subject; D: John Ford; W: Arthur Caesar (st & scr); Cast: Otto Matieson, Natalie Golitzen, Frank Reicher, Helen Ware, Philippe De Lacy, D'Arcy Corrigan, Russ Powell, Michael Mark, Buddy Roosevelt • Napoleon anonymously stops into a barber shop and the barber spouts off about what is wrong with the general's policies, not knowing to whom he is speaking. Napoleon leaves without revealing his identity. 32 min.

THE DIPLOMATS (Feb. 17, 1929) Short subject; D: Norman Taurog; W: Arthur Caesar (st & scr), Bobby Clark (st & scr), Paul McCullough (st & scr); Cast: Bobby Clark, Paul McCullough, Marguerite Churchill, Andrés de Segurola, Cissy Fitzgerald, John St. Polis, John Baston, Andre Cheron, Joe Smith Marba • No other information available for this short subject.

MAKING THE GRADE (Feb. 17, 1929); D: Alfred E. Green; W: Harry Brand, Edward Kaufman, Malcolm Stuart Boylan (dial & titles), George Ade (article); C: L.W. O'Connell, Norman Devol; E: J. Edwin Robbins; M: Erno Rapée; Cast: Edmund Lowe, Lois Moran, Lucien Littlefield, Albert Hart, James Ford, Rolfe Sedan, John Alden, Sherman Ross, Gino Conti, Mary Ashley, Lia Tora • Herbert (Lowe), the son of a wealthy small-town family, tries to prove himself but fails at everything he tries. He falls in love with a tea room waitress (Moran) and finally proves his mettle. 5,903' (Talking sequences and music; also released as a silent)

NEW YEAR'S EVE (Feb. 24, 1929); D: Henry Lehrman; W: Dwight Cummins, William Kernell (titles), Richard Connell (article); C: Conrad Wells; M: S.L. Rothafel; Cast: Mary Astor, Charles Morton, Earle Foxe, Florence Lake, Arthur Stone, Helen Ware, Freddie Frederick, Jane La Verne, Sumner Getchell, Stuart Erwin • Marjorie (Astor), saddled with the care of her younger brother (Frederick), visits a gambler, who is killed while she is in his presence. The police charge her with murder. The murderer later falls to his death and evidence is uncovered that exonerates Marjorie. 5,984' (Music and sound effects; also released as a silent)

THE GHOST TALKS (Feb. 24, 1929); D: Lewis Seiler; W: Frederick Hazlitt Brennan (scr), Harlan Thompson (dial), Max Marcin & Edward Hammonds (play); C: George Meehan; E: Ralph Dietrich; Cast: Helen Twelvetrees, Charles Eaton, Stepin Fetchit, Carmel Myers, Earle Foxe, Henry Sedley, Joe Brown, Clifford Dempsey, Baby Mack, Bess Flowers • A hotel night clerk (Eaton) with a correspondence diploma in detective work helps a young lady (Twelvetrees) track down $1 million in bonds stolen from her uncle by a gang of crooks and wins the lady in the process. 6,482' (Music and sound effects; also released as a silent)

ROUGH RIDING ROMANCE (March 3, 1929) Reissue — Silent

STRONG BOY (March 3, 1929); D: John Ford; W: James Kevin McGuinness (scr), Andrew Bennison (scr), John McLain (scr), Frederick Hazlitt Brennan (st), Malcolm Stuart Boylan (titles); C: Joseph August; Cast: Victor McLaglen, Leatrice Joy, Farrell MacDonald, Clyde Cook, Kent Sanderson, Douglas Scott, Slim Summerville, Tom Wilson, Eulalie Jensen, David Torrence • A baggage handler, Strong Boy (McLaglen), is promoted to the lost-and-found department after saving a railroad executive's son. He is promoted again when he returns a valuable necklace to a movie star. As a fireman on a locomotive, he prevents a holdup and is reunited with an engineer's daughter (Joy) who had walked out on him. 5,567' (Music and effects; also released as a silent)

HEARTS IN DIXIE (March 10, 1929); D: Paul Sloane; W: Walter Weems; C: Glen MacWilliams; E: Alexander Troffey; Cast: Clarence Muse, Eugene Jackson, Stepin Fetchit, Bernice Pilot, Clifford Ingram, Mildred Washington, Zack Williams, Gertrude Howard, C.H. Billbrew • A poor Negro farmer, Nappus (Muse), works in his old age to help his daughter, Chloe (Pilot), and her shiftless husband, Gummy (Fetchit). When Chloe and her daughter, Trailia (Washington), die because Gummy took them to a voodoo woman (Billbrew) instead of a white doctor, Nappus sells his farm to send his grandson Chiquapin (Jackson) north to study medicine, so he can then return to the South to help his people. 6,644' (All-talkie; also released as a silent)

BLUE SKIES (March 17, 1929); SP: Jeff Lazarus; D: Alfred L. Werker; W: John Stone, Malcolm Stuart Boylan (titles), Frederick Hazlitt Brennan (article); C: L.W. O'Connell; Cast: Helen Twelvetrees, Frank Albertson, Rosa Gore, William Orlamond, E.H. Calvert, Evelyn Hall, Claude King, Adele Watson, Helen Jerome Eddy • Two childhood sweetheart orphans grow up and leave the orphanage. Richard (Albertson) is the lost son of a millionaire, but he tries to transfer an inheritance to his true love, Dorothy (Twelvetrees), and is branded a criminal before all is straightened out. 5,408' (All-talkie)

SPEAKEASY (March 24, 1929); D: Benjamin Stoloff; W: Frederick Hazlitt Brennan, Edwin Burke, Edward Knoblock and George Rossner (novel); C: Joseph A. Valentine; E: J. Edwin Robbins; Cast: Lola Lane, Paul Page, Sharon Lynn, Warren Hymer, Helen Ware, Henry B. Walthall, Stuart Erwin, James Guilfoyle, Erville Anderson, Joseph Cawthorn • A female reporter, Alice Woods (Lane), does her best to get an interview with an ex-champion boxer, Paul Martin (Page), but is rebuffed. Alice fabricates a story that Martin is planning a comeback and soon falls for the champ. She proves that his manager (Hymer) is crooked and gets Martin back into the ring, where he regains his middleweight crown. 5,775' (All-talkie; also released as a silent)

GIRLS GONE WILD (March 24, 1929); D: Lewis Seiler; W: Beulah Marie Dix, Bertram Millhauser, Malcolm Stuart Boylan (titles); C: Arthur Edeson, Irving Rosenberg; Cast: Sue Carol, Nick Stuart, William Russell, Roy D'Arcy, Leslie Fenton, Hedda Hopper, John Darrow, Matthew Betz, Edmund Breese, Minna Ferry • Babs Holworthy (Carol), a wealthy young lady, goes dancing with a notorious bootlegger, who is shot by a rival gang. Her ex-boyfriend, Buck (Stuart), happens to be in the hall, and the two are kidnapped by the gang. The boyfriend's father (Russell), a motorcycle cop, gives chase and is wounded, but his son saves the day and regains Babs's love. 5,305' (All-talkie)

TRENT'S LAST CASE (March 31, 1929); D: Howard Hawks; W: Scott Darling (scr), Beulah Marie Dix Adpt), Malcolm Stuart Boylan (titles), Edmund Clerihew Bentley (novel); C: Harold Rosson; Cast: Donald Crisp, Raymond Griffith, Raymond Hatton, Marceline Day, Lawrence Gray, Nicholas Soussanin, Anita Garvin, Ed Kennedy • Sigsbee Manderson (Crisp) is apparently murdered and an inspector (Kennedy) lines up suspects, including the man's wife (Day), male secretary, uncle, butler and maid. While the secretary looks guilty, another detective proves that the man committed suicide in a way to frame the secretary, who was in love with his wife. 5,834' (Part-talkie with music and sound effects; also released as a silent)

THE LAST OF THE DUANES (Apr. 7, 1929) Reissue — Silent

NOT QUITE DECENT (Apr. 7, 1929); P: James K. McGuinness; D: Irving Cummings; W: Marion Orth (scr), Edwin Burke (dial), Malcolm Stuart Boylan (titles), Wallace Smith (article); C: Charles G. Clarke; E: Paul Weatherwax; Cast: Louise Dresser, June Collyer, Allan Lane, Oscar Apfel, Paul Nicholson, Marjorie Beebe, Ben Hewlett, Jack Kenney • A nightclub singer in New York, Mame Jarrow (Dresser), meets young stage performer Linda (Collyer), whom she realizes is her long-lost daughter. Not revealing her identity and trying to keep the girl from hooking up with the wrong type of man, she sends for the girl's small-town boyfriend, Jerry (Lane), who takes her home. 4,965' (Part-talkie with music and sound effects; also released as a silent)

THE VEILED WOMAN (Apr. 14, 1929); D: Emmett Flynn; W: Douglas Z. Doty (scr), Julio De Moraes (st), Lia Tora (st); C: Charles G. Clarke; Cast: Lia Tora, Paul Vicenti, Walter McGrail, Josef Swickard, Kenneth Thomson, Andre Cheron, Ivan Lebedeff, Maude George, Lupita Tovar • In flashback, an innocent French girl, Nanon (Tora), tells the story of three men in her life, including one she married, who led her to unhappy circumstances. She later learns that a former gambling club owner, Pierre (Vincenti), who is now a taxi driver, sacrificed everything to cover up a shooting Nanon committed. She finally finds happiness with him. 5,192' (All-talkie; also released as a silent)

THRU DIFFERENT EYES (Apr. 24, 1929); D: John Blystone; W: Milton Herbert Gropper (dial & st), Tom Barry (dial), Edna Sherry (st); C: Ernest Palmer, Al Brick; E: Louis Loeffler; Cast: Mary Duncan, Edmund Lowe, Warner Baxter, Natalie Moorhead, Earle Foxe, Donald Gallagher, Florence Lake, Sylvia Sidney, Purnell Pratt, Stepin Fetchit • Harvey Manning (Lowe) is placed on trial for the murder of his best friend, Jack Winfield (Baxter). During the legal proceedings both sides present sharply different information about the alleged murderer and his wife, Viola (Duncan). When the jury convicts Manning, a young girl comes forward and confesses that she was the murderer. 5,166' (All-talkie; also released as a silent)

THE WOMAN FROM HELL (Apr. 21, 1929); SP: James K. McGuinness; D: A.F. Erickson; W: Ray Doyle (scr), Charles Kenyon (scr), George Scarborough (adpt), Annette Bay Scarborough (adpt), Lois Leeson (st), Jaime Del Rio (st); C: Conrad Wells; Cast: Mary Astor, Robert Armstrong, Dean Jagger, Roy D'Arcy, May Boley, James Bradbury, Sr. • A woman (Astor) playing the Devil at an amusement stand, meets and marries a lighthouse keeper (Jagger). She returns with him, but is pursued by the barker (D'Arcy), who wants her to return to work. Her jealous husband finally confronts the man, but eventually realizes his wife has been faithful to him. 5,442'

THE FAR CALL (Apr. 28, 1929); D: Allan Dwan; W: Seton I. Miller (scr), Walter Woods (adpt), H.H. Caldwell (titles), Edison Marshall (article); C: Hal Rosson; E: H.H. Caldwell; Cast: Charles Morton, Leila Hyams, Arthur Stone, Warren Hymer, Dan Wolheim, Stanley J. Stanford, Ullrich Haupt, Charles Middleton, Pat Hartigan • Pal Loring (Morton), a potential thief of a seal hatchery, is revealed by a young woman (Hyams) to be the son of a deceased, well-respected member of the community. When Pal gives up the crime, his former henchman (Haupt) decides to rob the hatchery. Pal fights him off and protects the baby seals. 5,313' (Music and sound effects)

SOFT BOILED (May 5, 1929) Reissue — Silent

PROTECTION (May 5, 1929); D: Benjamin Stoloff; W: Frederick Hazlitt Brennan (scr), J. Clarkson Miller (st); C: Joseph Valentine; Cast: Robert Elliott, Paul Page, Dorothy Burgess, Ben Hewlett, Dorothy Ward, Joe Brown, Roy Stewart, William H. Tooker, Arthur Hoyt • While writing a story about a bootlegger, a reporter (Page) uncovers a protection racket involving city officials. His story is quashed by the powerful bootlegger; he then joins a crusading newspaper, which publishes the report and breaks up corruption. 5,536' (Music and sound effects; also released as a silent)

JOY STREET (May 12, 1929); D: Raymond Cannon; W: Charles Condon (scr & adpt), Frank Gay (scr & adpt), Raymond Cannon (st); C: Ernest Miller; Cast: Lois Moran, Nick Stuart, Rex Bell, Jose Crespo, Dorothy Ward, Ada Williams, Maria Alba, Sally Phipps, Florence Allen, Mabel Vail, Carol Wines, John Breeden • An unsophisticated young girl, Mimi (Moran), inherits a fortune and adopts the carefree life of a flapper. She meets a down-to-earth young man, Joe (Stuart), who tries to set her straight. After a serious accident in a joy ride, Mimi gives up her wild life and marries her boyfriend. 5,748' (Music and sound effects)

THE VALIANT (May 19, 1929); D: William K. Howard; W: John Hunter Booth, Tom Barry, Holworthy Hall and Robert Middlemass (play); C: Lucien Andriot, Glen MacWilliams; E: Jack Dennis; Cast: Paul Muni, John Mack Brown, Edith Yorke, Richard Carlyle, Marguerite Churchill, De Witt Jennings, Clifford Dempsey, Henry Kolker, Don Terry • After the World War, James Dyke (Muni) kills an old friend then gives himself up to the police. Dyke is sentenced to death. Dyke's mother (Yorke) sends her daughter Mary (Churchill) to see if Dyke, in a poorly reproduced newspaper photo, is her missing son. Dyke convinces Mary that he is a friend of her brother who died as a war hero. Dyke then goes to his death. 5,537' (Talking sequences)

FOX MOVIETONE FOLLIES OF 1929 (May 26, 1929); D: David Butler; W: David Butler (st), William K. Wells (dial); C: Charles Van Enger; E: Ralph Dietrich; Cast: Sue Carol, Dixie Lee, John Breeden, Lola Lane, De Witt Jennings, Sharon Lynn, Arthur Stone, Stepin Fetchit, Warren Hymer, Archie Gottler, Arthur Kay • A Southern boy (Breeden) catches up with his girlfriend (Lane) to convince her to abandon a stage career. He ends up buying a controlling interest in the show. On opening night, she replaces the star and becomes a hit. The boyfriend is able to sell the show back to the producer, who had designs on his girl. 7,522' (All-talkie; Technicolor sequence)

THE ONE WOMAN IDEA (June 2, 1929); SP: Philip Klein; D: Berthold Viertel; W: Marion Orth, Alan Williams (article); C: L. William O'Connell; M: Arthur Kay; Cast: Rod LaRocque, Marceline Day, Shirley Dorman, Sharon Lynn, Sally Phipps, Ivan Lebedeff, Douglas Gilmore, Gino Corrado, Joseph W. Girard, Arnold Lucy • An Oxford-educated Persian prince, Ahmed (LaRocque), meets a British Lady Alicia (Day), whose unfaithful husband (Gilmore) is a villainous Lord. A triangle develops and the prince ends up helping Alicia, with whom he has fallen in love. 6,111' (Music and sound effects; also released as a silent) • Viertel was a well-known Berlin stage director; this was his first American film.

THE BLACK WATCH (June 2, 1929); D: John Ford; W: John Stone (scr), James K. McGuinness (dial), Talbot Mundy (novel); C: Joseph August; E: Alexander Troffey; Cast: Victor McLaglen, Myrna Loy, David Rollins, Lumsden Hare, Roy D'Arcy, Mitchell Lewis, Cyril Chadwick, Claude King, Francis Ford, Walter Long • Captain Gordon King (McLaglen) of the Black Watch regiment in India, thought to be a coward, quells a revolt of tribesmen after he angers them for winning the affection of a girl, Yasmani (Loy), whom they look upon as a goddess. 8,487' (All-talkie; also released as a silent)

THE EXALTED FLAPPER (June 9, 1929); SP: Kenneth Hawks; D: James Tinling; W: Matt Taylor (scr), Ray Harris (adpt), H.H. Caldwell (titles), Will Irwin (article); C: Charles G. Clarke; E: H.H. Caldwell; M: Arthur Kay; Cast: Sue Carol, Barry Norton, Irene Rich, Albert Conti, Sylvia Field, Stuart Erwin, Lawrence Grant, Charles Clary, Michael Visaroff • In a fictional kingdom, Princess Izola (Carol) refuses to be "sacrificed" in a marriage of duty to foreign Prince Boris (Norton). She inadvertently meets and falls in love with the prince as he travels incognito. Her mother (Rich), unaware of Boris's identity, has him kidnapped, but Izola helps him escape and they are finally married. 5,806' (Music and sound effects; also released as a silent)

MASKED EMOTIONS (June 23, 1929); D: David Butler, Kenneth Hawks; W: Harry Brand, Benjamin Markson, Douglas Z. Doty (titles), Ben Ames Williams (article); C: Sidney Wagner; Cast: George O'Brien, Nora Lane, J. Farrell MacDonald, David Sharpe, James Gordon, Edward Pell, Sr., Frank Hagney • Two brothers, Bram (O'Brien) and Thad (Sharpe), are on a sloop owned by retired Capt. Goodell (Gordon). They run into opium smuggler Lee Wing (Peil Sr.), who kidnaps and later stabs Thad. Bram sets out to find the guilty party, and circumstances implicate Bram's girlfriend Emily Goodell (Lane). Bram catches up with Lee Wing and there is a finale with a fight atop the mast of a schooner. Bram rescues Thad and returns to Emily. 5,419' (Music and sound effects; also released as a silent)

BEHIND THAT CURTAIN (June 30, 1929); D: Irving Cummings; W: Sonya Levien, Clarke Silvernail, Wilbur Morse Jr. (titles), Earl Derr Biggers (article); C: Conrad Wells, Dave Ragin, Vincent Farrar; E: Alfred De Gaetano; Cast: Warner Baxter, Lois Moran, Gilbert Emery, Claude King, Philip Strange, Boris Karloff, Jamiel Hasson, Peter Gawthorne, John Rogers, Montague Shaw • Eve Mannering (Moran), the daughter of a wealthy Englishman (King), marries a fortune hunter, Durand (Strange), who kills an investigator looking into his past for her father. A Scotland Yard detective (Emery), intrigued by the case, follows a clue of the victim's Chinese slippers. This leads him to the murderer, Durand, who is killed while evading the law. 8,320' (All-talkie; also released as a silent)

BLACK MAGIC (July 7, 1929); SP: Bertram Millhauser; D: George B. Seitz; W: Beulah Marie Dix, Katherine Hilliker (titles), Walter Archer Frost and Paul Dickey (play); C: Glen MacWilliams; E: Katherine Hilliker; Cast: Josephine Dunn, Earle Foxe, John Holland, Henry B. Walthall, Dorothy Jordan, Fritz Feld, Sheldon Lewis, Ivan Linow, Blue Washington • Three men from different parts of the world find refuge on a South Seas island. They get together to swindle a white trader out of his pearls, then are cursed by a voodoo woman who makes them believe their deaths are imminent. 5,855' (Music and sound effects; also released as a silent)

PLEASURE CRAZED (July 7, 1929); SP: Philip Klein; D: Donald Gallaher; W: Douglas Z. Doty (scr), Clare Kummer (dial), Monckton Hoffe (play); C: Ernest Palmer, Glen MacWilliams; E: J. Edwin Robbins; Cast: Marguerite Churchill, Kenneth MacKenna, Dorothy Burgess, Campbell Gullan, Douglas Gilmore, Henry Kolker, Frederick Graham, Rex Bell, Charlotte Merriam • A young woman, Nora (Churchill), is placed as a housekeeper in the rented home of a wealthy couple, Capt. Anthony Dean (MacKenna) and Alma Dean

(Burgess), by crooks who are out to rob them. Nora grows fond of Anthony, and, when Alma strays, she is able to thwart the gang and end up with the husband. 5,460' (All-talkie; also released as a silent)

MASQUERADE (July 14, 1929); D: Russell J. Birdwell; W: Frederick Hazlitt Brennan, Malcolm Stuart Boylan, Louis Joseph Vance (novel); C: Charles G. Clarke, Don Anderson; E: Ralph Dietrich; Cast: Alan Birmingham, Leila Hyams, Arnold Lucy, Clyde Cook, Farrell MacDonald, George Pierce, Rita Le Roy, Frank Richardson, John Breeden, Jack Pierce • Young Sylvia Graeme (Hyams) breaks into world traveler Dan Maitland's (Birmingham) apartment to retrieve some papers that will free her father, Andrew (Pierce), from jail. A crook, Dan Anisty (Birmingham), after the same papers, assumes Maitland's identity, but is still unable to convince Sylvia to give them back. When Maitland takes Anisty's identity, everyone is confused until a showdown settles the affair. 5,694' (All-talkie; also released as a silent)

CHASING THROUGH EUROPE (Aug. 4, 1929); D: David Butler, Alfred L. Werker; W: Andrew Bennison, John Stone; C: Sidney Wagner, Lucien Andriot, L.W. O'Connell; Cast: Sue Carol, Nick Stuart, Gustav von Seyffertitz, Gavin Gordon, E. Alyn Warren • Newsreel photographer Dick Stallings (Stuart) meets wealthy American Linda Terry (Carol) in London, and they travel around Europe together, meeting Mussolini and the Prince of Wales. They are also pursued by a small-time crook, Don Merrill (Gordon), who attempts to kidnap Linda. This is foiled by Dick, who takes her back to America to get married. 5,581' (Part-talkie with music and sound effects; also released as a silent)

LUCKY STAR (Aug. 18, 1929); D: Frank Borzage; W: Sonya Levien (scr), John Hunter Booth (dial), Katherine Hilliker (titles), H.H. Caldwell (titles), Tristram Tupper (article); C: Chester Lyons, William Cooper Smith; E: Katherine Hilliker, H.H. Caldwell; Cast: Charles Farrell, Janet Gaynor, Guinn "Big Boy" Williams, Paul Fix, Hedwig Reicher, Gloria Grey, Hector V. Sarno • A young woman, Mary (Gaynor), is encouraged by her mother (Reicher) to marry Martin (Williams), a soldier returning from the war, who has a decent job. The man Mary really loves, Timothy (Farrell), has come back paralyzed from a war injury and is relegated to menial jobs at home. Just as Mary is about to wed her mother's choice, Timothy struggles to regain his ability to walk. In the end, he marries her. 8,784' (Part-talkie with music and sound effects; also released as a silent)

WORDS AND MUSIC (Aug. 18, 1929); AP: Chandler Sprague; D: James Tinling; W: Frederick Hazlitt Brennan (st), Jack McEdwards (st), Andrew Bennison (dial); C: Charles G. Clarke, Charles Van Enger, Don Anderson; E: Ralph Dixon; Cast: Lois Moran, David Percy, Helen Twelvetrees, William Orlamond, Elizabeth Patterson, Duke Morrison, Ward Bond, Richard Keene, Frank Albertson • Fraternity brothers, Phil Denning (Percy) and Pete Donahue (Morrison), compete to win a popular girl, Mary Brown (Moran), to lead their musical numbers in a college revue. However, Mary plays a practical joke on the dean of women (Patterson) and ruins Pete's chance to win the contest. 6,500' (All-talkie; also released as a silent) • Duke Morrison was an early screen name for John Wayne.

WHY LEAVE HOME? (Aug. 25, 1929); AP: Malcolm Stuart Boylan; D: Raymond Cannon; W: Robert S. Carr (adpt), Walter Catlett (dial), Russell G. Medcraft and Norma Mitchell (play); C: Daniel Clark; E: Jack Murray; Cast: Sue Carol, Nick Stuart, Dixie Lee, Jean Barry, Richard Keene, David Rollins, Jed Prouty, Walter Catlett, Gordon De Main, Ilka Chase, Dot Farley, Laura Hamilton • Three coquettish chorus girls, Mary (Carol), Billie (Lee) and Jackie (Barry), get dates with fraternity brothers, Dick (Stuart), José (Keene) and Oscar (Rollins), instead of seeing stepping-out husbands George (Prouty), Elmer (Catlett) and Roy (De Main). The men's wives, Ethel (Chase), Susan (Farley) and Maude (Hamilton), coincidentally hire the three college boys as escorts and everyone ends up at the same roadhouse. The confusion eventually gets sorted out. 6,388' (All-talkie)

SALUTE (Sept. 1, 1929); D: John Ford; W: James K. McGuinness (scr & dial), Tristram Tupper (st), John Stone (st), Wilbur Morse Jr. (titles); C: Joseph August; E: Alex Troffey; Cast: George O'Brien, Helen Chandler, Frank Albertson, William Janney, Clifford Dempsey, Lumsden Hare, Joyce Compton, David Butler, Stepin Fetchit, Rex Bell, John Breeden, John Wayne, Ward Bond • Army-Navy rivalry between the grandfathers of two military families is played out by brothers, Cadet John Randall (O'Brien), a football player for the Army, and Paul Randall (Janney), on the Annapolis team. Paul decides to leave school after a hazing incident, but is convinced to return by his girlfriend, Nancy Wayne (Chandler). When Paul gets into the Army-Navy football game, the game ends with a 6–6 tie, with both brothers scoring points for each side. 7,610' (All-talkie)

THEY HAD TO SEE PARIS (Sept. 9, 1929); D: Frank Borzage; W: Sonya Levien (scr), Owen Davis (dial), Wilbur Morse Jr. (titles), Homer Croy (novel); C: Chester Lyons, Al Brick; E: Margaret V. Clancey; Cast: Will Rogers, Irene Rich, Owen Davis, Jr., Marguerite Churchill, Fifi D'Orsay, Rex Bell, Ivan Lebedeff, Edgar Kennedy, Bob Kerr, Christiane Yves • An Oklahoma garage owner, Pike Peters (Rogers), strikes it rich in oil and his wife (Rich) insists the family visit Paris. While Mrs. Peters tries to marry off her daughter, Opal (Churchill), to a mercenary Marquis de Brissac (Lebedeff), Pike conjures up a phony affair with a singer, Claudine (Dorsay), to get everyone to return home. 8,602' (All-talkie; also released as a silent) • This was Will Rogers's first talking picture. It was a huge success, paving the way for more productions.

4 DEVILS (Sept. 15, 1929); D: F.W. Murnau; W: Carl Mayer (scr), Berthold Viertel (adpt), Marion Orth (adpt), John Hunter Booth (dial), Herman Joachim

Bang (novel); C: Ernest Palmer. L.W. O'Connell; E: Harold Schuster; Cast: Janet Gaynor, J. Farrell MacDonald, Charles Morton, Nancy Drexel, Anders Randolf, Claire McDowell, Barry Norton, Jack Parker, Philippe De Lacy • The circus trapeze act members, known as the "Four Devils," have been together since childhood. Two members of the group, Charles (Morton) and Marion (Gaynor), are engaged, but while performing in Paris, Charles becomes infatuated with a vamp (Duncan). Working without a net, Marion falls and is not killed, which brings Charles to his senses. (Originally released with music and effects, Oct. 1928; talking sequences were added for the 1929 release.) 9,469' • The original ending in which Marion dies was found to be too downbeat when shown to test audiences and was reshot.

THE GIRL FROM HAVANA (Sept. 22, 1929); D: Benjamin Stoloff; W: John Stone (st), Edwin Burke (titles); C: Joseph A. Valentine; E: Paul Weatherwax; M: S.L. Rothafel; Cast: Lola Lane, Paul Page, Kenneth Thompson, Natalie Moorhead, Warren Hymer, Joseph Girard, Adele Windsor, Marcia Chapman, Dorothy Brown, Juan Sedillo • Female detective Joan (Lane) poses as a chorus girl to capture a gang of jewel thieves. On a steamer to Havana, she falls in love with one of the suspected crooks (Page), who is actually a jeweler's son, tracking down the gang to find his father's murderer. 5,986' (All-talkie; also released as a silent)

BIG TIME (Sept. 29, 1929); AP: Chandler Sprague; D: Kenneth Hawks; W: Sidney Lanfield (adpt & dial), William K. Wells (dial), William Wallace Smith (article); C: L. William O'Connell; E: Al De Gaetano; Cast: Lee Tracy, Mae Clarke, Daphne Pollard, Josephine Dunn, Stepin Fetchit, John Ford • When vaudevillian Lily (Clarke) is having her baby, another woman, Gloria (Dunn) gets into the act with her husband, Eddie (Tracy). While the act is on the downswing, Lily becomes a movie star. Eddie eventually ends up as an extra in a film starring Lily, and the couple reunites. 7,480' (All-talkie; also released as a silent)

THE RIVER (Oct. 6, 1929); D: Frank Borzage; W: Philip Klein (scr), Dwight Cummins (scr), John Hunter Booth (dial), Tristram Tupper (novel); C: Ernest Palmer; E: Barney Wolf; M: Erno Rapée, Maurice Baron; Cast: Charles Farrell, Mary Duncan, Ivan Linow, Margaret Mann, Alfred Sabato, Bert Woodruff • Rosalee (Duncan), the mistress of a jailed murderer, meets a young man, Allen (Farrell), traveling the river on his barge. Rosalee is drawn to his innocence, but when her former lover returns, there is a fight and Allen frees the girl of any previous commitments, whereupon they continue downriver on the barge. 6,536' (Part-talkie with music and sound effects; also released as a silent)

FROZEN JUSTICE (Oct. 13, 1929); W: Allan Dwan; W: Sonya Levien (scr), Owen Davis (dial), Ejnar Mikkelsen (novel); C: Harold Rosson; E: Harold Schuster; Cast: Lenore Ulric, Robert Frazer, Louis Wolheim, Ullrich Haupt, Laska Winter, El Brendel, Tom Patricola, Alice Lake, Adele Windsor, Warren Hymer • A halfcaste, Talu (Ulric), whose mother was Eskimo, leaves her husband, Lanak (Frazer), for Nome with a ruthless trader, Capt. Jones (Haupt). Jones's first mate, Duke (Wolheim), falls in love with Talu and tries to return her to Lanak, but is shot by Jones. Pursued by Lanak in a sled chase, Talu and Jones tumble into a canyon. Jones is killed and Talu dies in her husband's arms. 7,170' (All-talkie; also released as a silent) • The trade ads featured the ballyhoo, "Punctuated with tribal lays and roustabout ballads, this picture has all the gaiety and lust for living of Klondike days where passion sizzled in the frigid air." This was originally announced as a John Ford production.

THE COCK-EYED WORLD (Oct. 20, 1929); D: Raoul Walsh; W: Raoul Walsh (scr), William K. Wells (dial), Wilbur Morse Jr. (titles), based on characters by Laurence Stallings and Maxwell Anderson; C: Arthur Edeson; E: Jack Dennis; Cast: Victor McLaglen, Edmund Lowe, Lily Damita, Lelia Karnelly, El Brendel, Bob Burns, Jeanette Dagna, Joe Brown, Stuart Erwin, Ivan Linow, Jean Barry • The continuing adventures of rivals Quirt (Lowe) and Flagg (McLaglen) take them, and their sidekick Olson (Brendel), from Siberia to Brooklyn to Nicaragua, fighting all the while for the love of Elenita (Damita). 10,611' (All-talkie; also released as a silent)

MARRIED IN HOLLYWOOD (Oct. 27, 1929); D: Marcel Silver; W: Harlan Thompson (adpt & dial), Leopold Jacobson and Bruno Hardt-Warden (play), Oskar Strauss (operetta); C: Charles Van Enger, Sol Halprin; E: Dorothy Spencer; Cast: J. Harold Murray, Norma Terris, Walter Catlett, Irene Palasty, Lennox Pawle, Tom Patricola, Evelyn Hall, John Garrick, Douglas Gilmore, Gloria Grey • The heir to a Balkan throne, Prince Nicholai (Murray), falls in love with an American operetta singer, Mary Lou (Terris), who is touring in Europe. He is about to renounce his position when his mother (Hall) has Mary Lou shipped back home, where she is discovered by a movie producer. Nicholai is forced to leave his country during a revolution and meets up with his love in Hollywood. 9,700' (All-talkie; also released as a silent) Part color

LOVE, LIVE AND LAUGH (Nov. 3, 1929); D: William K. Howard; W: Dana Burnet (scr), Edwin Burke (dial), George Jessel (dial), Leroy Clemens and John B. Hymer (play); C: Lucien Andriot; E: Al De Gaetano; Cast: George Jessel, Lila Lee, David Rollins, Henry Kolker, John Loder, John Reinhardt, Dick Winslow Johnson, Henry Armetta, Marcia Manon, Jerry Mandy • An Italian immigrant in New York, Luigi (Jessel), is called back to Italy and ends up in the war. He is blinded and spends three years in a prison camp before returning to his wife, Margharita (Lee), in America. Thinking Luigi was dead, Margharita has married a doctor (Loder), who cures Luigi's blindness without knowing who he is. When Margharita is about to reveal Luigi's identity to her new husband, Luigi decides to preserve her new life and moves on. 8,090'

A SONG OF KENTUCKY (Nov. 10, 1929); AP: Chandler Sprague; D: Lewis Seiler; W: Frederick Hazlitt Brennan; C: Charles G. Clarke; E: Carl Carruth; Cast: Joseph Wagstaff, Lois Moran, Dorothy Burgess, Douglas Gilmore, Herman Bing, Hedda Hopper, Edwards Davis, Bert Woodruff • A young songwriter, Jerry (Wagstaff), falls in love with a wealthy Southern girl, Lee (Moran), who is being forced to marry fortune hunter Kane Pitcairn (Gilmore). Pitcairn pays Nancy (Burgess), a female former vaudeville partner of Jerry's, to make Lee think he is unfaithful. Returning to Kentucky, Lee is about to marry when she happens upon a concert where Jerry is conducting his symphony. They reconnect and she finds out about the set-up. 7,125' (All-talkie)

ROMANCE OF RIO GRANDE (Nov. 11, 1929); D: Alfred Santell; W: Marion Orth, Katherine Fullerton Gerould (novel); P: Arthur Edeson; E: Paul Weatherwax; Cast: Warner Baxter, Mona Maris, Mary Duncan, Antonio Moreno, Robert Edeson, Agostino Borgato, Albert Roccardi, Soledad Jimenez, Majel Coleman • Pablo (Baxter), the supervisor of a railroad crew, is injured during an attack by bandits and recovers at the ranch of the Mexican grandfather (Edeson) he hates. There, Pablo falls in love with Manuelita (Maris) and has a rival relative for her affection, Juan (Moreno). Pablo eventually makes amends with his grandfather and wins the girl. 8,640' (All-talkie)

NIX ON DAMES (Nov. 24, 1929); AP: George Middleton; D: Donald Gallaher; W: Maude Fulton (scr & dial & st), Frank Gay (st); C: Charles G. Clarke; E: Dorothy Spencer; Cast: Mae Clarke, Robert Ames, William Harrigan, Maude Fulton, George MacFarlane, Frederick Graham, Camille Rovelle, Grace Wallace, Louise Beavers • Two acrobats, Bert (Ames) and Johnny (Harrigan), both of whom hate women, suddenly become rivals when they each fall in love with Jackie (Clarke) at a theatrical boardinghouse. The partners split up over the girl, but eventually reunite. 5,998' (All-talkie)

SEVEN FACES (Dec. 1, 1929); AP: George Middleton; D: Berthold Viertel; W: Dana Burnet, Richard Connell (article); C: Joseph August, Al Brick; E: Edwin Robbins; Cast: Paul Muni, Marguerite Churchill, Lester Lonergan, Russell Gleason, Gustav von Seyffertitz, Eugenie Besserer, Walter Rogers, Walka Stenermann • A caretaker at a Paris wax museum, Papa Chibou (Muni), tries to steal a figure of Napoleon when the museum is sold. He is arrested and brought to trial. Chibou dreams that the beloved historical figures from the museum come to life in his image. Chibou has also been advising lovers Georges, a lawyer (Gleason), and Helene (Churchill), who have been meeting secretly at the museum. Judge Berthelot (Lonergan), who is hearing Chibou's case, is Helene's father and she and Georges appeal to her father for a suspended sentence. They also arrange for him to get the wax figure of Napoleon. 7,750' (All-talkie; also released as a silent) • Paul Muni played seven different roles in the dream sequence, including a prizefighter, Don Juan, Franz Schubert and Napoleon.

SOUTH SEA ROSE (Dec. 8, 1929); D: Allan Dwan; W: Sonya Levien (scr), Elliott Lester (dial), Tom Cushing (play); C: Harold Rosson; E: Harold Schuster; Cast: Lenore Ulric, Charles Bickford, Kenneth MacKenna, Farrell MacDonald, Elizabeth Patterson, Tom Patricola, Ilka Chase, George MacFarlane, Ben Hall, Daphne Pollard • On a South Sea island, an unscrupulous trader, Capt. Briggs (Bickford), tricks an orphan, Rosalie (Ulric), who has a fortune waiting for her in France, into marrying him. Briggs realizes he really loves Rosalie, but almost loses her until she finds out his love is genuine. 6,500' (All-talkie; also released as a silent)

CHRISTINA (Dec. 15, 1929); D: William K. Howard; W: Marion Orth (scr), Tristram Tupper (st), S.K. Lauren (dial), Katherine Hilliker (titles), H.H. Caldwell (titles); C: Lucien Andriot; E: Katherine Hilliker, H.H. Caldwell; Cast: Janet Gaynor, Charles Morton, Rudolph Schildkraut, Harry Cording, Lucy Dorraine • The daughter of a toymaker in Holland, Christina (Gaynor), falls in love with Jan (Morton), a young man in a traveling carnival. The jealous carnival owner, Madame Bosman (Dorraine), does her best to separate the two, but after some time apart, they are romantically reunited. 7,651 (Part-talkie; also released as a silent)

HOT FOR PARIS (Dec. 22, 1929); D: Raoul Walsh; W: Charles J. McGuirk (adpt), Raoul Walsh (st), William K. Wells (dial); C: Charles Van Enger; E: Jack Dennis; Cast: Victor McLaglen, Fifi D'Orsay, El Brendel, Polly Moran, Lennox Pawle, August Tollaire, George Fawcett, Charles Judels, Eddie Dillon, Rosita Marstini • A gruff sailor, John Duke (McLaglen), misinterprets efforts by Paris officials to inform him that he has won the Grand Prix. He has various humorous adventures with his sidekick, Axel (Brendel), before he receives the money, then he celebrates with his French friends, including the seductive Fifi (D'Orsay). 6,570' (All-talkie; also released as a silent)

SUNNY SIDE UP (Dec. 29, 1929); P: David Butler, Buddy G. DaSylva; D: David Butler; W: Buddy G. DaSylva (st & dial), Ray Henderson (st & dial), Lew Brown (st & dial), David Butler (adpt); C: Ernest Palmer; E: Irene Morra; Cast: Janet Gaynor, Charles Farrell, Marjorie White, El Brendel, Mary Forbes, Peter Gawthorne, Sharon Lynn, Henry Armetta, Jackie Cooper (UC) • A department store worker, Molly (Gaynor), meets John (Farrell), a young society man, spending the summer in the Hamptons, at a 4th of July party. Molly, a tenement resident, makes John's flapper girlfriend, Bee (White), jealous and succeeds in winning him. 12,000' (All-talkie; also released as a silent) • The combination of Gaynor and Farrell and popular songs made this early talkie Fox's highest grossing release in the company's history at $3,500,000 in domestic rentals.

1930 Releases

THE LONE STAR RANGER (Jan. 5, 1930); AP: James Kevin McGuinness; D: A.F. Erickson; W: Seton I.

Miller (scr), John Hunter Booth (dial), Zane Grey (novel); C: Daniel P. Clark; E: Jack Murray; Cast: George O'Brien, Sue Carol, Walter McGrail, Warren Hymer, Russell Simpson, Roy Stewart, Lee Shumway, Colin Chase • A cowboy (O'Brien) joins the Texas Rangers to prove himself innocent of various charges against him. He rounds up a gang of cattle rustlers and wins a girl (Carol) from the East, who turns out to be the ringleader's (Simpson) daughter. 5,736' (All-talkie; also released as a silent) • This is a remake of the 1923 version.

CAMEO KIRBY (Jan. 12, 1930); D: Irving Cummings; W: Marion Orth, Booth Tarkington and Harry Leon Wilson (play); C: George Eastman, L. William O'Connell; E: Alex Troffey; M: Edgar Leslie; Cast: J. Harold Murray, Norma Terris, Douglas Gilmore, Robert Edeson, Myrna Loy, Charles Morton, Stepin Fetchit, George MacFarlane, Carrie Daumery • Cameo Kirby (Murray), an honest riverboat gambler, rescues Adele (Terris) and then wins back the deed to her father's plantation. Her father (Edeson), however, thinking he has lost the property, commits suicide. Kirby's reputation has been tarnished in Adele's eyes by a rival gambler (Gilmore), who ends up being killed in a duel, and Kirby is exonerated. 5,910' (All-talkie) • This is a remake of the 1923 version.

HARMONY AT HOME (Jan. 19, 1930); D: Hamilton MacFadden; W: William Collier Sr. (adpt & cont), Clare Kummer (adpt & cont), Charles J. McGuirk (adpt & cont), Seton I. Miller (adpt & cont), Edwin Burke (add'l dial), Elliott Lester (add'l dial), Harry Delf (play); C: Daniel Clark; E: Irene Morra; Cast: Marguerite Churchill, Rex Bell, Charlotte Henry, Charles Eaton, Dixie Lee, William Collier, Sr., Elizabeth Patterson, Dot Farley • Louise, the daughter (Churchill) of henpecked Joe Haller (Collier, Sr.) who has just gotten a promotion, meets a young man (Bell), whom she brings to her parents' home. Her overbearing mother (Henry) continues to make her life miserable until Joe, with new confidence since his promotion, takes the situation in hand. 6,295' (All-talkie)

THE SKY HAWK (Jan. 26, 1930); D: John G. Blystone; W: Llewellyn Hughes (scr & dial & article); C: Conrad Wells; E: Ralph Dietrich; Cast: Helen Chandler, John Garrick, Gilbert Emery, Lennox Pawle, Lumsden Hare, Billy Bevan, Daphne Pollard, Joyce Compton, Percy Challenger • When his plane crashes, a young English pilot (Garrick) is accused of cowardice by everyone except his girlfriend (Allan) and mechanic (Bevan). Although partially paralyzed, he constructs an airplane from wreckages and singlehandedly brings down a German zeppelin. 6,888' (All-talkie)

LET'S GO PLACES (Feb. 2, 1930); D: Frank R. Strayer; W: William K. Wells (scr & dial), Andrew Bennison (st); C: Conrad Wells; E: Al De Gaetano; M: Arthur Kay; Cast: Joseph Wagstaff, Lola Lane, Sharon Lynn, Frank Richardson, Walter Catlett, Dixie Lee, Ilka Chase, Charles Judels, Larry Steers, Betty Grable (UC) • Paul (Wagstaff), a singer sets out for a career in Hollywood while occupying the mansion of a famous opera singer (Judels). He falls in love a girl (Lane) he met en route, but his ruse is upended when the opera singer's wife (Chase) finds out what he's doing. By then, he already has a Hollywood career and turns out to be the famous man's long-lost nephew. 6,442'

MEN WITHOUT WOMEN (Feb. 9, 1930); AP: James Kevin McGuinness; D: John Ford; W: Dudley Nichols (scr & dial), James Kevin McGuinness (st), John Ford (st); C: Joseph H. August; E: Walter Thompson; Cast: Kenneth MacKenna, Frank Albertson, J. Farrell MacDonald, Warren Hymer, Paul Page, Walter MacGrail, Stuart Erwin, George LaGuere, John Wayne (UC) • An American submarine is hit by a freighter and sinks in the China Sea. A British officer (MacKenna), thought to be a coward, brings a ship and remains behind to rescue the last American through a torpedo tube. 7,774' (All-talkie)

CITY GIRL (Feb. 16, 1930); D: F.W. Murnau; W: Berthold Viertel (adpt), Marion Orth (adpt), Elliott Lester (dial & play); C: Ernest Palmer; E: H.H. Caldwell, Katherine Hilliker; Cast: Charles Farrell, Mary Duncan, David Torrence, Edith Yorke, Anne Shirley, Tom McGuire, Richard Alexander, Roscoe Ates • A farmer's son (Farrell), sent to Chicago to sell his wheat crop, meets and marries a waitress (Duncan), to the chagrin of his father (Torrence), who will have nothing to do with her. However, she eventually wins over her father-in-law. 6,171' (Part-talkie; also released as a silent)

THE BIG PARTY (Feb. 23, 1930); D: John G. Blystone; W: Harlan Thompson; C: George Schneiderman; E: J. Edwin Robbins; Cast: Dixie Lee, Walter Catlett, Frank Albertson, Richard Keene, Sue Carol, Douglas Gilmore, Ilka Chase, Elizabeth Patterson • An ambitious five-and-dime clerk, Kitty Collins (Lee), gets a job in a fancy dress shop, where she meets the wealthy owner (Catlett), who makes advances on her. She then returns, penitent, to her old boyfriend, Jack (Albertson), convinced that a poor but honest life is best of all. 6,520' (All-talkie; also released as a silent)

HAPPY DAYS (March 2, 1930); D: Benjamin Stoloff; W: Sidney Lanfield, Edwin J. Burke; C: Lucien Andriot, John Schmitz, J.O. Taylor (Grandeur); E: Clyde Carruth; M: Harry Stoddard; Cast: Janet Gaynor, Charles Farrell, Victor McLaglen, El Brendel, William Collier, Sr., George Jessel, Dixie Lee, Rex Bell, Will Rogers, Edmund Lowe, Walter Catlett, Frank Richardson, Warner Baxter, Charles E. Evans, Marjorie White, Richard Keene, Stuart Erwin, Martha Lee Sparks • Margie (White), a singer on Col. Billy's failing Mississippi showboat, is in love with the colonel's grandson Dick (Keene). To save the showboat, Margie heads to New York and enlists all the famous performers who started out with the colonel. 7,514' (35 mm) All-talkie 35 mm and Grandeur 70 mm • With virtually every star on the Fox Hills lot assigned to appear in this film, all other production work ceased during the second week of October 1929.

SUCH MEN ARE DANGEROUS (March 9, 1930); D: Kenneth Hawks; W: Ernest Vajda, Elinor Glyn; C: George Eastman, L. William O'Connell; E: Harold Schuster; M: George Gramlich, Albert Hay Malotte, Dave Stamper; Cast: Warner Baxter, Catherine Dale Owen, Albert Conti, Hedda Hopper, Claude Allister, Bela Lugosi • A Belgian financier, Ludwic (Baxter), with a disfigured face, marries the beautiful Elinor (Owen). When Elinor, who was forced to marry Ludwic for his wealth, deserts him, he goes to Germany, leaving behind evidence of his suicide. He has plastic surgery to correct his face, then returns to take revenge on his wife. However, he falls in love with her again and forgives the past. 7,400' (All-talkie; also released as a silent) • During the shooting of an aerial scene for this movie on January 2, 1930, a camera plane crashed into another plane over the Pacific, killing director Kenneth Hawks, cameraman Conrad Wells and eight others.

THE GOLDEN CALF (March 16, 1930); AP: Ned Marin; D: Millard Webb; W: Marion Orth (dial), Harold Atteridge (dial), Aaron Davis (article); C: Lucien N. Andriot; E: Alexander Troffey; M: Jimmy Monaco, Cliff Friend; Cast: Jack Mulhall, Sue Carol, El Brendel, Marjorie White, Richard Keene, Paul Page, Walter Catlett, Ilka Chase • A commercial illustrator (Mulhall) places an advertisement in a frantic quest to find the "perfect leg," and inadvertently discovers that the ideal limb belongs to none other than his secretary (Carol), who is in love with him. 6,552'

HIGH SOCIETY BLUES (March 23, 1930); D: David Butler; W: Harold J. Green, David Burnet; C: Charles Van Enger; E: Irene Morra; Cast: Janet Gaynor, Charles Farrell, William Collier, Sr., Hedda Hopper, Joyce Compton, Lucien Littlefield, Louise Fazenda, Brandon Hurst, Gregory Gaye • A millionaire's family moves next door to a pretty young society girl, Eleanor (Gaynor), who is engaged to a French count (Gaye). Her mother (Hopper) is dismayed when she falls for the new neighbor, Eddie (Farrell), instead. Eleanor eventually elopes with her new-found love, embarrassing her mother. 9,328' (All-talkie) • This was a follow-up to the highly successful Farrell/Gaynor film, *Sunnyside Up.*

CRAZY THAT WAY (March 30, 1930); D: Hamilton MacFadden; W: Marion Orth (scr & dial), Hamilton MacFadden (scr & dial), Vincent Lawrence (play); C: Joseph Valentine; E: Ralph Dietrich; Cast: Kenneth MacKenna, Joan Bennett, Regis Toomey, Jason Robards, Sr., Sharon Lynn, Lumsden Hare, Baby Mack • An engaged woman, Ann (Bennett), is pursued wherever she goes by Robert (Toomey), to the consternation of her fiancé, Frank (Robards). Tired of arguing with Frank, and as her other boyfriends fight over her, she falls in love with Jack (MacKenna), a friend of her father's. 5,800' (All-talkie; also released as a silent) • A remake of the 1925 film, *In Love with Love.*

THE THREE SISTERS (Apr. 6, 1930); D: Paul Sloane; W: James K. McGuinness (scr & dial), George S. Brooks (scr & dial), Marion Orth (st); C: L. William O'Connell; M: Abel Baer, L. Wolfe Gilbert; Cast: Louise Dresser, Tom Patricola, Kenneth MacKenna, Joyce Compton, June Collyer, Addie McPhail, Clifford Saum, Sidney De Gray, Paul Porcasi • An Italian mother, Marta (Dresser), faces hardships as a result of her three daughters: Carlotta (Compton) stabs a banker and escapes with her sister Antonia (McPhail); and Elena (Collyer) marries a count (MacKenna), but dies in childbirth. When the count is killed in the war, Marta has to give up the child, and ends up as a dishwasher. She is finally rescued from poverty by her other daughters, Carlotta and Antonia, who have prospered in America. 6,442' (All-talkie; also released as a silent) • Yet another variation on the 1921 melodramatic hit, *Over the Hill to the Poorhouse.*

TEMPLE TOWER (Apr. 13, 1930); D: Donald Gallaher; W: Llewellyn Hughes (adpt & dial), Herman Cyril McNeile (novel); C: Charles G. Clarke; E: Clyde Carruth; Cast: Kenneth MacKenna, Marceline Day, Henry B. Walthall, Cyril Chadwick, Peter Gawthorne, Ivan Linow, Frank Lanning, Yorke Sherwood • Bulldog Drummond (MacKenna) goes after a notorious criminal (Walthall), who, hidden under a mask, avenges members of his gang who have double-crossed him. 5,200' (All-talkie; also released as a silent)

DOUBLE CROSS ROADS (Apr. 20, 1930); D: George Middleton, Alfred L. Werker; W: Howard Estabrook (scr & dial), George S. Brooks (adpt), William R. Lipman (novel); C: Joseph H. August, Sol Halprin; E: Jack Dennis; Cast: Robert Ames, Lila Lee, Edythe Chapman, Montagu Love, Ned Sparks, Thomas E. Jackson, Charlotte Walker • David (Ames), an ex-convict, goes straight and falls in love with Mary (Lee). He is convinced by his old mob to pull off a jewel robbery. Mary, who turns out to be part of the gang, wants David let go after the robbery, but is double crossed. Another gang horns in on the spoils and both shoot it out from speeding cars, ultimately clearing the way for David and Mary. 5,800' (All-talkie; also released as a silent)

THE ARIZONA KID (Apr. 27, 1930); D: Alfred Santell; W: Joseph Wright, Ralph Block; C: Glen MacWilliams; E: Paul Weatherwax; Cast: Warner Baxter, Mona Maris, Carole Lombard, Theodore von Eltz, Hank Mann, Wilfred Lucas, James Gibson • The Kid (Baxter) is a bandit hero with many girlfriends. His romance is sidelined by an attractive Eastern girl, Virginia (Lombard), who is in league with her crooked brother, Nick (von Eltz), to raid the Kid's mine. When two of his workers are killed, his Mexican girlfriend, Lorita (Maris), helps him bring the culprits to a showdown. 7,902' (All-talkie; also released as a silent)

FOX MOVIETONE FOLLIES OF 1930 (May 4, 1930); AP: Al Rockett; D: Benjamin Stoloff; W: William K. Wells; C: L. William O'Connell; E: Milton Carruth; Cast: El Brendel, Marjorie White, Frank Richardson, William Collier, Jr., Miriam Seegar, Paul Nicholson, Huntley Gordon, Betty Grable (UC) • A rich man's do-nothing nephew, Conrad (Collier, Jr.), who secretly loves showgirls, gets his actress girlfriend Mary (Seegar) to keep a date by hiring her group to put on a show at his uncle's estate. Complications ensue for him when his valet, Axel (Brendel), tries to pass himself off as a millionaire. 7,522' (All-talkie)

BORN RECKLESS (May 11, 1930); AP: James K. McGuinness; D: John Ford; W: Dudley Nichols, Donald Henderson Clarke (novel); C: George Schneiderman; E: Frank E. Hull; M: Peter Brunelli, George Lipschultz, Albert Hay Malotte, Jean Talbot; Cast: Edmund Lowe, Catherine Dale Owen, Lee Tracy, Marguerite Churchill, Warren Hymer, Pat Somerset, William Harrigan, Randolph Scott (UC), John Wayne (UC) • Italian gangster Louis Beretti (Lowe), sent to fight in the war after being charged with robbery, returns and opens a nightclub. He gets back in with a gang when Big Shot (Hymer) settles his account with Ritzy Reiller (Page), who squealed on him. Later, Beretti rescues friend Jean Sheldon's (Owen) kidnapped child and is killed in the ensuing shoot-out. 7,400' (All-talkie; also released as a silent)

ON THE LEVEL (May 18, 1930); AP: James K. McGuinness; D: Irving Cummings; W: William K. Wells (scr & dial & st), Andrew Bennison (scr & st & dial), Dudley Nichols (adpt); C: L. William O'Connell, Dave Ragin; E: Alfred DeGaetano; Cast: Victor McLaglen, William Harrigan, Lilyan Tashman, Fifi D'Orsay, Arthur Stone, Leila McIntyre, Mary McAllister, Ben Hewlett • An iron riveter, Biff (McLaglen), falls for Lynn (Tashman), a glamorous decoy for racketeers. Lynn convinces Biff to sell phony options on a property to his friends. When he realizes what they have done, he overtakes the racketeers, returns the money and returns to his honest girlfriend, Mimi (D'Orsay). 5,815' (All-talkie; also released as a silent)

NOT DAMAGED (May 25, 1930); D: Chandler Sprague; W: Frank Gay (adpt & cont), Harold Atteridge (dial), Richard Connell (article); C: Chester Lyons; E: Alexander Troffey; Cast: Lois Moran, Walter Byron, Robert Ames, Inez Courtney, George Corcoran, Rhoda Cross, Ernest Wood • Gwen (Moran), a sales clerk engaged to the floorwalker at a department store, Charlie (Ames), falls for the less than honorable but wealthy Kirk (Byron). While making plans with her fiancé for their future, she ends up spending the night in Kirk's bed. However, Kirk insists he spent the night in another room, assuring her nothing untoward occurred. 6,500' • From this release on, Fox made all-talking films without silent versions.

WOMEN EVERYWHERE (June 1, 1930); AP: Ned Marin; D: Alexander Korda; W: Lajos Biro (scr & dial), Harlan Thompson (scr & dial), George Grossmith (st), Zoltan Korda (st); C: Ernest Palmer; E: Harold Schuster; Cast: J. Harold Murray, Fifi D'Orsay, George Grossmith, Clyde Cook, Ralph Kellard, Rose Dione, Walter McGrail • Charlie Jackson (Murray), a gun runner in Morocco, loves cabaret singer Lili (D'Orsay). When he escapes from the police, he hides out in her dressing room. Lili disguises him as a Legionnaire, but he is caught again and is sent to the desert to fight Arabs. Charlie later returns and wins Lili's admiration. 7,500'

SO THIS IS LONDON (June 8, 1930); D: John G. Blystone; W: Sonya Levien (scr), Owen Davis (adpt & dial), Arthur F. Goodrich (novel); C: Charles G. Clarke; E: Jack Dennis; M: James F. Hanley; Cast: Will Rogers, Irene Rich, Frank Albertson, Maureen O'Sullivan, Lumsden Hare, Mary Forbes, Bramwell Fletcher • A wealthy Texan (Rogers) who hates the stuffy English, visits London where his son (Albertson) falls in love with a well-bred girl (O'Sullivan). The son tries to have his parents make a good impression on the girl's mother (Forbes) and father (Hare), a Lord and Lady, but the uncouth Texan is incorrigible. When he meets his son's girlfriend he realizes he has been wrong. 8,300'

ROUGH ROMANCE (June 15, 1930); D: A.F. Erickson; W: Elliott Lester (scr), Donald Davis (dial), Kenneth B. Clarke (article); C: Dan Clark; E: Paul Weatherwax; M: Johnny Burke, George A. Little; Cast: George O'Brien, Helen Chandler, Antonio Moreno, Roy Stewart, Harry Cording, David Hartford, Eddie Borden, Frank Lanning • Interspersed with songs, this is the story of two Oregon lumberjacks: Billy West (O'Brien), who is honest a hard worker, and Loup Latour (Moreno), a menacing desperado. 4,800'

CHEER UP AND SMILE (June 22, 1930); AP: Al Rockett; D: Sidney Lanfield; W: Richard J. Green, Richard Connell (article); C: Joseph A. Valentine; E: Ralph Dietrich; Cast: Dixie Lee, Arthur Lake, Olga Baclanova, "Whispering" Jack Smith, Johnny Arthur, Charles Judels, John Darrow, Sumner Getchell, Franklin Pangborn • College student Eddie Fripp (Lake), expelled because of a fraternity prank, leaves his girlfriend, Margie (Lee), and heads to New York, where he gets a job as a nightclub singer. He proves to be a sensation. Margie comes to New York, and, after some complications, she marries him. 5,730'

GOOD INTENTIONS (June 29, 1930); D: William K. Howard; W: George Mankers Watters (scr), William K. Howard (st & dial); C: George Schneiderman; E: Jack Murray; Cast: Edmund Lowe, Marguerite Churchill, Regis Toomey, Earle Foxe, Eddie Gribbon, Robert McWade, Georgia Caine, J. Carrol Naish • David Cresson (Lowe), a gentleman in society circles, is really a thief. He romances Helen Rankin (Churchill) who has no idea about his real nature. When Helen's innocent boyfriend (Toomey) is taken hostage by another thief (Foxe), David sacrifices his life for him. 6,340'

WILD COMPANY (July 6, 1930); AP: Al Rockett; D: Leo McCarey; W: Bradley King (adpt & dial), John Stone (st), Philip Hurn (novel); C: L. William O'Connell; E: Clyde Carruth; M: Cliff Friend, Jack Meskill, Jimmy Monaco; Cast: H.B. Warner, Frank Albertson, Sharon Lynn, Joyce Compton, Claire McDowell, Mildred Van Dorn, Richard Keene, Kenneth Thomson, Bela Lugosi • Larry (Albertson), the son of an influential citizen (Warner), gets involved with a racketeer (Thomson) through a seductive singer (Lynn) he meets at a speakeasy. After a roadhouse robbery, Larry's father gets him to confess that the culprits were his girlfriend and the mobster. 6,666'

ONE MAD KISS (July 13, 1930); D: James Tinling, Marcel Silver; W: Dudley Nichols (adpt & dial), Adolf Paul (st); C: Ross Fisher, Charles Van Enger; E: Louis Loeffler; M: William Kernell, José Mojica, Dave Stamper; Cast: José Mojica, Mona Maris, Antonio Moreno, Tom Patricola • A Spanish outlaw (Mojica) clashes with the governor (Moreno), who has designs on a dancehall girl (Maris). When the outlaw is arrested, the girl feigns affection for the governor and smuggles in a gun, allowing an escape for the man she really loves. 5,786'

COMMON CLAY (Aug. 17, 1930); D: Victor Fleming; W: Jules Furthman, Cleves Kinkead (novel); C: Glen MacWilliams; E: Irene Morra; M: Arthur Kay; Cast: Constance Bennett, Lew Ayres, Tully Marshall, Matty Kemp, Purnell Pratt, Beryl Mercer, Charles McNaughton, Hale Hamilton, Genevieve Blinn • After being arrested in a nightclub raid, Ellen Neal (Bennett) starts a new life as a maid for a prominent family. She has an affair with the young son (Ayres), which results in a child. When she refuses to turn over the child, the family investigates her past and discovers that she is illegitimate. She ultimately turns out to be the daughter of the family's lawyer. 7,961'

MAN TROUBLE (Aug. 24, 1930); D: Berthold Viertel; W: George Manker Watters (adpt & dial), Edwin Burke (dial), Marion Orth (adpt), Ben Ames William (article); C: Joseph August; E: J. Edwin Robbins; M: R.H. Bassett, Richard Fall, Emil Gerstenberger, Glen Knight (all UC); Cast: Milton Sills, Dorothy Mackaill, Kenneth MacKenna, Sharon Lynn, Roscoe Karns, Oscar Apfel, James Bradbury, Jr., Harvey Clark, Edythe Chapman, Lew Harvey • A New York bootlegger, Mac (Sills), saves a down-and-out singer, Joan (Mackaill), and gives her a job in his club. Although grateful to him, Joan becomes romantically involved with George (MacKenna), a newspaper columnist. Jealous at first, Mac ends up fatally wounded in a shoot-out and gives Joan his blessing to marry George. 7,800'

DEL MISMO BARRO (Aug. 24, 1930) Spanish version — Common Clay; P: John Stone; D: David Howard; W: Jules Furthman (scr), Cleves Kinkead (novel), Francisco More de la Torre (Spanish version); C: Ross Fisher; E: Louis R. Loeffler; Cast: Mona Maris, Juan Torena, Luana Alcañiz, Rene Cardona, Carlos Villarías, Vicente Padula, Roberto E. Guzman, Maria Calvo, Rafael Valverde. • 93 min.

LAST OF THE DUANES (Aug. 31, 1930); AP: Edward Butcher, Harold B. Lipsitz; D: Alfred L. Werker; W: Ernest Pascal, Zane Grey (novel); C: Daniel B. Clark; E: Ralph Dietrich; Cast: George O'Brien, Lucille Brown, Myrna Loy, Walter McGrail, Clara Blandick, James Bradbury, Jr., Frank Campeau, Natalie Kingston, Nat Pendleton (UC) • A cowboy (O'Brien) breaks a promise to his mother to hang up his guns and takes off after the man who killed his father. He escapes the posse then helps a cattle rustler (McGrail) rescue a girl (Brown) and rounds up the band of outlaws. 5,500' • This is a remake of the 1924 Tom Mix version, with songs added.

SONG O' MY HEART (Sept. 7, 1930); D: Frank Borzage; W: Sonya Levien (cont), Tom Barry (st & dial); C: Al Brick, Chester A. Lyons, J.O. Taylor (Grandeur); E: Margaret V. Clancey; Cast: John McCormack, Maureen O'Sullivan, John Garrick, J.M. Kerrigan, Alice Joyce, Tommy Clifford, J. Farrell McDonald, Effie Elsher • A talented singer (McCormack) in an Irish village, who gave up his career when the woman he loved married a wealthy man, finds happiness in being able to help her children when their father deserts them. 7,740' • Borzage spent six weeks shooting scenes in Ireland with McCormack. This film was photographed in the Grandeur 70 mm format, but was inexplicably released only in standard 35 mm prints.

ON YOUR BACK (Sept. 14, 1930); AP: George Middleton; D: Guthrie McClintic; W: Howard J. Green, Rita Weiman (article); C: Joseph August; E: Frank Hull; Cast: Irene Rich, Raymond Hackett, H.B. Warner, Wheeler Oakman, Marion Shilling, Ilka Chase, Charlotte Henry • On the advice of a gambler (Oakman), Julianne (Rich) has her broker, Raymond (Warner), set up a usurious loan business. Through her fashionable Fifth Avenue salon, she extends credit to struggling showgirls. One of those girls, Jeanne (Shilling), who is having an affair with Raymond, becomes engaged to Julianne's son, Harvey (Hackett), a college student. To break up the relationship, Julianne calls in Jeanne's loan and threatens to expose Jeanne's affair to Harvey. Jeanne counters with the threat of an exposé of Julianne's illegal sideline business. Julianne relents and accepts Jeanne as a daughter-in-law. 6,600'

THE SEA WOLF (Sept. 21, 1930); D: Alfred Santell; W: Ralph Block (scr), S.N. Behrman (dial), Jack London (novel); C: Glen MacWilliams; E: Paul Weatherwax; Cast: Milton Sills, Jane Keithley, Raymond Hackett, Mitchell Harris, Nat Pendleton, John Rogers, Harold Kinney • Fearsome Captain Wolf Larsen (Sills) is unable to attract prostitute Lorna Marsh (Keith) to his ship until he shanghais Allen Rand (Hackett), the man she loves. Larsen treats Rand badly at first, but eventually promotes him. When a rival ship attacks, Larsen is badly injured and overcomes his jealousy to let the couple escape. 8,000' • This was another version of the London classic, made only four years after the 1926 Ralph Ince version. It was also Milton Sills's last film. He suffered a heart attack and died at age 48.

EL ÚLTIMO DE LOS VARGAS (Sept. 21, 1930) Spanish version — Last of the Duanes; P: Edward Butcher, William Goetz, Harold B. Lipsitz; D: David Howard; W: Francisco More de la Torre, Ernest Pascal, Zane Grey (novel); C: Sidney Wagner; Cast: Jorge Lewis, Luana Alcañiz, Vicente Padula, Carmen Rodriguez, Christina Montt, Martin Garralaga, Juan de Landa, Max Wagner, Hipolito Mora. • 61 min.

SOUP TO NUTS (Sept. 28, 1930); P: A. L. Rockett; D: Benjamin Stoloff; W: Rube Goldberg (scr & st & dial),

Howard J. Green (scr); C: Joseph A. Valentine; E: Clyde Carruth; M: Cliff Friend, James Monaco; Cast: Ted Healy, Frances McCoy, Stanley Smith, Lucile Browne, Charles Winninger, Hallam Cooley, William H. Tooker, Larry Fine, Moe Howard, Curly Howard • There is little coherence in this attempt to translate Rube Goldberg's comics to the movies. There are vaudeville-style gags about inept firemen but the real interest is in the first screen appearance of Ted Healy and his Stooges. 6,340'

LILIOM (Oct. 5, 1930); D: Frank Borzage; W: S.N. Behrman (scr & dial), Sonya Levien (cont), Ferenc Molnar (play); C: Chester Lyons; E: Margaret Clancey; M: Richard Fall; Cast: Charles Farrell, Rose Hobart, Estelle Taylor, H.B. Warner, Lee Tracy, Walter Abel, Mildred Van Dorn, Lillian Elliott, Guinn "Big Boy" Williams, Anne Shirley • A Hungarian merry-go-round barker, Liliom (Farrell), marries Julie (Hobart) and robs a bank cashier to provide for his baby. Liliom kills himself when the robbery fails and he's taken to Heaven, where he is given another ten years on earth, unrecognizable as his former self. Liliom eventually realizes Julie and his daughter will be happiest only if he leaves them. 8,472' • This story was remade by Fox in a more critically successful French version in 1934, starring Charles Boyer and directed by Fritz Lang.

EL BARBERO DE NAPOLEON (Oct. 5, 1930) Spanish version — Napoleon's Barber; D: Sidney Lanfield; W: Arthur Caesar; Cast: Juan Aristi Eulate, Nelly Fernandez, Manuel Paris

UP THE RIVER (Oct. 12, 1930); D: John Ford; W: Maurine Dallas Watkins; C: Joseph H. August; E: Frank E. Hull; Cast: Spencer Tracy, Claire Luce, Warren Hymer, Humphrey Bogart, William Collier, Sr., Joan Marie Lawes, George MacFarlane, Morgan Wallace • Steve (Bogart), a convict out on parole, returns to his home in New England. Con man Frosby (Wallace) coerces him to co-operate in swindling his mother out of some bonds, or have his background exposed. Steve reluctantly goes along. However, two prison buddies, St. Louis (Tracy) and Dan (Hymer), break out during the annual prison show and return the stolen goods to Steve's mother. 8,280'

SCOTLAND YARD (Oct. 19, 1930); P: Ralph Block; D: William K. Howard; W: Garret Fort, Denison Clift (play); C: George Schneiderman; E: Jack Murray; M: Hugo Friedhofer, Emil Gerstenberger, Arthur Kay, Glen Knight; Cast: Edmund Lowe, Joan Bennett, Donald Crisp, Georges Renavent, Lumsden Hare, David Torrence, Barbara Leonard, Halliwell Hobbes (UC), J. Carrol Naish (UC) • Criminal Dakin Barrolles (Lowe) escapes Scotland Yard detectives and joins the army. He is badly wounded in France, and his face is restored to resemble a wealthy Englishman, Sir John Lasher (Lowe), who has been killed. He uses his new identity to rob the family's wealth, but falls in love with Xandra (Bennett), who was married to his alter ego. 6,750'

EL VALIENTE (Oct. 26, 1930) Spanish version — The Valiant; P: John Stone; D: Richard Harlan; W: John Hunter (scr), Salvador Martin (Spanish version), Francisco More de la Torre (Spanish version), Manuel Paris (Spanish version), Paul Perez (Spanish version), Halworthy Hall & Robert Middlemass (play); C: Sidney Wagner; Cast: Juan Torena, Angelita Benitez, Carlos Villarías, Maria Calvo, Ralph Navarro, Rafael Callol, Max Wagner, Juan de Landa, Julio Villareal, Jacinto Jaramillo. 8 reels

RENEGADES (Oct. 26, 1930); D: Victor Fleming; W: Jules Furthman, Andre Armandy (novel); C: L. William O'Connell; E: Harold D. Schuster; M: R.H. Bassett, Emil Gerstenberger, Arthur Kay, George Lipschultz, Albert Hay Malotte, Jean Talbot (all UC); Cast: Warner Baxter, Myrna Loy, Noah Beery, Gregory Gaye, George Cooper, C. Henry Gordon, Colin Chase, Bela Lugosi, Noah Beery, Jr. (UC), Victor Jory (UC) • Four rebellious French legionnaires, Deucalion (Baxter), Machwurth (Beery), Biloxi (Cooper) and Vologuine (Gaye), escape and win military honors for bravery. Deucalion later becomes leader of an Arab tribe, kidnaps his disloyal ex-lover, Eleanore (Loy), and treats her as a servant. When the tribe plans an attack on Deucalion's old fort, he saves his former fellow officers by sacrificing his own life. 8,400'

THE BIG TRAIL (Nov. 2, 1930); P: Raoul Walsh; D: Raoul Walsh; W: Jack Peabody (scr & dial), Marie Boyle (scr & dial), Florence Postal (scr & dial), Fred Serser (scr), Hal G. Evarts (st); C: (35 mm version) Lucien Andriot, Don Anderson, Bill McDonald, Roger Sherman, Bobby Mack, Henry Pollack, (Grandeur 70 mm) Arthur Edeson, Dave Ragin, Sol Halprin, Curt Fetters, Max Cohn, Harry Smith, L. Kunkel, Harry Dawe; E: Jack Dennis; M: Arthur Kay; Cast: John Wayne, Marguerite Churchill, El Brendel, Tully Marshall, Tyrone Power, Sr., David Rollins, Frederick Burton, Ian Keith, Russ Powell, Charles Stevens • A wagon train of pioneers, led by scout Breck Coleman (Wayne), travels west along the Oregon Trail. Enamored of Ruth Cameron, Breck wins her love from rival Bill Thorpe (Keith) and gets even with Red Flack (Power), who killed his friend. 11,314' (35 mm) • This was the final production filmed in the Grandeur process.

THE DANCERS (Nov. 9, 1930); D: Chandler Sprague; W: Edwin J. Burke (adpt), George DuMaurier and Viola Tree (play); C: Arthur Todd; E: Alex Troffey; Cast: Lois Moran, Phillips Holmes, Walter Byron, Mae Clarke, Tyrell Davis, Mrs. Patrick Campbell • Three childhood friends in Canada go their own way in adult life. Diana (Moran) pursues a thrill-seeking career as a nightclub dancer, while Maxine (Clarke) becomes a professional dancer. The male of the group, Tony (Holmes), returns to England and becomes a lord, but his passion for the fast-living Diana is not fulfilled. Diana later admits that their childhood vow of love and honor has been violated. Tony ends up marrying the more down-to-earth Maxine. 7,500' • A remake of the 1925 movie of the same title, with the setting changed from South America to Canada.

A DEVIL WITH WOMEN (Nov. 16, 1930); AP: George Middleton; D: Irving Cummings; W: Henry Johnson, Dudley Nichols, Clements Ripley (article); C: Al Brick, Arthur L. Todd; E: Jack Murray; Cast: Victor McLaglen, Mona Maris, Humphrey Bogart, Luana Alcañiz, Michael Vavitch, Soledad Jimenez, Mona Rico, John St. Polis, Robert Edeson • An American captain, Jerry Maxton (McLaglen), a military hero in a Central American republic, is assigned to capture the notorious bandit Morloff (Vavitch). He teams up with an annoying friend, Tom (Bogart), and they become rivals for the same woman, Rosita (Maris). They make amends after being rescued from a firing squad by Rosita. Jerry then leaves Tom with Rosita. 5,750

JUST IMAGINE (Nov. 23, 1930); AP: Lew Brown, Buddy G. DeSylva, Ray Henderson; D: David Butler; W: DeSylva, Brown & Henderson (st & dial), David Butler (cont); C: Ernest Palmer; E: Irene Morra; Cast: El Brendel, Maureen O'Sullivan, John Garrick, Marjorie White, Frank Albertson, Hobart Bosworth, Kenneth Thomson, Mischa Auer, Ivan Linow, Joyzelle Joyner • A man (Brendel), hit by lightning in 1930, awakens in 1980 in time to become involved with a young aviator (Garrick), trying to prove himself by piloting a rocket ship to Mars, accompanied by his girlfriend (O'Sullivan). 10,200'

LIGHTNIN' (Dec. 7, 1930); P: John Golden, Henry King; D: Henry King; W: S.H. Behrman, Sonya Levien, Frank Bacon (play), Winchell Smith (play); C: Chester A. Lyons; E: Louis R. Loeffler; M: Arthur Kay; Cast: Will Rogers, Louise Dresser, Joel McCrea, Helen Cohan, Jason Robards Sr., Luke Cosgrove, J.M. Kerrigan, Ruth Warren, Sharon Lynn, Joyce Compton, Rex Bell • A slow-moving man, Lightnin' Bill Jones (Rogers), who owns a hotel, half in California and half in Nevada, is great at giving people advice. He's called to account in court when his wife (Dresser) sues him for divorce and her lawyer calls Jones a liar. Lightnin' interrogates the attorney and uses his smarts to turn the tables and win everyone's affection. 8,500' • This is a remake of the 1925 film of the same title.

OH, FOR A MAN (Dec. 14, 1930); D: Hamilton McFadden; W: Philip Klein, Lynn Starling, Mary T. Watkins (article); C: Charles G. Clarke; E: Alfred DeGaetano; M: Arthur Kay; Cast: Jeanette MacDonald, Reginald Denny, Warren Hymer, Marjorie White, Alison Skipworth, Albert Conti, Bela Lugosi, Andre Cheron, William B. Davidson • An opera singer, Carlotta (MacDonald), catches burglar Barney (Denny) in the act and thinks that he has possibilities for a singing career. However, he has little talent and realizes Carlotta is in love with him. They marry and move to Italy, where Barney is unhappy and leaves Carlotta. She returns to New York, performs poorly and Barney shows up again and encourages her to do better. 7,800'

THE PRINCESS AND THE PLUMBER (Dec. 21, 1930); P: Al Rockett; D: Alexander Korda, John G. Blystone (UC); W: Howard J. Green (scr & dial), Alice Duer Miller (article); C: L. William O'Connell, Dave Ragin; E: Margaret Clancey; M: Arthur Kay; Cast: Charles Farrell, Maureen O'Sullivan, H.B. Warner, Joseph Cawthorn, Bert Roach, Lucien Prival, Murray Kinnell, Louise Closser Hale, Arnold Lucy • An unsophisticated princess, Louisa (O'Sullivan), is visiting Switzerland with a baron (Prival) and a rich young American, Albert (Roach). Albert rescues her from the baron's advances, but the latter spreads a rumor to her father (Warner) that Albert has despoiled her. Her father demands that the couple marry, which is fine with them, since they have fallen in love. 6,480'

PART TIME WIFE (Dec. 28, 1930); D: Leo McCarey; W: Howard J. Green, Leo McCarey, Raymond L. Schrock, Stewart Edward White (article); C: George Schneiderman; E: Jack Murray; Cast: Edmund Lowe, Leila Hyams, Tommy Clifford, Walter McGrail, Louis Payne, Sam Lufkin, Bodil Rosing, George Corcoran, Bill Elliott (UC), George Irving (UC) • An oil tycoon, Jim Murdock (Lowe), splits up with his wife, Betty (Hyams), because she prefers playing golf. By chance, Jim's doctor recommends golf for his health and he later understands why his marriage failed. When Jim is accidentally matched with Betty on the course, reconciliation occurs. 6,500'

1931 Releases

IL GRANDE SENTIERO (Jan. 1, 1931) Italian version — The Big Trail; D: Louis Loeffler-Franco Corsaro, Luisa Caselotti, Guido Trento, Franco Puglia, Agostino Borgato, Lucino Garuffi, Violet Galeotti • This is the Italian version of The Big Trail.

LA PISTE DES GÉANTS (Jan. 1, 1931) French version — The Big Trail; D: Pierre Couderc; Cast: Gaston Glass, Jeanne Helbling, Margot Rousseroy, Raoul Paoli

UNDER SUSPICION (Jan. 4, 1931); AP: James K. McGuinness; D: A.F. Erickson; W: Tom Barry; C: George Schneiderman; E: J. Edwin Robbins; Cast: J. Harold Murray, Lois Moran, J.M. Kerrigan, Marie Saxon, Lumsden Hare, George Brent, Erwin Connelly, Rhoda Cross, Vera Gerald, Herbert Bunston • In the Canadian Northwest after the World War, Alice Freil (Moran) stands up for a shadowy ace pilot, John Smith (Murray), who rescues her when her canoe is heading for the rapids. Inspector Turner (Brent) is jealous of Smith and becomes suspicious when he discovers a dishonorable war record. It is later revealed, after Smith does some ace flying to rescue Alice's father (Hare), that the only stain on his record was trying to keep his brother free from blame in a wartime incident. 64 min.

THE MAN WHO CAME BACK (Jan. 11, 1931); D: Raoul Walsh; W: Edwin Burke (scr), John Fleming Wilson (novel), Jules Eckert Goodman (play); C: Arthur Edeson; E: Harold Schuster; Janet Gaynor, Charles Farrell, Kenneth MacKenna, William Holden, Mary Forbes, Ullrich Haupt, William Worthington, Peter Gawthorne, Leslie Fenton • Stephen (Farrell), the wastrel son of a New York millionaire, Thomas Randolph (Holden), has been cut off from his family's money and is in love with Angie (Gaynor), a cabaret singer who promises to follow him anywhere. To teach Stephen a lesson, his father has him shanghaied and taken to China. Angie follows and pretends to be hooked on opium to get Stephen back into her life. They move to Hawaii where Angie "wins the affection" of Captain Trevelyan (MacKenna) who has been sent by Stephen's father to confirm Angie's fidelity to Stephen. Thomas invites the couple to return to New York and the family. 87 min.

MEN ON CALL (Jan. 18, 1931); D: John Blystone; W: James K. McGuinness, Basil Woon; C: Charles Clarke, Glen MacWilliams; E: Paul Weatherwax; Cast: Edmund Lowe, Mae Clarke, William Harriman, Sharon Lynn, Warren Hymer, Ruth Warren, Leon Worth, Eric Mack, George Magrill, Tom Shirley, Stanley Blystone • Distraught over his girlfriend, Helen (Clarke), previously involved in a scandalous divorce, Chuck (Lowe), a railroad engineer, wrecks his train. He later joins the Coast Guard, befriends Cap (Harrigan), and, when they rescue a drowning woman, it turns out to be Helen. She explains that she was guiltless in the divorce, but Chuck makes her leave anyway. Cap and Chuck have it out over her departure, but Chuck later rescues Cap from a freighter fire. Helen shows up again and Chuck realizes that he loves her. 66 min.

ONCE A SINNER (Jan. 25, 1931); D: Guthrie McClintic; W: George Middleton; C: Arthur L. Todd; E: Ralph Dietrich; Cast: Dorothy Mackaill, Joel McCrea, John Halliday, C. Henry Gordon, Ilka Chase, Sally Blane, Nadia Faro, Clara Blandick, Myra Hampton, George Brent, Theodore Lodi • Diana (Mackaill), a New York society woman, marries small-town inventor Tommy (McCrea). Their marriage is disrupted when Tommy suspects a New York investor (Halliday) of being Diana's former lover. After they separate, Diana goes to Paris and is romanced by a notorious womanizer (Gordon). Tommy shows up, and, after some misunderstandings, he and Diana are reconciled. 70 min.

FAIR WARNING (Feb. 1, 1931); P: Harold B. Lipsitz, Edmund Grainger; D: Alfred L. Werker; W: Ernest Pascal, Max Brand (novel); C: Ross Fisher; Cast: George O'Brien, Louise Huntington, George Brent, Mitchell Harris, Nat Pendleton, John Sheehan, Eric Connelly, Willard Robertson, Alphonse Ethier, Ernest Adams • Dan (O'Brien), a cowboy with a soft spot for wild animals, gets into a bar fight when the till is being robbed by a gang headed by Lee Haines (Brent). Dan is later thought to be dead after being caught in a fire, but is rescued by a horse and dog that he had tamed. Dan then teams up with the marshal (Robertson) to capture the gang that has kidnapped Kate (Huntington), his sweetheart. 62 min. • This is a remake of the Brand novel *The Untamed*, which was filmed in 1920, and starred Tom Mix.

GIRLS DEMAND EXCITEMENT (Feb. 8, 1931); P: Ralph Block; D: Seymour Felix; W: Harlan Thompson; C: Charles Clarke; E: Jack Murray; Cast: Virginia Cherrill, John Wayne, Marguerite Churchill, Edward Nugent, Helen Jerome Eddy, Terrance Ray, Martha Sleeper, William Janney, Ralph Welles, George Irving • A battle of the sexes erupts at a college where Peter (Wayne), president of the Spartan Club, is trying to return the school to men only, while his on-again off-again girlfriend, Joan (Cherrill), rallies for the girls. Hijinks occur as both try to win the vote for their side. It all climaxes with a male-versus-female basketball game. Romance blossoms anew for the couple and the school stays co-ed. 66 min.

LA GRAN JORNADA (Feb. 13, 1931) Spanish version — *The Big Trail*; SP: William Goetz; D: David Howard; W: Hal G. Evarts (st), Francisco Moré de la Torre (Spanish version); C: Sidney Wagner; E: Jerry Webb; Cast: Jorge Lewis, Carmen Guerrero, Roberto Guzman, Martin Garralaga, Allan Garcia, Charles Stevens, Tito Davison, Carlos Villarías, Adriana Delano, Julio Villareal

DON'T BET ON WOMEN (Feb. 15, 1931); P: John W. Considine, Jr.; D: William K. Howard; W: Lynn Starling (scr & dial), Leon Gordon (scr & dial), William Anthony McGuire (st); C: Lucien Andriot; E: Harold Schuster; Cast: Edmund Lowe, Jeanette MacDonald, Roland Young, J.M. Kerrigan, Una Merkel, Helene Millard, Henry Kolker, Louise Beavers • Divorced Roger Fallon (Lowe), who fends off women, has a $10,000 bet with his friend Drake (Young) that he can kiss the first woman who enters their yacht within 48 hours. The woman turns out to be Drake's faithful wife, Jeanne (MacDonald), who learns of the bet and decides to take advantage of the situation. After flirting with Roger, she returns to her husband. 70 min.

BODY AND SOUL (Feb. 22, 1931); D: Alfred Santell; W: Jules Furthman, Elliott White Springs and A.E. Thomas (short story); C: Glen MacWilliams; E: Paul Weatherwax; Cast: Charles Farrell, Elissa Landi, Myrna Loy, Humphrey Bogart, Donald Dillaway, Pat Somerset, Ian MacLaren, Crauford Kent, Dennis D'Auburn, Douglas Dray • Mal (Farrell), an American squadron pilot in England, tells Carla (Landi) of the air battle death of her husband (Bogart). They become romantically involved until Carla is suspected of being a spy and responsible for the death of another pilot (Dillaway). Mal is about to shoot her when she exposes the real spy (Loy). 83 min. • Viennese-born Elissa Landi made her American debut in this movie.

DEL INFIERNO AL CIELO (Feb. 22, 1931) Spanish version — *The Man Who Came Back*; P: Raoul Walsh; D: Richard Harlan; W: Edwin J. Burke (st), Paul Perez (Spanish dial), Francisco de la Torre (Spanish version), John Fleming Wilson (novel); Cast: Juan Torena, Maria Alba, Carlos Villarías, Ralph Navarro, Carmen Rodriguez, Lucio Villegas, Juan Aristi Eulate, Ramon Peon, Virginia Ruiz

EAST LYNNE (March 8, 1931); P: A.L. Rockett; D: Frank Lloyd; W: Bradley King, Tom Barry, Mrs. Henry Wood (novel); C: John Seitz; E: Margaret Clancy; Cast: Ann Harding, Clive Brook, Conrad Nagel, Cecelia Loftus, Beryl Mercer, O.P. Heggie, Flora Sheffield, David Torrence, Wallie Albright, Jr., Ronald Cosbey, Eric Mayne • Cornelia (Loftus), the disagreeable sister of happily married Robert Carlyle (Nagel), plants seeds of mistrust about his wife, Lady Isabel (Harding) and diplomat Capt. Levison (Brook), who once loved her. Although the relationship was innocent, Isabel is divorced from Carlyle. She spends years abroad with Levison, who loses his job after taking a bribe. They are caught up in the Franco-Prussian war, during which a bomb kills Levison and leaves Isabel blind. Isabel returns to England to be with her son one last time, but her remarried husband finds her. Isabel, not wanting to be discovered, runs away and falls over a cliff to her death. 102 min.

NOT EXACTLY GENTLEMEN (March 8, 1931); AP: Edmund Grainger; D: Benjamin Stoloff; W: William Conselman (scr), Dudley Nichols (scr), Emmett Flynn (cont), Herman Whitaker (novel); C: Daniel Clark; E: Clyde Carruth; Cast: Victor McLaglen, Fay Wray, Lew Cody, Robert Warwick, Edward Gribbon, David Worth, Joyce Compton, Louise Huntington, Franklyn Farnum, Carol Wines • Three rogues, Bull Stanley (McLaglen), Ace Beaudry (Cody) and Bronco Dawson (Gribbon), rescue Lee Carleton (Wray) and her wagon from a gang of horse thieves. They take a liking to her, and, instead of stealing her map to a gold mine, they become her protectors. While finding a good husband (Worth) for her, they keep another gang from stealing the map. 62 min. • This is a remake of John Ford's *Three Bad Men*, released in 1926.

DOCTORS' WIVES (March 15, 1931); P: John W. Considine Jr.; D: Frank Borzage; W: Maurine Watkins, Henry and Sylvia Lieferant (novel); C: Arthur Edeson; E: Jack Dennis; Cast: Warner Baxter, Joan Bennett, Victor Varconi, Cecilia Loftus, Paul Porcasi, Minna Gombell, Helene Millard, John St. Polis, George Chandler, Violet Dunn, Ruth Warren • Nina (Bennett), a lab assistant, really wants to become a doctor but is relegated to marrying one, Dr. Penning (Baxter). She later leaves Penning when, suspicious of his constant absences, she discovers he is having an affair. A male friend of hers, Dr. Kane Ruyter (Varconi), becomes seriously ill and Penning saves his life by performing a delicate surgical procedure, even though he is jealous of the man. Kane is ultimately able to convince Penning that Nina still loves him. 82 min.

MR. LEMON OF ORANGE (March 22, 1931); D: John Blystone; W: Eddie Cantor (dial), Edwin Burke (dial), Jack Hays (play); C: Joseph August; E: Ralph Dixon; Cast: El Brendel, Fifi D'Orsay, William Collier, Sr., Donald Dillaway, Joan Castle, Ruth Warren, John Rutherford, Eddie Gribbon, Nat Pendleton, Lew Meehan • The Swedish simpleton Oscar Lemon (Brendel) is a lookalike to gangster Silent McGee (Brendel). Oscar is mistakenly picked up by a seductive Julie LaRue (D'Orsay), who wants revenge on the racketeer for killing her brother. She takes him to a speakeasy, where he is told about his likeness and escapes. There is a confrontation between the two lookalikes and Oscar captures McGee and earns a $10,000 reward. 67 min. • In an attempt to make El Brendel a leading comedy star, Fox provided this vehicle, which gave ample opportunity for his brand of silliness.

EL IMPOSTOR (March 22, 1931) Spanish version—*Scotland Yard*; D: Lewis Seiler; W: Garrett Fort (scr), Matias Cirici Ventallo (Spanish version), Denison Clift (play); C: Sidney Wagner; Cast: Juan Torena, Blanca de Castejon, Carlos Villarías, Julio Villareal, Juan Aristi Eulate, Andre Cheron, Emma Roldan, Antonio Vidal, Roberto Guzman, Rafael Alvir. 9 reels

SEAS BENEATH (March 29, 1931); D: John Ford; W: Dudley Nichols (scr & dial), Commodore James Parker (st); C: Joseph August; E: Frank E. Hull; Cast: George O'Brien, Marion Lessing, Mona Maris, Walter C. Kelly, Warren Hymer, Gaylord Pendleton, Walter McGrail, Larry Kent, Henry Victor, John Loder • The skipper of a mystery ship, Lt. Kingsley (O'Brien), puts into a neutral port where a German U-Boat waits to sink it. He befriends two attractive women, Lolita (Maris), a spy, and Anna Marie, who turns out to be the sister of a German U-Boat commander. Kingsley later finds out about the German plan and has most of his crew evacuated while he stalks the U-Boat, which he sinks. 101 min.

A CONNECTICUT YANKEE (Apr. 5, 1931); D: David Butler; W: William Conselman (adpt & dial), Mark Twain (novel); C: Ernest Palmer; E: Irene Morra; Cast: Will Rogers, William Farnum, Maureen O'Sullivan, Myrna Loy, Frank Albertson, Brandon Hurst, Mitchell Harris, Ward Bond • A radio expert (Rogers) is knocked out and awakens to find himself in King Arthur's (Farnum) Court. The story was adapted to Will Rogers's particular brand of humor, with satirical references to modern-day life and was also updated to include helicopters, radios and cars. 96 min. • This is a remake of the 1921 version.

CHARLIE CHAN CARRIES ON (Apr. 12, 1931); D: Hamilton MacFadden; W: Philip Klein (scr & dial), Barry Conners (scr & dial), Earl Derr Biggers (novel); C: George Schneiderman; E: Al De Gaetano; Cast: Marguerite Churchill, John Carrick, Warner Oland, Warren Hymer, Marjorie White, C. Henry Gordon, William Holden, George Brent, Peter Gawthorne, John T. Murray • In Honolulu, a Scotland Yard detective (Gawthorne) enlists his friend Charlie Chan (Oland) to help solve several murders that started off with a wealthy American on a round-the-world tour. After going through several suspects in the tour group, Chan writes identical letters to all of them and draws out the murderer. 69 min.

THREE GIRLS LOST (Apr. 19, 1931); P: A.L. Rockett; D: Sidney Lanfield; W: Bradley King, Robert D. Andrews (article); C: L.W. O'Connell; E: Ralph Dietrich; Cast: Loretta Young, Lew Cody, John Wayne, Joan Marsh, Joyce Compton, Paul Fix, Katherine Clare Ward, Ward Bond, Bert Roach • Three attractive young women, Norene (Young), Marcia (Marsh) and Edna (Joyce), from small towns, meet and room together in Chicago. They vie for jobs and men. Marsha becomes involved with an architect, Gordon (Wayne), and then goes for a mobster (Cody), so Norene makes a play for Gordon but eventually ends up with Tony (Fix), who was her fiancé back in Fremont, Minnesota. 71 min. • This was John Wayne's last film for Fox. He was reportedly unhappy with the roles he was getting and the studio canceled his contract.

THE SPY (Apr. 26, 1931); P: Ralph Block; D: Berthold Viertel, Hamilton MacFadden (retakes); W: Ernest Pascal; C: Lucien Andriot; E: J. Edwin Robbins; Cast: Kay Johnson, Neil Hamilton, John Halliday, Milton Holmes, Freddie Frederick, Austen Jewell, Henry Kolker, Douglas Haig, David Durand, Mischa Auer • A Russian aristocrat, Ivan (Hamilton), returns from exile in Paris to assassinate the Soviet leader to protect his wife (Johnson) and son (Frederick). He learns that his wife, who has taken up with political rival Sergei (Halliday) for her protection, has innocently informed on Ivan. Both become involved in the plot when Sergei is murdered, but Ivan is later spared a death sentence and is exiled to Siberia for ten years. 58 min.

ARE YOU THERE? (May 3, 1931); D: Hamilton MacFadden; W: Harlan Thompson; C: Joseph Valentine; E: Al De Gaetano; M: Arthur Kay; Cast: Beatrice Lilly, John Garrick, Olga Baclanova, George Grossmith, Jillian Sand, Roger Davis, Gustav von Seyffertitz, Nicholas Soussanin, Henry Victor, Lloyd Hamilton • Lord Geoffrey Troon (Garrick), concerned about his father's (Grossmith) engagement to a phony Russian countess, Helenka (Baclanova), enlists the help of bumbling female detective, Shirley Travis (Lilly). The "countess" tries to upend Travis, but is unsuccessful. Various attempts are then made by both sides to compromise the other. Eventually, Geoffrey's father, the Duke, falls in love with Travis. 60 min.

QUICK MILLIONS (May 3, 1931); D: Rowland Brown; W: Rowland Brown (scr), Courtenay Terrett (scr), John Wray (add'l dial); C: Joseph August; E: Harold Schuster; Cast: Spencer Tracy, Marguerite Churchill, John Wray, Warner Richmond, Sally Eilers, Robert Burns, George Raft, John Swor, Edgar Kennedy, Harry Myers, Dixie Lee • Bugs Raymond (Tracy) wants to get rich quick. He joins up with thug Nails Markey (Richmond), and uses strong-arm techniques to organize all the produce trucks. Bugs falls in love with Dorothy (Churchill), a society girl, and gains respectability by helping her father (Wray) complete a construction project. However, Nails sets up a murder and Bugs gets the rap. Finally, Bugs is not warned by Dorothy that Nails is out to kill him. Bugs is shot in front of the church where Dorothy is marrying another man. 70 min.

SIX CYLINDER LOVE (May 10, 1931); P: John W. Considine Jr.; D: Thornton Freeland; W: William Conselman, (adpt & dial), William Anthony McGuire (play); C: Ernest Palmer; E: J. Edwin Robbins; Cast: Spencer Tracy, Sidney Fox, Edward Everett Horton, Lorin Raker, William Collier, Sr., Una Merkel, Bert Roach, Ruth Warren, William Holden, El Brendel • An aggressive car salesman, Donroy (Tracy), keeps on helping people sell the same car after it brings them financial trouble. Newlyweds Gil (Raker) and Marilyn Sterling (Fox) agree to buy the car that has led their neighbor (Collier, Sr.) to financial ruin. The vehicle brings them bad luck as well. The Sterlings have to sell their house and move to an apartment. Donroy ends up selling the car to Axel (Brendel), the apartment janitor. 70 min. • This is a remake of a 1923 Fox film.

YOUNG SINNERS (May 17, 1931); D: John Blystone; W: William Conselman, Elmer Harris (play); C: John Seitz; E: Ralph Dixon; Cast: Hardie Albright, Thomas Meighan, Dorothy Jordan, Cecelia Loftus, James Kirkwood, Edmund Breese, Lucien Prival, Edward Nugent, Gaylord Pendleton, David Rollins • Keeping daughter Connie (Jordan) away from her dissolute boyfriend Gene (Albright), Caroline (Loftus) arranges an engagement to a German baron (Prival). Gene finds out about Connie and goes on a drinking binge. Gene's father (Kirkwood) sends him to a resort in the Adirondacks for rich men's sons. Gene, rehabilitated, is visited by Connie, who attempts to seduce him. Resisting her seduction, Gene earns Connie's respect. The baron turns out to be a phony and both families welcome the engagement of Connie and Gene. 70 min.

ALWAYS GOODBYE (May 24, 1931); AP: John W. Considine, Jr.; D: William C. Menzies, Kenneth MacKenna; W: Lynn Starling (cont & dial), Kate McLaurin (st); C: Arthur Edeson; Cast: Elissa Landi, Lewis Stone, Paul Cavanaugh, John Garrick, Frederick Kerr, Lumsden Hare, Herbert Bunston, Beryl Mercer • Attractive Lila Banning (Landi) turns down several offers of marriage. She takes up with a jewel thief (Cavanaugh), posing as his wife to steal a valuable diamond from a wealthy older man, John Graham (Stone), at his villa in Lake Como. Lila eventually falls in love and marries Graham. 60 min.

WOMEN OF ALL NATIONS (May 31, 1931); D: Raoul Walsh; W: Barry Conners, Maxwell Anderson and Lawrence Stallings (orig. characters); C: Lucien Andriot; E: Jack Dennis; M: Carli Elinor; Cast: Victor McLaglen, Edmund Lowe, Greta Nissen, El Brendel, Fifi D'Orsay, Marjorie White, Jesse De Vorska, Marion Lessing, T. Roy Barnes, Ruth Warren, Bela Lugosi • Another Quirt (Lowe) and Flagg (McLaglen) romp, this one starts out in Sweden with their buddy Olsen (Brendel). Quirt and Flagg fight over Elsa (Nissen), a country girl. They all end up in Turkey, where Elsa has become the favorite harem girl of Prince Hassam (Lugosi). The marines rescue Elsa from the harem and, once again, Quirt and Flagg swear off women. 73 min.

CUERPO Y ALMA (June 5, 1931) Spanish version—*Body and Soul*; D: David Howard; W: Jules Furthman (scr), Matias Cirici-Ventallo (Spanish version); Cast: Jorge Lewis, Ana Maria Custodio, José Alcantara, José Nieto, Enriqueta Soler, Rafael Calvo, Carlos Villarías, Felix de Pomes, Martin Garralaga, Max Baron. • 96 min.

DADDY LONG LEGS (June 7, 1931); D: Alfred Santell; W: Sonya Levien (scr & dial), S.N. Behrman (add'l dial); C: Lucien Andriot; E: Ralph Dietrich; Cast: Janet Gaynor, Warner Baxter, Una Merkel, John Arledge, Claude Gillingwater, Effie Ellsler, Kendall McComas, Kathlyn Williams, Elizabeth Patterson, Louise Closser Hale • Wealthy Jervis Pendleton (Baxter) secretly sponsors a young orphan, Judy (Gaynor), through college. Judy later meets and falls in love with Jervis without realizing his true identity. The truth is revealed, and both end up together. 80 min. • This is a remake of the non–Fox silent version starring Mary Pickford.

ANNABELLE'S AFFAIRS (June 14, 1931); AP: William Goetz; D: Alfred Werker; W: Leon Gordon (adpt & dial), Clare Kummer (play); C: Charles Clarke; E: Margaret Clancy; Cast: Victor McLaglen, Jeanette MacDonald, Roland Young, Sam Hardy, William Collier, Sr., Sally Blane, Joyce Compton, Ruth Warren, George Andre Beranger, Hank Mann • A brusque, rarely sober miner, John Rawson (McLaglen), returns unrecognized to find his estranged wife, Annabelle (MacDonald), working for millionaire Roland Wimbleton (Young). When Wimbleton discovers Annabelle owns stock in a mine that is worth millions, both he and Rawson woo her to get control of it. After several misunderstandings, through which Annabelle remains faithful to her wedding vows, John presents himself as her husband; they reunite. 75 min.

THE BLACK CAMEL (June 21, 1931); AP: William Sistrom; D: Hamilton MacFadden; W: Barry Conners (scr & dial), Philip Klein (scr & dial), Hugh Strange (adpt), Earl Derr Biggers (novel); C: Joseph August, Daniel Clark; E: Al De Gaetano; Cast: Warner Oland, Sally Eilers, Bela Lugosi, Dorothy Revier, Victor Varconi, Murray Kinnell, William Post Jr., Robert Young, Violet Dunn, J.M. Kerrigan, Dwight Frye • Charlie Chan (Oland) investigates the murder of an actress (Revier) in his home town of Honolulu. A beach bum (Kinnell) becomes a suspect until he, too, is murdered. Chan figures out that the killer of the actress was the jealous wife (Dunn) of a co-star, and the beach bum was shot by a butler (Frye), who felt he knew too much. 72 min.

GOLDIE (June 28, 1931); P: A.L. Rockett; D: Benjamin Stoloff; W: Gene Towne (adpt & dial), Paul Perez (adpt & dial); C: Ernest Palmer; E: Alex Troffey; Cast: Spencer Tracy, Warren Hymer, Jean Harlow, Jesse De Vorska, Lina Basquette, Eleanor Hunt, Maria Alba, Lelia Karnelly, Ivan Linow, Eddie Kane, George Raft, Billy Barty • Bill (Tracy) and Spike (Hymer), two brawling, womanizing sailors, end up in Calais, where they meet Goldie (Harlow), a beautiful carnival diver. Slow-witted Spike falls for Goldie, but Bill is convinced she is a tramp who only wants his money. Goldie convinces Spike that Bill tried to rape her, and the two have a bar-room brawl. They later make up and swear off women. 65 min. • Based on the 1928 film, *A Girl in Every Port.* 20th Century–Fox attempted to get a certificate for the film's reissue in 1937, but was turned down by the Breen Office because of the film's "vulgarity and low moral tone."

ESCLAVAS DE LA MODA (July 3, 1931) Spanish version—*On Your Back*; D: David Howard; W: Howard J. Green (apt. & dial), Matias Cirici Ventallo (Spanish version), Rita Weiman (article); C: Sidney Wagner; Cast: Carmen Larrabeiti, Julio Peña, Blanca de Castejon, Ralph Navarro, Felix de Pomes, Enriqueta Soler, Paco Moreno, Rafael Calvo, Robert Cartier, Nelly Fernandez • 75 min.

HUSH MONEY (July 5, 1931); P: A.L. Rockett; D: Sidney Lanfield; W: Dudley Nichols (dial), Sidney Lanfield (st), Philip Klein (st), Courtenay Terrett (st),; C: John Seitz; E: Irene Morra; Cast: Joan Bennett, Hardie Albright, Owen Moore, Myrna Loy, C. Henry Gordon, Donald Cosgrove, George Raft, Huey White, George Byron, Andre Cheron, Henry Armetta • Joan (Bennett), released from prison after serving a sentence for criminal activity with a gang, is offered help by Dan Emmett (Cosgrove), the detective who originally arrested her. She marries wealthy Stuart Elliott (Albright) and is advised by Emmett not to mention her past. When another gang member (Moore) is released, he blackmails Joan into letting him steal a $5,000 necklace. Emmett is able to retrieve it and return it to Joan before Stuart learns about her sordid background. 68 min.

THEIR MAD MOMENT (July 12, 1931); P: A.L. Rockett; D: Chandler Sprague, Hamilton MacFadden (retakes); W: Leon Gordon, Eleanor Mercein (novel); C: Dan Clark; E: Alexander Troffey; Cast: Dorothy Mackaill, Warner Baxter, ZaSu Pitts, Nance O'Neil, Lawrence Grant, Leon Janney, John St. Polis, Nella Walker, Mary Doran • Emily Stanley (Mackaill) is brought by her stepmother (Walker) to Biarritz to look for a suitable husband. She is driven into an engagement with wealthy Sir Harry Congers (Grant), but Emily is in love with a poor Basque boatman, Esteban (Baxter), who would only bring her a life of hardship. Just before she is about to marry Sir Harry, Emily discovers that Esteban is not poor at all, but very wealthy. Esteban rows them in his boat to a yacht, and they leave for England. 57 min.

A HOLY TERROR (July 19, 1931); P: Edmund Grainger; D: Irving Cummings; W: Alfred A. Cohn (scr), Ralph Block (adpt & cont), Max Brand (novel); C: George Schneiderman; E: Ralph Dixon; Cast: George O'Brien, Sally Eilers, James Kirkwood, Rita La Roy, Humphrey Bogart, Stanley Fields, Robert Warwick, Richard Tucker, Earl Pingree, Jay Wilson, Charles Whitaker • Tony Bard (O'Brien), a champion polo player from the East, goes west to solve his wealthy father's murder. He begins investigating on a Wyoming ranch, where he meets Jerry Foster (Eilers). Tony is kidnapped, but escapes and solves the mystery by finding his true father (Kirkwood) and learning that he had been raised by an impostor (Warwick), who had fallen in love with his mother. 53 min. • This was originally filmed as a Tom Mix western in 1921.

HAY QUE CASAR AL PRINCIPE (July 24, 1931) Spanish version—*Paid to Love*; D: Lewis Seiler; W: William Kernell (adpt & dial), Paul Perez (adpt & dial), Matilas Cirici Ventallo (Spanish version), Harry Carr (st); C: Glen MacWilliams; E: Fred Burnworth; Cast: José Mojica, Conchita Montenegro, Miguel Ligero, Manuel Arbo, José Alcantara, Carlos Villarías, Paco Moreno, Rafael Calvo • 73 min.

YOUNG AS YOU FEEL (Aug. 23, 1931); D: Frank Borzage; W: Edwin Burke (adpt), George Ade (play); C: Chester Lyons; E: Margaret Clancy; Cast: Will Rogers, Fifi D'Orsay, Lucien Littlefield, Donald Dillaway, Terrance Ray, Lucille Brown, Rosalie Roy, Gregory Gaye, John T. Murray, Brandon Hurst, C. Henry Gordon • A Chicago meatpacking company owner, Lemuel Morehouse, is tied to his business while his sons, Billy (Dillaway) and Tom (Ray), enjoy themselves. The situation is reversed when Lemuel decides to enjoy himself at sporting events, outwits an art swindler (Murray), and runs around with a married French singer, Fleurette (D'Orsay). Finally, Lemuel admits that he wanted to teach his sons a lesson, but he learned that "anyone is dead who lets life pass him by." 78 min.

TRANSATLANTIC (Aug. 30, 1931); D: William K. Howard; W: Guy Bolton (st), Lynn Starling (add'l dial); C: James (Wong) Howe; E: Jack Murray; M: Carli Elinor; Cast: Edmund Lowe, Greta Nissen, John Halliday, Myrna Loy, Jean Hersholt, Lois Moran, Earle Foxe, Billy Bevan, Henry Sedley, Louis Natheaux, Ruth Donnelly • An ocean liner makes the trip from New York to England with an assorted group of scoundrels on board, including gambler Monty Greer (Lowe), dancer Sigrid (Nissen), who is thought to be the mistress of banker Henry Graham (Halliday), and Handsome, a thief (Foxe) who is trying to steal Graham's securities. Greer offers to help Graham's daughter Judy (Moran) after her father is shot and killed by an unknown assailant. Greer identifies and fights the villainous Handsome into a confession of murder in the ship's engine room. 73 min.

MERELY MARY ANN (Sept. 6, 1931); D: Henry King; W: Jules Furthman, Israel Zangwill (play); C: John Seitz; E: Frank Hall; Cast: Janet Gaynor, Charles Farrell, Beryl Mercer, G.P. Huntley Jr., Lorna Balfour, Arnold Lucy, J.M. Kerrigan, Tom Whitely, Harry Rosenthal • An orphan girl, Mary Ann (Gaynor), works at a London boardinghouse where she meets John Lonsdale (Farrell), an aspiring musician who broke off with his wealthy family. She falls in love with John, but when she suddenly inherits enormous wealth, John breaks off the relationship because of the difference in their social status. When John becomes a popular composer, they reunite. 75 min. • This was the third time Fox filmed this story.

¿CONOCES A TU MUJER? (Sept. 11, 1931) Spanish version—*Don't Bet on Women*; D: David Howard; W: Leon Gordon (scr), Lynn Starling (scr), Matias Cirici-Ventalio (Spanish version); C: Sidney Wagner; Cast: Carmen Larrabeiti, Rafael Rivelles, Ana Maria Custodio, Manuel Arbo, Miguel Ligero, Enriquta Soler, Rafael Calvo, Raul Lechuga, Hipolito Mora, Emma Roldan • 6,867'

BAD GIRL (Sept. 13, 1931); D: Frank Borzage; W: Edwin Burke, Vina Delmar (novel), Vina Delmar and Brian Marlowe (play); C: Chester Lyons; E: Margaret Clancy; Cast: James Dunn, Sally Eilers, Minna Gombell, William Pawley, George Irving, Frank Darien, Sue Borzage • Eddie (Dunn), a young man who works in a radio store, has ambitions to start a business, but instead spends his savings on furnishing an apartment to impress his new wife, Dorothy (Eilers). Their ups and downs as newlyweds entail the many personal and financial sacrifices Eddie must endure to honor Dorothy's wish to secure the best doctor (Irving) to deliver their baby. 90 min.

THE BRAT (Sept. 20, 1931); D: John Ford; W: S.N. Behrman (adpt & cont), Sonya Levien (adpt & cont), Maude Fulton (play); C: Joseph August; E: Alex Troffey; Cast: Sally O'Neil, Allan Dinehart, Frank Albertson, William Collier, Sr., Virginia Cherrill, June Collyer, J. Farrell MacDonald, Mary Forbes, Albert Gran, Margaret Mann • Bailed out of jail, a 17-year-old street urchin (O'Neil), becomes the subject for novelist Mac Forrester (Dinehart). Living at his country estate, she falls in love with Mac, but it is his brother, Steve (Albertson), who falls for the brat. When the family is going to sell Steve's ranch in the West, the brat intervenes to protect it and finds that she loves Steve and not Mac. 60 min.

MAMÁ (Sept. 25, 1931) Spanish Language; P: Gregorio Martinez Sierra, Benito Perojo; D: Bert E. Sebell; W: José López Rubio, Gregorio Martinez Sierra (play); C: Sidney Wagner, Daniel Clark; E: Dorothy Spencer; Cast: Catalina Bárcena, Rafael Rivelles, Maria Luz Calleio, Julio Peña, José Nieto, Andrés de Segurola, Felix de Pomes, José Alcantara, Ralph Navarro, Rafael Calvo, Enriqueta Soler • At her daughter Cecelia's (Callejo) debutante ball, socialite wife Mercedes (Bárcena) is propositioned by a caddish Alfonso (Nieto), to whom she owes a large sum of money. Determined to swindle the family, Alfonso then courts Cecelia, who tries to pay back her mother's debt but is unable to raise the funds. Mercedes son, José (Peña), arranges to pay back Alfonso and expels him from the family circle. Meanwhile, Mercedes realizes that her husband, Santiago (Rivelles), caused all her misery by sending their children away to college, which left a void in her life, filled with a valueless social schedule. 7,240'

THE SPIDER (Sept. 27, 1931); P: William Sistrom; D: William C. Menzies; W: Barry Conners (dial & cont), Philip Klein (dial & cont), Fulton Oursler (play); C: James (Wong) Howe; E: Al De Gaetano; M: Carli Elinor; Cast: Edmund Lowe, Lois Moran, El Brendel, John Arledge, George E. Stone, Earle Foxe, Manya Roberti, Howard Phillips, Purnell Pratt, Jesse De Vorska, Ruth Donnelly • A magician, Chartrand the Great (Lowe), takes on the case of discovering an amnesiac's (Phillips) past by hypnotizing him during his show. A murder takes place, which panics the audience and leaves Chartrand to solve the crime. 59 min.

WICKED (Oct. 4, 1931); AP: John W. Considine, Jr.; D: Allan Dwan; W: Kathryn Scola (dial & cont), Kenyon Nicholson (dial & cont), Adela Rogers St. Johns (adpt); C: Peverell Marley; E: Jack Dennis; M: Carli Elinor; Cast: Elissa Landi, Victor McLaglen, Una Merkel, Irene Rich, Allan Dinehart, Theodore von Eltz, Oscar Apfel, Mae Busch, Ruth Donnelly, Eileen Percy, Joseph W. Reilly • Margot (Landi) is involuntarily involved in the aftermath of a bank robbery committed by her husband (von Eltz), who is shot by police. Margot is later convicted for the attempted murder of a police officer while her husband was being pursued. In jail, Margot gives birth to a daughter, who is taken from her and adopted by a wealthy couple, Judge Luther (Apfel) and his wife (Rich). Scott (McLaglen), a former suitor, is able to win Margot's freedom and to help her reunite with her child. 57 min.

LA LEY DEL HAREM (Oct. 9, 1931) Spanish version—*Fazil*; D: Lewis Seiler; W: William Kernell (scr), Matias Cirici-Ventallo (Spanish version), Pierre Frondaie (novel); C: Sidney Fox; E: Jerry Webb; M: Hugo Friedhofer; Cast: José Mojica, Carmen Larrbeiti, Maria Alba, Ralph Navarro, Julio Villareal, Rafael Calvo, Raul Figarola, Miguel Ligero, Virginia Arbo, Paco Moreno, Alfredo del Diestro • 77 min.

SKYLINE (Oct. 11, 1931); AP: John W. Considine, Jr.; D: Sam Taylor; W: Dudley Nichols (scr & dial), Kenyon Nicholson (scr & dial), William Anthony McGuire (add'l dial), Felix Riesenberg (novel); C: John Mescall; E: Harold Schuster; M: George Lipschultz; Cast: Thomas Meighan, Hardie Albright, Maureen O'Sullivan, Myrna Loy, Stanley Fields, Jack Kennedy, Robert McWade, Donald Dillaway, Alice Ward, Minna Gombell • An East River barge boy, John (Albright), fascinated by the skyscrapers of New York, leaves his drunken stepfather (Fields) to pursue his dream of becoming an architect. He meets a famous architect, McLellan (Meighan), who makes him his protégé. After becoming a father figure to John and helping the young man with his romances, Mac confesses that he is John's real father. 70 min.

RIDERS OF THE PURPLE SAGE (Oct. 18, 1931); AP: Edmund Grainger; D: Hamilton MacFadden; W: Philip Klein (dial & cont), Barry Connors (dial & cont), John F. Goodrich (adpt), Zane Grey (novel); C: George Schneiderman; E: Al De Gaetano; Cast: George O'Brien, Marguerite Churchill, Noah Beery, Yvonne Pelletier, James Todd, Stanley Fields, Lester Dorr, Shirley Nails, Frank McGlynn, Jr. • Lassiter (O'Brien), a cowboy in search of his sister who was lured away from her husband by Judge Dyer (Beery), meets Jane Withersteen (Churchill), whose ranch is the target of a tough gang. The pair is chased by the gang and escape by causing a landslide, which leaves them in a valley. 57 min. • This is the third time Fox produced this story.

SOB SISTER (Oct. 25, 1931); D: Alfred Santell; W: Edwin Burke (scr), Mildred Gilman (novel); C: Glen MacWilliams; E: Ralph Dietrich; Cast: James Dunn, Linda Watkins, Minna Gombell, Howard Phillips, George E. Stone, Molly O'Day, Eddie Dillon, George Byron, Lex Lindsay, Harold Waldridge, Neal Burns • A columnist, Jane (Watkins), steals scoops from Garry (Dunn), a reporter for a rival tabloid, but a love interest gradually develops between the two. There is a misunderstanding when Garry thinks Jane has stolen information from a murderer's diary that is in his possession. A confession by a photographer (Dillon) who took the diary clears Jane. Jane is later kidnapped by gangsters, but Garry and other reporters come to her rescue. 71 min.

THE CISCO KID (Nov. 11, 1931); AP: William Goetz; D: Irving Cummings; W: Al Cohn, O. Henry (based on character); C: Barney McGill; E: Alex Troffey; M: George Lipschultz; Cast: Warner Baxter, Edmund Lowe, Conchita Montenegro, Nora Lane, Frederick Burt, Willard Robertson, James Bradbury, Jr., Jack Dillon, Charles Stevens, Chris Martin • The Cisco Kid (Baxter) frustrates his nemesis, Sgt. Mickey Dunn (Lowe), by escaping once again near the Mexico border. Later, Cisco gets away with a café singer (Montenegro) after taunting the local sheriff. Dunn shows up and wounds Cisco during his escape. Cisco recovers, helping the family that is sheltering him to keep their ranch by robbing the bank that is about to foreclose. When Dunn catches up and finds out what Cisco has done, he congratulates him and lets him go. 61 min.

HEARTBREAK (Nov. 8, 1931); AP: William Goetz; D: Alfred Werker; W: William Conselman, Llewellyn Hughes (article); E: Margaret Clancy; M: George Lipschultz; Cast: Charles Farrell, Madge Evans, Paul Cavanaugh, Hardie Albright, John Arledge, Claude King, John St. Polis, Albert Conti, Theodore von Eltz, Wilson Benge • John (Farrell), an American embassy attaché in Vienna, is in love with the beautiful Countess Vilma (Evans), but he is drawn into battle as war breaks out. On the Italian border, he shoots down an Austrian aviator, Count Carl Walden (Albright), in an air fight. Walden turns out to be Vilma's twin brother. Only after the war does Vilma soften her anger towards John, and the couple reunites. 59 min.

THE YELLOW TICKET (Nov. 15, 1931); D: Raoul Walsh; W: Jules Furthman (scr), William Conselman (new ending), Guy Bolton (add'l dial), Michael Morton (play); C: James (Wong) Howe; E: Jack Murray; M: Carli Elinor; Cast: Elissa Landi, Lionel Barrymore, Laurence Olivier, Walter Byron, Arnold Korff, Mischa Auer, Edwin Maxwell, Rita La Roy, Sarah Padden, Boris Karloff, Alex Melesh • A Jewess, Marya Kalish (Landi), is forced to accept a "yellow ticket," which brands her a woman of the streets, in order to cross the Russian border to visit her imprisoned father. She meets English war correspondent Julian Rolfe (Olivier), who falls in love with her. Saving Julian from being sent to Siberia, Marya shoots the womanizing Chief of Police Andreeff (Barrymore). Julian later gets Marya to the English embassy and they escape just as war breaks out. 83 min.

AMBASSADOR BILL (Nov. 22, 1931); D: Sam Taylor; W: Guy Bolton, Vincent Sheean (article); C: John Mascall; E: Harold Schuster; Cast: Will Rogers, Marguerite Churchill, Greta Nissen, Tad Alexander, Ray Milland, Gustav von Seyffertitz, Arnold Korff, Ferdinand Munier, Edwin Maxwell, Ernest Wood • American ambassador Bill (Rogers) arrives in a foreign monarchy during a revolution and discovers that the king (Alexander) has been exiled through a double cross on the part of a prince (von Seyffertitz) who is plotting to seize the throne. After being set up in a compromising position in Countess Ilka's (Nissen) bedroom by the prince, Bill upends the scheme and gets the country back on track. 70 min.

MI ÚLTIMO AMOR (Nov. 28, 1931) Spanish version—*Their Mad Moment*; D: Lewis Seiler; W: Leon Gordon (adpt), José López Rubio (Spanish translation); Cast:

José Mojica, Ana Maria Custodio, Mimi Aguglia, Andrés de Segurola, Carmen Rodriguez, Elvira Morla, Nancy Torres, Robert Cartier, Paco Moreno • 9 reels

OVER THE HILL (Nov. 29, 1931); D: Henry King; W: Tom Barry, Jules Furthman, Will Carleton (poems); C: John Seitz; E: Frank Hull; M: George Lipschultz; Cast: Mae Marsh, James Dunn, Sally Eilers Edward Crandall, Claire Maynard, James Kirkwood, Joe Hachey, Tom Conlon, Julius Molnar, Olin Howland, Billy Barty • Ma Shelby (Marsh) a loyal wife, slaves away to support her lazy husband (Kirkwood). One of her sons, Johnny (Conlon), takes the blame for his father's stolen liquor rap to protect his mother. Pa Shelby dies before he can tell Ma the truth. Of all the children, Johnny, his life ruined by his prison time, is still the most loyal, while the others have abandoned their mother. Suffering miserably from the marital problems of her children, Ma Shelby is finally saved by Johnny, who finds her working as a washerwoman at a boarding house. 89 min. • This is a remake of the 1920 version, one of Fox's biggest silent successes.

ERAN TRECE (Dec. 4, 1931) Spanish version—*Charlie Chan Carries On*; D: David Howard; W: Barry Conners (scr), Philip Klein (scr), José López Rubio (Spanish dial), Earl Der Biggers (novel); C: Sidney Wagner; Cast: Juan Torena, Ana Maria Custodio, Rafael Calvo, Raúl Roulien, Blanca Castejon, Manuel Ligero, Amalia Santee, Carmen Rodriguez, Julio Villareal, Lia Tora • 79 min.

SURRENDER (Dec. 6, 1931); D: William K. Howard; W: S.N. Behrman, Sonya Levien, Pierre Benoit (novel); C: James (Wong) Howe; E: Paul Weatherwax; M: Carli Elinor; Cast: Warner Baxter, Leila Hyams, C. Aubrey Smith, Ralph Bellamy, Alexander Kirkland, William Pawley, Howard Phillips, George Andre Beranger, Bodil Rosing, Bert Hanlon • During World War I, at the castle of Prussian Count Reichendorf (Smith), a disfigured Capt. Elbing (Bellamy) courts Reichendorf's ward, Axelle (Hyams). When she is attracted to French Sgt. Dumaine (Baxter), who is being held prisoner at the castle, Elbing becomes jealous. He sentences Dumaine to be executed despite Axelle's pleas, but the Armistice brings an end to the war. Losing his purpose in the military, Elbing commits suicide, leaving Axelle free to continue her romance with Dumaine. 69 min.

GOOD SPORT (Dec. 13, 1931); AP: William Goetz; D: Kenneth MacKenna; W: William Hurlbut (scr), Gene Towne (st); C: Charles Clarke; E: Alex Troffey; M: George Lipschultz; Cast: Linda Watkins, John Boles, Greta Nissen, Minna Gombell, Hedda Hopper, Alan Dinehart, Claire Maynard, Louise Beavers, Sally Blane, Betty Francisco, Ethel Kenyon • Marilyn Parker (Watkins) inadvertently discovers her husband's vacated love nest when Rex (Dinehart) is out of town, and takes it over to understand the life of a mistress. Marilyn meets Boyce Cameron (Boles), who lectures her about the life she is leading. While Boyce tries to reform Marilyn, he falls in love with her. After complications, Marilyn leaves Rex, whom she blames for the failure of their marriage, and realizes she loves Boyce. 68 min.

DELICIOUS (Dec. 27, 1931); D: David Butler; W: Guy Bolton (adpt & st), Sonya Levien (adpt); C: Ernest Palmer; E: Irene Morra; M: George and Ira Gershwin; Cast: Janet Gaynor, Charles Farrell, El Brendel, Raúl Roulien, Lawrence O'Sullivan, Manya Roberti, Virginia Cherrill, Olive Tell, Mischa Auer, Marvine Maazel, Jeanette Gegna • A Scottish girl, Heather (Gaynor), rejected entry into the U.S., hides in a horse crate and ends up at the home of wealthy Larry Beaumont (Farrell). Fearing deportation, Heather runs off and has various adventures. In the end, Larry, who has fallen in love with Heather, snubs his socialite fiancée (Cherrill) and boards the ship on which Heather has been deported. He proposes to Heather, and they plan to be married by the ship's captain. 106 min.

1932 Releases

THE RAINBOW TRAIL (Jan. 3, 1932); P: Edmund Grainger; D: David Howard; W: Philip Klein (adpt & dial), Barry Conners (adpt & dial), Zane Grey (novel); C: Daniel Clark; E: Al De Gaetano; Cast: George O'Brien, Cecilia Parker, Minna Gombell, Roscoe Ates, J.M. Kerrigan, James Kirkwood, W.L. Thorne, Robert Frazer, Ruth Donnelly, Niles Welch • Cowboy Shefford (O'Brien) is seeking a gold treasure in a secluded gorge and agrees to rescue a group of travelers who were trapped there 15 years earlier. 60 min. • This is the third remake and first sound version of this story.

STEPPING SISTERS (Jan. 10, 1932); P: William Goetz; D: Seymour Felix; W: William Conselman (scr), Howard Warren Comstock (play); C: George Schneiderman; E: Jack Murray; Cast: Louise Dresser, Minna Gombell, Jobyna Howland, William Collier, Sr., Stanley Smith, Barbara Weeks, Howard Phillips, Ferdinand Munier, Mary Forbes, Robert Greig • Cissie Ramsay (Dresser), a former burlesque queen who has married into society, bumps into Rosie (Gombell) and Queenie (Howland), friends from 20 years earlier who have also taken on society airs. Comedic situations ensue as Cissie tries to keep her past from daughter Norma (Weeks). When the truth is eventually exposed, Norma defends her mother's past to their society friends. 59 min.

DANCE TEAM (Jan. 17, 1932); D: Sidney Lanfield; W: Edwin Burke; C: James Wong Howe; E: Margaret Clancy; Cast: James Dunn, Sally Eilers, Ralph Morgan, Minna Gombell, Nora Lane, Harry Beresford, Claire Maynard, Edward Crandall, Charles Williams • Jimmy Mulligan (Dunn), a street-wise guy who is constantly getting into fights, teams up with Poppy Kirk (Eilers) to form a dance team. After several gigs, they split up and date other people in high society. Eventually, they are brought back together, but Jimmy almost ruins everything by getting into yet another fight. 57 min.

CHARLIE CHAN'S CHANCE (Jan. 24, 1932); D: John Blystone; W: Barry Conners (scr), Philip Klein (scr),

Earl Der Biggers (novel); C: Joseph August; E: Alex Troffey; Cast: Warner Oland, Alexander Kirkland, H.B. Warner, Marian Nixon, Linda Watkins, James Kirkwood, Ralph Morgan, James Todd, Herbert Bunston, James Wang, Joe Brown • The famed Honolulu criminologist, Charlie Chan (Oland), detects foul play in the death of the former head of Scotland Yard and ends up exposing a gang of murderers who use poison gas. 71 min. • "This is unexpected as squirt from aggressive grapefruit."—Charlie Chan

THE SILENT WITNESS (Feb. 7, 1932); D: Marcel Varnel; W: Douglas Doty (scr), Jack De Leon & Jack Celestin (play); C: Joseph August; E: Jack Murray; Cast: Lionel Atwill, Greta Nissen, Weldon Heyburn, Helen Mack, Bramwell Fletcher, Montague Shaw, Wyndham Standing, Alan Mowbray, Herbert Mundin, Billy Bevan • Anthony Howard (Fletcher), son of London barrister, Sir Austin Howard (Atwill), chokes a girl (Nissen) of dubious virtue to death for cheating on him. Feeling responsible for pampering his son, Sir Austin confesses to the crime. A forger (Bevan), who witnessed the murder because he was going to carry out a crime against the Howards, reveals that Anthony indeed choked her but did not kill her. The girl's estranged husband (Heyburn) arrived and carried out the murder. Anthony reconciles with his girlfriend (Mack). 73 min.

CHEATERS AT PLAY (Feb. 14, 1932); D: Hamilton MacFadden; W: Malcolm Stuart Boylan (scr), Louis Joseph Vance (article); C: Ernest Palmer; E: Irene Morra; Cast: Thomas Meighan, Charlotte Greenwood, William Bakewell, Ralph Morgan, Barbara Weeks, Linda Watkins, Olin Howland, William Pawley, James Kirkwood • A former thief, Michael Lanyard (Meighan), helps an old friend (Greenwood) retrieve $350,000 in emeralds, which were stolen from her on an ocean liner bound for America. In exposing the thief, Lanyard discovers it was his son (Bakewell) who wanted to equal his father's exploits. He later has to rescue the son, who has become the target of another jewel thief (Morgan). 73 min.

SHE WANTED A MILLIONAIRE (Feb. 21, 1932); D: John Blystone; W: William Anthony McGuire (scr), Sonya Levien (st); C: John Seitz; E: Louis Loeffler; Cast: Joan Bennett, Spencer Tracy, Una Merkel, James Kirkwood, Dorothy Peterson, Douglas Cosgrove, Donald Dillaway, Tetsu Komai, Constantine Romanoff, Anita Barnes • Railroad worker Bill (Tracy) is sidelined from wooing Jane (Bennett) when she meets millionaire Roger (Kirkwood), who helps her win a Miss America pageant. Jane marries Roger but, aside from his money, there is little happiness for her. Roger eventually tries to strangle her, but she is rescued and returns to Bill, who has worked his way up to an executive position with the railroad. 74 min. • Winfield Sheehan is credited as a contributing, but unbilled, writer. Atlantic City was recreated in Redondo Beach for the pageant sequence.

THE GAY CABALLERO (Feb. 28, 1932); P: Edmund Grainger; D: Alfred Werker; W: Philip Klein, Barry Conners; C: George Schneiderman; E: Al De Gaetano; Cast: George O'Brien, Victor McLaglen, Conchita Montenegro, Linda Watkins, C. Henry Gordon, Weldon Heyburn, Martin Garralaga, Willard Robertson, Juan Torena • A former football star, Ted Radcliffe (O'Brien), returns to his ranch in the West and learns that his fortune has been diminished by Paco Morales (Gordon), a ruthless Mexican cattle king. He teams up with El Coyote (McLaglen), a Robin Hood–style sharpshooter to end Morales's reign. 60 min.

BUSINESS AND PLEASURE (March 6, 1932); P: A.L. Rockett; D: David Butler, Sam Taylor; W: William Conselman (adpt & dial), Booth Tarkington (novel), Arthur Goodrich (play); C: Ernest Palmer; E: Irene Morra; M: George Lipschultz; Cast: Will Rogers, Jetta Goudal, Joel McCrea, Dorothy Peterson, Peggy Ross, Cyril Ring, Jed Prouty, Oscar Apfel, Vernon Dent, Boris Karloff • While on a business trip in the Middle East to find the secret of Damascus steel, an Oklahoma razor-blade king, Earl Tinker (Rogers), is lured away from his wife (Peterson) by a seductive Madame Momora (Goudal), who is really a spy for a rival razor-blade company. Earl is kidnapped and in danger of execution, but Momora is eventually arrested, and all ends well. 79 min.

AFTER TOMORROW (March 13, 1932); D: Frank Borzage; W: Sonya Levien (adpt), John Golden & Hugh Stange (play); C: James (Wong) Howe; E: Margaret Clancy; Cast: Charles Farrell, Marian Nixon, Minna Gombell, William Collier, Sr., Josephine Hull, William Pawley, Greta Granstedt, Ferdinand Munier, Nora Lane • Peter Piper (Farrell) and Sidney Taylor (Nixon) are trying to save enough money to get married, but they are thwarted in their efforts by the selfishness of Mrs. Taylor (Gombell), who is carrying on an illicit romance, Mrs. Piper (Hull) who finds it impossible to part with her son, and Mr. Taylor, whose heart attacks drain the couple's funds. A sudden windfall, the result of an investment, allows Peter to pay for their wedding and honeymoon. 79 min.

DISORDERLY CONDUCT (March 20, 1932); D: John W. Considine Jr.; W: William Anthony McGuire (st & dial), Del Andrews (cont); C: Ray June; E: Frank Hull; Cast: Spencer Tracy, Sally Eilers, El Brendel, Dickie Moore, Ralph Bellamy, Ralph Morgan, Allan Dinehart, Frank Conroy, Cornelius Keefe, Claire Maynard, Nora Lane • Dick Fay (Tracy), a motorcycle cop, refuses a bribe from Phyllis (Eilers), who was speeding. Dick is demoted because Phyllis's father is influential politician James Crawford (Morgan). With nothing to lose, Dick then takes graft from Tony (Conroy), a bootlegger, and is fired. However, there is a gun battle when Tony thinks Dick double-crossed him. Dick survives and later rehabilitates himself when he proves Crawford paid him $10,000 to protect Phyllis's reputation after she was arrested in a speakeasy raid. 82 min. • Winfield Sheehan is credited, without billing, as a contributing writer.

DEVIL'S LOTTERY (March 27, 1932); D: Sam Taylor; W: Guy Bolton (scr), Nalbro Bartley; C: Ernest Palmer;

E: Harold Schuster; Cast: Elissa Landi, Victor McLaglen, Alexander Kirkland, Ralph Morgan, Paul Cavanaugh, Barbara Weeks, Beryl Mercer, Herbert Mundin, Halliwell Hobbes, Lumsden Hare • Two winners of the Calcutta Sweepstakes are invited to the horse owner's (Hobbes) country estate. One is Evelyn (Landi), a fallen young woman, and the other is Mrs. Meech (Mercer), the mother of a former fighter, Jim (McLaglen). Evelyn's live-in lover (Cavanaugh), a card cheat, shows up and gambles with Jim, who ends up killing him. 77 min.

CARELESS LADY (Apr. 3, 1932); P: William Goetz; D: Kenneth MacKenna; W: Guy Bolton, Reita Lambert (article); C: John Seitz, George Schneiderman; E: Alex Troffey; Cast: Joan Bennett, John Boles, Minna Gombell, Weldon Heyburn, Nora Lane, Raoul Roulien, J.M. Kerrigan, John Arledge, Fortunio Bonanova, Josephine Hull • A dowdy young woman, Sally (Bennett), decides to spruce herself up as a blonde in fancy dresses to get some "experience." Through a mix-up, Sally ends up in Paris under the name of Mrs. Stephen Ilington. Ilington (Boles), at the same hotel, is attracted to her. Back home, Sally now attracts much attention due to her reported "marriage separation." Stephen follows Sally and makes her jealous by pursuing her cousin (Lane), but romance blossoms in the end. 67 min.

AMATEUR DADDY (Apr. 10, 1932); D: John Blystone; W: Doris Malloy (scr), Frank Dolan (scr), William Conselman (dial), Mildred Cram (novel); C: James Wong Howe; E: Louis Loeffler; Cast: Warner Baxter, Marian Nixon, Rita LaRoy, William Pawley, Lucille Powers, David Landau, Clarence Wilson, Frankie Darro, Joan Breslaw, Gail Kornfeld, Joe Hachey • Jim (Baxter), a construction engineer in Oklahoma, fulfills a promise to take care of his late co-worker's orphaned children. The ranch on which the poverty-stricken family lives is actually sitting on an oil reserve, and a nasty neighbor (Landau) is trying to buy it. Jim has to deal with the neighbor's efforts to run him out of town, fend off the oldest daughter's (Nixon) puppy love, and deal with the fact he has adopted the wrong Smith family, but all ends well. 74 min. • This was an attempt to cash in on the popularity of Baxter's role in *Daddy Long Legs*.

YOUNG AMERICA (Apr. 17, 1932); D: Frank Borzage; W: William Conselman; C: George Schneiderman; E: Margaret Clancy; Cast: Spencer Tracy, Doris Kenyon, Ralph Bellamy, Tommy Conlon, Raymond Borzage, Beryl Mercer, Sarah Padden, Robert Homans, Dawn O'Day • Jack (Tracy), a druggist, is begged by his wife, Edith (Kenyon), to hire an orphan, Arthur (Conlon), for after-school work. Art has an unjustified reputation for being bad, and, after a few run-ins, is abandoned by his mean-spirited aunt (Padden). Art is reluctantly taken in by Jack, at Edith's request, but Jack is unable to trust him. Later, in trying to fight off hold-up men at the pharmacy, Art is taken and, after a car chase, prevents one of the thugs from shooting Jack. Art is then adopted by Jack and Edith. 70 min. • John Ford was originally set to direct this film as a comedy.

THE TRIAL OF VIVIENNE WARE (May 1, 1932); D: William K. Howard; W: Philip Klein (scr), Barry Connors (scr), Kenneth M. Ellis (novel); C: Ernest Palmer; E: Ralph Dietrich; Cast: Joan Bennett, Donald Cook, Richard Gallagher, ZaSu Pitts, Lillian Bond, Allan Dinehart, Herbert Mundin, Howard Phillips, William Pawley, Jameson Thomas • Socialite Vivienne Ware (Bennett) is arrested for the murder of her fiancé, Damon Fenwick (Thomas). John Sutherland (Cook), who thought he was going to marry Vivienne, acts as her defense attorney. In a very detailed trial, John fights hard for Vivienne and finally proves that the murder was perpetrated by a jealous lover of Fenwick's former girlfriend. 58 min.

WHILE PARIS SLEEPS (May 8, 1932); P: William Sistrom; D: Allan Dwan; W: Basil Woon; C: Glen MacWilliams; E: Paul Weatherwax; Cast: Victor McLaglen, Helen Mack, William Bakewell, Jack La Rue, Rita La Roy, Maurice Black, Dot Farley, Lucille La Verne, Paul Porcasi, Eddie Dillon, Arthur Stone • Manon (Mack), living in the Paris slums, fights for her right to love and live with dignity. Her father, Jacques (McLaglen), whom she thought had died in the war, shows up on the run from the law. He does not reveal who he is and ends up saving Manon and her lover Paul (Bakewell) from a tough Apache gang of thugs, who are after them. 67 min. • Scenes were re-shot after the Hays Office rejected the film on the basis of its treatment of white slavery. The script had not been submitted to the Hays Office before filming. When Fox submitted the film for a reissue certification, it was turned down for a "number of definitely unacceptable details."

THE WOMAN IN ROOM 13 (May 15, 1932); D: Henry King; W: Guy Bolton, Samuel Shipman & Max Marcin & Percival Wilde (play); C: John Seitz; E: Al De Gaetano; Cast: Elissa Landi, Ralph Bellamy, Neil Hamilton, Myrna Loy, Gilbert Roland, Walter Walker, Luis Alberni, Charles Grapewin • Laura (Landi), a faithful, estranged wife of the philandering Maj. Bruce (Bellamy), a mayoral candidate, admits she has fallen in love with another man, Paul (Hamilton), whom she marries. Bruce's detective firm is later hired to watch over Laura by her new father-in-law (Walker). When Laura is tied to the shooting death of a womanizer (Alberni), Paul takes the blame and is sentenced harshly. A gloating Bruce gets his revenge for the divorce when he shows up to tell Laura that another woman he was tailing did the shooting. A detective happens to have a recording machine that captures Bruce's confession, exonerating Paul. 67 min.

MAN ABOUT TOWN (May 22, 1932); D: John Francis Dillon; W: Leon Gordon (scr), Denison Clift (novel); C: James Wong Howe; E: Frank Hull; M: George Lipschultz; Cast: Warner Baxter, Karen Morley, Conway Tearle, Alan Mowbray, Leni Stengel, Lilian Bond, Lawrence Grant, Halliwell Hobbes, Charles Gerrard,

Noel Madison • In Washington D.C., Stephen (Baxter), a former government agent, gives up the gambling casino he's running when he bumps into Helena (Morley), whom he loved and lost in Budapest and who is engaged to his best friend, Bob (Tearle). Stephen does not come between them, but their paths cross again when Helena's sister's former lover (Mowbray), now a Russian spy, is murdered. Helena is the prime suspect. Stephen finds evidence to the contrary but in the process, is shot by police. Bob gives him a reason to live by saying that Helena will be prosecuted if he dies. Stephen and Helena are reunited. 76 min.

SOCIETY GIRL (May 29, 1932); D: Sidney Lanfield; W: Elmer Harris (scr), John Larkin Jr. & Charles Beahan (play); C: George Barnes; E: Margaret Clancy; M: George Lipschultz; Cast: James Dunn, Peggy Shannon, Spencer Tracy, Bert Hanlon, Walter Byron, Marjorie Gateson, Anne O'Neal, Eula Guy Todd, Eric Wilton • A pug, Johnny Malone (Dunn), is about to fight a championship bout when he meets society debutante Judy (Shannon), who sidetracks his training. Johnny argues with his manager (Tracy) and they split up. Judy walks out just before the fight and does not return, causing Pug to lose, but the couple is reconciled in the end. 74 min.

DIE GROSSE FAHRT (June 2, 1932) German version — *The Big Trail*; D: Lewis Seiler; Cast: Theo Small, Marion Lessing, Ulrich Haupt, Arnold Korff • Dialogue for the German version was written by Fred Zinnemann.

MYSTERY RANCH (June 12, 1932); D: David Howard; W: Al Cohn (scr), Stewart Edward White (short story); C: Joseph August, George Schneiderman; E: Paul Weatherwax; M: George Lipschultz; Cast: George O'Brien, Cecilia Parker, Charles Middleton, Charles Stevens, Forrester Harvey, Noble Johnson, Roy Stewart, Betty Francisco, Rusty Powell • Bob (O'Brien), a Texas Ranger, comes up against Steele (Middleton), a tyrannical Arizona rancher who wants to take over an entire valley. When he rescues Steele's niece Jane (Parker) from a horse fall, she writes him a desperate note to get her away from her uncle. Bob escapes Steele's henchmen, saves a servant loyal to Jane, then goes through blazing action to get rid of Steele and return ownership of the ranch to Jane. 54 min.

WEEK ENDS ONLY (June 19, 1932); D: Alan Crosland; W: William Conselman (scr), Warner Fabian (novel); C: Hal Mohr; E: Louis Loeffler; M: George Lipschultz; Cast: Joan Bennett, Ben Lyon, John Halliday, Halliwell Hobbes, Walter Byron, Henry Armetta, John Arledge, John Elliott, Berton Churchill • Venetia (Bennett), who works at a ritzy club, makes extra money by playing hostess at wealthy Arthur Ladden's (Halliday) country place on weekends. She falls in love with penniless, young artist Jack (Lyon), but keeps her weekend work a secret. When her "profession" is discovered, Jack thinks the worst of her and leaves. Venetia takes Arthur's offer to sail to Europe, but before they leave Jack rescues her from being a kept woman. 70 min.

BACHELOR'S AFFAIRS (June 26, 1932); D: Alfred Werker; W: Barry Conners (scr), Philip Klein (scr), James Forbes (play); C: Norbert Brodine; E: Al De Gaetano; M: George Lipschultz; Cast: Adolphe Menjou, Minna Gombell, Arthur Pierson, Joan Marsh, Allan Dinehart, Irene Purcell, Herbert Mundin, Don Alvarado, Rita LaRoy • Andrew (Menjou), an older New York millionaire, marries young gold-digger Eva (Marsh), to the disappointment of his secretary, Jane (Purcell). On his very active honeymoon, Andrew finds that he cannot to keep up with his effervescent wife. Andrew's partner (Dinehart) works up a plan to get Eva interested in a young architect (Pierson). Eva's sister (Gombell), enjoying Andrew's money, tries to prevent a break-up, but the young lovers plan to elope. Andrew gladly pays whatever is necessary to get himself out of the mess and gets together with the more sedate Jane. 64 min.

REBECCA OF SUNNYBROOK FARM (July 3, 1932); D: Alfred Santell; W: S.N. Berhman (scr), Sonya Levien (scr), Kate Douglas Wiggin & Charlotte Thompson (play); C: Glen MacWilliams; E: Ralph Dietrich; M: George Lipschultz; Cast: Marian Nixon, Ralph Bellamy, Mae Marsh, Louise Closser Hale, Alan Hale, Sarah Padden, Alphonz Ethier, Eula Guy, Ronald Harris, Willis Marks, Charlotte Henry • Do-gooder Rebecca (Nixon), daughter of a poor woman, sets out to help everyone, including rich aunts Jane (Marsh) and Miranda (Closser Hale), who have taken her in. By persistence, she encourages the atheistic Zion Simpson (Hale) to marry his common-law wife, Mary (Guy), by presenting him with a wedding ring as Mary gives birth to an out-of-wedlock baby. Rebecca also falls in love with the town doctor (Bellamy), who ends up saving Miranda's life. 77 min.

ALMOST MARRIED (July 17, 1932); AP: William Sistrom; D: William Cameron Menzies; W: Wallace Smith (scr), Guy Bolton (scr), Andrew Soutar (novel); C: John Mescall, George Schneiderman; E: Harold Schuster; M: George Lipschultz; Cast: Violet Heming, Ralph Bellamy, Allan Dinehart, Herbert Mundin, Maria Alba, Gustav von Seyffertitz, Tempe Pigott, Eva Dennison, Grace Hampton, Herbert Bunston • Anita Mellikovna (Heming), the wife of insane musician Louis Capristi (Kirkland), escapes from him in Paris then has to flee the secret police in Russia by marrying an Englishman (Bellamy), who takes her to London. Capristi comes after her, murders another girl (Alba) to keep his identity secret then stalks Anita but is prevented by Scotland Yard from murdering her. 51 min.

THE CRY OF THE WORLD (July 24, 1932); E: Louis de Rochemont • This is a compilation of Movietone News footage, covering the devastation of World War I and the political developments following the Armistice. 7,093'

THE FIRST YEAR (July 31, 1932); D: William K. Howard; W: Lynn Starling (scr), John Golden & Frank Craven (play); C: Hal Mohr; E: Jack Murray; M: George Lipschultz; Cast: Janet Gaynor, Charles Farrell,

Minna Gombell, Dudley Digges, Leila Bennett, Robert McWade, George Meeker, Maude Eburne, Henry Kolker, Elda Vokel • Before Grace (Gaynor) and Tommy Tucker's (Farrell) first year of marriage is over, they are behind in their rent and constantly bickering. Tommy, a real estate salesman, has scrimped to buy some land that the railroad wants. With a $100,000 offer for the land, it appears all is well until Grace's former suitor Dick (Meeker) enters the picture, making Tommy jealous and resulting in a separation. Grace learns that she is pregnant and, after a fist fight between Tommy and Dick, the couple is reunited. 80 min. • This is a sound remake of the 1926 Fox release.

CONGORILLA (Aug. 7, 1932); P: Martin Johnson, Osa Johnson; C: Martin Johnson, Richard Maedler; E: Truman Talley • This film is a documentary of the Johnsons' expedition to the Belgian Congo to study the habits of local gorillas. 72 min.

A PASSPORT TO HELL (Aug. 14, 1932); D: Frank Lloyd; W: Bradley King (scr), Leon Gordon (scr), Harry Hervey (st); C: John Seitz; E: Harold Schuster; M: George Lipschultz; Cast: Elissa Landi, Paul Lukas, Warner Oland, Alexander Kirkland, Donald Crisp, Earle Foxe, Yola d'Avril, Ivan Simpson, Eva Dennison, William Von Brincken • Around the time of the World War, a British woman, Myra (Landi), is deported from West Africa to the German sector because of a scandal. She marries Erich von Sydow (Kirkland) to get into the colony, but his father, Baron Von Sydow (Oland), the commanding officer, is furious with what Erich has done and assigns his son to the jungle. Erich commits suicide when Myra leaves him for another man, Kurt (Lukas). Myra tries to leave the colony but is unfairly lured into a trap, which makes her look like a spy. She is finally exonerated and returns to Kurt. 75 min.

THE PAINTED WOMAN (Aug. 21, 1932); D: John Blystone; W: Guy Bolton (scr), Leon Gordon (scr), Alfred C. Kennedy (play); C: Ernest Palmer; E: Alex Troffey; M: George Lipschultz; Cast: Spencer Tracy, Peggy Shannon, William Boyd, Irving Pichel, Raúl Roulien, Murray Kinnell, Laska Winter, Chris Pin-Martin, Paul Porcasi, Stanley Fields, Wade Boteler • Kiddo (Shannon), a loose woman who lives on the waterfront in the Orient, is involved with several men but finally meets Tom Brian (Tracy), an ex-marine with whom she falls in love. Capt. Boynton (Boyd), a lover from her past, returns and becomes an obstacle to her happiness. When Boynton is stabbed to death by Jim (Roulien) while he is attacking Kiddo, she is blamed and put on trial. Kiddo is eventually set free to be with Tom. 72 min.

DOWN TO EARTH (Sept. 4, 1932); D: David Butler; W: Edwin Burke (scr & dial), Homer Croy (st); C: Ernest Palmer; E: Irene Morra; M: George Lipschultz; Cast: Will Rogers, Dorothy Jordan, Irene Rich, Matty Kemp, Mary Carlisle, Brandon Hurst, Theodore Lodi, Clarence Wilson, Louise Mackintosh, Harvey Clark • A newly wealthy man, Pike Peters (Rogers), rails against his wife's (Rich) wasteful extravagance in a mansion with three butlers. The stock market crashes and renders Pike almost bankrupt. He uses the opportunity to rid himself of the large house staff and his wife's parasitic friends. The Peters family returns to their modest home in Oklahoma. Pike also helps his son Ross choose a girl with simple tastes (Jordan) over one whose family is wealthy (Carlisle). 80 min.

CHANDU, THE MAGICIAN (Sept. 16, 1932); D: Marcel Varnel; W: Barry Conners (scr), Philip Klein (scr), Harry A. Earnshaw & Vera M. Oldham & R.R. Morgan (creators); C: James (Wong) Howe; E: Harold Schuster; M: Louis De Francesco; Cast: Edmund Lowe, Irene Ware, Bela Lugosi, Herbert Mundin, Henry B. Walthall, Weldon Heyburn, June Vlasek, Nestor Abel, Virginia Hammond, Nigel de Brulier • Chandu (Lowe) uses all his magical skills to rescue an inventor (Walthall) of a death ray who has been kidnapped by the evil Roxor (Lugosi). Roxor wants to use the ray to destroy the world. Along the way, Chandu buys a scantily clad princess (Ware) from evil auctioneers then has to overcome informers and Roxor's henchmen. Roxor is killed by an explosion of the death ray. 74 min.

MARIDO Y MUJER (Sept. 25, 1932) Spanish version — *Bad Girl*; D: Bert E. Sebell; W: José López Rubio (Spanish dial), Eugene Delmar (novel), Vina Delmar (play); Cast: Conchita Montenegro, Jorge Lewis, Rosita Granada, Al Ernest Garcia, José Nieto, Mimi Aguglia, José López Rubio • 10 reels

HAT CHECK GIRL (Sept. 25, 1932); D: Sidney Lanfield; W: Barry Conners (scr), Philip Klein (scr), Arthur Kober (scr); C: Glen MacWilliams; E: Paul Weatherwax; M: George Lipschultz; Cast: Sally Eilers, Ben Lyon, Ginger Rogers, Arthur Pierson, Purnell Pratt, Noel Madison, Monroe Owsley, Dewey Robinson, Eulalie Jensen, Harold Goodwin • Gerry (Eilers), an innocent hat check girl, is pursued by a sleazy tabloid columnist (Owsley). She meets a young bachelor (Lyon) and becomes romantically involved with him. At a party, the columnist threatens to expose information about Gerry and a "murder" game turns into the real thing with Gerry's boyfriend becoming the suspect. However, the murderer is a man who was being blackmailed by the writer. 65 min.

WILD GIRL (Oct. 9, 1932); D: Raoul Walsh; W: Doris Anderson (scr), Edwin Justus Mayer (dial & adpt), Bret Harte (short story); C: Norbert Brodine; E: Jack Murray; M: Louis De Francesco; Cast: Charles Farrell, Joan Bennett, Ralph Bellamy, Eugene Pallette, Irving Pichel, Minna Gombell, Willard Robertson, Sarah Padden, Morgan Wallace, Ferdinand Munier • In a western town, Salomy Jane (Bennett), a tomboy, refuses the men who propose marriage. She eventually falls for a young stranger (Farrell) from Virginia, who has come to avenge his sister's suicide, precipitated by the scoundrel Baldwin (Wallace). The stranger kills Baldwin then makes a daring escape with Jane just as he is about to be hanged. He eludes the law with Jane's help until the matter is straightened out. 78 min. • Location work was filmed at Sequoia National Park, in California.

SIX HOURS TO LIVE (Oct. 16, 1932); D: William Dieterle; W: Bradley King (scr), Gordon Morris (st), Morton Barteaux (st); C: John Seitz; E: Ralph Dixon; M: Louis De Francesco; Cast: Warner Baxter, Miriam Jordan, John Boles, George Marion, Sr., Halliwell Hobbes, Irene Ware, Beryl Mercer, Edward McWade, John Davidson, Edwin Maxwell • Paul (Baxter), a statesman who is going to veto an international trade bill based on greed, is strangled. A doctor (Marion, Sr.) uses a ray he has invented to bring him back to life for six hours. In that time, Paul sets things right in his life, exposes the man in his own delegation who plotted against him, and casts a "no" vote for his country. He bids farewell to his true love, Val (Jordan), then dies, holding a flower she gave him. 80 min.

RACKETY RAX (Oct. 23, 1932); D: Alfred Werker; W: Ben Markson (scr), Lou Breslow (scr), Joel Sayre (short story); C: L.W. O'Connell; E: Robert Bischoff; Cast: Victor McLaglen, Greta Nissen, Nell O'Day, Arthur Pierson, Allan Dinehart, Allen Jenkins, Vincent Barnett, Marjorie Beebe, Esther Howard, Ivan Linow, Stanley Fields • "Knuckles" McGloin (McLaglen) has a racketeering enterprise and is on the lookout for a fast buck. After dodging a murder rap, McGloin gets in on football by taking over the mortgage of a local college. He hires thugs for his team. His moll (Nissen) chooses team colors and hires nightclub dancers as his cheerleaders. A rival racketeer (Fields) gets into the game and, when both teams face off, it is a free-for-all with guns, gas bombs and explosives. Both racketeers end up becoming partners. 65 min.

THE GOLDEN WEST (Oct. 30, 1932); D: David Howard; W: Gordon Rigby (scr), Zane Grey (novel); C: George Schneiderman; E: Ralph Dietrich; M: Arthur Lange; Cast: George O'Brien, Janet Chandler, Marion Burns, Arthur Pierson, Onslow Stevens, Emmett Corrigan, Bert Hanlon, Edmund Breese, Julia Swayne Gordon • Dave Lynch (O'Brien) leaves Kentucky and his sweetheart, Betty Summers (Chandler), because of a feud and heads west. Wounded in a duel in which Betty's brother is accidentally killed (Pierson), Dave is nursed by Helen (Burns), whom he rescued from a buffalo stampede. He later marries Helen, but they are killed in an Indian attack and their infant son is captured. Twenty years later, Dave's son, Motano (O'Brien), has become an Indian chief who leads raids against the railroad. The daughter (Chandler) of his father's one-time fiancée is captured by the Indians. After an Indian battle she falls in love with Motano who returns to white man's society. 70 min.

SHERLOCK HOLMES (Nov. 6, 1932); D: William K. Howard; W: Bertram Millhauser (scr), William Gillette (play) Arthur Conan Doyle (short story); C: George Barnes; E: Margaret Clancy; M: George Lipschultz; Cast: Clive Brook, Miriam Jordan, Ernest Torrence, Herbert Mundin, Reginald Owen, Howard Leeds, Alan Mowbray, Montague Shaw, Ivan Simpson, Stanley Fields • Evil Professor Moriarty (Torrence), sentenced to death, escapes from prison, killing his guards and later murders the judge (Shaw) who sentenced him. When Moriarty gets involved with American gangsters, Sherlock Holmes (Brook) comes out of retirement to recapture the malevolent criminal. In a cat-and-mouse game, Holmes finally puts an end to Moriarty's crime spree by shooting him during a bank robbery. Holmes then makes plans to marry his fiancée, Alice (Jordan). 71 min.

TOO BUSY TO WORK (Nov. 13, 1932); D: John Blystone; W: Barry Conners (scr), Philip Klein (scr), Ben Ames Williams (article); C: Charles G. Clarke; E: Alex Troffey; M: George Lipschultz; Cast: Will Rogers, Marian Nixon, Dick Powell, Frederick Burton, Charles Middleton, Louise Beavers, Constantine Romanoff, Douglas Cosgrove, John O'Hara, Bert Hanlon • Jubilo (Rogers), a hobo, whose wife ran off with another man while he was fighting in the war, tramps off in search of revenge. When he finally meets the culprit, Judge Hardy (Burton), he learns that Hardy has adopted his daughter Rose (Nixon). Rose is in love with a nice young man (Powell), and not wanting to disrupt her happiness, Jubilo changes his mind about revenge. He disappears before Rose can learn his identity. 70 min.

EL CABALLERO DE LA NOCHE (Nov. 19, 1932) Spanish version — *Dick Turpin*; D: James Tinling; W: William Kernell (adpt), José López Rubio (Spanish version), Paul Perez (adpt); C: Sidney Wagner; Cast: José Mojica, Mona Maris, Andres de Segurola, Romualdo Tirado, Manuel Paris, Lita Santos • 8 reels

TESS OF THE STORM COUNTRY (Nov. 20, 1932); D: Alfred Santell; W: S.N. Behrman (scr), Sonya Levien (scr), Rupert Hughes (play), Grace Miller White (novel); C: Hal Mohr; E: Ralph Dietrich; M: Louis De Francesco; Cast: Janet Gaynor, Charles Farrell, Dudley Digges, June Clyde, Claude Gillingwater, George Meeker, Sarah Padden, Edward Pawley, Professor Peppy, Matty Kemp • A retired skipper (Digges) wants to settle on land but his tomboyish, good-hearted daughter, Tess (Gaynor), insists on going out to illegally net-fish. Tess rescues Fred (Farrell), a wealthy young man, from his capsized motorboat, but learns that his father (Gillingwater) was responsible for burning down her house. Angered at first, Tess later softens and protects the womanizing Fred from a father with a shotgun. Tess secretly adopts Fred's sister Teola's (Clyde) baby when the real father (Meeker) is murdered. This complicates Tess' life, but all is finally resolved when Teola reclaims the baby. Fred and Tess are finally united. 75 min. • Janet Gaynor took over yet another role made famous by Mary Pickford in two silent versions, one produced in 1914 and the other in 1922.

CALL HER SAVAGE (Nov. 27, 1932); AP: Sam E. Rork; D: John Francis Dillon; W: Edwin Burke (scr), Tiffany Thayer (novel); C: Lee Garmes; E: Harold Schuster; M: Louis De Francesco; Cast: Clara Bow, Gilbert Roland, Thelma Todd, Monroe Owsley, Estelle Taylor, Weldon Heyburn, Willard Robertson, Anthony Jowitt, Fred Kohler, Russell Simpson • The father (Robertson) of Nasa (Bow), a tempestuous young woman in the Southwest, sends her to Chicago, where she marries a wealthy but irresponsible man (Owsley), who leaves her on their wedding night. Nasa earns her money on the street and lives in a slum flat, where her baby dies in a fire. After several other misfortunes, Nasa returns to her family and is romanced by Moonglow (Roland), a half-breed Indian. Nasa learns that her mother, too, was an Indian, and finally sees the prospect of a happy marriage. 85 min.

ME AND MY GAL (Dec. 4, 1932); D: Raoul Walsh; W: Arthur Kober (scr), Philip Klein (st), Barry Conners (st); C: Arthur Miller; E: Jack Murray; M: George Lipschultz; Cast: Spencer Tracy, Joan Bennett, Marion Burns, George Walsh, J. Farrell MacDonald, Noel Madison, Bert Hanlon, Adrian Morris, George Chandler, Will Stanton, Hank Mann • Fast-talking Detective Dolan (Tracy) works Pier 13, where he meets cynical chowder house waitress, Helen (Bennett), who reluctantly agrees to see him. Helen's newly married sister, Kate (Burns), is mixed up with her former suitor, Duke Castanega (Walsh), an escaped crook whose gang robs the bank where she works. Dolan helps apprehend Castanega, saves Kate's life and marries Helen. 79 min. • The story for this film was based in part on an episode from the 1920 Fox Film, *While New York Sleeps*.

HANDLE WITH CARE (Dec. 25, 1932); D: David Butler; W: Frank Craven (scr), Sam Mintz (scr), David Butler (st); C: John Schmitz; E: Irene Morra; M: George Lipschultz; Cast: James Dunn, Boots Mallory, El Brendel, Victor Jory, Buster Phelps, George Ernest, Arthur Vinton, Pat Hartigan, Frank O'Connor, Louise Carver • District Attorney Bill Gordon (Dunn) reunites with high-school friend Helen (Mallory), but the two nephews in her care, Tommy (Phelps) and Charlie (Ernest), become jealous. Neighborhood gangsters order Helen to warn Bill to stay out of a pending legal case. After Helen and Bill split up over Tommy and Charlie, the youngsters try to get them together again, but are kidnapped by the gangsters. Bill helps in rescuing the boys, who now accept him as a husband for their aunt. 77 min.

1933 Releases

ROBBERS' ROOST (Jan. 1, 1933); D: Louis King; W: Dudley Nichols; C: George Schneiderman; M: George Lipschultz; Cast: George O'Brien, Maureen O'Sullivan, Walter McGrail, Maude Eburne, Reginald Owen, William Pawley, Clifford Stanley, Robert Greig, Doris Lloyd, Gilbert Holmes • Jim Wall (O'Brien), a sharpshooting cowboy, is hired to combat cattle rustling. Jim meets the English ranch owner's (Owen) sister, Helen (O'Sullivan), and becomes romantically involved with Helen after rescuing her from a stampede. Jim is captured by a crooked ranch hand, Hays (Pawley), and Helen is kidnapped when she tries to help him. Getting away, Jim returns in time to rescue Helen from the foreman. The ensuing shoot-out brings the crooks to justice. 64 min.

SECOND HAND WIFE (Jan. 8, 1933); D: Hamilton MacFadden; W: Hamilton MacFadden, Kathleen Norris (novel); C: Charles Clarke; E: Alex Troffey; M: Louis De Francesco; Cast: Sally Eilers, Ralph Bellamy, Helen Vinson, Victor Jory, Karol Kay, Esther Howard • Carter (Bellamy) falls in love with his secretary, Sandra (Eilers), divorces his wife, Betty (Vinson), and remarries. However, Betty stubbornly retains custody of their young son and this almost ruins Carter's marriage to Sandra. Sandra discovers that Betty falsified facts in the divorce and reunites the son with his father. 70 min.

HOT PEPPER (Jan. 15, 1933); D: John Blystone; W: Barry Conners (scr), Phillip Klein (scr), Dudley Nichols (st), Bert Hanlon (add'l dial), Thomas Dugan (add'l dial); C: Charles Clarke; E: Alex Troffey; M: George Lipshultz; Cast: Edmund Lowe, Lupe Velez, Victor McLaglen, El Brendel, Lilian Bond, Boothe Howard, Gloria Roy, Andre Cheron • Quirt (Lowe) and Flagg (McLaglen) enter civilian life, with Flagg running a restaurant. A boatload of bootleg liquor arrives and so does a stowaway named Pepper (Velez). Quirt and Flagg fight over Pepper's affection. They also have to fend off a hoodlum (Howard), whom Quirt cheated in a card game. In the end, they swear off girls once again and join the Chinese army. 76 min.

FACE IN THE SKY (Jan. 15, 1933); D: Harry Lachman; W: Humphrey Pearson (scr), Myles Connolly (st); C: Lee Garmes; E: Ralph Dietrich; M: Louis De Francesco; Cast: Spencer Tracy, Marian Nixon, Stuart Erwin, Sam Hardy, Lila Lee, Sarah Padden, Russell Simpson, Frank McGlynn, Jr., Billy Platt, Guy Usher • Madge (Nixon), the young foster daughter of a brutal farmer (Simpson), is protected by Joe (Tracy) and Lucky (Erwin), who paint beauty preparation advertisements on the sides of barns. Joe heads off to New York to become famous, while Madge is kept behind to be forced into marriage with Jim (McGlynn Jr.). She runs away to the city to find Joe. Meanwhile, Joe has painted Madge's face on a billboard instead of the assigned model. When Madge finds him, he thinks he will be fired so they head out on the open road together. 77 min.

EL ÚLTIMO VARÓN SOBRE LA TIERRA (Jan. 30, 1933) Spanish version — *It's Great to Be Alive*; D: James Tinling; W: William Kernel (scr), Paul Perez (scr), José López Rubio (Spanish version), John D. Swain (article); C: Ray June; Cast: Raúl Roulien, Rosita Moreno, Mimi Aguglia, Carmen Rodriguez, Romualdo Tirado, Hilda Moreno, Antonio Vidal, Luz Segovia • 7 reels

DANGEROUSLY YOURS (Feb. 2, 1933); D: Frank Tuttle; W: Horace Jackson (scr), Paul Hervey Fox (st); C: John Seitz; E: Harold Schuster; Cast: Warner Baxter, Miriam Jordan, Herbert Mundin, Florence Eldridge, Florence Roberts, William Davidson, Arthur Hoyt, Mischa Auer, Nella Walker, Tyrell Davis • A suave jewel thief (Baxter) presents himself as a society gentleman with a man-servant (Mundin), who is really his accomplice. While on a big heist, he falls in love with a woman (Jordan) who happens to be a detective. He kidnaps her, but she escapes and eventually reforms him. 73 min.

INFERNAL MACHINE (Feb. 10, 1933); D: Marcel Varnel; W: Arthur Kober (scr), Carl Sloboda (play and novel); C: George Schneiderman; E: Ralph Dixon; M: Samuel Kaylin; Cast: Chester Morris, Genevieve Tobin, Victor Jory, Elizabeth Patterson, Edward Van Sloan, Josephine Whittell, James Bell, Arthur Hohl, Robert Littlefield, J. Carrol Naish • Robert (Morris), a stowaway who is pursuing Elinor (Tobin), a girl he met in Paris, finds out the transatlantic ship they are on will blow up at midnight. After panic settles down, the captain and a few others try to figure out who the anarchists are and how to find the "infernal machine." Robert lies that he is involved in the plot as a ploy to spend some time with Elinor in her room. However, he is innocent of wrongdoing and figures out who the actual perpetrator is. The guilty man is an anarchist writer (Bell) who made up a story about destroying the ship; he is led off in a straightjacket. 65 min.

STATE FAIR (Feb. 10, 1933); P: Winfield Sheehan; D: Henry King; W: Sonya Levien (scr), Paul Green (scr), Philip Stong (novel); C: Hal Mohr; E: R.W. Bischoff; M: Louis De Francesco; Cast: Janet Gaynor, Will Rogers, Lew Ayres, Sally Eilers, Norman Foster, Louise Dresser, Frank Craven, Victor Jory, Frank Melton, Erville Alderson • The Frake family sets off for the annual state fair, each member with an objective. Dad Abel (Rogers) wants to win the hog contest, Mom Melissa (Dresser) wants to win a baking prize, and son Pat (Ayres) and daughter Margy (Gaynor) are both looking for romance. Everyone gets something out of the fair, and all return home wiser and happier. 100 min.

SMOKE LIGHTNING (Feb. 17, 1933); P: Sol M. Wurtzel; D: David Howard; W: Gordon Rigby (scr), Sidney Mitchell (scr), Zane Grey (story); C: Sidney Wagner; E: Jack Murray; M: Arthur Lange; Cast: George O'Brien, Nell O'Day, Betsy King Ross, Frank Atkinson, Clarence Wilson, Morgan Wallace, Virginia Sale, George Burton, E.A. Warren, Douglas Dumbrille • Smoke Mason (O'Brien), passing through a small California town, wins a 5,000-acre ranch in a poker game by cheating to keep dishonest Sheriff Kyle (Wallace) from winning. Smoke tries to return the deed but the owner, Blake (Warren), has committed suicide. He then signs the deed over to the man's daughter, Betsy (Ross) and becomes her guardian. While Smoke romances Betsy's teacher, Dorothy (O'Day), Kyle arrests him for Blake's death. Smoke breaks out of jail and foils Kyle's plan to have an impostor become Betsy's guardian. 61 min.

PRIMAVERA EN OTOÑO (Feb. 19, 1933) Spanish language; P: John Stone; D: Eugene Forde; W: José López Rubio (adpt), John Reinhardt (adpt), Gregorio Martinez Sierra (play); C: Robert H. Planck; Cast: Raúl Roulien, Luana Alcañiz, Julio Peña, Antonio Moreno, Catalina Bárcena, Maria Calvo, Agostino Borgato, Hilda Moreno, Romualdo Tirado • Elena Montero (Bárcena) is an opera star in Madrid, leading a separate life from her husband, Enrique (Moreno), who is a rancher. Problems arise for daughter Agustina (Alcañiz), whose boyfriend Manolo (Peña) is very conservative and does not like Elena's influence over his girlfriend. Agustina becomes enamored of Juan (Roulien), an attaché of the Brazilian embassy and a friend of Elena's. When Enrique sees Juan with Elena, he assumes a romance and has a jealous fit. Meanwhile, he learns that Juan has proposed to Agustina. Elena and Enrique make up and agree to live together half of the year in Madrid and half on the ranch. 75 min.

BROADWAY BAD (Feb. 24, 1933); D: Sidney Lanfield; W: Arthur Kober (scr), Maude Fulton (scr), William R. Lipman (st), A.W. Pezet (st); C: George Barnes; E: Paul Weatherwax; M: Arthur Lange; Cast: Joan Blondell, Ricardo Cortez, Ginger Rogers, Adrienne Ames, Allen Vincent, Francis McDonald, Frederick Burton, Ronald Cosbey, Donald Crisp, Phil Tead • Bob (Vincent), the rich husband of rising stage star Tony Landers (Blondell), walks out on her, wrongly suspecting an affair with her producer, Craig (Cortez). Tony then puts on airs of being "bad" to promote her career. Secretly, she is a devoted mother, protecting her young son (Cosbey) from a husband who is now in debt to underworld figures. Bob tries to use blackmail to get custody of the boy and almost wins a court hearing. However, Tony lies that Craig is the boy's father and to help her, he goes along. Tony wins the custody battle. 59 min.

HUMANITY (March 3, 1933); D: John Francis Dillon; W: Bradley King (scr), Harry Fried (st); C: L.W. O'Connell; E: Frank Hull; M: Louis De Francesco; Cast: Ralph Morgan, Boots Mallory, Alexander Kirkland, Irene Ware, Noel N. Madison, Wade Boteler, Christian Rub, Betty Jane Graham, Ferike Boros, George Irving • "Doc" MacDonald (Morgan) goes to a medical conference and leaves his son Bill (Kirkland), recently back from medical school in Vienna, in charge of his practice. Bill's socialite fiancée, Olive (Ware), does not approve of him serving the poor community. Bill finances a Park Avenue practice by illegally patching up gangsters' gun wounds. Bill gets Doc involved in one case with a gangster friend and then confesses all to his father. To save Bill, Doc takes the blame for the infractions and loses his license. When Doc dies, Bill is compelled to tell the truth, but he is deterred because his skills can now follow in his father's footsteps and help the poor. 70 min.

SAILOR'S LUCK (March 10, 1933); D: Raoul Walsh; W: Marguerite Roberts (st & scr), Charlotte Miller (st & scr), Bert Hanlon (add'l dial), Ben Ryan (add'l dial); C: Arthur Miller; E: Jack Murray; M: Samuel Kaylin; Cast: James Dunn, Sally Eilers, Victor Jory, Sammy Cohen, Frank Moran, Esther Muir, Will Stanton, Curley Wright, Jerry Mandy, Lucien Littlefield, Buster Phelps • Young Sally (Eilers), who wants to avoid sailors, slowly gives Jimmy (Dunn) a chance and gets to like him. She ends up not having a place to stay and Jimmy offers her his hotel room but makes inappropriate advances. When Jimmy's ship sails unexpectedly, Sally thinks he abandoned her. After a variety of misunderstandings, Jimmy returns to reunite with Sally in the middle of a marathon dance. 78 min.

AFTER THE BALL (March 17, 1933) British-made; P: Michael Balcon; D: Milton Rosmer; W: J.O.C. Orton (scr), H.M. Harwood (adpt), based on a German film written by Jacques Bachrach, Ida Jenbach and Max Neufeld; C: Percy Strong; Cast: Esther Ralston, Basil Rathbone, Marie Burke, Jean Adrienne, George Curzon, Clifford Heatherley • Jack (Rathbone), a womanizing courier for the British government, follows Elissa (Ralston), a diplomat's wife, to her home after a masked ball. Jack makes love to the woman and is boasting about his conquest to his best friend, Peter (Curzon), when he discovers that the woman he was with is Peter's wife. In a series of complications, it is explained that Elissa slipped out of the room and let her maid re-enter in her clothes. 70 min.

PLEASURE CRUISE (March 24, 1933); D: Frank Tuttle; W: Guy Bolton (scr), Austin Allen (play); C: Ernest Palmer; E: Alex Troffey; M: Louis De Francesco; Cast: Genevieve Tobin, Roland Young, Ralph Forbes, Una O'Connor, Herbert Mundin, Minna Gombell, Theodor von Eltz, Frank Atkinson, Robert Greig, Arthur Hoyt • Tired of her husband Andrew's (Young) insane jealousy, Shirley (Tobin) decides to take a cruise, but Andrew goes along disguised as the ship's barber so he can spy on her. Many men flirt with Shirley, but one in particular (Forbes) tries to convince her to leave her stateroom door unlocked. Overhearing this, Andrew slips in and spends the night with her. Shirley claims she knew who it was all the time. 72 min.

BONDAGE (March 31, 1933); D: Alfred Santell; W: Arthur Kober (scr), Doris Malloy (scr), Grace Sothcote Leake (novel); C: Lucien Andriot; E: Jack Murray; M: Samuel Kaylin; Cast: Dorothy Jordan, Alexander Kirkland, Merle Tottenham, Nydia Westman, Jane Darwell, Isabel Jewell, Dorothy Libaire, Rafaela Ottiano, Clarence H. Wilson • Judy (Jordan) falls for a popular crooner (Woods), who leaves her unwed and pregnant. She ends up in a "house of refuge" where she is mistreated. She later attacks the cruel matron when her baby is taken from her for adoption and she takes to the streets. She is ultimately rescued by a compassionate doctor (Kirkland) from the home. 65 min.

HELLO, SISTER! (Apr. 14, 1933); D: Alan Crosland, Erich von Stroheim (UC), Alfred Werker (UC — retakes), Edwin Burke (UC — retakes); W: Erich von Stroheim (UC), Leonard Spigelgass (UC), Geraldine Norris (UC); C: James Wong Howe (UC) Arthur Miller (UC — retakes); E: Frank Hull; Cast: James Dunn, Boots Mallory, ZaSu Pitts, Minna Gombell, Terrance Ray, Will Stanton, Henry Kolker, Walter Walker, Astrid Allwyn, Claude King, Wade Boteler • Attractive Peggy (Mallory) and ungainly Millie (Pitts) meet two young men on the streets of New York. Jimmy (Dunn) is decent and Mac (Ray) is a cad. Mac attempts to rape Peggy, and, when she becomes pregnant, he tells Jimmy that the baby is his. Angry that Jimmy believed the lies, Peggy does not dispute him. Millie tells Jimmy the truth and while he fights with Mac, there is an explosion in the building. Jimmy rescues Peggy from the burning building. 61 min.

CAVALCADE (Apr. 15, 1933); P: Winfield Sheehan; D: Frank Lloyd; W: Reginald Berkeley (scr), Sonya Levien (st), Noel Coward (play); C: Ernest Palmer; E: Margaret Clancey; M: Louis De Francesco; Cast: Diana Wynyard, Clive Brook, Una O'Connor, Herbert Mundin, Beryl Mercer, Irene Browne, Tempe Pigott, Merle Tottenham, Frank Lawton, Ursula Jeans • Personal and historical events are intertwined in this story of two families, one aristocratic, and the other their servants, through a period from 1899 to 1933, with particular emphasis on the Great War. 110 min.

TRICK FOR TRICK (Apr. 21, 1933); D: Hamilton MacFadden; W: Howard J. Green (scr), Vivian Cosby (play), Shirley Warde (play), Harry Wagstaff Gribble (play), Fulton Oursler (play); C: L.W. O'Connell; E: Robert Bischoff; M: Samuel Kaylin; Cast: Ralph Morgan, Victor Jory, Sally Blane, Tom Dugan, Luis Alberni, Edward Van Sloan, Willard Robertson, Dorothy Appleby, Boothe Howard, Clifford Jones • A detective (Howard), searching for clues in the death of magician Azrah's (Morgan) assistant, goes to a séance, during which a rival magician (Jory) is exposed as the woman's murderer. The girl's father kills the rival after first thinking Azrah was guilty. 69 min.

ZOO IN BUDAPEST (Apr. 28, 1933); P: Jesse L. Lasky; D: Rowland V. Lee; W: Dan Totheroh (scr), Louise Long (scr), Rowland V. Lee (scr), Melville Baker (st), James Kirkland (st); C: Lee Garmes; E: Harold Schuster; M: Louis De Francesco; Cast: Loretta Young, Gene Raymond, O.P. Heggie, Wally Albright, Paul Fix, Murray Kinnell, Ruth Warren, Roy Stewart, Frances Rich, Niles Welch, Lucille Ward • An idealistic zookeeper, Zani (Raymond), who has never been outside the zoo, meets a teenaged runaway girl (Young) and romance blossoms. He also shelters a young boy (Albright) who hides in the zoo at night and accidentally opens the tiger's cage, which creates chaos as many animals escape. Zani rescues the boy and returns him to his wealthy parents, who gratefully provide a cottage for Zani and his new bride. 85 min.

THE WARRIOR'S HUSBAND (May 12, 1933); P: Jesse Lasky; D: Walter Lang; W: Ralph Spence (adpt & dial), Sonya Levien (cont), Julian Thompson (play); C: Hal Mohr; E: Ralph Dietrich; M: Louis De Francesco; Cast: Elissa Landi, Marjorie Rambeau, Ernest Truex, David Manners, Helen Ware, Maude Eburne, Claudia Coleman, Ferdinand Gottschalk, John Sheehan, Lionel Belmore • Hippolyta (Rambeau), queen of the ancient, female-dominated Pontus, returns home from battle with Greek male prisoners. Antiope (Landi) is attracted to Theseus (Manners) and later, rather than have to kill him, she allows him to carry her off. Hippolyta's effeminate son gets some courage and wants to lead Pontus's men in revolt. The Greek army conquers the Pontus Amazons and put women in their "rightful" place in society, and the women are shown to enjoy the new order. 75 min.

ADORABLE (May 19, 1933); D: Wilhelm Dieterle; W: George Marion, Jr. (scr), Jane Storm (scr), based on a German film written by Robert Leibmann, Paul Frank and Billie (Billy) Wilder; C: John Seitz; E: Irene Morra, R.W. Bischoff; M: Louis De Francesco, Werner Richard Heymann; Cast: Janet Gaynor, Henry Garat, C. Aubrey Smith, Herbert Mundin, Blanche Friderici, Hans von Twardowski, James Marcus, Sterling Holloway • European Princess Mitzi (Gaynor), posing as a manicurist to get a taste of a commoner's life, meets and falls in love with Karl (Garat), a delicatessen owner, really a lieutenant in disguise. She finally reveals her true identity and the lieutenant suddenly feels he can no longer romance her because of his lowly position. When a prince — the intended marriage match for Mitzi — bows out, the king, Mitzi's younger brother, makes Karl a prince so he can marry her. 83 min.

EL REY DE LOS GITANOS (May 26, 1933) Spanish language; D: Frank Strayer; W: Llewellyn Hughes (scr), Paul Perez (scr), José López Rubio (Spanish version); C: Robert Planck; Cast: José Mojica, Rosita Moreno, Julio Villareal, Romualdo Tirado, Ada Lozano, Antonio Vidal, Martin Garralaga, Paco Moreno • Princess Maria (Moreno) goes to the fair incognito and meets Karol (Mojica) a Gypsy king. Her fiancé, the Grand Duke Alejandro (Villareal), is jealous and arrests Karol for kissing the princess. Karol, serving his sentence, gets into a fight with Alejandro then kidnaps Maria, who goes along willingly, and takes her to his gypsy camp. While soldiers enter the camp, Alejandro fights a duel with Karol then runs off after missing his shot. Karol bids farewell to Maria and says his gypsies must move on. 82 min.

HOLD ME TIGHT (May 26, 1933); D: David Butler; W: Gladys Lehman (scr), Gertrude Rigdon (st); C: Arthur Miller; E: Irene Morra; M: Samuel Kaylin; Cast: James Dunn, Sally Eilers, Frank McHugh, June Clyde, Kenneth Thomson, Noel Francis, Dorothy Peterson, Clay Clement • Department store workers Chuck (Dunn) and Molly (Eilers) decide to marry and, for marital harmony, Chuck insists Molly quit her job. Molly finds out Chuck will be laid off and keeps her job in secret. Molly, fired following a customer complaint, discovers she is pregnant and tries to poison herself. Chuck unwittingly gets involved with Dolan (Thomson), the store's crooked detective, in a plot to steal furs. Molly, rehired by Dolan, who desires her, alerts the police to the crime and prevents Chuck from being shot. Chuck earns a better job so Molly can stay home and raise a family. 71 min.

CUANDO EL AMOR RIE (May 27, 1933) Spanish language; D: David Howard; W: Lynn Starling (st & scr), Francisco Moré de la Torre (Spanish version); C: Lucien Andriot; E: Ralph Dixon; Cast: José Mojica, Mona Maris, Carlos Villarías, Carmen Rodriguez, Rene Cardona, Rosita Granada, Rafael Valverde • Emilio (Mojica), a wild horse trainer, works on Don José's (Villarías) ranch in California. Emilio finds out that Manuel (Cardona), the fiancé of Don José's daughter, Elvira (Maris), has been carrying on with Anita (Granada) and that they have a daughter together. Emilio falls in love with Elvira, but social barriers keep them apart. Just before Elvira's wedding to Manuel, Anita visits her and reveals all. Don José finally allows Emilio to marry his daughter. 57 min.

IT'S GREAT TO BE ALIVE (June 2, 1933); D: Alfred Werker; W: Paul Perez (adpt), Arthur Kober (dial), John D. Swain (article); C: Robert Planck; E: Barney Wolf; M: Samuel Kaylin; Cast: Raúl Roulien, Gloria Stuart, Edna May Oliver, Herbert Mundin, Joan Marsh, Dorothy Burgess, Emma Dunn, Edward Van Sloan, Robert Grieg, Gloria Roy • Carlos (Roulien), an inveterate seducer of women, decides to take a Pacific flight when Dorothy (Stuart) breaks her engagement with him. His plane disappears and several years later, after "masculitis" has wiped out every man on earth, Carlos is found. His return begins as a dream come true. He is surrounded and pampered by beautiful women, but he eventually wants to marry Dorothy. The couple has to escape and they are pursued by the Navy and Air Force. Finally, a world congress convenes to determine that they can marry. 68 min. • This is a remake of the 1924 film, *The Last Man on Earth*.

I LOVED YOU WEDNESDAY (June 16, 1933); D: Henry King; W: Philip Klein (scr), Horace Jackson (scr), Molly Ricardel and William DuBois (play); C: Hal Mohr; E: Frank Hull; M: Louis De Francesco; Cast: Warner Baxter, Elissa Landi, Victor Jory, Miriam Jordan, Laura Hope Crews, June Vlasek, Fox Movietone Studio Dancers • A Parisian dancer (Landi) is deserted by her married American boyfriend (Jory), and rushes off to South America. She meets an engineer (Baxter) and they return to New York together, but she returns to her dancing career abroad. When she becomes famous, she returns to New York, but her former lover shows up and becomes a rival of the engineer who eventually wins her love. 75 min.

UNA VIUDA ROMÁNTICA (June 18, 1933) Spanish language; D: Louis King; W: José López Rubio (scr), Paul Perez (scr), Gregorio Martinez Sierra (play); C: Robert Planck; Cast: Catalina Bárcena, Gilbert Roland, Mona Maris, Juan Torena, Julio Peña, Fernando de Toledo, Julia Bejarano, Maria Calvo, Romualdo Tirado, Juan Martinez Pia • A chance meeting between Rosario (Bárcena) and author Luis Felipe (Gilbert) leads to the woman getting a job as the writer's secretary. Complications result when Rosario's three protective brothers, Mario (Toreno), Pepe (Peña) and Emilio (de Toledo), get involved because they think Luis Felipe is a threat to their sister's virtue. The author's lover, Estrella (Maris), an American dancer, also gets into the mix when Rosario goes to a costume ball in an outfit designed for Estrella. All is sorted out when Luis Felipe proposes to Rosario, and she accepts. 73 min.

BEST OF ENEMIES (June 23, 1933); D: Rian James; W: Sam Mintz (scr), Rian James (dial); C: L.W. O'Connell; E: Margaret Clancy; M: Arthur Lange; Cast: Buddy Rogers, Marian Nixon, Frank Morgan, Joseph Cawthorn, Greta Nissen, Arno Frey, William Lawrence, Anders Van Haden • A young aspiring musician, Jimmie (Rogers), is sent to study in Germany and meets his childhood friend Lena Schneider (Nixon). In love with Lena, Jimmie gets a job in a band at her father's (Cawthorn) beer garden. Jimmie's father (Morgan), visiting Germany, finds Jimmie and this renews a feud between the two fathers, which started over a business deal involving a beer garden. Lena is forbidden from seeing Jimmie. The couple elopes on a ship to America, with the fathers following them. However, a truce is made when both men decide to open a brewery together. 71 min.

ARIZONA TO BROADWAY (June 30, 1933); D: James Tinling; W: William Conselman (scr), Henry Johnson (scr); C: George Schneiderman; E: Louis Loeffler; M: Arthur Lange; Cast: James Dunn, Joan Bennett, Herbert Mundin, Sammy Cohen, Theodore von Eltz, Merna Kennedy, Earle Foxe, David Wengren, J. Carrol Naish, Max Wagner, Walter Catlett • Unregenerate con-man Smiley (Dunn), traveling with his entourage, meets Lynn (Bennett) who is on the trail of three men who swindled her brother out of $20,000. Smiley convinces his partners they can track down the swindlers and end up with the money. Through a convoluted scheme, Smiley gets involved with a New York gangster (Naish) and retrieves the money, but when Lynn is captured with one of his co-conspirators, she learns about his true motives. Luckily, Smiley calls in a rival gang to get them out of the mess they are in. His entire crew then goes straight. 66 min.

LIFE IN THE RAW (July 7, 1933); P: Sol M. Wurtzel; D: Louis King; W: Stuart Anthony (scr), Zane Grey (article); C: Robert Planck; E: Barney Wolf; M: Arthur Lange; Cast: George O'Brien, Claire Trevor, Greta Nissen, Francis Ford, Warner Richmond, Gaylord Pendleton, Alan Edwards, Nigel De Brulier • Judy (Trevor), a visitor to Arizona, is lost in the desert when Jim (O'Brien), a wanderer, offers to help her find directions to her brother's ranch. Brother Tom (Pendleton) has been coerced into committing a robbery after losing his ranch to a notorious gambler (Edwards). Jim is later arrested for the robbery. Judy vouches for him and he infiltrates the gang under an assumed identity, rescues Judy and Tom from abduction, and brings the criminals to justice. 62 min.

THE MAN WHO DARED (July 14, 1933); P: Sol M. Wurtzel; D: Hamilton MacFadden; W: Lamar Trotti (scr), Dudley Nichols (scr); C: Arthur Miller; E: Al DeGaetano; M: Samuel Kaylin; Cast: Preston Foster, Zita Johann, Joan Marsh, Irene Biller, Clifford Jones, June Vlasek, Leon Ames, Douglas Cosgrove, Douglas Dumbrille, Frank Sheridan, Leonid Snegoff • Anton Cermak (Foster) rises from the coal mines to become the mayor of Chicago. With all the gang violence of the 1920s, Cermak determines to restore law and order to his city. Attending a public rally with President Roosevelt, Cermak is felled by an assassin's bullet. 75 min.

LA MELODÍA PROHIBIDA (July 16, 1933) Spanish language; D: Frank Strayer; W: Paul Perez (scr), Enrique Jardiel Poncela (scr), William Kernell (cont), Eve Unsell (st); C: Harry Jackson; M: Samuel Kaylin; Cast: José Mojica, Conchita Montenegro, Mona Maris, Romualdo Tirado, Juan Martinez Pia, Carmen Rodriguez, Antonio Vidal, Ralph Navarro • At a South Pacific marriage ceremony of two natives, Kalu (Mojica) and Tuila (Montenegro), Kalu sings the "Forbidden Melody," which can only be sung on the night of a man's wedding. The next day Kalu meets Peggy (Maris), a wealthy American tourist, and she implores him to sing the song. Tuila finds out about this and orders Peggy to leave Kalu alone. Peggy lures Kalu to San Francisco, where he becomes a singer. After being abandoned by Peggy, Kalu becomes despondent, especially when he hears his "Forbidden Melody" on the radio. Thinking he hears Tuila calling him, he runs into the street and is struck by a fire engine and killed. 8 reels

THE DEVIL'S IN LOVE (July 21, 1933); P: Al Rockett; D: Wilhelm Dieterle; W: Howard Estabrook (scr), Harry Hervey (st); C: Hal Mohr; E: Ralph Dietrich; M: Louis De Francesco; Cast: Victor Jory, Loretta Young, Vivienne Osborne, David Manners, C. Henry Gordon, Herbert Mundin, Emil Chautard, J. Carrol Naish, Robert Barrat, Akim Tamiroff • André (Jory), a doctor accused of poisoning a Foreign Legion captain at Fort Rondet, practices in Port Zamba to escape execution. He becomes enamored of a visiting girl (Young) who happens to be engaged to his best friend (Manners). Learning that a fever epidemic has broken out at Rondet, he risks his life to return and save his friend. In tending to the legionnaires, one man on his deathbed admits to poisoning the captain, exonerating André. 71 min.

F.P. 1 (July 28, 1933); P: Erich Pommer; D: Karl Hartl; W: Walter Reisch (st & scr), Curt Siodmak (scr & novel), Robert Stevenson (dial), Peter MacFarlane (dial); C: Gunther-Rittau, Konstantin Tachet; M: Allan Gray; Cast: Conrad Veidt, Leslie Fenton, Jill Esmond, George Merritt, Donald Calthrop, Nicholas Hannen, William Freshman, Warwick Ward, Alexander Field, Francis L. Sullivan • A privately financed floating platform is constructed as an artificial island, anchored in the mid–Atlantic, for airships to land and refuel. A rival business interest conspires to destroy the platform and bankrupt the company, but is foiled in their attempt. 93 min. • This was originally a German film, made by Ufa, that was so successful it was remade as a British-Gaumont production.

EL PRECIO DE UN BESO (Aug. 10, 1933) Spanish version—*One Mad Kiss*; D: James Tinling; W: Dudley Nichols (scr), Adolph Paul (st), Francisco Moré de la Torre (Spanish version); C: Ross Fisher; E: Louis Loeffler; Cast: José Mojica, Mona Maris, Antonio Moreno, Tomas Patricola, Fred Malatesta, Juan Torena, Carlos

Villarías, Enrique Acosta, Martin Garralaga, Eumenio Blanco • 71 min.

SHANGHAI MADNESS (Aug. 11, 1933); P: Al Rockett, Winfield Sheehan; D: John Blystone; W: Austin Parker (scr & adpt), Gordon Wong Wellesley (adpt), Frederick Hazlitt Brennan (article); C: Lee Garmes; E: Margaret Clancy, Alexander Troffey; M: Louis De Francesco; Cast: Spencer Tracy, Fay Wray, Ralph Morgan, Eugene Pallette, Herbert Mundin, Reginald Mason, Arthur Hoyt, Albert Conti, Maude Eburne, William von Brincken • Lieutenant Pat Jackson (Tracy), dismissed from the Navy and unable to find work in Shanghai, is offered a job by Li Po Chang (Morgan) as gunner on an arms-smuggling ship. Young Wildeth (Wray), enamored of Pat, sneaks aboard the ship as well. Pat deposits her at an American mission, where the communists attack. Returning to retrieve her, Pat forces the ship's weak-hearted captain (Pallette) to protect the mission and rescue Wildeth. 68 min.

PILGRIMAGE (Aug. 18, 1933); D: John Ford; W: Philip Klein (scr), Barry Conners (scr), Dudley Nichols (dial), I.A.R. Wylie (article); C: George Schneiderman; E: Louis Loeffler; M: Samuel Kaylin; Cast: Henrietta Crossman, Heather Angel, Norman Foster, Marian Nixon, Maurice Murphy, Lucille La Verne, Charley Grapewin, Hedda Hopper, Robert Warwick, Betty Blythe • Hannah (Crossman), who allowed her son Jim (Foster) to enter the war to break up his romance, now feels responsible for his death. She saves a young man (Murphy) in Paris from suicide; he is despondent because his mother (Hopper) will not let him marry his pregnant girlfriend (Angel). Hannah convinces the boy's mother to permit the marriage, then returns home and makes amends with Mary (Nixon) who cares for an illegitimate child because Hannah would not let Jim marry her. 90 min.

THE LAST TRAIL (Aug. 25, 1933); P: Sol M. Wurtzel; D: James Tinling; W: Stuart Anthony (scr), Zane Grey (novel); C: Arthur Miller; E: Barney Wolf; M: Arthur Lange; Cast: George O'Brien, Claire Trevor, El Brendel, Matt McHugh, J. Carrol Naish, George Reed, Lucille La Verne, Ruth Warren, Luis Alberni, Edward LeSaint • Tom (O'Brien), a cowboy, returns to the contemporary west to take over his late uncle's large ranch. With the help of an undercover agent (Trevor) and an old pal (Brendel), Tom is able to root out a gangster (McHugh) who is planning to steal the ranch by pulling off a scheme in which someone else poses as Tom. 60 min.

PADDY, THE NEXT BEST THING (Sept. 1, 1933); P: Winfield Sheehan; D: Harry Lachman; W: Edwin Burke (scr), Gertrude Page (novel); C: John Seitz; E: Margaret Clancy; M: Louis De Francesco; Cast: Janet Gaynor, Warner Baxter, Walter Connolly, Harvey Stephens, Joseph M. Kerrigan, Fiske O'Hara, Claire McDowell, Merle Tottenham, Roger Imhof, Trevor Bland • To save her father (Connolly) from foreclosure, Eileen (Lindsay) agrees to marry wealthy Lawrence Blake (Baxter). Her mischievous sister, Paddy (Gaynor), tries to break up the romance by telling Blake her sister is mentally unbalanced. Paddy makes an effort to win Blake's love and succeeds, but when her father dies, she goes to work for her uncle. Blake finally finds her and schemes with Eileen's suitor, Jack (Stephens), to make both sisters jealous so that Eileen will marry Jack and Paddy will marry him. 76 min.

THE GOOD COMPANIONS (Sept. 8, 1933) British-Gaumont Production; P: Michael Balcon; D: Victor Saville; W: W.P. Lipscomb (scr), J.B. Priestley (novel); C: Bernard Knowles; Cast: Jessie Matthews, Edmund Gwenn, Mary Glynne, John Gielgud, Percy Parsons, A.W.K. Baskcomb, Dennis Hoey, Viola Compton, Richard Dolman, Finlay Currie • Two men, Jess (Gwenn) and Inigo (Gielgud), and Miss Trant (Glynne), a lady in search of adventure, meet a stranded music hall troupe. Trant uses a small inheritance to stake the troupe and a promising singer, Susie Dean (Matthews). After the money is exhausted, it looks like all are out of luck, until an important London producer happens to see the show and signs a contract with them. 113 min.

CHARLIE CHAN'S GREATEST CASE (Sept. 15, 1933); P: Sol M. Wurtzel; D: Hamilton MacFadden; W: Lester Cole (scr), Marion Orth (scr), Earl Der Biggers (novel); C: Ernest Palmer; E: Alex Troffey; M: Samuel Kaylin; Cast: Warner Oland, Heather Angel, Roger Imhof, John Warburton, Ivan Simpson, Virginia Cherrill, Francis Ford, Robert Warwick, Frank McGlynn, Clara Blandick, Claude King • Chan (Oland) works on a case in Honolulu involving the stabbing of a local bachelor (Warwick) who has made a lot of money, but some of it has come from criminal enterprises. The culprit turns out to be the man's lawyer (Byron), who was the victim of blackmail, uncovered by a tan line on his arm left by a watch which became evidence in the murder. 71 min.

DOCTOR BULL (Sept. 22, 1933); P: Winfield Sheehan; D: John Ford; W: Paul Green (scr), Jane Storm (cont), James G. Cozzens (novel); C: George Schneiderman; E: Louis Loeffler; M: Samuel Kaylin; Cast: Will Rogers, Vera Allen, Marian Nixon, Howard Lally, Barton Churchill, Louise Dresser, Andy Devine, Rochelle Hudson, Tempe Pigott, Elizabeth Patterson • A small-town doctor (Rogers), who has served his community for 20 years, is threatened with removal by those who do not like his frankness and honest criticism of hypocrisy. In the wake of a typhoid epidemic, caused by the town not heeding his warnings about waste from a power plant, he stays in his position and concocts a serum that helps a newly wed man (Lally) walk again. The town then rallies to his side. 77 min.

MY WEAKNESS (Sept. 29, 1933); D: David Butler; W: B.G. DeSylva (st & dial), David Butler (cont), Bert Hanlon (add'l dial), Ben Ryan (add'l dial); C: Arthur Miller; E: Irene Morra; M: Arthur Lange; Cast: Lilian Harvey, Lew Ayres, Charles Butterworth, Harry Langdon, Sid Silvers, Irene Bentley, Henry Travers, Adrian Rosley, Mary Howard, Irene Ware, Barbara Weeks • A hotel maid, Looloo (Harvey), overhearing Ronnie (Ayres) claim he could mold any girl into a socialite, begs to be his subject. Ronnie vows to marry her to his friend Gerald (Butterworth). In transforming Looloo, Ronnie falls in love with her and has to win her for himself. 74 min.

THE POWER AND THE GLORY (Oct. 6, 1933); P: Jesse L. Lasky; D: William K. Howard; W: Preston Sturges (scr); C: James Howe; E: Paul Weatherwax; M: Louis De Francesco; Cast: Spencer Tracy, Colleen Moore, Ralph Morgan, Helen Vinson, Clifford Jones, Henry Kolker, Sarah Padden, Billy O'Brien, Cullen Johnston, J. Farrell McDonald • Following his friend's death, Henry (Morgan) narrates the story of much-maligned Tom Garner (Tracy). He tells how Garner worked his way up from unschooled laborer to the tycoon president of railroads. Deserting his first wife (Moore) for Eve (Vinson), Tom is later driven to suicide by Eve's infidelity and the fact that his own son (Jones) from his first marriage figured into that breach. 76 min.

WALLS OF GOLD (Oct. 13, 1933); P: Sol M. Wurtzel; D: Kenneth MacKenna; W: Lester Cole (scr), Wallace Sullivan (adpt), Edmond Seward (adpt) Kathleen Norris (novel); C: George Schneiderman; M: Samuel Kaylin; Cast: Sally Eilers, Norman Foster, Ralph Morgan, Rosita Moreno, Rochelle Hudson, Frederic Santley, Marjorie Gateson, Mary Mason, Margaret Seddon, Gloria Roy • The owner of an employment agency, Jeanie (Eilers), falls in love with Barnes Ritchie (Foster), who introduces her to his wealthy playboy uncle, Gordon (Morgan). When Jeanie accepts expensive gifts from Gordon, Barnes gets angry and marries Jeanie's sister (Mason). As revenge, Jeanie marries Gordon and is miserable. Later, Barnes's wife dies and Gordon, in a dispute with one of his mistresses, has a heart attack and dies. Jeanie and Barnes finally get together. 70 min.

THE WORST WOMAN IN PARIS? (Oct. 20, 1933); P: Jesse L. Lasky; D: Monta Bell; W: Monta Bell (scr & adpt), Marion Dix (adpt), Martin Brown (dial); C: Hal Mohr; E: Paul Weatherwax; M: Louis De Francesco; Cast: Benita Hume, Adolphe Menjou, Harvey Stephens, Helen Chandler, Margaret Seddon, Adele St. Maur, Leonard Carey, Maidel Turner, George Irving, Jack Irwin • Socialite Peggy Vane (Hume), who has a scandalous reputation, is rescued from a train wreck by schoolteacher John (Stephens), who takes her to his small Kansas town. She falls in love with him and is enjoying small-town life when she learns that Adolphe (Menjou), her playboy friend in Paris, is destitute. Realizing she must help Adolphe, she returns to Paris and leaves John to the local woman (Chandler) who really loves him. 78 min.

THE MAD GAME (Oct. 27, 1933); D: Irving Cummings; W: William Conselman (scr & st), Henry Johnson (scr); C: Arthur Miller; M: Samuel Kaylin; Cast: Spencer Tracy, Claire Trevor, Ralph Morgan, Howard Lally, J. Carrol Naish, John Miljan, Matt McHugh, Kathleen Burke, Mary Mason, Willard Robertson • A bootlegger, Edward Carson (Tracy), betrayed by his fellow gangster, Chopper (Naish), his girlfriend (Burke) and his lawyer (Miljan), is sent to the penitentiary. While he is away, Chopper takes over the gang and turns to kidnapping. Seeking revenge, Carson convinces the warden to let him retrieve a judge's (Lally) son and daughter-in-law. With the help of a newspaper reporter (Trevor), Carson infiltrates the gang and succeeds, but loses his life. 65 min. • This film was given the approval by the Hays Office for the way it handled the subject of kidnapping, which was not permitted to be portrayed irresponsibly.

YO, TÚ Y ELLA (Oct. 29, 1933) Spanish language; D: John Reinhardt; W: José López Rubio (scr), John Reinhardt (scr), Gregorio Martinez Sierra (play); C: Robert Planck; Cast: Catalina Bárcena, Gilbert Roland, Rosita Moreno, Mona Maris, Valentin Parera, Julio Peña, Romualdo Tirado, Rosita Granada, José Peña Pepet • Estrella (Bárcena) leaves her husband, Gabriel (Roland), because of an affair he had. While she is in Venice, Gabriel is staying at the same hotel with his new wife, Laura (Maris). Estrella then becomes acquainted with Laura and finally tells her about her marriage to the unfaithful Gabriel. When Gabriel leaves Laura, he pursues Estrella once more until he finally convinces her to marry again. 8 reels

NO DEJES LA PUERTA ABIERTA (Nov. 3, 1933) Spanish version — *Pleasure Cruise*; D: Lewis Seiler; W: Paul Perez (scr), José López Rubio, Austen Allen (play); C: L. William O'Connell; M: Samuel Kaylin; Cast: Raúl Roulien, Rosita Moreno, Mona Maris, Jorge Lewis, Romualdo Tirado, Ralph Navarro, Rosita Granada, Alfredo Sabato, Martin Garralaga, Manuel Noriega • 76 min.

BERKELEY SQUARE (Nov. 3, 1933); P: Jesse L. Lasky; D: Frank Lloyd; W: Sonya Levien (scr), John L. Balderston (scr & play), J.C. Squire (play); C: Ernest Palmer; E: Harold Schuster; M: Louis De Francesco; Cast: Leslie Howard, Heather Angel, Valerie Taylor, Irene Browne, Beryl Mercer, Colin-Keith Johnston, Alan Mowbray, Juliette Compton, Ferdinand Gottschalk • American architect Peter Standish (Howard) travels back in time to 1784 and is mistaken for a descendant. His modern ways confound the people of the past and he eventually tires of the social restrictions. Engaged to Kate (Taylor), he falls in love with Helen (Angel), but is aware that their involvement would alter history. Peter returns to the present, in love with Helen, and confident they will be together at some time. 90 min.

MY LIPS BETRAY (Nov. 10, 1933); D: John Blystone; W: Hans Kraly (scr), Jane Storm (scr), S.N. Behrman (dial), Attila Orbok (play); C: Lee Garmes; E: Alex Troffey, Moe Kauffman; M: Samuel Kaylin, Hugo Friedhofer (UC); Cast: Lilian Harvey, John Boles, El Brendel, Irene Browne, Maude Eburne, Henry Stephenson, Herman Bing, Dewey Robinson • Lili (Harvey), a café singer in Ruthania, is told by his chauffeur that she is the king's favorite singer. Rumors spread of an affair and the king (Boles), who is a composer, investigates, although Lili does not know who he is. Lili, meanwhile, becomes famous from the rumors and the king does fall in love with her. To keep the country out of bankruptcy, the king has agreed to marry the princess of Moravia but, at the last minute, the princess runs off with someone else and geologists discover oil in the kingdom. 79 min.

OLSEN'S BIG MOMENT (Nov. 17, 1933); D: Malcolm St. Clair; W: Henry Johnson (scr), James Tynan (scr), George Marshall (st); C: L.W. O'Connell; M: Samuel Kaylin; Cast: El Brendel, Walter Catlett, Barbara Weeks, Susan Fleming, John Arledge, Maidel Turner, Edward Pawley, Joseph Sauers, Harvey Clark, O.G. Hendrian • An apartment janitor, Olsen (Brendel), helps tenant Jane (Weeks) meet the man she really loves, Harry (Arledge), even though she is engaged to the wealthy Robert Brewster (Catlett). The drunken Brewster drags Olsen to a speakeasy, where they get involved with gangsters. The leader of the gang (Pawley) plans to rob the guests at Brewster and Jane's wedding. Harry, not able to live without Jane, threatens to kill Jane and Brewster if Olsen cannot prevent the wedding. With all the chaos converging on the wedding, Olsen saves the day by foiling the gangsters and making sure Jane is able to marry Harry. 66 min.

JIMMY AND SALLY (Nov. 24, 1933); D: James Tinling; W: Paul Schofield (scr), Marguerite Roberts (scr), William Conselman (dial); C: Joseph Valentine; E: Ralph Dixon; M: Arthur Lange; Cast: James Dunn, Claire Trevor, Harvey Stephens, Lya Lys, Jed Prouty, Gloria Roy, Alma Lloyd, John Arledge, James Burke, Louise Beavers, Joseph Sauers, Matt McHugh • Jimmy (Dunn), the cocky, loudmouth publicity director of a meat-packing plant, holds onto his job because of ideas fed to him by his secretary, Sally (Trevor). When he loses the job, he leaves town, figuring he can make it on his own. He returns, somewhat humbled, to be offered a job by the now-elevated Sally, who ultimately breaks an engagement to someone else to be with Jimmy. 68 min.

HOOPLA (Nov. 30, 1933); P: Al Rockett; D: Frank Lloyd; W: Bradley King (scr), Joseph Moncure March (scr), John Kenyon Nicholson (play); C: Ernest Palmer; E: Margaret Clancy; M: Louis De Francesco; Cast: Clara Bow, Preston Foster, Richard Cromwell, Herbert Mundin, James Gleason, Minna Gombell, Roger Imhof, Florence Roberts, Harry Wood, Harvey Perry, Doc McKay • On a bet, a carnival dancer (Bow) seduces the barker's son (Cromwell) and suddenly finds that she has fallen in love with him. The couple marries, but the barker (Foster) is furious. The dancer takes a job in another town to put her husband through law school and, through her sacrifice, reconciles with the boy's father. 78 min. • This is a remake of the First National 1928 part-talkie, *The Barker*.

SMOKY (Dec. 8, 1933); P: Sol M. Wurtzel, John Stone; D: Eugene Forde; W: Stuart Anthony (scr), Paul Perez (scr), Will James (novel); C: Daniel B. Clark; M: Arthur Lange; Cast: Victor Jory, Irene Bentley, Frank Campeau, Hank Mann, LeRoy Mason, Leonid Snegoff, Will James, Wally Albright, Francis Ford • A strong-spirited horse, Smoky, grows to maturity and develops a trust for Clint (Jory), who lovingly trains him. When Smoky is stolen by an abusive half-breed (Mason), Clint sets out to find him. Unsuccessful, Clint takes over the ranch and marries Betty (Bentley). Later, someone spots Smoky, who is being led to the slaughterhouse, but Clint is able to save him in time. 69 min.

I WAS A SPY (Dec. 15, 1933) British-made; P: Michael Balcon; D: Victor Saville; W: W.P. Lipscomb (scr & dial), J.H. Beith (add'l dial), Ian Hay (add'l dial), Marthe Cnockaert McKenna (article); C: Charles Van Enger; E: Frederick Y. Smith; Cast: Madeleine Carroll, Herbert Marshall, Conrad Veidt, Gerald Du Maurier, Edmund Gwenn, Donald Calthrop, Anthony Bushell, Eva Moore, Martita Hunt, Nigel Bruce • In this true story of World War I, Marthe Cnockaert (Carroll), a Belgian nurse during the war, becomes a spy for the allies and falls into a romance with a German Commandant Oberaertz (Veidt), who is really a leader of the liberation movement. When she is captured by the Germans, Oberaertz takes the blame and she escapes death. 89 min.

MR. SKITCH (Dec. 22, 1933); D: James Cruze; W: Ralph Spence (scr), Sonya Levien (scr), Anne Cameron (article); C: John Seitz; E: Irene Morra; M: Louis De Francesco; Cast: Will Rogers, ZaSu Pitts, Rochelle Hudson, Florence Desmond, Harry Green, Charles Starrett, Eugene Pallette, Morgan Wallace, Wally Albright • Mr. Skitch (Rogers), a handyman, sets out for California with his wife (Pitts) and daughter (Hudson), after being forced out of his house because the local bank failed. His positive attitude helps his family through the hard times and bumps in the road. The daughter's boyfriend (Starrett) turns out to be wealthy and sets up an auto park for Mr. Skitch in his home town. 70 min.

AS HUSBANDS GO (Dec. 29, 1933); P: Jesse L. Lasky; D: Hamilton MacFadden; W: Sonya Levien (scr), Sam Behrman (add'l dial), Rachel Crothers (play); C: Hal Mohr; E: Dorothy Spencer; M: Louis De Francesco; Cast: Warner Baxter, Helen Vinson, Warner Oland, Catherine Doucet, G.P. Huntley Jr., Frank O'Connor, Eleanor Lyn, Jay Ward, Irene Biller, Greta Meyer • After having met charming continental gentlemen in Paris, Lucille (Vinson) and Emmie (Doucet) make a pact to pursue these men, especially when they learn both are following them to America. Lucille's boring Dubuque husband, Charles (Baxter), meets Ronald (Huntley) and does not realize his interest in Lucille. Becoming good friends, they take a fishing trip, during which Ronald admits that Lucille is not as glamorous at home as she was in Paris. Emmie successfully stays with Hippolitus (Oland), but Ronald returns to Europe, making Lucille realize the value of her marriage. 78 min.

1934 Releases

I AM SUZANNE! (Jan. 5, 1934); P: Winfield R. Sheehan, Jesse L. Lasky; D: Rowland V. Lee; W: Rowland V. Lee (st & scr), Edwin Justus Mayer (st & scr); C: Lee Garmes; E: Harold Schuster; M: Louis De Francesco; Cast: Lilian Harvey, Gene Raymond, Leslie Banks, Georgia Caine, Murray Kinnell, Geneva Mitchell, Halliwell Hobbes, Edward Keane, Lionel Belmore • A famous dancer, Suzanne (Harvey), who has agreed to marry her mentor, Baron Herring (Banks), has an accident which prevents her from continuing her career; she is then abandoned by the baron. A local puppeteer, Tony (Raymond), is smitten by Suzanne and fashions a puppet after her. Jealous of the puppet, Suzanne shoots it and then has a nightmare about being placed on trial by puppets. She apologizes to Tony and they put on a successful show together. 98 min.

ORIENT EXPRESS (Jan. 12, 1934); P: Winfield Sheehan; D: Paul Martin; W: Paul Martin (scr), Carl Hovey, (scr), Oscar Levant (scr), William Conselman (dial), Graham Greene (novel); C: George Schneiderman; M: Arthur Lange; Cast: Heather Angel, Norman Foster, Ralph Morgan, Herbert Mundin, Una O'Connor, Irene Ware, Dorothy Burgess, Lisa Gore, William Irving, Roy D'Arcy, Perry Ivins • A dancer, Coral (Angel), falls in love with a young date merchant, Carlton (Foster), aboard a train from Belgium to Constantinople. Also on board is a disguised revolutionary, Czinner (Morgan), who wants to foment more unrest in the Balkans. When Coral is arrested along with Czinner, because she accepted a letter to his people, she escapes from jail with a murderer (D'Arcy) who was on the train. Carlton eventually rescues Coral and they flee to safety. 72 min. • Author Graham Greene wrote "It was a bad film, one of the worst I had ever seen; the direction was incompetent, the photography undistinguished, the story sentimental."

FRONTIER MARSHAL (Jan. 19, 1934); D: Lew Seiler; W: William Conselman (scr), Stuart Anthony (scr), Stuart Lake (novel); C: Robert Planck; M: Arthur Lange; Cast: George O'Brien, Irene Bentley, George E. Stone, Alan Edwards, Ruth Gillette, Berton Churchill, Frank Conroy, Ward Bond, Edward LeSaint, Russell Simpson, Jerry Foster • Newcomer to Tombstone, Michael Wyatt (O'Brien), fearless and handy with a six-shooter, is offered the job of marshal. Wyatt rescues and befriends another newcomer, Mary (Bentley), stands up to the tough but terminally ill "Doc" Warren (Edwards), and then joins with Warren in a battle against a gang of crooks. 66 min.

SLEEPERS EAST (Jan. 26, 1934) EP: Winfield R. Sheehan; P: Sol M. Wurtzel; D: Kenneth MacKenna; W: Lester Cole (scr), Frederick Nebel (novel); C: Ernest Palmer; M: Samuel Kaylin; Cast: Wynne Gibson, Preston Foster, Mona Barrie, Harvey Stephens, Roger Imhof, J. Carrol Naish, Howard Lally, Suzanne Kaaren • On parole, Lena (Gibson), a good-time girl with gangster connections, is at a gambling club when witnesses a shooting committed by the mayor's son (Lally). Lena, promising not to talk, leaves town and teams up with her hometown boyfriend, Jason (Foster). She is later pursued by a lawyer (Stephens) looking for some political dirt. In an escape, Jason is mistakenly shot for a bank robber. When Lena is about to testify, the mayor's son shoots himself. 69 min.

CAROLINA (Feb. 2, 1934); P: Winfield Sheehan; D: Henry King; W: Reginald Berkeley (scr), Paul Green (play); C: Hal Mohr; E: Robert Bassler; M: Louis De Francesco; Cast: Janet Gaynor, Lionel Barrymore, Robert Young, Henrietta Crosman, Richard Cromwell, Mona Barrie, Stepin Fetchit, Russell Simpson, Ronnie Cosbey • In post–civil war Carolina, Will Connelly (Young), son of a proud, once-prominent family, falls in love with Joanna (Gaynor), daughter of a Yankee. Joanna saves the Connelly estate and restores the family fortune by convincing Will to plant tobacco, something his mother (Crosman) thinks is undignified. Overcoming the mother's attempts to break up the romance — something she had done to her brother-in-law Bob (Barrymore) many years earlier — Joanna ends up with Will. 82 min.

EVER SINCE EVE (Feb. 9, 1934); P: John Stone; D: George Marshall; W: Henry Johnson (scr), Stuart Anthony (scr), Paul Armstrong (play); C: Arthur Miller; M: Samuel Kaylin; Cast: George O'Brien, Mary Brian, Herbert Mundin, Betty Blythe, Roger Imhof, Russell Simpson, George Meeker, James Wang, Yorke Sherwood, Bill Franey • Neil (O'Brien) travels to New York to buy some equipment for a mine. One of the owners (Mundin) accompanies him to keep him away from women. Nevertheless, he meets and marries Elizabeth (Brian). Neil is later trapped in a mine explosion and, in a delirium, sends Elizabeth back to New York. When he regains his memory, he is unsuccessful in finding her, and goes to China. Elizabeth returns, pregnant, and is finally reunited with Neil. 72 min.

LA CIUDAD DE CARTÓN (Feb. 15, 1934) Spanish language; D: Louis King; W: Gregorio Martinez Sierra (st & scr), John Reinhardt (scr); M: Samuel Kaylin; Cast: Antonio Moreno, Catalina Bárcena, José Crespo, Andrés de Segurola, Luis Alberni, José Rubio, Rudolph Anders, Carlos Villarías, Julio Peña, Ralph Navarro • Craig (Alberni), a publicity agent, arrives on the scene of a train wreck, looking for European movie star Diane Dane. He decides that Teresa (Bárcena), a passenger on the train suffering from amnesia, is Dane. Craig brings Teresa to Hollywood, where she meets Janet Gaynor, Robert Young and Lionel Barrymore. She also meets and falls in love with rising star Clarence Williams (Crespo). Meanwhile, Teresa's rancher husband, Fred (Moreno), sees a picture of Diane Dane and realizes it's his wife. When Teresa regains her memory, her acting ability disappears. She is reunited with Fred, who gets a movie job and does a dangerous stunt so well that Craig gives him a contract. 76 min.

DEVIL TIGER (Feb. 16, 1934); D: Clyde Elliott; W: James O. Spearing (st & cont), Russell Shields (st & cont), Lew Lehr (st & cont); C: Richard Maedler, John Brockhurst; E: Truman Talley; Cast: Marion Burns, Kane Richmond, Harry Woods, Ah Lee, Devil Tiger • Bob Eller arrives in Malaysia and joins up with hunter

Doyle (Woods), who is on a quest to track down a tiger that has been killing natives. They are joined by Mary (Burns), whose father was killed by the "devil tiger." 60 min. • This is one of many features from the early 1930s that blended great amounts of often violent wildlife footage into a thin storyline.

HOLD THAT GIRL (Feb. 16, 1934); P: Sol M. Wurtzel; D: Hamilton MacFadden; W: Dudley Nichols, Lamar Trotti; C: George Schneiderman; E: Alex Troffey; M: Samuel Kaylin; Cast: James Dunn, Claire Trevor, Alan Edwards, Gertrude Michael, John Davidson, Robert McWade, Effie Ellsler, Jay Ward • A feisty female reporter for a New York tabloid, Tony Bellamy (Trevor), in the interest of getting a juicy story, becomes a party to a jewel robbery and ends up being taken to the gang leader (Edwards), who had previously proposed to marry her. In over her head, and with her life in danger, she is rescued by a detective (Dunn), whom she befriended in a previous entanglement. 66 min.

I BELIEVED IN YOU (Feb. 23, 1934); P: Sol M. Wurtzel; D: Irving Cummings; W: William Conselman (scr), William Anthony McGuire (st); C: Barney McGill; E: Al De Gaetano; M: Samuel Kaylin; Cast: Rosemary Ames, Victor Jory, John Boles, Gertrude Michael, George Meeker, Leslie Fenton, Joyzelle, Jed Prouty, Morgan Wallace, Luis Alberni, Jack Luden • A small town girl, True Merrill (Ames), associates with her much-admired artistic denizens of Greenwich Village. Wealthy Michael Harrison (Boles) tries to convince her of their worthlessness and agrees to finance their endeavors to show her that they will amount to nothing. True takes him up on the wager, which he wins. 68 min.

DAVID HARUM (March 2, 1934); P: Winfield R. Sheehan; D: James Cruze; W: Walter Woods (scr), Edward Noyes Westcott (novel); C: Hal Mohr; E: Jack Murray; M: Louis De Francesco; Cast: Will Rogers, Louise Dresser, Evelyn Venable, Kent Taylor, Stepin Fetchit, Noah Beery, Roger Imhof, Frank Melton, Charles Middleton, Sarah Padden, Lillian Stuart • A small-town banker and horse trader, David Harum (Rogers), has several back-and-forth encounters with his rival, the usurious Deacon Perkins (Middleton). He buys a horse that Perkins unloads as worthless and sells it to Ann (Venable). Ann's boyfriend, John (Taylor), makes a ten-to-one racing bet on the horse and wins. This gives David a victory over the sour deacon and provides John with money to marry. 83 min.

COMING OUT PARTY (March 9, 1934); P: Jesse L. Lasky; D: John Blystone; W: Gladys Unger (st & scr), Jesse Lasky Jr. (scr), Becky Gardiner (st),; C: John Seitz; E: Dorothy Spencer; M: Louis De Francesco; Cast: Frances Dee, Gene Raymond, Alison Skipworth, Nigel Bruce, Harry Green, Gilbert Emery, Marjorie Gateson, Clifford Jones, Jessie Ralph, Germaine de Neel • Mr. and Mrs. Stanhope (Emery, Gateson) spend $50,000 on their daughter Joy's (Dee) social debut, at which she is to announce her engagement. However, her once-poor, violinist fiancé Chris (Raymond) has just signed a contract to go abroad. The debutante impulsively decides to marry Jimmy Wolverton (Jones) instead. When Chris finds out that Joy is married, he appeals to the Stanhopes to annul the marriage, but they are displeased by his low social standing. Joy's husband, however, realizes the mistake he made and agrees to an annulment. 79 min.

GEORGE WHITE'S SCANDALS (March 16, 1934); P: Robert T. Kane; D: George White, Thornton Freeland, Harry Lachman; W: George White (st), Jack Yellen (add'l dial); C: Lee Garmes, George Schneiderman; E: Paul Weatherwax; M: Louis De Francesco; Cast: Rudy Vallee, Jimmy Durante, Alice Faye, Adrienne Ames, Gregory Ratoff, Cliff Edwards, Dixie Dunbar, George White, Gertrude Michael, Warren Hymer • George White gets involved in the romantic lives of his stars, Jimmy (Vallee), Kitty (Faye), Happy (Durante) and Patsy (Dunbar), while assembling his musical revue. A wedding number for Jimmy and Kitty at the finale turns out, to their surprise, to be the real thing. 80 min. • "Entire Production Conceived, Created and Directed by George White."

THREE ON A HONEYMOON (March 23, 1934); P: John Stone; D: James Tinling; W: Edward T. Lowe (scr), Raymond Van Sickle (scr), Ishbel Ross (novel); C: Joseph Valentine; E: Alex Troffey; M: Samuel Kaylin; Cast: Sally Eilers, ZaSu Pitts, Henrietta Crossman, Charles Starrett, Irene Hervey, John Mack Brown, Russell Simpson, Cornelius Keefe • A cruise line president's spoiled daughter, Joan (Eilers), is watched over by ship officer Dick (Starrett) to keep her out of trouble on a Mediterranean cruise. Aside from several misadventures, Joan protects another young woman on the ship from a blackmailer and later apologizes to Dick for her behavior, leading the way to romance. 65 min.

THE CONSTANT NYMPH (March 23, 1934); D: Basil Dean; W: Dorothy Farnum (scr), Margaret Kennedy (dial & play), Basil Dean (dial & play); C: Mutz Greenbaum; M: Louis Levy; Cast: Brian Aherne, Victoria Hopper, Peggy Blythe, Jane Baxter, Jane Cornell, Beryl Laverick, Lyn Harding, Mary Clare, Leonora Corbett, Fritz Schultz • In the Austrian Alps, a slightly mad composer has three difficult daughters, all half-sisters. One of the young daughters, Tessa (Hopper), falls madly in love with an adult, composer Lewis Dodd (Aherne). Lewis marries a respectable English cousin, Florence (Corbett), and moves to London, but soon realizes he should have waited for the young Tessa to come of age. Defying convention, Lewis returns to Tessa, but she dies from a heart ailment. 85 min.

ON A VOLÉ UN HOMME (March 24, 1934) French-made; P: Erich Pommer; D: Max Ophuls; W: Rene Pujol, Hans Willhelm; C: Rene Colas; M: Iurmann and Kaper; Cast: Lili Damita, Charles Fallot, Pierre Labry, Raoul Marco, Henry Garat, Nina Myral, Robert Goupil, Pierre Pierade, Fernand Fabre • On a train from Paris to the French Riviera, a young banker, Jean de Lafaye (Garat) flirts with and then is kidnapped by a beautiful woman, Annette (Damita), who is working for his business rivals. During his sequestration, the couple falls in love. 60 min.

BOTTOMS UP (March 30, 1934); P: B.G. DeSylva; D: David Butler; W: B.G. DeSylva (st & scr), David Butler (st & scr), Sid Silvers (st & scr); C: Arthur Miller; E: Irene Morra; M: Constantine Bakaleinikoff; Cast: Spencer Tracy, "Pat" Paterson, John Boles, Sid Silvers, Herbert Mundin, Harry Green, Thelma Todd, Robert Emmett O'Connor, Dell Henderson, Suzanne Kaaren • A Hollywood con man, Smoothie (Tracy), meets aspiring actress Wanda (Paterson) and plots to make her a star. Smoothie's friend Limey (Mundin) impersonates a lord, supposedly Wanda's father. A real star, Judith Marlowe (Todd), throws a party at which Wanda meets producer Hal Reed (Boles). A love triangle develops among Wanda, Smoothie and Hal. Wanda does become a star because of Hal, and Smoothie gives her up, claiming he is not the marrying kind. 85 min.

MURDER IN TRINIDAD (Apr. 6, 1934); P: Sol M. Wurtzel; D: Louis King; W: Seton I. Miller (scr), John W. Vandercook (novel); C: Barney McGill; E: Al De Gaetano, Alex Troffey; M: Samuel Kaylin; Cast: Nigel Bruce, Heather Angel, Victor Jory, Murray Kinnell, Douglas Watson, J. Carrol Naish, Claude King, Pat Somerset, Francis Ford, John Davidson, Noble Johnson • Bertram Lynch (Bruce) arrives in Trinidad to investigate diamond smuggling from Brazil. Young Joan (Angel) discovers diamonds in her father's (Kinnell) room and convinces him to leave to avoid arrest. Two murders occur and Lynch has several suspects, including a swamp dwelling smuggler (Naish). However, the culprit (Jory) turns out to be the head of an oil-leasing company. 74 min.

ALL MEN ARE ENEMIES (Apr. 20, 1934); P: Al Rockett; D: George Fitzmaurice; W: Samuel Hoffenstein (scr & dial), Lenore Coffee (scr & dial), Richard Aldington (novel); C: John Seitz; E: Harold Schuster; M: Louis De Francesco; Cast: Hugh Williams, Helen Twelvetrees, Mona Barrie, Herbert Mundin, Harry Stephenson, Walter Byron, Una O'Connor, Matt Moore, Halliwell Hobbes, Rafaela Ottiano • The son of an aristocratic English family, Tony (Williams), falls in love but is separated from Katha (Twelvetrees), the Austrian woman he loves, when war is declared. After the armistice, the lovers are unable to find each other and Tony marries a childhood sweetheart, Margaret (Barrie). Tony has a loveless marriage and finds Margaret in the arms of another man. Margaret later admits that Katha tried to find Tony but Margaret lied that she and Tony were married. Tony returns to where he first met Katha, and the lovers are happily reunited. 79 min. • The original novel was hailed in England as "the greatest love story since Tristan and Isolde."

HEART SONG (Apr. 27, 1934); P: Erich Pommer; D: Friedrich Hollaender; W: John Heygate (scr), Robert Stevenson (scr), Robert Liebmann (st), Walter Reisch (st), Felix Salten (st); C: Friedl Behn-Grund; M: Friedrich Hollaender, Franz Waxman; Cast: Lilian Harvey, Charles Boyer, Mady Christians, Maurice Evans, Friedel Schuster, Ernest Thesiger, Julius Falkenstein, Huntley Wright, Ruth Maitland • In 1890, a German duke falls in love with the voice of a woman, who turns out to be a hairdresser, rather than the empress. 84 min. • Although much effort and expense went into this UFA-Gaumont-British production, it yielded paltry domestic rentals of $31,000.

STAND UP AND CHEER (May 4, 1934); P: Winfield Sheehan; AP: Lew Brown; D: Hamilton MacFadden; W: Ralph Spence (dial), Will Rogers (st), Philip Klein (st); C: Ernest Palmer, L.W. O'Connell; E: Margaret Clancy; M: Arthur Lange; Cast: Warner Baxter, Madge Evans, James Dunn, Sylvia Froos, John Boles, Arthur Byron, Shirley Temple, Ralph Morgan, "Aunt Jemima," Mitchell & Durant, Nick Foran • A famous Broadway producer (Baxter) is assigned by President Roosevelt to raise the spirits of Americans during the Depression. Some evil businessmen, who are making money from the failed economy, get together to discredit the producer so that his plan will fail. Auditions continue and the show is a success. President Roosevelt calls the producer to congratulate him and then makes an announcement that the Depression is over. 80 min. • This was Shirley Temple's first appearance in a Fox feature release; it led to a long-term contract.

SUCH WOMEN ARE DANGEROUS (May 4, 1934); P: Al Rockett; D: James Flood; W: Jane Storm (scr), Oscar M. Sheridan (scr), Vera Caspary (st), Lenore Coffee (add'l dial); C: L.W. O'Connell; E: Dorothy Spencer; M: Louis De Francesco; Cast: Warner Baxter, Rosemary Ames, Rochelle Hudson, Mona Barrie, Herbert Mundin, Henrietta Crossman, Lily D. Stuart, Irving Pichel, Jane Barnes, Matt Moore • A best-selling writer, Michael (Baxter), romances opera singer Wanda (Barrie). Verne (Hudson), a young fan from Indiana, infatuated with Michael, is crushed when she sees him kissing Wanda. Michael's secretary Helen (Ames) is also in love with him. Verne conspires to win Michael and eventually threatens to do something dangerous. When Verne is found dead, Michael becomes the prime suspect. However, a note turns up which proves that Verne committed suicide. 81 min.

LA CRUZ Y LA ESPADA (May 5, 1934) Spanish language; D: Frank Strayer; Cast: José Mojica, Juan Torena, Anita Campillo, Lucio Villegas, Carmen Rodriguez, Paco Moreno, Carlos Montalban, Martin Garralaga, Julian Rivero, F.A. Armenta • In 18th-century California, Fra Francisco (Mojica), after rescuing Carmela (Campillo) from bandits, is tempted to take her from his friend, José Antonio (Torena). Francisco also discovers a cave with gold which increases the temptation. Overcoming these urges, he writes to José and tells him where to find the gold. However, José believes that Francisco has been flirting with Carmela and attacks him with a knife. Francisco denies the rumors and José begs his forgiveness. Francisco sings at the wedding of José and Carmela. 73 min.

NOW I'LL TELL (May 11, 1934); P: Winfield Sheehan; D: Edwin Burke; W: Mrs. Arnold Rothstein (st); C:

Ernest Palmer; E: Harold Schuster; M: Arthur Lange; Cast: Spencer Tracy, Helen Twelvetrees, Alice Faye, Robert Gleckler, Henry O'Neill, Hobart Cavanaugh, G.P. Huntley Jr., Shirley Temple, Ronnie Cosbey, Ray Cooke • A racetrack gambler, Murray Golden (Tracy), marries Virginia (Twelvetrees), who has no idea how he makes his money. Eventually, Murray owns a gambling house and meets a singer, Peggy (Faye), who is a mobster's (Gleckler) girlfriend. He later fixes a championship fight against the mobster, who kidnaps Virginia as revenge. Freed unharmed, Virginia leaves Murray and seeks a divorce. Murray, who has lost $200,000 worth of her jewelry, takes out an insurance policy and arranges to have the mobster shoot him so he can pay his wife back. 87 min. • This story is based on Mrs. Arnold Rothstein's mob kingpin husband, who is best known for fixing the 1919 World Series.

LILIOM (May 12, 1934) French version; D: Fritz Lang; W: Robert Leibmann (adpt), Bernard Zimmer (dial), Ferenc Molnar (play); C: Rudolph Maté, Louis Née; M: Jean Lenoir, Franz Waxman; Cast: Charles Boyer, Madeleine Ozeray, Robert Arnoux, Alexandre Rignault, Henri Richard, Barencey, Raoul Marco, Antonin Artaud, Léon Arvel, René Stern, Maximillienne • 120 min.

CHANGE OF HEART (May 18, 1934); P: Winfield Sheehan; D: John G. Blystone; W: Sonya Levien (scr), James Gleason (scr), Samuel Hoffenstein (add'l dial), Kathleen Norris (novel); C: Hal Mohr; E: Margaret Clancy; M: Louis De Francesco; Cast: Janet Gaynor, Charles Farrell, James Dunn, Ginger Rogers, Nick Foran, Beryl Mercer, Gustav von Seyffertitz, Kenneth Thomson, Theodor von Eltz, Shirley Temple • Of four college graduates who go to New York together, Madge (Rogers) wants to be a stage performer, Catherine (Gaynor) a journalist, Chris (Farrell) a lawyer, and Mack (Dunn) a radio crooner. They mix and match their romantic and professional lives in various configurations before finally settling down. 76 min.

SPRINGTIME FOR HENRY (May 25, 1934); P: Jesse L. Lasky; D: Frank Tuttle; W: Keene Thompson (scr), Frank Tuttle (scr), Benn W. Levy (play); C: John Seitz; E: Jack Murray; M: Louis De Francesco; Cast: Otto Kruger, Nancy Carroll, Nigel Bruce, Heather Angel, Herbert Mundin, Arthur Hoyt, Geneva Mitchell • An avowed playboy bachelor, wealthy Henry (Kruger), owner of the country's largest car company, tries to get as far as he can with every woman. He is in love with Julia (Carroll), who is married to his childhood friend (Bruce). Henry's new secretary, Miss Smith (Angel), vows to change his habits. After Miss Smith succeeds, she falls in love with Julia's husband, Johnny (Bruce). Through various complications, Henry makes a business deal with Johnny and ends up with Julia. 73 min.

CALL IT LUCK (June 1, 1934); P: John Stone; D: James Tinling; W: Dudley Nichols (st & scr), Lamar Trotti (scr), George Marshall (st), Joseph Cunningham (adpt), Harry McCoy (adpt); C: Joseph Valentine; E: Alex Troffey; M: Samuel Kaylin; Cast: "Pat" Paterson, Herbert Mundin, Charles Starrett, Gordon Westcott, Georgia Caine, Theodor von Eltz, Reginald Mason, Ernest Wood, Ray Mayer, Susan Fleming • A London cabbie, Herbert Biggelwade (Mundin), who won the sweepstakes, visits America with his niece Pat (Paterson), a singer, and a horse he believes is a racing champion. In New York, two con men, Luke (Westcott) and Nat (von Eltz), impersonate city officials and fleece Herbert of his winnings. Pat meets a Harvard graduate cab driver (Starrett), who provides them with a place to stay at his boardinghouse. Amy (Caine), the boardinghouse owner, gives them $25,000 to bet on the horse, which runs incredibly fast when he hears a bugle and wins the race with Herbert riding him. 64 min.

WILD GOLD (June 8, 1934); P: Sol M. Wurtzel; D: George Marshall; W: Lester Cole (scr), Henry Johnson (scr), Dudley Nichols (st), Lamar Trotti (st); C: Joseph Valentine; E: Fred Allen; M: Samuel Kaylin; Cast: John Boles, Claire Trevor, Harry Green, Roger Imhof, Ruth Gillette, Monroe Owsley, Edward Gargan, Suzanne Kaaren, Wini Shaw, Blanca Vischer, Elsie Larson • Jerry (Trevor), a showgirl from Reno, meets Steve (Boles), a construction engineer, after a car accident outside a small mining town. Jerry's good-for-nothing husband, Walter (Owsley), follows her to the town and causes the death of Steve's friend, Pop Benson (Imhof). Steve wants to avenge Benson's death, but Jerry prevents him. When a rainstorm washes out the local dam, flooding the town, Walter is killed. Steve and Jerry leave for San Francisco. 77 min.

BABY TAKE A BOW (June 22, 1934); P: John Stone; D: Harry Lachman; W: Philip Klein (scr), E.E. Paramore Jr. (scr), James P. Judge (play); C: L.W. O'Connell; E: Al De Gaetano; M: Samuel Kaylin; Cast: Shirley Temple, James Dunn, Claire Trevor, Alan Dinehart, Ray Walker, Dorothy Libaire, Ralf Harolde, James Flavin, Richard Tucker, Olive Tell • Two ex-cons, Eddie (Dunn) and Larry (Walker), are chauffeurs for a wealthy family. When the family's jewels are stolen, both men are suspects. The real thief gives the jewels to Eddie's young daughter, Shirley (Temple), who puts them in Eddie's pocket. The thief returns to get the jewels but Shirley keeps moving them to other places. Eddie's wife, Kay (Trevor), tries to find the jewels when the thief returns and gets to them first. Shirley retrieves them from the thief and the family gets a $5,000 reward. 73 min.

SHE LEARNED ABOUT SAILORS (June 29, 1934); P: John Stone; D: George Marshall; W: William Conselman (scr), Henry Johnson (scr), Randall H. Faye (st); C: Harry Jackson; E: Fred Allen; M: Samuel Kaylin; Cast: Lew Ayres, Alice Faye, Frank Mitchell, Jack Durant, Harry Green, Wilma Cox, Paul McVey, June Vlasek, Ray McClennan • Larry (Ayres), a sailor on leave in Shanghai, meets a club singer, Jean (Faye), who agrees to date him as long as he does not make any passes at her. Larry is miserable when he must ship out to Honolulu and leave Jean behind, but his buddies, Peanuts (Mitchell) and Eddie (Durant), arrange for them to be reunited. After several misunderstandings and split-ups, the couple is married. 76 min.

CHARLIE CHAN'S COURAGE (July 6, 1934); P: John Stone; D: George Hadden, Eugene Forde; W: Seton I. Miller (scr), Earl Derr Biggers (novel); C: Hal Mohr, Arthur Miller; E: Alex Troffey; M: Samuel Kaylin; Cast: Warner Oland, Drue Leyton, Donald Woods, Paul Harvey, Murray Kinnell, Reginald Mason, Virginia Hammond, Si Jenks, Harvey Clark, Jerry Jerome, Jack Carter • When Charlie Chan (Oland) disguises himself as a servant and delivers a pearl necklace as a favor to a friend in Honolulu, he gets involved in the murder of millionaire J.P. Madden (Harvey). Chan snoops around and discovers that a look-alike (Harvey), in cahoots with the millionaire's secretary (Kinnell), impersonated Madden and that the millionaire is still alive. 71 min.

GRANADEROS DEL AMOR (July 7, 1934) Spanish language; P: John Stone; D: John Reinhardt; W: William Kernell (orig), John Reinhardt (orig), José López Rubio (Spanish version); C: Robert Planck; M: Samuel Kaylin; Cast: Raúl Roulien, Conchita Montenegro, Valentin Parera, Andrés de Segurola, Romualdo Tirado, Maria Calvo, Carlos Villarías, Lucio Villegas, Paco Moreno, Fred Malatesta • Austrian playwright Erich (Roulien) looks for inspiration to write his next musical play. Visiting a castle in the Tyrol, he imagines himself as a Napoleonic-era French colonel who falls in love with a baroness (Montenegro), engaged to a nobleman (Parera). The colonel convinces the woman to escape the war with him, but they are caught and only saved from execution by a truce. The film ends with a scene from the hit play being performed. 80 min.

SHE WAS A LADY (July 20, 1934); P: Al Rockett; D: Hamilton MacFadden; W: Gertude Purcell (scr), Elisabeth Cobb (novel); C: Bert Glennon; E: Dorothy Spencer; M: Louis De Francesco; Cast: Helen Twelvetrees, Donald Woods, Ralph Morgan, Monroe Owsley, Irving Pichel, Doris Lloyd, Kitty Kelly, Halliwell Hobbes, Mary Forbes, Jackie Searl, Barbara Weeks • Shunned English aristocrat's daughter, Sheila (Twelvetrees), works at a dude ranch in Montana and meets Tommy (Woods), a playboy who proposes to her. She rejects him and returns to England but is not welcomed back into the family. In New York, she is rejected by Tommy's father (Morgan) as marriage material. Reduced to working at a gambling club, Tommy finds her and gets into a fight with her boss (Owsley). Sheila takes Tommy home and his father agrees that she is the best wife for his son. 77 min.

HANDY ANDY (July 27, 1934); P: Sol M. Wurtzel; D: David Butler; W: William Conselman (scr), Henry Johnson (scr), Kubec Glasmon (adpt), Lewis Beach (play); C: Arthur Miller; E: Irene Morra; M: Samuel Kaylin; Cast: Will Rogers, Peggy Wood, Conchita Montenegro, Roger Imhof, Mary Carlisle, Robert Taylor, Paul Harvey, Grace Goodall, Gregory Gaye, Frank Melton, Jessie Pringle • Hard-working druggist Andy (Rogers), after selling his shop at his wife's (Wood) insistence, is not able to find anything he enjoys as much. On a trip to New Orleans for Mardi Gras, Andy meets druggist Pierre (Gaye) and his wife, Fleurette (Montenegro), who conspire with him to get his shop back. When Andy and his wife return home, they discover the stock that Andy received for his store is worthless. Luckily, Andy sold the stock and bought back his shop while they were away. 81 min.

GRAND CANARY (Aug. 17, 1934); P: Jesse L. Lasky; D: Irving Cummings; W: Ernest Pascal (scr), A.J. Cronin (novel); P: Bert Glennon; E: Jack Murray; M: Louis De Francesco; Cast: Warner Baxter, Madge Evans, Marjorie Rambeau, Zita Johann, Roger Imhof, H.B. Warner, Barry Norton, Juliette Compton, Gilbert Emery, John Rogers • Dr. Leith (Baxter), demonized for using an experimental serum on his patients, joins a mission on Grand Canary Island run by Suzan (Johann). He selflessly helps the locals when a yellow fever epidemic breaks out and personally cares for wealthy, married Lady Fielding (Evans), who is in love with him, arousing jealousy in Suzan. Leith uses his serum to save Fielding and later returns to England and is honored for his service. 74 min.

THE CAT'S PAW (Aug. 24, 1934); D: Sam Taylor; W: Sam Taylor (scr), Clarence Budington Kelland (novel); P: Walter Lundin; E: Bernard Burton; M: Alfred Newman; Cast: Harold Lloyd, Una Merkel, George Barbier, Nat Pendleton, Grace Bradley, Alan Dinehart, Grant Mitchell, Fred Warren, Warren Hymer, J. Farrell MacDonald • A missionary's son (Lloyd), naïve in western ways, returns from China, and finds lodgings in a boardinghouse. Through several confluent circumstances, he is convinced to run for mayor by power brokers who see him as a pawn. However, he impresses his girlfriend (Merkel) and disrupts the power elites by running things his own way. 100 min.

PURSUED (Aug. 24, 1934); P: Sol Wurtzel; D: Louis King; W: Lester Cole (scr), Stuart Anthony (scr), Larry Evans (article); C: L.W. O'Connell; E: Al De Gaetano; M: Samuel Kaylin; Cast: Rosemary Ames, Victor Jory, Pert Kelton, Russell Hardie, George Irving, Torben Meyer, Jimmie Dime, John Gough, Allan Sears, Elsie Larson, Virginia Hills, Lucille Miller • Arriving in North Borneo to take over his late uncle's plantation, David (Hardie) is beaten up by thugs sent by the neighboring plantation owner, Beauregard (Jory). David, temporarily blinded, is nursed by a temptress, casino singer Mona (Ames), who has been saving her money to return to San Francisco. When David can see again, he proposes to Mona, but Beauregard kidnaps her and holds her on his plantation. When David returns to his own property, Beauregard sends Hansen (Meyer) to kill him. Mona intervenes and shoots Beauregard, then is reunited with David. 70 min.

UN CAPITÁN DE COSACOS (Aug. 29, 1934) Spanish language; D: John Reinhardt; W: José López Rubio (scr), Joaquin Artegas (st); C: Harry Jackson; E: Ernest Nims; Cast: José Mojica, Rosita Moreno, Tito Coral,

Mona Maris, Andrés de Segurola, Julio Peña, Paco Moreno, Martin Garralaga, Roberto Guzman, José Maria Sanchez Garcia • Olga (Maris), the mistress of Russian General Petrovich (de Segurola), is kidnapped and held for ransom. Sergio (Mojica), an officer exiled to Siberia for a romantic affair, follows and rescues Olga, but is soon suspected of flirting with her by Petrovich. When the kidnappers are freed so they can be tracked to other revolutionaries, Sergio becomes involved with one of them, Tanya (Moreno). Sergio is arrested, then leads the prisoners in revolt. Petrovich is arrested but allowed to leave with Olga, while Sergio stays with Tanya. 8 reels

THE WORLD MOVES ON (Aug. 31, 1934); P: Winfield R. Sheehan; D: John Ford; W: Reginald Berkeley (st & scr); C: George Schneiderman; E: Paul Weatherwax; M: Arthur Lange; Cast: Madeleine Carroll, Franchot Tone, Reginald Denny, Siegfried Rumann, Louise Dresser, Raúl Roulien, Lumsden Hare, Dudley Digges, Frank Melton, Brenda Fowler • Several threads are intertwined in this epic story. A business that united families in the U.S., England, France and Prussia, healing the animosity created by the War of 1812, is disrupted by World War I. 104 min.

SERVANTS' ENTRANCE (Sept. 7, 1934); P: Winfield Sheehan; D: Frank Lloyd; W: Samson Raphaelson (scr), Sigrid Boo (novel); C: Hal Mohr; E: Margaret Clancy; M: Arthur Lange; Cast: Janet Gaynor, Lew Ayres, Ned Sparks, Walter Connolly, Louise Dresser, G.P. Huntley Jr., Astrid Allwyn, Siegfried Rumann, John Qualen, Catherine Doucet • Hedda (Gaynor), the daughter of a once-wealthy Swedish family takes a job as a servant for retired brewer Hans (Rumann) and meets his chauffeur, Eric (Ayres), an aspiring engine designer. Hedda's father informs her he has regained his wealth. She uses her father's resources to search out Eric and proposes to him. 88 min.

CHARLIE CHAN IN LONDON (Sept. 14, 1934); P: John Stone; D: Eugene Forde; W: Philip MacDonald (scr), Earl Derr Biggers (orig. character); C: L.W. O'Connell; M: Samuel Kaylin; Cast: Warner Oland, Drue Leyton, Raymond Milland, Mona Barrie, Alan Mowbray, Murray Kinnell, Douglas Walton, Walter Johnson, E.E. Clive, George Barraud, Madge Bellamy • Chan (Oland) is hired by Englishwoman Pamela Gray (Leyton) and her fiancé Neil (Milland), to find the man who murdered an Air Force captain on her family's country estate. Although Pam's brother is under arrest, she is certain he is innocent. Several suspects develop in a fox hunt and there are attempts on Chan's life, but the wily detective figures out that the deceased was developing plans for a new kind of pistol and the murderer was a family friend (Mowbray), who is exposed as a spy. 77 min.

THE DUDE RANGER (Sept. 21, 1934) Atherton Productions; P: Sol Lesser; D: Edward F. Cline; W: Barry Barringer (st & scr), Zane Grey (st); C: Frank B. Good; E: Donn Hayes; Cast: George O'Brien, Irene Hervey, LeRoy Mason, Sid Saylor, Henry Hall, James Mason, Sid Jordan, Alma Chester, Lloyd Ingraham • Ernest Selby (O'Brien) travels west to sell the ranch he inherited, but discovers that half of the cattle are gone. Keeping his identity secret, he accepts a job offer from the ranch boss (Hall) and is attracted to his daughter Ann (Hervey). Resisting threats to his safety and Hyslip (Mason), a rival for Ann, Selby suspects Ann's father. After being set up as the guilty party himself, Selby reveals his true identity and proves Hyslip to be behind all the crimes being committed. 65 min.

LOVE TIME (Sept. 21, 1934); P: John Stone; D: James Tinling; W: William Conselman (scr), Henry Johnson (scr), Richard Carroll (st), Lynn Starling (adpt), Sally Sandlin (adpt); C: Arthur Miller; E: Alex Troffey; M: Samuel Kaylin; Cast: "Pat" Paterson, Nils Asther, Herbert Mundin, Harry Green, Henry B. Walthall, Lucien Littlefield, Henry Kolker, Albert Conti, Herman Bing, Roger Imhof, James Burke • Unaware that she is descended from Austrian nobility, Valerie (Paterson) lives in the country. She meets Franz Schubert (Asther), a music teacher, who teaches her to play violin. Valerie runs away and follows Schubert to Vienna and nurses him back to health from a serious illness. Discovering her true identity, Valerie tries to get permission from the emperor to marry Franz and convinces the court to hear his musical compositions. Franz is permitted to play if he agrees to give up Valerie. Her persistence, however, is rewarded when she is reunited with Franz. 73 min.

JUDGE PRIEST (Sept. 28, 1934); P: Sol M. Wurtzel; D: John Ford; W: Dudley Nichols (scr), Lamar Trotti (scr), Irvin S. Cobb (orig. character); C: George Schneiderman; E: Paul Weatherwax; M: Samuel Kaylin; Cast: Will Rogers, Tom Brown, Anita Louise, Henry B. Walthall, David Landau, Rochelle Hudson, Roger Imhof, Frank Melton, Charley Grapewin, Berton Churchill • Judge Priest (Rogers) leads a bucolic existence in his Kentucky town, in 1890. He presides over his son's (Brown) romantic involvement with Ellie May (Louise). When there is a dispute between two locals over a knife fight, the judge is forced to step down from the case because of political pressure. In the end, a man who has been demonized is happily rehabilitated by Southern justice. 79 min.

CARAVAN (Oct. 5, 1934); P: Robert T. Kane; D: Erik Charell; W: Samson Raphaelson (scr & dial), Robert Liebmann (cont), Melchior Lengyel (novel); C: Ernest Palmer, Theodor Sparkuhl; E: Robert Bischoff; M: Louis De Francesco; Cast: Charles Boyer, Loretta Young, Jean Parker, Phillips Holmes, Louise Fazenda, Eugene Pallette, C. Aubrey Smith, Charley Grapewin, Noah Beery, Dudley Digges • A gypsy violinist, Lazi (Boyer), is entrusted with playing music while grapes are harvested for the Tokay wine season. When the newly returned Countess Wilma (Young) has to marry to inherit the estate, she hears Lazi's music and chooses him. However, the marriage does not work out and Lazi gives Wilma her freedom. She rides off with Lieutenant von Tokay (Holmes) while Lazi continues to play his music for the harvest. 101 min.

CARAVANE (Oct. 5, 1934) French version *Caravan*; SP: Andre Daven; P: Robert Kane; D: Erik Charell; W: Bernard Zimmer (scr & dial), Robert Liebmann (cont), Melchior Lenyel (novel); C: Ernest Palmer, Theodore Sparkuhl; Cast: Annabella, Charles Boyer, Conchita Montenegro, Pierre Brasseur, Andre Berley, Carrie Daumery, Jules Raucourt, Luis Alberni, George Davis, Robret Graves, Armand Kaliz

365 NIGHTS IN HOLLYWOOD (Oct. 12, 1934); P: Sol M. Wurtzel; D: George Marshall; W: William Conselman (scr), Henry Johnson (scr), Jimmie Starr (short stories); C: Harry Jackson; M: Samuel Kaylin; Cast: James Dunn, Alice Faye, Frank Mitchell, Jack Durant, John Bradford, Frank Melton, John Qualen, Ray Cooke, Tyler Brooke, Paul McVey, Al Klein • Aspiring movie actress Alice (Faye) takes acting lessons and is discovered by teacher Jimmie (Dunn) to have singing talent. Alice's friends (Mitchell & Durant) convince wealthy Frank (Melton) to finance a film. Jimmie directs Alice and, although they are romantically involved, the leading man Adrian Almont (Bradford) becomes a rival. The film almost does not get finished, but a final fist fight between Jimmie and Adrian is captured by the camera and completes their movie. Jimmie and Alice end up together. 74 min.

NADA MÁS QUE UNA MUJER (Oct. 14, 1934) Spanish language—*Only a Woman*; D: Harry Lachman; W: Raymond Van Sickle (scr), John Reinhardt (scr), Manuel de Zarraga (Spanish version), Larry Evans (article), C: Rudolph Maté; Cast: Berta Singerman, Alfredo del Diestro, Luana Alcañiz, Lucio Villegas, Carmen Rodriguez, Julian Rivero • 81 min.

DOS MÁS UNO, DOS (Oct. 15, 1934) Spanish language; D: John Reinhardt; W: Anthony Coldeway (scr), Hilda Hess (scr), José López Rubio (Spanish version); C: Harry Jackson; E: Fred Allen; M: Samuel Kaylin; Cast: Rosita Moreno, Valentin Parera, Andrés de Segurola, Carmen Rodriguez, Rafael Storm, Carlos Montalban, Lucio Villegas, Carlos Villarías • In England, Carlos Bentley (Parera), an archeologist who prefers old-fashioned women, meets Elena (Moreno), a flapper who pretends to be a Victorian lady. While she loves Carlos, she wants him to love her for whom she is, a modern lady. She concocts a plan with Carlos's uncle (de Segurola) to create an alter-ego, "Peggy," and make Carlos fall in love her. This leads to endless complications when she has to keep both personas alive. 76 min.

PECK'S BAD BOY (Oct. 19, 1934); P: Sol Lesser; D: Edward F. Cline; W: Marguerite Roberts (scr), Bernard Schubert (scr), George W. Peck (orig. characters); C: Frank B. Good; E: Donn Hayes; M: Hugo Riesenfeld; Cast: Jackie Cooper, Thomas Meighan, Jackie Searl, Dorothy Peterson, O.P. Heggie, Charles Evans, Gertrude Howard, Larry Wheat, Harvey Clark • A snooty lad, Horace (Searl), and his mother, Lily (Peterson), come to live with their cousin Bill (Cooper). Horace does not make a smooth transition into his surroundings and Bill gets blamed for his cousin's mishaps. Fed up with his cousin and aunt, Bill trounces Horace in a fight and is then slapped by Lily. Bill's father (Meighan) finally sends the unwanted relatives on their way. 70 min.

MARIE GALANTE (Oct. 26, 1934); P: Winfield Sheehan; D: Henry King; W: Reginald Berkeley (scr), Jacques Deval (novel); C: John Seitz; E: Harold Schuster; M: Arthur Lange; Cast: Spencer Tracy, Ketti Gallian, Ned Sparks, Helen Morgan, Siegfried Rumann, Leslie Fenton, Arthur Byron, Robert Loraine, Jay C. Flippen, Frank Darien, Stepin Fetchit • A French girl, Marie (Gallian), is shanghaied to the Panama Canal. In an effort to earn passage back to France, she takes a singing job and gets involved with shady characters and international intrigue. Brogard (Rumann) is planning to blow up American Navy ships and Marie is naïvely lured into his plot. Crawbett (Tracy), an undercover American service agent who at first thinks Marie is a loose woman, finally realizes her innocence in the plot. With the help of Crawbett and Tenoki (Fenton), a Japanese agent, Marie is rescued. 88 min.

GAMBLING (Nov. 2, 1934); P: Harold B. Franklin; D: Rowland V. Lee; W: Garrett Graham (scr), George M. Cohan (play); C: Jack MacKenzie; M: Frank Tours; Cast: George M. Cohan, Wynne Gibson, Dorothy Burgess, Theodore Newton, Harold Healy, Walter Gilbert, Cora Witherspoon, Joseph Allen, Percy Ames • In the world of gambling dens, professional gambler Al Draper (Cohan), whose adopted daughter was killed, is upset when the accused Braddock (Newton), a notorious playboy who was the girl's fiancé, is acquitted. Al flirts with Dorothy (Burgess), Braddock's ex-girlfriend, and falls for her, but discovers that she is already married to Braddock. Suspecting Dorothy of murder, Al exposes the guilty party, Braddock, who accidentally killed the girl. 80 min. • Producer Harold B. Franklin had been president of Fox West Coast Theaters in the 1920s, then formed his own chain. This film was shot at Astoria Studios in New York.

ELINOR NORTON (Nov. 2, 1934); P: Sol M. Wurtzel; D: Hamilton MacFadden; W: Rose Franken (scr), Philip Klein (scr), Mary Roberts Rinehart (novel); C: George Schneiderman; M: Samuel Kaylin; Cast: Claire Trevor, Gilbert Roland, Henrietta Crosman, Hugh Williams, Norman Foster, Eula Gay, Carlisle Tupper, Cora Sue Collins, Antoinette Lees, Guy Usher • While her jealous husband, Tony (Williams), is away in battle, Elinor (Trevor), a nurse, meets Brazilian René Alba (Gilbert). When the injured Tony returns, he is suspicious that Elinor is seeing Bill (Foster), who is in love with her, but she is secretly seeing René. For Tony's health, Elinor moves to a ranch in the west, and René follows. After befriending René, Tony realizes he is a rival for Elinor. Tony attempts to shoot Elinor, but a struggle results and he only wounds her. Their marriage over, Elinor leaves with René, and Tony finally wishes them well. 72 min.

HELL IN THE HEAVENS (Nov. 9, 1934); P: Al Rockett; D: John Blystone; W: Byron Morgan (scr), Ted Parsons (scr), Jack Yellen (add'l dial), Hermann Rossman (play), Miles Malleson (play); C: Bert Glennon; E: Margaret Clancy; M: Louis De Francesco; Cast: Warner Baxter, Conchita Montenegro, Russell Hardie, Herbert Mundin, Andy Devine, William Stelling, Ralph Morgan, Vince Barnett, William Stack, Arno Frey • Steve Warner (Baxter), an American flyer in the Lafayette Escadrille, becomes first in command and vows to bring down the dreaded Baron (Frey). Meanwhile, Steve falls in love with a French girl, Aimee (Montenegro). When a report comes in about the location of the Baron, Steve, against Aimee's pleas, heads into the air. When he spots the ace's plane, his gun jams and he flies into the Baron's plane. Both planes crash to the ground and Steve captures the Baron. 80 min.

THE WHITE PARADE (Nov. 16, 1934); P: Jesse L. Lasky; D: Irving Cummings; W: Sonya Levien (scr), Ernest Pascal (scr), Rian James (adpt & novel), Jesse Lasky, Jr. (adpt); C: Arthur Miller; E: Jack Murray; M: Louis De Francesco; Cast: Loretta Young, John Boles, Dorothy Wilson, Muriel Kirkland, Astrid Allwyn, Frank Conroy, Jane Darwell, Frank Melton, Walter Johnson, Sara Haden, Joyce Compton • June (Young), Zita (Wilson), Glenda (Allwyn), Una (Compton) and Lucy (Gittelson) all become friends at a three-year nursing school program, in 1907. Their experiences, professional and personal, tragic and uplifting, are documented as they work their way through the program. 83 min.

THE FIRST WORLD WAR (Nov. 23, 1934); P: Truman Talley; W: Laurence Stallings (commentary); E: Bonney Powell, Louis de Rochemont, Russell Shields, Lew Lehr; M: John Rochetti • This is a compilation of Movietone News footage covering the war in Europe from its origins to its close. 78 min.

BACHELOR OF ARTS (Nov. 23, 1934); P: John Stone; D: Louis King; W: Lamar Trotti (scr), John Erskine (novel); C: L.W. O'Connell; M: Samuel Kaylin; Cast: Tom Brown, Anita Louise, Henry B. Walthall, Mae Marsh, Arline Judge, Frank Albertson, George Meeker, Frank Melton, Berton Churchill, Stepin Fetchit • Wealthy freshman Alec Hamilton (Brown) proposes to Mimi (Louise), who is working her way through college and only agrees to date. Mimi is convinced that Alec is spoiled. After Alec exhibits some irresponsible behavior, Mimi gets his father to cut off any money which forces him to get a job. Alec redeems himself by becoming responsible and uses his remaining money to help a professor's (Walthall) ailing wife. 74 min.

LAS FRONTERAS DEL AMOR (Dec. 1, 1934) Spanish language; D: Frank Strayer; W: Winifred Dunn (scr), Bernice Mason (st), Miguel de Zarraga (Spanish version); C: Arthur Martinelli; E: Ernest Nims; M: Samuel Kaylin; Cast: José Mojica, Rosita Moreno, Rafael Corio, Juan Martinez Pia, Alma Real, Rudolf Amendt, Chito Alonso, Gloria de la Vega, Lola Montero, Jesus Macias • Returning to his ranch in Mexico, opera singer Miguel (Mojica) meets California socialite Alice (Moreno), whose plane has run out of fuel. Thinking he is only a worker, Alice agrees to stay in his cabin for the night. Falling in love with Miguel, Alice leaves him because of social differences. She accepts a marriage proposal from Otto (Amendt), but Miguel finds out about the engagement and ends up marrying Alice. 82 min.

MUSIC IN THE AIR (Dec. 7, 1934); P: Erich Pommer; D: Joe May; W: Howard I. Young (scr), Billie Wilder (scr), Robert Liebmann (cont), Jerome Kern and Oscar Hammerstein II (operetta); C: Ernest Palmer; M: Louis de Francesco, Franz Waxman; Cast: Gloria Swanson, John Boles, Douglass Montgomery, June Lang, Al Shean, Reginald Owen, Joseph Cawthorn, Hobart Bosworth, Sara Haden, Roger Imhof, Jed Prouty • Karl (Montgomery), a schoolteacher in the Bavarian Alps, writes songs with Dr. Lessing (Shean) and is in love with his daughter, Sieglinde (Lang). Lessing convinces opera singer Frieda (Swanson) and librettist Bruno (Boles) to come to the town. This sets off a romantic conflict when Frieda becomes interested in Karl, and Bruno falls for Sieglinde. They all end up in Munich, but the young couple tires of the sophisticates, and, after numerous misunderstandings, return to the village to hear Karl's song on the radio. 81 min.

HELLDORADO (Dec. 21, 1934); P: Jesse L. Lasky; D: James Cruze; W: Frances Hyland (scr), Frank Mitchell Dazey (st), Rex Taylor (adpt); C: John Seitz; M: Louis De Francesco; Cast: Richard Arlen, Madge Evans, Ralph Bellamy, James Gleason, Henry B. Walthall, Helen Jerome Eddy, Gertrude Short, Patricia Farr, Stanley Fields, Lucky Hurlic, Stepin Fetchit • Art Ryan (Arlen) hitchhikes with society girl Glenda (Evans) and her fiancé (Bellamy), ending up stranded in a ghost town called Helldorado. With help from an old hermit, Abner (Walthall), Art uncovers a gold mine discovered by Abner and Art's grandfather. Art heads to the next town and announces his strike and plans for the Helldorado's future, but the ore turns out to be "fool's gold." Glenda, who has fallen in love with Art, is able to find the location of the real gold mine from Abner. 74 min.

BRIGHT EYES (Dec. 28, 1934); P: Sol M. Wurtzel; D: David Butler; W: William Conselman (scr), David Butler (st), Edwin Burke (st); C: Arthur Miller; M: Samuel Kaylin; Cast: Shirley Temple, James Dunn, Jane Darwell, Judith Allen, Lois Wilson, Charles Sellon, Walter Johnson, Jane Withers, Theodor von Eltz, Dorothy Christy, Brandon Hurst • Young Shirley Blake (Shirley) lives with a snooty family, for whom her mother, Mary (Wilson), works as a maid. When Mary is killed in a car accident, Shirley has to endure the family's cruel, spoiled daughter (Withers), but is favored by a crabby wheelchair-bound Uncle Ned (Sellon). Shirley spends much time with her late aviator father's best friend, Loop Merritt (Dunn), who eventually decides to marry his girlfriend, Adele (Allen), and both go to court to get custody of Shirley. 83 min. • This film launched Jane Withers's career as a star in Fox films.

SEÑORA CASADA NECESITA MARIDO (Dec. 30, 1934) Spanish language; D: James Tinling; W: José López

Rubio (scr); C: Daniel Clark; M: Samuel Kaylin; Cast: Catalina Bárcena, Antonio Moreno, José Crespo, Valentin Parera, Barbara Leonard, Romulado Tirado, Mimi Aguglia, Tito Coral, José Peña Pepet • In Budapest, Irma Karen (Bárcena) will grant her attorney husband, Tomas (Moreno), a divorce only if he can find her a new husband. However, Tomas starts getting jealous when new men enter the picture. Irma goes away alone and meets playwright Alejandro (Crespo) on her way to Zurich. When Tomas joins her, he is jealous again. A misunderstanding brings Alejandro, whose girlfriend has run off, and Irma close to marriage. Tomas once again injects himself and agrees to get back together with an understanding that arguments, which Irma enjoys, will only take place on Thursday from three to five. 72 min.

1935 Releases

LOTTERY LOVER (Jan. 4, 1935); P: Al Rockett; D: William Thiele; W: Franz Schultz (scr), Billie (Billy) Wilder (scr), Siegfried M. Herzig (st), Maurice Hanline (st), Sam Hellman (dial); C: Bert Glennon; E: Dorothy Spencer; M: Arthur Lange; Cast: Lew Ayres, "Pat" Paterson, Peggy Fears, Sterling Holloway, Walter King, Alan Dinehart, Reginald Denny, Eddie Nugent, Nick Foran, Rafaela Ottiano • Frank Harrington (Ayres), an American sailor on leave in Paris, wins a pool to romance well-known French dancer Gaby (Fears). Inexperienced in such matters, Frank is coached by an American guide, Tank (Dinehart), and a Canadian chorus girl, Patty (Paterson). Frank soon becomes more interested in Patty. When some sailors brag to French soldiers about Frank's conquest of Gaby, they challenge the Americans to a duel at dawn. Gendarmes break up the duel and Frank admits he was with Patty, not Gaby, the night before. 82 min.

THE COUNTY CHAIRMAN (Jan. 11, 1935); P: Edward Butcher; D: John Blystone; W: Sam Hellman (scr), Gladys Lehman (scr), George Ade (play); C: Hal Mohr; M: Arthur Lange; Cast: Will Rogers, Evelyn Venable, Kent Taylor, Louise Dresser, Mickey Rooney, Berton Churchill, Frank Melton, Robert McWade, Russell Simpson, William V. Mong • In the early 1900s, a young small-town Wyoming lawyer, Ben Harvey (Taylor), accepts a nomination as public prosecutor to keep his law partner, Jim Hackler (Rogers), from being humiliated. Ben's opponent is Elias Rigby (Churchill), father of his girlfriend, Lucy (Venable). Ben absorbs personal criticism from Rigby but fights back when any aspersions are cast on Jim. Outraged, Lucy agrees to marry Henry (Melton), son of a newspaper publisher, who can help her father defeat Ben. Although the race is heated, tempers calm afterwards and Lucy is reunited with Ben, who wins the election. 78 min.

MYSTERY WOMAN (Jan. 18, 1935); P: John Stone; D: Eugene Forde; W: Philip MacDonald (scr), Dudley Nichols (st), E.E. Paramore Jr. (st); C: Ernest Palmer; M: Samuel Kaylin; Cast: Mona Barrie, Gilbert Roland, John Halliday, Rod La Roque, Mischa Auer, Billy Bevan, William Faversham, Howard Lang, George Barraud, Arno Frey, Hal Boyer • French Captain Benoit (La Roque) is unfairly sentenced to life on Devil's Island for allegedly turning a valuable document over to the enemy. To exonerate him, his wife, Margaret (Barrie), suspects that millionaire Theodore Van Wyke (Halliday) has the document and follows him on an ocean liner to New York. Another passenger, Juan Santanda (Roland), is also after the document. Margaret has to cultivate a friendship with Juan to retrieve the evidence. Margaret is able to get the entire document, but Juan is shot by his enemies. She returns to France to free Benoit. 69 min.

CHARLIE CHAN IN PARIS (Jan. 25, 1935); P: John Stone; D: Lewis Seiler; W: Edward T. Lowe (scr), Stuart Anthony (scr), Philip MacDonald (st), Earl Der Biggers (character); C: Ernest Palmer; M: Samuel Kaylin; Cast: Warner Oland, Mary Brian, Thomas Beck, John Miljan, Murray Kinnell, Minor Watson, John Qualen, Keye Luke, Henry Kolker, Dorothy Appleby, Ruth Peterson, Perry Ivins • Chan (Oland) visits Paris to investigate forged bonds when an Apache dancer is murdered. This leads him to Albert Dufresne (Miljan), who is threatening to blackmail Yvette (Brian), whose fiancé (Beck) works at a bank. Dufresne, who is also suspected of issuing the forged bonds, is murdered. Yvette is arrested. Chan solves the forgeries and the murders by revealing that three bank employees, who have a counterfeiting operation in the sewers, have created a fictional character, Xavier, a disabled, shell-shocked vagrant, but all three had used the same disguise when needed to commit murder. 70 min.

UNDER PRESSURE (Feb. 1, 1935); P: Robert T. Kane; D: Raoul Walsh; W: Borden Chase (scr), Noel Pierce (scr), Lester Cole (scr), Borden Chase and Edward Doherty (novel); C: Hal Mohr, L.W. O'Connell; E: Robert Bischoff; Cast: Edmund Lowe, Victor McLaglen, Florence Rice, Marjorie Rambeau, Charles Bickford, Siegfried Rumann, Roger Imhof, George Walsh, Warner Richmond, Jack Wallace • Two "sand hogs," Shocker (Lowe) and Jumbo (McLaglen), head a team digging a tunnel under the East River in New York City. The digging team from the other side of the river is headed by Nipper Moran (Bickford), their bitter rival, and the leaders get into wild fights. Shocker and Jumbo also vie for the affection of a reporter, Pat (Rice), who decides to write a story about them. A tunnel flood sends Shocker in to rescue his friend and, when Jumbo recovers, he has to rescue Shocker. In the process, Jumbo's leg is paralyzed. A $5,000 bonus to eliminate the gap in the tunnel induces Shocker to push his team so Jumbo can have an operation. 71 min.

BABOONA (Feb. 8, 1935); SP: Truman Talley; P: Martin Johnson, Osa Johnson; C: Martin Johnson; E: Lew Lehr, Russell Shields, Lillian Seebach • This documentary, produced by the Johnsons, highlights wildlife and the tribes of Kenya from the ground and the air. 72 min.

ONE MORE SPRING (Feb. 15, 1935); P: Winfield Sheehan; D: Henry King; W: Edwin Burke (scr & dial),

Robert Nathan (novel); C: John Seitz; E: Harold Schuster; M: Arthur Lange; Cast: Janet Gaynor, Warner Baxter, Walter King, Jane Darwell, Roger Imhof, Grant Mitchell, Rosemary Ames, John Qualen, Nick Foran, Astrid Allwyn, Lee Kohlmar • An easygoing, formerly rich man, Otkar (Baxter), a temperamental musician, Morris Rosenberg (King), and an out-of-work chorus girl, Elizabeth (Gaynor), are all squatters in Central Park. Otkar rescues a banker, Sheridan (Mitchell), planning to commit suicide because his bank is going to fail. In the spring, Sheridan gets the government to protect his depositors and backs Otkar in a new venture. Otkar proposes to Gaynor, and King gets a job. After a difficult winter, spring brings new hope for all. 87 min.

WHEN A MAN'S A MAN (Feb. 15, 1935) Atherton Productions; P: Sol Lesser; D: Edward F. Cline; W: Agnes Christine Johnston (adpt & scr), Frank M. Dazey (adpt & scr), Harold Bell Wright (novel); C: Frank B. Good; E: Donn Hayes; Cast: George O'Brien, Dorothy Wilson, Paul Kelly, Harry Woods, Jimmy Butler, Richard Carlyle, Clarence Wilson, Edgar Norton • Larry Knight (O'Brien) is an Easterner who has lost his money and goes west. He goes to work on Dean Baldwin's (Carlyle) ranch. Cambert (Woods), a neighboring rancher who has cut off Baldwin's water supply, is trying to force Dean and his daughter Kitty (Wilson) to sell off their land for pennies. Larry devises a plan to draw water from underneath Cambert's property, but Baldwin's foreman, Phil (Kelly), who is a rival for Kitty, tells Cambert about the plan. Finally, Kitty decides to use dynamite to get their water supply back and, in an action-packed ending, Larry has to rescue her from the explosion. Phil captures Cambert and Larry and wins Kitty's affection. 68 min.

THE LITTLE COLONEL (Feb. 22, 1935) B.G. DeSylva Production; D: David Butler; W: William Conselman (scr & adpt), Anne Fellows Johnston (novel); C: Arthur Miller, William Skall (Technicolor photography); E: Irene Morra; M: Arthur Lange, Cyril J. Mockridge; Cast: Shirley Temple, Lionel Barrymore, Evelyn Venable, John Lodge, Sidney Blackmer, Alden Chase, William Burress, Frank Darien, Robert Warwick, Hattie McDaniel • Following the Civil War, Elizabeth (Venable), the daughter of an embittered southern colonel (Barrymore), is forced to return home after her marriage to a Northerner (Lodge) goes badly. Her young daughter (Temple), initially disliked by the colonel, finally wins him over and patches up the family. 80 min. • This was Fox's first use of the new three-strip Technicolor process in the final two minutes of the film.

¡ASEGURE A SU MUJER! (March 1, 1935) Spanish language; D: Lewis Seiler; W: Enrique Jardiel Poncela (adpt), Robert Ellis (adpt), Helen Logan (adpt); C: Daniel Clark; M: Samuel Kaylin; Cast: Raúl Roulien, Conchita Montenegro, Antonio Moreno, Mona Maris, Luis Alberni, Barbara Leonard, Carlos Villarías, José Peña Pepet, Blanca Vischer, Gloria Roy • To save a failing insurance company, an idea man with many former mistresses, Ricardo (Roulien), comes up with a scheme to sell policies to protect husbands from unfaithful wives. This leads to complications in a romantic relationship with his secretary, Camelia (Montenegro). Ricardo is caught up in a husband's attempt to frame his wife to collect insurance, and a disgruntled wife (Maris) helps set up Ricardo so the program will be scrapped. 83 min.

THE GREAT HOTEL MURDER (March 8, 1935); P: John Stone; D: Eugene Forde; W: Arthur Kober (scr), Vincent Starrett (short story); C: Ernest Palmer; E: Fred Allen; M: Samuel Kaylin; Cast: Edmund Lowe, Victor McLaglen, Rosemary Ames, Mary Carlisle, Henry O'Neill, C. Henry Gordon, William Janney, Charles C. Wilson, John Qualen, Madge Bellamy • A house detective at a fancy hotel, Andy McCabe (McLaglen), is assigned to figure out what caused the death of J.C. Blake in one of the rooms. To McCabe's dismay, mystery author Roger Blackwood (Lowe) barges into the investigation. Dr. Temple (Gordon), a toxicologist visiting for a convention, believes it was a suicide. Other suspects include Elinor Blake (Ames), the dead man's wife, and Claude Harvey (O'Neill), a banker who Blake had discovered with Elinor. After Mac and Roger trip over each other in the investigation, they discover that Harvey put some of Dr. Temple's poison in a cigarette given to Blake. 70 min.

JULIETA COMPRA UN HIJO (March 15, 1935) Spanish language; AP: John Stone; D: Louis King; W: José López Rubio (adpt), Gregorio Martinez Sierra (play); C: Daniel Clark; M: Samuel Kaylin; Cast: Catalina Bárcena, Gilbert Roland, Luana Alcañiz, Julio Peña, Soledad Jimenez, Barbara Leonard, Antonio Vidal, Tina Menard, Agostino Borgato, Rosa Rey • On a cruise ship, handsome but financially weak Jack Aranda (Roland) meets Julieta Albornoz (Bárcena), who is despondent over an untrustworthy fiancé. Jack woos her because of her wealth, even though he loves another. Julieta offers to pay Jack a large sum if he will marry her and provide her with a son. In the initially loveless marriage, Julieta gives birth to a daughter, which she feels does not fulfill their contract. Jack then returns her check and they both agree to have a real marriage. 74 min.

LIFE BEGINS AT 40 (March 22, 1935); P: Sol M. Wurtzel; D: George Marshall; W: Lamar Trotti (scr), Walter B. Pitkin (novel); C: Harry Jackson; E: Alexander Troffey; M: Samuel Kaylin; Cast: Will Rogers, Richard Cromwell, George Barbier, Rochelle Hudson, Jane Darwell, Slim Summerville, Sterling Holloway, Thomas Beck, Roger Imhof, Charles Sellon • A small-town newspaper editor, Kennesaw Clark (Rogers), helps Lee Austin (Cromwell), who was in prison, by hiring him. Col. Abercrombie (Barbier) dislikes Lee and takes the paper back from Clark. The colonel also publicly criticizes Adele (Hudson) for dating Lee. Abercrombie gets more resistance from Kennesaw in a local political race when the editor backs the colonel's rival, a lazy, wood-whittling T. Watterson Merriwether (Summerville). After much local commotion and a near-riot, Kennesaw eventually gets some dirt on Abercrombie. He then wins back his paper and sees Adele and Lee happy together. 79 min.

GEORGE WHITE'S 1935 SCANDALS (March 29, 1935); D: George White; W: Jack Yellen (scr), Patterson McNutt (scr); C: George Schneiderman; E: Robert Bischoff; M: Louis De Francesco; Cast: Alice Faye, James Dunn, Ned Sparks, Cliff Edwards, Arline Judge, Eleanor Powell, Emma Dunn, George White, The Scandals Beauties • Traveling to Florida, George White stops at a small town and sees a local show which features Honey Walters (Faye) and her songwriter boyfriend, Eddie (Dunn). White hires them and they become a hit in New York. However, both are eventually fired. When Honey's aunt Jane (Emma Dunn) comes to town, White searches around frantically to find the pair and get them back on stage. 83 min.

$10 RAISE (Apr. 5, 1935); P: Joseph Engel; D: George Marshall; W: Henry Johnson (scr), Lou Breslow (scr), Lamar Trotti (add'l dial), Peter B. Kyne (short story); C: Harry Jackson; E: Alex Troffey; M: Samuel Kaylin; Cast: Edward Everett Horton, Karen Morley, Alan Dinehart, Glen Boles, Berton Churchill, Rosina Lawrence, Ray Walker, Frank Melton, William Benedict, Jed Prouty • After working as a bookkeeper for many years, Hubert Wilkins (Horton) is prodded by his fiancée and co-worker, Emily (Morley), to ask his boss, Bates (Churchill), for a raise. Emily is fired because Bates's son Don (Boles) has become engaged to her sister (Lawrence). Hubert is later fired as well, but after being conned into buying marsh land, he makes a fortune from the mineral water there and buys Bates's company. 70 min.

IT'S A SMALL WORLD (Apr. 12, 1935); P: Edward Butcher; D: Irving Cummings; W: Sam Hellman (scr), Gladys Lehman (scr), Albert Treynor (short story); C: Arthur Miller; E: Jack Murray; M: Arthur Lange; Cast: Spencer Tracy, Wendy Barrie, Raymond Walburn, Virginia Sale, Astrid Allwyn, Irving Bacon, Charles Sellon, Nick Foran, Belle Daube, Frank McGlynn, Sr., Frank McGlynn, Jr. • On vacation in New Orleans, society girl Jane (Barrie) crashes into Bill Shevlin's (Tracy) car. Jane flirts with the locals and has a judge fine Bill for recklessness. Jane uses parts from Bill's car but is unable to pay, so Bill, under Napoleonic law, seizes the debtor. Bill and Jane, after much bickering, fall in love and drive off in a car fixed with their united parts. 71 min.

PECHMARIE (Apr. 15, 1935) German production; D: Erich Engel; Jenny Jugo, Friedrich Benfer, Willy Schur, Mally Georgi, E.G. Schiffner, Gerhard Bienert, Karl Hannemann, Hans V. Zeditz, Lewis Brody; W: Eva Leidmann, Erich Engel; C: Willy Winterstein; M: Theo Mackeben • An unlucky young woman, who works at her newsstand in Berlin, ends a relationship with a painter over a misunderstanding over her kindness toward an elderly man. The old man then tells her that she is holding a winning lottery ticket. She reconciles with the painter and they are able to buy a home with the winnings. 82 min.

SPRING TONIC (Apr. 19, 1935); P: Robert T. Kane; D: Clyde Bruckman; W: Patterson McNutt (scr), H.W. Hanemann (scr), Howard I. Young (adpt), Ben Hecht and Rose Caylor (play); C: L.W. O'Connell; E: Harold Schuster; M: Arthur Lange; Cast: Lew Ayres, Claire Trevor, Walter King, ZaSu Pitts, Jack Haley, Tala Birell, Siegfried Rumann, Frank Mitchell, Jack Durant, Herbert Mundin, Henry Kolker • Driving off on an impulse before her marriage, socialite Betty (Trevor) ends up at a lodge, where she is romanced by José (King). Her maid, Maggie (Pitts), reports their location to Betty's milquetoast fiancé, Caleb (Ayres). Caleb arrives and keeps a nosy reporter, Sykes (Haley), from calling in a story about the breakup. Caleb then returns José to his lover, Lola (Birell), and rescues Betty from an escaped tiger. He uses the same whip he used on the tiger to order Betty to kiss him. 58 min.

LADIES LOVE DANGER (May 3, 1935); D: H. Bruce Humberstone; W: Samson Raphaelson (scr), Ilya Zorn (st), Robert Ellis (adpt), Helen Logan (adpt); C: Daniel B. Clark; E: Fred Allen; M: Samuel Kaylin; Cast: Mona Barrie, Gilbert Roland, Donald Cook, Adrienne Ames, Hardie Albright, Herbert Mundin, Nick Foran, Marion Clayton, Ray Walker, Henry Kolker, Russell Hicks • A wealthy New York play angel, José Lopez (Kolker), who was about to marry ex-chorus girl Adele (Ames), is murdered. A playwright and amateur sleuth, Ricky Alonzo (Roland), gets involved with a mysterious woman, Rita (Barrie), who is really a reporter, and together they solve the convoluted crime. An actor, Phil (Albright), who secretly married Lopez' daughter Helen (Clayton), found out she was disinherited and then killed her father. Trying to find the will, he was seen by Adele and her lover, Tom Lennox (Cook), who then tried to blackmail him, so he killed them as well. Ricky is able to overcome Phil and prevent him from shooting Rita. 69 min.

COWBOY MILLIONAIRE (May 10, 1935) Atherton Productions; P: Sol Lesser; D: Edward F. Cline; W: George Waggner (scr), Dan Jarrett (scr); C: Frank B. Good; E: Donn Hayes; Cast: George O'Brien, Evalyn Bostock, Edgar Kennedy, Maude Allen, Alden Chase, Dan Jarrett, Lloyd Ingraham, Dean Benton, Thomas Curran • Englishwoman Pamela Barclay (Bostock) meets cowboy Bob Walker (O'Brien), who entertains visitors by staging phony stagecoach hold-ups on the way to an Arizona dude ranch. Pamela falls in love with Bob, but there is a misunderstanding when Pamela is led to believe that Bob is wooing her just to win a bet. In tears, Pamela packs up her things and returns to England. Meanwhile, Thornton (Chase), a con man traveling with Pamela, arranges to get control of a valuable mine owned by Bob and his partner, Persimmon (Kennedy). Bob gets on the ship, regains control of his mine and reunites with Pamela. 65 min.

OUR LITTLE GIRL (May 17, 1935); P: Edward Butcher; D: John Robertson; W: Stephen Avery (scr & adpt), Allen Rivkin (scr), Florence Leighton Pfalzgraf (short story); C: John Seitz; E: Margaret Clancey; M: Oscar Bradley; Cast: Shirley Temple, Rosemary Ames, Joel

McCrea, Lyle Talbot, Erin O'Brien-Moore, J. Farrell MacDonald, Poodles Hanneford, Margaret Armstrong, Rita Owin • Small-town physician Don Middleton (McCrea) has his marriage disrupted when playboy Rolfe Brent (Talbot) confesses his love for Don's wife, Elsa (Ames). At the same time, Don's nurse, Sarah (Moore), is in love with him. Molly (Temple), the Middletons' young daughter, senses the tension and is upset by it. The marital discord drives Molly to run away, but she meets a tramp (MacDonald), who tells Don where Molly went. Elsa also realizes her place is with her family, and all are reunited. 65 min.

THE DARING YOUNG MAN (May 24, 1935); P: Robert T. Kane; D: William A. Seiter; W: William Hurlbut (scr), Claude Binyon (st), Sidney Skolsky (st); C: Merritt Gerstad; E: Ernest Nims; M: Arthur Lange; Cast: James Dunn, Mae Clarke, Neil Hamilton, Sidney Toler, Warren Hymer, Stanley Fields, Madge Bellamy, Frank Melton, Raymond Hatton, Arthur Treacher, Robert Gleckler • A confirmed bachelor, reporter Don McLane (Dunn), changes his mind when he meets rival reporter Martha Allen (Clarke). Their plans to marry are interrupted when Mac's editor, Hooley (Gleckler), sends him undercover to a prison to expose corruption. Mac finds that Warden Palmer (Toler) is taking kickbacks. Meanwhile, stood up at the altar, Martha accepts another suitor's (Hamilton) proposal. Martha finds out that Mac is on the inside and goes to the prison when the mayor and commissioner are coming for a surprise inspection. Palmer tries to hide bags of cash but they break open and money flies all over. Reunited, Mac and Martha rush to get married, but both agree to postpone the nuptials to call in a juicy story. 75 min.

UNDER THE PAMPAS MOON (May 31, 1935); P: B.G. DeSylva; D: James Tinling; W: Ernest Pascal (scr), Bradley King (scr), Gordon Morris (st), Henry Johnson (add'l dial); C: Chester Lyons; E: Robert Simpson; M: Arthur Lange, Cyril J. Mockridge; Cast: Warner Baxter, Ketti Gallian, Veloz and Yolanda, John Miljan, J. Carrol Naish, Soledad Jimenez, Jack La Rue, George Irving, Blanca Vischer, Rita Cansino, Armida, Ann Codée • Argentine gaucho Cesar (Baxter) meets French singer Yvonne (Gallian), but when she leaves for Buenos Aires, her manager, Gregory (Miljan), steals Cesar's prized racehorse. Cesar heads for the big city and finds his horse, but Gregory gives him some money so he can enter the horse in a race. Cesar lives the high life in a fancy hotel but ultimately realizes that Gregory wants to ship the horse to France. Cesar steals his horse and, although he thinks Yvonne was in on the scheme, she convinces him of her innocence and they all return to the Pampas. 78 min.

DOUBTING THOMAS (June 7, 1935); D: David Butler; W: William Conselman (scr), Bartlett Cormack (adpt), George Kelly (play); C: Joseph Valentine; E: Irene Morra; M: Arthur Lange; Cast: Will Rogers, Billie Burke, Alison Skipworth, Sterling Holloway, Andrew Tombes, Gail Patrick, Frances Grant, Frank Albertson, Helen Flint, Johnny Arthur, John Qualen • Bitten by the acting bug, Paula Brown (Burke) tells her husband Thomas (Rogers), president of a breakfast sausage company, that she wants to pursue a career in Hollywood. When a famous director, Von Blitzen (Qualen), comes to town and sees a screen test he made of Thomas, he is impressed and implores Thomas to sign a contract. Thomas now turns the tables on Paula and says acting is more important than his marriage. However, the whole thing is a ruse and Paula is chastened. Thomas's son Jimmy (Albertson) also calms his girlfriend's (Grant) acting fever at the same time. 73 min.

BLACK SHEEP (June 14, 1935); P: Sol M. Wurtzel; D: Allan Dwan; W: Allen Rivkin (scr), Allan Dwan (st); C: Arthur Miller; E: Alexander Troffey; M: Samuel Kaylin; Cast: Edmund Lowe, Claire Trevor, Tom Brown, Eugene Pallette, Adrienne Ames, Herbert Mundin, Ford Sterling, Jed Prouty, Billy Bevan, David Torrence • A professional gambler, John Dugan (Lowe), on an ocean liner, makes a career of winning from businessmen and socialites. On a trip, he befriends a debutante Janette (Trevor), and helps a young man, Fred Curtis (Brown), who has been blackmailed into stealing jewels from a passenger to pay a gambling debt. The repayment gets complicated because other people are involved, but Dugan pulls it off because he has realized that Fred is his estranged son from a failed marriage. 75 min.

CHARLIE CHAN IN EGYPT (June 21, 1935); P: Edward T. Lowe; D: Louis King; W: Robert Ellis (scr), Helen Logan (scr), Earl Derr Biggers (character); C: Daniel B. Clark; E: Al De Gaetano; M: Samuel Kaylin; Cast: Warner Oland, "Pat" Paterson, Thomas Beck, Rita Cansino, Stepin Fetchit, Jameson Thomas, Frank Conroy, Nigel de Brulier, James Eagles. Paul Porcasi, Arthur Stone • Traveling to Egypt, Chan (Oland) investigates the death of a famed archeologist who is found wrapped up in a mummy's bandages in the tomb he uncovered. The archeologist's son, Barry (Eagles), fears that the tomb's curse will bring death to his entire family, including his sister Carol (Paterson) and her boyfriend, Tom (Beck). Barry is the next to die. A secret treasure room is the reason for the murders and the guilty party, Prof. Thurston (Conroy), had been illegally selling artifacts to museums. Chan reveals that the method of death was a drug that causes hallucinations and death. 72 min.

GINGER (July 5, 1935); P: Sol M. Wurtzel; D: Lewis Seiler; W: Arthur Kober (st & scr); C: Bert Glennon; E: Fred Allen; M: Samuel Kaylin; Cast: Jane Withers, O.P. Heggie, Jackie Searl, Katharine Alexander, Walter King, Donald Haines, Charles Lane, Arthur Hoyt, Tommy Bupp, Johnnie Pirrone, Jr. • A precocious eight-year-old, Ginger (Withers), who lives with her drunken uncle Rex (Heggie), an out-of-work Shakespearean actor, is caught stealing and turned over to the custody of a society woman, Mrs. Parker (Alexander). Ginger befriends her well-mannered son, Hamilton (Searl), and teaches him some street smarts, realigning Mrs. Parker's notions about children. Ginger eventually returns to Uncle Rex with Hamilton after being insulted by Mrs. Parker. All are reunited in the end. 74 min.

ORCHIDS TO YOU (July 12, 1935); P: Robert T. Kane; D: William A. Seiter; W: William Hurlbut (scr), Bartlett Cormack (scr), Gordon Rigby (st), Robert Dillon (st), Howard Estabrook (adpt); C: Merritt Gerstad; E: Ernest Nims; M: Arthur Lange; Cast: John Boles, Jean Muir, Charles Butterworth, Ruthelma Stevens, Harvey Stephens, Arthur Lake, Spring Byington, Sidney Toler, John Qualen, Patricia Farr • Tom Bentley (Boles), lawyer for an exclusive New York skyscraper, is charged with convincing florist Cammelia Rand (Muir) to move out of the premises to make room for a bank. Cammelia has two aces up her sleeve. She is constantly proposed marriage by the befuddled majority partner (Butterworth) in the building and she knows that a customer, George Draper (Stephens), is having an affair with Tom's wife (Stevens). Since discretion is important to Cammelia, she will not reveal the correspondent in a divorce trial involving Tom's wife, and ends up spending time in jail. Tom later gets a divorce and ends up marrying Cammelia. 75 min.

SILK HAT KID (July 19, 1935); P: Joseph Engel; D: H. Bruce Humberstone; W: Edward Eliscu (scr), Lou Breslow (scr), Dore Schary (scr), Gerald Beaumont (short story); C: Daniel Clark; E: Fred Allen; M: Samuel Kaylin; Cast: Lew Ayres, Mae Clarke, Paul Kelly, Ralf Harrolde, William Harrigan, Billy Lee, John Qualen, Warren Hymer, Vince Barnett, William Benedict • Eddie Howard (Ayres), a former champion boxer, shows up for a "protection" job at a legitimate New York casino owned by Tim Martin (Kelly). Because of schoolteacher Laura Grant (Clarke), he becomes a boxing instructor at a community center run by Brother Joe (Harrigan). However, Tim is in love with Laura and threatens to cut off funding for the center unless Joe fires Eddie. Tim and Eddie end up fighting it out with Brother Joe as a referee and are able to resolve their differences and allow kids to continue to benefit from the center. 67 min.

CURLY TOP (July 26, 1935); P: Winfield Sheehan; D: Irving Cummings; W: Patterson McNutt (scr), Arthur Beckhard (scr); C: John Seitz; E: Jack Murray; M: Oscar Bradley; Cast: Shirley Temple, John Boles, Rochelle Hudson, Jane Darwell, Rafaella Ottiano, Esther Dale, Etienne Girardot, Arthur Treacher, Maurice Murphy, Billy Gilbert • Elizabeth (Temple), a tot with musical talent, has lived at an orphanage since her parents were killed in a car accident. Mrs. Higgins (Ottiano), the stern matron, insists that Elizabeth's pony and duck must be sold, but a wealthy trustee, Edward (Boles), adopts Elizabeth, her pets and her older sister Mary (Hudson), under an assumed name and moves them into his summer estate. Mary is courted by wealthy Jimmie (Murphy), but ultimately marries Edward. 75 min.

THE FARMER TAKES A WIFE (Aug. 2, 1935); P: Winfield Sheehan; D: Victor Fleming; W: Edwin Burke (scr) Walter D. Edmonds, Max Gordon, Marc Connelly, Frank B. Eiser (play); C: Ernest Palmer; E: Harold Schuster; M: Oscar Bradley; Cast: Janet Gaynor, Henry Fonda, Charles Bickford, Slim Summerville, Andy Devine, Roger Imhof, Jane Withers, Margaret Hamilton, Siegfried Rumann, John Qualen • Boaters on the Erie Canal in 1853 are threatened by the encroaching railroads. Farmer Dan Harrow (Fonda) meets Molly Larkin (Gaynor), cook and romantic interest of boater Jotham Klore (Bickford), but insults her when he vouches for rail transport. They meet again when Molly is fed up with Jotham's drinking. Dan, who has won a lottery, proposes to Molly, but when Jotham finds out, he comes after Dan. When they get into a fistfight, Dan wins. He and Molly decide to go their separate ways because she prefers canal boats to farming, but she ultimately joins Dan on his farm. 91 min.

WELCOME HOME (Aug. 9, 1935) A B.G. DeSylva Production; D: James Tinling; W: Marion Orth (scr), Arthur T. Horman (st & scr), Paul Gerard Smith (add'l dial); C: Arthur Miller; E: Robert Simpson; M: Oscar Bradley; Cast: James Dunn, Arline Judge, Raymond Walburn, Rosina Lawrence, William Frawley, Charles Sellon, Charles Ray, Frank Melton, George Meeker, James Burke • Race track tout Dickie Foster (Dunn) and his tough associate, Gorgeous (Judge), return to their home town for a high school reunion. Dickie tries to help the chamber of commerce retrieve an investment of $10,000 in phony bonds, sold to them by his crooked friend. Although Dickie fails at first, he ends up convincing another wealthy alumnus to build a factory in the town, and ends up becoming its manager. Although Dickie is initially enamored of another local girl, he and Gorgeous plan to marry. 72 min.

DRESSED TO THRILL (Aug. 16, 1935); P: Robert T. Kane; D: Harry Lachman; W: Samson Raphaelson (scr); C: Rudolph Maté; E: Margaret Clancey; M: Louis De Francesco; Cast: Tutta Rolf, Clive Brook, Robert Barrat, Nydia Westman, George Hassell, Mme. Smirnova, Leonid Snegoff, G.P. Huntley Jr., Nenette Lafayette • After her lover, a Canadian soldier named Bill Trent (Brook), does not show up at the end of the World War, Colette Dubois (Rolf), a French dressmaker, becomes a traveling singer and changes her name to Nadia. Fame comes to Nadia quickly and she is tempted to marry Lord Penfield (Huntley Jr.) until she reads that Bill Trent is to marry a Parisian heiress. She returns to Paris and finds him, but he sees her only as the famous singer, Nadia. Colette wants Bill to love her for herself and goes through an elaborate ruse to win him back. 68 min.

DANTE'S INFERNO (Aug. 23, 1935); P: Sol M. Wurtzel; D: Harry Lachman; W: Philip Klein (scr), Robert M. Yost (scr); C: Rudolph Maté; E: Al De Gaetano; M: Samuel Kaylin; Cast: Spencer Tracy, Claire Trevor, Henry B. Walthall, Alan Dinehart, Scotty Beckett, Robert Gleckler, Rita Cansino, Gary Leon, Willard Robertson, Morgan Wallace • Ambitious ne'er-do-well Jim Carter (Tracy) takes over his father-in-law's (Walthall) carnival show, "Dante's Inferno," and turns it into an extravagant casino. Jim alienates Betty (Trevor), Jim's wife, by promoting gambling and vice. Ignoring safety reports, Jim bribes an inspector and then is prosecuted after a cave-in at his club. Jim then buys a cruise ship, but cuts corners and a fire breaks out. Jim discovers his young son, Alex (Beckett), is on board and has to rescue him. When Betty, who was planning to divorce Jim, meets him at the ship, he admits that he has made his own hell and vows to reform. 88 min. • Spencer Tracy was quoted as saying that this was "one of the worst pictures ever made anywhere, anytime."

REDHEADS ON PARADE (Aug. 30, 1935) A Jesse L. Lasky Production; P: Jesse L. Lasky; D: Norman Z. McLeod; W: Don Hartman (st & scr), Rian James (scr), Gertrude Purcell (st), Jay Gorney (st); C: John Seitz, Barney McGill; E: Dorothy Spencer; M: Louis De Francesco; Cast: John Boles, Dixie Lee, Jack Haley, Raymond Walburn, Alan Dinehart, Patsy O'Connor, Herman Bing, William Austin, Wilbur Mack, Anne Nagel • John Bruce (Boles) is a washed-up actor in a half-finished movie "Beauties on Parade," when his producer, George Magnus (Dinehart), and publicity agent, Peter Mathews (Haley), have to find a new backer to finish the film. A beauty shop operator, Ginger Blair (Lee), suggests they approach Augustus Twill (Walburn), the manufacturer of a red hair dye, for financing. John tells them to change the title to "Redheads on Parade." Twill agrees, but has his eyes on Ginger. John becomes jealous and the film's sole print is stolen by some rivals on the night of the premiere. All ends well when Ginger finds the film in time for the showing, and the audience goes wild. 78 min.

ANGELINA O EL HONOR DE UN BRIGADIER (Sept. 6, 1935) Spanish language; D: Louis King; W: Betty Reinhardt (scr), Enrique Jardiel Poncela (scr); C: Daniel Clark; E: Ernest Nims; M: Troy Sanders, Edward Kilenyi; Cast: Rosita Diaz, José Crespo, Enrique de Rosas, Julio Peña, Rina de Liguoro, Juan Torena, Andrés de Segurola, Romualdo Tirado, Ligia de Golconda • Don Marcial (Rosas) disagrees with his wife Marcela (Liguoro) and approves of daughter Angelina's (Diaz) sweetheart, Rodolfo (Peña), a romantic poet. Marcela's lover, the sophisticated Germán (Crespo), comes to the house and falls in love with Angelina. Germán talks Angelina into accompanying him to an inn, and, although there was nothing improper, a furious Don Marcial bursts in and challenges him to a duel. Rodolfo is also annoyed with Angelina. Germán is fatally wounded, which exposes Marcela's relationship. Don Marcial is unforgiving, but finally takes his wife back and they celebrate the wedding of Angelina and Rodolfo. 79 min.

STEAMBOAT 'ROUND THE BEND (Sept. 6, 1935); P: Sol M. Wurtzel; D: John Ford; W: Dudley Nichols (scr), Lamar Trotti (scr), Ben Lucien Burman (novel); C: George Schneiderman; E: Al De Gaetano; M: Samuel Kaylin; Cast: Will Rogers, Anne Shirley, Irvin S. Cobb, Eugene Pallette, John McGuire, Berton Churchill, Francis Ford, Roger Imhof, Raymond Hatton, Hobart Bosworth • Doc Pearly (Rogers), a riverboat captain on the Mississippi River in the 1890s, is trying to find a half-crazed evangelist (Churchill), who is the only witness to prevent Doc's nephew Duke (McGuire) from a hanging verdict in a murder case. In the process of heading downriver, Doc is forced to get into a steamboat race with Captain Eli, with the winner to take both boats. Doc wins the race by not refueling and instead sacrifices a wax museum he acquired as well as a stash of rum which he has been selling as tonic. Doc finds the evangelist, lassos him off the dock and gets the governor to grant a pardon for Duke. 80 min. • This feature was released shortly after Will Rogers's death.

THE GAY DECEPTION (Sept. 13, 1935); P: Jesse L. Lasky; D: William Wyler; W: Stephen Avery (scr), Don Hartman (scr); C: Joseph Valentine; E: Robert L. Simpson; M: Louis De Francesco; Cast: Francis Lederer, Frances Dee, Benita Hume, Alan Mowbray, Lennox Pawle, Adele St. Maur, Akim Tamiroff, Luis Alberni, Lionel Stander, Ferdinand Gottschalk • Small-town stenographer Mirabel (Dee), disappointed that she has not had an exciting time in New York, is asked to dinner by Prince Allesandro (Lederer), whom she has mistaken for a hotel bellboy. Mirabel is then invited to a society ball by Cordelia Channing (Hume) and her boyfriend, Lord Clewe (Mowbray). In need of an escort, Allesandro promises that Mirabel will attend the party with a prince, but when she realizes he is the escort, she gets angry. There are further complications when Allesandro is thought to be an impostor, but Mirabel finally realizes that he really is a prince and they unite at the end. 76 min.

THUNDER IN THE NIGHT (Sept. 20, 1935); P: John Stone; D: George Archainbaud; W: Frances Hyland (scr), Eugene Snow (scr), Ladislas Fodor; C: Bert Glennon; E: Alex Troffey; M: Samuel Kaylin; Cast: Edmund Lowe, Karen Morley, Paul Cavanaugh, Una O'Connor, Gene Lockhart, John Qualen, Russell Hicks, Arthur Edmund Carew, Bodil Rosing, Cornelius Keefe • In Budapest, Count Alvinczy (Cavanaugh), who has just been elected to the cabinet, is about to become the victim of a blackmailer, Szegedy (Keefe). When the blackmailer is killed, Police Captain Torok (Lowe) has to prove that his friends, the Count and his wife, Madalaine (Morley), are not responsible. Torok proves that Szegedy's mistress, Katherine (Roy), a sharpshooter, shot him from the police station window. 67 min.

THUNDER MOUNTAIN (Sept. 27, 1935) Atherton Productions; P: Sol Lesser; D: David Howard; W: Dan Jarrett (scr), Don Swift (scr), Zane Grey (novel); C: Frank B. Good; E: Frank Crandall; Cast: George O'Brien, Barbara Fritchie, Frances Grant, Morgan Wallace, George F. Hayes, Edward LeSaint, Dean Benton, William Norton Bailey, Sid Jordan • Prospector Kal (O'Brien) gets a grubstake from Sam Blair (LeSaint) and his daughter Sydney (Fritchie). When Kal and Sydney, now in love, reach the mother lode, Rand Leavitt (Wallace) has already staked his claim by waylaying

Kal's partner. Kal is ready to fight the claim jumper, but Sydney sides with Leavitt, who claims he located the mine first and offers her a share. Kal rallies other miners who dislike Leavitt and, with testimony from his partner, Steve (Benton), he confronts Leavitt in a fight on the cliff side of the mountain. Leavitt falls to his death. Kal walks away from Sydney and returns to his dance hall girl, Nugget (Grant). 58 min.

PIERNAS DE SEDA (Oct. 4, 1935) Spanish version — *Silk Legs*; D: John J. Boland; W: Paul Perez (scr), Frederica Sagor (st), José López Rubio (Spanish version); C: Harry Jackson; E: Nick De Maggio; M: Samuel Kaylin; Cast: Rosita Moreno, Raúl Roulien, Enrique de Rosas, Paco Moreno, Romualdo Tirado, Manuel Peluffo, Rodolfo Hoyos, Manuel Paris, Antonio Vidal, Rosita Granada • 80 min.

HERE'S TO ROMANCE (Oct. 4, 1935) Jesse L. Lasky Production; D: Alfred E. Green; W: Ernest Pascal (st & scr), Arthur Richman (scr), Sonya Levien (st); C: L.W. O'Connell; E: Irene Morra; M: Louis De Francesco; Cast: Nino Martini, Genevieve Tobin, Anita Louise, Maria Gambarelli, Reginald Denny, Vicente Escudero, Ernestine Schumann-Heink, Adrian Rosley, Mathilde Comont • Nino Donelli (Martini) is sponsored by the wife (Tobin) of his philandering music teacher, Emery (Denny), to study singing in Paris. Nino falls in love with Lydia (Louise), a ballerina who is upset that he is being sponsored by Kathleen, so she accepts Emery's offer to go to America. This causes Nino to ruin his debut performance in Paris. Disgraced, Nino ends up in New York, singing at a sheet music counter. Kathleen admits to Lydia that Nino did not know of her machinations. Nino is discovered by the head of the Metropolitan Opera. 86 min.

CHARLIE CHAN IN SHANGHAI (Oct. 11, 1935); P: John Stone; D: James Tinling; E: Edward T. Lowe (st & scr), Gerard Fairlie (st & scr), Earl Der Biggers (character); C: Barney McGill; E: Nick De Maggio; M: Samuel Kaylin; Cast: Warner Oland, Irene Hervey, Charles Locher, Russell Hicks, Keye Luke, Halliwell Hobbes, Frederick Vogeding, Neil Fitzgerald, Max Wagner • As Charlie Chan (Oland) gets to Shanghai, his friend Sir Stanley opens a box and is shot from a gun inside it. Stanley's personal secretary (Locher), a gang leader (Vogeding), and a secret agent from Washington (Hicks) are all suspects. Ducking attempts on his life, Chan, along with help from son Lee (Luke) and Stanley's daughter, Diana (Hervey), figures out that the American killed Stanley because of his co-operation with British authorities to ferret out an opium-smuggling gang. 70 min.

ROSA DE FRANCIA (Oct. 15, 1935) Spanish language; P: John Stone; D: Gordon Wiles; W: José López Rubio (scr), Helen Logan (cont); C: Joseph P. MacDonald; E: Nick De Maggio; M: Samuel Kaylin; Cast: Rosita Diaz, Julio Peña, Antonio Moreno, Consuelo Frank, Don Alvarado, Enrique de Rosas, Maria Calvo, Martin Garralaga, Rubi Gutierrez, Jinx Falkenburg • The irreverent Princess Luisa (Diaz), the Rose of France, marries Luis (Peña), a Spanish prince at a country estate, but his mother Queen Farnesio (Frank), will not allow her son to consummate the marriage until she is certain of Luisa's trustworthiness. A nobleman (de Rosas) feels the marriage needs to be consummated to assure Spain a strong monarchy. He gets the Marquis of Magny (Alvarado) to make overtures to Luisa to arouse Luis's jealousy. Luis, instead of becoming jealous, orders Luisa to leave for Madrid. Luis, who enjoys walking incognito among his people, meets Luisa, disguised as a common woman in the city, and falls in love with her. Luisa is arrested by the king (Moreno), but Luis recognizes her and takes her back to the palace bedroom. 80 min.

THIS IS THE LIFE (Oct. 18, 1935); P: Joseph Engel; D: Marshall Neilan; W: Lamar Trotti (scr), Arthur Horman (scr), Gene Towne (st), Graham Baker (st); C: Daniel B. Clark; E: Fred Allen; M: David Buttolph; Cast: Jane Withers, John McGuire, Sally Blane, Sidney Toler, Gloria Roy, Gordon Westcott, Francis Ford, Emma Dunn • A child performer, Geraldine (Withers), tired of being bound by her career, meets Michael (McGuire), who is running from the police and trying to prove his innocence on an embezzlement charge. Overhearing her aunt Diane (Roy) and uncle Ed (Westcott) planning to swindle her out of money, Geraldine dresses as a boy and escapes with Michael. The two of them encounter many adventures together and meet Helen (Blane), who hides Geraldine on her ranch, while Michael turns himself in. Michael is released when another man confesses to the crime and poses as an investigator to get Diane and Roy to release Geraldine into his and Helen's custody. 65 min.

BAD BOY (Oct. 25, 1935); P: Edward Butcher; D: John Blystone; W: Allen Rivkin (scr), Vina Delmar (st); C: Bert Glennon; E: Margaret Clancey; M: Arthur Lange; Cast: James Dunn, Dorothy Wilson, Louise Fazenda, Victor Kilian, John Wray, Luis Alberni, Beulah Bondi, Allen Vincent • Sally Larkin (Wilson) is keeping her romance with pool hustler Eddie Nolan (Dunn) a secret from her mother. Eddie agrees to get a job when they marry. Unable to find work, and with their marriage a secret, Sally's mother (Bondi) tries to convince her to marry Bob (Vincent). Depressed, Eddie burns their marriage certificate, but before he leaves, he manages to foil a kidnapping and is shot. Sally drives by and sees him lying in the street. She rushes over and tells her mother that they are married. Eddie, now a hero, gets a job selling pool tables. 56 min.

WAY DOWN EAST (Oct. 25, 1935); P: Winfield R. Sheehan; D: Henry King; W: Howard Estabrook (scr), William Hurlbut (scr), Joseph R. Grismer (play); C: Ernest Palmer; E: Robert Bischoff; M: Oscar Bradley; Cast: Rochelle Hudson, Henry Fonda, Slim Summerville, Edward Trevor, Margaret Hamilton, Andy Devine, Russell Simpson, Spring Byington, Astrid Allwyn • Penniless Anna Moore (Hudson) is hired by Squire Bartlett (Simpson), who runs a strict household on his New England farm. Bartlett's son, David (Fonda), who is to marry his cousin Kate (Allwyn), prefers Anna. The town gossip (Hamilton), seeing David and Anna together, spreads rumors about Anna's past. Anna is forced to leave the farm in the midst of a blizzard. David rescues Anna from a slab of ice flowing downriver toward rocks. When David berates his father for self-righteousness, the squire finally accepts Anna for David's wife. 84 min. • Janet Gaynor was originally in the lead but was injured in a car accident just after shooting started and had to be replaced.

TE QUIERO CON LOCURA (Nov. 1, 1935) Spanish language; D: John J. Boland; W: José López Rubio (scr & dial), Paul Perez (scr); C: Joseph P. MacDonald; E: Nick De Maggio; M: Edward Kilenyi; Cast: Rosita Moreno, Raúl Roulien, Enrique de Rosas, Juan Torrena, Carlos Villarías, Romualdo Tirado, Lucio Villegas, Nenette Noriega, Martin Garralaga • Norma (Moreno) has herself committed to an insane asylum to keep from marrying a cousin (Peluffo). Alberto (Roulien) has also committed himself to escape his mistress's husband, Hugo (de Rosas). Norma is cautious of Alberto at first, but they sneak out of the sanitarium for a night at a local cabaret. Hugo spots them and chases Alberto, wrecking the cabaret. In court with Norma's uncle (Villegas), Hugo, and the cabaret owner, a judge orders mental evaluations for Norma and Alberto. The psychologists declare that the couple is in love, but those who are after them are judged insane and are committed. 70 min.

MUSIC IS MAGIC (Nov. 1, 1935); P: John Stone; D: George Marshall; W: Edward Eliscu (scr), Lou Breslow (scr), Gladys Unger & Jesse Lasky Jr. (play); C: L.W. O'Connell; E: Alexander Troffey; M: Samuel Kaylin; Cast: Alice Faye, Ray Walker, Bebe Daniels, Frank Mitchell, Jack Durant, Rosina Lawrence, Thomas Beck, Andrew Tombes, Luis Alberni, Hattie McDaniel • Singer Peggy Harper (Faye) decides to try her luck in Hollywood, with promoter Jack Lambert (Walker). Unemployed in the movie capital, Peggy teams up with her two former knockabout partners, Peanuts (Mitchell) and Eddie (Durant), and they get a contract from producer Ben Pomeroy (Tombes), who is dealing with temperamental star Diane De Valle (Daniels). Jack reappears and gets Peggy a chance to audition. When De Valle decides to go back east for her daughter's benefit, Peggy gets a leading role in a musical. 66 min.

IN OLD KENTUCKY (Nov. 22, 1935); P: Edward Butcher; D: George Marshall; W: Sam Hellman (scr), Gladys Lehman (scr), Henry Johnson (add'l dial), Charles T. Dazey (play); C: L.W. O'Connell; E: Jack Murray; M: Arthur Lange; Cast: Will Rogers, Dorothy Wilson, Russell Hardie, Charles Sellon, Louise Henry, Esther Dale, Alan Dinehart, Charles Richman, Etienne Girardot, John Ince, Bill Robinson • Steve Tapley (Rogers), horse trainer for wealthy Pole Shattuck (Richman), is fired for protecting Ezra (Sellon), the cantankerous head of the Martingale family, who have been feuding with the Shattucks. Steve trains the Martingale horse for free so he can help Nancy (Wilson), Ezra's granddaughter. After complications because of the feud, Steve, with the help of his sidekick, Wash (Robinson), and a zany rainmaker (Girardot), is able to get the track muddy and allow their horse to beat the Shattuck's entry. 85 min. • This was Will Rogers's last feature.

NAVY WIFE (Nov. 29, 1935); P: Sol M. Wurtzel; D: Allan Dwan; W: Sonya Levien (scr), Edward T. Lowe (add'l dial), Kathleen Norris (novel); C: John Seitz, Rudolph Maté; E: Al De Gaetano; M: David Buttolph; Cast: Claire Trevor, Ralph Bellamy, Jane Darwell, Warren Hymer, Ben Lyon, Kathleen Burke, George Irving, Ann Howard • A widowed Navy doctor, Quentin Hardin (Bellamy), falls for Nurse Vicky Blake (Trevor) at a San Diego hospital. Vicky and Quentin meet again when both are stationed in Honolulu, and she accepts his marriage proposal. When Vicky takes Quentin's daughter (Howard) to Los Angeles for medical treatment, Quentin becomes familiar with Serena (Burke), which causes problems when his wife returns. Although there are rumors about Quentin and Serena, the latter turns out to be a spy and shoots Quentin. Vicky discovers that Quentin has broken up a spy ring. 72 min. • Lillian Wurtzel, Sol Wurtzel's daughter was listed as contributing to screenplay construction, but was not credited.

Chapter Notes

Chapter 1

1. Glendon Allvine, *The Greatest Fox of Them All* (New York: Lyle Stuart, 1969), p. 9.
2. Upton Sinclair, *Upton Sinclair Presents William Fox* (Los Angeles: published by the author, 1933), p. 25.
3. Ibid., p. 47.
4. Ibid., p. 18.
5. *The Film Yearbook 1926* (New York: Film Daily Publishers), p. 43.
6. Sinclair, p. 35.
7. *The Story of the Films*, ed. Joseph P. Kennedy (Chicago: A.W. Shaw, 1927), pp. 301–302.
8. Sinclair, p. 38.
9. *Motion Picture Studio Directory and Trade Annual, 1920* (New York: Motion Picture News), pp. 342–343.
10. Sinclair, p. 46.
11. *Variety Film Reviews 1907–1920* (New York: Garland, 1983), Nov. 21, 1914.
12. *The Story of the Films*, pp. 302–303.
13. *Variety Film Reviews 1907–1920*, Feb. 12, 1915.
14. Sinclair, p. 5.
15. Ibid., p. 48.
16. *1930 Motion Picture News Blue Book* (New York: Motion Picture News), p. 240.
17. *Fortune Magazine* (New York: Time, Inc., May 1930), p. 49.

Chapter 2

1. Allvine, pp. 21–22.
2. Richard Koszarski, *An Evening's Entertainment: The Age of the Silent Feature Picture, 1915–1928* (New York: Scribner's, 1990), p. 83.
3. Sinclair, p. 57.
4. *Exhibitors Trade Review* (New York: Exhibitors Trade Review, Inc., June 16, 1923), p. 112.
5. *Film Daily* (New York: Wid's Films and Film Folks, June 15, 1924), pp. 1, 4.
6. *New York Times Film Reviews, 1913–1931* (New York: New York Times and Arno Press, 1970), p. 22.
7. *New York Clipper* (New York: April 25, 1917), p. 33.
8. Lillian Wurtzel Semenov and Carla Winter, *William Fox, Sol M. Wurtzel and the Early Fox Film Corporation, Letters 1913–1923* (Jefferson, NC: McFarland, 2001), p. 23.
9. *Variety Film Reviews*, Aug. 3, 1917.
10. *New York Times Film Reviews 1913–1931*, p. 30.
11. *Variety Film Reviews 1907–1920*, Feb. 16, 1917.
12. Ibid., Nov. 16, 1917.
13. Semenov, p. 49.
14. Ibid., p. 50.
15. Ibid., p. 109.
16. Ibid., p. 110.
17. Ibid., p. 50.
18. Robert S. Birchard, *King Cowboy: Tom Mix and the Movies* (Burbank: Riverwood Press, 1993), p. 20.
19. Ibid., p. 46.
20. Ibid., p. 50.
21. Ibid.
22. Ibid., p. 34.
23. Ibid., p. 36.
24. Ibid., p. 39.
25. Ibid., p. 47.
26. Ibid.
27. Ibid., p. 53.
28. Ibid., p. 68.
29. Ibid., p. 81.
30. Koszarski, p. 10.

Chapter 3

1. Howard T. Lewis, *The Motion Picture Industry* (New York: D. Van Norstrand, 1933), p. 17.
2. *Eighty-Second Variety Annual* (New York, Jan. 20, 1988), pp. 93–95.
3. *Moving Picture World* (New York: Chalmers, June 7, 1919), 1471–1472.
4. Semenov, p. 73.
5. Ibid., p. 93.
6. Ibid., p. 97.
7. *New York Times Film Reviews, 1913–1931*, p. 60.
8. *Variety Film Reviews 1907–1920*, Feb. 7, 1919.
9. Semenov, p. 97.
10. Ibid., p. 68.
11. Ibid., p. 74.
12. Ibid., p. 73.
13. Ibid., p. 87.
14. Ibid., pp. 72–73.
15. *Motion Picture Studio Directory and Trade Annual 1920*, pp. 354–355.
16. Semenov, p. 80.
17. Ibid., p. 87.
18. *Variety Film Reviews 1907–1920*, Jan. 31, 1919.
19. Ibid., June 6, 1919.
20. Ibid., Oct. 11, 1918.
21. Ibid., March 26, 1920.
22. Ibid., May 28, 1920.
23. Semenov, p. 118.
24. *Variety Film Reviews 1907–1920*, Feb. 13, 1920.
25. Ibid., March 19, 1920.
26. Semenov, p. 129.
27. Ibid., p. 93.
28. Ibid., p. 118.
29. Ibid., p. 119.
30. Ibid., p. 118.
31. *Variety Film reviews 1907–1920*, June 11, 1920.
32. Ibid., April 30, 1920.
33. Semenov, pp. 120–121.
34. Daniel Blum, *A Pictorial History of the Silent Screen* (New York: Grosset & Dunlap, 1953), p. 201.
35. Ibid., p. 205.
36. *Variety Film Reviews, 1907–1920*, July 2, 1920.
37. *Wid's Daily*, Jan. 9, 1921, p. 14.
38. Semenov, p. 123.
39. Ibid., pp. 131–132.
40. *Wid's Daily*, March 15, 1921, p. 4.

Chapter 4

1. *The Film Yearbook 1926*, p. 43.
2. *Wid's Daily*, Jan. 19, 1921, p. 3.
3. Lewis, p. 18.
4. *The Story of the Films*, p. 71.
5. *Wid's Daily*, Jan. 21, 1921, pp. 1, 6.
6. Ibid., Feb. 17, 1921, p. 2.

7. *The Story of the Films*, p. 245.
8. Semenov, pp. 135–136.
9. Ibid., p. 140.
10. Sinclair, p. 59.
11. Ibid., p. 60.
12. *Variety Film Reviews 1907–1920*, Sept. 24, 1920.
13. *New York Times Film Reviews 1913–1931*, p. 79.
14. *Wid's Daily*, March 16, 1921, p. 4.
15. *Wid's Yearbook 1920–21* (New York: Wid's Films and Film Folks), p. 285.
16. *Wid's Daily*, Jan. 16, 1921, p. 23.
17. *Variety Film Reviews 1921–1925* (New York: Garland, 1983), May 26, 1922.
18. *York Times Film Reviews 1913–1931*, p. 121.
19. *Variety Film Reviews 1921–1925*, May 26, 1922.
20. *Wid's Daily*, April 24, 1921, p. 82.
21. *Variety Film Reviews 1921–1925*, Nov. 10, 1922.
22. Ibid., Aug. 18, 1922.
23. *New York Times Film Reviews 1913–1931*, p. 127.
24. Ibid., May 21, 1924.
25. Richard Koszarski, *An Evening's Entertainment: The Age of the Silent Feature Picture, 1915–1928* (New York: Scribner's, 1990), p. 116.
26. *The Story of the Films*, pp. 103–104.
27. Blum, p. 243.
28. Dan Ford, *Pappy: The Life of John Ford* (Englewood Cliffs, NJ: Prentice Hall, 1979), pp. 30–31.
29. *Variety Film Reviews 1921–1925*, Sept. 3, 1924.
30. *New York Times Film Reviews 1913–1931*, p. 209.
31. *Film Daily*, Oct. 11, 1925, p. 5.
32. Ibid., May 16, 1924, pp. 1, 7.
33. Ibid.
34. Ibid., June 8, 1924, p. 7.
35. Ibid., June 20, 1924, pp. 1, 7.
36. Ibid., March 24, 1925, p. 1.
37. Ibid., May 27, 1924, p. 7.
38. *The Film Year Book 1925* (New York: Film Daily), p. 554.
39. Ibid., p. 3.

Chapter 5

1. *Film Daily*, March 4, 1925, p. 1.
2. Ibid., June 14, 1925, p. 1.
3. Ibid., Sept. 8, 1925, p. 1.
4. *The Film Year Book 1925*, pp. III, VIII.
5. *Film Daily*, March 27, 1925.
6. Ibid., May 10, 1925, p. 10.
7. Ibid., June 16, 1925, pp. 1, 3.
8. Ibid., June 21, 1925, p. 1.
9. Ibid., Jan. 12, 1926, p. 1.
10. Ibid., Sept. 18, 1925, p. 3.
11. *The Film Yearbook 1926*, p. 17.
12. *Variety Film Reviews 1921–1925*, April 15, 1925.
13. *Film Daily*, May 10, 1925, p. 5.
14. *New York Times Film Reviews 1913–1931*, p. 246.
15. *Film Daily*, June 7, 1925, p. 19.
16. Ibid., Feb. 10, 1926, pp. 1, 11.
17. Ibid., Aug. 24, 1925, p. 1.
18. Ibid., June 14, 1925, pp. 6–7.
19. Ibid., June 21, 1925, p. 38.
20. *The Story of the Films*, p. 156.
21. *Film Daily*, July 7, 1925, p. 1.
22. *The Film Yearbook 1926*, p. 31.
23. Ibid., p. 457.
24. Ibid., p. 426.
25. *Film Daily*, Feb. 8, 1926, p. 1.
26. Semenov, p. 59.
27. Ibid., p. 61.
28. *Film Daily*, Oct. 7, 1925, p. 1.
29. *The Film Yearbook 1925*, p. 719.
30. *The Film Yearbook 1926*, p. 293.
31. *Film Daily*, Nov. 12, 1925, p. 11.
32. Ibid., Nov. 6, 1925, pp. 1, 6.
33. Ibid., Nov. 8, 1925, p. 1.
34. *The Story of the Films*, p. 32.
35. Ibid., p. 207.
36. Ibid., p. 218.
37. *Film Daily*, June 14, 1925, p. 3.
38. Ibid., March 24, 1926, p. 1.
39. Ibid., March 29, 1926, pp. 1, 4.
40. Ibid., May 14, 1926, p. 5.
41. Ibid., May 27, 1926, p. 1.
42. Janet Bergstrom, *William Fox Presents F. W. Murnau and Frank Borzage* (Twentieth Century–Fox Home Entertainment, 2008), p. 10.
43. *Film Daily*, Sept. 25, 1927, p. 1.
44. Ibid., July 16, 1926, pp. 9–10.
45. Ibid., June 2, 1926, p. 8.
46. *Historic Property Survey Report for Twentieth Century–Fox* (Los Angeles: Historic Resources Group, Oct. 12, 1990), p. 14.
47. *Exhibitors Trade Review*, p. 112.
48. *Film Daily*, Sept. 22, 1926, p. 10.
49. Ibid., July 9, 1926, p. 1.

Chapter 6

1. *Film Daily*, Aug. 1, 1926, p. 4.
2. Ibid., Oct. 24, 1926, p. 5.
3. Ibid., Feb. 6, 1927, p. 4.
4. Ibid., Nov, 1, 1925, p. 4.
5. Ibid., Oct. 7, 1926, pp. 8–9.
6. Ibid., Oct. 17, 1926, p. 4.
7. Ibid., June 18, 1929, p. 6.
8. Ibid., July 1, 1926, p. 1.
9. *Variety Film Reviews 1926–1929*, July 7, 1926.
10. Ibid., July 21, 1926.
11. Ibid., Aug. 25, 1926.
12. Ibid., Oct. 24, 1926.
13. Ibid., Nov. 10, 1926.
14. *Film Daily*, Oct. 14, 1926, p. 1.
15. Ibid., Oct. 21, 1926, p. 9.
16. Ibid., Sept. 27, 1926, pp. 4, 6.
17. Ibid., Sept. 26, 1926, p. 13.
18. Ibid., Nov. 26, 1926, p. 6.
19. Ibid., p. 1.
20. Ibid., June 21, 1927, pp. 1, 8.
21. Ibid., Aug. 16, 1927, p. 2.
22. Ibid., Aug. 2, 1927, p. 5.
23. Ibid., June 2, 1927, pp. 1, 6.
24. Ibid., Jan. 3, 1927, p. 1.
25. Ibid., p. 6.
26. Ibid.
27. Ibid., Feb. 3, 1927, p. 1.
28. Ibid., March 2, 1927, p. 1.
29. Ibid. March 20, 1927, p. 3.
30. Ibid., June 18, 1929, p. 6.
31. Ibid., March 27, 1927, p. 4.
32. Ibid., March 28, 1927, p. 1.
33. Sinclair, p. 314.
34. *Film Daily*, Aug. 22, 1927, p. 1.
35. Ibid., Sept. 30, 1927, p. 5.
36. Ibid., April 19, 1927, p. 1.
37. Ibid., May 13, 1927, pp. 1, 6.
38. Ibid., June 16, 1927, p. 3.
39. Ibid., May 29, 1927, p. 1.
40. Ibid., May 4, 1927, p. 1.
41. Ibid., Dec. 20, 1927, p. 4.
42. Ibid., April 11, 1927, p. 1.
43. Ibid., March 16, 1927, p. 6.
44. Ibid., Aug. 18, 1927, p. 9.
45. Ibid., Oct. 5, 1927, p. 1.

Chapter 7

1. *Film Daily*, Jan. 3, 1926, p. 1.
2. Sinclair, p. 62.
3. *The Story of the Films*, p. 326.
4. *Film Daily*, Nov. 30, 1925, p. 4.
5. Sinclair, p. 63.
6. *Film Daily*, Aug, 8, 1926, p. 3.
7. Ibid., Sept. 27, 1927, p. 4.
8. Ibid., July 30, 1926, p. 3.
9. Ibid., Aug. 8, 1926, p. 1.
10. Ibid., Aug. 8, 1926, p. 3.
11. Ibid., May 9, 1926, p. 1.
12. Sinclair, pp. 62–63.
13. *The Film Yearbook 1926*, p. 427.
14. Sinclair, p. 64.
15. *Film Daily*, Sept. 20, 1926, pp. 1, 7.
16. Ibid., May 22, 1929, p. 8.
17. Ibid., Nov. 7, 1930, pp. 1–2.
18. Ibid., Feb. 13, 1927, p. 1.
19. Ibid., Feb. 23, 1927, p. 5.
20. Ibid., Feb. 25, 1927, p. 1.
21. Ibid., p. 7.
22. Ibid., pp. 7–8.
23. Ibid., May 29, 1927, p. 5.
24. Ibid., March 4, 1927, pp. 1–2.
25. Ibid., Aug. 12, 1928, p. 9.
26. Sinclair, p. 64.
27. *Film Daily*, April 25, 1927, pp. 1–2.
28. Ibid., May 6, 1927, pp. 4–5.
29. Ibid., June 16, 1927, pp. 1, 5.
30. Ibid., Aug. 7, 1927, p. 16.
31. Ibid., Sept. 1, 1929, p. 9.
32. *New York Times Film Reviews, 1913–1931*, p. 455.
33. *Exhibitors Daily Review* (New York: Picture Publishers, Nov. 2, 1928), p. 4.
34. *Film Daily*, Oct. 27, 1927, pp. 1–2.
35. Ibid., Sept. 25, 1927, p. 1.
36. Ibid., Nov. 27, 1927, p. 12.
37. Ibid., July 26, 1927, p. 10.

38. *Exhibitors Daily Review*, Dec. 20, 1928, p. 1.
39. *Film Daily*, Jan. 10, 1929, p. 1.
40. Ibid., June 24, 1930, p. 1.
41. *Variety Film Reviews 1926–1929*, Oct. 12, 1927.
42. *Film Daily*, Nov. 7, 1927, pp. 1–2.
43. Ibid., Jan. 9, 1928, p. 5.
44. Ibid., March 18, 1928, p. 3.
45. *Variety Film Reviews 1926–1929*, March 21, 1928.
46. *Historic Property Survey for Twentieth Century–Fox*, p. 20.
47. *Film Daily*, Sept. 30, 1928, p. 4.
48. Ibid., June 18, 1929, p. 76.
49. Ibid., Sept. 30, 1928, p. 4.
50. Ibid., May 27, 1930, p. 71.
51. *Exhibitors Daily Review*, Oct. 29, 1928, p. 3.
52. *Film Daily*, May 27, 1930, p. 72.
53. *Variety Film Reviews 1926–1929*, July 11, 1928.
54. *Film Daily*, July 22, 1929, p. 2.
55. Ibid., Aug. 22, 1928, p. 4.
56. *Variety Film Reviews 1926–1929*, July 11, 1928.
57. *Film Daily*, Feb. 21, 1928, p. 12.
58. Ibid., May 21, 1928, p. 3.
59. Ibid., Aug. 7, 1928, p. 1.
60. Ibid., June 5, 1928, p. 12.
61. Ibid., Aug. 8, 1929, p. 10.
62. Ibid., May 27, 1928, p. 4.
63. Ibid., July 25, 1929, pp. 1, 5.
64. Ibid., Sept. 16, 1928, p. 6.
65. Ibid., June 18, 1929, p. 76.
66. Ibid., July 29, 1928, p. 7.
67. *Variety Film Reviews 1926–1929*, Jan. 23, 1929.
68. *New York Times Film Reviews 1913–1931*, p. 499.
69. *Film Daily*, May 27, 1930, p. 72.
70. Ibid., June 18, 1929, p. 76.
71. *Variety Film Reviews 1926–1929*, May 29, 1929.
72. *Film Daily*, July 26, 1928, p. 1.
73. Ibid., Sept. 9, 1928, p. 7.
74. Ibid., Jan. 17, 1929, p. 9.
75. Ibid., March 25, 1929, p. 1.

Chapter 8

1. *Film Daily*, Dec. 6, 1927, p. 3.
2. Ibid., Feb. 17, 1928, p. 4.
3. *Variety Film Reviews 1926–1929*, May 11, 1927.
4. *New York Times Film Reviews 1913–1931*, p. 367.
5. *Variety Film Reviews 1926–1929*, Sept. 28, 1927.
6. *New York Times Film Reviews Appendix Index* (New York: New York Times and Arno Press, 1970), p. 3835.
7. *Film Daily*, Sept. 25, 1927, p. 4.
8. Ibid., Dec. 11, 1927, p. 10.
9. Ibid., Jan. 24, 1928, p. 6.
10. *Time*, Jan. 13, 1930, time.com, article/0.9171.789097.00.
11. *Film Daily*, Oct. 20, 1927, p. 3.
12. Ibid., Jan. 10, 1928, p. 3.
13. Ibid., Jan. 27, 1928, p. 10.
14. Ibid., June 11, 1928, p. 1.
15. Ibid., Jan. 29, 1928, pp. 1, 3.
16. Ibid., May 31, 1928, pp. 1–2.
17. Ibid., April 4, 1928, p. 1.
18. Ibid., March 12, 1927, p. 4.
19. *Exhibitors Daily Review*, Sept. 4, 1928, pp. 1, 4.
20. *Film Daily*, April 24, 1928, pp. 1, 3.
21. Ibid., Jan. 10, 1929, p. 1.
22. Ibid., Jan. 11, 1928, p. 4.
23. Ibid., Nov. 18, 1927, p. 8.
24. Ibid., Nov. 21, 1927, p. 8.
25. Ibid., Nov. 27, 1927, p. 4.
26. *Exhibitors Daily Review*, Sept. 13, 1928, p. 5.
27. *Film Daily*, May 24, 1928, p. 3.
28. *Variety Film Reviews 1926–1929*, Feb. 15, 1928.
29. *New York Times Film Reviews 1913–1931*, p. 424.
30. *Variety Film Reviews 1926–1929*, April 11, 1929.
31. *New York Times Film Reviews 1913–1931*, p. 437.
32. *Variety Film Reviews 1926–1929*, May 23, 1929.
33. *New York Times Film Reviews 1913–1931*, p. 446.
34. Ibid., p. 472.
35. *Variety Film Reviews 1926–1929*, Oct. 10, 1929.
36. *Motion Picture Times* (Dallas: Associated Publications), Jan. 19, 1929.

Chapter 9

1. *Film Daily*, May 9, 1930, p. 1.
2. Sinclair, pp. 78–79.
3. Ibid., p. 65.
4. Ibid.
5. *Film Daily*, Sept. 18, 1929, p. 8.
6. Ibid., Feb. 6, 1930, p. 1.
7. *Exhibitors Daily Review*, Nov. 26, 1928, p. 1.
8. *Film Daily*, Feb. 28, 1929, p. 1.
9. Ibid., March 1, 1928, p. 11.
10. Ibid., March 1, 1929, pp. 1–2.
11. Ibid., April 18, 1929, p. 1.
12. Ibid., March 10, 1929, p. 1.
13. Sinclair, p. 82.
14. *Film Daily*, Dec. 10, 1928, p. 1.
15. Ibid., Feb. 28, 1929, p. 30.
16. Ibid., Sept. 13, 1929.
17. *Motion Picture Daily* (New York: Quigley Publications), Nov. 24, 1933, p. 7.
18. *Film Daily*, March 19, 1929, p. 9.
19. Ibid., Sept. 9, 1929, p. 1.
20. Ibid., Oct. 22, 1929, p. 1.
21. Ibid., Dec. 31, 1929, p. 3.
22. *Exhibitors Daily Review*, Oct. 10, 1928, p. 1.
23. *Film Daily*, July 18, 1929, 6. [Reported as "J. Carol Nase, an actor of New York."]
24. Ibid., July 21, 1929, p. 3.
25. Ibid., Oct. 11, 1929, p. 1.
26. Ibid., Oct. 14, 1929, p. 7.
27. Ibid., Jan. 3, 1930, p. 1.
28. Allvine, Glendon, pp. 129–130.
29. *Time*, Dec. 4, 1933, time.com/article/0,9171,746432,00.
30. *Film Daily*, Jan. 13, 1930, p. 1.
31. Ibid., Jan. 19, 1930, p. 11.
32. Ibid., Jan. 21, 1930, p. 1.
33. Ibid., Jan. 28, 1930, p. 1.
34. Ibid., Feb. 4, 1930, p. 1.
35. Ibid., Feb. 10, 1930, p. 12.
36. Ibid., Feb. 20, 1930, p. 7.
37. Ibid., Feb. 21, 1930, p. 7.
38. Ibid., March 6, 1930, p. 1.
39. Ibid.
40. Ibid. March 25, 1930, p. 11.
41. Ibid. March 31, 1930, p. 1.
42. Ibid., April 8, 1930, p. 1.
43. *Motion Picture Daily*, Nov. 22, 1933, p. 8.
44. *Time*, Dec. 4, 1933, time.com/article/0,9171,746432,00.
45. *Film Daily*, April 9, 1930, p. 1.
46. Ibid., June 17, 1931, pp. 1, 12.
47. Ibid., Oct. 22, 1931, p. 1.
48. *Time*, July 11, 1932, time.com/article/0,9171,743997-2,00.
49. Ibid., Oct. 24, 1934, www.time.com/article 0,9171,882284,00.
50. *Film Daily*, March 6, 1935, p. 1.
51. *Time*, Sept. 7, 1936, time.com/article/0,9171,847834,00.
52. *Brooklyn Eagle* (Brooklyn, New York), Oct. 21, 1941, p. 3.

Chapter 10

1. *Variety*, Aug. 13, 1930, p. 5.
2. *Film Daily*, Nov. 10, 1930, p. 1.
3. Ibid., July 18, 1930, p. 1.
4. Ibid., July 24, 1930, p. 1.
5. *Variety*, Aug. 27, 1930, p. 2.
6. *Film Daily*, Aug. 4, 1930, p. 2.
7. Ibid., Sept. 16, 1930, p. 10.
8. Ibid., April 18, 1930, p. 3.
9. *Time*, April 28, 1930, time.com, article 0,9171,752468,00.
10. *Film Daily*, June 16, 1930, pp. 1, 41.
11. Ibid., July 29, 1930, p. 1.
12. Ibid., March 6, 1931, p. 12.
13. Ibid., Sept. 5, 1930, p. 1.
14. Ibid., May 7, 1930, p. 1.
15. Ibid., May 8, 1930, p. 6.
16. Ibid., April 21, 1930, p. 1.
17. Ibid., May 27, 1930, p. 74.
18. Ibid., Sept. 23, 1930, p. 8.
19. Ibid., Feb. 9, 1931, p. 1.
20. Ibid., Jan. 28, 1931, p. 1.
21. Ibid., May 12, 1930, p. 1.
22. Ibid., July 6, 1930, p. 1.
23. Ibid., Sept. 3, 1930, p. 11.
24. Ibid., Sept. 4, 1930, p. 1.
25. Ibid., July 1, 1930, p. 1.
26. *Harrison's Reports* (New York: P.S. Harrison Publisher), April 25, 1934, p. 68A.
27. Ibid., Jan. 24, 1931, p. 13.
28. *Film Daily*, May 27, 1930, p. 74.

29. Ibid., June 25, 1930, p. 8.
30. Ibid., Aug. 18, 1930, p. 8.
31. Ibid., May 27, 1930, p. 74.
32. Ibid., Jan. 14, 1931, p. 1.
33. Ibid., July 31, 1930, pp. 1, 2.
34. Ibid., Jan. 6, 1931, p. 6.
35. Ibid., May 21, 1930, p. 9.
36. *New York Times Film Reviews, 1913–1931*, p. 602.
37. *Film Daily*, July 8, 1930, p. 1.
38. Ibid., Sept. 24, 1930, p. 5.
39. Ibid., Aug. 25, 1930, p. 5.
40. Ibid., Jan. 13, 1931, p. 1.
41. Ibid., Nov. 12, 1930, p. 1.
42. *Hollywood Reporter* (Hollywood: The Wilkerson Daily Corp.), March 9, 1934, p. 1.
43. *Film Daily*, April 14, 1931, p. 2.
44. Ibid., Jan. 18, 1931, p. 2.
45. Ibid., Dec. 31, 1930, p. 4.
46. Ibid., Jan. 29, 1931, pp. 1, 6.
47. Ibid., April 2, 1930, p. 8.
48. Ibid., April 8, 1931, p. 1.
49. Ibid., April 9, 1931, p. 8.
50. Ibid., May 1, 1931, pp. 1, 11.
51. Ibid., May 17, 1931, p. 12.
52. Ibid., April 16, 1931, pp. 1, 11.
53. Ibid., Aug. 6, 1931, p. 1.
54. Ibid., Aug. 6, 1931, p. 1.
55. Ibid., April 26, 1931, pp. 1, 9.
56. Ibid., May 1, 1930, p. 8.
57. Sinclair, p. 328.
58. *Motion Picture Daily*, Nov. 11, 1933, p. 1.
59. Ibid., Nov. 24, 1933, p. 1.
60. Ibid., June 22, 1931, p. 1.
61. Ibid., June 9, 1931, pp. 1, 4.
62. Ibid., July 1, 1931, p. 12.
63. Ibid., July 3, 1931, p. 2.
64. Ibid., July 9, 1931, pp. 1–2.
65. Ibid., Oct. 3, 1931, p. 1.
66. Ibid., Nov. 28, 1933, p. 3.
67. *Film Daily*, July 16, 1931, p. 13.
68. Ibid., Aug. 11, 1931, p. 1.
69. *Daily Variety* (Hollywood: Daily Variety Ltd.), Sept. 29, 1931, p. 4.
70. Ibid., Nov. 3, 1931, p. 2.
71. *Film Daily*, Aug. 7, 1931, p. 4.
72. Ibid., Oct. 22, 1931, p. 1.
73. Ibid., Nov. 17, 1931, p. 8.
74. Ibid., Nov. 19, 1931, p. 8.

Chapter 11

1. *Variety*, Dec. 29, 1931, p. 169.
2. *Film Daily*, Jan. 11, 1932, p. 1.
3. Ibid., March 22, 1932, p. 1.
4. Ibid., April 27, 1932, p. 1.
5. Ibid., Jan. 3, 1932, p. 3.
6. Ibid., Jan. 12, 1932, p. 1.
7. Ibid., Jan. 13, 1932, pp. 1, 5.
8. Ibid., Nov. 25, 1931, p. 1.
9. Ibid., Jan. 4, 1931, pp. 1, 8.
10. *Daily Variety*, Dec. 8, 1931, p. 5.
11. *Film Daily*, Jan. 11, 1932, pp. 1, 7.
12. Ibid., Jan. 11, 1932, pp. 1, 7.
13. *Daily Variety*, Jan. 12, 1932, p. 3.
14. Ibid.
15. *Film Daily*, March 2, 1932, p. 1.
16. Ibid., April 18, 1932, p. 1.
17. Ibid., Jan. 26, 1932, p. 1.
18. Ibid., Jan. 20, 1932, p. 1.
19. Ibid., Feb. 1, 1932, p. 2.
20. Ibid., Jan. 27, 1932, p. 6.
21. Ibid., Feb. 7, 1932, p. 1.
22. Ibid., April 14, 1932, p. 2.
23. *Hollywood Herald* (Hollywood: Quigley Publishing), Jan. 22, 1932, p. 1.
24. *Film Daily*, Jan. 17, 1932, p. 1.
25. Ibid., Jan. 12, 1932, p. 8.
26. Ibid., Feb. 17, 1932, p. 1.
27. Ibid., Feb. 25, 1932, pp. 1, 4.
28. Ibid., Jan. 20, 1932, pp. 4–5.
29. *New York Clipper* (New York), April 25, 1917, p. 33.
30. *Film Daily*, March 23, 1932, p. 3.
31. Ibid., April 20, 1932, p. 7.
32. Ibid., June 22, 1933, p. 1.
33. Ibid., April 1, 1932, pp. 1, 8.
34. Ibid., Feb. 14, 1932, p. 10.
35. *New York Times Film Reviews, 1932–1938*, p. 804.
36. *Film Daily*, April 3, 1932, p. 10.
37. *New York Times Film Reviews, 1932–1938*, p. 805.
38. *Film Daily*, April 17, 1932, p. 10.
39. Ibid., May 1, 1932, p. 10.
40. Ibid., May 29, 1932, p. 10.
41. *New York Times Film Reviews, 1932–1938*, p. 808.
42. Ibid., p. 915.
43. *Hollywood Reporter*, Jan. 3, 1934, pp. 1, 4.
44. *Film Daily*, April 19, 1932, p. 1.
45. Ibid., May 17, 1932, p. 63.
46. Ibid., May 18, 1932, pp. 1, 5.
47. Ibid., May 19, 1932, pp. 1–2.
48. *Motion Picture Daily*, May 17, 1932, p. 7.
49. *Film Daily*, May 27, 1932, pp. 14–15.
50. Ibid., April 14, 1933, p. 11.
51. Ibid., June 22, 1932, p. 1.
52. Ibid., April 3, 1932, p. 1.
53. Ibid., Feb. 9, 1932, p. 1.
54. Ibid., May 31, 1932, pp. 1, 3.
55. Ibid., Nov. 15, 1932, p. 1.
56. Ibid., Nov. 14, 1932, p. 1.
57. Ibid., Sept. 16, 1932, p. 1.
58. Ibid., Nov. 14, 1932, p. 2.
59. Ibid., Aug. 5, 1932, p. 1.
60. Ibid., Aug. 10, 1932, p. 7.
61. Ibid., June 16, 1932, p. 1.
62. Ibid., Aug. 31, 1932, p. 1.
63. Ibid., Oct. 23, 1932, p. 1.
64. *Variety*, Oct. 25, 1932, p. 5.
65. *Film Daily*, Oct. 7, 1932, p. 1.
66. *Motion Picture Daily*, Oct. 28, 1933, p. 3.
67. *Film Daily*, Aug. 18, 1932, p. 1.
68. Ibid., Dec. 2, 1932, p. 3.
69. *Hollywood Reporter*, Jan. 10, 1933, p. 4.
70. Ibid., Jan. 12, 1933, pp. 1–2.
71. *Film Daily*, Oct. 13, 1932, p. 6.
72. Ibid., June 20, 1932, p. 1.
73. Ibid., Jan. 12, 1933, p. 4.

Chapter 12

1. *Hollywood Reporter*, Jan. 3, 1933, p. 3.
2. *Film Daily*, Jan. 11, 1933, p. 13.
3. Ibid., Feb. 1, 1933, p. 8.
4. *Hollywood Reporter*, Jan. 14, 1933, p. 1.
5. *New York Times Film Reviews, 1933–1938*, p. 903.
6. *Film Daily*, Feb. 2, 1933, p. 8.
7. *Hollywood Reporter*, Jan. 12, 1933, p. 3.
8. Ibid., Feb. 19, 1933, pp. 1, 4.
9. Ibid., April 4, 1933, p. 2.
10. Ibid., Feb. 10, 1933, p. 1.
11. *Film Daily*, Feb. 23, 1933, p. 4.
12. *Hollywood Reporter*, Feb. 28, 1933, p. 1.
13. Ibid., March 13, 1933, p. 3.
14. Ibid., April 12, 1933, p. 6.
15. Ibid., April 14, 1933, p. 1.
16. Ibid., April 28, 1933, p. 3.
17. Ibid., May 10, 1933, p. 1.
18. Ibid., May 6, 1933, p. 2.
19. *Film Daily*, April 5, 1933, p. 2.
20. *Hollywood Reporter*, May 8, 1933, p. 3.
21. Ibid., April 18, 1934, p. 7.
22. Ibid., June 5, 1933, p. 1.
23. Ibid., June 13, 1933, p. 3.
24. Ibid., June 16, 1933, p. 6.
25. Ibid., May 19, 1933, p. 4.
26. Ibid., June 5, 1933, p. 8.
27. *Daily Variety*, Nov. 20, 1934, p. 6.
28. *Film Daily*, March 4, 1933, p. 1.
29. Ibid., p. 6.
30. Ibid., Feb. 14, 1933, p. 4.
31. Ibid., Feb. 16, 1933, p. 8.
32. *Harrison's Reports*, April 8, 1933, p. 56.
33. *Motion Picture Herald* (New York: Quigley Publishing), Feb. 18, 1933, p. 11.
34. *Hollywood Reporter*, May 12, 1933, p. 2.
35. *Film Daily*, May 29, 1933, p. 1.
36. *Hollywood Reporter*, June 1, 1933, p. 2.
37. Ibid., June 23, 1933, p. 3.
38. Ibid., May 2, 1933, p. 2.
39. *Film Daily*, May 12, 1933, p. 7.
40. *Hollywood Reporter*, June 17, 1933, p. 1.
41. Ibid., May 31, 1933, p. 4.
42. *New York Times Film Reviews, 1932–1938*, p. 970.
43. *Hollywood Reporter*, June 20, 1933, p. 3.
44. Ibid., June 29, 1933, p. 9.
45. *Motion Picture Daily*, Oct. 28, 1933, p. 3.
46. *Hollywood Reporter*, May 26, 1933, p. 1.
47. *Film Daily*, March 29, 1933, p. 4.

48. *Hollywood Reporter*, June 15, 1934, p. 1.
49. *Motion Picture Daily*, Oct. 3, 1933, p. 7.
50. Ibid., Dec. 1, 1933, pp. 24–25.
51. Ibid., Oct. 25, 1933, p. 1.
52. Ibid., Nov. 3, 1933, p. 1.
53. Ibid., Nov. 8, 1933, p. 1.
54. Ibid., Oct. 26, 1933, p. 1.
55. Ibid., Dec. 12, 1933, p. 1.

Chapter 13

1. Henry Wales, Studio Staff Writer, *Fox Film Corporation Studio Press Release* (Los Angeles), December 1933, pp. 1–4.

Chapter 14

1. *Hollywood Reporter*, June 19, 1934, p. 1.
2. *Motion Picture Daily*, Oct. 13, 1933, p. 6.
3. Ibid., Oct. 12, 1933, pp. 4–5.
4. *Daily Variety*, July 25, 1934, p. 1.
5. *Motion Picture Daily*, Dec. 12, 1933, p. 1.
6. Ibid., Dec. 22, 1933, p. 1.
7. Ibid., Dec. 21, 1933, p. 8.
8. Ibid., Dec. 22, 1933, p. 6.
9. *Hollywood Reporter*, Jan. 3, 1934, pp. 1, 4.
10. Ibid., Jan. 13, 1934, p. 1.
11. *Film Facts: Exhibitor Choices in Motion Pictures*, New York: Motion Picture Producers and Distributors Association of America, 1938, Exhibit B
12. *Hollywood Reporter*, Jan. 22, 1934, p. 7.
13. Ibid., Jan. 15, 1934, p. 3.
14. Ibid., March 31, 1934, p. 2.
15. Ibid., Feb. 9, 1934, p. 3.
16. Ibid., Feb. 22, 1934, p. 2.
17. Ibid., March 10, 1934, p. 2.
18. Ibid., June 15, 1934, p. 2.
19. Ibid., April 10, 1934, p. 3.
20. Ibid., May 12, 1934, p. 12.
21. Ibid., June 14, 1934, p. 3.
22. Ibid., March 16, 1934, p. 3.
23. Ibid., March 3, 1934, p. 1.
24. Ibid., Feb. 28, 1934, p. 3.
25. Ibid., March 19, 1934, p. 3.
26. Ibid., April 24, 1934, p. 2.
27. Ibid., April 28, 1934, p. 3.
28. Ibid., Feb. 19, 1934, p. 2.
29. Ibid., Jan. 16, 1934, p. 1.
30. Ibid., Feb. 13, 1934, p. 3.
31. Ibid., June 13, 1934, p. 1.
32. Ibid., Feb. 23, 1934, p. 2.
33. Ibid., Jan. 31, 1934, p. 1.
34. Ibid., Jan. 27, 1934, p. 3.
35. Ibid., Feb. 1, 1934, p. 1.
36. Ibid., March 23, 1934, p. 1.
37. Ibid., June 14, 1934, p. 1.
38. Ibid., June 4, 1934, p. 1.
39. Ibid., May 29, 1934, p. 1.
40. Ibid., Feb. 21, 1934, p. 1.
41. Ibid., Feb. 26, 1934, p. 1.
42. Ibid., March 15, 1934, p. 1.
43. Ibid., April 27, 1934, p. 1.
44. Ibid., April 30, 1934, p. 1.
45. Ibid., Feb. 14, 1934, p. 1.
46. Ibid., June 29, 1934, p. 4.
47. *Daily Variety*, July 7, 1934, p. 2.
48. Ibid., Sept. 18, 1934, p. 8.
49. *Hollywood Reporter*, May 29, 1934, p. 7.
50. *Daily Variety*, July 2, 1934, p. 1.
51. Ibid., July 19, 1934, p. 4.
52. *Hollywood Reporter*, Feb. 26, 1934, p. 1.
53. Ibid., March 1, 1934, p. 1.
54. Ibid., March 12, 1934, p. 3.
55. Ibid., March 19, 1934, p. 3.
56. Ibid., May 2, 1934, p. 3.
57. Ibid., April 11, 1934, p. 6.
58. Ibid., March 27, 1934, p. 1.
59. Ibid., June 26, 1934, p. 1.
60. Ibid., May 31, 1934, p. 13.
61. Ibid., June 2, 1934, p. 1.
62. Ibid., May 26, 1934, p. 1.
63. *Daily Variety*, July 12, 1934, p. 3.
64. Ibid., July 9, 1934, p. 3.
65. *Hollywood Reporter*, June 18, 1934, p. 1.
66. Ibid., June 1, 1934, p. 4.
67. Ibid., June 4, 1934, p. 3.
68. *Daily Variety*, July 6, 1934, p. 2.
69. Ibid., Dec. 3, 1934, p. 6.
70. Ibid., Dec. 11, 1934, p. 3.
71. Ibid., July 21, 1934, p. 1.
72. Ibid., July 23, 1934, p. 7.
73. Ibid., July 24, 1934, p. 1.
74. Ibid., Aug. 16, 1934, p. 3.
75. Ibid., Dec. 5, 1934, p. 3.
76. Ibid., Nov. 1, 1934, p. 1.
77. Ibid., Sept. 10, 1934, p. 7.
78. Ibid., Dec. 5, 1934, p. 3.
79. *Film Daily*, Jan. 5, 1935, p. 4.
80. *Daily Variety*, Dec. 11, 1934, p. 1.
81. Ibid., Aug. 31, 1934, p. 5.
82. Ibid., July 30, 1934, p. 1.
83. Ibid.
84. Ibid., Aug. 4, 1934, p. 1.
85. Ibid., Nov. 6, 1934, p. 1.
86. Ibid., Aug. 7, 1934, p. 1.
87. *Harrison's Reports*, Dec. 9, 1934, p. 208.
88. *Daily Variety*, Nov. 23, 1934, p. 2.
89. Ibid., Dec. 21, 1934, p. 1.
90. Ibid., Sept. 15, 1934, p. 4.
91. Ibid., Nov. 13, 1934, p. 1.
92. Ibid., Nov. 19, 1934, p. 3.
93. *Daily Variety*, July 3, 1934, p. 1.
94. Ibid., Aug. 14, 1934, p. 1.
95. Ibid., Nov. 30, 1934, p. 3.
96. *Film Daily*, March 22, 1935, p. 1.
97. Ibid., Mar 22, 1935, p. 6.
98. Ibid., May 13, 1935, p. 1.
99. *Daily Variety*, Dec. 24, 1934, p. 1.
100. *Film Daily*, Jan. 23, 1935, p. 1.
101. Ibid., Feb. 9, 1935, p. 1.
102. Ibid., May 8, 1935, p. 9.

Chapter 15

1. *Film Daily*, Nov. 15, 1925, p. 8.
2. Ibid., Oct. 14, 1928, p. 1.
3. Ibid., May 19, 1931, p. 1.
4. Ibid., Jan. 7, 1933, p. 1.
5. *Hollywood Reporter*, Jan. 19, 1933, p. 1.
6. Ibid., Jan. 26, 1933, pp. 1–2.
7. Ibid., Jan. 20, 1933, p. 1.
8. *Variety*, Nov. 29, 1932, p. 45.
9. *Hollywood Reporter*, Feb. 1, 1933, p. 1.
10. Ibid., Feb. 27, 1933, p. 1.
11. Ibid., April 15, 1933, p. 1.
12. Ibid.
13. Ibid.
14. Ibid., 5.
15. Ibid., April 17, 1933, p. 3.
16. *Variety*, April 25, 1933, p. 5.
17. Leonard Mosley, *Zanuck: The Rise and Fall of Hollywood's Last Tycoon* (Boston: Little, Brown, 1984), p. 129.
18. George F. Custen, *Twentieth Century's Fox: Darryl F. Zanuck and the Culture of Hollywood* (New York: Basic Books), p. 176.
19. *Hollywood Reporter*, May 15, 1933, p. 1.
20. Aubrey Solomon, *Twentieth Century-Fox: A Corporate and Financial History* (Metuchen, NJ: Scarecrow Press, 1988), p. 20.
21. *Hollywood Reporter*, April 28, 1933, p. 1.
22. *Variety*, April 25, 1933, p. 5.
23. *Hollywood Reporter*, April 28, 1933, p. 1.
24. Ibid., May 22, 1933, p. 1.
25. Ibid., June 5, 1933, p. 7.
26. Ibid., June 12, 1933, p. 5.
27. Ibid., June 6, 1933, p. 12.
28. Ibid., June 19, 1933, p. 4.
29. Ibid., June 17, 1933, p. 11.
30. Ibid., May 25, 1933, p. 6.
31. Ibid., June 1, 1933, p. 1.
32. *Time*, June 10, 1935, www.time.com/article/0,9171,883461,00.
33. *Harrison's Reports*, Sept. 2, 1933, p. 140.
34. *Hollywood Reporter*, June 10, 1933, p. 2.
35. Ibid., June 16, 1933, p. 1.
36. Ibid., Jan. 8, 1934, p. 10.
37. Ibid., June 10, 1933, p. 2.
38. *Motion Picture Daily*, Dec. 4, 1933, p. 13.
39. Ibid., Oct. 11, 1933, pp. 8–9.
40. Ibid., Dec. 13, 1933, p. 2.
41. *Motion Picture Herald*, Aug. 3, 1935, p. 30.
42. *Hollywood Reporter*, Jan. 17, 1934, p. 3.
43. Ibid., Jan. 27, 1934, p. 4.
44. Ibid., Feb. 1, 1934, p. 2.

45. Ibid., Jan. 22, 1934, p. 3.
46. Ibid., March 27, 1934, p. 1.
47. Ibid., March 29, 1934, p. 1.
48. Ibid., May 12, 1934, p. 1.
49. Ibid., Jan. 29, 1934, p. 1.
50. Ibid., March 29, 1934, p. 2.
51. Ibid., March 7, 1934, p. 1.
52. Ibid., May 8, 1934, p. 6.
53. Ibid., May 9, 1934, p. 2.
54. Ibid., May 8, 1934, p. 3.
55. Ibid., June 4, 1934, p. 1.
56. Ibid., June 6, 1934, p. 2.
57. *Daily Variety*, Aug. 11, 1934, p. 5.
58. *Hollywood Reporter*, June 9, 1934, p. 2.
59. *Daily Variety*, Aug. 21, 1934, p. 1.
60. Ibid., Aug. 22, 1934, p. 1.
61. Ibid., p. 4.
62. Ibid., Dec. 6, 1934, p. 2.
63. Ibid., Dec. 13, 1934, p. 1.
64. *Film Daily*, Jan. 7, 1935, pp. 4–5.
65. Ibid., March 29, 1935, p. 1.
66. *Time*, June 10, 1935, www.time.com/article/0,9171,883461,00.
67. *Film Daily*, April 17, 1935, p. 8.
68. Ibid., April 19, 1935, p. 4.
69. Ibid., May 28, 1935, p. 1.
70. Ibid., May 29, 1935, p. 1.

Chapter 16

1. *International Motion Picture Almanac 1936–37* (New York: Quigley Publishing, 1936), pp. 933–934.
2. *Film Daily*, June 15, 1935, p. 1.
3. Solomon, p. 41.
4. A. Scott Berg, *Goldwyn: A Biography* (New York: Alfred A. Knopf, 1989), p. 273.
5. *Time*, June 10, 1935, time.com/article/0,9171,883461,00.
6. *Film Daily*, May 31, 1935, p. 6.
7. Ibid., June 17, 1935, p. 17.
8. Ford, p. 94.
9. *Time*, July 29, 1935, time.com/article/0,9171,847487,00.
10. *Motion Picture Herald*, July 31, 1935, p. 25.
11. *Harrison's Report*, July 27, 1935, p. 117.
12. Ibid., Aug. 10, 1935, p. 128.
13. Ibid., Aug. 24, 1935, p. 137.
14. *The Motion Picture Herald*, July 17, 1935, p. 36.
15. Ibid., July 24, 1935, p. 4.

Bibliography

Allvine, Glendon. *The Greatest Fox of Them All*. New York: Lyle Stuart, 1969.
American Film Institute Catalog of Motion Pictures Produced in the United States, 1921–1930. New York: R.R. Bowker, 1971.
Bergstrom, Janet. *William Fox Presents F.W. Murnau and Frank Borzage*. Twentieth Century–Fox Home Entertainment LLC, 2008.
Birchard, Robert S. *King Cowboy: Tom Mix and the Movies*. Burbank: Riverwood Press, 1993.
Blum, Daniel. *A Pictorial History of the Silent Screen*. New York: Grosset & Dunlap, 1953.
Daily Variety, 1931–1935.
Exhibitors Daily Review, 1928.
Exhibitors Trade Review.
Film Daily, 1925–1935.
Film Daily Year Book 1920. New York: Quigley, 1921.
Film Year Book 1925. New York: Film Daily, 1926.
Film Year Book 1926. New York: Film Daily, 1927.
Ford, Dan. *Pappy: The Life of John Ford*. Englewood Cliffs, NJ: Prentice Hall, 1979.
Fortune Magazine, May 1930.
Harrison's Reports, 1934–1935.
Historic Property Survey Report for Twentieth Century–Fox. Los Angeles: Historic Resources Group, Oct. 12, 1990.
Hollywood Herald.
Hollywood Reporter.
International Motion Picture Almanac 1936–37. New York: Quigley, 1936.
Koszarski, Richard. *An Evening's Entertainment: The Age of the Silent Feature Picture, 1915–1928*. New York: Scribner's, 1990.
Lewis, Howard T. *The Motion Picture Industry*. New York: D. Van Norstrand, 1933.
Motion Picture News Blue Book, 1930.
Motion Picture Daily, 1928–1933.
Motion Picture Herald, 1935.
Motion Picture Studio Directory and Trade Annual, 1920.
Motion Picture Times.
Moving Picture World.
Griffith, Richard, and Arthur L. Mayer. *The Movies*. New York: Simon & Schuster, 1957.
New York Times Film Reviews (1913–1931). New York: The New York Times and Arno Press, 1970.
New York Times Film Reviews (1932–1938). New York: The New York Times and Arno Press, 1970.
Semenov, Lillian Wurtzel, and Carla Winter. *William Fox, Sol M. Wurtzel and the Early Fox Film Corporation, Letters 1913–1923*. Jefferson, NC: McFarland, 2001.
Sinclair, Upton. *Upton Sinclair Presents William Fox*. Los Angeles: published by the author, 1933.
Solomon, Aubrey. *Twentieth Century–Fox: A Corporate and Financial History*. Metuchen, NJ: Scarecrow Press, 1988.
Kennedy, Joseph P. *The Story of The Films*. Chicago & New York: A.W. Shaw, 1927.
Time magazine, 1930–1935.
Variety Film Reviews 1907–1920. New York and London: Garland, 1983.
Variety Film Reviews 1921–1925. New York and London: Garland, 1983.
Variety Film Reviews 1926–1929. New York and London: Garland, 1983.
Variety Film Reviews 1930–1933. New York and London: Garland, 1983.
Variety Film Reviews 1934–1937. New York and London: Garland, 1983.
Variety, various years.
Wid's Daily, 1918–1924.

Index

Abraham Lincoln (1924) 68
Abraham Lincoln (1930) 149
Academy of Motion Pictures Arts and Sciences 121, 141, 158, 172
Ace High (1918) 42, 247
Acord, Art 87
Adolfi, John G. 21, 25, 207
Adorable (1933) 164, 340
Adorée, Renée 59, 125
The Adventurer (1920) 261
Advice to the Lovelorn (1933) 211; see also *Miss Lonelyhearts*
Affairs of Cellini (1934) 214
After the Ball (1933) 165, 189, 339
After Tomorrow (1932) 162, 332
After Your Own Heart (1921) 272
Against All Odds (1924) 288
Ah, Wilderness (1935) 192
The Air Circus (1928) 109, 120, 310
Aladdin and the Wonderful Lamp (1917) 27, 242–243
Alba, Maria 119
Albee Theaters 69
Alcañiz, Luana 144
Ali Baba and the Forty Thieves (1918) 27, 28, 251
Alias the Night Wind (1923) 283
Alicoate, Jack 127, 133, 138, 159
All-Continent Corporation 134, 223
All for a Husband (1917) 243
All Men Are Enemies (1934) 202, 347
All Quiet on the Western Front (1930) 149
Allain, Marcel 57
Allen, Elizabeth 175
Allison, May 79
Allvine, Glendon 68, 109
Almost Married (1932) 164, 334
Aloma of the South Seas (1926) 98
Always Goodbye (1931) 327
Amateur Daddy (1932) 168, 333
Ambassador Bill (1931) 330
Ambition (1916) 234
Ameche, Don 220, 224
Ameranglo Corporation 133
America (1924) 66, 68
American Broadcasting Company 124
American Buds (1918) 246–247
American Methods (1917) 239
American Telephone and Telegraph Company 123, 127–128, 132, 177

Les Amours d'Elizabeth (1912) 13; see also *Queen Elizabeth*
The Ancient Mariner (1926) 75, 296
Anderson, Judith 211
Angel, Heather 171
Angelina o el honor de un brigadier (1935) 358
The Animal Kingdom (1932) 175
Ankles Preferred (1927) 302
Ann Vickers (1933) 191
Anna Christie (1930) 146, 149
Anna Karenina (1915) 20, 228
Anna Karenina (1935) 201
Annabelle's Affairs (1931) 328
anti-trust litigation 51, 128; see also consent decree
Any Wife (1922) 275
Apfel, Oscar 21, 23
Arabia (1922) 60, 280
Arabian Love (1922) 59, 276–277
Arbuckle, Roscoe "Fatty" 6, 15, 19, 56, 60
Archainbaud, George 63, 204
Architectural Forum 67
Are You There? (1931) 155, 327
The Arizona Express (1924) 287
The Arizona Kid (1930) 131, 139, 320
The Arizona Romeo (1925) 291
Arizona to Broadway (1933) 341
The Arizona Wildcat (1927) 306
Arlen, Richard 199
Arliss, George 149, 209, 212, 215, 217
Arrowsmith (1931) 191
Artclass 74
Arthur, Harry 159
The Artist (1923) 49
As Husbands Go (1933) 180, 181, 344
Ascher Theaters 69, 71, 76
¡*Asegure a su mujer!* (1935) 354
Associated Producers 52
Asther, Nils 125
Astor, Mary 120, 125
Atherton Productions 219
Atlas Distributors 74
The Auctioneer (1927) 77, 83, 112, 302
Audubon Theater 12
Ayres, Lew 141, 175, 188

Babbitt (1934) 191
The Babes in the Woods (1917) 27, 243–244

Baboona (1935) 353
Baby Face (1933) 196
Baby Take a Bow (1934) 201, 204, 348
Bachelor of Arts (1934) 352
Bachelor's Affairs (1932) 164, 334
Bacon, Lloyd 197, 207
Bad Boy (1935) 359
Bad Girl (1931) 155, 329
Bagnall, George N. 137, 160, 167
Baker, Graham 192
Baker, Phil 216
Balaban & Katz 69, 70, 93
Balboa Amusement Producing Company 13, 23
Balfour, Boardman and Company 193
Bank of America 129, 136, 150, 216, 217
Bankers Trust Company 128
Bankhead, Tallulah 146
Banks, Leslie 214
Banks, Monty 87
Banky, Vilma 107
Banner 74
Bar Nothin' (1921) 273
Bara, Theda (Theodosia Goodman) 6, 15, 19, 20, 21, 22, 23, 25, 27, 29, 30, 32, 34, 40, 41, 87
Barbary Coast (1935) 201
El barbero de Napoleon (1930) 323; see also *Napoleon's Barber*
Bárcena, Catalina 145
Bard, Ben 120
Bare Knuckles (1921) 269
Bari, Lynn 204
The Barker (1929) 175
Barrie, Mona 220
Barrymore, John 6, 62, 87, 97, 107, 176, 193
Barrymore, Lionel 87, 120, 125, 176
Barsky 74
Barthelmess, Richard 48, 60, 87, 193
Bartholomew, Freddie 222
Baruch, Bernard 129
Bassler, Robert 200
The Battle of Hearts (1916) 234
The Battle of Life (1916) 237
The Battling Butler (1926) 83
Baum, Lou 94
Baxter, Warner 125, 131, 139, 141, 152, 154, 155, 164, 168, 176, 184, 186, 196, 198, 204, 217, 220, 222

369

Be a Little Sport (1919) 41, 256
Beal, Frank 46
The Beast (1916) 234, 259
Beau Brummel (1924) 68
Beau Geste (1927) 82
Beaudine, William 125
Beaumont, Harry 84, 85
Beebe, Marjorie 125
Beery, Wallace 60, 146, 176, 193, 209, 210, 216, 222
Behind That Curtain (1929) 315
Behind the Front (1926) 83
Belasco, David 14, 15, 94
Bell, Rex 119, 120
Bell Telephone Laboratories 96
Bellamy, Madge 73, 75, 83, 87, 95, 119
Bellamy, Ralph 164, 167
La Belle Russe (1919) 15, 257
Belle of Samoa (1928) 110
Belle of the Nineties (1934) 201
Bells of San Juan (1922) 279
Ben-Hur (1925) 81–82, 98, 201
Bennett, Belle 79, 87
Bennett, Constance 141, 193, 212, 215
Bennett, Enid 48
Bennett, Joan 131, 164, 168, 175
Bennison, Andrew 111
Berger, Ludwig 115
Berkeley, Busby 197
Berkeley Square (1933) 178, 180, 186, 343
Bernhardt, Sarah 13, 20, 90
Bernie, Ben 101, 103
Bernstein, David M. 125
Bernstein, Henri 115
Bertha, the Sewing Machine Girl (1926) 83, 301
The Best Bad Man (1925) 296
Best of Enemies (1933) 165, 341
Betrayed (1917) 241
The Better 'Ole (1927) 97
Betty Boop 157
Beware of the Bride (1920) 266
Beyond Price (1921) 270
Big Broadcast of 1936 (1936) 201
Big Dan (1923) 284–285
The Big House (1930) 146, 149
The Big Parade (1925) 59, 70, 81–82, 83, 98
The Big Party (1930) 319
The Big Punch (1921) 268
Big Time (1929) 317
Big Town Ideas (1921) 270
Big Town Round-Up (1921) 272
The Big Trail (1930) 124, 147, 148–149, 150, 323
A Bill of Divorcement (1932) 175
Biograph 11
Biophone 107
The Bird of Prey (1918) 248
The Birth of a Nation (1915) 5–6, 15, 23, 38
Bischoff, R.W. 145
The Bitter Truth (1917) 237
The Black Camel (1931) 328
Black Jack (1927) 305
Black Magic (1929) 315
Black Paradise (1926) 299

Black Shadows (1920) 261
Black Sheep (1935) 356
The Black Watch (1929) 315
Blackton, J. Stuart 10
Blazing Love (1916) 233
Blind Wives (1920) 49
Blindfold (1928) 312
The Blindness of Devotion (1915) 230
Blindness of Divorce (1918) 32, 246
The Blizzard (1924) 287
Block, Ralph 139
Blockade (1928) 108
block-booking 51, 88, 187
Blondell, Joan 146
Blood Money (1933) 211
Blood Will Tell (1927) 95, 306
Bloom, Edgar S. 124
Blue, Monte 87
Blue Blood and Red (1916) 233, 273
The Blue Eagle (1926) 83, 85, 300
Blue Skies (1929) 313
The Blue Streak (1917) 238
Blue-Eyed Mary (1918) 247
Blumenthal, A.C. 95, 126, 165, 224
The Blushing Bride (1921) 269
Blystone, John G. 43, 44, 63, 84, 154, 159, 164, 182, 189, 197
Blythe, Betty 53
Body and Soul (1931) 142, 325
Bogart, Humphrey 141, 143, 148, 167
Boles, John 164, 220
Boleslavsky, Richard 197
Bolton, Guy 75
Bondage (1933) 165, 339
The Bondman (1916) 36, 232–233, 247
Bonnie Annie Laurie (1918) 249
The Book Agent (1917) 239
Borden, Olive 79, 87
Born Reckless (1930) 131, 321
Born to Be Bad (1934) 215
Borzage, Frank 62, 73, 80, 83, 85, 94, 114, 115, 121, 122, 125, 138, 148, 155, 162
Bosko 157
Boss of Camp 4 (1922) 280
Boston Blackie (1923) 283
Boston Evening American 170, 212, 215
Bottoms Up (1934) 183, 190, 196, 347
Bow, Clara 83, 164, 168, 175, 181
The Bowery (1933) 210, 211
Box Office Attraction Film Rental Company 13, 15, 18, 20, 44, 50
Boyer, Charles 193
Boylan, Malcolm Stuart 191
Brabin, Charles J. 40, 49, 125
Bracken, Bertram 14, 27, 35
Bradley, Grace 201
Brand, Harry 209
The Branded Sombrero (1928) 307
A Branded Soul (1917) 29, 243
The Brass Bowl (1924) 290
Brass Commandments (1923) 281–282
The Brat (1931) 154, 329
Brave and Bold (1918) 247
Breen, Joseph I. 197, 215
Bren, J.R. 210, 212

Brendel, El 141, 143, 147, 148, 164, 175, 192
Brenon, Herbert 20, 23, 24
Bride #13 (1920) 57, 265
The Bride of Fear (1918) 246
Bright Eyes (1934) 201, 204, 222, 352
Bring 'Em Back Alive (1932) 169
Bristolphone 107
British Gaumont Company 123, 160, 167, 173, 179, 193
Broadway Bad (1932) 162, 165, 338
Broadway Melody (1929) 112
The Broadway Peacock (1922) 276
The Broadway Sport (1917) 240
Broadway Through a Keyhole 211
Brockwell, Gladys 15, 29, 32, 35, 38, 41, 45, 46
Broken Commandments (1919) 257
The Broken Law (1915) 20, 230–231, 252
The Broncho Twister (1927) 303
Bronson, Betty 73
Brook, Clive 107, 204
Brown, Clarence 125, 197
Brown, Johnny Mack 125
Brown, Lew 119, 148, 195–196
Browning, Tod 125
Brush, Matthew C. 137
Buchanan's Wife (1918) 251
Buchman, Sidney 166
Bucking the Barrier (1923) 282
Bucking the Line (1921) 274
Buddy 157
Buel, Kenean 27
Bulldog Drummond Strikes Back (1934) 215
Burger, Paul 155
Burke, Edwin 176
Burke, James 126
Burman, Ben Lucien 219
Burnett, W.R. 174
Burns, Frank 43
The Bush Leaguer (1927) 83
Business and Pleasure (1932) 161, 168, 332
The Buster (1923) 282
Butcher, Edward W. 139, 158, 159, 167, 188, 192, 198, 219, 222
Butler, David 95, 125, 141, 143, 174, 197

El caballero de la noche (1932) 336; see also *Dick Turpin*
The Cabinet of Dr. Caligari (1927) 115
Cagney, James 146, 193, 205
The Caillaux Case (1918) 34, 249
A California Romance (1922) 280–281
Call Her Savage (1932) 164, 175, 181, 336–337
Call It Luck (1934) 189, 192, 348
The Call of the Soul (1919) 252
The Call of the Wild (1935) 215, 216
Calvert's Valley (1922) 279
Cameo Kirby (1923) 60, 88, 285, 304
Cameo Kirby (1930) 319
Camille (1917) 242
The Camille of the Yukon 36, 263; see also *Silent Lie*

A Camouflage Kiss (1918) 246
Campbell, Evelyn 75
Campeau, Frank 79
Canfield, Mark 205
Cannon, Raymond 120
Cantor, Eddie 87, 210
The Canyon of Light (1926) 301
Un capitán de cosacos (1934) 349–350
Capra, Frank 166, 196
Caprice of the Mountains (1916) 234, 274
Caprice, June 25, 29, 33
Captain Blood (1935) 201
Captain Lash (1929) 312
Captured (1933) 207
Caravan (1934) 193–195, 350
Caravane (1934) 351
Cardinal Richelieu (1935) 215, 216
Careless Lady (1932) 162, 333
Carewe, Edwin 58, 201
Carleton, Will 53
Carlos, Abraham 23, 25
Carmen, Jewel 32, 35, 74
Carmen (1915) 20, 23, 230, 272
Carol, Sue 109, 125
Carolina (1934) 182, 195, 202, 345
Carr, Mary 54, 58
Case Research Laboratories 98
Case, Theodore 96, 98, 100
Casey at the Bat (1927) 83
Catch My Smoke (1922) 281
The Cat's Paw (1934) 349
Caught in the Act (1918) 251
Cavalcade (1933) 164, 170, 178, 179, 182, 183, 186, 188, 193, 339
A Celebrated Scandal (1915) 20, 228
censorship 65, 146, 196–197, 215
Chadwick Productions 73, 94
Chadwick, Ike 94
Chain Lightning (1927) 304
The Challenge of the Law (1920) 266
The Champion of Lost Causes (1925) 292
Chandu, the Magician (1932) 164, 335
Chaney, Lon 60, 62, 73, 87, 125
Change of Heart (1933) 195, 202, 348
Chaplin, Charlie 6, 19, 30, 43, 45, 48, 49, 52, 56, 60, 73, 136, 156, 165, 219
Chaplin, Lita Grey 165
Chaplin, Sydney 87, 97, 205
Charell, Erik 193–195
Charlie Chan (series) 152, 169, 202, 204, 219, 222
Charlie Chan Carries On (1931) 326
Charlie Chan in Egypt (1935) 356
Charlie Chan in London (1934) 350
Charlie Chan in Paris (1935) 353
Charlie Chan in Shanghai (1935) 359
Charlie Chan's Chance (1932) 331–332
Charlie Chan's Courage (1934) 349
Charlie Chan's Greatest Case (1933) 342
Chase, Charley 66
Chase (National) Bank 156, 173, 180, 181, 188, 193, 200, 216, 217

Chase Securities Corporation 150
Chasing Rainbows (1919) 258
Chasing the Moon (1922) 276
Chasing Through Europe (1929) 110, 316
The Chauffeur (1921) 49
The Cheat (1931) 146
The Cheater Reformed (1921) 268
Cheaters at Play (1932) 162, 332
Cheating Herself (1919) 256
Cheating the Public (1918) 32, 245
Checkers (1919) 21, 34, 257
Cheer Up and Smile (1930) 321
Chevalier, Maurice 193, 196
Chicken à la Cabaret (1920) 44
Chicken a la King (1928) 309
A Child of the Wild (1917) 238
Children of the Ghetto (1915) 15, 228
Children of the Night (1921) 272
Christie Comedies 111
Christina (1929) 318
Chuck Conners 210
Churchill, Marguerite 125, 143, 168
Cimarron (1931) 158
Cinderella of the Hills (1921) 273
Cinephone 107
The Circus Ace (1927) 304
The Circus Cowboy (1924) 287–288
The Circus Kid (1928) 108
The Cisco Kid (1931) 184, 330
Citizen Kane (1941) 179
The City (1926) 77, 89, 301
City Girl (1930) 148, 319
City Lights (1931) 158
La ciudad de cartón (1934) 345
Clancy's Kosher Wedding (1927) 82
The Clansman 23
Clark, John D. 110, 167
Clark, Marguerite 48
Clark, Robert 125
Clarke, Eric T. 82
Clarke, Harley L. 123, 124, 132, 133, 135, 136–137, 138–139, 140, 145, 146–147, 148–149, 150–152, 153–154, 156, 158, 159, 160, 162–163, 167, 173, 177, 187
Clarke, Mae 141
Clayton, Ethel 48
The Clemenceau Case (1915) 20, 36, 228
Cleopatra (1917) 21, 30, 36, 248–249, 261
Cleopatra (1934) 201
Clift, Denison 21, 36, 43, 47
Clifton, Elmer 66
Cline, Eddie 43, 84
Clive of India (1934) 214, 216
Clyde, Andy 158
Cochrane, Robert H. 52, 94
The Cock-Eyed World (1929) 115, 137, 150, 153, 186, 317
Cohan, George M. 192, 220
Cohen, Emanuel 172
Cohen, Sammy 122, 125
The Cohens and the Kellys (1926) 82
Cohn, Harry 50, 172, 208
Cohn, Jack 50
Colbert, Claudette 215
Cole, Lester 201
Coleman, Judge Frank J. 131

Colleen (1927) 304
Collier Sr., William 141
Collins, Fred 188
Collins, Joan 34
Collyer, June 120, 125
Colman, Ronald 107, 212, 215, 217
color film production 214
Colorado Fuel & Iron Company 161
Colorado Pluck (1921) 270
Columbia Pictures 50, 94, 109, 133, 157, 166, 169, 197, 212
Columbo, Russ 211
Come to My House (1927) 306–307
The Coming of the Law (1919) 42, 255
Coming Out Party (1934) 180, 182, 183, 189, 346
Common Clay (1930) 141, 144, 147, 149, 322
competing sound systems 107
Compson, Betty 60
Coneybear, John F. 143
Coneyvear, William 135
Confession (1918) 247
Congorilla (1932) 164, 335, 169
Conklin, Chester 44
A Connecticut Yankee in King Arthur's Court (1921) 56, 272–273, 297
A Connecticut Yankee in King Arthur's Court (1931) 144, 147, 155, 186, 326
¿Conoces a tu mujer? (1931) 329; see also *Don't Bet on Women*
The Conqueror (1917) 242, 289
Conscience (1917) 242
Conselman, William M. 191
consent decree 88
Considine, John, Jr. 139
Consolidated Film Industries 133, 207
The Constant Nymph (1934) 346
Conway, Jack 63, 125
Cook, Clyde 49, 56
Cook, Joe 180–181
Coolidge, Calvin 129
Cooney Theaters 76
Cooper, Courtney Riley 219
Cooper, Jack 49
The Corsican Brothers 192
Cortellaphone 107
Cosmopolitan Pictures 66
cost cutting 88–89
Costain, Thomas 200
Costello, Dolores 87, 104, 205
Costello, Helene 106
The Country Beyond (1926) 80, 300
The County Chairman (1935) 223, 353
Courcier, Bud 43
The Covered Wagon (1923) 61, 62, 70, 81, 84
Coward, Noël 164
Cowardice Court (1919) 255
The Cowboy and the Countess (1926) 297
The Cowboy Kid (1928) 309
Cowboy Millionaire (1935) 355
The Cradle Snatchers (1927) 77, 303
Craven, Frank 75

Crawford, Joan 125, 146, 176, 193
Crazy That Way (1930) 131, 320
The Criminal Code (1914) 13, 14
The Crimson Runner (1925) 83
Crosman, Henrietta 171
Cross, Victoria 14
Crossed Wires (1924) 66; *see also Daughters of the Night*
Crossman, Melville 205
The Crusader (1922) 279
The Crusades (1935) 201
La cruz y la Espada (1934) 347
Cruze, James 61, 62, 70, 174, 197
Cry of the World (1932) 164, 334
Cuando el amor rie (1933) 340
Cuerpo y Alma (1931) 327; *see also Body and Soul*
Cummings, Constance 208, 211
Cummings, Irving 80, 83, 84, 120, 125, 141, 189
Cummings, Robert 196
Cupid's Fireman (1923) 286
Cupid's Roundup (1918) 32, 35, 244
Curly Top (1935) 222, 357
Curlytop (1924) 291
Curtis, Edward 204
Curtiz, Michael 197, 205, 207
Curwood, James Oliver 75
The Custard Cup (1923) 281
The Cyclone (1920) 47, 260
The Cyclone Rider (1924) 289

Daddy Long Legs (1931) 155, 327
Dames (1934) 201
Dana, Violet 60
Dance Team (1932) 331
The Dancers (1925) 292
The Dancers (1930) 323
The Danger Zone (1918) 251–252
Dangerously Yours (1933) 164, 337–338
Daniels, Bebe 87
Dannenberg, Joe 68, 69
Dante's Inferno (1911) 38
Dante's Inferno (1924) 65–66, 223, 289
Dante's Inferno (1935) 196, 201, 202, 204, 219, 357–358
The Daredevil (1920) 46, 261
Daredevil Kate (1916) 235, 275
Daredevil's Reward (1928) 307
The Daring Young Man (1935) 202, 356
The Dark Angel (1925) 83
The Darlings of Paris (1917) 237, 253
Darnell, Linda 225
Darwin Was Right (1924) 290
A Daughter of France (1918) 246
A Daughter of the Gods (1916) 23, 24, 65, 236, 261
Daughters of the Night (1924) 290
David Copperfield (1935) 201
David Harum (1934) 346
Davies, Marion 38, 66, 87, 125, 146
Davis, Bette 146
Davis, Judge J. Warren 134
Davis, Will S. 21
Davis Distributors 74
Day, Marceline 120
The Dead Line (1920) 262–263

The Deadwood Coach (1924) 291, 311
The Debt of Honor (1918) 246
Dee, Frances 198
De Forest, Dr. Lee 98–99, 104
Del infierno al cielo (1931) 325; *see also The Man Who Came Back*
Del mismo Barro (1931) 144, 322; *see also Common Clay*
Del Rio, Dolores 79, 87, 102, 112
Del Ruth, Hampton 31, 43, 44, 49, 56
Del Ruth, Roy 43, 94, 216
Delafield, Edward C. 129
Delicious (1931) 152, 155, 331
Delmar, Vina 219
DeMille, Cecil Blount 13, 26, 61, 62, 70, 82, 88, 125
DeMille, William C. 125
Dempsey, Jack 83
Denny, Reginald 87, 143
Depinet, Ned 94
The Derelict (1917) 239
Desert Blossoms (1921) 274
The Desert Fox (1951) 214
Desert Love (1920) 262
The Desert Outlaw (1924) 288
Desert Valley (1926) 301
The Desert's Price (1925) 296
Destruction (1915) 20, 231
De Sylva, B.G. "Buddy" 119, 148, 183, 193, 195–196, 200, 203–204, 219, 222
Devil Is a Woman (1935) 201
Devil Tiger (1934) 345–346
A Devil with Women (1930) 324
The Devil Within (1921) 274
The Devil's Daughter (1915) 20, 229
The Devil's in Love (1933) 165, 341
The Devil's Lottery (1932) 162, 168, 186, 332–333
The Devil's Riddle (1920) 46, 261
The Devil's Wheel (1918) 246
Dick Turpin (1925) 73, 292
Dickson, W.K.L. 10
Dietrich, Marlene 146
Dietz, Howard 126
Dillon, John Francis 164
Dillon, Read & Company 129, 136, 150
Dinner at Eight (1933) 176
The Diplomats (1929) 313
Disney, Walt 157
Disorderly Conduct (1932) 162, 332
The Divorce Trap (1919) 255
The Divorcée (1930) 146, 149
Dix, Richard 83, 87
The Dixie Merchant (1926) 297
Dixon, Thomas 23
Do and Dare (1922) 279
Doctor Bull (1933) 186, 342
Dr. Jekyll and Mr. Hyde (1932) 197
Dr. Rameau (1915) 36, 229
Doctors' Wives (1931) 326
Does It Pay? (1923) 284
Doing Their Bit (1918) 248
Don Juan (1926) 97, 118
Don Q. Son of Zorro (1925) 73
Donovan, William J. 126, 129
Don't Bet on Women (1931) 325

Don't Marry (1928) 115, 121, 309
Doorway to Hell (1930) 205
Doran, D.A. 167
Dorman, Shirley 120
Dorothy Vernon of Haddon Hall (1924) 61, 66
Dos más uno, dos (1934) 351
double bills 38
Double Cross Roads (1930) 320
Doubting Thomas (1935) 223, 356
Dover, William 207, 209
Down to Earth (1932) 164, 168, 335
Doyle, Laird 209
Dracula (1931) 108
Drag Harlan (1920) 266, 292
Dressed to Kill (1928) 307–308
Dressed to Thrill (1935) 357
Dresser, Louise 109, 125
Dressler, Marie 30, 107, 146, 176
Drexel, Nancy 120
Dry Martini (1928) 120, 310
The Dude Ranger (1934) 350
Dumas, Alexandre 14, 192
Duncan, Mary 120, 125
Dunlap, Scott 43, 46, 84
Dunn, James 141, 147, 155, 164, 168, 193, 201, 202, 220
DuPar, E.B. 43
Dupont, E.A. 78
Durand of the Bad Lands (1917) 32, 241, 262
Durand of the Bad Lands (1925) 295
Durant, Jack 191–192
Durham, Fay 43
Duval, M. 215
Dwan, Allan 78, 83, 94, 125, 138
Dynamite Allen (1921) 269

The Eagle and the Hawk (1933) 197
Early to Wed (1926) 298
East Coast Distribution 74
East Lynne (1916) 234
East Lynne (1925) 71, 73, 75, 296
East Lynne (1931) 325–326
East Side, West Side (1927) 152, 305
Eastman Kodak Company 124, 143
Eastward Ho! (1919) 259
Éclair Studio, New Jersey 14
Edison, Thomas Alva 10, 96, 100
Educational Pictures 71–72, 107, 111, 157, 195, 211
Edwards, J. Gordon 14, 23, 24, 27, 30, 43, 53, 58, 63, 66
Eilers, Sally 141, 155, 164, 168, 188
Eisele, John C. 19, 38
Electrical Research Products Incorporated (ERPI) 99, 103, 128, 134, 169
The Eleventh Hour (1923) 283
Elinor Norton (1934) 351
Ellis, Earl 43
Elman, Mischa 97
Elope If You Must (1922) 276
Elwell, C.F. 96
The End of the Trail (1916) 235, 290
Engel, Joseph P. 90, 204, 219
Engel, Samuel G. 207
Engl, Dr. J. 98
Enright, Ray 207
Equity Pictures Corp. 52

Eran Trece (1931) 331; *see also Charlie Chan Carries On*
The Escape (1928) 308
Esclavas de la moda (1931) 328; *see also On Your Back*
The Eskimo (1922) 49
Essanay 11, 12
Estabrook, Howard 210
The Eternal Sapho (1916) 233
Evangeline (1919) 44, 257
Ever Since Eve (1921) 272
Ever Since Eve (1934) 345
The Everlasting Whisper (1925) 295
Every Girl's Dream (1917) 241
Every Man's Wife (1925) 293–294
Every Mother's Son (1919) 34, 253
The Exalted Flapper (1929) 315
Excellent Pictures 94
Exhibitors Daily Review 118
The Exiles (1923) 284
The Exquisite Sinner (1926) 83
Extra! Extra! (1922) 276
Eyes of the Forest (1923) 286

Face at Your Window (1920) 48, 266
Face in the Sky (1933) 164, 170, 337
The Face on the Barroom Floor (1923) 281
Fair, Elinor 44
Fair Warning (1931) 325
Fairbanks, Douglas 6, 19, 37, 45, 48, 60, 61, 73, 211, 219
Faith (1920) 260
The Fallen Angel (1918) 248
The Fallen Idol (1919) 255
Fame and Fortune (1918) 42, 251
The Family Stain (1915) 230
The Family Upstairs (1926) 77, 84, 85, 299
Famous Players Film Company 13, 23
Famous Players-Lasky 14, 37, 45, 50, 51, 61, 62, 68, 69, 70, 71, 77, 80, 91, 93
Fan Fan (1918) 28, 250
Fantomas (1920) 57, 267–268
The Far Call (1929) 314
A Farewell to Arms (1932) 197
The Farmer Takes a Wife (1935) 200, 203, 219, 223, 357
The Farmer's Daughter (1928) 311
Farnum, Dustin 32, 53
Farnum, William 15, 20, 23, 25, 29, 32, 33, 34, 35, 41, 44, 47, 48, 53, 148
Farrar, Geraldine 23, 45
Farrell, Charles 87, 102, 115, 119, 120, 122, 125, 137, 138, 142, 143, 146, 147, 148, 150, 152, 155, 164, 168, 195
The Fast Mail (1922) 278
Faye, Alice 204, 217, 220, 225
Fazenda, Louise 87, 205
Fazil (1928) 120, 152, 310
Federation of Women's Clubs 196
Feist, Felix 94
Felix, Seymour 141
Fenton, Leslie 79
Ferguson, Elsie 48
Fetchit, Stepin 125, 192, 199

The Feud (1919) 259
Feyder, Jacques 125
Fields, W.C. 87
Fig Leaves (1926) 77, 84, 85, 299
Fighting Blood (1916) 23, 232, 251
The Fighting Buckaroo (1926) 298
Fighting for Gold (1919) 254
The Fighting Heart (1925) 71, 83, 295
The Fighting Streak (1922) 277
Film Booking Office (F.B.O.) 82, 88, 108
film booking substitutions 142
The Film Daily 68, 84, 86, 87, 91, 92, 103, 104, 107, 114, 119, 125, 126, 127, 132, 133, 138, 142, 157, 159, 164, 167, 170, 177, 199, 204, 205
film piracy 67
Film Securities Corporation 181
Film Year Book 73
Filmophone 100
The Final Payment (1917) 240
Fine, Larry 157
Finkelstein and Ruben Theaters 92, 117, 128
The Firebrand (1918) 247
Firebrand Trevison (1920) 265
Fires of Conscience (1916) 235
Firnatone 106
First Division Pictures, Inc. 133
First National Pictures 37, 44, 51, 65, 66, 69, 77, 80, 82, 83, 87, 88, 90, 106, 108, 109, 117, 126–128, 139, 151, 154, 157, 169, 205, 208, 221–222
First National Theaters 91, 93
The First World War (1934) 352
The First Year (1926) 71, 75, 297
The First Year (1932) 164, 168, 334–335
Fitzpatrick & McElroy Theaters 76
Five Star Final (1931) 158
Flaherty, Robert J. 125
Flame of Youth (1920) 267
Flames of Desire (1924) 291
Flames of the Flesh (1920) 46, 260
Flaubert, Gustave 28
Fleetwing (1928) 309
Fleischer, Max 157
Fletcher, Brooks 178
Flying "A" Studios 23
The Flying Horseman (1926) 299–300
Flynn, Emmett J. 63
Flynn, Ray 95
Foch, Marshal 101
Folies Bergère (1935) 215
The Folly of Vanity (1925) 292
Folly Theater 11
Fonda, Henry 217, 225
The Fool (1925) 66, 71, 295–296
A Fool There Was (1915) 19, 36, 227–228, 247
Foolish Wives (1922) 52
The Fool's Revenge (1916) 232
Footfalls (1921) 274
Footlight Parade (1933) 196
The Footlight Ranger (1923) 281
The Fourth Estate (1916) 231–232
For Big Stakes (1922) 278

For Freedom (1918) 251
For Heaven's Sake (1926) 98
For Liberty (1917) 35, 244
The Forbidden Path (1918) 245
The Forbidden Room (1919) 253
Forbidden Trails (1920) 263
Ford, Harrison 48
Ford, John (Jack) 58–59, 60, 64–65, 71, 73, 80, 83, 84, 85, 87, 89, 94, 120, 125, 131, 138, 143, 154, 190, 191, 197, 202, 216, 220, 222
Forde, Eugene 166, 173
foreign production 58, 78, 95, 179, 198
foreign versions 144–145, 149, 172, 198
Fortune Magazine 6, 19
42nd Street (1933) 222
Foster, Preston 175
4 Devils (1928) 115, 121, 138, 148, 316–317
Four Horsemen of the Apocalypse (1921) 52
Four Sons (1928) 94, 120, 310
Fowler, Gene 214
Fox, Aaron 137
Fox, Belle 134
Fox, Eve (Leo) 10, 17, 18, 134, 223–224
Fox, Mona 134
Fox, Mrs. Aaron 133
Fox, William: acquisition of Loew's, Inc. 124–125, 126–127, 151, 181; acquisition of theaters 12, 36, 51–52, 69–72, 76, 90, 91–93, 98, 100, 101, 117–118, 123, 124, 125, 126; auto accident 127; death of 134; 150, 151–152, 153, 154; early career 9–19; efforts to retrieve Fox Films 160; 167, 173–174, 181, 200, 204, 219, 225; financial problems 127–134; and Fox Film Corp. 19–29, 31–37, 38–39, 42–43, 49–50, 53–63, 64–65, 66, 68, 75, 78–79, 80, 82, 83, 84, 85, 94, 115, 117, 119; height of success 121–122; and sound 95–100, 102–103, 109
Fox-Case Corporation 98, 100, 101, 124, 126
Fox Film Corporation: becoming a public company 69–70; directors 26, 35, 62–63, 78–79, 83–84, 125, 197; early productions 19–25; effects of Depression 135–140, 155–157; effects of NRA 187–188; executive changes 131–133, 139–140, 151, 156, 160, 161, 220; foreign markets 37; incorporation 19; kiddie features 27–28; lagging behind other studios 47–48, 73, 152, 169, 175–176, 188–189; merger with 20th Century 215–225; mismanagement 151–152, 153–155, 158, 161; musical productions 119, 142–143, 200; production facilities 14, 19, 23, 38–39, 43–44, 52, 66, 77, 79–80, 84, 90, 105–106; program of releases 19, 29–31, 39–41, 49–50, 52–56, 63–64, 66, 70–71, 75, 77, 83, 94–95, 120, 152; recovering

profitability 202; refinancing 173, 180–181; and sound 100, 109–112, 113–117, 148; stars 19–20, 22, 29–30, 32–34, 41–43, 48, 59–60, 62, 87, 118–119, 125, 141, 152, 175, 191, 192, 199, 204; story department 28, 39, 47, 166, 191, 196, 200, 201; studio politics 174
Fox Film Realty Corporation 91
Fox Film Stock Company 204
Fox Hills Studio (Pico Boulevard) 79, 84, 85, 90, 94, 105–106, 123, 220, 222
Fox Metropolitan Playhouses 122, 123, 126, 139, 200
Fox Midwesco 123, 139
Fox Movietone Follies of 1929 (1929) 110, 112, 138, 142, 315
Fox Nature Color 124, 143
Fox Newsreels 86, 217
Fox-Poli circuit 139
Fox Studio (New York) 98, 100, 169
Fox Theater Corporation 9, 32, 90, 103, 91, 93, 122, 123, 125, 126, 129, 132, 135, 137, 149, 153, 156, 160, 167, 173
Fox Varieties (short subjects) 71, 85
Foxe, Earle 71, 119, 125
F.P. 1 (1933) 341
Francis, Alec 79
Franey, Billy 44
Frankenstein (1931) 146
Franklin, Chester 27–28, 35
Franklin, Harold B. 117, 139
Franklin, Sidney A. 27–28, 35
Frazer, Robert 79
Frederick, Pauline 60
A Free Soul (1931) 158
Freedman, William 135
The Freshman (1925) 73
Fried, Harry 196
Friedland, Anatole 101
Friendly Enemies (1925) 83
A Friendly Husband (1923) 281
Frisco Sally Levy (1927) 82
Frohman and Erlanger 38
From Now On (1920) 265
From the Valley of the Missing (1915) 228
Las fronteras del Amor (1934) 352
Frontier Marshal (1934) 189, 345
Frozen Justice (1929) 94, 138, 317
Frye, W.C. 23
Fuchs, Anna 9
Fuchs, Michael 9
Fugitives (1929) 312
Furthman, Jules G. 21

Gable, Clark 167, 193, 209, 215
Gaiety Theater 11
Gain, J.J. 167
Gallant Lady (1934) 211
The Galley Slave (1915) 20, 231
Gallian, Ketti 175, 204
Gambling (1934) 351
Gambling in Souls (1919) 253
Gang War (1928) 108
Garat, Henry 164, 171, 186
Garbo, Greta 107, 125, 146, 176, 193, 201

Gardner, Jack 139
Gates, Bill 6
The Gateway to the Moon (1928) 307
Gaumont, Leon 100
The Gay Caballero (1932) 162, 332
The Gay Deception (1935) 198, 358
The Gay Retreat (1927) 305
Gaynor, Janet 75, 85, 87, 107, 112, 114, 115, 119, 121, 122, 125, 137, 138, 143, 146, 147, 148, 150, 152, 155, 164, 166, 168, 171, 184, 186, 188, 193, 195, 196, 198, 202, 221, 224
Gaynor, William J. 18
Gell, W.J. 167
General Film Company 12, 161
General Theaters Equipment Company 124, 133, 136, 137, 146, 151, 152, 153, 155, 160, 181
Gentle Cyclone (1926) 299
Gentle Julia (1923) 286
George White's 1935 Scandals (1935) 355
George White's Scandals (1934) 182, 195–196, 201, 202, 346
Gerald Cranston's Lady (1924) 290
German cinema 78–79, 81, 94
German production 79, 94, 179
Gershwin, George 152
Gershwin, Ira 152
Get Your Man (1921) 270
The Ghost Talks (1929) 313
Giannini, Dr. A.H. 207, 217
The Giant Swing 174
Gibson, Hoot 87
Gifford, Walter S. 124
Gilbert, Florence 79
Gilbert, John (Jack) 59–60, 62, 87, 88, 125, 167
The Gilded Butterfly (1926) 75, 296–297
A Gilded Fool (1915) 20, 228
Ginger (1935) 356–357
The Girl from Havana (1929) 317
The Girl I Left Behind Me (1915) 15, 228
A Girl in Bohemia (1919) 258
A Girl in Every Port (1928) 115, 119, 121, 307
The Girl in the Red Velvet Swing (1955) 34
Girl of My Heart (1920) 266
Girl Shy (1924) 68
The Girl with Champagne Eyes (1918) 35, 245–246
The Girl with No Regrets (1919) 252
Girls Demand Excitement (1931) 325
Girls Gone Wild (1929) 313–314
Gish, Dorothy 48, 66
Gish, Lillian 45, 60, 62, 66, 87
Glaum, Louise 46
Glazer, Benjamin 121
Gleam O'Dawn (1922) 59, 275
Gleason, James 210
Glennon, Bert 189
Godfrey, Samuel 154, 158
Goetz, William B. 139, 160, 171, 207, 208, 219
Going Crooked (1926) 77, 301
Gold and the Girl (1925) 75, 293

Gold and the Woman (1916) 232
The Gold Diggers (1923) 61
Gold Diggers of 1933 (1933) 207
Gold Heels (1925) 291
The Gold Rush (1925) 73, 81
Goldberg, Rube 79
Golden, Max 173
The Golden Calf (1930) 320
The Golden Strain (1925) 75, 296
The Golden West (1932) 336
Goldie (1931) 155, 328
Goldwyn, Samuel 9, 193, 201, 208, 210, 219
Goldwyn Film Company 37, 50, 61, 157
Goldwyn Girls 198
Gombell, Minna 164
Gone with the Wind (1939) 5
Good, Frank 43
Good As Gold (1927) 304
Good-by Girls! (1923) 282
The Good Companions (1933) 342
Good Intentions (1930) 321
Good Sport (1931) 331
Gordon, Max 200
Gore Brothers Enterprises 51
Gotham Productions 94
Gottler, Archie 119
The Governor's Lady (1923) 286
Grable, Betty 224
The Grail (1923) 284
Grainger, Edmund 154, 160
Grainger, James R. 69, 71, 90, 91, 92, 95, 113, 117, 119, 120, 126, 127, 132, 145, 147, 154, 157, 159, 160–161, 165, 167
La Gran Jornada (1931) 325; see also *The Big Trail*
Granaderos del amor (1934) 349
Grand Canary (1934) 180, 189, 191, 349
Grand Hotel (1932) 176
Il Grande Sentiero (1931) 324; see also *The Big Trail*
Grandeur 123–124, 127, 133, 146–147, 149, 150, 152
Grant, Cary 215
The Grapes of Wrath (1940) 214, 222
Grauman's Chinese Theater 212
Graves, Ralph 66
Great Depression 151, 157, 196–187, 216, 217
Great Diamond Mystery (1924) 289
Great Hotel Mystery (1935) 202, 354
The Great K&A Train Robbery (1926) 90, 300
The Great Nickel Robbery (1920) 44
The Great Night (1922) 280
The Great Train Robbery (1903) 10
The Great White North (1928) 120, 312
The Greater Glory (1926) 83
Greater New York Film Rental Company 12, 13
Greater Than a Crown (1925) 294
Green, Alfred E. 78, 83, 84
The Green-Eyed Monster (1916) 231
Grey, Zane 219
Griffith, Corinne 62, 83, 87, 107

Griffith, D.W. 5, 13, 15, 26, 30, 45, 52, 66, 82, 178
Griffith, Raymond 73, 207, 208
Grinde, Nick 125
Die Grosse Fahrt (1932) 334; see also *The Big Trail*
The Guide (1921) 49
Guizar, Tito 219
The Gunfighter (1923) 283–284
The Gunfighter (1950) 23

Hackett, Raymond 141
Haines, William 125
Haley, Jack 204, 220
Hall, Mordaunt 102
Halliday, John 143
Halperin, Victor 111
Halsey, Stuart and Company 91, 123, 128, 131–133, 136, 150
Hamilton, Lloyd 30
Hamilton, Neil 143
Hammeras, Ralph 184
Hammerstein, Elaine 48
Hammons, Earle W. 71–72, 94, 157
Hamper, Genevieve 15
Hamrick Theaters 69
Handle with Care (1932) 164, 337
Hands Off (1921) 269
Handy Andy (1934) 190, 202, 204, 222, 349
Hangman's House (1928) 119, 122, 308
Happy Days (1930) 124, 147, 319
Harbaugh, Carl 27
Hard Boiled (1926) 299
Harding, Ann 193, 211
Hardy, Oliver 108
Harlow, Jean 155, 167, 176
Harman/Ising 157
Harmony at Home (1930) 319
Harris, Elmer 212
Harrison, Pete 142, 177–178, 200, 210, 220–221
Harrison's Reports 142, 177–178, 198, 210, 211, 220–221
Hart, William S. 6, 19, 40, 45, 48
Harvey, Lilian 168, 170, 175, 179, 180, 183, 192
Hat Check Girl (1932) 164, 335
Hathaway, Henry 197
Haver, Phyllis 125
Havoc (1925) 71, 73, 83, 294–295
Hawks, Howard 83, 109, 120, 125
Hay que casar al principe (1931) 328; see also *Paid to Love*
Hayes, Helen 167
Hays, Will H. 60, 65, 97, 115, 187–188, 196, 207
Hays office 146, 164, 172, 192
Healy, Ted 141
Hearst, William Randolph 66
Hearst International Newsreel 101
Heart and Soul (1917) 239
The Heart Buster (1924) 288
The Heart of a Lion (1917) 244
The Heart of Romance (1918) 245
The Heart of Salome (1927) 303
Heart Song (1934) 347
Heart Strings (1920) 260
Heartbreak (1931) 330

Hearts and Spurs (1925) 294
Hearts in Dixie (1929) 110, 138, 313
Hearts of Oak (1924) 289
Hearts of Youth (1921) 270
A Heart's Revenge (1918) 245
Hecht, Ben 166
Heisler, Frank 43
Hell in the Heavens (1934) 351–352
Hell Roarin' Reform (1919) 42, 253
The Hell Ship (1920) 261
Helldorado (1934) 199, 352
Hello Cheyenne (1928) 308
Hello, Sister (1933) 164, 175, 339; see also *Walking Down Broadway*
Hell's Angels (1930) 149, 155
Hell's 400 (1926) 298
Hell's Hole (1923) 284
Help! Help! Police! (1919) 254
Henderson, Ray 119, 148
Henie, Sonja 224
Her Double Life (1916) 23, 235
Her Elephant Man (1920) 260
Her Greatest Love (1917) 238–239
Her Honor the Mayor (1920) 264
Her One Mistake (1918) 247
Her Price (1918) 248
Her Temptation (1917) 29, 239
Here's to Romance (1935) 198, 359
Hickville to Broadway (1921) 272
High Finance (1917) 238
High School Hero (1927) 95, 305–306
High Society Blues (1930) 148, 320
Hill, Edwin C. 77
Hill, George 125
Hilliard, Robert 19
Hills of Peril (1927) 303
Hillyer, Lambert 84
His Greatest Sacrifice (1921) 270
His Mother's Secret (1915) 231
Hit of the Show (1928) 108
Hoblitzelle, Karl 101
Hold Me Tight (1933) 164, 178, 340
Hold That Girl (1934) 346
Holiday (1930) 149
The Hollywood Reporter 163, 167, 170, 174, 179, 180, 188, 189, 190, 191, 192, 195, 206, 209, 210, 211, 212, 214–215
A Holy Terror (1931) 328
Homesick (1928) 312
Honesty–the Best Policy (1926) 299
Honor Among Men (1924) 64, 289
Honor Bound (1928) 308
Honor First (1922) 59, 278, 305
The Honor System (1917) 30, 32, 241, 261
Hoodman Blind (1923) 286, 298; see also *A Man of Sorrow*
Hoopla (1933) 175, 181, 344
Hoover, Herbert 124, 126, 129, 178
Hope, Bob 158
Horkheimer, Elwood 13
Horkheimer, Herbert 13
A Horseman of the Plains (1928) 307
Horton, Edward Everett 220
Hostettler Theaters 76
Hot for Paris (1929) 318
Hot Pepper (1933) 164, 190, 337
Hough, R.L. 154, 158, 172

House of Rothschild (1934) 210, 212, 214
Houston, Claudius 126
How Green Was My Valley (1941) 222
How to Marry a Millionaire (1953) 214
Howard, Curly 157
Howard, E. Percy 102
Howard, Leslie 176
Howard, Moe 157
Howard, William K. 125, 141, 164, 197
Hoxie, Jack 87
Hoyt Theaters 137, 160
Hubbard, Lucien 125, 205
Hudson, Rochelle 220
Hughes, Howard 149, 155
Hugo, Victor 28
Humanity (1932) 165, 338
The Hunchback of Notre Dame (1917) 28
The Hunted Woman (1925) 293
The Huntsman (1920) 49
Husband Hunter (1920) 265
Hush Money (1931) 328
Hyams, Leila 125
Hyland, Peggy 33, 38, 40
Hymer, Warren 125
Hypocrisy (1916) 234

I Am a Fugitive from a Chain Gang (1932) 205
I Am Suzanne! (1934) 179, 180, 181, 344–345
I Believed in You (1934) 346
I Loved You Wednesday (1933) 164, 175, 340
I Want to Forget (1918) 251
I Was a Spy (1933) 344
Ibáñez, Vicente 52
The Idler (1914) 227
If I Were King (1920) 48, 264
If Winter Comes (1923) 283
I'll Say So (1918) 251
Imitation of Life (1934) 201
Imperial Comedies 71
El impostor (1931) 326; see also *Scotland Yard*
In Love with Love (1924) 291
In Old Arizona (1929) 109–110, 139, 141, 185, 312
In Old Kentucky (1935) 222, 223, 360
Independent Theater Owners of America 197–198
Infernal Machine (1933) 165, 338
Infidelity 36, 252; see also *Dr. Rameau*
The Informer (1935) 191
Ingram, Rex 20, 62
The Innocent Sinner (1917) 240–241
Inspiration Pictures 111
International Projector Company 123
Interstate Amusement Corp. 101
Interstate Equities Corp. 153
Intolerance (1916) 30
The Iron Heart (1920) 47, 263
The Iron Horse (1925) 62, 64–65, 70, 71, 73, 84, 295

The Iron Rider (1920) 267
Iron to Gold (1922) 276
Is Zat So? (1927) 77, 83, 303
Isadore Ostrer 123, 167
The Island of Desire (1917) 237
It Had to Happen (1936) 215
It Happened One Night (1934) 215
It Is the Law (1924) 63, 66, 289
It's a Small World (1935) 355
It's Great to Be Alive (1933) 165, 178, 340
I've Got Your Number (1934) 211

Jaccard, Jacques 46
Jack and the Beanstalk (1917) 27, 32, 241–242
Jack Spurlock — Prodigal (1918) 245
Jackie (1921) 58, 274
Jacks, Ben 79
Jackson, Ben 84, 159
Jackson, Helen Hunt 201
James, Rian 174
James, William 71
Janice Meredith (1924) 66
Jannings, Emil 73
Janns Corporation 79
The Jazz Singer (1927) 6, 103–104, 205
Jealousy (1916) 236
Jesse James (1939) 214
Jimmy and Sally (1933) 164, 181, 344
Jiulieta compra un hijo (1935) 354
Jobs, Steve 6
Johnson, Adrian 21
Johnson, Hugh 187
Johnson, Joseph 140, 159
Johnson, Julian 166, 171, 175, 191, 200
Johnson, Kay 143
Johnson, Nunnally 214
The Johnstown Flood (1926) 71, 87, 297
Jolson, Al 103, 205
The Jolt (1921) 274
Jones, Charles "Buck" 46–47, 53, 58, 59, 60, 62, 71, 73, 75, 77, 78, 87, 95, 148
Jones Family 222
Jordan, Miriam 164, 168
Jory, Victor 168
José, Edward 14
Journey's End (1930) 149
Joy, Col. Jason 192, 197
The Joy Girl (1927) 305
Joy Street (1929) 314
The Joyous Troublemaker (1920) 263
Judels, Charles 109
Judge Priest (1934) 199, 202, 204, 222, 350
The Judge's Wife (1914) 13
Julian, Rupert 125
The Jungle Trail (1919) 41, 44, 254
Just Imagine (1930) 148, 149, 324
Just Off Broadway (1924) 286
Just Pals (1920) 58, 267
Just Tony (1922) 60, 278, 312

Kahane, B.B. 172
Kalem 11, 12
Kalich, Bertha 22

Kalmus, Herbert T. 96
Kane, Robert T. 179, 180, 182, 200
Kathleen Mavourneen (1919) 40, 258
Kathodophone 98
Katz, Sam 70, 172
Kaufman, Rita 184
Kaye, Danny 158
Keaton, Buster 83, 87, 125, 158
Keeler, Ruby 205
Keeney, Frank A. 74
Keith Theaters 69
Keith-Albee-Orpheum Theaters 93, 157
Kelland, Clarence Buddington 219, 220
Kellerman, Annette 24, 65
Kelly, Paul 210, 211, 220
Kempner, Alec 135
Kennedy, Edgar 44, 56
Kennedy, Joseph P. 94
Kent, Sidney R. 94, 161, 163, 164, 165, 166–167, 173, 174, 175, 176, 178–179, 188, 193, 195, 196, 197, 198–199, 200, 202, 204, 205, 215, 216, 217, 219, 220, 223, 224
Kentucky Days (1923) 285
Kentucky Jubilee Choir 101
Kentucky Pride (1925) 71, 73, 294
Kenyon, Charles 21
Kerr, Sophie 219
Kerrigan, J.M. 154, 158
The Kid (1921) 52
The Kid Is Clever (1918) 248
Kid Millions (1934) 201
Kinegraphone 107
King, Henry 62, 148, 182, 197
King Alfonso XIII of Spain 102
King Bozo (1926) 85
King George V of England 102
King Kong (1933) 179, 197
King of Jazz (1930) 112
The King of Kings (1927) 82
The Kingdom of Love (1917) 244, 274
Kingston, Samuel F. 38
Kinograms 101
Kipling, Rudyard 19
Kirkland, Alexander 168
Kirkwood, James 60
The Kiss Barrier (1925) 293
Kiss Me Again (1925) 73
Kiss Me Quick (1920) 49
Klein, Philip 175
Kleine 12
Knickerbocker Cloth Examining and Shrinking Company 10
Knockout Reilly (1927) 83
Know Your Men (1921) 269
Knox, Judge John C. 132, 151, 181
Kober, Arthur 173
Kosher Kitty Kelly (1926) 82
Krazy Kat 157
Kreutzer Sonata (1915) 228
Kultur (1918) 250
Kuser, Anthony Mrs. 129
Kyne, Peter B. 75

La Cava, Gregory 209, 214, 216
Lachman, Harry 196, 204
Ladies' Home Journal 191

Ladies Love Danger (1935) 355
Ladies Must Dress (1927) 306
Ladies of Leisure (1930) 146
Ladies to Board (1924) 287
Lady Audley's Secret (1915) 15, 20, 229
The Lady from Longacre (1921) 273
Laemmle, Carl 9, 12, 37, 98, 172
La Marr, Barbara 62
The Lamplighter (1921) 269
The Land of Jazz (1920) 267
Land of the Free (1918) 249; *see also Why America Will Win*
Landi, Elissa 152, 164, 165, 168, 175
Landis, Cullen 106
Lane, Lola 120
Lanfield, Sidney 164, 209
Lang, Walter 209, 212
Langdon, Harry 66, 158
Lantz, Walter 157
LaPlante, Laura 87
LaRoque, Rod 120
Lasky, Jesse L. 45, 166–167, 172, 175, 179–180, 182, 187, 188, 189, 195, 198–199, 200, 202, 203, 219
Lasky, Jesse L., Jr. 71, 172
Lasky's Redheads 198
The Last Days of Pompeii (1935) 201
The Last Gentleman (1934) 215
The Last Laugh (1924) 73, 78, 115
The Last Man on Earth (1924) 178, 290
The Last of the Duanes (1919) 41, 258
The Last of the Duanes (1924) 288–289, 314
Last of the Duanes (1930) 144, 322
The Last Straw (1920) 260–261
The Last Trail (1921) 274
The Last Trail (1927) 302
The Last Trail (1933) 164, 342
Laughton, Charles 215
Laurel, Stan 66, 108
Lawless Love (1918) 249
Lawrence, Gertrude 101, 103
Lawson, John Howard 172
Lazybones (1925) 62, 71, 73, 295
Leave It to Me! (1920) 262
Lederer, Francis 198
Lee, Dixie 125
Lee, Dorothy 44
Lee, Irene 173
Lee, Jane 27, 40, 42
Lee, Katherine 27, 40
Lee, Rowland V. 216
Lee, Sammy 183, 184
Leeper, Dwight C. 94
Legion of Decency 197
Lehman Bros. 129, 136–137
Lehrman, Henry 30, 44
Leni, Paul 78
Leo, Ben 135
Leo, Jack 18, 38, 96, 98, 117, 126, 127, 129, 133, 137, 151
Leo, Joe 18, 135, 139
Leonard, Robert Z. 125
Leroux, Gaston 112
LeRoy, Mervyn 197, 205
LeSaint, Edward J. 27, 35, 43
Lesser, Sol 51, 219

Lester, Elliott 94
Let's Go Places (1930) 319
Levine, Charles S. 135, 137
Lewis, Albert 144, 146, 153, 166
Lewis, George 144
Lewis, Mitchell 104
Lewis, Sinclair 191, 204
Lewis J. Selznick Enterprises 37, 52
La ley del harem (1931) 330; see also *Fazil*
The Liar (1918) 249
Lichtman, Al 219
Life Begins at 40 (1935) 201, 204, 222, 354–355
Life in the Raw (1933) 164, 341
Life of An American Fireman (1903) 10
Life's Shop Window (1914) 14, 227
The Light (1919) 252
Lightner, Winnie 101
Lightnin' (1925) 71, 294
Lightnin' (1930) 148, 324
The Lights of New York (1922) 280
The Lights of New York (1928) 106–107
Lights of the Desert (1922) 278
Liliom (1930) 148, 323
Liliom (1933) 348
Lillie, Beatrice 141, 155
The Lily (1926) 300
Lily Turner (1933) 196
Lincoln, Caryl 119
The Lincoln Highwayman (1919) 260
Lindbergh, Charles 101, 102
Linow, Ivan 125
Lipsitz, Harold P. 90, 139, 172–173
Little Annie Rooney (1925) 73
Little Caesar (1930) 153, 174, 205
The Little Colonel (1935) 201, 222, 354
The Little Grey Mouse (1920) 266
The Little Gypsy (1915) 230
The Little Minister (1934) 201
Little Miss Happiness (1916) 235
Little Miss Hawkshaw (1921) 273
Little Miss Marker (1934) 195
Little Miss Smiles (1922) 275
The Little Wanderer (1920) 264
The Littlest Rebel (1935) 222–223
Live Wires (1921) 272
Lives of a Bengal Lancer (1935) 201
Livingston, Margaret 79
Lloyd, Frank 25, 27, 35, 62, 176, 182, 186, 193
Lloyd, Harold 30, 48, 56, 60, 73, 87
Loeb, Edward 159
Loeb, Jack 135
Loeb, Walker, & Loeb 159
Loeffler, Louis 145
Loew, Arthur M. 125
Loew, Marcus 9, 125
Loew, Mrs. Carrie 125
Loew's Incorporated 6, 9, 45, 61, 68, 71, 91, 116, 124–125, 126, 128–129, 138, 150–151, 156, 165, 173, 181, 224
Loew's Theaters 9, 37, 137
London, Jack 148
The Lone Chance (1924) 288

The Lone Star Ranger (1919) 41, 256, 273
The Lone Star Ranger (1923) 284
The Lone Star Ranger (1930) 318–319
Long, Harold 209
Long, Ray 188, 191
Looking for Trouble (1933) 211, 212; see also *Trouble-Shooters*
Lord, Delmar 43
Los Angeles Times 106
Lost at the Front (1927) 83
Lost Money (1919) 259
The Lost Patrol (1934) 191
The Lost Princess (1919) 257
The Lost World (1925) 73
Lottery Lover (1935) 198, 353
Love, Bessie 79, 125
Love and Secret (1916) 236
The Love Auction (1919) 252–253
The Love Gambler (1922) 280
Love Hungry (1928) 308
Love Is Love (1919) 41, 44, 256
Love Letters (1924) 287
Love, Live and Laugh (1929) 317
Love Makes 'Em Wild (1927) 302–303
The Love Parade (1929) 112
The Love That Dares (1919) 254
The Love Thief (1916) 23, 36, 237; see also *The She Tiger*
Love Time (1934) 350
Lovebound (1923) 282
Lovelace, Hunter 200
Love's Harvest (1920) 263
Love's Law (1917) 238
Loves of Carmen (1927) 112, 114, 305
Lovetime (1921) 272
Lowe, Edmund 63, 71, 75, 86, 87, 89, 107, 112, 115, 119, 120, 125, 131, 137, 143, 146, 147, 152, 164, 192, 199, 201, 202, 204
Lowe, Edward T. 204, 219
Loy, Myrna 167, 175
Lubin, Herbert 92
Lubin 11, 12
Lubitsch, Ernst 62, 146
Lubliner & Trinz Theaters 76
Lucas, George 20
Luce, Claire 141
Luck and Pluck (1919) 252
Lucky Horseshoe (1925) 294
Lucky Star (1929) 138, 316
Lure of Ambition (1919) 40, 259
Lyon, Ben 164

MacDonald, J. Farrell 79, 87, 125
MacDonald, Jeannette 119, 143, 148, 167
MacDonald, Katherine 48
MacFadden, Hamilton 141, 143, 197
Mack Sennett Studios 19, 32
Mack, Helen 154
Mackaill, Dorothy 87
MacKenna, Kenneth 141, 197
MacMahon, Aline 205, 210
The Mad Game (1933) 343
Madame Bovary 28
Madame DuBarry (1917) 21, 244
Madame Sans-Gene (1925) 73

Madame Wants No Children (1927) 114, 303
Madness of Youth (1923) 282
Magic Carpet of Movietone 158
Magnificent Obsession (1934) 201
Maid of the West (1921) 272
Making the Grade (1929) 120, 313
Mallory, Boots 164
Mamá (1931) 145, 154, 329
Man About Town (1932) 162, 333–334
A Man Four-Square (1926) 298
The Man from Bitter Roots (1916) 234
The Man Hunter (1919) 41, 253, 291
A Man of Sorrow (1916) 233
A Man of Sorrow (1926) 298; see also *Hoodman Blind*
Man Trouble (1930) 322
Man Who Broke the Bank at Monte Carlo (1935) 216, 222, 223
The Man Who Came Back (1924) 64, 288
Man Who Came Back (1931) 143, 144, 150, 324–325
The Man Who Dared (1920) 264–265
The Man Who Dared (1933) 165, 175, 341
The Man Who Played Square (1924) 290
The Man Who Won (1923) 283
The Man Without a Country (aka *As No Man Has Loved*, 1925) 71, 294
A Manhattan Knight (1920) 261–262
Manhattan Melodrama (1934) 197
Mankiewicz, Herman 166
Mankiewicz, Joseph 166
Mann, Hank 49
Mann, Margaret 120–121
A Man's Mate (1924) 60, 287
Man's Size (1923) 281
The Marble Heart (1916) 232
March, Fredric 212, 215, 216, 217
Marcus, Lee 94
Marido y mujer (1932) 335; see also *Bad Girl*
Marie Galante (1934) 175, 199, 202, 351
Marin, Ned 139
Maris, Mona 144
Marriage (1927) 302
The Marriage Circle (1924) 68
Marriage in Transit (1925) 293
Marriage License? (1926) 77, 80, 84, 85, 300
Marriages Are Made (1918) 250
Married Alive (1927) 304
Married in Haste (1919) 41, 254
Married in Hollywood (1929) 317
Married Life of Helen and Warren (1926) 71
Marshal Neilan Productions 69
Marshall, George 77, 95, 175, 197
Martini, Tito 219
Marveltone 107
Marx Theaters 76
Mary of Scotland (1936) 191
Maselle, J. 98

Masked Emotions (1929) 315
Mason, Shirley 53, 58, 59, 60, 75
Masquerade (1929) 316
Mata Hari (1932) 197
Mayer, Carl 115
Mayer, Edith 139
Mayer, Louis B. 60, 118, 124, 125, 126, 128–129, 133, 151, 166, 172, 207, 224
Mayo, Archie 197
The Mayor of Hell (1933) 196
McAvoy, May 79, 107, 205
McBride, James E. 38
McCarthy, Charles 167
McCarthy, J.J. 82
McClintic, Guthrie 141, 143
McConnell, Gladys 79
McConville, Bernard 35, 56
McCormack, John 119, 141, 148
McCoy, Tim 125
McCrea, Joel 125, 167
McCullough, Paul 110, 125
McDermott, Marc 49
McGill, Barney 189
McGrail, Walter 79
McGuinness, James Kevin 139
McIntyre, D.E. 160
McLaglen, Victor 86, 87, 107, 112, 115, 119, 122, 125, 137, 146, 147, 152, 165, 168, 192, 201, 202
McLeod, Norman 125
McNamara, Ted 122
Me and My Gal (1932) 164, 337
Me, Gangster (1928) 120, 310–311
The Mediator (1916) 23, 236
Meehan, M.J. "Mike" 133
Mehaffey, Blanche 87
Meighan, Thomas 48
Meistertone 107
Melford, George H. 84
Méliès 12
Meller, Racquel 100, 101, 103
Melting Millions (1917) 238
The Men of Zanzibar (1922) 277
Men on Call (1931) 325
Men Without Women (1930) 149, 319
Mendes, Lothar 78
Menjou, Adolphe 87
Mercer, Beryl 141
Meredyth, Bess 215
Merely Mary Ann (1916) 22, 232
Merely Mary Ann (1920) 265
Merely Mary Ann (1931) 155, 329
Merivale, Philip 171
The Merry-Go-Round (1919) 257
The Merry Widow (1925) 73, 98
The Merry Widow (1935) 201
Merton of the Movies (1924) 61
Metro-Goldwyn-Mayer 6, 50, 62, 69, 77, 79, 80, 81, 82, 83, 87, 88, 93, 108, 109, 112, 114, 118, 124, 125, 126, 133, 136, 137, 138, 139, 143, 146, 154, 156, 157, 160, 166, 167, 176, 179, 192, 197, 201, 209, 211, 212, 217, 224, 225
Metro Pictures Corporation 23, 45, 50, 52, 66, 157
Metropolis (1927) 148
Metropolitan (1935) 222, 223

Metzger, Lou 94
Mi último amor (1931) 330–331; see also *Their Mad Moment*
Michael Shayne 222
Michel, W.C. 159, 160
Mickey Mouse 157
Middleton, George 139
The Midnight Kiss (1926) 77, 87, 300
Miens, Gus 43
The Mighty Barnum (1934) 210, 214, 215
Mile-A-Minute Romeo (1923) 285
Miles, Harry 5, 12
Millarde, Harry 27, 33, 54, 66
Miller, Charlotte 173
Min and Bill (1931) 158
The Mind Reader (1933) 208
miniature golf 135
Minter, Mary Miles 48, 61
Mintz, Sam 174
Miranda, Carmen 224–225
The Mischief Maker (1916) 236
Les Miserables (1918) 245
Les Miserables (1935) 215, 216, 217
Miss Adventure (1919) 254
Miss Innocence (1918) 248
Miss Lonelyhearts 210; see also *Advice to the Lovelorn*
Miss U.S.A. (1917) 243
Mr. Lemon of Orange (1931) 192, 326
Mr. Logan, U. S. A. (1918) 249
Mr. Moto 222
Mr. Skitch (1933) 181, 344
Mitchell, Frank 191–192
Mitchell, Howard 43, 45
Mitchell, Sidney 119
Mitchell, William D. 128
Mitchell Camera Company 124
Mix, Tom 6, 32, 36, 38, 39, 40, 42, 43, 44, 46–47, 48, 53, 59, 60, 63, 71, 73, 77, 78, 79, 87, 90, 113–114, 119, 148, 149, 184, 199
Mixed Faces (1922) 279–280
A Modern Cinderella (1917) 237
A Modern Thelma (1916) 233
Mojica, José 144, 166
Molly and I (1920) 45, 262
Mona Vanna (1923) 284
Money to Burn (1922) 277
The Monkey Talks (1927) 77, 83, 112, 302
Monogram Picture Corp. 133
Monroe, Marilyn 225
Monsieur Beaucaire (1924) 66, 67
Monte Cristo (1922) 59–60, 88, 278–279
Montgomery, Robert 125, 146
Moonshine Valley (1922) 278
Moore, Colleen 73, 87, 179
Moore, Tom 48
The Moral Law (1918) 15, 245
Moran, Lois 119, 120, 121, 125, 143
Moran, Polly 56, 125
More Pay, Less Work (1926) 299
Moreno, Antonio 144
Morgan, Ralph 153–154
Morley, Karen 204
Morocco (1930) 146
Morosco, Walter 171

Mortimer, Edmund 63
Morton, Charles 120, 125
Moskowitz, Charles C. 137
Moss Theaters 69
Moss-Sapiro Theaters 117
The Mother Heart (1921) 270
Mother Knows Best (1928) 109, 120, 311
Mother Machree (1928) 77, 83, 85, 109, 120, 311
Mother of His Children (1920) 45, 262
Motion Picture Code Administration 197, 215
Motion Picture Daily 211
Motion Picture Herald 211
Motion Picture Patents Company 12, 38, 131
Motion Picture Producers Association 60, 97, 209
Mott, John 200
The Mountain Woman (1921) 268
Movietone City 105–106, 125, 137, 158, 160, 166, 172, 182–186, 204, 216, 221
Movietone Entertainments 111
Movietone Follies of 1930 (1930) 131, 320–321
Movietone News 101–103, 136, 178
Movietone sound system 6, 99–105, 109, 112, 123, 124, 169
Muldorfer, C.H. 105
Mundin, Herbert 189, 192, 220
Muni, Paul 125, 141, 143
Murder in Trinidad (1934) 347
Murillo, Mary 21, 22, 23
Murnau, Borzage and Fox (2008) 132
Murnau, F.W. 73, 83, 102, 114, 115, 121, 122, 125, 138, 148
Murphy, Edna 57
Murray, Charlie 83
Murray, J. Harold 101, 119, 141, 142, 147
Murray, Mae 87
Music in the Air (1934) 202, 352
Music Is Magic (1935) 360
The Music Master (1927) 77, 114, 302
Mussolini, Benito 101, 111
Mutiny on the Bounty (1935) 193, 201
Mutt & Jeff cartoons 50
My Darling Clementine (1946) 222
My Friend, the Devil (1922) 280
My Husband's Wives (1924) 290
My Lips Betray (1933) 182, 343–344
My Little Sister (1919) 255
My Own Pal (1926) 90, 297
My Weakness (1933) 175, 342–343
Myers, Harry 87
Mystery Ranch (1932) 164, 334
Mystery Woman (1935) 353

Nada más que una mujer (1934) 351
Nagel, Conrad 104, 125
Nansen, Betty 20
Napoleon's Barber (1929) 110, 313
National Board of Review 73

National Recovery Act 181, 186–188, 192–193
National Theaters 69, 200, 202, 219
National Theatre Supplies 123, 139, 140, 150
A Naughty Wink (1920) 44
Navy Wife (1935) 360
Negri, Pola 62
Neill, Roy William 63, 84
Nero (1922) 58, 60, 77, 279
Nesbit Thaw, Evelyn 34, 40, 44
Nestor 23
The Net (1923) 285–286
Never Say Quit (1919) 253
The New Commandment (1925) 83
The New Klondike (1926) 83
The New Teacher (1922) 278
New Year's Eve (1929) 313
New York Academy of Music 12
New York Globe 56
New York Graphic 107
New York Herald-Tribune 107, 170, 178, 189, 212
New York News 189, 212
The New York Peacock (1917) 238
New York Post 170, 189, 212
New York Sun 107, 212
New York Times 54, 58, 64, 71, 114, 121, 147, 160, 162, 170, 178, 189, 212
New York World-Telegram 189, 211, 212, 215
The News Parade (1928) 110, 122, 309
Niblo, Fred 62, 125
Nichols, Dudley 173, 190–191
The Nigger (1915) 15, 228
Nigh, William 125
The Night Horsemen (1921) 273
Nilsson, Anna Q. 87
Nissen, Greta 164, 168
Nix on Dames (1929) 318
Nixon, Marian 164
No dejes la puerta abierta (1933) 343; see also *Pleasure Cruise*
No Man's Gold (1926) 299
No Mother to Guide Her (1923) 285
No Other Woman (1928) 309
Nolan, H.T. 65
None but the Brave (1928) 309
Normand, Mabel 30, 49, 56, 60
Norris, Kathleen 219
North, Robert 160
North of 53 (1917) 242
North of Hudson's Bay (1923) 285
Northwest Theaters 69
Norton, Barry 120
Not a Drum Was Heard (1924) 286
Not Damaged (1930) 321
Not Exactly Gentlemen (1931) 326
Not Quite Decent (1929) 314
Novak, Eva 87
Novarro, Ramon 87
Now I'll Tell (1934) 195, 347–348
Number 17 (1920) 267

Oath-Bound (1922) 278
Oberon, Merle 215
O'Brien, Eugene 48
O'Brien, George 63–65, 78, 79, 83, 87, 119, 120, 125, 154, 164, 173
O'Connor, Una 171
Oh, for a Man (1930) 143, 148, 324
Oh, You Tony! (1924) 289
Oland, Warner 152
Old English (1930) 149
Old Ironsides (1926) 82
Oldknow, Oscar S. 139, 140, 149, 153
Oliver Twist, Jr. (1921) 269
Olsen's Big Moment (1933) 164, 175, 192, 344
On a volé un homme (1934) 346–347
On the Jump (1918) 250
On the Level (1930) 321
On with the Show (1929) 112
On Your Back (1930) 322
On Your Toes (1927) 83
Once a Sinner (1931) 144, 325
One Hour with You (1932) 146
One Increasing Purpose (1927) 77, 85, 113, 301
One Mad Kiss (1930) 144, 148, 322
The One-Man Trail (1921) 269
One More Spring (1935) 198, 353–354
One Touch of Sin (1917) 29, 237–238
The One Woman Idea (1929) 315
O'Neill, Eugene 192
O'Neill, James 59
Orchestraphone 107
Orchids to You (1935) 357
Orient Express (1934) 189, 345
The Orphan (1920) 47, 262
Orphans of the Storm (1921) 178
Orpheum Theaters 69
O'Sullivan, Maureen 148, 152, 167
Oswald the Rabbit 157
Other Men's Daughters (1918) 248
Otterson, John E. 124, 128, 129, 131–132, 134
Our Gang 66
Our Little Girl (1935) 203, 222, 355–356
Out of the Inkwell 157
Outlaws of Red River (1927) 303
The Outsider (1926) 297
Over the Hill (1931) 152, 155, 331
Over the Hill to the Poorhouse (1921) 53, 58, 112, 271–272, 297

Paddy, the Next Best Thing (1933) 186, 342
Page, Anita 125
Page, Paul 120
Paid to Love (1926) 83, 304
The Painted Lady (1924) 289
The Painted Madonna (1917) 243
Painted Post (1928) 309
The Painted Veil (1934) 201
The Painted Woman (1932) 165, 186, 335
Pajamas (1927) 307
The Palace of Pleasure (1926) 75, 297
Pallotophone 107
Pantages Theaters 69
Paramount-Famous Lasky 88
Paramount Pictures 14, 45, 61, 62, 77, 78, 82, 83, 88, 93, 94, 95, 105, 108, 109, 112, 114, 116, 118, 126, 143, 146, 149, 151, 154, 155, 156, 157, 161, 165, 166, 167, 169, 172, 179, 195, 196, 201, 202, 209, 216, 217
Paramount-Publix 70, 149
Paramount Theater, New York 92–93, 117
Pardon My Nerve (1922) 276
A Parisian Romance (1916) 231
Parrott, James 125
Part Time Wife (1930) 324
Partners of Fate (1921) 268
A Passport to Hell (1932) 164, 165, 335
Pathé 11, 12, 37, 66–67, 82, 87, 108, 109, 149, 150, 151, 154
Pathé News 101
Paths to Paradise (1925) 73
Patricola, Tom 144
Patsy (1917) 240
Patzek, Erika 212
Pawn Ticket 210 (1922) 281
Pearson, Virginia 15, 22, 30, 32, 87
Pechmarie (1935) 355
Peck, Gregory 23
Peck, Lydell 171
Peck's Bad Boy (1934) 351
Peg of the Pirates (1918) 247
Peña, Julio 199
percentage bookings 135–136
Percy, Eileen 53, 87
Perez, Paul 173
The Perfect Crime (1928) 108
Perjury (1921) 274
Perry, Kathryn 79
Pershing, Major General John J. 31
Peter Ibbetson (1935) 201
Peter Pan (1924) 73
The Phantom of the Opera (1925) 73, 81, 112
Philbin, Mary 87
Phipps, Sally 95, 120, 122, 125
Phonofilm 98–99, 104
Photophone 109, 133–134
Photoplay Magazine 73, 120
Pickford, Mary 6, 19, 33, 43, 45, 48, 60, 66, 209–210, 211, 219
Pierce, Noel 201
Piernas de seda (1935) 359
Pilgrimage (1933) 186, 190, 342
Pincus, Joe 144
The Pinhead (1924) 49
Pioneer Film Corp. 52
La Piste des géants (1931) 324; see also *The Big Trail*
Pitfalls of a Big City (1919) 254
Pitts, ZaSu 164, 189
Plastered in Paris (1928) 120, 310
The Play Girl (1928) 308
Play Square (1921) 272
Pleasure Crazed (1929) 315–316
Pleasure Cruise (1933) 165, 339
The Plunderer (1915) 36, 229
The Plunderer (1924) 287
The Plunger (1920) 266–267
Poli Theaters 69
Pollard, Snub 66
Pommer, Erich 179, 198, 204

Popeye 157
Porter, Cole 215
Porter, Edwin S. 10, 90
Ports of Call (1925) 292
Powell, Dick 205, 222
Powell, William 79, 193
Power, Tyrone 224
The Power and the Glory (1933) 179, 180, 343
Prairie Trails (1920) 268
Praskins, Leonard 212
El precio de un beso (1933) 341–342; see also *One Mad Kiss*
Prendergast, Frank 140
Prep and Pep (1928) 311
The Price of Silence (1917) 237
Price, Waterhouse & Company 151
Pride of New York (1917) 244
The Primal Law (1921) 272
Primavera en otoño (1933) 338
The Primitive Call (1917) 237
Prince of Wales 111
The Princess and the Plumber (1930) 324
Princess Romanoff (1915) 228–229
Pringle, Aileen 125
The Prisoner of Shark Island (1936) 214, 216
Private Izzy Murphy (1926) 82
Producers Distributing Corporation 83
production shortage 157
Professional Soldier (1936) 216, 222
Protection (1929) 314
The Prussian Cur (1918) 34, 249
Public Enemy (1931) 153, 197, 205
Publicity Madness (1927) 305
Publix Theater Corporation 69, 91, 116, 165
Pursued (1934) 349
Putting One Over (1919) 255–256
Pynchon & Company 151

Queen Elizabeth (1912) 90; see also *Les Amours d'Elizabeth*
The Queen of Hearts (1918) 249–250
The Queen of Sheba (1921) 53, 275
Queen of the Sea (1918) 249
Queenie (1921) 273
Quick Millions (1931) 327
Quinlan, Walter 185

Rackety Rax (1932) 164, 336
radio 95–96
Radio City Music Hall 133, 170, 178
Radio Corporation of America (R.C.A.) 105, 133
Radio-Keith-Orpheum (RKO) 108, 112, 126, 149, 150, 153, 155, 157, 165, 169, 172, 191, 201, 216
Radio Pictures 109, 175, 179, 192, 197, 208, 212
Raft, George 209, 210, 215
The Ragged Heiress (1922) 276
Ragged Princess (1916) 236
The Rainbow Trail (1918) 35, 250, 268
The Rainbow Trail (1925) 293
The Rainbow Trail (1932) 331
Raine, Norman Reilly 192

Ramona (1928) 200
Ramona (1936) 219, 220
Ramsaye, Terry 178
Rapée, Erno 86, 103
Rapf, Harry 126
Raphaelson, Samson 204
Ratoff, Gregory 192
Ray, Albert 38, 41–42, 44
Ray, Charles 48
Rayart Pictures 74, 94, 109
Raymond, Gene 179
Rebecca of Sunnybrook Farm (1932) 164, 168, 334
The Rebellious Bride (1919) 254
The Red Dance (1928) 102, 120, 311–312
Red Wine (1928) 312
Redheads on Parade (1935) 198, 203, 358
Regeneration (1915) 229–230, 252
Reid, Wallace 6, 48
reissues 36, 153
Reliance Motion Pictures 23
Reliance Picture Corp. 133
remakes 22, 148, 152
Renegades (1930) 323
Return of Peter Grimm (1926) 77, 80, 85, 87, 301
Revnes, Maurice 73, 79
El rey de los gitanos (1933) 340
Reynolds, Lynn 47
Rice, Florence 201
Rice, Maitland 159
Rich, Vivian 46
Rich, Walter J. 96
Rich but Honest (1927) 303
A Rich Man's Plaything (1917) 242
Riders of the Purple Sage (1918) 249, 269
Riders of the Purple Sage (1925) 75, 292
Riders of the Purple Sage (1931) 152, 330
A Ridin' Romeo (1921) 270
Riding with Death (1921) 274
Rienhardt, John 199
Riley the Cop (1928) 311
Rin-Tin-Tin 87, 205
Rio Rita Girls 101
Riskin, Robert 166
Ritz Brothers 158, 225
The River (1929) 138, 317
The River Pirate (1928) 120, 122, 310
Roach, Anthony 43
Roach, Hal 66, 108
The Road Demon (1921) 268–269
Road House (1928) 309
The Road to Glory (1926) 297
roadshow presentation 5, 38, 70, 81–82
Roaring Lions and Wedding Bliss (1917) 30
Robbers Roost (1932) 164, 337
Robbins, Herman 38
Roberta (1935) 201
Roberts, Marguerite 173
Robertson-Cole Productions 52
Robin Hood (1922) 38
Robinson, Edward G. 146, 192, 205, 210

Roche, John 79
Rockett, Al 139, 154, 159, 160, 172, 188, 198
Rogers, Charles "Buddy" 108
Rogers, Charles R. 172
Rogers, Gregory 205
Rogers, Saul E. 127, 132, 137, 152, 165
Rogers, Will 56, 66, 87, 107, 138, 144, 148, 152, 155, 160, 161, 164, 166, 168, 170, 173, 181, 184, 186, 188, 190, 191, 192, 193, 195, 196, 199, 201, 202, 216, 217, 220, 221, 222, 223
Roland, Gilbert 220
Rolf, Tutta 204, 219
Rollins, David 109
Romance Land (1923) 282
Romance of the Rio Grande (1929) 318
Romance of the Underworld (1928) 120, 311
Romance Ranch (1924) 288
Romeo and Juliet (Fox, 1916) 21, 22, 236
Romeo and Juliet (Metro, 1916) 23
Romola (1925) 66
The Roof Tree (1921) 275
Roosevelt, Franklin Delano 152, 177, 186–187
Rosa de francia (1935) 359
The Rose of Blood (1917) 243
Rose of Nome (1920) 264
Rose of the West (1919) 44, 256, 273
Roseman, Edward 57
Rosenberg, Irving 43
Rosenblatt, Sol A. 187
Rosenbluth, Leo 135
Rosher, Charles 121
Rothafel, S.P. "Roxy" 37, 91–92, 95, 140
Rough and Ready (1918) 246, 275, 292
The Rough Diamond (1921) 274
Rough House Rosie (1927) 83
The Rough Riders (1927) 82
Rough Riding Romance (1919) 44, 46, 256–257, 313
Rough Romance (1930) 321
Rough Shod (1922) 277
The Roughneck (1924) 291
Roulien, Raúl 166, 199
Rowland, Richard A. 52, 66, 82, 136, 154, 159, 160, 166, 167, 175
Roxie Hart (1942) 214
Roxy Theater 9, 37, 91–93, 118, 124, 127, 140, 141, 153, 157, 163, 165, 167, 211
Royal Romance (1917) 239
Royce, Edward 119
Rubens, Alma 73, 75, 84, 87, 89
Rubin, J. Robert 126, 224
Rubinstein, Jacob 127
Rubio, José López 173
The Ruling Passion (1916) 23, 232
Runyon, Damon 191
Russell, Rosalind 215
Russell, William 53, 60
Rustling for Cupid (1926) 298

Ruth, Babe 83
Ryan, James 173

Sacred Silence (1919) 258
Saenger Theaters 69
The Sailor (1921) 49
Sailor's Luck (1933) 164, 338–339
St. Clair, Malcolm 175
St. Elmo (1914) 14
St. Elmo (1923) 284, 305
St. John, Al 49
St. Polis, John 79
Sale, Charles "Chic" 100, 101, 103
Sally (1925) 73
Salome (1919) 21, 40, 44, 252, 261, 281
Salute (1929) 316
Samson (1915) 20, 227
Sand, Jillian 141
Sandlin, Sally 196
Sandy (1926) 87, 298
Santschi, Tom 79
Sardou, Victorien 14
Sarfer, Charles 58
Savoir, Alfred 204
Sax, Sam 89, 94
Sayre, Joel 191
Scandal Proof (1925) 293
Scaramouche (1924) 67
Scarface (1932) 197
The Scarlet Honeymoon (1925) 292–293
The Scarlet Letter (1917) 238, 274
The Scarlet Pimpernel (1917) 243
The Scarlet Road (1918) 248
Schenck, Joseph M. 118, 139, 179, 207, 208, 209, 210, 211, 214, 215, 216, 217, 219, 223, 224
Schenck, Nicholas M. 68, 125, 126, 128, 160
Schertzinger, Victor 63, 80, 84, 85, 89
Schine Theaters 76
Schneiderman, George 43, 58
Schnitzer, Joseph 94
Schoedsack, Ernest B. 43
Schulberg, B.P. 136, 172
Schumann-Heink, Ernestine 219
Schuster, Harold 154, 158
Scotland Yard (1930) 323
Scott, William 46
Scrappy 157
Screen Writers' Guild 172
The Scuttlers (1920) 267, 290
The Sea Hawk (1924) 66, 67
The Sea Wolf (1930) 148, 186, 322
Searl, Jackie 220
Seas Beneath (1931) 190, 326
Seastrom, Victor 125
Sebell, Bert 154, 158
Second Hand Love (1923) 283
Second Hand Wife (1933) 164, 337
The Secret Studio (1927) 304
Secrets (1924) 68
Sedgwick, Edward 125
Seiler, Lewis 43, 63, 74, 84, 109, 120, 125, 220
Seitz, George B. 125
A Self-Made Man (1922) 278
Selig 11, 12

Selig Studio 32
Semon, Larry 83
Sennett, Mack 30, 32, 49, 56, 66
Señora casada necesita marido (1934) 352–353
serials 57
The Serpent (1916) 36, 232
Sersen, Fred 184
Servant's Entrance (1934) 193, 202, 350
Seven Faces (1929) 318
7th Heaven (1927) 71, 77, 83, 85, 87, 103, 112, 114, 115, 118, 119, 121, 162
Shackles of Gold (1922) 277
Shadow of the East (1924) 287
Shame (1921) 59, 273, 306
The Shamrock Handicap (1926) 87, 298
Shanghai Madness (1933) 164, 175, 342
Shannon, Peggy 164
Shapiro, Victor M. 160
The Shark (1920) 260
Sharp Shooters (1928) 307
Shaw, George Bernard 102
Shaw, Oscar 79
She (1917) 239
She (1935) 201
The She-Devil (1918) 251
She Done Him Wrong (1933) 189
She Learned About Sailors (1934) 348–349
The She Tiger (1920 re-issue of *The Love Thief*) 36, 262
She Wanted a Millionaire (1932) 161, 168, 332
She Was a Lady (1934) 349
She Wolves (1925) 293
Shearer, Douglas 109
Shearer, Norma 62, 87, 107, 125, 146, 193
Sheehan, Clayton 58, 91, 118, 132, 145
Sheehan, Howard 57
Sheehan, Winfield R. 18, 25, 31, 37, 38, 47, 49, 57, 59, 65, 69, 71, 72, 77, 79, 83, 84–87, 89, 90, 92, 94, 95, 103, 110, 112, 114–116, 117, 118, 119–121, 122–123, 126, 127, 129, 130–131, 132–133, 137, 139, 140, 141, 144, 145, 146, 150, 153, 154, 158, 160, 162–163, 164, 165, 166, 168–169, 170, 173, 174, 176, 177, 180, 181, 185, 187, 188, 192, 193, 195–196, 198–199, 201, 204, 215, 216, 217, 220–223
The Sheik (1921) 59
Sheldon, E. Lloyd 21
Sheldon, Eldon Brewster 15
The Shepherd King 285
Sherlock Holmes (1932) 165, 185, 336
Shirley of the Circus (1922) 280
Shod with Fire (1920) 261
Should a Husband Forgive? (1919) 258
Should a Mother Tell? (1915) 20, 229
Show Boat (1929) 112
Show Them No Mercy (1935) 222, 223
Showboat (1936) 201

Shubert brothers 38
Shubert Playhouses 38
Shurtleff, A.D. 159
Siberia (1926) 71, 89, 298
Sidney, George 83
Sidney, Sylvia 125
Sierra, Gregorio Martinez 173
Sigvard, Prince of Sweden 212
Silent Command (1923) 284
The Silent Lie (1917) 36, 240; see also *Camille of the Yukon*
The Silent Witness (1931) 154, 332
Silk Hat Kid (1935) 357
Silk Legs (1927) 112, 306
Sills, Milton 30, 60, 62, 66, 87, 143, 148
Silly Symphonies 157
Silver, Marcel 125
The Silver Treasure (1926) 299
Silver Valley (1927) 305
Silver Wings (1922) 58, 278
Simmons, Martin L. 210
Simon, Simone 219
Sin (1915) 20, 230
The Sin of Madelon Claudet (1931) 158
The Sin Sister (1929) 312–313
Sinclair, Upton 19, 53–54, 151, 177–178
Singed (1927) 304
Singin' in the Rain (1952) 107
The Singing Fool (1928) 104, 112
Singing River (1921) 272
The Sink or Swim 36, 264; see also *Yankee Way*
Sins of Her Parents (1916) 15, 236
Sins of Men (1916) 15, 233–234
The Siren (1917) 240
The Siren's Song (1919) 40, 254–255
Sister Against Sister (1917) 15, 238
A Sister of Salome (1920) 264
Sistrom, William 154
Six Cylinder Love (1923) 285
Six Cylinder Love (1931) 327
Six Hours to Live (1932) 164, 186, 336
Six Shooter Andy (1918) 42, 245
Skid Proff (1923) 283
Skippy (1931) 158
Skirts (1921) 56, 269–270
Skouras, Charles 160, 200
Skouras, George 160
Skouras, Spyros 160, 163, 200
Skouras Theaters 69
The Sky Hawk (1930) 319
Sky High (1922) 60, 275, 312
Skyline (1931) 152, 330
The Skywayman (1920) 265
Slander (1916) 233
The Slave (1917) 240
Slaves of Beauty (1927) 303
Sleepers East (1934) 345
Slide, Kelly, Slide (1927) 83
The Small Town Girl (1917) 239
Smeck, Roy 97
Smiles (1919) 41, 253
Smiles Are Trumps (1922) 275–276
Smith, Cliff 43
Smith, Courtland 127
Smith, E.A. Yerby 43

Smith, Howard 209
Smith, Winchell 71
Smoke Lightning (1933) 164, 173, 338
Smoky (1933) 181, 344
Snares of Paris (1919) 258
The Sneak (1919) 42, 256
Snowdrift (1923) 282
So Big (1925) 73
So This Is London (1930) 148, 321
Sob Sister (1931) 330
Society Girl (1932) 334
Soft Boiled (1923) 283, 314
Soft Living (1928) 307
A Soldier's Oath (1915) 20, 36, 231
Solomon, B.R. 210
Some Boy! (1917) 240
Song O' My Heart (1930) 148, 149, 322
The Song of Hate (1915) 20, 229
A Song of Kentucky (1929) 318
Sorrows of Satan (1926) 82
The Soul of Broadway (1915) 230, 253
The Soul of Buddha (1918) 21, 246
The Soul of Satan (1917) 29, 241
Soup to Nuts (1930) 322–323
South Sea Love (1923) 285
South Sea Rose (1929) 318
Southern Enterprises Incorporated 51
Souvestre, Pierre 57
Spanish language films 144–145, 149, 154, 166, 198, 199, 201
Sparks Theaters 76
Speakeasy (1929) 313
The Speed Maniac (1919) 36, 258
Spence, Ralph 21
The Spider (1931) 143, 329
The Spider and the Fly (1916) 234
Spielberg, Steven 20
Spigelgass, Leonard 164, 175
The Spirit of Good (1920) 264
The Splendid Sin (1919) 257
Sponable, Earl 98
Sporting Blood (1916) 235
Spring Tonic (1935) 355
Springtime for Henry (1934) 180, 195, 348
Spuds (1927) 83
The Spy (1917) 241
The Spy (1931) 143, 327
Square Crooks (1928) 307
The Square Shooter (1920) 264
The Square Triangle (1914) 13
Stage Madness (1927) 302
A Stage Romance (1922) 276
Stagecoach (1939) 149, 191
Stahl, John M. 78
Stand Up and Cheer (1934) 190, 195, 196, 347
Stanley Theaters 69, 91, 93, 108, 117, 128
Stanton, Richard 27
Stanwyck, Barbara 146
The Star Dust Trail (1926) 75, 292
State Fair (1933) 164, 170, 182, 186, 188, 189, 338
Steamboat Round the Bend (1935) 191, 204, 220, 222, 223, 358

Steamboat Willie 107
Steger, Julius 66
Stein, Modest 119
Steincamp, William 158
Steiner 74
Stella Dallas (1925) 98
Sten, Anna 210
Steppin' Fast (1923) 283
Stepping Sisters (1932) 331
Stewart, Anita 48, 79
stock market crash 127, 151
Stolen Honor (1918) 244
Stoll Film Corp. 52
Stoloff, Benjamin 84, 120, 125
Stone, John (Jack Strumwasser) 111, 144, 145, 199, 201, 204, 219
Stone, Lewis 125, 176
Stong, Philip 188
The Story of Temple Drake (1933) 196
Straight from the Shoulder (1921) 270–271
The Straight Way (1916) 235
Strange Idols (1922) 277
The Strange Woman (1918) 251
Strauss, Florence 166, 167
Street Angel (1928) 115, 120, 122, 309–310
Street Scene (1931) 158
Strength of the Pines (1922) 275
Strong Boy (1929) 138, 313
The Strongest (1920) 261
Struss, Karl 121
Stuart, Charles B. 137
Stuart, Harry 137
Stuart, Nick 95, 111, 120, 122, 125
Such Men Are Dangerous (1930) 131, 320
Such Women Are Dangerous (1934) 189, 347
Sue, Eugene 219, 220
Summer Bachelors (1926) 83, 301
Summerville, Slim 49, 56
Sunny Side Up (1929) 112, 137, 148, 149, 153, 318
Sunrise (A Trip to Tilsit, 1928) 78, 83, 102, 114, 115, 120, 121, 122, 138, 148, 311
Sunset Sprague (1920) 266
Sunshine Comedies 23, 30–31, 43, 49–50, 56, 63, 66, 74
Supernatural (1933) 189
Suratt, Valeska 19, 27, 29–30, 46
Surrender (1931) 331
Sutherland, Edward 197
Sutter's Gold (1935) 201
Swain, Mack 49
Swanson, Gloria 48, 60, 62, 73
Swat the Spy (1918) 42, 250
Swerling, Jo 166
Syncopation (1929) 112

A Tailor-Made Man (1922) 61
Taking a Chance (1928) 311
A Tale of Two Cities (1917) 15, 176, 238, 261
Talking Picture Epics, Inc. 133
Talley, Marion 97
Talmadge, Constance 45, 48, 53, 60, 87

Talmadge, Norma 45, 48, 60, 62, 87
Tangled Lives (1917) 15, 239
Tarasova, Nina 101
Tarkington, Booth 219
Tarnish (1924) 61
Tarzan and His Mate (1934) 201
Tarzan, the Ape Man (1932) 169
The Tattlers (1920) 262
Taurog, Norman 125, 197
Taxi 13 (1928) 108
Taylor, Estelle 48, 49
Taylor, Sam 162
Taylor, Samuel Taylor Coleridge 75
Taylor, William Desmond 14
Te quiero con locura (1935) 360
Teare, Ethel 44
technical advances 96
Technicolor 9, 96, 111, 124, 220
Teeth (1924) 290
Teffeau, George 43
Tell It to the Marines (1918) 42, 250
Tellegen, Lou 79
Temple, Gertrude 195
Temple, Shirley 190, 195, 196, 201, 203, 217, 220, 221, 222, 223
The Temple of Venus (1923) 285
Temple Tower (1930) 320
Ten Cents a Dance (1931) 146
The Ten Commandments (1923) 61, 70, 81
Tenderloin (1928) 104
$10 Raise (1935) 355
The Terror (1920) 263
The Terror (1928) 107
Terry, Paul 158
Terrytoons 158
Tess of the Storm Country (1932) 164, 336
The Test of Manhood (1914) 13
The Texan (1920) 266
Thalberg, Irving 126, 166, 168, 204, 205, 217, 224
Thank You (1925) 71, 295
Thanks a Million (1935) 222, 223
That French Lady (1924) 288
Thaw, Russell 34
theater chain consolidation 68–70
theater construction 52
Their Mad Moment (1931) 328
They Had to See Paris (1929) 138, 316
The Thief (1914) 227
The Thief (1920) 267
Thief in the Dark (1928) 308
The Thief of Bagdad (1924) 61, 67, 81
Thieves (1919) 259
30 Below Zero (1926) 300–301
This Freedom (1923) 286
This Is the Life (1917) 243
This Is the Life (1935) 359
Thompson, Harland 119
Thou Shalt Not (1919) 253–254
Thou Shalt Not Steal (1917) 242
Three Bad Men (1926) 71, 77, 84, 85, 89, 300
Three Girls Lost (1931) 326
Three Gold Coins (1920) 47, 263–264
365 Nights in Hollywood (1934) 351

Three Jumps Ahead (1923) 282
The Three Musketeers (1935) 201
Three on a Honeymoon (1934) 189, 346
Three on a Match (1933) 196
The Three Sisters (1930) 320
Three Stooges 141, 157
Three Who Paid (1923) 281
Thru Different Eyes (1929) 314
Thunder in the Night (1935) 204, 358
Thunder Mountain (1925) 295
Thunder Mountain (1935) 358–359
Thunderclap (1921) 273
Tibbett, Lawrence 216, 223
Tiffany Pictures 149, 154
Tiger Rose (1923) 61
The Tiger Woman (1917) 21, 238
The Tiger's Cub (1920) 266
Tillie's Punctured Romance (1914) 30
Timber Wolf (1925) 294
Time magazine 116, 133, 212, 219, 220
Times Have Changed (1923) 284
Tin Pan Alley (1919) 41, 260
Tinker, Edward R. 129, 153, 156, 158, 159, 160, 161, 163, 170, 188
Tinling, James 95, 115, 125, 145, 193, 197
To a Finish (1921) 272
To Honor and Obey (1917) 29, 240
To Love and to Hold (1914) 13
Todd, David 160
Tolstoy, Leo 14
The Tomboy (1921) 270
Tony Runs Wild (1926) 298
Too Busy to Work (1932) 168, 336
Top Hat (1935) 201
Tora, Lia 119
The Toreador (1921) 49
Torena, Juan 144, 199
Torrence, Ernest 125
Torres, Raquel 125
A Tortured Heart (1916) 234
Tottenham, Merle 171
Touche, Niven & Company 151
The Town That God Forgot (1923) 282
Towne, Gene 192
Tracy, Lee 141, 211
Tracy, Spencer 148, 152, 155, 164, 168, 170, 175, 179, 199, 201, 202
Trader Horn (1931) 169
The Trail Rider (1925) 292
Trailin' (1921) 275
Transatlantic (1931) 329
Traverse, Madlaine 38, 41, 44, 46, 47
Treasure Island (1918) 27
Treat 'Em Rough (1919) 252
Trent's Last Case (1929) 314
Trevor, Claire 220
The Trial of Vivienne Ware (1932) 162, 333
Trick for Trick (1933) 164, 339
Tri-Ergon process 98, 123, 133–134
A Trip to Chinatown (1926) 87, 299
Trooper O'Neill (1922) 278
Trotti, Lamar 191
The Trouble Shooter (1924) 287

Trouble-Shooters 210; see also *Looking for Trouble*
Troublemakers (1917) 27, 244
Troubles of a Bride (1924) 291
Truart 74
True Blue (1918) 247
True Heaven (1929) 312
Truxton King (1923) 282, 306
Tryon, Glenn 87
Tumbling River (1927) 304
Tunberg, Karl 200
Turn to the Right (1922) 61
Turpin, Ben 30, 56, 66
Twain, Mark 56
Twelvetrees, Helen 125
Twentieth Century–Fox 218–225
Twentieth Century Pictures 133, 139, 179, 207–218, 219, 224
20,000 Years in Sing Sing (1933) 205
Twins of Suffering Creek (1920) 263
2 Girls Wanted (1927) 305
Two Little Imps (1917) 27, 240
Two Moons (1920) 268
The Two Orphans (1915) 20, 36, 229

Ufa Studio 78, 94
El último de los Vargas (1930) 322; see also *Last of the Duanes*
El último varón sobre la Tierra (1933) 337; see also *It's Great to Be Alive*
Uncle Tom's Cabin (1927) 82
Under Pressure (1935) 201, 353
Under Suspicion (1931) 324
Under the Pampas Moon (1935) 204, 356
Under the Yoke (1918) 247–248
Under Two Flags (1916) 234–235, 252
Under Two Flags (1936) 219
The Unfaithful Wife (1915) 231
The Unholy Three (1925) 73
Union Depot (1932) 222
United Artists 50, 61, 108, 124, 149, 153, 155, 157, 169, 179, 201, 207, 208, 209–210, 211, 212, 214, 215, 216–217, 219, 220–221
United States Department of Justice 51, 126–127
Universal Chain Theaters 76, 93
Universal Pictures 12, 23, 50, 52, 58, 75, 78, 82, 88, 93, 95, 105, 108, 109, 112, 124, 133, 146, 179, 197, 201, 212
The Unknown Soldier (1926) 83
Unknown 274 (1917) 244
The Untamed (1920) 265
Untermeyer, Samuel 130, 131, 132
The Unwelcome Mother (1916) 235
Up and Going (1922) 276
Up the River (1930) 143, 148, 149, 323
Upstream (1927) 80, 302
Upton Sinclair Presents William Fox 177–178
Urban, Joseph 144, 184
Utilities Power & Light Corporation 123

Vagabond Luck (1919) 259
The Vagabond Trail (1924) 287

Valentino, Rudolph 52, 59, 62, 66, 83
The Valiant (1929) 314–315
El Valiente (1930) 323; see also *The Valiant*
Valli, Virginia 79, 83, 84, 87
Van Beuren studios 157
Van Bibber comedies 71, 85
Van Dyke, Woodbridge Strong 63, 125, 197
Van Loan, H.H. 36, 43, 46
Vanderbilt, Cornelius Jr. 219
Variety 14, 15, 30, 44, 48, 54, 58, 59, 64, 71, 84, 104, 106, 109, 114, 120, 121, 156, 198
Variety (1925) 78
Varnel, Marcel 154, 158
Varsity (1928) 108
vaudeville 136
Veidt, Conrad 87
The Veiled Woman (1929) 119, 314
Very Confidential (1927) 95, 306
Very Truly Yours (1922) 277
The Victim (1916) 237
Vidor, Florence 60
Vidor, King 100, 125
Viertel, Berthold 120, 125, 143
The Village Blacksmith (1923) 58, 281
Villarías, Carlos 108
A Virgin Paradise (1921) 272
The Virginian (1923) 61
Vitagraph 10, 11, 12, 33, 37, 50, 161
Vitaphone 6, 96–98, 99, 100, 101, 102, 103–104, 106–107, 108, 109, 118, 123
Una Viuda romantica (1933) 340
The Vixen (1916) 23, 236–237
Vocaphone 107
Vogt, H. 98
The Volga Boatman (1927) 82
Von Stroheim, Erich 52, 62, 164

Wages for Wives (1925) 62, 71, 75, 296
Walker, Jimmy 140
Walker, Johnnie 57
Walker, Ray 204
Walking Down Broadway (1933) 164; see also *Hello, Sister*
Wall Street Journal 70, 85
Wallace, Richard 192
Walling, Richard 79, 87
Wallis, Hal 205, 207
Walls of Gold (1933) 343
The Walls of Jericho (1914) 14, 227
Walsh, George 23, 29, 32, 41, 53, 64, 150
Walsh, Raoul 21, 23, 25, 27, 30, 35, 41, 83, 125, 141, 149, 174, 192, 201
Wanamaker, John 122
Wanamaker, Rodman 122
The Wanderer (1925) 61
The War Bride's Secret (1916) 236
The War Horse (1927) 302
Warner, Albert 156–157
Warner, H.B. 141
Warner, Harry M. 96, 102, 165, 206, 210
Warner, Jack 107, 172, 205, 207, 209

Warner Brothers 50, 88, 96–98, 103, 105, 106–107, 108, 109, 124, 126–127, 128, 146, 151, 153, 154, 156–157, 166, 169, 172, 179, 195, 196, 201, 205–207, 209, 210, 211, 212, 214, 216, 217, 221–222
The Warrens of Virginia (1924) 66, 290
The Warrior's Husband (1933) 164, 178, 339–340
Washburn, Bryant 48
Way Down East (1920) 52, 61
Way Down East (1935) 219, 220, 223, 359–360
Wayne, John 149
We Live Again (1934) 201
We Should Worry (1918) 247
The Web of Chance (1919) 259
Weber & Fields 10
Weekends Only (1932) 164, 334
Weeks, H. Keith 105, 158
Welcome Home (1935) 193, 357
Weldie, Max 215
Wellman, William 63, 197, 212
Werker, Alfred 125
Wesco Holding Company 117, 202
West, Mae 196
West, Nathanael 211
West Coast Theaters 51, 69, 91, 117, 118, 123, 128, 137, 139, 147, 151, 156, 160, 172, 181, 199–200, 202
West of Chicago (1922) 279
Western Blood (1918) 42, 246
Western Electric 96, 103, 109, 133–134, 137, 157, 169, 172
Western Luck (1924) 288
Western Speed (1922) 277
What Love Will Do (1921) 272
What Price Glory (1926) 74, 77, 79, 80, 82, 83, 86, 91, 92, 98, 103, 112, 114, 115, 118, 122, 137, 186, 220, 304–305
What Would You Do? (1920) 260
Whatever She Wants (1921) 275
The Wheel (1925) 294
When a Man Loves (1927) 97
When a Man Sees Red (1917) 242, 268
When a Man's a Man (1935) 354
When a Woman Sins (1918) 250
When False Tongues Speak (1917) 242
When Fate Decides (1919) 255
When Knighthood Was in Flower (1922) 38
When Men Desire (1919) 21, 40, 253
When Odds Are Even (1923) 285
When the Door Opened (1926) 75, 296
Where Love Leads (1916) 235
While Justice Waits (1922) 280
While New York Sleeps (1920) 48, 49, 265
While Paris Sleeps (1932) 333
While the Devil Laughs (1921) 268
Whispering Sage (1927) 298
Whispering Wires (1926) 77, 80, 300
White, George 182, 195, 196
White, Marjorie 141
White, Pearl 48, 53, 60
White, Stanford 34

White Lies (1920) 263
The White Moll (1920) 264
The White Parade (1934) 180, 202, 352
Whitman, P.D. 43
Who Are My Parents? (1922) 280
Why America Will Win (1918) 34, 249; see also *Land of the Free*
Why I Would Not Marry (1918) 32, 250, 275
Why Leave Home? (1929) 316
Why Sailors Go Wrong (1928) 122, 308
Why Trust Your Husband? (1921) 268
Wicked (1931) 329
Widmark, Richard 225
Wife Number Two (1917) 28, 241
A Wife's Sacrifice (1916) 23, 233
Wild Company (1930) 321–322
Wild Girl (1932) 152, 164, 335
Wild Gold (1934) 189, 348
Wild Waves and Women (1919) 44
Wild West Romance (1928) 309
The Wilderness Trail (1919) 256
Wiles, Gordon 200
Wilkerson, W.R. 170, 174, 192, 206–207
William, Warren 205, 208
William Fox Studio (Western Avenue) 23, 25, 84, 85, 95, 115, 124, 125, 137, 172, 196, 199, 222, 223
Williams, Earle 48
Williams, Walter 43
Win That Girl (1928) 120, 310
Winchell, Walter 211
The Winding Star (1925) 295
Wing Toy (1921) 268
Wings (1927) 82
Wings of the Morning (1919) 259
Wings of the Storm (1926) 301
Wings of Youth (1925) 87, 293
Winner Take All (1924) 289–290
The Winning of Barbara Worth (1926) 61, 98
The Winning Streak (1919) 257
Winning with Wits (1922) 275
Winninger, Charles 141
The Witch (1916) 232
With Byrd at the South Pole (1930) 149
Withers, Jane 220
Without Compromise (1922) 280
Without Fear (1922) 277
Witte, Lou 184
The Wizard (1927) 112, 306
Wolf, Barney 173
Wolf, Marco 140
Wolf Fangs (1927) 119, 306
The Wolf Man (1924) 287
The Wolf's Claw (1919 re-issue of *The Serpent*) 36, 252
Wolfson-Meyer Theaters 70
Wolves of the Night (1919) 41, 256, 288
Woman and the Law (1918) 32, 246
The Woman from Hell (1929) 314
The Woman He Wronged (1914) 13
The Woman in Room 13 (1932) 333
A Woman There Was (1919) 40
The Woman Who Gave (1918) 34, 250–251
Woman Wise (1928) 307

Woman! Woman! (1919) 44, 252
Womanpower (1926) 85, 300
A Woman's Honor (1916) 23, 234
A Woman's Past (1915) 230
A Woman's Resurrection (1915) 20, 229
Women Everywhere (1930) 321
Women of All Nations (1931) 155, 327
Wonder Bar (1934) 201
The Wonderful Adventure (1915) 15, 20, 230
Wood, Sam 125, 197
Words and Music (1929) 316
Words and Music By— (1919) 255
The World Moves On (1934) 197, 202, 350
A World of Folly (1920) 263
World Wide Pictures 109, 169
Wormwood (1915) 229
The Worst Woman in Paris? (1933) 175, 180, 343
Would You Forgive? (1920) 46, 262
The Wrath of Love (1917) 241
Wray, Fay 175
Wray, John Griffith 84
Wurtzel, Ben 158, 159
Wurtzel, Lillian 196
Wurtzel, Sam 166, 173
Wurtzel, Sol M. 18, 25, 26, 27–28, 31, 32, 33, 35–36, 38, 41, 42–43, 44, 46–47, 49, 52, 57, 59, 63, 64, 66, 74, 77, 79, 83, 85, 94–95, 122–123, 134, 137, 139, 141, 146, 154, 158, 159, 160, 163, 165, 166, 172–173, 191, 196, 198, 199, 200, 204, 217, 219, 220, 222, 223
W.W. Hodkinson Corp. 52

The Yankee Senor (1926) 297
The Yankee Way (1917) 36, 242
Yellow Dog Catcher (1919) 44
Yellow Fingers (1926) 298
The Yellow Stain (1922) 59, 277
The Yellow Ticket (1931) 152, 330
Yo, tú y ella (1933) 343
Yolanda (1924) 66
The Yosemite Trail (1922) 279
Yost, Robert M. 160, 172
You Can't Get Away with It (1923) 286
Young, Clara Kimball 48
Young, Loretta 180, 193, 209, 212, 215, 217, 220
Young America (1932) 333
Young as You Feel (1931) 328–329
Young Sinners (1931) 327
Youth Must Have Love (1922) 279

Zanft, John 123, 127
Zangwill, Israel 14, 15, 22
Zanuck, Darryl Francis 108, 139, 166, 172, 179, 196, 204–217, 219, 220–225
Ziegfeld, Florenz 119
Ziegfeld Follies 143
Zierler, Sam 94
Zimbalist, Efrem 97
Zinnemann, Fred 147
Zoo in Budapest (1933) 165, 178, 179–180, 186, 339
Zukor, Adolph 13, 45, 51, 70, 90, 161, 166, 209

www.ingramcontent.com/pod-product-compliance
Lightning Source LLC
Chambersburg PA
CBHW060257240426
43661CB00060B/2813